Fodor's Affordable Europe

New THIRD EDITION

"These books succeed admirably; easy to follow and use, full of cost related information, practical advice and recommendations...maps are clear and easy to use."

—*Travel Books Worldwide*

"Good helpmates for the cost-conscious traveler."
—*Detroit Free Press*

"Concentrates on life's basics...without skimping on literary luxuries."
—*New York Daily News*

"The Fodor's series puts a premium on showing its readers a good time."
—*Philadelphia Inquirer*

Portions of this book appear in *Fodor's Europe*.

Fodor's Travel Publications, Inc.
New York • Toronto • London • Sydney • Auckland

Fodor's Affordable Europe

Editor: Linda Cabasin
Editorial Contributors: Steven Amsterdam, Rob Andrews, Barabara Walsh Angelillo, Corky Bastlund, Robert Blake, Toula Bogdanos, Rodney Bolt, Hannah Borgeson, Jules Brown, Roderick Conway-Morris, Samantha Cook, Fionn Davenport, Giuliano Davenport, Mario Falzon, Nigel Fisher, Robert I. C. Fisher, George Hamilton, Emma Harris, Simon Hewitt, Catherine Hill-Herndon, Joel Honig, Alannah Hopkin, Anto Howard, Laura M. Kidder, Ky Krauthamer, Corinne LaBalme, David Lakein, Lisa Leventer, David Low, Deborah Luhrman, Amy McConnell, Anne Midgette, Rebecca Miller, Anastasia Mills, Kristen Perrault, Karina Porcelli, Mark Potok, Kathryn Sampson, Mary Ellen Schultz, M.T. Schwartzman, Kate Sekules, George Semler, Eric Sjogren, Fiona Smith, Timea Spitka, Dinah Spritzer, Katherine Tagge, Robert Tilley, Julie Tomasz, Ivanka Tomova, Meltem Türköz, Nancy van Itallie, Greg Ward, Daniel Williams.
Creative Director: Fabrizio La Rocca
Cartographer: David Lindroth
Cover Design: Tigist Getachew/Guido Caroti
Cover Photograph: Catherine Karnow/Woodfin Camp

Design: Vignelli Associates

Contents

How This Guide Will Save You Money

If you're one of the rock-bottom-budget travelers who sleep on park benches to save money and would never, ever dress up for duck à l'orange at Jean-Louis, then look to another guidebook for your travel information.

But if you're among those who budget some of the finer things into their traveling life, if you would stay home before spending a night in a hostel dormitory, and if you're willing to pay a little more for crisp sheets, a firm bed, and a really superb dining experience every now and again, read on. It's for you that Fodor's team of savvy, budget-conscious writers and editors have prepared this book.

We share your traveling style and your champagne tastes, and we know that saving money means making choices. Some of us do it by sticking to public transportation and picnic lunches. Others splurge on a hotel with amenities but forgo fancy meals. Still others take the hostel route in order to go on a shopping spree.

In this guide, we've tried to include enough options so that all of you spend time and money in the ways you most enjoy. The hotels we suggest are good values, and there are no dives, thank you—only clean, friendly places with an acceptable level of comfort, convenience, and charm. We also recommend a range of inexpensive and moderately priced restaurants where you can eat well in pleasant surroundings. You'll read about the best budget shopping and how to make the arts-and-nightlife scene without breaking the bank. And we'll tell you how to get around by public transportation.

As for planning what to see and do, you'll find the same lively writing and authoritative background information available in Fodor's renowned Gold Guides.

Please Write to Us

Everyone who has contributed to *Affordable Europe* has worked hard to make the text accurate. All prices and opening times are based on material supplied to us at press time, and Fodor's cannot accept responsibility for any errors that may have occurred. The passage of time always brings changes, so it's a good idea to call ahead to confirm information when it matters—particularly if you're making a detour to visit specific sights or attractions. When making reservations at a hotel or inn, be sure to speak up if you have a disability or are traveling with children, if you prefer a private bath or a certain type of bed, or if you have specific dietary needs or any other concerns.

Do let us know about your trip. Was your hotel comfortable and were the museums you visited worthwhile? Did you happen upon a treasure that we haven't included? We would love to have your feedback, positive and negative. If you have suggestions or complaints, we'll look into them and revise our entries when it's the right thing to do. So please send us a letter or postcard (we're at 201 East 50th Street, New York, New York 10022). We look forward to hearing from you. In the meantime, have a wonderful trip!

Karen Cure
Editorial Director

1 Essential Information

Important Contacts

No single travel resource can give you every detail about every topic that might interest or concern you at the various stages of your journey—when you're planning your trip, while you're on the road, and after you get back home. The following organizations, books, and brochures will supplement the information in *Affordable Europe*. For related information, including both basic tips on visiting Europe and background information on many of the topics below, study Smart Travel Tips, the section that follows Important Contacts.

Air Travel

Carriers U.S. airlines that serve major European cities include **American Airlines** (tel. 800/433–7300); **Continental** (tel. 800/231–0856); **Delta** (tel. 800/241–4141); **Northwest** (tel. 800/447–4747); **TWA** (tel. 800/892–4141); and **United** (tel. 800/538–2929).

European national airlines that fly directly from the United States: **Austria:** Austrian Airlines (tel. 800/843–0002); **Belgium:** Sabena Belgian World Airlines (tel. 800/955–2000); **Czech Republic and Slovakia:** Czechoslovak Airlines (CSA, tel. 212/765–6022); **Denmark:** Scandinavian Airlines (SAS, tel. 800/221–2350); **Finland:** Finnair (tel. 800/950–5000); **France:** Air France (tel. 800/237–2747); **Germany:** Lufthansa (tel. 800/645–3880); **Great Britain:** British Airways (tel. 800/247–9297); Virgin Atlantic (tel. 800/862–8621); **Greece:** Olympic Airways (tel. 212/838–3600 or 800/223–1226 outside NY); **Holland:** KLM Royal Dutch Airlines (tel. 800/374–7747); **Hungary:** Malév Hungarian Airlines (tel. 212/757–6446); **Ireland:** Aer Lingus (800/223–6537); **Italy:** Alitalia (tel. 800/223–5730); **Malta:** Air Malta (tel. 415/362–2929); **Norway:** Scandinavian Airlines (SAS, tel. 800/221–2350); **Poland:** LOT Polish Airlines (tel. 212/869–1074); **Portugal:** TAP Air Portugal (tel. 800/221–7370); **Romania:** Tarom Romanian Airlines (tel. 212/687–6013); **Spain:** Iberia Airlines (tel. 800/772–4642); **Sweden:** Scandinavian Airlines (tel. 800/221–2350); **Switzerland:** Swissair (tel. 800/221–4750); and **Turkey:** THY Turkish Airlines (tel. 212/986–5050).

Offices of major European national airlines in or near London: **Austria:** Austrian Airlines (tel. 0171/434–7300); **Czech Republic and Slovakia:** Czechoslovak Airlines (CSA, tel. 0171/255–1898); **Denmark:** Scandinavian Airlines (SAS, tel. 0171/734–4020); **Finland:** Finnair (tel. 0171/408–1222); **France:** Air France (tel. 0181/742–6600); **Germany:** Lufthansa (tel. 0181/750–3520 or 0345/737747); **Great Britain:** British Airways (tel. 0181/897–4000); Virgin Atlantic (tel. 01293/747747); **Greece:** Olympic Airways (tel. 0171/409–3400); **Holland:** KLM Royal Dutch Airlines (tel. 0171/750–9000); **Ireland:** Aer Lingus (tel. 0181/899–4747); **Italy:** Alitalia (tel. 0171/602–7111); **Malta:** Air Malta (tel. 0171/785–3177); **Norway:** Scandinavian Airlines (SAS, tel. 0171/734–4020); **Poland:** LOT Polish Airlines (tel. 0171/580–5037); **Portugal:** TAP Air Portugal (tel. 0171/828–0262); **Romania:** Tarom Romanian Airlines (tel. 0171/224–3693); **Spain:** Iberia Airlines (tel. 0171/413–1201); **Sweden:** Scandinavian Airlines (tel. 0171/734–4020); **Switzerland:** Swissair (tel. 0171/434–7300); and **Turkey:** THY Turkish Airlines (tel. 0171/499–9249).

Charters Although charter companies often deal only with travel agencies, some, such as **Martinair** (tel. 800/627–8462) and **New Frontiers** (tel. 800/677–0720) will ticket individuals directly.

Complaints To register complaints about charter and scheduled airlines, contact the U.S. Department of Transportation's **Office of Consumer Affairs** (400 7th St. NW, Washington, DC 20590, tel. 202/366–2220 or 800/322–7873).

Consolidators Established consolidators selling to the public include **Euram Tours** (1522 K St. NW, Suite 430, Washington DC, 20005, tel. 800/848–6789); **TFI Tours International** (34 W. 32nd St., New York, NY 10001, tel. 212/736–1140 or 800/745–8000); and **Travac** (989 6th Ave., New York, NY 10018, tel. 800/872–8800). One in Great Britain is **Trailfinders** (42–50 Earls Court Rd., London W8 6FT, tel. 0171/937–5400).

Publications For general information about charter carriers, ask for the Office of Consumer Affairs brochure **"Plane Talk: Public Charter Flights."** The Department of Transportation also publishes a 58-page booklet, **"Fly Rights"** (Consumer Information Center, Dept. 133-B, Pueblo, CO 81009; $1.75).

For other tips and hints, consult the Consumers Union's monthly **"Consumer Reports Travel Letter"** (Box 53629, Boulder, CO 80322, tel. 800/234–1970; $39 annually) and the newsletter **"Travel Smart"** (40 Beechdale Rd., Dobbs Ferry, NY 10522, tel. 800/327–3633; $37 annually); *The Official Frequent Flyer Guidebook,* by Randy Petersen (4715-C Town Center Dr., Colorado Springs, CO 80916, tel. 719/597–8899 or 800/487–8893; $14.99 plus $3 shipping); *Airfare Secrets Exposed,* by Sharon Tyler and Matthew Wonder (Universal Information Publishing; $16.95 plus $3.75 shipping from Sandcastle Publishing, Box 3070-A, South Pasadena, CA 91031, tel. 213/255–3616 or 800/655–0053); and *202 Tips Even the Best Business Travelers May Not Know,* by Christopher McGinnis (Irwin Professional Publishing, 1333 Burr Ridge Pkwy., Burr Ridge, IL 60521, tel. 708/789–4000 or 800/634–3966; $10 plus $3 shipping).

Better Business Bureau

For local contacts in the home town of a tour operator you may be considering, consult the **Council of Better Business Bureaus** (4200 Wilson Blvd., Arlington, VA 22203, tel. 703/276–0100).

Bus Travel

From the U.K. **Eurolines** links London with the English Channel ferry ports and Amsterdam, Paris, Antwerp, Brussels, and other points farther afield in Germany, France, and Italy. Night service to Paris takes about eight hours; the overnight journey time to Amsterdam is about 12 hours. **Citysprint** uses the Dover–Calais Hovercraft service en route to Amsterdam to reduce travel time to about 10 hours. **National Express** uses Sealink ferries (*see* Ferry Travel, *below*) to the Republic of Ireland. A connecting bus service in Ireland is operated by Bus Éireann. Sailings are from Fishguard to Rosslare—a 3½-hour crossing. Eurolines services can be booked in person at **National Express** offices at Victoria Coach Station or at 52 Grosvenor Gardens, London SW1W 0AU, opposite Victoria Rail Station (tel. 0171/730–8235), at any National Express agent throughout Britain, and at **Eurolines** (23 Crawley Rd., Luton LU1 1HX, tel. 01582/404511). **Citysprint** services can be booked at Victoria Coach Station or by calling 01304/240241.

Car Rental

Major car-rental companies represented in Europe include **Alamo** (tel. 800/327–9633, 0800/272-2000 in the United Kingdom); **Avis** (tel. 800/331–1084, 800/879–2847 in Canada); **Budget** (tel. 800/527–0700, 0800/181–181 in the United Kingdom); **Hertz** (tel. 800/654–3001, 800/263–0600 in Canada, 0181/679–1799 in the United Kingdom); and **National** (sometimes known as Europcar InterRent outside North America; tel. 800/227–3876), 0181/950–5050 in the United Kingdom).

Car rental prices vary considerably throughout Europe, as does tax. Rates in London begin at $21 a day and $126 a week for an economy car with unlimited mileage (plus 17.5% tax). Rates in Paris begin at $180 a week for an economy car with unlimited mileage (plus 18.6% tax). In Madrid, rates start at $24 a day and $167 a week (plus 16% tax). In Rome, rates begin at $48 a day and $185 a week for an economy car with unlimited mileage (plus 19% tax). Many car rental agencies in Rome impose mandatory theft insurance on all rentals. Coverage costs $10–$15 a day.

Rental Wholesalers
Contact **Auto Europe** (Box 7006, Portland, ME 04112, tel. 207/828–2525 or 800/223–5555); **Europe by Car** in New York City (write 1 Rockefeller Plaza, 10020; visit 14 W. 49th St.; or call 212/581–3040, 212/245–1713, or 800/223–1516) or Los Angeles (9000 Sunset Blvd., 90069, tel. 800/252–9401 or 213/272–0424 in CA); **Foremost Euro-Car** (5658 Sepulveda Blvd., Suite 201, Van Nuys, CA 91411, tel. 818/786–1960 or 800/272–3299); or the **Kemwel Group** (106 Calvert St., Harrison, NY 10528, tel. 914/835–5555 or 800/678–0678).

The Channel Tunnel

For information, contact **Le Shuttle** (tel. 0990/353535 in the United Kingdom, 800/388–3876 in the United States), which transports cars, or **Eurostar** (tel. 01233/617575 in the United Kingdom, 800/942–4866 in the United States), the high-speed train service between London (Waterloo) and Paris (Gare du Nord). Eurostar tickets are available in the United Kingdom through **British Rail International** BritRail (Victoria Station, London, tel. 0171/834–2345 or 01233/617575 for credit-card bookings), and in the United States through **Rail Europe** (tel. 800/942–4866 or 800/438–7245) and **BritRail Travel** (1500 Broadway, New York, NY 10036, tel. 212/575–2667 or 800/677–8585).

Children and Travel

Flying
Look into **"Flying With Baby"** (Third Street Press, Box 261250, Littleton, CO 80126, tel. 303/595–5959; $5.95 plus $1 shipping), cowritten by a flight attendant. **"Kids and Teens in Flight,"** free from the U.S. Department of Transportation's Office of Consumer Affairs, offers tips for children flying alone. Every two years the February issue of *Family Travel Times* (*see* Know-How, *below*) details children's services on three dozen airlines.

Know-How
Family Travel Times, published 10 times annually by Travel With Your Children (TWYCH, 45 W. 18th St., New York, NY 10011, tel. 212/206–0688; annual subscription $55), covers destinations, types of vacations, and modes of travel.

The *Family Travel Guides* catalogue (tel. 510/527–5849; $1 postage) lists about 200 books and articles on family travel. Also check *Take Your Baby and Go! A Guide for Traveling with Babies, Toddlers and Young Children,* by Sheri Andrews, Judy Bordeaux, and Vivian Vasquez (Bear Creek Publications, 2507 Minor Ave., Seattle, WA 98102, tel. 206/322–7604 or 800/326–6566; $5.95 plus $1.50 shipping). *Innocents Abroad: Traveling with Kids in Europe,* by Valerie Wolf Deutsch and Laura Sutherland (Penguin USA, 120 Woodbine St., Bergenfield, NJ 07621, tel. 201/387–0600 or 800/253–6476; $15.95 or $4.95 paperback), covers child- and teen-friendly activities, food, and transportation.

Lodging
Novotel hotels (tel. 800/221–4542) permit up to two children to stay free in their parents' room. **Sofitel** hotels (tel. 800/221–4542) offer a free second room for children during July and August and over the Christmas holiday. **Holiday Fun with Kids,** with more than 100 properties in Switzerland, offers programs for children at reduced prices; contact the Swiss National Tourist Office (608 5th Ave., New

York, NY 10019, tel. 212/757–5944) for a brochure. The **Sol and Melia chains** (tel. 800/336–3542) in Spain permit children 12 and under to stay free with their parents. **Italy's CIGA hotels** (reservations, tel. 800/221–2340) welcome families as well.

Resorts **Club Med** (40 W. 57th St., New York, NY 10019, tel. 800/258–2633) has "Baby Clubs" (from age four months), "Mini Clubs" (for ages four to six or eight, depending on the resort), and "Kids Clubs" (for ages eight and up during school holidays) at many of its resort villages in France, Italy, Switzerland, and Spain.

Tour Contact **Grandtravel** (6900 Wisconsin Ave., Suite 706, Chevy Chase,
Operators MD 20815, tel. 301/986–0790 or 800/247–7651), which has tours for people traveling with grandchildren ages 7 to 17; **Families Welcome!** (21 W. Colony Pl., Suite 140, Durham, NC 27705, tel. 919/489–2555 or 800/326–0724); or **Rascals in Paradise** (650 5th St., Suite 505, San Francisco, CA 94107, tel. 415/978–9800 or 800/872–7225).

If you're outdoorsy, look into **American Wilderness Experience** (Box 1486, Boulder, CO 80306, tel. 303/444–2622 or 800/444–0099); the **American Museum of Natural History** (79th St. and Central Park W, New York, NY 10024, tel. 212/769–5700 or 800/462–8687); and **Wildland Adventures** (3516 N.E. 155th St., Seattle, WA 98155, tel. 206/365–0686 or 800/345–4453).

Customs

U.S. Citizens The **U.S. Customs Service** (Box 7407, Washington, DC 20044, tel. 202/927–6724) can answer questions on duty-free limits and publishes a helpful brochure, "Know Before You Go." For information on registering foreign-made articles, call 202/927–0540.

Canadians Contact **Revenue Canada** (2265 St. Laurent Blvd. S, Ottawa, Ontario, K1G 4K3, tel. 613/993–0534) for a copy of the free brochure **"I Declare/Je Déclare"** and for details on duties that exceed the standard duty-free limit.

U.K. Citizens **HM Customs and Excise** (Dorset House, Stamford St., London SE1 9NG, tel. 0171/202–4227) can answer questions about U.K. customs regulations and publishes **"A Guide for Travellers,"** detailing standard procedures and import rules.

For Travelers with Disabilities

Complaints To register complaints under the provisions of the Americans With Disabilities Act, contact the U.S. Department of Justice's **Public Access Section** (Box 66738, Washington, DC 20035, tel. 202/514–0301, fax 202/307–1198, TTY 202/514–0383).

Organizations Contact the **American Academy of Otolaryngology** (1 Prince St., Al-
Hearing exandria, VA 22314, tel. 703/836–4444, fax 703/683–5100, TTY 703/
Impairments 519–1585).

Mobility Contact the **Information Center for Individuals with Disabilities**
Impairments (Fort Point Pl., 27–43 Wormwood St., Boston, MA 02210, tel. 617/727–5540, 800/462–5015 in MA, TTY 617/345–9743); **Mobility International USA** (Box 10767, Eugene, OR 97440, tel. and TTY 503/343–1284, fax 503/343–6812), the U.S. branch of an international organization based in Belgium (*see below*) that has affiliates in 30 countries; **MossRehab Hospital Travel Information Service** (1200 W. Tabor Rd., Philadelphia, PA 19141, tel. 215/456–9603, TTY 215/456–9602); the **Society for the Advancement of Travel for the Handicapped** (347 5th Ave., Suite 610, New York, NY 10016, tel. 212/447–7284, fax 212/725–8253); the **Travel Industry and Disabled Exchange** (TIDE, 5435 Donna Ave., Tarzana, CA 91356, tel. 818/344–3640, fax 818/344–0078); and **Travelin' Talk** (Box 3534, Clarksville, TN 37043, tel. 615/552–6670, fax 615/552–1182).

Vision Impairments Contact the **American Council of the Blind** (1155 15th St. NW, Suite 720, Washington, DC 20005, tel. 202/467–5081, fax 202/467–5085) or the **American Foundation for the Blind** (15 W. 16th St., New York, NY 10011, tel. 212/620–2000, TTY 212/620–2158).

Publications Several free publications are available from the U.S. Information Center (Box 100, Pueblo, CO 81009, tel. 719/948–3334): **"New Horizons for the Air Traveler with a Disability"** (address to Dept. 355A), describing legally mandated changes; the pocket-size **"Fly Smart"** (Dept. 575B), good on flight safety; and the Airport Operators Council's worldwide **"Access Travel: Airports"** (Dept. 575A).

The 500-page *Travelin' Talk Directory* (Box 3534, Clarksville, TN 37043, tel. 615/552–6670; $35) lists people and organizations who help travelers with disabilities. For specialist travel agents worldwide, consult the *Directory of Travel Agencies for the Disabled* (Twin Peaks Press, Box 129, Vancouver, WA 98666, tel. 206/694–2462 or 800/637–2256; $19.95 plus $2 shipping).

In the U.K. Contact the **Royal Association for Disability and Rehabilitation** (RADAR, 12 City Forum, 250 City Rd., London EC1V 8AF, tel. 0171/250–3222) or **Mobility International** (Rue de Manchester 25, B1070 Brussels, Belgium, tel. 00–322/410–62–97), an international clearinghouse of travel information for people with disabilities.

Travel Agencies and Tour Operators The Americans with Disabilities Act requires that travel firms serve the needs of all travelers. However, some agencies and operators specialize in making group and individual arrangements for travelers with disabilities, among them **Access Adventures** (206 Chestnut Ridge Rd., Rochester, NY 14624, tel. 716/889–9096), run by a former physical-rehab counselor. In addition, many general-interest operators and agencies (*see* Tours Operators, *below*) can arrange vacations for travelers with disabilities.

Developmental Disabilities Contact the nonprofit **New Directions** (5276 Hollister Ave., Suite 207, Santa Barbara, CA 93111, tel. 805/967–2841).

Mobility Impairments A number of operators specialize in working with travelers with mobility impairments: **Accessible Journeys** (35 W. Sellers Ave., Ridley Park, PA 19078, tel. 610/521–0339 or 800/846–4537, fax 610/521–6959), a registered nursing service that arranges vacations; **Flying Wheels Travel** (143 W. Bridge St., Box 382, Owatonna, MN 55060, tel. 507/451–5005 or 800/535–6790), a travel agency that specializes in European cruises and tours; **Hinsdale Travel Service** (201 E. Ogden Ave., Suite 100, Hinsdale, IL 60521, tel. 708/325–1335 or 800/303–5521), a travel agency that will give you access to the services of wheelchair traveler Janice Perkins; **Nautilus Tours** (5435 Donna Ave., Tarzana, CA 91356, tel. 818/344–3640 or 800/345–4654); and **Wheelchair Journeys** (16979 Redmond Way, Redmond, WA 98052, tel. 206/885–2210), which can handle arrangements worldwide.

Discounts

Options include **Entertainment Travel Editions** (Box 1068, Trumbull, CT 06611, tel. 800/445–4137; fee $28–$53, depending on destination); **Great American Traveler** (Box 27965, Salt Lake City, UT 84127, tel. 800/548–2812; $49.95 annually); **Moment's Notice Discount Travel Club** (163 Amsterdam Ave., Suite 137, New York, NY 10023, tel. 212/486–0500; $25 annually, single or family); **Privilege Card** (3391 Peachtree Rd. NE, Suite 110, Atlanta GA 30326, tel. 404/262–0222 or 800/236-9732; $74.95 annually); **Travelers Advantage** (CUC Travel Service, 49 Music Sq. W, Nashville, TN 37203, tel. 800/548–1116 or 800/648–4037; $49 annually, single or family); and **Worldwide Discount Travel Club** (1674 Meridian Ave., Miami Beach, FL 33139, tel. 305/534–2082; $50 annually for family, $40 single).

The ***Entertainment Europe Book*** (Entertainment Publications, 2125 Butterfield Rd., Troy, MI 48084, tel. 800/477–3234; $63 plus postage and handling) includes a directory of some 750 hotels in 38 countries. You can receive discounts of up to 50% at these hotels, but you may be able to get some of these on your own. Bear in mind that many establishments offer only a limited number of rooms at discount prices, and for limited times of year.

Driving

Auto Clubs In the United Kingdom, the **Automobile Association** (Box 128, FREEPOST, Basingstoke, Hampshire RG21 1BR; tel. 0345/555577) and the **Royal Automobile Club** (RAC Travel Services, Box 499, Croydon CR2 6ZH, tel. 0800/550–550) operate on-the-spot breakdown and repair services across Europe. Replacement cars can be provided in case of accidents. U.S. citizens cannot use these services on the Continent.

Electricity

Send a SASE to the **Franzus Company** (Customer Service, Dept. B50, Murtha Industrial Park, Box 142, Beacon Falls, CT 06403, tel. 203/723–6664) for a copy of the free brochure "Foreign Electricity Is No Deep Dark Secret."

Ferry Travel

Ferry service from the United Kingdom to many European countries is provided by: **Brittany Ferries** (Millbay Docks, Plymouth PL1 3EW, tel. 01705/827701; to France and Spain); **Color Line** (International Ferry Terminal, Royal Quays, North Shields NE29 6EE, tel. 01912/961313; to Norway); **Eurolink Ferries** (Ferry Terminal, Sheerness, Kent ME12 1RX, tel. 01233/617575; to Germany and Holland); **Hoverspeed** (International Hoverport, Marine Parade, Dover, Kent CT17 9TG, tel. 01304/240241; to France); **Irish Ferries** (150 New Bond St., London W1Y 0AQ, tel. 0171/491–8682; to Ireland); **North Sea Ferries** (King George Dock, Hedon Rd., Hull HU9 5QA, tel. 01482/795141; to Holland); **P&O European Ferries** (Channel House, Channel View Rd., Dover, Kent CT17 9TJ, tel. 01304/203388 or 0181/575–8555 in London; to France, Spain, and Northern Ireland); **Sally Line** (Argyle Centre, York St., Ramsgate CT11 9DS, tel. 01843/595522; to Belgium and France); **Scandinavian Seaways** (Scandinavia House, Parkeston Quay, Harwich, Essex CO12 4QG, tel. 01255/240240; to Denmark, Germany, and Sweden); **Sealink** (Charter House, Park St., Ashford, Kent TN24 8EX, tel. 01233/647047; to France, Germany, Holland, and Ireland); and **Swansea Cork Ferries** (Kings Dock, Swansea SA1 8RU, tel. 01792/456116; to Ireland).

Gay and Lesbian Travel

Organization The **International Gay Travel Association** (Box 4974, Key West, FL 33041, tel. 800/448–8550), a consortium of 800 businesses, can supply names of travel agents and tour operators.

Publications The premiere international travel magazine for gays and lesbians is *Our World* (1104 N. Nova Rd., Suite 251, Daytona Beach, FL 32117, tel. 904/441–5367; $35 for 10 issues). The 16-page monthly **"Out & About"** (tel. 212/645–6922 or 800/929–2268; $49 for 10 issues), covers gay-friendly resorts, hotels, cruise lines, and airlines.

Tour Operators Cruises and resort vacations are handled by **RSVP Travel Productions** (2800 University Ave. SE, Minneapolis, MN 55414, tel. 800/328–7787) for gays, **Olivia** (4400 Market St., Oakland, CA 94608, tel. 800/631–6277) for lesbian travelers. For mixed gay and lesbian travel, contact **Hanns Ebensten Travel** (513 Fleming St., Key West, FL

33040, tel. 305/294–8174), one of the nation's oldest operators in the gay market, and **Toto Tours** (1326 W. Albion Suite 3W, Chicago, IL 60626, tel. 312/274–8686 or 800/565–1241), which has group tours worldwide.

Travel Agencies The largest agencies serving gay travelers are **Advance Travel** (10700 Northwest Freeway, Suite 160, Houston, TX 77092, tel. 713/682–2002 or 800/695–0880); **Islanders/Kennedy Travel** (183 W. 10th St., New York, NY 10014, tel. 212/242–3222 or 800/988–1181); **Now Voyager** (4406 18th St., San Francisco, CA 94114, tel. 415/626–1169 or 800/255–6951); and **Yellowbrick Road** (1500 W. Balmoral Ave., Chicago, IL 60640, tel. 312/561–1800 or 800/642–2488). **Skylink Women's Travel** (746 Ashland Ave., Santa Monica, CA 90405, tel. 310/452–0506 or 800/225-5759) works with lesbians.

Health Issues

Finding a Doctor For members, the **International Association for Medical Assistance to Travellers** (IAMAT, 417 Center St., Lewiston, NY 14092, tel. 716/754–4883; 40 Regal Rd., Guelph, Ontario, Canada N1K 1B5, tel. 519/836–0102; 1287 St. Clair Ave., Toronto, Ontario, Canada M6E 1B8, tel. 416/652–0137; 57 Voirets, 1212 Grand-Lancy, Geneva, Switzerland; membership free) publishes a worldwide directory of English-speaking physicians who meet IAMAT standards.

Medical-Assistance Companies Contact **International SOS Assistance** (Box 11568, Philadelphia, PA 19116, tel. 215/244–1500 or 800/523–8930; Box 466, Pl. Bonaventure, Montréal, Québec, Canada H5A 1C1, tel. 514/874–7674 or 800/363–0263); **Medex Assistance Corporation** (Box 10623, Baltimore, MD 21285, tel. 410/296–2530 or 800/573-2029); **Near Services** (Box 1339, Calumet City, IL 60409, tel. 708/868–6700 or 800/654–6700); and **Travel Assistance International** (1133 15th St. NW, Suite 400, Washington, DC 20005, tel. 202/331–1609 or 800/821–2828). Because these companies also sell death-and-dismemberment, trip-cancellation, and other insurance coverage, there is some overlap with the travel-insurance policies sold by the companies listed under Insurance, *below.*

Warnings The **National Centers for Disease Control** (Center for Preventive Services, Division of Quarantine, Traveler's Health Section, 1600 Clifton Rd., MSE03, Atlanta, GA 30333, automated hot line 404/332–4559) provides information on health risks abroad and vaccination requirements and recommendations.

Insurance

Travel insurance covering baggage, health, and trip cancellation or interruptions is available from **Access America** (Box 90315, Richmond, VA 23286, tel. 804/285–3300 or 800/284–8300); **Carefree Travel Insurance** (Box 9366, 100 Garden City Plaza, Garden City, NY 11530, tel. 516/294–0220 or 800/323–3149); **Near Services** (Box 1339, Calumet City, IL 60409, tel. 708/868–6700 or 800/654–6700); **Tele-Trip** (Mutual of Omaha Plaza, Box 31716, Omaha, NE 68131, tel. 800/228–9792); **Travel Insured International** (Box 280568, East Hartford, CT 06128, tel. 203/528–7663 or 800/243–3174); **Travel Guard International** (1145 Clark St., Stevens Point, WI 54481, tel. 715/345–0505 or 800/826–1300); and **Wallach & Company** (107 W. Federal St., Box 480, Middleburg, VA 22117, tel. 703/687–3166 or 800/237–6615).

In the U.K. The **Association of British Insurers** (51 Gresham St., London EC2V 7HQ, tel. 0171/600–3333; 30 Gordon St., Glasgow G1 3PU, tel. 0141/226–3905; Scottish Provident Building, Donegall Sq. W, Belfast BT1 6JE, tel. 01232/249176; call for other locations) gives advice by phone and publishes the free **"Holiday Insurance,"** which sets out typical policy provisions and costs.

Lodging

Apartment and Villa Rental Among the companies to contact are **At Home Abroad** (405 E. 56th St., Suite 6H, New York, NY 10022, tel. 212/421–9165); **Europa-Let** (92 N. Main St., Ashland, OR 97520, tel. 503/482–5806 or 800/462–4486); **Hometours International** (Box 11503, Knoxville, TN 37939, tel. 615/588–8722 or 800/367–4668); **Interhome** (124 Little Falls Rd., Fairfield, NJ 07004, tel. 201/882–6864); **Property Rentals International** (1008 Mansfield Crossing Rd., Richmond, VA 23236, tel. 804/378–6054 or 800/220–3332); **Rental Directories International** (2044 Rittenhouse Sq., Philadelphia, PA 19103, tel. 215/985–4001); **Rent-a-Home International** (7200 34th Ave. NW, Seattle, WA 98117, tel. 206/789–9377 or 800/488–7368); **Vacation Home Rentals Worldwide** (235 Kensington Ave., Norwood, NJ 07648, tel. 201/767–9393 or 800/633–3284); **Villas and Apartments Abroad** (420 Madison Ave., Suite 1105, New York, NY 10017, tel. 212/759–1025 or 800/433–3020); and **Villas International** (605 Market St., Suite 510, San Francisco, CA 94105, tel. 415/281–0910 or 800/221–2260). Members of the travel club **Hideaways International** (767 Islington St., Portsmouth, NH 03801, tel. 603/430–4433 or 800/843–4433; $99 annually) receive two annual guides plus quarterly newsletters, and arrange rentals among themselves.

Home Exchange Principal clearinghouses include **HomeLink International/Vacation Exchange Club** (Box 650, Key West, FL 33041, tel. 305/294–1448 or 800/638–3841; $60 annually), which gives members four annual directories, with a listing in one, plus updates; **Intervac International** (Box 590504, San Francisco, CA 94159, tel. 415/435–3497; $65 annually), which has three annual directories; and **Loan-a-Home** (2 Park La., Apt. 6E, Mount Vernon, NY 10552, tel. 914/664–7640; $35–$45 annually), which specializes in long-term exchanges.

Hotel Brokers For lodging in major cities, you can check prices with a hotel broker, who is assigned to sell a block of rooms at selected hotels. Two are **Hotels Plus** (2205 Thames Dr., Conyers, GA 30208, tel. 770/929–1102 or 800/235–0909) and **Travel Bound** (599 Broadway, 12th Floor, New York, NY 10012, tel. 212/334–1358 or 800/456–8656).

Reservations Services Moderately priced hotels can be found in unexpected sources. The prestigious **Steigenberger Reservation Service** (in the United States and Canada, tel. 800/233–5652; in Great Britain, tel. 0171/486–5754 or 0800/289392), best known for booking luxury hotels worldwide, now represents less expensive properties with a touch of character.

Money Matters

ATMs For foreign **Cirrus** locations, call 800/424–7787; for foreign **Plus** locations, consult the Plus directory at your local bank.

Currency Exchange If your bank doesn't exchange currency, contact **Thomas Cook Currency Services** (41 E. 42nd St., New York, NY 10017 or 511 Madison Ave., New York, NY 10022, tel. 212/757–6915 or 800/223–7373 for locations) or **Ruesch International** (tel. 800/424–2923 for locations).

Wiring Funds Funds can be wired via **American Express MoneyGram**^{SM} (tel. 800/926–9400 from the United States and Canada for locations and information) or **Western Union** (tel. 800/325–6000 for agent locations or to send using MasterCard or Visa, 800/321–2923 in Canada).

Passports and Visas

U.S. Citizens For fees, documentation requirements, and other information, call the **Office of Passport Services** information line (tel. 202/647–0518).

Canadians For fees, documentation requirements, and other information, call the Ministry of Foreign Affairs and International Trade's **Passport Office** (tel. 819/994–3500 or 800/567–6868).

U.K. Citizens For information on fees and documentation requirements or to get an emergency passport call the **London passport office** (tel. 0171/ 271–3000).

Photo Help

The **Kodak Information Center** (tel. 800/242–2424) answers consumer questions about film and photography. The *Kodak Guide to Shooting Great Travel Pictures* explains techniques for getting the best shots (Fodor's Travel Publications, tel. 800/533–6478; $16.50).

Rail Travel

Discount Passes An excellent value if you plan to rack up the miles, **EurailPasses** provide unlimited first-class rail travel during their period of validity in Austria, Belgium, Denmark, Finland, France, Germany, Greece, Hungary, the Irish Republic, Italy, Luxembourg, the Netherlands, Norway, Portugal, Spain, Sweden, and Switzerland (but not England, Scotland, Northern Ireland, and Wales). Standard passes are available for 15 days ($498), 21 days ($648), one month ($728), two months ($1,098), and three months ($1,398). **Eurail Saverpasses** valid for 15 days cost $430 per person, for 21 days $550, for one month $678 per person; you must do all your traveling with at least one companion (two companions from April through September). **Eurail Youthpasses,** which cover second-class travel, cost $578 for one month, $768 for two months; you must be under 26 on the first day you travel. **Eurail Flexipasses** allow you to travel first class for 5 ($348), 10 ($560), or 15 ($740) days within any two-month period. **Eurail Youth Flexipasses,** available to those under 26 on their first travel day, allow you to travel second class for 5 ($255), 10 ($398), or 15 ($540) days within any two-month period. Another option is the **Europass,** featuring a minimum of 5 and a maximum of 15 days (within a two-month period) of unlimited rail travel in your choice of three to all five of the participating countries (France, Germany, Italy, Spain, and Switzerland); the cost for five days is $280 first class, $198 second class (three countries); for 8 days, $394 first class, $284 second class (four countries), and for 11 days, $508 first class, $366 second class (all five countries). Each extra rail day costs $38 for first class and $28 for second class. With Europass, if two people travel together first-class, the second receives a half-price pass. The second-class **Youth Europass,** for travelers under 26, covers four countries for the price of three countries for 5–10 days' travel; a fifth country is free with 11–15 days' travel within a two-month period. Europass and Europass Youth purchasers can also receive discounts on Eurostar, the Channel Tunnel train. Apply through your travel agent or **Rail Europe** (226–230 Westchester Ave., White Plains, NY 10604, tel. 800/438–7245 or 800/848–7245 or 2087 Dundas E, Suite 105, Mississauga, Ontario, Canada L4X 1M2, tel. 416/602–4195); **DER Tours** (Box 1606, Des Plaines, IL 60017, tel. 800/782–2424, fax 800/282–7474); or **CIT Tours Corp.** (342 Madison Ave., Suite 207, New York, NY 10173, tel. 212/697–2100 or 800/248–8687; 310/670–4269 or 800/248–7245 in western United States).

Rail Europe also sells single-country passes for Austria, Bulgaria, the Czech Republic, Finland, France, Germany, Greece, Hungary, Norway, Poland, Portugal, Romania, Russia, Spain, and Switzerland, as well as multicountry passes that cover Britain and France jointly, all of Scandinavia, and the Benelux nations. Typically these are flexipasses, valid for 5, 10, 15, or other specified number of days, within a longer time period; rail-and-drive schemes are also available.

Travelers under 26 who have resided in Europe for at least six months qualify for the **Inter Rail Card.** There are 15-day and one-month cards that allow for unlimited travel in 24 countries for £180 and £260, respectively, as well as half-price travel within the United Kingdom and discounts of up to 50% on some ferry services to and from the United Kingdom. All cards are available from rail stations.

If you plan to do a lot of rail traveling in Great Britain, look into the many **BritRail Passes** offered by **BritRail Travel International** (1500 Broadway, New York, NY 10036, tel. 212/575–2667 or 800/677–8585 or 94 Cumberland St., Toronto, Ontario, Canada M5R 1A3, tel. 416/482–1777).

Senior Citizens

Educational Travel
The nonprofit **Elderhostel** (75 Federal St., 3rd Floor, Boston, MA 02110, tel. 617/426–7788), for people 60 and older, has offered inexpensive study programs since 1975. The nearly 2,000 courses cover everything from marine science to Greek myths and cowboy poetry. Fees for two- to three-week international trips—including room, board, and transportation from the United States—range from $1,800 to $4,500.

For people 50 and over and their children and grandchildren, **Interhostel** (University of New Hampshire, 6 Garrison Ave., Durham, NH 03824, tel. 603/862–1147 or 800/733–9753) runs 10-day summer programs involving lectures, field trips, and sightseeing. Most last two weeks and cost $2,125–$3,100, including airfare.

Organizations
Contact the **American Association of Retired Persons** (AARP, 601 E St. NW, Washington, DC 20049, tel. 202/434–2277; $8 per person or couple annually). Its Purchase Privilege Program gets members discounts on lodging, car rentals, and sightseeing.

For more information on lodging, car rental, and other travel-product discounts, along with magazines and newsletters, contact the **National Council of Senior Citizens** (1331 F St. NW, Washington, DC 20004, tel. 202/347–8800; membership $12 annually) and *Mature Outlook* (6001 N. Clark St., Chicago, IL 60660, tel. 312/465–6466 or 800/336–6330; subscription $9.95 annually).

Publications
The 50+ Traveler's Guidebook: Where to Go, Where to Stay, What to Do, by Anita Williams and Merrimac Dillon (St. Martin's Press, 175 5th Ave., New York, NY 10010, tel. 212/674–5151 or 800/288–2131; $12.95), offers many useful tips. "The Mature Traveler" (Box 50400, Reno, NV 89513; $29.95, tel. 702/786–7419), a monthly newsletter, covers travel deals.

Students

Groups
Major tour operators include **Contiki Holidays** (300 Plaza Alicante, Suite 900, Garden Grove, CA 92640, tel. 714/740–0808 or 800/466–0610) and **AESU Travel** (2 Hamill Rd., Suite 248, Baltimore, MD 21210, tel. 410/323–4416 or 800/638–7640).

Hosteling
Contact **Hostelling International–American Youth Hostels** (733 15th St. NW, Suite 840, Washington, DC 20005, tel. 202/783–6161) in the United States; **Hostelling International–Canada** (205 Catherine St., Suite 400, Ottawa, Ontario K2P 1C3, tel. 613/237–7884) in Canada; and the **Youth Hostel Association of England and Wales** (Trevelyan House, 8 St. Stephen's Hill, St. Albans, Hertfordshire AL1 2DY, tel. 01727/855215 and 01727/845047) in the United Kingdom. Membership ($25 in the United States, C$26.75 in Canada, and £9 in the United Kingdom) gets you access to 5,000 hostels worldwide that charge $7–$20 nightly per person.

ID Cards
For discounts on transportation and admissions, get the **International Student Identity Card** (ISIC) if you're a bona fide student or the **International Youth Card** (IYC) if you're under 26. In the United States, the ISIC and IYC cards cost $16 each and include basic travel

accident and illness coverage, plus a toll-free travel hot line. Apply through the Council on International Educational Exchange (*see* Organizations, *below*). Cards are available for $15 each in Canada from **Travel Cuts** (187 College St., Toronto, Ontario M5T 1P7, tel. 416/979–2406 or 800/667–2887) and in the United Kingdom for £5 each at student unions and student travel companies.

Organizations   A major contact is the **Council on International Educational Exchange** (CIEE, 205 E. 42nd St., 16th Floor, New York, NY 10017, tel. 212/661–1450), with locations in Boston (729 Boylston St., Boston, MA 02116, tel. 617/266–1926); Miami (9100 S. Dadeland Blvd., Miami, FL 33156, tel. 305/670–9261); Los Angeles (1093 Broxton Ave., Los Angeles, CA 90024, tel. 310/208–3551); 43 college towns nationwide; and the United Kingdom (28A Poland St., London W1V 3DB, tel. 0171/437–7767). Twice a year, it publishes *Student Travels* magazine. The CIEE's Council Travel Service is the exclusive U.S. agent for several student-discount cards.

Campus Connections (325 Chestnut St., Suite 1101, Philadelphia, PA 19106, tel. 215/625–8585 or 800/428–3235) specializes in discounted accommodations and airfares for students. The **Educational Travel Centre** (438 N. Frances St., Madison, WI 53703, tel. 608/256–5551) offers rail passes and low-cost airline tickets, mostly for flights departing from Chicago. For air travel only, contact **TMI Student Travel** (100 W. 33rd St., Suite 813, New York, NY 10001, tel. 800/245–3672).

In Canada, also contact **Travel Cuts** (*see* ID cards, *above*).

Publications   See the *Berkeley Guide to Europe* (Fodor's Travel Publications, tel. 800/533–6478 or from bookstores; $18.95).

Telephone Matters

For local access numbers abroad, contact **AT&T** USA Direct (tel. 800/874–4000), **MCI** Call USA (tel. 800/444–4444 or 800/444–4141 for automated hot line), or **Sprint** Express (tel. 800/793–1153).

Tour Operators

Group tours and independent vacation packages can be bargains depending on what they include (*see* Packages and Tours *in* Smart Travel Tips, *below*). Among the companies selling tours and packages to Europe, the following have a proven reputation, are nationally known, and have plenty of options to choose from.

Group Tours   For deluxe tours, try **Tauck Tours** (11 Wilton Rd., Westport CT 06881, tel. 203/226–6911 or 800/468–2825) or **Maupintour** (Box 807, Lawrence KS 66044, tel. 913/843–1211 or 800/255–4266). Another operator falling between deluxe and first-class is **Globus** (5301 S. Federal Circle, Littleton, CO 80123, tel. 303/797-2800 or 800/221–0090). For first-class and first-class superior programs, try **Caravan Tours** (401 N. Michigan Ave., Chicago, IL 60611, tel. 312/321–9800 or 800/227–2826); **Trafalgar Tours** (21 E. 26th St., New York, NY 10010, tel. 212/689–8977 or 800/854–0103); **Brendan Tours** (15137 Califa St., Van Nuys, CA 91411, tel. 818/785–9696 or 800/421–8446); and **Insight International** (745 Atlantic Ave., Boston, MA 0211, tel. 617/482-2000 or 800/582–8380). For budget and tourist-class programs, contact **Cosmos** (*see* Globus, *above*).

Single Travelers   Because tour prices are usually based on two sharing a room, you may be charged a single supplement if you're on your own. Several companies help match up companions; one of them is **Travel Companion Exchange** (Box 833, Amityville, NY 11701, tel. 516/454–0880).

Organizations   The **National Tour Association** (546 E. Main St., Lexington, KY 40508, tel. 606/226–4444 or 800/682–8886) and **United States Tour**

Operators Association (211 E. 51st St., Suite 12B, New York, NY 10022, tel. 212/750–7371) can provide lists of member operators and information on booking tours.

Packages Just about every airline that flies to Europe sells independent vacation packages that include round-trip airfare and hotel accommodations. Among U.S. carriers, contact **American Airlines Fly AAway Vacations** (tel. 800/321–2121), **Continental Airlines Grand Destinations** (tel. 800/634–5555), **Delta Dream Vacations** (tel. 800/872–7786), and **United Airlines Vacation Planning Center** (tel. 800/328–6877). Independent packages are also available from leading tour operators. Contact **CIE Tours** (108 Ridgedale Ave., Box 2355, Morristown, NJ 07962, tel. 201/292–3899 or 800/243–8687); **DER Tours** (11933 Wilshire Blvd., Los Angeles, CA 90025, tel. 310/479–4140 or 800/782–2424); and **Jet Vacations** (1775 Broadway, New York, NY 10019, tel. 212/474–8740 or 800/538–2762).

Publications Consult the brochures **"Worldwide Tour & Vacation Package Finder"** from the National Tour Association (*see* Organizations, *above*) and the Better Business Bureau's **"Tips on Travel Packages"** (Publication No. 24-195; 4200 Wilson Blvd., Arlington, VA 22203; $2).

Theme Trips Theme trips are, by their nature, more expensive than a general-interest tour or package, but they still may be a better deal than arranging everything on your own.

Travel Contacts (45 Idmiston Rd., London SE27 9HL, tel. 011/44–81766–7868, fax 011/44–81766–6123), which has 135 member operators, can satisfy just about any special interest in Europe.

Adventure From rafting on Turkey's Coruh River to climbing the Austrian Alps, adventure travel in Europe can mean hiking, walking, skiing, cycling—you name it. Contact **All Adventure Travel** (5589 Arapahoe, No. 208, Boulder, CO 80303, tel. 800/537–4025); **Mountain Travel-Sobek** (6420 Fairmount Ave., El Cerrito, CA 94530, tel. 510/527–8100 or 800/227–2384); **Wilderness Travel** (801 Allston Way, Berkeley, CA 94710, tel. 510/548–0420 or 800/368–2794); **Himalayan Travel** (112 Prospect St., Stamford, CT 06901, tel. 800/225–2380, fax 203/359–3669); or **Uniquely Europe** (2819 First Ave., No. 280, Seattle, WA 98121, tel. 206/441–8682 or 800/426–3610).

In the United Kingdom, **Top Deck Travel** (131–135 Earl's Court Rd., London SW5 9RH, tel. 0171/244–8641) offers tours to Europe, with activities including flotilla sailing and a variety of water sports, including rafting.

Art and Architecture For a variety of programs, contact **4th Dimension Tours** (1150 N.W. 72nd Ave., Suite 250, Miami, FL 33126, tel. 305/477–1525 or 800/343–0020); **Five Star Touring** (60 E. 42nd St., Suite 612, New York, NY 10165, tel. 212/818–9140 or 800/792–7827); **Esplanade Tours** (581 Boylston St., Boston, MA 02116, tel. 617/266–7465 or 800/628–4893); **Archeological Tours** (271 Madison Ave., New York, NY 10016, tel. 212/986–3054, fax 212/370–1561); and the **Smithsonian Institution's Study Tours and Seminars** (1100 Jefferson Dr. SW, Room 3045, Washington, DC 20560, tel. 202/357–4700).

In the United Kingdom, contact **Prospect Music & Art Tours Ltd.** (454–458 Chiswick High Rd., London W4 5TT, tel. 0181/995–2151) and **Swann Hellenic Treasures Tours** (77 New Oxford St., London WC1A 1PP, tel. 0171/800–2300).

Ballooning **European Bombard Balloon Adventures** (855 Donald Rd., Juno Beach, FL 33408, tel. 407/775–0039 or 800/862–8537) operates balloon holidays in France, Italy, Austria, Turkey, the Czech Republic, and Switzerland.

In the United Kingdom, **Air 2 Air** (Vauxhall House, Coronation Rd., Bristol BS3 1RN, tel. 0117/963–3333), a clearinghouse for balloon activities in Britain, has information about what's happening on the Continent.

Barge Travel For barge vacations in Europe, contact **Avalon Tours** (1909 Alden Landing, Portsmouth, RI 02871, tel. 401/683–1782 or 800/662–2628) and **Barge & Voyage** (140 E. 56th St., Suite 4C, New York, NY 10022, tel. 800/438–4748).

Bicycling Bike tours are available from **Backroads** (1516 5th St., Suite A550, Berkeley, CA 94710, tel. 510/527–1555 or 800/462–2848); **Euro-Bike** (Box 990-P, De Kalb, IL 60115, tel. 800/321–6060, fax 815/758–8851); and **Classic Adventures** (Box 153, Hamlin, NY 14464, tel. 800/777-8090, fax 716/964-7297).

Cruising **EuroCruises** (303 W. 13th St., New York, NY 10014, tel. 212/691–2099 or 800/688–3876) represents more than 20 European-based cruise lines and 60 ships, ranging from 32-passenger yachts to 2,500-passenger ocean liners.

Fishing **Fishing International** (Box 2132, Santa Rosa, CA 95405, tel. 800/950–4242, fax 707/539–1320) has trout and salmon fishing packages in Ireland, France, and Norway.

Folk Art **The Texas Connection** (207 Arden Grove, San Antonio, TX, tel. 210/980–9538) visits tapestry and embroidery workshops; leather and ceramic studios; and famous markets in Spain, Portugal, Morocco, Great Britain, Hungary, Romania, Greece, and Turkey.

History History buffs should contact **Herodot Travel** (7 S. Knoll Rd., Mill Valley, CA 94941, tel. and fax 415/381–4031).

Horseback Riding **FITS Equestrian** (685 Lateen Rd., Solvang, CA 93463, tel. 805/688–9494, fax 805/688–2943) has tours for every level of rider.

Horticulture Amateur and professional gardeners alike should contact **Expo Garden Tours** (145 4th Ave., Suite 4A, New York, NY 10003, tel. 212/677–6704 or 800/448–2685).

Motorcycle **Beach's Motorcycle Adventures** (2763 W. River Pkwy., Grand Island, NY 14072, tel. 716/773–4960, fax 716/773–5227) can take you on Alpine adventures through Germany, Austria, Italy, France, Switzerland, and Lichtenstein.

Music **Dailey-Thorp Travel** (330 W. 58th St., New York, NY 10019, tel. 212/307–1555; book through travel agents) specializes in classical music and opera programs throughout Europe; its packages include tickets that are otherwise very hard to get. Also try **Keith Prowse Tours** (234 W. 34th St., Suite 1000, New York, NY 10036, tel. 212/398–1430 or 800/669–8687).

In the United Kingdom, **Travel for the Arts** (117 Regent's Park Rd., London NW1 8UR, tel. 0171/483–2290) takes groups to visit the musical highlights of regions throughout Europe. **Prospect Music & Art Tours** (*see* Art and Architecture, *above*) has tours to many of the famous annual festivals—Savonlinna, Prague, Bregenz, and Munich among them.

Natural History **Questers Worldwide Nature Tours** (257 Park Ave. S, New York, NY 10010, tel. 800/468–8668) explores the wild side of Europe in the company of expert guides. **Earthwatch** (680 Mt. Auburn St., Watertown, MA 02272, tel. 617/926–8200) recruits volunteers to serve in its EarthCorps as short-term assistants to scientists or research expeditions.

In the United Kingdom, **Ramblers Holidays Ltd.** (Box 43, Welwyn Garden City, Hertfordshire AL8 6PQ, tel. 01707/331–133) arranges walking tours within Europe with guides who point out natural features of interest.

Singles and Young Adults Travelers 18–35 looking to join a group should try **Club Europa** (802 W. Oregon St., Urbana, IL 61801, tel. 217/344–5863 or 800/331–

1882) and **Contiki Holidays** (*see* Groups *in* Students, *above*). **Trafalgar Tours** (*see* Group Tours *in* Tour Operators, *above*) has a "Club 21" program of escorted bus tours through Europe and Great Britain for travelers ages 21 to 35.

Sports **Golf International** (275 Madison Ave., New York, NY 10016, tel. 212/986–9176 or 800/833–1389) has golf packages to the United Kingdom, Ireland, and France. For other participant and spectator sports, contact **Keith Prowse & Co.** (234 W. 44th St., Suite 100, New York, NY 10036, tel. 800/669–7469) or **Travel Concepts** (62 Commonwealth Ave., Suite 3, Boston, MA 02116, tel. 617/266–8450), which packages prestigious sporting events and can also enroll you in an English polo school or a Swedish tennis clinic.

In the United Kingdom, **Green Card Golf Holidays** (11a Queensdale Rd., London W11 4QF, tel. 0171/727–7287) arranges visits to greens and amateur tournaments suitable for every level of handicap throughout Western Europe. Companies offering Alpine skiing packages include **Top Deck Ski** (131 Earls Court Rd., SW5 9RH, tel. 0171/244–8641) and **Crystal Holidays** (Arlington Rd., Surbiton KT6 6BW, tel. 0181/399–5144), both with a wide range of resorts at competitive prices.

Walking For walking tours of England, France, and Italy, contact **Backroads** (*see* Bicycling, *above*).

Wine and Food For a culinary adventure, try **Annemarie Victory Organization** (136 E. 64th St., New York, NY 10021, tel. 212/486 0353, fax 212/751–3149) or **Travel Concepts** (*see* Sports, *above*). To attend a cooking school in England, France, or Italy, contact **Cuisine International** (7707 Willow Vine Ct., Suite 219, Dallas, TX 75230, tel. 214/373–1161, fax 214/373–1162) or **Endless Beginnings** (9825 Dowdy Dr., Suite 105, San Diego, CA 92126, tel. 619/566–4166 or 800/822–7855).

In the United Kingdom, **Alternative Travel Group, Ltd.** (69–71 Banbury Rd., Oxford OX2 6PE, tel. 01865/310–334) has wine-tasting tours of France in the region of Alsace, as well as other countries. They also stage orchid, truffle, and mushroom hunts in Italy, France, and Portugal.

Travel Agencies

For names of reputable agencies in your area, contact the **American Society of Travel Agents** (1101 King St., Suite 200, Alexandria, VA 22314, tel. 703/739–2782).

U.S. Government Travel Briefings

The U.S. Department of State's Overseas Citizens Emergency Center (Room 4811, Washington, DC 20520; enclose SASE) issues **Consular Information Sheets,** which cover crime, security, political climate, and health risks as well as embassy locations, entry requirements, currency regulations, and other routine matters. (Travel Warnings, which counsel travelers to avoid a country entirely, are issued in extreme cases.) For the latest information, stop in at any U.S. passport office, consulate, or embassy; call the interactive hot line (tel. 202/647–5225, fax 202/647-3000); or, with your PC's modem, tap into the Bureau of Consular Affairs' computer bulletin board (tel. 202/647–9225).

Visitor Information

Austrian National Tourist Office. In the United States: Telephone inquiries only, 500 5th Ave., Suite 2022, New York, NY 10110, tel. 212/944–6880, fax 212/730–4568; 11601 Wilshire Blvd., Suite 2480, Los Angeles, CA 90025, tel. 310/477–3332, fax 310/477–5141. In

Canada: 2 Bloor St. E, Suite 3330, Toronto, Ontario M4W 1A8, tel. 416/967–3381, fax 416/967–4101. In the United Kingdom: Telephone inquiries only, 30 St. George St., London W1R 0AL, tel. 0171/629–0461, fax 0171/499–6038.

Belgian National Tourist Office. In the United States and Canada: 780 3rd Ave., New York, NY 10017, tel. 212/758–8130, fax 212/355–7675. In the United Kingdom: 29 Princes St., London W1R 7RE, tel. 01891/887799 (per-minute charge), fax 0171/629–0454.

British Tourist Authority. In the United States: 551 5th Ave., Suite 701, New York, NY 10179, tel. 212/986–2200, fax 212/986–1188; 625 N. Michigan Ave., Suite 1510, Chicago, IL 60611, tel. 312/787–0490, fax 312/787–7746; World Trade Center, 350 S. Figueroa St., Suite 450, Los Angeles, CA 90071, tel. 213/628–3525, fax 213/687–6621; 2850 Cumberland Pkwy., Suite 470, Atlanta, GA 30339, tel. 404/432–9635, fax 404/432–9641. In Canada: 111 Avenue Rd., Suite 450, Toronto, Ontario M5R 3J8, tel. 416/925–6326. In the United Kingdom: Thames Tower, Black's Rd., Hammersmith, London W6 9EL, tel. 0181/846–9000.

Bulgarian National Tourist Office. In the United States and Canada: Balkan Holidays (authorized agent), 41 E. 42nd St., Suite 508, New York, NY 10017, tel. 212/573–5530, fax 212/573–5538. In the United Kingdom: For information, call Balkan Holidays, 19 Conduit St., London W1R 9TD, tel. 0171/491–4499.

Czech Travel Bureau and Tourist Office (Čedok). In the United States and Canada: 10 E. 40th St., New York, NY 10016, tel. 212/689–9720. In the United Kingdom: 49 Southwark St., London SE1 1RU, tel. 0171/378–6009, fax 0171/403–2321; the Czech Center, 30 Kensington Palace Gardens, London W8 4QY, tel. 0171/243–7981, fax 0171/727–9589.

Danish Tourist Board. In the United States: 655 3rd Ave., New York, NY 10017, tel. 212/949–2333, fax 212/983–5260. In Canada: c/o Helen Bergstrom, Box 636, Streetsville, Mississauga, Ontario, L5M 2C2, tel. 519/576–6213, fax 519/576–7115. In the United Kingdom: 55 Sloane St., London SW1X 9SY, tel. 0171/259–5959, fax 0171/259–5955.

Finnish Tourist Board. In the United States and Canada: 655 3rd Ave., New York, NY 10017, tel. 212/949–2333, fax 212/983–5260; 1900 Ave. of the Stars, Suite 1070, Los Angeles, CA 90067, tel. 310/277–5226. In the United Kingdom: 30–35 Pall Mall, London SW1Y 5LP, tel. 0171/839–4048, fax 0171/321–0696.

French Government Tourist Office. In the United States: Nationwide, tel. 900/990–0040 (costs 50¢ per minute); 444 Madison Ave., 16th Floor, New York, NY 10022, tel. 212/838–7800, fax 212/247–6468; 645 N. Michigan Ave., Chicago, IL 60611, tel. 312/337–6301, fax 312/337–6339; 2305 Cedar Springs Rd., Dallas, TX 75201, tel. 214/720–4010, fax 214/720–0250; 9454 Wilshire Blvd., Beverly Hills, CA 90212, tel. 310/271–2358, fax 310/276–2835. In Canada: 1981 McGill College Ave., Suite 490, Montréal, Québec H3A 2W9, tel. 514/288–4264, fax 514/845–4868; 30 St. Patrick St., Suite 700, Toronto, Ontario M5T 3A3, tel. 416/593–4723, fax 416/979–7587. In the United Kingdom: 178 Piccadilly, London W1V OAL, tel. 01891/244123 (per-minute charge).

German National Tourist Office. In the United States: 122 E. 42nd St., New York, NY 10168, tel. 212/661–7200, fax 212/661–7174; 11766 Wilshire Blvd., Suite 750, Los Angeles, CA 90025, tel. 310/575–9799, fax 310/575–1565. In Canada: 175 Bloor St. E, Suite 604, Toronto, Ontario M4W 3R8, tel. 416/968–1570. In the United Kingdom: Nightingale House, 65 Curzon St., London W1Y 7PE, tel. 01891/600100 (per-minute charge).

Gibraltar Government Tourist Office. In the United States and Canada: 1155 15th St. NW, Room 710, Washington, DC 20005, tel. 202/452–1108, fax 202/872–8543. In the United Kingdom: Arundel Great Court, 179 The Strand, London WC2R 1EH, tel. 0171/836–0777.

Greek National Tourist Organization. In the United States: 645 5th Ave., New York, NY 10022, tel. 212/421–5777, fax 212/826–6940; 611 W. 6th St., Suite 2198, Los Angeles, CA 90017, tel. 213/626–6696, fax 213/489–9744; 168 N. Michigan Ave., Suite 600, Chicago, IL 60601, tel. 312/782–1084, fax 312/782–1091. In Canada: 1233 Rue de la Montagne, Suite 101, Montréal, Québec H3G 1Z2, tel. 514/871–1535, fax 514/871–1498; 1300 Bay St., Toronto, Ontario M5R 3K8, tel. 416/968–2220, fax 416/968–6533. In the United Kingdom: 4 Conduit St., London W1R 0DJ, tel. 0171/734–5997.

Hungarian National Tourist Office (IBUSZ). In the United States and Canada: 150 E. 58th St., New York, NY 10155, tel. 212/586–5230. In the United Kingdom: Box 4336, London SW18 4XE, tel. 01891/171200 (per-minute charge), fax 01891/669970.

Irish Tourist Board. In the United States: 345 Park Ave., New York, NY 10154, tel. 212/418–0800 or 800/223–6470, fax 212/371–9052. In Canada: 160 Bloor St. E, Suite 1150, Toronto, Ontario M4W 1B9, tel. 416/929–2777, fax 416/929–6783. In the United Kingdom: Ireland House, 150 New Bond St., London W1Y 0AQ, tel. 0171/493–3201, fax 0171/493–9065.

Italian Government Travel Office (ENIT). In the United States: 630 5th Ave., Suite 1565, New York, NY 10111, tel. 212/245–4822, fax 212/586–9249; 12400 Wilshire Blvd., Suite 550, Los Angeles, CA 90025, tel. 310/820–0098, fax 310/820–6357. In Canada: 1 Pl. Ville Marie, Suite 1914, Montréal, Québec H3B 3M9, tel. 514/866–7667. In the United Kingdom: 1 Princes St., London W1R 8AY, tel. 0171/408–1254.

Luxembourg Tourist Information Office. In the United States and Canada: 17 Beekman Pl., New York, NY 10022, tel. 212/935–8888, fax 212/935–5896. In the United Kingdom: 122 Regent St., London W1R 5FE, tel. 0171/434–2800.

Malta National Tourist Office. In the United States and Canada: 350 5th Ave., Suite 4412, New York, NY 10118, tel. 212/695–9520, fax 212/695–8229. In the United Kingdom: Mappin House, Suite 300, 4 Winsley St., London W1N 7AR, tel. 0171/323–0506.

Monaco Government Tourist and Convention Bureau. In the United States and Canada: 845 3rd Ave., New York, NY 10022, tel. 212/759–5227, fax 212/754–9320. In the United Kingdom: 3–18 Chelsea Garden Market, Chelsea Harbour, London SW10 0XE, tel. 0171/352–9962.

Netherlands Board of Tourism. In the United States: 225 N. Michigan Ave., Suite 326, Chicago, IL 60601, tel. 312/819–0300, fax 312/819–1740. In Canada: 25 Adelaide St. E, Suite 710, Toronto, Ontario M5C 1Y2, tel. 416/363–1577, fax 416/363–1470. In the United Kingdom: 25–28 Buckingham Gate, London SW1E 6LD, tel. 01891/200277 (per-minute charge).

Norwegian Tourist Board. In the United States and Canada: 655 3rd Ave., New York, NY 10017, tel. 212/949–2333, fax 212/983–5260. In the United Kingdom: Charles House, 5–11 Lower Regent St., London SW1Y 4LR, tel. 0171/839–6255.

Polish National Tourist Office. In the United States and Canada: 275 Madison Ave., Suite 1711, New York, NY 10016, tel. 212/338–9412, fax 212/338–9283. In the United Kingdom: 82 Mortimer St., London W1N 8HN, tel. 0171/580–8028, fax 0171/436–6558.

Portuguese National Tourist Office. In the United States: 590 5th Ave., 4th Floor, New York, NY 10036, tel. 212/354–4403, fax 212/764–6137. In Canada: 60 Bloor St. W, Suite 1005, Toronto, Ontario M4W 3BS, tel. 416/921–7376, fax 416/921–1353. In the United Kingdom: 22–25A Sackville St., London W1X 1DE, tel. 0171/494–1441.

Romanian National Tourist Office. In the United States and Canada: 342 Madison Ave., Suite 210, New York, NY 10173, tel. 212/697–6971, fax 212/697–6972. In the United Kingdom: 83A Marylebone High St., London W1M 3DE, tel. 0171/224–3692.

Slovakia. In the United States and Canada: Viktor Corporation, 10 E. 40th St., Suite 3601, New York, NY 10016, tel. 212/213–3862, fax 212/213–4461. In the United Kingdom: Embassy of the Slovak Republic, Information Dept., 25 Kensington Palace Gardens, London W8 4QY, tel. 0171/243–0803, fax 0171/727–5821.

Spanish National Tourist Office. In the United States: 665 5th Ave., New York, NY 10022, tel. 212/759–8822, fax 212/980–1053; 845 N. Michigan Ave., Chicago, IL 60611, tel. 312/642–1992, fax 312/642–9817; San Vicente Plaza Bldg., 8383 Wilshire Blvd., Suite 960, Beverly Hills, CA 90211, tel. 213/658–7188, fax 213/658–1061; 1221 Brickell Ave., Suite 1850, Miami, FL 33131, tel. 305/358–1992, fax 305/358–8223. In Canada: 102 Bloor St. W, Suite 1400, Toronto, Ontario M5S 1M8, tel. 416/961–3131, fax 416/961–1992. In the United Kingdom: 57–58 St. James's St., London SW1A 1LD, tel. 0171/499–0901, fax 0171/629–4257.

Swedish Travel and Tourism Council. In the United States and Canada: 655 3rd Ave., 18th Floor, New York, NY 10017, tel. 212/949–2333, fax 212/983–5260. In the United Kingdom: 73 Welbeck St., London W1M 8AN, tel. 0171/935–9784, fax 0171/935–5853.

Swiss National Tourist Office. In the United States: 608 5th Ave., New York, NY 10020, tel. 212/757–5944, fax 212/262–6116; 222 N. Sepulveda Blvd., Suite 1570, El Segundo, CA 90245, tel. 310/335–5980, fax 310/335–5982; 150 N. Michigan Ave., Suite 2930, Chicago, IL 60601, tel. 312/630–5840, fax 312/630–5848. In Canada: 154 University Ave., Suite 610, Toronto, Ontario M5H 3Y9, tel. 416/971–9734. In the United Kingdom: Swiss Centre, 1 New Coventry St., London W1V 8EE, tel. 0171/734–1921.

Turkish Tourist Office. In the United States and Canada: 821 UN Plaza, New York, NY 10017, tel. 212/687–2194, fax 212/599–7568; 1717 Massachusetts Ave. NW, Suite 306, Washington, DC 20036, tel. 202/429–9844, fax 202/429–5649. In Canada: c/o Turkish Embassy, 197 Wurtemburg St., Ottawa, Ontario K1N 8L9, tel. 613/789–4044. In the United Kingdom: 170–173 Piccadilly, 1st Floor, London W1V 9DD, tel. 0171/734–8681.

Weather

For current conditions and forecasts, plus the local time and helpful travel tips, call the **Weather Channel Connection** (tel. 900/932–8437; 95¢ per minute) from a Touch-Tone phone.

Smart Travel Tips

The more you travel, the more you know about how to make trips run like clockwork. To help make your travels hassle-free, Fodor's editors have rounded up dozens of tips from our contributors and travel experts all over the world, as well as basic information on visiting Europe. For names of organizations to contact and publications that can give you more information, *see* Important Contacts, *above*.

Air Travel

If time is an issue, **always look for nonstop flights,** which require no change of plane and make no stops. If possible, **avoid connecting flights,** which stop at least once and can involve a change of plane, although the flight number remains the same; if the first leg is late, the second waits.

Aloft
Airline Food

If you hate airline food, **ask for special meals when booking.** These can be vegetarian, low cholesterol, or kosher, for example; commonly prepared to order in smaller quantities than standard catered fare, they can be tastier.

Jet Lag

To avoid this syndrome, which occurs when travel disrupts your body's natural cycles, try to maintain a normal routine. At night, **get some sleep.** By day, move about the cabin to **stretch your legs, eat light meals, and drink water—not alcohol.**

Smoking

Smoking is banned on all flights within the United States of less than six hours' duration and on all Canadian flights; the ban also applies to domestic segments of international flights aboard U.S. and foreign carriers. Delta has banned smoking system-wide. On U.S. carriers flying to Europe and other destinations abroad, a seat in a no-smoking section must be provided for every passenger who requests one, and the section must be enlarged to accommodate such passengers if necessary as long as they have complied with the airline's deadline for check-in and seat assignment. If smoking bothers you, request a seat far from the smoking section.

Foreign airlines are exempt from these rules but do provide no-smoking sections. British Airways has banned smoking, as has Virgin Atlantic, on most international flights; some nations have banned smoking on all domestic flights, and others may ban smoking on some international flights. Talks continue on the feasibility of broadening no-smoking policies.

Cutting Costs

The Sunday travel section of most newspapers is a good source of deals. *See* also Travel Passes, *below.* Major airlines might be advertising special deals; the newer, lower-overhead airlines often run cheap rates; and you might learn about a charter flight that's going where you want when you want.

Charter Flights

Charters usually have the lowest fares and the most restrictions. Departures are limited and seldom on time, and you can lose all or most of your money if you cancel. (The closer to departure you cancel, the more you lose, although sometimes you will be charged only a small fee if you supply a substitute passenger.) The flight may be canceled for any reason up to 10 days before departure (after that, only if it is physically impossible to operate). The charterer may also revise the itinerary or increase the price after you have bought the ticket, but only if the new arrangement constitutes a "major change" do you have the right to a refund. Before buying a charter ticket, **read the fine print** about the company's refund policies. Money for charter flights is usually paid into a bank escrow account, the name of which should be on the contract, and if you don't pay by credit card, **make your check payable to the carrier's escrow account** (unless you're dealing with a travel agent, in which case, his or her check should be payable to the escrow account). The U.S. Department of Transportation's Office of Consumer Affairs has jurisdiction.

Charter operators may offer flights alone or with ground arrangements that constitute a charter package. You typically must book charters through your travel agent.

Consolidators

Consolidators, who buy tickets at reduced rates from scheduled airlines, sell them at prices below the lowest available from the airlines directly—usually without advance restrictions. Sometimes you can even get your money back if you need to return the ticket. Carefully read the fine print detailing penalties for changes and cancellations. If you doubt the reliability of a consolidator, **confirm your reservation with the airline.**

Major Airlines   The least-expensive airfares from the major airlines are priced for round-trip travel and are subject to restrictions. You must usually **book in advance and buy the ticket within 24 hours** to get cheaper fares, and you may have to **stay over a Saturday night.** The lowest fare is subject to availability, and only a small percentage of the plane's total seats are sold at that price. It's good to **call a number of airlines**—and **when you are quoted a good price, book it on the spot**— the same fare on the same flight may not be available the next day. Airlines generally allow you to change your return date for a $25 to $50 fee, but most low-fare tickets are nonrefundable. However, if you don't use your ticket, you can apply the cost toward the purchase price of a new one, again for a small charge.

Try to **arrange your flights to match the best airfares.** If you plan to visit both London and Paris, for example, you'll find that it's generally cheaper to fly to London first. Airline prices swing up and down with the seasons, too. June through mid-September is the most expensive time to travel to Europe, so **consider travel during the shoulder seasons** of spring (April and May) and fall (mid-September and October). In winter, flights may be cheaper, except to ski resorts. Airfares are usually higher on weekends, so **fly midweek.**

Travel Passes   You can **save on air travel** within Europe if you plan on traveling to and from Europe aboard Air France (to Paris), Sabena (to Brussels), or Czechoslovak Airlines (to Prague). As part of their Euro Flier program, you can then buy between three and nine flight coupons, which are valid on those airlines' flights to more than 100 European cities. At $120 each, these coupons are a good deal, and the fine print still allows you plenty of freedom.

Within   Air travel within the EU countries was deregulated in 1993, spur-
Europe ring a slew of special deals from national carriers and from charter operators that now offer scheduled flights. The best require a round-trip purchase and Saturday night stay-over. For one-way or midweek travel, the smaller airlines generally offer better prices. For air travel within one country, **check with your transatlantic carrier.** Many carriers offer an air travel pass at a reasonable price that is good for numerous domestic flights.

Airlines are developing hub-style services. The idea is that you take a transatlantic flight to an airline's hub, then continue on its service to other European cities. SAS is developing Copenhagen as a Scandinavian hub; KLM is doing the same at Amsterdam's Schiphol (and is working with Northwest to ease transatlantic connections); British Airways at London's Heathrow and Gatwick; and Lufthansa at Frankfurt. If you plan to fly to other European cities, **choose an airline with the most cost-efficient connections,** but remember that these may not be the most direct.

Before booking an internal flight, **compare different modes of transportation.** Flights from London to Edinburgh take about one hour— airport to airport—while the BritRail InterCity train takes just over 4 hours. But if you add in the hour needed to get from central London to the airport, the need to check in as much as one hour before departure, the inevitable flight delays, the time spent waiting for luggage, and the transfer time back into town from Edinburgh Airport—you'll find you may not have saved more than half an hour for a considerably higher fare.

For scheduled flights, you will be asked to check in at least one hour before departure; for charter flights, generally two hours. If you are traveling with just hand luggage, it is possible to check in as late as 30 minutes before takeoff.

The Green Channel/Red Channel customs system in operation at most western European airports and other borders is basically an honor system. If you have nothing to declare, walk through the Green Channel, where there are only spot luggage checks; if in doubt, go through the Red Channel. If you fly between two EU-member countries, you may go through the new Blue Channel, where there are no customs officers except the one who glances at baggage labels to make sure only people off EU flights get through.

Bicycling

Some ferry lines transport bicycles free, others charge a nominal fee. Shop around. You can also transport your bicycle by air as checked baggage—you usually won't have to pay extra as long as you are within the 44-pound total baggage allowance.

Most European rail lines will transport bicycles free of charge or for a nominal fee, though you may have to book ahead. Check with the main booking office.

Local and regional tourist information offices will have information about renting bicycles. For bike tours of Europe, *see* Tour Operators *in* Important Contacts A to Z, *above*.

Budget

Make a budget, providing for accommodations, food, transportation, and cultural and recreational activities. Each day, **allow yourself a certain amount of spending money** and try not to exceed that limit. There's no reason to set the same limit every day; you may want to live the spartan life for a while, then indulge yourself later. Nor can a budget be the same for every place: A visit to a major city may be more expensive than a trip to a small provincial town. And you need to decide whether it's worth extra money to pay for convenience and comfort in a particular locale.

Bus Travel

In Britain, France, Germany, and Holland, bus travel was, until recently, something of a poor man's option—slow, uncomfortable, but cheap. Today, though, fast modern buses travel on excellent highways and offer standards of service and comfort comparable to those on trains—but still at generally lower fares. Between major cities and over long distances, trains are almost always faster; but buses will take you to places that trains often do not reach.

In several southern European countries—including Portugal, Greece, much of Spain, and Turkey—the bus has supplanted the train as the main means of public transportation, and is often quicker and more comfortable, with more frequent service, than the antiquated national rolling stock. Unless there is a particular scenic rail route you want to see, **choose the bus over the train in southern Europe**—but be prepared to discover that the bus is more expensive. Competition among lines is keen, so **ask about air-conditioning and reclining seats** before you book.

National or regional tourist offices have information about bus services. For reservations on major lines before you go, contact your travel agent at home; do your legwork so you know the different services available.

Cameras, Camcorders, and Computers

Laptops Before you depart, **check your portable computer's battery,** because you may be asked at security to turn on the computer to prove that it is what it appears to be. At the airport, you may prefer to **request a manual inspection,** although security X-rays do not harm hard-disk or floppy-disk storage. Also, **register your foreign-made laptop with U.S. Customs.** If your laptop is U.S.-made, call the consulate of the country you'll be visiting to find out whether or not it should be registered with local customs upon arrival. You may want to **find out about repair facilities at your destination** in case you need them.

Photography If your camera is new or if you haven't used it for a while, **shoot and develop a few rolls of film** before you leave. Always **store film in a cool, dry place**—never in the car's glove compartment or on the shelf under the rear window.

Every pass through an X-ray machine increases film's chance of clouding. To protect it, carry it in a clear plastic bag and **ask for hand inspection at security.** Such requests are virtually always honored at U.S. airports, and usually are accommodated abroad. Don't depend on a lead-lined bag to protect film in checked luggage—the airline may increase the radiation to see what's inside.

Video Before your trip, **test your camcorder, invest in a skylight filter to protect the lens, and charge the batteries.** (Airport security personnel may ask you to turn on the camcorder to prove that it's what it appears to be.) The batteries of most newer camcorders can be recharged with a universal or worldwide AC adapter charger (or multivoltage converter), usable whether the voltage is 110 or 220. All that's needed is the appropriate plug.

Videotape is not damaged by X-rays, but it may be harmed by the magnetic field of a walk-through metal detector, so **ask that videotapes be hand-checked.** Videotape sold in Europe is based is based on the PAL standard, which is different from the one used in the United States (NTSC). You will not be able to view your tapes through the local TV set or view movies bought there in your home VCR. Blank tapes bought in Europe can be used for camcorder taping, but they are pricey. Some U.S. audiovisual shops convert foreign tapes to U.S. standards; contact an electronics dealer to find the nearest.

Camping

If you enjoy the outdoors, spend some of your nights at the affordable campsites throughout Europe (individual chapters have information). Camping equipment is likely to be more expensive abroad, so **bring what you need from home.**

The Channel Tunnel

The Channel Tunnel provides the fastest route across the Channel—25 minutes from Folkestone to Calais, or 60 minutes from motorway to motorway. It consists of two large, 50-kilometer-long (31-mile-long) tunnels for trains, one in each direction, linked by a smaller service tunnel running between them.

Le Shuttle, a special car, bus, and truck train, operates continuously, with trains departing every 15 minutes at peak times and at least once an hour through the night. No reservations are necessary, although tickets may be purchased in advance from travel agents. Most passengers travel in their own car, staying with the vehicle throughout the "crossing," with progress updates via radio and display screens. Motorcyclists park their bikes in a separate section with its own passenger compartment, and foot passengers must book passage by coach. At press time, prices for a one-day round-trip ticket began at £107–£154 for a car and its occupants. Prices for a five-day round-trip ticket began at £115.

Eurostar operates high-speed passenger-only trains, which whisk riders between new stations in Paris (Gare du Nord) and London (Waterloo) in 3 hours and between London and Brussels (Midi) in 3¼hours. At press time, fares were $154 for a one-way, first-class ticket and $123 for an economy fare.

The Tunnel is reached from exit 11a of the M20. Tickets for either Tunnel service can be purchased in advance (*see* Important Contacts, *above*.)

Children and Travel

Baby-Sitting   For recommended local sitters, **check with your hotel desk.**

Driving   If you are renting a car, **arrange for a car seat when you reserve.** Sometimes they're free.

Flying   Always **ask about discounted children's fares.** On international flights, the fare for infants under age 2 not occupying a seat is generally either free or 10% of the accompanying adult's fare; children ages 2 through 11 usually pay half to two-thirds of the adult fare. On domestic flights, children under 2 not occupying a seat travel free, and older children currently travel on the "lowest applicable" adult fare.

Baggage   In general, the adult baggage allowance applies for children paying half or more of the adult fare. Before departure, **ask about carry-on allowances,** if you are traveling with an infant. In general, those paying 10% of the adult fare are allowed one carry-on bag, not to exceed 70 pounds or 45 inches (length + width + height) and a collapsible stroller; you may be allowed less if the flight is full.

Facilities   When making your reservation, **ask for children's meals or a free-standing bassinet** if you need them; the latter are available only to those with seats at the bulkhead, where there's enough legroom. If you don't need the bassinet, **think twice before requesting bulkhead seats**—the only storage for in-flight necessities is in the inconveniently distant overhead bins.

Safety Seats   According to the Federal Aviation Administration (FAA), it's good to **use safety seats aloft.** Airline policy varies. U.S. carriers allow FAA-approved models, but airlines usually require that you buy a ticket, even if your child would otherwise ride free, because the seats must be strapped into regular passenger seats. Foreign carriers may not allow infant seats, may charge the child's rather than the infant's fare for their use, or may require you to hold your baby during takeoff and landing, thus defeating the seat's purpose.

Lodging   Most hotels allow children under a certain age to stay in their parents' room at no extra charge, while others charge them as extra adults; be sure to **ask about the cut-off age.**

Credit Cards

The following abbreviations are used: **AE,** American Express; **DC,** Diners Club; **MC,** MasterCard; and **V,** Visa.

Customs and Duties

In Europe   See individual country chapters for limits on imports.

Back Home   You may bring home $400 worth of foreign goods duty-free if you've
In the U.S.   been out of the country for at least 48 hours and haven't already used the $400 exemption, or any part of it, in the past 30 days.

Travelers 21 or older may bring back 1 liter of alcohol duty-free, provided the beverage laws of the state through which they reenter the United States allow it. In addition, 100 non-Cuban cigars and 200 cigarettes are allowed, regardless of your age. Antiques and works of art more than 100 years old are duty-free.

Duty-free, travelers may mail packages valued at up to $200 to themselves and up to $100 to others, with a limit of one parcel per addressee per day (and no alcohol or tobacco products or perfume valued at more than $5); outside, identify the package as being for personal use or an unsolicited gift, specifying the contents and their retail value. Mailed items do not count as part of your exemption.

In Canada Once per calendar year, when you've been out of Canada for at least seven days, you may bring in C$300 worth of goods duty-free. If you've been away less than seven days but more than 48 hours, the duty-free exemption drops to C$100 but can be claimed any number of times (as can a C$20 duty-free exemption for absences of 24 hours or more). You cannot combine the yearly and 48-hour exemptions, use the C$300 exemption only partially (to save the balance for a later trip), or pool exemptions with family members. Goods claimed under the C$300 exemption may follow you by mail; those claimed under the lesser exemptions must accompany you.

Alcohol and tobacco products may be included in the yearly and 48-hour exemptions but not in the 24-hour exemption. If you meet the age requirements of the province through which you reenter Canada, you may bring in, duty-free, 1.14 liters (40 imperial ounces) of wine or liquor *or* 24 12-ounce cans or bottles of beer or ale. If you are 16 or older, you may bring in, duty-free, 200 cigarettes, 50 cigars or cigarillos, and 400 tobacco sticks or 400 grams of manufactured tobacco. Alcohol and tobacco must accompany you on your return.

An unlimited number of gifts valued up to C$60 each may be mailed to Canada duty-free. These do not count as part of your exemption. Label the package "Unsolicited Gift—Value under $60." Alcohol and tobacco are excluded.

In the U.K. If your journey was wholly within EU countries, you no longer need to pass through customs when you return to the United Kingdom. If you plan to bring large quantities of alcohol or tobacco, check in advance on EU limits.

From countries outside the EU, you may import duty-free 200 cigarettes, 100 cigarillos, 50 cigars or 250 grams of tobacco; 1 liter of spirits or 2 liters of fortified or sparkling wine; 2 liters of still table wine; 60 milliliters of perfume; 250 milliliters of toilet water; plus £136 worth of other goods, including gifts and souvenirs.

Dining

Cutting Costs Dining is one of the great pleasures of travel; it can also be costly. Fortunately, you can eat well but still save money at reasonably priced pubs, bistros, and brasseries, as well as at restaurants serving ethnic cuisines. You can **look for less expensive restaurants** on the outskirts of town or in the countryside. Another option is to **buy your food at a store or market** and have a picnic; the shopping alone can be a great experience. Wine, too, is cheaper if you can buy your own. Unless board is included with your room, **start the day with something from a local bakery,** and pick up coffee from a local shop. Individual chapters have additional suggestions.

A good cost-saver is to **plan on lunch being your main meal,** at least part of the time. Many European restaurants offer several-course luncheons that are cheaper than dinner menus, so you may not have to pass up a place just because it seems too costly at night.

For Travelers with Disabilities

When discussing accessibility with an operator or reservationist, **ask hard questions.** Are there any stairs, inside *or* out? Are there grab bars next to the toilet *and* in the shower/tub? How wide is the doorway to the room? To the bathroom? For the most extensive facilities, meeting the latest legal specifications, **opt for newer facilities,** which more often have been designed with access in mind. Older properties or ships must usually be retrofitted and may offer more limited facilities as a result. Be sure to **discuss your needs before booking.**

Discount Clubs

Travel clubs offer members unsold space on airplanes, cruise ships, and package tours at as much as 50% below regular prices. Membership may include a regular bulletin or access to a toll-free hot line giving details of available trips departing from three or four days to several months in the future. Most also offer 50% discounts off hotel rack rates. Before booking with a club, **make sure the hotel or other supplier isn't offering a better deal.**

Driving

Borders Many European countries have a relatively casual approach to border controls for drivers. At many frontiers, you may simply be waved through. There are, however, spot checks at all borders, and at some—particularly those checkpoints used by heavy commercial truck traffic—there can be long delays at peak times. Ask tourist offices or motoring associations for latest advice on ways to avoid these tie-ups.

Documentation If you are driving a rented car, the rental company will have provided you with all the necessary papers; if the vehicle is your own, you will need proof of ownership, certificate of roadworthiness (known in the United Kingdom as a Ministry of Transport, or MOT, road vehicle certificate), up-to-date vehicle tax, and a Green Card proof of insurance, available from your insurance company (fees vary depending on destination and length of stay).

Rules of the Road Speed limits in most countries are set much higher than those in the United States. Even on British motorways, where the upper limit is a very conservative 112 kph (70 mph), it is not uncommon to be passed by vehicles traveling 24–32 kph (15–20 mph) faster than that. On German autobahns, French autoroutes, or Italian autostradas, cars in the fast lane are often moving at speeds of 167 kph (100 mph) and faster. Always **stay in the slower lane unless you want to pass,** and be sure to make way for faster cars wanting to pass you. Much of the time traffic is heavier than is common on U.S. freeways outside major city rush hours.

Most tourists will find it more rewarding to avoid the freeways and use the alternative main routes. Traffic moves more slowly, and this can also save money; many European freeways (such as those of France, Spain, Italy, and Greece) are toll roads, and a day's drive on them can be expensive. Wherever you're driving, be sure to carry a good map.

In the United Kingdom, the Republic of Ireland, Malta, and Gibraltar, cars drive on the left. In other European countries, traffic is on the right. Beware the transition when coming off ferries from Britain or Ireland to the Continent (and vice versa).

Traffic During peak vacation periods, main routes can be jammed with holiday traffic. In the United Kingdom, try to avoid driving during any of the long bank-holiday (public holiday) weekends, when motorways can be clogged. In France, Spain, and Italy, huge numbers of people still take a fixed one-month vacation in August, so avoid driving during *le départ*, the first weekend in August, when vast numbers of drivers head south; or *le retour*, when they head back.

Entertainment

Cutting Costs Before shelling out money on high-price theater and concert tickets, **look into what's free.** You may find performances in churches or sound-and-light extravaganzas staged outdoors in summer. Be ready to **ask about discounts**—not all are advertised, so inquire before paying. Try for weekend rates, student and age-related price reductions, and promotional deals. Admission to movies in Paris, for instance, is reduced for Monday shows. Half-price theater tickets for same-day performances are fairly common in most European cities. Avoid cabarets, nightclubs, and even relatively modest discos, which tend to be expensive. If you visit these establishments, always **check the cover price and the cost of drinks before you order.**

Ferry Travel

Ferry routes for passengers and vehicles link the North Sea, English Channel, and Irish Sea ports with almost all of Britain's maritime neighbors. For ferry operators, *see* Important Contacts, *above*.

Insurance

Travel insurance can protect your investment, replace your luggage and its contents, or provide for medical coverage should you fall ill during your trip. Most tour operators, travel agents, and insurance agents sell specialized health-and-accident, flight, trip-cancellation, and luggage insurance as well as comprehensive policies with some or all of these features. Before you make any purchase, **review your existing health and homeowner policies** to find out whether they cover expenses incurred while traveling.

Baggage Airline liability for your baggage is limited to $1,250 per person on domestic flights. On international flights, the airlines' liability is $9.07 per pound or $20 per kilogram for checked baggage (roughly $640 per 70-pound bag) and $400 per passenger for unchecked baggage. However, this excludes valuable items such as jewelry and cameras that are listed in your ticket's fine print. You can buy additional insurance from the airline at check-in, but first **see if your homeowner's policy covers lost luggage.**

Flight You should **think twice before buying flight insurance.** Often purchased as a last-minute impulse at the airport, it pays a lump sum when a plane crashes, either to a beneficiary if the insured dies or sometimes to a surviving passenger who loses eyesight or a limb. Supplementing the airlines' coverage described in the limits-of-liability paragraphs on your ticket, it's expensive and basically unnecessary. Charging an airline ticket to a major credit card often automatically entitles you to coverage and may also embrace travel by bus, train, and ship.

Health If your own health insurance policy does not cover you outside the United States, **consider buying supplemental medical coverage.** It can provide from $1,000 to $150,000 worth of medical and/or dental expenses incurred as a result of an accident or illness during a trip. These policies also may include a personal-accident or death-and-dismemberment provision (pays a lump sum ranging from $15,000 to $500,000 to your beneficiaries if you die or to you if you lose one or more limbs or your eyesight) and a medical-assistance provision, which may either reimburse you for the cost of referrals, evacuation, or repatriation and other services or may automatically enroll you as a member of a particular medical-assistance company. (*See* Health Issues *in* Important Contacts, *above.*)

Trip Without insurance, you will lose all or most of your money if you must cancel your trip due to illness or any other reason. Especially if your airline ticket, cruise, or package tour is nonrefundable and cannot be changed, it's essential that you **buy trip-cancellation-and-interruption insurance.** When considering how much coverage you need, look for a policy that will cover the cost of your trip plus the nondiscounted price of a one-way airline ticket should you need to return home early. Read the fine print carefully, especially sections defining "family member" and "preexisting medical conditions." Also **consider default or bankruptcy insurance,** which protects you against a supplier's failure to deliver. However, such policies often do not cover default by a travel agency, tour operator, airline, or cruise line if you bought your tour and the coverage directly from the firm in question.

For U.K. You can buy an annual travel-insurance policy valid for most vaca-
Travelers tions during the year in which it's purchased. If you go this route, make sure it covers you if you have a preexisting medical condition or are pregnant.

Lodging

Apartment If you want a home base that's roomy enough for a family and comes
and Villa with cooking facilities, **consider a furnished rental.** It's generally
Rentals cost-wise, too, although not always—some rentals are luxury properties (economical only when your party is large). Home-exchange directories do list rentals—often second homes owned by prospective house swappers—and some services search for a house or apartment for you (even a castle if that's your fancy) and handle the paperwork. Some send an illustrated catalogue and others send photographs of specific properties, sometimes at a charge; up-front registration fees may apply.

Cutting Costs There are ways to save money on lodging even if you are traveling in the peak summer season rather than in the shoulder seasons of spring and fall. You can **look for substantial discounts or special packages from large hotel chains;** these can top 50%. Since hotels are often filled with business travelers during the week, you may save money by visiting on weekends.

The individual country chapters in this guide also describe an array of inexpensive lodgings other than hotels, from bed-and-breakfasts and small inns to farmhouses. In the country, you may see signs for rooms for rent; in addition, **check local tourist offices** for listings of accommodations and information about any discounts. And remember that in Europe it's always acceptable to **look at your room before checking in;** don't hesitate to ask for another or to decline the accommodation.

If you're willing to take a chance, you can **save money by showing up at the last minute.** Even in high season, rooms can be available at the end of the day, and if you show up in mid-afternoon, you may get the room discounted. Show up in early evening, however, and a discount is less likely, because desk clerks assume you really need the room.

Home If you would like to find a house, an apartment, or other vacation
Exchange property to exchange for your own while on vacation, **become a member of a home-exchange organization,** which will send you its annual directories listing available exchanges and will include your own listing in at least one of them. Arrangements for the actual exchange are made by the two parties to it, not by the organization.

Medical Assistance

No one plans to get sick while traveling, but it happens, so **consider signing up with a medical-assistance company.** These outfits provide referrals, emergency evacuation or repatriation, 24-hour hot lines for medical consultation, dispatch of medical personnel, relay of medical records, cash for emergencies, and other personal and legal assistance.

Money and Expenses

ATMs Chances are that you can **use your bank card at ATMs** to withdraw money from an account and get cash advances on a credit-card account if your card has been programmed with a personal identification number, or PIN. Before leaving home, **check in on frequency limits** for withdrawals and cash advances. Also **ask whether your card's PIN must be reprogrammed** for use in Europe. Four digits are commonly used overseas. Note that Discover is accepted only in the United States.

On cash advances you are charged interest from the day you receive the money from ATMs as well as from tellers. Although transaction fees for ATM withdrawals abroad may be higher than fees for withdrawals at home, Cirrus and Plus exchange rates are excellent because they are based on wholesale rates only offered by major banks.

Exchanging Currency For the most favorable rates, **change money at banks.** You won't do as well at exchange booths in airports, rail, and bus stations, nor in hotels, restaurants, and stores, although you may find their hours more convenient. To avoid lines at airport exchange booths, **exchange a small amount of currency before you leave home.**

Traveler's Checks Whether or not to buy traveler's checks depends on where you are headed; **take cash to rural areas and small towns, traveler's checks to cities.** The most widely recognized are American Express, Citicorp, Thomas Cook, and Visa, which are sold by major commercial banks for 1% to 3% of the checks' face value—it pays to **shop around.** Both American Express and Thomas Cook issue checks that can be countersigned and used by you or your traveling companion, and they both provide checks, at no extra charge, denominated in various non-U.S. currencies. You can **cash them in banks** without paying a fee (which can be as much as 20% elsewhere) and use them as readily as cash in many hotels, restaurants, and shops. So you won't be left with excess foreign currency, **buy a few checks in small denominations** to cash toward the end of your trip. Record the numbers of the checks, cross them off as you spend them, and keep this information separate from your checks.

Wiring Money You don't have to be a cardholder to send or receive funds through MoneyGram℠ from American Express. Just go to a MoneyGram agent, located in retail and convenience stores and in American Express Travel Offices. Pay up to $1,000 with cash or a credit card, anything over that in cash. The money can be picked up within 10 minutes in the form of U.S. dollar traveler's checks or local currency at the nearest MoneyGram agent, or, abroad, at the nearest American Express Travel Office. There's no limit, and the recipient need only present photo identification. The cost runs from 3% to 10%, depending on the amount sent, the destination, and how you pay.

You can also send money using Western Union. Money sent from the United States or Canada will be available for pickup at agent locations in 100 countries within 15 minutes. Once the money is in the system, it can be picked up at any one of 25,000 locations. Fees range from 4% to 10%, depending on the amount you send.

Packages and Tours

A package or tour to Europe can make your vacation less expensive and more convenient. Firms that sell tours and packages purchase airline seats, hotel rooms, and rental cars in bulk and pass some of the savings on to you. In addition, the best operators have local representatives to help you out at your destination.

A Good Deal? The more your package or tour includes, the better you can predict the ultimate cost of your vacation. Make sure you know exactly what is included, and **beware of hidden costs.** Are taxes, tips, and service charges included? Transfers and baggage handling? Entertainment and excursions? These can add up.

Most packages and tours are rated deluxe, first-class superior, first class, tourist, and budget. The key difference is usually accommodations. If the package or tour you are considering is priced lower than in your wildest dreams, **be skeptical.** Also, **make sure your travel agent knows the hotels** and other services. Ask about location, room size, beds, and whether the hotel has a pool, room service, or programs for children, if you care about these. Has your agent been there or sent others you can contact?

Buyer Beware Each year consumers are stranded or lose their money when operators go out of business—even very large ones with excellent reputations. If you can't afford a loss, take the time to **check out the operator**—find out how long the company has been in business, and ask several agents about its reputation. Next, **don't book unless the firm has a consumer-protection program.** Members of the United States Tour Operators Association and the National Tour Association are required to set aside funds exclusively to cover your payments and travel arrangements in case of default. Nonmember operators may instead carry insurance; look for the details in the operator's brochure—and the name of an underwriter with a solid reputation. Note: When it comes to tour operators, **don't trust escrow accounts.** Although there are laws governing those of charter-flight operators, no governmental body prevents tour operators from raiding the till.

Next, **contact your local Better Business Bureau and the attorney general's office** in both your own state and the operator's; have any complaints been filed? Last, **pay with a major credit card.** Then you can cancel payment, provided that you can document your complaint. Always **consider trip-cancellation insurance** (*see* Insurance, *above*).

Big vs. Small An operator that handles several hundred thousand travelers annually can use its purchasing power to give you a good price. Its high volume may also indicate financial stability. But some small companies provide more personalized service; because they tend to specialize, they may also be experts on an area.

Using an Travel agents are an excellent resource. In fact, large operators accept bookings only through travel agents. But it's good to **collect brochures from several agencies,** because some agents' suggestions may be skewed by promotional relationships with tour and package firms that reward them for volume sales. If you have a special interest, **find an agent with expertise in that area;** the American Society of Travel Agencies (*see* Travel Agents *in* Important Contacts, *above*) can give you leads in the United States. (Don't rely solely on your agent, though; agents may be unaware of small niche operators, and some special-interest travel companies only sell direct.

Single Prices are usually quoted per person, based on two sharing a room.
Travelers If traveling solo, you may be required to pay the full double occupancy rate. Some operators eliminate this surcharge if you agree to be

matched up with a roommate of the same sex, even if one is not found by departure time.

Packing for Europe

What you pack depends more on the season than on any particular dress code. In general, northern and central Europe have cold, snowy winters, and the Mediterranean countries have mild winters, though parts of southern Europe can be bitterly cold, too. In the Mediterranean resorts you may need a warm jacket for mornings and evenings, even in summer. The mountains usually are warm on summer days, but the weather, especially in the Alps, is unpredictable, and the nights are generally cool.

For European cities, **pack as you would for an American city**; formal outfits for first-class restaurants and nightclubs, casual clothes elsewhere. Jeans are as popular in Europe as they are in the rest of the world and are perfectly acceptable for sightseeing and informal dining. Sturdy walking shoes are appropriate for the cobblestone streets and gravel paths that fill many of the parks and surround some of the historic buildings. For visits to churches, cathedrals, and mosques, avoid shorts and immodest outfits. Italians are especially strict, insisting that women cover their shoulders and arms (a shawl will do). Women, however, no longer need to cover their heads in Roman Catholic churches. In Turkey, though, women must have a head covering; a long-sleeved shirt and a long skirt are also required.

To discourage purse snatchers and pickpockets, **take a handbag with long straps** that you can sling across your body, bandolier-style, and with a zippered compartment for money and other valuables.

If you stay in budget hotels, **take your own soap:** Many do not provide soap, and those that do often give guests only one tiny bar per room. Pack an extra pair of eyeglasses or contact lenses in your carry-on luggage, and if you have a health problem, **bring enough medication** to last the trip or have your doctor write a prescription using the drug's generic name, because brand names vary from country to country (you'll then need a prescription from a doctor in the country you're visiting). In case your bags go astray, **don't put prescription drugs or valuables in luggage to be checked.** To avoid problems with customs officials, carry medications in original packaging. Also, don't forget the addresses of offices that handle refunds of lost traveler's checks.

Electricity To use your U.S.-purchased electric-powered equipment, **bring a converter and an adapter.** The electrical current in Europe is 220 volts, 50 cycles alternating current (AC). Wall outlets in most of Europe take plugs with two round prongs; Great Britain uses plugs with two oversize round prongs.

If your appliances are dual voltage, you'll need only an adapter. Hotels sometimes have 110-volt outlets for low-wattage appliances marked "For Shavers Only" near the sink; don't use them for high-wattage appliances like blow-dryers. If your laptop computer is older, carry a converter; new laptops operate equally well on 110 and 220 volts, so you need only an adapter.

Luggage Free airline baggage allowances depend on the airline, the route,
Regulations and the class of your ticket; ask in advance. In general, on domestic flights and on international flights between the United States and foreign destinations, you are entitled to check two bags—neither exceeding 62 inches, or 158 centimeters (length + width + height), or weighing more than 70 pounds (32 kilograms). A third piece may be brought aboard; its total dimensions are generally limited to less than 45 inches (114 centimeters), so it will fit easily under the seat in front of you or in the overhead compartment. In the United States,

the FAA gives airlines broad latitude to limit carry-on allowances and tailor them to different aircraft and operational conditions. Charges for excess, oversize, or overweight pieces vary.

If you are flying between two foreign destinations, note that baggage allowances may be determined not by piece but by weight—generally 88 pounds (40 kilograms) in first class, 66 pounds (30 kilograms) in business class, and 44 pounds (20 kilograms) in economy. If your flight between two cities abroad *connects* with your transatlantic or transpacific flight, the piece method still applies.

Safeguarding Your Luggage Before leaving home, **itemize your bags' contents** and their worth, and label them with your name, address, and phone number. (If you use your home address, cover it so that potential thieves can't see it.) Inside your bag, **pack a copy of your itinerary.** At check-in, **make sure that your bag is correctly tagged** with the airport's three-letter destination code. If your bags arrive damaged or not at all, file a written report with the airline before leaving the airport.

Passports and Visas

If you don't already have one, **get a passport.** While traveling, **keep a photocopy of the data page** separate from your wallet and leave another copy with someone at home. If you lose your passport, promptly call the nearest embassy or consulate and the local police; having the data page can speed replacement.

U.S. Citizens All U.S. citizens, even infants, need a valid passport to enter the countries covered in this guide. See the individual country chapters for any visa requirements or limits on the length of your stay. New and renewal application forms are available at any of the 13 U.S. Passport Agency offices and at some post offices and courthouses. Passports for adults are valid for 10 years and are usually mailed within four weeks; allow five weeks or more in spring and summer.

Canadians You need a valid passport to enter the countries covered in this guide. See the individual country chapters for any visa requirements or limits on the length of your stay. Application forms are available at 28 regional passport offices as well as post offices and travel agencies. Whether for a first or a subsequent passport, you must apply in person. Children under 16 may be included on a parent's passport but must have their own to travel alone. Passports are valid for five years and are usually mailed within two to three weeks of application.

U.K. Citizens Citizens of the United Kingdom need a valid passport to enter the countries covered in this guide. See the individual country chapters for any visa requirements or limits on the length of your stay. Applications for new passports are available from main post offices as well as at the passport offices in Belfast, Glasgow, Liverpool, London, Newport, and Peterborough. You may apply in person at all passport offices, or by mail to all except the London office. Renewal passports must be applied for in person at passport offices. Children under 16 may travel on an accompanying parent's passport. All passports are valid for 10 years. Allow a month for processing.

Public Transportation

To save money if you're staying in a major city, **consider a public transit pass.** In most European cities, you can buy passes for unlimited travel on municipal buses and trains, good for a certain number of days. There may also be discounts on tickets purchased in quantity.

Rail Travel

To save money, **look into rail passes** (*see* Rail Travel *in* Important Contacts, *above*). But be aware that if you don't plan to cover many miles, you may come out ahead by buying individual tickets for each leg of your trip.

Many travelers assume that rail passes guarantee them seats on the trains they wish to ride. Not so. You need to **book seats ahead even if you are using a rail pass;** seat reservations are required on some European trains, particularly high-speed trains, and are a good idea on trains that may be crowded—particularly in summer on popular routes. You will also need a reservation if you purchase overnight sleeping accommodations.

You can also **save money by traveling overnight on the train,** since you sleep there instead of in a hotel. If you do spend the night on a train, take precautions against theft—sleep on top of your wallet or valuables, or take shifts with a companion.

From the U.K. Boat trains timed to meet ferries at Channel ports leave London and connect with onward trains at the main French and Belgian ports. Calais and Boulogne have the best quick connections for Paris (total journey time about six to seven hours using the cross-Channel Hovercraft); the Ramsgate–Oostende Jetfoil provides the fastest rail-sea connection to Brussels (about 5½ hours, station to station), with good rail connections to Germany and points east.

Boat trains connecting with ferries from Harwich to the Dutch and Danish North Sea ports leave from London/Liverpool Street; there are good rail connections from the Dutch ports to Amsterdam and onward to Germany and Belgium and south to France.

For the Republic of Ireland, trains connecting with the ferry services across the Irish Sea leave from London/Euston and London/Paddington.

Within Europe International trains link most European capitals, including those of Eastern Europe; service is offered several times daily. Generally, customs and immigration formalities are completed on the train by officials who board when it crosses the frontier.

France, Germany, and the United Kingdom have all developed high-speed trains, although the latter has fallen behind the other two. The French National Railroad's (SNCF's) Train à Grande Vitesse (TGV), for example, takes just 4½ hours to cover the 871 kilometers (540 miles) from Paris to Marseille on the Mediterranean.

A number of European airlines and railways operate fast train connections to hub airports, and these can sometimes be booked through the airline's reservation service.

Most European systems operate a two-tier class system. The few advantages of first class are outweighed by its substantially greater cost, so **travel second class whenever practical.** Some of the poorer European countries retain a third class, but avoid it unless you are on a rock-bottom budget.

For additional information on rail services and special fares, contact the national tourist office of the country (*see* Visitor Info *in* Important Contacts, *above*).

Renting a Car

Cutting Costs To get the best deal, **book through a travel agent and shop around.** If you want to lock in the rates in dollars, **rent before you travel.** You may also be able to **tie a rental in with your airline ticket or tour package.** When pricing cars, **ask where the rental lot is located.** Some off-airport locations offer lower rates—even though their lots are only minutes away from the terminal via complimentary shuttle. You may also want to **price local car-rental companies,** whose rates may be lower still, although service and maintenance standards may not be up to those of a national firm. Also **ask your travel agent about a company's customer-service record.** How has it responded to late plane arrivals and vehicle mishaps? Are there often lines at the rental counter, and, if you're traveling during a holiday period, does a confirmed reservation guarantee you a car?

Always **find out what equipment is standard** at your destination before specifying what you want; **do without automatic transmission or air-conditioning** if they're optional. In Europe, manual transmissions are standard and air-conditioning is rare and often unnecessary.

Also in Europe, **look into wholesalers**—companies that do not own their own fleets but rent in bulk from those that do and often offer better rates than traditional car-rental operations. Prices are best during low travel periods, and rentals booked through wholesalers must be paid for before you leave the United States. If you use a wholesaler, **know whether the prices are guaranteed** in U.S. dollars or foreign currency, and if unlimited mileage is available; find out about required deposits, cancellation penalties, and drop-off charges; and confirm the cost of any required insurance coverage.

Insurance When you drive a rented car, you are generally responsible for any damage or personal injury that you cause as well as damage to the vehicle. Before you rent, **see what coverage you already have** by means of your personal auto-insurance policy and credit cards. For about $14 a day, rental companies sell insurance, known as a collision damage waiver (CDW), that eliminates your liability for damage to the car; it's always optional and should never be automatically added to your bill.

Requirements Your driver's license is acceptable; an International Driver's Permit, available from the American or Canadian Automobile Association, is a good idea. Check the individual country chapters or call the country's tourist office for further information.

Surcharges Before picking up the car in one city and leaving it in another, **ask about drop-off charges or one-way service fees,** which can be substantial. Note, too, that some rental agencies charge extra if you return the car before the time specified on your contract. To avoid a hefty refueling fee, **fill the tank just before you turn in the car.**

Senior-Citizen Discounts

To qualify for age-related discounts, **mention your senior-citizen status up front** when booking hotel reservations, not when checking out, and before you're seated in restaurants, not when paying your bill. Note that discounts may be limited to certain menus, days, or hours. When renting a car, **ask about promotional car-rental discounts**—they can net lower costs than your senior-citizen discount.

Shopping

Shop wisely. For bargains, **seek out small crafts and antiques shops,** where owners are sometimes amenable to negotiating. Ask at your hotel or the tourist bureau about flea markets. Wherever possible, **take advantage of the various countries' VAT refund schemes.** At many stores, if you spend more than a specific amount on a given purchase, you can claim a refund; be sure to ask about this. It's always good to **take a calculator;** you'll know what the dollar-equivalent is, and you can always hold it up if you're trying to bargain in a foreign language.

Sightseeing

Cutting Costs It doesn't always take great effort to **plan less-expensive activities,** such as walking, hiking, and bicycling, that are often more rewarding than typical sightseeing. You may be able to **hop on a local bus or tram** for a ride through some of a city's most appealing areas. And remember that while admission charges to castles, châteaus, and monuments have been increasing, you can visit the churches, cathedrals, and formal gardens in most towns and cities at no charge. Museums may be costly to enter—but visiting art galleries is free. In many countries in Europe, **look for reduced museum admission fees** on Sundays and occasionally Wednesdays; you should also **check out combination passes for museums and other attractions.**

Students on the Road

To save money, **look into deals available through student-oriented travel agencies.** To qualify, you'll need to have a bona fide student ID card. Members of international student groups also are eligible. *See* Students *in* Important Contacts, *above.*

Telephones

Long Distance The long-distance services of AT&T, MCI, and Sprint make calling home relatively convenient and let you avoid often hefty hotel surcharges; typically, you dial an 800 number in the United States and a local number abroad. Also check with your hotel to see whether there is a flat fee on calls using these services. If so, head to the nearest public telephone. Before you go, **find out the local access codes** for your destinations.

If you do not use these services, prepare yourself with change or a phone card—sold at newsstands and tobacconists in many European countries—and dial direct at a pay phone to save money.

When to Go

For information about travel seasons and for the average daily maximum and minimum temperatures of the major European cities, *see* Essential Information *in* each country chapter.

2 Austria

Once one of Europe's cheapest vacation lands, Austria has catapulted into the ranks of the most expensive, certainly in dollar terms. Nevertheless, there are still bargains, at least by Austrian standards, to be found, and discovering them can be one of the diversions of a vacation in Austria. The country is highly accessible by public transport of one form or another. The rail network is well maintained, and trains are fast, comfortable, and punctual. Highways are superb and well marked. Public transportation in the cities, although not cheap, is safe, clean, and convenient. In short, the visitor to Austria spends more time having fun than coping with the logistics of getting from A to B.

What Austria lacks in size, it more than makes up for in diversity. Its Alps and mountain lakes in the central and southern provinces rival those of neighboring Switzerland, the vast Vienna Woods reminds some of the Black Forest, the steppes of the province of Burgenland blend with those across the border in Hungary, and the vineyards along the Danube easily compare with those of the Rhine and Mosel river valleys. In addition, nowhere else is there a Vienna or a Salzburg—or such pastry shops!

Austrians are for the most part friendly and welcoming. They are an outdoor people, given to heading off to the ski slopes, mountains, lakes, and woods at the first snowflake or crocus. At the same time, they can be as melancholy as some of the songs of their wine taverns would suggest. Communication is seldom a problem, since most Austrians speak another language, usually English, besides their native German.

What you'll discover in conversation with Austrians is that they are more for evolution than revolution, so change is gradual, and old values tend to be maintained. Graceful dancers do execute the tricky "left waltz" on balmy summer evenings in Vienna, and you may find an entire town celebrating some event, complete with brass band in lederhosen, affordable entertainment at its cheapest and most glorious.

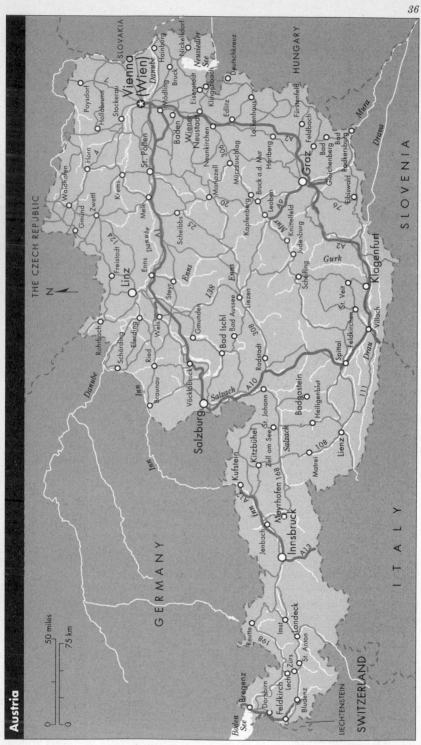

Austria

36

Essential Information

Before You Go

When to Go Austria has two main tourist seasons. The summer season starts at Easter and runs to about mid-October. The most pleasant months weather-wise are May, June, September, and October. June through August are the peak tourist months, and aside from a few overly humid days when you may wish for the wider use of air-conditioning, even Vienna is pleasant; the city literally moves outdoors in summer. The winter cultural season starts in October and runs into June; the winter sports season gets under way in December and lasts until the end of April, although you can ski in selected areas well into June and on some of the highest glaciers year-round. Some events—the Salzburg Festival is a prime example—make a substantial difference in hotel and other costs. Nevertheless, bargains are available in the off-seasons, from mid-January to early May (except Easter), and mid-September to November.

Climate Summer can be warm; winter, bitterly cold. The southern region is usually several degrees warmer in summer, several degrees colder in winter. Winters north of the Alps can be overcast and dreary, whereas the south basks in winter sunshine.

The following are the average daily maximum and minimum temperatures for Vienna.

Jan.	34F	1C	May	67F	19C	Sept.	68F	20C
	25	- 4		50	10		53	11
Feb.	38F	3C	June	73F	23C	Oct.	56F	14C
	28	- 3		56	14		44	7
Mar.	47F	8C	July	76F	25C	Nov.	45F	7C
	30	- 1		60	15		37	3
Apr.	58F	15C	Aug.	75F	24C	Dec.	37F	3C
	43	6		59	15		30	- 1

Currency The unit of currency is the Austrian schilling (AS), divided into 100 groschen. There are AS 20, 50, 100, 500, 1,000, and 5,000 bills; AS 1, 5, 10, and 20 coins; and 1-, 2-, 10-, and 50-groschen coins. The 1- and 2-groschen coins are scarce, and the AS20 coins are unpopular—though useful for some cigarette machines. The 500- and 100-schilling notes look perilously similar; confusing the two can be an expensive mistake.

At press time (summer 1995), there were about AS10.91 to the dollar and about AS15.46 to the pound sterling. Credit cards are widely used throughout Austria, although not all establishments take all cards, nor are cards graciously accepted, particularly for smaller amounts, by many establishments. American Express has money machines in Vienna at Parkring 10 (actually in Liebenberggasse, off Parkring) and at the airport. Visa cards work in most bank machines; these are marked, but you will need an acceptable PIN (Personal Identification Number) code. Check with your home bank before departing, and expect to pay a hefty fee on cash withdrawals. Bank Austria will give cash against Visa cards.

Cash traveler's checks at a post office, major bank (Bank Austria, Creditanstalt, BAWAG, or Erste Österreichische Spar-Casse), or American Express office to get the best rate. All charge a small commission; some smaller banks or "change" offices may give a poorer rate *and* charge a higher fee. All change offices at airports and the main train stations in major cities cash traveler's checks. Bank-operated change offices in Vienna with extended hours are located on Stephansplatz and in the Westbahnhof and Südbahnhof rail stations. The Bank Austria machines on Stephansplatz and at Kärntnerstrasse 51 (to the right of the opera) and at the Raiffeisenbank on Kohlmarkt (at Michaelerplatz) change bills in other currencies into schillings, but rates are poor and a hefty commission is automatically deducted.

What It Will Cost Austria is not inexpensive, but a low rate of inflation keeps prices fairly stable. Vienna and Salzburg are the most expensive cities. Many smaller towns offer virtually identical facilities at half the price. Austrian prices are inclusive: Service and tax are included.

Sample Prices Cup of coffee, AS25; half-liter of draft beer, AS27–AS40; glass of wine, AS35; Coca-Cola, AS25; open sandwich, AS25; theater ticket, AS200–upward; concert ticket, AS250–upward; opera ticket, AS600–upward; 1-mile taxi ride, AS35.

Customs on Arrival Austria's duty-free allowances are as follows: 200 cigarettes or 100 cigars or 250 grams of tobacco, 2 liters of wine and 1 liter of spirits, one bottle of toilet water (about 300-milliliter size), 50 milliliters of perfume for those aged 18 and over arriving from other European countries. Visitors arriving from the United States, Canada, or other non-European points may bring in twice the above amounts.

Language German is the official national language. In larger cities and most resort areas, you will have no problem finding those who speak English; hotel and restaurant staff, in particular, speak English reasonably well. Most younger Austrians speak at least passable English, and fluency is improving, particularly in the cities.

Getting Around

By Train Trains in Austria are fast and efficient, and most lines have now been electrified. Hourly express trains run on the key Vienna–Salzburg route. All principal trains have first- and second-class cars, as well as smoking and no-smoking areas. Overnight trains have sleeping compartments, and most trains have dining cars, although quality is inverse to the prices. If you're traveling at peak times, a reserved seat—available for a small additional fee—is always a good idea, particularly in the more crowded second-class coaches; first-class is an unnecessary extravagance.

Fares If you're visiting other European countries, a **Eurail Pass** (*see* Getting Around Europe, in Chapter 1, for details), valid throughout most of Europe, is the best deal. Austria has only two discount tickets. A **Bundesnetzkarte** offers unlimited travel for a month and costs AS5,400 for first class and AS3,600 for second class. The alternative is a **Domino** card, which is good for unlimited travel on any 3, 5, or 10 days within a 30-day period. The cost is AS2,100 (3 days), AS2,440 (5 days), and AS4,820 (10 days) for first class and AS1,400 (3 days), AS1,830 (5 days), and AS2,920 (10 days) for second class unless you're under 27, in which case **Domino-Junior** costs AS1,100 (3 days), AS1,220 (5 days), AS2,240 (10 days) for second class. Check on rates because they are subject to change; special deals are available. Full details are available from travel agents or from the Austrian National Tourist Office.

By Bus Service is available to virtually every community accessible by highway. Winter buses have ski racks. Vienna's central bus terminal (Wien-Mitte/Landstrasse Hauptstrasse, opposite the Hilton) is the arrival/departure point for international bus routes; in most other cities the bus station is adjacent to the train station.

By Boat Boats ply the Danube from Passau in Germany all the way to Vienna and from Vienna to Bratislava (Slovakia), Budapest (Hungary), and the Black Sea. Only East European boats run beyond Budapest. Overnight boats have cabins; all have dining. The most scenic stretches in Austria are from Passau to Linz and through the Wachau Valley (Melk, Krems). Make reservations from **DDSG** (the

Danube Steamship Company) in Vienna (tel. 0222/727–50–0) or travel agents.

By Bicycle Bicycles can be rented at many train stations and returned to that station or, by prior arrangement, to any other that also rents. Since the railroad bicycle rentals are the cheapest available (particularly if you have a rail ticket for that day), demand is heavy, so reserve in advance at the nearest station. Most trains and some postal buses will take bikes as baggage. Bikes can be taken on the Vienna subway on weekends and during off-peak hours on weekdays. Marked cycling routes parallel most of the Danube.

Staying in Austria

Telephones Pay telephones take AS 1, 5, 10, and 20 coins. A three-minute local
Local Calls call costs AS1. Emergency calls are free. Instructions are in English in most booths. Add AS1 when time is up to continue the connection. If you will be phoning frequently, get a phone "credit card" at a post office. This works in all *Wertkartentelefon* phones; the cost of the call will be deducted from the card automatically. Cards cost AS95 for AS100 worth of phoning, AS48 for calls totaling AS50. Phone numbers throughout Austria are being changed. A sharp tone indicates no connection or that the number has been changed. For information call 08 or, in Vienna, 1611.

International It costs more to telephone *from* Austria than it does to telephone *to*
Calls Austria. Calls from post offices are the least expensive. Hotels time all calls and charge a "per unit" fee according to their own tariff, which can add AS100 or more to your bill. To avoid this charge, call overseas and ask to be called back. To make a collect call—you can't do so from pay phones—dial the operator and ask for an *R Gespräch* (pronounced air-ga-*shprayk*). To reach an **AT&T** long-distance operator, dial 022/903–0111; for **MCI,** dial 022/903–012; for **Sprint,** dial 022/903–014.

International Dial 08 or, in Vienna, 1614, 1612 for Germany information, 1613 for
Information other European countries. Most operators speak English; if yours doesn't, you'll be passed to one who does.

Country Code The country code for Austria is 43.

Mail Airmail letters to the United States and Canada cost AS11.50 mini-
Postal Rates mum; postcards cost AS8.50. Airmail letters to the United Kingdom cost AS7; postcards cost AS6. An aerogram costs AS12.

Receiving Mail American Express offices in Vienna, Linz, Salzburg, and Innsbruck will hold mail at no charge for those carrying an American Express credit card or American Express traveler's checks.

VAT Refunds Value-added tax (VAT) at 20% is charged on all sales and is automatically included in prices. If you purchase goods worth AS1,000 or more, you can claim the tax back as you leave or once you've reached home, unless you're a citizen or resident of a European Union (EU) country. Ask shops where you buy the goods to fill out and give you the necessary papers. Get the papers stamped at the airport or border by customs officials (who may ask to see the goods). You can get an immediate refund of the VAT at the airport or at main border points, less a service charge, or you can return the papers by mail to the shop(s), which will then deal with the details. The VAT refund can be credited to your credit-card account or paid by check.

Opening and **Banks.** Doors open weekdays 8–noon or 12:30 and 1:30–3 or 4. Hours
Closing Times vary from one city to another. All banks are closed on Saturdays; only American Express and some exchange offices are open.

Museums. Opening days and times vary considerably from one city to another and depend on the season, the size of the museum, budgetary constraints, and other factors. Your hotel or the local tourist office will have current details.

Shops. These open weekdays from 8 or 9 until 6 and Saturday until noon or 1 only, except the first Saturday of every month, when they stay open until 5. A few shops in larger cities are open on Thursday evenings until 8 PM. Many smaller shops close for one or two hours at midday.

National Holidays In 1996: January 1 (New Year's); January 6 (Epiphany); April 7–8 (Easter); May 1 (May Day); May 16 (Ascension); May 26–27 (Pentecost); June 6 (Corpus Christi); August 15 (Assumption); October 26 (National Day); November 1 (All Saints' Day); December 8 (Immaculate Conception); December 25–26. Changing holidays in 1997: March 30–31 (Easter); May 8 (Ascension); May 18–19 (Pentecost); May 29 (Corpus Christi).

Dining Take your choice of sidewalk *Würstl* (frankfurter) stands, *Imbissstube* (the correct spelling is *Imbißstube*, but we don't use the double s symbol) (quick-lunch stops), cafés, *Heuriger* wine restaurants, self-service restaurants, modest *Gasthäuser* (neighborhood establishments with local specialties), and full-fledged restaurants in every price category. Most establishments post their menus outside. Shops that sell coffee beans (such as Eduscho) also offer coffee by the cup at prices that are considerably lower than those in a café. Many Anker bakery shops also offer full and inexpensive breakfasts as well as tasty *Schmankerl* (snacks) and coffee, and often butcher shops sell a variety of cooked meats—a great basis for a picnic lunch. Butcher shops (*Fleisher* or *Fleischhauer*) may also offer soup and a main course at noon; these frequently provide excellent value but the trade-off is usually a lack of sit-down comfort. A growing number of shops and snack bars sell pizza by the slice.

Mealtimes Austrians often eat up to five meals a day: a very early Continental breakfast of rolls and coffee; a slightly more substantial breakfast (*Gabelfrühstück*) with eggs or cold meat, possibly even a small goulash, at mid-morning (understood to be 9, sharp); a main meal at noon; afternoon coffee *(Jause)* with cake at teatime; and, unless dining out, a light supper to end the day. Cafés offer breakfast; most restaurants open somewhat later. Lunches usually cost more in cafés than in restaurants, but set lunch menus often are an excellent value. You'll save by taking your main meal at noon when restaurants and cafés offer their midday specials. Use the Wiener schnitzel (pork, not authentic veal) to judge prices: If it's offered for AS65 or less, you've found yourself a budget eatery—but quality, of course, may vary.

What to Wear Casual dress is acceptable, although in Vienna formal dress (jacket and tie) is preferred in some moderate restaurants at dinner. When in doubt, it's best to dress up.

Ratings Prices are per person and include soup and a main course, usually with salad, and a small beer or glass of wine. Prices also include taxes and service (but a small tip of 4–5% is customary, in addition). Best bets are indicated by a star ★.

Category	Major City	Other Areas
$$	AS200–AS400	AS170–AS350
$	AS150–AS200	AS130–AS170
¢	under AS150	under AS130

Lodging Austrian hotels and pensions are officially classified using from one to five stars. These grades broadly coincide with our own four-way rating system. No matter what the category, standards for service and cleanliness are high. All hotels in the $ category have either a bath or shower in the room; all but the very cheapest of the ¢ accommodations provide hot and cold water, with bath and toilets down the hall. Accommodations include conventional hotels, country inns (Gasthöfe), motels (considerably less frequent), and the more modest pensions. In the summer season, student dorms are opened up to the public and are a best bet. If you'll be satisfied with a private room or quarters rock-bottom in price (and probably comfort, using communal bath and toilet), check the tourist office or the *Zimmernachweis* (accommodations bureau) at the railroad station; most private accommodations have less than a handful of rooms and you can waste a lot of time and money trying to find one with available space. In any case, be sure to book ahead for the cheaper accommodations, even if it's just a phone call from your previous stopover. Note that very few of the lower-price accommodations accept credit cards.

Ratings   All prices quoted here are for two people in a double room. Though exact figures vary, a single room generally costs more than 50% of the price of a comparable double room. Breakfast—which can be anything from a simple roll and coffee to a full and sumptuous buffet—is usually included in the room rate. Best bets are indicated by a star ★.

Category	Major City	Other Areas
$$	AS900–AS1,250	AS700–AS1,000
$	AS700–AS900	AS600–AS700
¢	under AS700	under AS600

Tipping   Railroad porters get AS10 per bag. Hotel porters or bellhops get AS5–AS10 per bag. Doormen get AS10 for hailing a cab and assisting. Room service gets AS10 for snacks and AS20 for full meals. Maids get no tip unless your stay is a week or more or special service is rendered. In restaurants, 10% service is included. Add anything from AS5 to AS50 or 5–7%, depending on the restaurant and the size of the bill.

Vienna

Arriving and Departing

By Plane   All flights use Schwechat Airport, about 16 kilometers (10 miles) southwest of Vienna (tel. 0222/711–10–2231).

Between the   Buses leave from the airport for the city air terminal (tel. 0222/
Airport and   5800–35404) located by the Hilton on Wien-Mitte-Landstrasse
Downtown   Hauptstrasse every half hour from 5 to 6:30 AM and every 20 minutes from 6:50 AM to 11:30 PM, then every half hour to 1:30 AM, hourly April–October to 5 AM. Buses also run every hour from the airport to the Westbahnhof (west train station) and the Südbahnhof (south train station). Be sure you get on the right bus! The one-way fare for all buses is AS60.

By Train   Vienna has four train stations. The principal station, Westbahnhof, is for trains to and from Linz, Salzburg, and Innsbruck. Trains from Germany and France arrive here, too. The Südbahnhof is for trains to and from Graz, Klagenfurt, Villach, and Italy. Franz-Josefs-Bahnhof is for trains to and from Prague, Berlin, and Warsaw. Go to Wien-Mitte (Landstrasse) for local trains to and from the north of the city. Budapest trains use the Westbahnhof and Südbahnhof, and Bratislava trains use Wien-Mitte and Südbahnhof, so check.

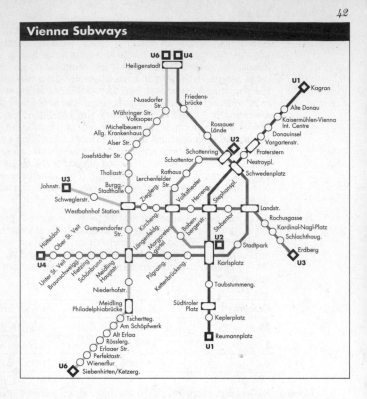

Vienna Subways

By Bus   If you arrive by bus, it will probably be at the central bus terminal, Wien-Mitte, opposite the city air terminal (and the Hilton).

By Boat   All Danube riverboats dock at the DDSG terminal on Mexikoplatz. There's an awkward connection with the U-1 subway from here. Some boats also make a stop slightly upstream at Heiligenstadt, Nussdorf, from which there is an easier connection to the U-4 subway line.

Getting Around

Vienna is fairly easy to explore on foot; indeed, much of the heart of the city—the area within the Ring—is largely a pedestrian zone. The Ring itself was once the city ramparts, torn down over a century ago to create today's broad, tree-lined boulevard.

After hours of walking, however, travelers will opt for public transportation, which is comfortable, convenient, and frequent, though not cheap. Tickets for the bus, subway, and streetcar are available in most subway (U-Bahn) stations. Tickets in multiples of five are sold at cigarette shops, known as Tabak-Trafik, or at the window marked "Vorverkauf" at central stations, such as Karlsplatz or Stephansplatz. A block of five tickets costs AS85, a single ticket AS20. If you plan to use public transportation frequently, get a **24-hour ticket** (AS50), a **three-day tourist ticket** (AS130), or an **eight-day ticket** (AS265). Maps and information are available at the Stephansplatz, Karlsplatz, and Praterstern U-Bahn stations.

By Bus or   Inner-city buses are numbered 1A through 3A and operate week-
Streetcar   days to about 7:40 PM, Saturdays until 2 PM. Reduced fares (buy a **Kur zstreckenkarte;** it gives four trips for AS34) are available for these routes, as well as designated shorter stretches (roughly two to four stops) on all other bus or streetcar lines. Streetcars and buses are numbered or lettered according to route, and they run until about

midnight. Night buses, marked N, follow special routes every half hour; the fare is AS25. The Nos. 1 and 2 streetcar lines run the circular route around the Ring, clockwise and counterclockwise, respectively.

By Subway Subway lines (U-Bahn; stations are marked with a huge blue "U") are designated U-1, U-2, U-3, U-4, and U-6 and are clearly marked and color-coded. Additional services are provided by a fast suburban train, the S-Bahn, indicated by a stylized blue "S" symbol. Both are tied into the general city-fare system.

Important Addresses and Numbers

Tourist Information City Tourist Office (Kärntnerstr. 38, behind the opera, tel. 0222/ 513–8892). Open daily 9–7.

Embassies U.S. (Gartenbaupromenade 2 [Marriott Bldg., Parkring 12a], tel. 0222/31339). Canadian (Fleischmarkt 19/Laurenzerberg 2, tel. 0222/ 531–380). U.K. (Jauresg. 12, tel. 0222/713–1575).

Emergencies Police (tel. 133), Ambulance (tel. 144), Doctor: ask your hotel or in an emergency, phone your consulate.

Exploring Vienna

Vienna has been described as an "old dowager of a town," not a bad description for this onetime center of empire. It's not just the aristocratic and courtly atmosphere, with monumental doorways and stately facades of former palaces at every turn. Nor is it just that Vienna has a higher proportion of middle-aged and older citizens than any other city in Europe, with a concomitant sense of stability, quiet, and respectability. Rather, it's these factors, combined with a love of music; a discreet weakness for rich food (especially cakes); an adherence to old-fashioned and formal forms of address; a high, if unadventurous, regard for the arts; and a gentle mourning for lost glories, that produce a stiff but elegant, slightly otherworldly, sense of dignity. Note, however, that this conservative outlook occasionally translates into a negative attitude toward backpackers and those whose dress, appearance, or behavior doesn't match up to the self-set standards of the older Viennese.

The Heart of Vienna Most main sights are in the inner zone, the oldest part of the city, encircled by the Ring, once the city walls and today a broad boulevard. Before setting out, be sure to check opening times of museums carefully; they can change unpredictably. Carry a ready supply of AS10 coins; many places of interest have coin-operated tape machines that provide English commentaries.

Numbers in the margin correspond to points of interest on the Vienna map.

Vienna's role as imperial city is preserved in the complex of buildings that make up the former royal palace. Start your tour at Albertinaplatz, behind the opera house. Head down Augustinerstrasse. To the right is the "Memorial to Victims of Fascism," disputed, in part, because the sculptor was once an admitted Communist. On your left is the **Albertina,** home to the world's largest collection of drawings, sketches, engravings, and etchings. There are works here by Dürer—these are perhaps the highlight of the collection—Rembrandt, Michelangelo, Correggio, and many others. *Augustinerstr. 1, tel. 0222/534830. Closed for renovations, but check to see if parts of the collection are being shown elsewhere.*

Beethoven was a regular visitor at the Palais Lobkowitz across the street on Lobkowitzplatz. The renovated palace now houses the **Theater Museum.** Exhibits cover the history of theater in Vienna and the rest of Austria. A children's museum in the basement is

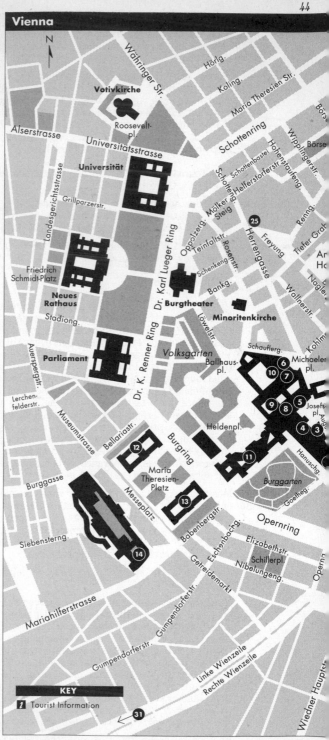

Vienna

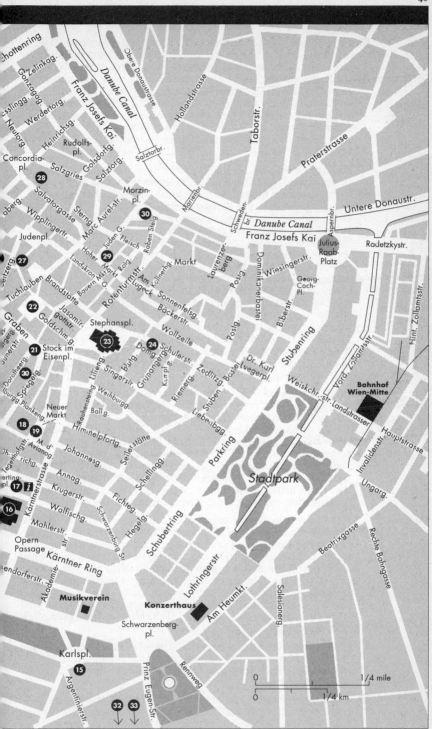

reached by a slide! *Lobkowitzpl. 2, tel. 0222/512–8800. Admission: AS40 adults, AS20 students, children free. Open Tues.–Sun. 10–5.*

❸ Go back to Augustinerstrasse to the 14th-century **Augustinerkirche,** a favorite on Sundays, when the 11 AM mass is sung in Latin. The Hapsburg rulers' hearts are preserved in a chamber here. Nearby is ❹ the **Nationalbibliothek** (the National Library), with its stunning Baroque great hall. Don't overlook the fascinating collection of globes on the third floor. *Josefsplatz 1, tel. 0222/534–10–397. Admission: AS20 adults, children free. Opening hrs may vary, but generally open May–Oct., Mon.–Sat. 10–4, Sun. and holidays 10–1; Nov.–Apr., Mon.–Sat. 11–noon. Globe museum: tel. 534–10–297. Admission: AS10. Open Mon.–Wed., Fri. 11–12, Thurs. 2–3.*

Josefsplatz is where much of *The Third Man* was filmed, specifically in and around the Palais Pallavicini across the street. The entrance ❺ to the **Spanische Reitschule,** the Spanish Riding School, is here, too, though the famed white horses are actually stabled on the other side of the square. During renovations to the Hofburg, the entrance to the school has been relocated to the main courtyard next to the Swiss Gate, through the Michaelertor rotunda dome. For tickets, write to the Spanische Reitschule (Hofburg, A-1010 Vienna) or Austrian Tourist Office (Friedrichstr. 7, A-1010 Vienna) *at least* three months in advance. Get the detailed schedule, but generally there are performances on Sunday at 10:45 AM from March through June, and from September through October. Evening performances are occasionally given on Wednesdays at 7 PM. Tickets for the few short training performances on Saturday mornings at 10 AM are available only from ticket offices and travel agencies. You can watch the 10 AM–noon training sessions Tuesday to Saturday during much of the performance season; tickets are available only at the door (Burghof, Inner Court; AS80 adults, AS20 children).

From here, you're only a few steps from Michaelerplatz, the circular ❻ square that marks the entrance to the **Hofburg,** the royal palace. On one side of the square, opposite the entrance, on the corner of Herrengasse and Kohlmarkt, is the **Loos building** (1911), designed by Adolf Loos. Step inside—it's now a bank—to see the remarkable restoration of the foyer. Outside, it's no more than a simple brick-and-glass structure, but architectural historians point to it as one of the earliest "modern" buildings in Europe—a building where function determines style. In striking contrast is the Baroque **Michaelertor,** opposite, the principal entrance to the Hofburg.

Head under the domed entrance of the Michaelertor to visit the ❼ **imperial apartments** of Emperor Franz Josef and Empress Elisabeth. Among the exhibits is the exercise equipment used by the beautiful empress. Here, too, is the dress she was wearing when she was stabbed to death by a demented Italian anarchist on the shores of Lake Geneva in 1898; the dagger marks are visible. *Michaelerplatz 1, tel. 0222/587–5554–515. Admission: AS40 adults, AS20 children; combined ticket with the Court Silver and Tableware Museum, AS90 adults, AS45 children. Open Mon.–Sat. 8:30–noon, 12:30–4; Sun., holidays 8:30–12:30.*

❽ Be sure to see the **Schatzkammer,** the imperial treasury, home of the magnificent crown jewels. *Hofburg, Schweizerhof, tel. 0222/533–7931. Admission: AS60 adults, AS30 children. Open Wed.–Mon. 10–6, Thurs. 10–9.*

❾ The **Hofburgkapelle,** the court chapel, is where the Vienna Boys Choir sings mass at 9:15 AM on Sundays mid-September through June. You'll need tickets to attend; they are available at the chapel from 5 PM Friday (line up by 4:30 and expect long delays) or by writing two months ahead to Hofmusikkapelle, Hofburg, Schweizerhof, A-1010 Vienna. The city tourist office can sometimes help with ticket applications.

⑩ Diagonally across the main courtyard is the new **Court Silver and Tableware Museum,** a brilliant showcase of imperial table settings sparkling with light and mirrors, reflecting period elegance. *Burghof, inner court, tel. 0222/523–4240. Admission: AS70 adults, AS35 children; combination ticket with imperial apartments, AS90 adults, AS45 children. Open daily 9–5.*

Head south to Heldenplatz, the vast open square punctuated by oversize equestrian statues of Prince Eugene and Archduke Karl, in
⑪ front of the **Neue Hofburg Museums.** The ponderously ornate 19th-century edifice—Hitler announced the annexation of Austria from the balcony in 1938—now houses a series of museums. Highlights are the Waffensammlung (the weapons collection, with far more armor than arms, even suits of armor for children and horses); the collections of musical instruments (you hear the various instruments—and explanatory text in German—on wireless headphones as you go from room to room); the ethnographic museum, and the exciting Ephesus museum, with finds from the excavations at that ancient site. *Neue Hofburg, Heldenpl. 1, tel. 0222/521770. Admission: AS30 adults, AS15 children. Open Tues.–Sun. 10–6.*

Walk west again under the unmonumental Hero's Monument archway and across the Ring, the broad boulevard encircling the inner
⑫ city, to the museum complex. The **Naturhistorisches Museum** (Natural History Museum) is on your right, the **Kunsthistorisches**
⑬ **Museum** (Art History Museum) is on your left. The latter is one of the world's great art museums; this is not a place to miss. The collections focus on old-master painting, notably Brueghel, Cranach, Titian, Canaletto, Rubens, and Velázquez. But there are important Egyptian, Greek, Etruscan, and Roman exhibits, too. *Burgring 5, tel. 0222/521770. Admission: AS45 adults, AS30 children. Open Tues.–Sun. 10–6; limited galleries also open Thurs. 10–9.*

At the Mariahilferstrasse end of the Messepalast complex is the
⑭ small and fascinating **Tabak Museum,** the Tobacco Museum. *Mariahilferstr. 2, tel. 0222/526–1716. Admission: AS20 adults, AS10 children. Open Tues.–Fri. 10–5, weekends 10–2.*

Head east down the Getreidemarkt, with the Kunsthistorisches Museum on your left. Looming up ahead, with the gilt, cauliflower-shape dome, is the Sezession and beyond it, a huge yellow-and-blue container. Both are art museums with changing exhibits. Beyond them, over Karlsplatz, is the heroic facade and dome, flanked by
⑮ vast twin columns, of the **Karlskirche.** It was built around 1715 by Fischer von Erlach. The oval interior is surprisingly small, given the monumental facade: One expects something on the scale of St. Peter's in Rome. The ceiling has airy frescoes, and stiff shafts of gilt radiate like sunbeams from the altar.

Take the pedestrian underpass back under the Ring to Opernplatz.
⑯ This is the site of the **Staatsoper,** one of the best opera houses in the world and a focus of Viennese social life. Tickets are expensive and rare, so you may have to settle for a backstage tour. The tour schedule for the day is posted outside the door under the right front arcade on the Kärntnerstrasse side and will depend on the activities going on inside. Standing-room tickets for performances are a bargain. You line up in advance for an authorization number and again, before the performance, to get a ticket and compete for a nonreserved place. In both cases, the earlier you get there the better.

Head up Kärntnerstrasse, Vienna's main thoroughfare, now a busy pedestrian mall. Directly behind the opera in the Philharmoniker-
⑰ strasse to your left is the creamy facade of the **Sacher Hotel.** Take a look inside at the plush red-and-gilt decor, a fin de siècle masterpiece. The hotel is also the home of the original Sachertorte—the ultimate chocolate cake. Back on Kärntnerstrasse, around the cor-

ner from the Sacher, is the city tourist office. Leading off Kärntnerstrasse, to the left, is the little Marco d'Aviano-Gasse. Follow it to **Kapuzinerkirche,** in whose crypt, called the **Kaisergruft** or imperial vault, the serried ranks of long-dead Hapsburgs lie. The oldest tomb is that of Ferdinand II; it dates from 1633. The most recent tomb is that of Empress Zita, widow of Austria's last kaiser, dating from 1989. *Neuer Markt 1, tel. 0222/512-6853-12. Admission: AS30 adults, AS20 children. Open daily 9:30-4.*

In the center of the square is the ornate 18th-century **Donner Brunnen,** the Providence Fountain. The figures represent main rivers that flow into the Danube; Empress Maria Theresa thought the figures were obscene and wanted them removed or properly clothed. Turn north into Plankengasse, then, at the bright yellow Protestant churches, head east into the narrow Dorotheergasse.

On your right, in the former Eskeles palace, is the **Jewish Museum.** Permanent and changing exhibits take a more global look at Judaism and so fail to reflect the rich Jewish culture and heritage of Vienna and Austria. There's a good café and reading room, but don't consider this museum a priority if you're pressed for time. *Dorotheergasse 11, tel. 0222/535-0431. Admission: AS50 adults, AS25 children. Open Sun.-Wed. and Fri. 10-6, Thurs. 10-9.*

Continue on Dorotheergasse to reach pedestrians-only Graben. The **Pestsäule,** or Plague Column, shoots up from the middle of the street, looking like a geyser of whipped cream touched with gold. It commemorates the Black Death of 1697; look at the graphic depictions of those who fell victim to its ravages. A small turning to the right, just past the column, leads to the Baroque **Peterskirche.** The little church, the work of Johann Lukas von Hildebrandt, finished in about 1730, has what is probably the most theatrical interior in the city. The pulpit is especially fine, with a highly ornate canopy, but florid and swirling decoration is everywhere.

Walk down Goldschmiedgasse to Stephansplatz, site of the **Stephansdom** (St. Stephen's Cathedral). Its towering Gothic spires and gaudy 19th-century tiled roof still dominate Vienna's skyline. The oldest part of the building is the 13th-century entrance, the soaring **Riesentor,** or Giant Doorway. Inside, the church is mysteriously dark, filled with an array of monuments, tombs, sculptures, paintings, and pulpits. Despite extensive wartime damage—and numerous Baroque additions—the building radiates an authentically medieval atmosphere. Climb up the 345 steps of **Alte Steffl,** Old Steven, the south tower, for a stupendous view over the city. An elevator goes up the north tower to **Die Pummerin,** the Boomer, a 22-ton bell first cast in 1711 from cannons captured from the Turks. Take a 30-minute tour of the crypt to see the copper urns in which the entrails of the Hapsburgs are carefully preserved.

On a narrow street east of the cathedral is the house where Mozart lived from 1784 to 1787. Today it's the **Mozart Erinnerungsräume,** the Mozart Museum. It was here that the composer wrote *The Marriage of Figaro*—thus the nickname Figaro House—and here, some say, that he spent the happiest years of his life. *Domg. 5, tel. 0222/ 513-6294. Admission: AS15 adults, AS5 children. Open Tues.-Sun. 9-12:15 and 1-4:30.*

Other Corners of Vienna Walk back down the Graben and the narrow Naglergasse and turn left into the Freyung. On your left is the **Palais Ferstl,** now a stylish shopping arcade. At the back is the skillfully restored **Café Central,** once headquarters for Vienna's leading literary figures. Next door to Palais Ferstl is **Palais Harrach,** part of which is now an outpost of the Museum of Fine Arts for special exhibits and the overflow of tapestries and paintings from the main house. Cross the Freyung to the dominant **Schottenkirche.** The monks who were brought to found it were actually Irish, not Scottish. The Benedictines have installed a small but worthwhile museum of mainly religious art, including a late Gothic winged altar removed from the church when it received a Baroque overlay in the mid-1600s. Enter through the courtyard to the left. *Freyung 6, tel. 0222/534-98-600. Admission: AS40 adults, AS20 children. Open Thurs.-Sat. 10-5, Sun. 12-5.*

Turn back through the Freyung to **Am Hof,** a remarkable square with the city's Baroque central fire station, possibly the world's most ornate. You'll find occasional flea markets in the square on Thursdays and Fridays in summer plus seasonal markets at other times. Cross the square to the **Kirche am Hof.** The interior is curiously reminiscent of many Dutch churches.

Continue to Judenplatz and turn right into Parisergasse to the **Uhrenmuseum** (Clock Museum), located in a lovely Renaissance house. *Schulhof 2, tel. 0222/533-2265. Admission: AS30 adults, AS10 children. Open Tues.-Sun. 9-4:30.*

Turn down the Kurrentgasse and, via Fütterergasse, cross the Wipplingerstrasse into Stoss im Himmel (literally, a "thrust to heaven"). To your left down Salvatorgasse is **Maria am Gestade,** originally a church for fishermen on the nearby canal. Note the ornate "folded hands" spire. Return along Wipplingerstrasse, across Marc-Aurel-Strasse, to **Hoher Markt,** with a central monument celebrating the betrothal of Mary and Joseph. Roman ruins are displayed in the museum on the south side of the square. *Hoher Markt 3, tel. 0222/535-5606. Admission: AS15 adults, AS5 children; free on Fri. morning. Open Tues.-Sun. 9-12:15 and 1-4:30.*

On the north side of Hoher Markt is the amusing **Anker-Uhr,** a clock that tells time by figures moving across a scale. They are identified on a plaque at the lower left of the clock; it's well worth passing by at noon to catch the show, when all the figures go past. Go through Judengasse to the **Ruprechtskirche** (St. Rupert's). The oldest church in Vienna, dating from the 11th century, is small, damp, dark, and, unfortunately, usually closed, though you can peek through a window.

Vienna Environs

It's a 15-minute ride from the city center on subway line U-4 (stop either at Schönbrunn or Hietzing) to **Schönbrunn Palace,** the magnificent Baroque residence built between 1696 and 1713 for the Hapsburgs. Here Kaiser Franz Josef I was born and died. His "office" (kept as he left it in 1916) is a touching reminder of his spartan life; other rooms, however, reflect the elegance of the monarchy. The ornate public rooms are still used for state receptions. A guided tour covers 45 of the palace's 1,441 rooms; among the curiosities are the Chinese room and the gym fitted out for Empress Elisabeth, where she exercised daily to keep her figure. Ask about ground-floor rooms open independent of the main tour, but don't pass up the primary tour. *Schönbrunner Schlossstr., tel. 0222/81113-238. Admission: AS95 adults, AS40 children with guided tour. AS80 adults, AS30 children without tour, but not all rooms are accessible. Open Nov.-Mar., daily 9-4:30; Apr.-Oct., daily 8:30-5.*

Once on the grounds, don't overlook the **Tiergarten** (Zoo). It's Europe's oldest menagerie and, when established in 1752, was intended to amuse and educate the court. It contains an extensive assortment of animals, some of them in their original Baroque enclosures. *Tel. 0222/877-9294-0. Admission: AS80 adults, AS60 children. Open Nov.-Jan., daily 9-4:30; Feb. and Oct., daily 9-5; Mar., daily 9-5:30; Apr., daily 9-6; May-Sept., daily 9-6:30.*

Follow the pathways up to the **Gloriette,** that Baroque ornament on the rise behind Schönbrunn, and enjoy superb views of the city. Originally this was to have been the site of the palace, but projected construction costs were considered too high. *Admission: AS20* *adults, AS10 children. Open May–Sept., daily 9–6 and Oct., daily 9–5.*

③② Take the D streetcar toward the Südbahnhof to reach **Schloss Belvedere** (Belvedere Palace), a Baroque complex often compared to Versailles. It was commissioned by Prince Eugene of Savoy and built by Johann Lukas von Hildebrandt in 1721–22. The palace comprises two buildings, one at the foot and the other at the top of a hill. The lower tract was first built as residential quarters; the upper buildings were reserved for entertaining. The gardens in between are among the best examples of natural Baroque ornamentation found anywhere. Both sections now house outstanding art museums: the gallery of 19th- and 20th-century art in the Upper Belvedere (Klimt, Kokoschka, Schiele, Waldmüller, Markart) and the Baroque museum (including medieval Austrian art) in the Lower Belvedere. *Prinz-Eugen-Str. 27, tel. 0222/798–4158–0. Admission: AS60 adults, AS30 children. Open Tues.–Sun. 10–5.*

③③ Continue across the Gürtel from the Upper Belvedere southward to the **20th Century Museum**, containing a small but extremely tasteful modern art collection. *Schweizer Garten, tel. 0222/799–6900–0. Admission: AS45 adults, AS25 children. Open Tues.–Sun. 10–6.*

You can reach a small corner of the **Vienna Woods** by streetcar and bus. Take a streetcar or the U-2 subway to Schottentor/University and, from there, the No. 38 streetcar (Grinzing) to the end of the line. Grinzing itself is out of a picture book; alas, much of the wine offered in the taverns is less enchanting. (For better wine and ambience, try the area around Pfarrplatz/Probusgasse in Hohe Warte [No. 37 streetcar, Bus 39A] or the suburb of Nussdorf, reached by streetcar D.) To get to the woods, change in Grinzing to Bus 38A. This will take you to Kahlenberg, which provides a superb view over the Danube and the city. You can take the bus or hike to Leopoldsberg, the promontory over the Danube from which Turkish invading forces were repulsed during the 16th and 17th centuries.

Shopping

Shopping Districts Tourists gravitate to the (generally expensive) **Kärntnerstrasse, Graben, and Kohlmarkt,** but moneywise Viennese do most of their shopping on the **Mariahilferstrasse.**

Department Stores **Steffl,** on the Kärntnerstrasse, and **Gerngross, Herzmansky,** and **Stafa** on the Mariahilferstrasse are the major outlets.

Food and Flea Markets The **Naschmarkt** (between Rechte and Linke Wienzeile; weekdays 6 AM–mid-afternoon, Sat. 6–1) is a sensational open-air food market, offering specialties from around the world. The **Flohmarkt** (flea market) operates year-round beyond the Naschmarkt (subway U-4 to Kettenbrückengasse) and is equally fascinating (Sat. 8–4). Bargaining here goes on in any number of languages. An **Arts & Crafts Market** with better offerings operates on Saturday (2–6) and Sunday (10–6) alongside the Danube Canal near the Salztorbrücke.

Dining

The simpler restaurants and Gasthäuser usually offer the best value. Look for blackboards outside listing daily specials, often a midday menu of soup and a main course, and possibly a dessert as well. Follow local habits—have your main meal at noon, a lighter meal in the evening—and you'll economize. Generally the farther you get from the first district, the more modest the restaurants. Restaurants around the university cater to students' tastes and budgets. For details and price-category definitions, *see* Dining *in* Staying in Austria, *above.*

$$ Imperial Café. In the Imperial Hotel, the café is much more than just a (very good) meeting spot for coffee or *Torte* (cake); both lunch and after-concert supper are popular and reasonably priced. The rooms are understated by local standards; crystal and velvet are evident but not overdone. The city's politicians, attorneys, and business types gather here for solid Viennese fare, selecting either from the choice daily specialties, which generally include a superb cream soup, or relying on such standards as *Leberknödelsuppe* (liver dumpling soup) and *Tafelspitz* (Viennese boiled beef). In summer, the terrace outside is enticing but noisy. The wine list includes French and German selections, but many prefer an open wine by the glass. *Kärntner Ring 16, tel. 0222/501–10–359, fax 0222/501–10–410. Reservations recommended. Jacket and tie. AE, DC, MC, V.*

$$ Kaiserwalzer. The "old Vienna" atmosphere is a bit heavy, but puts the menu—focusing on Austrian and Hungarian specialties—in just the right setting. Come for red beet soup, Wiener schnitzel, or *Fogosch*, the tasty Danube fish. Service is attentive and open wines are fine. *Esterházygasse 9, tel. 0222/587–0494, fax 0222/587–0494. Reservations advised. Jacket and tie. AE, DC, MC, V. Closed lunch and Sun.*

$ Bastei-Beisl. A comfortable, wood-paneled restaurant offering good traditional Viennese fare. Outdoor tables are particularly pleasant on summer evenings. *Stubenbastei 10, tel. 0222/512–4319. AE, DC, MC. Closed Sun.*

$ Bei Max. The decor is somewhat bland, but the tasty Carinthian
★ specialties—*Kasnudeln* (cheese dumplings) and *Fleischnudeln* (meat dumplings) in particular—keep this friendly restaurant packed. *Landhausgasse 2/Herrengasse, tel. 0222/533–7359. Reservations advised. No credit cards. Closed Sat., Sun., last wk in July, 1st 3 wks in Aug.*

$ Gigerl. It's hard to believe you're right in the middle of the city at
★ this imaginative and charming wine restaurant that serves hot and cold buffets. The rooms are small and cozy but may get smoky and noisy when the place is full—which it usually is. The food is typical of wine gardens on the city's fringe: roast meats, casserole dishes, cold cuts, salads. The wines are excellent. The surrounding narrow alleys and ancient buildings add to the charm of the outdoor tables in summer. *Rauhensteingasse 3, tel. 0222/513–4431. Reservations advised. AE, DC, MC, V.*

$ Königsbacher bei der Oper. The suite of smallish rooms or, better,
★ the outside garden tables, set the perfect atmosphere for Viennese standards such as roast pork or schnitzel. The daily special is a bargain; look for the week's listing posted by the door. Choose German beer or any of the excellent wines as accompaniment. *Walfischgasse 5, tel. 0222/513–1210. Reservations advised. No credit cards. Closed Sat. dinner, Sun.*

$ Ofenloch. This place is always packed, which speaks well not only of
★ the excellent specialties from some Viennese grandmother's cookbook but also of the atmosphere. Waitresses are dressed in appropriate period costumes, and the furnishings add to the color. At times the rooms may be too smoky and noisy for some tastes. If you like garlic, try *Vanillerostbraten*, a rump steak with as much garlic as you request. *Kurrentgasse 8, tel. 0222/533–8844. Reservations essential. AE, DC, MC, V.*

$ Stadtbeisl. Good standard Austrian fare is served at this popular eatery, which is comfortable without being pretentious. The service suffers as the place fills up, but if you are seated outside in summer, you probably won't mind. *Naglergasse 21, tel. 0222/533–3507. Reservations advised. V.*

$ Zu den drei Hacken. This is one of the few genuine Viennese Gasthäuser in the city center; like the place itself, the fare is solid if not elegant. Legend has it that Schubert dined here; the ambience probably hasn't changed much since then. There are tables outside in summer, although the extra seating capacity strains both the kitchen and the service. *Singerstr. 8, tel. 0222/512–5895. No reservations. AE, DC, MC, V. Closed Sun.*

$ **Zu ebener Erde und erster Stock.** Ask for a table upstairs in this exquisite, tiny, utterly original Biedermeier house, which serves good, standard Austrian fare; the cheaper downstairs space is really more for snacks. *Burggasse 13, tel. 0222/523–6254. Reservations advised. AE. Closed Sat. lunch, Sun., and Mon. late July–late Aug.*

¢ **Einstein.** Diners—predominantly students—are seated at one of a warren of semiprivate booths, set off with dark-wood dividers in the restaurant section, or at typical small tables in the café area. The fare is mainly Austrian, with occasional international touches. Try the excellent cream of garlic soup or the *Suppentopf*, a thick stew that's a meal in itself, and have a genuine (Czech) *Budweiser* beer on the side. *Rathausstr. 4, tel. 0222/422626. No reservations. No credit cards. Open weekdays 7 AM–2 AM, Sat. 10 AM–2 AM, Sun. 10 AM–midnight.*

¢ **Gulaschmuseum.** From the traditional Hungarian *guylás* to the North American version—chili con carne—you'll find ample and tasty portions along with noontime specials during the week. Although this stylish restaurant is based on the theme of goulash— with a dozen variations on the theme—the menu offers other items as well. *Schulerstr. 20, tel. 0222/512–1017. No credit cards.*

¢ **Inigo.** The crowd is mixed in this somewhat plain but popular restaurant run by the Catholic charities. Prices are low, and one of the two bargain daily specials is vegetarian, for example, tofu-filled cabbage roll. *Bäckerstr. 18, tel. 0222/512–7451. No reservations. No credit cards. Closed Sat. lunch and Sun.*

¢ **Lustig Essen.** The principle in these unadorned modern rooms is
★ smaller portions (but not that small) and thus a chance to sample more of the excellent international and Austrian meat and fish dishes, as well as desserts. *Salvatorgasse 6, tel. 0222/533–3037. No credit cards.*

¢ **Naschmarkt.** These informal cafeteria-style restaurants, done in pseudo–Art Deco, are run (quite well) by the city and offer daily specials of prepared and grilled-to-order dishes plus regular features, such as sandwich platters and a good salad bar. Soups are excellent, particularly the goulash in winter, gazpacho in summer. *Schwarzenbergplatz 16, tel. 0222/505–3115. No reservations. No credit cards. Open weekdays 6:30 AM–10:30 PM, weekends 9–10:30. Schottengasse 1, tel. 0222/533–5186. No reservations. No credit cards. Open weekdays 10:30–7:30, weekends 10:30–3.*

¢ **Rosenberger Markt-Restaurant.** Downstairs under a huge artificial tree, a cluster of cafeteria-style food stations offers soups, excellent grilled specialties, salads, and desserts, all attractively presented and prepared to order. Look for seasonal specialties, such as asparagus and fresh chilled melon. *Maysedergasse 2/Fürichgasse 3, tel. 0222/512–3458. No reservations. Open daily 11–11. Café open 8 AM– 11 PM. No credit cards.*

¢ **Schnitzelhaus.** This local self-service chain specializes in pork schnitzel (pork cutlet breaded and deep-fried), but you can have a turkey schnitzel, schnitzel cordon bleu, or a schnitzelburger as alternative. There are smaller portions for children. The red, white, and gray decor is unornamented, the fragrance of fat may hang in the air, but the schnitzels are certainly not bad (choose fries over the mushy potato salad) and prices are rock-bottom. All items are available for take-out. *Kettenbrückengasse 19, tel. 586–1774; Billrothstr. 18; Favoritenstr. 145; Brigittaplatz 22, tel. 330–5322. No credit cards. Open daily 10–10.*

Lodging

Vienna's inner city is the best base for visitors because it's so close to most of the major sights, restaurants, and shops. This accessibility translates, of course, into higher prices, although there are still values to be found. Without wandering too far or sacrificing too much in the way of comfort, you can still find budget lodgings, and the efficient public transportation can deliver you to still-cheaper accommodations outside the center.

The youth hostel is in a delightful location overlooking the city but far from the center (you need an hour or more by public transport), and there's an early curfew. The listed seasonal hotels (student dorms) are better located but available only from July to September. The tourist office can help you with private rooms or the very cheapest accommodations; most of these places are too small to list. For details and price-category definitions, *see* Lodging *in* Staying in Austria, *above.*

$$ **Hotel-Pension Zipser.** This 1904 house, with an ornate facade and
★ gilt-trimmed coat of arms, is one of the city's better hotel values. It's in a fascinating district of small cafés, shops, jazz clubs, and excellent restaurants, yet within steps of the J streetcar line direct to the city center. The rooms are newly redone in browns and beiges, with modern furniture to match; the baths are elegant and well lit. The balconies of some of the back rooms overlook tree-filled neighborhood courtyards. The restyled lobby lounge is fresh and inviting. The friendly staff will help get theater and concert tickets. Book ahead a month or two to be sure of a room. *Lange Gasse 49, A–1080, tel. 222/404–54–0, fax 0222/408–5266–13. 47 rooms with bath or shower. Facilities: coffee shop, parking. AE, DC, MC, V.*

$$ **Post.** Taking its name from the city's main post office, opposite, this
★ is an older but updated hotel that has a fine location, a friendly staff, and a good café. *Fleischmarkt 24, tel. 0222/515830, fax 0222/515–83808. 107 rooms, 77 with bath or shower. AE, DC, MC, V.*

$ **Cyrus.** Rooms on the side or back of this converted block of apartments are quieter, but the trade-off for a front room could be luxurious space, if not overly elegant with somewhat worn furnishings. Rooms are neat and clean, and the Iranian family management is friendly. You're two blocks away from Keplerplatz, a pedestrian zone with a lot of shops, on the U-1 line, three stops to Karlsplatz, four to Stephansplatz/City. *Laxenburger Str. 14, tel. 0222/604–4288, fax 0222/604–4288. 20 rooms, 16 with bath or shower. Facilities: bar, TV room. No credit cards.*

$ **Kirschbichler.** Rooms in this simple, tidy family-run pension are freshly done with dark-wood furniture against beige walls. You're one subway stop from the *Wien-Mitte* station here. Ask for one of the rooms on the courtyard side: they're quieter. There's no breakfast, but tea and coffee are provided. *Landstrasser Hauptstr. 33, tel. 0222/712–1068. 15 rooms with shower. No credit cards.*

$ **Kugel.** You're halfway between the Westbahnhof and the city center
★ in this older but recently redecorated hotel. The breakfast/TV room is somewhat shabby, but the guest rooms are furnished in modern, light-wood pieces; those with the attractively tiled full baths will push the price up somewhat, those with only a shower remain comfortably within budget range. *Siebensterngasse 43, corner Neubaugasse 46, tel. 0222/933355 or 0222/931330, fax 0222/931678. 38 rooms, most with shower or full bath. Facilities: bar, TV room. No credit cards.*

¢ **Accordia.** This new seasonal hotel is within an easy 10–15-minute walk from the city center. Rooms are typical for student quarters (unadorned but neat and functional). *Grosse Schiffgasse 12, tel. 0222/212–1668, fax 0222/212–1670. 122 rooms with bath. AE, MC, DC, V.*

¢ **Aramis.** Rooms are comfortable in this seasonal hotel directly on the No. 37 streetcar line, which will take you to the university/Schottentor, fairly close to the center, in about 20 minutes. The area is primarily residential although dotted with occasional small local *Heuriger* (wine houses); some of the vineyards are not distant. Accommodations are normally student quarters in a fairly new building tucked away in delightful quiet behind a facade of apartments. *Döblinger Hauptstr. 55, tel. 0222/369–8673, fax 0222/512–1968. 58 rooms, all with bath. Facilities: restaurant, bar, TV room, garden. MC, V.*

¢ **Falstaff.** Family management sets the tone at this pension on two floors of an older apartment building on a quiet side street easily reached by streetcar D from the city center. Rooms are spacious (singles less so) and comfortable if unadorned, with modest but adequate furnishings in dark wood, in pleasing contrast to the brightness of the rooms themselves. *Müllnergasse 5, tel. 0222/317–9127 or 0222/317–9186, fax 0222/317–9186–4. 17 rooms, 11 with bath or shower. V.*

¢ **Haus Döbling.** Of the seasonal hotels, this is considerably the cheapest, dating from a time when neither students nor those who used the facility during holiday periods expected luxuries such as a shower or bath in the room. Facilities are modest, 1950s modern but adequate, and transportation to the center via Streetcar 38 or Bus 40A is easy and fast. There's parking for bicycles and cars. *Gymnasiumstr. 85, tel. 0222/347631, fax 0222/347631–25. 194 rooms, none with bath. MC, V.*

¢ **Hospiz.** YMCA ownership guarantees immaculate if somewhat spartan rooms, but this doesn't bother the youthful guests. Personnel is particularly friendly and helpful with sightseeing, tickets, and advice. You're within walking distance of the Westbahnhof, and there's space for bikes and car parking as well. The U-3 subway whisks you to the city center in about 10 minutes. *Kenyongasse 15, tel. 0222/523–1304, fax 0222/523–1304–13. 23 rooms, 7 with shower. MC, V.*

¢ **Koper.** Two floors in Haus Klaret, basically a student dorm, offer compact but clean, functional rooms year-round. A bed, a desk, and a clothes closet are it for the furnishings, which are adequate and a good value for the money. Each floor has a kitchen with stoves and a refrigerator where guests can prepare snacks. Administration is in Korotan, a block away at Albertgasse 48. *Bennogasse 21, tel. 0222/ 403–4193, fax 0222/403–4193–99. 16 rooms, 8 with shower. AE, MC, V.*

¢
★ **Wild.** This friendly, family-run pension on several floors of an older apartment house offers the best value in town. The rooms are simple but modern, with furniture made from light-colored woods and pine-paneled ceilings. Each cluster of rooms has a kitchenette where you can prepare coffee and snacks. The breakfast room-TV lounge is bright and attractive, and the hotel is near the major museums. *Lange Gasse 1, tel. 0222/435174, fax 0222/433408. 14 rooms, none with bath. Facilities: sauna, solarium, fitness room. AE, DC, MC, V.*

¢ **Wilhelmshof.** Behind a florid 19th-century facade, this family-run, friendly hotel near the great Ferris wheel in the Prater has comfortable older rooms plus a fresh new up-to-date section. Furnishings are in dark oak with red upholstery accents. Corner Room 123 is particularly appealing for its arrangement. You're three subway stops on the U-1 line from the city center. There's parking for both cars and bicycles. *Kleine Stadtgutgasse 4, tel. 0222/214–5521, fax 0222/214–5521–17. 62 rooms, 40 with bath. Facilities: bar, TV room, parking. No credit cards.*

Seasonal hotels. A number of student dormitories are opened up to the public during the July–September holiday season. Unless you have a specific location in mind, the easiest way to check availabilities is to call the Albertina central administration office at 0222/512–7493, fax 0222/521–1968, or the Rosen-Hotel group, 0222/597–0680–0, fax 0222/597–0689–89, but note that the Rosen group includes more expensive quarters in addition to seasonal hotels; be sure to determine the price category in advance of booking. Many seasonal hotels will take credit cards.

The Arts

Theater and Opera Check the monthly program published by the city; posters also show opera and theater schedules. Tickets for the Opera, Volksoper, and the Burg and Akademie theaters are available at the central ticket office to the left rear of the Opera (**Bundestheaterkassen**, Hanuschgasse 3, tel. 0222/514–44–0, fax 0222/514–44–2969; open weekdays Mon.–Fri. 8 AM–6 PM, Sat., Sun., holidays 9 AM–noon. New information office in the opera arcades (Kärntnerstrasse) open Mon.–Fri. 10 AM to one hour before performance; Sat. 10 AM–noon, closed Sun. and holidays. Telephone ticket sales (credit card) 0222/513–1513. Tickets go on advance sale a week before performances. Unsold tickets can be obtained at the evening box office. Plan to be there at least one hour before the performance; students can buy remaining tickets at lower prices, so they are usually out in force. Tickets can be ordered six days in advance from anywhere in the world by phone (tel. 0222/513–1513; AE, DC, MC, V). The bargain way to attend an opera performance is to join the crowd in standing room; numbered entitlement tickets are given out in advance; with these, you line up an hour before the performance to buy the standing-room ticket itself. Theater is offered in English at **Vienna English Theater** (Josefsgasse 12, tel. 0222/402–1260) and **International Theater** (Porzellangasse 8 Müllnergasse, tel. 0222/319–6272).

Music Most classical concerts are in either the **Konzerthaus** (Lothringerstr. 20, tel. 0222/712–1211, fax 0222/713–1709) or **Musikverein** (Dumbastr. 3, tel. 0222/505–8190, fax 0222/505–9409). Tickets can be bought at the box offices (AE, DC, MC, V). Pop concerts are scheduled from time to time at the **Austria Center** (Am Hubertusdamm 6, tel. 0222/236–9150; U-1 subway to Vienna International Center stop). Tickets to various musical events are available via Vienna Ticket Service, tel. 0222/587–9843, fax 0222/587–9844 or at the "Salettl" gazebo ticket office on the Kärntnerstrasse next to the opera, where after 2 PM you can get remaining tickets to evening musicals and other events at half price (tel. 0222/588–85–0, AE, DC, MC, V).

Film Films are shown in English at **Burg Kino** (Opernring 19, tel. 0222/587–8406), **de France** (Schottenring 5, tel. 0222/317–5236), **English Cinema Haydn** (Mariahilferstr. 57, tel. 0222/587–2262), **Top Kino** (Rahlgasse 1, tel. 0222/587–5557), and **Film Museum** (Augustinerstr. 1, tel. 0222/533–7054). To find English-language movies, look for "OF" (*Originalfassung*, original language) or "OmU" (original with subtitles) in the newspaper listings.

Jazz **Jazzland** (Franz Josefs-Kai 29, tel. 0222/533–2575) is the enduring center for Dixie and traditional jazz, with top performers regularly, including such artists as Art Farmer; around the corner at **Roter Engel** (Rabensteig 5, tel. 0222/535–4105) you'll find impromptu sessions; a relative newcomer to the modern jazz scene is **Porgy & Bess** (Spiegelgasse 2, tel. 0222/512–8438–0).

Nightlife

Cabarets Most cabarets are expensive and unmemorable. Two of the best are **Casanova** (Dorotheergasse 6, tel. 0222/512–9845), which emphasizes striptease, and **Moulin Rouge** (Walfischgasse 11, tel. 0222/512–2130).

Discos **Atrium** (Schwarzenbergpl. 10, tel. 0222/505–3594) is open Thursday through Sunday and draws a lively younger crowd. **Queen Anne** (Johannesgasse 12, tel. 0222/512–0203) is central, popular, and always packed. The **U-4** (Schönbrunnerstr. 222, tel. 0222/858307) ranks high among the young set.

Nightclubs A casual '50s atmosphere pervades the popular **Café Volksgarten** (Burgring 1, tel. 0222/533–0518), situated in the city park of the same name; tables are set outdoors in summer. Live bands, dancing, and snacks are offered at **Chattanooga** (Graben 29, tel. 0222/533–5000).

Wine Taverns For a traditional Viennese night out, head to one of the city's atmospheric wine taverns, some of which date as far back as the 12th century. You can often have full meals at these taverns, but the emphasis is mainly on drinking. **Melker Stiftskeller** (Schottengasse 3, tel. 0222/533–5530) is one of the friendliest and most typical of Vienna's wine taverns. Other well-known ones: **Augustinerkeller** (Augustinerstr. 1, tel. 0222/533–1026), open at lunchtime as well as during the evenings, with good food and wine and reasonable prices, in the same building as the Albertina collection; **Esterhazykeller** (Haarhof 1, tel. 0222/533–3482), a particularly mazelike network of rooms; and **Zwölf-Apostelkeller** (Sonnenfelsgasse 3, tel. 0222/512–6777), deep underground near St. Stephen's Cathedral.

Salzburg

Arriving and Departing

By Plane For information, phone Salzburg airport, tel. 0662/852091.

Between the Airport and Downtown Buses leave for the Salzburg train station at Südtirolerplatz every 15 minutes during the day, every half hour at night. Journey time is 18 minutes.

By Train Salzburg's main train station is at Südtirolerplatz. Train information, tel. 0662/1717; ticket orders and seat reservations, tel. 0662/1700.

By Bus The central bus terminal (information: tel. 0662/167 for postal buses, 0662/872150 for railroad buses) is in front of the train station, although during construction of the underground local railroad station in front of the main rail station, various bus stops may be scattered around the square.

Getting Around

By Bus and Trolleybus Service is frequent and reliable; route maps are available from the tourist office or your hotel. Save money by buying a block of five single tickets (AS15 each) or a 24-hour ticket (AS32) that is good on all trolley and bus lines, on the funicular up to the fortress, on the Mönchsberg lift, and on the rail line north to Bergheim; half-price tickets for children 6–15. Local transportation information, tel. 0662/620551–31.

Tourist Information

Salzburg's official tourist office, **Stadtverkehrsbüro,** has an **information center** at Mozartplatz 5, tel. 0662/847568, and at the main train station, tel. 0662/871712. The main office is at Auerspergstrasse 7, tel. 0662/88987–0.

Exploring Salzburg

Numbers in the margin correspond to points of interest on the Salzburg map.

Salzburg is best known as the birthplace of Wolfgang Amadeus Mozart and receives its greatest number of visitors during the annual Music Festival in July and August. Dominated by a fortress on one side and a minimountain (Kapuzinerberg) on the other, this Baroque city is best explored on foot. Many areas are pedestrian precincts. Some of the most interesting boutiques and shops are found in the dozens of alleys and passageways that link streets and squares. And take an umbrella: Salzburg is noted for sudden, brief downpours that start as abruptly as they stop.

The Salzach River separates the old and new towns; for the best perspective on the old, climb the **Kapuziner** hill (pathways from the Linzerstrasse or Steingasse). Once back down at river level, walk up
❶ through Markartplatz to the **Landestheater,** where opera and operettas are staged during the winter months; the larger houses used during the festival are closed most of the year. Just across the street is the newly reconstructed **Mozart Residence,** now housing archives, audiovisual facilities, and a small recital hall. Wander through the Baroque **Mirabell** gardens in back of the theater and enjoy a dramatic view of the Old City, with the castle in the background. If you are
❷ pressed for time, you can pass up the **Baroque Museum.** *Admission: AS40 adults, AS20 children. Open Tues.–Sat. 9–noon and 2–5, Sun. 9–noon.*

❸ However, be sure to look inside **Schloss Mirabell.** It houses public offices, including that of the city's registrar; many couples come here for the experience of being married in such a sumptuous setting. The foyer and staircase, decorated with cherubs, are good examples of Baroque excess. Chamber music concerts are given in the Baroque hall upstairs in summer. *Mirabellpl., tel. 0662/8882–2258. Open Mon.–Thurs. 8–4, Fri. 8–1.*

Head left down Schwarzstrasse, back toward the center of the city.
❹ On your left is the famed **Mozarteum,** a music academy (Schwarzstr. 26, tel. 0662/88940–0) whose courtyard encloses the summerhouse in which Mozart wrote *The Magic Flute.* Cross over the Markartsteg footbridge to the Old City side of the Salzach River.
❺ Turn right and walk a short distance up the Kai to the **Carolino Augusteum Museum.** This is the city museum, whose collections include art and archaeology. *Museumspl. 1, tel. 0662/843145. Admission: AS40 adults, AS15 children; combined ticket with toy museum in Bürgerspital (see below), cathedral excavations, and Folklore Museum: AS60 adults, AS20 children. Open Tues. 9–8, Wed.–Sun. 9–5.*

❻ Follow the Gstättengasse to the **Bürgerspital,** which houses a toy and musical instruments museum within its Renaissance arcades. *Bürgerspitalpl. 2, tel. 0662/847560. Admission: AS30 adults, AS10 children, or combined ticket with Carolino Augusteum. Open Tues.–Sun. 9–5.*

Ahead is Herbert-von-Karajan-Platz, whose central **Pferdeschwemme** (Horse Fountain) is its most notable feature. Built into
❼ the side of the mountain itself is the **Festspielhaus,** a huge complex where Salzburg's annual festival, the Festspiel, is held. *Hofstallgasse 1, tel. 0662/8045–0.*

From the Festspielhaus, turn left into the Wiener-Philharmoniker-
❽ Strasse. The **Kollegienkirche** (Collegiate Church) on the left is the work of Fischer von Erlach and is one of the best examples of Baroque architecture anywhere; be sure to look inside. On weekday mornings the Universitätsplatz, in front of the church, is crowded with market stands. Cut under the covered passageway and turn right into Sigmund-Haffner-Gasse. At the corner on the left stands
❾ the 13th-century **Franziskanerkirche** (Franciscan Church), an eclectic mix of architectural styles, with Romanesque and Gothic ac-
❿ cents. Nearby, at Domplatz, is the Salzburg **Dom** (cathedral), a magnificently proportioned building; note the great bronze doors as you enter.

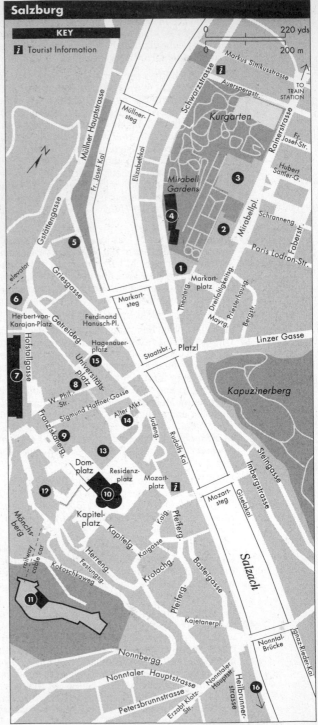

To reach the fortress on the hill above, walk under the arcade to the right side of the church and up the narrow Festungsgasse at the back end of Kapitalplatz. From here, you can either follow the footpath up the hill or take a five-minute ride on the Festungsbahn, the inclined railway cable car. On a sunny day, a far more pleasurable— and strenuous—route is to hike up the Festungsgasse, turning frequently to enjoy the changing panorama of the city below.

⑪ Once you've reached the **Festung Hohensalzburg** itself, you can wander around on your own (admission: AS30 adults, AS15 children) or take a tour (admission and tour: AS60 adults, AS55 senior citizens, AS35 children). The views from the 12th-century fortress are magnificent in all directions. The main attraction is **St. George's Chapel,** built in 1501. A year later the Festung acquired the 200-pipe barrel organ, which plays daily in summer at 7 AM, 11 AM, and 6 PM. *Mönchsberg, tel. 0662/8042–2133. Open July–Sept., daily 8–7; Apr.–June, Oct., daily 9–6; Nov.–Mar., daily 9–5. Guided tour schedule varies.*

⑫ Back down in the city, follow the wall to **Stiftskirche St. Peter** (St. Peter's Abbey). The cemetery lends an added air of mystery to the monk's caves cut into the cliff. The catacombs attached to the church can be visited by guided tour. *Just off Kapitalplatz, tel. 0662/ 844578–0. Admission: AS12 adults, AS8 children. Tours May– Sept., daily 10–5, Oct.–Apr., daily 11–noon and 1:30–3:30. Check tour schedules on the notice board.*

Head around the cathedral to the spacious Residenzplatz, a vast and
⑬ elegant square. The **Residenz** itself includes prince-archbishop's living quarters and representative rooms. *Residenzpl. 1, tel. 0662/ 8042–2690. Admission: AS45 adults, AS35 senior citizens, children AS15. Tours Sept.–June, weekdays at 10, 11, 12, 2, and 3; July– Aug., daily every 30 mins. from 10 to 4:30.*

The **Residenzgalerie,** in the same building complex, has an outstanding collection of 16th- to 19th-century European art. *Residenzpl. 1, tel. 0662/8042–2270. Admission: AS45 adults, AS35 senior citizens, AS15 children. Combined ticket with state rooms: AS70. Open daily 10–5. Closed on Wed. Oct.–Mar.*

⑭ From the lower end of Residenzplatz, cut across into the **Alter Markt,** which still serves as an open market. Salzburg's narrowest house is squeezed into the north side of the square. Turn left into Getreidegasse, a tiny street packed with boutiques and fascinating
⑮ shops. At the head of the tiny Rathausplatz is **Mozart's birthplace,** now a museum. *Getreidegasse 9, tel. 0662/844313. Admission: AS62 adults, AS47 senior citizens, AS17 children. Open daily 9–6; during the festival, daily 9–7.*

⑯ One popular excursion from Salzburg is to **Schloss Hellbrunn,** about 5 kilometers (3 miles) outside the city. Take Bus 55. The castle was built during the 17th century, and its rooms have some fine trompe l'oeil decorations. The castle's full name is Lustschloss Hellbrunn— Hellbrunn Pleasure Castle. It was designed for the relaxation of Salzburg's prince-bishops and includes the **Wasserspiele,** or fountains, conceived by someone with an impish sense of humor. Expect to get sprinkled as water shoots up from unlikely spots, such as the center of the table at which you're seated. The Baroque fountains are also fascinating. Both the castle and the fountain gardens can be included on a tour. *Tel. 0662/820372. Admission: AS48 adults, AS24 children. Tours Apr. and Oct., daily 9–4:30; May–Sept., daily 9–5. Evening tours July–Aug. at 6, 7, 8, 9, and 10 PM.*

Dining

$$ **Zum Eulenspiegel.** Salzburgers claim that the food here is not as
★ good as elsewhere and that the place is too full of tourists. They're

partly right, but the restaurant, on four floors of a narrow old house, has numerous intimate corners, a winding staircase, and delicately elegant decor that make it one of the most romantic places around. It's right in the middle of town, the friendly staff speaks English, and the food is certainly nothing to complain about. With dishes such as suckling pig with potato strudel, and pickled salmon trout with honey-mustard sauce, it should be on your agenda. *Hagenauerplatz 2, tel. 0662/843180-0. Reservations advised. MC, V. Closed Sun. except during the festival; also closed Jan.–mid-Mar.*

$$ **Zum Mohren.** Good food, a central location by the river, a welcoming
★ atmosphere, friendly service, and reasonable prices have made Zum Mohren a favorite with both Salzburgers and tourists. The restaurant is in the basement of a 15th-century house: atmospheric but a little cramped. If this bothers you, try for a table in the room to the right as you enter. The menu always offers at least one vegetarian item and several fish dishes among a selection of Austrian specialties like sautéed veal liver and roast hare. *Judengasse 9/Rudolfskai 20, tel. 0662/842387. Reservations advised. No credit cards. Closed Sun. and holidays; June; and 1 wk in Nov.*

$ **Stiftskeller St. Peter.** Choose the garden or one of the less formal
★ rooms in what is said to be Europe's oldest Gasthaus. You'll come in under budget if you stick to standards such as *Leberknödelsuppe* (liver dumpling soup) and roast pork; the open house wines are excellent, particularly the white *Grüner Veltliner Prälatenwein*. *St. Peter district I4, tel. 0662/841268. Reservations advised, particularly in festival season. AE, DC, MC, V.*

$ **Wilder Mann.** The atmosphere may be too smoky for some (choose
★ the outside courtyard in summer), but the beamed ceiling and antlers are genuine, as are the food and value. Try the *Tellerfleisch* (boiled beef) or game in season. *Getreidegasse 20/Griesgasse 17 (passageway), tel. 0662/841787. Reservations advised. No credit cards. Closed Sun.*

$ **Zipfer Bierhaus.** This traditional Gasthaus dates from the 1600s and offers standard Austrian favorites, such as roast chicken, veal, and game in season. Mozart's sister Nannerl lived upstairs in the 1700s; look down the 16th-century well between the two sections of the restaurant. *Sigmund-Haffner-Gasse 12/Universitätspl. 19, tel. 0662/840745. Reservations advised. No credit cards. Closed Sun. and holidays.*

¢ **Augustiner Bräu.** Bring your own picnic or select your food, from grilled chicken to salads, at one of the nine stands, then enjoy your choice along with the excellent house beer, either at one of the wooden tables or, in summer, outdoors in the popular garden. *Augustinergasse 4, tel. 0662/431246. No reservations. No credit cards. Open daily 3–11.*

¢ **Bürgerwehr-Einkehr.** The location atop Mönchsberg (hike up, or take the elevator) overlooking the city adds that special touch to the basic Gasthaus fare of roast meats or chicken. Either wine or beer is the right accompaniment. *Mönchsberg 19c, tel. 0662/841729. No reservations. No credit cards. Closed mid-Oct.–April.*

¢ **Fasties.** There are two branches of this starkly modern, friendly
★ snack bar, where you'll find foods ranging from sandwiches and salads to tasty hot noodle dishes with Italian overtones. The high stools are not the most comfortable, but that's the trade-off for the quality of food and the reasonable prices. The Pfeifergasse location, just off Mozartplatz, is more of a bistro and has more comfortable seating. *Lasserstr. 19, tel. 0662/873876. Open weekdays 11–7:30. Pfeifergasse 3, tel. 0662/844774. Open weekdays 8 AM–8 PM, Sat. 8–3; 8 AM–9 PM Mon.–Sat., mid-June–mid-Oct. No credit cards.*

¢ **Humboldt-Stuben.** The hunting-lodge atmosphere in the main room
★ seems just right for any of the Austrian standards such as pork with sauerkraut or pork schnitzel, served until 1:30 AM, long after most restaurants have closed. The daily specials are usually excellent and

good value. Alternatively, tackle the enormous salad bar. *Gstätten-gasse 6, tel. 0662/843171. Reservations advised. No credit cards.*

¢ **Sternbräu.** During the summer, the spacious self-service garden is a favorite in this complex of restaurants, but there's atmosphere to spare in the other rooms, such as the wood-paneled wine *keller* (tavern). Try any of the typical Austrian specialties, such as sausages or *Stelze* (knuckle of pork). *Griesgasse 23, tel. 0662/842140–0. No reservations. No credit cards. Open daily 9 AM–11 PM.*

¢ **Zum fidelen Affen.** If you don't have a reservation, you'll have to
★ fight Salzburg's young businesspeople for a table in this popular but somewhat smoky beer bar–restaurant, decked out with rough wooden floors and tables. Try the filling *Schinkenfleckerl* (a baked ham and pasta dish) or ask for the vegetarian specialties, such as spinach strudel. *Preisterhausgasse 8, tel. 0662/877361. Reservations advisable. No credit cards. Open Mon.–Sat. 5:30–11 PM.*

Lodging

Reservations are always advisable and are essential at festival time (both Easter and summer), particularly for scarce low-price accommodations. High season is mid-July to mid- or late August, and regular guests book a year or more in advance. Cheaper accommodations fill quickly; if you don't have a booking, check the tourist office at the rail station or at Mozartplatz. Be sure to get confirmation of reservations in writing. For available private rooms, also try Eveline Truhlar at Bob's Special Tours (0662/859411–0). Most private rooms are somewhat out of the center so you'll be dependent on bus schedules and need travel time. Driving a car into the city is unwise, and parking garages are expensive. For details and price-category definitions, *see* Lodging *in* Staying in Austria, *above.*

$$ **Amadeus.** Rooms in this family-run house are tasteful and spacious,
★ if simple, with natural wood and rustic accessories. Skillful renovations behind the period pink facade have turned a building that dates from the 1500s into a modern hotel that retains its intriguing winding stone stairs and original narrow hallways. It's centrally located and within a couple of minutes' walk of the sites across the river. *Linzer Gasse 43–45, tel. 0662/871401, fax 0662/876163–7. 23 rooms with bath or shower. AE, DC.*

$$ **Wolf.** The embodiment of Austrian gemütlichkeit, just off the
★ Mozartplatz, the Wolf offers spotlessly clean and cozy rooms at reasonable prices. The rooms in this small family-run hotel are idiosyncratically arranged on several upper floors, connected by narrow, winding stairs, and are decorated with a pleasing Salzburg mix of rag rugs and rural furniture. The staff is friendly and helpful; the only problem is getting a room here. *Kaigasse 7, tel. 0662/843453–0, fax 0662/842423. 12 rooms. AE. Closed mid-Feb.–mid-Mar.*

$ **Haus Wartenberg.** This rambling older house offers spacious double rooms along with tiny singles and doubles at yet lower prices, all pleasantly furnished in rustic country style. You're a brisk 10-minute walk or a short ride on the 1, 2, or 15 O-Bus lines from the center. *Riedenburger Str. 2, tel. 0662/844284, fax 0662/844284–5. 18 rooms, 10 with bath. Facilities: restaurant, garage. DC.*

$ **Markus Sittikus.** Rooms here are light and attractive, and many on
★ the top floor get lovely morning sunlight. The train station is nearby, and the staff is friendly and helpful. This is a popular hotel, so book early, particularly for the cheaper rooms; otherwise prices are above the $ category. *Markus-Sittikus-Str. 20, tel. 0662/871121–0, fax 0662/871121–58. 41 rooms with bath or shower. AE, DC, MC, V.*

$ **Schwarzes Rössl.** This onetime traditional Gasthof is now a seasonal hotel outside of the school year, when it is not occupied by students. Rooms are fresh and immaculate if not elegant, and the location is excellent, close to nighttime action and only a couple of minutes' walk across the bridge to the old city. *Priesterhausgasse 6, tel. 0662/ 874426, fax (reservations) 0222/401–7620. 51 rooms with bath. AE, DC, MC, V. Closed Oct.–June.*

$ **Traube.** Another of the city's former traditional hotels is open as seasonal accommodation during summer school holidays. Rooms are varied in size and the spacious baths are mainly down the hall, but the Traube still retains a quaint charm and the location is splendid. *Linzer Gasse 4, tel. 0662/88960–1, fax 0662/878671. 40 rooms, 14 with bath. AE, DC, MC, V. Closed Oct.–June.*

$ **Trumer Stube.** Guests repeatedly recommend this family-run pen-
★ sion, mentioning the friendly atmosphere and helpful staff. It's in a well-kept old building down a narrow, winding street near Mirabellplatz. The breakfast room is bright and cheerful; the simple but pleasant guest rooms are scrupulously clean and are redecorated every four years. Ask for a room in the lower price category; the best rooms are beyond the $ prices. *Bergstr. 6, tel. 0662/874776, fax 0662/874326. 22 rooms with shower. No credit cards.*

¢ **Bergland.** You're a bit farther from the city center in this simple pension, but still within walking distance of the main sights. If Bergland is full, you'll probably be referred to one of the other nearby, but slightly more expensive, pensions. *Rupertgasse 15, tel. 0662/872318, fax 0662/872318–8. 18 rooms with shower. No credit cards. Closed Nov.–Dec. 20.*

¢ **Jahn.** The upstairs rooms (street level is a Chinese restaurant) are clean if modest. The railroad station is two blocks away, and you can walk into the city center if you don't want to take a bus. Rooms with bath are just above the ¢ category. *Elisabethstr. 31, tel. 0662/ 871405, fax 0662/875535. 21 rooms, 15 with bath. Facilities: parking. MC, V.*

¢ **Römerwirt.** Some of the rooms in this friendly Gasthof have views up to the back side of the fortress. Accommodation is simple but clean, and there's a pleasant garden in the inner court. Bus 5 will take you to the center; it's a bit of a hike but possible. *Nonntaler Hauptstr. 47, tel. 0662/829423. 35 rooms, 15 with bath. No credit cards. Closed Oct.–Mar.*

¢ **Überfuhr.** This friendly, family-run Gasthof is directly on the river about 2 kilometers (1 ¼ miles) south of the city. A room with bath will tip the price just over the $ category. Front rooms have a view of the fortress but also have traffic noise, which fortunately is fairly light. You can walk to town or hike a longish two blocks and take the No. 49 bus to the center. The popular house restaurant (closed Mon.) offers Austrian standards and moves into the garden in summer. *Ignaz-Rieder-Kai 43, tel. 0662/623010–0, fax 0662/623010–4. 20 rooms, 13 with bath. AE, DC, MC, V. Closed Feb.*

The Arts

Festivals   Tickets for performances are almost impossible to get once you are in Salzburg. Write ahead to **Salzburger Festspiele** (Postfach 140, A-5010 Salzburg, fax 0662/846682).

Opera, Music,   Theater and opera are presented in the **Festspielhaus** (*see* Explor-
and Art   ing, *above*), opera and operetta at the **Landestheater** (Schwarzstr. 22, tel. 0662/871512–0), and concerts at the **Mozarteum** (Schwarzstr. 26, tel. 0662/873154–0). Chamber music—in costume—is performed in **Schloss Mirabell**. Special art exhibits in the **Carolino Augusteum** (*see* Exploring, *above*) are often outstanding.

Innsbruck

Arriving and Departing

By Plane   The airport is 3 kilometers (2 miles) west of the city. For flight information, phone 0512/22525–304.

Between the Airport and Downtown   Buses (Line F) to the city center (Maria-Theresien-Str.) run every 20 minutes and take about 20 minutes. Get your ticket from the bus driver; it costs AS18.

By Train   All trains stop at the city's main station at Südtiroler-Platz. Connections are available to Munich, Vienna, Rome, and Zurich. For information, phone 0512/1717. Ticket reservations, tel. 0512/1700.

By Bus   The terminal is to the right of the main train station.

Getting Around

By Bus and Streetcar   Most bus and streetcar routes begin or end at Südtiroler-Platz, site of the main train station. The bus is the most convenient way to reach the six major ski areas outside the city. Many hotels offer free transportation with direct hotel pickup; for those staying in the Old City, the buses leave from in front of the Landestheater. Check with your hotel or the tourist offices for schedules.

Tourist Information

The city's two main tourist offices are at Burggraben 3 (tel. 0512/5356, fax 0512/5356–43—Innsbruck) and Wilhelm-Greil-Strasse 17 (tel. 0512/5320–170, fax 0512/5320–174—Tirol). Ask about the Club-Innsbruck pass, which opens the door to a number of discounts.

Exploring Innsbruck

Numbers in the margin correspond to points of interest on the Innsbruck map.

At the center of the province of Tirol lies the quaint and well-preserved capital city of Innsbruck. Squeezed by the mountains and sharing the valley with the Inn River, Innsbruck is compact and very easy to explore on foot. The ancient city—it received its municipal charter in 1239—no doubt owes much of its fame and charm to its unique situation. To the north, the steep, sheer sides of the Alps rise like a shimmering blue-and-white wall from the edge of the city, an awe-inspiring backdrop to the mellowed green domes and red roofs of the picturesque Baroque town.

Modern-day Innsbruck retains close associations with three historical figures: Emperor Maximilian I and Empress Maria Theresa, both of whom are responsible for much of the city's architecture, and Andreas Hofer, a Tirolean patriot. You will find repeated references
① to them as you tour the city. A good starting point is the **Goldenes Dachl** (the Golden Roof), which made the ancient mansion whose balcony it covers famous. (It's actually made of copper tiles, gilded with 14 kg [31 lbs.] of gold.) The building now houses an **Olympic Museum,** which features videotapes of the Innsbruck winter Olympics. *Herzog-Friedrich-Str. 15, tel. 0512/5360–575. Admission: AS22 adults, AS11 children. Open daily 9:30–5:30. Closed on Mon., Nov.–Feb.*

② A walk up the Hofgasse brings you to the **Hofburg,** the Rococo imperial palace, with its ornate reception hall decorated with portraits of Maria Theresa's ancestors. *Rennweg 1, tel. 0512/587186. Admis-*

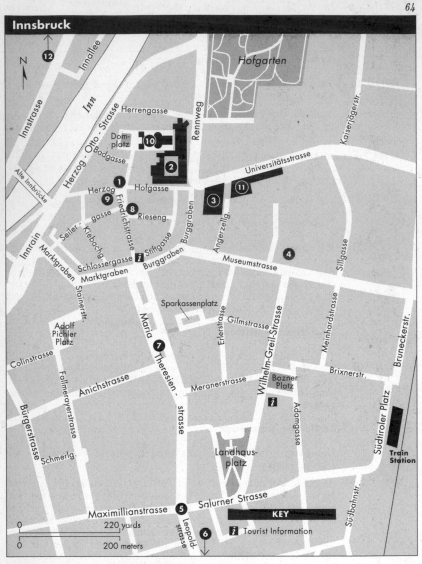

Innsbruck

Hofgarten

Herrengasse
Rennweg
Universitätsstrasse

Dom-
platz

Herzog - Otto - Strasse

Badgasse

Hofgasse

Herzog Friedrichstrasse

Rieseng.

Seiler - Kiebachg.

Stiftgasse

Burggraben

Angerzellg.

Kaiserjägerstr.

Schlossergasse

Burggraben

Museumstrasse

Stillgasse

Marktgraben

Marktgraben

Innrain

Stainerstr.

Sparkassenplatz

Erlerstrasse

Gilmstrasse

Meinhardstrasse

Bruneckerstr.

Adolf
Pichler
Platz

Maria

Theresien-

strasse

Wilhelm-Greil-Strasse

Colinstrasse

Fallmerayerstrasse

Anichstrasse

Meranerstrasse

Bozner
Platz

Brixnerstr.

Südtiroler Platz

Bürgerstrasse

Schmerlg.

Landhaus-
platz

Adamgasse

Train
Station

Süd-bahnstr.

Maximillianstrasse

Salurner Strasse

Leopold-
strasse

0   220 yards

0   200 meters

KEY

i   Tourist Information

Inn

Innallee

Innstrasse

Alte Innbrücke

N

Major Attractions
Annasäule, **7**
Ferdinandeum, **4**
Goldenes Dachl, **1**
Grassmayr Bell
Museum, **6**
Hofburg, **2**
Hofkirche, **3**
Triumphpforte, **5**

Other Attractions
Alpine Zoo, **12**
Dom zu St. Jakob, **10**
Helblinghaus, **9**
Stadtturm, **8**
Tiroler Volkskunst-
museum, **11**

sion: AS50 adults, AS10 children. Open mid-May–mid-Oct., daily 9–5; mid-Oct.–mid-May, Mon.–Sat. 9–5.

❸ Close by is the **Hofkirche,** the Imperial Church, built as a mausoleum for Maximilian. The emperor is surrounded by 24 marble reliefs portraying his accomplishments, as well as 28 oversize statues of his ancestors, including the legendary King Arthur. The above-mentioned Andreas Hofer is also buried here. Don't miss the silver chapel with its ornate altar. The **Tiroler Volkskunstmuseum** (Tirolean Folk Art Museum) is housed in the Hofkirche, too, and shows costumes, rustic furniture, and farmhouse rooms decorated in styles ranging from Gothic to Rococo. *Universitätsstr. 2, tel. 0512/584302. Admission: Hofkirche AS20 adults, AS10 children; Volkskunstmuseum AS40 adults, AS15 children; combined ticket: AS50 adults. Hofkirche open Sept.–June, daily 9–5; July–Aug., daily 9–5:30; Volkskunstmuseum open Sept.–June, Mon.–Sat. 9–5, Sun. 9–noon; July–Aug., Mon.–Sat. 9–5:30, Sun. 9–noon.*

❹ Follow Museumstrasse to the **Ferdinandeum,** which houses Austria's largest collection of Gothic art, as well as paintings from the 19th and 20th centuries. *Museumstr. 15, tel. 0512/594–8971. Admission: AS50 adults, AS40 senior citizens, AS20 children. Open May–Sept., daily 10–5, Thurs. eve. 7–9; Oct.–Apr., Tues.–Sat. 10–noon and 2–5, Sun. and holidays 10–1.*

❺ Cut back down Wilhelm-Greil-Strasse to the **Triumphpforte** (Triumphal Arch), built in 1765. For an unusual treat, turn left to visit the **❻** **Grassmayr Bell Museum** to see how bells are made. *Leopoldstr. 53, tel. 0512/59416–34. Admission: AS20 adults, AS10 children. Open Mon.–Fri. 9–6, Sat. 9–12.*

❼ Walk up Maria-Theresien-Strasse past the **Annasäule** (Anna Column) for a classic "postcard" view of Innsbruck with the Alps in the background.

Shopping

Shopping Districts Many shops are found in the historic streets of Maria-Theresien-Strasse, Museumstrasse, Brixnerstrasse, Meranerstrasse, and among the arcades of Herzog-Friedrich-Strasse.

Gift Ideas The best-known and best-loved local specialties include Tirolean hats (those gray or green felt ones, garnished with a feather), loden cloth, lederhosen, dirndls, wood carvings, and mountain and skiing equipment.

Dining

For details and price-category definitions, *see* Dining *in* Staying in Austria, *above.*

$$ **Hirschenstuben.** These rustic rooms are just right for the game,
★ trout, and other local specialties served in this ancient house. The Italian dishes, such as osso buco, are also excellent. *Kiebachgasse 5, tel. 0512/582979. Reservations advised. AE, DC, MC, V. Closed Sun. and Mon. lunch; 2nd ½ of Jan., mid-June–early July.*

$ **Engl.** This is a Gasthaus in the true sense of the word: a simple setting, moderately attentive but overworked personnel, and large helpings of delicious food. Look for pork and chicken dishes here, but check the daily specials as well. *Innstr. 22, tel. 0512/283112. No reservations. AE, DC, MC, V. Closed Sun.*

$ **Ottoburg.** A rabbit warren of rooms, in a 13th-century building, the
★ Ottoburg is exactly right for an intimate, cozy lunch or dinner. Looks are not deceiving; the country decor you see upstairs is genuine, although you'll find the less intimate Stüberl on the lower level of the ground floor to be less expensive. The daily specials are excellent value; otherwise, you can be tempted over the $$ range here.

Herzog-Friedrich-Str. 1, tel. 0512/574652. Reservations advised. AE, DC, MC, V. Closed 2 wks in Nov.

$ Stieglbräu. Lovers of good beer will be delighted to find this popular rustic spot, which, in addition to its thirst-quenching brews, provides good, solid Austrian fare. Portions are substantial, the garden exceptionally pleasant. The noonday specials are excellent, but so are the traditional pork, beef, and chicken entrées. *Wilhelm-Greil-Str. 25, 0512/584338. No credit cards.*

$ Weisses Rossl. A friendly family atmosphere with a Tirolean accent marks this pleasant restaurant. The food is simple but excellent; *Tiroler G'röstl,* a tasty hash, is a good example, but check the daily specials first. *Kiebachgasse 8, tel. 0512/583057. AE, MC, V. Closed Sun., holidays, early Nov., mid-Apr.*

¢ Gasthaus Steden. The substantial portions and unassuming (if occasionally smoky) atmosphere attract businessmen as well as regulars to this thoroughly authentic Gasthaus. The roast pork is particularly tasty, and the daily specialties are a good value. *Anichstr. 15, tel. 0512/580890. No credit cards. Closed Sun., holidays.*

¢ Inn 95. The diners in this casual spot, mainly from the adjacent hostel, are mostly young and not very critical, but you'll still find fair value in the daily noontime specials. The *Knödel* (dumplings) are filling and good. *Innstr. 95, tel. 0512/86515. No credit cards. Closed Sun., holidays.*

¢ Schnitzelparadies. The specialty is schnitzel and variations, but the mixed grill and salads are good, too. The atmosphere is casual Old London, with Tiffany lamps, oak floors, and even an English phone booth. *Innrain 25, tel. 0512/572972. No reservations. No credit cards. Closed Sun., holidays.*

¢ Wienerwald. The grilled and fried chicken here are outstanding. You'll find other specialties as well, although most are beyond the $ category. The open wines are excellent, and there are salad bars. In summer, the gardens of both locations are particularly pleasant and stay open to 11 PM. *Maria-Theresien-Str. 12, tel. 0512/584165-0, and Museumstr. 24, tel. 0512/588994. Reservations advised. AE, DC, MC, V.*

Lodging

The best accommodation bargains during the winter are those included in ski package deals; during the summer, student dorms are transformed into modest hotels, though they are not necessarily the cheapest or most central. During the school year, the overflow of students occupies well over half of the private rooms as well; much of what's left, even students won't take. Most private accommodations have less than a handful of rooms. Rather than phoning around for a bargain vacancy, you'll save time and probably money as well by going directly to the city-run room-booking office (*Zimmernachweis*) in the rail station or the tourist office in Burggraben.

For details and price-category definitions, *see* Lodging *in* Staying in Austria, *above.*

$$ Weisses Kreuz. At first encounter, you'll fall in love with this hotel, set over the stone arcades in the heart of the old city. It has seen massive renovations since the first Gasthof stood on this site in 1465, and the rooms are simple but comfortable, with mainly rustic furniture and lots of light wood. The service is friendly and accommodating; there are special rooms on the ground floor in which you can keep your skis; hotel reception and a restaurant are upstairs. *Herzog Friedrich-Str. 31, A-6020, tel. 0512/59479-0, fax 0512/59479-90. 39 rooms, 28 with bath or shower. Facilities: 2 restaurants. AE, V.*

$ ★ Binder. A short streetcar (Line 3) trip from the center of town shouldn't be too high a price to pay for less costly comfort at this small, friendly hotel. The family management is particularly outgoing. Rooms are immaculate if not luxurious. *Dr.-Glatz-Str. 20, tel. 0521/33436–0, fax 0512/33436–99. 32 rooms, most with bath or shower. Facilities: bar, parking, garage. AE, MC, V.*

$ **Rössl in der Au.** This student dorm offers convenient, reasonably priced quarters in summer, plus views across the river to the old city. The rooms are modern, if somewhat spartan. Check prices, as some are above the $ category. *Höttinger Au 34, tel. 0512/286846 or 0512/226460, fax 0512/293850. 140 rooms with bath. Facilities: garage, parking. AE, DC, MC, V. Open July–Sept.*

$ **Tautermann.** This family-run, friendly hotel in a converted villa
★ above the city offers informal but complete comfort other than an elevator. The rooms are in natural woods against white; the upper rooms on the west side have gorgeous views of the nearby mountains. Bus A to Höttinger Kirchenplatz gets you to within a short block. Some rooms are priced above the $ range. *Stamser Feld 5, tel. 0512/281572, fax 0512/281572–10. 28 rooms with bath or shower. Facilities: parking. AE, DC, MC, V.*

¢ **Innbrücke.** The pink facade of this 550-year-old house on the river across from the old city conceals simple but attractive rooms furnished in light wood, with patterned wallpaper and carpeting; those in front, which have bay windows, are particularly appealing. *Innstr. 1, tel. 0512/281934. 20 rooms, some with bath. AE, DC, MC, V.*

¢ **Internationales Studentenhaus.** This is the best-located and cheapest of the seasonal hotels; it's a student dorm during the academic year. Accommodations are clean and adequate. *Rechengasse 7, tel. 0512/59477–0, fax 0512/59477–15. 275 rooms with shower. Facilities: parking. AE, DC, MC, V. Closed Sept.–June.*

¢ **Paula.** The trade-off to being outside of town is a lovely villa; you're in peaceful "green" territory, and most rooms have balconies. The K bus line gets you close to this friendly, highly personal pension. *Weiherburggasse 3, tel. 0512/292262. 12 rooms with bath or shower. Facilities: parking. No credit cards.*

¢ **Riese Haymon.** Facilities are modest, but most rooms in this former
★ cloister south of the town center near Wilten are fairly spacious. A few have showers, furnishings are eclectic, but the feature here is value and a friendly management. Buses J, K, and S take you virtually to the door. *Haymongasse 4, tel. 0512/589837, fax 0512/586190. 22 rooms, 7 with shower. Facilities: restaurant, café, parking. No credit cards.*

Nightlife

Innsbruck at night is livelier than first appearances indicate. Check **Café Brasil** (Leopoldstr. 7, tel. 0512/583466), with its stylishly shabby furnishings. **Das Büro** (Badgasse 3, tel. 0512/575633) is cool modern. The **Fischerhäusl** (Herrengasse 8, tel. 0512/583535) behind the cathedral is usually packed, and the action at the **Hofgarten Café** (Rennweg 6a, tel. 0512/588871) in the Hofgarten can go on well into the morning hours. The **Blue Chip** disco (Wilhelm-Greil-Str. 17, tel. 0512/565000) and **Jimmy's Bar** upstairs (Wilhelm-Greil-Str. 19, tel. 0512/570473) are current hot spots.

3   Belgium

Good things come in small packages. Belgium, which occupies the stretch of land bordering the North Sea between France and Holland, measures just under 320 kilometers (200 miles) from Oostende in the west to the German border, less than 160 kilometers (100 miles) from Antwerp in the north to the French border. This is good news for the budget-conscious traveler because it means that virtually all points of interest can be reached on one-day rail trips from the capital. With more than 10 million people, Belgium is the second most densely populated country in the world. Although influenced by the Dutch and the French, Belgium has a distinctive culture, or rather, two: Flemish and Walloon. The Flemish, who speak Dutch (Flemish), inhabit the northern half of the country and account for 56% of the population. The French-speaking Walloons live in the other half. The capital, Brussels, is officially designated a dual-language area.

In the course of history, the Belgians have been ruled by the Romans, French, Spanish, Austrians, Dutch, English, and Germans. Many of Europe's greatest battles have been fought on Belgian soil—from Waterloo and earlier to the long-slogging encounters of World War I. During World War II, this territory witnessed both the initial blitzkrieg of Nazi Panzer units and Hitler's final desperate counterattack against the advancing Allies in the Ardennes—an offensive that has gone down in history as the Battle of the Bulge.

Brussels stands in the very center of the country. A booming, expanding, and often expensive city, it is now the capital of Europe. Here the European Union (EU) has its headquarters. Over the past few years a number of new hotels have been constructed in Brussels for budget travelers. Away from the capital hotel prices are at least 20% lower, with particularly advantageous prices at resort hotels on the coast and in the Ardennes.

The south of the country is a wild, wooded area, with mountains rising to more than 620 meters (2,000 feet). In the Dutch-speaking north, on the other hand, the land is flat and heavily cultivated, much as it is in neighboring Holland. Here stand the medieval Flem-

Belgium

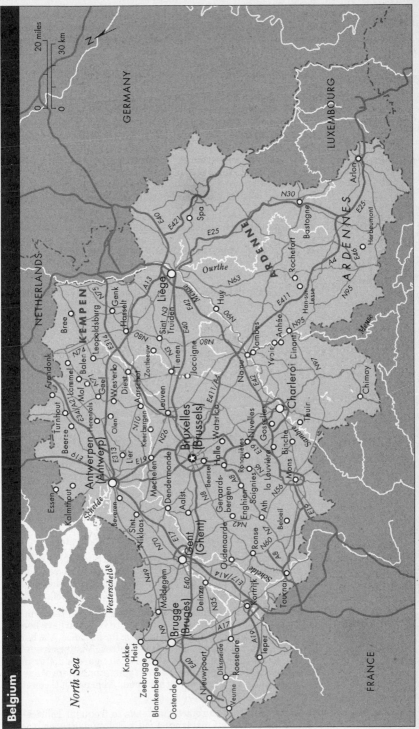

ish cities of Ghent and Brugge (Bruges), with their celebrated carillons and canals—not to mention the 68 kilometers (42 miles) of sandy beaches that make up the country's northern coastline. Due north of Brussels lies Antwerp, the country's dynamic seaport. This city, where the painter Rubens lived, is now the world's leading diamond-cutting center.

Essential Information

Before You Go

When to Go The tourist season runs from early May to late September and peaks in July and August, when the weather is warmest. May and September offer the advantage of generally clear skies and smaller crowds. In the coastal resorts, some hotels and restaurants remain open all year.

Climate Temperatures range from around 65°F in May to an average 73°F in July and August. In winter, temperatures drop to an average of about 40° to 45°F. Snow is unusual except in the mountains of the Ardennes, where cross-country skiing is a popular sport in February and March.

The following are the average daily maximum and minimum temperatures for Brussels.

Jan.	40F	4C	May	65F	18C	Sept.	69F	21C
	30	- 1		46	8		51	11
Feb.	44F	7C	June	72F	22C	Oct.	60F	15C
	32	0		52	11		45	7
Mar.	51F	11C	July	73F	23C	Nov.	48F	9C
	36	2		54	12		38	3
Apr.	58F	14C	Aug.	72F	22C	Dec.	42F	6C
	41	5		54	12		32	0

Currency The unit of currency in Belgium is the franc. There are bills of 100, 500, 1,000, 2,000, and 10,000 francs in addition to coins of 1, 5, 20, and 50 francs. At press time (summer 1995), the exchange rate was about BF32 to the dollar and BF45 to the pound sterling.

What It Will Cost A recent study suggested that the cost for a prudent but not penny-pinching week in Brussels will come to about $650 per person. This includes two gourmet meals, five prix-fixe menus, seven light meals, and a shared double room in a moderately priced hotel. Major Brussels hotels also offer substantially reduced summer rates.

Sample Prices A cup of coffee in a café will cost BF45–BF60; a glass of beer, BF35–BF85; and a glass of wine, about BF100. Train travel averages BF6 per mile, the average bus/metro/tram ride costs BF50, theater tickets cost about BF500, and movie tickets cost about BF250.

Customs on Arrival Since the introduction of the European Single Market, the limits for what visitors from EU countries may bring to Belgium have become generous to the point of being meaningless; for instance, 120 bottles of wine, 10 liters of alcohol, and 800 cigarettes. Visitors from non-EU countries can bring in 200 cigarettes or 50 cigars or 250 grams of tobacco, 2 liters of still wine and 1 liter of spirits or 2 liters of aperitif wine, and 50 grams of perfume. Other goods from non-EU countries may not exceed BF2,000 in value.

Language Language is a sensitive subject that leads to frequent political crises. There are three national languages in Belgium: French, spoken primarily in the south of the country (Wallonia); Dutch, spoken in the north; and German, spoken in a small area in the east. Brussels is bilingual, with both French and Flemish officially recognized, though French predominates. Many people speak English in Brussels and in the north (Flanders). If your French is good but your Flemish is nonexistent, it is politic to speak English to Flemings, especially in Antwerp or Flanders. In Wallonia you may have to muster whatever French you possess, but in tourist centers you will be able to find people with at least basic English.

Getting Around

By Train Fast and frequent trains connect all main towns and cities. If you intend to travel frequently, buy a **Benelux Tourrail Ticket,** which allows unlimited travel in Belgium, Luxembourg, and the Netherlands for any five days during a one-month period. If you are over 26, the cost of the five-day pass is BF4,040 second-class. For those under 26, the pass costs BF3,030 second-class. The **Belgian Tourrail Ticket** allows unlimited travel for five days in a one-month period at a cost of BF1,980 second-class. Young people from 12 to 26 can purchase a **Go Pass** for BF1,290, valid for 10 one-way trips in a six-month period on the Belgian rail network. All of the above are available at any Belgian train station.

Special weekend round-trip tickets are valid from Friday noon to Monday noon: A 40% reduction is available on the first traveler's ticket and a 60% reduction on companions' tickets. During the tourist season there are similar weekday fares to the seaside and the Ardennes.

By Bus There is a wide network of local and regional buses throughout Belgium. Details of services are available at train stations and tourist offices. Intercity bus service is almost nonexistent.

By Bicycle You can rent a bicycle from Belgian railways at 48 stations throughout the country; train travelers get reduced rates. Mountain bikes can be rented at bike shops in most tourist centers. Bicycling is especially popular in the flat northern and coastal areas. Bicycle lanes are provided in many Flemish cities, but bicycling in Brussels is madness.

Staying in Belgium

Telephones Pay phones work with 5- and 20-franc coins or with telecards, avail-
Local Calls able in a number of denominations starting from BF200. The telecards can be purchased at any post office and at many newsstands. Most phone booths that accept telecards have a list indicating where these cards are sold. An average local call costs BF20.

International The least expensive method is to buy a high-denomination telecard
Calls and make a direct call from a phone booth. A five-minute phone call to the United States at a peak time will cost about BF750 by this method. To reach an **AT&T** long-distance operator, dial 078/11–0010; for **MCI,** 0800–10012; for **Sprint,** 0800–10014.

Operators The numbers for operator assistance and information vary from one city to another; it's best to ask at a hotel or post office or to consult a telephone directory.

Country Code The country code for Belgium is 32.

Mail Airmail letters and postcards to the United States cost BF38 for the
Postal Rates first 10 grams and BF4 more for each additional 5 grams. Airmail letters to the United Kingdom are BF16 for the first 20 grams.

Receiving Mail If you're uncertain where you'll be staying, have mail sent in care of **American Express** (pl. Louise 1, B-1000 Brussels). Cardholders are spared the $2-per-letter charge.

Shopping
Sales-Tax
Refunds
When you buy goods for export, you can ask most shops to fill out special forms covering VAT or sales tax. An itemized invoice showing the amount of VAT will also do. When you leave Belgium, you must declare the goods at customs and have the customs officers stamp the documents. Once you're back home, you simply send the stamped forms back to the shop, and your sales tax will be refunded. This facility is available in most boutiques and large stores and covers most purchases of more than BF2,000. There's a simpler option, but it requires a bit of trust. At the time of purchase by credit card, you pay only the price without VAT, but you also sign, with your card, a guarantee in the amount of the sales tax. Have the invoice stamped by customs when you leave the last European Union country on your itinerary. You have three months to return the stamped invoice to the store, where the guarantee is then disposed of. If you fail to do so, you forfeit the guarantee.

Opening and
Closing Times
Banks are open weekdays from 9 to 4; some close for an hour at lunch. Exchange facilities are usually open on weekends, but you'll get a better rate during the week.

Museums are generally open from 10 to 5 six days a week. Closing day is Monday in Brussels and Antwerp, Tuesday in Brugge. Check individual listings.

Shops are open weekdays and Saturdays from 10 to 6 and generally stay open later on Friday. Hours vary from store to store, so it's best to check in advance. Bakeries and some small food shops are open on Sunday.

National
Holidays
In 1996: January 1; April 8 (Easter Monday); May 1 (May Day); May 16 (Ascension); May 27 (Pentecost Monday); July 21 (National Holiday); August 15 (Assumption); November 1 (All Saints' Day); November 11 (Armistice); December 25. Changing holidays for 1997: March 31 (Easter Monday); May 8 (Ascension); May 19 (Pentecost Monday).

Dining
Nearly all Belgians take eating seriously and are discerning about fresh produce and innovative recipes. Prix-fixe menus are available in virtually all restaurants and often represent very considerable savings. Menus and prices are always posted outside. Belgian specialties include *lapin à la bière* (rabbit in beer), *faisan à la brabançonne* (pheasant with chicory), *waterzooi* (a rich chicken or fish hotpot), and *carbonnades* (chunky stews).

Belgian snacks are equally appetizing. The waffle *(gaufre/wafel)* has achieved world fame, but *couques* (sweet buns), *speculoos* (spicy gingerbread biscuits), and *pain d'amandes* (nutty after-dinner biscuits) are less well known. For lunch, cold cuts, rich pâtés, and *jambon d'Ardenne* (Ardenne ham) are popular, often accompanied by goat cheese and rye or whole-wheat bread.

Mealtimes
Most hotels serve breakfast until 10. Belgians usually eat lunch between 1 and 3, some making it quite a long, lavish meal. However, the main meal of the day is dinner, which most Belgians eat between 7 and 10; peak dining time is about 8.

What to Wear
Belgians tend to be fairly formal and dress conservatively when dining out in the evenings. Younger Belgians favor stylish, casual dress in most restaurants.

Ratings
Prices are per person and include a first course, main course, dessert, 20.5% VAT, and 16% service charge. Beverage is not included. Best bets are indicated by a star ★.

Category	Cost
$$	BF1,500–BF2,500
$	BF500–BF1,500
¢	under BF500

Lodging You can trust Belgian hotels, almost without exception, to be clean and of a high standard. The more modern hotels in city centers can be very expensive, but there are smaller, well-appointed hotels, offering lodging at excellent rates. The family-run establishments in out-of-the-way spots, such as the Ardennes, can be surprisingly inexpensive.

Youth Hostels For information about youth hostels, contact **Fédération Belge des Auberges de la Jeunesse** (tel. 02/215–31–00). For sources of information in the United States and Great Britain, *see* Student and Youth Travel *in* Chapter 1, The Gold Guide.

Camping Belgium is well supplied with camping and trailer sites. For details, contact the **Royal Camping and Caravaning Club of Belgium** (av. des Villas 5, B-1060 Brussels, tel. 02/537–36–81).

Ratings Hotel prices are inclusive and are usually listed in each room. All prices are for two people in a double room. Best bets are indicated by a star ★.

Category	Cost
$$	BF3,500–BF6,000
$	BF2,500–BF3,500
¢	under BF2,500

Tipping Tipping has been losing its hold in Belgium over the past few years because a service charge is almost always figured into the bill. For example, a tip of 16% is included in all restaurant and café bills. The tip is also included in taxi fares. Porters in railway stations ask a fixed per-suitcase price, BF30 in the day and BF35 at night. For moderately priced hotels, BF50 should be an adequate tip for bell-hops and doormen. At the movies, tip the usher BF20, whether or not he or she shows you to your seat. In restaurants, cafés, movie theaters, theaters, train stations, and other public places, you should tip the washroom attendant BF10.

Brussels

Arriving and Departing

By Plane All international flights arrive at Brussels's Zaventem Airport, a 16-minute train trip from the city center. **Sabena, American, Delta, TWA,** and **United** all fly into Brussels from the United States. **Sabena, British Airways,** and **British Midland** dominate the short-haul London (Heathrow)–Brussels route. **Air UK** flies to Brussels from London (Stansted), and **British Airways** flies from London (Gatwick). Several regional centers in Great Britain also have direct flights to Brussels.

Between the There is regular train service from the airport to the Gare du Nord
Airport and (North Station) and the Gare Centrale (Central Station), which
Downtown leaves every 20 minutes. The trip takes 16 minutes and costs BF140 (second-class round-trip); you can buy a ticket at a booth in the luggage area. The first train from the airport runs at 6:09 AM and the last one leaves at 11:46 PM.

By Train and The opening of the Channel Tunnel under the English Channel has
Boat/Jetfoil created a whole new ball game. **Eurostar** trains link London's Waterloo station with Brussels' Gare du Midi in 3 ¼ hours. Prices are volatile in the new competitive situation. For information, call 02/224–
88–56.

Traditional train service from London connects with the Ramsgate–
Oostende ferry or jetfoil, and from Oostende the train takes you to
Brussels. The Channel crossing takes about two hours by jetfoil, 4 ½
hours by ferry. Total train time on both sides of the Channel is close
to three hours. For information, call **British Rail International** in
London (tel. 0171/834–2345) or **Sally Line** (tel. 01843/595522). In
Belgium, tickets are available at railway stations and from travel
agents; for information, call 02/219–26–40.

By Bus and From London, the Hoverspeed City Sprint bus connects with the
Hovercraft Dover–Calais Hovercraft, and the bus then takes you on to rue Antoine Danseart 101 in Brussels. The journey takes 6 ½ hours; for reservations and times, contact **Hoverspeed** (tel. 01304/240241) in Great
Britain; call 02/513–93–40 in Brussels.

Getting Around

By The metro, trams (streetcars), and buses run as part of the same
Metro, Tram, system. All three are clean and efficient, and a single ticket costs
and Bus BF50. The best buy is a 10-trip ticket, which costs BF310, or a one-
day card costing BF120. You need to stamp your ticket in the appropriate machine on the bus or tram; in the metro, your card is
stamped as you pass through the automatic barrier. You can purchase these tickets in any metro station or at newsstands. Single
tickets can be purchased on the bus. All services are few and far between after 10 PM.

Detailed maps of the Brussels public transportation network are avail-
able in most metro stations and at the Brussels tourist office in the
Grand' Place (tel. 02/513–89–40). A free map accompanies the new
Tourist Passport (also available at the tourist office), which costs
BF200 and gives you one day's public transportation and museum
admissions worth BF1,000.

Important Addresses and Numbers

Tourist The **Tourist Information Brussels (TIB)** office is in the Hôtel de Ville
Information on the Grand' Place (tel. 02/513–89–40), open April–November, daily 9–6; November–April, limited Sunday hours 10–2; December–
February, closed Sunday. The main tourist office for the rest of **Belgium** is near the Grand' Place (rue Marché-aux-Herbes 63, tel. 02/
504–03–90) and is open weekdays 9–7, weekends 9–1 and 2–7 (in
winter, the office closes at 6 PM and is not open Sunday morning).
There is a tourist office at **Waterloo** (chaussée de Bruxelles 149, tel.
02/354–99–10); it is open April–November 15, daily 9:30–6:30 and
November 16–March, daily 10:30–5.

Embassies U.S. (blvd. du Régent 27, B–1000 Brussels, tel. 02/513–38–30). **Canadian** (av. de Tervuren 2, B–1040 Brussels, tel. 02/741–06–11).
U.K. (rue d'Arlon 85, B–1040 Brussels, tel. 02/287–62–11).

Emergencies **Police** (tel. 101); **Accident** (tel. 100); **Ambulance** (tel. 100); **Doctor**
(tel. 02/648–80–00 and 02/479–18–18); **Dentist** (tel. 02/426–10–26).

Exploring Brussels

Brussels mixes the provincial and the international. Underneath the
bureaucratic surface, the city is a subtle meeting of the Walloon and
Flemish cultures. As the heart of the ancient Duchy of Brabant,
Brussels retains its old sense of identity and civic pride. A stone's

throw from the steel-and-glass towers, there are cobbled streets and forgotten spots where the city's eventful and romantic past is plainly visible through its 20th-century veneer.

Numbers in the margin correspond to points of interest on the Brussels map.

The Grand' Place Begin in the **Grand' Place,** one of the most ornate market squares in Europe. There is a daily flower market and a colorful Sunday-morning bird market. On summer nights, the entire square is flooded with music and colored light. The Grand' Place also comes alive during local pageants, such as the *Ommegang,* a splendid historical pageant (early July); the biennial *Tapis de Fleurs,* when the entire square is covered by a carpet of flowers (mid-August); and the traditional Christmas illumination, when there is also a life-size crib and real animals.

The bombardment of the city by Louis XIV's troops left only the **Hôtel de Ville** (town hall) standing. Civic-minded citizens started rebuilding the Grand' Place immediately, but the highlight of the square remains the Gothic town hall. The central tower, combining boldness and light, is topped by a statue of St-Michel, the patron saint of Brussels. Among the magnificent rooms are the Salle Gothique, with its beautiful paneling; the Salle Maximilienne, with its superb tapestries; and the Council Chamber, with a ceiling fresco, *Assembly of the Gods,* painted by Victor Janssens in the early 15th century. *Tel. 02/512-75-54. Admission: BF80. English-speaking tours Tues. 11:30 and 3:15, Wed. 3:15, Sun. 12:15. No individual visits.*

Opposite the town hall is the **Maison du Roi** (King's House)—though no king ever lived there—a 16th-century palace housing the **City Museum.** The collection includes important ceramics and silverware—Brussels is famous for both—church sculpture, and statues removed from the facade of the town hall, as well as an extravagant collection of costumes for Manncken Pis (*see below*). *Grand' Place, tel. 02/511-27-42. Admission: BF80. Open weekdays 10-12:30 and 1:30-5, weekends 10-1.*

Southwest of the town hall, on the corner of the rue de l'Etuve and rue du Chêne, stands the famous **Manneken Pis,** a fountain with a small bronze statue of a chubby little boy urinating. Made by Jerome Duquesnoy in 1619, the statue is known as "Brussels's Oldest Citizen" and is often dressed in costumes that are kept in the City Museum. The Manneken was kidnapped by 18th-century invaders (soldiers, not tourists!) but was returned promptly.

Leaving the Manneken, cross the Grand' Place in the direction of the Marché-aux-Herbes. If you are planning to visit the rest of Belgium, stop in at the regional tourist office (rue Marché-aux-Herbes 63).

Opposite the tourist office, take the Petite rue des Bouchers, the main restaurant street in the heart of the tourist maelstrom. Each restaurant advertises its wares by means of large signs and carts packed with a selection of game and seafood. As a general rule, however, remember that the more lavish the display, the poorer the cuisine. From here, explore the network of galleries called **Galeries St-Hubert,** which includes the Galerie de la Reine, Galerie du Roi, and Galerie des Princes, all built in 1847. The motto on the central galleries, "Omnibus Omnia," is not altogether appropriate, given the designer prices.

Head south along the rue du Marché-aux-Herbes and the rue Madeleine until you come to the equestrian **statue of King Albert.** To the left of the statue is the Central Station and to the right, the **Bibliothèque Nationale** (National Library). Walk through the formal gardens next to the National Library and look back at the ornate clock,

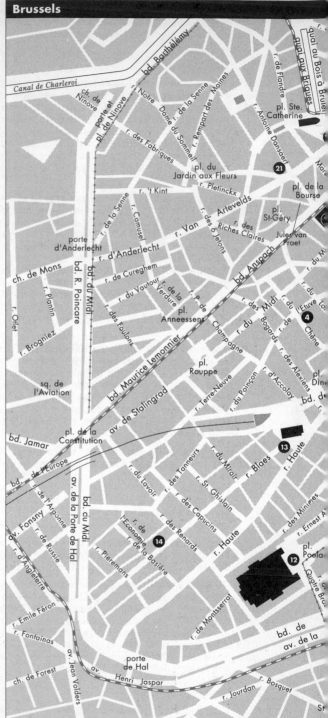

Brussels

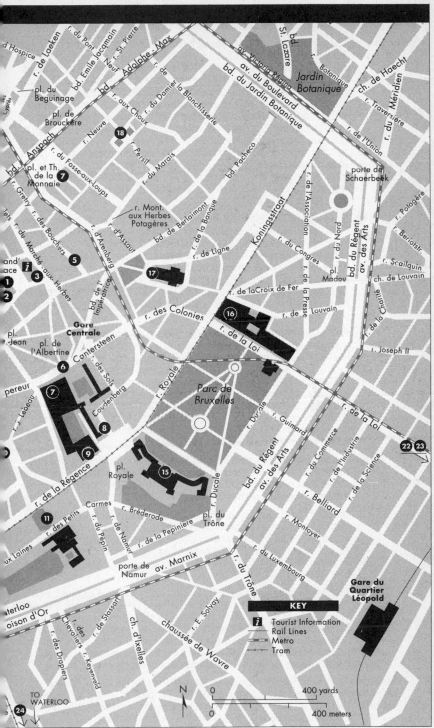

KEY

i	Tourist Information
	Rail Lines
	Metro
	Tram

Jardin Botanique

Parc de Bruxelles

Gare Centrale

Gare du Quartier Léopold

TO WATERLOO

N

0   400 yards

0   400 meters

with moving figures, over the lower archway. Try to hear—and see—it at noon, when it strikes the hour.

Place Royale If you continue walking through the gardens, you will arrive at the **place Royale,** the site of the Coudenberg palace, where the sovereigns once lived. Here you have a superb view over the lower town.

❽ On the northwest corner of the square is the **Musée d'Art Moderne** (Museum of Modern Art), housed in an exciting feat of modern architecture. On entry, a vertiginous descent into the depths reveals a sudden well of natural light. The paintings are displayed with the light and space they deserve. Although there are a few paintings by Matisse, Gauguin, Degas, and Dali, the surprise lies in the quality of Belgian modern art. See Magritte's luminous fantasies, James Ensor's masks and still lifes, and Spilliaert's coastal scenes. Do not miss Permeke's deeply brooding *Fiancés* or Delvaux's Surrealist works. *Pl. Royale 1, tel. 02/508–32–11. Admission free. Open Tues.–Sun. 10–1 and 2–5.*

❾ Next door is the **Musée Royale d'Art Ancien** (Royal Museum of Ancient Art). Here the collection is of Flemish and Dutch paintings, ranging from magnificent 15th- and 16th-century works—Cranach, Matsys, and Brueghel the Elder, among them—to Rubens (several fine canvases), Van Dyck, and David. Do not miss Brueghel's dramatic *La Chute d'Icare (The Fall of Icarus)* or Hieronymous Bosch's *Le Dernier Jugement (The Last Judgment)*, a malevolent portrait of humanity. *Rue de la Régence 10, tel. 02/508–32–11. Admission free. Open Tues.–Sun. 10–12 and 1–5.*

From the square at the neoclassical **Place Royale,** with its attractive white buildings (the town's center during the years of Austrian rule in the 18th century), the Rue de la Régence runs toward the Palais de Justice. The Sablon lies along this street, on the right. The **Grand Sablon,** the city's most sophisticated square, is alive with cafés, restaurants, and antiques shops. Toward the end of the square is the **church of Notre Dame du Sablon,** built in flamboyant Gothic style. Although much of the original workmanship was lost in restoration, it remains one of the city's best-loved churches. The stained-glass windows are illuminated from within at night.

⓫ A small garden square, the **Petit Sablon** is surrounded by 48 statues representing Brussels's medieval guilds. Each craftsman carries an object that reveals his trade: The furniture maker holds a chair, for instance; the wine merchant, a goblet.

On the Petit Sablon is the **Musée Instrumental** (Museum of Musical Instruments). A huge collection of over 1,000 musical instruments is on display. Half of them are unique, and a few go back to the Bronze Age. The guide can often be persuaded to play one of the pianos. *Petit Sablon 17, tel. 02/511–35–95. Admission free. Open Tues.–Sun. 2:30–4:30.*

Immediately behind the Petit Sablon is the **Palais d'Egmont,** at different times the residence of Christina of Sweden, Louis XV, and Voltaire. It is now used by the Belgian Ministry of Foreign Affairs for official meetings. If security allows, you can enter the Jardin d'Egmont, another small park, on this side. Come out of the entrance on rue du Grand Cerf and turn left toward the boulevard de Waterloo, a wide street full of bars and designer shops.

Palais de Justice to the Black Tower At the end of the rue de la Régence is the **Palais de Justice,** constructed under the empire builder, Leopold II. Often described as the ugliest building in Europe, the palais is designed to impress upon you the majesty of justice. It's located on the site of the former Gallows Hill.

Down a rather steep hill from the Palais de Justice is the working-class **Marolles** district, where the artist Pieter Brueghel died in 1569. His imposing marble tomb is in **Notre Dame de la Chapelle,** his

local church on rue Haute. From place de la Chapelle, take rue Blaes
to the flea market in **place du Jeu de Balle.** On the way, you will pass a
number of rough Belgian bars and North African food shops. Until
this century, bourgeois Belgians considered this labyrinth of small
alleys a haven for thieves and political refugees. Although the
Marolles continues to welcome immigrants and outsiders, it has lost
its danger but kept its slightly raffish character.

Return via the Sablon to the place Royale. Directly ahead of you is
the **Parc de Bruxelles** (Brussels Park) with the **Palais Royal** (Royal
Palace) at the end closer to you. (The palace is open for visits from
July 22 to early September.) You can walk through the park to the
Palais de la Nation (Palace of the Nation) at the opposite end, where
the two houses of the Belgian Parliament meet. When Parliament is
not sitting, you can visit the building. *Tel. 02/519–81–36. Admission
free. Guided tours weekdays 9:30–noon.*

Surrounding the park are elegant turn-of-the-century houses. The
prime minister's office is next to the Parliament building. A walk
downhill (rue des Colonies) toward the downtown area and a short
right-hand detour bring you to the **Cathédrale St-Michel et Ste-
Gudule.** The cathedral's chief treasure is the beautiful stained-glass
windows designed by Bernard van Orley, an early 16th-century
painter at the royal court. In summer the great west window is
floodlit from inside to reveal its glories. In the crypt, you can see the
remnants of the original 12th-century church.

Situated between the cathedral and the galleries is **La Mort Subite**
(Sudden Death) (rue Montagne-aux-Herbes-Potagères 7, tel. 02/
513–13–18), the city's most genuine beer hall. Locals sit on long
benches and select drinks from the best beer list in Brussels, including foamy *bière blanche* (white lager beer), strong *trappiste* (brewed
by monks), *framboise* (made with raspberries), and heady *kriek* (a
cherry beer).

Continue downhill to the **place des Martyrs,** a dignified square over a
mass grave for local patriots who died in the 1830 battle to expel the
Dutch. Renovation of this nobly proportioned square is now in prog-
ress. Cross the rue Neuve and continue on to the boulevard
Adolphe-Max. Turn left and then right, in front of the imposing
Bourse (stock exchange), to place Ste-Catherine.

The 12th-century **Tour Noir** (Black Tower) here is part of the city's
first fortifications. Archaeological excavations have begun under
this shamefully neglected monument. Under the square runs the
river Senne, channeled underground in the last century when the
pollution of the canal basins and the stench from the open sewers became too great. As a result of its watery past, place Ste-Catherine
and the old fish market (quai aux Briques) that extends north from it
still have the city's best seafood restaurants. Return to the Bourse
via the **rue Antoine Dansaert,** which has lately become a trendy
shopping street with boutiques, galleries and cafés.

**Parc du
Cinquantenaire
and Bois de la
Cambre**
To see the **European Commission Headquarters** at the Rond Point
Schuman, take the metro (Line 1) from the center. The vast 13-story
cruciform building is now undergoing restoration to remove asbes-
tos ceilings and partitions. The Council offices are located nearby.
The new European Parliament building is a couple of blocks away.

The **Cinquantenaire** is a huge, decorative archway, built in 1905 in a
pleasant park. The buildings on either side of the archway house the
Musées Royaux d'Art et d'Histoire (Royal Museums of Art and History). Displays include Greek, Roman, and Egyptian artifacts and
toys. Large-scale temporary exhibitions are also mounted here.
*Parc du Cinquantenaire 10, tel. 02/741–72–11. Admission free.
Open weekdays 9:30–5, weekends 10–5.*

The new **Autoworld Museum,** also in the Cinquantenaire, has one of the world's most handsome collections of vintage cars. *Parc du Cinquantenaire 11, tel. 02/736–41–65. Admission: BF150. Open daily 10–6 (Nov.–Mar., until 5).*

㉔ South of the Palais de Justice is the **Bois de la Cambre,** a popular, rambling park on the edge of town. Take Tram 94 from Sablon or place Stéphanie for a pleasant 10-minute ride along avenue Louise. Just before the bois is the former **Abbaye de la Cambre,** a 14th-century church with cloisters, an 18th-century courtyard, and a terraced park. The Bois de la Cambre is a good place for a family outing, with a lake, boat trips, pony rides, and an outdoor roller-skating rink.

Waterloo   No history buff can visit Brussels without making the pilgrimage to the site of the **Battle of Waterloo,** where Napoleon was finally defeated on June 18, 1815. It is easily reached from the city and lies 19 kilometers (12 miles) to the south of the Forêt de Soignes; take a bus from place Rouppe or a train from Gare Centrale to Waterloo station.

Wellington's headquarters, now a museum, presents the complex battle through illuminated 3-D maps, scale models, and military memorabilia, including the general's personal belongings. *Chaussée de Bruxelles 149, tel. 02/354–78–06. Admission: BF70. Open Apr.–Oct., daily 9:30–6:30; Nov.–Mar., daily 10:30–5.*

Just south of town is the actual battlefield. Start at the **visitor center,** which has an audiovisual presentation with scenes of the battle. You can also book guides to take you around the battlefield. *Route du Lion 252–254, tel. 02/385–19–12. Admission: BF300. Open Apr.–Oct., 9:30–6:30; Nov.–Mar., 10:30–5. Guides 1815: Route du Lion 250, tel. 02/385–06–25. 1-hr tour BF1,400; 3-hour tour BF2,200.*

Overlooking the battlefield is the **Butte du Lion,** a pyramidal monument erected by the Dutch. After climbing its 226 steps, you will be rewarded with a splendid view of the battlefield. The old fortified farms, the scenes of intense hand-to-hand fighting, are still standing.

The Battle of Waterloo is reenacted every five years (next time in 2000) around June 15. A thousand local citizens dress as French, Prussian, and English soldiers and realistically shoot one another with old muskets.

Off the Beaten Track

The **Maison d'Erasme** is a beautifully restored 15th-century house where Erasmus, the great humanist, lived in 1521. Every detail of this atmospheric house is authentic, with period furniture; paintings by Holbein, Dürer, and Hieronymous Bosch; and early editions of Erasmus's works, including *In Praise of Folly. Rue du Chapitre 31, tel. 02/521–13–83. Admission: BF50. Open Wed.–Thurs. and Sat.–Mon., 10–noon and 2–5. Metro: Saint-Guidon.*

The **Centre Belge de la Bande Dessinée** (Belgian Comic-Strip Center) celebrates the comic strip, emphasizing such famous Belgian graphic artists as Hergé, Tintin's creator. Hergé apparently invented the *ligne claire,* a simple, bold style of drawing. The display is housed in Victor Horta's splendid Art Nouveau building, once a department store. Horta's juggling of steel, glass, and light has created an exciting backdrop. *Rue des Sables 20, tel. 02/219–19–80. Admission: BF150. Open Tues.–Sun. 10–6. Trams 92, 93. Metro: Botanique.*

Shopping

Gift Ideas
Chocolates For "everyday" chocolate, try the Côte d'Or variety, available in any chocolate shop or larger store. For the delicious pralines—rich chocolates filled with every fruit, liqueur, or nut imaginable—try the brands made by Godiva, Neuhaus, or Leonidas, available at shops scattered throughout the city. Godiva is the best known, Neuhaus the best tasting, and Leonidas the best value for your money.

Lace To avoid disappointment, ask the store assistant outright whether the lace is handmade Belgian or made in the Far East. As preparation, visit the **Lace Museum** (rue de la Violette 6, near the Grand' Place). **La Maison F. Rubbrecht,** on the Grand' Place, sells authentic, handmade Belgian lace. For a large choice of old and modern lace, try **Manufacture Belge de Dentelles** (Galerie de la Reine 6–8).

Shopping
Districts For boutiques and stores, the main districts are in the **ville basse** (low town), the **Galeries St-Hubert** (luxury goods or gift items), **rue Neuve** (inexpensive clothes), and **City 2** and the **Anspach Center** (large covered shopping complexes).

You'll find designer names and department stores (such as **Sarmalux**) in the **ville haute** (high town). **Avenue Louise** is its center, complete with covered galleries; **Galerie Louise;** and **Galerie de la Toison d'Or,** the appropriately named street of the Golden Fleece!

Markets On Saturdays (9–5) and Sundays (9–1), the Sablon square is transformed into an **antiques market.** In early December it runs a traditional **European Christmas Market** with crafts from many countries. The **flower market** on the Grand' Place (Tuesday–Sunday 8–4) is a colorful diversion. **Midi Market** (by Gare du Midi train station) is far more exotic. On Sunday morning (5 AM–1 PM) the whole area becomes a colorful souk as the city's large North African community gathers to buy and sell exotic foods and household goods. The **Vieux Marché** (Old Market) in place du Jeu de Balle is a rough flea market worth visiting for the authentic atmosphere of the working-class Marolles district. The market is open daily 7–2. To make real finds, get there as early in the morning as you can.

Dining

Servings are plentiful everywhere. Most places feature a plat du jour (daily special) at a reasonable price. If you are interested in local gourmet restaurants, ask the tourist office on the Grand' Place for its booklet "Gourmet Restaurants" (BF50), updated annually; it includes many affordable places.

For details and price-category definitions, *see* Dining *in* Staying in Belgium, *above*.

$$ **Aux Armes de Bruxelles.** This restaurant is one of the few to escape the "tourist trap" label in this hectic little street. Inside, a lively atmosphere fills three rooms. Service is fast and friendly, and portions are large. Specialties include *waterzooi de volaille* (a rich chicken stew) and *moules au vin blanc* (mussels in white wine). *Rue des Bouchers 13, tel. 02/511–21–18. Reservations advised. AE, DC, MC, V. Closed Mon. and June.*

$$ **Brasserie Georges.** Open every night until midnight, this hugely popular restaurant was the first of its kind in Brussels and is still the best. The brasserie formula calls for a big display of shellfish at the entrance, an art deco interior, friendly service by waitresses in black and white, and traditional fare such as sauerkraut, sausage and potato salad, and poached cod. Some 25 wines are sold by the glass. *Av. Winston Churchill 259, tel. 02/347–21–00. Reservations advised. AE, DC, MC, V.*

$$
★ **La Quincaillerie.** The name means "the hardware store"—and the character has been retained, with tables perched on the balcony and

a zinc oyster bar downstairs. The three-course prix-fixe menu is a bargain. Excellent game dishes are nicely presented by staff members who, like the clientele, are young and pleasant. *Rue du Page 45, tel. 02/538–25–53. Reservations advised. AE, DC, MC, V.*

$ **Adrienne.** Just around the corner from avenue de La Toison d'Or, this buffet restaurant serves cold cuts, vegetables, salads, and a separate dessert buffet. On warm days you can sit on the terrace. *Rue Capitaine Crespel 1a, tel. 02/511–93–39. Reservations advised lunch. AE, DC, MC, V.*

$ **Au Vieux Saint Martin.** When neighboring eateries on Grand Sablon are empty, this one remains full, and you're equally welcome whether you order a full meal or a cup of coffee. The short menu features Belgian specialties, including a splendid *filet américain* (steak tartare); portions are huge. Wines are sold by the glass or bottle. Bright contemporary paintings hang on the walls, and picture windows overlook the pleasant square. *Grand Sablon 38, tel. 02/512–64–76. Open daily noon–midnight. No reservations. No credit cards.*

$ **Chez Leon.** This hundred-year-old restaurant continues to do a vigorous business, even though prices have been edging upward lately. Over the years it has expanded into a row of eight old houses. Heaping plates of mussels and other Belgian specialties, like eels in a green sauce, are served nonstop from noon to midnight all year round. The french fries are arguably the best in town. *Rue des Bouchers 18, tel. 02/511–14–15. No reservations. AE, DC, MC, V.*

$ **Falstaff.** Some things never change, and Falstaff is one of them. This
★ huge tavern, with an interior that is pure Art Nouveau, fills up for lunch and keeps going until 5 AM, with an ever-changing crowd from students to pensioners. Cheerful waitresses punch in your orders for onion soup, filet mignon, salads, and other straightforward dishes on electronic order pads. Falstaff II, at No. 25, has the same food but not the ambience. *Rue Henri Maus 19, tel. 02/511–87–89. Reservations advised. AE, DC, MC, V.*

¢ **Boccaccio.** At this super-friendly hole-in-the-wall, the Moroccan owner and his Swedish wife serve up generous portions of pasta and other Italian specialties. *Rue du Marché-aux-Fromages 14, tel. 02/512–29–29. AE, DC, MC, V.*

¢ **Le Faste Fou.** On a side street near place Louise, this eatery has counter service downstairs and table service in the sparsely furnished upstairs dining room. Generous salads predominate, with hot meals a bit more expensive. *Rue du Grand-Cerf 21, tel. 02/511–38–32. AE, DC, MC, V.*

¢ **Le Pain Quotidien.** The "Daily Bread," basically a down-home bake-
★ ry, is a great success story; branches have opened all over the city. Each centers around a big refectory table where open sandwiches are served on hearty breads; toppings include Brie and walnuts or carpaccio with basil and Parmesan. Huge salads and generous slices of pie are also on offer. All open for breakfast at 8 AM and close at 7 PM. *Rue Antoine Dansaert 16, tel. 02/502–23–61; place du Grand Sablon 11, tel. 02/502–70–73; chaussée de Waterloo 515, tel. 02/343–33–59; and other locations. No reservations. No credit cards.*

The city has a large number of snack bars, some of them serving quite good food. The **Poechenellekelder** (rue du Chêne 5, tel. 02/511–92–62) serves a variety of cream cheese sandwiches, accompanied by an even larger choice of beers. Virtually all cafés also serve simple fare, like spaghetti or omelets.

Lodging

The annual hotel guide published by Tourist Information Brussels provides the most reliable and up-to-date information on prices and services. Avoid the cheap hotel districts near Gare du Midi and Gare du Nord train stations. Hotels can be booked at the tourist office on the Grand' Place (tel. 02/513–89–40), and a deposit is required (deductible from the final hotel bill).

For details and price-category definitions, *see* Lodging *in* Staying in Belgium, *above.*

$$ Alfa Louise. Opened in 1994 on prestigious avenue Louise, this hotel offers large rooms with office-size desks and a sitting area. Bathrobes and room safes are additional amenities. There's a jazz piano bar off the lobby, but no restaurant. *Av. Louise 212, tel. 02/644–29–29, fax 02/644–18–78. 40 rooms with bath. Facilities: piano bar-breakfast room, meeting rooms, parking. AE, DC, MC, V.*

$$ Beau Site. Gleaming white and with flower boxes suspended from the windowsills, this appealing 1993 hotel has reasonably spacious rooms that come in different shapes rather than the standard cube. The complimentary buffet includes bacon and eggs. The location, just a block from avenue Louise, is another plus. *Rue de Longue Haie 76, tel. 02/640–88–89, fax 02/640–16–11. 38 rooms with bath. Facilities: breakfast room. AE, DC, MC, V.*

$ Matignon. Only the Belle Epoque facade of this family-owned and-operated hotel, opposite the Bourse and a couple of blocks from the Grand Place, was preserved when it was converted into a hotel in 1993. The lobby is tiny, to make room for the large café-brasserie. Rooms are small but have large beds. The five duplex suites are a good value for families. *Rue de la Bourse 10, tel. 02/511–08–88, fax 02/513–69–27. 17 rooms with bath, 5 suites. Facilities: bar, café (closed Mon.). AE, DC, MC, V.*

$ Mozart. The entrance to the Mozart is between two Greek pita joints, and the reception area is up a flight of stairs; there's no elevator. The attractive oak-beam rooms, in shades of salmon, are spacious, and each comes with refrigerator and shower. Complimentary breakfast is served in a cozy nook. The proprietors also own and manage the Boccacio restaurant across the street. *Rue Marché-aux-Fromages 15a, tel. 02/502–66–61, fax 02/502–77–58. 23 rooms with bath. Facilities: breakfast room. AE, DC, MC, V.*

$ Orion. Located in the old fish market (now a lively restaurant district), this residential hotel contains two-person studios and four-person apartments that can be booked per night, with rebates for stays of a week or more. In principle, you make your own bed and do your own cleaning, but a small supplement adds these services. All rooms have fully equipped kitchenettes; there's also a breakfast room downstairs. *Quai au Bois-à-Brûler 51, tel. 02/221–14–11, fax 02/221–15–99. 169 rooms with bath. Facilities: breakfast room, parking. AE, DC, MC, V.*

¢ Sabina. At this well-located hotel, where the wallpaper and carpets make a bit of a fusty impression, the rooms are small but cozy. *Rue du Nord 78, tel. 02/218–26–37, fax 02/219–32–39. 24 rooms, 20 with bath or shower.*

¢ Saint Nicolas. The entrance to this 1994 hotel is bright and airy, and an attractive breakfast room adjoins the lobby. Rooms are relatively basic, but all come with a private bathroom. Triple rooms are available. *Rue Marché-aux-Poulets 32, tel. 02/219–04–40, fax 02/219–17–21. 50 rooms with bath or shower. Facilities: breakfast room. AE, DC, MC, V.*

¢ Welcome/Truite d'Argent. ★ The smallest hotel in Brussels, in a quiet street off the fish market, has modern, well-equipped rooms and two restaurants: a small bistro, Les Caprices de Sophie, reserved for residents at dinner, and an expensive fish restaurant around the corner. *Rue du Peuplier 5, tel. 02/219–95–46, fax 02/217–18–87. 6 rooms with bath. Facilities: 2 restaurants, meeting rooms, parking. AE, DC, MC, V.*

Two modern youth hostels feature double rooms. They are the **Auberge Bruegel** (rue St. Esprit 2, tel. 02/511–04–36) and the **Auberge Jacques Brel** (rue de la Sablonniere 30, tel. 02/218–01–87). A new, well-appointed youth hostel, **Auberge Jean Nihon** (rue de l'Elephant 4, tel. 02/410–38–58, fax 02/410–39–05) opened in 1992.

The Arts

The traditional performing arts—ballet, opera, theater—are well represented in Brussels. There is also a wide range of English-language entertainment, including movies and, on occasion, theater. The best way to find out what's going on is to buy a copy of the English-language weekly magazine *The Bulletin*. It's published every Thursday and sold at newsstands for BF80.

Music   Major classical music concerts are generally held at the **Palais des Beaux-Arts** (rue Ravenstein 23, tel. 02/507–82–00). Alternatively, there are many free Sunday morning concerts at various churches, including the **Cathédrale St-Michel et Ste-Gudule** and the **Petite Église des Minimes** (rue des Minimes 62). Major rock and pop concerts are given at **Forest National** (av. du Globe 36, tel. 02/347–03–55).

Theater   At Brussels's 30 theaters, actors perform in French, Flemish, and occasionally in English. Puppet theater is a Belgian experience not to be missed. In Brussels, visit the intimate **Théâtre Toone VII** (impasse Schuddeveld, petite rue des Bouchers 21, tel. 02/511–71–37). In this atmospheric medieval house, satirical plays are performed in a Bruxellois dialect.

Film   Movies are mainly shown in their original language, so many are in English. **The UCG Acropole** (Galeries de la Toison d'Or, tel. 02/511–43–28) and the **UCG de Brouckère** complex (place de Brouckère, tel. 02/218–06–07) feature comfortable armchairs and first-run movies. For unusual movies or screen classics, visit the **Musée du Cinéma** (Cinema Museum) (rue Baron Horta 9, tel. 02/507–83–70); five movies are shown daily, at only BF80 each (BF50 for tickets bought 24 hours in advance).

Nightlife

Discos   **Griffin's** (rue Duquesnoy 5, tel. 02/505–55–55), at the Royal Windsor Hotel, appeals to young adults and business travelers. **Le Garage** (rue Duquesnoy 16, tel. 02/512–66–22) draws a younger crowd.

Bars   The diversity is greater here than in many other European capitals. These are just a few of the best: **La Fleur en Papier Doré** (rue des Aléxiens 53, tel. 02/511–16–59) is a quiet bar that attracts an artistic audience to drink local beer and look at the ancient walls covered with surreal paintings and old etchings. **Cirio** (rue de la Bourse 18, tel. 02/512–13–95) is a pleasantly quiet bar with nice decor. **Rick's Café** (av. Louise 344, tel. 02/647–75–30) is as popular with homesick Americans as it is with the British expatriate community. It serves fairly expensive American and Tex-Mex food. **Henry J. Bean's** (rue du Montagne-aux-Herbes-Potagères 40, tel. 02/219–28–28) is a 1950s-style bar and grill frequented by the younger set.

Jazz   Among the best venues are **Travers** (rue Traversière 11, tel. 02/218–40–86), and **Preservation Hall** (pl. de Londres 4, tel. 02/502–15–97), and **Sounds** (rue de la Tulipe 28, tel. 02/512–92–50).

Antwerp

Arriving and Departing

By Plane   Antwerp International Airport (tel. 03/218–12–11), just 3 kilometers (2 miles) southeast of the city, is served by a small number of flights from neighboring countries. Most visitors fly into Brussels

National Airport, 50 minutes away; bus service to Antwerp runs hourly.

Between the Airport and Downtown   Buses bound for Antwerp's central train station leave about every 20 minutes; travel time is around 15 minutes. Taxis are readily available as well.

By Train   Express trains run between Antwerp and Brussels; the trip takes 35 minutes. Antwerp Central Station is at Koningin Astridplein 27 (tel. 03/233–39–15). There are four trains an hour in each direction.

Getting Around

By Streetcar   In the downtown area, the streetcar (or tram) is the best, and most common, means of transportation. Some lines have been rebuilt underground (look for signs marked "M"); the most useful line runs between the central station (metro: Diamant) and the Groenplaats (for the cathedral). A single ride costs BF40, a 10-ride ticket BF250, and a day pass BF100. For detailed maps of the transportation system, stop at the tourist office.

Tourist Information

The **Toerisme Stad Antwerpen** (Antwerp City Tourist Office) is near the cathedral (Grote Markt 15, tel. 03/232–01–03, fax 03/231–19–37). It is open Monday–Saturday 9–6, Sunday 9–5. A booklet with self-guided tours, including the famous "Rubens Walk," is available from the tourist office. Various other popular walks are signposted throughout the city.

Exploring Antwerp

Antwerp, lying on the Scheldt River 50 kilometers (31 miles) north of Brussels, is the world's fifth-largest port and the main city of Belgium's Flemish region. Its name, according to legend, is derived from *handwerpen*, or "hand throwing." A Roman soldier, it seems, cut off the hand of a malevolent giant and flung it into the river; his feat is commemorated by a statue on the Grote Markt. In the 16th century, Emperor Charles V made Antwerp the world's most important trading center, and a century later Rubens and other painters made their city an equally important center of the arts. Diamond cutting in Antwerp started at about this time, and the city is still a world leader in the diamond trade. Antwerp's latest wave of prosperity dates back to 1863, when an international treaty obliged the Dutch (who controlled the mouth of the Scheldt River) to allow freedom of navigation on the Scheldt. Much of the glory that was Antwerp has been preserved, and Antwerp's year as Cultural Capital of Europe for 1993 left a much-improved cultural infrastructure behind.

Numbers in the margin correspond to points of interest on the Antwerp map.

1 Antwerp's **Centraalstation** is a good place to start exploring the city. This elegant neoclassical building was built a hundred years ago as a **2** "railway cathedral." To the east of the station is **Antwerp Zoo**, a huge, well-designed complex that also includes a winter garden, a planetarium, a good restaurant, and two natural-history museums. *Koningin Astridplein 26, tel. 03/231–16–40. Admission: BF390 adults, BF240 children. Open July–Aug., daily 8:30–6:30; Sept.–Feb., daily 9–5; Mar.–June, daily 8:30–6.*

Near the central station, along the Pelikaanstraat and the streets running off it, lies the **Diamond Quarter.** You can visit the diamond exhibition and see diamond cutters at work at the **Provinciaal 3 Diamantmuseum** (Diamond Museum). *Lange Herentalsestraat 31–*

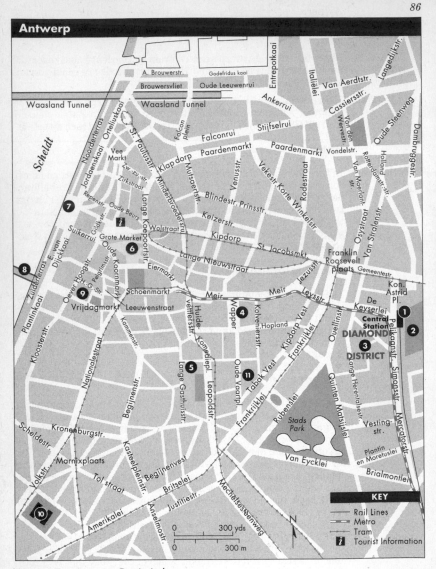

Antwerp

Antwerp Zoo, **2**

Centraalstation, **1**

Koninklijk Museum voor Schone Kunsten, **10**

Museum Mayer van den Bergh, **5**

Onze-Lieve-Vrouwekathedraal, **6**

Plantin-Moretus Museum, **9**

Provinciaal Diamantmuseum, **3**

Rubenshuis, **4**

St. Annatunnel, **8**

Steen, **7**

Vogelmarkt, **11**

33. Admission free. Open daily 10–5. Cutting and polishing demonstrations Sat. 2–5.

The broad De Keyserlei leads west from the central station to the main shopping area, the **Meir.** South of the Meir, on Wapper, is **❹ Rubenshuis** (Rubens House). The artist lived here from 1610 until his death in 1640. It's a patrician's home, enriched with paintings by Rubens and his contemporaries. *Wapper 9. Admission: BF75. Open Tues.–Sun. 10–4:45.*

Turn left at the 24-story **Torengebouw,** and you find yourself in a shopping district where windows display the fashion designs of the **❺** "Antwerp Six." A few blocks south is the **Museum Mayer van den Bergh,** whose greatest treasure is Brueghel's *Dulle Griet* (often referred to in English as "Mad Meg"), a powerful antiwar allegory. *Lange Gasthuisstraat 19, tel. 03/232–42–37. Admission: BF75. Open Tues.–Sun. 10–4:45.*

❻ Turn back, and let the 400-foot spire lead you to the **Onze-Lieve-Vrouwekathedraal** (Cathedral of Our Lady). This Gothic church, just renovated, is the largest in the Low Countries. Its art treasures include four Rubens altarpieces. *Groenplaats 21, tel. 03/231–30–33. Admission: BF60. Open weekdays 10–5, Sat. 10–3, Sun. 1–4.*

The **Grote Markt,** flanked by the 16th-century City Hall and surrounded by old guild houses, is just a few steps north of the cathedral. The area north of the square, with its narrow streets, churches, and old merchants' houses, is the heart of old Antwerp.

Returning to the cathedral, walk the short distance west along the **❼** Suikerrui to the river. To your right is the fortresslike **Steen,** the oldest building in Antwerp, dating from the 12th century. From the terrace you can watch the old port and the passing river traffic.

Walking along the river south of the Steen, you come to a foot tunnel, **❽** the **St. Annatunnel,** leading to the left bank of the river. Turn east, and explore St. Jans Vliet, Hoogstraat, and Reyndersstraat, an area of old Antwerp full of shops, authentic bars, and excellent restaurants. Via Heilig Geeststraat, you reach Vrijdagmarkt and the **❾ Plantin-Moretus Museum,** a famous printing works founded in the 16th century. The building is a fine example of Renaissance architecture and is magnificently furnished. Among its treasures are many first editions, engravings, and a copy of Gutenberg's Bible, the *Biblia Regia. Vrijdagmarkt 22, tel. 03/233–02–94. Admission: BF75. Open Tues.–Sun. 10–5.*

From the Plantin, walk through the Vrijdagmarkt, where there is a **furniture and secondhand market** every Wednesday and Friday morning. Continue up the Oude Koornmarkt to the Groenplaats and **❿** catch a tram to the **Koninklijk Museum voor Schone Kunsten** (Royal Museum of Fine Arts). It lies in the southern part of the city and houses more than 1,500 paintings by old masters, including a magnificent array of works by Rubens, Van Dyck, Hals, and Brueghel. The second floor houses one of the best collections of the Flemish school anywhere in the world. The first floor is given over to more modern paintings. The neoclassical building also has an adequate snack bar. *Leopold de Waelplaats 1–9. Admission free. Open Tues.–Sun. 10–4:45.*

⓫ On Sunday morning you can see the famous **vogelmarkt,** or bird market, a few blocks south of Rubenshuis on the Oude Vaartplaats. You'll find everything from birds and domestic pets to plants, clothes, and food.

Dining

Local specialties include herring and eel dishes and *witloof* (endives) cooked in a variety of ways. As for drink, there are 20 local beers; a city gin called *jenever;* and a strong liqueur, *Elixir d'Anvers.*

For details and price-category definitions, *see* Dining *in* Staying in Belgium, *above.*

$$ **Neuze Neuze.** Five tiny houses have been cobbled together to create
★   this handsome, split-level restaurant. Dishes like warm smoked salmon served with endives in a white beer sauce or monkfish rolls with a little bit of caviar are executed with the flair of pricier establishments. *Wijngaardstraat 19, tel. 03/232–57–83. Reservations advised. AE, DC, MC, V. Closed Sun. and the last 2 wks of July.*

$$ **Sir Anthony Van Dijck.** In 1992 the owner-chef cut prices in half; increased the number of tables; and introduced simpler, brasserie-type dishes based on less expensive products. Still, the food, including duck à l'orange and tuna steak, is quite good. The antiques-filled interior is the same, and so is its setting in the charming Vlaaykensgang alley. *Oude Koornmarkt 16, tel. 03/231–61–70. AE, DC, MC, V. Closed Sun. and most of Aug.*

$ **Jan Zonder Vrees.** Named for the legendary Jan Without Fear, this attractive restaurant is in a 14th-century house, formerly a brothel. Now it serves waterzooi, rabbit in beer, and other specialties. *Krabbenstraat 2, tel. 03/232–90–80. Reservations accepted. AE, V.*

$ **Zuiderterras.** A stark glass-and-black-metal construction, this riverside café and restaurant was designed by avant-garde architect bOb (his spelling) Van Reeth. There's a view of the river on one side and the cathedral and old town on the other. *Ernest Van Dijckkaai, tel. 03/234–12–75. AE, DC, MC, V.*

¢   **Panaché.** This Antwerp institution serves the best sandwiches in town and, in the back room, simple but satisfying fare. *Statiestraat 17, tel. 03/232–69–05. No reservations. AE, DC, MC, V.*

¢   **Pelgrom.** Situated in interconnecting 16th-century cellars, Pelgrom is open every day from noon to midnight, serving predominantly Flemish dishes at budget prices. More expensive menus are also available. *Pelgrimstraat 15, tel. 03/234–08–09. AE, DC, MC, V.*

Lodging

All hotels are modern, so expect comfort, rather than period charm. For details and price-category definitions, *see* Lodging *in* Staying in Belgium, *above.*

$$ **Prinse.** Opened in 1990, the Prinse occupies a 400-year-old building surrounding an interior courtyard. Rooms are a neutral modern, with black leather furnishings, soft blue tones, and all-tile baths. Those on the top floor, with exposed beams, have more character. Although close to both sightseeing and shopping districts, this hotel offers peace and quiet. *Keizerstraat 63, tel. 03/226–40–50, fax 03/ 225–11–48. 30 rooms with bath. Facilities: breakfast room, meeting rooms, parking. AE, DC, MC, V.*

$ **Cammerpoorte.** All modern but nestled in the old town, this simple hotel opened in 1990. Rooms are slick, with all-weather carpeting and graphite-look laminate. The breakfast buffet is served in a conference-room atmosphere. *Nationalestraat 38–40, tel. 03/231–97– 36, fax 03/226–29–68. 46 rooms with bath. Facilities: breakfast room. AE, DC, MC, V.*

$ **Waldorf.** This pleasant, modern hotel is near the diamond center, and most of the guests are in the diamond business. The smallish rooms are attractively decorated in gray and brown. *Belgielei 36, tel. 03/230–99–50, fax 03/230–78–70. 100 rooms with bath. Facilities: restaurant, bar. AE, DC, MC, V.*

¢ **Pension Cammerpoorte.** Owned by the same family as the hotel of the same name (*see above*), this small pension has been scrubbed and decorated with enthusiasm. The brick-and-lace café downstairs provides the buffet breakfast that's included in the price, while rooms–on landings up the narrow staircase–are full of bright pastels and sad-clown art. *Steenhouwersvest 55, tel. 03/231–28–36, fax 03/226–29–68. 9 rooms with toilet and shower. Facilities: café. AE, DC, MC, V.*

¢ **Scoutel.** This new, clean, and well-managed place is officially a youth hostel, but it is open to all comers; the rooms are doubles or triples. It is close to the central train station and next to the diamond district. *Stoomstraat 3–7, tel. 03/226–46–06, fax 03/232–63–92. 24 rooms with shower. No credit cards.*

Brugge

Arriving and Departing

By Train Trains run hourly at 28 and 59 minutes past the hour from Brussels (Gare du Midi) to Brugge. The London–Brussels service stops here as well. The train station is south of the canal that surrounds the downtown area; for information, tel. 050/38–24–06. Travel time from Brussels is 53 minutes.

Getting Around

On Foot By far the easiest way to explore the city is on foot, because bus access is restricted and the downtown sights are fairly close together. You can also rent bicycles; ask the tourist office for information.

Guided Tours

Boat Trips Boat trips along the city canals are run by several companies and depart from five separate landings. Boats ply the waters March–November, 10–6. There is no definite departure schedule; boats leave when enough people have gathered, but you'll never have to wait more than 15 minutes or so.

Orientation Tours Fifty-minute minibus trips of the city center leave every hour on the hour from the Market Square in front of the post office. Tours are given in seven languages (individual headphones) and cost BF330 (children BF200).

Tourist Information

Toerism Brugge (Brugge Tourist Office) (Burg 11, tel. 050/44–86–86) is on a central square.

Exploring Brugge

Brugge (also known by its French name, Bruges) is an exquisitely preserved medieval town. It was Brugge's good fortune to be linked with the sea by a navigable waterway, and the city became a leading member of the Hanseatic League in the 13th century. Europe's first stock exchange was established here. Brugge was ignored for centuries after the Zwin silted up in the 15th century, but this past misfortune is its present glory. Little has changed in this city of interlaced canals, overhung with humpbacked bridges and weeping willows. The Burg, an intimate medieval square, is the inspiring setting for summer classical concerts.

Numbers in the margin correspond to points of interest on the Brugge map.

❶ The best place to start a walking tour is the **Markt** (Market Square).
❷ From the top of the **Belfort** (belfry) there's a panoramic view of the town. The belfry has a carillon notable even in Belgium, where they are a matter of civic pride. On summer evenings, the Markt is brightly lit. *Belfort admission: BF100. Open Apr.–Sept., daily 9:30–5; Oct.–Mar., daily 9:30–12:30 and 1:30–5. Carillon concerts Oct.–mid-June, Sun., Wed., and Sat. 2:15–3; mid-June–Sept., Mon., Wed., and Sat. 9–10 PM, Sun. 2:15–3.*

❸ On the eastern side of the Markt stands the **Provinciaal Hof,** the neo-Gothic provincial government building. Walk east from the Markt along Breidelstraat, to the Burg, a square at the center of ancient
❹ Brugge. On the left is the **Proostdijg** (Provost's House), built in 1665. Across the square is a row of magnificent buildings—the
❺ **Stadhuis** (town hall), dating from the 14th century, its wonderfully
❻ ornate facade covered with statues; **Oude Griffie,** the former Recorder's House dating from the 1530s and ornamented with impres-
❼ sive windows; and the **Heilig-Bloed Basiliek** (the Basilica of the Holy Blood), a 12th-century Romanesque chapel built to enshrine a relic believed to contain Jesus's blood. Here, too, is a **Heilig-Bloed Museum** (Museum of the Holy Blood), with many treasures associated with the cult. The Procession of the Holy Blood on Ascension Day (in 1996 it will be held on May 16) is a major pageant that combines religious and historical elements. *Stadhuis admission: BF60. Open Apr.–Sept., daily 9:30–5; Oct.–Mar. daily 9:30–12:30 and 2–5. Heilig-Bloed Museum admission: BF40. Open Apr.–Sept., daily 9:30–noon and 2–6; Oct.–Mar., daily 10–noon and 2–4. Closed Wed. afternoon.*

❽ Walk through a passage between the town hall and the Oude Griffie and you'll come to the **Dijver,** the city canal. Canal boat trips leave from here. *Boats leave on demand. Average trip 30 mins. Cost: BF150.*

❾ Walking south along the Dijver, you'll soon reach a group of museums. The **Groeninge Museum,** on the Dijver Canal, has a very rich, wide-ranging collection of Flemish masterpieces, with works by Van Eyck, Memling, Bosch, and Bruegel, among many others, plus some contemporary works. *Dijver 12, tel. 050/33–99–11. Admission: BF130; combination ticket for BF350 covers the Groeninge, Brangwyn, Gruuthuse, and Memling museums (see below). Open Apr.–Sept., daily 9:30–5; Oct.–Mar., Wed.–Mon. 9:30–12:30 and 2–5.*

The **Brangwyn Museum,** next door, is named for the artist Frank Brangwyn (1867–1956) and contains hundreds of his Brugge-inspired works, as well as a fine collection of old lace. *Dijver 16, tel. 050/33–99–11. Admission: BF130. Open Apr.–Sept., daily 9:30–5; Oct.–Mar., Wed.–Mon. 9:30–noon and 2–5.*

❿ The **Gruuthuse Museum,** in the 15th century a palace of the aristocratic Gruuthuse family, contains archaeological exhibitions and a large collection of Flemish sculpture, paintings, furniture, altarpieces, and tapestries. *Dijver 17, tel. 050/33–99–11. Admission: BF130. Open Apr.–Sept., daily 9:30–5; Oct.–Mar., Wed.–Mon. 9:30–12:30 and 2–5.*

⓫ Here, too, is the **Memling Museum,** dedicated to the work of one of Brugge's most famous sons, the painter Hans Memling (1430–90), and housed in the former Sint Jans Hospital (Hospital of St. John), where the artist was nursed back to health after being wounded in France. *Mariastraat 38, tel. 050/33–25–62. Admission: BF130. Open Apr.–Sept., daily 9:30–5; Oct.–Mar., Thur.–Tues. 9:30–12:30 and 2–5.*

⓬ Next to the Memling Museum is the **Onze-Lieve-Vrouwekerk** (Church of Our Lady), with a notable collection of paintings and

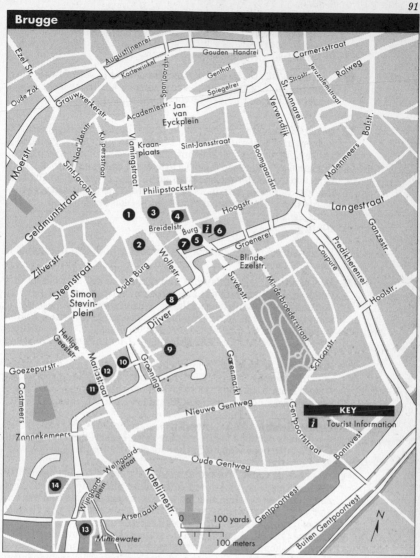

Brugge

Begijnhof, **14**
Belfort, **2**
Dijver, **8**
Groeninge Museum, **9**
Gruuthuse Museum, **10**
Heilig-Bloed Basiliek, **7**

Markt, **1**
Memling Museum, **11**
Minnewater, **13**
Onze-Lieve-Vrouwekerk, **12**
Oude Griffie, **6**
Proostdijg, **4**
Provinciaal Hof, **3**
Stadhuis, **5**

carvings—especially Michelangelo's small *Madonna*—and some splendidly colorful tombs. *Admission to mausoleum: BF30. Open weekdays 10–11:30 and 2:30–5, Sun. 2:30–5. (Oct.–Mar. the church closes at 4:30.) No visits during services.*

 Continue south to the enchanting **Minnewater** (Lake of Love) park. From the Minnewater visit the adjoining 16th-century lockkeeper's house, usually surrounded by contented white swans, the symbol of the city.

⑭ Beside Minnewater, a picturesque bridge leads to the **Begijnhof,** the former almshouses and the most serene spot in Brugge. Founded in 1245 by the countess of Constantinople, the Béguinage was originally a home for widows of fallen Crusaders. These women took partial vows and lived a devout life while serving the community. Although the last Béguines left in 1930, a Benedictine community has replaced them. The Béguinage has kept its cloistered charm.

Dining

For details and price-category definitions, *see* Dining *in* Staying in Belgium, *above.*

$$ **De Castillion.** This restaurant and hotel occupies an 18th-century building. Predinner drinks are served in a handsome Art Deco salon; notable dishes include a fillet of venison and a fricassee of turbot and salmon. The hotel side comprises 18 rooms and 2 suites. *Heilige Geeststraat 1, tel. 050/34–30–01, fax 050/33–94–75. Reservations advised. Jacket and tie. AE, DC, MC, V. Closed Tues. and first ½ of Jan.*

$ **Steakhouse de Tassche.** A husband-and-wife team runs this place, and the cooking comes from the heart. A wide range of simple dishes, from steak and fries to grilled sole, are served in a setting of pink damask and copper. *Oude Burg 11, tel. 050/33–12–82. DC, MC, V.*

$ **Straffe Hendrik.** On an attractive square near the Béguinage, this tap room is part of a family-run brewery. It serves a cold lunch buffet, Flemish beer soup, and other specialties. *Walplein, tel. 050/33–26–97. No credit cards.*

¢ **Staminee de Garre.** Tucked in an alley off one of the busiest tourist streets, this tiny, two-tiered coffeehouse offers Mozart and magazines along with coffee and 136 brands of beer. Simple cold platters and grilled sandwiches are attractively presented. *Off Breidelstraat, tel. 050/34–10–29. No credit cards.*

¢ **Taverne Curiosa.** A steep flight of stairs takes you down from one of the main shopping streets to this medieval cellar. A smoked seafood platter is always on the menu, and other specialties include inventive omelets. The ambience is pleasantly relaxed. *Vlamingstraat 22, tel. 050/34–23–34. V. Closed July.*

Lodging

In proportion to its size, Brugge has a large number of hotels—in fact, many more than Antwerp. For details and price-category definitions, *see* Lodging *in* Staying in Belgium, *above.*

$$ **Oud Huis Amsterdam.** Two 16th-century town houses have been
★ combined to create this hotel, overlooking the canal near Jan Van Eyckplein. The rooms, all different, are large and modern. In the evening guests are provided with free transportation by horse-drawn coach to the romantic (but expensive) restaurant 't Bourgoensche Cruyce. *Spiegelrei 3, tel. 050/34–18–10, fax 050/33–88–91. 19 rooms with bath. AE, DC, MC, V.*

$ **Ter Brughe.** If it's atmosphere and period charm you want, you won't be disappointed by this delightful canalside hotel, a 15th-century survival, with friendly service and a cozy atmosphere. There's no restaurant. *Oost-Gistelhof 2, tel. 050/34–03–24, fax 050/33–88–73. 24 rooms with bath. DC, MC, V. Closed Jan.–Feb.*

¢ **De Pauw.** At this spotless, family-run hotel, the warmly furnished rooms have names rather than numbers, and breakfast comes with six kinds of bread, cold cuts, and cheese. *St. Gilliskerkhof 8, tel. 050/ 33–71–18. 8 rooms, 6 with bath. AE, DC, MC, V.*

¢ **Fevery.** You're made to feel a personal guest in this friendly hotel. There's even a baby monitor to enable parents to relax downstairs. Rooms have been upgraded with new carpets and chenille bedspreads. *Collaert Mansionstraat 3, tel. 050/33–12–69, fax 050/33–17–91. 11 rooms with bath. Facilities: bar. AE, DC, MC, V.*

¢ **Jacobs.** This hotel is on the same square as De Pauw and shares many of its characteristics. It is larger, however, and the clientele are a bit younger. The rooms have blond-wood furniture, and although not large are quite comfortable. *Baliestraat 1, tel. 050/33–98–31. 26 rooms, 24 with bath. Facilities: bar, breakfast room. AE, MC, V.*

4 **Bulgaria**

Bulgaria is a small, austere country that lies in the eastern half of the Balkan Peninsula. It is a land whose mountains, seascapes, and rustic beauty have attracted European travelers for centuries. From the end of World War II until recently, it was the closest ally of the former Soviet Union and presented a rather mysterious image to the Western world. This era ended in 1989 with the overthrow of Communist party head Todor Zhivkov. Since then, Bulgaria has gradually opened itself to the West as it struggles along the path toward democracy and a free-market economy.

Endowed with long Black Sea beaches, the rugged Balkan range in its interior, and fertile Danube plains, Bulgaria has much to offer the tourist year-round. Its tourist industry is quite well developed and is being restructured to shield visitors better from shortages of goods and services and the other legacies of rigid central planning.

The Black Sea coast along the country's eastern border is particularly attractive, with secluded coves and old fishing villages, as well as wide stretches of shallow beaches that have been developed into self-contained resorts. The interior landscape offers great scenic beauty, and the traveler who enters it will find a tranquil world of forested ridges, spectacular valleys, and rural communities where folklore is a colorful part of village life.

The capital, Sofia, is picturesquely situated in a valley near Mount Vitosha. There is much of cultural interest here, and the city has good hotels and restaurants serving international cuisine. The other major draw is Varna, the site of one of Europe's first cultural settlements and the most important port in Bulgaria.

Essential Information

Before You Go

When to Go The ski season lasts from mid-December through March, while the Black Sea coast season runs from May to October, reaching its

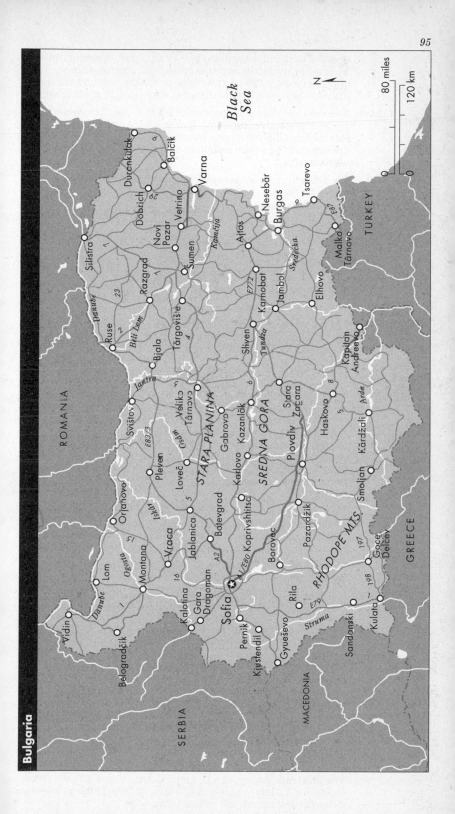

Bulgaria

Black Sea

TURKEY

ROMANIA

SERBIA

MACEDONIA

GREECE

STARA PLANINA

SREDNA GORA

RHODOPE MTS.

80 miles
120 km

Durcnkulak
Balčik
Varna
Vetrino
Nesebǎr
Tsarevo
Burgas
Ajtos
Dobrich
Novi Pazar
Sumen
Kamčija
Malko
Tǎrnovo
Silistra
Razgrad
Kapitan
Andreevo
Ruse
Bjala
Tǎrgovište
Veliko
Tǎrnovo
Sliven
Karnobat
Jambol
Elhovo
Svištov
Gabrovo
Kazanlǎk
Stara
Zagara
Haskovo
Kǎrdžali
Pleven
Loveč
Katlovo
Plovdiv
Smoljan
Orjahovo
Botevgrad
Koprivshtitsa
Pazardžik
Goce
Delčev
Vraca
Jablanica
Borovec
Montana
Lom
Kalotina
Gara
Dragoman
Pernik
Rila
Kulata
Sandanski
Vidin
Belogradčik
Sofia
Kjustendil
Gyueševo
Struma

Danube
Bǎli Lom
Iantra
Osǎm
Isḱǎr
Ogosta
Danube
Tundža
Arda
Sreděcka
E772
E83/3
A1/E80
A2
E79
E87

crowded peak in July and August. Fruit trees blossom in April and May; in May and early June the blossoms are gathered in the Valley of Roses (you have to be up early to watch the harvest); the fruit is picked in September, and in October the fall colors are at their best.

Climate Summers are warm, winters are crisp and cold. The coastal areas enjoy considerable sunshine; March and April are the wettest months inland. Even when the temperature climbs, the Black Sea breezes and the cooler mountain air prevent the heat from being overpowering.

The following are the average daily maximum and minimum temperatures for Sofia.

Jan.	35F	2C	May	69F	21C	Sept.	70F	22C
	25	– 4		50	10		52	11
Feb.	39F	4C	June	76F	24C	Oct.	63F	17C
	27	– 3		56	14		46	8
Mar.	50F	10C	July	81F	27C	Nov.	48F	9C
	33	1		60	16		37	3
Apr.	60F	16C	Aug.	79F	26C	Dec.	38F	4C
	42	5		59	15		28	– 2

Currency The unit of currency in Bulgaria is the lev (plural leva), divided into 100 stotinki. There are bills of 1, 2, 5, 10, 20, 50, 100, 200, 500, 1,000, and 2,000 leva; coins of 1, 2, and 5 leva; and coins of 5, 10, 20, and 50 stotinki. At press time (summer 1995), as part of efforts at economic reform, hard-currency payments for goods and services are no longer permitted. The only legal tender for commercial transactions and tourist services in Bulgaria is the lev. These services include air, train, and long-distance bus travel; all accommodations, from camping to hotels; and car rentals and Balkantourist package tours. You may import any amount of foreign currency, including traveler's checks, and exchange it at branches of the Bulgarian State Bank, commercial banks, Balkantourist hotels, airports, border posts, and other exchange offices, which quote their daily selling and buying rates. The rate quoted by the Bulgarian State Bank at press time is 66 leva to the U.S. dollar, 106 leva to the pound sterling.

It is forbidden either to import or to export Bulgarian currency. Unspent leva must be exchanged at frontier posts on departure before you go through passport control. You will need to present your official exchange slips to prove that the currency was legally purchased.

The major international credit cards are accepted in some of the larger stores, hotels, and restaurants.

What It Will Cost Prices in Bulgaria have been low for years, but this is changing as the government tries to revive the economy and open it up to the West. If you choose the more moderate hotels, accommodations won't be very expensive. It is possible to cut costs even more by staying in a private hotel or private room in a Bulgarian house or apartment—also arranged by Balkantourist or other tourism companies—or by camping. The favorable cash exchange rate, linked to foreign-currency fluctuations, makes such expenses as taxi and public transport fares, museum and theater admission, and meals in most restaurants seem comparatively low by international standards. A little hard currency, exchanged at this rate, goes a long way. Shopping for imported and domestic wares in the duty-free shops also helps to keep travel expenses down. The following price list, correct as of spring 1995, can therefore be used only as a rough guide.

Sample Prices Trip on a tram, trolley, or bus, 5 leva; theater ticket, 40 leva–60 leva; coffee in a moderate restaurant, 5 leva–20 leva; bottle of wine in a moderate restaurant, 120 leva–200 leva.

Museums Museum admission is very inexpensive, ranging from 30 leva to 50 leva (less than $1).

Visas All visitors need a valid passport. Those traveling in groups of six or more do not require visas, and many package tours are exempt from the visa requirement. Americans do not need visas when traveling as tourists. Other tourists, traveling independently, should inquire about visa requirements at a Bulgarian embassy or consulate before entering the country, since fees may be higher for visas obtained at the border.

Customs on Arrival You may import duty-free into Bulgaria 250 grams of tobacco products, plus 1 liter of hard liquor and 2 liters of wine. Items intended for personal use during your stay are also duty-free. Travelers are advised to declare items of greater value—cameras, tape recorders, etc.—so there will be no problems with Bulgarian customs officials on departure.

Language The official language, Bulgarian, is written in Cyrillic and is very close to Old Church Slavonic, the root of all Slavic languages. English is spoken in major hotels and restaurants, but is unlikely to be heard elsewhere. It is essential to remember that in Bulgaria, a nod of the head means "no" and a shake of the head means "yes."

Getting Around

By Train Buy tickets in advance at a ticket office—there is one in each of the major centers—and avoid long lines at the station. Trains are very busy; seat reservations are obligatory on expresses. All medium- and long-distance trains have first- and second-class carriages and limited buffet services; overnight trains between Sofia and Black Sea resorts have first- and second-class sleeping cars and second-class couchettes. From Sofia there are six main routes—to Varna and to Burgas on the Black Sea coast, to Plovdiv and on to the Turkish border, to Dragoman and the Yugoslav border, to Kulata and the Greek border, and to Ruse on the Romanian border. The main line is powered by electricity. Plans to electrify the rest are under way.

By Plane **Balkanair** (Balkan Bulgarian Airlines) has regular services to the Black Sea ports of Varna and Burgas. Book through Balkantourist offices, though this can take time, and overbooking is not unusual. Group travel and air-taxi services are available through the privately run Hemus Air and Air Via. Business flights to other destinations in the country are also arranged by Hemus Air.

By Bus The routes of the crowded buses are mainly planned to link towns and districts not connected by rail. Within the cities a regular system of trams and trolley buses operates for a single fare of 5 leva. Ticket booths, at most tram stops, sell single or season tickets; you can also pay the driver. The tourist information offices have full details of routes and times.

By Boat Modern luxury vessels cruise the Danube from Passau in Austria to Ruse. Hydrofoils link main communities along the Bulgarian stretches of the Danube and the Black Sea, and there are coastal excursions from some Black Sea resorts. A ferry from Vidin to Calafat links Bulgaria with Romania.

Staying in Bulgaria

Telephones Calls can be made from hotels or from public telephones in the post office in each major town or resort. To place a call to the United States via an **AT&T** international operator, dial 00–1800–0010; for **Sprint,** dial 00–800–0877. There is a new system of international telephones—modern, direct-dial phones with no coin slots—that operate only with special cards paid for in leva. Directions for buying the cards are given, often in English, on the phones.

Mail Letters and postcards to the United States cost 7 leva, 15 leva to the United Kingdom.

Opening and Closing Times **Banks** are open weekdays 9–3.

Museums are usually open 9–6:30 but are often closed on Monday or Tuesday.

Shops are open Monday–Saturday 9–7. Many shops are open on Sunday as well.

National Holidays In 1996: January 1 (New Year's Day); March 3 (Independence Day); April 14 and 15 (Orthodox Easter); May 1 (Labor Day); May 24 (Bulgarian Culture Day); December 24, 25, 26 (Christmas). Changing holiday in 1997: April 26 and 27 (Orthodox Easter).

Dining There is a choice of hotel restaurants with their international menus (not listed below), Balkantourist restaurants, or the inexpensive restaurants and cafeterias run privately and by cooperatives. The best bets are the small folk-style restaurants that serve national dishes and local specialties. The word *picnic* in a restaurant name means that the tables are outdoors. Standards have improved, but food is still rarely served piping hot, and visitors should be prepared for loud background music.

Specialties Balkan cooking revolves around lamb and pork, sheep cheese, potatoes, peppers, eggplant, tomatoes, onions, carrots, and spices. Fresh fruit, vegetables, and salads are particularly good in season, and so are the soups. Bulgaria invented yogurt (*kiselo mleko*), with its promise of good health and longevity, and there are excellent cold yogurt soups (*tarator*) during the summer. Rich cream cakes and syrupy baklava are served to round out a meal.

Bulgarian wines are good, usually full-bodied, dry, and inexpensive. The national drink is *rakia*—a plum or grape brandy called *slivova* or *grosdova*—but vodka is popular, too. Coffee is strong and is often drunk along with a cold beverage, such as cola or a lemon drink. Tea is taken with lemon instead of milk.

What to Wear In Sofia, casual dress is appropriate at $$, $, and ¢ restaurants.

Ratings Prices are per person and include a first course, main course, dessert, and tip, but no alcohol. Best bets are indicated by a star ★.

Category	Cost
$$	300 leva–600 leva
$	150 leva–300 leva
¢	100 leva–150 leva

Credit Cards Increasingly, even restaurants in the $$ category are accepting credit cards, although the list of cards accepted may not always be correctly posted. Before you place an order, check to see whether you can pay with your card.

Lodging There is a wide choice of accommodations, ranging from hotels—most of them dating from the '60s and '70s—to apartment rentals, rooms in private homes, hostels, and campsites. Although hotels are improving, they still tend to suffer from temperamental wiring and erratic plumbing, and it is a good idea to pack a universal drain plug, since plugs are often missing in hotel bathrooms. In moderate and inexpensive hotels, bathrooms often look unusual. Don't be surprised if strangely placed plumbing turns the entire bathroom into a shower. Because of power cuts in the winter, flashlights and other battery-powered appliances are strongly recommended if you're traveling off-season.

Hotels Until recently, most hotels used by Western visitors were owned by Balkantourist and Interhotels. At press time (summer 1995), many of the government-owned or operated hotels listed below were on the verge of privatization. The conversion is expected to take up to five years. Hotels may be closed for renovation for extended periods or may be permanently shut down. Visitors are strongly urged to call hotels ahead to get the latest information. Some hotels were always privately run or run by municipal authorities or organizations catering to specific groups (Shipka for motorists, Orbita for young people, Pirin for hikers). Most have restaurants and bars; the large, modern ones have swimming pools, shops, and other facilities. Some coastal resorts have complexes where different categories of hotels are grouped, each with its own facilities.

Private Lodgings Staying in private homes, arranged by Balkantourist, is becoming a popular alternative as a means not only of cutting costs but of offering increased contact with Bulgarians. There are one-, two- and three-star private accommodations. Some offer a bed or bed and breakfast only; some provide full board. Three-star rooms are equipped with kitchenettes. Booking offices are located in most main tourist areas. In Sofia, contact **Balkantourist** at 1 Vitosha Blvd. (tel. 2/43331) or go to the private accommodations office at 27 Stambolijski Boulevard, (tel. 2/88–52–56 or 2/88–44–30).

Hostels Hostels are basic, but clean and cheap. Contact **Orbita** (48 Hristo Botev Blvd., Sofia, tel. 2/80–01–02).

Campsites There are more than 100 campsites, many near the Black Sea coast. They are graded one, two, or three stars, and the best of them offer hot and cold water, grocery stores, and restaurants. Balkantourist provides a location map.

Ratings The following hotel categories are for two people in a double room with half board (breakfast and a main meal). Best bets are indicated by a star ★. You must show your exchange slips to prove that your money was legally changed.

Category	Sofia	Other Areas
$$	2,500–6,000 leva	2,000–4,000 leva
$	800–2,500 leva	500–2,000 leva
¢	under 800 leva	under 800 leva

Tipping To tip, round out your restaurant bill 3%–5%.

Sofia

Arriving and Departing

By Plane All international flights arrive at Sofia airport. For information on international flights, tel. 2/79–80–35 or 2/72–06–72; domestic flights, tel. 2/79–32–21.

Between the Airport and Downtown Bus 84 serves the airport. Fares for taxis taken from the airport taxi stand run about 150 leva for the 10-kilometer (6-mile) ride into Sofia. Avoid the taxi touts; they tend to overcharge or to insist on payment in hard currency.

By Train The central station is at the northern edge of the city. For information, tel. 2/3–11–11 or 2/843–33–33. The ticket offices in Sofia are in the underpass of the National Palace of Culture (1 Bulgaria Sq., tel. 2/843–42–92) or at the Rila International Travel Agency (5 Gurko St., tel. 2/87–07–77). There is a taxi stand at the station.

Getting Around

By Bus Buses, trolleys, and trams run fairly often. Buy a ticket from the ticket stand near the streetcar stop and punch it into the machine as you board. (Watch how the person in front of you does it.) For information, tel. 2/312–42–63.

On Foot The main sites are centrally located, so the best way to see the city is on foot.

Important Addresses and Numbers

Since late 1990, a national commission has been working to rename cities, streets, and monuments throughout the country. Names given in the following sections were correct as of summer 1995 but are subject to change.

Tourist **Balkantourist Head Office** (tel. 2/43331) is at 1 Vitosha Boulevard;
Information the tourist and accommodations office (tel. 2/88–52–56 or 2/88–44–30) is at 27 Stambolijski Boulevard. It also has offices or desks in all the main hotels.

Embassies U.S. (1 Suborna St., tel. 2/88–48–01). U.K. (38 Levski Blvd., tel. 2/88–53–61).

Emergencies **Police:** Sofia City Constabulary (tel. 166); **ambulance** (tel. 150); **fire** (tel. 160); **doctor:** Clinic for Foreign Citizens (Mladost 1, 1 Eugeni Pavlovski St., tel. 2/77–95–18); **"Pirogov"** Emergency Hospital (tel. 2/5–15–31).

Exploring Sofia

Sofia is set on the high Sofia Plain, ringed by mountain ranges: the Balkan range to the north; Lyulin Mountains to the west; part of the Sredna Gora Mountains to the southeast; and, to the southwest, Mount Vitosha, the city's playground, which rises to 2,325 meters (7,500 feet). The area has been inhabited for about 7,000 years, but the visitor's first impression is of a modern city with broad streets, light traffic, spacious parks, and open-air cafés. As recently as the 1870s it was part of the Ottoman Empire, and one mosque still remains. Most of the city, however, was planned after 1880.

Numbers in the margin correspond to points of interest on the Sofia map.

① **Ploshtad Sveta Nedelya** (St. Nedelya Square) is a good starting point for an exploration of the main sights. The south side of the square is **②** dominated by the 19th-century **Tzarkva Sveta Nedelya** (St. Nedelya Church). Go behind it to find Vitosha Boulevard, a lively pedestrian street with plenty of stores, cafés, and dairy bars.

The first building along this boulevard, on the west side of the **③** street, is the former Courts of Justice, now the **Natzionalen Istoricheski Musei** (National History Museum). Its vast collections, vividly illustrating the art history of Bulgaria, include priceless Thracian treasures, Roman mosaics, enameled jewelry from the First Bulgarian Kingdom, and glowing religious art that survived the years of Ottoman oppression. The courts are due to return to this location as soon as a new home is found for the National History Museum collection. *Vitosha Blvd., tel. 2/88–41–60. Open Mon.–Fri. 9:30–4:30.*

Return to the southeast side of St. Nedelya Square, and in the court **④** yard of the Sheraton Sofia Balkan Hotel you will see the **Rotonda Sveti Georgi** (rotunda of St. George). Built in the 4th century as a Roman temple, it has served as a mosque and church, and recent restoration has revealed medieval frescoes. It is not open to the public. Head east to the vast Alexander Batenberg Square, which is domi-

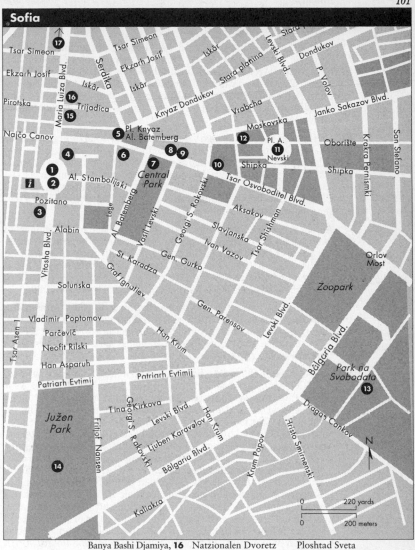

Sofia

Banya Bashi Djamiya, **16**
Borisova Gradina, **13**
Hram-pametnik
Alexander Nevski, **11**
Mavsolei Georgi
Dimitrov, **7**
Natzionalen
Archeologicheski
Musei, **6**

Natzionalen Dvoretz
na Kulturata,**14**
Natzionalen
Etnografski Musei, **8**
Natzionalen
Istoricheski Musei, **3**
Natzionalna
Hudozhestvena
Galeria, **9**
Partiyniyat Dom, **5**

Ploshtad Sveta
Nedelya, **1**
Rotonda Sveti Georgi, **4**
Tsentralen Universalen
Magazin, **15**
Tsentralni Hali, **17**
Tzarkva Sveta
Nedelya, **2**
Tzarkva Sveta Sofia, **12**
Tzarkva Sveti
Nikolai, **10**

⑤ nated by the **Partiyniyat Dom** (the former headquarters of the Bulgarian Communist party).

Facing the square, but entered via Alexander Stambolijski Boulevard, is the former Great Mosque, which now houses the ⑥ **Natzionalen Archeologicheski Musei** (National Archaeological Museum). The 15th-century building itself is as fascinating as its contents, which illustrate the culture of the different peoples who inhabited Bulgaria up to the 19th century. *Tel. 2/88–24–06. Closed for renovations.*

⑦ On the next block to the east is the former **Mavsolei Georgi Dimitrov** (Georgi Dimitrov Mausoleum), which until 1990 contained the embalmed body of the first general secretary of the Bulgarian Communist party, who died in Moscow in 1949 and was known as the "Father of the Nation." His remains have been moved to the Central Cemetery, and there is talk of converting the mausoleum into a museum or of destroying it.

Across from the mausoleum is the former palace of the Bulgarian ⑧ tsar, which currently houses the **Natzionalen Etnografski Musei** (National Ethnographical Museum), with displays of costumes, handicrafts, and tools that illustrate the agricultural way of life of the country people until the 19th century. *1 Alexander Batenberg Sq., tel. 2/87–41–91. Open Wed.–Sun. 10–noon and 1:30–5:30.*

⑨ In the west wing of the same building is the **Natzionalna Hudozhestvena Galeria** (National Art Gallery). It houses a collection of the best works of Bulgarian artists, as well as a foreign art section that contains some graphics of famous artists. *1 Alexander Batemberg Sq., tel. 2/89–28–41. Open Tues.–Sun. 10:30–6.*

⑩ Nearby stands the ornate Russian **Tzarkva Sveti Nikolai** (Church of St. Nicholas), erected 1912–14. From here you'll enter Tsar Osvoboditel Boulevard, with its monument to the Russians, topped by the equestrian statue of Russian Tsar Alexander II. It stands in front of the National Assembly. Behind the National Assembly you'll be confronted by the neo-Byzantine structure with glittering onion domes whose image you may recognize from almost every piece of tourist literature and which really does dominate the city. ⑪ This is the **Hram-pametnik Alexander Nevski** (Alexander Nevski Memorial Church), built by the Bulgarian people at the beginning of this century as a mark of gratitude to their Russian liberators. Inside are alabaster and onyx, Italian marble and Venetian mosaics, magnificent frescoes, and space for a congregation of 5,000. Attend a service to hear the superb choir, and, above all, don't miss the fine collection of icons in the **Crypt Museum**. *Admission: 50 leva. Open Wed.–Mon. 10:30–5.*

Cross the square to the west to pay your respects to the much older ⑫ **Tzarkva Sveta Sofia** (Church of St. Sofia), which dates from the 6th century, though remains of even older churches have been found during excavations. Its age and simplicity are in stark contrast to its more glamorous neighbor.

Return to Tsar Osvoboditel Boulevard and continue east to the ⑬ **Borisova Gradina** (Boris's Garden), with its lake and fountains, woods and lawns, huge sports stadium, and open-air theater. From the park take Dragan Tsankov west (back toward St. Nedelya Square) briefly, before going left on Patriarh Evtimij, toward Južen Park. The formal gardens and extensive woodlands here are to be extended as far as Mount Vitosha.

At the entrance to the park stands a large modern building, the ⑭ **Natzionalen Dvoretz na Kulturata** (National Palace of Culture), with its complex of halls for conventions and cultural activities. Its underpass, on several levels, is equipped with a tourist information office, shops, restaurants, discos, and a bowling alley. *1 Bulgaria Sq., tel. 2/51501. Admission: 50 leva. Open 10:30–6:30.*

⑮ Back at St. Nedelya Square, follow Knyaginya Maria-Luiza Boulevard to the train station. The large building on the right is the recently refurbished **Tsentralen Universalen Magazin** (Central Department Store). *2 Knyaginya Maria-Luiza Blvd. Open Mon.– Sat. 8–8.*

⑯ Just beyond is a distinctive building, a legacy of Turkish domination, the **Banya Bashi Djamiya** (Banja Basi Mosque); it is closed to visitors. Nearby you will see the Public Mineral Baths. Across the boul-
⑰ evard is the busy **Tsentralni Hali** (Central Market Hall), which is closed for renovations.

Shopping

Gifts and Souvenirs There are good selections of arts and crafts at the shop of the **Union of Bulgarian Artists** (6 Shipka St.). Try also the Bulgarian Folk Art Shop (14 Vitosha Blvd.). You will find a range of souvenirs at **Sredec** (7 Lege St.). **Souvenir Store** (7 Stambolijski Blvd.) has more of the same. Another is **Prizma Store** (1 Vasil Levski St.). If you are interested in furs or leather, try the shops along **Vitosha Blvd., Levski Blvd.,** or **Tsar Osvoboditel Blvd.** For recordings of Bulgarian music, go to the **National Palace of Culture** (1 Bulgaria Sq., on the underground level).

Shopping Districts The latest shopping center is in the underpass of the modern **National Palace of Culture,** where stores sell fashions, leather goods, and all forms of handicrafts. The pedestrians-only area along **Vitosha Boulevard** features many new, privately owned shops. The colorful small shops along **Graf Ignatiev Street** also deserve attention.

Department Stores Sofia's largest department store is the **Central Department Store** at 2 Knyaginya Maria-Luiza Boulevard.

Dining

Eating in Sofia can be enjoyable and even entertaining if the restaurant has a nightclub or folklore program. Be prepared to be patient and make an evening of it, since service can be slow at times. Or try a *mehana,* or tavern, where the atmosphere is informal and service sometimes a bit quicker. For details and price-category definitions, *see* Dining *in* Staying in Bulgaria, *above.*

$$ Boyansko Hanche. Local and national specialties are the main features in this restaurant and folklore center, 10 kilometers (6 miles) from downtown (take Bus 64 or 107). *Near Bojanska church, tel. 2/ 56–30–16. No credit cards.*

$$ Club-Restaurant. Bulgarian and European cuisines at their best are served in this elegant new place. *15 Dimitar Nestorov Blvd., tel. 2/ 59–50–21. No credit cards.*

$$ Eddy's Diner. This is the home of American cooking in the center of Sofia. The charming restaurant offers a variety of salads, burgers, sandwiches, and grilled steaks. *4 Vitosha Blvd., tel. 2/87–67–83. No credit cards.*

$$ The Golden Dragon. This new restaurant, centrally located, is very popular for its wide selection of Chinese dishes. *86 Rakovski St., no phone. No credit cards.*

$$ Phenyan. This place is known for its Far Eastern ambience and Korean specialties. *24 Assen Zlatarov St., tel. 2/44–34–36. No credit cards.*

$$ Rubin. This eating complex in the center of Sofia has a snack bar and an elegant restaurant that serves Bulgarian and international food. A full meal can sometimes push the cost into a higher price category. *4 St. Nedelya Sq., tel. 2/87–47–04. AE, DC, MC, V.*

$ **Chinese Restaurant.** Located in a village 16 kilometers (10 miles)
★ south of Sofia, this place is known for its very good Chinese cuisine
and exotic atmosphere. *Dolni Lozen, tel. 2/26–16–02. No credit
cards.*

$ **Party Club Restaurant.** An unusual mix of Continental and Chinese
dishes is the main draw here. *3 Vasil Levski Blvd., tel. 2/81–05–44 or
2/81–43–43. AE, DC, MC, V.*

$ **Vodeničarski Mehani.** The English translation is "Miller's Tavern,"
which is appropriate, since it's made up of three old mills linked together. It is at the foot of Mount Vitosha and features a folklore
show and a menu of Bulgarian specialties. The nightclub is open till 4
AM. *Dragalevci District (Bus 64), tel. 2/67–10–21. No credit cards.*

$ **Zheravna.** This is a small, cozy place with a homey atmosphere. It
serves tasty Bulgarian food. *67 Levski Blvd., tel. 2/87–21–86. No
credit cards.*

$ **Zlatnite Mostove.** This restaurant, on Mount Vitosha, has live music
in the evenings. *Vitosha District, 19 km (12 mi) from the city center,
no phone. No credit cards.*

¢ **Sofiisko Pivo.** This large restaurant, 15 kilometers (10 miles) from
★ the center of town, serves Bulgarian food and a wide selection of
beer. *Vladaya District, tel. 2/57–82–18. No credit cards.*

¢ **Vkusnoto Kebapche.** The name of this small, family place comes from
the tasty, grilled meatballs that are the specialty of the restaurant.
20 San Stefano St., tel. 2/46–20–27.

Also recommended are the moderate and friendly club-restaurants,
which have been open to nonmembers since 1991: **Klub na
Jurnalistite** (Club of the Journalists, 4 Graf Ignatiev St., tel. 2/87–
30–83), **Klub na Pisatelite** (Writers Club, 5 Angel Kanchev St., tel.
2/88–00–31), **Klub na Hudojnicite** (Artists Club, 6 Shipka St., tel.
2/43–431), and **Klub na Filmovite Deici** (Filmmakers Club, 37
Ekzarh Yosif St., tel. 2/80–22–25).

Lodging

The following hotels maintain a high standard of cleanliness and are
open year-round unless otherwise stated. If you arrive in Sofia without reservations, go to Interhotels Central Office (2 Sveta Sofia St.),
Balkantourist (1 Vitosha Blvd.), Bureau of Tourist Information and
Reservations (22–24 Lavele St.), the National Palace of Culture (1
Bulgaria Sq.), or the central railroad station. For details and price-
category definitions, *see* Lodging *in* Staying in Bulgaria, *above.*

$$ **Bulgaria.** Despite its central location, this small hotel is quiet and a
bit old-fashioned. *4 Tsar Osvoboditel Blvd., tel. 2/88–22–11. 85
rooms, some with bath or shower. Facilities: restaurant, tavern, cof-
fee shop, bar. AE, DC, MC, V.*

$$ **Deva-Spartak.** This small hotel is behind the National Palace of Cul-
★ ture. It offers excellent sports facilities. *4 Arsenalski Blvd., tel. 2/
66–12–61. 13 rooms. Facilities: restaurant, indoor and outdoor
swimming pools, Spartak sports complex, shop. AE, DC, MC, V.*

$$ **Hemus.** This is a smaller place near the Vitosha Hotel. Guests can
take advantage of the facilities of its larger neighbor while saving
money for the casino or nightclub. *31 Cherni Vrah Blvd., tel. 2/6–
39–51. 240 rooms, most with bath or shower. Facilities: restaurant,
folk tavern, nightclub, shops. AE, DC, MC, V.*

$$ **Pliska-Cosmos.** Part of the Balkan Airlines hotel chain, the Pliska-
Cosmos, at the entrance to the city, has been recently renovated. *87
Tsarigradsko Shose Blvd., tel. 2/71281. 200 rooms with shower. Fa-
cilities: restaurant, bar, shops. AE, DC, MC, V.*

$$ **Rila.** A convenient, central downtown location makes it a low-cost
alternative to the Sheraton. *6 Kaloyan St., tel. 2/88–18–61. 120
rooms with shower. Facilities: restaurant, folk tavern, art gallery.
AE, DC, MC, V.*

$ **Rai-90.** This small, private hotel is not far from the center of the city. *13 Lidize St., tel. 2/72–96–90. 10 rooms with bath or shower. Facilities: coffee shop. No credit cards.*

$ **Serdika.** The centrally located Serdika has an old Berlin-style restaurant that serves German specialties. *2 Yanko Sakazov Blvd., tel. 2/44–34–11. 140 rooms, most with shower. DC, MC, V.*

¢ **Prostor.** The airy winter garden is a particularly pleasant public
★ room. Nestled high atop Mount Vitosha, 20 kilometers (12 miles) from the city, Prostor provides excellent views of Sofia. Take Bus 66 to the National Park Vitosha. *Tel. 2/67–11–73. 107 rooms with bath. Facilities: restaurant, bar, nightclub, pool, fitness center, shop. AE, DC, MC, V.*

¢ **Sevastopol.** This is a quiet, small hotel on one of Sofia's most attractive streets. *116 Rakovski St., tel. 2/87–59–41. 60 rooms with showers on the floor. Facilities: restaurant, nightclub, gift shop. No credit cards.*

¢ **Shipka.** This downtown hotel is popular with locals because of its restaurants and disco. *34 Totleben Blvd., tel. 2/54941. 160 rooms with bath or shower. Facilities: 2 restaurants, bar, disco. No credit cards.*

¢ **Slavjanska Beseda.** This centrally located hotel is close to all the city's theaters. *3 Slavjanska St., tel. 2/88–04–41 or 2/88–36–91. 50 rooms, most with shower. No credit cards.*

The Arts

The standard of music in Bulgaria is high, whether it takes the form of opera, symphonic, or folk music, which has just broken into the international scene with its close harmonies and colorful stage displays. Contact Balkantourist or the **Concert Office** (2 Tsar Osvoboditel Blvd., tel. 2/87–15–88) for general information.

You don't need to understand Bulgarian to enjoy a performance at the **Central Puppet Theater** (14 Gen. Gurko St., tel. 2/88–54–16) or at the **National Folk Ensemble** (check with the tourist office for details).

There are a number of fine art galleries: The art gallery of the **Sts. Cyril and Methodius International Foundation** (Alexander Nevski Sq., tel. 2/88–49–22; open Wed.–Mon. 10:30–6) has a collection of Indian, African, Japanese, and Western European paintings and sculptures. The art gallery of the **Union of Bulgarian Artists** (6 Shipka St., tel. 2/44–61–15; open daily 10:30–6) has exhibitions of contemporary Bulgarian art.

Nightlife

Nightclubs The following hotel bars have floor shows and a lively atmosphere: **Bar Sofia** (Grand Hotel Sofia, 4 Narodno Sobranie Sq., tel. 2/87–88–21), **Bar Variety Ambassador** (Vitosha Hotel, 100 James Boucher Blvd., tel. 2/2511), **Bar Variety** (Park Hotel Moskva, 25 Nezabravka St., tel. 2/1261), and **Bar Fantasy** (Sheraton Sofia Hotel Balkan, 5 St. Nedelya Sq., tel. 2/87–65–41).

Discos There is a disco, nightclub, and bowling alley at the **National Palace of Culture** (1 Bulgaria Sq.). **Orbylux** (76 James Boucher Blvd., tel. 2/63939) is known as the classiest disco in town. **Excalibur** (Kliment Ohridsky St., no phone) is a popular new disco in the underpass of Sofia University.

Gamblers can try their luck at the casino in the **Vitosha Hotel** (100 James Boucher Blvd., tel. 2/2511) or at the **Sheraton Sofia Hotel** (5 St. Nedelya Sq., tel. 2/87–65–41).

The Black Sea Golden Coast

Bulgaria's most popular resort area attracts visitors from all over Europe. Its sunny, sandy beaches are backed by the easternmost slopes of the Balkan range and by the Strandja Mountains. Although the tourist centers tend to be huge state-built complexes with a somewhat lean feel, they have modern amenities. Sunny Beach, the largest of the resorts, with more than 100 hotels, has plenty of children's amusements and play areas; baby-sitters are also available. The historic port of Varna is a good center for exploration. It is a focal point of land and sea transportation and has museums, a variety of restaurants, and some nightlife. The fishing villages of Nesebâr and Sozopol are more attractive. Lodgings tend to be scarce in these villages, so private accommodations, arranged on the spot or by Balkantourist, are a good option. Whatever resort you choose, all offer facilities for water sports and some have instructors. Tennis and horseback riding are also available.

Getting Around

Buses make frequent runs up and down the coast and are inexpensive. Buy your ticket in advance from the kiosks near the bus stops. **Cars** and **bicycles** can be rented; bikes are particularly useful for getting around such spreading resorts as Sunny Beach. A **hydrofoil** service links Varna, Nesebâr, Burgas, and Sozopol. A regular **boat** service travels the Varna–Sveti Konstantin (St. Konstantin)–Golden Sands–Albena–Balčik route.

Tourist Information

There is a Balkantourist office in most towns and resorts.

Albena (tel. 057/2721); **Burgas** (Hotel Primorets, 1 Knyaz Batemberg St., tel. 056/45496); **Nesebâr** (tel. 0554/5830 or 0554/5833); **Slânčev Brjag** (tel. 0554/2325 or 0554/2510); **Sveti Konstantin and Zlatni Pjasâci** (tel. 052/86–10–45 or 052/85–53–02); **Varna** (main office, 3 Moussala Sq., tel. 052/22–34–84; private accommodations office, 3 Moussala Sq., tel. 052/22–55–24).

Exploring the Black Sea Golden Coast

Varna **Varna,** Bulgaria's third-largest city, is easily reached by rail (about 7½ hours by express) or road from Sofia. There is plenty to see in the port city of Varna. The ancient city, named Odessos by the Greeks, became a major Roman trading center and is now an important shipbuilding and industrial city. The main sights can be linked by a planned walk.

Begin with the **Museum of History and Art,** one of the great—if lesser known—museums of Europe. The splendid collection includes the world's oldest gold treasures from the Varna necropolis of the 4th millennium BC, as well as Thracian, Greek, and Roman treasures and richly painted icons. *41 Osmi Primorski Polk Blvd., tel. 052/23–70–57. Open Tues.–Sat. 10–5.*

Near the northeastern end of Osmi Primorski Polk Boulevard are numerous shops and cafés; the western end leads to Mitropolit Simeon Square and the monumental **Cathedral** (1880–86), whose lavish murals are worth a look. Running north from the cathedral is Vladislav Varnenchik Street, with shops, movie theaters, and eateries. Opposite the cathedral, in the City Gardens, is the **Old Clock Tower,** built in 1880 by the Varna Guild Association. On the

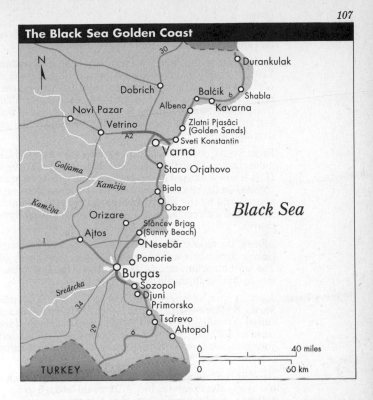

The Black Sea Golden Coast

N

30

Durankulak

Dobrich

Balčik   Shabla

Albena

Kavarna

Novi Pazar

Vetrino

A2

Zlatni Pjasâci
(Golden Sands)

Sveti Konstantin

Varna

Goljama

Staro Orjahovo

Kamčija

Bjala

Kamčija

Obzor

Black Sea

Orizare

Slânčev Brjag
(Sunny Beach)

Ajtos

Nesebâr

1

Pomorie

Burgas

Sredecka

Sozopol

34

Djuni

Primorsko

Tsârevo

29

6

Ahtopol

0   40 miles

TURKEY

0   60 km

---

south side of the City Gardens, on Nezavisimost Square, stands the magnificent Baroque **Stoyan Buchvarov National Theater.**

Leave the square to the east and walk past the Moussala Hotel. The tourist information office is at 3 Moussala Square (tel. 052/22–34–84). Nearby, on the corner of Knyaz Boris I Boulevard and Shipka Street, are the remains of the **Roman fortress wall** of Odessos. Knyaz Boris I Boulevard is another of Varna's shopping streets where you can buy handcrafted souvenirs.

Walk south along Odessos Street to Han Krum Street. Here you'll find the Holy Virgin Church of 1602 and the substantial remains of the **Roman Thermae**—the public baths, dating from the 2nd to the 3rd century AD. Buy the excellent English guidebook here to get the most out of your visit.

Not far from the baths, moving west, is old Drăzki Street, recently restored and comfortingly lined with restaurants, taverns, and coffeehouses.

Head toward the sea. At 41 Osmi Primorski Polk Boulevard is the **Archaeological Museum** (open Tues.–Sat. 10–5). Continue along Primorski Boulevard and follow it, with the sea on your right, to No. 2 for the **Naval Museum** (tel. 052/22–26–55; open weekdays 8–4), with its displays of the early days of navigation on the Black Sea and the Danube. The museum is at the edge of the extensive and luxuriant **Marine Gardens,** which command a wide view over the bay. In the gardens there are restaurants, an open-air theater, and the fascinating **Copernicus Astronomy Complex** (tel. 052/22–28–90; open weekdays 8–noon and 2–5) near the main entrance.

Sveti Konstantin   Eight kilometers (5 miles) north along the coast from Varna is **Sveti Konstantin,** Bulgaria's oldest Black Sea resort. Small and intimate, it spreads through a wooded park near a series of sandy coves. Today this luxury resort offers hydrotherapy on the spot where warm mineral springs were discovered in 1947.

In contrast to the sedate atmosphere of **Sveti Konstantin** is lively **Zlatni Pjasâci** (Golden Sands), a mere 8 kilometers (5 miles) to the north, with its extensive leisure amenities, mineral-spring medical centers, and sports facilities. Just over 4 kilometers (2 miles) inland from Golden Sands is **Aladja Rock Monastery,** one of Bulgaria's oldest, cut out of the cliff face and made accessible to visitors by sturdy iron stairways.

From Sveti Konstantin, if time permits, take a trip 16 kilometers (10 miles) north to **Balčik.** Part of Romania until just before World War II, it is now a relaxed haven for Bulgaria's writers, artists, and scientists. On its white cliffs are crescent-shaped tiers populated with houses, and by the Balčik Palace, the beautiful **Botanical Gardens** are dotted with curious buildings, including a small Byzantine-style church.

Albena, the newest Black Sea resort, is located between Balčik and Golden Sands. It is well known for its long, wide beach and clean sea. The most luxurious among its 35 hotels is the **Dobrudja,** with extensive hydrotherapy facilities.

Slânčev Brjag   Another popular resort, this time 36 kilometers (22 miles) south of Varna, is **Slânčev Brjag** (Sunny Beach). It is enormous and especially suited to families because of its safe beaches, gentle tides, and facilities for children. During the summer there are kindergartens for young vacationers, children's concerts, and even a children's discotheque.

Nesebâr is 5 kilometers (3 miles) south of Sunny Beach and accessible by regular excursion buses. It would be hard to find a town that exudes a greater sense of age than this ancient settlement, founded by the Greeks 25 centuries ago on a rocky peninsula reached by a narrow causeway. Among its vine-covered houses are richly decorated medieval churches. Don't miss the frescoes and the dozens of small, private, cozy pubs.

Continue traveling south along the coast. The next town of any size is **Burgas,** Bulgaria's second main port on the Black Sea. Burgas is rather industrial, with several oil refineries, though it does have a pleasant **Maritime Park** with an extensive beach below. For a more appealing stopover, continue for another 32 kilometers (20 miles) south to **Sozopol,** a fishing port with narrow cobbled streets leading down to the harbor. This was Apollonia, the oldest of the Greek colonies in Bulgaria. It is now a popular haunt for Bulgarian and, increasingly, foreign writers and artists who find private accommodations in the rustic Black Sea–style houses, so picturesque with their rough stone foundations and unpainted wood slats on the upper stories.

Dining and Lodging

For details and price-category definitions, *see* Dining and Lodging *in* Staying in Bulgaria, *above.* Gradually, even restaurants in the $$ category are beginning to accept credit cards. Check with a restaurant before ordering.

Albena   **Bambuka** (Bamboo Tree). This open-air restaurant serves interna-
Dining   tional and Bulgarian cuisine and seafood. *Albena Resort, tel. 0572/ 2404. No credit cards. $$*
Gergana. This cozy beachside restaurant serves grilled seafood from the Black Sea and Bulgarian dishes, such as white sheep's cheese cooked in a clay pot with eggs, vegetables, and spices. *Albena Resort, tel. 0572/2910. No credit cards. ¢*
★ **Orehite.** Enjoy Bulgarian specialties and seafood while you watch

Orehite's famous fire-dancing show. *Albena Resort, tel. 0572/2250. No credit cards. ¢*

Lodging **Dobrudja Hotel.** This is a big, comfortable hotel with a mineral-wa-
★ ter health spa. *Albena Resort, tel. 0572/2020. 272 rooms with bath. Facilities: 2 restaurants, nightclub, coffee shop, 3 bars, shops, in-door and outdoor swimming pools, fitness center, hydrotherapy. AE, DC, MC, V. $$*

Kardam. This hotel, near the center of the resort, offers basic, no-frills accommodations. *Albena Resort, tel. 0572/2927. 115 rooms with bath. Facilities: bar. AE, DC, MC, V. ¢*

Mura. One of the largest hotels in Albena, Mura is an exceptional budget establishment in that it accepts credit cards. It is located in the center, near many sports facilities and discos. *Albena Resort, tel. 0572/2236. 173 rooms with bath. Facilities: restaurant, bar, shop. AE, DC, MC, V. ¢*

Burgas **Starata Gemia.** The name of this restaurant translates as "old boat,"
Dining appropriate for a beachfront restaurant featuring fish specialties. *Next to Primorets Hotel, tel. 056/45708. No credit cards. $$*

Lodging **Bulgaria.** The Bulgaria is a high-rise Interhotel in the center of town. It features its own nightclub with floor show and a restaurant set in a winter garden. *21 Aleksandrovska St., tel. 056/42820. 200 rooms, most with bath or shower. AE, DC, MC, V. $$*

Slânčev Brjag **Hanska Šatra.** Situated in the coastal hills behind the sea, this com-
Dining bination restaurant and nightclub has been built to resemble the
★ tents of the Bulgarian hans of old. It has entertainment well into the night. *4.8 km (3 mi) west of Slânčev Brjag Resort, tel. 0554/2811. No credit cards. $$*

Ribarska Hiza. This lively beachside restaurant specializes in fish and has music until 1 AM. *Northern end of Slânčev Brjag Resort, tel. 0554/2186. No credit cards. $*

Viatarna Melnica. National dishes, such as *kavarma* (spicy minced pork or beef and vegetables in a sauce of fried onions, thyme, mint, and red pepper, all baked in a clay pot), are served at this restau-rant, the "Wind Mill," 2 kilometers (1.3 miles) from the center of the resort. *Slânčev Brjag Resort, tel. 0554/2812. No credit cards. ¢*

Yujni Noshti. Relax on the beach in wicker furniture at this restau-rant whose name means "Southern Nights." International dishes and Bulgarian meals make up the bill of fare. *Slânčev Brjag Resort, tel. 0554/2851. No credit cards. ¢*

Lodging **Burgas.** Large and comfortable, this hotel lies at the southern end of the resort. *Slânčev Brjag Resort, tel. 0554/2358 or 0554/2721. 250 rooms with bath or shower. Facilities: restaurant, 2 pools, sports hall, coffee shop, bar. AE, DC, MC, V. $$*

★ **Globus.** Considered by many to be the best in the resort, this hotel combines a central location with modern facilities. *Slânčev Brjag Resort, tel. 0554/2245 or 0554/2018. 100 rooms with bath or shower. Facilities: indoor pool, restaurant, sports hall, coffee shop, bar. AE, DC, MC, V. $$*

Kuban. Near the center of the resort, this large establishment is just a short stroll from the beach. *Slânčev Brjag Resort, tel. 0554/2309 or 0554/2307. 216 rooms, most with bath or shower. Facilities: restaurants, coffee shop. AE, DC, MC, V. $$*

Čajka. This hotel offers the best location at a low cost. *Slânčev Brjag Resort, tel. 0554/2308. 36 rooms, some with bath or shower. No cred-it cards. $*

Shipka. A superb location in the heart of Slânčev Brjag makes this large high-rise hotel a standout. *Slânčev Brjag Resort, tel. 0554/2848. 143 room with bath. Facilities: bar, shop. AE, DC, MC, V. ¢*

Trakia. A 20-minute walk from the beach, this somewhat character-less low-rise hotel outside the center can be reached by an electric train that stops nearby. The ride takes five minutes. *Slânčev Brjag*

Resort, tel. 0554/2747. 182 rooms with bath. Facilities: restaurant, bar, shop. AE, DC, MC, V. ¢

Sveti Konstantin

Dining

★ **Bulgarska Svatba.** This folk-style restaurant with dancing is on the outskirts of the resort; charcoal-grilled meats are especially recommended. *Sveti Konstantin Resort, tel. 052/86–12–83. No credit cards. $$*

Manastirska Izba. Centrally located, this eatery is a modest but pleasant restaurant with a sunny terrace. *Sveti Konstantin Resort, tel. 052/86–20–36. No credit cards. $$*

Lodging **Čajka.** Čajka means "seagull" in Bulgarian, and this hotel has a bird's-eye view of the entire resort from its perch above the northern end of the beach. *Sveti Konstantin Resort, tel. 052/86–13–32. 130 rooms, most with bath or shower. No credit cards. $$*

Narcis. In a park near the sea, this spa hotel offering balneotherapy is open year-round. Other treatments available include bioenergy therapy, mineral-mud applications, and underwater massage. *Sveti Konstantin Resort, tel. 052/86–12–25. 60 rooms with bath. Facilities: indoor mineral-water pool, whirlpool. No credit cards. ¢*

Varna

Dining **Morsko Kazino.** This spacious restaurant offers Bulgarian and international cuisine, including seafood. *In Marine Garden, tel. 052/22–21–49. No credit cards. $$*

Okean. Fish and seafood specialties are served in this restaurant in the center of the city. *4 San Stefano St., tel. 052/23–94–07 or 052/24–10–62. No credit cards. $$*

Lodging **Odessa.** Expect just the basics at this four-story hotel next to the
★ Marine Garden. *1 Slivnitsa Blvd., tel. 052/22–83–81. 93 rooms with bath. Facilities: restaurant, bar, shops. No credit cards. $*

5 The Czech Republic

J ust three years after the dramatic but peaceful revolution that overthrew a Communist regime that had been in power for 40 years, Czechoslovakia again made world headlines in 1993 when its two constituent republics, Czech and Slovak, officially parted ways to form independent countries. To observers from abroad, the rush to split the republics following federal elections in 1992 came as something of a surprise. Formed from the ruins of the Austro-Hungarian empire at the end of World War I, *Czecho-Slovakia* had portrayed itself to the world as a modern-day success story: a union of two peoples that had managed to overcome divisive nationalism in the higher interest of stabilizing a potentially volatile region.

Popular perceptions were reinforced by a long list of achievements. During the difficult 1930s, the Czechoslovak republic was the model democracy in Central Europe. The 1968 Prague Spring, an intense period of cultural renewal when Communists spoke openly of creating a more humane socialism, was centered largely on Czech territory, but was led by a courageous Slovak, Alexander Dubček. In 1989 the Communists were brought down by students and opponents of the regime in Prague and Bratislava who shared a similar faith in the power of democracy and freedom.

The forces of separation, however, proved in the end to be too powerful. For all its successes, Czechoslovakia was ultimately an artificial creation, masking important and longstanding cultural differences between two outwardly similar peoples. The Czech Republic, linking the old Austrian crown lands of Bohemia and Moravia, can look to a rich cultural history going back some 600–700 years when the Bohemian Kingdom played a pivotal role in shaping Central Europe's history and helped ignite the great religious and social conflicts of European history.

Slovakia, by contrast, languished for nearly a millennium as an agrarian outpost of the Hungarian empire. The two nations still have much in common, however. They share similar languages and cuisines, and they present layer upon layer of historical beauty, en-

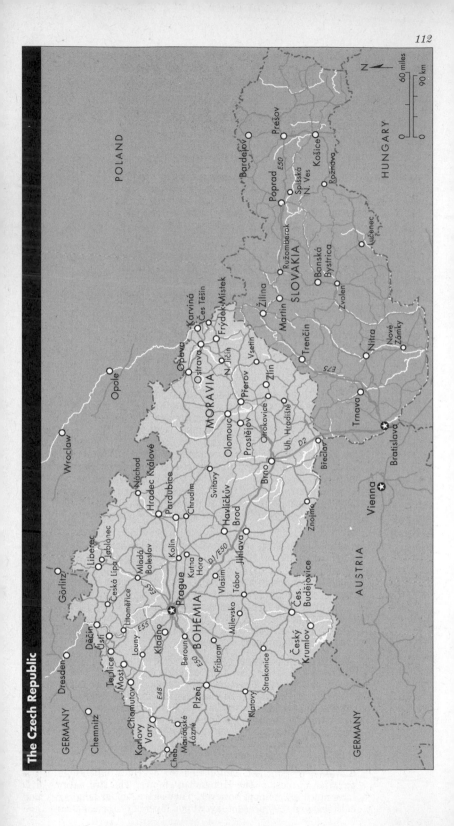

The Czech Republic

livened by cultural treasures and a rapidly changing social scene, all at prices that make even the most cost-conscious tourist feel wealthy.

Essential Information

Before You Go

When to Go Organized sightseeing tours run from April or May through October (year-round in Prague). Some monuments, especially castles, either close entirely or open for shorter hours during the winter. Hotel rates drop during the off-season except during festivals. May, the month of fruit blossoms, is the time of the Prague Spring Music Festival. During the fall, when the forests are glorious, Brno holds its music festival.

Climate The following are the average daily maximum and minimum temperatures for Prague.

Jan.	36F	2C	May	66F	19C	Sept.	68F	20C
	25	- 4		46	8		50	10
Feb.	37F	3C	June	72F	22C	Oct.	55F	13C
	27	- 3		52	11		41	5
Mar.	46F	8C	July	75F	24C	Nov.	46F	8C
	32	0		55	13		36	2
Apr.	58F	14C	Aug.	73F	23C	Dec.	37F	3C
	39	4		55	13		28	- 2

Currency The unit of currency in the Czech Republic is the Czech crown, or koruna, written as Kč, and divided into 100 hellers. There are bills of 20, 50, 100, 200, 500, and 1,000 Kč and coins of 10, 20, and 50 hellers and 1, 2, 5, 10, 20, and 50 Kč. At press time (summer 1995), the koruna was trading at around 21 Kč to the dollar and 36 Kč to the pound.

Credit cards are widely accepted in establishments used by foreign tourists.

What It Will Cost Costs are highest in Prague and only slightly less in the Bohemian resorts and main spas, though even in these places you can now find very reasonable accommodations in private rooms. The least expensive areas are northern Bohemia and northern Moravia.

Sample Prices Cup of coffee, 10 Kc; beer (½ liter), 10 Kc–25 Kc; Coca-Cola, 20 Kc; ham sandwich, 30 Kc; 1-mile taxi ride, 100 Kc.

Museums Admission to museums, galleries, and castles ranges from 5 Kc to 80 Kc.

Visas U.S. and British citizens do not need visas to enter the Czech Republic. Visa requirements have been temporarily reintroduced for Canadian citizens; check whether this is still the case with the consulate. Apply to the Embassy of the Czech Republic, 541 Sussex Drive, Ottowa, Ontario K1N 6Z6, tel. 613/562–3875, fax 613/562–3878.

Customs *On Arrival* Valuable items should be entered on your customs declaration. You can bring in 200 cigarettes, 100 cigars, 1 liter of alcohol, and gifts to the value of 1,000 Kc.

On Departure Only antiques bought at specially appointed shops may be exported—ask before you buy. To be on the safe side, hang on to all receipts.

Language English is spoken fairly widely among both the young and those associated with the tourist industry. You will come across English speakers elsewhere, though not frequently. German is widely understood throughout the country.

Getting Around

By Train There is an extensive rail network throughout the country. As elsewhere in Eastern Europe, fares are low and trains are often crowded. Most long-distance trains have dining cars; overnight trains between main centers have sleeping cars.

By Plane Internal air service links Prague with Ostrava and, in Slovakia, Bratislava, Košice, and Poprad (for the High Tatras). Prices are reasonable. Make reservations at Čedok offices or directly at ČSA, Czechoslovak Airlines (tel. 02/24815110).

By Bus A wide-ranging bus network provides quicker service than trains at somewhat higher prices (though they are still very low by Western standards). Buses are always full, and, on long-distance routes especially, reservations are advisable.

Staying in the Czech Republic

Telephones
Local Calls Most public telephones take phone cards, sold at post offices and newsstands starting at 100 Kc for 50 units. Local calls use a minimum of one unit. To make a call, lift the receiver, insert the card, and dial.

International Calls There's automatic dialing to many countries, including those in North America and the United Kingdom. The international dialing code is 00, followed by the country code. Direct or collect calls can be made from some coin phones and most card phones, but your best bet is to go to the main post office (Jindřišská 14, near Wenceslas Square). For international inquiries, dial 0132 for the United States, Canada, or the United Kingdom. To reach an **AT&T** international operator, dial 0042–000101; for **MCI,** dial 0042–000112; for **Sprint,** dial 0042–087187.

Country Code The country code for the Czech Republic is 42.

Mail
Postal Rates Airmail letters to the United States and Canada cost 11 Kc up to 20 grams, postcards 6 Kc. Airmail letters to the United Kingdom cost 8 Kc up to 20 grams, postcards 5 Kc.

Receiving Mail Mail can be sent to Poste Restante at the main post office in Prague (Jindřišská 14, window 28) or to any other main post office. There's no charge. The American Express office on Wenceslas Square in Prague will hold letters addressed to cardholders or holders of American Express traveler's checks for up to one month free of charge.

Opening and Closing Times **Banks and Museums.** Banks are open weekdays 8–5. Museums are usually open Tuesday–Sunday 10–5.

Shops are generally open weekdays 9–6; some close between noon and 2. Many are also open till noon or later on Saturday.

National Holidays In 1996: January 1; April 8 (Easter Monday); May 1; May 8 (Liberation Day); July 5–6; December 25, 26. Changing holiday in 1997: March 31 (Easter Monday).

Dining You can choose among restaurants, wine cellars *(vinárna),* the more down-to-earth beer taverns *(pivnice),* cafeterias, and a growing number of coffee shops and snack bars. Eating out is popular, and in summer you should reserve in advance. Privatization's legacy is more restaurants and more kinds of cuisine, especially in Prague.

Prague ham makes a favorite first course, as does soup, which is less expensive. The most typical main dish is roast pork (or duck or goose) with sauerkraut and dumplings. Dumplings in various forms, generally with a rich gravy, accompany many dishes.

Mealtimes Lunch is usually from 11:30 to 2 or 3; dinner from 6 to 9:30 or 10. Some places are open all day, and you may find it easier to find a table in off-hours.

What to Wear A jacket and tie are recommended for expensive restaurants. Informal dress is appropriate elsewhere.

Ratings Prices are reasonable by American standards, even in the more expensive restaurants. Czechs don't normally go in for three-course meals, and the following prices apply only if you're having a first course, main course, and dessert (excluding wine and tip). Best bets are indicated by a star ★ .

Category	Prague	Other Areas
$$	200 Kc–350 Kc	100 Kc–250 Kc
$	125 Kc–200 Kc	60 Kc–100 Kc
¢	under 125 Kc	under 60 Kc

Lodging There's a choice of hotels, motels, private accommodations, hostels, and campsites. Many older properties are gradually being renovated, and the best have great character and style. There is still an acute shortage of hotel rooms during the peak season, so make reservations well in advance. Many private room agencies are now in operation, offering a variety of lodgings. The standards of facilities and services hardly match those in the West, so don't be surprised by faulty plumbing or indifferent reception clerks.

Hotels These are officially graded with from one to five stars. Many hotels used by foreign visitors are affiliated with Čedok and are mainly in the three- to five-star categories. These will have all or some rooms with bath or shower. Čedok can also handle reservations for some non-Čedok hotels.

Hotel bills can be paid in crowns, though some hotels still try to insist on hard currency.

Private Lodgings Prague is full of travel agencies offering accommodations in private homes. These accommodations are invariably cheaper and often more comfortable than hotels, though you may have to sacrifice something in privacy. The largest room-finding service is probably **AVE** (tel. 02/24223226) in the main and Holešovice train stations and the airport (all open 7 AM–11 PM) and other locations. Insist on a room in the center, however, or you may find yourself in a dreary, far-flung suburb. Two other helpful agencies are **Hello Ltd.** (Senovážné nám. 3, Prague 1, tel. 02/24214212) and **Stop City** (Vinohradská 24, Prague 2, tel. 02/24231233, open daily 11–8, 10–9 in summer). Elsewhere, look for signs declaring "Room Free" or, more frequently, in German, "Zimmer Frei" or "Privatzimmer" along main roads. Čedok and PIS offices can also frequently help you locate private accommodations.

In summer, dozens of hostels operate in university dormitories and sports clubs. AVE (*see above* under Private Accommodations) offers hostel lodging starting at 200 Kc per person.

Ratings Prices are for double rooms, generally including breakfast. Prices at the lower end of the scale apply to low season. At certain periods, such as Easter or during festivals, there may be an increase of 15%–25%. Best bets are indicated by a star ★ .

Category	Prague	Other Areas
$$	1500 Kc–3000 Kc	750 Kc–1500 Kc
$	1000 Kc–1500 Kc	350 Kc–750 Kc
¢	under 1000 Kc	under 350 Kc

Tipping Czechs are not usually blatant about the fact that tips are expected. As a rule of thumb, in $$ or $ restaurants, add a few Kc; in more expensive ones, add 10%. For taxis, add 10 Kc. In $$ or $ hotels, you carry baggage yourself.

Prague

Arriving and Departing

By Plane All international flights arrive at Prague's Ruzyně Airport, about 20 kilometers (12 miles) from downtown. For arrival and departure times, tel. 02/367814 or 02/367760.

Between the Airport and Downtown A shuttle bus links the airport with Czechoslovak Air Lines' (ČSA's) Town Terminal Vltava (Revoluční 25). Buses depart every 20 minutes during the day, every half hour evenings and on weekends. The trip into Prague costs 30 Kc and takes about 30 minutes. The cheapest way to get into Prague is by regular Bus 119; the cost is 6 Kc, but you'll need to change to the subway at the Dejvická station to reach the center. By taxi, expect to pay 300 Kc and up.

By Train The main station for international and domestic routes is Hlavní nádraží (tel. 02/24217654), ul. Wilsonova, not far from Wenceslas Square. Some international trains arrive and depart from Nádraží Holešovice (tel. 02/24615865), on the same metro line (C) as the main station.

By Bus The main bus station is Florenc (at Na Florenci, tel. 02/24211060), not far from the main train station (metro line B or C to the Florenc station).

Getting Around

Public transportation is a bargain. *Jízdenky* (tickets) cost 6 Kc and can be bought at hotels and newsstands and from dispensing machines in the metro stations. For the metro, punch the ticket in the station before descending the escalators; for buses and trams, punch the ticket inside the vehicle. You can also buy one-day passes allowing unlimited use of the system for 50 Kc, two-day passes for 85 Kc, three-day passes for 110 Kc, and five-day passes for 170 Kc. The passes can be purchased at the main metro stations and at certain newsstands.

By Subway Prague's three modern subway lines are easy to use and relatively clean and safe. They provide the simplest and fastest means of transportation, and most new maps of Prague mark the routes.

By Tram/Bus You need to buy a new ticket every time you change vehicles. Trams 50–59 and Buses 500 and above run all night after the metro shuts down at midnight.

Important Addresses and Numbers

Tourist Information The main Čedok office (Na příkopě 18, tel. 02/24197111) is close to Wenceslas Square. Next door is the **Prague Information Service (PIS)** (Na příkopě 20, tel. 02/544444).

Prague Metro

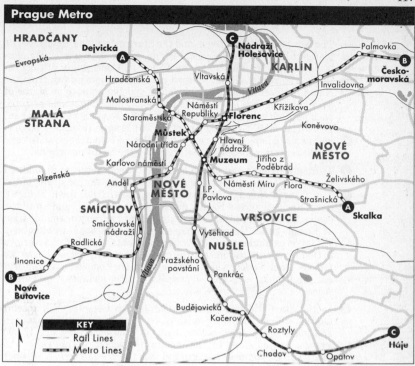

HRADČANY

Dejvická **A**

Evropská

C Nádraží
Holešovice

Palmovka

B

Česko-
moravská

KARLÍN

Hradčanská

Vltavská

Vltava

Invalidovna

Malostranská

Náměstí
Republiky **Florenc**

Křížíkova

MALÁ
STRANA

Staroměstská

Koněvova

Můstek

Národní třída

Hlavní
nádraží

NOVÉ
MĚSTO

Karlovo náměstí

Muzeum

Jiřího z
Poděbrad

Plzeňská

Anděl

NOVÉ
MĚSTO

Náměstí Míru

Flora

Želivského

I.P.
Pavlova

Strašnická

SMÍCHOV

VRŠOVICE

Skalka **A**

Smíchovské
nádraží

Vyšehrad

NUSLE

Radlická

Jinonice

Pražského
povstání

Pankrác

B

Nové
Butovice

Vltava

Budějovická

Kačerov

N

KEY

Roztyly

Chodov

Opatov

Háje **C**

Rail Lines

Metro Lines

Embassies U.S. (Tržiště 15, Malá Strana, tel. 02/24510847). **Canadian** (Mic-
kiewiczova 6, Hradčany, tel. 02/24311108). **U.K.** (Thunovská 14,
Malá Strana, tel. 02/24510439).

Emergencies **Police** (tel. 158 or 2121), **Ambulance** (tel. 155), **Doctor: Foreigners'
Department** of **Na Homolce Hospital** (Roentgenova 2, Prague 5,
weekdays tel. 02/5292–2146, evenings and weekends tel. 02/5292–
2191); **First Medical Clinic of Prague** (Vyšehradská 35, Prague 2, tel.
02/292286, 298978, 24-hr emergency tel. 02/7921692, 02/0601–
225050); **24-Hour Pharmacies** (two close to the center are at
Štefánikova 6, Prague 5, tel. 02/24511112, and Koněvova 210,
Prague 3, tel. 02/6441895). **Lost credit cards:** American Express (02/
24219992); Diners Club, Visa (02/24125353); MasterCard/EuroCard
(02/24423135).

Exploring Prague

Prague is one of the most enchanting cities in Europe. Like Rome,
Prague is built on seven hills, which slope gently or precipitously
down to the Vltava River. The riverside location, enhanced by a series of graceful bridges, makes a great setting for two of the city's
most notable features: its extravagant, fairy-tale architecture and
its memorable music. Mozart claimed that no one understood him
better than the citizens of Prague, and he was only one of several
great masters who lived or lingered here.

Prague escaped serious wartime damage, but it didn't escape neglect. Because of the long-term restoration program now under
way, some part of the city is always under scaffolding. But what's
completed—which is nearly all that's described in the following itineraries—is hard to find fault with as an example of sensitive and
painstaking restoration.

*Numbers in the margin correspond to points of interest on the
Prague map.*

**The Nové
město and
Staré město**

❶

❷ ❸

❹

The Nové město (New Town) and the Staré město (Old Town) are the
places to discover the heart of Prague. **Václavské náměstí** (Wenceslas Square) is the Times Square of Prague. Confusingly, it's not actually a square at all but a broad boulevard sloping down from the
Národní muzeum (National Museum) and the equestrian **statue of
St. Wenceslas**. The lower end is where all the action is. Na příkopě,
once part of the moat surrounding the Old Town, is now an elegant
pedestrian mall. Čedok's main office and Prague Information Service are along here, on your way to the **Prašná brána** (Powder Tower),
a 19th-century neo-Gothic restoration of the medieval original.

❺

❻
❼

Turn into Celetná and you're on the old **Royal Route,** once followed
by coronation processions past the foreboding Gothic spires of the
Týn Church through **Staroměstské náměstí** (Old Town Square),
down **Karlova**, across **Karlův most** (Charles Bridge), and up to the
castle. Along this route, you can study every variety or combination
of Romanesque, Gothic, Renaissance, and Baroque architecture.
Two good examples are the town buildings at Celetná 12 and Karlova
8. On Staroměstské náměstí, the crowds regularly gather below the
famous **Clock Tower,** where, on the hour, the complex five-century-
old mechanism activates a procession that includes the Twelve
Apostles.

❽

❾

In the **Starý židovský hřbitov** (Old Jewish Cemetery) in **Josefov**
(Joseph's Town, the old Jewish quarter), ancient tombstones lean
and jostle each other; below them, in a dozen layers, are 12,000
graves. As you stand by the tomb of the scholar Rabbi Löw, who
died in 1609, you may see, stuffed into the cracks, scraps of paper
bearing prayers and requests. Be sure to visit the tiny Gothic
Staronová synagóga (Old-New Synagogue), as well as the several
other synagogues and exhibitions comprising the **Státní židovské
muzeum** (National Jewish Museum of Prague). *Červená 101, tel. 02/
24810099. Museum admission: 80 Kč. Open Sun.–Fri. 9–6 (9–4:30
in winter; last tour of cemetery at 3 in winter); closed Sat. and religious holidays.*

When you stand on Charles Bridge, you'll see views of Prague that
would still be familiar to the sculptors who added the 30 Baroque
statues in the early 18th century. They're worth a closer look, especially the 12th on the left, starting from the Old Town side of the
bridge (St. Luitgarde, by Matthias Braun, circa 1710), and the 14th
on the left (in which a Turk guards suffering saints, by F. M.
Brokoff, circa 1714). Most of the statues are copies of the pollution-
damaged originals.

❿

The **Betlémská kaple** (Bethlehem Chapel) has been completely reconstructed since Jan Hus thundered his humanitarian teachings
from its pulpit in the early 15th century to congregations that could
number 3,000. But the little door through which he came to the pulpit is original, as are some of the inscriptions on the wall. *Betlémské
nám. Open daily 9–6.*

**Malá Strana
and Hradčany
(Lesser
Quarter
and Castle
Area)**

⓫

Cross Charles Bridge and follow Mostecká up to Malostranské
náměstí. After the turbulence of the Counter-Reformation at the
start of the 17th century, Prague witnessed a great flowering of
what became known as Bohemian Baroque. The architects
(Dientzenhofer, father and son) of the **Chrám svatého Mikuláše**
(Church of St. Nicholas) were among its most skilled exponents. If
you're in Prague when a concert is being given in this church, fight
for a ticket. The lavish sculptures and frescoes of the interior make
for a memorable setting. *Malostranské nám. Open daily 10–4 (9–6
in summer).*

On busy Letenská Street a small door admits visitors to the large,
⑫ formal **Wallenstein Gardens,** part of the huge palace built in the
1620s by the Hapsburgs' victorious commander, Albrecht of Wallenstein. A high-arching, covered outdoor stage in late-Renaissance
style dominates its western end. Music and theater pieces are occasionally performed here. *Admission free. Open May–Sept., daily
9–7.*

⑬ The monumental complex of **Pražský hrad** (Prague Castle) has witnessed the changing fortunes of the city for more than 1,000 years.
The castle's physical and spiritual core is the **Cathedral of St. Vitus.**
It took from 1344 to 1929 to build, so you can trace the whole gamut
of styles from high Gothic to Art Nouveau. This is the final resting
place for numerous Bohemian kings. Charles IV lies in the crypt.
"Good King" Wenceslas (in reality a mere prince, later canonized)
has his own chapel in the south transept. Knightly tournaments often accompanied coronation ceremonies in the **Royal Palace,** next to
the cathedral, hence the broad Riders' Staircase leading up to the
grandiose **Vladislav Hall** of the Third Courtyard. Oldest of all the
buildings, though much restored, is the Romanesque complex of **St.
George's Basilica and Convent.** Behind a Baroque facade, it houses a
superb collection of Bohemian art from medieval religious sculptures to Baroque paintings. *Admission: 80 Kc. Open Tues.–Sun.
9–5 (9–4 in winter).*

⑭ The Baroque church and shrine of **Loreto** is named for the Italian
town to which the Virgin Mary's House in Nazareth was supposedly
transported by angels to save it from the infidel. The crowning glory
of its fabulous treasury is the glittering monstrance of the *Sun of
Prague,* set with 6,222 diamonds. Arrive on the hour to hear the 27-
bell carillon. *Loretánské nám. 7. Admission: 30 Kc. Open Tues.–
Sun. 9–noon and 1–4:30.*

Shopping

Specialty Look for the name **Dílo** for objets d'art and prints; **Lidová Řemesla**
Shops for folk art. **Moser** (Na příkopě 12) is the most famous for glass and
porcelain. Shops specializing in Bohemian crystal, porcelain, ceramics, and antiques abound.

Shopping Many of the main shops are in and around Wenceslas Square
Districts (Václavské náměstí) and Na příkopě, as well as along Celetná and
Pařížská.

Department Three central stores are **Bílá Labut'** (Na poříčí 23), **Krone** (Václavské
Stores nám. 21), and **Kotva** (Nám. Republiky 8).

Dining

Eating out in Prague is a very popular pastime, so it's advisable to
make reservations whenever possible, especially for dinner. For details and price-category definitions, *see* Dining in Staying in the
Czech Republic, *above.*

$$ **Myslivna.** They took the antlers off the walls of this rustic restaurant
a year or so after the Velvet Revolution, but the cooks still know
their way around boar, pheasant, and quail. Try leg of venison in
wine sauce with walnuts or wild boar, all prepared to please the eye
and palate, if a touch on the pricey side. *Jagellonská 21, Vinohrady,
tel. 02/6270209. Reservations advised. AE, V.*

$$ **Penguin's.** Fairly standard Czech and international food is served in
a room where you'd expect to pay more for the ambience and the
service. The muted mauve-and-matte-black walls make for casual
elegance. *Zborovská 5, tel. 02/545660. Reservations advised. AE,
MC, V.*

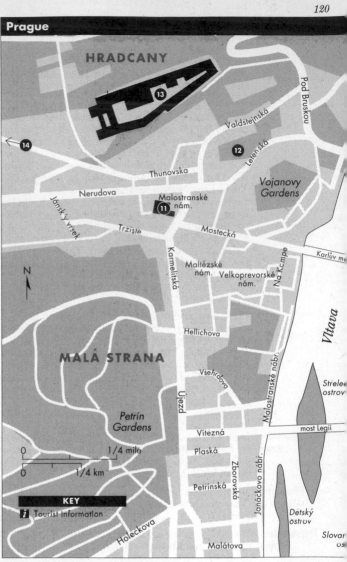

Prague

HRADCANY

MALÁ STRANA

Petřín Gardens

Vojanovy Gardens

Vltava

KEY

ℹ️ Tourist Information

Betlémská kaple, **10**
Chrám svatého Mikuláše, **11**
Karluv most, **7**
Loreto, **14**
Národní muzeum, **2**
Prašná brána, **4**
Prazský hrad (Prague Castle), **13**

Royal Route, **5**
Staroměstské náměstí, **6**
Starý zidovský hřbitov, **8**
Státní zidovské muzeum, **9**
Statue of St.Wenceslas, **3**
Václavské náměstí, **1**
Wallenstein Gardens, **12**

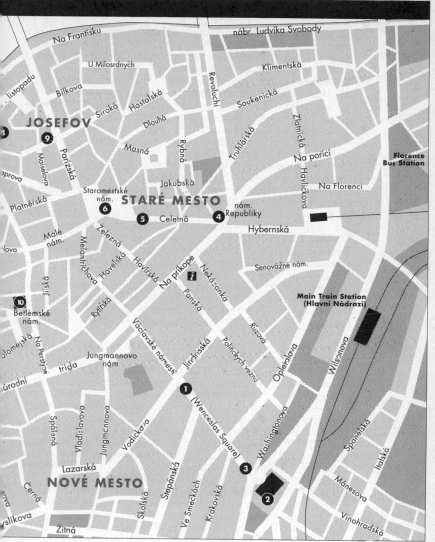

Na Frantisku

nábr. Ludvíka Svobody

U Milosrdných

Klimentská

listopadu

Bílkova

Siroká

Haštalská

Soukenická

JOSEFOV

Dlouhá

Revoluční

Zlatnická

Florence
Bus Station

Maiselova

Pařížská

Masná

Rybná

Truhlářská

Na poříčí

Na Florenci

aprova

Platnérská

Jakubská

Havlíčkova

Staroměstské
nám.

STARÉ MESTO

nám.
Republiky

Zelezná

Celetná

Hybernská

Malé
nám.

Melantrichova

Havelská

Havířská

Na příkopě

Nekázanka

Senovážné nám.

lova

Rytířská

Panská

Main Train Station
(Hlavní Nádraží)

Betlémské
nám.

Václavské náměstí

Jungmannovo
nám

Jindřišská

Politických vezňů

Ruzová

Opletalova

Wilsonova

Spálená

Vladislavova

Jungmannova

Vodičkova

Washingtonova

Spanelská

Italská

Lazarská

NOVÉ MESTO

Stepánská

Ve Smečkách

Krakovská

Mánesova

Vinohradská

Zitná

$$ Pezinok. You'll get good, hearty fare served in a relaxed, no-frills atmosphere at this "House of Slovak Culture," located behind Národní Třída in the New Town. The homemade sausage, accompanied by hearty Slovak wine, is excellent. The large *palačinky* (crepes) for dessert are some of the best in Prague. *Purkyňova 4, tel. 02/291996. Reservations advised. AE, MC, V.*

$$ Restaurace U Supa. Good solid Czech food and beer attract Czechs and foreigners to this friendly and comfortable restaurant. The high vaulted ceiling in the front room gives an Old World air to the place, and in the back room a sad-faced musician plays your favorite synthesized polkas. *Celetná 20. AE, DC, MC, V.*

$$ U Lorety. Sightseers will find this an agreeable spot—peaceful except for the welcoming carillon from neighboring Loreto Church. The service here is discreet but attentive, the tables are private, and the food is consistently excellent. Venison and steak are specialties. *Loretánské nám. 8, near the Castle, tel. 02/24510191. Reservations advised. No credit cards.*

$ Na Zvonařce. This bright beer hall serves very good traditional fare at unbeatable prices. Sit on the terrace during the summer to escape the noisy crowd. Noteworthy dishes include real fried chicken and English roast beef. Fruit dumplings for dessert are a rare treat. The service is slow. *Šafaříkova 1, tel. 02/254534. Reservations advised. No credit cards.*

$ U Koleje. The friendly staff at this popular neighborhood restaurant, suitable for the whole family, serves good traditional pork and beef dishes and excellent beer. You may have to share a table. *Slavíkova 24, tel. 02/6274163. Reservations advised. No credit cards.*

$ U Medvídků. Enjoy Bohemian specialties here in a noisy but jolly atmosphere. Try the goulash with sliced bread dumplings. *Na Perštýně 7, Staré město, tel. 02/24211916. AE, DC, MC, V.*

$ V Krakovské. This clean pub, noted for its excellent traditional food, is the place to try Bohemian duck: It's cooked just right and offered at an excellent price. Wash it down with good light or dark Braník beer. *Krakovská 20, tel. 02/261537. No credit cards.*

$ Vltava. This riverside retreat has a snug dining room and a summertime patio. Chicken and steak are on the menu, but the specialties are carp and trout, served in large portions and prepared in many ways. *Rašínovo nábřeží between Jiráskův and Palackého bridges, tel. 02/294964. Reservations advised. No credit cards.*

¢ Demínka. With its chandeliers and lofty ceilings, this restaurant has a low-key elegance, and the standard Czech fare served here is of unusually high quality. There is seating outdoors in the summer, but only for beer. It's a short walk from Wenceslas Square, behind the National Museum. *Škrétova 1, 12000, tel. 02/24223383. Reservations advised. MC, V.*

¢ Novoměstský Pivovar. What's old is new here: "Gothic" wall frescoes in one of the many rooms, each decorated in a different style, are only a couple of years old, and the beer is brewed on the premises, an age-old practice revived at this labyrinthine pub. You can eat standard and satisfying pub dishes, such as fried cheese, goulash, and pork schnitzel. *Vodičkova 20, Nové město, 11000. AE, MC.*

¢ Saté Grill. Indonesian noodles, pork and chicken saté, and tasty rice dishes go for $1 to $3 each. Outdoor seating offers a sliver of a view down the Hradčany slope. Menus are available in English. *Pohořelec 3, above Loretánské nám, tel. 02/532113. No credit cards.*

¢ U Vejvodů. Hidden in the tiny streets of the Old Town, this pub serves excellent beer and the usual variations on pork, cabbage, and dumplings. The front room is reserved for nonsmokers. *Jilská 4, tel. 02/24210591. No credit cards.*

¢ U Zlatého Tygra. This impossibly crowded hangout is the last of a breed of authentic Czech pivnice. The smoke and stares preclude a long stay, but it's still worth dropping in for typical pub staples like ham and cheese plates or roast pork. The service is surly, but the beer is good. *Husova 17, Staré město. No reservations. No credit cards. Evenings only.*

Lodging

The cheaper hotels in Prague can be a little on the shabby side. Private accommodations are often a better option. *See* Private Accommodations under Essential Information, *above,* for the names of organizations offering private rooms.

$$ **Axa.** Funky and functional, this Modernist high-rise, built in 1932, was a mainstay of the budget-hotel crowd until reconstruction forced a price hike. The rooms, now with color TV sets and modern plumbing, are certainly improved; the lobby and public areas look tacky, though, with plastic flowers and glaring lights. *Na poříčí 40, 11000, tel. 02/24812580, fax 02/2322172. 133 rooms, most with bath. Facilities: restaurant, bar, nightclub, swimming pool, exercise room. AE, DC, MC, V.*

$$ **Central.** It lives up to its name, with a site near Celetná Street and Náměstí Republiky. Rooms are sparsely furnished, but all have baths. The Baroque glories of the Old Town are steps away. *Rybná 8, 11000, tel. 02/24812041, fax 02/2328404. 62 rooms with bath. Facilities: restaurant, nightclub. MC, V.*

$$ **Kampa.** In this early Baroque armory-turned-hotel, tucked away in a shady corner of Malá Strana, the rooms are clean, if spare; the bucolic setting compensates for any discomforts. The late-Gothic vaulting looms over patrons in the massive dining room. *Všehrdova 16, 11000, tel. 02/24510409, fax 02/24510377. 85 rooms with bath. Facilities: restaurant, café. AE, DC, MC, V.*

$$ ★ **Opera.** When this hotel opened in the 1890s, it may have been the hospice of choice for divas performing at the nearby State (Státní) Theater. In the intervening years, though, a four-lane highway was constructed between the buildings, and the two went their separate ways. Decent rooms, friendly staff, and plenty of fin-de-siècle charm are helping to restore this hotel's former luster. *Těšnov 13, 11000, tel. 02/2315609, fax 02/2311477. 66 rooms, most with bath. Facilities: restaurant, snack bar. AE, DC, MC, V.*

$ **Apollo.** A standard, no-frills box of a hotel, offering decent, clean rooms at a fair price, the Apollo is about 20 minutes outside the center by public transportation. *Kubišova 23, 17000, tel. 02/66410628, fax 02/66414570. Metro Holešovice, then Tram 5, 12, 17, or 25 to Hercovka. 35 rooms with bath or shower. AE, MC, V.*

$ **Balkán.** This no-frills hotel is in the busy west-bank neighborhood of Smíchov, with its good, inexpensive restaurants and handy access to tourist sites by foot or public transport. The rooms are clean and adequate to the task of providing a night's sleep; the street can be noisy. *Svornosti 28, 15000, tel. 02/540777, fax 02/540670. 24 rooms, most with bath. Facilities: restaurant. AE.*

$ **Hybernia.** The train-station flophouse appearance hides what is actually a respectably clean, secure hotel. The rooms are of the cookie-cutter two-bed-and-a-table variety, but perfectly adequate for a short stay. The location, next to Masarykovo train station and a short walk from the main station, is excellent for the money. *Hybernská 24, 11000, tel. 02/24210439, fax 02/24211513. 70 rooms, some with bath. Facilities: restaurant, bar, lounge. No credit cards.*

$ **Pension Janata.** Catering mostly to German motorists, this pension in outer Žižkov has small rooms with shared bathrooms clustered around the courtyard. You can cook your own meals in one of the kitchens. The management works hard to keep the place clean and efficient. It's 15 minutes by tram from the town center. *Hájkova 19, 13000, tel./fax 02/278455. 7 rooms, 2 with bath. From main train station, Tram 5 or 9 to Biskupcova stop; walk left on Koněvova 2 blocks to Hájkova. Facilities: restaurant, parking. AE, MC, V.*

¢ **Hostel Estec.** This hostel's two best features are that accommodation is in double rooms rather than barracks-style sleeping quarters, and that it stays open year-round. It's in an array of university dormitories atop Petřín Hill, near the Strahov Stadium. The cost is less than $10 per person. *Vaníčkova 5, 16000, tel. 02/527344, fax 02/ 527343. From metro station Dejvická (line A), take Bus 143, 149, or 217 to Koleje Strahov stop; hostel is across street. 40 rooms year-round, 200 in summer; none with bath. AE, MC, V.*

¢ **Pension Březina.** A basic pension, it divides its rooms between two locations, one on Legerova, near the I. P. Pavlova metro station, and the other, quieter and much more central, on Krocínova in the Old Town. Breakfast is available only at the Legerova location. *Legerova 41, 12000, tel. 02/293639, fax 02/298482. 7 rooms at each location, some with bath. AE, DC, MC, V.*

¢ **Pension Unitas.** Operated by the Christian charity Unitas in an Old Town convent, this well-run establishment's accommodations include an interrogation cell once unwillingly occupied by Václav Havel. Conditions are much more comfortable nowadays, though hardly luxurious. No alcohol or tobacco is permitted. *Bartolomějská 9, Staré město, 11000, tel. 02/2327700, fax 02/ 2327709. 40 rooms, none with bath. Breakfast included. AE, MC, V.*

The Arts

Prague's cultural life is one of its top attractions, and its citizens like to dress up for it, but performances are usually booked far ahead. You can get a monthly program of events from the Prague Information Service, Čedok, or many hotels. The English-language newspapers, *The Prague Post* and *Prognosis*, carry detailed entertainment listings. The main ticket agencies are **Bohemia Ticket International** (Salvátorská 6, tel. 02/24227832) and **Tiketpro** (main outlet, Štěpánská 61, Lucerna Passage, tel. 02/24232110, fax 02/24232021; credit card orders accepted). For major concerts, opera, and theater, it's much cheaper, however, to buy tickets at the box office.

Concerts Performances are held in nearly every church in town, it seems, and in quite a few ornate palaces as well, notably the **churches of St. Nicholas** in both the Old Town Square and Malá Strana; **St. James's Church** on Malá Stupartská in the Old Town, where the organ plays amid a flourish of Baroque statuary; the giant **Wallenstein Palace** in Malá Strana; and in the castle's **Garden on the Ramparts,** where music comes with a view.

The Czech Philharmonic, Prague Symphony, and Czech Radio Orchestra play in the intimate, lavish **Dvořák Hall** in the **Rudolfinum** (Nám. Jana Palacha, tel. 02/24893111). The other main concert venue, **Smetana Hall,** along with the rest of the Obecní dům building on Náměstí Republiky, will remain closed for repairs into 1997.

Opera and Ballet Opera is of an especially high standard in Prague. The main venues in the grand style of the 19th century are the beautifully restored **National Theater** (Národní třída 2, tel. 02/24912673) and the **State Opera Prague** (Wilsonova 4, tel. 02/24227693; formerly the Smetana Theater). The even older **Theater of Estates** (Ovocný třída 1, tel. 02/ 227281; formerly the Týl Theater) hosts opera, ballet, and theater performances.

Theater Diverse kinds of multimedia theater, "black theater" (motion, dance, music performed in black costumes), mime, and other nonverbal forms abound. Most famous is **Laterna Magika** (Magic Lantern, Národní třída 4, tel. 02/24914129), a popular extravaganza combining live actors, mime, and sophisticated film techniques.

Puppet Shows This traditional form of Czech popular entertainment has been given new life thanks to productions at the **National Marionette Theater** (Žatecká 1) and the **Magic Theater of the Baroque World** (Celetná 13).

Nightlife

Cabaret **The Alhambra** (Václavské nám. 5, tel. 02/24193692) has a three-part floor show. More moderately priced is **Variété Praha** (Vodičkova 30, tel. 02/24215945).

Discos Discos catering to a young crowd (mostly 14–18-year-olds) line Wenceslas Square. The best bet is to stroll down the square and listen for the liveliest music. For excellent jazz try **Reduta** (Národní třída 20, tel. 02/24912246). **Agharta** (Krakovská 5, tel. 02/24212914) is another good jazz club. For live rock, check out the **Rock Cafe** (Národní třída 20, tel. 02/24914416). You can also rock at **Malostranská Beseda** (Malostranské nám. 21, tel. 02/539024).

Bohemian Spas

The Bohemian countryside is a restful world of gentle hills and thick woods. It is especially beautiful during fall foliage or in May, when the fruit trees that line the roads are in blossom. In such settings lie the two most famous of the Czech Republic's scores of spas: Karlovy Vary and Mariánské Lázně. During the 19th and early 20th centuries, the royalty and aristocrats of Europe who came to ease their overindulged bodies (or indulge them even more!) knew these spas as Karlsbad and Marienbad.

To the south, the higher wooded hills of Šumava, bordering Germany, have their own folklore and give rise to the headwaters of the Vltava. You'll follow its tortuous course as you enter South Bohemia, which has probably spawned more castles than any other region of comparable size. The medieval towns of South Bohemia are exquisite, though be prepared to find them in various stages of repair or decay. In such towns the Hussite reformist movement was born during the early 15th century, sparking off a series of religious conflicts that eventually embroiled all Europe.

Getting Around

There are excellent and very cheap bus connections to Karlovy Vary and Mariánské Lázně from the Florenc bus station in Prague. Train service between the two towns is also frequent. Train service to Karlovy Vary is slower (and only slightly cheaper); trains leave Prague from the Masarykovo station. Most trains to Germany pass through Mariánské Lázně. Trains for Mariánské Lázně leave Prague from the main station, Hlavní nádraží.

Exploring Bohemian Spas

Karlovy Vary, or Karlsbad, was named after Charles IV, who, while out hunting, was supposedly led to the main thermal spring of Vřídlo by a fleeing deer. In due course, the spa drew not only many of the crowned heads and much of the blue blood of Europe but also leading musicians and writers. The same parks, promenades, and colonnades still border the little river Teplá, beneath wooded hills. For all its later buildings and proletarian patients, Karlovy Vary still has a great deal of elegance. The waters from the spa's 12 springs are uniformly foul tasting. The thing to do is sip them from traditionally shaped cups while nibbling rich Karlovy Vary wafers *(oplatky)*, then resort to the "13th spring," Karlovy Vary's tangy herbal liqueur called *Becherovka*.

Karlovy Vary and **Mariánské Lázně** have Czechoslovakia's two best golf courses. As a spa, Mariánské Lázně is younger and smaller, yet its more open setting gives it an air of greater spaciousness. It was much favored by Britain's Edward VII, though from all accounts, he didn't waste too much time on strict diets and rigorous treatments.

Dining and Lodging

In many parts of Bohemia, the only real options for dining are the restaurants and cafés at the larger hotels. For details and price-category definitions, *see* Dining and Lodging in Staying in the Czech Republic, *above*.

Karlovy Vary
Dining and Lodging

Adria. Conveniently located by the bus station and small train station, this is a faded but adequate relic of the spa's glorious past. After a remodeling that pushed prices up, all rooms now have a toilet and shower. *Západní 1, 36000, tel. 017/3223765. 30 rooms with bath. Facilities: restaurant. No credit cards. $$*

Pension Malta. Spacious rooms and a location just across the river from the colonnade are the draws at this small hotel. The rooms are furnished simply, but all have a bath, a television, and a refrigerator. *I.P. Pavlova 16, 36000, tel. 017/3223137, fax 017/3228741. 15 rooms with bath. Facilities: restaurant. AE, MC, V. $$*

Lodging

Astoria. This older private spa is now trying to make it as a hotel and will probably succeed, given its excellent location near the "Sprudel" and main colonnade. In keeping with spa tradition, the rooms and public areas are comfortable but sterile. *Vřídelní 23, 36000, tel. 017/3228224, fax 017/3224368. 96 rooms with bath. MC, V. $$*

Turist. This older hotel offers just the basics, but it's near both train stations, the bus station, and the bustling pedestrian shopping zone just north of the spa district. *Dr. Davida Bechera 18, 36000, tel. 017/26837. 20 rooms without bath. No credit cards. $*

Mariánské Lázně
Dining and Lodging

Evropa. This former workers' spa-retreat is now a pleasant turn-of-the-century hotel, conveniently located downtown. The hotel restaurant is German, with game dishes, such as wild boar and venison. *Třebízského 101, 35301, near Čedok, tel. 0165/2064, fax 0165/5408. 94 rooms, some with bath. Facilities: restaurant (reservations advised). No credit cards. $–$$*

Lodging

Pacifik. The lavish facade of this matronly spa-hotel, with its twin angelic musicians on the roof, commands a view of the main street. Rooms are large, high-ceilinged, and functional. Should you desire the complete spa treatment, prices here are lower than most. *Mírové nám. 84, 35301, tel. 0165/3006, fax 0165/2645. 75 rooms, some with bath. DC, MC, V. $–$$*

Kossuth. This is another complex of former union houses offering convenience and moderate prices. More modest than the Evropa, this slightly worn-out hotel, on a quiet street, houses tourists mostly from within the country and the Eastern bloc. *Ruská 77, 35301, tel. 0165/2861, fax 0165/2862. 211 rooms, most without bath. No credit cards. $*

6   Denmark

While it's true that Denmark is one of the world's most expensive countries, your visit needn't be. Seeing the country as the Danes themselves do, through the window of a small café and from the seat of a bicycle, costs little more than a visit in other parts of Europe.

The Danes are friendly and helpful folk who have even coined a term—*hyggelig*—for the feeling of well-being that comes from their own brand of cozy hospitality. The stereotype of melancholic Scandinavia doesn't hold here: not in the café-studded streets of the larger cities, where musicians and fruit vendors hawk their wares to passersby; not in the tiny coastal towns, where the houses are the color of ice-cream flavors; not in the jam sessions that erupt in the Copenhagen jazz clubs, nor in the equally joyous "jam" sessions involved in the production of *smørrebrød* (the famous open-face Danish sandwich). Even the country's indoor-outdoor museums, where history is reconstructed through full-scale dwellings out in the open, indicate that Danes don't wish to keep life behind glass.

Denmark is the only Scandinavian country without wild tracts of forest and lake. This is a land of cultivated woodlands and well-groomed agriculture, where every acre is rich in orchard and field. Nowhere are you far from water, as you drive on and off the ferries and bridges linking the three regions of Jutland, Funen, and Zealand.

Long one of the world's most liberal countries, Denmark has a highly developed social welfare system. The hefty taxes are the subject of grumbles and jokes, but Danes remain proud of their state-funded medical and educational systems, as well as their high standard of living.

The country that gave the world Isak Dinesen, Hans Christian Andersen, and Søren Kierkegaard has a long-standing commitment to culture and the arts. In what other nation does the royal couple translate the writings of Simone de Beauvoir or the queen design postage stamps for Christmas? The Danish Ballet, founded in Co-

Denmark

North Sea

Skagerrak

TO GREENLAND

TO FAROE ISLANDS

SWEDEN

Skagen

Hirtshals

Hjørring

Frederikshavn

Sæby

Brønderslev

Hanstholm

Læsø

Thisted

Lim-fjord

Limfjord

Aalborg

Nykøbing

Hadsund

Aalborg Bugt

Kattegat

Lemvig

Skive

Anholt

Struer

Viborg

Holstebro

Randers

Jylland

Grenå

Ringkøbing

Herning

Silkeborg

Århus

Ebeltoft

Skanderborg

Samsø

Grindsted

Horsens

Tisvildeleje

Hornbæk

Skjern

Vejle

Nykøbing

Helsingør

Billund

Samsøbælt

Frederikssund

Hillerød

Esbjerg

Holsted

Fredericia

Kalundborg

Holbæk

Fanø

Middelfart

Store-bælt

Jyderup

Copenhagen

Ribe

Kolding

Odense

Kerteminde

Roskilde

Amager

Rømø

Vojens

Assens

Fyn

Slagelse

Ringsted

Køge Bugt

Skærbæk

Haderslev

Nyborg

Korsør

Køge

Tønder

Åbenrå

Fåborg

Lillebælt

Næstved

St. Heddinge

Als

Svendborg

Karrebæksminde

Sønderborg

Troense

Tranekær

Langeland

Vordingborg

Ærøskøbing

Rudkøbing

Stege

Møn

Ærø

Marstal

Nakskov

Nykøbing

Falster

Rødby

Maribo

Rønne

Lolland

Nysted

Sjælland

Ostsee

GERMANY

N

SWEDEN

Baltic Sea

Bornholm

Rønne

TO BORNHOLM

0   50 miles

0   75 km

penhagen in 1722, is world renowned, while the provinces have numerous theater groups and opera houses.

Perhaps Denmark's greatest charm is its manageable size—about half that of Maine. This feature, combined with one of the world's largest concentrations of bicycles and a flat landscape, will lead the visitor to the same conclusion reached by Danes long ago: The best way to explore this country is atop a bike, spinning through colorful Copenhagen and the peaceful island of Funen.

Essential Information

Before You Go

When to Go Most travelers visit Denmark during the warmest months, July and August, but there are advantages to going in May, June, or September, when sights are less crowded and many establishments offer off-season discounts. However, few places in Denmark are ever unpleasantly crowded, and when the Danes make their annual exodus to the beaches, the cities have even more breathing space.

Climate The following are the average daily maximum and minimum temperatures for Copenhagen.

Jan.	36F	2C	May	61F	16C	Sept.	64F	18C
	28	- 2		46	8		51	11
Feb.	36F	2C	June	67F	19C	Oct.	54F	12C
	28	- 2		52	11		44	7
Mar.	41F	5C	July	71F	22C	Nov.	45F	7C
	31	- 1		57	14		38	3
Apr.	51F	11C	Aug.	70F	21C	Dec.	40F	4C
	38	3		56	14		34	1

Currency The monetary unit in Denmark is the krone (kr., Dkr., or DKK), which is divided into 100 øre. At press time (summer 1995), the krone stood at 5.1 kr. to the dollar and 8.57 kr. to the pound sterling. Most well-known credit cards are accepted in Denmark.

What It Will Cost Denmark's economy is stable, and inflation remains reasonably low, without wild fluctuations in exchange rates. While Denmark is slightly cheaper than Norway and Sweden, the standard and cost of living are nonetheless high, especially for such luxuries as alcohol. Prices are highest in Copenhagen, while the least-expensive areas are Funen and Jutland.

Sample Prices Cup of coffee, 14–20 kr.; bottle of beer, 15–25 kr.; soda, 10–15 kr.; ham sandwich, 20–40 kr.; 1-mile taxi ride, 3 kr.

Customs on Arrival If you purchase goods in a country that is a member of the European Union (EU) and pay that country's value-added tax (VAT) on those goods, you may import duty-free 1½ liters of liquor or 3 liters of strong wine (under 22%), plus 5 liters of other wine and 300 cigarettes or 150 cigarillos or 75 cigars or 400 grams of tobacco. Other articles may be brought in up to a maximum of 2,800 kr.; you are also allowed 50 grams of perfume.

If you purchase goods in a country that is a member of the European Union (EU) and pay that country's value-added tax (VAT) on those goods, you may import duty-free 1½ liters of liquor; 300 cigarettes or 150 cigarillos or 75 cigars or 400 grams of tobacco. If you are entering Denmark from a non-EU country or if you have purchased your goods on a ferryboat or in an airport not taxed in the EU, you must pay Danish taxes on any amount of alcoholic beverages greater than 1 liter of liquor or 2 liters of strong wine, plus 2 liters of table wine. For tobacco, the limit is 200 cigarettes or 100 cigarillos or 50 cigars or 250 grams of tobacco. You are also allowed 50 grams of perfume. Other articles (including beer) are allowed up to a maximum of 1,350 kr.

Language Danish is a difficult tongue for foreigners, except those from Norway and Sweden, to understand, let alone speak. Danes are good linguists, however, and almost everyone, except elderly people in rural areas, speaks English well.

Getting Around

By Train and Bus Traveling by train or bus is easy because Danish State Railways (DSB, tel. 33/14–17–01) and a few private companies cover the country with a dense network of train services, supplemented by buses in remote areas. Hourly intercity trains connect the main towns in Jutland and Funen with Copenhagen and Zealand, using high-speed diesels, called IC–3s, on the most important stretches. All these trains make the one-hour ferry crossing of the Great Belt (Store Bælt), the waterway separating Funen and Zealand. You can reserve seats on intercity trains and IC–3s, and you *must* have a reservation if you plan to cross the Great Belt. Buy tickets at stations for trains, buses, and connecting ferry crossings. You can usually buy tickets on the buses themselves. For most cross-country trips, children between four and 11 travel free when accompanying an adult, though they must have a seat reservation (30 kr.). Ask about discounts for senior citizens and groups.

Fares Only the five-day **Scanrail pass** can be purchased in Denmark. Call either RailEurope (800/849–7245) or DER Tours (800/782–2424). The Scanrail pass available in Denmark is a good buy for 21 days of unlimited travel by rail and on most sea routes in Denmark, Norway, Sweden, and Finland. For details, call DER, RailEurope, or your travel agent. DSB also offers other discounts, including those on "inexpensive" days, as well as reductions for students, children, seniors, and groups of three or more. For discounts, ask, ask, ask!

By Boat Denmark has an excellent ferry service, with both domestic and international routes. There is frequent service to Germany, Poland, Sweden, Norway, and the Faroe Islands (in the Atlantic Ocean, north of Scotland), as well as to Britain. Domestic ferries provide services between the three areas of Jutland, Funen, and Zealand and to the smaller islands, 100 of which are inhabited. Danish State Railways and several private shipping companies publish timetables in English, and you should reserve on domestic as well as overseas routes. Ask about off-season discounts.

By Bicycle It is said that the Danes have the greatest number of bikes per capita in the world, and indeed, with its flat landscape and uncrowded roads, Denmark is a cycler's paradise. You can rent bikes at some train stations and many tourist offices, as well as from private firms. Additional information on cycling can be supplied by the **Danish Cyclists' Association** (Dansk Cyklist Forbund) (Rømersgade 7, DK 1362 Copenhagen, tel. 33/32–31–21). Danish tourist offices publish the pamphlet *Cycling Holiday in Denmark*.

Staying in Denmark

Telephones
Local calls Pay phones take 1-, 5-, and 10-kr. coins. Dial first, then insert your coins when you make your connection. You must use the area codes even when dialing a local number. Calling cards, which can be purchased at DSB stations, post offices, and some kiosks, cost 25, 50, or 100 kr. and can be used at special phones.

International Calls Dial 00, then the country code, the area code, and the number. To reach an **AT&T** long-distance operator, dial 8001–0010; for **MCI,** dial 8001–0022; and for **Sprint,** 8001–0877.

Operators and To speak to an operator, most of whom speak English, dial 118; for
Information an international operator, dial 113.

Country Code Denmark's international country code is 45.

Mail Surface and airmail letters, as well as aerograms, to the United
Postal Rates States cost 5 kr. for 20 grams; postcards also cost 5 kr. Letters and
postcards to the United Kingdom and other EU countries cost 3.75
kr. You can buy stamps at post offices or from shops that sell postcards.

Receiving Mail If you do not know where you will be staying, have mail sent to
American Express or Poste Restante at any post office. American
Express charges noncardholders 10 kr. for each letter. If no post office is specified, letters will be sent to the main post office in Copenhagen (Tietgensgade 37, DK 1704).

Shopping Visitors from a non-EU country can save 20% by obtaining a refund
VAT Refunds of the value-added tax (VAT) at over 1,500 shops displaying a Tax
Free sign on the window. If the shop sends your purchase directly to
your home address, you pay only the sales price, exclusive of VAT,
plus dispatch and insurance costs. If you want to take the goods
home yourself, pay the full price in the shop and get a VAT refund at
the Danish duty-free shopping center at the Copenhagen airport.
You can obtain a copy of the *Tax-Free Shopping Guide* from the tourist office.

Opening and **Banks.** In Copenhagen, banks are open weekdays 9:30–3 and
Closing Times Thursdays until 6. Several *bureaux de change*, including the ones at
Copenhagen's central station and airport, stay open until 10 PM.
Outside Copenhagen, banking hours vary, so check locally.

Museums are generally open 10–3 or 11–4 and are closed on Mondays. In winter museums are open for fewer hours, and some close
for the season.

Shops are generally open weekdays 9–5:30; most stay open on
Thursdays and Fridays until 7 or 8 and close on Saturdays at 1 or 2.
The first Saturday of every month, most shops stay open until 4 or 5.
Grocery stores stay open until 8 PM on weekdays. Saturday after-
noons and Sundays, everything is closed except flower shops and bake-
ries.

National For 1996: January 1, April 4–8 (Easter), May 3 (Common Prayer),
Holidays May 16 (Ascension), May 26–27 (Pentecost), June 5 (Constitution
Day, shops close at noon), and December 24–26 (Christmas). For
1997 the movable ones are: March 27–31 (Easter), April 25 (Common Prayer), May 8 (Ascension), May 18, 19 (Pentecost).

Dining Danes take their food seriously, and Danish food, however simple, is
excellent, with an emphasis on fresh ingredients and careful presentation. Fish and meat are both of top quality in this farming and fishing country, and both are staple ingredients of the famous
smørrebrød. Some smørrebrød are huge meals in themselves: Inno-
cent snackers can find themselves faced with a dauntingly large (but
nonetheless delicious) mound of fish or meat, slathered with pickle
relish, all atop *rugbrød* (rye bread) and *franskbrød* (wheat bread).
Another specialty is *wiener brød* (a Danish pastry), an original far
superior to anything that dares call itself "Danish pastry" elsewhere.

All Scandinavian countries have versions of the cold table, but
Danes claim that theirs, *det store kolde bord*, is the original and the
best. It's a celebration meal; the setting of the long table is a work of
art—often with paper sculpture and silver platters—and the food
itself is a minor miracle of design and decoration. In hotels and restaurants the cold table is served at lunch only, though you will find a
more limited version at hotel breakfasts—a good bet for budget
travelers.

Liquid refreshment is top-notch. Denmark boasts more than 50 varieties of beer made by as many breweries; the best known come from Carlsberg and Tuborg. Those who like harder stuff should try *snaps*, the aquavit traditionally drunk with cold food. Do as the locals do, and knock it back after eating some herring. The Danes have a saying about the herring-snaps combo: "The fish should be swimming."

What to Wear The Danes are a fairly casual lot, and few restaurants require a jacket and tie. Even in the most chic establishments, the tone is elegantly casual.

Ratings Meal prices vary little between town and country. Prices are per person and include a first course, main course, and dessert, plus taxes and tip, but not wine. Best bets are indicated by a star ★.

Category	Cost
$$	120–200 kr.
$	80–120 kr.
¢	under 80 kr.

Lodging Accommodations in Denmark range from the spare and comfortable to the resplendent. Even inexpensive hotels offer simple designs in good materials and good, firm beds. Many Danes prefer a shower to a bath, so if you particularly want a tub, ask for it, but be prepared to pay more. Farmhouse and *kro* (inn) accommodations offer a terrific alternative to more traditional hotels. Except in the case of rentals, breakfast and taxes are usually included in prices, but check when making a reservation.

Hotels While luxury hotels in the city or countryside offer rooms of a high standard, less-expensive accommodations are uniformly clean and comfortable.

Inns A cheaper and charming alternative to hotels are the old stagecoach kro inns scattered throughout Denmark. You can save money by contacting **Kro Ferie** (Vejlevej 16, 8700 Horsens, tel. 75/64–87–00) to invest in a book of Inn Checks, valid at 86 inns. Each check costs 375 kr. per person or 550 kr. per couple and includes one overnight stay in a double room with bath, breakfast included. Family checks, for three (595 kr.) and four (685 kr.) persons are also available. Order a free catalogue from Kro Ferie, and choose carefully. The organization includes some chain hotels that would be hard-pressed to demonstrate a modicum of inn-related charm. Note that some establishments also tack on an additional 100-kr. surcharge to the price of a double.

Youth Hostels The 100 youth hostels in Denmark are excellent, and they're open to everyone regardless of age. If you have an International Youth Hostels Association card (obtainable before you leave home), the average rate is 60 kr. Without the card, there's a surcharge of 25 kr. For more information on youth hostels, contact **Danmarks Vandrehjem** (Vesterbrogade 39, DK 1620 V, tel. 31/31–36–12).

Camping Denmark has over 500 approved campsites, with a rating system of one, two, or three stars. You need an International Camping Carnet or Danish Camping Pass (available at any campsite and valid for one year). For more details on camping and discounts for groups and families, contact **Campingrådet** (Hesseløgade 10, DK 2100 Copenhagen, tel. 39/27–88–44).

Ratings Prices are for two people in a double room and include service and taxes and usually breakfast. Best bets are indicated by a star ★.

Category	Copenhagen	Other Areas
$$	670–800 kr.	450–650 kr.
$	600–670 kr.	400–450 kr.
¢	under 600 kr.	under 400 kr.

Tipping The egalitarian Danes do not expect to be tipped. Service is included in bills for hotels, bars, and restaurants. The exception is hotel porters, who get around 5 kr. per bag; you should also leave 1 or 2 kr. for the use of a public toilet if an attendant is present.

Copenhagen

Arriving and Departing

By Plane The main airport for both international and domestic flights is Copenhagen Airport, 10 kilometers (6 miles) from the center of town.

Between the Airport and Downtown There is frequent bus service to the city; the airport bus to the central station leaves every 15 minutes, and the trip takes about 25 minutes. You pay the 30-kr. fare on the bus. Public buses cost 15 kr. and run as often, but take twice as long. Bus 250S takes you to Rådhus Pladsen, the city-hall square.

By Train Copenhagen's central station is the hub of the train networks. Express trains leave every hour, on the hour, from 6 AM to 10 PM for principal towns in Funen and Jutland. Find out more from **DSB Information** at the central station (tel. 33/14–17–01). You can make reservations at the central station (tel. 33/14–88–00) and most other stations and through travel agents. In Copenhagen, public shower facilities are open at the Main Train Station, 4:30 AM–2 AM and cost 15 kr. Bring a towel.

Getting Around

By Bus and Suburban Train The best bet for visitors is the **Copenhagen Card,** affording unlimited travel on buses and suburban trains (S-trains), admission to over 60 museums and sights around Zealand, and a reduction on the ferry crossing to Sweden. You can buy the card, which costs about 140 kr. (one day), 230 kr. (two days), or 295 kr. (three days), half price for children 5–11, at tourist offices and hotels and from travel agents.

Buses and suburban trains operate on the same ticket system and divide Copenhagen and the surrounding areas into three zones. Tickets are validated on the time system: On the basic ticket, which costs 10 kr. for an hour, you can travel anywhere in the zone in which you started. You can obtain a discount by buying a card of 10 basic tickets for 70 kr. Get zone information from the 24-hour information service: tel. 36/45–45–45 for buses, 33/14–17–01 for S-trains. Buses and S-trains run from 5 AM (6 AM on Sundays) to 12:30 AM. Infrequent buses run through the night.

By Bicycle More than half the 5 million Danes are said to ride bikes, which are popular with visitors as well. Bike rental costs 30–50 kr. a day, with a deposit of 100–200 kr. Contact **Danwheel-Rent-a-Bike** (Colbjørnsensgade 3, tel. 31/21–22–27) or **Urania Cykler** (Gammel Kongevej 1, tel. 31/21–80–88).

Important Addresses and Numbers

Tourist Information The main tourist information office is **Danmarks Turistråd** (Danish Tourist Board) (Bernstoffsgade 1, DK 1577 V, tel. 33/11–13–25). Located on the Tivoli grounds, it is open May, weekdays 9–6, Sat.

9–2, Sun. 9–1; June–Sept., daily 9–6; Oct.–Apr., weekdays 9–5, Sat. 9–noon, closed Sun. There are also offices at Elsinore, Hillerød, Køge, Roskilde, Gilleleje, Hundersted, and Tisvildeleje. Youth information in Copenhagen is available at **Huset** (Rådhusstraede 13, tel. 33/15–65–18).

Embassies **U.S.** (Dag Hammarskjöldsallé 24, tel. 31/42–31–44). **Canadian** (Kristen Benikowsgade 1, tel. 33/12–22–99). **U.K.** (Kastelsvej 40, tel. 35/26–46–00).

Emergencies **Police, Fire, Ambulance** (tel. 112). **Doctor** (after hours, tel. 33/12–00–41). Fees payable in cash only; night fees around 400–500 kr.). **Dentist: Dental Emergency Service,** Tandlægevagten, 14, Oslo Plads, near Østerport station (no telephone; emergencies only; cash only).

Exploring Copenhagen

When Denmark ruled Norway and Sweden in the 15th century, Copenhagen was the capital of all three countries. Today it is still the liveliest Scandinavian capital, with about 1 million inhabitants. It's a city meant for walking, the first in Europe to recognize the value of pedestrian streets in fostering community spirit. If there's such a thing as a cozy metropolis, you'll find it here.

Rådhus *Numbers in the margin correspond to points of interest on the*
Pladsen and *Copenhagen map.*
Slotsholmen
The best place to start a stroll is the Rådhus Pladsen (City Hall Square), the hub of Copenhagen's commercial district. The mock-Renaissance building dominating it is the **Rådhus** (city hall), completed in 1905. A statue of Copenhagen's 12th-century founder, Bishop Absalon, sits atop the main entrance. Inside you can see the first World Clock, an astrological timepiece invented and built by Jens Olsen and put in motion in 1955. If you're feeling energetic, take a guided tour up the 350-foot tower for a panoramic view. *Rådhus Pladsen, tel. 33/66–25–82. Open Mon.–Wed., Fri. 9:30–3, Thur. 9:30–4, Sat. 9:30–1. Tours in English: weekdays at 3, Sat. at 10. Tower tours: Mon.–Sat. at noon; additional tours June–Sept. at 10, noon, and 2. Admission: tour 20 kr., tower 10 kr.*

❷ On the right of Rådhus Pladsen is **Lurblæserne** (Lur Blower's Column), topped by two Vikings blowing an ancient trumpet called a *lur*. The artist took a good deal of artistic license—the lur dates from the Bronze Age, 1500 BC, while the Vikings lived a mere 1,000 years ago. The monument is a starting point for sightseeing tours of the city.

If you continue to the square's northeast corner and turn right, you will be in Frederiksberggade, the first of the five pedestrian streets
❸ that make up the **Strøget,** Copenhagen's shopping district. Walk past the cafés and trendy boutiques to the double square of **Gammel and Nytorv,** where, farther along, the street has been hand inlaid with mosaic tiles. While Strøget is famous as a shopping area, and elegant stores abound, it's also where Copenhagen comes to stroll. Outside the posh displays of the fur and porcelain shops, the sidewalks have the festive aura of a street fair.

Turn down Rådhusstræde toward Frederiksholms Kanal and continue to Ny Vestergade. Here you'll find the entrance to the
❹ **Nationalmuseet** (National Museum), with extensive collections that chronicle Danish cultural history to modern times and display Egyptian, Greek, and Roman antiquities. Viking enthusiasts will want to see the Runic stones in the Danish cultural history section. *Ny Vestergade 10, tel. 33/13–44–11. Admission: 30 kr. adults, 20 kr. students and senior citizens, free for children under 16. Open Tues.–Sun. 10–5.*

❺ Cross Frederiksholms Kanal to the massive gray **Christiansborg Slot** (Christiansborg Castle). The complex, which contains the Folketinget (Parliament House) and the Royal Reception Chambers, is situated on the site of the city's first fortress, built by Bishop Absalon in 1167. While the castle that stands was being built at the turn of the century, the National Museum excavated the ruins beneath the site. *Christiansborg ruins, tel. 33/92–64–92. Admission: 12 kr. adults, 5 kr. children. Open May–Sept., daily 9:30–3:30; closed Oct.–Apr., Mon. and Sat. Folketinget, tel. 33/37–55–00. Admission free. Tours every hr (except noon) on Sun., 10–4. Reception Rooms. Admission: 27 kr. adults, 10 kr. children. Open May–Dec. and Feb.–Sept., Tues.–Sun., English tours at 10, noon, and 2; Oct.–Dec. and Feb.–Apr., Tues.–Thurs., and Sun., English tours at 11 and 3.*

❻ Just north of the castle is **Thorvaldsens Museum.** The 19th-century Danish sculptor Bertel Thorvaldsen, buried at the center of the museum, was greatly influenced by the statues and reliefs of classical antiquity. In addition to his own works, there is a collection of paintings and drawings by other artists illustrating the influence of Italy on Denmark's Golden Age artists. *Porthusgade 2, tel. 33/32–15–32. Admission free. Open Tues.–Sun. 10–5.*

❼ Nearby, **Det Kongelige Bibliotek** (Royal Library) houses the country's largest collection of books, newspapers, and manuscripts. Look for early records of the Viking journeys to America and Greenland and the statue of the philosopher Søren Kierkegaard in the garden. *Christians Brygge 8, tel. 33/93–01–11. Admission free. Open weekdays 9–7, Sat. 10–7.*

❽ Close to the library is the **Teaterhistorisk Museet** (Theater History Museum), in the Royal Court Theater of 1767. You can see extensive exhibits on theater and ballet history, then wander around the boxes, stage, and dressing rooms to see where it all happened. *Christiansborg Ridebane 18, tel. 33/11–51–76. Admission: 20 kr. adults, 10 kr. senior citizens and students, 5 kr. children. Open Wed. 2–4, Sun. noon–4.*

Also at this address are the **Royal Stables**, which display vehicles used by the Danish monarchy from 1777 to the present. *Tel. 33/12–38–15. Admission: 10 kr. adults, 5 kr. children 6–15. Open Oct.–Apr., Sat.–Sun. 2–4; May–Sept., Fri.–Sun. 2–4.*

❾ Across the street that bears its name is **Tøjhusmuseet** (Royal Armory), with impressive displays of uniforms, weapons, and armor in an arched hall 200 yards long. *Tøjhusgade 3, tel. 33/11–60–37. Admission: 20 kr. adults, 5 kr. children 6–17. Open mid-Sept.–mid-June, Tues.–Fri. 1–3, weekends noon–4; mid-June–mid-Sept., Tues.–Sun. 10–4.*

❿ A few steps from Tøjhuset is the old stock exchange, **Børsen,** believed to be the oldest still in use—although it functions only on special occasions. It was built by the 16th-century monarch King Christian IV, a scholar and warrior, and architect of much of the city. The king is said to have had a hand at twisting the tails of the four dragons that form the structure's distinctive green copper spire. With its steep roofs, tiny windows, and gables, the building is one of Copenhagen's treasures.

From Børsen, look east across the drawbridge (Knippelsbro) that connects Slotsholmen with Christianshavn, one of the oldest parts **⓫** of Copenhagen, to the green-and-gold spire of **Vor Frelsers Kirke** (Our Savior's Church). The Gothic structure was built in 1696. Local legend has it that the staircase encircling it was built curling the wrong way around and that when its architect reached the top and saw what he had done, he jumped. Unfortunately, the delicate steeple is under repair (and scaffolding) until spring 1995 at the earliest.

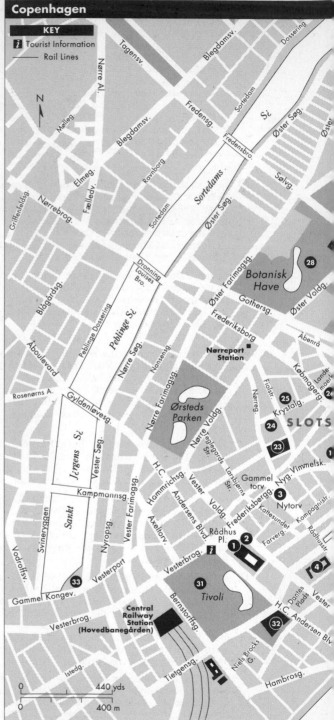

Copenhagen

KEY

i Tourist Information

Rail Lines

Skt. Annægade, tel. 31/57–27–98. Admission: 10 kr. adults, 4 kr. children. Open Mar. 15–May, Mon.–Sat. 9–3:30, Sun. noon–3:30; June–Sept., Mon.–Sat. 9–4:30, Sun. noon–4:30; Oct.–Mar. 14, Mon.–Sat. 9–3:30, Sun. noon–4:30. Tower closed; once it opens, there will be a separate admission fee.

Head back to Strøget, turning left along the Amagertov section. Toward the end and to the right (5 Niels Hemmingsens Gade) is the 18th-century **Helligånds Kirken** (Church of the Holy Ghost). The choir contains a marble font by the sculptor Thorvaldsen.

In Østergade, the easternmost of the streets that make up Strøget, you cannot miss the green spire of **Nikolaj Kirke** (Nikolaj Church). The building that currently stands was built in the 20th century; the previous structure, which dated from the 13th century, was destroyed by fire in 1728. Today the church's role is secular—it's an art gallery and an exhibition center.

Royal Palace Area Kongens Nytorv (the King's New Market) is the square marking the end of Strøget. The **Kongelige Teater** (Danish Royal Theater), home of Danish opera and ballet as well as theater, sits on the south side. The Danish Royal Ballet remains one of the world's great companies, with a repertoire ranging from classical to modern. On the western side of the square you'll see the stately facade of the hotel D'Angleterre, the grande dame of Copenhagen hotels.

The street leading southeast from Kongens Nytorv is **Nyhavn**. The recently gentrified canal was a longtime haunt of sailors. Now restaurants and boutiques outnumber the tattoo shops, but on hot summer nights the area still gets rowdy, with Scandinavians reveling amid a fleet of old-time sailing ships and well-preserved 18th-century buildings. Hans Christian Andersen lived at both Nos. 18 and 20.

Turn left at the end of Nyhavn to see the harbor front and then make an immediate left onto Sankt Annæ Plads. Take the third right onto Amaliegade. Continue straight ahead for **Amalienborg Palace**, the principal royal residence since 1784. When the royal family is in residence during the fall and winter, the Royal Guard and band march through the city at noon to change the palace guard. The second division of the Royal Collection (the first is at Rosenborg) is at Amalienborg. Among the museum's highlights are the study of King Christian IX (1818–1906) and the drawing room of his wife, Queen Louise. The collection also includes Rococo banquet silver, highlighted by a flamboyant Viking ship centerpiece, and a small costume collection. *Amalienborg Museum, tel. 33/12–21–86. Admission: 35 kr. adults, 5 kr. children. Open Mar.–Oct., daily 11–4; late-Oct.–Feb., Tues.–Sun. 11–4.*

Rest a moment on the palace's harbor side, amid the trees and fountains of **Amaliehavn Gardens**. Across the square, it's just a step to Bredgade and **Marmorkirken** (the Marble Church), a 19th-century Baroque church with a dome that looks several sizes too large for the building beneath it.

Bredgade is also home to the exotic onion domes of the **Russiske Ortodoks Kirke** (Russian Orthodox Church). Farther on is the **Kunstindustrimuseet** (Museum of Decorative Art), with a large selection of European and Oriental handicrafts, as well as ceramics, silver, and tapestries. *Bredgade 68, tel. 33/14–94–52. Admission: 30 kr. adults, 20 kr. students and senior citizens, children under 16 free. Permanent exhibition open Tues.–Sun. 1–4; special exhibitions open Tues.–Sat. 10–4, Sun. 1–4.*

A little farther, turn right onto Esplanaden and you'll come to **Frihedsmuseet** (Liberty Museum), situated in Churchill Parken. It gives an evocative picture of the heroic Danish Resistance movement during World War II, which managed to save 7,000 Jews from the Nazis by hiding them in homes and hospitals, then smuggling them across to Sweden. *Churchillparken, tel. 33/13–77–14. Admission free. Open Sept. 16–April, Tues.–Sat. 11–3, Sun. 11–4; May–Sept. 15, Tues.–Sat. 10–4, Sun. 10–5.*

At the park's entrance stands the English church, St. Alban's, and, in the center, the **Kastellet** (Citadel), with two rings of moats. This was the city's main fortress in the 18th century, but, in a grim reversal during World War II, the Germans used it as the headquarters of their occupation of Denmark. *Admission free. Open 6 AM–sunset.*

Continue on to the Langelinie, which on Sunday is thronged with promenading Danes, and at last to **Den Lille Havfrue (the Little Mermaid),** the 1913 statue commemorating Hans Christian Andersen's lovelorn creation, and the subject of hundreds of travel posters.

Around Strøget From Langelinie, take the train or bus from Østerport station back to the center. Walk north from Strøget on Nørregade until you reach **Vor Frue Kirke** (The Church of Our Lady), Copenhagen's cathedral since 1924. The site itself has been a place of worship since the 13th century, when Bishop Absalon built a chapel here. The spare neo-classical facade is a 19th-century revamp that repaired the damage incurred during Nelson's famous bombing of the city in 1801. Inside are Thorvaldsen's marble sculptures of Christ and the Apostles. *Opening times are irregular. Call for details. Nørregade, Frue Plads, tel. 33/15–10–78.*

Head north up Fjolstraede until you come to the main building of **Københavns Universitet** (Copenhagen University), built in the 19th century on the site of the medieval bishops' palace. Past the university, turn right onto Krystalgade. On the left is the arklike **Københavns Synagoge** (Copenhagen Synagogue), designed by the famous contemporary architect Gustav Friedrich Hetsch. Hetsch drew on the Doric and Egyptian styles to create the arklike structure.

Just across Købmagergade is the **Rundetårn,** a round tower built as an observatory in 1642 by Christian IV. It is said that Peter the Great of Russia drove a horse and carriage up the 600 feet of the inner staircase. You'll have to walk, but the view is worth it. *Købmagergade, tel. 33/93–66–60. Admission: 12 kr. adults, 5 kr. children. Open Dec.–May and Sept.–Oct., Mon.–Sat. 10–5, Sun. noon–4; June–Aug., Mon.–Sat. 10–8, Sun. noon–8. Mid-Oct.–mid-Mar. the old observatory, with a giant telescope and an astronomer on hand to answer questions, is open Tues. and Wed., 7–10 PM.*

Turn right at Runde Tårn onto Landemærket, then left onto Åbenrå. If your appetite for museums is not yet sated, turn right out of Åbenrå until you reach Gothersgade, where another right, onto Øster Voldgade, will bring you to **Rosenborg Slot.** This Renaissance castle—built by Renaissance man Christian IV—houses the Crown Jewels, as well as a collection of costumes and royal memorabilia. Don't miss Christian IV's pearl-studded saddle. *Øster Voldgade 4A, tel. 33/15–32–86. Admission: 40 kr. adults, 5 kr. children. Castle open end-Oct.–Apr., Tues., Fri., and Sun. 11–2; treasury open daily 11–3. Both open May, Sept.–end-Oct., daily 11–3; June–Aug., daily 10–4.*

The palace is surrounded by gardens, and just across Øster Voldgade is the **Botanisk Have,** Copenhagen's 25 acres of botanical gardens, with a rather spectacular Palm House containing tropical and subtropical plants. *Admission free. Open May–Aug., daily 8:30–6; Sept.–Apr., daily 8:30–4. Palm House open daily 10–3.*

Leave the gardens through the north exit to get to the **Statens Museum for Kunst** (National Art Gallery), where the collection ranges from modern Danish art to works by Rubens, Dürer, and the Impressionists. Particularly fine are the museum's 20 Matisses. *Sølvgade 48–50, tel. 33/91–21–26. Admission: 20 kr. adults, chil-*

*dren under 16 free; extra for special exhibits. Open Tues.–Sun. 10–
4:30, Wed. until 9 PM.*

30 A nearby building houses the **Hirschsprungske Samling** (Hirsch-
sprung Collection) of Danish 19th-century art. The cozy museum
features works from the Golden Age, in particular those by a group
of late-19th-century painters called the Skagen school.
*Stockholmsgade 20, tel. 31/42–03–36. Admission: 20 kr. adults, 10
kr. students and senior citizens, children under 16 free; extra for
special exhibits. Open (tentatively) Mon., Thurs.–Sun. 10–5, Wed.
10–10; call first to confirm.*

From Stockholmsgade, turn right onto Sølvgade and then left onto
Øster Søgade, just before the bridge. Continue along the canal (the
street name will change from Øster Søgade to Nørre Søgade to
Vester Søgade) until you reach the head of the harbor. Walk straight
ahead and turn left onto Vesterbrogade.

31 On the right lies Copenhagen's best-known attraction, **Tivoli.** In the
1840s, the Danish architect Georg Carstensen persuaded King
Christian VIII that an amusement park was the perfect opiate of the
masses, preaching that "when people amuse themselves, they forget
politics." In the comparatively short season, from May to September, about 4 million people come through the gates. Tivoli is more
sophisticated than a mere funfair: It boasts a pantomime theater
and open-air stage; elegant restaurants; and numerous classical,
jazz, and rock concerts. On weekends there are elaborate fireworks
displays and maneuvers by the Tivoli Guard, a youth version of the
Queen's Royal Guard. Try to see Tivoli at least once by night, when
the trees are illuminated along with the Chinese Pagoda and the
main fountain. *Admission: 40 kr. adults, 20 kr. children. Open mid-
Apr.–mid-Sept., daily 10 AM–midnight.*

At the southern end of the gardens, on Hans Christian Andersens
32 Boulevard, is the **Ny Carlsberg Glyptotek** (New Carlsberg Picture
Hall). This elaborate neoclassical building houses a collection of
works by Gauguin and Degas and other Impressionists, as well as
Egyptian, Greek, Roman, and French sculpture. *Dantes Plads 7,
tel. 33/91–10–65. Admission: 15 kr. adults, children free; adults
free on Wed. and Sun. Open Sept.–Apr., Tues.–Sat. noon–3, Sun.
10–4; May–Aug., Tues.–Sun. 10–4.*

Tucked between St. Jorgens Lake and the main arteries of
33 Vesterbrogade and Gammel Kongevej is the **Tycho Brahe Planetarium.** The modern cylindrical building is filled with astronomy exhibitions and an Omnimax Theater, which takes visitors on a visual
journey up through space and down under the seas. *Gammel
Kongevej 10, tel. 33/12–12–24. Admission: 65 kr. for exhibition and
theater; exhibition only, 15 kr. Reservations advised for theater.
(Because the films can be disorienting, planetarium officials discourage them for children under 7.) Open daily 10:30–9.*

Excursions from Copenhagen

Helsingør– Shakespeare immortalized the town and castle when he chose
Kronborg **Kronborg Castle** as the setting for *Hamlet.* Finished in 1585, the ga-
Castle bled and turreted structure is about 600 years younger than the fortress we imagine from the setting of Shakespeare's tragedy. Well
worth seeing is the 200-foot-long dining hall, the luxurious chapel,
and the royal chambers. The ramparts and 12-foot walls are a reminder of the castle's role as coastal bulwark—Sweden is only a few
miles away. The town of **Helsingør**—about 29 miles north of Copenhagen—has a number of picturesque streets with 16th-century
houses. There is frequent train service to Helsingør station.
Helsingør, tel. 49/21–30–78. Admission: 30 kr. adults, 10 kr. chil-

dren. Open Easter and May–Sept., daily 10:30–5; Oct. and Apr., Tues.–Sun. 11–4; Nov.–Mar., Tues.–Sun. 11–3.

Louisiana A world-class modern art collection is housed in a spectacular building on the "Danish Riviera," the North Zealand coast. Even those who can't tell a Rauschenberg from a Rembrandt should make the 35-kilometer (22-mile) trip to see the setting: It's an elegant, rambling structure set in a large park. In the permanent collection, Warhols vie for space with Giacomettis and Picassos. There are temporary exhibits, as well as concerts and films. In the summer, Danes bring their children and picnic in the sculpture garden. There's also a cafeteria, where you get a great view of the Calder mobile; the sound; and, on a clear day, Sweden. The new children's wing has pyramid-shape chalkboards, kid-proof computers, and weekend activities under the guidance of an artist or museum coordinator.

Louisiana is well worth the half-hour train ride from Copenhagen to Humlebæk. The museum is a 10-minute walk from the station. *Gammel Strandvej 13, Humlebæk, tel. 42/19–07–19. Admission: 48 kr. adults, 15 kr. children. Open Mon., Tues., Thurs., and Fri. 10–5, Wed. 10–10, weekends 10–6. (Combined train from Copenhagen and admission ticket, 77 kr., available from DSB. Higher admission prices for special exhibits.*

Roskilde History enthusiasts should take advantage of the frequent train service from Copenhagen to the bustling market town of **Roskilde,** 30 kilometers (19 miles) west of the city. A key administrative center during Viking times, it remained one of the largest towns in northern Europe through the Middle Ages. Its population has dwindled, but the legacy of its 1,000-year history lives on in the spectacular cathedral. Built on the site of Denmark's first church, the **Domkirke** (cathedral) has been the burial place of Danish royalty since the 15th century. Inside, four chapels house 38 kings and queens. Strewn with marble tombs, the interior has the feeling of a stately but surreal warehouse. *Domkirkeplasden, Roskilde. Admission: 5 kr. adults, 2 kr. children. Open Apr.–Sept., weekdays 9–4:45; Oct.– Mar., weekdays 10–2:45. May–Aug., weekdays and Sat. 9–4:45, Sun. 12:30–4:45; Sept.–Apr., Sun. 12:30–3:45. For Sat. times, which vary, and to confirm opening times, call the tourist board at 42/35–27–00.*

A 10-minute walk south and through the park takes you to the water and to the **Viking Ship Museum.** Inside are five Viking ships, discovered at the bottom of the Roskilde Fjord in 1962. Detailed placards in English chronicle Viking history. There are also English-language films on the excavation and reconstruction. *Strandengen, Roskilde, tel. 42/35–65–55. Admission: 30 kr. adults, 20 kr. children. Open Apr.–Oct., daily 9–5; Nov.–Mar., daily 10–4.*

Shopping

Gift Ideas While Copenhagen is a mecca for shoppers in search of impeccable designs and top-notch quality, budget shoppers may find bargains elusive. Several ideas for inexpensive gifts include simple table decorations—a porcelain or glass candle holder or long-lasting candles, often handmade. Denmark also produces tasteful reproductions of Viking ornaments and jewelry, in bronze as well as silver and gold.

Specialty Shops Synonymous with shopping are Strøget's pedestrian streets. For glass, try **Holmegaard** (Østergade 15, tel. 33/12–44–77), where hand-crafted items are available. Just off the street is Pistolstræde, a typical old courtyard that's been lovingly restored and filled with intriguing boutiques. **Magasin** (Kongens Nytorv 13, tel. 33/11–44–33) is one of the largest department stores in Scandinavia. **Illum** (Østergade 52, tel. 33/14–40–02) is a department store with an eating arcade. Don't confuse Illum with **Ilums Bolighus** (Amagertorv

10, tel. 33/14–19–41), where swanky items for the home, quality clothing, and gifts are displayed in gallery-style surroundings. **Royal Copenhagen Porcelain** (Amagertorv 6, tel. 33/13–71–81) carries porcelain; bargain hunters should head for the seconds emporium on the top floor. **Georg Jensen**, with its two shops (Amagertorv 4 and Østergade 40, tel. 33/11–40–80), is one of the world's finest silversmiths. Off the eastern end of Strøget the **Tin Centret** (Ny Østergade 2, tel. 33/14–82–00) has a large pewterware collection (tin means pewter in Danish). Finally, if everything seems too pricey, walk down Strøget to **Søstrene Grene** (Amagertorv 29, tel. 33/14–19–48), a phenomenally popular penny mart where even the most devout tightwads cannot resist parting with their kroner.

Dining

Food remains one of the great pleasures of a stay in Copenhagen, a city with over 2,000 restaurants. Traditional Danish fare spans all the price categories: You can order a light lunch of the traditional smørrebrød, snack from a *store-kolde bord* (cold buffet), or dine out on lobster and Limfjord oysters. If you are strapped for cash, you can enjoy fast food Danish style, in the form of *pølser* (hot dogs) sold from trucks on the street.

For details and price-category definitions, *see* Dining in Staying in Denmark, *above*.

$$ **Copenhagen Corner.** Diners get a great view of the Rådhus Pladsen here, and terrific smørrebrød besides for reasonable prices—both of which compensate for often slack service provided by an overworked staff. Plants hang from the ceiling; waiters hustle platters of herring, steak, and other Danish-French dishes; and businesspeople clink glasses. In summer you can eat outside. *Rådhus Pladsen, tel. 33/91–45–45. Reservations advised. AE, DC, MC, V. Closed Dec. 24.*

$$ **El Meson.** Ceiling-hung pottery, swarthy waiters, and a top-notch
★ menu make this Copenhagen's best Spanish restaurant. Choose carefully for a moderately priced meal, which may include beef spiced with spearmint, lamb with a honey sauce, or paella valenciana for two. *Hauser Plads 12, tel. 33/11–91–31. Reservations advised. AE, DC, MC, V. Dinner only; closed Sun.*

Havfruen. A life-size wooden mermaid swings langorously from the ceiling in this snug fish restaurant in Nyhavn. Copenhagen natives love the maritime-bistro ambience and the French-inspired fish specialties. *Nyhavn 39, tel. 33/11–11–38. Reservations advised. DC, MC, V. Closed Sun.*

$$ **Ida Davidsen.** Five generations old, this world-renowned lunch place
★ has become synonymous with smørrebrød. Choose from creative open-face sandwiches, piled high with such ingredients as pâté, bacon, and steak tartare, as well as smoked duck, served with a beet salad and potatoes. *Skt. Kongensgade 70, tel. 33/91–36–55. Reservations advised. DC, MC, V. Lunch only. Closed weekends and July.*

$$ **Peder Oxe.** In a 17th-century square in the old center of town, the Peder Oxe is classically elegant, with whitewashed walls, wooden floors, a 15th-century Portuguese tiled kitchen, and crisp damask tablecloths. It's usually crowded with diners from every walk of life. Their mainly grilled fish and beef menu also includes an excellent all-you-can-eat salad bar. *Gråbrødretorv 11, tel. 33/11–00–77. DC, MC, V.*

$$ **Victor.** This French-style corner café offers great people-watching and bistro food. It's best during weekend lunches, when young and old gather for specialties like rib roast, homemade pâté, smoked salmon, and cheese platters. The menu changes—and becomes pricier after 6. *Ny Østergade 8, tel. 33/13–36–13. Reservations advised. AE, DC, MC, V.*

$ **Bacchullus.** Located off Strøget and backed with a small courtyard, Bacchullus is fashionably rustic and a mecca for the health-conscious. Well-dressed bohemians duck in here for the soothing music and the vegetarian choices such as hummus and warm pita bread, organic pizza, stuffed eggplant, and other healthful options from a buffet that relies heavily on grains, natural sweeteners, fresh fruit, and vegetables. *Grønnegade 12–14, tel. 33/15–16–90. Reservations accepted. D, MC, V. Closed Sun. lunch.*

$ **El Greco II.** The atmosphere, dutifully consisting of island-blue everything and tourist posters, is standard Greek-restaurant, but the food is the attraction. A lunch and dinner all-you-can-eat buffet includes potato and tomato stew, moussaka, calamari, mashed potatoes and garlic, oven-baked lamb, beef in red wine and onions, stuffed peppers, bean salads, cucumbers and yogurt, and more. One of the partners, Billy, is wont to meander from table to table like a swarthy mother hen, cajoling already stuffed diners to clean their plates. *Vesterbrogade 94, tel. 31/23–10–45 (El Greco I, Skindergade 20, tel. 33/32–93–44). Reservations required. AE, DC, MC, V.*

$ **Flyvefiske.** Silvery stenciled fish swim along blue-and-yellow walls in this funky Thai eatery. Among the city's more experimental (and spicy) restaurants, it offers chicken with cashew nuts, spicy shrimp soup with lemongrass, and herring shark in basil sauce. There is also a less expensive café in the basement that falls into the budget category. *Lars Bjørnstræde 18, tel. 33/14–95–15. AE, DC, MC, V. Closed Sun.*

$ **Krasnapolsky.** It's near the university, and there's a brooding youth at every table. The food is light and inventive—market-fresh produce is used religiously. Not as healthy as the quiches and sandwiches, but equally delicious, are the cakes and tarts, made in-house. *Vestergade 10, tel. 33/32–88–00. Reservations accepted. No credit cards.*

¢ **Quattro Fontane.** Chatty Italian waiters and a very affordable menu make one of Copenhagen's best Italian restaurants a boisterous affair, packed tight with locals and students. The list of homemade pastas includes cheese or beef ravioli or cannelloni and linguine topped with a variety of sauces. The pizza is excellent, the ice cream, shameless—and both are also available from the carryout in Frederiksberg. (Falkonér Allé, tel. 38/39–49–82). *Guldbergsgade 3, tel. 31/39–39–31. Reservations advised, especially on weekends. No credit cards.*

¢ **Riz Raz.** Located on a corner off Strøget, this Middle Eastern restaurant is a favorite with locals, who pack it to bursting on weekends. The all-you-can-eat buffet is heaped with lentils, tomatoes, potatoes, olives, hummus, warm pita bread, *kufte* (Middle Eastern meatballs), yogurt and cucumbers, pickled vegetables, bean salads, and occasionally even pizza. *Kompagnistræde 20, tel. 33/15–05–75. Reservations advised, essential on weekends. DC, MC, V. Closed Dec. 24–25, Jan. 1.*

Lodging

Copenhagen is well served by a wide range of hotels, and you can expect your accommodations to be clean, comfortable, and well run. Most Danish hotels include a substantial breakfast in the room rate, but this isn't always the case: Inquire when making reservations. During summer, reservations are always recommended, but if you should arrive without one, try the booking service at the *Vaerelseavivisning kiosk* (Rooms Service booth) in the central station. This service will also locate rooms in private homes, with rates starting at about 140 kr. for a single.

For details and price-category definitions, *see* Lodging in Staying in Denmark, *above*.

Splurge **Cab-Inn Copenhagen.** Copenhagen's answer to Japanese-style hotel minirooms is more cozy than futuristic, with shiplike "berths" brightly decorated. All offer standard hotel furnishings, including private shower and, albeit their small size, wall-hangable desks and chairs. *Vodroffsvej 55, 1900 FR C, tel. 35/36–11–11, fax 35/36–11–14. 201 rooms with shower. Facilities: café, exercise room (Also 86-room location, Danasvej 32, tel. 31/21–04–00, fax 31/21–74–09.) AE, DC, MC, V.*

Splurge **Skovshoved.** After thorough renovations in 1994, this 400-year-old gingerbread villa-hotel moved up into the splurge category, but its fishing-village surroundings and art-packed atmosphere make it worthwhile. The rooms differ in size and decor, but all are furnished in bright, modern prints and a mix of modern and antique furniture. The modern art-filled lobby and adjacent sitting room are similarly tropical. The hotel is 15 miles from the center of Copenhagen; Bus. 6 takes 45 minutes to the Town Hall Square. The restaurant provides gourmet dishes but ranks in the $$$ category; a pub serves more inexpensive sandwiches and light fare. *Strandvejen 267, 2920 Charlottenlund, tel. 31/64–00–28, fax 31/64–06–72. 20 rooms with bath. Facilities: meeting room. AE, DC, MC, V.*

$$ **Ascot.** A charming old building in the city's downtown area, this family-owned hotel has a classical columned entrance and an excellent breakfast buffet. The rooms have colorful geometric-pattern bedspreads and cozy bathrooms. Many have been remodeled; a few have kitchenettes. They also vary in size and decor, but all are so homey that repeat guests often ask for their regular rooms. *Studiestræde 61, 1554 KBH V, tel. 33/12–60–00, fax 33/14–60–40. 143 rooms, 30 apartments, all with bath. Facilities: meeting rooms, restaurant (breakfast only), bar. AE, DC, MC, V.*

$$ **Copenhagen Admiral.** A five-minute stroll from Nyhavn, this converted 18th-century granary has a massive and imposing exterior. Inside, sturdy wooden beams harmonize with an ultramodern decor. A few duplex suites are in the $$$ category, but for the most part, this is one of the less expensive top hotels, cutting both frills and prices. *Toldbodogade 24–28, 1253 KBH K, tel. 33/11–82–82, fax 33/32–55–42. 365 rooms with bath. Facilities: restaurant, bar, café, sauna. AE, MC, V.*

$$ **Mayfair.** Like its neighbors, the Webers and the Triton, this hotel is near Copenhagen's half-hearted red-light district and busy, shop-lined Vesterbrogade. Guests are greeted by an austere, English-style lobby where they can sip complimentary coffee before heading to rooms decorated with dark-wood furniture and gold-toned upholstery. *Helgolandsgade 3, 1653 KBH V, tel. 31/31–48–01, fax 31/23–96–86. 102 rooms with bath, 4 suites. Facilities: meeting room, breakfast. AE, DC, MC, V.*

$$ **Sophie Amalie Hotel.** While the D'Angleterre hotel is deliciously palatial, its smaller sister hotel is commonsense and no-frills. The pretty, pink lobby has a fountain and bar, and the cozy, pastel-toned rooms overlook the harbor, Amalienborg Palace, or the modest town skyline. *Skt. Annæ Plads 21, 1250 KBH K, tel. 33/13–34–00, fax 33/11–77–07. 134 rooms with bath, 17 suites. Facilities: restaurant, bar, meeting rooms, parking, sauna. AE, DC, MC, V.*

$$ **Triton.** Streamlined and modern, the Triton has a cosmopolitan clientele and a central location. The large rooms, in blond wood and warm tones, are equipped with every modern convenience, and most of the bathrooms have been modernized. The buffet breakfast is exceptionally generous. *Helgolandsgade 7–11, 1653 KBH V, tel. 31/31–32–66, fax 31/31–69–70. 123 rooms with bath. Facilities: restaurant (breakfast only), bar. AE, DC, MC, V.*

$$ **Webers Hotel.** This recently renovated hotel offers downtown style and conveniences, like classical decor and a small gym, in the working-class neighborhood of Vesterbro. Crystal chandeliers flash in the lobby, while guest rooms are bright and new, with zippy geometric upholstery and posters. *Vesterbrogade 11B, 1620 KBH V, tel.*

31/31–14–32, fax 31/31–14–41. 100 rooms with bath. Facilities: bar, meeting rooms, sauna, exercise room, breakfast. AE, DC, MC, V.

$ **Missionhotellet Nebo.** This hotel is comfortable and even prim, despite the dubious location, between the main train station and Istedgade's seediest porn shops. Well maintained by a friendly staff, the guest rooms are furnished with industrial carpeting and polished pine furniture. Half the rooms have baths, the others share baths and toilets in the hallway; downstairs there's a breakfast restaurant with a tiny courtyard. *Istedgade 6, 1650 KBH V, tel. 31/21–12–17, fax 31/23–47–74. Facilities: breakfast.*

$ **Verstersøhus.** What this hotel lacks in charm, it makes up for in location: It's across the street from swan-filled lakes and just a 10-minute walk to Strøget. The rooms are simple, with '60s-style furniture, but they're also convenient, especially for budget-minded families who want an apartment with a kitchenette. *Vestersøgade 58, 1601 KBH V, tel. 33/11–38–70, fax 33/11–00–90. 44 rooms, 35 with shower, 15 with kitchenette. Facilities: breakfast. AE, DC, MC, V. Closed Dec. 24–Jan. 2.*

$ **Viking.** A comfortable, century-old former mansion close to Amalienborg Castle, Nyhavn, and the Little Mermaid, the Viking is convenient to most sights and public transportation. The rooms are surprisingly spacious. *Bredgade 65, 1260 KBH K, tel. 33/12–45–50, fax 33/12–46–18. 89 rooms, 19 with bath. Facilities: restaurant (breakfast only). AE, DC, MC, V.*

¢ **Missionshotelet Ansgar.** The neighborhood, Copenhagen's red-light district, is nothing to write home about, but accommodations are clean and sufficient if you value function over form. The location may be, er, colorful, but it is convenient—around the corner from the main train station and a 10-minute walk to Tivoli. *Colbjørnsensgade 29, 1653 KBH V, tel. 31/21–21–96, fax 31/21–61–91. 87 rooms, 68 with shower. Facilities: breakfast. AE, DC, MC, V. Closed Dec. 24–Jan. 2.*

The Arts

Copenhagen This Week has good information on musical and theatrical events, as well as special events and exhibitions. Concert and festival information is available from the **Dansk Musik Information Center (DMIC,** Vimmelskaftet 48, tel. 33/11–20–66). **Billetnet** (tel. 35/28–91–83), the post office box office, has tickets for most major events. Keep in mind that same-day purchases at the box office **ARTE** (near the Nørreport Station) will give you half off. Copenhagen's main theater and concert season runs from September through May, and tickets can be obtained either directly from theaters and concert halls or from ticket agencies; ask your hotel concierge for advice.

Music Tivoli Concert Hall (Vesterbrogade 3, tel. 33/15–10–12), home of the Zealand Symphony Orchestra, offers more than 150 concerts (many free of charge) each summer, featuring a host of Danish and foreign soloists, conductors, and orchestras.

Theater, The **Royal Theater** (Kongens Nytorv, tel. 33/14–10–02) regularly
Opera, and holds performances alternating among theater, ballet, and opera.
Ballet For English-language theater, call either the professional **London Toast Theatre** (tel. 33/33–80–25) or the amateur **Copenhagen Theatre Circle** (tel. 31/62–86–20).

Nightlife

Many of the city's restaurants, cafés, bars, and clubs stay open after midnight, some as late as 5 AM. Copenhagen is famous for jazz, but you'll find night spots catering to musical tastes ranging from bop to ballroom music. Younger tourists should make for the district around the Nikolaj Kirke, which has scores of trendy discos and dance spots.

Privé (Ny Østergade 14), tel. 33/13–75–20) is a Euro-techno-pop disco favored by the young and painfully chic. **Rosie McGee's** (Vesterbrogade 2A, tel. 33/32–19–23) is hugely popular with a mixed crowd of both young and old, who come for the international pop and rock, cavernous English-pub atmosphere, and good-natured rowdiness.

A few streets behind the railway station is Copenhagen's red-light district, where sex shops share space with Asian grocers. While the area is fairly well lighted and lively, women may feel uncomfortable going there alone at night.

Nightclubs Probably the most exclusive nightclub is **Fellini's** in the SAS Royal (Hammerichsgade 1, tel. 33/93–32–39). Jet-setters and 007-wannabes now head to the **Copenhagen Casino** at the SAS Scandinavia Hotel (Amager Blvd. 70, tel. 33/11–23–24).

Jazz Copenhagen has a worldwide reputation for sophisticated jazz clubs, though, sadly, many have closed in the past couple of years. **La Fontaine** (Kompagnistræde 11) is Copenhagen's quintessential jazz dive; the bordello atmosphere and Scandinavian jazz talent make this a must. **Copenhagen Jazz House** (Niels Hemmingsensgade 10, tel. 33/15–26–00) is more upscale than La Fontaine, attracting European and some international names. **Jazzhus Slukefter** (Vesterbrogade 3, tel. 33/11–11–13), Tivoli's jazz club, lures some of the biggest names in the world.

Odense

It was Hans Christian Andersen, the region's most famous native, who dubbed Funen (Fyn in Danish) "The Garden of Denmark." Part orchard, part farmland, Funen is sandwiched between Zealand and Jutland, and with its tidy, rolling landscape, seaside towns, manor houses, and castles, it is one of Denmark's loveliest islands. Its capital is 1,000-year-old Odense in the north, one of Denmark's best-known cities and the birthplace of Hans Christian Andersen. It has two museums detailing his life and works.

Getting Around

Frequent trains link Copenhagen and Odense; the trip takes between two and three hours. Most of the sights are in the old heart of town, within a mile radius. For those sights a bit out of the way, like the open-air Funen Village, there are local buses and, where appropriate, boat service.

Tourist Information

The tourist office at **Odense** (Rådhuset, tel. 66/12–75–20) can provide information about the **Odense Eventyr Pass** (Adventure Pass), which provides admission to most museums and sights, free bus transportation, and discounts for city tours and plays. The two-day pass costs 100 kr. for adults and 50 kr. for children under 14.

Exploring Odense

Plan on spending at least one night here in Denmark's third-largest city. In addition to its museums and pleasant pedestrian streets, Odense gives one a good feel for a provincial capital.

If you can't take quaintness, don't go to the **H. C. Andersens Hus** (Hans Christian Andersen Museum). The surrounding area has been carefully preserved, with cobbled pedestrian streets and low houses with lace curtains. Inside, the detailed exhibits use photos, diaries, drawings, and letters to convey a sense of the man and the time in which he lived. Among the most evocative rooms is one furnished exactly like his Copenhagen study; notice the immense size of his long, narrow boots, casually tossed into a corner. *Ramsherred, tel. 66/13-13-72, ext. 4662. Admission: 20 kr. adults, 10 kr. children under 14. Open May and Sept., daily 10-5; June-Aug., daily 9-6.*

Nearby is the **Carl Nielsen Museum,** a modern structure with multimedia exhibits on Denmark's most famous composer (1865–1931) and his wife, the sculptor Anne Marie Carl-Nielsen. *Claus BergsGade 11, tel. 66/13-13-72, ext. 4671. Admission: 15 kr. adults, 5 kr. children. Open daily 10-4.*

Brandt's Passage, off Vestergade, is a heavily boutiqued walking street. At the end of it, in what was once a textile factory, is a four-story art gallery, the Brandts Klædefabrik, incorporating the **Museum for Photographic Art,** the **Graphic Museum,** and other spaces, with temporary exhibits for video art. It's well worth the short walk to see Funen's version of a Soho loft. *37-43 Brandts Passage, tel. 66/13-78-97. Admission: 20-25 kr. to each museum; 40 kr. for entrance to both. Open Tues.-Fri. 10-5, weekends 11-5.*

Don't neglect **Den Fynske Landsby** (Funen Village), 3 kilometers (2 miles) south; an enjoyable way of getting there is to travel down the Odense River by boat. The open-air museum-village is made up of 20 farm buildings, including workshops, a vicarage, a water mill, and a windmill. There's a theater, too, which in summer stages adaptations of Andersen's tales. *Sejerskovvej 20, tel. 66/13-13-72, ext. 4642. Admission: 20 kr. adults, 10 kr. children. Open Apr.-mid-May and mid-Sept.-end-Oct., daily 10-5; mid-May-mid-Sept., daily 10-7.*

Dining and Lodging

Odense boasts a wide range of hotels and inns, many of which offer off-season (October through May) rates, as well as special weekend deals. The city is also endowed with campsites and a youth hostel set in an old manor house. For details and price-category definitions, *see* Dining and Lodging in Staying in Denmark, *above*.

Dining

$$
★
Frank A. Guarded by a meter-tall wooden bulldog named Tobias, this merry meeting place is dominated by its display of high-kitsch curios and paintings and an unfathomable collection of bric-a-brac. Friendly waiters serve drinks and French-inspired Danish dishes like ham schnitzel with creamed potatoes and pepper steak flambé to a mostly local crowd. *Jernbanegade 4, tel. 66/12-27-57. Reservations accepted. DC, MC, V.*

$$ **Restaurant Provence.** Tucked a few minutes from the pedestrian street, this cozy, blue-and-white dining room puts a Danish twist on Provençal cuisine. Specialties include venison with blackberry sauce and duck breast cooked in sherry. *Pogstræde 31, tel. 66/12-12-96. Reservations advised. DC, MC, V.*

$ **Air Pub.** This friendly, airplane-theme bar and restaurant is one of Odense's most popular meeting places. Because it's also on one of the pedestrian streets, it's the perfect lunch spot for a quick sandwich and beer. *Kongensgade 41, tel. 66/14-66-08. No reservations. No credit cards.*

$ **Den Grimme Ælling.** The name of this chain restaurant, translated as the Ugly Duckling, really isn't appropriate here. The family-style interiors are homey, with pine furnishings. Thanks to an all-you-can-eat buffet heaped with cold and warm dishes, it's very popular with locals and visitors. *Hans Jensens Stræde 1, tel. 65/91-70-30. Reservations advised. DC, MC.*

¢ **Målet.** A spirited local clientele frequents this sports club and restaurant filled with soccer memorabilia. Schnitzels are the specialty, prepared with mushrooms, paprika, or even Italian and Madagascar style. *Jernbanegade 17, tel. 66/17–82–41. No reservations. No credit cards.*

Lodging   **Missionshotellet Ansgar.** The rooms are a trifle boxlike, but clean
    $$ and comfortable nonetheless. This hotel offers solid lodgings (with
satellite television) near the station. *Østre Stationsvej 32, 5000
Odense C, tel. 66/11–96–93, fax 66/11–96–75. 44 rooms with bath.
MC, V.*

    $ **Ydes Hotel.** This bright, colorful hotel is a good bet for students and
budget-conscious travelers tired of barrack-type accommodations.
The plain, white, hospital-style rooms are clean and comfortable.
*Hans Tausensgade 11, 5000 Odense C, tel. 66/12–11–31, fax 66/12–
17–82. 28 rooms, 19 with shower. Facilities: breakfast, bar. AE, DC,
MC, V.*

7 Finland

Prices in Finland have dropped with respect to the other Nordic countries. Still, the dollar's recent tumble has been especially rough here. Although prices—like weather—are subject to change, budget travelers can still head to Finland now, while the living is relatively easy.

If you like majestic open spaces, fine architecture, and civilized living, then Finland is for you. It is a land of lakes—187,888 at the last count—and forests. It is a land where nature is so prized that even the design of city buildings reflects the soaring spaces of the countryside.

The music of Sibelius, Finland's most famous son, tells you what to expect from this Nordic landscape. Both can swing from the somber nocturne of midwinter darkness to the tremolo of sunlight slanting through pine and bone-white birch or from the crescendo of a sunset before it fades into the next day's dawn. Similarly, the Finnish people reflect the changing moods of their land and climate. They can get annoyed when described as "children of nature," but the description is apt. Their affinity with nature has produced some of the world's greatest designers and architects.

Until 1917, Finland (the Finns call it *Suomi)* was under the domination of its nearest neighbors, Sweden and Russia, which fought over it for centuries. After more than 600 years under Swedish rule and 100 under the czars, the country inevitably bears many traces of these two cultures, including a small (6%) but influential Swedish-speaking population and a scattering of Russian Orthodox churches.

But the Finns themselves are neither Scandinavian nor Slavic. All that is known of their origins—they speak a Finno-Ugric tongue, part Finnish, part Hungarian—is that they are descended from wandering groups of people who probably came from west of the Ural Mountains before the Christian era and settled on the swampy shores of the Gulf of Finland.

There is a tough, resilient quality in the Finns. No other people fought the Soviets to a standstill as the Finns did in the Winter War

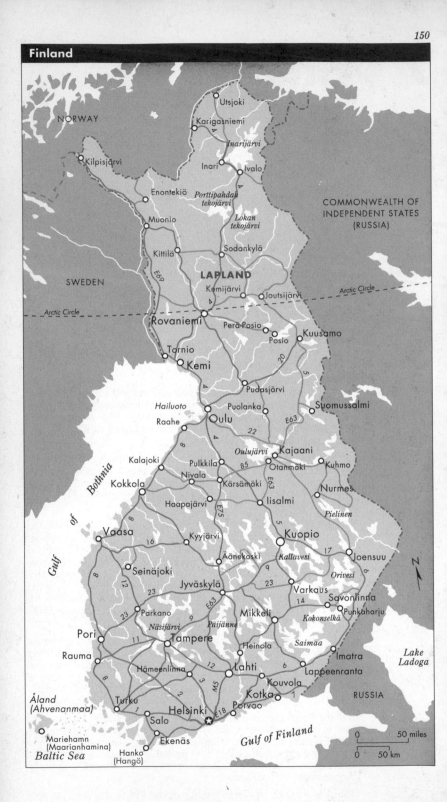

of 1939–40. This resilience, in part, stems from the turbulence of the country's past, but also comes from the people's strength and determination to work the land and survive the long winters. No wonder there is a poet-philosopher lurking in most Finns, one who sometimes drowns his melancholic, darker side in the bottle. For Finns are in a state of constant confrontation—with the weather, the land, and an eastern neighbor that is engulfed in political and economic turmoil. Finns are stubborn, patriotic, and self-sufficient, yet not aggressively nationalistic. On the contrary, rather than being proud of past battles, Finns are proud of finding ways to live in peace. Their country's independence and their own personal freedom are what they tenaciously hold on to and will never easily relinquish.

The average Finn doesn't volunteer much information, but that's due to reserve, not indifference. Make the first approach and you may have a friend for life. Finns like their silent spaces, though, and won't appreciate back-slapping familiarity—least of all in the sauna, still regarded by many as a spiritual, as well as a cleansing, experience.

Essential Information

Before You Go

When to Go The tourist summer season runs from mid-June until mid August, a magnificently sunny and generally dry time marked by unusually warm temperatures in recent years. This is when most Finns move to summer homes, called *kesämökki*, at the seaside or lakefront to enjoy the "white nights," the long days of the midnight sun. Outside this period, many amenities and attractions either close or operate on much reduced schedules. But there are advantages to visiting Finland off-season, not the least being that you avoid the mosquitoes, which can be fearsome, especially in the north. The fall colors (from early September in the far north, October in the south) are spectacular. January through March (through April in the north) is the main cross-country skiing season, and in the lengthening spring days you can get a great suntan. Spring is brief but magical, as the snows melt, the ice breaks up, and nature explodes into life almost overnight.

Climate Generally speaking, the spring and summer seasons begin a month earlier in the south of Finland than they do in the far north. You can expect warm (not hot) days in Helsinki from mid-May. The midnight sun can be seen from May to July, depending on the region. In midwinter there is a corresponding period in the north when the sun does not rise at all, but it is possible to see magnificent displays of the Northern Lights. Even in Helsinki, summer nights are brief and never really dark, whereas in midwinter daylight lasts only a few hours.

The following are average daily maximum and minimum temperatures for Helsinki.

Jan.	26F	-3C	**May**	56F	13C	**Sept.**	56F	13C
	17	-8		44	6		46	8
Feb.	26F	-3C	**June**	66F	19C	**Oct.**	49F	9C
	17	-8		51	10		39	4
Mar.	34F	1C	**July**	73F	23C	**Nov.**	39F	4C
	23	-5		57	14		30	- 1
Apr.	44F	6C	**Aug.**	66F	19C	**Dec.**	32F	0C
	32	0		55	13		21	- 6

Currency The unit of currency in Finland is the Finnmark (FIM), divided into 100 penniä. There are bills of FIM 20, 50, 100, 500, and 1,000. Coins are 10 and 50 penniä, and FIM 1, FIM 5, and FIM 10. At press time (summer 1995), the exchange rate was about FIM 3.9 to the dollar and about FIM 6.59 to the pound sterling. Credit cards are widely accepted, even in many taxicabs. Traveler's checks can be changed only in banks.

What It Will Cost Prices are highest in Helsinki; otherwise they vary little throughout the country. Taxes are already included in hotel and restaurant charges, and there is no airport departure tax. However, the price of many goods includes an 18% sales tax, less on food (*see* Shopping in Staying in Finland, *below*).

Sample Prices Cup of coffee, FIM 5; glass of beer, FIM 10–FIM 20; Coca-Cola, FIM 7; ham sandwich, FIM 15–FIM 20; 1-mile taxi ride, about FIM 20.

Customs on Arrival Visitors to Finland may import goods for their own use from another EU country duty-free, with the exception of alcohol and tobacco. Visitors over 22 years old may bring in 1 liter of spirits or 3 liters of aperitives (over 22 percent alcohol by volume) or 3 liters of sparkling wines, plus 5 liters of table wine and 15 liters of beer. Spirits containing over 60 percent alcohol by volume may not be brought into Finland. Visitors aged 18–22 years old may not bring in spirits, but may import other drinks listed above. If the items were purchased in a duty-free shop at an airport or harbor, or onboard an airplane or ship, visitors may bring in 1 liter of spirits, 2 liters of aperitives or sparkling wines, 2 liters of table wine and 15 liters of beer. Visitors over 17 years old may bring in 300 cigarettes, 75 cigars, or 400 grams of tobacco (about 13 ounces). If the items were purchased at a duty-free shop, 200 cigarettes, 50 cigars, or 250 grams (about 8 ounces) of tobacco are allowed. Goods up to a value of FIM 1,100 may be imported, but be sure to check restrictions on the amount and type of foodstuffs allowed. Dogs and cats may be brought into Finland quarantine-free when they have a veterinarian's certificate stating that they have had an antirabies vaccine at least 30 days and not more than 12 months prior to importation.

Language The official languages of Finland are Finnish and Swedish, though only a small minority (about 6%) speak Swedish. English is widely spoken among people in the travel industry and by many younger Finns, though they're often shy about using it. Nearly all tourist sites and attractions provide texts in English.

Getting Around

By Train Finland's extensive rail system reaches all main centers of the country and offers high standards of comfort and cleanliness.

Fares A Finnrail pass entitles you to 3, 5, or 10 days of travel in a four-week period. On the days you travel, you may go round-trip or one-way. Second-class prices are FIM 505 (three travel days), FIM 685 (five days), and FIM 945 (10 days); first-class tickets are FIM 760 (three travel days), FIM 1030 (five days), and FIM 1420 (10 days). Children under 17 years old pay half fare. These tickets can be purchased in and out of the country. In Finland, the Finnrail Pass is available from Finnish state railways (VR, tel. 90/100123; in Helsinki, 0100123). In the United States and Canada, call **Rail Europe** (tel. 914/682–2999, fax 914/682–2821); in the United Kingdom, contact **Finlandia Travel** (tel. 071/409–7334). Other discounts apply to children, groups, and senior citizens. Reservations are essential on special fast trains.

By Plane Finnair (tel. 90/818800) operates a network of flights linking 25 towns in Finland. For $377, a **Holiday Ticket** includes 10 flight coupons valid for any domestic Finnair flight. Finnair grants visitors under 25 years old a 60% **Youth Discount** on flights booked ahead. Senior citizens, children, and groups are eligible for other discounts. Tickets are available in most countries. In Finland, they can be purchased at major travel agencies and Finnair offices.

By Bus Bus travel plays a leading role in Finland, and the country's bus system provides the most extensive travel network of all; it can take you virtually anywhere. A **Coach Holiday Ticket,** available from bus stations and travel agencies, entitles you to 1,000 kilometers (625 miles) of bus travel for FIM 320 for two weeks. The Holiday Ticket is ⅔ off the normal price. Schedule information is available from Oy Matkahuolto Ab (tel. 358/0/613681).

By Boat Helsinki and Turku have regular sea links with the Åland Islands in the Baltic Sea. From mid-June to mid-August you can cruise the labyrinthine lakes of the Finnish interior. Try to include at least one of these trips in your itinerary. Complete timetables are available from the Finnish Tourist Board.

By Bicycle Planned bicycle routes are provided in many areas. The main advantages for the cyclist are the lack of steep hills and the absence of heavy traffic. Bikes can be rented in most youth hostels. The Finnish **Youth Hostel Association** (Yrjönkatu 38B, Helsinki, tel. 90/694–0377) offers accommodation packages of 4, 7, or 14 days to tie in with visitors' cycling tours.

Staying in Finland

Telephones To avoid exorbitant hotel surcharges on calls, use the public pay
Local Calls phones. Have some FIM 1 and FIM 5 coins ready. Note that the Finnish letters å, ä, and ö come at the end of the alphabet; this may be useful when looking up names in the telephone book. For information about telephone charges, dial 92020; for number inquiries, dial 118.

International You can dial directly to Britain and the United States from any-
Calls where in Finland. Calls to other countries can be made from a telegraph office; these are marked LENNÄTIN or TELE and usually adjoin the post office. An operator will assign you a private booth and collect payment at the end of the call. To dial the numbers listed in this guide from outside of Finland, omit the "9" at the beginning of the city code. To make a direct international phone call from Finland, dial 990, then the appropriate country code and phone number. For an **AT&T** long-distance operator, dial 9800–10010; for **MCI,** 9800–10280; for **Sprint,** 9800–10284.

Country Code The country code for Finland is 358.

Mail At press time (summer 1995), airmail rates to North America were
Postal Rates FIM 3.40 for a letter of up to 20 grams. Letters to the United Kingdom cost FIM 2.90.

Receiving Mail If you're uncertain about where you'll be staying, be sure that mail sent to you is marked "Poste Restante" and addressed to the Main Post Office, Mannerheimintie 11, 00100 Helsinki, or to major post offices in other towns. American Express (AREA Matkatoimisto Oy, Pohjoisesplanadi 2, tel. 90/628788) offers a free clients' mail service and will hold mail for up to one month. The Finland Travel Bureau also provides a free mail service for foreigners: Mail should be addressed to its Mail Department, Box 319, 00101 Helsinki, and collected from the office at Kaivokatu 10A.

Shopping If you purchase goods worth more than FIM 100 in any of the many
Sales Tax shops marked "tax-free for tourists," you can get a 12%–16% refund
Refunds when you leave Finland. Show your passport and the store will give you a check for the appropriate amount that you can cash at most departure points from the EU. This refund is available for non-EU residents only.

Opening and Closing Times

Banks. Open weekdays 9:15–4:15.

Museums. Opening hours vary considerably, so check individual listings. Most close one day a week, usually Monday. Many museums in the countryside are open only during the summer months.

Shops. Most are open weekdays 9–6, Saturday 9–2. Department stores and supermarkets sometimes stay open until 8 from Monday through Friday.

National Holidays

In 1996: January 1, January 6 (Epiphany), Good Friday, Easter, and Easter Monday (April 5, April 7–8), May 1 (May Day), May 16 (Ascension), May 26 (Pentecost), Midsummer's Eve and Day (June 20–21), November 1 (All Saints' Day), December 6 (Independence Day), December 25–26. Changing holidays in 1997: Good Friday, Easter, and Easter Monday (March 28, March 30–1), May 8 (Ascension), May 18 (Pentecost), Midsummer's Eve and Day (June 19–20).

Dining

Most restaurants offer lunch specials and/or set business lunches that are up to 50% cheaper than their à la carte menus. Eating your main meal at lunchtime rather than in the evening is a money-saving strategy that will allow you to eat in some of Helsinki's better restaurants quite reasonably. You can find bargain meals at Finland's many cafes and *grilli* (grills), although quality varies considerably. Most large supermarkets and indoor market halls sell prepared food perfect for picnicking. Finland's high standards of hygiene make it possible for visitors to eat out at grill stands. At budget prices, these offer basic Finnish fast food at its best, including hamburgers and sausages.

As in other parts of Scandinavia, the *voileipäpöytä* (cold table) is often a work of art as well as a feast. It's sometimes available at lunchtime. Special Finnish dishes include *poronkäristys* (reindeer casserole); salmon, herring, and various freshwater fish; and *lihapullia* (meatballs) with a tasty sauce. Crayfish parties are popular between the end of July and early September. For a delicious dessert, try cloudberries (related to blackberries).

Mealtimes

The Finns eat early; lunch runs from 11 or noon to 1 or 2, dinner from 4 to 7 (a bit later in Helsinki).

What to Wear

Except for the most elegant restaurants, where a jacket and tie are preferred, casual attire is acceptable for restaurants in all price categories.

Ratings

Prices are per person and include first course, main course, dessert, and service charge—but not wine. All restaurant checks include a service charge (*sisältää palvelupalkkion*). If you want to leave an additional tip—though it really isn't necessary—it's enough to round the figure off to the nearest FIM 5 or FIM 10. Best bets are indicated by a star ★.

Category	Helsinki	Other Areas
$$	over FIM 80	over FIM 70
$	FIM 40–FIM 80	FIM 40–FIM 70
¢	under FIM 40	under FIM 40

Lodging

The range of accommodations available in Finland includes hotels, motels, boarding houses, private homes, rented chalets and cottages, farmhouses, youth hostels, and campsites. There is no official system of classification, but standards are generally high. If you haven't reserved a room in advance, you can make reservations at the **Hotel Booking Center** at Helsinki's Railway Station (Rautatieasema, tel. 90/171133) or through a travel agency; the booking fee is FIM 10. Don't forget that hotel rates are usually 30%–40% cheaper in the summer than in the winter months. There are also special weekend rates.

Hotels Nearly all hotels in Finland are modern or will have been recently renovated; a few occupy fine old manor houses. Most have rooms with bath or shower. Prices generally include breakfast and often a morning sauna and swim. The **Finncheque** voucher system, operating in many hotels from June through August, offers good discounts. Only the first night can be reserved, but subsequent reservations can be made free from any Finncheque hotel. For additional information, inquire at the Hotel Booking Center or Finnish Tourist Board, Eteläesplanadi 4, Helsinki, tel. 90/403011.

Several hotel groups, such as Cumulus, Sokos-Hotels, Rantasipi, and Arctia, offer special packages, and unless there's a festival going on, some hotels reduce their prices substantially in July.

Summer Hotels University students' accommodations are turned into "summer hotels" from June through August; they offer modern facilities at slightly lower-than-average prices.

Boarding Houses These provide the least-expensive accommodations and are found only outside Helsinki. Local tourist offices have lists.

Rentals The choice is huge, and the chalets and cottages are nearly always in delightful lakeside or seashore settings. For comfortable (not luxurious) accommodations, count on paying FIM 1,000–FIM 3,500 for a four-person weekly rental. A central reservations agency is **Lomarengas** (Malminkaari 23C, Helsinki, tel. 90/3516–1321, or Eteläesplanadi 4, Helsinki, tel. 90/170611).

Youth Hostels These range from empty schools to small manor houses. There are no age restrictions, and prices range from FIM 45 to FIM 200 per bed. The Finnish Tourist Board can provide a list of hostels.

Camping There are about 350 Finnish campsites, all classified into one of three grades. All offer showers and cooking facilities, and many include cottages for rent. A list is available from the Finnish Tourist Board.

Ratings Prices are for two people in a double room and include breakfast and service charge. Best bets are indicated by a star ★.

Category	Helsinki	Other Areas
$$	over FIM 375	over FIM 300
$	FIM 200–FIM 375	FIM 175–FIM 300
¢	under FIM 200	under FIM 175

Tipping The Finns are less tip conscious than other Europeans. (For restaurant tips, *see* Dining, *above*.) Train and airport porters have a fixed charge. The obligatory checkroom fee of about FIM 5 is usually posted; if not, give FIM 5–FIM 10, depending on the number in your party.

Helsinki

Arriving and Departing

By Plane All international flights arrive at Helsinki's Vantaa Airport, 20 kilometers (12 miles) north of the city. For arrival and departure information, call 9700–8100.

Between the Airport and Downtown Finnair buses leave two to four times an hour for the city terminals, located at the Inter-Continental hotel (Töölönkatu 21, tel. 90/40551) and the Railway Station. The trip takes about 30 minutes and costs

FIM 22. A local bus service (No. 615), which takes about 40 minutes, goes to the Railway Station and costs FIM 15.

By Train Helsinki's Railway Station is in the heart of the city. For train information, phone 90/100121 (from Helsinki, 0100121).

By Bus The terminal for many local buses is the Railway Station square, Rautatientori. The main long-distance bus station is located off Mannerheimintie between Salomonkatu and Simonkatu. For information, phone 90/9600–4000.

By Sea The Silja Line terminal for ships arriving from Stockholm is at Olympialaituri, on the west side of the South Harbor. Ferries and hydrofoils arriving from Tallinn also dock at the Olympialaituri or the adjacent Makasiinilaituri. The Finnjet-Silja Line and Viking Lines terminal for ships arriving from Travemünde and Stockholm is at Katajanokka, on the east side of the South Harbor.

Getting Around

The center of Helsinki is compact and best explored on foot. However, the Helsinki City Tourist Office provides a free Helsinki route map that shows all public transportation. As far as public transportation tickets go, your best buy is the **Helsinki Card,** which gives unlimited travel on city public transportation, as well as free entry to many museums, a free sightseeing tour, and a variety of other discounts. It's available for one, two, or three days (FIM 95, FIM 135, and FIM 165); about half price for children). You can buy it at most hotels and at the Helsinki City Tourist Office. The **Helsinki City Transport Tourist Ticket** entitles visitors to unlimited travel on all public transportation. The ticket is FIM 25 (one day), FIM 50 (two days), or FIM 75 (three days). Children are half fare.

By Subway Helsinki's only subway line runs from Ruoholahti, just west of the city center, to Mellunmaki, in the eastern suburbs. It runs from 5:15 AM (later on weekends) to 11:30 PM. Rides within Helsinki cost FIM 9; tickets are sold at stations. Transfers are free within one hour of the start of travel. You can also buy a 10-trip ticket for FIM 75 at **R-Kiosks** and shops showing the Helsinki transport logo (a yellow circle with two curving arrows).

By Streetcar These run from 6 AM to 1:30 AM, depending on the line. They can be handy, and route maps and schedules are posted at most downtown stops. Tickets are the same as for the subway; single tram tickets are also sold onboard by drivers. Ten-trip tickets are also available as for the Metro. The Helsinki City Tourist Office distributes a pamphlet called "Helsinki Sightseeing: 3T" which describes points of interest along the 3T tram's downtown route.

By Boat In summer there are regular boat services from the South Harbor market square to the islands of Suomenlinna and Korkeasaari.

Important Addresses and Numbers

Tourist Information The **Helsinki City Tourist Office** is near the South Harbor (Pohjoisesplanadi 19, tel. 90/169–3757); open May 2–Sept., weekdays 8:30–6, weekends 10–3; Oct.–April, 8:30–4, closed weekends. The **Finnish Tourist Board's Tourist Information Office** (covering all Finland) is nearby at Eteläesplanadi 4, tel. 90/4030–1211 or 90/4030–1300; open June–August, weekdays 8:30–5, Sat. 10–2: from September–May, weekdays 8:30–4, closed weekends.

Embassies U.S. (Itäinen Puistotie 14, tel. 90/171931). **Canadian** (Pohjoisesplanadi 25B, tel. 90/171141). **U.K.** (Itäinen Puistotie 17, tel. 90/661293).

Emergencies General (tel. 112); Police (tel. 112); Ambulance (tel. 112); Doctor (tel. 10023); Dentist (tel. 90/736166).

Exploring Helsinki

Helsinki is a city of the sea, built on peninsulas and islands along the
Baltic shoreline. Streets curve around bays, bridges arch over to
nearby islands, and ferries carry traffic to destinations further off-
shore. Helsinki has grown dramatically since World War II, and now
makes up about ⅙ of Finland's population. The city covers a total of
433 square miles and includes 315 islands. Most sights, hotels and
restaurants, however, are on one peninsula—it forms a compact hub
of special interest to the visitor.

Helsinki is a relatively young city compared to other European capitals. In the sixteenth century, the Swedish king, Gustavus Vasa,
whose rule included present-day Finland, decided to woo trade from
the Estonian city of Tallinn, and thus challenge the Hanseatic
League's monopoly on Baltic trade. The city was founded on June
12, 1550, at the rapids of the Vantaa River, by people from four Finnish towns ordered to move there by the king.

Over the next three centuries, Helsinki (Helsingfors in Swedish)
had its ups and downs, suffering several fires and epidemics. Turku,
on Finland's west coast, was the capital and intellectual center. Helsinki did not take center stage until Finland was ceded by Sweden to
Russia in 1809. The Russian czar, Alexander I, made Finland an au-
tonomous grand duchy of Russia; he proclaimed Helsinki the capital
in 1812. About the same time, much of Turku burned to the ground,
forcing the university to move to Helsinki as well. From then on,
Helsinki's position as Finland's first city was guaranteed.

Fire also played a role in Helsinki's fortunes. Just before the czar's
proclamation, a fire destroyed many of Helsinki's traditional wood-
en buildings, necessitating the construction of a new city center.
The German-born architect Carl Ludvig Engel was commissioned to
rebuild the city, and, as a result, Helsinki has some of the purest neoclassical architecture in the world. Add to this foundation the stunning outlines of the Jugend period (early 20th century) and the
modern buildings designed by talented Finnish architects, and you
have a European capital city that is as architecturally eye-catching
as it is different from its Scandinavian neighbors or the rest of Europe.

*Numbers in the margin correspond to points of interest on the
Helsinki map.*

❶ Across from the city tourist office and beside the South Harbor is
the **Kauppatori,** frequented by Finns and tourists alike. All around
are stalls selling everything from colorful, freshly cut flowers to ripe
fruit, from vegetables trucked in from the hinterland to handicrafts
made in small villages. Look at the fruit stalls—mountains of straw-
berries, raspberries, blueberries, and, if you're lucky, *lakka* (cloudberries), which grow largely above the Arctic Circle in the midnight
sun. Closer to the dock are fresh fish, caught that morning in the
Baltic Sea and still flopping. The market is a hive of activity and, in a
sense, the heartbeat of everyday life in Helsinki. The market ends at
2 PM, and, in the summer, the fruit and vegetable stalls are replaced
with arts-and-crafts stalls. This happens at 3:30 PM and lasts until
about 8 PM.

❷ Across the street is the political center of Finland, the **Presidentin-
linna** (Presidential Palace), built as a private home in 1818 and converted for use by the czars in 1843. It was the official residence of
Finnish presidents from 1919 to 1993. It still houses President
Martti Ahtisaari's offices and is the scene of official receptions. Just
up the street is the city hall. Across from the palace is the waterfront, where ferries and sightseeing boats set out into the bay. On a
summer's day it is a sailor's vision: sails hoisted and taut to the wind
and island waters to explore. The redbrick edifice perched above the

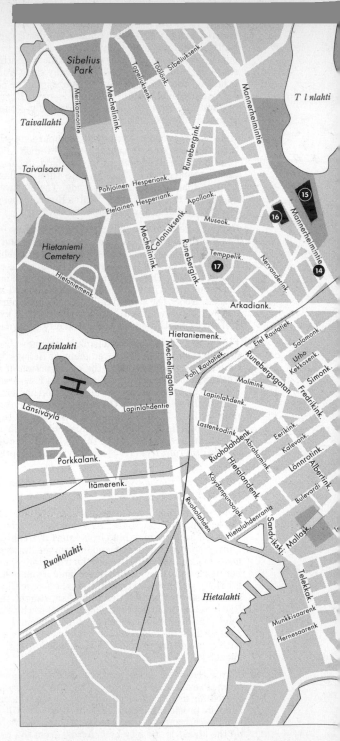

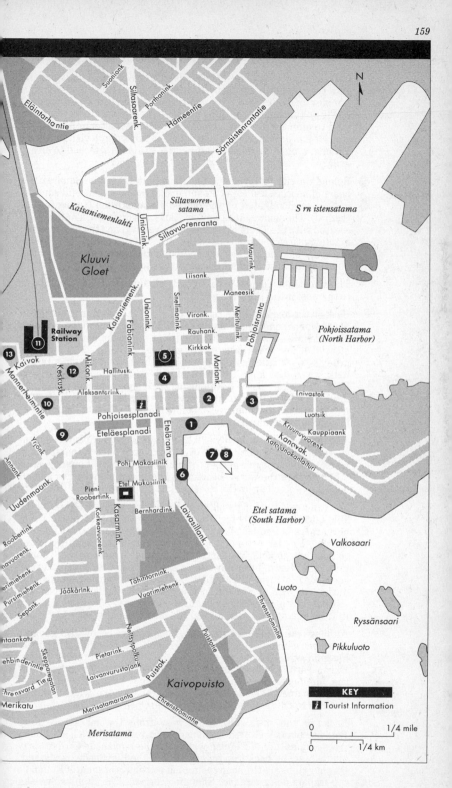

N

Suonionk.

Eläintarhantie

Siltasaarenk.

Porthaninik.

Hämeentie

Sörnäistenrantatie

S rn istensatama

Kaisaniemenlahti

Unionink.

Siltavuoren-
satama

Siltavuorenranta

Kluuvi
Gloet

Maurink.

Liisank.

Maneesik.

Pohjoissatama
(North Harbor)

Snellmanink.

Vironk.

Meritullink.

Kaisaniemenk.

**Railway
Station**

Fabianink.

Unionink.

Rauhank.

Kirkkok.

Pohjoisranta

13

Kaivok.

Mikonk.

11

12

Keskusk.

Hallitusk.

Aleksanterink.

5

4

Mariank.

Laivastok.

3

Luotsik.

Kruunuvuorenk.

Kauppiaank.

2

Mannerheimintie

10

Pohjoisesplanadi

Eteläesplanadi

1

Etelä:an a

Konevak.

Katajanokanlaituri

9

Yrjönk.

Annank.

7 **8**

Pohj Makasiinik.

6

Etel satama
(South Harbor)

Pieni
Roobertink.

Etel Mukasiinik.

Uudenmaank.

Bernhardink.

Kasarmink.

Laivasillank.

Valkosaari

Roobertink.

Korkeavuorenk.

navuorenk.

erimiehenk.

Pursimiehenk.

Jääkärlnk.

Tähtitorink.

Luoto

Ryssänsaari

Sepank.

Vuorimiehenk.

Neitsypolku

Puistok.

Pikkuluoto

htaankatu

Pietarink.

Ehrenströmintie

ehbinderintie

Skepparegatan

Laivanvarustajank.

Puistotie

Ehrensvard Tie egatan

Kaivopuisto

Merikatu

Merisalamaranta

Ehrenströmintie

KEY

ℹ️ Tourist Information

Merisatama

0   1/4 mile

0   1/4 km

❸ east side of the market is the Orthodox **Uspenskin Katedraali** (Uspenski Cathedral); its terrace affords a beautiful view of the bay.

Just behind the cathedral is the district of **Katajanokka.** Here the 19th-century brick warehouses are slowly being renovated to form a complex of boutiques, arts-and-crafts studios, and restaurants. You'll find innovative designs at these shops, and the restaurants tend to offer lighter fare, which can make this a tempting area to stop for lunch. While in Katajanokka, you may enjoy a visit to **Wanha Satama,** a small complex of cafés and food stores attached to an art gallery.

❹ Behind the city hall, you will find **Senaatintori** (Senate Square), the heart of neoclassical Helsinki and one of the most graceful squares **❺** in Europe, dominated by the domed **Tuomiokirkko** (Lutheran Cathedral). The square is the work of Carl Ludvig Engel. The harmony created with the Tuomiokirkko, the university, and the state council building places you amid one of the purest styles of European architecture. Senaatintori has a dignified, stately air, enlivened by the bustle around the Kiseleff Bazaar on the square's south side.

The streets leading off Senaatintori contain government buildings; to the west is the University of Helsinki.

Back on the market, head southward along the western shore of the South Harbor on Eteläranta Street. You'll soon come to the old brick **❻** **Market Hall**—it's worth taking a look at the voluminous displays of meat, fish, and other gastronomic goodies (open weekdays 8–5, Saturday 8–2). A little farther on are the **Makasiini and Olympia Terminals,** where the huge ferries from Sweden, Estonia, and Poland berth. Beyond this is **Kaivopuisto,** the elegant parkland district much favored by Russian high society during the 19th century. It is now popular as a strolling ground for Helsinki's citizens and as a residential area for diplomats.

Just around the headland you'll spot a peculiarly Finnish tradition: special platforms jutting out over the water (either the sea or a lake), on which people gather to scrub their carpets. Laundry, as in other parts of the world, becomes a lively, communal affair and an occasion to catch up on the latest gossip.

You can avoid the long walk back by cutting across Kaivopuisto to Tehtaankatu and catching Streetcar 3T to the marketplace. From **❼** here, there is frequent ferry service to **Suomenlinna,** or "Finland's Castle." Finnish units of the Swedish army began construction of this fortress in 1748. The fortress' six islands, known as the "Gibraltar of the North," were Sweden's shield against Russia until their surrender to Russia, without a fight, by the Swedish commander during the War of Finland in 1808. The commander's motives are still not fully understood by historians. A heavy British naval attack in 1855, during the Crimean War, damaged the fortress.

Although still a military garrison, Suomenlinna is now also a collection of museums and parks. In early summer, it is engulfed in purple lilacs introduced from Versailles by the Finnish architect Augustin Ehrensvärd. Children enjoy exploring the nooks and crannies of the fortifications. One museum you may wish to visit is the **❽** **Pohjoismainen Taidekeskus** (Nordic Arts Center), which exhibits work by Nordic artists. *Admission free. Open Tues.–Sun. 11–6.*

Back on the mainland, head west from the marketplace up **Pohjoisesplanadi** (North Esplanade). To your left, the leafy linden trees and statues of Finnish writers in the Esplanade gardens provide a peaceful backdrop for concerts at the Esplanade bandstand. On your right are the showrooms and boutiques of some of Finland's **❾** top fashion designers (*see* Shopping, *below*). The circular **Svenska Teatern** (Swedish Theater) marks the junction of the Esplanade and Helsinki's main artery, Mannerheimintie.

⑩ If you take a right up Keskuskatu, you'll come to **Stockmann's,** Helsinki's most famous department store, well worth a shopping
⑪ stop. Next you'll come to the **Railway Station** and its square, the bustling commuting hub of the city. The station's huge red-granite figures are by Emil Wikström, but the solid building they adorn was designed by Eliel Saarinen, one of the founders of the early 20th-
⑫ century National Romantic style. The **Ateneumin Taidemuseo,** Finland's central art museum, is on the south side of the square facing the **National Theater.** *Admission: FIM 10 adults, children free. Open year-round Tues., Thurs., and Fri. 9–5; Wed. 9–9; weekends 11–5.*

⑬ In front of the main post office west of the station is the **statue of Marshal Mannerheim** gazing down Mannerheimintie, the major thoroughfare named in his honor. Perhaps no man in Finnish history is so revered as Marshal Baron Carl Gustaf Mannerheim, the military and political leader who guided Finland through much of the turbulent 20th century. When he died in Switzerland on January 28, 1951, his body was flown back to his native land to lie in state in the cathedral. For three days, young war widows, children, and soldiers filed past his bier by the thousands. In 1994, plans to move the statue to build a new museum were met with a public outcry that forced architects back to the drawing board.

⑭ About half a mile along, past the colonnaded red-granite **Parliament**
⑮ **House,** stands **Finlandiatalo** (Finland Hall), one of the last creations of Alvar Aalto. Behind the hall lies the inland bay of Töölönlahti and,
⑯ almost opposite, the **Suomen Kansallismuseo** (National Museum), another example of National Romantic exotica in which Eliel Saarinen played a part. *Admission: FIM 15 adults, children free. Open June–Aug., Tues. 11–8, Wed.–Sun. 11–5; Sept.–May, Tues. 11–8, Wed.–Sun. 11–4.*

⑰ Tucked away in a labyrinth of streets to the west is the strikingly modern **Temppeliaukion Kirkko** (Temple Square Church). Carved out of solid rock and topped with a copper dome, this Helsinki landmark is a center for religious activities, church services, and concerts. From here it's only a short distance back to Mannerheimintie, where you can pick up any streetcar for the downtown area. *Lutherinkatu 3. Open year-round 11–8. Closed Tues. 1–2, during concerts and services.*

Shopping

Shopping Districts and Specialty Shops Helsinki's prime shopping districts run along **Pohjoisesplanadi** (North Esplanade) and **Aleksanterinkatu** in the city center. The streets around **Iso Roobertinkatu,** a pedestrian street near the center, are also full of a variety of shops. The **Forum** (Mannerheimintie 20) is a modern, multi-story shopping center for clothing, gifts, books, toys, etc. You can also make purchases until 10 PM daily in the shops along the Tunneli underpass underneath the Railway Station.

Some shops in the **Kiseleff Bazaar Hall** (Aleksanterinkatu 28), which once housed Stockmann's department store and now has shops selling handicrafts, toys, and knitwear, are open on Sundays from noon to 4 in the summer. Along Pohjoisesplanadi, and the other side of the street, Etelaesplanadi, you will find Finland's design houses. **Hackman Arabia** (Pohjoisesplanadi 25) sells Finland's well-known china, Iittala glass and other items. The **Arabia Factory Shop** (Hameentie 135, tel. 90/393–9303), north of the city center, is out of the way but offers factory seconds and special sales of many Hackman-Arabia products and is open on Sundays year-round. **Pentik** (Pohjoisesplanadi 27) features beautifully made leather goods. **Aarikka** (Pohjoisesplanadi 25–27 and Etelaesplanadi 8) offers wooden jewelry, toys, and gifts. **Artek** (Etelaesplanadi 18) is known for its Alvar Alto–designed furniture and ceramics. **Marimekko** (Pohjoisesplanadi 31, Etelaesplanadi 18) sells women's clothing, household items, and gifts made from its famous textiles. **Design Forum Finland** (Etelaesplanadi 8), which often hosts exhibits of the latest Finnish design innovations, can provide more information.

Department Stores   **Stockmann's,** a huge store that fills an entire block between Aleksanterinkatu, Mannerheimintie, and Keskuskatu, is your best bet if you want to find everything under one roof.

Markets   The **Kauppatori market** beside the South Harbor (*see* Exploring Helsinki, *above*) is an absolute must year-round. In favorable weather, there is a variety of goods to be explored at the **Hietalahti flea market,** at the west end of Bulevardi on Hietalahti. (Open Mon.–Sat. 8 AM–2 PM.) The more basic Hakaniemi Kauppahalli is just north of the center on Hakaniemi Tori (Square). Upstairs, there are several small shops, some selling gifts and crafts. (Open Mon.–Thurs. 8–5, Fri. 8–6, Sat. 8–3.)

Dining

For details and price-category definitions, *see* Dining in Staying *in* Finland, *above*.

$$ **Asia King.** The Asia King offers generous portions of authentic Indian food. *Sepankatu 19, tel. 90/664521. Reservations advised. AE, DC, MC, V. Closed Christmas, Midsummer.*

$$ **Kaksi Kanaa.** The Kaksi Kanaa, in a renovated warehouse in Katajanokka, has live music in the evenings as well as an extensive menu and wine list. The restaurant also has excellent, low-price daily luncheon specials. *Kanavakatu 3, tel. 90/669260. Reservations required. AE, DC, MC, V. Closed Christmas, Easter, Midsummer.*

$$ **Kynsilaukka (Garlic).** Garlic is the pungent theme of this restaurant, where the rustic decor suits the menu. *Fredrikinkatu 22, tel. 90/651939. Reservations advised. AE, DC, MC, V.*

$$ **Omenapuu.** Omenapuu's central location and varied menu make it a lunchtime favorite for shoppers and business people. *Keskuskatu 6, 2nd Floor, tel. 90/630205. Reservations advised for lunch. AE, DC, MC, V. Closed Christmas.*

$$ **Perho Mechelin.** This is the restaurant connected with Helsinki's catering school; the menu includes several Finnish specialties. *Mechelininkatu 7, tel. 90/405–6210. Reservations advised. AE, DC, MC, V. Closed Christmas, Midsummer.*

$$ **Restaurant Maxill.** Minimalist yet stylish decor sets off Maxill's creative, bistro-inspired menu. *Korkeavuorenkatu 4A, tel. 90/638873. Reservations advised. AE, DC, MC, V. Closed during Christmas, and for 3 wks at Midsummer.*

$ **Café København.** Generous open-face sandwiches are the specialty of Café København, Helsinki's only Danish restaurant; the menu includes other traditional Scandanavian dishes as well. *Tehtaankatu 21, tel. 90/633997. Reservations not required. DC, V. Closed Christmas, Easter.*

$ **Mexicana.** This small restaurant serves Helsinki's most authentic Mexican food, as well as some nicely priced lunch specials. *Pursiemiehenkatu 5, tel. 90/666797. AE, MC, V. Closed Christmas, Midsummer.*

$ **Pikku Satama.** The casual Pikku Satama, in the renovated warehouse complex Wanha Satama in Katajanokka, serves a variety of food—pizza, baked potatoes with a selection of interesting toppings, and hot dishes. Pikku Satama serves both lunch and dinner specials. *Pikku Satamakatu 3, tel. 90/174093. AE, DC, MC, V. Closed Finnish holidays.*

$ **Via Veneto.** Via Veneto's homey atmosphere provides a colorful background for this Italian restaurant's extensive selection of pastas, Italian-style pizza, and other dishes. *Iso Roobertinkatu 35–37,* *tel. 90/179904. MC, V. Closed Christmas, and for 6 wks beginning at Midsummer.*

¢ **Forum.** In the lower level of the Forum shopping center, there are several fast food restaurants where you can eat cheaply. *Mannerheimintie 20, tel. 90/642210. Restaurants may be closed Christmas, Easter, Midsummer.*

¢ **Kasvisravintola.** This cafeteria-style vegetarian restaurant serves lunch and dinner specials for FIM 38 weekdays, FIM 42 on weekends. The hearty entrees come with bread, salad, and milk. *Korkeavuorenkatu 3, tel. 90/179212. DC, MC, V. Closed Christmas, Easter, Midsummer.*

¢ **Suola ja Pippuri.** An attractive eatery near the University, Suola ja Pippuri serves daily specials for both lunch and dinner mainly in the FIM 30–45 range. *Snellmaninkatu 17, tel. 90/135–6651. AE, DC, MC, V. Closed Christmas, Midsummer.*

Lodging

For details and price-category definitions, *see* Lodging *in* Staying in Finland, *above.*

$$ **Arthur.** On a quiet, central street, the Arthur is unpretentious but comfortable. *Vuorikatu 17b, tel. 90/173441, fax. 90/626880. 143 rooms with bath or shower. Facilities: sauna, restaurant. AE, DC, MC, V. Sometimes closed during Christmas.*

$$ **Aurora.** Close to the city center and right across the Linnanmäki amusement park is Aurora. Reasonable prices, cozy rooms, and good facilities have made the hotel popular, especially with families. *Helsinginkatu 50, tel. 90/717400, fax 90/714240. 70 rooms with shower, 6 with bath. Facilities: restaurant, sauna, squash courts, health spa, solarium. AE, DC, MC, V. Usually open Christmas.*

$$ **Omapohja.** This bed-and-breakfast is just behind the Railway Station. The rooms are modest but clean; the lobby has turn-of-the-century charm. Rooms without baths are less expensive. *Itainen Teatterinkuja 3, tel. 90/666211. 15 rooms, 3 with bath. MC, V. Closed at Christmas.*

$$ **Seurahuone Socis.** This Helsinki landmark, partially renovated in 1992, is across the street from the Railway Station. Its restaurant is a popular downtown lunch spot. *Kaivokatu 12, tel. 90/69141, fax 90/691–4010. 118 rooms with shower. Facilities: restaurant, café, sauna, conference rooms. AE, DC, MC, V.*

$ **Academica.** This summer hostel is a student dormitory during the year. Each room has a kitchen and bath. *Hietaniemenkatu 14, tel. 90/402–0206, fax 90/441201. 115 rooms with bath. Facilities: sauna, pool, café. AE, DC, MC, V. Closed Sept.–May.*

$ **Erottajanpuisto Matkailukoti.** This hostel is centrally located in Helsinki's shopping district. It has clean rooms; none with bath. Discounts are given to youth hostel card holders. *Uudenmankatu 9, tel. 90/642169, fax. 90/680–2757. 15 rooms without bath. Facilities: self-service kitchen. MC, V.*

$ **Finnapartments Fenno.** This hotel, a few blocks north of the Hakaniemi market square, has rooms either with or without a private bath. *Franzeninkatu 26, tel. 90/773–1661, fax 90/701–6889. 100 rooms, 68 with shower. Facilities: café, sauna. AE, DC, MC, V.*

$ **Satakuntatalo.** Satakuntatalo is only a five-minute walk from the Railway Station. Friendly service and clean rooms (without shower) have made it popular among Americans. Some rooms can get traffic noise. Breakfast is included. *Lapinrinne 1A, tel. 90/695851, fax 90/694–2226. 64 rooms, 5 with shower. Facilities: restaurant, saunas, self-service laundry. AE, MC, V. Open June 1–Aug. 31.*

$ **Skatta.** Modest Skatta is located in the elegant neighborhood of Katajanokka Island, and 2 kilometers (1¼ miles) from the Railway Station. Each room has a kitchenette. *Linnankatu 3, tel. 90/659233 or 90/669984, fax 90/631352. 24 rooms with shower. Facilities: café,* *sauna, kitchenettes, exercise room. AE, DC, MC, V. Sometimes closed during Christmas.*

¢ **Stadionin Maja.** Three kilometers (1.8 miles) from the Railway Station, this modest youth hostel is the cheapest place in town to sleep. There are good bus and streetcar connections. *Pohjois Stadiontie 3B, tel. 90/496071, fax 90/496466. 23 rooms without bath. Facilities: self-service kitchen, laundry, breakfast room. No credit cards. Closed Christmas.*

¢ **Vantaa Hostel.** This hostel is conveniently located only 5 kilometers (3 miles) from the Helsinki-Vantaa Airport. A section of the hostel offers 24 rooms with private shower at higher rates. *Valkoisenlähteentie 52, tel. 90/839–3310. 7 rooms. Facilities: breakfast room. No credit cards. Sometimes closed during Christmas.*

The Arts

For a list of events, pick up the free publications *Helsinki This Week*, available in hotels and tourist offices. A central reservations office for all events is **Lippupalvelu,** Mannerheimintie 5, tel. 9700–4700 or 90/664466 when calling from abroad. Call **Tiketti,** Yrjönkatu 29C, tel. 90/9700–4204, to book tickets for small concerts at clubs and restaurants.

Theater Although all performances are in Finnish or Swedish, summertime productions in such bucolic settings as **Suomenlinna Island, Kekuspuisto Park, Mustikkamaa Island,** the **Rowing Stadium** (operettas), **Indoor Ice Rink** (rock concerts), and the **Savoy Theater** (ballet and music performances) make enjoyable entertainment. The splendid new **Kansallisooppera** (Finnish National Opera, tel. 90/4030–2211, fax 90/4030–2210) opened in 1993 in a waterside park by **Töölönlahti** just a few hundred feet from Finlandia Hall.

Concerts The main locations for concerts are **Finlandia Hall** (tel. 90/40241), **Temppeliauko Church** (*see* Exploring, *above*), and the **Sibelius Academy** (tel. 90/405441).

Festivals Finland holds many festivals throughout the country, especially during the summer months. The **Helsinki Festival** is said to be the biggest in Scandinavia. For more than two weeks during August to September, the city is turned over to the arts. Scores of musical happenings and art exhibitions are organized throughout Helsinki. Contact Helsinki Festival, Rauhankatu 7E, tel. 90/135–4522. For more information on festivals, call Finland Festivals, Mannerheimintie 40, B49, tel. 90/445686, fax 90/445117.

Nightlife

The price of drinks at nightclubs and discos can be expensive when compared to continental Europe. The high price of alcohol is attributable to the Finnish (and Nordic) alcohol policy, which is strictly controlled by the state. Those who do not want to spend a lot of money on alcohol when visiting one of these establishments should just order a bottle of beer. For information about what is happening in Helsinki, see **Helsinki This Week,** available at most hotels, travel agencies and the Helsinki City Tourist Office.

Bars and One of the most popular nightspots in Helsinki is **Happy Days**
Lounges (Pohjoisesplanadi 2, tel. 90/657700), known for its hamburgers and outdoor terrace. The historic **Kappeli Café-Brasserie** (Eteläesplanadi 1, tel. 90/179242) brews its own beer. **Kaarle XII** (Kasarmikatu 40, tel. 90/171312) is in one of Helsinki's striking Jugendstyle buildings. **Cantina West** (Kasarmikatu 23, tel. 90/622–1500) is a popular Tex-Mex bar and restaurant with good food and live music nightly.

Jazz   For live jazz, try **Storyville Happy Jazz Club** (Museokatu 8, tel. 90/408007), which features Finnish and foreign jazz musicians and New Orleans–style cuisine. The **Hot Tomato Jazz Café** (Annankatu 6, tel. 90/680–1701) is popular with young people.

Nightclubs   **Cafe Adlon** (Fabianinkatu 14, tel. 90/664611) is one of the most popular discos in town. **Fennia** (Mikonkatu 17, tel. 90/666355) boasts dancing and live music on the weekends, as well as a restaurant. **Hesperia Nightclub** (Hotel Hesperia, Kivelänkatu 2, tel. 90/43101) is another well-known and long-standing Helsinki hotspot. **Kaivohuone** (Kaivopuisto Park, tel. 90/177881), with its attractive park setting, is a summertime favorite.

The Lakelands

In southeastern and central Finland, the light has a softness that seems to brush the forests, lakes, and islands, changing the landscape throughout the day. For centuries, though, this beautiful region was actually a buffer between the warring empires of Sweden and Russia. The Finns of the Lakelands prevailed by sheer *sisu* (guts), and now their descendants live peacefully amid the rough beauty of the terrain.

Getting Around

Savonlinna is a good starting point to begin exploring Finland's Lakeland district. You can fly to the Savonlinna area from Helsinki in 40 minutes; a connecting bus takes you the remaining 16 kilometers (10 miles) into town. By train, the journey takes 5½ hours; by bus, six hours. Take advantage of the excellent network of air, rail, bus, and boat transportation. Take the boat from Savonlinna to Kuopio in 12 hours (**Roll Line**, tel. 971/262–6744). From Kuopio, take the 320-kilometer (200-mile) cross-country bus ride via Jyväskylä to Tampere. Continue by boat to Hämeenlinna in about eight hours (**Finnish Silverline**, tel. 931/2124803). The final leg by bus or train back to Helsinki takes about one hour.

Tourist Information

Savonlinna (Puistokatu 1, tel. 957/273492). Open June and August, daily 9–6; July, daily 8 AM–10 PM; September–May, weekdays 9–4 PM, closed weekends.

Exploring the Lakelands

Savonlinna   The center of **Savonlinna** is a series of islands linked by bridges. First, stop at the tourist office for information; then cross the bridge east to the **open-air market** that flourishes alongside the main passenger quay. It's from here that you can catch the boat to Kuopio. In days when waterborne traffic was the major form of transportation, Savonlinna was the central hub of the passenger fleet serving Saimaa, the largest lake system in Europe. Now the lake traffic is dominated by cruise and sightseeing boats.

A 10-minute stroll from the quay to the southeast brings you to Savonlinna's most famous sight, the castle of **Olavinlinna**. First built in 1475 to protect Finland's eastern border, the castle retains its medieval character and is one of Scandinavia's best-preserved historic monuments. Still surrounded by water that once formed part of its defensive strength, the fortress rises majestically out of the lake. The Savonlinna Opera Festival is held in the courtyard each July. The combination of music and setting is spellbinding. You will need to make reservations well in advance (tel. 957/514700 fax 957/21866), both for tickets and for hotel rooms, since Savonlinna becomes a mecca for music lovers. *Castle admission: FIM 20 adults, FIM 10 children, guided tours every hr. Open June–Aug., daily 10 AM–5 PM; Sept.–May, daily 10–3.*

Close to the castle are three 19th-century steam schooners: *Salama, Savonlinna,* and *Mikko.* **Salama** houses an excellent museum on the history of lake traffic, including the fascinating floating timber trains that are still a common sight on Saimaa today. *Admission: FIM 15 adults, FIM 5 children. Open June and Aug., daily 11–5, July, daily 10–8. Closed Sept.–May.*

The most popular excursion from Savonlinna is to **Retretti.** You can take either a two-hour boat ride or a 30-minute, 29-kilometer (18-mile) bus trip. The journey by bus takes you along the 8-kilometer (5-mile) ridge of **Punkaharju.** This amazing ridge of pine-covered rocks, which rises out of the water and separates the lakes on either side, predates the Ice Age. At times it narrows to only 25 feet, yet it still manages to accommodate a road and train tracks. *Admission: FIM 60 adults, FIM 25 children 7–16, FIM 145 family (2 adults plus 2 or more children). Open May 24–June 23 and Aug., daily 10–6; June 24–July, daily 10–7.*

Dining and Lodging

For details and price-category definitions, *see* Dining and Lodging *in* Staying in Finland, *above.*

Savonlinna **Juanita.** The family-run Juanita is located in the heart of
Dining Savonlinna. The restaurant emphasizes classic Continental-style cooking. *Olavinkatu 44, tel. 957/514531. Reservations recommended in the summer months. MC, V. $$*

Majakka. Centrally located, Majakka delivers home cooking in a family atmosphere. *Satamakatu 11, tel. 957/21456. Reservations required during festival season. AE, V. $$*

Ravintola Hopeasalmi. Right next to the market square is a 100-year-old steamboat that has been converted into a restaurant. Ravintola Hopeasalmi is divided into three sections: a dining room, a pizzeria (which is inexpensive), and a pub. The restaurant in the dining section specializes in such local fish dishes as the delicious *muikku,* a small, local freshwater fish. *Kauppatori, tel. 957/21701. Reservations advised during July. AE, V. Open daily from May 1 to mid-Sept.; closed rest of the year. $$*

Ravintola Retretti. Popular in summer when tourists visit the Retretti Art Center, the restaurant specializes in Finnish fare. Buffets are regularly offered June to August. *Punkaharju, tel. 957/644161. Reservations advised during summer months. DC, MC, V. Closed Jan. $$*

Paviljonki. Paviljonki is connected with the Savonlinna restaurant school. Located 1 kilometer (½ mile) west of the city center, the restaurant serves homemade Finnish dishes. *Rjalahdenkatu 4, tel. 957/520960. DC, V. $*

Uskudar Kebab. This is Savonlinna's only fast-food kebab-café (baari) that also serves pizza. *Pilkkakoskenkatu 3, tel. 957/514206. No reservations. No credit cards. Closed Christmas, Midsummer. ¢*

Lodging **Hospits.** On Lake Saimaa in the city center, Hospits is owned by the YMCA. *Linnankatu 20, tel. 957/515661, fax 957/515120. 22 rooms, 10 with shower. Facilities: restaurant, sauna. V. $$*

Malakias. About 2 kilometers (1.2 miles) from the center of town is Malakias, a student dormitory converted into a hotel in the summer (July 1–Aug. 7). The rooms are basic; all share a bath and kitchenette with one other room. *Pihlajavedenkuja 6, tel. 957/57500, fax 957/272524. 220 rooms. AE, DC, MC, V. $$*

Pietari Kylliainen. Pietari Kulliainen is centrally located; some rooms can get traffic noise. Room prices are higher in July during the Opera Festival. *Olavinkatu 15, tel. 957/575–0500, fax 957/24873.*

48 rooms with shower. Facilities: restaurant, café, sauna. AE, DC, MC, V. Closed for 2 wks during Christmas. $$

Vuorilinna Summer Hotel. Guests at this hotel have access, for a fee, to the facilities of the nearby Casino Spa Hotel, including the pool. Some rooms have a private bath, most share a bath and kitchenette with one other room. *Kasinonsaari, tel. 957/57500, or 957/739–5430 (reservations), fax 957/272524. 220 rooms, 60 with shower. AE, DC, MC, V. Closed Sept.–May. $$*

Vuorilinna Youth Hostel. Part of the Vuorilinna Summer Hotel is run as a youth hostel. All rooms share a bath and kitchenette with one other room. *Kasinonsaari, tel. 957/57500 or 957/739–5430 (reservations), fax 957/272524. 25 rooms. AE, DC, MC, V. Closed Sept.–May. $*

8 France

Hotels and restaurants in France offer some of the best value in Western Europe—and the French economy hasn't suffered as much as its neighbors', with inflation climbing less than 3% a year. Even in the heart of Paris it is possible to find a double room with shower for less than $80 a night; good-value hotels abound in every country town. You can have a fine three-course meal in a restaurant for less than $20.

France's rail system is another plus for the budget traveler. Not only is the network comprehensive, but trains run on time and are comfortable, fast, and relatively cheap. Travel in France is geared to train lovers; drivers have to face highway tolls and exorbitant gas prices, and car rentals are expensive, as in the rest of Europe. Domestic air travel is also costly. Long-distance buses are almost non-existent, and hitchhiking is difficult.

One thing the French do well—probably because it's instinctive and they don't need to think about it—is live. The essence of French *savoir-vivre*, or knowing how to live, is simplicity. Everyday things count: eating, drinking, talking, dressing, shopping. Daily rituals are meant to be enjoyed. Dining is the best example. The French don't like rushing their meals. They plan them in advance, painstakingly prepare them, look forward to them over an aperitif, admire the loving presentation of each dish, savor each mouthful. The pace is unhurried, and the wine flows steadily.

Make the most of the simple pleasure to be had from basking in the sunshine outside a café. Admire the casual elegance of the passersby or the old men in their time-honored berets. Even the most mundane things can become objects of beauty in French eyes. The daily market is a festival of colors and textures, with fruit and vegetable stalls artistically and imaginatively composed. Shop windows are works of art.

Most French towns and villages are quietly attractive and historic. Chances are that the ornate *hôtel-de-ville* (town hall) has been there since the Revolution, and the church or cathedral since the Middle Ages. The main streets tend to be lined with sturdy trees planted before living memory. The 20th century is kept firmly at bay. Modern buildings—such as supermarkets—are banished to the outskirts or obliged to fit in with the architecture of the town center.

Whatever you may have been led to believe, France is a welcoming country. Don't be misled by the superficial coldness of the French: They are a formal people who don't go out of their way to speak to strangers (except in anger). Above all, don't suppose that all Frenchmen are like Parisians—it's not true. Most of the French are more approachable and friendly.

Still, deep down, most of the French are chauvinists who are proud of *La douce France* (sweet France), worship Napoléon, and feel that the Liberty-Equality-Fraternity motto of the French Revolution confers moral superiority upon their country.

Essential Information

Before You Go

When to Go
On the whole, June and September are the best months to be in France. Both months are free of the mid-summer crowds. June offers the advantage of long daylight hours, while slightly cheaper prices and frequent Indian summers (often lasting well into October) make September an attractive proposition. Try to avoid the second half of July and all of August, or be prepared for inflated prices and huge crowds on the beaches. Don't travel on or around July 14 or August 1, 14, or 31. In addition, July and August heat can be stifling in southern France. Paris can be stuffy in August, too. But, on the other hand, it's pleasantly deserted (although many restaurants, theaters, and small shops are closed).

The skiing season in the Alps and Pyrénées lasts from Christmas through Easter—steer clear of February (school vacation time) if you can. Anytime between March and November will offer you a good chance to soak up the sun on the Riviera. If you're going to Paris or the Loire, remember that the weather is unappealing before Easter. If you're dreaming of Paris in the springtime, May (not April) is your best bet.

Climate
Be prepared for changes in climate if you wish to visit different parts of France. North of the Loire (including Paris), France has a northern European climate—cold winters, pleasant if unpredictable summers, and frequent rain. Southern France has a Mediterranean climate: mild winters, long, hot summers, and sunshine throughout the year. The more continental climate of eastern and central France is a mixture of these two extremes: Winters can be very cold and summers very hot. France's Atlantic coast has a temperate climate even south of the Loire, with the exception of the much warmer city of Biarritz.

The following are the average daily maximum and minimum temperatures for Paris.

Jan.	43F	6C	May	68F	20C	Sept.	70F	21C
	34	1		49	10		53	12
Feb.	45F	7C	June	73F	23C	Oct.	60F	16C
	34	1		55	13		46	8
Mar.	54F	12C	July	76F	25C	Nov.	50F	10C
	39	4		58	14		40	5
Apr.	60F	16C	Aug.	75F	24C	Dec.	44F	7C
	43	6		58	14		36	2

The following are the average daily maximum and minimum temperatures for Marseille.

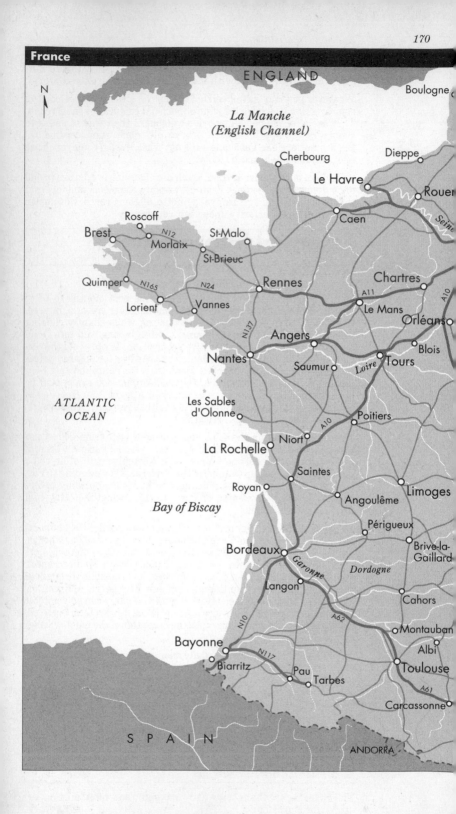

Jan.	50F	10C	May	71F	22C	Sept.	77F	25C
	35	2		52	11		58	14
Feb.	53F	12C	June	79F	26C	Oct.	68F	20C
	36	2		58	14		51	10
Mar.	59F	15C	July	84F	29C	Nov.	58F	14C
	41	5		63	17		43	6
Apr.	64F	18C	Aug.	83F	28C	Dec.	52F	11C
	46	8		63	17		37	3

Currency The unit of French currency is the franc, subdivided into 100 centimes. Bills are issued in denominations of 50, 100, 200, and 500 francs (frs); coins are 5, 10, 20, and 50 centimes and 1, 2, 5, 10, and 20 francs. The small, copper-color 5-, 10-, and 20-centime coins have considerable nuisance value, but can be used for tips in bars and cafés.

International credit cards and traveler's checks are widely accepted throughout France, except in rural areas. At press time (summer 1995), the dollar was worth 4.5 frs, and the pound sterling was worth 7.6 frs.

What It Will Cost Gasoline prices are above the European average, and there are tolls on major highways. Train travel, though, is a good buy.

Hotel and restaurant prices compensate for travel expenses. Prices are highest in Paris, on the Riviera, and in the Alps during the ski season. But even in these areas, you can find pleasant accommodations and excellent food for surprisingly reasonable prices.

All taxes must be included in posted prices in France. The initials TTC (*toutes taxes comprises*—taxes included) are sometimes included on price lists but, strictly speaking, they are superfluous. Restaurant and hotel prices must *by law* include taxes and service charges: If they are tacked onto your bill as additional items, you should complain.

Sample Prices Prices vary greatly depending on the region, proximity to tourist sites, and—believe it or not—whether you're standing up or sitting down in a café! Here are some samples: cup of coffee, 5–10 frs; glass of beer, 10–13 frs; soft drink, 10–15 frs; ham sandwich, 14–20 frs; 1-mile taxi ride, 35 frs.

Visas Citizens of the United States, Canada, and Britain do not require a visa to visit France.

Customs on Arrival There are two levels of duty-free allowance for travelers entering France: one for goods obtained (tax paid) within another EU country and the other for goods obtained anywhere outside the EU or for goods purchased in a duty-free shop within the EU.

In the first category, you may import duty-free: 300 cigarettes, or 150 cigarillos, or 75 cigars, or 400 grams of tobacco; 5 liters of table wine and (1) 1½ liters of alcohol over 22% volume (most spirits), (2) 3 liters of alcohol under 22% by volume (fortified or sparkling wine), or (3) 3 more liters of table wine; 90 milliliters of perfume; 375 milliliters of toilet water; and other goods to the value of 2,400 francs (620 frs for those under 15).

In the second category, you may import duty-free: 200 cigarettes, or 100 cigarillos, or 50 cigars, or 250 grams of tobacco (these allowances are doubled if you live outside Europe); 2 liters of wine and (1) 1 liter of alcohol over 22% volume, (2) 2 liters of alcohol under 22% volume, or (3) 2 more liters of table wine; 60 milliliters of perfume; 250 milliliters of toilet water; and other goods to the value of 300 francs (150 frs for those under 15).

Language The French study English for a minimum of four years at school, but few are fluent in their conversation. English is widely understood in major tourist areas, and in most tourist hotels there should be at least one person who can converse with you. Even if your own French is rusty, try to master a few words: The French are more cooperative when they think you are at least making an effort to speak their language.

Getting Around

By Train **SNCF,** the French national railroad, is generally recognized as Europe's best national train service: fast, punctual, comfortable, and comprehensive. The high-speed TGVs, with a top speed of 190 mph, are the best domestic trains, heading southeast from Paris to Lyon, the Riviera, and Switzerland; west to Nantes; southwest to Bordeaux; and north to Lille. Most TGVs require passengers to pay a supplement—usually 20–40 frs, but a bit more during peak periods. Also, you need a seat reservation—easily obtained at the ticket window or from an automatic machine. Seat reservations are reassuring but seldom necessary on other French trains, except at certain busy holiday times.

You must punch your train ticket in one of the waist-high orange machines you'll encounter alongside platforms. Slide your ticket in faceup and wait for a "clink" sound. If nothing happens, try another machine. (The small yellow tickets and automatic ticket barriers used for most suburban Paris trains are similar to those in the métro/RER.) The ticket collectors will present you with an on-the-spot fine of 100 frs if your ticket hasn't been validated before you board.

It is not necessary to take an overnight train, even if you are traveling from one end of France to the other; but if you take one, you have a choice between *wagons-lits* (sleeping cars), which are expensive, and *couchettes* (bunks), which sleep six to a compartment (sheet and pillow provided) and are more affordable (around 90 frs). Ordinary compartment seats do not pull together to enable you to lie down. In summer there are special night trains from Paris to Spain and the Riviera geared for a younger market, with discos and bars.

Fares Various reduced-fare passes are available from major train stations in France and from travel agents acting as agents for SNCF. If you are planning a lot of train travel, we suggest that you buy a special **France Vacances** card (around 1,400 frs for nine days). Families and couples are also eligible for big discounts. So are senior citizens (over 60) and young people (under 26), who qualify for different discount schemes (**Carte Vermeil** and **Carrissimo**). Having paid for your pass, you can get 50% reductions during blue periods (most of the time) and 20% most of the rest of the time (white periods: noon Friday to noon Saturday; 3 PM Sunday to noon Monday). A calendar showing the white and blue periods is available at any station. The **Carte Kiwi** (280 frs) enables children and up to four accompanying adults to travel half price on four trips. Note that there is no reduction for booking an *aller-retour* (round-trip) ticket rather than an *aller simple* (one-way).

By Plane France's domestic airline service is called **Air Inter.** Most domestic flights from Paris leave from Orly. Contact your travel agent or Air Inter (tel. 45–46–90–00). Train service is nearly always cheaper and may be faster, though, particularly when you consider time spent traveling to and from the airport.

By Bus Because of excellent train service, long-distance buses are rare and found mainly where train service is inadequate. Bus tours are organized by the **SNCF** and other tourist organizations, such as **Horizons Européens:** Ask for their brochures at any major travel agent, or contact France-Tourisme at 3 rue d'Alger, 75001 Paris, tel. 42–61–85–50.

By Boat   France has Europe's most extensive inland waterway system. Canal and river vacations are popular: Visitors can either take an organized cruise or rent a boat and plan their own leisurely route. Contact a travel agent for details or ask for a *Tourisme Fluvial* brochure in any French tourist office. Some of the most picturesque stretches are to be found in Brittany, Burgundy, and the Midi. The Canal du Midi between Toulouse and Sète, constructed in the 17th century, is a historic marvel. Additional information is available from French national tourist offices or **Bourgogne Voies Navigables** (1 quai de la République, 89000 Auxerre, tel. 86–52–18–99).

By Bicycle   With plenty of wide, empty roads and rolling countryside, there is no shortage of suitable biking terrain. The French themselves are great cycling enthusiasts—witness the Tour de France. Bikes can be rented from a total of 260 train stations for around 40 frs a day; you need to show your passport and leave a deposit of about 500 frs (unless you have a Visa or MasterCard). You do not always need to return the bike to the same station. Bikes may be sent as accompanied luggage from any station in France; some trains in rural areas don't even charge to transport bikes. Tourist offices will supply details on the more than 200 local shops that have bikes for rent, or obtain the SNCF brochure "Guide du Train et du Vélo" from any station.

Staying in France

Telephones   The French telephone system is modern and efficient. Phone booths
Local Calls   are plentiful; they are nearly always available at post offices and cafés. A local call in France costs 80 centimes for three minutes; half-price rates apply between 9:30 PM and 8 AM and between 1:30 PM Saturday and 8 AM Monday.

Some French pay phones work with 1-, 2-, and 5-fr coins (1 fr minimum), but most phones are now operated by *télécartes* (phone cards), sold in post offices, métro stations, and *tabacs* (cost: 40 frs for 50 units; 96 frs for 120).

All French phone numbers have eight digits; a code is required only when calling the Paris region from the provinces (dial 16–1 and then the number) and for calling the provinces from Paris (dial 16, then the number). Because more phone lines are needed, in October 1996 all numbers will get a prefix of two new digits. In Paris and Ile de France, 01 will precede the number (replacing the 16–1); in the northwest, 02; in the northeast, 03; in the southeast, 04; and in the southwest, 05.

International   Dial 19 and wait for the tone, then dial the country code (1 for the
Calls   United States and Canada, 441 for the United Kingdom), area code (minus any initial 0), and number. If you make phone calls from your hotel room, expect to be greatly overcharged. To reach an **AT&T** long-distance operator, dial 19–0011; for **MCI,** dial 19–0019; and for **Sprint,** 19–0087. Dial 12 for a local operator.

Country Code   France's country code is 33.

Mail   Airmail letters to the United States and Canada cost 4.30 frs for 20
Postal Rates   grams. Letters to the United Kingdom cost 2.80 frs for up to 20 grams, as they do within France. Postcards cost 2.40 frs within France and if sent to EU countries (2.40 frs for surface or 3.80 frs for airmail to North America). Stamps can be bought in post offices and tabacs.

Receiving Mail   If you're uncertain where you'll be staying, have mail sent to American Express (if you're a cardmember) or Thomas Cook; mail labeled "poste restante" is also accepted at most French post offices.

Shopping   A number of shops, particularly large stores in cities and holiday re-
VAT Refunds   sorts, offer value-added tax (VAT) refunds to foreign shoppers. You

are entitled to an export discount of 18.6%, depending on the item purchased, though this often applies only if your purchases in the same store reach a minimum 2,800 frs (for residents of EU countries) or 1,200 frs (all others).

Bargaining Shop prices are clearly marked, and bargaining is not a way of life. Still, at outdoor markets, flea markets, and in antiques stores, you can try your luck. If you're thinking of buying several items in these places, you have nothing to lose in cheerfully suggesting to the proprietor, *"Vous me faites un prix?"* ("How about a discount?").

Hours **Banks** are generally open weekdays 9:30–4:30. Most close for an hour to an hour and a half for lunch.

Museums are closed one day a week (usually Tuesday) and on national holidays. Usual times are from 9:30 to 5 or 6. Many museums close for lunch (noon–2); on Sunday many are open afternoons only.

Shops in big towns are open from 9 or 9:30 to 7 or 8 without a lunch break and have recently begun to open on Sunday. Smaller shops often open earlier and close later, but take a lengthy lunch break (1–4). This siesta-type schedule is more typical in the south of France. Corner grocery stores frequently stay open until around 10 PM.

National In 1996: January 1, April 7 and 8 (Easter Sunday and Monday), May
Holidays 1 (Labor Day), May 8 (Fête de la Victoire 1945), May 16 (Ascension), May 26 and 27 (Whit Sunday and Monday), July 14 (Bastille Day), August 15 (Assumption), November 1 (All Saints' Day), November 11 (Armistice), December 25. Changing holidays in 1997: March 31 and April 1 (Easter Monday and Tuesday), May 8 (Ascension), May 18 and 19 (Whit Sunday and Monday).

Dining Eating in France is serious business, at least for two of the three meals each day. For a light meal, try a brasserie (steak and french fries remain the classic) or a picnic (a baguette loaf with ham, cheese, or pâté makes a perfect combination).

French breakfasts are relatively modest—strong coffee, fruit juice if you insist, and croissants. International chain hotels are likely to offer American or English breakfasts, but in cafés you will probably be out of luck if this is what you want.

Mealtimes Dinner is the main meal and usually begins at 8. Lunch begins at 12:30 or 1.

What to Wear Jacket and tie are recommended at some of the more stylish $$ restaurants. When in doubt, it's best to dress up. Otherwise casual dress is appropriate.

Precautions Tap water is perfectly safe, though not always very palatable (least of all in Paris). Mineral water is a good alternative; there is a vast choice of *eaux plates* (plain) as well as *eaux gazeuses* (fizzy).

Ratings Prices are per person and include a first course, main course, and dessert plus taxes and service (which are always included in displayed prices), but not wine. Best bets are indicated by a star ★.

Category	Cost
$$	175 frs–300 frs
$	100 frs–175 frs
¢	under 100 frs

Lodging France has a wide range of accommodations, from rambling old village inns to stylishly converted châteaus. Prices must, by law, be posted at the hotel entrance and should include taxes and service. Prices are always by room, not per person. Ask for a *grand lit* if you want a double bed. Breakfast is not always included in this price, but you are usually expected to have it and often are charged for it whether you partake or not. In smaller rural hotels, you may be expected to have your evening meal at the hotel, too.

The quality of rooms, particularly in older properties, can be uneven; if you don't like the room you're given, ask to see another. If you want a private bathroom, state your preference for *douche* (shower) or *baignoire* (bath)—the latter always costing more. Tourist offices in major train stations can reserve hotels for you, and so can tourist offices in most towns.

Hotels Hotels are officially classified from one-star to four-star-deluxe. France has—but is not dominated by—big hotel chains: Examples in the upper price bracket include Frantel, Holiday Inn, Novotel, and Sofitel. The Ibis and Climat de France chains are more moderately priced. Chain hotels, as a rule, lack atmosphere, with the following exceptions:

Logis de France. This is a group of small, inexpensive hotels that can be relied on for comfort, character, and regional cuisine. Look for its distinctive yellow and green sign. The Logis de France paperback guide is widely available in bookshops (cost: around 75 frs) or from Logis de France (83 av. d'Italie, 75013 Paris, tel. 45–84–83–84, fax 44–24–08–74).

France-Accueil is another chain of friendly low-cost hotels. You can get a free booklet from France-Accueil (163 av. d'Italie, 75013 Paris, tel. 45–83–04–22, fax 45–86–49–82).

Rentals *Gîtes Ruraux* offers families or small groups stays in a furnished cottage, chalet, or apartment. These can be rented by the week or month. Contact either the **Maison des Gîtes de France,** 35 rue Godot-de-Mauroy, 75009 Paris, tel. 49–70–75–75, fax 49–70–75–76 (indicate the region that interests you), or the French Government Tourist Office in New York or London (*see* Visitor Info *in* Chapter 1).

Bed-and- Known in France as *chambres d'hôte*, these are increasingly popular
Breakfasts in rural areas, and can be a great bargain. Check local tourist offices for details.

Youth Hostels With inexpensive hotel accommodations in France so easy to find, you may want to think twice before staying in a youth hostel—especially as standards of French hostels don't quite approximate those in neighboring countries. Contact **Fédération Unie des Auberges de Jeunesse** (27 rue Pajol, 75018 Paris, tel. 44–89–87–27, fax 44–89–87–10).

Camping French campsites have a good reputation for organization and amenities but are crowded in July and August. Many welcome advance reservations, and if you're traveling in summer, it makes sense to book in advance. A guide to France's campsites is published by the **Fédération Française de Camping et de Caravaning,** 78 rue de Rivoli, 75004 Paris, tel. 42–72–84–08. They'll send it to you directly for 121 francs (includes shipping).

Ratings Prices are for double rooms and include all taxes. Best bets are indicated by a star ★.

Category	Paris, Ile de France, the Riviera	Other Areas
$$	500 frs–800 frs	350 frs–500 frs
$	300 frs–500 frs	200 frs–350 frs
¢	under 300 frs	under 200 frs

Tipping The check in a bar or restaurant will include service, but it is customary to leave some small change unless you're dissatisfied. The amount varies, from 30 centimes for a beer to a few francs after a meal. Tip taxi drivers and hairdressers about 10%. Give ushers in theaters 1–2 frs. Cloakroom attendants will expect nothing if there is a sign saying POURBOIRE INTERDIT (no tip); otherwise give them 5 frs. Washroom attendants usually get 5 frs—a sum that is often posted.

Bellhops should get 10 frs per item. If you stay in a moderately priced hotel for more than two or three days, it is customary to leave something for the chambermaid—perhaps 10 frs per day. Expect to tip 10 frs for room service—but nothing is expected if breakfast is routinely served in your room.

Service station attendants get nothing for giving you gas or oil, and 5 or 10 frs for checking tires. Train and airport porters get a fixed sum (6–10 frs) per bag. Museum guides should get 5–10 frs after a guided tour. It is standard practice to tip guides (and bus drivers) after an excursion.

Paris

Arriving and Departing

By Plane International flights arrive at either Charles de Gaulle Airport (Roissy), 26 kilometers (16 miles) northeast of Paris, or at Orly Airport, 16 kilometers (10 miles) south of the city. For information on arrival and departure times, call individual airlines.

Between the **From Charles de Gaulle:** Buses operated by **Air France** leave every
Airport and 15 minutes from 5:40 AM to 11 PM. The fare is 48 frs, and the trip
Downtown takes 40 minutes (up to 1½ hours during rush hour). You arrive at the Arc de Triomphe or Porte Maillot, on the Right Bank by the Hôtel Concorde-Lafayette. Alternatively, the **Roissybus,** operated by RATP, runs directly to and from rue Scribe at the Paris Opéra every 15 minutes and costs 35 frs.

From Orly: Buses operated by **Air France** leave every 12 minutes from 6 AM to 11 PM and arrive at the Air France terminal near Les Invalides on the Left Bank. The fare is 44 frs, and the trip takes between 30 and 60 minutes, depending on traffic. RATP also runs the **Orlybus** to and from Denfert-Rochereau and Orly every 15 minutes for 30 frs.

Both airports have their own train stations, from which you can take the RER service to Paris. The advantages of this are speed, price (44 frs to Paris from Charles de Gaulle, 50 frs from Orly on the shuttle-train **Orlyval**), and the fact that the RER trains link up directly with the métro system. The disadvantage is having to lug your bags around. Taxi fares from airports to Paris range from 150 to 230 frs, with a 5-fr surcharge per bag.

A new **Paris Airports Service** takes you by eight-passenger van to your destination in Paris from either airport; from de Gaulle: $26 (one person) or $32 (two); Orly: $25 (one), $26 (two); less for groups. To book ahead (English-speaking clerks), call 33–1/49–62–78–78, fax 33–1/49–11–18–82; on arrival, 09–14–16–93.

By Train Paris has five international stations: Gare du Nord (for northern France, northern Europe, and England via Calais, Boulogne, or the Channel Tunnel); Gare de l'Est (for Strasbourg, Luxembourg, Basel, and central Europe); Gare de Lyon (for Lyon, Marseille, the Riviera, Geneva, Italy); Gare d'Austerlitz (for the Loire Valley, southwest France, Spain); Gare St-Lazare (for Normandy, England via Dieppe). The Gare Montparnasse serves western France (mainly Nantes and Brittany) and is the terminal for TGV Atlantique service from Paris to Bordeaux. For train information, tel. 45–82–50–

50. You can reserve tickets at any Paris station regardless of the destination. Go to the Grandes Lignes counter for travel within France or to the Billets Internationaux (international tickets) desk if you're heading out of France.

By Bus Long-distance bus journeys within France are uncommon, which may be why Paris has no central bus depot. The leading Paris-based bus company is **Eurolines** (28 av. du Général-de-Gaulle, Bagnolet, tel. 49–72–51–51).

Getting Around

Paris is relatively small as capital cities go, and most of its prize monuments and museums are within walking distance of one another. A river cruise is a pleasant way to get an overview. The most convenient form of public transportation is the métro; buses are a slower alternative, though they do allow you to see more of the city. Taxis are not expensive but not always easy to hail, either. Car travel within Paris is best avoided because parking is chronically difficult.

By Métro There are 13 métro lines crisscrossing Paris and the nearby suburbs, and you are seldom more than a five-minute walk from the nearest station. It is essential to know the name of the last station on the line you take, as this name appears on all signs within the system. A connection (you can make as many as you please on one ticket) is called a *correspondance*. At junction stations, illuminated orange signs, bearing the names of each line terminal, appear over the corridors leading to the various correspondances. Illuminated blue signs, marked *sortie*, indicate the station exit.

The métro runs from 5:30 AM to 1:15 AM. Some lines and stations in the seedier parts of Paris are a bit risky at night—in particular Line 2 (Porte-Dauphine–Nation) and the northern section of Line 13 from St-Lazare to St-Denis/Asnières. The long, bleak corridors at Jaurès and Stalingrad are a haven for pickpockets and purse snatchers. But the Paris métro is relatively safe, as long as you don't walk around with your wallet hanging out of your back pocket or travel alone (especially women) late at night.

The métro network connects at several points in Paris with RER trains that race across Paris from suburb to suburb: RER trains are a sort of supersonic métro and can be a great time-saver. All métro tickets and passes are valid for RER and bus travel within Paris. Métro tickets cost 7 frs each, though a *carnet* (10 tickets for 41 frs) is a far better value. If you're staying for a week or more, the best deal is the *coupon jaune* (weekly) or *carte orange* (monthly) ticket, sold according to zone. Zones 1 and 2 cover the entire métro network (cost: 63 frs per week or 219 frs per month). If you plan to take a suburban train to visit monuments in the Ile de France, you should consider a four-zone ticket (Versailles, St-Germain-en-Laye; 113 frs per week) or a six-zone ticket (Rambouillet, Fontainebleau; 150 frs per week). For these weekly or monthly tickets, you need to obtain a pass (available from train and major métro stations) and provide a passport-size photograph.

Alternatively there are one-day (Formule 1) and three- and five-day (Paris Visite) unlimited travel tickets for the métro, bus, and RER. The advantage is that unlike the coupon jaune, which is good from Monday morning to Sunday evening, the latter are valid starting any day of the week and give you admission discounts to a limited number of museums and tourist attractions. The prices are 38, 95, and 150 frs for Paris only; 95, 210, and 285 frs for the suburbs including Versailles, St-Germain-en-Laye, and Disneyland Paris.

Access to métro and RER platforms is through an automatic ticket barrier. Slide your ticket in flat and pick it up as it pops up farther along. Keep your ticket; you'll need it again to leave the RER system.

By Bus Most buses run from around 6 AM to 8:30 PM; some continue until midnight. Night buses operate from 1 AM to 6 AM between Châtelet and nearby suburbs. They can be stopped by hailing them at any point on their route. You can use your métro tickets on the buses, or you can buy a single-ride ticket on board. You need to show weekly/monthly/special tickets to the driver as you get on; if you have individual yellow tickets, you should state your destination and be prepared to punch one or more tickets in the red and gray machines on board the bus.

Important Addresses and Numbers

Tourist Information Paris Tourist Office (127 av. des Champs-Elysées, 75008 Paris, tel. 49–52–53–54). Open daily 9–8 (except Dec. 25, Jan 1). Offices in major train stations are open daily 8–8.

Embassies U.S. (2 av. Gabriel, 75008 Paris, tel. 42–96–12–02). Canada (35 av. Montaigne, 75008 Paris, tel. 44–43–29–00). U.K. (35 rue du Faubourg St-Honoré, 75008 Paris, tel. 42–66–91–42).

Emergencies Police: dial 17 for emergencies. Automatic phone booths can be found at various main crossroads for use in police emergencies *(Police-Secours)* or medical help *(Services Médicaux)*; ambulance (tel. 15 or 45–67–50–50); doctor (tel. 43–37–77–77); hospitals: American Hospital (63 blvd. Victor-Hugo, Neuilly, tel. 47–45–71–00); British Hospital (3 rue Barbès, Levallois-Perret, tel. 47–58–13–12); dentist (tel. 43–37–51–00; open 24 hours). Pharmacies: Dhéry (Galerie des Champs, 84 av. des Champs-Elysées, tel. 45–62–02–41; open 24 hours); Drugstore (corner of blvd. St-Germain and rue de Rennes; open until 2 AM); Pharmacie des Arts (106 blvd. Montparnasse; open until midnight).

English-Language Bookstores W. H. Smith (248 rue de Rivoli); Galignani (224 rue de Rivoli); Brentano's (37 av. de l'Opéra); Shakespeare & Co. (rue de la Bûcherie).

Most newsstands in central Paris sell *Time, Newsweek,* and the *International Herald Tribune,* as well as the English dailies.

Travel Agencies American Express (11 rue Scribe, 75009 Paris, tel. 47–77–77–07). Wagons-Lits (32 rue du Quatre-Septembre, 75002 Paris, tel. 42–66–15–80).

Guided Tours

Orientation Tours Bus tours of Paris offer a good introduction to the city. The two largest operators are Cityrama (4 pl. des Pyramides, tel. 44–55–61–00) and Paris Vision (214 rue de Rivoli, tel. 42–60–31–25). Tours start from their respective offices. Both are in the 1er arrondissement (ward), opposite the Tuileries Gardens (toward the Louvre end). Tours are generally given in double-decker buses with either a live guide or tape-recorded commentary. They last two to three hours and cost about 150 frs. The same operators also offer a variety of other theme tours (historic Paris, modern Paris, Paris by night) that last from 2½ hours to all day and cost between 150 and 450 frs. For a more intimate tour of the city, Cityrama also runs minibus excursions that pick you up and drop you off at your hotel. Costs run between 210 and 350 frs per person; reservations are necessary.

Boat Trips Boat trips along the Seine are a must for first-time Paris visitors. The two most famous services are the Bâteaux-Mouches, which leaves from the Pont de l'Alma, at the end of the avenue George V, and the Vedettes du Pont-Neuf, which sets off from the square du

Paris Métro

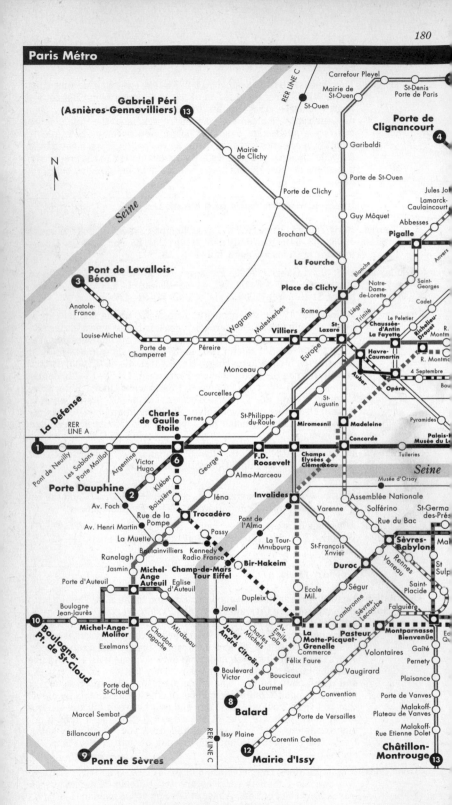

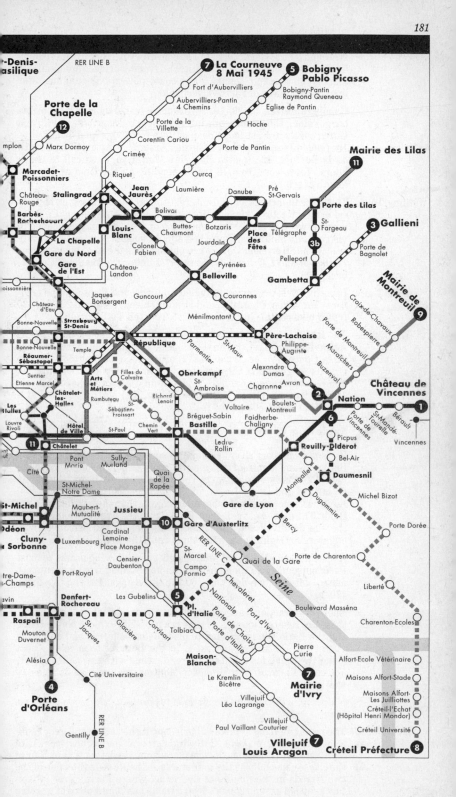

Vert Galant, on the western edge of the Ile de la Cité. Price per trip is around 40 frs. Boats depart in season every half hour from 10:30 to 5 (slightly less frequently in winter). Evening cruises are available most of the year and, thanks to the boats' powerful floodlights, offer unexpected views of Paris's riverbanks.

Canauxrama (tel. 42–39–15–00) organizes canal tours in flat-bottom barges along the picturesque but relatively unknown St-Martin and Ourcq canals in East Paris. Departures from 5 bis quai de la Loire, 19e (métro Jaurès), or the Bassin de l'Arsenal, opposite 50 boulevard de la Bastille, 12e (métro Bastille). Times vary, so call to check hours. Tours cost from 75 frs, depending on the time of day and length of trip.

Walking Tours There are numerous special-interest tours concentrating on historical or architectural topics. Most are in French, however. Charges vary between 40 and 60 frs, depending on fees that may be needed to visit certain buildings. Tours last about two hours and are generally held in the afternoon. Details are published in the weekly magazines *Pariscope* and *L'Officiel des Spectacles* under the heading "Conférences."

Bike Tours Paris by Cycle organizes daily bike tours around Paris and the environs (Versailles, Chantilly, and Fontainebleau) for about 220 frs, 120 frs for bike rental (78 rue de l'Ouest, 14e, tel. 43–35–28–63).

Excursions The **RATP** organizes many guided excursions in and around Paris. Ask at its tourist service on the place de la Madeleine (north of place de la Concorde), or at the RATP office at St-Michel (53 quai des Grands-Augustins). **Cityrama** and **Paris Vision** (*see* Orientation Tours, *above*) organize half- and full-day trips to Chartres, Versailles, Fontainebleau, the Loire Valley, and Mont St-Michel at a cost of between 150 and 750 frs.

Exploring Paris

Paris is a compact city. With the possible exception of the Bois de Boulogne and Montmartre, you can easily walk from one sight to the next. Paris is divided in two by the River Seine, with two islands (Ile de la Cité and Ile St-Louis) in the middle. The south—or Left—Bank has a more intimate, bohemian flavor than the haughtier Right Bank. The east–west axis from Châtelet to the Arc de Triomphe, via the rue de Rivoli and the Champs-Elysées, is the principal thoroughfare for sightseeing and shopping on the Right Bank.

A special **Carte Musécs et Monuments** pass, allowing access to most Paris museums and monuments, can be obtained from museums or métro stations (one-day pass, 60 frs; three days, 120 frs; five days, 170 frs).

Though attractions are grouped into four logical touring areas, there are several "musts." If time is a problem, explore Notre Dame and the Latin Quarter; head to place de la Concorde and enjoy the vista from the Champs-Elysées to the Louvre; then take a boat along the Seine for a waterside rendezvous with the Eiffel Tower. You could finish off with dinner in Montmartre and consider it a day well spent.

Numbers in the margin correspond to points of interest on the Paris map.

Notre Dame/ The most enduring symbol of Paris, and its historical and geograph-
Left Bank ic heart, is **Notre Dame Cathedral,** around the corner from Cité métro station. This is the logical place from which to start any tour of
➊ the city—especially as the tour starts on the **Ile de la Cité,** one of the two islands in the middle of the Seine, where Paris's first inhabitants settled around 250 BC. Notre Dame has been a place of worship for more than 2,000 years; the present building is the fourth on this

site. It was begun in 1163, making it one of the earliest Gothic cathedrals, although it was not finished until 1345. The facade seems perfectly proportioned until you notice that the north (left) tower is wider than the south. The interior is at its lightest and least cluttered in the early morning. Bay-by-bay cleaning is gradually revealing the original honey color of the stone. Window space is limited and filled with shimmering stained glass; the circular rose windows in the transept are particularly delicate. The 387-step climb up the towers is worth the effort for a perfect view of the famous gargoyles and the heart of Paris. *Admission to the cathedral is free. Admission to towers: 31 frs adults, 20 frs students, 7 frs children. Open 9:30–12:15 and 2–6 (2–5 in winter). Treasury (religious and vestmental relics) open weekdays 9:30–6, Sun. 2–6. Admission: 15 frs adults, 10 frs students, 5 frs children.*

The pretty garden to the right of the cathedral leads to a bridge that crosses to the city's second and smaller island, the **Ile St- Louis,** barely 650 yards long and an oasis of inner-city repose.

The rue des Deux-Ponts bisects the island. Head south over the Pont de la Tournelle. To your left is the **Tour d'Argent,** one of the city's most famous restaurants.

Continue along quai de la Tournelle past Notre Dame, then turn left at rue St-Jacques. A hundred yards ahead, on the right, is the back end of the **Eglise St-Séverin,** an elegant and unusually wide 16th-century church. Note the spiraling column among the forest of pillars behind the altar.

Turn left out of the church, cross the bustling boulevard St-Germain, and take rue de Cluny to the left. This leads to the **Hôtel de Cluny,** which houses the **Musée National du Moyen-Age,** a museum devoted to the late Middle Ages and Renaissance. Look for the *Lady with the Unicorn* tapestries and the beautifully displayed medieval statues. *6 pl. Paul-Painlevé. Admission: 27 frs adults, 18 frs students and children; 18 frs for all on Sun. Open Wed.–Mon. 9.30–5:15.*

Head up rue de la Sorbonne to the **Sorbonne,** Paris's ancient university. Students here used to listen to lectures in Latin, which explains why the surrounding area is known as the **Quartier Latin** (Latin Quarter). The Sorbonne is the oldest university in Paris—indeed, one of the oldest in Europe—and has for centuries been one of France's principal institutions of higher learning.

Walking up rue Victor-Cousin and turning left into rue Cujas, you come to the **Panthéon.** Its huge dome and elegant colonnade are reminiscent of St. Paul's in London but date from a century later (1758–89). The Panthéon was intended to be a church, but during the Revolution it was swiftly earmarked as a secular hall of fame. Its crypt contains the remains of such national heroes as Voltaire, Rousseau, and Zola. The interior is empty and austere, with principal interest centering on Puvis de Chavanne's late 19th-century frescoes, relating the life of Geneviève, patron saint of Paris. *Admission: 26 frs adults, 17 frs senior citizens, 6 frs children. Open daily 10–5:30.*

Behind the Panthéon is **St-Etienne du Mont,** a church with two claims to fame: its ornate facade and its curly Renaissance rood-screen (1521–35), the only one of its kind in Paris. Don't forget to check out the fine 17th-century glass in the cloister at the back of the church.

Take the adjoining rue Clovis, turn right into rue Descartes, then left at the lively place de la Contrescarpe down rue Rollin. Cross rue Monge to rue de Navarre. On the left is the **Arènes de Lutèce** (always open during daylight hours, admission free), a Gallo-Roman arena rediscovered only in 1869; it has since been landscaped and exca-

Paris

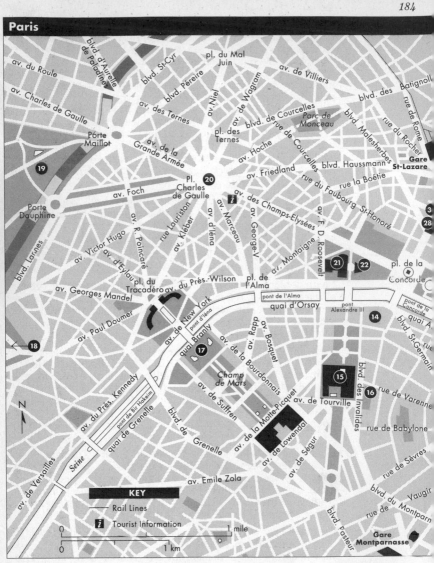

KEY

— Rail Lines

🛈 Tourist Information

0 ___ 1 mile
0 ___ 1 km

Arc de Triomphe, **20**
Arènes de Lutèce, **7**
Bois de Boulogne, **19**
Centre Pompidou, **39**
Eglise de la
Madeleine, **28**
Eglise St-Séverin, **3**
Eiffel Tower, **17**

Fauchon's, **29**
Grand Palais, **21**
Hédiard's, **30**
Hôtel de Cluny, **4**
Hôtel de Ville, **44**
Jardin des Plantes, **8**
Jardin des
Tuileries, **23**
Les grands
magasins, **34**
Les Halles, **38**

L'Hôtel des
Invalides, **15**
Louvre, **24**
Louvre des
Antiquaires, **36**
Moulin Rouge, **27**
Musée d'Orsay, **13**
Musée Marmottan, **18**
Musée Picasso, **40**

Musée Rodin, **16**
Notre Dame
Cathedral, **1**
Opéra, **33**
Palais Bourbon, **14**
Palais de Justice, **46**
Palais du
Luxembourg, **10**
Palais-Royal, **35**
Panthéon, **6**
Petit Palais, **22**

vated to reveal parts of the original amphitheater, and counts as one of the least-known points of interest in Paris.

8 Rue de Navarre and rue Lacépède lead to the **Jardin des Plantes** (Botanical Gardens), which have been on this site since the 17th century. The gardens have what is reputedly the oldest tree in Paris, a robinia planted in 1636 (allée Becquerel), plus several natural history museums, a zoo, alpine garden, hothouses, aquarium, and maze. Natural science enthusiasts will be in their element at the various museums, devoted to insects (Musée Entomologique), fossils and prehistoric animals (Musée Paléontologique), and minerals (Musée Minéralogique). The Grande Galerie de l'Evolution, with its mind-boggling collection of stuffed creatures (some now extinct), reopened in 1994 to great acclaim. *Admission: 12–40 frs. Museums open Wed.–Mon. 9–11:45 and 1–4:45.*

Head back up rue Lacépède from the Jardin des Plantes. Turn left into rue Gracieuse, then right into rue Ortolan, which soon crosses the **rue Mouffetard**—site of a colorful market and many restaurants. Continue along rue du Pot-de-Fer and rue Rataud. At rue Claude-Bernard, turn right; then make your first left up rue St-Jacques.

9 Set slightly back from the street is the **Val de Grâce,** a domed church designed by the great architect Jules Hardouin-Mansart and erected in 1645–67 (after the Sorbonne church but before the Invalides). Its two-tiered facade, with capitals and triangular pedestals, was directly inspired by the Counter-Reformation Jesuit architectural style found more often in Rome than in Paris. The Baroque style of the interior is epitomized by the huge twisted columns of the baldachin (ornamental canopy) over the altar.

Continue to the **Closerie des Lilas** along nearby boulevard de Port-Royal. This celebrated brasserie—and former haunt of such literary figures as Baudelaire, Verlaine, Hemingway, and Apollinaire—retains more style than some of its cousins farther down the once bohemian, now unexciting, boulevard du Montparnasse, whose modern landmark, the 656-foot Tour Montparnasse, is visible in the distance.

From the crossroads by the Closerie des Lilas there is an enticing view down the tree-lined avenue de l'Observatoire toward the **Palais du Luxembourg.** The palace was built by Queen Marie de' Médicis at the beginning of the 17th century in answer to Florence's Pitti Palace. It now houses the French Senate and is not open to the public. In the surrounding gardens, mothers push their baby carriages along tree-lined paths among the majestic fountains and statues.

Head through the gardens to the left of the palace into rue de Vaugirard. Turn left, then right into rue Madame, which leads down to the enormous 17th-century church of **St-Sulpice.** Stand back and admire the impressive, though unfinished, 18th-century facade, with its unequal towers. The interior is overwhelmingly impersonal, but the wall paintings by Delacroix, in the first chapel on the right, are worth a visit.

Rue Bonaparte descends to boulevard St-Germain. You can hardly miss the sturdy pointed tower of **St-Germain-des-Prés,** the oldest church in Paris (begun around 1160, though the towers date to the 11th century). Note the colorful nave frescoes by the 19th-century artist Hippolyte Flandrin, a pupil of Ingres.

The spirit of writers Jean-Paul Sartre and Simone de Beauvoir still haunts the **Café de Flore** opposite the church, though this, and the neighboring **Les Deux Magots,** have more tourists than literary luminaries these days. Still, you can linger over a drink while watching what seems to be all of Paris walking by.

Rue de l'Abbaye runs along behind St-Germain-des-Prés to place Fürstemberg, a charming little square where fiery Romantic artist Eugène Delacroix (1798–1863) had his studio. If you go there on a summer evening, you'll sometimes find young Frenchmen singing love songs. Turn left into rue Jacob and continue along rue de l'Université. You are now in the heart of the Carré Rive Gauche, the Left Bank's district of art dealers and galleries.

⑬ About a quarter of a mile along rue de l'Université, turn down rue de Poitiers. Ahead is the sandstone bulk of the **Musée d'Orsay.** Follow it around to the left to reach the main entrance. The new Musée d'Orsay—opened in late 1986—is already one of Paris's star tourist attractions, thanks to its imaginatively housed collections of the arts (mainly French) spanning the period 1848–1914. Exhibits take up three floors, but the visitor's immediate impression is one of a single, vast hall. This is not surprising: The museum was originally built in 1900 as a train station. The combination of hall and glass roof with narrow, clanky passages and intimate lighting lends Orsay a human, pleasantly chaotic feel.

The chief artistic attraction, of course, is the Impressionist collection, transferred from the inadequate Jeu de Paume museum across the river. Other highlights include Art Nouveau furniture, a faithfully restored Belle Epoque restaurant (formerly part of the station hotel), and a model of the Opéra quarter beneath a glass floor. *1 rue Bellechasse, tel. 40–49–48–14. Admission: 35 frs adults; 24 frs senior citizens, students, and children. Open Tues., Wed., Fri., Sat. 10–5:30; Thurs. 10–9:30; Sun. 9–5:30.*

If the lines outside the Musée d'Orsay prove daunting, take a peek into the **Légion d'Honneur** museum across the way, a stylish mansion with a collection of French and foreign medals and decorations. *Admission: 10 frs. Open Tues.–Sun. 2–5.*

⑭ Farther along on rue de l'Université is the 18th-century **Palais Bourbon,** home of the French National Legislature (Assemblée Nationale). The colonnaded façade commissioned by Napoléon is a sparkling sight after a recent cleaning program (jeopardized at one stage by political squabbles as to whether cleaning should begin from the left or the right). There is a fine view across to place de la Concorde and the Madeleine.

Follow the Seine down to the exuberant **Pont Alexandre III.** The Grand and Petit Palais are to your right, across the river. To the left, ⑮ the silhouette of **L'Hôtel des Invalides** soars above expansive if hardly manicured lawns. The Invalides was founded by Louis XIV in 1674 to house wounded (or "invalid") war veterans. Although only a few old soldiers live here today, the military link remains in the form of the **Musée de l'Armée**—a vast collection of arms, armor, uniforms, banners, and pictures. The **Musée des Plans-Reliefs** contains a fascinating collection of scale models of French towns made by the military architect Vauban in the 17th century.

The museums are far from being the only reason for visiting the Invalides. It is an outstanding Baroque ensemble, designed by Bruand and Mansart, and its church possesses the city's most elegant dome as well as the tomb of Napoléon, whose remains are housed in a series of no fewer than six coffins within a tomb of red porphyry. A son-et-lumière (sound and light) performance in English is held in the main courtyard on evenings throughout the summer (admission: 40 frs). *Admission to museums and church: 34 frs adults, 24 frs children. Open daily 10–6 (10–5 in winter).*

⑯ Alongside is the **Musée Rodin.** Together with the Picasso Museum in the Marais, this is one of the most charming of Paris's individual museums, consisting of an old house (built 1728) with a pretty garden, both filled with the vigorous sculptures of Auguste Rodin (1840–

1917). The garden also has hundreds of rosebushes, with dozens of different varieties. *77 rue de Varenne. Admission: 27 frs, 18 frs Sun. Open Tues.–Sun. 10–5.*

⑰ Take avenue de Tourville to avenue de La Motte-Picquet. Turn left, and in a few minutes you will come face-to-face with the **Eiffel Tower,** built by Gustave Eiffel for the World Exhibition of 1889. Recent restorations haven't made the elevators any faster—long lines are inevitable—but decent shops and two good restaurants have been added. Consider coming in the evening, when every girder is lit in glorious detail. Such was Eiffel's engineering precision that even in the fiercest winds the tower never sways more than a few centimeters. Today, of course, it is the best-known Parisian landmark. Standing beneath it, you may have trouble believing that it nearly became 7,000 tons of scrap-iron when its concession expired in 1909. Only its potential use as a radio antenna saved the day; it now bristles with a forest of radio and television transmitters. If you're full of energy, you can stride up the stairs as far as the tower's third floor, but only the elevator will take you right to the top. The view from 1,000 feet up will enable you to appreciate the city's layout and proportions. *Admission: on foot, 12 frs; elevator, 20–53 frs, depending on the level. Open July–Aug., daily 9 AM–midnight; Sept.–June, Sun.–Thurs. 9 AM–11 PM, Fri., Sat. 9 AM–midnight.*

West Paris and the Louvre

⑱ Our second itinerary starts at the **Musée Marmottan.** To get there, take the métro to La Muette, then head down chaussée de la Muette, through the small Ranelagh park to the corner of rue Boilly and avenue Raphaël. The museum is a sumptuous, early 19th-century mansion, replete with many period furnishings, and probably is the most underestimated museum in Paris. It houses a magnificent collection of paintings by Claude Monet, along with other Impressionist works and some delicately illustrated medieval manuscripts. *2 rue Louis-Boilly. Admission: 35 frs adults, 15 frs children and senior citizens. Open Tues.–Sun. 10–5:30.*

⑲ Continue along rue Boilly and turn left on boulevard Suchet. The next right takes you into the **Bois de Boulogne.** Class and style have been associated with "Le Bois" (The Woods) ever since it was landscaped into an upper-class playground by Haussmann in the 1850s. The attractions of this sprawling 2,200-acre wood include cafés, restaurants, gardens, waterfalls, and lakes. You could happily spend a day or two exploring, but for the moment we suggest that you pass Auteuil racetrack on the left and then walk to the right of the two lakes. An inexpensive ferry crosses frequently to an idyllic island. Rowboats can be rented at the far end of the lake. Just past the boathouse, turn right on the route de Suresnes and follow it to Porte Dauphine, a large traffic circle.

⑳ Cross over to avenue Foch, with the unmistakable silhouette of the Arc de Triomphe in the distance. Keep an eye out for the original Art Nouveau iron-and-glass entrance to Porte Dauphine métro station, on the left. Then continue along avenue Foch, the widest and grandest boulevard in Paris, to the **Arc de Triomphe.** This 164-foot arch was planned by Napoléon to celebrate his military successes. Yet when Empress Marie-Louise entered Paris in 1810, it was barely off the ground and an arch of painted canvas had to be strung up to save appearances. Napoléon had been dead for more than 20 years when the Arc de Triomphe was finally finished in 1836.

Place Charles de Gaulle, referred to by Parisians as **L'Etoile** (The Star), is one of Europe's most chaotic traffic circles. Short of a death-defying dash, your only way to get over to the Arc de Triomphe is to take the pedestrian underpass from either the Champs-Elysées (to your right as you arrive from avenue Foch) or avenue de la Grande Armée (to the left). France's Unknown Soldier is buried beneath the archway; the flame is rekindled every evening at 6:30.

From the top of the Arc you can see the "star" effect of Etoile's 12 radiating avenues and admire two special vistas: one down the Champs-Elysées toward place de la Concorde and the Louvre, and the other down avenue de la Grande Armée toward La Tête Défense, a severe modern arch surrounded by imposing glass and concrete towers. Halfway up the Arc is a small museum devoted to its history. *Museum and platform admission: 31 frs adults, 20 frs senior citizens, 6 frs children. Open daily 10–5:30; 10–5 in winter.*

The **Champs-Elysées** is the site of colorful national ceremonies on July 14 and November 11; its trees are often decorated with French tricolors and foreign flags to mark visits from heads of state. It is also where the cosmopolitan pulse of Paris beats strongest. The gracefully sloping 2-kilometer (1¼-mile) boulevard was originally laid out in the 1660s by André Le Nôtre as a garden sweeping away from the Tuileries. There is not much sign of that as you stroll past the cafés, restaurants, airline offices, car showrooms, movie theaters, and chic arcades that occupy its upper half, although the avenue was spruced up in the early 1990s, with wider sidewalks and an extra row of trees. Farther down, on the right, is the **Grand Palais,** ㉑ which plays host to Paris's major art exhibitions. Its glass roof makes its interior remarkably bright. *Admission varies. Usually open daily 10:30–6:30.*

The Grand Palais also houses the **Palais de la Découverte,** with scientific and mechanical exhibits and a planetarium. Entrance is in the avenue Franklin-Roosevelt. *Admission: 25 frs adults, 15 frs students; additional 15 frs (10 frs students) for planetarium. Open Tues.–Sat. 9:30–6, Sun. 10–7.*

Directly opposite the main entrance to the Grand Palais is the **Petit** ㉒ **Palais,** built at the same time (1900) and now home to an attractively presented collection of French paintings and furniture from the 18th and 19th centuries. *Admission: 26 frs adults, 14 frs students. Open Tues.–Sun. 10–5:40.*

Continue down to place de la Concorde, built around 1775 and scene of more than a thousand deaths at the guillotine, including those of Louis XVI and Marie Antoinette. The obelisk, a gift from the viceroy of Egypt, was erected in 1833.

㉓ To the east of the place de la Concorde is the **Jardin des Tuileries:** formal gardens with trees, ponds, and statues, currently undergoing renovations as part of the Grand Louvre Project. Standing guard on either side are the **Jeu de Paume** and the **Orangerie,** identical buildings erected in the mid-19th century. The Jeu de Paume, home of an Impressionist collection before its move to the Musée d' Orsay, has been completely transformed. Its spacious, austere, white-walled rooms now house temporary exhibits of contemporary art, usually at its most brazen. The Orangerie contains fine early 20th-century French works by Monet (including his *Water Lilies*), Renoir, Marie Laurencin, and others. *Admission to Jeu de Paume: 35 frs adults, 25 frs students. Open Tues. noon–9:30, Wed.–Fri. noon–7, weekends 10–7. Admission to Orangerie: 27 frs adults, 18 frs students, senior citizens, and on Sun. Open Wed.–Mon. 9:45–5:45.*

Pass through the Tuileries to the Arc du Carrousel, a rather small triumphal arch erected more quickly (1806–08) than its big brother at the far end of the Champs-Elysées. Towering before you is the ㉔ **Louvre,** with its glass pyramids. The Louvre, originally a royal palace, is today the world's largest and most famous museum. I. M. Pei's pyramids are the highlight of a major modernization program begun in 1984 and scheduled for completion in 1996. The plans include the extension of the museum collections into the Richelieu wing and cleaning of the facades, restoration of the gardens between the Louvre and the Tuileries, and the construction of an underground garage and shopping arcade, the **Carrousel du Louvre.** In the course of construction, the medieval foundations of the palace were unearthed and are maintained and displayed as an integral part of the museum's collection.

The Louvre was begun as a fortress in 1200 (the earliest parts still standing date from the 1540s) and completed under Napoléon III in the 1860s. The Louvre used to be even larger; a wing facing the Tuileries Gardens was razed by rampaging revolutionaries during the bloody Paris Commune of 1871.

Whatever the aesthetic merits of Pei's new-look Louvre, the museum has emerged less cramped and more rationally organized. Yet its sheer variety can seem intimidating. The main tourist attraction is Leonardo da Vinci's *Mona Lisa* (known in French as *La Joconde)*, painted in 1503. The latest research, based on Leonardo's supposed homosexuality, would have us believe that the subject was actually a man! The *Mona Lisa* may disappoint you; it's smaller than most imagine, it's kept behind glass, and it's invariably encircled by a mob of tourists.

Turn your attention instead to some of the less-crowded rooms and galleries nearby, where Leonardo's fellow Italians are strongly represented: Fra Angelico, Giotto, Mantegna, Raphael, Titian, and Veronese. El Greco, Murillo, and Velázquez lead the Spanish; Van Eyck, Rembrandt, Frans Hals, Brueghel, Holbein, and Rubens underline the achievements of northern European art. English paintings are highlighted by works of Lawrence, Reynolds, Gainsborough, and Turner. Highlights of French painting include works by Poussin, Fragonard, Chardin, Boucher, and Watteau—together with David's *Coronation of Napoleon*, Géricault's *Raft of the Medusa*, and Delacroix's *Liberty Guiding the People.*

Famous statues include the soaring *Victory of Samothrace* (3rd century BC), the celebrated *Venus de Milo* (end of 2nd century BC), and the realistic Egyptian *Seated Scribe* (circa 2000 BC). New rooms for sculpture were opened in the Denon Wing's former imperial stables in 1994. Be sure to inspect the Gobelins tapestries, the Crown Jewels (including the 186-carat Regent diamond), and the 9th-century bronze statuette of Emperor Charlemagne. *Admission 40 frs adults, 20 frs students and for all after 3 PM and Sun., children under 18 free. Open Mon. and Wed. 9–9:45 PM, Thurs.–Sun. 9–6.*

Montmartre If you start at the Anvers métro station and head up rue de Steinkerque, with its budget clothing shops, you will be greeted by the most familiar and spectacular view of the Sacré-Coeur basilica ㉕ atop the Butte Montmartre. The **Sacré-Coeur** was built in a bizarre, mock-Byzantine style between 1876 and 1910. It is no favorite with aesthetes, yet it has become a major Paris landmark. It was built as an act of national penitence after the disastrous Franco-Prussian War of 1870—a Catholic show of strength at a time when conflict between Church and State was at its most bitter.

The large, rather gloomy interior is short on stained glass but long on golden mosaics; *Christ in Glory*, above the altar, is the most impressive. The basilica's many cupolas are dominated by a dome and a 260-foot bell tower that contains the Savoyarde, one of the world's largest bells, cast in Annecy, Savoy, in 1895.

㉖ Around the corner is the **place du Tertre,** full of would-be painters and trendy, overpriced restaurants. The painters have been setting up their easels on the square for years; don't be talked into having your portrait done unless you really want to—in which case, check the price first.

Despite its eternal tourist appeal and ever-growing commercialization, Montmartre has not lost all its traditional bohemian color. Walk down rue Norvins and descend the bustling rue Lepic to place Blanche and one of the favorite haunts of Toulouse-Lautrec and other luminaries of the Belle Epoque—the legendary **Moulin Rouge** cabaret.

Montmartre is some distance from the rest of the city's major attractions, so go left up boulevard de Clichy as far as **place Pigalle,** then take the métro to Madeleine.

Central Paris The **Eglise de la Madeleine,** with its array of uncompromising columns, looks like a Greek temple. The only natural light inside comes from three shallow domes; the walls are richly but harmoniously decorated, with plenty of gold glinting through the dim interior. The church was designed in 1814 but not consecrated until 1842, after efforts to turn the site into a train station were defeated. The portico's majestic Corinthian colonnade supports a huge pediment with a sculptured frieze of the *Last Judgment*. From the top of the steps you can admire the vista down rue Royale across the Seine. Another vista leads up boulevard Malesherbes to the dome of **St-Augustin,** a mid-19th-century church notable for its innovative use of iron girders as structural support.

 Place de la Madeleine is in the heart of Paris's prime shopping district: Jewelers line rue Royale; **Fauchon's** and **Hédiard's,** behind the Madeleine, are high-class delicatessens. Alongside the Madeleine is a **ticket kiosk** (open Tues.–Sat. 12:30–8) selling tickets for same-day theater performances at greatly reduced prices.

Continue down boulevard de la Madeleine and turn right into rue des Capucines. This nondescript street leads to rue de la Paix. Immediately to the right is **place Vendôme.** This is one of the world's most opulent squares, a rhythmically proportioned example of 17th-century urban architecture that shines in all its golden-stone splendor since being sandblasted several years ago. Other things shine here, too, in the windows of jewelry shops that are even more upscale (and understated) than those in rue Royale—fitting neighbors for the top-ranking **Ritz** hotel. The square's central column, topped by a statue of Napoléon, is made from the melted bronze of 1,200 cannons captured at the Battle of Austerlitz in 1805.

Rue de la Paix leads to the place de l'Opéra. Dominating the northern side of the square is the imposing **Opéra,** the first great work of the architect Charles Garnier, who in 1860 won the contract to build the opera house. He used elements of neoclassical architecture—bas-reliefs on facades and columns—in an exaggerated combination that borders on parody. The lavishly upholstered auditorium, with its delightful ceiling painted by Marc Chagall in 1964, seems small—but this is because the stage is the largest in the world, accommodating up to 450 players. *Tel. 47–42–57–50. Admission: 30 frs adults, 18 frs students and children. Open daily 10–4:30.*

Behind the Opéra are *les grands magasins,* Paris's most venerable department stores. The nearer of the two, the **Galeries Lafayette,** is the more outstanding because of its elegant turn-of-the-century glass dome. But **Printemps,** farther along boulevard Haussmann to the left, is better organized and has an excellent view from its rooftop cafeteria.

Take the métro at Chaussée d'Antin, near the Galeries Lafayette, and travel three stops (direction Villejuif) as far as **Palais-Royal.** This former royal palace, built in the 1630s, has a charming garden, bordered by arcades and boutiques, that many visitors overlook.

On the square in front of the Palais-Royal is the **Louvre des Antiquaires,** a chic shopping mall full of antiques dealers. It deserves a browse whether you intend to buy or not. Afterward, head east along rue St-Honoré and left into rue du Louvre. Skirt the circular **Bourse du Commerce** (Commercial Exchange) and head toward the

③⑦ imposing church of **St-Eustache** (1532–1637), an invaluable testimony to the stylistic transition between Gothic and Classical architec-

③⑧ ture. It is also the "cathedral" of **Les Halles**—the site of the central market of Paris until the much-loved glass-and-iron sheds were torn down in the late '60s. The area has since been transformed into a trendy—and already slightly seedy—shopping complex, Le Forum.

Head across the topiary garden and left down rue Berger. Pass the square des Innocents, with its Renaissance fountain, to boulevard de Sébastopol. Straight ahead lies the futuristic, funnel-topped

③⑨ **Beaubourg** (a.k.a. the Pompidou Center)—a must for lovers of modern art. The Beaubourg was built in the mid-1970s and named in honor of former French president Georges Pompidou (1911–74). Always crowded, this "cultural Disneyland" houses a **Museum of Modern Art,** a huge library, experimental music and industrial design sections, a children's museum, and a variety of activities and exhibitions. Musicians, magicians, fire-eaters, and other street performers fill the large forecourt near the entrance. *Plateau Beaubourg, tel. 42–77–12–33. Admission free. Art museum admission: 30 frs; 20–50 frs for special exhibitions; 50 frs for daily pass covering all sectors of the center. Open Mon., Wed.–Fri. noon–10; weekends 10– 10. Guided tours in English in summer and the Christmas season: weekdays 3:30 PM and weekends 11 AM.*

Note, on the right side of the Beaubourg as you face it, the large digital clock, dubbed the **Genitron,** which counts down the seconds to the year 2000 at what seems like an apocalyptic pace. Peek into the café-lined **square Stravinsky** just to the right; kids will delight in the lively fountain animated by the colorful and imaginative sculptures and aquatic mechanisms by French artists Niki de Saint-Phalle and Jean Tinguely.

Continue east to the **Marais,** one of the most historic quarters of Paris. The spacious affluence of its 17th-century mansions *(hôtels particuliers),* many beautifully restored, contrasts with narrow winding streets full of shops and restaurants. Rue de Rambuteau leads from the Beaubourg into rue des Francs-Bourgeois. Turn left on rue Elzévir—via the **Musée Cognacq-Jay,** devoted to the arts of the 18th century—to rue Thorigny, where you will find the Hôtel

④⓿ Salé and its **Musée Picasso.** This is a convincing experiment in modern museum layout, whether you like Picasso or not. Few of his major works are here, but many fine, little-known paintings, drawings, and engravings are on display. *5 rue Thorigny, tel. 42–71–25–21. Admission: 26 frs adults, 17 frs senior citizens and for all on Sun., under 18 free. Open Wed.–Mon. 9:30–6.*

Double back down rue Elzévir and turn left along rue des Francs-

④① Bourgeois until you reach the **place des Vosges.** Built in 1605, this is the oldest square in Paris. Its harmonious proportions, soft pink brick, and cloisterlike arcades give the square an aura of calm. In the far corner is the **Maison de Victor Hugo,** containing souvenirs of the great poet's life and many of his surprisingly able paintings and ink drawings. *6 pl. des Vosges. Admission: 12 frs adults, 6.50 frs students and children. Open Tues.–Sun. 10–5:40.*

Rue Birague leads from the middle of the place des Vosges down to rue St-Antoine. About 250 yards along to the left is the **place de la**

④② **Bastille.** Unfortunately, there are no historic vestiges here; not even the soaring column, topped by the figure of Liberty, commemorates the famous storming of the Bastille in 1789 (the column stands in memory of Parisians killed in the uprisings of 1830 and 1848). Only the **Opéra de la Bastille,** which opened in 1989, can be said to mark the bicentennial.

Retrace your steps down rue St-Antoine as far as the large Baroque church of **St-Paul-St-Louis** (1627–41). Then continue down the rue de Rivoli to the **Hôtel de Ville.** This magnificent city hall was rebuilt in its original Renaissance style after being burned down in 1871, during the violent days of the Paris Commune. The vast square in front of its ornate facade is laid out with fountains and bronze lamps.

Avenue de Victoria leads to place du Châtelet. On the right is the **Tour St-Jacques.** This richly worked 170-foot stump is all that remains of a 16th-century church destroyed in 1802.

From Châtelet take the pont-au-Change over the Seine and back to the Ile de la Cité and the **Palais de Justice** (law courts). Visit the turreted **Conciergerie,** a former prison with a superb vaulted 14th-century hall (Salles des Gens d'Armes) that often hosts temporary exhibitions. The **Tour de l'Horloge** (clock tower) near the entrance on the quai de l'Horloge has a clock that has been ticking off time since 1370. Around the corner in the boulevard du Palais, through the imposing law court gates, is the **Sainte-Chapelle,** built by St-Louis (Louis IX) in the 1240s to house the Crown of Thorns he had just bought from Emperor Baldwin of Constantinople. The building's lead-covered wood spire, rebuilt in 1854, rises 246 feet. The somewhat garish lower chapel is less impressive than the upper one, whose walls consist of little else but dazzling 13th-century stained glass. *Conciergerie and Sainte-Chapelle. Admission: joint ticket 40 frs, single ticket 26 frs, 17 frs students. Open daily 9:30–6:30; winter 10–5.*

From boulevard du Palais turn right on quai des Orfèvres. This will take you past the quaint place Dauphine to the **square du Vert Galant** at the westernmost tip of the Ile de la Cité. Here, above a peaceful garden, you will find a statue of the Vert Galant: gallant adventurer Henry IV, king from 1589 to 1610.

Off the Beaten Track

Cemeteries aren't every tourist's idea of the ultimate attraction, but **Père Lachaise** is the largest, most interesting, and most prestigious in Paris. It forms a veritable necropolis with cobbled avenues and tombs competing in pomposity and originality. Steep slopes and lush vegetation contribute to a powerful atmosphere; some people even bring a picnic lunch. Leading incumbents include Chopin, Molière, Proust, Oscar Wilde, Sarah Bernhardt, Jim Morrison, Yves Montand, and Edith Piaf. Get a map at the entrance and track them down. *Av. du Père-Lachaise. Open daily 8–6, winter 8–5. Métro: Gambetta.*

Shopping

Gift Ideas Paris is the home of fashion and perfume. Old prints are sold in *bouquinistes* (stalls) along the Left Bank of the Seine. For classic reproduction home decorations, the shop in the **Musée des Arts Décoratifs** in the Louvre (107 rue de Rivoli) is well worth visiting. Regional specialty foods, herbs, and pâtés can be found at **Fauchon** and **Hédiard,** two upscale grocers at, respectively, 30 and 21 place de la Madeleine, 8e.

Boutiques Only Milan can compete with Paris for the title of Capital of European Chic. The top shops are along both sides of the Champs-Elysées and along the avenue Montaigne and the rue du Faubourg St-Honoré. The neighborhood around **place des Victoires** is a good place to look for avant-garde dress shops, as is the Marais. **St.-Germain-des-Prés, rue de Grenelle,** and **rue de Rennes** on the Left Bank are centers for small specialty shops, antiques galleries, and boutiques. If you're on a tight budget, search for bargains along the shoddy streets around the foot of Montmartre (*see* Exploring, *above*), or near **Barbès-Rochechouart** métro station. The streets to the north of the Marais, close to **Arts-et-Métiers** métro, are historically linked to the cloth trade, and many shops offer garments at wholesale prices.

Department Stores   The most famous department stores in Paris are **Galeries Lafayette** and **Printemps,** on boulevard Haussmann. Others include **Au Bon Marché** on the Left Bank (métro: Sèvre-Babylone) and the **Samaritaine,** overlooking the Seine east of the Louvre (métro: Pont-Neuf).

Food and Flea Markets   The sprawling **Marché aux Puces de St-Ouen,** just north of Paris, is one of Europe's largest flea markets. Best bargains are to be had early in the morning (open Sat.–Mon.; métro: Porte de Clignancourt). There are smaller flea markets at the Porte de Vanves and Porte de Montreuil (weekends only).

Dining

Eating out in Paris should be a pleasure, and there is no reason why choosing a less expensive restaurant should spoil the fun. After all, Parisians themselves eat out frequently and cannot afford five-star dining every night, either. For details and price-category definitions, *see* Dining *in* Staying in France, *above.*

Left Bank   **Les Bookinistes.** Talented chef Guy Savoy's fifth bistro annex—his
$$ first on the Left Bank—is a big success with the locals. The cheery,
★   peach-color postmodern room, with red, blue, and yellow wall sconces, looks out on the Seine. Savoy's menu of French country cooking changes seasonally, and might include a mussel and pumpkin soup, ravioli stuffed with chicken and celery, or baby chicken roasted in a casserole with root vegetables. The reasonable prices are challenged by a somewhat pricey wine list. The service is friendly and efficient. *53 quai des Grands-Augustins, 6e, tel. 43–25–45–94. Reservations advised. AE, DC, MC, V. Closed Sun., no lunch Sat. Métro: St-Michel.*

$$ **Campagne et Provence.** This small establishment on the quay across
★   from Notre Dame specializes in country cooking. The Provençal-inspired menu includes assorted vegetables stuffed with *brandade* (creamed salt cod), ratatouille, and beer *daube* (stew) with olives. You'll find some reasonably priced regional wines to accompany your always fresh, colorful meal here. *25 quai de la Tournelle, 5e, tel. 43–54–05–17. Reservations advised. MC, V. Closed Sun. No lunch Mon. or Sat. Métro: Maubert-Mutualité.*

$ **Le Petit St-Benoît.** This bare-bones bistro has been nurturing poor
★   students and travelers for more than 125 years. Classics of the *cuisine bourgeoise* are served by frequently sassy waitresses in a communal atmosphere. Try the veal roast, blanquette, or *hachis Parmentier* (ground-beef-and-mashed-potato pie). *4 rue St-Benoît, 6e, tel. 42–60–27–92. Reservations advised. No credit cards. Closed weekends. Métro: St-Germain-des-Prés.*

$ **Le Tout Petit Plat.** This charming and conveniently located wine bar, where the food's as good as the wine, occupies the tiny former quarters of the very popular Le Petit Plat. All the dishes are paired with a suggested glass of wine, allowing you to discover such mellifluous combinations as a plate of country ham, nutty *tête-de-moine* (monk's-head cheese), and a glass of crisp Vouvray. Other light, savory offerings include tomatoes and fennel *à la provençale*, and a delicious stewed chicken with five spices. *3 rue des Grands-Degrés, 5e, tel. 40–46–85–34. Reservations advised. MC, V. Closed Thurs. Métro: Maubert-Mutualité.*

$ **Vagenende.** This is a kind of poor man's Maxim's, with an equally gorgeous Belle Epoque interior—but without the pretense. Classic dishes include the house foie gras, sea trout with red-wine sauce, pot-au-feu, and *baba au rhum* (rum-soaked cake). Service can be inept when the large restaurant is full. Prix-fixe menus keep meals in this price range; à la carte is higher. Service until 1 AM. *142 blvd. St-Germain, 6e, tel. 43–26–68–18. Reservations advised. AE, MC, V. Métro: Odéon.*

¢ **Au Sauvignon.** A young, modish, intellectual crowd fills this tiny
★ wine bar, where you'll find the usual limited menu of *tartines,* or open-face sandwiches, on the famous Poilâne loaf, topped with good-quality charcuterie, cheese, or both. The colorful murals will amuse you, but it's even more fun to people-watch from one of the tables set on the narrow sidewalk. *80 rue des Saints-Pères, 7e, tel. 45–48–04–69. No reservations. No credit cards. Closed Sat. eve., Sun., Aug., Christmas wk, and Easter. Métro: Sèvres-Babylone.*

¢ **Thoumieux.** Virtually everything at this third-generation restaurant is made on the premises, including the foie gras, *rillettes* (minced, potted meat), duck confit, cassoulet, and the homey desserts. The red velour banquettes, mellow yellow walls, and bustling waiters in long white aprons are delightfully Parisian, but you'll hear a lot of English spoken here. *79 rue St-Dominique, 7e, tel. 47–05–49–75. Reservations advised. MC, V. Métro: Invalides.*

West Paris **Le Cercle Ledoyen.** This luxurious brasserie sits below the landmark
$$ restaurant Ledoyen. For about $50 a dinner—wine included—you can sample chef Ghislaine Arabian's cooking, including her specials served at Ledoyen. The handsome, curved dining room affording a view of the surrounding park is a pleasure year-round, and the terrace is a special treat in warm weather. *Carré des Champs-Elysées, 8e, tel. 47–42–23–23. Reservations advised. AE, DC, MC, V. Closed Sun. Métro: Champs-Elysées-Clemenceau.*

$ **Bistrot d'André.** This classic bistro stands close to the former site of the Citroën automobile factory, and car mementos—mainly plaques and old photos—line the walls. The wooden chairs and maroon-velvet benches conjure up a mood of prewar Paris, and jovial Hubert Gloaguen, the moustached patron, hosts half the quartier most nights. Bistro cooking at its sturdiest and most reliable includes snails, andouillette, confit *de canard* (duck), and chicken with tarragon. An aperitif (try the kir with red wine) and four courses plus coffee comes to under 150 francs, and a decent bottle of Burgundy won't push your check skyward either. *232 rue St-Charles, 15e, tel. 45–57–89–14. Reservations advised. MC, V. Closed Sat. lunch and Sun. Métro: Charles-Michel.*

¢ **Le Suffren.** Next to the Ecole Militaire, at the far end of the Champ de Mars, is this archetypal brasserie: lively, good value, with oysters, fish, and other seafood in abundance. Foreigners are treated with a welcome lack of condescension. *84 av. de Suffren, 15e, tel. 45–66–97–86. Reservations accepted. V. Closed Mon. Métro: Ecole-Militaire.*

Montmartre **Brasserie Flo.** This, the first of brasserie king Jean-Paul Bucher's
and Central seven Paris addresses, is hard to find down its passageway near the
Paris Gare de l'Est, but it's worth the effort. The rich wood and stained-
$$ glass interior is typically Alsatian, the service enthusiastic, and the brasserie standards, such as shellfish, steak tartare, and *choucroute,* savory. Order one of the carafes of Alsatian wine. An à la carte meal is outside our price range, but two lunch menus are under 175 francs, as is the after-11 PM Faim de Nuit menu. *7 cour des Petites-Ecuries, 10e, tel. 47–70–13–59. Reservations advised. AE, DC, MC, V. Métro: Château d'Eau.*

$$ **Chardenoux.** A bit off the beaten track, this cozy neighborhood bis-
★ tro with amber walls, etched-glass windows, dark bentwood furniture, tile floors, and a long zinc bar attracts a cross section of savvy Parisians with its first-rate, traditional cooking. Start with one of the delicious salads, such as the green beans and foie gras, and then try the veal chop with morels, or a game dish. Savory desserts and a nicely chosen wine list with several excellent Côtes-du-Rhônes complete the experience. *1 rue Jules-Vallés, 11e, tel. 43–71–49–52. Res-*

ervations advised. AE, V. Closed Sat., Sun., and Aug. Métro: Charonne.

$$ **Le Restaurant.** Here's a real oasis just steps from place Pigalle, an area where it's not easy to find a good meal. The simply decorated storefront dining room is popular with the artists and media types who've been quietly moving into this otherwise touristy and slightly tawdry neighborhood. The food is interesting and generally good; try the omelet of oysters, or lamb with fennel and black olives. For dessert, the shortbread tart filled with melted chocolate is delicious. The service is often slow, though, especially on weekends. *32 rue Véron, 18e, tel. 42–23–06–22. Reservations advised. AE, MC, V. Closed Mon. Métro: Abbesses.*

$ **Jo Goldenberg.** The doyen of Jewish eating places in Paris, Jo Goldenberg is in the heart of that most Jewish district, the Marais. Its two-level restaurant, with modern paintings, is always good-natured and crowded. The food is solid and cheap and heavily influenced by Central Europe (ground beef and salami), and there are a fair number of kosher dishes. This makes it a great place to dine on a winter evening, but a bit heavy going in summer. The Israeli and Eastern European wines are rarely available elsewhere in France. *7 rue des Rosiers, 4e, tel. 48–87–20–16. Reservations advised. AE, DC, V. Métro: St-Paul.*

¢ **Chartier.** People come here more for the bonhomie than the food, which is often rather ordinary. This cavernous, turn-of-the-century restaurant enjoys a huge following among the budget-minded, including students, solitary bachelors, and tourists. You may find yourself sharing a table with strangers as you study the long, old-fashioned menu of such favorites as hard-boiled eggs with mayonnaise, pâté, and roast veal with spinach. *7 rue du Faubourg-Montmartre, 9e, tel. 47–70–86–29. No reservations. No credit cards. Métro: Rue Montmartre.*

¢ **L'Ebauchoir.** Trendy, laid-back locals who know a bargain when they see one frequent this old-fashioned bistro with a classic, prewar decor. Don't expect dainty service, but come instead for a hearty feed and good, inexpensive wines. The salad with poached eggs and bacon bits and the confit de canard are delicious, as are the steaks and the homemade dessert tarts. *43–45 rue de Citeaux, 12e, tel. 43–42–49–31. Reservations advised. MC, V. Closed Sun. Métro: Faidherbe-Chaligny.*

Lodging

Paris is popular throughout the year, so make reservations early. For details and price-category definitions, *see* Lodging *in* Staying in France, *above.*

Left Bank **Elysa Luxembourg.** The Elysa is what the French call *un hôtel de*
$$ *charme.* Though the building is not large, most rooms are surpris-
★ ingly spacious, and all are exquisitely maintained and refurbished yearly. Cream-color furniture is set against pale blue or pink fabrics. You'll find a minibar in every room and a breakfast lounge serving Continental or buffet breakfasts. This is one of the rare hotels in the city with a sauna. *6 rue Gay-Lussac, 75005, tel. 43–25–31–74, fax 46–34–56–27. 25 rooms with bath, 5 with shower. Facilities: sauna. AE, MC, V. Métro: Luxembourg.*

$$ **Panthéon.** In a handsome 18th-century building facing the Panthé-
★ on, this excellent hotel has prices that range from $ to $$. Some of the charming rooms have exposed beams, balconies, and stunning views that stretch all the way to Sacré-Coeur; a vaulted breakfast room and impressive lobby are added attractions. The desk staff is very helpful. *19 pl. du Panthéon, 75005, tel. 43–54–32–95, fax 43–26–64–65. 34 rooms with bath. Facilities: breakfast room, air-conditioning. AE, DC, V. Métro: Luxembourg.*

$ **Esméralda.** You'll either love this hotel or hate it. The Esméralda, which boasts a fine (though noisy) location in a fusty 17th-century building across from Notre Dame, is famed for its cozy, eccentric charm. Some closet-size rooms are nearly overpowered by gaudy imitation antiques, and there's usually an assemblage of dogs and cats snoozing in the (tiny) lobby. Request a room with a view of the cathedral. Single rooms with showers on the landings are very cheap. *4 rue St-Julien-le-Pauvre, 75005, tel. 43–54–19–20, fax 40–51–00–68. 15 rooms with bath, 4 with shower on the landing. No credit cards. Métro: St-Michel.*

$ **Familia.** The hospitable Gaucheron family runs this comfortable ho-
★ tel with great panache. A mural painted by a local art student adorns the lobby, and the 30 rooms are clean, neat, and equipped with cable TV (with CNN) and hair dryers in the bathrooms. Rooms overlooking the attractive Left Bank street have double-glazed windows. Seven rooms with balconies are highly prized and must be booked well in advance. *11 rue des Ecoles, 75005, tel. 43–54–55–27, fax 43–29–61–77. 14 rooms with bath, 16 with shower. Facilities: minibars. MC, V. Métro: Jussieu, Maubert-Mutualité, Cardinal-Lemoine.*

$ **Grandes-Ecoles.** This delightful hotel in three small, old buildings is
★ set far off the street in a beautiful garden. There are parquet floors, antiques, and a (nonworking) piano in the breakfast area. Most rooms have beige carpets and flowery wallpaper. You won't find a quieter, more charming hotel for the price. There's a faithful American clientele, including some backpackers. The rooms with bathroom facilities on the well-lighted landings are inexpensive. *75 rue du Cardinal-Lemoine, 75005, tel. 43–26–79–23, fax 43–25–28–15. 29 rooms with bath, 10 with shower, 9 with shared bath. AE, MC, V. Métro: Cardinal-Lemoine.*

West Paris **Keppler.** Ideally located on the edge of the 8e and 16e arrondisse-
$$ ments near the Champs-Elysées, this small hotel in a 19th-century building has many of the amenities of a larger hotel—room service, small bar—at extremely reasonable prices. The spacious, airy rooms are simply decorated with modern furnishings. Some rooms with shower are less expensive. *12 rue Keppler, 75016, tel. 47–20–65–05, fax 47–23–02–29. 31 rooms with bath, 18 with shower. Facilities: bar. AE, MC, V. Métro: Kléber, George V.*

$ **Argenson.** This friendly, family-run hotel provides what may well be
★ the best value in the swanky 8e arrondissement. Some of the city's greatest sights are just a 10-minute walk away. Old furniture, molded ceilings, and skillful flower arrangements add to the charm. The best rooms have full baths, but they are pricier; reserve well in advance for one of these. The smallest rooms have shared baths. *15 rue d'Argenson, 75008, tel. 42–65–16–87, fax 47–42–02–06. 27 rooms, 24 with bath or shower. MC, V. Métro: Miromesnil.*

¢ **Grand Hôtel Lévèque.** A superb location near the Ecole-Militaire and a charming welcome are the Lévèque's biggest assets. Many of the airy, high-ceiling rooms were recently renovated, and while rooms vary in size, all are immaculate, as are the tiled bathrooms. The bright front rooms overlook a pedestrians-only market street lined with enticing food shops. Rooms that open onto the back courtyard are a few francs cheaper. If you are burdened with heavy luggage, book a room on a lower floor, as there is no elevator. *29 rue Cler, 75007, tel. 47–05–49–15, fax 45–50–49–36. 35 rooms with shower, 15 with shared bath. Facilities: lounge. MC, V. Métro: Ecole-Militaire.*

Montparnasse **Istria.** This small, charming hotel was once an artists' hangout. To-
$$ tally rebuilt in 1988 around a flower-filled courtyard on a quiet
★ street, it is now a family-run establishment with simple, clean, and comfortable rooms decorated in soft, summery colors. *29 rue Campagne-Première, 75014, tel. 43–20–91–82, fax 43–22–48–45. 4 rooms with bath, 22 with shower. AE, MC, V. Métro: Raspail.*

$ **Daguerre.** This sparkling-clean hotel not far from the Montparnasse
★ cemetery opened in 1994. All rooms are equipped with TV (CNN),
safes, minibars, and hair dryers. Two ground-floor rooms are set up
for wheelchair users. The hotel has an elevator. *94 rue Daguerre,
75014, tel. 43–22–43–54, fax 43–20–66–84. 8 rooms with bath, 22
with shower. AE, MC, V. Métro: Gaîté, Denfert-Rochereau.*

Marais **Bretonnerie.** This lovely, small hotel is on a tiny street in the Marais,
and Central a few minutes' walk from Beaubourg. The snug rooms are decorated
$$ in Louis XIII style, but vary considerably in size from spacious to
cramped. Some have antiques, beamed ceilings, and marble bath-
rooms. There's a breakfast room in the vaulted cellar. *22 rue Ste-
Croix-de-la-Bretonnerie, 75004, tel. 48–87–77–63, fax 42–77–26–
78. 30 rooms with bath, 2 suites with bath. Facilities: breakfast
room. MC, V. Closed Aug. Métro: Hôtel de Ville.*

$$ **Britannique.** During WWI the Britannique was the headquarters
for a Quaker mission. Today it's a friendly, family-owned hotel in a
restored 19th-century building, with a handsome winding staircase
and nicely decorated, soundproof rooms. *20 av. Victoria, 75001, tel.
42–33–74–59, fax 42–33–82–65. 31 rooms with bath, 9 with shower.
AE, DC, MC, V. Métro: Châtelet.*

$ **Allegro République.** This neighborhood in the 11e is eccentric and
★ eclectic, a mixture of Turkish restaurants and lace-curtain bistros
(the famous Astier is across the street from the hotel). The Allegro,
which opened in 1994, has small, cheerful rooms with beige floral
bedspreads and apple-green tiled bathrooms. The management is
exceptionally friendly. *39 rue Jean-Pierre Timbaud, 75011, tel. 48–
06–64–97, fax 48–05–03–38. 6 rooms with bath, 36 rooms with shower. AE, MC, V. Métro: République, Parmentier.*

$ **Place des Vosges.** A loyal American clientele swears by this small ho-
★ tel on a charming street just off the exquisite square of the same
name. Oak-beam ceilings and rough-hewn stone in public areas and
some of the guest rooms add to the atmosphere. Ask for the top-floor
room, the hotel's largest, with a view of Marais rooftops. There's a
welcoming little breakfast room. *12 rue de Birague, 75004, tel. 42–
72–60–46, fax 42–72–02–64. 11 rooms with bath, 5 with shower. Facilities: breakfast room. AE, DC, V. Métro: Bastille.*

¢ **Castex.** This family-run hotel in a 19th-century building is a real
★ find. The decor is strictly functional, but the extremely friendly
owners, squeaky-clean rooms, and rock-bottom prices mean the
Castex is often fully booked months ahead. There's a large American clientele. The eight least expensive rooms, two per floor, share
toilets on the immaculate, well-lighted landings. There's no elevator, and TV is in the lobby only. *5 rue Castex, 75004, tel. 42–72–31–
52, fax 42–72–57–91. 4 rooms with bath, 23 with shower. MC, V.
Métro: Bastille.*

¢ **Le Fauconnier.** This youth hostel offers simple, clean beds in rooms
for two, four, or six at just over 100 francs per person per night. The
building, a lovely 17th-century town house, is on a small, quiet
street near the Seine. Breakfast is served in a pleasant ground-floor
room or, in summer, on a small patio. Most rooms have a shower or
wash basin; the toilet is down the hall. Guests must be between the
ages of 18 and 30. *11 rue du Fauconnier, 75004, tel. 42–74–23–45,
fax 40–27–81–64. 28 rooms with shower; toilets on landings. Facilities: breakfast room. No elevator. No credit cards. No reservations.
Métro: St-Paul.*

¢ **Lille.** You won't find a less expensive base for exploring the Louvre
than this hotel, located a short distance from the Cour Carrée. The
facade received a face-lift a few years ago, but the somewhat shabby
interior and minimal plumbing down long corridors were not upgraded. Hence the very low prices. Still, the Lille is a slice of Old
Paris. There's no elevator, and not all rooms have TVs or phones. *8
rue du Pélican, 75001, tel. 42–33–33–42. 6 rooms with shower, 7
with shared bath. No credit cards. Métro: Palais-Royal.*

The Arts

The monthly English-language magazine *Paris Boulevard* and the weekly magazines *Pariscope, L'Officiel des Spectacles,* and *Figaroscope* give detailed entertainment listings. The Paris Tourist Office has set up a **24-hour English-language hot line** (tel. 49–52–53–56) with information about weekly events. The best place to buy tickets is at the place of performance. Otherwise, try hotels, travel agencies (try **Paris-Vision** at 214 rue de Rivoli), and special ticket counters (**Alpha-FNAC,** 1–5 rue Pierre-Lescot, Forum des Halles, 3rd level down). Half-price tickets for same-day theater performances are available at the ticket stand at the **Kiosque Théâtre,** on the west side of the Madeleine church.

Theater   There is no Parisian equivalent to Broadway or the West End, although a number of theaters line the grand boulevards between Opéra and République. Shows are mostly in French; classical drama is at the distinguished **Comédie Française** (by the Palais-Royal). A completely different charm is to be found in the tiny **Théâtre de la Huchette,** near St-Michel, where Ionesco's short modern plays make a deliberately ridiculous mess of the French language.

Concerts   The principal venues for classical music are the **Salle Pleyel** (252 rue du Faubourg St-Honoré), near the Arc de Triomphe; the new **Opéra Bastille;** and the **Châtelet** theater (place Châtelet). You can also attend one of the many inexpensive organ or chamber music concerts in churches throughout the city.

Opera   The "old" **Opéra,** or **Opéra Garnier** (*see* Dance, *below*), ceded its role as Paris's main opera house to the **Opéra Bastille** (pl. de la Bastille, 12e, tel. 44–43 96–96 or 44–73–13–00), which stages both traditional opera and symphony concerts. Getting a ticket for an opera or ballet performance is not easy, though, and requires either luck, much planning, or a well-connected hotel receptionist. The **Opéra Comique** (the French term for opera with spoken dialogue), close by at 5 rue Favart (tel. 42 60–04–99) is more accessible.

Dance   The highlights of the Paris dance year usually take place at the **Opéra Garnier** (pl. de l'Opéra, 9e, tel. 47–42–53–71), which, in addition to being the sumptuous home of the well-reputed Paris Ballet, also bills dozens of major foreign troupes ranging from classical to modern. Other major venues include the **Théâtre de la Ville** (tel. 42–74–22–77) at place du Châtelet and the **Palais des Congrès** (tel. 40–68–00–05) at Porte Maillot.

Film   There are hundreds of movie theaters in Paris, and some of them, especially in principal tourist areas such as the Champs-Elysées and the boulevard des Italiens near the Opéra, run English films marked "V.O." *(version originale*—i.e., not dubbed). Admission is around 40 frs–50 frs, with reduced rates on Monday. Movie fanatics should check out the **Beaubourg** and **Musée du Cinéma** at Trocadéro, where old and rare films are often screened.

Nightlife

Cabaret   This is what Paris is supposed to be all about. Its nightclubs are household names—more so abroad than in France, it would seem, judging by the hefty percentage of foreigners present at most shows. Prices range from 200 frs (basic admission plus one drink) up to 700 frs (dinner included). For 350 frs–500 frs, you can get a good seat plus half a bottle of champagne.

The **Crazy Horse** (12 av. George-V, tel. 47–23–32–32) is one of the field leaders in pretty women and dance routines: It features lots of humor and a lot less clothes. The **Moulin Rouge** (pl. Blanche, tel. 46–06–00–19) is an old favorite at the foot of Montmartre. Nearby is the **Folies-Bergère** (32 rue Richer, tel. 42–46–77–11), which reopened at the end of 1993 with a new show recalling its music-hall origins. The **Lido** (116 bis av. des Champs-Elysées, tel. 40–76–56–10) is all razzle-dazzle after its $10 million facelift in 1994.

Bars and Nightclubs Upscale nightclubs are usually private, so unless you have a friend who is a member, forget it. Try the wildly popular **Niel's** (27 av. Ternes, 17e) or **Sheherazade** (93 rue de Liège, 9e) on weeknights only, or you run the risk of spending the evening waiting in line on the sidewalk.

The Pigalle area in Montmartre is becoming the place to be, despite its reputation as a seedy red-light district. Among hot places here are: **Moloko** (26 rue Fontaine, 9e), a smoky late-night bar; **Le Dépanneur** (next door at 27 rue Fontaine), which caters to more of a gin-drinking yuppie crowd; **Lili la Tigresse** (98 rue Blanche, 9e), a sexy bar with a trendy crowd; and—not to be missed—the brasserie **Pigalle** (22 blvd. de Clichy, 18e), whose '50s frescoes and ceramics have been classified as a national treasure.

The nightlife is still hopping in and around the Bastille: the **China Club** (50 rue de Charenton, 12e) is a trendy bar with an Orient Express theme; **Le Casbah** (18 rue de la Forge Royale, 11e) is a bar and dance club with a touch of Casablanca; and **Le Piston Pelican** (15 rue de Bagnolet, 20e), a favorite among Beaux-Arts students, has a laid-back ambience and occasional live music.

For a more leisurely experience in an atmosphere that is part bar and part gentlemen's club, try an old haunt of Hemingway, the Fitzgeralds, and Gertrude Stein: **Harry's Bar** (5 rue Daunou), a cozy, wood-paneled spot for Americans, journalists, and sportsmen.

Gay and Lesbian Gay and lesbian bars and clubs are mostly concentrated in the Marais and include some of the most happening addresses in the city. The very trendy **Banana Café** (13 rue de la Ferronnerie, 1er) attracts an energetic and scantily clad mixed crowd; dancing on the tables is the norm. For men, **Le Quetzal** (10 rue de la Verrerie, 4e), which features a chrome-and-blue-light atmosphere, gets very crowded and smoky on weekends; **The Trap** (10 rue Jacob, 6e) contains a ground-floor video bar with a staircase leading to a darker, more social area. For a more relaxed atmosphere try **Subway** (35 rue Ste-Croix-de-la-Bretonnerie, 4e), a popular hangout that has pinball and pool.

For women, **La Champmeslé** (4 rue Chabanais, 2e) is the hub of lesbian nightlife with a back room reserved for women only; **Le Memorie's** (2 pl. de la Porte-Maillot, 17e), though in a staid neighborhood, is Paris's most renowned lesbian dance club.

Jazz Clubs The Latin Quarter is a good place to track down Paris jazz, and the doyen of clubs is the **Caveau de la Huchette** (5 rue de la Huchette), where you can hear Dixieland in a hectic, smoke-filled atmosphere. **Le Slow Club** (130 rue de Rivoli), another favorite, tries to resurrect the style of early Bourbon Street, and nearly succeeds.

Rock Clubs **Le Sunset** (60 rue des Lombards) is a small, whitewashed cellar with first-rate live music and a clientele that's there to listen. **New Morning** (7 rue des Petites-Ecuries) is a top spot for visiting American musicians and good French bands.

Discos **Club Zed** (2 rue des Anglais off blvd. St-Germain, 5e) is the best place for rock and roll. The long-established **Balajo** (9 rue de Lappe, 11e) is crowded and lots of fun, with plenty of nostalgic '60s sounds often dominating the selection. **Memphis** (3 impasse Bonne-Nouvelle) boasts some impressive lighting and video gadgetry.

Ile de France

The area surrounding Paris is called the Ile (island) de France, reflecting the role it has played over the centuries as the economic, political, and religious center of the country. For many visitors to Paris, it is the first taste of French provincial life, with its slower pace and fierce devotion to the soil.

Although parts of the area are fighting a losing battle to resist the encroaching capital, you can still see the countryside that was the inspiration for the Impressionists and other 19th-century painters and is home to a wealth of architecture dating from the Middle Ages. The most famous buildings are Chartres—one of the most beautiful of French cathedrals—and Versailles, the monumental château of Louis XIV, the Sun King.

Before the completion of Versailles, king and court resided in the delightful château of St-Germain-en-Laye, west of Paris. This is within easy day-trip range from Paris, as are the châteaus of Vaux-le-Vicomte, Rambouillet, and Fontainebleau, and the newest Disney venture, Disneyland Paris.

Getting Around

The region is reached easily from Paris by car and by regular suburban train services, but you may find it convenient to group some sights together: Versailles, Rambouillet, and Chartres are all on the Paris–Chartres train line; Fontainebleau, Barbizon, and Vaux-le-Vicomte are all within a few miles of each other.

By Train Three lines connect Paris with Versailles; on each, the trip takes about 30 minutes. Best for the château is RER-C5 to Versailles Rive Gauche station. Trains from Gare St-Lazare go to Versailles Rive Droite. Trains from Gare Montparnasse go to Versailles Chantiers and then on to Rambouillet and Chartres. Fontainebleau is served by 20 trains a day from Gare de Lyon; buses for Barbizon leave from in front of the main post office in Fontainebleau. The RER-A4 line will take you to Disneyland Paris.

Guided Tours

Two private companies, **Cityrama** and **Paris Vision,** organize regular half-day and full-day tours from Paris with English-speaking guides. Times and prices are identical. Tours are subject to cancellation, and reservations are suggested. Cityrama tours depart from 4 place des Pyramides, 1er (tel. 44–55–61–00). Paris Vision leaves from 214 rue de Rivoli, 1er (tel. 42–60–31–25).

Versailles and Les Trianons. Daily excursions starting at 9:30 include a complete tour of Paris in the morning followed by an afternoon at Versailles. Half-day excursions of Versailles leave mornings and afternoons daily (9:30 and 2:30; 300 frs) and include a guided tour of the château, Hall of Mirrors, and Queen's Suite. On Thursday only, you can extend the morning tour (450 frs) to include an afternoon visit (starting 1:30) to the Trianons, or take a separate afternoon visit there (1:30; 220 frs).

Chartres. Both companies organize half-day tours to Chartres on Tuesday, Thursday, and Saturday afternoons (1:30; 270 frs) and **Versailles–Chartres** day trips on Tuesday and Saturday (9:30; 450 frs).

Fontainebleau and Barbizon. Half-day trips (1:30; 310 frs) on Wednesday, Friday, and Sunday run to Fontainebleau and nearby Barbizon (which is otherwise difficult to reach); these two can also be linked to a Versailles tour leaving at 9:30 on the same days.

Tourist Information

Barbizon (41 rue Grande, tel. 60–66–41–87).
Chartres (pl. de la Cathédrale, tel. 37–21–50–00).
Disneyland Paris (Central Reservations Office, Box 105, Marne-la-Vallée Cedex 4, 77777 France, tel. 60–30–60–30).
Fontainebleau (31 pl. Napoléon-Bonaparte, tel. 64–22–25–68).
Rambouillet (8 pl. de la Libération, tel. 34–83–21–21).
Versailles (7 rue des Réservoirs, tel. 39–50–36–22).

Exploring the Ile de France

Versailles   **Versailles** is the location of one of the world's grandest palaces and one of France's most popular attractions. Wide, tree-lined avenues, broader than the Champs-Elysées and bordered with massive 17th-century mansions, lead directly to the Sun King's château. From the imposing place d'Armes in front of the château, you enter the Cour des Ministres, a sprawling cobbled forecourt. Right in the middle, the statue of Louis XIV stands triumphant, surveying the town that he built from scratch to house those of the 20,000 noblemen, servants, and hangers-on who weren't lucky enough to get one of the 3,000 beds in the château.

The building of the château in its entirety took 50 years. Hills were flattened, marshes drained, forests transplanted, and water for the magnificent fountains was channeled from the Seine several miles away. Visit the **Grands Appartements,** the six salons that made up the royal living quarters, and the famous **Galerie des Glaces** (Hall of Mirrors). Both can be visited without a guide, but you can get a cassette in English. There are also guided tours of the **Petits Appartements,** where the royal family and friends lived in relative intimacy, and the miniature opera house—one of the first oval rooms in France, built on the *aile nord* (north wing) for Louis XV in 1770. *Grands Appartements and Galerie des Glaces admission: 40 frs adults, 26 frs students and senior citizens. Open Tues.–Sun. 9–6:30 (9–5:30 in winter).*

The château's vast grounds are masterpieces of formal landscaping. At one end of the Petit Canal, which crosses the Grand Canal at right angles, is the **Grand Trianon,** a scaled-down pleasure palace built in the 1680s. The **Petit Trianon,** nearby, is a sumptuously furnished 18th-century mansion, commissioned by Louis XVI for Marie Antoinette, who would flee here to avoid the stuffy atmosphere of the court. Nearby, she built the village, complete with dairy and mill, where she and her companions would dress as shepherdesses and lead a make-believe bucolic life. *Château grounds: admission free. Open 8:30–dusk. Grand Trianon admission: 21 frs adults, 14 frs children and senior citizens. Open June–Sept., daily 10–6:30; Oct.–May, daily 10–12:30 and 2–5:30. Petit Trianon admission: 12 frs adults, 8 frs children and senior citizens. Open June–Sept., daily 10–6:30; Oct.–May, daily 2–5:30.*

Rambouillet   Just a little more than 20 kilometers (12 miles) southwest of Versailles is the small town of **Rambouillet,** home of a château, adjoining park, and 34,000 acres of forest. Since 1897, the château has been a summer residence of the French president; today, it is also used as a site for international summits. You can visit the château only when the president is not in residence—fortunately, he's not there often.

French kings have lived in the château since it was built in 1375. Highlights include the **Appartements d'Assemblée,** decorated with finely detailed wood paneling, and Napoléon's bathroom, with its Pompeii-inspired frescoes. The park stretches way behind the château. Beyond the **Jardin d'Eau** (Water Garden) lies the English-style garden and the **Laiterie de la Reine** (Marie Antoinette's Dairy). This was another of her attempts to "get back to nature." *Tel. 34–83–00–*

Ile de France

25. *Admission: 27 frs adults, 17 frs children and senior citizens. Open Wed.–Mon. 10–11:30 and 2–4:30 (till 5:30 Apr.–Sept.). Park admission free. Open sunrise–sunset. Marie Antoinotte's Duiry admission: 13 frs. Open same hrs as château; closes at 4 in winter.*

Chartres   Long before you arrive you will see **Chartres's** famous cathedral towering over the plain of the Beauce, France's granary. The attractive old town, steeped in religious history and dating from before the Roman conquest, is still laced with winding medieval streets.

Today's Gothic cathedral, **Notre Dame de Chartres,** is the sixth Christian church to have been built on the site; despite a series of fires, it has remained virtually the same since the 12th century. The **Royal Portal** on the main facade, presenting "the life and triumph of the Savior," is one of the finest examples of Romanesque sculpture in the country. Inside, the 12th- and 13th-century rose windows come alive even in dull weather, thanks to the deep Chartres blue of the stained glass: Its formula remains a mystery to this day. *Cathedral tours available: Ask at the Maison des Clercs, 18 rue du Cloître Notre Dame. Tours in English daily noon and 2:45.*

As the rest of the tour is on another side of Paris, it is probably easiest to return to the capital to continue (*see* Getting Around Ile de France, *above*).

Fontainebleau   In the early 16th century, the flamboyant François I transformed the medieval hunting lodge of **Fontainebleau** into a magnificent Renaissance palace. His successor, Henry II, covered the palace with his initials, woven into the *D* for his mistress, Diane de Poitiers. When he died, his queen, Catherine de' Medici, carried out further alterations, later extended under Louis XIV. Napoléon preferred the relative intimacy of Fontainebleau to the grandeur of Versailles. Before he was exiled to Elba, he bade farewell to his Old Guard in the courtyard, now known as the **Cour des Adieux** (Farewell Court). The emperor also harangued his troops from the **Horseshoe Staircase.**

Ask the curator to let you see the **Cour Ovale** (Oval Court), the oldest and perhaps most interesting courtyard. It stands on the site of the original 12th-century fortified building, but only the keep remains today.

The **Grands Appartements** (royal suites and ballroom) are the main attractions of any visit to the château. The **Galerie de François I** is really a covered bridge (built 1528–30) looking out over the Cour de la Fontaine. The overall effect inside the Galerie—and throughout Fontainebleau—is one of classical harmony and proportion, combining to create a sense of Renaissance lightness and order. François I appreciated the Italian Renaissance, and the ballroom is decorated with frescoes by Primaticcio (1504–70) and his pupil, Niccolò dell'Abbate. If you're here on a weekday, you will also be able to join a guided tour of the Petits Appartements, used by Napoléon and Josephine. *Pl. du Général-de-Gaulle, tel. 64–22–27–40. Admission: 31 frs, 20 frs under 25 and for all on Sun. Open Wed.–Mon. 9:30–12:30 and 2–5.*

Barbizon The **Rochers des Demoiselles,** a rocky outcrop just south of town, are good for an afternoon stroll. The **Gorges d'Apremont,** which offer the best views of the rocks, are near **Barbizon,** on the edge of the forest, 10 kilometers (6 miles) northwest of Fontainebleau. This delightful little village is scarcely more than a main street lined with restaurants and boutiques, but a group of landscape painters put it on the map in the mid-19th century. Théodore Rousseau and Jean-François Millet both had their studios here. Sculptor Henri Chapu's bronze medallion, sealed to one of the famous sandstone rocks in the forest nearby, pays homage to the two leaders of what became known as the Barbizon group.

Drop in at the **Ancienne Auberge du Père Ganne** (rue Grande), where most of the landscape artists ate and drank while in Barbizon. They painted on every available surface, and even now you can see some originals on the walls and in the buffet.

Next to the church, in a barn that Rousseau used as a studio, you'll find the **Musée de l'Ecole de Barbizon** (Barbizon School Museum), containing documents of the village as it was in the 19th century as well as a few original works by Rousseau, Diaz, Troyon, and Charles Jacque. *55 rue Grande, tel. 60–66–22–38. Admission: 15 frs adults. Open Apr.–Sept., Wed.–Sun. 10:30–12:30 and 2–6; Oct–Mar., Wed.–Sun. 10:30–12:30 and 2–5.*

Disneyland Now you can get a dose of American pop culture in between visits to
Paris the Louvre and the Left Bank. In 1992, the **Disneyland Paris** (formerly Euro Disney) complex opened in Marne-la-Vallée, just 32 kilometers (20 miles) east of Paris. The complex is divided into several areas, including the pay-as-you-enter theme park that is the main reason for coming here. Occupying 136 acres, Disneyland is less than half a mile across and ringed by a railroad with whistling steam engines. Although smaller than its U.S. counterparts, Disneyland Paris was built with great attention paid to the tiniest detail. Smack in the middle of the park is the soaring Sleeping Beauty Castle, which is surrounded by a plaza from which you can enter the four "lands" of Disney: **Frontierland, Adventureland, Fantasyland,** and **Discoveryland.** In addition, Main Street U.S.A. connects the castle to the entrance, under the pointed pink domes of the Disneyland Hotel. In 1995, Disneyland Paris inaugurated its newest attraction, **Space Mountain,** aiming to catapult riders through the Milky Way. *Admission: 150–195 frs adults, 120–150 frs children under 12. Open Apr.–mid-June, weekdays 9–7, weekends 9–midnight; mid-June–Aug., daily 9–midnight; Sept.–Oct., weekdays 9–7, weekends 9–9; Nov.–Mar., weekdays 10–6, weekends 10–9.*

There are six hotels in the 4,800-acre Disneyland Paris complex, all just outside the theme park. The resort also comprises parking lots, a train station, and the Festival Disney entertainment center, with restaurants, a theater, dance clubs, shops, a post office, and a tourist office. Cheaper accommodations—log cabins and campsites—are available at Camp Davy Crockett, farther from the theme park.

Dining and Lodging

For details and price-category definitions, *see* Dining *and* Lodging *in* Staying in France, *above.*

Barbizon **Le Relais.** The delicious specialties—particularly the beef and the
Dining game (in season)—are served in large portions, and there is a good choice of prix-fixe menus. The Relais is spacious, with walls covered with paintings and hunting trophies, and there is a big open fire. The owner is proud of the large terrace, where you can eat in the shade of lime and chestnut trees. *2 av. du Charles-de-Gaulle, tel. 60–66–40–28. Weekend reservations required. MC, V. Closed Tues., Wed., 2nd ½ of Aug., most of Jan. $*

Dining and **Auberge des Alouettes.** This delightful 19th-century inn is set on two
Lodging acres of grounds. The interior has been redecorated in '30s style, but many rooms still have their original oak beams. The restaurant, with a large open terrace, features nouvelle cuisine in sizable portions. *4 rue Antoine-Barye, 77630, tel. 60–66–41–98, fax 60–66–20–69. 23 rooms with bath. Facilities: restaurant, tennis, parking. Reservations required for restaurant. AE, DC, MC, V. $*

Chartres **Le Buisson Ardent.** Set in an attractive, old, oak-beam building
Dining within sight of the cathedral's south portal, Buisson Ardent is a popular restaurant providing inexpensive prix-fixe menus (especially good on weekdays) and a choice of imaginative à la carte dishes with delicious sauces. The wine list is comprehensive. *10 rue au Lait, tel. 37–34–04–66. Reservations advised. AE, DC, MC, V. Closed Sun. evenings. $*

Dining and **La Poste.** This comfortable, traditional hotel—smarter these days
Lodging but still with a folksy charm to its rambling corridors and faded bedroom wallpaper—is reasonably priced and, above all, brilliantly situated between the station and the cathedral. The spacious dining room offers a choice of set menus, two of which fall in our $ category; the à la carte offerings are inventive but expensive. *3 rue du Général-Koenig, tel. 37–21–04–27. 59 rooms, some with shower. Facilities: restaurant. AE, DC, MC, V. $*

Lodging **Grand Monarque.** The most popular rooms in this 18th-century coaching inn are in a separate turn-of-the-century building overlooking a garden. Rooms have the level of comfort and consistency you would expect from a Best Western. The hotel also has an excellent, reasonably priced restaurant. *22 pl. des Epars, tel. 37–21–00–72. 54 rooms with bath or shower. Facilities: restaurant. AE, DC, MC, V. $$*

Disneyland **Disneyland** is peppered with places to eat, ranging from snack bars
Paris and fast-food joints to full-service restaurants—all with a distin-
Dining guishing theme. In addition, all Disney hotels have restaurants that are open to the public. As these are outside the theme park, it is not recommended that you waste time traveling to them for lunch. Disney now offers wine and beer at sit-down restaurants within the park. Eateries serve nonstop as long as the park is open. *For restaurant reservations, tel. 60–45–65–40. Sit-down restaurants (reservations advised; AE, DC, MC, V) $–$$; counter-service restaurants (no credit cards). ¢–$*

Fontainebleau **La Table des Maréchaux.** Right on the town's main street, just five
Dining minutes from the château, this lovely restaurant has two reasonably priced lunch menus (130 frs and 180 frs). Traditional French dishes

include gizzard salad and lamb with béarnaise sauce. *9 rue Grande, tel. 64–22–20–39. Reservations advised. AE, MC, V. $$*

Lodging **Londres.** The balconies of this tranquil, family-style hotel look out over the palace and the Cour des Adieux; the 19th-century facade is preserved by government order. Inside, the decor is dominated by Louis XV furniture. *1 pl. du Général-de-Gaulle, tel. 64–22–20–21, fax 60–72–39–16. 22 rooms with bath. Facilities: restaurant, tearoom, bar, parking. AE, DC, MC, V. Closed Dec. 20–Jan. 5. $*

Rambouillet **La Poste.** Traditional, unpretentious cooking is the attraction of this **Dining** former coaching inn, close to the château. The restaurant's two dining rooms are often packed with a lively group. The service is good, as is the selection of inexpensive prix-fixe menus, even on Sunday. *101 rue du Général-de-Gaulle, tel. 34–83–03–01. Reservations advised. AE, MC, V. Closed Mon. No dinner Sun. $*

Versailles **Quai No. 1.** Fish enthusiasts don't have to spend a fortune in Ver- **Dining** sailles, as a visit to this atmospheric restaurant—awash in wood and brass and decked out in seafaring paraphernalia—will underline. Smoked salmon is the house specialty, and crème brûlée the pick of the desserts. *1 av. de St-Cloud, tel. 39–50–42–26. Reservations advised. MC, V. Closed Mon. No dinner Sun. $$*
Londres. This is the place for lunch after a weary, foot-slogging visit to the château. Take a seat on the leafy terrace overlooking the esplanade and order langoustine in a vermouth sauce or rib of beef with marrow. *7 rue Colbert, tel. 39–50–05–79. Reservations advised. MC, V. Closed Mon. and Jan.–Feb. $*

Normandy

Jutting out into the Channel, Normandy has had more connections with the English-speaking world than any other part of France. The association continues today. Visitors flock to Normandy not only to see historic monuments but to relax in the rich countryside amid apple orchards, lush meadows, and sandy beaches.

The historic city of Rouen, capital of Upper Normandy, is full of churches, well-preserved buildings, and museums. Normandy also has one of France's most enduring tourist attractions: Mont-St-Michel, a remarkable Gothic abbey perched on a rocky mount off the Cotentin peninsula. This region is also recognized as one of France's finest gastronomic centers; try some of the excellent cheeses washed down with local cider, the apple brandy (Calvados), or the wide range of seafood dishes.

Getting Around

Trains run hourly from Paris (Gare St-Lazare) to Rouen (journey time 70 minutes). Three trains daily go from Rouen to Bayeux: Allow at least 2½ hours, including an obligatory change at Caen.

Tourist Information

Bayeux (Pont St-Jean, tel. 31–92–16–26).
Rouen (25 pl. de la Cathédrale, tel. 35–71–41–77).

Exploring Rouen, Bayeux, and Mont-St-Michel

Numbers in the margin correspond to points of interest on the Rouen map.

Rouen Rouen, the capital of Upper Normandy, has a remarkable number of
 historic churches, from the city's **Cathédrale Notre Dame**, dating from the 12th century, to the modern, fish-shape **Eglise Jeanne d'Arc** on the old market square, where Joan of Arc was burned at the stake

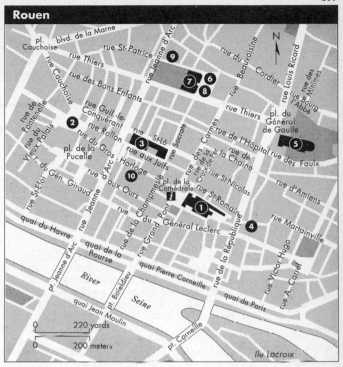

in 1431. The tourist office organizes a guided tour leaving from the place de la Cathédrale and visiting the city's main churches, the **③ Palais de Justice,** and the lively old quarter around the rue du Gros-Horloge, where you can see the giant Renaissance clock that was built in 1527. The most noteworthy churches are located on the right bank, around the old quarter, and can be visited on foot. Try to visit **④ ⑤ Eglise St-Maclou,** with its five-gabled façade; **Abbaye St-Ouen,** a **⑥** beautifully proportioned 14th-century abbey; and the **Eglise St-Godard,** with well-preserved stained-glass windows.

One ticket will get you into several of Rouen's best museums, **⑦** notably the **Musée des Beaux-Arts** near Eglise St-Godard (on square Vedral). This museum specializes in 17th- and 19th-century French paintings, with a particular emphasis on artists who lived and worked locally. There is an outstanding collection of macabre paintings by Romantic painter Géricault. Nearby museums include the **⑧ Musée Le Secq des Tournelles** (rue Jacques Villon, in the Eglise St-Laurent), which has an unusual collection of wrought iron; the **⑨ Musée de la Céramique** (rue Faucon), which now houses Rouen's por-**⑩** celain collections; and the **Musée du Gros-Horloge** (rue du Gros-Horloge), where you can study the mechanism of the Renaissance clock that gives its name to the museum. *Admission: 21 frs. Open Thurs.–Mon. 10–noon and 2–6, Wed. 2–6.*

Bayeux **Bayeux,** a few miles inland from the D-Day beaches via N13, was the first French town freed by the Allies in June 1944. But it is known primarily as the home of **La Tapisserie de la Reine Mathilde** (known to us as the Bayeux Tapestry), which tells the epic story of William's conquest of England in 1066. It is on show at the **Centre Culturel Guillaume le Conquérant** (William the Conqueror Cultural Center). *Rue St-Exupère. Admission: 32 frs adults, 15 frs students. Open June–Sept., daily 9–7; Oct.–May, daily 9:30–12:30 and 2–6.*

The **Musée de la Bataille de Normandie** (Museum of the Battle of Normandy) traces the history of the Allied advance against the Germans in 1944. It overlooks the British Military Cemetery. *Blvd. Général-Fabian-Ware. Admission: 24 frs adults, 12 frs students. Open June–Aug., daily 9–7; Sept.–mid-Oct. and mid-Mar.–May, daily 9:30–12:30 and 2:30–6:30; mid-Oct.–mid-Mar., daily 10–12:30 and 2–6.*

Mont-St-Michel You can glimpse spire-topped **Mont-St-Michel,** known as the Merveille de l'Occident (Wonder of the West), long before you reach the causeway that links it with the mainland. Its dramatic silhouette may well be your most lasting image of Normandy. The wonder of the abbey stems not only from its rocky perch a few hundred yards off the coast (it's cut off from the mainland at high tide), but from its legendary origins in the 8th century and the sheer exploit of its construction, which took more than 500 years, from 1017 to 1521. The abbey stands at the top of a 264-foot mound of rock, and the granite used to build it was transported from the Isles of Chausey (just beyond Mont-St-Michel Bay) and Brittany and laboriously hauled up to the site.

Legend has it that the Archangel Michael appeared to Aubert, bishop of Avranches, inspiring him to build an oratory on what was then called Mont Tombe. The original church was completed in 1144, but new buildings were added in the 13th century to accommodate the monks, as well as the hordes of pilgrims who flocked here even during the Hundred Years' War, when the region was in English hands. The Romanesque choir was rebuilt in an ornate Gothic style during the 15th and 16th centuries. The abbey's monastic vocation was undermined during the 17th century, when the monks began to flout the strict rules and discipline of their order, a drift into decadence that culminated in the monks' dispersal and the abbey's conversion into a prison well before the French Revolution. Only within the past 25 years have monks been able to live and work here once more.

A highlight of the abbey is the collection of 13th-century buildings on the north side of the mount. The exterior of the buildings is grimly fortresslike, but inside are some of Normandy's best examples of the evolution of Gothic architecture, ranging from the sober Romanesque style of the lower halls to the masterly refinement of the cloisters and the refectory.

The climb to the abbey is hard going, but worth it. Head first for the Grand Degré, the steep, narrow staircase on the north side. Once past the ramparts, you'll come to the pink-and-gray granite towers of the Châtelet and then to the Salle des Gardes, the central point of the abbey. Guided tours start from the Saut Gautier terrace (named after a prisoner who jumped to his death from it)—you must join one of them if you want to see the beautifully wrought Escalier de Dentelle (Lace Staircase) inside the church. *Admission: 32 frs adults, 18 frs students and senior citizens, 6 frs children under 12. Open mid-May–mid-Sept., daily 9:30–6; mid-Sept.–mid-May, daily 9:30–11:45 and 1:45–5 or 4:15, depending on month.*

Dining and Lodging

For details and price-category definitions, *see* Dining *and* Lodging *in* Staying in France, *above.*

Bayeux **L'Amaryllis.** This small, simply decorated restaurant produces good
Dining Norman fare at very reasonable prices. For 98 frs, a three-course dinner (with six or so choices for each course) will place before you such pleasures as a half dozen oysters, fillet of sole with a cider-based sauce, and pastries for dessert. *32 rue Saint-Patrice, tel. 31-22-47-94. AE, DC, MC, V. Closed Mon., and Dec. 20–Jan. 15. $*

Lodging **Notre-Dame.** It's difficult to find a better setting for a night in Bayeux than the Notre-Dame, on a charming cobbled street leading to the west front of the cathedral. You can sit outside on the terrace and drink in the scene with your evening aperitif. Rooms and cuisine are no more than average, but with rates starting at 150 francs, a lunchtime plat du jour for under 50 francs, and a set dinner menu at 90 francs, you can't complain. *44 rue des Cuisiniers, 14400, tel. 31–92–87–24, fax 31–92–67–11. 24 rooms, some with shower. Facilities: restaurant (closed Sun. evening and Mon.). DC, MC, V. Closed mid-Oct.–mid-Apr. ¢*

Rouen **Vieux Logis.** This tiny restaurant near the Hôtel de Ville, with ele-
Dining gant 18th-century-style furnishings, is the pride and joy of jolly Joseph Guillou. He treats visitors to a 70-franc menu that includes wine and coffee and goes down as the best value meal in Rouen. *5 rue Joyeuse, tel. 35–71–55–30. Reservations required. No credit cards. ¢*

Lodging **Hôtel de la Cathédrale.** Housed in a medieval building, and separated from the back of the cathedral by a narrow, pedestrians-only street, this hotel provides small but neat and comfortable rooms with either a private bath or shower. (No, the cathedral's bells do not boom out the hours throughout the night.) Breakfast only is served, in the wonderfully beamed *salle à manger.* The owner is very cordial, and will be happy to offer tips on exploring Rouen and to advise on dining options. *12 rue St-Romain, 76000, tel. 35–71–57–95, fax 35–70–15–54. 25 rooms with bath or shower. Facilities: breakfast room. MC, V. $–$$*

Mont-St- **Le Manoir de la Roche Turin.** An appealing alternative to the high-
Michel price hotels in Mont-St-Michel is this small, ivy-clad manor house 9
Dining and kilometers (6 miles) away. Rooms are pleasantly old-fashioned, but
Lodging the bathrooms are modern, and the owners run a delightful dining room. The *agneau pré-salé* (salt-meadow lamb) is superb, but lobster and fresh fish are also available on the 150-franc and 200-franc menus. *50220 Courtils, tel. 33–70–96–55, fax 33–48–35–20. 11 rooms with bath, 1 suite. Facilities: restaurant (closed Mon.), free parking. MC, V. Closed mid-Nov.–mid-Mar. $$*

Burgundy and Lyon

For a region whose powerful medieval dukes held sway over large tracts of Western Europe and whose current image is closely allied to its expensive wine, Burgundy is a place of surprisingly rustic, quiet charm.

The heart of Burgundy is the dark, brooding Morvan Forest. Dijon, the region's only city, retains something of its medieval opulence, although its present reputation is essentially gastronomic; fine restaurants abound, and local "industries" produce mustard, cassis (black-currant liqueur), snails, and—of course—wine. The vineyards that lead down toward the ancient town of Beaune are among the world's most distinguished and picturesque.

The vines continue to flourish as you head south along the Saône Valley, through the Mâconnais and Beaujolais, toward Lyon, one of France's most appealing cities. The combination of frenzied modernity and unhurried joie de vivre gives Lyon a sense of balance. The only danger is a temptation to overindulge in its rich and robust cuisine.

Getting Around

TGVs make the 95-minute run from Paris (Gare de Lyon) to Dijon every two hours. More traditional locomotives chug from Dijon to

Beaune (journey time 20 minutes) every 1½ hours or so. Six trains daily connect Beaune to Lyon, two hours away.

Tourist Information

Beaune (rue de l'Hôtel-Dieu, tel. 80–26–31–30).
Dijon (29 pl. Darcy, tel. 80–30–35–39).
Lyon (pl. Bellecoeur, tel. 78–42–25–75).

Exploring Burgundy and Lyon

Dijon   **Dijon** is the capital of both Burgundy and gastronomy. Visit its restaurants and the **Palais des Ducs** (Ducal Palace), testimony to bygone splendor and the setting for one of France's leading art museums (admission: 12 frs; open Wed.–Mon. 10–6). The tombs of Philip the Bold and John the Fearless head a rich collection of medieval objects and Renaissance furniture. Outstanding features of the city's old churches include the stained glass of **Notre Dame,** the austere interior of the **cathedral of St-Bénigne,** and the chunky Renaissance facade of **St-Michel.** Don't miss the exuberant 15th-century gateway at the **Chartreuse de Champmol**—all that remains of a former charterhouse—or the adjoining **Puits de Moïse,** the so-called Well of Moses, with six large, realistic medieval statues on a hexagonal base.

Beaune   The **Hospices** (or Hôtel-Dieu) **de Beaune** owns some of the finest vineyards in the region yet was founded in 1443 as a hospital. Its medical history is retraced in a **museum** that also features Rogier van der Weyden's medieval Flemish masterpiece *The Last Judgment,* plus a collection of tapestries, though a better series (late 15th century, relating the *Life of the Virgin*) hangs in Beaune's main church, the **Collégiale Notre Dame,** which dates from 1120. *Hospices de Beaune. Admission: 27 frs adults, 14 frs children. Open daily 9–11:30 and 2–5:30.*

The history of local wines can be explored at the **Musée du Vin de Bourgogne,** housed in a mansion built in the 15th and 16th centuries (admission: 10 frs; open Apr.–Oct., daily 9–noon and 1:30–6; Nov.–Mar., daily 10–noon and 2–5:30). The place to drink the stuff is in the candlelit cellars of the **Marché aux Vins** (wine market), on rue Nicolas Rolin, where you can taste as much as you please for around 40 francs.

Lyon   In recent years, **Lyon** has solidified its role as a commercial center, thanks to France's policy of decentralization and the TGV that puts Paris at virtual commuter distance (two hours). Much of the city has an appropriate air of untroubled prosperity, and you will have plenty of choices when it comes to good eating.

The clifftop **Notre Dame de Fourvière,** the city's most striking symbol, is an exotic mish-mash of styles with an interior that's pure decorative overkill. Climb the Fourvière heights for the view instead and then go to the nearby remains of two **Roman theaters.** *Théâtres Romains. Admission free. Open Mar.–Oct., weekdays 8–noon and 2–5, Sat. 9–noon and 3–6, Sun. 3–6; Nov.–Feb., weekdays 8–noon and 2–5.*

The pick of Lyon's museums is the **Musée des Beaux-Arts,** which houses sculpture, classical relics, and an extensive collection of Old Masters and Impressionists. Don't miss local artist Louis Janmot's 19th-century mystical cycle *The Poem of the Soul,* 18 canvases and 16 drawings that took nearly 50 years to complete. *20 pl. des Terreaux, tel. 78–28–81–11. Admission: 20 frs adults, 10 frs students. Open Wed.–Sun. 10:30–6.*

Dining and Lodging

For details and price-category definitions, *see* Dining *and* Lodging *in* Staying in France, *above.*

Beaune **La Grilladine.** This small restaurant can be recommended on three
Dining counts: The cooking, while not elaborate, produces good, hearty,
Burgundian dishes (boeuf bourguignon; eggs poached in a red wine
and bacon sauce); the prices are reasonable, with a three-course
meal starting at 78 francs; and the ambience is warm, intimate, and
cheerful. Of the two rooms here, the one on the right as you enter is
the cozier, with exposed stone walls, an ancient beam supporting
the ceiling, and tables set with rose-pink tablecloths. *17 rue
Maufoux, tel. 80–22–22–36. Reservations advised. MC, V. Closed
Mon.* $

Lodging **Hôtel de la Cloche.** Though some of the rooms here are on the small
side, all are neat and clean, all have private bath, and all are reasonably priced, ranging from about 290 francs to 360 francs (affordable
lodging is increasingly hard to find in the center of town). The hotel's
restaurant has good prices as well, and there are a couple of even less
expensive places to eat nearby. The staff is helpful, and there's a
parking lot across the street. *40–42 rue du Faubourg Madeleine,
21200, tel. 80–24–66–33, fax 80–24–04–24. 16 rooms, all with bath.
Facilities: restaurant. MC, V. Closed Dec. 20–Jan. 20.* $$

Dijon **Toison d'Or.** A collection of superbly restored 16th-century build-
Dining ings belonging to the Burgundian Company of Winetasters forms
the backdrop to this fine restaurant, which features a small wine
museum in the cellar. Toison d'Or is lavishly furnished and quaint
(candlelight is de rigueur in the evening). The food is increasingly
sophisticated. Try the langoustines with ginger and the nougat and
honey dessert. *18 rue Ste-Anne, tel. 80–30–73–52. Reservations ac-
cepted. Jacket required. AE, DC, MC, V. Closed Sat. lunch, Sun.,
part of Feb., most of Aug., and public holidays.* $$

Lodging **Central Urbis.** This central, long-established hotel has sound-proof,
air-conditioned rooms that offer a degree of comfort in excess of
their price. The adjoining grill room, the Central Grill Rôtisserie,
offers a good alternative to the gastronomic sophistication that is
difficult to avoid elsewhere in Dijon. *3 pl. Grangier, 21000, tel. 80–
30–44–00, fax 80–30–77–12. 90 rooms with bath. AE, DC, MC, V.
Facilities: restaurant (restaurant closed Sun.).* $

Lyon **A Ma Vigne.** Here is a restaurant that's popular with tourists; it pro-
Dining vides straightforward meals as a break from too much gourmet Lyonnais dining. French fries, *moules* (mussels), roast ham, and tripe
lead the menu. Locals appreciate this, too, so get there early, especially at lunchtime. *23 rue Jean-Larrivé, tel. 78–60–46–31. MC, V.
Closed Sun., Aug.* $

Bouchon de Fourvière. This wood-paneled restaurant, with a charming view over the Saône River, has won rave reviews for its spinach
salad with chicken liver, black pudding with apple, and stewed rabbit with pasta. Two excellent-value set menus and a good choice of
inexpensive local wines (mainly Côte du Rhône) make this an address to remember. *9 rue de la Quarantaine, Quai Fulchiron, tel.
72–41–85–02. Reservations advised. AE, MC, V. Closed Sun. and
Aug.* ¢

Lodging **Globe et Cécil.** You won't beat this strangely named hotel for value
and convenience in downtown Lyon: It lies just off place Bellecour
(Lyon's largest and most central square) in the heart of the city's
shopping district, halfway between the rivers Saône and Rhône and
a mere five-minute walk from historic Old Lyon at the foot of
Fourvière hill. The rooms are functional, the modern decor sober
and tasteful. Ask for a quieter room at the back of the hotel. *21 rue*

Gasparin, 69002, tel. 78–42–58–95, fax 72–41–99–06. 63 rooms, 48 with bath or shower. AE, DC, MC, V. $

Loire Valley

The Loire is the longest river in France, rising near Le Puy in the east of the Massif Central and pursuing a broad northwest curve on its 1,000-kilometer (620-mile) course to the Atlantic Ocean near Nantes. The region traditionally referred to as the Loire Valley—château country—is the 225-kilometer (140-mile) stretch between Orléans, 113 kilometers (70 miles) south of Paris, and Angers, 96 kilometers (60 miles) from the Atlantic coast. Thanks to its mild climate, soft light, and lush meadowland, this area is known as the Garden of France. Its leading actor—the wide, meandering Loire—offers two distinct faces: fast-flowing and spectacular in spring, sluggish and sandy in summer.

The Loire Valley's golden age came under François I (1515–47), France's flamboyant contemporary of England's Henry VIII. He hired Renaissance craftsmen from Italy and hobnobbed with the aging Leonardo da Vinci, his guest at Amboise. His salamander emblem is to be seen in many châteaus, including Chambord, the mightiest of them, begun in 1519.

Getting Around

Trains leave Paris (Gare d'Austerlitz) for Blois every couple of hours. The journey lasts 1½–2 hours. About eight trains daily connect Blois to Amboise, 20 minutes away, stopping en route near Chaumont (alight at Onzain Station). Frequent buses link Blois to Chambord and Cheverny; hiring a bike (available at most railway stations) is a good alternative here, as distances are short and the terrain undemanding.

Tourist Information

Blois (3 av. du Docteur Jean-Laigret, tel. 54–74–06–49).

Exploring Blois and Amboise

Blois **Blois** is the most attractive of the major Loire towns, with its tumbling alleyways and its **château**. The château is a mixture of four different styles: Feudal (13th century), Gothic-Renaissance transition (circa 1500), Renaissance (circa 1520), and Classical (circa 1635). *Admission: 30 frs. Open May–Aug., daily 9–6:30; Sept.–Apr., daily 9–noon and 2–5.*

Blois makes an ideal launching pad for a visit to the châteaus of Chambord and Cheverny. **Chambord** (begun 1519) is 18 kilometers (11 miles) east of Blois along D33, near Bracieux. It stands in splendid isolation in a vast forest and game park. There's another forest on the roof: 365 chimneys and turrets, representing architectural self-indulgence at its least squeamish. Grandeur or a mere 440-room folly? Judge for yourself, and don't miss the superb spiral staircase or the chance to saunter over the rooftop terrace. *Admission: 31 frs adults, 7 frs children. Open July–Aug., daily 9:30–6:30; Sept.–June, daily 9:30–11:45 and 2–sunset.*

A pleasant 20 kilometers (12 miles) through the forest leads you southwest to **Cheverny**. This white, symmetrical château, in the disciplined Classical style (built 1620–34), has ornate painted and gilded paneling on its walls and ceilings. Hunting buffs will thrill at the sight of the antlers of 2,000 hapless stags in the Trophy Room. Hordes of hungry hounds lounge around outside dreaming of their next kill. *Admission: 29 frs adults, 20 frs students and senior citi-*

zens. Open mid-June–mid-Sept., daily 9–6:30; mid-Sept.–mid-June, daily 9:30–noon and 2:30–5.

About 20 kilometers (12 miles) south of Blois stands the sturdy château of **Chaumont,** built between 1465 and 1510—well before Benjamin Franklin became a regular visitor. There is a magnificent Loire panorama from the terrace, and the stables—where thoroughbreds dined like royalty—show the importance attached to fine horses, for hunting or just prestige. *Admission: 25 frs adults, 13 frs students and senior citizens. Open Apr.–Sept., daily 9:30–12:30 and 2–4:30; Oct.–Mar., daily 9:30–12:30 and 2–3:30.*

Amboise Downstream (westward) another 16 kilometers (10 miles) lies the bustling town of **Amboise,** whose **château,** with charming grounds, a rich interior, and excellent views over the river from the battlements, dates from 1500. It wasn't always so peaceful: In 1560, more than 1,000 Protestant "conspirators" were hanged from these battlements during the Wars of Religion. *Admission: 30 frs adults, 20 frs students, 10 frs children. Open July–Aug., daily 9–6:30; Sept.–June, daily 9–noon and 2–5.*

The nearby **Clos-Lucé,** a 15th-century brick manor house, was the last home of Leonardo da Vinci, who was invited to stay here by François I. Leonardo died here in 1519, and his engineering genius is illustrated by models based on his plans and sketches. *Admission: 31 frs adults, 25 frs students and senior citizens. Same hrs as the château, but open till 6:30 in winter. Closed. Jan.*

Dining and Lodging

For details and price category definitions, *see* Dining *and* Lodging *in* Staying in France, *above.*

Amboise **Le Blazon.** This delightful small hotel, enlivened by the enthusiasm
Dining and of the owners, is behind the château, a four-minute walk from the
Lodging center of town. The old building has been well converted into guest rooms of different shapes and sizes, whose compact, prefabricated bathroom units have showers and toilets. Most rooms have twin beds, though a few have queens. Room 229, with exposed beams and a cathedral ceiling, has special charm; Room 109 is comfortably spacious and has a good view of the square. There's superior fare in the pretty little restaurant, with menus beginning at 95 francs. The menu changes with the seasons, and may include roast lamb with garlic and medallions of pork, and appetizers of salmon carpaccio with mustard dressing and air-dried duck breast scented with herbs and spices. *14 rue Joyeuse, 37400, tel. 47–23–22–41, fax 47–57–56–18. 29 rooms with bath. Facilities: restaurant. MC, V. $–$$*

Blois **Noë.** The pastel dining room at the "Noah," a half mile uptown from
Dining the château, is usually full of locals—always a good sign. They come to enjoy such inexpensive house specialties as chicken liver, duckling, and carp in a wine sauce. There are set menus at 100 francs and 150 francs. *10 bis av. de Vendôme. tel. 54–74–22–26. Reservations advised. MC, V. Closed Sat. lunch, Mon., Tues. evenings, and Sun. evenings in winter. $*

Dining and **Le Médicis.** Just 1,000 yards from the château, this smart, friendly
Lodging hotel is your best bet in Blois. The rooms, all with private bath, are roomy, air-conditioned, and sound-proof, and have been newly and individually redecorated. The one suite has a whirlpool. But the restaurant alone would make a stay here worthwhile. Chef-owner Christian Garanger brings an innovative touch to classic dishes. For example, there are *coquille Saint-Jacques* (scallops) with a pear fondue, and thin slices of roast hare with a black-currant sauce. His presentation, too, is admirable. The maître d' will happily guide you through the menu—indeed, the entire staff here is knowledgeable and helpful. *2 allée François Ier, 41000, tel. 54–43–94–04, fax 54–*

42–04–05. 12 rooms with bath, 1 suite. Facilities: restaurant (no dinner Sun. in low season). AE, DC, MC, V. Hotel closed Jan. 3–Jan. 24. $$

Chambord **Hôtel St-Michel.** Considering its location right across from the châ-
Lodging teau, the St-Michel offers good value. Some of its rooms afford splendid views of the château, its lawns, and the forest backdrop, as does the conveniently situated terrace, an ideal place for summer morning coffee before the tourist hordes arrive. *103 pl. St-Michel, 41250, tel. 54–20–31–31, fax 54–20–36–40. 39 rooms, 31 with bath. Facilities: restaurant, tennis court. MC, V. Closed mid-Nov.–mid-Dec. $*

The Riviera

Few places in the world have the same pull on the imagination as France's fabled Riviera, the Mediterranean coastline stretching from St-Tropez in the west to Menton on the Italian border. Cooled by the Mediterranean in the summer and warmed by it in winter, the climate is almost always pleasant. Avoid the area in July and August, however—unless you love crowds. To see the Riviera at its best, plan your trip in the spring or fall, particularly in May or September.

While the Riviera's coastal resorts seem to live exclusively for the tourist trade and have often been ruined by high-rise blocks, the hinterlands remain relatively untarnished. The little villages, perched high on the hills behind medieval ramparts, seem to belong to another century. One of them, St-Paul-de-Vence, is the home of the Maeght Foundation, one of the world's leading museums of modern art.

Artists, attracted by the light, have played a considerable role in popular conceptions of the Riviera, and their presence is reflected in the number of modern art museums: the Musée Picasso at Antibes, the Musée Renoir and the Musée d'Art Moderne Mediterranée at Cagnes-sur-Mer, and the Musée Jean Cocteau near the harbor at Menton. Wining and dining are special treats on the Riviera, especially if you are fond of garlic and olive oil. Bouillabaisse, a spicy fish stew, is the most popular regional specialty.

The tiny principality of Monaco, which lies between Nice and Menton, is included in this section despite the fact that it is a sovereign state. Although Monaco has its own army and police force, its language, food, and way of life are French. Its famous casino, the highly visible royal Grimaldi family, and the wealth of jetsetters, chic fashions, and opulent yachts all ensure that it maintains its reputation as a "golden ghetto."

Getting Around

By Train Six TGVs daily make the six- to seven-hour run from Paris (Gare de Lyon) to the Riviera, stopping at Cannes and Nice. Frequent local trains connect Nice to Monaco and Menton. Grasse is a 50-minute bus ride from Cannes.

Tourist Information

Cannes (Palais des Congrès, La Croisette, tel. 93–39–24–53).
Grasse (22 cours Honoré-Cresp, tel. 93–36–03–56).
Menton (Palais de l'Europe, tel. 93–57–57–00).
Monaco (2a blvd. des Moulins, tel. 92–16–61–16).
Nice (av. Thiers, tel. 93–87–07–07; 5 av. Gustave-V, tel. 93–87–60–60).

Exploring the Riviera

Cannes In 1834, a chance event was to change the lifestyle of **Cannes** forever. Lord Brougham, Britain's lord chancellor, was en route to Nice when an outbreak of cholera forced the authorities to freeze all travel. Trapped in Cannes, he fell in love with the place and built himself a house there as an annual refuge from the British winter. The English aristocracy, czars, kings, and princes soon caught on, and Cannes became a community for the international elite. Grand palace hotels were built to cater to them, and Cannes came to symbolize dignified luxury. Today, Cannes is also synonymous with the **International Film Festival.**

Cannes is for relaxing—strolling along the seafront on the **Croisette** and getting tanned on the beaches. Almost all the beaches are private, but that doesn't mean you can't use them, only that you must pay for the privilege. The Croisette offers splendid views of the **Napoule Bay.** Only a few steps inland is the old town, known as the **Suquet,** with its steep, cobbled streets and its 12th-century watchtower.

Grasse is perched in the hills behind Cannes. Follow your nose to the town that claims to be the perfume capital of the world. A good proportion of its 40,000 inhabitants work at distilling and extracting scent from the tons of roses, lavender, and jasmine produced here every year. The various perfumers are only too happy to guide visitors around their fragrant establishments. Fragonard is the best known (20 blvd. Fragonard, tel. 93–36–44–65). The old town is attractive, with its narrow alleys and massive, somber **cathedral.** Three of the paintings inside the cathedral are by Rubens and one is by Fragonard, who lived here for many years.

Nice With its population of 400,000, its own university, new congress hall, and nearby science park, **Nice** is the undisputed capital of the Riviera. Founded by the Greeks as Nikaia, it has lived through several civilizations and was attached to France only in 1860. It consequently boasts a profusion of Greek, Italian, British, and French styles. Tourism may not be the main business of Nice, but it is a deservedly popular center with much to offer. The double blessing of climate and geography puts its beaches within an hour-and-a-half's drive of the nearest ski resorts. There is an eclectic mixture of old and new architecture, an opera house, museums, flourishing markets, and regular concerts and festivals, including the Mardi Gras festival and the Battle of Flowers.

The **place Masséna** is the logical starting point for an exploration of Nice. This fine square was built in 1815 to celebrate a local hero: one of Napoléon's most successful generals. The **Promenade des Anglais,** built by the English community here in 1824, is only a short stroll past the fountains and the **Jardin Albert I**er. It now carries heavy traffic but still forms a splendid strand between town and sea. The narrow streets in the old town are the prettiest part of Nice: Take the rue de l'Opéra to see **St-François-de-Paule** church (1750) and the **opera house.** At the northern extremity of the old town lies the vast **place Garibaldi** —all yellow-ocher buildings and formal fountains.

The **Musée Chagall** is on the boulevard de Cimiez, near the Roman ruins. The museum was built in 1972 to house the Chagall collection, including the 17 huge canvases of *The Message of the Bible*, which took 13 years to complete. *Av. du Dr-Ménard, tel. 93–81–75–75. Admission: 27 frs adults, 18 frs students and senior citizens. Open July–Sept., Wed.–Mon. 10–7; Oct.–June, Wed.–Mon. 10–12:30 and 2–5:30.*

Monaco Sixteen kilometers (10 miles) along the coast from Nice is **Monaco.** For more than a century Monaco's livelihood was centered in its splendid copper-roof **casino.** The oldest section dates from 1878 and

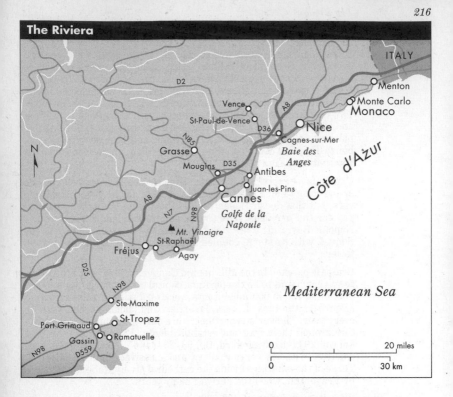

The Riviera

ITALY
Menton
Monte Carlo
Monaco
Nice
Cagnes-sur-Mer
Vence
St-Paul-de-Vence
Grasse
Mougins
Antibes
Juan-les-Pins
Cannes
Baie des Anges
Côte d'Azur
Golfe de la Napoule
Mt. Vinaigre
St-Raphaël
Fréjus
Agay
Mediterranean Sea
Ste-Maxime
St-Tropez
Port Grimaud
Gassin
Ramatuelle

0   20 miles
0   30 km

was conceived by Charles Garnier, architect of the Paris opera house. It's as elaborately ornate as anyone could wish, bristling with turrets and gold filigree, and masses of interior frescoes and bas-reliefs. There are lovely sea views from the terrace, and the gardens out front are meticulously tended. The main activity is in the American Room, where beneath the gilt-edged ceiling busloads of tourists feed the one-arm bandits. *Pl. du Casino, tel. 92–16–21–21. Persons under 21 not admitted. Admission 50 frs (American Room free). Open daily noon–4 AM. Closed May 1.*

The **Musée National des Automates et Poupées d'Autrefois** (Museum of Dolls and Automatons) has a compelling collection of 18th- and 19th-century dolls and mechanical figures, the latter shamelessly showing off their complex inner workings. It's magically set in a 19-century seaside villa (designed by Garnier). *17 av. Princesse-Grace, tel. 93–30–91–26. Admission: 26 frs adults, 15 frs children. Open daily 10–12:15 and 2:30–6:30.*

Monaco Town, the principality's old quarter, has many vaulted passageways and exudes an almost tangible medieval feel. The magnificent **Palais du Prince** (Prince's Palace), a grandiose Italianate structure with a Moorish tower, was largely rebuilt in the last century. Here, since 1297, the Grimaldi dynasty has lived and ruled. The spectacle of the **Changing of the Guard** occurs each morning at 11:55; inside, guided tours take visitors through the state apartments and a wing containing the **Palace Archives** and **Musée Napoléon.** *Pl. du Palais, tel. 93–25–18–31. Palace admission: 40 frs adults, 20 frs children. Open June–Oct., daily 9:30–12:30 and 2–6:30. Musée Napoléon and Palace Archives admission: 20 frs adults, 10 frs children. Open Tues.–Sun. 9:30–6:30.*

Monaco's **cathedral** (4 rue Colonel Bellando de Castro) is a late 19th-century neo-Romanesque confection in which Philadelphia-born Princess Grace lies in splendor, along with past members of the Grimaldi dynasty. Nearby is the **Musée Historial des Princes de Monaco** (Waxworks Museum), a Monégasque Madame Tussauds, with none-too-realistic wax figures stiffly portraying various episodes in the Grimaldi history. The waxworks may not convince, but the rue Basse is wonderfully atmospheric. *27 rue Basse, tel. 93–30–39–05. Admission: 24 frs. Open May–Sept., daily 9–8; Oct.–Dec., daily 10:30–5:30; Jan.–Apr., daily 9–6:30.*

Next to the **St-Martin Gardens**—which contain an evocative bronze monument in memory of Prince Albert I (Prince Rainier's great-grandfather, the one in the sou'wester and flying oil skins, benignly guiding a ship's wheel)—is the **Musée Océanographique** (Oceanography Museum and Aquarium). This museum is also an internationally renowned research institute founded by the very Prince Albert who is remembered for being an eminent marine biologist in his day; the well-known underwater explorer Jacques Cousteau is the present director. The aquarium is the undisputed highlight, however, where a collection of the world's fish and crustacea—some colorful, some drab, some the stuff nightmares are made of—live out their lives in public. *Av. St-Martin, tel. 93–30–15–14. Admission: 60 frs adults, 30 frs children. Open Sept.–Oct. and May–June, daily 9:30–7; Nov.–Apr., daily 9:30–6; July and Aug., daily 9–8.*

Before heading back inland, take a short stroll to the eastern tip of the rock, to the **Fort Antoine Theater** (av. de la Quarantaine, tel. 93–30–19–21), a converted 18th-century fortress that certainly looks a lot prettier now than it would have in more warlike times, covered as it is in ivy and flowering myrtle and thyme. In the summer, this is an open-air theater seating 350.

The Moneghetti area is the setting for the **Jardin Exotique** (Tropical Garden), where 600 varieties of cacti and succulents cling to the rock face, their improbable shapes and sometimes violent coloring a further testimony to the fact that Mother Nature will try anything once. Your ticket also allows you to explore the **caves**, next to the gardens, and to visit the adjacent **Museum of Prehistoric Anthropology.** *Blvd. du Jardin Exotique, tel. 93–30–33–65. Admission: 31 frs adults, 26 frs senior citizens, 15 frs children. Open Oct.–May, daily 9–5:30; June–Sept., daily 9–7.*

Dining and Lodging

For details and price-category definitions, *see* Dining *and* Lodging *in* Staying in France, *above.*

Cannes
Dining

Au Bec Fin. A devoted band of regulars will attest to the quality of this family-run restaurant near the train station. Don't look for a carefully staged decor: It's the spirited local clientele and the homey food that distinguish this cheerful bistro. The prix-fixe menu is a fantastic value at 80 francs; try the fish cooked with fennel or the *salade niçoise. 12 rue du 24-Août, tel. 93–38–35–86. Reservations advised. AE, DC, MC, V. Closed Sat. dinner, Sun., and Christmas–late Jan. ¢*

Lodging

Mondial. A three-minute walk from the beach takes you to this six-story hotel, a haven for the traveler seeking solid, unpretentious lodging in a town that leans more to tinsel. Many guest rooms offer sea views. There's no restaurant. *77 rue d'Antibes, 06400, tel. 93–68–70–00, fax 93–99–39–11. 23 rooms with bath. No credit cards. $$*

Beverly. Despite extensive renovations and a name change in 1993, the Beverly (formerly the Bristol) continues to offer an intimate, wallet-friendly contrast to the big names lurking nearby on La Croisette. Prices start at around 260 francs, but be prepared to go a bit higher if you fancy one of the 10 (quieter) rooms with a balcony at the back of the building. The beach, train station, and Palais des Festivals are all within a three-minute walk. *14 rue Hoche, 06400,* *tel. 93–39–10–66, fax 92–98–65–63. 19 rooms, 15 with bath or shower. AE, MC, V. Closed Dec.–mid-Jan. ¢*

Grasse
Lodging

Panorama. The excellent views of the Massif de l'Estérel and right across to Cannes are the vindication of this hotel's name. It is modern and well run and has ample parking. Most rooms have good views, but there is no restaurant. *2 pl. du Cours, 06130, tel. 93–36–80–80, fax 93–36–92–04. 36 rooms with bath. MC, V. $*

Monaco
Dining

Polpetta. This popular trattoria is close enough to the Italian border to pass for the real thing. It's excellent value for the money, with delicious home cooking to boot. *2 rue Paradis, tel. 93–50–67–84. Reservations required in high season. MC, V. Closed Tues., Feb. 15–Mar. 15, Oct. 15–30. No lunch Sat. $$*

Port. Harbor views from the terrace and top-notch Italian food make the Port a good choice. A large, varied menu includes shrimp, pasta, lasagna, fettuccine, fish risotto, and veal with ham and cheese. *Quai Albert Ier, tel. 93–50–77–21. Reservations advised. AE, DC, MC, V. Closed Mon. and Nov. $$*

Lodging

★

Alexandra. Shades of the Belle Epoque linger on in this comfortable hotel's spacious lobby and airy guest rooms. Tan and rose colors dominate the newer rooms. If you're willing to do without a private bath, this place sneaks into the $ category. The friendly proprietress, Madame Larouquie, makes foreign visitors feel right at home. *35 blvd. Princesse-Charlotte, 98000, tel. 93–50–63–13, fax 92–16–06–48. 55 rooms, 46 with bath. AE, DC, MC, V. $$*

Balmoral. Despite the name, there's nothing even vaguely Scottish about this somewhat old-fashioned hotel overlooking the harbor. The rooms are a reasonable size, if blandly decorated; many have balconies. *12 av. de la Costa, 98000, tel. 93–50–62–37, fax 93–15–08–69. 75 rooms with bath or shower, ½ with air-conditioning. Facilities: restaurant (closed Nov.). AE, DC, MC, V. $$*

France. The modest hotel France, near the train station, can't begin to compete with the opulence of some of the others in town, but it's one of the cheapest around and worth a look if you are on a tight budget. *6 rue de La Turbie, 98000, tel. 93–30–24–64, fax 92–16–13–34. 26 rooms with bath or shower. DC, MC, V. $*

Nice
Dining

La Mérenda. This noisy downtown bistro, with its down-to-earth Italo-Provençal food, is a good find. House specials include pasta with *pistou* (a garlic-and-basil sauce) and succulent tripe. *5 rue Gioffredo, tel. 93–85–55–95. No reservations. Closed Sat., Sun., Mon., Feb., and Aug. $$*

La Diva. This simply decorated restaurant in the old town, halfway between place Masséna and the seafront, provides cheerful service and two lunch menus at 115 francs and 150 francs that feature ravioli, mussels, and fillet of sea bream with basil. The dinner menu, similarly priced, might include such fish and pasta specialties as seafood stew, duck ravioli, or fettuccine with mushrooms. *4 rue de l'Opéra, tel. 93–85–96–15. MC, V. Closed Mon. $*

Lodging

La Mer. This small hotel is handily situated on place Masséna, close to the old town and seafront. The rooms are spartan (and carpets sometimes frayed), but all have a minibar and represent good value. Ask for a room away from the square to be sure of a quiet night. *4 pl. Masséna, 06000, tel. 93–92–09–10, fax 93–85–00–64. 12 rooms with bath or shower. $*

★

Little Palace. This place is the closest thing to a country-house hotel in Nice. The old-fashioned decor, the jumble of bric-a-brac, and the heavy wooden furniture lend an Old World air; some may say it's like stepping onto a film set. *9 av. Baquis, 06000, tel. 93–88–70–49, fax 93–88–78–89. 36 rooms, 31 with bath. MC, V. $*

9 Germany

A reunited Germany offers the traveler a unique experience. Today one country exists where there used to be two, and although the 40-year division was an artificial one, the differences that developed will take many years to even out. Travelers will notice the big gap in wealth between the two halves: In western Germany, a stable economy has resulted in cared-for cities, towns, and villages and in a manicured countryside; in eastern Germany, many cities and rural areas are scarred by a 19th-century approach to industrialization that had little or no concern for the environment. Still, the Communist authorities did attempt to preserve and renovate some historic buildings.

Rapid reunification has damaged the German economy, which had been unaffected by the recession in other parts of the western world. The bid to quickly rejuvenate former East Germany and provide its 17 million inhabitants with better living standards has so far proved difficult and has cost western German taxpayers thousands of millions of Deutschmarks. As late as January 1995, the government announced an additional 7.5% income tax (known as the solidarity tax), on top of the regular income tax, to pay for the staggering cost of reunification. Germans in the eastern part of the country still earn less than their fellow countrymen in the west. But some basic costs of living are lower. Apartment rents, for example, are often considerably less than what Germans in the west pay, although rent and utility costs are rising quickly.

Germans tend to rise very early and are hammering away at building sites by 7 AM or seated at their office desks by 8 AM, but they take their leisure time just as seriously. Annual vacations of up to six weeks are the norm, and secular and religious festivals occupy another 12 days. Every town and village and many city neighborhoods manage at least one "fest" a year, when the beer barrels are rolled out and sausages are thrown on the grill. The seasons have their own festivities: Fasching (Carnival) heralds the end of winter; countless beer gardens open up with the first warm rays of sunshine; fall is celebrated with the Munich Oktoberfest; and Advent brings Christkindlmarkt, colorful pre-Christmas markets held in town and city squares.

Germany

North Sea

Baltic Sea

HOLLAND

DENMARK

POLAND

Rügen

Fehmarn

Elbe

Ems

Oder

Neisse

100 miles

150 km

N

Flensburg

Husum

Kiel

Neustadt

Wismar

Lübeck

Schwerin

Ludwigslust

Neustadt-Gleve

Gistrow

Teterow

Waren

Schwerin

Rostock

Barth

Stralsund

Greifswald

Anklam

Neubrandenburg

Neustrelitz

Neuruppin

Prenzlau

Pritzwalk

Perleberg

Wittenberge

Oranienburg

Berlin

Potsdam

Brandenburg

Frankfurt an der Oder

Lübben

Cottbus

Wittenberg

Bitterfeld

Leipzig

Halle

Dessau

Bernburg

Magdeburg

Nordhausen

Wolfsburg

Braunschweig

Halberstadt

Hannover

Hildesheim

Göttingen

Stendal

Salzwedel

FORMER BORDER BETWEEN EAST AND WEST GERMANY

Hamburg

Bremen

Bremerhaven

Cuxhaven

Wilhelmshaven

Emden

Carolinensiel

Norden

Oldenburg

Meppen

Osnabrück

Rheine

Minden

Bielefeld

Münster

Dortmund

Hagen

Essen

Duisburg

The great outdoors have always been an important escape hatch for the Germans, and *Lebensraum* (living space) is even more highly prized in the era of high technology and pressurized urban life. Germany does its best to meet the needs of its hardworking inhabitants. A Bavarian mountain inn, the glow of its lights reflected on the blanket of snow outside, may be only a short drive from Munich. The busy industrial city of Stuttgart lies at the gateway to the Black Forest (Schwarzwald), the popular region of spas, hiking trails, and its tempting cake. Berlin is surrounded by its own lakes and green parklands.

Essential Information

Before You Go

When to Go   The main tourist season in Germany runs from May to late October, when the weather is at its best. In addition to many tourist events, this period has hundreds of folk festivals. The winter sports season in the Bavarian Alps runs from Christmas to mid-March. Prices everywhere are generally higher during the summer, so you may find considerable advantages in visiting out of season. Most resorts offer out-of-season (*Zwischensaison*) and "edge-of-season" (*Nebensaison*) rates, and tourist offices can provide lists of hotels offering special low-price inclusive weekly packages (*Pauschalangebote*). Similarly, many winter resorts offer lower rates for the periods immediately before and after the Christmas and New Year high season (*Weisse Wochen*, or "white weeks"). The disadvantages of visiting out-of-season, especially in winter, are that the weather is often cold and gloomy and tourist attractions, especially in rural areas, are closed. Ski resorts are an exception.

Climate   Germany's climate is generally temperate. Winters vary from mild and damp to very cold and bright. Particularly chilly regions include the Baltic coast, the Alps, the Harz Mountains, and the Black and Bavarian forests. Summers are usually sunny and warm, save a few cloudy and wet days. In Alpine regions, spring often comes late, with snow flurries well into April. Fall is sometimes spectacular in the south: warm and soothing.

The following are the average daily maximum and minimum temperatures for Munich.

Jan.	35F	1C	May	64F	18C	Sept.	67F	20C
	23	– 5		45	7		48	9
Feb.	38F	3C	June	70F	21C	Oct.	56F	14C
	23	– 5		51	11		40	4
Mar.	48F	9C	July	74F	23C	Nov.	44F	7C
	30	– 1		55	13		32	0
Apr.	56F	14C	Aug.	73F	23C	Dec.	36F	2C
	38	3		54	12		26	– 3

Currency   The unit of currency in Germany is the Deutschmark, written DM and generally referred to as the Mark. It is divided into 100 pfennig. There are bills of 5 (rare), 10, 20, 50, 100, 200, 500, and 1,000 Marks and coins of 1, 2, 5, 10, and 50 pf and 1, 2, and 5 Marks. At press time (summer 1995), the Mark stood at DM 1.30 to the dollar, DM 1.03 to the Canadian dollar, and DM 2.16 to the pound sterling.

The deutsche mark is legal tender throughout reunited Germany. The cost of living is still somewhat lower in the former GDR (German Democratic Republic), where most people earn slightly less than their western colleagues doing the same jobs, and some of these lower costs benefit tourists—for example, on public transportation, in cafés and beer restaurants, and in simple accommodations, such as country inns and private guest houses. But a growing number of places that cater specifically to visitors are now charging western rates.

Major credit cards are widely accepted in Germany, though not universally so. You can buy a seat on a Lufthansa flight with a credit card, but not on a German train, for example.

What It Will Cost
Inflation has crept up in the 1990s (at press time, the annual rate of inflation was more than 4%), primarily because of the cost of financing the rejuvenation and integration of former East Germany. For example, a "reunification" tax has been levied on basic commodities, such as gas, and telephone charges have risen. There were further modest increases in fares for most forms of public transportation.

The most expensive areas to visit are the major cities, notably Frankfurt, Hamburg, and Munich. Out-of-the-way rural regions, such as north and east Bavaria, the Saarland on the French border, and some parts of eastern Germany, offer the lowest prices.

Sample Prices
Cup of coffee in a café, DM 3.50, in a stand-up snack bar DM 1.80; mug of beer in a beer hall, DM 4.50, a bottle of beer from a supermarket, DM 1.50; soft drink, DM 2; ham sandwich, DM 4; 2-mile taxi ride, DM 12.

Visas
To enter Germany, only passports are required of visitors from the United States, Canada, and the United Kingdom, although U.S. citizens must obtain a visa if they plan to stay longer than three months.

Customs
Since 1993 and the start of a single, unrestricted market within the European Union (EU), there are no restrictions on importing items duty-free for citizens of the 12 member countries traveling among EU countries.

If you are entering Germany as a citizen of a country that does not belong to the EU, you may import duty-free (1) 200 cigarettes or 50 cigars or 250 grams of tobacco, plus (2) 1 liter of spirits more than 22% proof or 2 liters of spirits less than 22% proof and 2 liters of still wine, plus (3) 50 grams of perfume and ¼ liter of toilet water, plus (4) other goods to the value of DM 115.

Tobacco and alcohol allowances are for visitors aged 17 and over. Other items intended for personal use may be imported and exported freely. There are no restrictions on the import and export of German currency.

Language
Many people under age 40 speak some English, although the level of understanding varies considerably. English is not as widely understood in eastern parts of the country, where before the collapse of Communism Russian was the first foreign language taught in many schools.

Getting Around

By Train
Privatization of the German railway system began in 1994 and is expected to take at least six years to complete, so routes and timetables may still change in some areas. The separate rail networks of the former East and West Germany merged in 1994 into **Deutsche Bahn (DB)**, or German Rail, bringing Berlin and the cities of the old German Democratic Republic much closer to the main railheads of the west. Electrification and renovation of the ancient tracks in eastern Germany also made big strides forward, allowing the extension there of the high-speed InterCity Express (ICE) service. InterCity (IC) and EuroCity services were improved and expanded, and the regional InterRegio network was extended nationwide. Train travel times have been reduced so dramatically that journeys between many cities—Munich–Frankfurt, for example—are faster by

rail than by plane. All overnight InterCity services and the slower D-class trains have sleepers. All InterCity and InterCity Express trains have restaurant cars. A DM 6 surcharge is added to the ticket price on all InterCity and EuroCity journeys irrespective of distance (DM 12 round-trip), and InterCity Express fares are about 20% more expensive than normal ones. Seat reservations are free of charge. Bikes cannot be transported on InterCity Express trains, but InterCity and EuroCity and some D-class trains have special storage facilities aboard, and InterRegio trains have compartments where cyclists can travel next to their bikes.

Fares The **German Rail Pass,** not available to Germans, allows travel over the entire German rail network for 5, 10, or 15 days within a single month; the cost is $260, $410, and $530, respectively, in first class, and $178, $286, and $386 in second class (in Germany, the prices are DM 520, DM 720, and DM 900, and DM 350, DM 480, and DM 600). A **Twin Pass** discounts these rates for two people traveling together; the cost per person is $234, $369, and $477 for first class, and $160, $257, and $331 for second class (DM 400, DM 520, and DM 675, and DM 265, DM 360, and DM 450). A **Youth Pass,** sold to those aged 12–25 for second-class travel, costs $138–$238 (DM 270–DM 450). These passes are also valid on all buses operated by the Deutsche Bahn, as well as on tour routes along the Romantic and Castle roads served by **Deutsche Touring Gesellschaft,** or DTG (contact DTG, Am Römerhof 17, D-60486 Frankfurt/Main, tel. 069/79030 for reservations). Rhine, Main, and Mosel river cruises operated by the Köln-Düsseldorfer (KD) Line (*see* By Boat, *below*). Passes are sold by travel agents and DER Tours (Box 1606, Des Plaines, IL 60017, tel. 800/782–2424) in the United States and by Deutsche Bahn in Germany.

The EU is bringing greater cooperation between railroad authorities of individual countries, and new deals allowing more freedom and flexibility than ever have been introduced. In 1995 a more comprehensive version of the popular **InterRail** ticket became available. It's complicated, but young travelers (26 years old or younger) touring just one area of Europe can save big. The system divides Europe into seven zones, with different tariffs within each one. Germany belongs to Zone C, along with Switzerland, Austria, and Denmark. A one-month InterRail ticket for travel within this zone and an additional zone of your choice costs DM 500, and a two-week ticket DM 420. Young travelers touring only Germany can get an even better deal with a **Euro Domino** ticket, which allows rail travel on all German trains for 3, 5, or 10 days within one month (for DM 231, DM 257, and DM 378). No age limit is linked to other deals, such as the **Sparpreis** and **ICE-Super Sparpreis,** which offer big savings on return journeys made on off-peak days.

By Bus Long-distance bus services in Germany are part of the Europe-wide Europabus network. Services are neither as frequent nor as comprehensive as those on the rail system, so make reservations. Be careful in selecting the service you travel on: All Europabus services have a bilingual hostess and offer small luxuries that you won't find on the more basic, though still comfortable, regular services. For details and reservations, contact **DTG** (*see* By Train, *above*). Reservations can also be made at any of the Deutsche Touring offices in Cologne, Hanover, Hamburg, Munich, Nuremberg (Nürnberg), and Wuppertal and at travel agents.

Rural bus services are operated by local municipalities and some private firms, as well as by Deutsche Bahn and the post office. Services are variable, however, even when there is no other means to reach your destination by public transportation.

By Plane Germany's national airline, **Lufthansa,** serves all major cities. **LTU International Airways** (in the United States, tel. 800/546–7334; in

Germany, tel. 0221/941–8888) has connections between Düsseldorf and Munich and between Frankfurt and Munich. Regular fares are high, but you can save up to 40% with Flieg und Spar ("fly and save") specials; several restrictions apply, such as a DM 100 penalty for changing flights. Contact Lufthansa at Frankfurt International Airport (tel. 069/6907–1222; in the United States at tel. 800/645–3880; in Great Britain at tel. 0171/495–2044). **Deutsche BA,** a British Airways subsidiary, competes with Lufthansa on many domestic routes, including those between Berlin and Munich, and Köln/Bonn and Düsseldorf. Contact Deutsche BA in Berlin (tel. 030/4101–2647).

By Boat   For a country with such a small coastline, Germany is a surprisingly nautical nation: You can cruise rivers and lakes throughout the country. The biggest fleet, and most of the biggest boats, belongs to the Cologne-based KD line, the Köln-Düsseldorf Rheinschiffahrt. It operates services on the rivers Rhine, Moselle, and Main. For details, write **KD River Cruises of Europe** (Rhine Cruise Agency, 2500 Westchester Ave., Purchase, NY 10577, tel. 914/696–3600) or **KD German Rhine Line** (Frankenwerft 15, D-50667 Köln, tel. 0221/208–8288).

Services on the 160-kilometer (100-mile) stretch of the Danube (Donau) between the spectacular Kelheim gorge and Passau on the Austrian border are operated by **Donauschiffahrt Wurm & Köck** (Höllgasse 26, D-8390 Passau, tel. 0851/929–292). The company has daily summer cruises on the Rivers Danube, Inn, and Ilz, which meet at Passau. Bodensee (Lake Constance), the largest lake in Germany, located at the meeting point of Germany, Austria, and Switzerland, has up to 40 ships crisscrossing it in summer. Write **Deutsche Bahn,** Bodensee-Schiffsbetriebe, Hafenstrasse 6, D-7750 Konstanz.

By Bicycle   Bicycles can be rented at more than 370 train stations throughout Germany from April 1 to October 31. The cost is DM 11 or DM 13 (with gears) per day, DM 7 or DM 9 if you have a valid rail ticket. You can pick up a bike at one station and return it to another, provided the station rents bikes. Bavaria has the greatest number of stations offering this service. You will need to buy a *Fahrradkarte*, or bicycle ticket (DM 8.60 per journey) to take your bike on the train; Inter-City Express trains do not carry bikes. Full details are given in German Rail's brochure *Radler-Bahn*. Most cities also have bike-rental companies, usually priced about DM 15 per day or DM 80–DM 90 a week.

Staying in Germany

Telephones   Telephone lines between western and eastern Germany are now much improved after an initial period of difficulty following reunification. All but the more remote eastern regions can be reached by direct dialing; placing calls to a few rural districts may still require the assistance of an operator, reached at 010. For directory inquiries for numbers within Germany, dial 01188.

Since reunification, all phones in the east and west use the same coins: 10 pf, DM 1, and DM 5 for long-distance calls. A local call costs 30 pf and lasts six minutes. For all self-dial calls, lift the receiver, put the coins into the machine, and dial. Card phones are rapidly replacing coin-operated phones; cards cost DM 12 or DM 50 (for DM 60 worth of calls) and can be purchased at all post offices and many exchange places.

If you have no change, go to the local post office, where there are usually public booths; the counter clerk gets you a line, and you pay him or her afterward.

International   These can be made from public phones bearing the sign INLANDS UND
Calls   AUSLANDSGESPRÄCHE. Using DM 5 coins is best for long-distance dial-

ing; a four-minute call to the United States costs DM 15. To avoid weighing yourself down with coins, however, make international calls from post offices; even those in small country towns will have a special booth for international calls. To reach an **AT&T** long-distance operator, dial 0130–0010; for **MCI,** dial 0130–0012; for **Sprint,** 0130–0013. Dial 0010 for a local operator who handles international calls.

Country Code   Germany's country code is 49.

Mail   Airmail letters to the United States and Canada cost DM 3; postcards cost DM 2. Airmail letters to the United Kingdom cost DM 1; postcards cost 80 pf.

You can arrange to have mail sent to you in care of any German post office; have the envelope marked "Postlagernd." This service is free. Alternatively, have mail sent to any American Express office in Germany. There's no charge to cardholders, holders of American Express traveler's checks, or anyone who has booked a vacation with American Express. Otherwise, you pay DM 2 per collection (not per item).

Shopping   German goods carry a 15% value-added tax (VAT). You can claim this
VAT Refunds   back either as you leave the country or once you've returned home. When you make a purchase, ask the shopkeeper for a form known as an "Ausfuhr-Abnehmerbescheinigung"; he or she will help you fill it out. As you leave the country, give the form, plus the goods and receipts, to German customs. You will get an official export certificate or stamp. You then send the form back to the shop, and it will send the refund.

Opening and   **Banks.** Times vary from state to state and city to city, but banks are
Closing Times   generally open weekdays from 8:30 or 9 to 2 or 3 (5 or 6 on Thursday). Some banks close from 12:30 to 1:30. Branches at airports and main train stations open as early as 6:30 AM and close as late as 10:30 PM.

Museums. Museums are generally open Tuesday to Sunday 9–5. Some close for an hour or more at lunch, and some are open on Monday. Many stay open until 9 on Thursdays.

Shops. Times vary, but shops are generally open weekdays from 8:30 or 9 until 6:30 PM and Saturdays until 1 or 2 PM. On the first Saturday of each month, many larger shops and department stores in Germany are open until 6. In several cities large stores stay open until 8:30 PM on Thursdays.

National   In 1996: January 1, January 6 (Epiphany, Bavaria and Baden-
Holidays   Württenberg only), April 5 (Good Friday), April 8 (Easter Monday), May 1 (Worker's Day), May 16 (Ascension), May 27 (Pentecost Monday), June 6 (Corpus Christi, southern Germany only), August 15 (Assumption Day, Bavaria and Saarland only), October 3 (Germany Unity Day), November 1 (All Saints' Day), November 20 (Day of Prayer and Repentance), December 24–26 (Christmas); changing holidays in 1997: March 28 (Good Friday), March 31 (Easter Monday), May 8 (Ascension), May 19 (Pentecost), May 29 (Corpus Christi), November 19 (Day of Prayer and Repentance).

Dining   It's hard to generalize about German food beyond saying that standards are high and portions are large. In fact, the range of dining experiences is vast: everything from high-price nouvelle cuisine to hamburgers. As a visitor, you should search out local restaurants if atmosphere and regional specialties are your priority. Beer restaurants in Bavaria, *Apfelwein* taverns in Frankfurt, and *Kneipen*—the pubs on the corner cum local cafés—in Berlin nearly always offer best value and atmosphere. But throughout the country you'll find *Gaststätten* and/or *Gasthöfe*—local inns—where atmosphere and regional specialties are always available.

In larger towns and cities throughout the country, Germans like to nibble at roadside or market snack stalls, called *Imbisse*. Hot sausages, spicy meatballs (*Fleischpflanzerl*), meatloaf topped with a fried egg (*Leberkäs*), in the south, and sauerkraut are the tradition- al favorites. But more international foods eaten on the hoof are creeping in, too: french fries, pizzas, hamburgers, and the *Döner Kebab*, the Turkish gyro equivalent, which in many larger cities has become as much a part of the German diet as bratwurst.

The most famous German specialty is sausage. Everyone has heard of frankfurters, but if you're in Munich, try *Weisswurst*, a delicate white sausage traditionally eaten only between midnight and noon. Nürnberg's sausage favorite is the *Nürnberger Bratwurst*. Look for the "Bratwurststube" sign. Dumplings (*Knödel*) can also be found throughout the country, though their natural home is probably Ba- varia; farther north, potatoes often take their place.

The natural accompaniment to German food is either beer or wine. Munich is the beer capital of Germany, though there's no part of the country where you won't find the amber nectar. Say "Helles" or "Export" if you want light beer; "Dunkles" if you want dark beer. In Bavaria, try the sour but refreshing beer brewed from wheat, called *Weissbier*. Germany is also a major wine-producing country, and much of the wine is of superlative quality. You will probably be hap- py with the house wine in most restaurants or with one of those earthenware pitchers of cold Moselle wine. If you want something more expensive, remember that all wines are graded in one of three basic categories: *Tafelwein* (table wine), *Qualitätswein* (fine wines), and *Qualitätswein mit Prädikat* (top-quality wines).

Mealtimes Breakfast, served anytime from 6:30 to 10 (in some cafés and *Kneipen* until as late 2 or 4 PM), is often a substantial meal, with cold meats, cheeses, rolls, and fruit. Lunch is served from around 11:30 (es- pecially in rural areas) to around 2; dinner is generally from 6 until 9:30 PM, or earlier in some quiet country areas. Lunch tends to be the main meal, a fact reflected in the lunchtime *Tageskarte*, or suggested menu; try it if you want maximum nourishment for minimum outlay.

What to Wear Casual dress is appropriate for restaurants in this book.

Ratings Prices are per person and include a first course, main course, des- sert, and tip and tax. Best bets are indicated by a star ★.

Category	Major Cities and Resorts	Other Areas
$$	DM 50–DM 75	DM 35–DM 55
$	DM 30–DM 50	DM 20–DM 35
¢	under DM 30	under DM 20

Lodging The standard of German hotels is generally excellent. Prices are highest in big cities, where there are fewer budget options to choose from.

In addition to hotels proper, the country also has numerous *Gasthöfe* or *Gasthäuser* (country inns); pensions or *Fremdenheime* (guest houses); and, at the lowest end of the scale, *Zimmer*, meaning, quite simply, rooms, normally in private houses. Look for the sign "Zimmer frei" or "zu vermieten," meaning "for rent." A red sign reading "besetzt" means there are no vacancies.

Lists of hotels are available from the German National Tourist Of- fice (Beethovenstr. 69, D-60325 Frankfurt/Main, tel. 069/75720), and from all regional and local tourist offices. Tourist offices will also make reservations for you—they charge a nominal fee—but may have difficulty doing so after 4 PM in peak season and on week- ends. A reservations service is also operated by the German National

Tourist Office (Allgemeine Deutsche Zimmer-reservierung, Cornel-ius-str. 34, D-60325 Frankfurt/Main, tel. 069/740–767).

Most hotels have restaurants, but those describing themselves as *Garni* will provide breakfast only. Many larger hotels offer no-smoking rooms, so it's always worth asking for one when you check in.

Tourist accommodations in eastern Germany are beginning to blossom under free enterprise, although the choice and facilities are still far behind the western half of the country. Accommodations remain tight at the top- and middle-quality levels, so if you want to stay in good hotels in eastern Germany, book well in advance (Berlin is one notable exception). The real boom in lodgings has been at the inexpensive end of the market, where thousands of beds are now available for the adventurous traveler. For relatively few Marks every village can now provide somewhere for the tourist to put his or her head and perhaps offer a simple but wholesome evening meal. Many guest houses have sprung up under the enterprising stewardship of homemakers eager to supplement the family income. For a list of approved addresses, consult the local tourist office.

Pub Lodgings A group of more than 40 small, privately owned inns and pubs, many with a small house brewery attached, have banded together to produce a color guide to their location and services. Most are in the country and are moderately priced. Contact **Private Brauerigast-höfe,** Kloster-ring 1, D-87660 Irsee, tel. 08341/4321.

Rentals Apartments and hotel homes, most accommodating from two to eight guests, can be rented throughout Germany. Rates are low, with reductions for longer stays. Charges for gas and electricity, and sometimes water, are usually added to the bill. There is normally an extra charge for linen, but not if you bring your own. Local and regional tourist offices have lists of apartments in their areas; otherwise contact the **German National Tourist Office** (*see* Lodging *in* Staying in Germany, *above*).

Farm Vacations Taking an *Urlaub auf dem Bauernhof*, as the Germans put it, has increased dramatically in popularity over the past four or five years. Almost every regional tourist office has listings of farms by area offering bed-and-breakfast, apartments, or whole farmhouses to rent. Alternatively, contact the **German Agricultural Association** (DLG) (Eschborner Landstr. 122, D-60489 Frankfurt/Main, tel. 069/247–880). It produces an annual listing of more than 1,500 farms, all of them inspected and graded, that offer accommodations. The brochure costs DM 7.50.

Camping There are 2,600 campsites in Germany, about 1,600 of which are listed by the **German Camping Club** (DCC) (Mandlstrasse 28, D-80802, Munich, tel. 089/380–1420). The German National Tourist Office also publishes an annually updated listing of sites. Most sites are open from May through October, with about 400 staying open year-round. They tend to become crowded during the summer, so it's always worthwhile to make reservations a day or two ahead. Prices range from DM 15 to DM 20 per night for two adults, a car, and trailer (less for tents). If you want to camp away from an official site, you must get permission beforehand; if you can't find the owner, ask the police. You're allowed to spend no more than one night in parking lots on roadsides and in city parking lots if you're in a camper, and you may not set up any camping equipment.

Youth Hostels Germany's youth hostels—*Jugendherberge*—are probably the most efficient and up-to-date in Europe. There are 600 in all, many located in castles, adding a touch of romance to otherwise utilitarian accommodations. There's an age limit of 27 in Bavaria; elsewhere, there are no restrictions, though those under 20 take preference if space is limited. You'll need a Hostelling International card to stay in a German youth hostel; write **American Youth Hostels Association** (Box 37613, Washington, DC 20013) or **Canadian Hostelling Association** (333 River Rd., Ottawa, Ontario K1L 8H9). In Great Britain, contact the **Youth Hostels Association** (22 Southampton St., London WC2). The International Youth Hostel card can also be obtained from the **Deutsches Jugendherbergswerk Hauptverband** (Bismarckstr. 8, D-32754 Detmold, tel. 05231/74010) or one of its regional offices, which provides a complete list of German hostels for DM 6.50.

Hostels must be reserved well in advance for midsummer, especially in eastern Germany. Bookings for hostels can only be made by calling the hostels directly; telephone numbers are listed in Deutsches Jugendherbergwerk's listings (*see above*).

Ratings   Service charges and taxes are included in all quoted room rates. Similarly, breakfast is usually, but not always, included, so check before you book in Rates are often surprisingly flexible in German hotels, varying considerably according to demand. Major hotels in cities often have lower rates on weekends or other periods when business is quiet. If you're lucky, you can find reductions of up to 60%. Prices are for two people in a double room. Best bets are indicated by a star ★.

The following chart is for lodgings throughout Germany. Generally, accommodations in eastern Germany are less expensive than in western Germany.

Category	Major Cities or Resorts	Other Areas
$$	DM 140–DM 200	DM 100–DM 160
$	DM 100–DM 140	DM 80–DM 100
¢	under DM 100	under DM 80

Tipping   Service is almost always included in the bill at eating places (under the heading *Bedienung*, at the bottom of the check). Other than that there is no obligation to give a tip, especially if you were not satisfied. Nevertheless, it is customary to round out the check to the next Mark or two. For taxi drivers, also round out to the next Mark or two: for DM 11.20, make it DM 12; for DM 11.80, make it DM 13. Railway and airport porters (if you can find any) have their own scale of charges, but round out the requested amount to the next Mark.

Munich

Arriving and Departing

By Plane   Munich's Franz Josef Strauss (FJS) Airport, named after a former state premier, opened in May 1992. It is 28 kilometers (17½ miles) northeast of the city center.

Between the Airport and Downtown   The S-8 suburban train line links FJS Airport with the city's main train station (Hauptbahnhof). Trains depart in both directions every 20 minutes from 3:55 AM to 1:15 AM daily. Intermediate stops are made at Ostbahnhof (good for hotels located east of the River Isar) and city center stations, such as Marienplatz. The 38-minute trip costs DM 10 if you purchase a multi-use strip ticket (*see* Getting Around, *below*) and use 8 strips; otherwise an ordinary one-way ticket is DM 12.80 per person. A tip for families: Up to five people (maximum of two adults) can travel to or from the airport for only DM 20 by buying a Tageskarte (*see* Getting Around, *below*). This is particularly advantageous if you are arriving in Munich because you can continue to use the Tageskarte in the city for the rest of the day. The only restriction is that you cannot use this special day ticket before 9 AM weekdays.

An express bus also links the airport and Hauptbahnhof, departing in both directions every 20 minutes. The trip takes about 40 minutes and costs DM 15.

By Train All long-distance services arrive at and depart from the main train station, the Hauptbahnhof. Trains to and from destinations in the Bavarian Alps use the adjoining Starnbergerbahnhof. For information on train times, tel. 089/19419 or 592–991; English is spoken by most information office staff. For tickets and information, go to the station or to the ABR travel agency, right by the station on Bahnhofplatz.

By Bus Munich has no central bus station. Long-distance buses arrive at and depart from the north side of the train station on Arnulfstrasse. A taxi stand is 20 yards away.

Getting Around

Downtown Munich is only about 1 mile square, so it can easily be explored on foot. Other areas—Schwabing, Nymphenburg, the Olympic Park—are best reached on the efficient and comprehensive public transportation network. It incorporates buses, streetcars, subways (U-Bahn), and suburban trains (S-Bahn). Tickets are good for the entire network, and you can break your trip as many times as you like using just one ticket, provided you travel in one direction only and within a given time limit. If you plan to make only a few trips, buy strip tickets (Streifenkarten)—blue for adults, red for children. Adults get 12 strips for DM 15; children the same number for DM 8 (but these prices were expected to rise 15% by mid-1996). For adults, short rides that span up to four stations cost one strip; trips spanning more than four stations cost two strips. Children pay one strip per ride. All tickets must be validated by time-punching them in the automatic machines at station entrances and on all buses and streetcars. The best buy is the Tageskarte. Up to two adults and three children can use this excellent-value ticket for unlimited journeys between 9 AM and the end of the day's service (about 2 AM). It costs DM 10 for the inner zone, which covers central Munich. A Tageskarte for the entire system, extending to the Starnbergersee and Ammersee lakes, costs DM 20. Holders of a Eurail Pass, a Youth Pass, an InterRail Card, or a DB Tourist Card travel free on all S-Bahn trains.

Important Addresses and Numbers

Tourist Information The address to write to for information in advance of your visit is Fremdenverkehrsamt München, Sendlingerstr. 1, D-80313, München. This address also deals with lodging questions and bookings. Two other offices provide on-the-spot advice: at the Hauptbahnhof (tel. 089/239–1256), weekdays between 8 AM and 10 PM, Sun. and holidays 11–7 PM; and at the corner of Rindermarkt and Pettenbeckstrasse, behind Marienplatz (tel. 089/239–1272), open Mon.–Thurs. 8:30–4, Fri. 8:30–2.

Consulates **U.S. Consulate General** (Königinstrasse 5, tel. 089/28880). **British Consulate General** (Bürkleinstr. 10, tel. 089/211090). **Canadian Consulate** (Tal 29, tel. 089/222–661).

Emergencies **Police** (tel. 110). **Ambulance** and **emergency medical attention** (tel. 089/558–661). **Dentist** (tel. 089/723–3093).

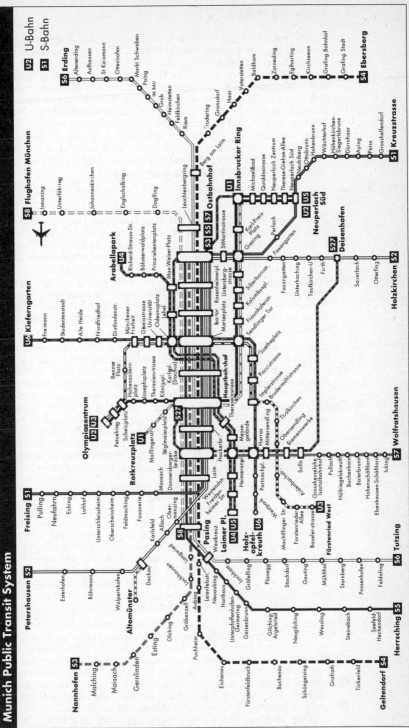

Munich Public Transit System

Exploring Munich

Germans in other parts of the country sometimes refer to Munich (München) as the nation's "secret capital." This sly compliment may reflect the importance of Munich—it's the number-one tourist destination in Germany, as well as the most attractive major German city—but there's nothing "secret" about the way Münchners make this brave claim. Flamboyant, easygoing Munich, city of beer and Baroque, is starkly different from the sometimes stiff Prussian influences to be found in Berlin, the gritty industrial drive of Hamburg, or the hard-headed commercial instincts of high-rise Frankfurt. This is a city to visit for its good-natured and relaxed charm—Gemütlichkeit, they call it here—and for its beer halls, its museums, its malls, its parks, and its palaces.

The Historic Heart *Numbers in the margin correspond to points of interest on the Munich map.*

❶ Begin your tour of Munich at the **Hauptbahnhof,** the main train station. The city tourist office is here, ready with information and maps. Cross the street and you're at the start of a kilometer (½ mile) of pedestrian shopping malls, the first being Schützenstrasse. Facing you are **Hertie,** Munich's leading department store, and ❷ **Karlsplatz** square, known locally as *Stachus*. The huge, domed building on your left is the late-19th-century **Justizpalast** (Palace of Justice). It's one of Germany's finest examples of *Gründerzeit*, the 19th-century versions of Medieval and Renaissance architectural styles.

Head down into the pedestrian underpass—it's another extensive shopping area—to reach the other side and one of the original city ❸ gates, **Karlstor.** The city's two principal shopping streets—**Neuhauserstrasse** and **Kaufingerstrasse**—stretch away from it on the other side. Two of the city's major churches are here, too: the ❹ ❺ **Bürgersaal** and the **Michaelskirche.** The latter is one of the most magnificent Renaissance churches in Germany, a spacious and handsome structure decorated throughout in plain white stucco. It was built for the Jesuits in the late 16th century and is closely modeled on their church of the Gesù in Rome. The intention was to provide a large preaching space, hence the somewhat barnlike atmosphere.

A block past the Michaelskirche to your left is Munich's late-15th-❻ century cathedral, the **Frauenkirche,** or Church of Our Lady. Towering above it are two onion-shape domes, symbols of the city (perhaps because they resemble brimming beer mugs, cynics claim). They were added in 1525 after the body of the church had been completed. Step inside and you'll be amazed at the stark simplicity of the church. This is partly the result of the construction that followed the severe bombing in World War II. The Frauenkirche underwent a second major postwar renovation during 1992–93, costing DM 26 million ($17 million) and was reopened in 1994 for celebrations marking the 500th anniversary of its consecration.

❼ From the Frauenkirche, walk to the **Marienplatz** square, the heart of the city, surrounded by shops, restaurants, and cafés. It takes its name from the 300-year-old gilded statue of the Virgin in the center. When it was taken down to be cleaned in 1960, workmen found a small casket containing a splinter of wood said to have come from the ❽ cross of Christ. The square is dominated by the 19th-century **Neues Rathaus,** the new town hall, built in the fussy, turreted style so ❾ loved by Ludwig II. The **Altes Rathaus,** or old town hall, a medieval building of great charm, sits, as if forgotten, in a corner of the square. At 11 AM and 9 PM daily (plus May–October, 5 PM), the **Glockenspiel,** or chiming clock, in the central tower of the town hall, swings into action. Two tiers of dancing and jousting figures perform their ritual display.

Heading south down Rosenstrasse to Sendlingerstrasse, you come
⑩ to the **Asamkirche** on your right. If you have any interest in church
architecture, this is a place you shouldn't miss. It was built around
1730 by the Asam brothers—Cosmas Damian and Egid Quirin—
next door to their home, the Asamhaus. They dedicated it to St.
John Nepomuk, a 14th-century Bohemian monk who was drowned in
the Danube. Pause before you go in to see the charming statue of angels carrying him to heaven from the rocky riverbank.

⑪ Go back to Marienplatz and turn right for the **Viktualienmarkt,** the
food market. Open-air stalls sell cheese, wine, sausages, fruit, and
flowers. Fortified with Bavarian sausage and sauerkraut, plunge
⑫ into local history with a visit to the **Residenz,** home of the
Wittelsbachs from the 16th century to their enforced abdication at
the end of World War I. From Max-Joseph-Platz you'll enter the
great palace, with its glittering Schatzkammer, or treasury, and
glorious Rococo theater, designed by court architect François
Cuvilliès. Also facing the square is the stern neoclassical portico of
⑬ the **Nationaltheater,** built at the beginning of the 19th century and
twice destroyed. *Residenz and Schatzkammer, Max-Joseph-Platz
3. Admission to each: DM 4 adults. Open Tues.–Sun. 10–4:30 PM.
Cuvilliès Theater admission: DM 2.50 adults. Open Mon.–Sat. 2–5,
Sun. 10–5.*

⑭ To the north of the Residenz is the **Hofgarten,** the palace gardens.
Two sides of the gardens are bordered by sturdy arcades designed
by Leo von Klenze, whose work for the Wittelsbachs in the 19th century helped transform the face of the city.

Odeonsplatz itself is dominated by two striking buildings. One is the
⑮ **Theatinerkirche,** built for the Theatine monks in the mid-17th century, though its handsome facade, with twin eye-catching domes, was
added only in the following century. Despite its Italian influences,
the interior, like that of the Michaelskirche, is austerely white. The
⑯ other notable building here is the **Feldherrnhalle,** an open loggia
built by Ludwig I and modeled on the Loggia dei Lanzi in Florence.
Next to it is the site of Hitler's unsuccessful putsch of 1923, later a
key Nazi shrine.

The Feldherrnhalle looks north along one of the most imposing boulevards in Europe, the **Ludwigstrasse,** which in turn becomes the
Leopoldstrasse. The state library and the university are located
⑰ along it, while halfway up it is the **Siegestor,** or Arch of Victory,
modeled on the Arch of Constantine in Rome. Beyond it is
Schwabing, once a student and artist quarter but now much glossier,
with a mix of bars, discos (*see* Nightlife, *below*), trendy cafés, and
boutiques.

Back on Leopoldstrasse, wander down to the university, turn on to
Professor-Huber-Platz (he was a Munich academic executed by the
Nazis for his support of an anti-Hitler movement), and take
Veterinärstrasse. It leads you to Munich's largest park, the magnifi-
⑱ cent **Englischer Garten.**

The Englischer Garten, 4½ kilometers (3 miles) long and over a ½
kilometer (¼ mile) wide, was laid out by Count Rumford, a refugee
from the American Revolutionary War. It wasn't Rumford's English
ancestry that determined the park's name as much as its open, informal nature, a style favored by 18th-century English aristocrats. You
can rent boats or bikes, visit beer gardens—the most famous is at
the foot of a Chinese Pagoda—or simply stroll around. Ludwig II
used to love to wander incognito along the serpentine paths. Late-
20th-century Germans have embraced nature worship with almost
pagan fervor, and large sections of the park have been designated
⑲ nudist areas. The biggest is behind the **Haus der Kunst,** Munich's
leading modern art gallery and a surviving example of Third Reich
architecture. The building underwent major renovations in 1992.

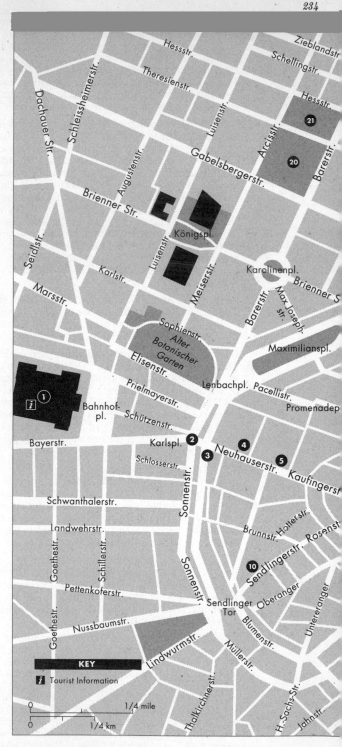

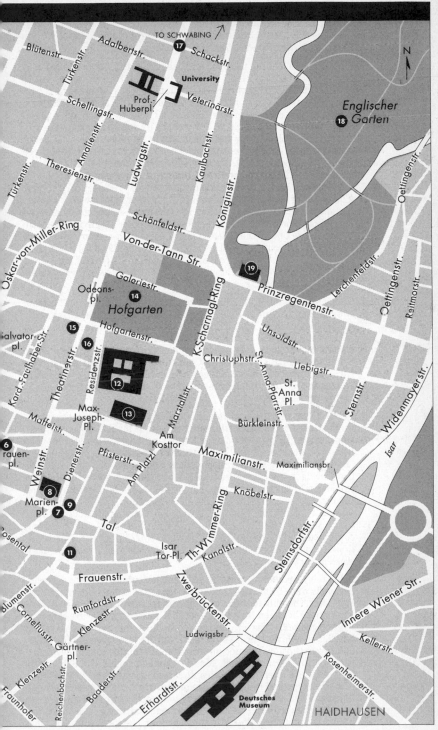

Part of the basement also houses one of the city's most exclusive discos, the PI. *Haus der Kunst, Prinzregentenstr. 1. Admission: DM 5 adults, DM 3 children; Sun. and holidays free. Open Tues.– Sun. 10–5, also Thurs. 10–8.*

㉑ Munich's two leading picture galleries, the Alte (meaning "old") and the Neue (meaning "new") Pinakothek, are on Barerstrasse, just to the west of the university. The **Alte Pinakothek** is not only the repository of some of the world's most celebrated Old Master paintings, but an architectural treasure in its own right, though much scarred from wartime bomb damage. It was built by von Klenze at the beginning of the 19th century to house Ludwig I's collections. The museum was closed in 1994 for renovations expected to take at least three **㉑** years. A selection of its finest paintings is on show at the **Neue Pinakothek.** This was another of Ludwig I's projects, built to house his "modern" collections, meaning, of course, 19th-century works. The building was destroyed during World War II, and today's museum opened in 1981. The low, brick structure—some have compared it with a Florentine palazzo—is an unparalleled environment in which to see one of the finest collections of 19th-century European paintings and sculpture in the world. *Barerstr. 29. Admission: DM 6 adults, DM 1 children; free Sun. and holidays. Open Tues.–Sun. 9–5; also Tues. 5–8 PM. Take the No. 18 streetcar from Karlsplatz for both the Alte and Neue Pinakotheks.*

Suburban Attractions There are a number of trips you can take to attractions not far from the city center. One is to the **Olympic Park,** a 10-minute U-Bahn ride (U-3); another is to **Nymphenburg,** 6 kilometers (4 miles) northwest and reached by the U-1 subway to Rotkreuzplatz, then the No. 12 streetcar. The town of Dachau is 20 minutes from Marienplatz on the S-2 line. To get to the **Dachau Concentration Camp Memorial** from the stop, take Bus 722 to Robert-Boschstrasse and walk along Alte Römerstrasse for 100 yards, or board Bus 720 and get off at Ratiborer Strasse.

Perhaps the most controversial buildings in Munich are the circus tent–shaped roofs of the **Olympic Park.** Built for the 1972 Olympics, the park, with its undulating, transparent tile roofs and modern housing blocks, represented a revolutionary marriage of technology and visual daring when first unveiled. Sports fans might like to join the crowds in the Olympic stadium when the local soccer team, Bayern Munich, has a home game. Call 089/699–310 for information and tickets. There's an amazing view of the stadium, the Olympic Park, and the city from the Olympic tower. An elevator speeds you to the top in seconds. *Tower admission: DM 5 adults, DM 2.50 children; combined tower and park tour (until 5 PM) DM 7 adults, DM 4 children. Open mid-Apr.–mid-Oct., daily 8 AM–midnight; mid-Oct.–mid-Apr., daily 9 AM–midnight.*

Schloss Nymphenburg was the Wittelsbach summer palace. The oldest parts date from 1664, but construction continued for more than 100 years, the bulk of the work being undertaken in the reign of Max Emmanuel between 1680 and 1730. The gardens, a mixture of formal French parterres (trim, ankle-high hedges and gravel walks) and English parkland, were landscaped over the same period. The interiors are exceptional, especially the Banqueting Hall, a Rococo masterpiece in green and gold. Make a point of seeing the Schönheits Galerie, the **Gallery of Beauties.** It contains more than 100 portraits of women who had caught the eye of Ludwig I; duchesses rub shoulders with butchers' daughters. Among them is Lola Montez. Seek out the **Amalienburg,** or Hunting Lodge, on the grounds. It was built by Cuvilliès, architect of the Residenz Theater in Munich. That the lodge was designed for hunting of the indoor variety can easily be guessed by the sumptuous silver-and-blue stucco and the atmosphere of courtly high life. The palace also contains the **Marstallmuseum** (the Museum of Royal Carriages), containing a sleigh that belonged to Ludwig II, among the opulently decorated vehicles, and, on the floor above, the **Nymphenburger Porzellan,** with examples of the porcelain produced here between 1747 and the 1920s. *Schloss Nymphenburg. Combined ticket to all Nymphenburg attractions: DM 6 adults, DM 4 children. Combined ticket to Schloss, Gallery of Beauties, Amalienburg, and Marstallmuseum: DM 2.50 adults, DM 2 children. Botanic gardens: DM 1.50. Children under 15 free. Open Apr.–Sept., Tues.–Sun. 9–12:30 and 1:30–5; Oct.– Mar., Tues.–Sun. 10–12:30 and 1:30–4. Amalienburg and gardens open daily.*

Although the 1,200-year-old town of **Dachau** attracted hordes of painters and artists from the mid-19th century until World War I, most people remember it as the site of Germany's first **concentration camp.** From its opening in 1933 until its capture by American soldiers in 1945, the camp took in more than 206,000 political dissidents, Jews, clergy, and other "enemies" of the Nazis; more than 32,000 prisoners died here. Photographs, contemporary documents, the few remaining cell blocks, and the grim crematorium create a somber and moving picture of the vicious living and working conditions at the camp. *Admission free. Open Tues.–Sun. 9–5; documentary (in English) shown at 11:30 and 3:30.*

Shopping

Gift Ideas Munich is a city of beer, and beer mugs and coasters make an obvious souvenir. There are many specialist shops in downtown Munich, but **Ludwig Mory,** in the town hall on Marienplatz, is about the best. Munich is also the home of the famous Nymphenburg porcelain factory; its major outlet is on Odeonsplatz. You can also buy direct from the factory, which is on the half-moon–shape road—Schlossrondell—in front of Nymphenburg Palace. *Tel. 089/1791–9710. Salesroom open Mon.–Fri. 8:30–noon and 12:30–5.*

Shopping Districts From Odeonsplatz you are poised to plunge into the heart of the huge pedestrian mall that runs through the center of town. The first street you come to, **Theatinerstrasse,** is also one of the most expensive. In fact, it has only one serious rival in the money-no-object stakes: **Maximilianstrasse,** the first street to your left as you head down Theatinerstrasse. Both are lined with elegant shops selling desirable German fashions and other high-price goods from around the world. Leading off to the right of Theatinerstrasse is **Maffeistrasse,** where **Loden-Frey** has Bavaria's most complete collection of traditional wear, from green loden to lederhosen. Maffeistrasse runs parallel to Munich's principal shopping streets: **Kaufingerstrasse** and **Neuhauserstrasse,** the one an extension of the other.

Department Stores All the city's major department stores—other than **Hertie** (*see* Exploring, *above*)—are along Maffeistrasse, Kaufingerstrasse, and Neuhauserstrasse. **Kaufhof** and **Karstadt-Oberpollinger** are probably the best.

Dining

Some of Europe's best chefs are to be found here, purveyors of French nouvelle cuisine in some of the most noted—and pricey— restaurants in Germany. But these restaurants are mainly for the gourmet. For those in search of the local cuisine, the path leads to Munich's tried-and-true wood-paneled, flagstone beer restaurants and halls, where the food is as sturdy as the large measure of beer that comes to your table almost automatically. Try the Weisswurst, brought to your table in a tureen of boiling water to keep them fresh and hot. They are served with a sweet mustard and pretzels and are a breakfast or midmorning favorite. Equally good is Leberkäs, wedges of piping-hot meat loaf with a fried egg on top and pan-fried potatoes.

For details and price-category definitions, *see* Dining *in* Staying in Germany, *above*.

$$ Augustiner Keller. The 19th-century Keller is the flagship beer restaurant of Munich's oldest brewery, Augustiner. The communal atmosphere of two baronial hall-like rooms make this a good place to meet locals. The emphasis is on polished woodwork, including the ornate floor. The daily changing menu offers a full range of Bavarian specialties, but see if you can get *Tellerfleisch*—cold roast beef with lashings of horseradish, served with salad on a big wooden board. Another recommendation: sauerbraten, roast pork in a spicy sauce with dumplings. *Arnulfstr. 52, tel. 089/594–393. No credit cards.*

$$ Nürnberger Bratwurst Glöckl. This is about the most authentic old-
★ time Bavarian sausage restaurant in Munich, and it's always crowded. Wobbly chairs, pitch-black wooden paneling, tin plates, monosyllabic waitresses, and, downstairs, some seriously Teutonic-looking characters establish an unbeatable mood. The menu is limited, with finger-size Nürnberger sausages and sauerkraut the staple offering. Beer is served straight from wooden barrels. The restaurant is right by the Frauenkirche—the entrance is set back from the street and can be hard to spot—and makes an ideal lunchtime layover. *Frauenplatz 9, tel. 089/220–385. Reservations advised. No credit cards. Closed Sun. and public holidays.*

$$ Spöckmeier. This rambling Bavarian beer restaurant, only 50 yards from Marienplatz, is spread over three floors and is a firm favorite with the locals. It is famous for its homemade Weisswurst, but the daily changing menu also offers more than two dozen solid main course dishes and a choice of four draft beers. The house *eintopf* (a rich broth of noodles and pork) is a meal in itself. *Rosenstr. 9, tel. 089/268–088. AE, DC, MC, V.*

$ Donisl. The two-story galleried interior of this centuries-old beer hall bustles with activity from early morning until midnight. During Fasching, Donisl serves Weissbier and Weisswurst all night to the fancy-dress-ball crowds. In summer, tables spill outside in front of the Rathaus on Marienplatz. Regulars on the menu include *Schweinshaxe* (pig's knuckle) and roast pork and dumplings. Traditional music performances start at 5 PM. *Weinstr. 1, tel. 089/220–184. No reservations. AE, DC, MC, V.*

$ Franziskaner. Vaulted archways, cavernous rooms interspersed with intimate dining areas, bold blue frescoes on the walls, and long wooden tables create a spick-and-span medieval atmosphere. Aside from the late-morning Weisswurst, look out for *Ochsenfleisch* (boiled ox meat) and dumplings. *Perusastr. 5, tel. 089/231–8120. No reservations. No credit cards.*

$ Hofbräuhaus. The heavy stone vaults of the Hofbräuhaus contain the city's most famous beer restaurants. Crowds of singing, shouting, swaying beer drinkers fill the cavernous, smoky hall. Picking their way past the tables are hefty waitresses in traditional garb bearing frothing steins. The menu is strictly solid Bavarian. If you're not here solely to drink, try the more subdued upstairs restaurant, where the service is not so brusque and less beer gets spilled. It's between Marienplatz and Maximillianstrasse. *Platzl 9, tel. 089/221–676. No reservations. No credit cards.*

$ Hundskugel. History practically oozes from the crooked walls at this tavern, Munich's oldest, which dates from 1440. The food is surprisingly good. If *Spanferkel*—roast suckling pig—is on the menu, make a point of ordering it. This is simple Bavarian fare at its best. *Hotterstr. 18, tel. 089/264–272. Reservations advised. No credit cards. Closed Sun.*

$ Lindwurm Stüberl. Locals in the know swear that this is the best
★ place in Munich to eat traditional Bavarian spit-roast chicken (*Brathendl*). Husband-and-wife kitchen duo Margot and Wolfram

Ensle use only fresh chickens, seasoned with pepper and parsley. But this old-fashioned Gaststätte also has a strong following for the many other traditional dishes that are fading from an increasingly "sophisticated" upscale market. Wolfram's special steamed suet pudding (*Dampfnudeln*) with vanilla sauce is made from a secret recipe that includes a dash of rum. Look out, too, for the Ensle's venison goulasch. Hot dishes are served from 10 AM to 9:30 PM. *Lindwurmstr. 32, tel. 089/534-638. Reservations advised. No credit cards. Closed Sun.*

$ **Pfälzer Weinprobierstube.** A warren of stone-vaulted rooms of vari-
★ ous sizes, wooden tables, glittering candles, dirndl-clad waitresses, and a vast range of wines add up to an experience as close to your picture of timeless Germany as you're likely to get. The food is reliable rather than spectacular. Local specialties predominate. *Residenzstr. 1, tel. 089/225-628. No reservations. No credit cards.*

$ **Zum Brez'n.** This hostelry is bedecked in the blue-and-white of the Bavarian flag. The eating and drinking are spread over three floors and cater to a broad clientele—from local business lunchers to hungry night owls emerging from Schwabing's bars and discos looking for a bite at 2 AM. Zum Brez'n offers a big all-day menu of traditional roasts, to be washed down with a choice of three draft beers. *Leopoldstrasse 72, tel. 089/390-092. No credit cards.*

¢ **Bella Italia.** The five branches of this Italian restaurant offer the same excellent, no-frills value, which makes them very popular, especially among students. The extensive menu of pasta dishes, priced under DM 10, range from spaghetti *bolognese* to cannelloni; there are also pizzas. Beer and wine prices are lower than elsewhere in Munich. *Sendlingerstr. 66 (near Karlsplatz); Weissenburgerstr. 2; Leopoldstr. 44; Türkenstr. 50; Bahnhofplatz 3, in Pasing, tel. 089/ 885-233. No reservations. No credit cards.*

¢ **Buxs.** If you've had your fill of schnitzel and roast pork and dumplings, head to this self-service vegetarian restaurant. Both the food and the beer are produced organically. A daily changing menu includes pastas and a huge salad selection. *Frauenstr. 9, tel. 089/229-482. No reservations. No dinner Sat., closed Sun. No credit cards.*

¢ **Nordsee Buffet.** Seafood is the specialty in this excellent, bustling stand-up cafe, where a large selection of fresh fish—from plaice to king prawns—is flown in daily. One of the best deals is from the bouillabaisse pot that simmers away behind the counter in the main window. In summer, customers take their meals outside and sit at tables in the adjacent beer garden. *Am Viktualienmarkt, no phone. No reservations. Open weekdays until 6:30 PM, no dinner Sat., closed Sun. and holidays. No credit cards.*

¢ **Oberpollinger Karstadt.** One of the best values in town is found next to the Karlstor city gate at Karlsplatz, at this department store self-service restaurant. Aside from such hot dishes as sausages with sauerkraut and Greek gyros, there is also a gourmet delicatessen snack bar serving oysters and lobster and a Japanese hot-food counter. A three-course traditional Bavarian lunch costs less than DM 20; mugs of freshly brewed coffee cost DM 2.50; late risers can buy a Continental breakfast for DM 4.50. *Neuhauserstr. 44, tel. 089/290-230. No reservations. Open weekdays 9:15 AM-6, Sat. 9:15-2. No credit cards.*

¢ **Sultan.** Discerning members of Munich's resident Turkish community dine regularly at Mehmet Altindag's restaurant-cum-takeout, where the big menu offers a taste of southern Turkey and Syria. Mehmet's lamb kebab, garnished with salad and yogurt on fresh-baked pita bread, is an unbeatable value at DM 6. For something more substantial, try one of his grilled lamb dishes with lemon, eggplant, and olives. *Corner of Goethestr. and Schwantalerstr., tel. 089/ 598-443. Reservations advised early evening. No credit cards. Open daily until 1 AM.*

Lodging

Make reservations well in advance and be prepared for higher-than-average rates. Though Munich has a vast number of hotels in all price ranges, most are full year-round; this is a major trade and convention city, as well as a prime tourist destination. If you plan to visit during the "fashion weeks" (Mode Wochen) in March and September or during Oktoberfest at the end of September, make reservations at least several months in advance. Munich's tourist offices will handle only written or personal requests for reservations assistance. Write to Fremdenverkehrsamt, Sendlingerstr. 1, D-80313 München, fax 089/239–1313. Your best bet for finding a room if you haven't reserved is the tourist office at the Hauptbahnhof, by the Bayerstasse entrance. The staff will charge a small fee.

Budget bargains can be obtained right in the heart of the city, but consider staying in a suburban hotel, where you will generally get better value for your money. A 15-minute train ride is no obstacle to serious sightseeing. Check out the city tourist office's "Key to Munich" packages. These include reduced-rate hotel reservations, sightseeing tours, theater visits, and low-cost travel on the U- and S-Bahn. Write to the tourist office (*see* Important Addresses and Numbers *in* Munich, *above*).

For details and price-category definitions, *see* Lodging *in* Staying in Germany, *above*.

$$ Alpen Hotel. The sturdy old "Alpen," a handsome corner house in Renaissance style, prides itself on its tradition of friendly management (it's been run by the same family for three generations) and high standards. Rooms come in a variety of styles, from Bavarian to sleek modern, and one suite has a romantic, canopied four-poster bed. The vaulted Stefan Restaurant, its walls inexplicably smothered with religious figures, is renowned for vegetarian food but also has a menu replete with such Bavarian specialties as pork knuckle. The hotel's location, midway between the main railway station and central Karlsplatz, couldn't be better. Families can take advantage of rooms with three beds, in which children under 10 are accommodated free of charge. *Adolf-Kolping-Str. 14, tel. 089/554–585, fax 089/550–3658. 60 rooms with bath or shower. Facilities: restaurant, parking. AE, DC, MC, V.*

$$ Arosa. This plain, well-worn but friendly lodging in the old town is just a five-minute walk to Marienplatz. If you're driving, make sure you reserve a spot in the hotel garage; parking in the area is difficult. Munich's oldest pub, the Hundskugel, is right down the street. *Hotterstr. 2, tel. 089/267087, fax 089/263–104. 75 rooms, 66 with bath. Facilities: restaurant, bar, garage. AE, DC, MC, V.*

$$ Gästehaus am Englischer Garten. Though the rooms are slightly basic, you need to reserve well in advance to be sure of getting one in this converted 200-year-old watermill. The hotel, complete with ivy-clad walls and shutter-framed windows, stands right on the edge of the Englischer Garten, no more than a five-minute walk from the bars and shops of Schwabing. Be sure to ask for a room in the main building; the modern annex down the road is cheaper but charmless. There's no restaurant, but in summer, breakfast is served on the terrace. *Liebergesellstr. 8, tel. 089/392–034. 34 rooms, some with bath. No credit cards.*

$$ Mayer. It's a 25-minute train ride from the city center, but this family-run hotel offers comforts and facilities that would cost twice as much in town. The style and furnishings are typical Bavarian country "rustic"; plenty of pine and green-and-red checkered fabrics. Owner-chef Rainer Radach was a student of Eckhart Witzigmann, one of Germany's most noted gourmet experts. The Mayer is a 10-minute walk, or short taxi ride, from Germering station, on the S-5 suburban line, eight stops west of the Hauptbahnhof. *Augsbur-*

gerstr. 45, 8034 Germering, tel. 089/844–071, fax 089/844–094. 56 rooms with bath. Facilities: restaurant, indoor pool. AE, MC.

$ **Am Markt.** Although its tucked away in a corner of the colorful Viktualienmarkt in the heart of the old town, this old-fashioned hotel has long ceased to be a secret. Its central location and slightly seedy charm make up for the lack of luxury. It's very popular, so book well in advance. Parking in the area is a problem. *Heiliggeistr. 6, tel. 089/225–014. 28 rooms, some with bath. No credit cards.*

$ **Hotel Kronprinz.** With a double room costing DM 80, the family-run "Crown Prince" offers unmatchable value just a two-minute walk from Karlsplatz and the shopping precincts. The grand entrance, complete with baroque lantern, isn't really matched by the guest rooms, which are basic but clean. One big plus: exceptionally friendly and helpful service. *Zweigstr. 10, tel. 089/593–606. 47 rooms, some with shower. AE, DC, MC, V.*

$ **Zur Post.** The Post is a comfortable family-run hostelry in the western district of Pasing, not far from Nymphenburg Palace and park. The rooms have Bavarian country-style furnishings and decor with lots of pine woodwork. The location is convenient to both the train and the streetcar routes to town. Traditional Bavarian food is served in the restaurant. *Bodenseestr. 4, tel. 089/886–772, fax 089/ 837–319. 96 rooms with bath. Facilities: restaurant. No credit cards.*

¢ **Am Kaiserplatz.** Set in a quiet and pretty tree-lined 19th-century square, this small family-run guest house, in the fashionable Schwabing district, is handy for exploring the nightlife scene, centered in nearby Münchener Freiheit on the U-3/6 subway lines. The rooms are furnished in a variety of styles, from Art Deco to Victorian. *Kaiserplatz 12, tel. 089/349–190, fax 089/339–316. 10 rooms, 6 with shower. No credit cards.*

¢ **Jugend-Gästehaus.** This excellently serviced modern lodging of the German Youth Hostels Association is five minutes by foot from the Thalkirchen U-Bahn station, 15 minutes from the city center. Accommodations range from double rooms (DM 58, without bath) to three- and four-bed rooms to segregated dormitories, with shared bathrooms on each floor. Rates include breakfast. *Miesingstr. 4, tel. 089/723–6550. 340 beds, 34 double rooms. No credit cards.*

¢ **Pension Diana.** Located in an 18th-century building in the jumble of winding old-town streets, the Diana is only a few steps from the pedestrianized city center (closest U-Bahn/S-Bahn station: Karlsplatz), with its many historic sights, including the twin-domed cathedral. It offers plainly furnished double and multibed rooms. *Altheimer Eck 15, tel. 089/260–3107, fax 089/263–934. No private baths. No credit cards.*

¢ **Strigl.** A bed-and-breakfast in a century-old terraced house in the fashionable district of Schwabing, the Strigl is just a short walk from the No. 18 tram stop at Elizabethplatz. The pension is run by a young family, one of whose members speaks English. The style of the rooms is turn-of-the-century, with rug-covered hardwood floors. Be forewarned: It's on the second floor and there is no elevator. *Elisabethstr. 11, tel. 089/271–3444, fax 089/271–6250. 10 rooms with sinks share 2 baths. No credit cards.*

The Arts

Details of concerts and theater performances are available from the *Monatsprogramm* booklets (DM 2.50) obtainable from hotels, guest houses, or newspaper kiosks. Use one of the ticket agencies in the city center: **Hieber Konzert Kasse** (Liebfrauenstr. 1, tel. 089/2900–8014) or the **Residenz Bücherstube** (Residenzstr. 1, tel. 089/220–868), concert tickets only. You can also book tickets at the two kiosks on the concourse below Marienplatz.

Concerts Munich's Philharmonic Orchestra entertains in Germany's biggest concert hall, the **Gasteig Cultural Center.** Tickets can be bought directly at the box office (the Gasteig center is on Rosenheimerstrasse, on a hill above the Ludwigsbrücke Bridge). The Bavarian Radio Orchestra performs Sunday concerts here. In summer, concerts are held at two Munich palaces, **Nymphenburg** and **Schleissheim,** and in the open-air interior courtyard of the **Residenz.**

Opera Munich's **Bavarian State Opera** company is world famous, and tickets for major productions in its permanent home, the State Opera House, are difficult to obtain. Book far in advance for the annual opera festival, held in July and August; contact the tourist office for the schedule of performances and ticket prices. The opera house box office (Maximilianstr. 11, tel. 089/2185–1920) takes reservations one week in advance only. It's open weekdays 10–1 and 2–6, Saturday 10–1.

Dance The ballet company of the Bavarian State Opera performs at the **State Opera House.** Ballet productions are also staged at the attractive late-19th-century **Gärtnerplatz Theater** (tel. 089/201–6767). A limited number of tickets at greatly reduced prices are sometimes released, allowing holders to stand at the back of these theaters during performances.

Film English-language films are shown regularly at the Europa film theater in the **Atlantik Palast** (Schwantalerstr. 2–6), **Cinema** (Nymphenburgerstr. 31), the **Film Museum** (St. Jakobs Platz), and the **Museum Lichtspiele** (Ludwigsbrücke).

Theater There are two state theater companies, one of which concentrates on the classics. Two English-language theater companies present regular productions: the Munich English Theatre (Theater in Karlshof, tel. 089/596–611) and the American Drama Group Europe (Theater an der Leopoldstrasse, tel. 089/343–803).

Nightlife

Bars, Cabaret, Nightclubs Although it lacks the racy reputation of Hamburg, Munich has something for just about all tastes. For spicy striptease, explore the train station district (Schillerstrasse, for example) or the neighborhood of the famous Hofbräuhaus (Am Platzl).

Jazz The best jazz can be heard at the **Allotria** (Oscar-von-Miller Ring 3), the **Unterfahrt** (Kirchenstr. 96), and the **Podium** (Wagnerstr. 1). Or try **Jenny's Place in the Blue Note** (Moosacherstr. 24, tel. 089/351–0520), named for an English singer who settled in Munich.

Discos Disco bars abound in the side streets surrounding Münchener Freiheit in Schwabing, especially on Occamstrasse. More upscale are **Nachtcafe** (Maximiliansplatz 5), open all night on weekends, and **Nachtwerk** (Landsbergerstr. 185), with everything from punk to avant-garde, plus live bands.

For Singles Every Munich bar is singles territory. Three you might like to try are **Schumann's** (Maximilianstr. 36) anytime after the curtain comes down at the nearby opera house; **Alter Simpl** (Türkenstr. 57) but not before midnight; and the trendy **Roxy** (Leopoldstr. 48), where being seen at a pavement table at 2 AM is the thing. For the student, beards, and pipe scene, try any of the trendy cafés on Turkenstrasse, behind the university.

Frankfurt

Arriving and Departing

By Plane Frankfurt airport, the busiest in mainland Europe, is about 10 kilometers (6 miles) southwest of the city.

Between the Airport and Downtown There are several ways to get into town. Two S-Bahn lines connect the airport and the center. The S-14 runs between the Hauptwache station and the airport, and the S-15 from the main train station, the Hauptbahnhof. The S-14 runs every 20 minutes and takes 15 minutes; the S-15 leaves every 10 minutes and takes 11 minutes. The trip costs DM 4.20 (DM 5.60 in rush hour, 6:30–8:30 AM and 4–6:30 PM). InterCity and high-speed InterCity Express trains also stop at Frankfurt airport train station on hourly direct runs to Cologne, Dortmund, Hamburg, and Munich. A No. 61 bus runs from the airport to the Südbahnhof station in Sachsenhausen, where there is access to the U-Bahn (subway) lines U-1 and U-3; the fare is DM 4.20 (DM 5.60 during rush hours). Taxi fare from the airport to downtown is about DM 40. By rented car, follow the signs to Frankfurt ("Stadtmitte") via the B43 main road.

By Train Frankfurt's main train station, the Hauptbahnhof, and the airport station are directly linked with all parts of the country by fast Euro-City and InterCity services and by the high-speed InterCity Express trains. For train information, tel. 069/19419. For tickets and general information, go directly to the station or to the DER travel office at the Hauptbahnhof.

By Bus Long-distance buses connect Frankfurt with more than 200 European cities. Buses leave from the south side of the Hauptbahnhof. Tickets and information are available from **Deutsche Touring GmbH** (Am Römerhof 17, tel. 069/790–3219).

Getting Around

By Public Transportation A combination of subway and suburban train, streetcar, and bus services provides speedy transportation. Tickets cover travel on the complete network, which is divided into tariff zones. A single ticket for travel within the city costs DM 2.20 (DM 2.80 during rush hour). Each trip you make is paid for when you cancel a strip in the automatic machines found on buses, streetcars, and subways. A day ticket (for use during one calendar day) offers unlimited journeys in the inner zone for DM 6. Buy all tickets at newspaper kiosks or from blue automatic dispensing machines. For further information or assistance, call 069/269–462.

Important Addresses and Numbers

Tourist Information There are three city information offices. One is at the Hauptbahnhof, across from platform 23 (tel. 069/213–8849). It's open Monday–Friday 8 AM–9 PM, Sat 8 AM–8 PM, Sunday and holidays 9:30 AM–8 PM. The other is in the town hall in the Old Town at Römerberg 27 (tel. 069/2123–8708). It's open daily 9 AM–6 PM. Both offices will help you find accommodations. A third information office (tel. 069/690–6211) is in the airport Arrival Hall B, daily 6:45 AM–10:15 PM. The DER Deutsches Reisebüro, Arrival Hall B6, can also help you find rooms. Open daily 8 AM–9 PM (tel. 069/693–071). For information in advance of your trip, contact the **Verkehrsamt Frankfurt/Main** (Kaiserstrasse 52, 60329 Frankfurt, tel. 069/212–38800).

Consulates U.S. (Siesmayerstrasse 21, tel. 069/75350). U.K. (Bockenheimer Landstrasse 42, tel. 069/170–0020).

Emergencies **Police** (tel. 110). **Fire** (tel. 112). **Doctor** (tel. 19292). **Dentist** (tel. 069/ 660–7271).

Exploring Frankfurt

Numbers in the margin correspond to points of interest on the Frankfurt map.

At first glance, Frankfurt-am-Main doesn't seem to have much to offer the tourist. Virtually flattened by bombs during the war, it now bristles with skyscrapers, the visible sign of the city's role as Germany's financial capital. Yet the inquisitive and discerning visitor will find many remnants of Frankfurt's illustrious past (besides being well placed for excursions to other historic cities, such as Heidelberg and Würzburg, and within easy reach of the Rhine).

Originally a Roman settlement, Frankfurt was later one of Charlemagne's two capitals (the other being Aachen). Still later, it was for centuries the site of the election and coronation of the emperors of that unwieldy entity, the Holy Roman Empire, which was the forerunner of a united Germany. It was also the birthplace of the poet and dramatist Goethe (1749–1832). The house in which he was born is one of many restored and reconstructed old buildings that inject a flavor of bygone days into the center of this busy modern city.

Although the true center of Frankfurt is its ancient **Römerberg Square,** where the election of Holy Roman emperors was traditionally proclaimed and celebrated, this tour of the city begins slightly to the north, at the **Hauptwache,** an 18th-century guardhouse that today serves a more peaceful purpose as a café. The ground floor houses Intertreff, an information office that assists young visitors with such tasks as finding moderately priced accommodations. *Open weekdays 10–6, Sat. 10–1.*

Head south along Kornmarkt, passing on the left the **Katerinenkirche** (Church of St. Catherine), the historic center of Frankfurt Protestantism, in whose 17th-century font Goethe was baptized. After crossing Berlinerstrasse, and still heading south, you'll pass the **Paulskirche** (Church of St. Paul). It was here that the first all-German parliament convened in 1848, and the church is therefore an important symbol of German unity and democracy. Continue down Buchgasse and within a few minutes you're on the north bank of the river **Main.** Turn left toward the iron foot bridge (the first suspension bridge in Europe) known as the **Eiserner Steg** and at the **Rententurm,** one of the city's medieval gates, bear left again and you'll arrive at the spacious **Römerberg,** center of Frankfurt's civic life over the centuries. In the center of the square stands the 16th-century **Fountain of Justitia** (Justice): At the coronation of Emperor Matthias in 1612, wine instead of water spouted from the stonework. Not long ago, city officials started restaging this momentous event for festive occasions, such as the annual Main Fest.

Compared with many city halls, Frankfurt's **Römer** is a modest affair, with a gabled Gothic facade. It occupies most of one side of the square and is actually three patrician houses (the Alt-Limpurg, the Römer—from which it takes its name—and the Löwenstein). The mercantile-minded Frankfurt burghers used the complex not only for political and ceremonial purposes, but for trade fairs and commerce.

The most important events to take place in the Römer, however, were the elections of the Holy Roman emperors. The **Kaisersaal** (Imperial Hall) was last used in 1792 to celebrate the election of Emperor Francis II, who was later forced to abdicate by egomaniac Napoleon Bonaparte. (The 16-year-old Goethe smuggled himself into the banquet celebrating the coronation of Emperor Joseph II in

1765 by posing as a waiter.) Today, visitors can see the impressive full-length 19th-century portraits of the 52 emperors of the Holy Roman Empire that line the walls of the banqueting hall. *Admission: DM 3 adults, DM 1 children. Open Tues.–Sun. 11–3.*

Charlemagne's son, Ludwig the Pious, established a church on the present site of the Römerberg in AD 850. His church was replaced by a much grander Gothic structure, one used for imperial coronations; it became known as the **Kaiserdom**, the Imperial Cathedral (although "Cathedral" is a courtesy title, since Frankfurt was never the seat of a bishopric). The cathedral suffered only superficial damage during World War II, and it still contains most of its original treasures, including a fine 15th-century altar.

On the south side of the square stands the 13th-century **Nikolaikirche** (St. Nicholas's Church). It's worth trying to time your visit to the square to coincide with the chimes of the glockenspiel carillon, which ring out three times a day. *Carillon chimes daily at 9, noon, and 5. Nikolaikirche open Mon–Sat. 10–5.*

From the Römerberg, stroll south toward the river, but turn right this time, past the riverside **Leonhardskirche** (St. Leonhard's Church), which has a fine 13th-century porch and a beautifully carved circa 1500 Bavarian altar, then into the narrow Karmelitergasse to the **Karmeliterkirche** (Carmelite Church and Monastery). Its quiet cloister contains the largest religious fresco north of the Alps, a 16th-century representation of the birth and death of Christ. The monastery itself has been renovated and expanded to house the **Museum of Prehistory and Early History** (Museum für Vor- und Frühgeschichte). *Admission: DM 5 adults, DM 2.50 children. Open Tues.–Sun. 10–5, Wed. until 8).*

From here, it's only a short way to the **Goethehaus und Goethemuseum** (Goethe's House and Museum). It was here that the poet was born in 1749, and though the house was destroyed by Allied bombing, it has been carefully restored and is furnished with pieces from Goethe's time, some belonging to his family. The adjoining museum is closed for renovations until 1997. *Grosser Hirschgraben 23, tel. 069/282–824. Admission: DM 4 adults, DM 3 children. Open Apr.–Sept., Mon.–Sat. 9–6, Sun. 10–1; Oct.–Mar., Mon.–Sat. 9–4, Sun. 10–1.*

From the Goethehaus, retrace your steps to the Hauptwache via Rossmarkt. From there, stroll past the elegant boutiques of Goethestrasse, which ends at Opernplatz and Frankfurt's reconstructed opera house, the **Alte Oper.** Wealthy Frankfurt businessmen gave generously for the construction of the opera house during the 1870s (provided they were given priority for the best seats), and Kaiser Wilhelm I traveled from Berlin for the gala opening in 1880. Bombed in 1944, the opera house remained in ruins for many years while controversy raged over its reconstruction. The new building, in the classical proportions and style of the original, was finally opened in 1981; it's now a prime venue for classical concerts and conferences, and even, occasionally, an opera.

From the steps of the opera house, you have a good view of the financial district's modern skyscrapers, many of them housing the headquarters of Germany's banks. Largest of all is the Deutsche Bank; its 155-meter building is on your right as you look out from the Alte Oper. Cross busy Opernplatz, head down Grosse Bockenheimer Strasse (known locally as Fressgasse—literally "Food Street"—because of its abundance of gourmet shops and restaurants), turn left into Börsenstrasse, and you'll hit the center of the financial district. Just around the corner from Fressgasse is the Frankfurt **Börse,** Germany's leading stock exchange and financial powerhouse. It was founded by Frankfurt merchants in 1558 to establish some order in

Frankfurt

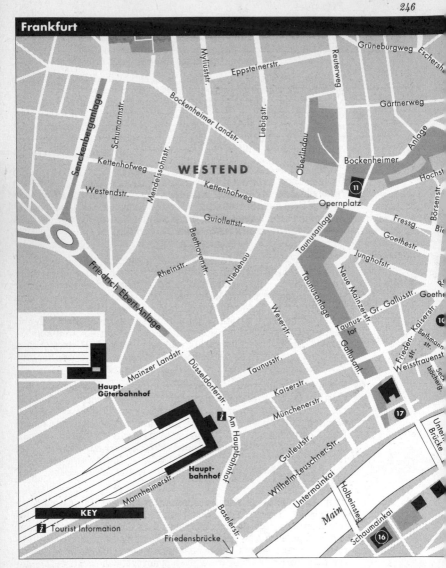

Alte Brücke, **14**
Alte Oper, **11**
Börse, **12**
Goethehaus und
Goethemuseum, **10**
Hauptwache, **1**
Jewish Museum, **17**
Kaiserdom, **6**

Karmeliterkirche, **9**
Katerinenkirche, **2**
Kuhhirtenturm, **15**
Leonhardskirche, **8**
Museum of Modern
Art, **13**
Nikolaikirche, **7**
Paulskirche, **3**
Römer, **5**
Römerberg, **4**
Städelsches
Kunstinstitut und
Städtische Galerie, **16**

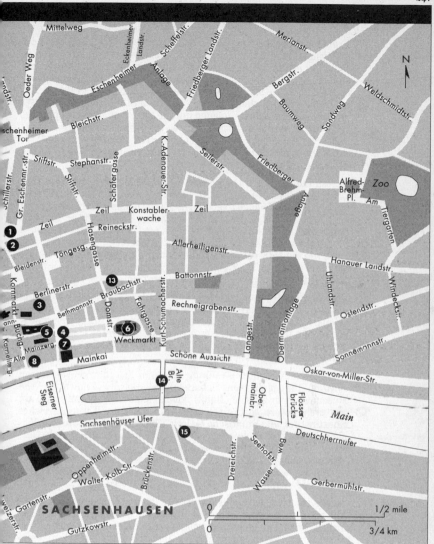

Mittelweg

Oeder Weg

Eckenheimer Landstr.

Scheffelstr.

Merianstr.

Eschenheimer Anlage

Friedberger Landstr.

Bergstr.

Baumweg

Sandweg

Weldschmidtstr.

Bleichstr.

eschenheimer Tor

K. Adenauer-Str.

Seilerstr.

Friedberger

Anlage

Alfred-Brehm-Pl.

Am Tiergarten

Zoo

Schillerstr.

Gr. Eschienmr-str.

Stiftstr.

Stephanstr.

Schäfergasse

Stiftstr.

Zeil

Konstabler-wache

Zeil

Reineckstr.

Zeil

Allerheiligenstr.

Hanauer Landstr.

Uhlandstr.

Windeckstr.

Bleidenstr.

Töngesg.

Hasengasse

Battonnstr.

Ostendstr.

Berlinerstr.

Braubachstr.

Rechneigrabenstr.

Obermainanlage

Sonnemannstr.

Bethmannstr.

Domstr.

Fahrgasse

Kurt-Schumacherstr.

Tangestr.

Mainzerg.

Weckmarkt

Schöne Aussicht

Oskar-von-Miller-Str.

Mainkai

Alle

Mainzerg

Alle

Eiserner Steg

Alte Br.

Main

Sachsenhäuser Ufer

Obermainbr.

Flössenbrücke

Deutschherrnufer

Oppenheimstr.

Walter-Kolb-Str.

Brückenstr.

Dreieichstr.

Seehofstr.

Wasser weg

Gerbermühlstr.

SACHSENHAUSEN

Gartenstr.

weizerstr.

Gutzkowstr.

0 1/2 mile

0 3/4 km

N

their often-chaotic dealings. *Admission free. Gallery open weekdays 11–1.*

From the Börse, turn right into Schillerstrasse, and within two minutes you're back at the Hauptwache. Here begins Frankfurt's main shopping street, the **Zeil,** which claims the highest turnover per square yard of stores in all Germany. Turn right into Hasengasse and you'll see the striking wedge form of Frankfurt's newest museum rising straight ahead of you. The **Museum of Modern Art** (Museum für Moderne Kunst), opened in June 1991, contains an important collection of works by such artists as Sia Armajani, Joseph Beuys, Walter de Maria, and Andy Warhol. *Domstr. 10, tel. 069/2123–8819. Admission: DM 7 adults, DM 3.50 children. Open Tues., Thurs., Fri., Sun. 10–5, Wed. 10–8, Sat. 12–7.*

Across the Main lies the district of **Sachsenhausen.** It's said that Charlemagne arrived here with a group of Saxon families during the 8th century and formed a settlement on the banks of the Main. It was an important bridgehead for the crusading Knights of the Teutonic Order and, in 1318, officially became part of Frankfurt. Cross to Sachsenhausen over the **Alte Brücke.** Along the bank to your left you'll see the 15th-century **Kuhhirtenturm,** the only remaining part of Sachsenhausen's original fortifications. The composer Paul Hindemith lived and worked in the tower from 1923 to 1927.

The district still has a medieval air, with narrow back alleys and quiet squares that have escaped the destructive tread of the city developer. Here you'll find Frankfurt's famous *Ebbelwei* taverns. A green pine wreath over the entrance tells passersby that a freshly pressed—and alcoholic—apple wine or cider is on tap. You can eat well in these little inns, too.

No fewer than eight top-ranking museums line the Sachsenhausen side of the Main, on **Schaumainkai** (locally known as the **Museumsufer** or Museum Bank). These range from exhibitions of art and architecture to the German Film Museum. The **Städelsches Kunstinstitut und Städtische Galerie** (Städel Art Institute and Municipal Gallery) has one of the most significant art collections in Germany, with fine examples of Flemish, German, and Italian Old Masters, plus a sprinkling of French Impressionists. *Schaumainkai 63. Admission: DM 6 (free from 4 PM on Wed., Sun., and public holidays); DM 3 children. Open Tues.–Sun. 10–5, Wed. until 8.*

Across the river from this impressive lineup of museums is Frankfurt's **Jewish Museum** (cross the Untermain Bridge to reach it). The fine city mansion houses a permanent exhibit tracing the history of Frankfurt's Jewish community; its library is Germany's main registry for Jewish history. *Untermainkai 14–15, tel. 069/2123–5000. Admission: DM 10 adults, DM 7 children. Open Tues.–Sun. 10–5, Wed. until 8.*

Dining

Several Frankfurt restaurants close for the school summer vacation break, a six-week period that falls between mid-June and mid-September. Always check to avoid disappointment.

For details and price-category definitions, *see* Dining *in* Staying in Germany, *above.*

$$ **Börsenkeller.** Solid Germanic food, with just a hint of French style, ★ is served here to fortify the business community from the nearby stock exchange (*Börse* means "money market"). Steaks are a specialty. *Schillerstr. 11, tel. 069/281–115. Reservations accepted. AE, DC, MC, V. Closed Sat. dinner and Sun.*

$$ **Operncafe.** A whiff of Paris wafts through this bistro-style café-restaurant, just across the square from the Frankfurt opera house. The

menu changes daily and has an unmistakable French touch. Breakfasts are also served, and the late-night opera crowd keeps the kitchen busy until the small hours. *Opernplatz 10, tel. 069/285–260. Credit cards accepted only during trade fairs.*

$$ Zur Müllerin. The *Müllerin* (miller's wife) is Lieselotte Müller, who has been running this restaurant since the 1950s. Her regulars are artists and actors from the nearby theaters; you'll find expressions of appreciation for the cooking skills of their beloved Müllerin decorating the restaurant walls. *Weissfrauenstr. 18, tel. 069/285–182. No credit cards. Closed for lunch on Sat. and Sun.*

$ Cafe GegenwART. *Gegenwart* means "the present," and the accent on ART here means regularly changing exhibitions by local artists on the walls of this friendly, noisy café-restaurant. It's frequented by a young crowd, and in the summer diners spill out onto the pavement, where Riviera-style tables brighten up the city scene. There's a French touch about the menu, too—the tomato fondue is a dream. *Berger Str. 6, tel. 069/497–0544. No credit cards. Open daily.*

$ Knoblauch. *Knoblauch* is German for "garlic," and that's the staple of many of the imaginative dishes served in this fashionable Frankfurt haunt. The oysters in garlic sauce have made the place famous. The clientele is young and arty, drawn not only by the menu, which changes daily, but by the small art gallery on the premises. *Staufenstr. 39, tel. 069/722–828. No credit cards.*

$ Lux. This stylish and reasonably priced café-bar-restaurant at the center of town pulls in a twenty something crowd. They come for the salads, afternoon snacks, or a cup of coffee as much as for the hearty evening meals. *Kornmarkt 11, tel. 069/281–529. No credit cards.*

$ Zum Gemalten Haus. This is the real thing, a traditional wine tavern
★ in the heart of Sachsenhausen. Its name means "At the Painted House," a reference to the frescoes that cover the place inside and out. In the summer and on fine spring and autumn days, the courtyard is the place to be (the inner rooms can get a bit crowded). But if you can't at first find a place at one of the bench-lined long tables, order an apple cider and hang around until someone leaves. It's worth the wait. *Schweizerstr. 67, tel. 069/614–559. No credit cards. Closed Mon. and Tues.*

$ Zum Schwarzen Stern. This is a colorful beer restaurant in the heart of the historic quarter. Schnitzel with mushrooms in cream sauce or roast hare in red wine are two examples of the solid and tasty local menu, washed down with good beer. It's a favorite haunt of newlyweds who come out of the Registry Office opposite. *Römerberg 6, tel. 069/291–979. AE, DC, MC, V. Open daily but closed 3–6 PM.*

¢ Grossenwahn. If you're in the neighborhood on a Sunday morning, stop here for a brunch washed down with Rheingau Sekt, perhaps in the garden if the weather is agreeable. Indoors, the walls are covered with modern paintings. For a late meal, this is also the place. *Lehnaustr. 97, tel. 069/599–356. Reservations advised. AE, MC, V. No lunch weekdays.*

¢ Melange. New owners of this popular restaurant have kept up its tradition of serving inexpensive but imaginative dishes from a daily-changing menu. Pink tablecloths drape the tables, and the clientele is drawn heavily from the nearby university. Vegetarians will find numerous choices. In summer, there's outdoor dining on the boulevard terrace. *Jordanstr. 19, tel. 069/701–287. Reservations advised. No credit cards.*

¢ Zitadelle. You won't find cheaper steaks anywhere else in Frankfurt, and they come with sauces to rival those in much more expensive restaurants. You'll have to fight for seating, though, at the rough pub-style tables, where you can stake your claim by ordering one of the excellent beers. *Falltorstr. 6, tel. 069/458–668. No credit cards. No lunch, closed weekends.*

Lodging

For details and price-category definitions, *see* Lodging *in* Staying in Germany, *above*.

$$ **Am Zoo.** This hotel provides modest but comfortable accommodations in Frankfurt's east end and, as the name suggests, is near the city's famous big zoo. *Alfred-Brehm-Platz 6, tel. 069/490–771, fax 069/439–868. 85 rooms with bath. Facilities: restaurant. AE, DC, MC, V. Closed Christmas.*

$$ **Hotel Ibis Frankfurt Friedensbrücke.** This modern hotel is situated on the north bank of the Main river, just five minutes' walk from the train station. It was recently acquired by the Ibis chain, which specializes in modern comfort at affordable prices. *Speicherstr. 3–5, tel. 069/273–030, fax 069/237–024. 200 rooms with bath. Facilities: restaurant, bar. AE, DC, MC, V.*

$$ **Hotel-Pension Sattler.** Frau Sattler runs her comfortable hotel-pension like a real home. The handsome turn-of-the-century building faces a tree-lined avenue in Frankfurt's Westend, a short walk from the fairgrounds and the Palmengarten. The rooms have high ceilings and are individually furnished, some with antiques. Some have balconies. There's no restaurant, but the immediate area is well served. *Beethovenstr. 46, tel. 069/746–091, fax 069/748–466. 25 rooms with bath or shower. Facilities: parking. AE, DC, MC, V.*

$$ **Hotelschiff Peter Schlott.** This hotel is actually a riverboat, moored near the Frankfurt suburb of Höchst. Few comforts are lacking, although the rooms are on the small side. Still, they offer fine views of the River Main, which laps outside the portholes. *Mainberg, tel. 069/315–480, fax 069/307–671. 19 rooms, about half with shower. Facilities: restaurant, parking. AE, MC.*

$$
★ **Maingau.** This excellent-value hotel is in the city's Sachsenhausen district, within easy reach of the downtown area and just a stone's throw from the lively Altstadt quarter and cheery apple-cider taverns. The rooms are spartanly furnished, though clean and comfortable, and some even have TV. *Schifferstr. 38–40, tel. 069/617–001, fax 069/620–790. 100 rooms with bath. Facilities: restaurant, garage. AE, MC.*

$ **Hotel Kautz.** Above Erwin Kautz's cozy beer tavern are clean, airy rooms, functionally furnished but perfectly comfortable. The hotel is in the heart of Sachsenhausen—just look for the distinctive beer barrels set in the outside wall. *Gartenstr. 17, tel. 069/618–061, fax 069/613–236. 15 rooms with shower. Facilities: restaurant, bar. AE, DC, MC, V.*

¢ **Pension Uebe.** Try for one of the mansard rooms in this friendly, centrally located pension—they are snug and furnished in Hessian farmhouse style, with rocking chairs and basketwork crafts. Chandeliers lend a touch of luxury to some of the larger rooms on the lower floors. *Grüneburgweg 3, tel. 069/591–209. 19 rooms, 17 with bath. Facilities: parking. AE, DC, MC, V.*

¢ **Waldhotel "Hensel's Felsenkeller."** Helmut Braun's traditional old hotel has the woods that ring Frankfurt as its backyard, yet the city center is just a 15-minute tram ride away (the nearest stop is a three-minute walk from the hotel). The rooms are quite basic, but there are plans to modernize them to add more comfort. *Buchrainstr. 95, tel. 069/652–086, fax 069/658–371. 15 rooms, 7 with bath. Facilities: restaurant, parking. MC.*

Hamburg

Arriving and Departing

By Plane Hamburg's international airport, Fuhlsbüttel, is 11 kilometers (7 miles) northwest of the city. Lufthansa flights connect Hamburg with all other major German cities and European capitals.

Between the Airport and Downtown An Airport-City-Bus between Hamburg's main train station (Hauptbahnhof) and the airport (stopping also at the Atlantic, Reichshof, and Plaza hotels and the fairgrounds) operates daily at 20-minute intervals between 5:40 AM and 10:30 PM. The first bus leaves the airport for the city at 6:30 AM. It takes about 25 minutes. One-way fare, including luggage, is DM 8. There is also an "Airport Express" bus, No. 110, which runs between the airport and the Ohlsdorf S-Bahn (suburban line) and U-Bahn (subway) station. The fare is DM 3.60. Taxi fare from the airport to the downtown area is about DM 30. By rented car, follow the signs to "Stadtmitte" (Downtown), which appear immediately outside the airport area.

By Train Hamburg is a terminal for mainline services to northern Germany; trains to Schleswig-Holstein and Scandinavia also stop here. There are two principal stations: Hauptbahnhof (the main train station) and Hamburg-Altona. Euro-City, InterCity and high-speed Inter-City Express (ICE) services connect Hamburg with all German cities and the European rail network. For train information, tel. 040/19419.

By Bus Hamburg's bus station, the Zentral-Omnibus-Bahnhof, is in Adenauerallee, behind the Hauptbahnhof. For tickets and information, contact the **Deutsche Touring Gesellschaft** (Am Römerhof 17, D-60486 Frankfurt/Main, tel. 069/79030).

Getting Around

By Public Transportation The comprehensive city and suburban transportation system includes a subway network (U-Bahn), which connects efficiently with S-Bahn (suburban) lines, and an exemplary bus service. Tickets cover travel by all three, as well as by harbor ferry. A ticket costs DM 2.30 (DM 3.60 for travel outside the inner city) and can be bought at the automatic machines found in all stations and most bus stops. A day ticket permitting unlimited travel in the entire Hamburg urban area from 9 AM to 1 AM for one adult and up to three children costs DM 6.90 (DM 12.20 for a group of up to four adults and three children); a three-day ticket costs DM 19. The all-night buses (Nos. 600–640) tour the downtown area, leaving the Rathausmarkt and the Hauptbahnhof every hour. The one- and three-day **Hamburg CARDs** allow free transport on all public transportation within the city, free admission to state museums, and approximately 30% discounts on most bus, train, and boat tours. For information about the Hamburg CARD inquire at tourist offices. Information about the public transportation system can be obtained from the **Hamburg Passenger Transport Board** (HHV), Steinstrasse 1, tel. 040/322–911; it's open daily 7 AM–8 PM.

Important Addresses and Numbers

Tourist Information The principal Hamburg tourist office is at Bieberhaus, Hachmannplatz, next to the Hauptbahnhof. It's open weekdays 7:30–6, Saturday 8–3 (tel. 040/3005–1244). There's also a tourist information center inside the Hauptbahnhof itself (open daily 7 AM–11 PM, tel. 040/3005–1230) and in the arrivals hall of Hamburg Airport (open daily from 8 AM to 11 PM, tel. 040/3005–1240). Other tourist offices can be found in the Hanse-Viertel shopping arcade (open week-

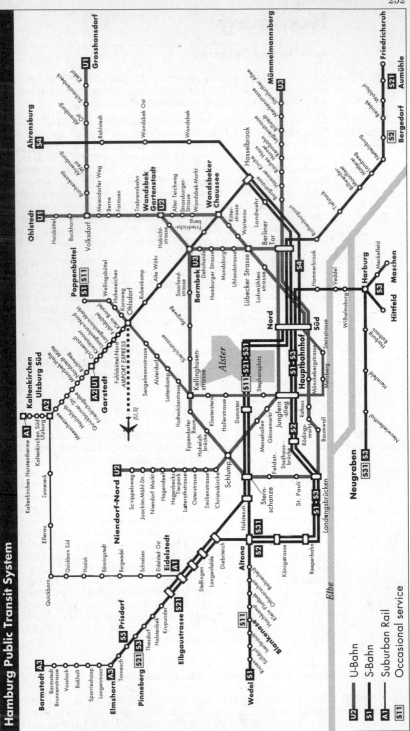

Hamburg Public Transit System

252

days 10–6:30, Sat. 10–3:30, Sun. 11–3 tel. 040/3005–1220) and at the Landungsbrücken (open daily 9:30–5:30, tel. 040/3005–1200). All centers will reserve hotel accommodations.

Consulates **U.S.** (Alsterufer 27, 1, (tel. 040/411–710). **U.K.** (Harvestehuder Weg 8a, tel. 040/448–0320).

Emergencies **Police** (tel. 110). **Doctor** (tel. 040/228–022). **Dentist** (tel. 11500). **Ambulance** (tel. 112).

Exploring Hamburg

The comparison that Germans like to draw between Hamburg and Venice is—like all such comparisons with the *Serenissima*—somewhat exaggerated. Nevertheless, Hamburg is, a city on water: the great river Elbe, which flows into the North Sea; the small river Alster, which has been dammed to form two lakes, the Binnenalster and Aussenalster; and many canals. Once a leading member of the Hanseatic League of cities, which dominated trade on the North Sea and the Baltic during the Middle Ages, Hamburg is still a major port, with 33 individual docks and 500 berths for oceangoing vessels.

Apart from its aquatic aspects, Hamburg's most striking aspect is its contradictions. Within the traces of its old city walls, Hamburg combines the seamiest, steamiest streets of dockland Europe with the sleekest avenues to be found anywhere between Biarritz and Stockholm. The result is a city that is, in parts, ugly, but still a fascinating mixture of old and new. It is also a city in which escaping the urban bustle is relatively easy, since it contains more than 800 kilometers (500 miles) of riverside and country paths within its boundaries.

Numbers in the margin correspond to points of interest on the Hamburg map.

❶ Hamburg's main train station, the **Hauptbahnhof,** is not only the start of the city tour but very much part of it—the rare train station that tempts you to linger. Originally built in 1906 and completely renovated in 1991, it has a remarkable spaciousness and sweep, accentuated by a 148-meter-wide (460-feet-wide) glazed roof, the largest unsupported roof in Germany. Gather city travel guides and maps from the city tourist office here and ride one stop on the S-Bahn (suburban railroad) to the Dammtor station. Compare this Art Nouveau–style building (built in 1903) with the one you've just left. You'll find splendid examples of Germany's version of Art Nouveau, the *Jugendstil,* throughout your tour of Hamburg.

The Dammtor station brings you out at the northern end of the **Wallringpark,** a stretch of parkland that runs for more than a kilometer alongside what was once the western defense wall of the city.
❷ The first two sections of the park—the **Alter Botanischer Garten**
❸ (Old Botanical Garden) and the **Planten un Blomen** (Plants and Flowers)—have lots to attract the attention of gardeners and flower lovers. In summer, the evening sky over the Planten un Blomen lake is lighted up by the colored waters of its fountain, dancing what the locals romantically call a "water ballet."

The section of the park known as **Grosse Wallanlagen**—to the southwest—is interrupted abruptly by the northern edge of the **St. Pauli** district and its most famous—or infamous—thoroughfare, the
❹ **Reeperbahn** (*see* Nightlife, *below*). Unlike other business sections of Hamburg, this industrious quarter works around the clock; although it may seem quiet as you stroll down its tawdry length in broad daylight, any tourist who stops at one of its bars will discover that many of the girls who work this strip are on a day shift.

Hamburg

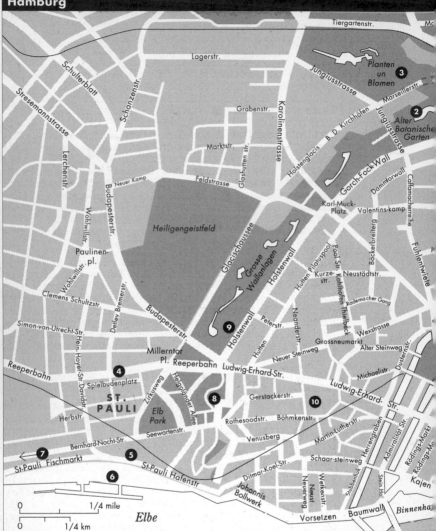

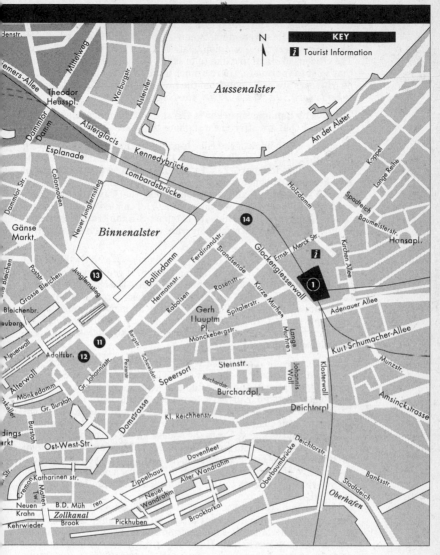

N

Aussenalster

Binnenalster

An der Alster

Kennedybrücke

Lombardsbrücke

Theodor Heusspl.

Mittelweg

Warburgstr.

Alsteruter

remers-Allee

Dammtor Damm

Alsterglacis

Esplanade

Colonnaden

Neuer Jungfernstieg

Gänse Markt.

Dammtor str.

Jungfernstieg

Potstr.

Grosse Bleichen

Ballindamm

Ferdinandstr.

Brandsende

Hermannstr.

Raboisen

Rosenstr.

Kurze Mühren

Glockengiesserwall

Ernst Merck Str.

Holzdamm

Koppel

Lange Reihe

Spadteich

Baumeisterstr.

Kirchen Allee

Hansapl.

Bleichenbr.

euborg

Neuerwall

Adolfsbr.

Alterwall

Mönkedamm

Gr. Burstah

Gr. Burstah

Burstah

Gr. Johannisstr.

Pezant

Bergstr.

Schauedstr.

Speersort

Gerh Hauptm Pl.

Spitalerstr.

Mönckebergstr.

Steinstr.

Burchardstr.

Burchardpl.

Lange Mühren

Johannis Wall

Adenauer Allee

Kurt Schumacher-Allee

Munzstr.

Amsinckstrasse

Klosterwall

Deichtorpl.

Domstrasse

Kl. Reichhenstr.

Ost-West-Str.

Dovenfleet

Deichtorstr.

Banksstr.

Oberbaumbrücke

Katharinen str.

Zippelhaus

Neuer Wandrahm

Alter Wandrahm

Stadtdeich

Oberhafen

dings rkt

Cremon

Mtaten Tw.

B.D. Müh ren

Brooktorkai

Neuen Krahn

Zollkanal

Brook

Pickhuben

Kehrwieder

⑭

⑬

⑪

⑫

①

⑤ If it's a Sunday morning, join the late revelers and the early joggers and dog-walkers for breakfast at the **Fischmarkt** (fish market), down at the Elbe riverside between the St. Pauli Landungsbrücken (the piers where the excursion boats tie up) and Grosse Elbstrasse. The citizens of Hamburg like to breakfast on pickled herring, but if that's not to your taste, there's much more than fish for sale, and the nearby bars are still open from the previous night. *The fish market is held every Sun., 5 AM–10 AM, starting at 7 in winter.*

⑥ The nearby **Landungsbrücken** is the start of the many boat trips of the harbor that are offered throughout the year.

Along the north bank of the Elbe is one of the finest walks Hamburg has to offer. The walk is long, about 13 kilometers (8 miles) from the St. Pauli Landungsbrücken to the attractive waterside area of **⑦** **Blankenese,** and that's only three-quarters of the route. But there are S-Bahn stations and bus stops along the way, to give you a speedy return to the downtown area. Do, however, try to reach Blankenese, even if you have to catch an S-Bahn train from downtown to Blankenese station and walk down to the riverbank from there.

Blankenese is another of Hamburg's surprises—a city suburb that has the character of a quaint fishing village. If you've walked all the way from St. Pauli, you may not be able to face the 58 flights of stairs (nearly 5,000 individual steps) that crisscross through Blankenese between its heights and the river. But by all means attempt an exploratory prowl through some of the tiny lanes, lined with the retirement retreats of Hamburg's sea captains and the cottages of the fishermen who once toiled here.

A ferry connects Blankenese with Hamburg's St. Pauli, although the S-Bahn ride back to the city is much quicker. Back at St. Pauli, resume your tour at the riverside and head back toward the downtown area through Elb Park, crossing Helgolander Allee to the **⑧** **Bismarckdenkmal** (Bismarck Memorial)—an imposing statue of the Prussian "Iron Chancellor," the guiding spirit of the 19th-century unification of Germany. Cross the square ahead of you and make for **⑨** the **Museum für Hamburgische Geschichte** at Holstenwall 24. A visit to this museum is highly recommended—it will give you an excellent perspective of the forces that guided Hamburg's development from its 9th-century origins to the present. The museum has a department (Historic Emmigration Office—at the St. Pauli Landungsbrücken, tel. 040/3005–1250) of great interest to American descendants of German immigrants, who can arrange to have called up from the microfilm files information about any ancestors who set out for the New World from Hamburg. Alternating collections close as an extensive renovation continues. *Holstenwall 24, tel. 040/3504–2360. Admission: DM 6 adults, DM 1 children. Open Tues.–Sun. 10–6.*

Cross Holstenwall to Peterstrasse, where you'll find a group of finely restored, 18th-century half-timbered houses. Turn right, go down Neanderstrasse, and cross Ludwig-Erhard-Strasse to Ham-**⑩** burg's principal Protestant church, the **Michaeliskirche** (St. Michael's Church), the finest Baroque church in northern Germany. Twice in its history, this well-loved 17th-century church has given the people of Hamburg protection—during the Thirty Years' War and again in World War II. From its 440-foot tower, there is a magnificent view of the city and the Elbe, and twice a day the watchman blows a trumpet solo from up there. *Elevator or staircase (449 steps) fee: DM 4 adults, DM 2.50 children.*

From the Michaeliskirche, return to Ludwig-Erhard-Strasse, turn right, then go left down Brunnenstrasse to Wexstrasse. Follow Wexstrasse to Grosse Bleichen, turn right down Heugberg and cross the Bleichenbrücke and Adolphsbrücke, over two of Hamburg's ca-

nals (known as the Fleete), turn left into Alter Wall, and you'll come
⑪ to the **Rathausmarkt,** the town hall square. The designers of the
square deliberately set out to create a northern version of the Piazza
San Marco in Venice and, to a certain extent, succeeded. The
rounded glass arcade bordered by trees was added in 1982. The 100-
⑫ year-old **Rathaus** is built on 4,000 wooden piles sunk into the marshy
ground beneath. It is the home not only of the city council but of the
Hamburg state government, for Hamburg is one of Germany's federal, semiautonomous states. The sheer opulence of its interior is
hard to beat. It has 647 rooms, six more than Buckingham Palace.
Although visitors can tour only the state rooms, the tapestries,
huge staircases, glittering chandeliers, coffered ceilings, and gilt-
framed portraits convey forcefully the wealth of the city in the last
century and give rich insight into bombastic municipal taste. *English-language tours: DM 1 adults, 50 pf children. Mon.–Thurs.,
hourly 10:15–3:15, Fri.–Sun., hourly 10:15–1:15.*

If you've had enough sightseeing by this time, you've ended up at the
right place, for an arcade at the western edge of the Rathausmarkt
signals the start of Europe's largest undercover shopping area,
nearly a kilometer of airy arcades, cool in summer and warm in winter, bursting with color and life. Mixed among the shops are expensive restaurants and cozy cafés, and one of the rare opportunities in
Germany (or anywhere) to eat lobster and sip good wine at a fast-
food outlet. It's easy to get lost here, but all the arcades lead at some
⑬ point to the wide, seasidelike promenade, the **Jungfernstieg,** which
borders Hamburg's smaller artificial lake, the **Binnenalster** (to its
north is the larger **Aussenalster**). Although called lakes, they are really dammed-up sections of the Alster River, which rises only 56 kilometers (35 miles) away in Schleswig Holstein. The original dam,
built at the beginning of the 13th century to form a millrace before
the river spilled into the Elbe, is today the elegant Jungfernstieg
promenade. From the Jungfernstieg, you can take a boat tour of the
two Alster lakes and the canals beyond, passing some of Hamburg's
most ostentatious homes, their extensive grounds rolling down to
the water's edge (the locals call it "Millionaires' Coast").

Hamburg has its share of millionaires, enriched by the city's thriving commerce and industry. But they, in turn, can claim to have enriched the artistic life of Hamburg. For example, it was a group of
wealthy merchants who, in 1817, founded the Kunstverein, from
which grew Hamburg's famous Kunsthalle collection. The
⑭ **Kunsthalle** is at the end of our Hamburg tour, next to the
Hauptbahnhof, and its collection of paintings is one of Germany's
finest. You'll find works by practically all the great northern European masters from the 14th to the 20th century, as well as by such
painters as Goya, Tiepolo, and Canaletto. For many visitors, the
highlight of the entire collection is the *Grabow Altarpiece,* painted
in 1379 by an artist known only as Master Bertram; the central scene
is the Crucifixion, but numerous side panels depict the story of humanity from Genesis to the Nativity. *Glockengiesserwall 1, tel. 040/
2486–2612. Admission: DM 6 adults, DM 1 children. Open Tues.–
Sun. 10–6, Thurs. 10–9.*

Dining

For details and price-category definitions, *see* Dining *in* Staying in
Germany, *above.*

$$ **Ahrberg.** Located on the river in Blankenese, the Ahrberg has a
★ pleasant terrace for summer dining and a cozy, wood-paneled dining
room for colder days. The menu features a range of traditional
German dishes and seafood specialties—often served together. Try
the shrimp and potato soup and fresh carp in season. *Strandweg 33,*

tel. 040/860–438. Reservations advised. AE, DC, MC, V. Closed Sun.

$$ Fisherhaus. Always busy (expect to share a table) and plainly decorated, this establishment offers time-honored Hamburg specialties. Fish from Hamburg's famous market, right outside, are responsible for the menu's variety and quality. It's hardly haute cuisine, but the standards, like the service, are ultrareliable. This is a great place to try eel soup. *St. Pauli Fischmarkt 14, tel. 040/314–053. Reservations advised. AE, DC, MC, V.*

$$ Tre Fontane. At this fine Italian restaurant, the lady of the house prepares all the dishes herself, and she is happy to advise guests on the specials of the day. Be prepared for big portions, but be sure to make a reservation first. *Mundsburger Damm 45, tel. 040/223–193. Reservations advised. No credit cards. Closed Tues.*

$ At Nali. This is one of Hamburg's oldest and most popular Turkish restaurants, and it stays open until 1 AM—handy for those hankering for a late-night kebab. Prices are low, service is reliable and friendly, and the menu is extensive. *Rutschbahn 11, tel. 040/410–3810. Reservations advised on weekends. AE, DC, MC, V.*

$ Avocado. This popular, modern restaurant offers excellent value and an imaginative vegetarian menu; it's also Hamburg's only no-smoking restaurant. Try the salmon in Chablis. *Kanalstr. 9, tel. 040/220–4599. Reservations required. No credit cards. Dinner only. Closed Mon.*

$ Restaurant Fischkajüte. This is Hamburg's oldest fish tavern, a few steps from the waterside at Pier 5. Eel soup is the house specialty, but all the dishes, including the traditional *Labskaus* (marinated beef cooked with egg and served with pickled herring and roast potatoes), have an individual flair. *St. Pauli Landungsbrücken, Brücke (pier) 5, tel. 040/314–162. Reservations advised on weekends. AE, DC, MC, V. Closed Wed., 3 wks in Oct.*

¢ Filmhaus. This favorite of local journalists and artists, in a municipal film center in the working-class district of Altona, has good daily specials. The cuisine is Italian and German with a Cameroonian accent: The various fish soups are particularly worth trying, as is the sliced beef and mushrooms in cream sauce. The atmosphere is light and modern, despite the old furniture. *Friedensallee 7, tel. 040/393–467. No reservations. No credit cards. Sat. and Sun. dinner only.*

¢ Max und Konsorten. Traditional German fare, such as *Leberkäse* (a sort of German pâté), and some Indian specialties are served at this cheap, cheerful, always crowded restaurant. Try the mussels in pepper sauce or the spicy chicken breast. Old tables and sideboards create a dark, woody atmosphere. Other perks: its location by the main train station and that it serves food until midnight. *Spadenteich 7, tel. 040/245–617. No reservations. No credit cards.*

¢ Opitz. North of the city center in the Eppendorf district is Opitz, a turn-of-the-century restaurant with old marble-top tables that serves hearty German fare and Hamburg specialties. Several varieties of Hamburg's ubiquitous pickled herring are served: Try the Labskaus. *Eppendorferlandstr. 165, tel. 040/47–65–98. Reservations advised. V. No lunch Sat.*

Lodging

For details and price-category definitions, *see* Lodging *in* Staying in Germany, *above.*

$$ Baseler Hof. Centrally located near the inner lake and the State Opera House, this hotel offers friendly, efficient service and neatly furnished rooms. There is no charge for children under 10 sharing a room with their parents. *Esplanade 11, tel. 040/359–060, fax 040/3590–6918. 140 rooms, most with bath. Facilities: 2 restaurants, bar, room service. AE, DC, MC, V.*

$$ Metro Merkur. Centrally located near Hamburg's main train station, the recently renovated Metro Merkur is a convenient, functional hotel. There is no restaurant, but the bar offers a selection of evening snacks and warm dishes. *Bremer Reihe 12–14, tel. 040/247–266, fax 040/240–284. 105 rooms, most with bath. Facilities: bar. AE, DC, MC, V.*

$$ Wedina. Fully renovated and refurbished by its new Swiss owners, the Wedina offers high-standard accommodations in two attractive city mansions on a quiet street running down to the Aussenalster. All rooms have contemporary furnishings and modern bathrooms. *Gurlittstr. 23, tel. 040/243–011, fax 040/280–3894. 27 rooms with bath or shower. Facilities: bar, small outdoor pool, sauna, garden. AE, DC, MC, V.*

$ Alameda. The Alameda offers guests good, basic accommodations. The upstairs rooms are nicer, but all have TVs, radios, and minibars. *Colonnaden 45, tel. 040/344–290, fax 040/343–439. 18 rooms all with shower. AE, DC, MC, V.*

$ Haus Emde. This small, friendly hotel can be reached from the S-1 line (Hamburg-Othmarschen stop). Although it's not central, the hotel offers suburban peace and quiet in a charming city mansion set on its own grounds. Rooms were recently renovated. *Lüdemannstr. 1, tel. 040/893–626, fax 040/810–0689. 10 rooms, 2 suites, with bath or shower. No credit cards.*

$ Steen's. This small, intimate hotel is decorated in a light, airy Scandinavian style. The rooms are clean, if modestly furnished, and all have TVs and a minibars. It is conveniently located, close to the main train station. *Holzdamm 43, tel. 040/244–642, fax 040/280–3593. 11 rooms with bath. No credit cards.*

¢ Hotel Terminus. In a 19th-century row house near the main train station (Hauptbahnhof), the Hotel Terminus is a small, old-style hotel with accommodations that are spartan, but clean. *Steindamm 5, tel. 040/280–3144, fax 040/241–518. 20 rooms. AE, DC, MC, V.*

¢ Hotel Zentrum. This fully renovated, 100-year-old hotel is run by a lively couple. The rooms are starkly decorated but comfortable. Also located just a few minutes from the Hauptbahnhof, the Hotel Zentrum's rooms can be noisy: Ask for a room facing the courtyard. *Bremer Reihe 23, tel. 040/280–2528, fax 040/246–019. 15 rooms, 5 with shower. No credit cards.*

Nightlife

Few visitors can resist taking a look at the **Reeperbahn,** if only by day. From 10 PM onward, however, the place really shakes itself into life, and *everything* is for sale. Among the Reeperbahn's even rougher side streets, the most notorious is the Grosse Freiheit, which means "Great Freedom." A stroll through this small alley, where the attractions are on display behind plate glass, will either tempt you to stay or send you straight back to your hotel. Three of the leading clubs on the Grosse Freiheit are the **Colibri** (No. 30, tel. 040/312–424), the **Safari** (No. 24, tel. 040/313–233), and the **Salambo** (No. 11, tel. 040/315–622).

The Reeperbahn area is not just a red-light district, however. Side streets are rapidly filling up with a mixture of yuppie bars, restaurants, and theaters that complement the seamen's bars and sex shops. The **Hans-Albers-Platz** is a center of this revival, where the stylish bar La Paloma provides contrast to the Hans-Albers-Ecke, an old sailors' bar. The **Theater Schmidt** (Spielbudenplatz 23, tel. 040/311–231) offers variety shows most evenings to a packed house.

A few tips for visiting the Reeperbahn: Avoid going alone; ask for a price list whenever you drink (legally, it has to be on display), and pay as soon as you're served; and if you have trouble, threaten to call the cops. If threats don't work—call the cops.

The Rhine

None of Europe's many rivers is so redolent of history and legend as the Rhine. For the Romans, who established forts and colonies along its western banks, the Rhine was the frontier between civilization and the barbaric German tribes. Roman artifacts can be seen in museums throughout the region. The Romans also introduced viticulture—a legacy that survives in the countless vineyards along the riverbanks—and later, Christianity. Throughout the Middle Ages, the river's importance as a trade artery made it the focus of sharp, often violent, conflict among princes, noblemen, and archbishops. Many of the picturesque castles that crown its banks were the homes of robber barons who held up passing ships and barges and exacted heavy tolls to finance even grander fortifications.

For poets and composers, the Rhine—or *"Vater* (Father) *Rhein,"* as the Germans call it—has been an endless source of inspiration. As legend has it, the Lorelei, a treacherous, craggy rock, was home to a beautiful and bewitching maiden who lured sailors to a watery grave. Wagner based four of his epic operas on the lives of the medieval Nibelungen, said to have inhabited the rocky banks.

The Rhine does not belong to Germany alone. Its 1,312-kilometer (820-mile) journey takes it from deep within the Alps, through Switzerland and Germany, into the Netherlands, and out into the North Sea. But it is in Germany—especially the stretch between Mainz and Köln (Cologne) known as the Middle Rhine—that the riverside scenery is most spectacular. This is the "typical" Rhine: a land of steep and thickly wooded hills, terraced vineyards, tiny villages hugging the banks, and brooding castles.

Getting Around

By Train A good way to visit the Rhineland in a limited time is to take the scenic train journey from Mainz to Köln along the western banks of the river. The views are spectacular, and the entire trip takes less than two hours. Choose an InterCity train for its wide viewing windows. If you're traveling north toward Köln, make sure you get a window seat on the right-hand side. Better still, sit in the restaurant car, where you can enjoy a meal or beverage while you watch the scenery unfold. Contact **German National Railways** in Frankfurt (Reisedienst, Friedrich-Ebert-Anlage 43, tel. 069/19419) or get details at any big train station travel office.

By Boat Passenger ships traveling up and down the Rhine and its tributaries offer a pleasant and relaxing way to see the region. **Köln-Düsseldorfer Steamship Company (KD)** operates a fleet of ships that travel daily between Düsseldorf and Frankfurt, from Easter to late October. It also offers cruises along the entire length of the Rhine. Passengers have a choice of buying an excursion ticket or a ticket to a single destination. For information about services, write to Frankenwerft 15, 50667 Köln 1, or tel. 0221/258–3001. This company also offers trips up the Mosel as far as Trier. From March through November, **Hebel-Line** (tel. 06742/2420) offers a scenic cruise of the Lorelei Valley; night cruises feature music and dancing. For information about Neckar River excursions, contact **Neckar Personen Schiffahrt** in Stuttgart (tel. 0711/541–073 or 0711/541–074).

Tourist Information

Koblenz (Fremdenverkehrsamt, Pavillon am Hauptbahnhof, tel. 0261/31304 and Fremdenverkehrsverband Rheinland-Pfalz, Löhrstrasse 103, tel. 0261/31079).
Köln (Verkehrsamt, Unter Fettenhennen 19, tel. 0221/221–3340).
Mainz (Verkehrsverein, Bahnhofstrasse 15, tel. 06131/286–210).

Exploring the Rhine

Köln   **Köln** (Cologne) is the largest city on the Rhine, marking the northernmost point of the river's scenic stretch before it becomes a truly industrial waterway through the Ruhr Valley. It's a very old city—first settled by the Romans in 38 BC—and today is a vibrant, zestful Rhineland center, with an active cultural life and a business and commercial infrastructure that supports trade fairs year-round.

By the Middle Ages, Köln was the largest city north of the Alps, and as a member of the powerful Hanseatic League, it was more important commercially than either London or Paris. Ninety percent of the city was destroyed in World War II, and in the rush to rebuild it many mistakes were made. But although today's Köln lacks the aesthetic unity of many other rebuilt German cities, the heart of the Altstadt (Old Town), with its streets that follow the line of the medieval city walls, has great charm and throbs with life at night.

Towering over the old town is the extraordinary Gothic cathedral, the **Kölner Dom,** dedicated to Sts. Peter and Mary. It's comparable to the best French cathedrals; a visit to it may prove a highlight of your trip to Germany. What you'll see is one of the purest expressions of the Gothic spirit in Europe. Spend some time admiring the outside of the building (you can walk almost all the way around it). Notice that there are practically no major horizontal lines—all the accents of the building are vertical. It may come as a disappointment to learn that the cathedral, begun in 1248, was not completed until 1880. Console yourself with the knowledge that it was still built to original plans. At 157 meters (515 feet) high, the two west towers of the cathedral were by far the tallest structures in the world when they were finished.

The cathedral was built to house what were believed to be the relics of the Magi, the three kings or wise men who paid homage to the infant Jesus. Today the relics are kept just behind the altar, in the same enormous gold-and-silver **reliquary** in which they were originally displayed. The other great treasure of the cathedral is the **Gero Cross,** a monumental oak crucifixion dating from 975. Impressive for its simple grace, it's in the last chapel on the left as you face the altar.

Other highlights are the stained-glass windows, some of which date from the 13th century; the 15th-century altar painting; and the early 14th-century high altar, with its surrounding arcades of glistening white figures and its intricate choir screens. The choir stalls, carved from oak around 1310, are the largest in Germany, seating 104 people. There are more treasures to be seen in the **Dom Schatzkammer,** the cathedral treasury, including the silver shrine of Archbishop Engelbert, who was stabbed to death in 1225. *Admission: DM 3 adults, DM 1.50 children. Open Mon.–Sat. 9–5, Sun. 1–5.*

Grouped around the cathedral is a collection of superb museums. If your priority is painting, try the ultramodern **Wallraf-Richartz-Museum** and **Museum Ludwig** complex (which includes the Philharmonic concert hall beneath its vast roof). Together, they form the largest art collection in the Rhineland. The Wallraf-Richartz-Museum contains pictures spanning the years 1300 to 1900, with Dutch and Flemish schools particularly well represented (Rubens, who spent his youth in Köln, has a place of honor, but there are also outstanding works by Rembrandt, Van Dyck, and Frans Hals). The Museum Ludwig is devoted exclusively to 20th-century art; its Picasso collection is so outstanding that a special museum is to be built for it. *Bischofsgartenstr. 1. Admission: DM 8 adults, DM 4 children. Open Tues.–Fri. 10–6, weekends 11–6.*

Opposite the cathedral is the **Römisch-Germanisches Museum,** built from 1970 to 1974 around the famous Dionysius mosaic that was uncovered at the site during the construction of an air-raid shelter in 1941. The huge mosaic, more than 91½ meters (100 yards) square, once covered the dining-room floor of a wealthy Roman trader's villa. Its millions of tiny earthenware and glass tiles depict some of the adventures of Dionysius, the Greek god of wine and, to the Romans, the object of a widespread and sinister religious cult. Bordering the museum on the south is a restored 82½-meter (90-yard) stretch of the old Roman harbor road. *Roncallipl. 4. Admission: DM 5 adults, DM 2.50 children. Open Tues.–Fri. 10–4, weekends 11–4.*

Now head south to the nearby **Alter Markt** and its **Altes Rathaus,** the oldest town hall in Germany (if you don't count the fact that the building was entirely rebuilt after the war). The square has a handsome assembly of buildings—the oldest dating from 1135—in a range of styles. Go inside to see the 14th-century **Hansa Saal,** whose tall Gothic windows and barrel-vaulted wood ceiling are potent expressions of medieval civic pride. The figures of the prophets, standing on pedestals at one end, are all from the early 15th century. Along the south wall are nine additional statues, the so-called *Nine Good Heroes,* carved in 1360. Charlemagne and King Arthur are among them. *Altes Rathaus, Alter Markt. Free guided tours of the Altes Rathaus (in German and English) on Mon., Wed., and Sat. at 3 PM. Praetorium. Open Tues.–Sun. 10–5.*

Now head across Unter Käster toward the river and one of the most outstanding of Köln's 12 Romanesque churches, the **Gross St. Martin.** Its massive 13th-century tower, with distinctive corner turrets and an imposing central spire, is another landmark of Köln. The church was built on the riverside site of a Roman granary.

Gross St. Martin is the parish church of Köln's colorful old city, the **Martinsviertel,** an attractive combination of reconstructed, high-gabled medieval buildings, winding alleys, and tastefully designed modern apartments and business quarters. The place comes to vibrant life at sunset.

To complete your daytime Köln tour, however, leave the Martinsviertel along Martinstrasse and turn right into Gürzenichstrasse, passing the crenellated Gothic-style Gürzenich civic reception-concert hall. Take a left turn into Hohestrasse and another right turn into Cäcilienstrasse. At No. 29, you'll find the 12th-century St. Cäcilien church, and within its cool, well-lit interior one of the world's finest museums of medieval Christian art, the **Schnütgen Museum.** The museum is named after the cathedral capitular Alexander Schnütgen, who bequeathed his collection of religious art to the city in 1906. Enlarged considerably over the years, the collection was moved to St. Cäcilien in 1956. Although the main emphasis of the museum is early and medieval sacred art, the collection also covers the Renaissance and Baroque periods. *Cäcilienstr. 29, tel. 0221/2310. Admission: DM 5 adults, DM 2.50 children. Open Tues.–Fri. 10–6, weekends 11–6. Guided tours on Sun. at 11 (in German).*

Koblenz   In the heart of the Middle Rhine region, at the confluence of the Rhine and Moselle rivers, lies the city of **Koblenz,** the area's cultural and administrative center and the meeting place of the two great wine-producing districts. It is also an important traffic point along the Rhine. Here you are ideally placed to sample and compare the light, fruity Moselle wines and the headier Rhine varieties. The city's tourist-oriented **Weindorf,** or wine village, just south of the **Pfaffendorfer Bridge,** consists of a number of taverns, where you can try the wines in traditional Römer glasses, with their symbolic amber and green bowls.

The city of Koblenz began as a Roman camp—Confluentes—more than 2,000 years ago. The vaults beneath **St. Florin's Church** contain an interesting assortment of Roman remains. In the 12th and 13th centuries, the city was controlled by the archbishop-electors of Trier, and a host of fine churches and castles were built.

A good place to begin your tour of Koblenz is the **Deutches Eck,** or "Corner of Germany," the tip of the sharp peninsula separating the Rhine and Moselle rivers. In the 12th century, the Knights of the Teutonic Order established their center here. The towering equestrian statue of Kaiser Wilhelm, destroyed by Allied bombs during World War II, was erected anew in 1993, despite many who felt that the statue was more a celebration of Prussian might than of German unity. On summer evenings, concerts are held in the nearby **Blumenhof Garden,** in front of the renovated 13th-century manor housing the new Museum Ludwig of contemporary art. Most of the city's historic churches are also within walking distance of the Deutsches Eck. The **Liebfrauenkirche** (Church of Our Lady), completed in the 13th century, incorporates Romanesque, late Gothic, and Baroque elements. **St. Florin,** a Romanesque church built around 1100, was remodeled in the Gothic style in the 14th century. Gothic windows and a vaulted ceiling were added in the 17th century. The city's most important church, **St. Kastor,** also combines Romanesque and Gothic elements and features some unusual altar tombs and rare Gothic wall paintings. These are dotted through Koblenz's attractively restored **Old Town,** much of which is now a pedestrian district. Many of the ancient cellars beneath the houses have been rediscovered and serve as wine bars and jazz clubs.

Koblenz also offers an assortment of castles and palaces. The former residence of the archbishop of Trier now houses the city administrative offices. The original 18th-century building was demolished during the war; today only the interior staircase remains. Across the river, on the Rhine's east bank, towers the city's most spectacular castle, the **Ehrenbreitstein.** Its fortifications date from the 1100s, although the bulk of it was built in the 16th and 17th centuries. To reach the fortress, cross the Rhine by bridge or ferry and take the cable car (*Sesselbahn*) or, if you're in shape, try walking up. The view alone is worth the trip. On the second Saturday in August, a magnificent fireworks display, "The Rhine Aflame," is presented here. The fortress contains an interesting museum, the **Landesmuseum,** with exhibits tracing the industrial and technological development of the Rhine Valley (among the displays are a reconstructed 19th-century tobacco factory and a pewter works). *Admission to the museum is free. Open early Mar.–mid-Nov., daily 9–12:30 and 1–5. Fortress open year-round.*

Mainz On the west side of the Rhine, south of Koblenz, stands the city of **Mainz,** an old university town that's the capital of the Rhineland-Palatinate state. During Roman times, Mainz was a camp called Moguntiacum. Later it was the seat of the powerful archbishops of Mainz. It's also the city in which, around 1450, printing pioneer Johannes Gutenberg established his first movable-type press. (He's such an important figure in Mainz that he has his own festival, celebrated in mid-June.) He is commemorated by a monument and square bearing his name and a museum containing his press and one of his Bibles. *Liebfrauenplatz 5. Admission free. Open Tues.–Sat. 10–6, Sun. and holidays 10–1. Closed Jan.*

Today, Mainz is a bustling, modern city of nearly 200,000. Although it was heavily bombed during World War II, many of the buildings have been faithfully reconstructed, and the pedestrian zones of the Old Town, lined with medieval-style buildings housing taverns and shops, exude charm. A focal point is the city's **Dom** (Cathedral), one of the finest Romanesque churches in Germany. On nearby Gutenbergplatz stand two fine Baroque churches, **Seminary Church** and **St. Ignatius.** The Old Town also boasts the country's oldest Renaissance fountain—**the Marktbrunnen**—and the **Dativius-Victor-Bogen Arch,** dating from Roman times. The **Römisch-Germanisches**

Museum, in the **Kurfürstliches Schloss** (Elector's Palace), contains a notable collection of archaeological finds. *Rheinstr. Admission free. Open Tues.–Sun. 10–6.* A newer touch is the Gothic church of St. **Stephan,** standing on a hilltop south of the Old Town; in the choir are six stained-glass windows by French artist Marc Chagall.

Dining and Lodging

The Rhineland has a number of regional specialties. Be sure to sample the wide variety of sausages available, the goose and duck dishes from the Ahr Valley, and Rhineland sauerbraten—accepted by many as the most succulent of pot roasts. Hotels in the Rhineland range from simple little inns to magnificent castle hotels. Many smaller towns have only small hotels and guest houses, some of which close during the winter months. During the peak summer season and in early autumn—wine festival time—accommodations are scarce, so it is advisable to reserve well in advance.

For details and price-category definitions, *see* Dining and Lodging *in* Staying in Germany, *above.*

Koblenz　**Weinhaus Hubertus.** This restaurant, named for the patron saint of
Dining　hunting, lives up to its sporting image. Its decor is 17th-century rustic, its specialty, fresh game in season. Guests enjoy generous portions and a congenial atmosphere. *Florinsmarkt 6, tel. 0261/31177. Reservations advised. No credit cards. $$*

Lodging　**Kleiner Riesen.** The Kleiner Riesen was one of the oldest hostelries in Koblenz, with a history stretching back three centuries. When it was destroyed in World War II, the owners converted their riverside home into a modern Kleiner Riesen—new, but with much of the old tradition of excellent service very much in evidence. Ask for a room with a Rhine view. *Kaiserin-Augusta-Anlagen 18, tel. 0261/32077, fax 0261/160–725. 27 rooms with bath. Facilities: parking. AE, DC, MC, V. $$*
Hotel Hoegg. Built in the shadow of the mighty Ehrenbreitstein fortress, the Hoegg is convenient for sightseeing on both sides of the Rhine. Rooms with views of the fortress are quieter. *Hofstrasse 282, Ehrenbreitstein, tel. 0261/73629, fax 0261/77961. 55 rooms with shower. AE, MC. ¢*
Zum Schwarzen Bären. This traditional old hotel, on the outskirts of the city, is on the high side of the budget category, but it's well worth the extra Marks and 15-minute bus trip to and from the city center. Rooms are small but comfortable and individually furnished. The ground-floor restaurant is one of the best in Koblenz. *Koblenzer Strasse 35, Moselweiss, tel. 0261/460–2700, fax 0261/4602713. 20 rooms with bath. Facilities: restaurant. AE, DC, MC, V. ¢*

Köln　**Gaffelhaus.** Köln is known for its local brew, called *Kölsch,* and
Dining　Gaffel is one of the leading brands. At the centrally located Gaffelhaus, you can sample glass after glass of this mild-flavor beverage, accompanied by Köln specialties in authentic surroundings. Meals are a bit pricier than the light offerings around the bar. Expect mobs in the evenings. *Alter Markt 20–22, tel. 0221/257–7692. Reservations advised. AE, DC, MC, V. $$*
★　**Gaststätte Früh am Dom.** For real down-home German food, there are few places to compare with this time-honored former brewery. Bold frescoes on the vaulted ceilings establish the mood, and such dishes as *Hämchen* (pork knuckle) provide an authentically Teutonic experience. The beer garden is delightful for summer dining. *Am Hof 12–14, tel. 0221/258–0397. Reservations advised. No credit cards. $$*
Alt Köln. You won't find pork knuckle outside Bavaria that's bigger or cheaper than in this bustling, friendly tavern-restaurant in the cathedral's shadow. The menu is crammed with Rhineland special-

ties (fish roulade, for instance), and the beer is the best local Kölsch. *Trankgasse 7–9, tel. 0221/134678. AE, MC. $*

Päffgen am Heumarkt. Popular with students, this hangout in the Martinsviertel neighborhood serves simple local specialties to filled houses. Kölsch is, as usual, the beverage of choice. *Heumarkt 62, tel. 069/257–7765. Reservations advised. No credit cards. Closed Mon. $*

Zum Treppchen. One of Köln's oldest hostelries (it dates from 1656), the Treppchen clings to tradition, serving the same dishes that have been served here for centuries. The smoked eel was a favorite among Rhineland fishermen when the Treppchen began business, and the roast beef is just as great-great-grandfather liked it. In summer, you can enjoy your meal on the terrace. *Kirchstr. 15, tel. 0221/392–179. No credit cards. ¢*

Lodging
★ **Altstadt.** Close to the river in the old town, this is the place for charm and low rates. Each room is furnished differently, and the service is impeccable—both welcoming and efficient. There's no restaurant. *Salzgasse 7, tel. 0221/257–7851, fax 0221/257–7853. 28 rooms with bath. Facilities: sauna. AE, DC, MC, V. Closed Christmas. $$*

Flandrischer Hof. To squeeze into the cheapest bracket here you'll have to accept one of the smaller rooms, but it will be as comfortable and as well appointed as the others. What the rooms lack in space is compensated for in the public rooms, where a log fire crackles in the open hearth of the lounge in winter. The city's pedestrian-only shopping area begins at the end of the street, and the city center is a 10-minute walk away. *Flandrische Str. 3–5, tel. 0221/252–095, fax 0221/251–052. 143 rooms with bath. Facilities: bar, parking, restaurant. AE, DC, MC, V. $$*

Im Stapelhäuschen. Cheaper rooms in this narrow, 13th-century, gabled house are small and don't share the Rhine view enjoyed by the larger and more expensive doubles, but the location—in the old city's former fish market—couldn't be better for the price. The ground-floor tavern-restaurant is a snug retreat from the city bustle; it's in a slightly higher price bracket, but does a respectable job with spruced-up versions of German classics. *Fischmarkt 1–3, tel. 0221/257–7863, fax 0221/257–4232. 35 rooms, 15 with bath. AE, DC, MC, V. $*

Hotel Rossner. Centrally located (a two minutes' walk from the train station), this hotel offers decent rooms (no shower) and breakfast for a truly bargain price. *Jakordenstr. 19, tel. 0221/122–703. 15 rooms without bath. No credit cards. Closed Dec. ¢*

Mainz
Dining
Rats und Zunftstuben Heilig Geist. Although the decor is predominantly modern, this popular restaurant also incorporates some Roman remains and offers a traditional atmosphere. The cuisine is hearty German fare. *Rentengasse 2, tel. 06131/225–757. AE, DC, MC, V. $$*

Lodging
Hotel Pfeil-Continental. The city tourist information office takes up the ground floor of this centrally located budget hotel, so you can collect pamphlets and maps on the way to checking in. Luxury takes second place to convenience here. There's no restaurant, but the immediate vicinity has many. *Bahnhofstr. 15, tel. 06131/232–179, fax 06131/286–2155. 31 rooms, 22 with bath or shower. AE, MC, V. $$*

Hotel Stadt Coblenz. In the heart of town, this attractive hotel offers budget rooms (bath in the hall) at budget prices—ask for a room facing the back. The rustic restaurant serves local and German specialties. *Rheinstr. 49, tel. 06131/227–602. 6 rooms, 1 with bath. Facilities: restaurant. No credit cards. $*

The Black Forest

Only a century ago, the Black Forest (Schwarzwald) was one of the wildest stretches of countryside in Europe. It had earned its somber name because of the impenetrable stretches of dark forest that clothed the mountains and shielded small communities from the outside world. Today, it's a friendly, hospitable region, still extensively forested, but with large, open valleys and stretches of verdant farmland.

The Black Forest is the southernmost German wine region and the custodian of some of the country's best traditional foods. (Black Forest smoked ham and Black Forest cake are world famous.) It retains its vibrant clock-making tradition, and local wood-carvers haven't yet died out. Best of all, though, it's still possible to stay overnight in a Black Forest farmhouse and eat a breakfast hearty enough to last the day, all for the price of an indifferent meal at a restaurant in, say, Munich or Frankfurt.

Getting Around

A main north–south train line follows the Rhine Valley, carrying Euro-City and InterCity trains that call at hourly intervals at Freiburg and Baden-Baden, connecting those two centers directly with Frankfurt and many other German cities. Local lines connect most Black Forest towns. For scenery buffs, there's the Black Forest Railway through the valley of Höllental (for information, call the Deutsche Bahn at 0761/19419). The nearest airports are at Stuttgart; Strasbourg, in the neighboring French Alsace; and the Swiss border city of Basel, just 64 kilometers (40 miles) from Freiburg.

Tourist Information

Baden-Baden (Augustaplatz 8, tel. 07221/275–200).
Freiburg (Rotteckring 14, tel. 0761/368–9090).

Exploring the Black Forest

The regional tourist authority has worked out a series of scenic routes covering virtually every attraction the visitor is likely to want to see (obtainable from the **Fremdenverkehrsverband**, Bertoldstr. 45, 79098 Freiburg, tel. 0761/31317). The routes are basically intended for the motorist, but most points can be reached by train or bus. The following itinerary is accessible by all means of transportation and takes in parts of the Black Forest High Road, Low Road, Spa Road, Wine Road, and Clock Road.

Freiburg Perched on the western slopes of the Black Forest, **Freiburg** was founded as a free market town in the 12th century. It was badly bombed in World War II, but has been carefully restored so that the narrow streets of the Old City have much of their original charm. The center of town is largely closed to car traffic, and the alleyways are crisscrossed with little canals, or *Bächle*, a Freiburg trademark. Towering over the city is its most famous landmark, the cathedral, or **Münster.** The cathedral took three centuries to build and has one of the finest spires in the world. April through October, English-language walking tours of the Old Town include an explanation of the Münster's numerous architectural styles. The two-hour tours are led Wednesday and Thursday at 10 AM and Monday, Friday, Saturday, and Sunday at 2:30 PM. *Admission: DM 8 adults, DM 2 children. (Contact tourist office; see above.)*

The square in front of the cathedral also serves as the city marketplace. A fitting backdrop to the colorful bustle of garlic vendors and sausage sellers is provided by **Kaufhaus,** the 16th-century market house.

Baden-Baden From Freiburg, head north to fashionable **Baden-Baden,** idyllically set in a wooded valley of the northern Black Forest. The town sits on top of extensive underground hot springs that gave the city its name (*Bad,* German for "spa"). The Romans first exploited the springs, which were then rediscovered by wealthy 19th-century travelers. By the end of the 19th century, there was scarcely a crowned head of Europe who had not dipped into the healing waters of Baden-Baden.

One of the grand buildings of Baden-Baden's Belle Epoque is the pillared **Kurhaus,** home of Germany's first casino, which opened its doors to the world's gamblers in 1853. Entrance costs a modest DM 5, though visitors are required to sign a declaration that they enter with sufficient funds to settle subsequent debts! *Jacket and tie. Passport necessary as proof of identity. Open Sun.–Fri. 2 PM–2 AM, Sat. 2 PM–3 AM. Daily tours (DM 3) from Apr.–Sept., daily 9:30–noon; Oct.–Mar., 10–noon.*

If jackets and ties are customary attire at the casino, no clothes at all are de rigueur at Baden-Baden's famous Roman baths, the **Friedrichsbad.** You "take the waters" here just as the Romans did nearly 2,000 years ago—nude. *Römerplatz 1, tel. 07221/275–920. Admission: DM 38 (includes massage). Children under 18 not admitted. Open Mon.–Sat. 9 AM–10 PM, Sun. 2–10 PM.*

The attractions of the Friedrichsbad are rivaled by the neighboring **Caracalla baths,** renovated and enlarged in 1985. The huge, modern complex has five indoor pools, two outdoor ones, numerous whirlpools, a solarium, and what is described as a "sauna landscape"—you look out through windows at the countryside while steaming. *Römerplatz 11, tel. 07221/275–940. Admission: DM 18 for 2 hrs, DM 24 for 3 hrs. Open daily 8 AM–10 PM.*

Dining and Lodging

For details and price-category definitions, *see* Dining and Lodging *in* Staying in Germany, *above.*

Baden-Baden **Gasthaus zur Traube.** Regional specialties, such as smoked bacon
Dining and homemade noodles, take pride of place in this cozy inn, south of the city center in the Neuweier district. You can also spend the night in one of the 18 neatly furnished rooms. *Mauerbergstr. 107, tel. 07223/57216. MC, V. Closed Wed. $$*
Bratwurstglöckle. Hunt out the large bronze bell—the *Glöckle*—that hangs outside this traditional beer and wine tavern. It signals good food and drink at reasonable prices. *Steinstr. 7, tel. 07221/2968. No credit cards. ¢*

Lodging **Deutscher Kaiser-Etol.** This centrally located, old, established hotel, a few minutes' stroll from the Kurhaus, offers homey and individually styled rooms at comfortable prices in an otherwise expensive town. All the doubles have balconies on a quiet street off one of the main thoroughfares. *Merkurstr. 9, tel. 07221/2700, fax 07221/270–270. 44 rooms with bath. Facilities: restaurant (closed Sun. dinner), bar, bicycle hire. AE, DC, MC, V. $$ and Splurge.*
Hotel am Markt. The Bogner family has run this 250-year-old hotel for more than 30 years. It's friendly, popular, and right in the center of town. *Marktplatz 17–18, tel. 07221/22747, fax 07221/391–887. 28 rooms, 14 with bath or shower. Facilities: restaurant, terrace. AE, DC, MC, V. $*
Hotel Bischoff. The Friedrichsbad Roman baths are right across the street, and most other attractions in Baden-Baden are only a short walk from this quiet fin-de-siècle villa-hotel. The guest rooms are basic, though adequately furnished. There's a cozy breakfast room,

but no restaurant. *Römerplatz 2, tel. 07221/22378, fax 07221/38308. 21 rooms with shower. AE, DC, MC, V. $*

Hotel Greiner. This 20-year-old hotel stands in its own grounds at the end of Baden-Baden's stately Lichtentaler Allee. Ask for one of the larger double rooms with balcony. *Lichtentaler Allee 88, tel. 07221/71135. 34 rooms, 18 with shower. Facilities: garden, parking. Closed mid-Nov.–mid-Dec. No credit cards. $*

Hotel Sonne. *Sonne* means sun in English, an appropriate name for a hotel that soaks up the sunshine on the wooded slopes outside Baden-Baden, at the start of the Schwarzwaldhochstrasse route through the Black Forest. The hotel is attractive and typical of the region, with flower-smothered wood balconies running along its snow-white facade. *Geroldsauerstr. 145, tel. 07221/7412. 18 rooms with bath. Facilities: restaurant, garden, parking. MC, V. ¢*

Freiburg **Enoteca.** Three dining possibilities are now offered by the refur-
Dining bished Enoteca. If you're trying to keep expenses down, eat in the crowded, friendly bistro, or go for a light meal at the bar, which is open until 1:30 AM. The adjacent restaurant is more elegant, and correspondingly pricey. Proprietor Manfred Schmitz is a respected local wine connoisseur, as well as an accomplished chef, and he can be relied on to recommend just the right vintage to accompany such specialties as veal roulade with gorgonzola. *Schwabentorplatz, tel. 0761/30751. Restaurant reservations advised. AE, DC, MC, V. Closed Sun. $$*

Oberkirchs Weinstuben. The landlord of this small hotel's tavern, which faces the cathedral, personally bags some of the game that ends up in the kitchen. Fresh trout is another specialty. In summer, the dark oak dining tables spill out onto a garden terrace. *Münsterplatz 22, tel. 0761/31011. V. Closed Sun., holidays, and 3 wks in Jan. $$*

Zur Trotte. For an atmospheric taste of Freiburg, look into this little *Weinstube.* You'll find simple, local specialties served for lunch and dinner, together with a wide variety of local wines, in a rustic interior featuring a big tile oven (*Kachelofen*). It's on the bank of a Freiburg canal, in the street where the river fishermen used to live, which is now lined with little rustic shops. *Fischerau, tel. 0761/30777. No credit cards. $*

Lodging **Gasthaus zum Kreuz.** It's a bit out of town, but the bus from the city center stops at this flower-bedecked 1755 farmhouse, and you pay rural prices for urban comforts. The Hug family has run the establishment since 1898; the youngest generation has added satellite TV in every room. *Grosstalstr. 28, 79117 Freiburg-Kappel, tel. 0761/62055, fax 0761/64793. 17 rooms with bath. Facilities: sauna, solarium, fitness room, TV in rooms, parking. MC. Closed 2 wks in Jan. $$*

Rappen Hotel. A farmhouse theme dominates here, with brightly painted rustic beds in every room. The Rappen is in the center of the traffic-free old city, overlooking the Cathedral and the marketplace (overhearing the bells of the former, the bustle of the latter). In the countrified but comfortable restaurant, patrons have the choice of more than 200 regional wines. *Am Münsterplatz 13, tel. 0761/31353, fax 0761/382–252. 25 rooms, 13 with bath. Facilities: bar-restaurant, terrace. AE, DC, MC, V. $$*

Hotel am Stadtgarten. The rooms are small and plain (although they each have a TV and phone), but the hotel is centrally located and a very good value. A good breakfast is included in the room rate. *Bernhardstr. 5, tel. 0761/282–9002, fax 0761/2829022. 24 rooms with bath or shower. Facilities: restaurant, parking. AE, MC, V. $*

Berlin

Berlin is now a united metropolis—again the largest in continental Europe—and only four small sections of the Wall have been left in place to remind visitors and residents alike of the hideous barrier that divided the city for nearly 30 years. Old habits die hard, however, and it will be a long time before Germans and even Berliners themselves can get accustomed to regarding Berlin as one entity with one identity. You'll still hear Berliners in the western, more prosperous half talking about "those over there" when referring to people in the still down-at-the-heels eastern part. All restrictions on travel within and beyond the city have, of course, disappeared, but there's still a strong feeling of passing from one world into another when crossing the scar that marks the line where the Wall once stood. It's not just the very visible differences between the glitter of West Berlin and the relative shabbiness of the east. Somehow the historical heritage of a long-divided city permeates the place and penetrates the consciousness of every visitor. You'll almost certainly arrive in and depart from the western part of Berlin, but just as surely your steps will lead you into the east.

Arriving and Departing

By Plane **Tegel Airport** (tel. 030/410–2306) is only 7 kilometers (4 miles) from downtown. Airlines flying to Tegel include Delta, United, Air France, British Airways, Lufthansa, Deutsche BA, and some charter specialists. Because of increased air traffic at Tegel following unification, the former military airfield at **Tempelhof** (even closer to downtown, tel. 030/691–510), is being used more and more. **Schönefeld** (tel. 030/67870) airport is about 24 kilometers (15 miles) outside the downtown area.

Between the Airports and Downtown Bus 109 runs every 10 minutes between Tegel Airport and downtown. The journey takes 30 minutes and the fare is DM 3.70 and covers public transportation throughout Berlin. A taxi will cost about DM 25. If you've rented a car at the airport, follow signs for the "Stadtautobahn" highway. Tempelhof is right on the U-6 subway line, in the center of the city. A shuttle bus leaves Schönefeld airport every 10–15 minutes for the nearby S-Bahn station. S-Bahn trains leave every 20 minutes for the Friedrichstrasse station. The trip takes about 30 minutes, and you can get off at whatever stop is nearest your hotel. The fare by bus or subway is DM 3.70. You can also take a taxi from the airport; the fare to your hotel will be about DM 40–DM 55, and the trip will take about 40 minutes. By car, follow the signs for "Stadtzentrum Berlin."

By Train There are six major rail routes to Berlin from the western half of the country (from Hamburg, Hannover, Köln, Frankfurt, Munich, and Nürnberg), and the network has expanded considerably, making the rest of eastern Germany more accessible. Service between Berlin and Eastern Europe has also improved significantly, resulting in shorter travelling times. For the latest information on routes, call **Deutsche Bahn** (tel. 030/19419), or inquire at the local main train station. Three people or more can often travel at discounted group rates.

Some trains now stop at and depart from all of Berlin's four main train stations, but generally north- and west-originated trains arrive at Friedrichstrasse and Zoologischer Garten, south- and east-originated trains at Hauptbahnhof and Lichtenberg.

By Bus Long-distance bus services link Berlin with numerous western German and other western European cities. For travel details, if you're in Berlin, call the main bus station (Messedam, tel. 030/301–

8028), or if you're in western Germany, inquire at the local tourist office.

Getting Around

By Public Transportation Berlin is large, and only the center can comfortably be explored on foot. Fortunately, the city is blessed with excellent public transportation, a combination of U-Bahn (subway) and S-Bahn (metropolitan train) lines, buses, streetcars (in east Berlin only), and even a ferry across the Wannsee lake. The nine U-Bahn lines alone have 164 stations. Extensive all-night bus and streetcar service (they are marked by the letter N next to their number) are in operation all week, and the subway lines U-9 and U-12 run all night on weekends. For DM 3.70 (DM 2.50 children) you can buy a ticket that covers travel on the entire system for 2 hours. A multiple ticket, valid for four trips, costs DM 12.50 (DM 8.50 children). Or, you can pay DM 15 for a **Day Card** (no children's discount), good for 30 hours of unlimited use (except on the Wannsee Lake ferries). The **Group Day Card,** for DM 20, offers the same benefits for two adults and up to three children. If you're staying for more than a few days, the week **Tourist Pass,** for DM 40, is the best bargain. The **BerlinWelcomeCard,** for DM 29, gives one adult and up to three children three days of unlimited travel as well as free admission to or reductions of up to 50% on sightseeing trips, museum admissions, theater tickets, and other events and attractions. Information can be obtained from all ticket booths or from the main office of the city transport authority, **BVG** (Berliner Verkehrsbetriebe, tel. 030/752–7020) at Hardenbergplatz, in front of the Bahnhof Zoo. If you're caught without any ticket the fine is DM 60.

Important Addresses and Numbers

Tourist Information The main tourist office, **Verkehrsamt Berlin,** is at the Europa Center (Budapesterstr., tel. 030/262–6031). It's open daily 8 AM–10:30 PM. There are other offices at the main hall of **Tegel Airport** (tel. 030/4101–3145, open daily 8 AM–11 PM) and at the **Zoologischer Garten** (tel. 030/313–9063, open daily 8 AM–11 PM); and at **Hauptbahnhof** (tel. 030/279–5209; open daily 8–8). Accommodations can be reserved at all offices, which also issue a free English-language information brochure, *Berlin Turns On.* Pretravel information on Berlin can be obtained by writing to the Verkehrsamt Berlin (Martin-Luthar Str. 105, 10825 Berlin). Berlin has an information center especially for women that helps with finding accommodations and information on upcoming events: **Fraueninfothek Berlin** (Kircksenstr. 47, tel. 030/282–3980; open Tues.–Sat. 9–9, Sun. and public holidays 9–3).

Tips for Travelers with Disabilities Many S- and U-Bahn stations have elevators and a few buses have hydrolic lifts. Check the public transportation maps or call the BVG (*see above*). **Servic-Ring-Berlin e.V.** (tel. 030/859–4010 or 030/9389–2410) and **Verband Geburts- und anderer Behinderter e.V.** (tel. 030/341–1797) provide information and van and wheelchair rentals.

Consulates **United States** (Clayallee 170, tel. 030/819–7454). **Canada** (International Trade Center, Friedrich Str. 95, tel. 030/261–1161). **Great Britain** (Unter den Linden 32–34, tel. 030/201–8401). **Ireland** (Ernst-Reuter-Pl. 10, tel. 030/3480–0822).

Emergencies **Police** (tel. 030/110). **Ambulance and emergency medical attention** (tel. 030/310031). **Dentist** (tel. 030/01141).

Exploring Berlin

Visiting Berlin is a bittersweet experience, since so many of the triumphs and tragedies of the past are tied up with the bustling present. The result can be either dispiriting or exhilarating. And by

European standards, Berlin isn't that old: Köln had existed for more than 1,000 years when Berlin was born from the fusion of two tiny settlements on islands in the Spree River. Although already a royal residence in the 15th century, Berlin really came into its own three centuries later, under the rule of King Friedrich II—Frederick the Great—whose liberal reforms and artistic patronage led the way as the city developed into a major cultural capital.

The events of the 20th century would have crushed the spirit of most other cities. Hitler destroyed the city's reputation for tolerance and plunged Berlin headlong into the war that led to the wholesale destruction of monuments and houses. And after World War II, Berlin was still to face the bitter division of the city and the construction of the infamous Wall in 1961. But a storm of political events, beginning in 1989, brought the downfall of the East German Communist regime; the establishment of democracy in the east; and, finally, in October 1990, the unification of Berlin and of all Germany. Now you can travel from one end of Berlin to the other and in and out of the long-isolated western part of the city as easily as you would in any other metropolis.

Numbers in the margin correspond to points of interest on the West Berlin map.

West Berlin The **Kurfürstendamm,** or Ku'damm as the Berliners call it, is one of Europe's busiest thoroughfares, throbbing with activity day and
❶ night. At its eastern end is the **Kaiser Wilhelm Gedächtniskirche** (Kaiser Wilhelm Memorial Church Tower). This landmark had come to symbolize not only West Berlin, and it still is a dramatic reminder of the futile destructiveness of war. The shell of the tower is all that remains of the church that was built at the end of the 19th century and dedicated to Kaiser Wilhelm. Inside is a historical exhibition of the devastation of World War II. *Admission free. Open Tues.–Sat. 10–5, closed holidays.*

❷ Cross Budapesterstrasse to enter the **Zoologischer Garten,** Berlin's zoo. It has the world's largest variety of individual types of fauna, along with a fascinating aquarium. *Admission to zoo only: DM 10 adults, DM 5 children; admission to aquarium only: DM 9 adults, DM 4.50 children. Combined admission for the aquarium and zoo: DM 15 adults, DM 7.50 children. Open daily from 9 AM to 6:30 PM or to dusk in winter.*

❸ Double back to the Kurfürstendamm to catch Bus 142 to Kemperplatz. Among the buildings that make up the **Kulturforum** (Cultural Forum) on the large square is the **Philharmonie** (Philharmonic Hall), home of the famous Berlin Philharmonic orchestra. You'll recognize it by its roof, which resembles a great wave. *Matthäkirchstr. 1, tel. 030/261–4383. Ticket office open weekdays 3:30–6 and weekends 11–2.*

Opposite is the **Kunstgewerbemuseum** (Museum of Decorative Arts), which displays arts and crafts of Europe from the Middle Ages to the present. Among its treasures is the Welfenschatz (Guelph Treasure), a collection of 16th-century gold and silver plate from Nürnberg. *Tiergartenstr. 6, tel. 030/266–2911. Admission: DM 4 adults, DM 2 children. Free Sun. Open Tues.–Fri. 9–5, weekends 10–5.*

Leave the museum and walk south past the mid-19th-century church of St. Matthaeus to the **Neue Nationalgalerie** (New National Gallery), a modern glass-and-steel building designed by Mies van der Rohe and built in the mid-1960s. The gallery's collection consists of paintings, sculpture, and drawings from the 19th and 20th centuries, with an accent on works by the Impressionists. *Potsdamerstr. 50, tel. 030/266–2666. Admission: DM 4 adults, DM 2 children. Free Sun. Open Tues.–Fri. 9–5, weekends 10–5.*

Berlin Public Transit System

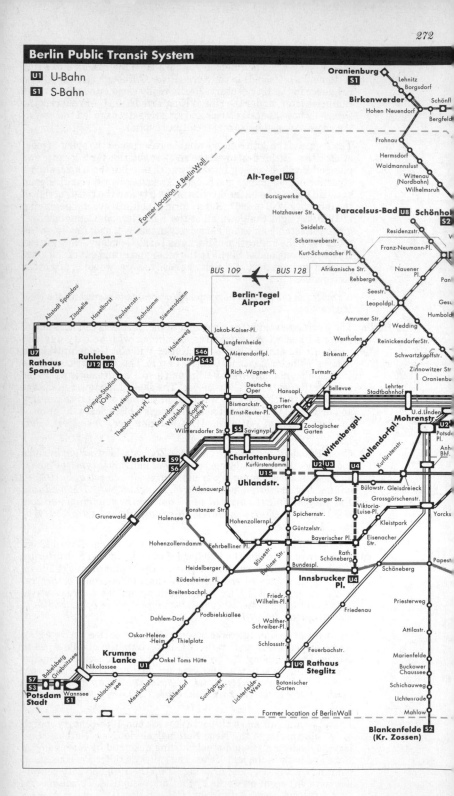

U1 U-Bahn
S1 S-Bahn

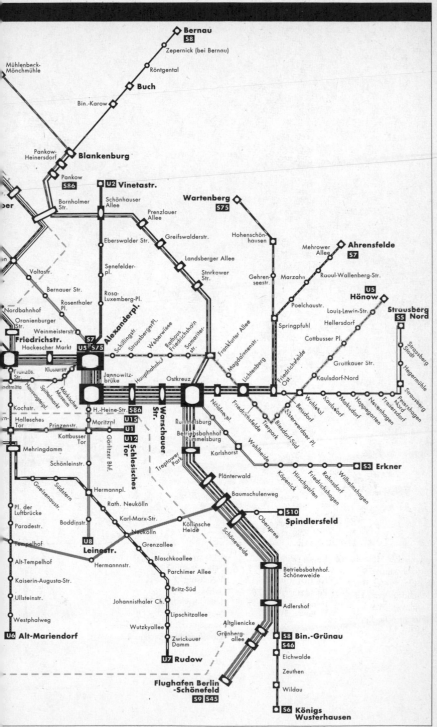

West Berlin

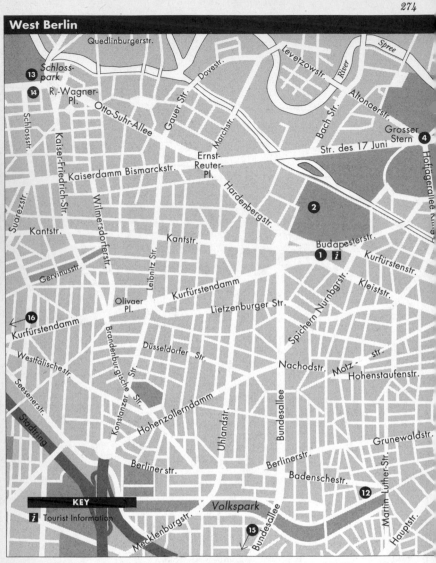

KEY

i Tourist Information

Ägyptisches Museum, **14**
Berliner Mauer, **9**
Brandenburger Tor, **6**
Gemäldegalerie, **15**
Grunewald, **16**
Haus am Checkpoint
Charlie, **11**

Kaiser Wilhelm
Gedächtniskirche, **1**
Kulturforum, **3**
Potsdamer Platz, **8**
Prince-Albert-
Gelände, **10**

Rathaus
Schöneberg, **12**
Reichstag, **7**
Schloss
Charlottenburg, **13**
Siegessäule , **4**
Sowjetisches Ehrenmal, **5**
Zoologischer Garten, **2**

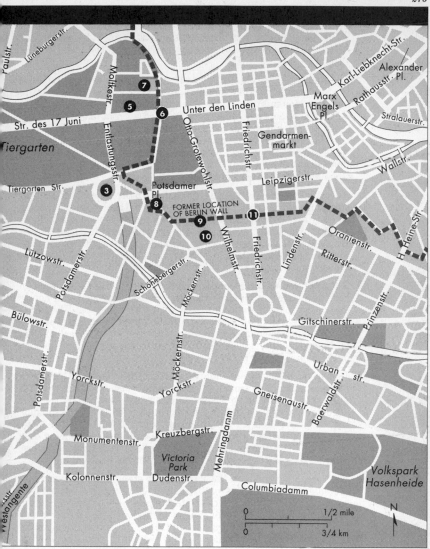

The Kulturforum is adjacent to the 255-hectare (630-acre) **Tiergarten Park,** which has at last recovered from the war, when it was not only ripped apart by bombs and artillery, but was stripped of its woods by desperate, freezing Berliners in the bitter cold of 1945–46.

④ The column in the center of a large traffic circle in the Tiergarten is the **Siegessäule** (Victory Column), erected in 1873 to commemorate four Prussian military campaigns against the French. The granite and sandstone monument originally stood in front of the Reichstag (parliament), but was moved to its present location in 1938 as part of the Nazi's grand architectural designs for Berlin. Climb the 285 steps to its 65-meter (210-foot) summit and you'll be rewarded with a fine view of Berlin. *Admission: DM 1.50 adults, DM 1 children. Open Mon. 3–6, Tues.–Sun. 9–6.*

⑤ At the base of the Siegessäule, go east down the wide Strasse des 17 Juni (June 17th Street), named in memory of the day, in 1953, when 50,000 East Germans staged an uprising that was put down by Soviet tanks. On the left, you'll pass the **Sowjetisches Ehrenmal** (Soviet Honor Memorial), a semicircular colonnade topped with a statue of a Russian soldier and flanked by what are said to be the first Soviet tanks to have fought their way into Berlin in 1945.

⑥ Ahead of you is **Brandenburger Tor** (Brandenburg Gate), built in 1788 as a victory arch for triumphant Prussian armies. The horse-drawn chariot atop the arch was reerected after the war. The monumental gate was cut off from West Berlin by the Wall, and it became a focal point of celebrations marking the unification of Berlin and of all Germany. It was here that German politicians formally sealed unification.

⑦ Just north of the Brandenburg Gate is the **Reichstag,** Germany's parliament building from its completion in 1894 until 1933, when it was gutted by fire under suspicious circumstances. When the federal government relocates to Berlin (scheduled for 2000), the Bundestag, or lower house of parliament, will convene here. At the Reichstag's northeastern corner, white wooden crosses hang on a low metal fence—grim reminders of the 80 East Germans who lost their lives trying to escape to the west after the Wall was built.

⑧ Walk south along where the Wall used to stand to **Potsdamer Platz** (Potsdam Square). It was one of Berlin's (and Europe's) busiest prewar squares, and then was the widest expanse of no-man's-land separating East and West Berlin. Follow farther along the Wall's former location to see the real thing, one of four still-standing segments of ⑨ ⑩ the famous **Berliner Mauer** (Berlin Wall), to find the **Prince-Albert-Gelände** (Prince Albert Grounds) along Niederdircherstrasse. Buildings that once stood here housed the headquarters of the Gestapo and other Nazi security organizations from 1933 until 1945. After the war, they were leveled and remained so until 1987, when what was left of the buildings was excavated and an exhibit documenting their history and Nazi atrocities opened. *Topography of Terrors, Stresemannstr. 110, tel. 030/2548–6703. Admission free. Open Tues.–Sun. 10–6. Tours by appointment only.*

⑪ The history of the hideous Berlin Wall can be followed in the museum that arose at the Checkpoint Charlie crossing point, at Friedrichstrasse, the second cross street heading east on Niederkircherstrasse. The crossing point disappeared along with the Wall, but the **Haus am Checkpoint Charlie** (House at Checkpoint Charlie–The Wall Museum) is still there. Be sure to give yourself at least a few hours to see the many excellent exhibits and films. *Friedrichstr. 44, tel. 030/251–4569. Admission: DM 7.50 adults, DM 4 children. Open daily 9 AM–10 PM.*

A short subway ride away is the Schöneberg district, where you'll
find **Rathaus Schöneberg** (Schöneberg City Hall, at U-4 subway stop
of same name), the former West Berlin city hall. (In 1991 the city administration moved back to the Rote Rathaus in Berlin Mitte.) In the
belfry of the Rathaus is a replica of the Liberty Bell, donated to
Berliners in 1950 by the United States and rung every day at noon.
The tower is open to visitors Wed. and Sun. only, 10–4.

Take the U-Bahn north one stop from Rathaus Schöneberg station
and change to the U-7 line for eight stops, to Richard-Wagner-Platz
station. From the station, walk east along Otto-Suhr-Allee to the
handsome **Schloss Charlottenburg** (Charlottenburg Palace) and its
beautiful, calming grounds, which have French and English gardens and a swan-filled pond. Built at the end of the 17th century by
King Frederick I for his wife, Queen Sophie Charlotte, the palace
was progressively enlarged for later royal residents. Frederick the
Great's suite of rooms can be visited. *Luisenplatz. Admission to
Galerie der Romantik: DM 4 adults, DM 2 children. Free Sun. Open
Tues.–Fri. 9–5, Sat. and Sun. 10–5.*

Opposite the palace is the **Ägyptisches Museum** (Egyptian Museum), home of perhaps the world's best-known portrait sculpture,
the beautiful Nefertiti. The 3,300-year-old Egyptian queen is the
centerpiece of a fascinating collection of Egyptology. *Schlosstr. 70.
Admission: DM 4 adults, DM 2 children. Free Sun. Open Mon.–
Thurs. 9–5, weekends 10–5. Closed Fri. Combined day pass to 4
Charlottenburg museums: DM 8 adults, DM 4 children.*

Take the U-7 back toward Schöneberg until Fehrbelliner Platz,
where you change to line U-1 southwest for five stops to Dahlem-
Dorf station. This is the stop for the magnificent **Dahlem museums,**
chief of which is west Berlin's leading picture gallery, the
Gemäldegalerie. The collection includes many works by the great
European masters, with 26 Rembrandts and 14 by Rubens.
*Arnimallee 23/27. Admission: DM 4 adults, DM 2 children. Free
Sun. Open Tues.–Fri. 9–5, weekends 10–5.*

No visit to west Berlin is complete without an outing to the city's
outdoor playground, the **Grunewald** park. Bordering the Dahlem
district to the west, the park is a vast green space, with meadows,
woodlands, and lakes. There are a string of 60 lakes within Berlin's
boundaries; some are kilometers long, others are no more than
ponds. The total length of their shorelines is longer than Germany's
Baltic Coast. There's even space for nudist beaches on the banks of
the Wannsee lake, and in winter a downhill ski run and even a ski
jump operate on the modest slopes of the Teufelsberg hill.

East Berlin The infamous Wall is gone, but the spirit of division remains in a city
that was physically split for 28 years. The stately buildings of the
city's past are not as overwhelmed by new high-rise construction as
in West Berlin, but East Berlin's postwar architectural blunders are
just as monumental in their own way.

*Numbers in the margin correspond to points of interest on the East
Berlin map.*

For a sense of times past, enter the eastern part of Berlin at
Checkpoint Charlie, the most famous crossing point between the two
Berlins during the Cold War; American and Soviet tanks faced each
other here during the tense months of the Berlin Blockade in 1948.
At this point both ends of Friedrichstrasse are lined with attractive
new shops and trendy restaurants. Turn right onto Mohrenstrasse
and you'll arrive at **Gendarmenmarkt,** with its beautifully reconstructed **Schauspielhaus**—built in 1818, and now the city's main concert hall—and the twin **German** (on the south, undergoing
restoration) and **French cathedrals.** In the latter, you'll find the
Huguenot Museum, which has some interesting collections of the

East Berlin

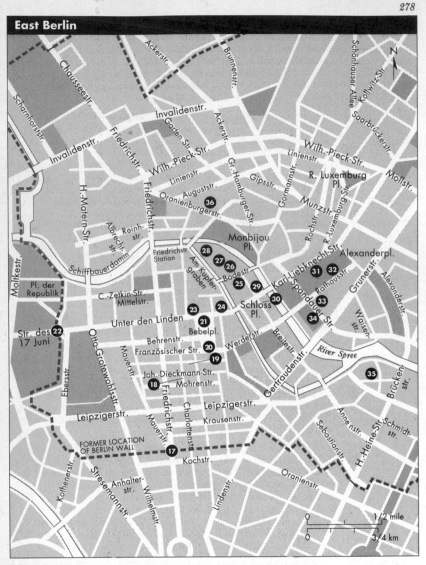

Altes Museum, **25**	Fernsehturm, **32**	Palast der Republik, **30**
Berliner Dom, **29**	Huguenot Museum, **19**	Pergamon Museum, **27**
Bodemuseum, **28**	Humboldt University, **23**	Rotes Rathaus, **33**
Brandenburger Tor, **22**	Marienkirche, **31**	Schauspielhaus, **18**
Checkpoint Charlie, **17**	Märkisches Museum, **35**	St. Hedwigs
Deutsche	Nationalgalerie, **26**	Kathedrale, **20**
Staatsoper, **21**	Neue Synagoge, **36**	
Deutsches Historisches	Nikolaikirche, **34**	
Museum, **24**		

history and art of the French Protestant Huguenots who took refuge in Germany after being expelled from Catholic France in 1685. *Gendarmenmarkt. Admission: DM2 adults, DM1 children. Tues., Wed.–Sat. 12–5, Sun. 1–5.*

Continue east along the Französischer Strasse and turn left into Hedwigskirchgasse to reach Bebelplatz. The peculiar round shape ❷⓿ of **St. Hedwigs Kathedrale** (St. Hedwig's Cathedral) calls to mind Rome's Pantheon. The tiny street named Hinter der Katholischen Kirche (Behind the Catholic Church) is a reminder that though Berlin was very much a Protestant city, St. Hedwig's was built (about 1747) for Catholics.

Walk north across Bebelplatz to Unter den Linden, the elegant cen-❷⓵ tral thoroughfare of Old Berlin. On your right is the **Deutsche Staatsoper,** the great opera house of Berlin, now with an entirely new interior. Just after Oberwallstrasse is the former crown prince's palace, the **Kronprinzenpalais,** now used to house official government visitors.

Look back down the street to the west and you'll see the monumental ❷⓶ **Brandenburger Tor** (Brandenburg Gate), its chariot-and-horses sculpture now turned to face the east. Cross Unter den Linden and ❷⓷ look into the courtyard of **Humboldt University.** It was built as a palace for the brother of Friedrich II of Prussia but became a university in 1810, and today is one of Germany's largest universities. Marx and Engels were its two most famous students. Beyond the war memori-❷⓸ al, housed in a onetime arsenal (built 1695–1730) is the **Deutsches Historisches Museum** (German Historical Museum), which has an exhibit tracing German history from the Middle Ages to the present on display. *Unter den Linden 2. Admission: DM 4 adults, DM 2 children. Open Thurs.–Tues. 10–6.*

Turning left along the Spree canal (along Am Zeughaus and Am Kupfergraben) will bring you to east Berlin's museum complex, at the northern end of what is known as **Museumsinsel** (Museum Is-❷⓹ land). The first of the Big Four that you'll encounter is the **Altes Museum** (entrance on Lustgarten), an austere neoclassical building just to the north of Schlossplatz. The collections here include postwar art from some of Germany's most prominent artists and numerous etchings and drawings from the Old Masters. Next comes the ❷⓺ **Nationalgalerie,** on Bodestrasse, which features 19th- and 20th-cen-❷⓻ tury painting and sculpture. The **Pergamon Museum,** on Am Kupfergraben, is one of Europe's greatest museums. Its name derives from the museum's principal exhibit and the city's number-one attraction, the Pergamon Altar, a monumental Greek altar dating from 180 BC that occupies an entire city block. Almost as impressive is the Babylonian Processional Way. The Pergamon Museum also houses vast Egyptian, early Christian, and Byzantine collections, plus a fine array of sculpture from the 12th to the 18th centuries. To ❷⓼ the north is the **Bodemuseum** (also on Am Kupfergraben, but with its entrance on Monbijoubrücke), with an outstanding collection of early Christian, Byzantine, and Egyptian art, as well as exhibits of Italian Old Master paintings. *Admission to each museum: DM 4 adults, DM 2 children. Combined day pass to 4 Museuminsel museums: DM 8 adults, DM 4 children. Free Sun. Museum complex open Tues.–Sun. 9–5.*

From the museum complex, follow the Spree canal south to Unter ❷⓽ den Linden and the vast and impressive **Berliner Dom** (Berlin Cathedral). The hideous modern building in bronze mirrored glass oppo-❸⓿ site is the **Palast der Republik** (Palace of the Republic), a postwar monument to socialist progress that also housed restaurants, a theater, and a dance hall. Since 1991 the Palast has been closed while the politicians argue about its fate. It formerly housed the Volkskammer, the East German People's Chamber (parliament).

Head east on Karl-Liebknecht-Strasse for a closer look at the 13th-
③ century **Marienkirche** (Church of St. Mary), especially noting its
late-Gothic *Dance of Death* fresco. You are now at the lower end of
③ Alexanderplatz. Just ahead is the massive **Fernsehturm** (TV Tower),
completed in 1969 and 1,198 feet high (not accidentally 710 feet higher than west Berlin's broadcasting tower). It offers the best view of
Berlin and the city's highest café. *Admission: 6 DM adults, 3 DM
children. Open daily 9 AM–midnight.*

③ The red building southwest of the tower is the **Rotes Rathaus** (Red
City Hall). The building's redbrick design and the frieze depicting
scenes from the city's history are impressive. In the fall of 1991 the
city administration and seat of the governing mayor were transferred from Rathaus Schöneberg back to the Rotes Rathaus, renew-
ing its prewar function. The adjacent area, known as the **Nikolai
Viertel** (Nikolai Quarter), has been handsomely rebuilt and is now
filled with delightful shops, cafés, and restaurants. On Probst-
③ strasse is **Nikolaikirche,** Berlin's oldest building. The church, dating
from 1230, was heavily damaged in the war, but has been beautifully
restored and is now a museum. Wander back down Muhlendamm
into the area around the Breitestrasse—there are some lovely old
buildings here—and on over to the **Fischerinsel** area. The throbbing
heart of Old Berlin of 750 years ago, Fischerinsel retains a tangible
medieval flavor.

③ Nearby is the **Märkisches Museum,** which has different exhibits on
Berlin's history in addition to an amusing section devoted to
automaphones—"self-playing" musical instruments, demonstrated
Sundays at 11 and Wednesdays at 3. Live bears—the city's symbol—are in a pit next to the museum. *Am Köllnischen Park 5. Admission: DM 3 adults, DM 1 children. Instrument demonstration:
DM 2. Open Tues.–Sun. 10–6.*

Take the U-2 subway from Märkisches Museum station three stops
to Stadtmitte, then change to the U-6, traveling three stops to
Oranienburger Tor. Walk a few blocks down Oranienburgerstrasse
③ to reach the **Neue Synagoge.** Completed in 1866, the synagogue was
one of Germany's most beautiful until it was seriously damaged on
November 9, 1938, the infamous *Kristalnacht* (crystal night) when
synagogues and Jewish stores were vandalized, looted, and burned.
Further destroyed by Allied bombing in 1943, it sat untouched until
restoration began under the East German regime in the mid-80's.
Today only the facade remains and it is connected to the Centrum
Judaicum (Jewish Center)—a center for Jewish culture and learning.

Shopping

Berlin is a city of alluring stores and boutiques. Despite the new capital's cosmopolitan gloss, prices are generally lower than in cities
like Munich and Hamburg.

Fine porcelain is still produced at the former Royal Prussian Porcelain Factory, now called **Königliche Porzellan Manufactur,** or KPM.
This delicate, handmade, hand-painted china is sold at KPM's store
at Kurfürstendamm 26A (tel. 030/881–1802), but it may be more fun
to visit the factory salesroom at Wegelystrasse 1, which also sells
seconds at reduced prices. If you long to have Queen Nefertiti on
your mantlepiece at home, try the **Gipsformerei der Staatlichen
Museen Preussicher Kulturbesitz** (Sophie-Charlotte-Str. 17, tel.
030/321–7011, open weekdays 9–4). It sells plaster casts of this and
other treasures from the city's museums.

Shopping The liveliest and most famous shopping area in west Berlin is the
Districts **Kurfürstendamm** and its side streets, especially between
Breitscheidplatz and **Oliver Platz**. The **Europa Center** at

Breitscheidplatz encompasses more than 100 stores, cafés, and restaurants—this is not a place to bargain-hunt, though! Running east from Breitscheidplatz is **Tauenzientstrasse,** another shopping street.

East Berlin's chief shopping areas are along the **Friedrichstrasse, Unter den Linden,** and in the area around **Alexanderplatz.** The **Berliner Markthalle** (corner of Karl-Liebknecht-Str. and Rosa-Luxembug-Str.) is one of the east's newest and largest malls.

Department Stores The classiest department store in Berlin is **KaDeWe,** the Kaufhaus des Western (Department Store of the West, as it's modestly known in English), at Wittenbergplatz. The biggest department store in continental Europe, KaDeWe is a grand-scale emporium in modern guise. Be sure to check out the food department, which occupies the whole sixth floor. The other main department store downtown is **Wertheim** on Ku'damm. Neither as big nor as attractive as the KaDeWe, Wertheim nonetheless offers a large selection of fine wares.

The main department store in east Berlin is **Kaufhof** (formerly Centrum), at the north end of Alexanderplatz. Under the old regime, you could find ridiculously cheap subsidized prices. Now it is filled with mainly Western-made products, superior, but more expensive.

Antiques On Saturdays and Sundays from 10 to 5, the colorful and lively antiques and handicrafts fair on Strasse des 17 Juni swings into action. Don't expect to pick up any bargains—or to have the place to yourself. Not far from Wittenbergplatz is **Keithstrasse,** a street given over to antiques stores. Another good street for antiques is **Suarezstrasse,** between Kandstrasse and Bismarckstrasse.

In east Berlin, antiques are sold in the Nikolai quarter, at the **Berliner Antikenmarkt** under the tracks at Friedrichstrasse, and in the restored Husemannstrasse. Some private stores along the stretch of Friedichstrasse north of the Spree Bridge offer old books and prints.

Dining

Dining in Berlin can mean sophisticated nouvelle creations in upscale restaurants with linen tablecloths and hand-printed porcelain plates or hearty local specialties in atmospheric yet inexpensive inns. The range is as vast as the city. Specialties include *Eisbein mit Sauerkraut,* knuckle of pork with pickled cabbage; *Rouladen,* rolled, stuffed beef; *Spanferkel,* suckling pig; *Berliner Schüsselsülze,* potted meat in aspic; *Schlachteplatte,* mixed grill; *Hackepeter,* ground beef; and *Kartoffelpuffer,* fried potato cakes. *Bockwurst* is a chubby frankfurter that's served in a variety of ways and sold in restaurants and at Bockwurst stands all over the city. *Schlesisches Himmerlreich* is roast goose or pork served with potato dumplings in rich gravy. *Königsberger Klopse* consists of meatballs, herring, and capers—it tastes much better than it sounds.

For details and price-category definitions, *see* Dining *in* Staying in Germany, *above.*

$$ Alt-Nürnberg. Step into the tavernlike interior and you could be in Bavaria: The waitresses even wear dirndls. Bavarian blue and white is everywhere, and such Bavarian culinary delights as *Schweinshaxe* (knuckle of pork) are well represented on the menu. If you prefer to eat in the Prussian style, the calves' liver *Berliner Art* is recommended. *Europa Center, tel. 030/261–4397. Reservations advised. AE, DC, MC, V.*

$$ Blockhaus Nikolskoe. Prussian King Wilhelm III built this Russian-
★ style wooden lodge for his daughter Charlotte, wife of Russia's Czar Nicholas I. It's in the southwest of the city, on the eastern edge of

Glienicke Park. In summer, you can eat on the open terrace over-looking the Havel River. In character with its history and appear-ance, the Blockhaus features game dishes. *Nikolskoer Weg, tel. 030/ 805–2914. Reservations advised. AE, DC, MC, V. Closed Thurs.*

$$ Ponte Vecchio. Delicious Tuscan food is served here in a handsome, light-wood dining room. Ask the friendly waiters for their recom-mendations—the food is excellent and simply presented. Try the delicate *vitello tonnato*, veal with a tuna sauce. *Spielhagenstr. 3, tel. 030/342–1999. Reservations required. DC. Dinner only (except Sun.). Closed Tues., 4 wks in summer, and Christmas.*

$$ Samâdhi. This quaint restaurant just north of Savigny Platz serves a wide variety of vegetarian Southeast Asian food. The soft light-ing, sparse interior, and friendly service don't exactly transport you to Asia, but you'll feel its presence once you sample some of the deli-cately prepared food. One of eight soups the restaurant offers—the Thai coconut soup with tofu—is smoothness embodied, and at DM 5 the fried banana dessert is a bargain. *Goethestr. 6, tel. 030/313– 1067. Reservations advised for dinner. No credit cards.*

$$ Turmstuben. Not for the infirm or those who afraid of heights, this restaurant is tucked away below the cupola of the French Cathedral, at the north side of the beautiful Gendarmenmarkt, and is reached by a long, winding staircase. The reward is a table in one of Berlin's most original and attractive restaurants. The menu is as short as the stairway is long, but there's an impressive wine list. *Gendarmenmarkt, tel. 030/229–3969. Weekend reservations strong-ly advised. MC, V.*

$ Alt-Cöllner Schankstuben. A charming, genuine old Berlin house is the setting for a restaurant and a *Kneipe* (pub), both of which pro-vide exceptionally friendly service. *Friedrichsgracht 50, tel. 030/ 242–5972. Reservations accepted. AE, DC, MC, V.*

$ Eierscale (II). Berlin is famous for its breakfast cafés, and this is one of the best—and the best located, on the corner of central Rankestrasse and the Ku'damm. It serves breakfast until 4 PM, but gets going in the evenings when jazz groups perform. The lunch and supper menus feature filling Berlin fare but the Mexican-style spare-ribs are especially recommended. Sunday morning live jazz accompa-nies the buffet brunch. *Rankestrasse 1, tel. 030/882–5305. AE, DC, MC, V.*

$ Thürnagel. The great vegetarian food here makes healthful eating fun. The *seitan* (vegetable protein) in sherry sauce or the tempeh curry are good enough to convert a seasoned carnivore. *Gneis-enaustr. 57, tel. 030/691–4800. Reservations advised. No credit cards. Dinner only.*

$ Zur Letzen Instanz. Established in 1525, this place combines charm-
★ ing old Berlin atmosphere with a limited (but tasty) choice of dishes. Napoléon is said to have sat alongside the tiled stove in the front room. The emphasis here is on beer, both in the recipes and in the mug. Service can be erratic, though engagingly friendly. *Waisenstr. 14–16, tel. 030/242–5528. Reservations advised for lunch and din-ner. AE, DC, MC, V.*

¢ Café Oren. This popular vegetarian eatery next to the Neue Synagoge buzzes with loud chatter all evening, and the atmosphere and service are welcoming and friendly. The intimate back court-yard is a wonderful place to enjoy a warm autumn afternoon. The extensive menu offers mostly Israeli and Middle Eastern fare, including the delicious filled "Moroccan Cigars," in addition to nu-merous desserts. *Oranienburgerstr. 28, tel. 030/282–8228. Reser-vations advised. No credit cards.*

¢ Deichgraf. Yuppies and blue-collar workers rub shoulders in this traditional restaurant in west Berlin's Wedding district. The experi-enced chefs serve up a wide selection of *neue deutsche Küche* (new German cuisine) dishes. The large beer garden is popular in the sum-mer. *Norufer 10, tel. 030/453–7613. No credit cards.*

¢ **Max and Moritz.** You can feast on traditional Berlin fare at this typical, old-style Kreuzberg restaurant, complete with dark-wood paneling and a smoky, casual atmosphere. Try the Königsberger Klopse. *Oranienstr. 162, tel. 030/614–1045. Reservations accepted. No credit cards.*

¢ **Orpheus.** This Kreuzberg bar-restaurant owes its popularity to its friendly service and diverse menu, which includes pizza and salads as well as typical local meat dishes. Dinner is served until 1 AM. *Katzbachstr. 17, tel. 030/785–7734. No credit cards.*

¢ **Reinhard's.** This popular Nikolai quarter restaurant is one of Berlin's newest. Friends meet here to enjoy carefully prepared entrées and sample spirits from the amply stocked bar, all served by friendly, bright-tie-wearing waiters. The honey-glazed breast of duck is a house specialty. *Poststr. 28, tel. 030/242–5295. Reservations advised for dinner. AE, DC, MC, V.*

¢ **Vineta.** Known among insiders as one of Berlin's least expensive restaurants, Vineta cooks up traditional German fare for prices below DM 10. The food is good, but don't expect much ambience; the restaurant is housed in a typically bland 1950s-style East German building, and the furnishings are spartan. *Berlinerstr., at the Pankow/Vinetastr. Subway station, tel. 030/472–4122. Reservations accepted. No credit cards.*

Lodging

Berlin lost all its grand old luxury hotels in the bombing during World War II; though some were rebuilt, many of the best hotels today are modern. Although they lack little in service and comfort, you may find some short on atmosphere. Eager for hard currency, the East German government built several elegant luxury hotels in East Berlin, all of which are very expensive. If you're seeking something more moderate, the better choice may be west Berlin, where there are large numbers of good-value pensions and small hotels, many of them in older buildings with some character. In east Berlin, however, the hotels run by the Evangelical Lutheran church offer outstanding value for your money.

Business conventions year-round and the influx of summer tourists mean that you should make reservations well in advance. If you arrive without reservations consult the board at Tegel Airport that shows hotels with vacancies or go to the tourist office.

For details and price-category definitions, *see* Lodgings *in* Staying in Germany, *above.*

$$ **Casino Hotel.** What was once the main quarters of Imperial officers has been skillfully converted into an appealing hotel with large, comfortable rooms, all tastefully furnished and well equipped—the Prussian soldiers never had it so good! The hotel is in the Charlottenburg district. *Königin-Elisabeth-Str. 47a, tel. 030/303–090. 23 rooms with bath. Facilities: 24-hr snack bar. AE, DC, MC, V.*

$$ **Charlottenhof.** This popular hotel-pension, ideally located on east Berlin's beautiful Gendarmenmarkt, was taken over by a large west German group in 1991. Luckily the room prices have remained moderate, and the homey, friendly nature of the original establishment has come through intact. Ask for the weekend bargain rates. *Charlottenstrasse 52, tel. 030/238–060. 86 rooms with bath. Facilities: restaurant. AE, DC, MC, V.*

$$ ★ **Econtel.** Families are well cared for at this hotel, and lone travelers also appreciate the touches in the single rooms, which come with trouser presses and hair dryers. The breakfast buffet offers a dazzling array of choices to fill you up for a day of sightseeing—perhaps at nearby Charlottenburg Palace. *Sommeringstr. 24, tel. 030/346–*

810. *205 rooms with bath or shower. Facilities: lobby bar. AE, MC, V.*

$$ Gendarm Garni Hotel. This well-run hotel is also by the Gendarmenmarkt. All the rooms are neat and pleasantly furnished. Ask for the corner suite facing the square; the view and the large living room (for DM 225) make it one of the better deals in town. *Charlottenstr. 60, tel. 030/200–4180. 25 rooms with bath, 4 suites. Facilities: lobby bar. AE, MC, V.*

$$ Hotel Gotland. Opened in 1987, the Gotland has modern rooms equipped with showers, radio, and cable TV. A breakfast buffet is included in the rates. The 20 rooms book up quickly, so be sure to make reservations. *Franzstr. 23, tel. 030/621–2094. 20 rooms with bath. Facilities: garage. No credit cards.*

$$ Hotel Müggelsee. Berlin's biggest and, some say, most beautiful lake is just beyond your balcony in this establishment, which was once a favorite among Communist leaders. The hotel can arrange for a forest picnic and even has a yacht for guests to use. *Am Grossen Müggelsee, tel. 030/658–820. 174 rooms with bath. Facilities: 4 restaurants, bar, nightclub, summer terrace, sauna, solarium, massage, fitness room, tennis court, boutiques. AE, DC, MC, V.*

$$ Mürkischer Hof. All of downtown old Berlin is within walking distance of this small hotel just off Friedrichstrasse. The rooms are fairly large and cheerfully furnished. *Linienstr. 133, tel. 030/282–7155. 20 rooms, most with bath. AE, MC, V.*

$$ Ravenna. This small, friendly hotel is in the Steglitz district, close to the Botanical Garden and the Dahlen Museum. All the rooms are well equipped, but Suite 111B is a bargain: It includes a large living room and kitchen for the rate of only DM 305. *Grunewaldstr. 8–9, tel. 030/790–910. 55 rooms with bath or shower. AE, DC, MC, V.*

$$ Riehmers Hofgarten. A few minutes walk from the Kreuzberg hill and surrounded by the colorful district's bars and restaurants, this hotel also has fast connections to the center of town. The 19th-century building's high-ceilinged rooms are elegantly furnished. *Yorckstr. 83, tel. 030/781–011. 21 rooms with bath or shower. AE, DC, MC, V.*

$ Alpenland. Near the fashionable Ku'damm, this small hotel offers comfort and quiet in a central location. Most rooms have private bathrooms. The Bavarian rustic-style restaurant downstairs serves wholesome German food. Room reservations are necessary. *Carmerstr. 8, tel. 030/312–3970 or 030/312–4898. 45 rooms, most with bath. Facilities: restaurant. MC, V.*

$ Hotel Merkur. This small hotel is in central east Berlin's Prenzlauer Berg district. The service is friendly, and the rooms are comfortable, equipped with such extras as minibar, safes, radios, and TVs. *Torstr. 156, tel. 030/282–8297. 16 rooms, some with bath. AE, DC, MC, V.*

$ Hotel Pension Neues Tor. Before the Wall was torn down, this little pension sat in the shadow of the Communist city checkpoint. Today the checkpoint is defunct, and the Neues Tor is conveniently close to several east Berlin museums. The atmosphere is friendly, and basic rooms have radios and TVs. Breakfast is included in the rates. *Invalidenstr. 102, tel. 030/282–3859. 7 rooms, some with bath. No credit cards.*

¢ Pension Elton. The city is at your doorstep when you stay in this cozy pension in the heart of west Berlin. You'll get a modest, comfortable room equipped with a telephone and a TV and breakfast for a very reasonable price. *Pariser Str. 9, tel. 030/883–6155. 8 rooms, some with bath. Facilities: elevator. AE, DC, MC, V.*

¢ Haus Schliebner Pension. The Wall used to cut through northern Berlin just a couple of blocks from this tiny pension. Today the whole city is freely and easily accessible from the nearby S-Bahn station. The rooms are simply furnished and have washbasins but no showers. *Dannenwalder Weg 95, tel. 030/416–7997. 7 rooms without bath. No credit cards.*

¢ **Hotel Transit.** This large, nondescript hotel is in the lively, colorful Kreusberg district. The rooms are blandly furnished, but are equipped with minibars and there's a TV room. The Yorckstrasse S-Bahn station is just a short walk away. *Hagelberger Str. 53–54, Kreuzberg, tel. 030/785–5051. 49 rooms with bath. Facilities: snack bar, laundry facilities. AE, DC, MC, V.*

¢ **Pension Berliner Bar.** With only the most basic furnishings and decor—traditional socialist style—this pension is no lap of luxury, and breakfast is not included. What it does have going for it is location. You'll be staying right on Friedrichstrasse, with all of downtown east Berlin at your feet and all points west quickly reachable by subway. Be sure to ask for a per night discount if you stay more than a few days. *Friedrichstr. 124, tel. 030/282–9352. 15 rooms, none with bath. No credit cards.*

¢ **Pension 22.** Tucked away in the beautiful outlying district of Kladow, this little pension is ideal for those who like to escape the noise and bustle of the central city. The rooms are comfortable and pleasingly decorated; some are equipped with showers. *Schambachweg 22, tel. 030/365–5230. 5 rooms, some with bath. No credit cards.*

The Arts

Today's Berlin has a tough task in trying to live up to the reputation it gained from the film *Cabaret,* but if nightlife is a little toned down since the '20s, the arts still flourish. The quality of opera and classical concerts in Berlin is high. Tickets are available at the theaters' own box offices, either in advance or an hour before the performance, at many hotels, and at numerous ticket agencies, including **Ticket Counter** (in Europa Center, tel. 030/264–1138); **Hekticket** (Alexanderpl.); **Theaterkasse Centrum** (Meinekestr. 25, tel. 030/882–7611); and the **Top Ticket** branches (in all major stores, such as Hertie, Wertheim, and KaDeWe). Check the monthly publication *Berlin Programm* for a detailed guide to what's going on in the arts while you're there.

Concerts The Berlin Philharmonic, one of the world's leading orchestras, performs in the **Philharmonie** (Matthaikirchstr. 1, tel. 030/261–4383). It plays a major role in the annual festival months of August, September, and October. The east's venue is **Konzerthaus Berlin** (in Schauspielhaus at Gendarmenmarkt, tel. 030/2030–92100).

Opera and The **Deutsche Oper** (Opera House, Bismarckstr. 35, tel. 030/341–
Ballet 0249), by the U-Bahn stop of the same name, is the home of opera and ballet companies. Other performances are given at **Deutsche Staatsoper** (Unter den Linden 7, tel. 030/200–4762) and **Komische Oper** (Behrenstr. 55–57, tel. 030/229–2555).

Musicals **Metropol Theater** (Friedrichstr. 101, tel. 030/2036–4117).

Nightlife

Nightlife in west Berlin is no halfhearted affair. It starts late (from 9 PM) and runs until breakfast. Almost 50 Kneipen have live music of one kind or another, and there are numerous small cabaret clubs and discos. The heart of this nocturnal scene is the Kurfürstendamm, but some of the best bars and discos are around Nollendorfplatz (try **Metropol** for late-night dancing on weekends, Nollendorfpl. 5) in Schöneberg, and along Oranienstrasse and Wienerstrasse in Kreuzberg (head straight for the secret back room at **Bierhimmel,** Oranienstr. 183).

West Berlin is still Germany's drag-show capital, as you'll see if you go to **Chez Nous** (Marburgerstr. 14). It's essential to book ahead (tel. 030/213–1810). The women are for real next door (No. 15) at the **Scotch Club 13.**

Berlin is a major center for jazz in Europe. If you're visiting in the fall, call the tourist office for details of the annual international Jazz Fest. Throughout the year a variety of jazz groups appear at the **Eierschale** (Podbielskiallee 50) and **Quasimodo** (Kantstr. 12a).

Nightlife in east Berlin offers just as much excitement and variety as that in the west, and new bars and clubs open almost weekly. Most of the action is in Mitte along Oranienburgerstrasse and points north—**Zosch** (Tucholskystr. 30) has a great basement bar—and in Prenzlauerberg along Knaackstrasse and around Kollwitzplatz **Café Westfall** (Kollwitzstr. 64) is one of few places left over from Communist days. For clubs with music and atmosphere, try one of the following: **Checkpoint** (Leipzigerstr. 55); **Franz** (Schönhauser Allee 36–39); **Knaack** (Greifswalderstr. 224); **Sophienklubb** (Sophienstr. 6); **Tacheles** (Oranienburgerstr. 53–56).

Saxony and Thuringia

Saxony and Thuringia—just their names conjure up images of kingdoms and forest legends, of cultural riches and booming industrial enterprises. Today's reality is markedly less glamorous. Isolated from the West for decades, these two regions in eastern Germany are now struggling to make the transition from state-planned economies to a free-market system. Slowly, progress is being made, thanks to massive injections of cash from the federal government and the arrival of foreign and western German investors. But many people have been made jobless in the process. In January 1992, the opening up of the "Stasi" secret police files revealed the full horror and extent of former East Germany's monitoring of its citizens' lives. Closely tied politically and economically to the former Soviet Union for 45 years, many eastern Germans remain uncomfortable with their newly won freedoms and uncertain about the future. In Saxony, though, people seem happy enough with their new "Freistaat Sachsen" title, something they share with the Free State of Bavaria.

Dresden was once the capital of the kingdom of Saxony, and no city could be prouder of its history. The sculpture of August the Strong atop his horse was back in its original place many years before East Berlin, remembering its Prussian past, removed the statue of Frederick the Great from its hiding place and put it back on the Unter den Linden in the late 1970s. Even in its darker postwar moments, the glory of Saxony was never completely extinguished. Dresden now attracts millions of visitors from around the world, all eager to view its cultural treasures.

Thuringia's fame, it is sometimes said, begins and ends with its vast green forests, an unfair assessment, given its many other historical facets and that for centuries it was the home of dozens of kingdoms. Back in the 14th century, Thuringia was known as the Rynestig or Rennsteig (literally, fast trail), when it attracted traders from the dark forested depths of the Thuringian Wald (Woods) to the prospering towns of Erfurt (today the state capital), Eisenach, and Weimar, then already 600 years old. It was in Weimar that the privy councillor and poet, Johann Wolfgang von Goethe, was inspired by the pristine beauties of the 168 kilometers (104 miles) of the Rennsteig in 1777 to write that "tranquility crowns all its peaks." Goethe enjoyed his time in Weimar—he stayed 57 years—as did his friend and contemporary Friedrich von Schiller, professor and poet, who taught history in Jena but preferred Weimar's cultured atmosphere in which to live with his family. The Hungarian composer Franz Liszt regularly spent the summer in Weimar, where he conducted the royal court's orchestra and championed the works of his friend and son-in-law, Richard Wagner, who was born in Leipzig. But it is Goethe who reigns supreme in Weimar. His face graces many a monument,

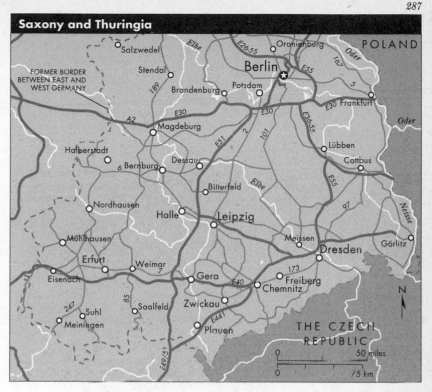

and his sayings adorn the town's libraries. Even Weimar's picturesque riverside park, the Park an der Ilm, was planned by him.

Tourist attractions in the east, many of them long neglected, are being given a face-lift by the eager tourist boards that replaced the unwieldy Communist-era bureaucracy. Hotels are popping up at a
giddy rate, and virtually all but the cheapest of them incorporate facilities still relatively rare in the West—fax and modem outlets in
each room, for instance, and satellite TV. The phone systems of re-
unified Germany have been completely integrated. Rail and road
communications are still being improved, however. Trains slow to an
amble where the lines are being replaced or electrification installed.
And long delays can occur on autobahns where major road works are
in progress. Rail and bus travel is cheaper in the east, although fare-
consolidation is progressing. Other prices have generally crept up to
western levels, although bargains can still be found: In country
districts, a lunch-time menu may cost less than DM 10. The changes
can mean that addresses and telephone and fax numbers differ from
those obtained by us at press time (many streets and squares named
after Communist-era events or personalities are being redesig-
nated, for example).

We suggest that you contact the German National Tourist Office for
the latest information or phone ahead to confirm information locally.

Getting Around

By Train In Saxony and Thuringia, there are generally two types of trains:
fast, shown as D in the timetables, and regular/local services, indicated with an E. But the Euro-City and InterCity services of the
Deutsche Bahn are being progressively incorporated into the system in eastern Germany. The fast categories have varying supple-
mentary fares; local trains do not. Most trains have first- and
second-class cars, and many have either dining or buffet cars. Long-

distance trains have first- and second-class sleeping compartments and couchettes. It is advisable to make advance reservations at major stations or through travel agents because trains are often full. Railway buffs will want to ride the narrow-gauge lines in the mountainous south.

By Bus and Streetcar Within Saxony and Thuringia, most areas are accessible by bus, but service is infrequent and serves chiefly to connect with rail lines. Check schedules carefully. In Dresden, Leipzig, and Weimar, public transport in the form of buses and streetcars is cheap and efficient.

Tourist Information

Dresden (Tourist Information, Pragerstr. 10–11, tel. 0351/495–5025). A museum card good for one day and covering admission to all museums in the Staatlichen Kunstsammlungen, including the museums at the Albertinum and the Zwinger, is available at the participating institutions. The card costs DM 8 for adults, DM 4 for children.

Weimar (Box 647, Markstr. 4, tel. 03643/24000).

Exploring Dresden

Dresden, superbly located on the banks of the river Elbe, suffered appalling damage during World War II, but has been lovingly rebuilt. The city is compact and easy to explore, with Italianate influences everywhere, most pronounced in the glorious Rococo and Baroque buildings in pastel shades of yellow and green.

The **Semper Opera House,** at Theaterplatz in the center of Dresden, is a mecca for music lovers. Named after its architect, Gottfried Semper, the theater has premiered Wagner's *The Flying Dutchman* and *Tannhäuser* (conducted by the composer) and nine operas of Richard Strauss, including *The Rosenkavalier*. Dating from 1871–78 (the first building by Semper burned down in 1869), the opera house fell victim to the 1945 bombings. Semper's architectural drawings had been preserved, so it was rebuilt on the same lines and reopened with much pomp in 1985. At concert intermissions, guests often mingle on the high-up balconies, which have breathtaking views of the city. Tickets are in great demand at the Semper (tel. 0351/48420, fax 0351/484–2692); try booking through your travel agent before you go or ask at your hotel. As a last resort, line up at the Abendkasse (Evening Box Office) half an hour before the performance—a limited number of tickets are always available.

From Theaterplatz, stroll down the Sophienstrasse to the largely 18th-century **Zwinger** palace complex, one of the city's cultural wonders in the heart of the Altstadt. Completely enclosing a central courtyard of lawns and pools, the complex consists of six linked pavilions decorated with a riot of garlands, nymphs, and other Baroque ornamentation and sculpture, all created under the direction of Matthaus Daniel Pöppelmann.

The southwestern side is taken up by another Semper creation, the **Sempergalerie,** with a collection of Old Master paintings, including important works by Correggio, Dürer, Holbein the Younger, Raphael, Rembrandt, and Vermeer. You'll also find examples of Canaletto's Dresden vistas. The two other museums within the complex are the Porzellansammlung (Porcelain Collection) and the Mathematisch-Physikalischer Salon, which displays fascinating old scientific instruments. *Sempergalerie admission: DM 7 adults, DM 1.50 children. Open Tues.–Sun. 10–6. Porzellansammlung admission: DM 3 adults, DM 1.50 children. Open Fri.–Wed. 10–6. Mathematisch-Physikalischer Salon admission: DM 3 adults, DM 1.50 children. Open Fri.–Wed. 9:30–5.*

After leaving the Zwinger, head eastward along Ernst-Thälmann-Strasse and turn into the **Neumarkt** (New Market), which is, despite its name, the historic heart of old Dresden. The ruined shell on the right is all that remains of the mighty Baroque **Frauenkirche,** once Germany's greatest Protestant church, after the bombing raids of February 1945. Its jagged, precariously tilting walls had been left as a memorial, a poignant reminder of the evils of war. The reconstruction in progress is scheduled for completion in 2000.

Behind the Frauenkirche looms Dresden's leading art museum, the **Albertinum.** This large, imperial-style building gets its name from Saxony's King Albert, who between 1884 and 1887 converted a royal arsenal into a convenient setting for the treasures he and his forebears had collected.

Permanent exhibits at the Albertinum include the **Gemäldegalerie Alte Meister/Neue Meister,** which displays outstanding 19th- and 20th-century European pictures that include French Impressionist and Postimpressionist works and Caspar David Friedrich's haunting *Das Kreuz im Gebirge.*

Despite the rich array of paintings, it is the **Grüne Gewölbe** (Green Vault) that invariably attracts the most attention. Named after a green room in the palace of August the Strong, this part of the Albertinum (entered from Georg-Treu-Platz) contains an exquisite collection of unique objets d'art fashioned from gold, silver, ivory, amber, and other precious and semiprecious materials. Among them is the world's biggest "green" diamond, 41 carats in weight, and a dazzling group of tiny, gem-studded figures, some of which can be admired only through a magnifying glass. Somewhat larger and less delicate is the drinking bowl of Ivan the Terrible, perhaps the most sensational of the treasures to be found in this extraordinary museum. Next door is the **Skulpturensammlung** (Sculpture Collection), which includes ancient Egyptian and classical objects and Italian Mannerist works. *Tel. 0351/495-3056. Albertinum admission: DM 7 adults, DM 3.50 children. Open Fri.–Wed. 10–6.*

The southern exit of the Albertinum, at Augustus-Strasse, brings you back to the Neumarkt and leads you to another former royal building now serving as a museum, the 16th-century **Johanneum,** once the royal stables. Instead of horses, the Johanneum now houses the Verkehrsmuseum (Transport Museum), a collection of historical vehicles, including vintage automobiles and engines. *Augustusstr. 1, tel. 0351/495-3002. Admission: DM 4 adults, DM 2 children. Admission half price on Fri. Open Tues.–Sun. 10–5.*

On the outside wall of the Johanneum is a prime example of Meissen porcelain art: a 102-meter-long (335-foot-long) painting on Meissen tiles of a royal procession. More than 100 members of the royal Saxon house of Wettin, half of them on horseback, are depicted on the giant jigsaw made up of 25,000 porcelain tiles, painted from 1904 to 1907.

Follow this unusual procession to the end and you arrive at the former royal palace, the **Herzogschloss,** now restored to its original Renaissance magnificence. The main gate of the palace, the Georgentor, has an enormous statue of the fully armed Saxon Count George. *Sophienstr., tel. 0351/495-3110. Admission: DM 5 adults, DM 2.50 children. Open Mon., Tues., Fri.–Sun. 9–5, Thurs. 9–6.*

Standing next to the Herzogschloss is the **Katholische Hofkirche,** also known as the Cathedral of St. Trinitas, Saxony's largest church. The son of August the Strong, Frederick Augustus II (ruled 1733–63) brought architects and builders from Italy to construct this Catholic church, consecrated in 1754, in a city that had been the first large center of Lutheranism. In the cathedral's crypt are the tombs of 49 Saxon rulers and a precious vessel containing the heart of August the Strong.

Moving away from the treasures near the river, along the St. Petersburger Strasse, make a left into Lingnerplatz. The **Deutsches Hygiene-Museum** (German Health Museum) reflects Dresden's important role in the history of medicine. The most famous object is a glass model of a human, which caused a sensation when it was first displayed in 1930. *Lingnerplatz 1, tel. 0351/48460. Admission: DM 4 adults, DM 2 children. Open Tues.–Sun. 9–5.*

Exploring Weimar

Weimar, wedged between Erfurt and Jena and southwest of Leipzig, sits prettily on the Ilm River between the Ettersberg and Vogtland hills and has a place in German political and cultural history out of all proportion to its size (population 63,000). Its civic history, not long by German standards, began as late as 1410, but by the early 19th century Weimar had become one of Europe's most important cultural centers, where Goethe and Schiller were neighbors; Carl Maria von Weber wrote some of his best music; and Liszt was director of music, presenting the first performance of Wagner's *Lohengrin*. Walter Gropius founded his Staatliche Bauhaus design school in Weimar in 1919, and it was there, in 1919–20, that the German National Assembly drew up the constitution of the Weimar Republic. After the collapse of the ill-fated Weimar government, Hitler chose the city as the site for the first national congress of his new Nazi party, and later built—or forced prisoners to build for him—the notorious Buchenwald concentration camp on the outskirts of Weimar.

Goethe spent 57 years in Weimar, 47 of them in the house that has since become a shrine for millions of visitors. **Goethehaus** is two blocks south of Theaterplatz on a street called Frauenplan. The museum it contains is testimony not only to the great man's literary might, but to his interest in the sciences, particularly medicine, and his administrative skills (and frustrations) as Weimar's exchequer. Here you find the desk at which Goethe stood to write (he liked to work standing up), his own paintings (he was an accomplished watercolorist), and the modest bed on which he died. *Frauenplan 1, tel. 03643/5450. Admission: DM 8 adults, children under 16 free. Open Mar.–Oct., Tues.–Sun. 9–5; Nov.–Feb., Tues.–Sun. 9–4.*

On a tree-shaded square around the corner from Goethe's house is Schiller's green-shuttered home, **Schillerhaus**, in which he and his family spent a happy, all-too-brief three years (Schiller died there in 1805). The poet and playwright's study, dominated by the desk where he probably completed *William Tell*, is tucked underneath the mansard roof. Much of the remaining furniture and the collection of books were added later, although they all date from around Schiller's time. *Neugasse 2, tel. 03643/62041. Admission: DM 6 adults, children under 16 free. Open Mar.–Oct., Wed.–Mon. 9–5; Nov.–Feb., Wed.–Mon. 9–4.*

Another historic house worth visiting is found on the **Marktplatz**, the central town square. It was the home of the painter Lucas Cranach the Elder, who lived there during his last year, 1552–53. Its wide, imposing facade, richly decorated, bears the coat of arms of the Cranach family. In its ground floor it houses a modern art gallery open to the public.

Around the corner and to the left is Weimar's 16th-century castle, the **Stadtschloss**, with its restored classical staircase, festival hall, and falcon gallery. The castle houses an impressive art collection, including several fine paintings by Cranach the Elder and many early 20th-century works by such artists as Böcklin, Liebermann, and Beckmann. *Burgplatz. Admission: DM 3 adults, DM 2 children. Open Tues.–Sun. 10–6.*

In Weimar's old, reconstructed town center stands the Late Gothic **Herderkirche,** with its large winged altarpiece started by Lucas Cranach the Elder and finished by his son in 1555. A short walk south, past Goethehaus and across Wieland Platz, brings you to the cemetery, **Historischer Friedhof** (Historic Cemetery), where Goethe and Schiller are buried. Their tombs are in the classical-style chapel. The Goethe-Schiller vault can be visited daily (except Tuesday) 9–1 and 2–5; winter 9–1 and 2–4.

On the other side of the Ilm, amid meadowlike parkland, is Goethe's beloved **Gartenhaus** (Garden House), where he wrote much poetry and began his masterpiece *Iphigenie auf Tauris* (admission: DM 4 adults, DM 1.50 children; open daily 9–noon and 1–5, winter 9–noon, 1–4). Goethe is said to have felt very close to nature here, and you can soak up the same rural atmosphere today on footpaths along the peaceful little river, where time seems to have stood still. Just across the river from the Gartenhaus is a generous German tribute to another literary giant, William Shakespeare: a 1904 statue that depicts him jauntily at ease on a marble plinth, looking remarkably at home in his foreign surroundings.

North of Weimar, in the Ettersberg Hills, is a blighted patch of land that contrasts cruelly with the verdant countryside that so inspired Goethe: **Buchenwald,** where, from 1937 to 1945, 65,000 men, women, and children from 35 countries met their deaths through disease, starvation, and gruesome medical experiments. Each person is commemorated today by a small stone placed on the outlines of the former barracks (no longer existing) and by a massive memorial tower. A free bus to Buchenwald leaves from Weimar's main train station. Also leaving from the station are bus tours of the camp, organized by the Weimar tourist information office. The buses depart hourly from 9 to 4 daily. *Campsite admission free. Open Tues.–Sun. 9:45–4:30.*

Dining and Lodging

Many of the best restaurants in Saxony and Thuringia are in the larger hotels. You can expect hearty food in both regions. Roast beef, venison, and wild boar are often on Saxon menus, and in the Vogtland you'll find *Kaninchentopf* (rabbit stew). In Thuringia, regional specialties include *Thüringer Rehbraten* (roast venison); roast mutton served in a delicate cream sauce; tasty grilled Thuringian sausages; *Thüringer Sauerbraten mit Klössen* (roast corned beef with dumplings); *Börenschinken* (cured ham); and roast mutton shepherd-style, with beans and vegetables. The light Meissner Wein, wine from the Meissen region, is splendid.

The choice of hotels in Saxony and Thuringia remains limited, and although private householders may now rent rooms, these are also hard to come by, because the demand is far greater than the supply. Contact the local tourist information offices for names of bed-and-breakfasts. Very few inexpensive hotels exist in Weimar. Your best bet is to arrange a private room through the local tourist office.

For details and price-category definitions, *see* Dining and Lodging *in* Staying in Germany, *above*.

Dresden **Kügelnhaus.** A combination grill–coffee shop–restaurant–beer cel-
Dining lar, Kügelnhaus is extremely popular, so get there early or reserve your table in advance. You'll find the usual hefty local dishes, but prepared with a deft touch. *Hauptstr. 13, tel. 0351/52791. Reservations advised. AE, DC, MC, V. $$*
Haus Altmarkt. The choice of cuisine in this busy corner of the colonnaded Altmarkt is enormous—from McDonald's to the upscale Amadeus restaurant on the first floor. In between are a jolly bistrolike café and an atmospheric vaulted beer tavern, Zum

Humpen, with a secluded, intimate bar. Wherever you choose to eat you'll find midday menus under DM 20. In warm weather you can eat outside on a terrace and watch the marketplace bustle. *Am Altmarkt 1, tel. 0351/495–1212. No reservations. No credit cards. $–$$*

Dining and **Linie 6.** The "Line 6" takes its name from the tram line outside the
Lodging front door that provided some of the ancient tram cars in this highly original hotel's museum. Tram-car anecdotes also form the basis of a very amusing nightly cabaret program in the hotel's nightclub (although proficiency in German helps you enjoy the show in full). The Linie 6 restaurant is famous beyond Dresden, chiefly for its seemingly endless Saxon buffet, with fine regional specialties and contrastingly huge joints of meat. Advance reservations for the hotel are essential. *Schaufussstrasse 24, tel. and fax 0351/30268. 3 rooms, 4 suites. AE, MC. $$*

Pillnitzer Elbblick. This is an "insider's address," so advance reservation is essential. The best way to arrive is by boat, at the Weisse Flotte landing stage in front of the hotel. Reserve a room overlooking the Elbe and Dresden's Elbe island or the neighboring Pillnitz palace, and book a window table in the Zum Dampschiff ("Steamship") restaurant. Don't let the view distract you, though, from the European specialties, from Hungarian paprika-risotto to Greek-style lamb. Germany makes its contribution with fresh fish. *Söbringenerstr. 2, tel. 0351/39286, fax 0351/39222. 7 rooms with bath. AE, MC. $$*

Lodging **Ibis Hotels Bastei/Königstein/Lilienstein.** This is three hotels in one, all fronting Dresden's central pedestrian mall. The Ibis group, since acquiring the Communist-era high-rise hotels, has accomplished a major transformation, making the rooms stylish and comfortable, with friendly pastel tones matched by light wood veneers and bright prints on the walls. All of them have satellite TV. Nonsmokers can choose from more than 60 special rooms. *Prager Str. 3–9, tel. 0351/485–6666, fax 0351/485–6667. 897 rooms, 21 suites, all with bath. Facilities: 3 restaurants, bar. AE, DC, MC, V. $$*

Weimar **Ratskeller.** This historic restaurant is in the cellar of the Stadthaus
Dining (City House), a Renaissance building dating from the 17th century. The wholesome regional fare includes grilled sausages with sauerkraut and onions and Thuringian onion soup. *Markt 10, tel. 03643/64142. AE, DC, MC, V. $$*

Dining and **Hotel Thüringen.** The plush elegance of the Thüringen's restaurant,
Lodging complete with velvet drapes and chandeliers, makes it seem expensive, but the menu of international and regional dishes is moderately priced. An excellent Thüringen roast beef, for instance, costs less than DM 20. There are 29 comfortable rooms, all of them also in the same price bracket. *Brennerstr. 42, tel. 03643/3675 or 62900. AE, DC, MC, V. $$*

Lodging **Hotel Amalienhof.** The historic Amalienhof (built in 1826 and now protected by a preservation order) is run by a church-based organization, though only a discreetly placed crucifix betrays the fact. Otherwise, this moderately priced hotel is a worldly and comfortable retreat with a quiet location only a few steps from Weimar's main attractions. Rooms are tastefully decorated and furnished in pastel shades and cherry wood, with a choice antique or two placed here and there. *Amalienstr. 2, tel. 03643/5490, fax 03643/549–110. 22 rooms with shower. Facilities: restaurant, wine cellar. MC. $$*

10 Great Britain

Great Britain can be an expensive destination for a vacation, but you don't have to rule it out. There are many ways to make your budget more elastic, and now that the dollar-pound exchange rate has swung back to a slightly more realistic level for Americans, this has become easier.

To make a trip work at a reasonable cost, here are two very important strategies: Book as many lodgings as far ahead as you possibly can. Hotel space will be the biggest component of your travel costs. Believe us, you can mortgage your soul at British hotels. They are among the highest priced in the world and far too often do not give true value for the exorbitant sums they charge. If you manage to find reasonable places and book most of them ahead, then you already have one foot up in controlling your vacation costs. Keep the B&B scene in mind when searching for lodgings. In Britain, B&Bs tend not to be the chichi upscale option they are in the States, but range from guest rooms in somebody's home to fairly modest hotels with few facilities. The second saving point is to invest in a BritRail Pass before you leave home (a Eurail Card, too, if you are going on to mainland Europe). The economy in travel costs and in freedom of movement the passes can represent is enormous.

Great Britain is an ideal holiday destination for anyone with a feeling for the past. Here you'll find soaring medieval cathedrals, tributes to the faith of the churchmen and craftsmen who built them, but terribly heavy financial burdens for their descendents; grand country mansions of the aristocracy, filled with treasures, among them paintings, furniture, and tapestries, and set in elegantly landscaped grounds; grim fortified castles, their gray stone walls still fronting a dangerous world; and endless gardens, rich with lilies and roses, tended by generations of dedicated gardeners who spend more time and money on the plants than they do on their houses.

All these can be visited by everyone, either free or for only a small entrance fee. Make sure, though, before you start on your trip, that you are equipped with as many membership tickets as you can get, from English Heritage, National Trust, and so on. The saving in en-

Great Britain

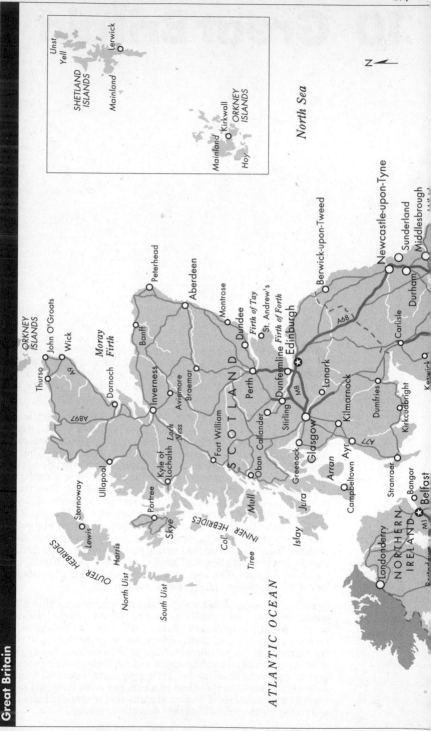

N

SHETLAND ISLANDS

Unst
Yell
Lerwick

Mainland

ORKNEY ISLANDS
Mainland Kirkwall
Hoy

North Sea

Berwick-upon-Tweed

Newcastle-upon-Tyne
Sunderland
Middlesbrough

Durham

A68

Carlisle

Keswick

Peterhead

Aberdeen

Montrose

Banff

Dundee
Firth of Tay
St. Andrew's
Firth of Forth
Edinburgh

ORKNEY ISLANDS
John O'Groats
Wick
Thurso

Moray Firth

Dornoch

A9

A897

Inverness
Aviemore
Braemar
Loch Ness

S C O T L A N D

Perth
Dunfermline
M9

Lanark

Kyle of
Lochalsh
Fort William

Stirling
Glasgow
Kilmarnock

Ullapool

Oban Callander

Dumfries

Portree

Greenock
Ayr

Kirkcudbright

Skye

Mull

Jura

Arran
A77

INNER HEBRIDES

Islay

Campbeltown

Stranraer

Bangor

Col

Tiree

Londonderry

N O R T H E R N
I R E L A N D

Belfast

M1

OUTER HEBRIDES

Stornoway
Lewis
Harris

North Uist

South Uist

A T L A N T I C   O C E A N

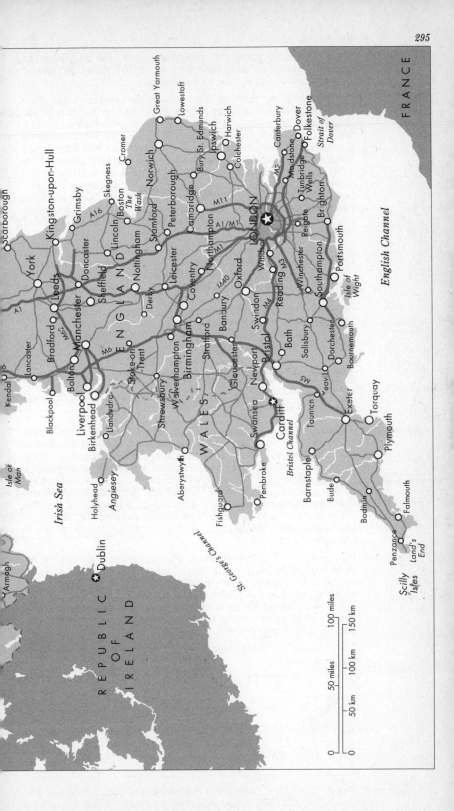

trance fees to the properties under the control of these groups can be significant. Most cathedrals are free, though even they request contributions to offset their vast expenses.

But Britain is not just one huge historic theme park. Many of its most profound pleasures are to be found in wandering through the changing countryside, at any season of the year. Taking a bus for a few hours deep into the open spaces outside a main town can reveal much about the essence of the land and its people. A short ride, for instance, from York, will take you through long stretches of wild, heather-covered moorland, ablaze with color in the fall, or past the steep, sheep-covered mountainsides of the Dales, cut by deep valleys and scattered with stone-built hamlets. If you take a bus from Stratford, you will find a secret world of villages hidden in orchards and surrounded by fields that have been worked for hundreds of years.

If you are centering your trip on London, you can see a lot for free, from the famous parks to some of the world's greatest art collections. The city's museums are starting to charge for entry, but the costs of admission are unlikely to become too burdensome. Try the theater ticket booth in Leicester Square for cut-price tickets, not for the sellout shows, but for some good runners-up. And you will be surprised, too, how reasonably priced many of the concerts are when you compare them with similar tickets back home—even after taking the rate of exchange into account.

Essential Information

Before You Go

When to Go The main tourist season runs from mid-April to mid-October. In recent years, however, parts of the winter—especially December—have been almost as busy. Winter is also the height of London's theater, ballet, and opera season. Springtime reveals the countryside at its most verdant and beautiful, while fall offers soft vistas of muted, golden color. September and October are the months to visit the northern moorlands and Scottish highlands, while June is best for Wales and the Lake District. Most British people take their vacations during July and August, when costs are high and accommodations are at a premium.

Climate On the whole, Britain's climate is a temperate one, although summers have been fairly hot in recent years. Wherever you are and whatever the season, be prepared for sudden changes. What begins as a brilliant, sunny day often turns into a damp and dismal one by lunchtime. Take an umbrella and raincoat wherever you go, particularly in Scotland, where the temperatures are somewhat cooler and the rainfall is more plentiful.

The following are the average daily maximum and minimum temperatures for London.

Jan.	43F	6C	May	62F	17C	Sept.	65F	19C
	36	2		47	8		52	11
Feb.	44F	7C	June	69F	20C	Oct.	58F	14C
	36	2		53	12		46	8
Mar.	50F	10C	July	71F	22C	Nov.	50F	10C
	38	3		56	13		42	6
Apr.	56F	13C	Aug.	71F	22C	Dec.	45F	7C
	42	6		56	13		38	3

Currency The British unit of currency is the pound sterling, divided into 100 pence (p). Bills are issued in denominations of 5, 10, 20, and 50 pounds (£). Coins are £1, 50p, 20p, 10p, 5p, 2p, and 1p. Scottish banks issue Scottish currency, of which all coins and notes—with the exception of the £1 notes—are accepted in England. At press time (summer 1995), the exchange rate was approximately $1.60 to the pound.

Traveler's checks are widely accepted in Britain, and many banks, hotels, and shops offer currency-exchange facilities. You will probably lose from 1¢ to 4¢ on the dollar, however, depending on where you change them; banks offer the best rates. In London and other big cities, bureaux de change abound, but it definitely pays to shop around: They usually have a minimum charge of £1 and often a great deal more. Credit cards are universally accepted. The most popular are MasterCard and Visa.

What It Will Cost In general, transportation in Britain is expensive in comparison with other countries. You would be well advised to take advantage of the many reductions and special fares available on trains, buses, and subways. Always ask about them when you buy your ticket. Gasoline prices are about the same as those on the Continent.

London now ranks with Tokyo as one of the world's most expensive hotel capitals. Finding budget accommodations—especially during July and August—can be difficult. Many London hotels offer special off-season (October–March) rates, however, and the recession has forced them into offering special rates all year round. Dining out, even in moderate restaurants, can be startlingly expensive, but a large number of pubs offer excellent food at reasonable prices, and fast-food facilities are widespread. Many ethnic restaurants also tend to be better value for your money.

Remember that the gulf between prices in the capital and outside is wide. Be prepared to pay a value-added tax (VAT) of 17½% on almost everything you buy; in most cases it is added to the advertised price.

Sample Prices For London: cup of coffee, £1–£2; pint of beer, £1.70–£2.20; glass of wine, £2–£5; soda, 60p; 1-mile taxi ride, £2.50; ham sandwich, £1.75.

Customs on Arrival There are two levels of duty-free allowance for people entering the United Kingdom: one, for goods bought outside the European Union (EU) or for goods bought in a duty-free shop within the EU; the other, for goods bought in an EU country but not in a duty-free shop.

In the first category, you may import duty-free 200 cigarettes or 100 cigarillos or 50 cigars or 250 grams of tobacco *(Note:* If you live outside Europe, these allowances are doubled), plus 1 liter of alcoholic drinks over 22% volume or 2 liters of alcoholic drinks not over 22% volume or fortified or sparkling wine, plus 2 liters of still table wine, plus 60 cc/ml of perfume, plus 250 cc/ml of toilet water, plus other goods to the value of £36.

In the second category you may import duty-free a considerable amount of liquor and tobacco—almost as much as you could possibly want—for example, 800 cigarettes and 110 liters of beer! New regulations in January 1993 removed almost all customs barriers within the EU.

In addition, no animals or pets of any kind may be brought into the United Kingdom without a six-month quarantine.

Getting Around

By Train Although it has the (recently less deserved) reputation of being unreliable, and is shamefully overpriced, Britain's rail service is one of the fastest, safest, and most comfortable in the world. At press time, trains were still run by the state-owned **British Rail,** although this is due to change, as the various routes are sold off to private operators. British Rail expects half its lines to be franchised by mid-1996.

The country's principal—and most efficient—service is the Inter-City network, linking London with every major city in the country. The most modern trains travel up to 125 mph and offer comfortable, air-conditioned cars, with restaurant or buffet facilities. Local train services are not quite as reliable, particularly around congested city centers such as London. In general, seat reservations are not necessary except during peak vacation periods and on popular medium- and long-distance routes. Reserving a standard-class seat costs £1.

Fares British Rail fares are expensive. However, the network does offer a wide range of ticket reductions, and these can make a tremendous difference. The information office in each station is generally the most reliable source of information. Information and tickets can also be obtained from British Rail Travel Centers within the larger train stations and from travel agents displaying the British Rail logo.

One of the best bargains available to overseas visitors is the **BritRail Pass** or the **BritRail Youth Pass,** the U.K. equivalent of the Eurail Pass. It provides unlimited travel over the entire British Rail network (and associated ferry and bus routes) for periods of 8, 14, or 22 days, or one month. The cost of a **BritRail Adult Pass** for 8 days is $230 standard and $315 first class; for 15 days, $355 standard and $515 first class; for 22 days, $445 and $645; and for a month, $520 and $750. The **Youth Pass,** for those aged 16 to 25, provides unlimited second-class travel and costs $189 for 8 days, $280 for 15 days, $355 for 22 days, and $415 for one month. The **Senior Citizen Pass,** for passengers over 60, costs $209 for 8 days (first class $295), $320 for 15 days (first class $479), $399 for 22 days (first class $585), and $465 for one month (first class $675). There is also a **Flexi Pass,** which allows 4, 8, or 15 days' travel in one month. These passes can be purchased only outside Britain, either in the United States, before you leave, or in one of 46 other countries. British Rail has its own information offices in New York, Los Angeles, Chicago, Dallas, Vancouver, and Toronto. The quoted prices are in U.S. dollars. Canadian tickets are slightly higher-priced.

Note that the Eurail Pass is not valid for travel in Britain.

If you are planning to travel only short distances, be sure to buy inexpensive same-day return tickets. These cost only slightly more than ordinary one-way, standard-class tickets but can be used only after 9:30 AM and on weekends. Other special offers are regional **Rover** tickets, giving unlimited travel within local areas, and **Saver** returns, allowing greatly reduced round-trip travel during off-peak periods. For information about routes and fares, contact the **British Travel Centre** (12 Regent Street, London SW1Y 4PQ, no phone). Also inquire at main rail stations for details about reduced-price tickets to specific destinations.

By Plane For a comparatively small country, Britain offers an extensive network of internal air routes. These are run by half a dozen airlines. Hourly shuttle services operate every day between London and Glasgow, Edinburgh, Belfast, and Manchester. Seats are available on a no-reservations basis, and you can generally check in about half an hour before flight departure time. Keep in mind, however, that Britain's internal air services are not as competitive as those in the United States. And with modern, fast trains and relatively short distances, it is often much cheaper—and not much more time consuming—to travel by train.

By Bus Buses provide the most economical form of public transportation in Britain. Prices are invariably half that of train tickets, and the network is just as extensive. In recent years, both short- and long-distance buses have improved immeasurably in speed, comfort, and frequency. There is one important semantic difference to keep in mind when discussing bus travel in Britain. Buses (either double- or single-decker) are generally part of the local transportation system in towns and cities and make frequent stops. Coaches, on the other hand, are comparable to American Greyhound buses and are used only for long-distance travel.

National Express offers the largest number of routes of any coach operator in Britain. It also offers a variety of discount tickets, including the **BritExpress Card** for overseas visitors, which covers all the National Express and Scottish Citylink services, costs £7, and entitles you to 30% off standard fares throughout England and Wales and selected services in Scotland. You can buy it from travel agents in the United States; in London, at the Victoria Coach Station, Buckingham Palace Road, SW1 9TP; or at main train stations in Edinburgh and Glasgow. Call the National Express Information Office at Victoria Coach Station (tel. 0171/730–0202) or **Eastern Scottish** (St. Andrew Sq., Edinburgh, tel. 0131/556–8464) for information.

One bargain that is well worth considering is the **Tourist Trail Pass.** It provides *unlimited* travel for 3, 5, 8, or 15 days, and costs £49, £79, £119, and £179, respectively (using the BritExpress Card: £39, £65, £95, and £145). There are time limits for completion of travel.

The bus companies of Britain have been denationalized for some years now, and they often duplicate routes. However, they almost all offer *Rover* or *Explorer* tickets to their areas, which can be a significant savings.

By Boat Britain offers more than 2,400 kilometers (1,500 miles) of navigable inland waterways—rivers, lakes, canals, locks, and loughs—for leisure travel. Particular regions, such as the Norfolk Broads in East Anglia, the Severn Valley in the West Country, and the sea lochs and canals of Scotland, are especially popular among the nautically minded. Although there are no regularly scheduled waterborne services, hundreds of yachts, canal boats, and motor cruises are available throughout the year. The **British Tourist Authority's** booklet *U.K. Waterway Holidays* is a good source of information. You can also contact the **Inland Waterways Association** (114 Regents Park Rd., London NW1 8UQ, tel. 0171/586–2510) or the **British Waterways Board** (Willow Grange, Church Rd., Watford WD1 3QA, tel. 01923/226422). A knowledgeable British company is **UK Waterway Holidays** (1 Port Hill, Hertford SG14 1PJ), which is in touch with several U.S. firms, and does cruises on waterways all over England and Wales.

By Bicycle Cycling provides an excellent way to see the countryside, and most towns—including London—offer bike-rental facilities. Any bike shop or tourist information center should be able to direct you to the nearest rental firm. Rental fees generally run from £15 per day, plus a fairly large deposit, though this can often be put on your credit card. If you're planning a tour and would like information on rental shops and special holidays for cyclists, contact a British Tourist Authority office in the United States before you leave home. Another source for maps and lists of cycle-rental shops is the **Cyclists' Touring Club** (Cotterell House, 69 Meadowrow, Godalming, Surrey GU7 3HS, tel. 01483/417217).

On Foot Many organizations conduct group walking holidays during the summer months. These are especially popular in the Welsh mountains, the Lake District, Dartmoor, and Exmoor. Details are available from the British Tourist Authority. **The Countryside Commission** (John Dower House, Crescent Place, Cheltenham Glos., GL50 3LR, tel. 01242/521381) also has many useful publications and information about national trails.

Staying in Great Britain

Telephones   In spring 1995, an extra digit was added to telephone numbers throughout Britain (five cities got a brand new area code). This may not yet be reflected on every business card or listing, so if a phone number doesn't work, try adding a "1" after the initial "0."

Local Calls   Public telephones are plentiful in British cities, especially London, and you will find fewer these days out of order. Other than on the street, the best place to find a bank of pay phones is in a hotel or large post office; pubs usually have a pay phone, too. As part of Telecom's modernization efforts, the distinctive red phone booths are gradually being replaced by glass and steel cubicles, but the red boxes still remain in a lot of the country. The workings of coin-operated telephones vary, but there are usually intructions in each unit. Most take 10p, 20p, 50p, and £1 coins. A Phonecard is also available; it comes in denominations of 10, 20, 40, and 100 units and can be bought in a number of retail outlets. Cardphones are clearly marked with a special green insignia, and they will not accept coins.

A local call before 6 PM costs 15p for three minutes. It will cost 47p a minute to call the United States during the day. Each large city or region in Britain has its own numerical prefix, which is used only when you are dialing from outside the city. In provincial areas, the dialing codes for nearby towns are often posted in the booth, and some even list international codes.

International   The cheapest way to make an overseas call is to dial it yourself. But
Calls   be sure to have plenty of coins or Phonecards close at hand. After you have inserted the coins or card, dial 010, the international code, then the country code—for the United States, it is 1—followed by the area code and local number. To reach an **AT&T** long-distance operator, dial 0500–890011; for **MCI**, dial 0800890202, and for **Sprint**, dial 0800–890877 (from a British Telecom phone) or 0500890877 (from a Mercury Communications phone). To make a collect or other operator-assisted call, dial 155.

Country Code   When you're dialing overseas, the United Kingdom's country code is 44.

Operators and   For information anywhere in Britain, dial 192. For the operator, dial
Information   100, or 155 for the international operator.

Mail   Airmail letters to the United States and Canada cost 41p; postcards,
Postal Rates   35p; aerograms, 36p. Letters and postcards to Europe weighing up to 20 grams cost 30p (25p to EU-member countries). Letters within the United Kingdom: first class, 25p; second class and postcards, 19p. These rates may have increased by early 1996.

Receiving Mail   If you're uncertain where you'll be staying, you can arrange to have your mail sent to American Express, 6 Haymarket, London SW1Y 4BS. The service is free to cardholders; all others pay a small fee. You can also collect letters at London's main post office. Ask to have them sent to Poste Restante, Main Post Office, London. The point of collection is King Edward Building, King Edward Street, London EC1A 1AA, tel. 0171/239–5047. Hours are Monday, Tuesday, Thursday, and Friday 8:30 AM–6:30 PM; Wednesday 9 AM–6:30 PM; closed weekends. You'll need your passport or other official form of identification.

Shopping   Foreign visitors can avoid Britain's crippling 17½% value-added tax
VAT Refunds   (VAT) by taking advantage of a variety of special refund and export schemes. The easiest and most common way of getting a refund is the Over-the-Counter method. To qualify for this, you must buy goods worth £50 or more (stores vary; if you are from the EU, it can be as much as £420). The shopkeeper will attach a special paper—Form VAT 407—to the invoice, and upon leaving the United Kingdom, you present the goods, form, and invoice to the customs officer.

Allow plenty of time to do this at the airport. There are often long lines. The form is then returned to the store, and the refund forwarded to you, minus a small service charge. The Direct Export method is another option. With this method, you are also issued Form VAT 407, but your purchases are sent home separately, and upon returning home, you must have the form certified by customs or a notary public. You then return the form to the store, and your money is refunded.

Opening and Closing Times

Banks. Most banks are open weekdays 9:30–4:30. Some have extended hours on Thursday evenings, and a few are open on Saturday mornings.

Museums. Museum hours vary considerably from one part of the country to another. In large cities, most open on weekdays 10–5; many are also open on Sunday afternoons. The majority close one day a week. Holiday closings vary, so be sure to check individual listings. Be sure, also, to double-check the opening times of historic houses, especially if the visit involves a difficult trip. A considerable saving, if you are traveling with the family, is a **family ticket,** sold by many sites. This ticket usually covers two adults and two children at a greatly reduced fee.

Shops. Usual business hours are Monday–Saturday 9–5:30, but the relaxation of archaic Sunday trading laws in late 1994 means that shops may now open seven days a week, and many stores of all sizes have taken advantage of this opportunity. Outside the main centers, most shops observe an early closing day once a week, often Wednesday or Thursday; they close at 1 PM and do not reopen until the following morning. In small villages, many also close for lunch. In large cities—especially London—department stores stay open for late-night shopping (usually until 7:30 or 8) one day midweek.

National Holidays

In 1996: **England and Wales:** January 1, April 5 (Good Friday), April 8 (Easter Monday), May 1 (May Day), May 6 (Spring Bank Holiday), August 26 (Summer Bank Holiday), December 25–26. **Scotland:** January 1–2; April 5, 8; May 1 (May Day); May 27 (Spring Bank Holiday); August 26; December 25–26. Changing holidays in 1997 for **England and Wales:** March 28 (Good Friday), March 31 (Easter Monday), May 5 (May Day), May 26 (Spring Bank Holiday), August 25 (Summer Bank Holiday). **Scotland:** March 28, 31; May 5 (May Day); May 26 (Spring Bank Holiday); August 4 (Summer Bank Holiday).

Guided Tours

Guide Friday is one of Britain's leading guided tour operators. It has tours of all the towns we list outside London–Bath, Cambridge, Edinburgh, Oxford, Stratford-upon-Avon, Windsor, and York. Prices vary with the complexity of the route, but they are usually £4 or £4.50 for adults, £1 for children, and £3.50 for senior citizens. More than a million visitors take tours, which are an excellent way of seeing the sights in a short time. If you buy a Great British Cities ticket, you can take in five cities for £19, including London. Guide Friday telephone numbers are Bath, 01225/444102; Cambridge, 01223/62444; Edinburgh, 0131/556–2244; Stratford, 01789/294466; Windsor, 01753/855755; and York, 01904/640896.

Dining

British food at its best takes advantage of fresh, local ingredients, like wild salmon, spring lamb, orchard apples, plums, and pears, and endless varieties of seasonal vegetables. Good food can prove expensive, so check the prices displayed by law outside restaurants before committing yourself. Remember to explore pubs, B&Bs, ethnic restaurants—especially Indian ones—and the better chain restaurants for dining bargains.

Mealtimes

These vary somewhat, depending on the region of the country you are visiting. But in general, breakfast is served between 7:30 and 9 and lunch between noon and 2. Tea—a British tradition and often a meal in itself—is generally served between 4 and 5:30. Dinner or supper is served between 7:30 and 9:30, sometimes earlier, but rarely later outside the metropolitan areas. High tea, at about 6, replaces dinner in some areas, and in large cities, after-theater suppers are often available.

What to Wear Jacket and tie are suggested for the more formal restaurants in the top-price categories, but, in general, casual chic or informal dress is acceptable in almost all our affordable-choice restaurants.

Ratings Prices quoted here are per person and include a first course, a main course, and dessert, but not wine or service. Best bets are indicated by a star ★.

Category	London and Southern England	Other Areas
$$	£20–£30	£15–£25
$	£12–£20	£10–£15
¢	under £12	under £10

Lodging Britain offers a wide variety of accommodations, ranging from enormous, top-quality, top-price hotels to simple, intimate farmhouses and guest houses.

Hotels Expensive is practically the rule in Britain. You can pay an arm and a leg for a night's lodging if you don't check the prices in advance. We have included some hotels within a moderate price range among our selections: These tend to be guest houses masquerading under the name "hotel," but none the worse for that. You have to make a decision. Do you want to pay through the nose for a night's oblivion in fancy, overpriced surroundings, or would you rather spend your money while conscious. You will find that guest houses and B&Bs offer you the best value around.

A useful budget tip is to be sure to ask for a hotel's weekend rates. Hotels often reduce their rates by as much as a half on weekends, when their business guests have gone home to their families, leaving the hotels with many empty rooms. That way you can stay at a notable hotel in splendid comfort that you would not otherwise even contemplate.

Bed-and-Breakfasts B&Bs and their slightly snootier cousins, guest houses, are, generally speaking, private houses that take in guests. The heaviest concentrations of them in Britain are in the resorts where the Brits normally take their holidays: Brighton, Blackpool, Penzance, for example, but they are to be found everywhere in lesser numbers. Many of them are in big Victorian houses, built before the days of family planning, when there were bedrooms for rafts of children.

Many of our selections have only half the number of baths and showers than bedrooms, or even less. All these places will have communal bathrooms, and you can greatly reduce your expenditure by going for a room without bath. All rooms will almost certainly have a washbasin. You should work out the room-to-bath ratio. Three or four rooms to a bath is acceptable, six or more probably isn't.

B&Bs, as their name tells you, will provide breakfast, often far better than you will get in a full-fledged hotel. You will be fueled for a lot of sightseeing by an English breakfast!

All tourist offices have lists of B&Bs and guest houses, and the central organizations produce national lists. The English Tourist Board has an annual *Hotels and Guesthouses of England*, and a *Bed and Breakfast, Farmhouses, Inns and Hostels;* Wales does a *Bed and Breakfast* guide; Scotland's is called *Hotels and Guest Houses.*

Farmhouses Such accommodations have become increasingly popular in recent years. Farmhouses rarely offer professional hotel standards, but they have a special appeal: the rustic, rural experience. Prices are generally very reasonable. Ask for the British Tourist Authority booklets *Farmhouse Vacations* and *Stay on a Farm*. A car is vital for a successful farmhouse stay.

Holiday Furnished apartments, houses, cottages, and trailers are available
Cottages for weekly rental in all areas of the country. These vary from quaint, cleverly converted farmhouses to brand-new buildings set in scenic surroundings. For families and large groups, they offer the best value-for-money accommodations. Lists of rental properties are available free of charge from the British Tourist Authority. Discounts of up to 50% apply during the off-season (October to March).

University In larger cities and in some towns, certain universities offer their
Housing residence halls to paying vacationers. The facilities available are usually compact sleeping units, and they can be rented on a nightly basis. For information, contact the **British Universities Accommodation Consortium** (Box 880, University Park, Nottingham NG7 2RD, tel. 01602/504571).

Youth Hostels There are more than 350 youth hostels throughout England, Wales, and Scotland. They range from very basic to very good. Many are located in remote and beautiful areas; others can be found on the outskirts of large cities. Despite the name, there is no age restriction. The accommodations are inexpensive and generally reliable and usually include cooking facilities. For additional information, contact the **YHA Headquarters** (Trevelyan House, 8 St. Stephen's Hill, St. Albans, Hertfordshire AL1 2DY, tel. 01727/55215).

Camping Britain offers an abundance of campsites. Some are large and well equipped; others are merely small farmers' fields, offering primitive facilities. For information, contact the British Travel Authority in the United States or the **Camping and Caravan Club, Ltd.** (Greenfields House, Westwood Way, Coventry CV4 8JH, tel. 01203/694995).

Ratings Prices are for two people in a double room and include all taxes. Best bets are indicated by a star ★.

Category	London and Southern England	Other Areas
$$	£60–£80	£50–£60
$	£40–£60	£40–£50
¢	under £40	under £40

Tipping Some restaurants and most hotels add a service charge of 10%–15% to the bill. If this has been done, you are under no obligation to tip further. If no service charge is indicated, add 10%–15% to your total bill. Taxi drivers should also get 10%–15%. You are not expected to tip theater or movie ushers, elevator operators, or bartenders in pubs. Hairdressers and barbers should receive 10%–15%.

London

Arriving and Departing

By Plane International flights to London arrive at either Heathrow Airport, 19.4 kilometers (12 miles) west of London, or at Gatwick Airport, 40.3 kilometers (25 miles) south of the capital (only American Airlines flights from Chicago arrive at the third airport, Stansted). Most—but not all—flights from the United States go to Heathrow, while Gatwick generally serves European destinations, often with charter flights.

Between the Airport and Downtown The Piccadilly Line serves Heathrow (all terminals) with a direct Underground, or tube (subway), link. The 40-minute ride costs £3.10. Three special buses also serve Heathrow: A1 leaves every 30 minutes for Victoria Station; A2 goes to Euston Station every 30 minutes; and bus 390 departs eight times daily for Victoria, near the station. The one-way cost for all these services is £5–£6; journey time is approximately 80 minutes.

From Gatwick, the quickest way to London is the nonstop rail Gatwick Express, costing £8.90 one-way and taking 30 minutes to reach Victoria Station. Greenline Coaches runs the Flightline 777 to Victoria Station; it takes about 70 minutes and costs £6 one-way.

Cars and taxis drive from Heathrow into London on the M4; the trip can take more than an hour, depending on traffic, and the taxi fare will be at least £25. From Gatwick, the traffic can be very bad, making a taxi ride a bad bet. The fare will be at least £35.

By Train London is served by no fewer than 15 train stations, so be absolutely certain of the station for your departure or arrival. All have Underground stations either in the train station or within a few minutes' walk from it, and most are served by several bus routes. British Rail controls all major services. The principal routes that connect London to other major towns and cities are on an InterCity network; unlike its European counterparts, British Rail makes no extra charge for the use of this express service network.

Seats can be reserved by phone only with a credit card. You can, of course, apply in person to any British Rail Travel Centre or directly to the station from which you depart. Below is a list of the major London rail stations and the areas they serve.

Charing Cross (tel. 0171/928–5100) serves southeast England, including Canterbury, Margate, Dover/Folkestone.
Euston/St. Pancras (tel. 0171/387–7070) serves East Anglia, Essex, the Northeast, the Northwest, and North Wales, including Coventry, Stratford-upon-Avon, Birmingham, Manchester, Liverpool, Windermere, Glasgow, and Inverness.
King's Cross (tel. 0171/278–2477) serves the east Midlands; the Northeast, including York, Leeds, and Newcastle; and north and east Scotland, including Edinburgh and Aberdeen.
Liverpool Street (tel. 0171/928–5100) serves Essex and East Anglia.
Paddington (tel. 0171/262–6767) serves the south Midlands, west and south Wales, and the west country, including Reading, Bath, Bristol, Oxford, Cardiff, Swansea, Exeter, Plymouth, and Penzance.
Victoria (tel. 0171/928–5100) serves southern England, including Gatwick Airport, Brighton, Dover/Folkestone (from May), and the south coast.
Waterloo (tel. 0171/928-5100) serves the southwestern United Kingdom, including Salisbury, Bournemouth, Portsmouth, Southampton, Isle of Wight, Jersey, and Guernsey.

Fares The fare structures are likely to change if the proposed selling off of nationalized British Rail to various independent operators goes ahead. Even if that happens (at press time, British Rail estimated the process might be halfway through by mid-1996), it will doubtless still be less expensive to buy a return (round-trip) ticket. You should always ask about discount fares for your proposed trip— "Supersavers" and similar tickets typically cost about half the full fare. You can hear a recorded summary of timetable and fare information to many InterCity destinations by dialing the appropriate "dial and listen" numbers listed under British Rail in the telephone book.

Channel   For details on travel between Great Britain and the Continent via
Tunnel   the Channel Tunnel, *see* The Channel Tunnel *in* Chapter 1.

By Bus   The **National Express** coach service has routes to over 1,000 major
towns and cities in the United Kingdom. It's considerably cheaper
than the train, although the trips usually take longer. National Express
press offers two types of service: an ordinary service, which makes
frequent stops for refreshment breaks, and a Rapide service, which
has hostess and refreshment facilities on board. Day returns are
available on both, but booking is advised on the Rapide service. National Express
tional Express coaches leave Victoria Coach Station (Buckingham
Palace Rd.) at regular intervals, depending on the destination. For
travel information and credit card reservations, dial 0171/730–0202.

Getting Around

By   Known as "the tube," London's extensive Underground system is by
Underground   far the most widely used form of city transportation. Trains run
both beneath and above ground out into the suburbs, and all stations
are clearly marked with the London Underground circular symbol.
(A "subway" sign refers to an under-the-street crossing.) Trains are
all one class; smoking is *not* allowed on board or in the stations.

There are 10 basic lines—all named—plus the East London line,
which runs from Shoreditch and Whitechapel across the Thames
south to New Cross, and the Docklands Light Railway, which runs
from Stratford in London's East End to Greenwich, with an extension
sion to the Royal Docks to be completed. The Central, District,
Northern, Metropolitan, and Piccadilly lines all have branches, so
be sure to note which branch is needed for your particular
distination. Electronic platform signs tell you the final stop and
route of the next train, and most signs also indicate how many minutes
utes you'll have to wait for the train to arrive.

From Monday to Saturday, trains begin running around 5:30 AM; the
last services leave central London between midnight and 12:30 AM. On
Sundays, trains start two hours later and finish about an hour earlier.
The frequency of trains depends on the route and the time of day, but
normally you should not have to wait more than 10 minutes in central
areas.

A pocket map of the entire tube network is available free from most
Underground ticket counters. There should also be a large map on the
wall of each platform—though often these are defaced beyond
recognition.

Fares   For both buses and tube fares, London is divided into six concentric
zones; the fare goes up the farther afield you travel. Ask at Underground
ground ticket counters for the London Transport (LT) booklet *Tickets*,
ets, which gives details of all the various ticket options and bargains
for the tube; after some experimenting, you'll soon know which ticket
et best serves your particular needs. Till then, here is a brief summary
mary of the major ticket categories, but note that these prices are
subject to increases.

Singles and Returns. For one trip between any two stations, you can
buy an ordinary single for travel anytime on the day of issue; if
you're coming back on the same route the same day, then an ordinary
nary return costs twice the single fare. Singles vary in price from £1
in the central zone to £3.10 for a six-zone journey—not a good option
for the sightseer who wants to make several journeys.

One-Day Travelcards. These allow unrestricted travel on the tube,
most buses, and British Rail trains in the Greater London zones and
are valid weekdays after 9:30 AM, weekends, and all public holidays.
They cannot be used on airbuses, night buses, nor for certain special
services. The price is £2.80–£3.80.

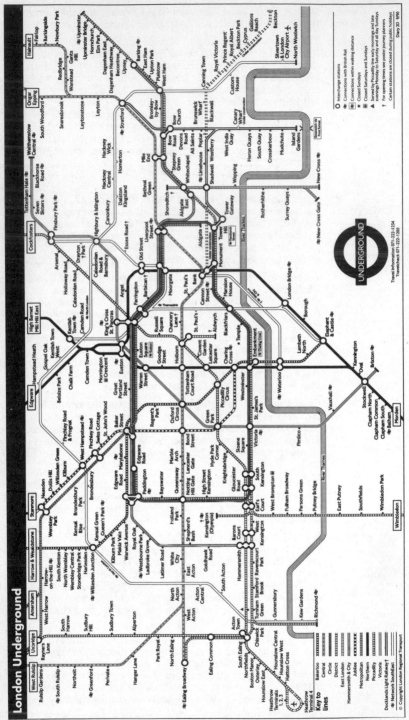

London Underground

LRT Registered User No. 96/2190

Visitor's Travelcard. These are the best bet for visitors, but they must be bought before leaving home and are available both in the United States and Canada. They are valid for periods of three, four, or seven days ($25, $32, $49; $11, $13, $21 children) and can be used on the tube and virtually all buses and British Rail services in London. This card also includes a set of money-saving discounts to many of London's top attractions. Apply to travel agents or to BritRail Travel International (1500 Broadway, NYC 10036, tel. 212/382–3737). One-day passes can also be bought at London hotels for £3.90.

For more information, there are **LT Travel Information Centres** at the following tube stations: Euston (*open Sat.–Thurs. 7:15–6, Fri. to 7:30*); King's Cross (*open Sat.–Thurs. 8:15–6, Fri. to 7:30*); Oxford Circus (*open Mon.–Sat. 8:15–6*); Piccadilly Circus (*open Mon.–Sun. 8:15–6*); Victoria (*open Mon.–Sun. 8:15–9:30*); and Heathrow (*open Mon.–Sun. [to 9 or 10 PM in Terminals 1 and 2]*). For information on all London bus and tube times, fares, etc., dial 0171/222–1234; the line is operated 24 hours a day.

By Bus London's bus system consists of bright red double- and single-deckers, plus other buses of various colors. Destinations are displayed on the front and back, with the bus number on the front, back, and side, though not all buses run the full length of their route at all times. Some buses still have a conductor whom you pay after finding a seat, but most these days are one-man buses, in which you pay the driver upon boarding.

Buses stop only at clearly indicated stops. Main stops—at which the bus should stop automatically—have a plain white background with a red LT symbol on it. There are also request stops with red signs, a white symbol, and the word "Request" added; at these you must hail the bus to make it stop. Smoking is not allowed on any bus. Although you can see much of the town from a bus, *don't* take one if you want to get anywhere in a hurry; traffic often slows travel to a crawl, and during peak times you may find yourself waiting at least 20 minutes for a bus and not being able to get on it once it arrives. If you intend to go by bus, ask at a Travel Information Centre for free London Bus Maps.

Fares Single fares start at 50p for short distances (90p in the central zone). Travelcards are good for tube, bus, and British Rail trains in the Greater London Zones. There are also a number of bus passes available for daily, weekly, and monthly use, and prices vary according to zones. A photograph is required for weekly or monthly bus passes; this also applies to children and older children who may need a child-rate photocard to avoid paying the adult rate.

Important Addresses and Numbers

Tourist Information The main **London Tourist Information Centre** at Victoria Station Forecourt provides details about London and the rest of Britain, including general information; tickets for tube and bus; theater, concert, and tour bookings; and accommodations. Open Monday–Saturday 9–7, Sunday 9–5.

Other information centers are located in **Harrods** (Brompton Rd., SW1 7XL) and **Selfridges** (Oxford St., W1A 2LR) and are open store hours only; and at **Heathrow Airport** (Terminals 1, 2, and 3) and **Gatwick Airport** (International Arrivals Concourse).

The **British Travel Centre** (12 Regent St., SW1Y 4PQ) provides details about travel, accommodations, and entertainment for the whole of Britain. Open weekdays 9–6:30 and weekends 10–4. Phone information about a wide variety of topics is available on an automated information system. **VisitorCall** (tel. 01839/123456 for menu) costs 39p after 6PM, or 49p between 9AM and 6PM.

Embassies and Consulates **American Embassy** (24 Grosvenor Sq., W1A, 1AE, tel. 0171/499–9000). Located inside the embassy is the **American Aid Society,** a charity set up to help Americans in distress. Dial the embassy number and ask for extension 570 or 571.

Canadian High Commission (McDonald House, 1 Grosvenor Sq., W1, tel. 0171/258–6600).

Emergencies For police, fire brigade, or ambulance, dial 999.

The following **hospitals** have 24-hour emergency rooms: **Charing Cross** (Fulham Palace Rd., W6, tel. 0181/846–1234); **Guys** (St. Thomas St., SE1, tel. 071/955–5000), **Royal Free** (Pond St., Hampstead, NW3, tel. 071/794–0500), **St. Thomas's** (Lambeth Palace Rd., SE1, tel. 071/928–9292).

Credit Cards Should your credit cards be lost or stolen, here are some numbers to dial for assistance: **Access (MasterCard)** (tel. 0181/450–3122); **American Express** (tel. 0171/222–9633, 24 hrs, or 01273/696933 8–6 only for credit cards, tel. 01800/521313 for traveler's checks); **Barclaycard (Visa)** (tel. 01604/230230); and **Diners Club** (tel. 01252/516261).

Exploring London

Traditionally London has been divided between the City, to the east, where its banking and commercial interests lie, and Westminster to the west, the seat of the royal court and of government. In these two areas stand the Tower of London and St. Paul's Cathedral, Westminster Abbey and the Houses of Parliament, Buckingham Palace, and the older royal palace of St. James's. Other parts of London worth exploring include Covent Garden, where a former fruit and flower market has been converted into a lively shopping area; Hyde Park and Kensington Gardens, which cut a great swathe of green parkland across the city center; the museum district of South Kensington; the South Bank Arts Complex; and Hayward Gallery. The views from the gallery are stunning—to the west are the Houses of Parliament and Big Ben, to the east the dome of St. Paul's is just visible on London's changing skyline.

Numbers in the margin correspond to points of interest on the London map.

Westminster **Westminster** is the royal backyard—the traditional center of the royal court and of government. Here, within a kilometer or so of each other, are virtually all London's most celebrated buildings (St. Paul's Cathedral and the Tower of London excepted), and there is a strong feeling of history all around you. Generations of kings and queens and their offspring have lived here since the end of the 11th century, in no less than four palaces, three of which (Buckingham, St. James's, and Westminster) still stand.

❶ Start at **Trafalgar Square,** which is on the site of the former Royal Mews. Both the square's name and its present appearance date from about 1830. A statue of Lord Nelson, victor over the French in 1805 at the Battle of Trafalgar, at which he lost his life, stands atop a column. Lions guard the base of the column, which is decorated with four bronze panels depicting naval battles against France and cast from French cannons captured by Nelson. The bronze equestrian statue on the south side of the square is of the unhappy Charles I; he is looking down Whitehall toward the spot where he was executed in 1649.

❷ In the **National Gallery,** which occupies the long neoclassical building on the north side of the square, is a comprehensive collection of paintings, with works from virtually every famous artist and school from the 14th to the 19th century. The gallery is especially strong on Flemish and Dutch masters, Rubens and Rembrandt among them, and on Italian Renaissance works. The Sainsbury Wing houses the early Renaissance collection. *Trafalgar Sq., tel. 0171/839–3321; 0171/839–3526 (recorded information). Admission free; charge for Sainsbury Wing exhibitions. Open Mon.–Sat. 10–6, Sun. 2–6; June–Aug., Wed. until 8.*

③ Around the corner, at the foot of Charing Cross Road, is a second major art collection, the recently renovated **National Portrait Gallery,** which contains portraits of well-known (and not so well-known) Britons, including monarchs, statesmen, and writers. *2 St. Martin's Pl., tel. 0171/930–1552. Admission free. Open weekdays 10–5, Sat. 10–6, Sun. 2–6.*

④ The Gallery's entrance is opposite the distinctive neoclassical church of **St. Martin-in-the-Fields,** built in about 1730. Regular lunchtime music recitals are held here, often free of charge.

⑤ **Admiralty Arch** guards the entrance to **The Mall,** the great ceremonial way that leads alongside **St. James's Park** to Buckingham Palace. The Mall takes its name from a game called "pell mell," a version of croquet that society people, including Charles II and his courtiers, used to play here in the late 1600s. The park, with its duck-filled lake, deck chairs and bandstand, and perfectly maintained flowerbeds, was developed by successive monarchs, most recently by George IV in the 1820s, having originally been used for hunting by Henry VIII. Join office workers relaxing with a lunchtime sandwich, or stroll here on a summer's evening when the illuminated fountains play and Westminster Abbey and the Houses of Parliament beyond the trees are floodlit.

⑥ On the other side of the Mall, you'll pass along the foot of the imposing **Carlton House Terrace,** built in 1827–32 by John Nash. A right turn up Marlborough Road brings you to the complex of royal and government buildings known collectively as **St. James's Palace.**
⑦ Although the earliest parts of this lovely brick building date from the 1530s, it had a relatively short career as the center of royal affairs, from the destruction of Whitehall Palace in 1698 until 1837, when Victoria became queen and moved the royal household down the road to Buckingham Palace. It is, however, the London residence of the Prince of Wales. Also, a number of royal functionaries have offices here, and various court functions are held in the state rooms. Foreign ambassadors are still accredited to the "Court of St. James's."

⑧ At the end of Marlborough Road, beyond the open-sided **Friary Court,** turn left along **Cleveland Row** and walk past **York House,** the sometime London home of the duke and duchess of Kent. Another
⑨ left turn into **Stable Yard Road** takes you to **Lancaster House,** built for the duke of York by Nash in the 1820s and used today for government receptions and conferences. On the other side of Stable Yard is
⑩ **Clarence House,** so called because it was designed and built by Nash in 1825 for the duke of Clarence, who later became King William IV. It was restored in 1949 and is now the home of the Queen Mother. Inside the palace is the **Chapel Royal,** said to have been designed for Henry VIII by the painter Holbein; it was heavily redecorated in the mid-19th century. The ceiling still has the initials H and A, intertwined, standing for Henry VIII and his second wife, Anne Boleyn, the mother of Elizabeth I and the first of his wives to lose her head. The public can attend Sunday morning services here between the first week of October and Good Friday.

⑪ **Buckingham Palace,** at the end of the Mall, is the London home of the queen and the administrative hub of the entire royal family. When the queen is in residence (normally on weekdays except in January, August, September, and part of June), the royal standard flies over the east front. Inside there are dozens of splendid state rooms, used on such formal occasions as banquets for visiting heads of state. The private apartments of Queen Elizabeth and Prince

London

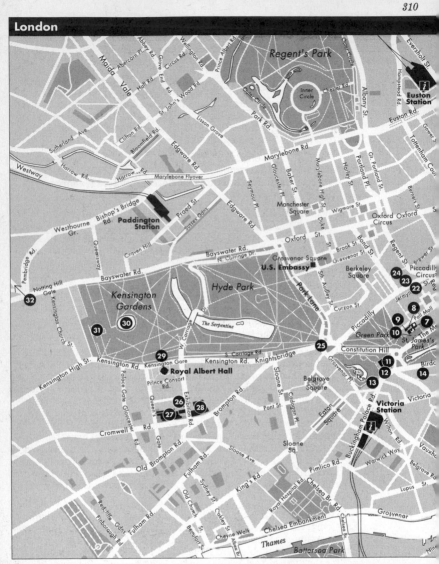

Albert Memorial, **29**
Bank of England, **45**
Banqueting House, **20**
Barbican, **42**
British Museum, **38**
Buckingham Palace, **11**
Cabinet War Rooms, **15**
Carlton House Terrace, **6**
Cenotaph, **19**

Clarence House, **10**
Covent Garden, **33**
Guildhall, **43**
Horse Guards Parade, **21**
Hyde Park, **25**
Kensington Palace, **31**
Lancaster House, **9**
Leadenhall Market, **48**
Lloyd's of London, **49**
London Transport Museum, **35**

The Mall, **5**
Mansion House, **47**
Museum of London, **41**
Museum of Mankind, **24**
National Gallery, **2**
National Portrait Gallery, **3**
Natural History Museum, **27**
Palace of Westminster, **17**

Parliament Square, **16**
Portobello Road, **32**
Queen's Gallery, **12**
Round Pond, **30**
Royal Academy of Arts, **23**
Royal Exchange, **46**
Royal Mews, **13**
Royal Opera House, **37**
St. James's Church, **22**
St. James's Palace, **7**

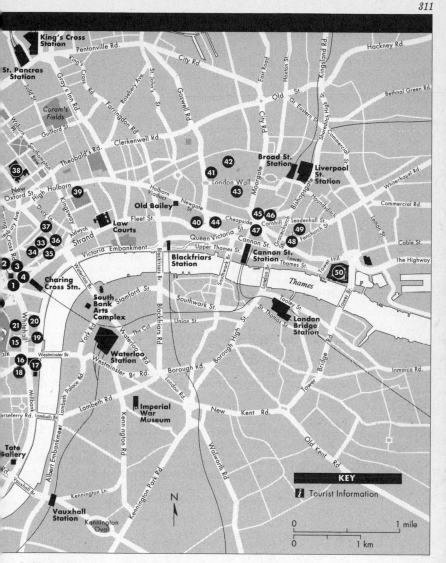

St. Martin-in-the-Fields, **4**

St. Mary-le-Bow, **44**

St. Paul's Cathedral, **40**

St. Paul's Church, **34**

Science Museum, **26**

Sir John Soane's Museum, **39**

Theatre Museum, **36**

Tower of London, **50**

Trafalgar Square, **1**

Victoria and Albert Museum, **28**

Wellington Barracks, **14**

Westminster Abbey, **18**

York House, **8**

Philip are in the north wing. Behind the palace lie some 40 acres of private gardens, a haven for wildlife in the midst of the capital.

The ceremony of the **Changing of the Guard** takes place in front of the palace at 11:30 daily, April through July, and on alternate days during the rest of the year. It's advisable to arrive early since people are invariably stacked several-deep along the railings, whatever the weather.

⑫ Parts of Buckingham Palace are open to the public during August and September, while the former chapel, bombed during World War II, rebuilt in 1961, and now the **Queen's Gallery,** shows paintings from the vast royal art collections from March through December. *Buckingham Palace Rd., tel. 0171/493–3175. Admission: Buckingham Palace, £8 adults, £4 children, £5.50 senior citizens; Queen's Gallery, tel. 0171/799–2331. Admission: £3 adults, £1.50 children, £2 senior citizens. Open Tues.–Sat. and bank holidays 10–5, Sun. 2–5; closed between exhibitions.*

⑬ Just along Buckingham Palace Road from the Queen's Gallery is the **Royal Mews,** where some of the queen's horses are stabled and the elaborately gilded state coaches are on view. *Tel. 0171/799–2331. Admission: £3 adults, £1.50 children under 16, £2 senior citizens; combined ticket with Queen's Gallery, £5 adults, £2.20 children, £3.50 senior citizens. Open Oct.–Mar., Wed. noon–4; Apr.–Sept., Tues.–Thurs. noon–4. Closed Mar. 25–30, Oct. 1–6, Dec. 23–Jan. 5.*

⑭ **Birdcage Walk,** so called because it was once the site of the royal aviaries, runs along the south side of St. James's Park, past the **Wellington Barracks.** These are the regimental headquarters of the Guards Division, the elite troops that traditionally guard the sovereign and mount the guard at Buckingham Palace. The **Guards Museum** relates the history of the Guards from the 1660s to the present; paintings of battle scenes, uniforms, and a cat-o'-nine-tails are among the items on display. *Tel. 0171/414–3428. Admission: £2 adults, £1 children under 16 and senior citizens. Open Sat.–Thurs. 10–4.*

⑮ The **Cabinet War Rooms,** between the Foreign Office and the Home Office, are the underground offices used by the British High Command during World War II. Among the rooms on display are the Prime Minister's Room, from which Winston Churchill made many of his inspiring wartime broadcasts, and the Transatlantic Telephone Room, from which he spoke directly to President Roosevelt in the White House. *Clive Steps, King Charles St., tel. 0171/930–6961. Admission: £3.90 adults, £1.90 children under 16, £3 senior citizens. Open daily 10–5:15.*

⑯ **Parliament Square** is flanked, on the river side, by the Palace of Westminster. Among the statues of statesmen long since dead are those of Churchill; Abraham Lincoln; and Oliver Cromwell, the Lord Protector of England during the country's sole, brief republican period (1648–60).

⑰ The **Palace of Westminster** was the monarch's main residence from the 11th century until 1512, when the court moved to the newly built Whitehall Palace. The only part of the original building to have survived, however, is **Westminster Hall,** which has a fine hammer-beam roof. The rest was destroyed in a disastrous fire in 1834 and was rebuilt in the newly popular mock-medieval Gothic style with ornate interior decorations. The architect, Augustus Pugin, provided many delightful touches, such as Gothic umbrella stands. In addition to Westminster Hall, which is used only on rare ceremonial occasions, the palace contains the debating chambers and committee rooms of the two Houses of Parliament—the Commons (whose members are elected) and the Lords (whose members are appointed or inherit their seats). There are no tours of the palace, but the public is admitted to the Public Gallery of each House; expect to wait in line for several hours (the line for the Lords is generally much shorter than that for the Commons).

The most famous features of the palace are its towers. At the south end is the 104-meter (336-foot) **Victoria Tower.** At the other end is **St. Stephen's Tower,** better known, but inaccurately so, as Big Ben. That is actually the nickname of the 13-ton bell in the tower on which the hours are struck; Big Ben himself was probably Sir Benjamin Hall, commissioner of works when the bell was installed in the 1850s. A light shines from the top of the tower during a night sitting of Parliament.

⑱ Westminster Abbey is the most ancient of London's great churches and the most important, for it is here that Britain's monarchs are crowned. It is unusual for a church of this size and national importance not to be a cathedral. The abbey dates largely from the 13th and 14th centuries, although **Henry VII's Chapel,** an exquisite example of the heavily decorated late Gothic style, was not built until the early 1600s, and the twin towers over the west entrance are an 18th-century addition. There is much to see inside, including the touching tomb of the Unknown Warrior, a nameless World War I soldier buried, in memory of the war's victims, in earth brought with his corpse from France; and the famous Poets' Corner, where England's great writers—Milton, Chaucer, Shakespeare, Blake, et al.—are memorialized and sometimes even buried. Behind the high altar are the royal tombs, including those of Queen Elizabeth I, Mary Queen of Scots, and Henry V. In the Chapel of Edward the Confessor stands the Coronation Chair. Among the royal weddings that have taken place here are those of the present queen and most recently, in 1986, the duke and duchess of York.

It is all too easy to forget, swamped by the crowds trying to see the abbey's sights, that this is a place of worship. Early morning is a good moment to catch something of the building's atmosphere. Better still, take time to attend a service. *Broad Sanctuary, tel. 0171/ 222–5152. Admission to the nave is free, to Poets' Corner and Royal Chapels, £4 adults, £1 children, students, and £2 senior citizens (Royal Chapels, free Wed. 6–7:45 PM). Open weekdays 9–4, Sat. 9–2 and 3:45–5; Sun. all day for services only; museum and cloisters open Sun.; closed weekdays to visitors during services; Royal Chapels closed Sun. No photography except Mon. evening.*

The Norman **Undercroft,** off the original monastic cloisters, houses a small museum with exhibits on the abbey's history. In the **Pyx Chamber** next door, the original strongroom, the Abbey's treasure is housed. The nearby **Chapter House** was where the English Parliament first met. *Tel. 0171/222–5152. Joint admission: £2.10 adults, £1.65 students and senior citizens, £1.05 children under 15. Open daily 10:30–1:45.*

⑲ From Parliament Square, walk up **Parliament Street** and **Whitehall** (this is a single street—its name changes), past government offices, toward Trafalgar Square. The **Cenotaph,** in the middle of the road, is the national memorial to the dead of both world wars. On the left is the entrance to **Downing Street,** an unassuming row of 18th-century houses. The prime minister's office is at No. 10 (he has a private apartment on the top floor). The chancellor of the exchequer, the finance minister, occupies No. 11.

⑳ On the right side of Whitehall is the **Banqueting House,** built by the architect Inigo Jones in 1625 for court entertainments. This is the only part of Whitehall Palace, the monarch's principal residence in the 16th and 17th centuries, that was not burned down in 1698. It has a magnificent ceiling by Rubens, and outside there is an inscription that marks the window through which King Charles I stepped to his execution. *Tel. 0171/930–4179. Admission: £2.90 adults, £2.20 students and senior citizens, £1.90 children under 16. Open Tues.– Sat. 10–5, Sun. 2–5.*

㉑ Opposite is the entrance to **Horse Guards Parade,** the former tilt yard of Whitehall Palace. This is the site of the annual ceremony of Trooping the Colour, when the queen takes the salute in the great military parade that marks her official birthday on the second Saturday in June (her real one is on April 21). There is also a daily guard-changing ceremony outside the guard house at 11 AM (10 on Sunday).

St. James's and Mayfair After such a concentrated dose of grand, historical buildings, it's time to explore two of London's elegant shopping areas. Start by walking west from Piccadilly Circus along **Piccadilly,** which contains some grand and very English shops (including **Hatchards,** the booksellers, **Swaine, Adeney Brigg,** the equestrian outfitters, and **Fortnum and Mason,** the department store that supplies the queen's groceries, and academic societies.

㉒ **St. James's Church** was designed by the 17th-century architect Christopher Wren and contains beautiful wood carvings by Grinling Gibbons.

㉓ On the north side of Piccadilly, **Burlington House** contains the offices of many learned societies and the headquarters of the **Royal Academy of Arts.** The RA, as it is generally known, stages major visiting art exhibitions. The best known is the Summer Exhibition (May–Aug.), featuring a chaotic hodgepodge of works by living British artists.

Burlington Arcade, beside the RA, is a covered walkway dating from 1819, whose quaint shops sell luxury goods, such as cashmere sweaters, silk scarves, handmade chocolates, and leather-bound books. A uniformed beadle is on duty to ensure that no one runs, whistles, or sings here.

㉔ The **Museum of Mankind,** behind the RA, contains the British Museum's ethnographic collection, though this will eventually be transferred to the British Museum when the British Library moves to its new premises in St. Pancras. There are displays on the South Seas, the Arctic, and other regions of the world. *6 Burlington Gardens, tel. 0171/437–2224. Admission free. Open Mon.–Sat. 10–5, Sun. 2:30–6.*

Some of the original 18th-century houses survive on the west side of **Berkeley Square.** Farther along is **Curzon Street,** which runs along the northern edge of **Shepherd Market,** a maze of narrow streets full of antiques shops, restaurants, and pubs that retain something of a village atmosphere.

Hyde Park and Beyond A great expanse of green parkland begins at **Hyde Park Corner** and cuts right across the center of London. **Hyde Park,** which covers ㉕ about 137 hectares (340 acres), was originally a royal hunting ground, while **Kensington Gardens,** which adjoins it to the west, started life as part of the royal Kensington Palace. These two parks contain many fine trees and are a haven for wildlife. The sandy track that runs along the south edge of the parks has been a fashionable riding trail for centuries. Though it's called **Rotten Row,** there's nothing rotten about it. The name derives from *route du roi* ("the King's Way")—the route William III and Queen Mary took from their home at Kensington Palace to the court at St. James's. There is boating and swimming in the **Serpentine,** the S-shape lake formed by damming a stream that used to flow here. Refreshments can be had at the lakeside tearooms, and the **Serpentine Gallery** (tel. 0171/402–6075) holds noteworthy exhibitions of modern art.

Leave the park at **Exhibition Road** and visit three of London's major
㉖ museums. The **Science Museum** is the leading national collection of
science and technology, with extensive hands-on exhibits on outer
space, astronomy, computers, transportation, and medicine. *Tel.
0171/938–8000; 0171/938–8123 (recorded information). Admission:
£4.50 adults, £2.40 children under 15 and senior citizens. Open
Mon.–Sat. 10–6, Sun. 11–6.*

㉗ The **Natural History Museum** is housed in an ornate late-Victorian
building with striking modern additions. As in the Science Museum,
its displays on topics such as human biology and evolution are designed to challenge visitors to think for themselves. *Cromwell Rd.,
tel. 0171/938–9123; 0142/692–7654 (recorded information). Admission: £5 adults, £2.50 children under 15 and senior citizens; free
weekdays 4:30–6. Open Mon.–Sat. 10–6, Sun. 2:30–6.*

㉘ The **Victoria and Albert Museum** (or V & A) originated in the 19th
century as a museum of decorative art and has extensive collections
of costumes, paintings, jewelry, and crafts from every part of the
globe. The collections from India, China, and the Islamic world are
especially strong. *Cromwell Rd., tel. 0171/938–8500; 0171/938–8441
(recorded information). Suggested voluntary contribution: £4.50
adults, £1 children and senior citizens. Open Mon.–Sat. 10–5:50,
Sun. 2:30–5:50.*

㉙ Back in Kensington Gardens, the **Albert Memorial** commemorates
Queen Victoria's much-loved husband, Prince Albert, who died in
1861 at the age of 42. The monument, itself the epitome of high Victorian taste, commemorates the many socially uplifting projects of
the prince, among them the Great Exhibition of 1851, whose catalogue he is holding. The Memorial, which has been badly eroded by
pollution, is currently being restored.

From the **Flower Walk,** behind the Albert Memorial, carefully
planted so that flowers are in bloom virtually throughout the year,
㉚ strike out across Kensington Gardens to the **Round Pond,** a favorite
place for children to sail toy boats.

㉛ **Kensington Palace,** across from the Round Pond, has been a royal
home since the late 17th century—and is one still, for the London
sojourns of Princess Margaret. From the outside it looks less like a
palace than a country house, which it was until William III bought it
in 1689. Inside, however, are state rooms on a grand scale, mostly
created in the early 18th century. Such distinguished architects as
Wren, Hawksmoor, Vanbrugh, and William Kent were all employed
here. Queen Victoria spent a less than ecstatic childhood at Kensington Palace, though she repaired to Buckingham Palace as soon
as she was crowned. Kensington Palace is currently closed for refurbishment. *Tel. 0171/937–9561.*

North of Kensington Gardens is the lively district of **Notting Hill,**
full of restaurants and cafés where young people gather. The best-
㉜ known attraction in this area is **Portobello Road,** where the lively antiques and bric-a-brac market is held each Saturday (arrive early in
the morning for the best bargains). The street is also full of regular
antiques shops that are open most weekdays.

Covent You could easily spend a half day exploring the block of streets north
Garden of the Strand known as **Covent Garden.** The heart of the area is a for-
㉝ mer wholesale fruit and vegetable market, established in 1656. The
market moved to more modern and accessible premises only in 1974.
The Victorian Market Building is now **The Piazza,** a vibrant shopping center with numerous boutiques, crafts shops, and cafés. On
the south side of the market building is the lively and much less formal **Jubilee Market,** full of assorted stalls selling clothes, crafts, jewelry, leather goods, and imported trinkets.

㉞ Look for the open-air entertainers performing under the portico of **St. Paul's Church**—you can enjoy an excellent show for the price of a few coins thrown in the hat that's passed among the onlookers. The church, entered from Bedford Street, is known as the Actors' Church, and inside are numerous memorials to theater people. The **Royal Opera House** and the **Theatre Royal Drury Lane,** two of London's oldest theaters, are close by.

For interesting specialty shops, head north of the Market Building. Shops on **Long Acre** sell maps, art books, and glass; shops on **Neal Street** sell clothes, pottery, jewelry, tea, housewares, and goods from the Far East.

㉟ The **London Transport Museum** is sparkling after its recent comprehensive renovation. It features live actors, touch-screen displays, and many hands-on exhibits, including a tube-driving simulator. The shop is popular for its historic London Transport posters. *The Piazza (southeast corner), tel. 0171/379–6344. Admission: £3.95 adults, £2.50 children 5–16 and senior citizens, children under 5 free. Open daily 10–5:15.*

㊱ The **Theatre Museum** contains a comprehensive collection of material on the history of the English theater—not merely the classic drama but also opera, music hall, pantomime, and musical comedy. Scripts, playbills, costumes, and props are displayed; there is even a re-creation of a dressing room filled with memorabilia of former stars. *Russell St., tel. 0171/836–7891. Admission: £3 adults, £1.50 students, senior citizens, and children under 14. Open Tues.–Sun. 11–7.*

㊲ On **Bow Street** is the **Royal Opera House,** home of the Royal Ballet and the Royal Opera Company. The plush interior captures the richness of Victorian England.

Bloomsbury **Bloomsbury** is a semiresidential district to the north of Covent Garden that contains some spacious and elegant 17th- and 18th-century squares. It could claim to be the intellectual center of London, since both the British Museum and the University of London are found here. The area also gave its name to the Bloomsbury Group, a clique of writers and painters who thrived here in the early 20th century. The antiquarian and specialist bookshops, publishing houses, restaurants, and pubs frequented by the local literati add to the academic-cum-bohemian ambience of the area.

㊳ The **British Museum** houses a vast and priceless collection of treasures, including Egyptian, Greek, and Roman antiquities; Renaissance jewelry; pottery; coins; glass; and drawings from virtually every European school since the 15th century. It's best to pick out one section that particularly interests you—to try to see everything would be an overwhelming and exhausting task. Some of the highlights are the **Elgin Marbles,** sculptures that formerly decorated the Parthenon in Athens; the **Rosetta Stone,** which helped archaeologists to interpret Egyptian script; a copy of the **Magna Carta,** the charter signed by King John in 1215 to which is ascribed the origins of English liberty; and the **Mildenhall treasure,** a cache of Roman silver found in East Anglia in 1842. *Great Russell St., tel. 0171/636–1555; 0171/580–1788 (recorded information). Admission free. Open Mon.–Sat. 10–5, Sun. 2:30–6.*

㊴ On the border of London's legal district, **Sir John Soane's Museum** is an eccentric and delightful collection of art and artifacts in the former home of the architect of the Bank of England, whose well-developed senses of humor and perspective are equally apparent. *13 Lincoln's Inn Fields, tel. 0171/405–2107. Admission free. Open Tues.–Sat. 10–5; closed national holidays.*

The City The **City,** the traditional commercial center of London, is the most ancient part of the capital, having been the site of the great Roman city of Londinium. Since those days, the City has been built and rebuilt several times. The wooden buildings of the medieval City were destroyed in the Great Fire of 1666. There were further waves of reconstruction in the 19th century, and then again after World War II, to repair the devastation wrought by air attacks. The 1980s have seen the construction of many mammoth office developments, some undistinguished, others incorporating adventurous and exciting ideas.

Throughout all these changes, the City has retained its unique identity and character. The lord mayor and Corporation of London are still responsible for the government of the City, as they have been for many centuries. Commerce remains the lifeblood of the City, which is a world financial center rivaled only by New York, Tokyo, and Zurich. The biggest change has been in the City's population. Until the first half of the 19th century, many of the merchants and traders who worked in the City lived there, too. Today, despite its huge daytime population, scarcely 8,000 people live in the 274 hectares (677 acres) of the City. Try, therefore, to explore the City on a weekday morning or afternoon. On weekends its streets are deserted, and many of the shops and restaurants, even some of the churches, are closed.

40 Following the Great Fire, **St. Paul's Cathedral** was rebuilt by Sir Christopher Wren, the architect who was also responsible for designing 50 City parish churches to replace those lost in the Great Fire. St. Paul's is Wren's greatest work. Fittingly, he is buried in the crypt, under the simple epitaph composed by his son, which translates as: "Reader, if you seek his monument, look around you." The cathedral has been the site of many famous state occasions, including the funeral of Winston Churchill in 1965 and the ill-fated marriage of the prince and princess of Wales in 1981. Note the fine choir stalls by the great 17th-century wood carver Grinling Gibbons—a rare decorative flourish in a surprisingly restrained interior, with relatively few monuments and tombs. Among those commemorated are George Washington; the essayist and lexicographer Samuel Johnson; and two military heroes—Nelson, victor over the French at Trafalgar in 1805, and Wellington, who defeated the French on land at Waterloo 10 years later. In the ambulatory (the area behind the high altar) is the American Chapel, a memorial to the 28,000 U.S. citizens stationed in Britain during World War II who lost their lives while on active service.

The greatest architectural glory of the cathedral is the dome. This consists of three distinct elements: an outer, timber-framed dome covered with lead; an interior dome built of brick and decorated with frescoes of the life of St. Paul by the 18th-century artist Sir James Thornhill; and, in between, a brick cone that supports and strengthens both. There is a good view of the church from the **Whispering Gallery,** high up in the inner dome. The gallery is so called because of its remarkable acoustics, whereby words whispered on one side can be clearly heard on the other, 35 meters (112 feet) away. Above this gallery are two others, both external, from which there are fine views over the City and beyond. *Tel. 0171/248–2705. Admission to cathedral free (donation requested); Ambulatory (American Chapel), Crypt, and Treasury: £3 adults, £2 children, £2.50 senior citizens; to galleries: £2.50 adults, £1.50 children, £2 senior citizens. Tours of the cathedral weekdays at 11, 11:30, 2, and 2:30, £5 adults, £2.50 children. Cathedral open Mon.–Sat. 7:30–6, Sun. 8–6; the Ambulatory, Crypt, and Galleries weekdays 10–4:15, Sat. 11–4:15.*

A short walk north of the cathedral, to **London Wall,** so called because it follows the line of the wall that surrounded the Roman settlement, brings you to the **Museum of London.** Its displays enable you to get a real sense of what it was like to live in London at different periods of history, from Roman times to the present day. Among the highlights are the Lord Mayor's Ceremonial Coach; an imaginative reconstruction of the Great Fire; and the Cheapside Hoard, jewelry hidden during an outbreak of the plague in the 17th century and never recovered by its owner. A new Introductory Gallery uses computer graphics to illustrate London's growth from prehistoric times to the present day. The 20th-century exhibits include a Woolworth's counter and elevators from Selfridges; both stores were founded by Americans and had an immense impact on the life of Londoners. *London Wall, tel. 0171/600–3699. Admission £3 adults, £1.50 children under 18 and senior citizens. Open Tues.–Sat. 10–6, Sun. 2–6.*

㊷ The **Barbican** is a vast residential complex and arts center built by the City of London. It takes its name from the watchtower that stood here during the Middle Ages, just outside the City walls. The arts center contains a concert hall, where the London Symphony Orchestra is based; two theaters; an art gallery; a movie theater; and several cafés and restaurants. The theaters are the London home of the Royal Shakespeare Company.

㊸ On the south side of London Wall stands **Guildhall**, the much-reconstructed home of the Corporation of London; the lord mayor of London is elected here each year with ancient ceremony. *King St., tel. 0171/606–3030. Admission free. Open weekdays 10–5.*

Now walk south to **Cheapside.** This was the chief marketplace of medieval London (the word *ceap* is Old English for "to barter"), as the street names hereabouts indicate: Milk Street, Ironmonger Lane, etc. Despite rebuilding, many of the streets still run on the

㊹ medieval pattern. The church of **St. Mary-le-Bow** in Cheapside was rebuilt by Christopher Wren after the Great Fire; it was built again after being bombed during World War II. It is said that to be a true Cockney, you must be born within the sound of Bow bells.

A short walk east along Cheapside brings you to a seven-way inter-

㊺ section. The **Bank of England,** which regulates much of Britain's financial life, is the large windowless building on the left. At the northern side of the intersection, at right angles to the bank, is the

㊻ **Royal Exchange,** originally built in the 1560s as a trading hall for merchants. The present building, opened in 1844 and the third on the site, is now occupied by the **London International Financial Futures Exchange.** *Tel. 0171/623–0444. Visitors' Gallery open by appointment to groups from relevant organizations.*

The third major building at this intersection, on its south side, is the

㊼ **Mansion House,** the official residence of the lord mayor of London.

Continue east along **Cornhill,** site of a Roman basilica and of a medieval grain market. Turn right into Gracechurch Street and then left

㊽ into **Leadenhall Market.** There has been a market here since the 14th century; the present building dates from 1881.

Just behind the market is one of the most striking pieces of contem-

㊾ porary City architecture: the headquarters of **Lloyd's of London,** built by the modernist architect Richard Rogers, whose other famous work is Paris's Pompidou Centre, and whose practice has also won the competition to redesign the South Bank Complex. The underwriters of Lloyd's provide insurance for everything imaginable, from oil rigs to a pianist's fingers, though they suffered a crash in 1993. Most of the so-called Names, whose millions formed the Lloyd's backbone, lost major money. *1 Lime St., tel. 0171/623–7100. Open by appointment to groups from recognized organizations.*

㊿ From here it's a short walk east to the **Tower of London,** one of London's most famous sights and one of its most crowded, too. Come as early in the day as possible and head for the Crown Jewels, so you can see them before the crowds arrive.

The tower served the monarchs of medieval England as both fortress and palace. Every British sovereign from William the Conqueror in the 11th century to Henry VIII in the 16th lived here, and it remains a royal palace, in name at least. The **History Gallery**, south of the White Tower, is a walk-through display designed to answer questions about the inhabitants of the tower and its evolution over the centuries.

The **White Tower** is the oldest and the most conspicuous building in the entire complex. Inside, the **Chapel of St. John** is one of the few unaltered parts. A structure of great simplicity, it is almost entirely lacking in ornamentation. The **Royal Armories,** England's national collection of arms and armor, occupies the rest of the White Tower. Armor of the 16th and 17th centuries forms the centerpiece of the displays, including pieces belonging to Henry VIII and Charles I.

Among other buildings worth seeing is the **Bloody Tower.** This name has been traced back only to 1571; it was originally known as the Garden Tower. Sir Walter Raleigh was held prisoner here, in relatively comfortable circumstances, between 1603 and 1616, during which time he wrote his *History of the World;* his rooms are furnished much as they were during his imprisonment. The little princes in the tower—the boy king Edward V and his brother Richard, duke of York, supposedly murdered on the orders of Gloucester, later crowned Richard III—certainly lived in the Bloody Tower and may well have died here, too. Another bloody death is alleged to have occurred in the **Wakefield Tower,** when Henry VI was murdered in 1471 during England's medieval civil war, the Wars of the Roses. It was a rare honor to be beheaded in private inside the tower; most people were executed outside on **Tower Hill,** where the crowds could get a much better view. Important prisoners were held in the **Beauchamp Tower;** the walls are covered with graffiti and inscriptions carved by prisoners.

The **Crown Jewels,** housed in the new **Jewel House** (with four times the capacity of the old one) is a breathtakingly beautiful collection of regalia, precious stones, gold, and silver. The Royal Scepter contains the largest cut diamond in the world. The Imperial State Crown, made for the 1838 coronation of Queen Victoria, contains some 3,000 precious stones, largely diamonds and pearls. Look for the ravens whose presence at the tower is traditional. It is said that if they leave, the tower will fall and England will lose her greatness. *Tower Hill, tel. 0171/709–0765. Admission: £7.95 adults, £5.95 students and senior citizens, £5.25 children under 16. Reduced admission charges apply during Feb. when the Jewel House is closed. Small additional admission charge to the Fusiliers Museum only. Open Mar.–Oct., Mon.–Sat. 9:30–5, Sun. 2–5; Nov.–Feb., Mon.– Sat. 9:30–4.*

Yeoman Warder guides conduct tours daily from the Middle Tower, no charge, but a tip is always appreciated. Subject to weather and the availability of guides, tours are conducted about every 30 min until 3:30 in summer, 2:30 in winter.

Off the Beaten Track

Greenwich The historical and maritime attractions at **Greenwich,** on the Thames, some 8 kilometers (5 miles) east of central London, make it an ideal place for a day out. You can get to Greenwich by riverboat from Westminster and Tower Bridge piers, by the high-speed riverbuses, or by train from Charing Cross station. You can also take the Docklands Light Railway from Tower Gateway to Island Gardens and walk a short distance along a pedestrian tunnel under the river.

Visit the **National Maritime Museum,** a treasure house of paintings; maps; models; sextants; and, best of all, ships from all ages, including the ornate royal barges. *Romney Rd., tel. 0181/858–4422. Admission: £4.95 adults, £2.95 children, £3.95 senior citizens. Open late Mar.–late Oct., Mon.–Sat. 10–6, Sun. 2–6; late Oct.–late Mar., Mon.–Sat. 10–5, Sun. 2–5.*

Two ships now in dry dock are the glorious 19th-century clipper ship *Cutty Sark* and the tiny *Gipsy Moth IV,* which Sir Francis Chichester sailed single-handedly around the world in 1966. *Cutty Sark, King William Walk, tel. 0181/858–3445. Admission: £3.25 adults, £2.25 children under 16 and senior citizens. Open late Mar.– Sept., Mon.–Sat. 10–5:30, Sun. noon–5:30; Oct.–Mar., Mon.–Sat. 10–4:30, Sun. noon–4:30. Gipsy Moth IV, King William Walk, tel. 0181/853–3589. Admission: 50p adults, 30p children and senior citizens. Open Apr.–Oct., Mon.–Sat. 10–5:30, Sun. noon–5:30.*

The **Royal Naval College** was built in 1694 as a home, or hospital, for old sailors. You can see the magnificent **Painted Hall,** where Nelson's body lay in state following the Battle of Trafalgar, and the College Chapel. *Tel. 0181/858–2154. Admission free. Open Fri.– Wed. 2:30–4:30.*

Behind the museum and the college is **Greenwich Park,** originally a royal hunting ground and today an attractive place in which to wander and relax. On top of the hill is the **Old Royal Observatory,** founded in 1675, where original telescopes and other astronomical instruments are on display. The prime meridian—zero degrees longitude—runs through the courtyard of the observatory. *Greenwich Park, tel. 0181/858–4422. Admission (includes National Maritime Museum and Queen's House): £4.95 adults, £2.95 children, £3.95 senior citizens. Open Apr.–Oct., Mon.–Sat. 10–6, Sun. 2–6; Nov.– Mar., Mon.–Sat. 10–5, Sun. 2–5.*

Shopping

Shopping is one of London's great pleasures, but you have to know where and when to go to pick up a bargain. In December to January, and again in June, when retailers clear the racks ready for next season's ranges, you'll find most goods in most shops on sale. Reductions typically start at 10% and go up to 75%.

Shopping Districts Certain areas can't be beat, but are strictly for window shopping, since they harbor London's highest price tags. These include **Bond Street,** where the big-name jewelers and couturiers are (plus **Fenwick's** fashion store, where prices are reasonable), and **Piccadilly,** with its beautiful **Arcades** and the food hall at **Fortnum & Mason.**

Up **Regent Street,** find **Hamleys** toy store, almost bigger than F.A.O. Schwarz, and **Liberty,** not inexpensive, but possibly the city's most appealing department store, with famous fabrics and a bazaar atmosphere. **Oxford Street** is packed with bargains and office workers. **John Lewis** ("never knowingly undersold") and rather staid **Selfridges** are two department stores worth checking out. **Marks & Spencer** is where all British people buy their underwear (and sweaters)—an essential stop.

Though his suits may be made in Savile Row, the English gentleman comes to **St. James's** for the rest of his outfit, which includes shoes, shirts, silk ties, hats, and all manner of accessories. The prices mirror the quality.

Knightsbridge, dominated by **Harrods,** also boasts many fine boutiques on **Beauchamp Place, Walton Street,** and **Sloane Street,** and **Harvey Nichols,** an excellent fashion store, where there's a permanent sale department.

Chelsea includes the famous, now tired, **King's Road** and borders **South Kensington,** where **Brompton Cross** is good for designer items of all categories. **Kensington Church Street** is full of exquisite, expensive antiques, while **Kensington High Street** has a good array of mid-priced clothes.

Over at **Covent Garden,** you'll find crafts, clothes, and ephemera of all sorts in a lively knot of streets around the **Piazza,** where the street entertainment is free—central London's best value.

Markets   Street markets are one aspect of London life not to be missed, especially if you're watching the pennies. Here are some of the more interesting markets:

Bermondsey. Arrive as early as possible for the best treasure. *Tower Bridge Rd., SE1. Open Fri. 4:30 AM–noon. Take the tube to London Bridge and walk or take the No. 15 or 25 bus to Aldgate and then a No. 42 bus over Tower Bridge to Bermondsey Square.*

Camden Lock. The youth center of the world, apparently, and good for cheap leather boots. The canalside antiques, crafts, and junk markets are also picturesque in their fashion, and very crowded. *Chalk Farm Rd., NW1. Open Sat.–Sun. 9:30–5:30. Take the tube or the No. 24 or 29 bus to Camden Town.*

Camden Passage. The rows of little antiques shops are a good hunting ground for silverware and jewelry. Saturday is the day for stalls; shops are open the rest of the week. *Islington, N1. Open Wed.–Sat. 8:30–3. Take the tube or No. 19 or 38 bus to the Angel.*

Petticoat Lane/Brick Lane. Look for leather goods, bargain-price fashions, household goods and linens, and bric-a-brac and antiques, plus CDs, cameras, videos, and stereos at budget prices. *Middlesex St., E1. Open Sun. 9–2. Take the tube to Liverpool Street, Aldgate, or Aldgate East.*

Portobello Market. Saturday is the best day to search the stalls for not-quite-bargain-price silverware, curios, porcelain, and jewelry. It's always crowded, with an authentic hustle-and-bustle atmosphere, and firmly on the tourist route. Past the fruit stalls, at the "Westway" (north) end, you'll find a good flea market. *Portobello Rd., W11. Open Fri. 5–3, Sat. 8–5. Take the tube or No. 52 bus to Notting Hill Gate or Ladbroke Grove or No. 15 bus to Kensington Park Road.*

Dining

For details and price-category definitions, *see* Dining *in* Staying in Great Britain, *above.*

Bloomsbury   **North Sea Fish Restaurant.** This is the place for good old British fish
¢   and chips—battered and deep-fried white fish with thick-cut fries. It's a bit tricky to find—three blocks south of St. Pancras station, down Judd Street. You can eat in or take out. *7–8 Leigh St., tel. 0171/ 387–5892. Reservations advised. AE, DC, MC, V. Closed Sun., holidays, 10 days at Christmas. Tube: Russell Square.*

¢   **Wagamama.** London is wild for Japanese noodles, and at this crowded, high-tech café, they come fast (the waitstaff have computerized order pads) and delicious. Ramen, in or out of soup, are topped with sliced meats or tempura, and there are rice and vegetable dishes, plus salads and curries. You'll probably be sharing a table. *4 Streatham St., tel. 0171/323–9223. No reservations. No credit cards. Closed Christmas. Tube: Tottenham Court Road.*

Chelsea   **PJ's Bar and Grill.** This is a very friendly place with polo memorabil-
$ ia, wooden floorboards, and stained-glass windows. Large amounts of all-American staples like soft-shell crab, gumbo, steak, and salads are offered, accompanied by any cocktail ever invented, mixed by expert bartenders. *52 Fulham Rd., tel. 0171/581–0025. Reserva-*

tions advised weekends. AE, DC, MC, V. Closed Christmas. Tube: South Kensington.

¢ **Chelsea Kitchen.** This café opened in the '60s to feed the crowds of hungry people searching for hot, filling, and inexpensive food. Expect nothing more fancy than pasta, omelets, salads, stews, and casseroles. The menu changes every day. *98 King's Rd., tel. 0171/589–1330. No credit cards. Closed Christmas. Tube: Sloane Square.*

¢ **Henry J. Bean's.** Hamburgers and Tex-Mex food are served to American oldies music. You order from the bar, then eat in the large and pleasant patio garden. *195–197 King's Rd., tel. 0171/352–9255. No reservations. No credit cards. Closed Dec. 25, 26, 31. Tube: Sloane Square.*

The City **Quality Chop House.** This trendy place, housed in a converted Vic-
$$ torian café, serves generous portions of exquisitely cooked, grease-free "caff" food, like homemade veal sausages with onion gravy and creamed potato. You may have to share one of the tables for six. *94 Farringdon Rd., tel. 0171/837–5093. Reservations advised. No credit cards. Closed Sun., Mon. dinner, Sat. lunch, Christmas. Tube: Farringdon.*

Covent **Bertorelli's.** Opposite the stage door of the Royal Opera House,
Garden Bertorelli's is a favorite with operagoers. Chic, postmodern decor
$$ complements Madalena Bonino's regional Italian food—such as
★ poached cotechino sausage with lentils and roquette and fontina risotto. *44a Floral St., tel. 0171/836–3969. Reservations advised. AE, DC, MC, V. Closed Sun., Dec. 25. Tube: Covent Garden.*

$–$$ **Joe Allen.** This brick-walled basement restaurant follows the style of its New York counterpart and is similarly frequented by theater folk. The barbecued ribs come these days with trendy wilted greens and black-eyed peas, but you can still get great burgers and fries, plus brownies and ice cream. *13 Exeter St., tel. 0171/836–0651. Reservations required. No credit cards. Closed Christmas. Tube: Covent Garden.*

$–$$ **Le Palais du Jardin.** This establishment is a fair imitation of a Parisian brasserie, complete with a seafood bar offering lobsters for a tenner, though there's plenty else—duck confit with apples and prunes, coq au vin, and tuna with a black olive potato cake. Not as chic nor as expensive as it looks, but always busy. *136 Long Acre, tel. 0171/379–5353. Reservations advised. AE, DC, MC, V. Closed Christmas. Tube: Covent Garden.*

$ **Maxwell's.** Its Hampstead sister was London's first burger place, and this younger branch near the tube also does the kind of food you're homesick for—quesadillas and nachos, Buffalo wings, barbecued ribs, cajun chicken and shrimp, chef salad, and a real New York City Reuben. *8–9 James St., tel. 0171/836–0303. Reservations advised weekends. AE, DC, V. Closed Christmas. Tube: Covent Garden.*

$ **Porters.** British food—especially pies (from steak and kidney to chicken and chili) and steamed sponge with custard for dessert—is served in the Earl of Bradford's good-value restaurant. *17 Henrietta St., tel. 0171/836–6466. Reservations necessary weekend dinner. AE, MC, V. Closed Christmas. Tube: Covent Garden.*

¢ **Diana's Diner.** Diana has moved elsewhere, and this superior café is now Italian-run but still serves enormous portions of well-cooked, homey food—roast chicken, stuffed baked potatoes, pasta, and risotto. It's very popular with local workers and residents, so it's always full. *39 Endell St., tel. 0171/240–0272. No credit cards. Closed after 7 PM, Sun. dinner. Tube: Covent Garden.*

¢ **Fatboy's Diner.** One for the kids, this is a 1941 trailer transplanted from the banks of the Susquehanna River in Pennsylvania. Fifties jukebox raves accompany the hot dogs, burgers, and fries. *21 Maiden La., tel. 0171/240–1902. No reservations. No credit cards. Closed Christmas. Tube: Covent Garden.*

¢ **Food for Thought.** This is a simple downstairs vegetarian restaurant
★ with seats for only 50, so there's almost always a waiting line. The
menu—stir-fries, casseroles, salads, and desserts—changes daily,
and each dish is freshly made. No alcohol is served here. *31 Neal St.,
tel. 0171/836–0239. No reservations. No credit cards. Closed Sun.,
Sat. after 4:30 PM, weekdays after 8 PM, 2 wks at Christmas, holidays.
Tube: Covent Garden.*

¢ **Rock & Sole Plaice.** The horrible pun announces exactly what is
served here—fish in the British fashion, dipped in batter and deep-
fried. Try banana fritters for dessert. *47 Endell St., tel. 0171/836–
3785. No credit cards. Closed Sun., Christmas. Tube: Covent Garden.*

Kensington **Lou Pescadou.** Walking into this little Provençal restaurant is like
$$ crossing the Channel to France. As befits the heavily boat-themed
decor, fish is the specialty: Try the *petite bouillabaisse* (fish soup) or
poached red mullet in tarragon sauce. *241 Old Brompton Rd., tel.
0171/370–1057. No reservations. AE, DC, MC, V. Closed Aug.,
Dec. 25. Tube: South Kensington.*

$$ **Wodka.** This modern Polish restaurant, in a quiet backstreet, serves
★ stylish food to stylish people and often has the relaxed atmosphere
of a dinner party. Try herring blinis, roast duck with figs and port,
and the several flavored vodkas. *12 St. Albans Grove W8, tel. 0171/
937–6513. Reservations advised. AE, DC, MC, V. Closed weekend
lunch, Dec. 25–26. Tube: Gloucester Road.*

Knightsbridge **St. Quentin.** This is a popular French spot, just a few blocks west of
$$ Harrods. Every inch of the Gallic menu is explored—Gruyère
quiche, escargots, cassoulet, lemon tart—in the bourgeois provin-
cial comfort so many London chains (the Dômes, the Cafés Rouges)
try hard, yet fail, to achieve. *243 Brompton Rd., tel. 0171/589–8005.
Reservations advised. AE, DC, MC, V. Closed Christmas. Tube:
South Kensington.*

¢ **Luba's Bistro.** Luba's, with its long wooden tables, plain decor, and
authentic Russian cooking, has been popular for decades. This is
where to find your favorite culinary clichés—chicken Kiev and beef
Stroganoff. *6 Yeoman's Row, tel. 0171/589–2950. MC, V. Closed
Sun., public holidays. Tube: Knightsbridge.*

¢ **Stockpot.** Speedy service is the mark of this large, jolly restaurant,
full of young people and middle-aged shoppers. The food is filling
and wholesome; try the homemade soups, the Lancashire hot pot, or
the apple crumble. Breakfast is also served Monday–Saturday.
There are other Stockpots at 40 Panton St. (tel. 0171/839–5142), 18
Old Compton St. (tel. 0171/287–1066), and 273 King's Rd. (tel. 0171/
823–3175). *6 Basil St., tel. 0171/589–8627. Reservations accepted.
No credit cards. Closed Dec. 25, New Year's Day. Tube: Knights-
bridge.*

Mayfair **Criterion.** This wonderful, palatial neo-Byzantine mirrored, marble
$–$$ hall, with its stunning gold mosaic ceiling, is a welcome point of light
in the Piccadilly desert. The Mediterranean menu (garlic roast
chicken, poached salmon with leeks and lemon, chocolate marquise)
is an especially good value if you take advantage of the two-courses-
for-£10 deal. *Piccadilly Circus, tel. 0171/925–0909. Reservations
advised. AE, DC, MC, V. Closed Christmas. Tube: Piccadilly Circus.*

$ **Smollensky's Balloon.** This American-style bar-restaurant is a fa-
vorite among families and has a children's Sunday lunch. The menu
has a few weekly specials, but your best bet is steak, which comes in
a choice of cuts and sauces accompanied by lots of good, thin fries. *1
Dover St., tel. 0171/491–1199. AE, DC, MC, V. Closed Christmas.
Tube: Green Park.*

¢ **Chicago Pizza Pie Factory.** Huge pizzas with salad and garlic bread
are served at reasonable prices at the Windy-City-in-a-basement,
complete with Chicago's WJMK in the air. These pies are American-

style with a thick chewy base; an enormous selection of cocktails further hinders digestion. *17 Hanover Sq., tel. 0171/629–2669. Reservations advised for lunch. No credit cards. Closed Dec. 25, 26. Tube: Oxford Circus.*

¢ **L'Artiste Musclé.** With two cramped floors of France in picturesque Shepherd Market, this place is eccentric, but well loved and of good value. Steak, baked potatoes, and salad are always available. The daily specials, of things like beef bourguignon, come heaped on large plates. You can sit outside in summer. *1 Shepherd Market, tel. 0171/493–6150. AE, MC, V. Closed Sun. lunch, Christmas. Tube: Green Park.*

Notting Hill Gate

$$ **The Belvedere.** In the middle of picturesque Holland Park, there could be no finer setting for a sunny Sunday brunch than a table here. The food is Mediterranean—lots of sun-dried tomatoes and shaved Parmesan. Book way ahead for the few balcony tables. *Holland Park, off Abbotsbury Rd., tel. 0171/602–1238. Reservations required weekends. AE, DC, MC, V. Closed Sun. dinner, Christmas. Tube: Holland Park.*

$$ ★ **192.** This raucus media-mafia hangout is both wine bar and restaurant, serving up-to-the-minute combinations of fresh ingredients, like a warm salad of duck marinated in Thai spices and lime or a saffron seafood risotto. Choosing two or three first courses instead of an entrée keeps the check reasonable. *192 Kensington Park Rd., tel. 0171/229–0482. Reservations advised. AE, MC, V. Closed Mon. lunch, public holidays. Tube: Notting Hill Gate.*

¢ **Tootsies.** Good burgers are cheerfully served in a dark restaurant, brightened by vintage advertisements and vintage rock music. Big salads, BLTs, chicken, and chili are also offered; pies and ice cream are the choices for dessert. *115 Notting Hill Gate, tel. 0171/727–6562; also at 120 Holland Park Ave., tel. 0171/229–8567. MC, V. Closed Christmas. Tube: Holland Park.*

St. James's

$$ **Café Fish.** This bustling restaurant has a wonderful selection of fish, from trout and halibut to turbot and shark, arranged on the menu according to cooking method—meunière, steamed, broiled, or baked. Other dishes include fresh seafood straight out of a Paris brasserie; smoked fish pâté and crusty bread are included in the cover, and there's often a pianist. *39 Panton St., tel. 0171/930–3999. Reservations advised. AE, DC, MC, V. Closed Sat. lunch, Sun., Christmas. Tube: Piccadilly Circus.*

$ **The Fountain.** At the back of Fortnum & Mason's famous store is this elegant and very English restaurant serving light meals, sandwiches, ice cream, cakes, and tea. Welsh rarebit, Fortnum's game pie, or filet steak are typical offerings, and the place is licenced, so you can have a glass of wine with your meal. *181 Piccadilly, tel. 0171/734–4938. Reservations accepted for dinner. AE, DC, MC, V. Closed Sun., public holidays. Tube: Green Park.*

Soho

$$ ★ **Bistrot Bruno.** A star chef in affordable guise (*see* The Canteen, in Chelsea, *above*), Bruno Loubet here offers his justly famous *cuisine de terroir.* Nonfoodies should steer clear of *fromage de tête* (brawn, or pig's head in aspic) and tripe niçoise (cow's stomach) and try, perhaps, duck leg confit with crushed potato and cèpe mushroom sauce. Next door is Café Bruno, an even better bargain. Also look out for Loubet's L'Odeon. *63 Frith St., tel. 0171/734–4545. Reservations essential. Closed Sat. lunch, Sun., Christmas. Tube: Leicester Square.*

$$ ★ **dell' Ugo.** Chef-restaurateur Antony Worrall Thompson has a knack of knowing what London wants to eat—and at this arty, three-floor Soho place, that's Mediterranean dishes like bruschetta, spicy sausages with white bean casserole, crunchy chicken with garlic potatoes, overstuffed deli sandwiches (at around £4), or just a kir and garlic bread. The ground floor is a café–wine bar. *56 Frith St., tel.*

0171/734–8300. Reservations advised for restaurant. AE, MC, V. Closed Sun., Christmas. Tube: Leicester Square.

$$ Soho Soho. You can't miss this lively place, which is located on a corner and apparently built of glass. The ground floor is a café-bar with a rotisserie at the rear (upstairs is a formal restaurant), serving flavorful Provençal-influenced food to match the decor. Omelets, charcuterie, and cheeses supplement dishes like wild mushroom risotto with shaved Parmesan. *11–13 Frith St., tel. 0171/494–3491. AE, DC, MC, V. Closed Sun., Christmas. Tube: Leicester Square.*

$ Deal's West. This restaurant is part-owned by Viscount Linley, but you'd never guess the royal connection from the party atmosphere and big, no-nonsense helpings in this wood-beamed diner. Choose salads, ribs, and burgers or Thai-influenced dishes, like the "DIY Deals," where you cook strips of marinated meat on your own hot brick. *14–16 Fouberts Pl., tel. 0171/287–1050. Reservations advised. AE, DC, MC, V. Closed Sun. dinner, Christmas. Tube: Oxford Circus.*

$ Tai Wing Wa. This newcomer does good Dim Sum for beginners—there's a menu, and it's in English, *and* the waiters are friendly. *7–9 Newport Pl., W1, tel. 0171/287–2702. Reservations advised. AE, DC, MC, V. Closed Sat., Christmas. Tube: Leicester Square.*

¢ Pollo. Are you a hip club animal or a fashion student? If you are, then come to the Soho Italian institution and stand on line for great pasta and people-watching. Otherwise come for lunch, when it's a little calmer, and stick to soup, pasta, or risotto—the meat dishes aren't so reliable. *20 Old Compton St., tel. 0171/734–5917. No credit cards. Closed Sun., public holidays. Tube: Leicester Square.*

Lodging

Although British hotels traditionally included breakfast in their nightly tariff, this is not to be taken for granted these days. Lodging in London is expensive, but money may often be saved by staying outside the center of town. For details and price category definitions, *see* Lodging *in* Staying in Great Britain, *above.*

Bayswater
$$
★ **Camelot.** This affordable hotel, recently refurbished and extended, has TVs, phones, and tea-coffeemakers in all rooms. An attractive brick-walled breakfast room has a large open fireplace and farmhouse tables. The bathless single rooms are great bargains; also ask about the discount for prepaid longer stays. *45–47 Norfolk Sq., W2 1RX, tel. 0171/723–9118, fax 0171/402–3412. 43 rooms, 33 with bath or shower. Facilities: lounge, free in-house videos. MC, V. Tube: Paddington.*

$ Columbia. This enormous, colonnaded Victorian edifice across the street from Kensington Gardens has large, tall rooms, a bar, and lounges that would not look out of place at twice the price. Slightly famous rock bands often stay here. *95–99 Lancaster Gate, W2 3NS, tel. 0171/402–0021, fax 0171/706–4691. 103 rooms with bath. AE, MC, V. Tube: Lancaster Gate.*

¢–$ Lancaster Hall Hotel. This modest place is owned by the German YMCA, which guarantees efficiency and spotlessness. There's a bargain 20-room "youth annex" offering basic rooms with shared baths. *35 Craven Terrace, W2, tel. 0171/723–9276, fax 0171/224–8343. 100 rooms, 80 with bath or shower. Facilities: restaurant, bar. MC, V. Tube: Lancaster Gate.*

Bloomsbury
$$ **Academy.** Convenient to the British Museum and area shops, the Academy is in a Georgian building and has a bar, library-lounge, and patio garden. *17–21 Gower St., WC1E 6HG, tel. 0171/631–4115, fax 0171/636–3442. 32 rooms, 24 with bath. AE, DC, MC, V. Tube: Russell Square.*

$
★ **Morgan.** This charming family-run hotel, in an 18th-century terrace house, has rooms that are small and comfortably furnished, but friendly and cheerful. The tiny paneled breakfast room is straight

out of a doll's house. There are also four apartments with eat-in kitchens and their own phone lines. *24 Bloomsbury St., WC1B 3QJ, tel. 0171/636–3735. 14 rooms with shower, 4 apartments. No credit cards. Tube: Russell Square.*

$ **Ruskin.** Immediately opposite the British Museum, the family-owned, well-run, and very popular Ruskin is both pleasant and quiet—all front windows are double-glazed. The bedrooms are clean, though nondescript; the back ones overlook a pretty garden. *23–24 Montague St., WC1B 5BN, tel. 0171/636–7388, fax 0171/323–1662. 35 rooms, 7 with shower. Facilities: lounge. AE, DC, MC, V. Tube: Tottenham Court Road.*

$ **St. Margaret's.** This guest house, on a tree-lined Georgian street conveniently close to Russell Square, has been run for many years by a friendly Italian family. You'll find spacious rooms, the back ones with a garden view. *24 Bedford Pl., WC1B 5JL, tel. 0171/636–4277. 64 rooms, 10 with bath or shower. Facilities: 2 lounges. No credit cards. Tube: Russell Square.*

¢–$ **Ridgemount.** The kindly owners, Mr. and Mrs. Rees, make you feel at home in this tiny hotel by the British Museum. There's a homey, cluttered feel in the public areas, and some bedrooms overlook a leafy garden. *65 Gower St., WC1E 6HJ, tel. 0171/636–1141. 15 rooms, none with bath. Facilities: lounge. No credit cards. Tube: Russell Square.*

¢ **Central Club.** This YWCA is slightly more expensive than the average, but an excellent location, the facilities, and standards make it worth the bit extra. There's free access to the sports center, with a large pool and gymnasium, and aerobics, yoga, and martial arts classes are included in the rate. Nobody under 18 years old admitted. *16–22 Great Russell St., WC1B 3LR, tel. 0171/636–7512 (ask for reservations manager), fax 0171/636–5278. 104 rooms, 25 shared bathrooms. Facilities: sports center, coffee shop, laundry, hairdresser. No credit cards. Tube: Tottenham Court Road.*

¢ **John Adams Hall.** This group of Georgian houses has been converted into student accommodations that are available at bargain rates during school vacations. There is nothing luxurious here, but it's a short walk to the British Museum and Euston Station is across the street. *15–23 Endleigh St., WC1H 0DH, tel. 0171/387–4086 or 4796. 148 rooms (126 are singles), 28 shared bathrooms. No credit cards. Tube: Euston.*

Chelsea and Kensington
$–$$
La Reserve. In the lively Fulham Broadway neighborhood, by the tube, find this unique, small hotel. Varnished floorboards, black Venetian blinds, contemporary paintings (for sale), and primary-color upholstery sets the sophisticated tone. The tranquil bedrooms have TVs, minibars, hair dryers, tea-coffeemakers, and phones. *422–428 Fulham Rd., SW6 1DU, tel. 0171/385–8561, fax 0171/385–7662. 37 rooms with bath. Facilities: restaurant, bar, lounge, satellite TV. AE, DC, MC, V. Tube: Fulham Broadway.*

$ **Abbey House.** Standards are high and the rooms unusually spacious in this hotel in a fine residential block near Kensington Palace and Gardens. *11 Vicarage Gate, W8 4AG, tel. 0171/727–2594. 15 rooms, none with bath. Facilities: orthopedic beds. No credit cards. Tube: Kensington High Street.*

$ **Periquito Queensgate.** When a hotel calls its own rooms "compact," you'd assume they're closet-size, and you'd be right. This place, one of a small chain, also has a jazzy purple, kingfisher and canary color scheme, to match its tropical parrot logo, and the Natural History Museum is across the street. Satellite TV's, tea-coffeemakers, and hair dryers are crammed into those teeny rooms. *68–69 Queen's Gate, London SW7 5JT, tel. 0171/370–6111, fax 0171/370–0932. 61 rooms with bath. Facilities: lounge, bar. AE, MC, V. Tube: Gloucester Road.*

$ **Vicarage Hotel.** This genteel establishment, run by the same husband-wife team for over 30 years, has high standards of cleanliness.

The bedrooms are traditional and comfortable, with solid English furniture. It attracts many repeat visitors from the United States and welcomes single travelers. *10 Vicarage Gate, W8 4AG, tel. 0171/ 229–4030. 20 rooms, none with bath. Facilities: small TV lounge. No credit cards. Tube: Gloucester Road.*

¢ **Holland Park Independent Hostel.** In this Edwardian house in an up-scale neighborhood, everything is friendly and relaxed, which is just as well, since guests sleep in dormitories and share a kitchen. Unlike many hostels, there is no curfew or lockout; rates are rock bottom. *31 Holland Park Gardens, W14, tel. 071/602–3369. 15 dormitory rooms (60 beds), 4 shared bathrooms. No credit cards. Tube: Holland Park.*

Splurge **The Gore.** Owned by the Hazlitt's people (*see* West End, *below*), this mansion-size town house by the Albert Hall has rooms above the $$ price range, but it is so unique, welcoming, and comfortable that it's worth it. All rooms are scattered with antiques and covered in prints and etchings, while some more expensive ones are utterly over the top, with Tudor-style wood paneling and a four-poster bed, for instance. Bistrot 190 downstairs is one of London's best brasseries. *189 Queen's Gate, SW7 5EX, tel. 0171/584–6601, fax 0171/589–8127. 54 rooms, all with bath. AE, DC, MC, V. Tube: Gloucester Road.*

Hampstead and Regent's Park **Swiss Cottage Hotel.** A charming, family-run hotel, formerly a retirement home, is stuffed with antiques and reproductions and staffed with very pleasant people. The bedrooms are freshly deco-

$$ rated in Victorian style, well sized, and comfortable. There's a restaurant, a cozy lounge, and a welcoming bar that opens onto the patio garden. It's about a 20-minute ride to the West End from here. *4 Adamson Rd., NW3 3HP, tel. 0171/722–2281, fax 0171/483–4588. 80 rooms, all with bath. AE, DC, MC, V. Tube: Swiss Cottage.*

$ **La Gaffe.** The bedrooms in this friendly, eccentric, Italian-run hotel in a row of converted shepherds' cottages are minute, but they're spotless and come complete with TV and phone. Downstairs is a wine bar–café that is popular with Hampstead locals and serves as the hotel lounge. *107–111 Heath St., NW3 6SS, tel. 0171/435–8965, fax 0171/794–7592. 14 rooms, all with shower. AE, MC, V. Tube: Hampstead.*

$ **Primrose Hill B&B.** Members of this small B&B agency believe that "traveling shouldn't be a ripoff" and invite guests into their beautiful homes at reasonable rates to prove it. All houses are in and around Primrose Hill and Hampstead, and guests receive a key. Booking well ahead is essential; phone or write for more details. *Gail O'Farrell, 14 Edis St., NW1 8LG, tel. 0171/722–6869. Around 15 rooms with varying facilities. No credit cards. Tube: varies.*

Knightsbridge and Victoria **The Bulldog Club.** You must join Amanda St. George's *very* exclusive B&B club before you are eligible to book a stay with some of

$$ London's grandest families. Many of the families have converted their now grown-up children's rooms; others have purpose-built guest annexes; all offer total comfort, with breakfast included and TV and tea-coffee facilities in your room—and a copy of the London *Times. For further details, contact 35 The Chase, SW4 0NP, tel. 0171/622–6935, fax 0171/491–1328. Facilities vary; most rooms have private bath/shower. AE, MC, V. Tube: varies.*

$$ **Claverley.** Located on a quiet, tree-lined street, the Claverley offers friendly, attractive surroundings, some four-poster beds, and the wealthy world of Knightsbridge shopping, just around the corner. *13–14 Beaufort Gdns., SW3 1PS, tel. 0171/589–8541, fax 0171/584– 3410. 31 rooms, all with bath. AE, V. Tube: Knightsbridge.*

$$ **Ebury Court.** This small, old-fashioned, country house–style hotel is near Victoria Station. The rooms are not large, but are characterful, with chintzes and antiques. Following refurbishment, there are now few rooms without private baths, and these remain good value; others slightly exceed this category. *26 Ebury St., SW1W 0LU, tel.*

0171/730–8147, fax 0171/823–5966. 45 rooms, 36 with bath. Facilities: restaurant, club with bar and lounge. DC, MC, V. Tube: Victoria.

Londonwide **London Homestead Services.** This family-run business offers bed
$ and breakfast in private homes, most of which are in quiet residential areas and provide first-floor bedrooms with shared bathrooms. Rates get higher the closer you get to central London, but all hosts provide you with a key and all homes have been evaluated by LHS staff. The minimum stay is three nights. Phone or write for more details. *Coombe Wood Rd., Kingston-upon-Thames, Surrey KT2 7JY, tel. 0181/949–4455, fax 0181/549–5492. About 500 rooms with varying facilities. MC, V. Tube: varies.*

Pimlico **Dolphin Square.** The profile of this unique Art Deco quadrangle on
$$ the Thames, five minutes from Westminster, recently rose several notches when Princess Anne moved in. It offers peaceful, modern, self-catering apartments, from studio size with kitchenette to two-bedroom. A large swimming pool, several squash courts, and a tennis court are at your disposal, and you have a very stylish brasserie and bar in-house. *Dolphin Sq., SW1V 3LX, tel. 0171/834–3800, fax 0171/798–8735. 152 apartments, all with bath. AE, DC, MC, V. Tube: Pimlico.*

West End **Bryanston Court.** Three 18th-century houses have been converted
$$ into a traditional English family-run hotel with open fires and comfortable armchairs; the bedrooms are small, pink, and clean. *56–60 Great Cumberland Pl., W1H 7FD, tel. 0171/262–3141, fax 0171/262–7248. 56 rooms with bath or shower. Facilities: restaurant, bar, lounge, satellite TV. AE, DC, MC, V. Tube: Marble Arch.*

$$ **Durrants.** A hotel since the late 18th century, Durrants is just a little shabby around the edges, but the location—in the heart of the West End just by the Wallace collection—is unbeatable. The decor is Olde English wood paneling with motel-like bedrooms, but everything is clean and comfortable. *George St., W1H 6BH, tel. 0171/935–8131, fax 0171/487–3510. 96 rooms, 85 with bath. Facilities: restaurant, bar, lounges. AE, MC, V. Tube: Bond Street.*

$$ **Fielding Hotel.** Tucked away in a quiet alley in Covent Garden, this
★   small hotel is adored by its regulars. The atmosphere is homey and welcoming; the bedrooms are all different and, though some are very small, all are comfortable. There are a lot of stairs in this labyrinthine conversion and no elevator. *4 Broad Court, Bow St., WC2B 5QZ, tel. 0171/836–8305, fax 0171/497–0064. 26 rooms, 1 with bath, 23 with shower. Facilities: bar, breakfast room. AE, DC, MC, V. Tube: Covent Garden.*

$ **Edward Lear.** The former home of Edward Lear, the artist and writer of nonsense verse, this hotel has an imposing entrance leading to a black-and-white tiled lobby and spotless bedrooms varying widely in size and slightly in price (bathless ones are bargains). Some family rooms are huge, and rooms at the back are far quieter. *28–30 Seymour St., W1H 5WD, tel. 0171/402–5401, fax 0171/706–3766. 32 rooms, 12 with bath or shower. V. Tube: Marble Arch.*

Splurge   **Hazlitt's.** It's an open secret that this, Soho's only hotel, is a unique place. Disarmingly friendly, full of antiques and character, Hazlitt's trademarks are its thousands of framed prints obscuring the walls and the Victorian claw-foot bath in every bathroom. Each room is different and all are heavily booked. Rooms here are just above the $$ price range. *6 Frith St., W1V 5TZ, tel. 0171/434–1771, fax 0171/439–1524. 23 rooms, all with bath. AE, DC, MC, V. Tube: Tottenham Court Road.*

The Arts

For a list of events in the London arts scene, visit a newsstand or bookstore to pick up the weekly magazine *Time Out*. The city's evening paper, the *Evening Standard,* carries listings, as do the major Sunday papers; the daily *Independent* and *Guardian;* and, on Friday, the *Times.*

Theater London's theater life can be broadly divided into three categories: the government-subsidized national companies; the commercial, or "West End," theaters; and the fringe.

The main national companies are the **National Theatre** (NT) and the **Royal Shakespeare Company** (RSC). Each has its own custom-designed facilities, in the South Bank arts complex and in the Barbican Arts Centre, respectively. Each presents a variety of plays by writers of all nationalities, ranging from the classics of Shakespeare and his contemporaries to specially commissioned modern works. Box office: NT, tel. 0171/928–2252; RSC, tel. 0171/638–8891.

The West End theaters largely stage musicals, comedies, whodunits, and revivals of lighter plays of the 19th and 20th centuries, often starring television celebrities. Occasionally there are more serious productions, including successful productions transferred from the subsidized theaters, such as RSC's *Les Liaisons Dangereuses* and *Les Misérables.*

The two dozen or so established fringe theaters, scattered around central London and the immediate outskirts, frequently present some of London's most intriguing productions if you're prepared to overlook occasional rough staging and uncomfortable seating. Fringe tickets are considerably less expensive than West End ones.

Most theaters have an evening performance at 7:30 or 8 daily, except Sunday, and a matinee twice a week (Wednesday or Thursday and Saturday). Expect to pay from £6 for a seat in the upper balcony to at least £20 for a good seat in the stalls (orchestra) or dress circle (mezzanine)—more for musicals. Tickets may be booked in person at the theater box office; over the phone by credit card; or through ticket agents, such as **First Call** (tel. 0171/497–9977). In addition, the ticket booth in Leicester Square sells half-price tickets on the day of performance for about 45 theaters; there is a small service charge. Beware of unscrupulous ticket agents who sell tickets at four or five times their box-office price (a small service charge is legitimate) and scalpers, who stand outside theaters offering tickets for the next performance. It's worth asking at the box office on the night of the performance—there will always be around 20 "returns" and nearly all theaters keep a row of "house seats" for emergencies or to sell at the last minute.

Concerts Ticket prices for symphony orchestra concerts are still relatively moderate—between £5 and £15, although you can expect to pay more to hear big-name artists on tour. If you can't book in advance, arrive half an hour before the performance for a chance at returns.

The London Symphony Orchestra is in residence at the **Barbican Arts Centre** (tel. 0171/638–8891), although other top symphony and chamber orchestras also perform here. The **South Bank arts complex** (tel. 0171/928–8800), which includes the **Royal Festival Hall** and the **Queen Elizabeth Hall,** is another major venue for choral, symphony, and chamber concerts. For less expensive concert going, try the **Royal Albert Hall** (tel. 0171/589–8212) during the summer Promenade season; special tickets for standing room are available at the hall on the night of performance. **The Wigmore Hall** (tel. 0171/935–2141) is a small auditorium, ideal for recitals. Inexpensive lunchtime concerts take place all over the city in smaller halls and churches, often featuring string quartets, singers, jazz ensembles, and gospel choirs. **St. John's, Smith Square** (tel. 0171/222–1061), a converted Queen Anne church, is one of the more popular venues. It has a handy crypt cafeteria.

Opera The **Royal Opera House** ranks alongside the New York Met. Prices range from as little as £8.50 (in the upper balconies, from which only a tiny portion of the stage is visible) to nearly £400 for a Grand Tier box. Bookings are best made at the box office (tel. 0171/240–1066). The **Coliseum** (tel. 0171/836–3161) is the home of the English National Opera Company; productions are staged in English and are often innovative and exciting. The prices, which range from £8 to £48, are much cheaper than those of the Royal Opera House.

Ballet The Royal Opera House also hosts the **Royal Ballet.** The prices are slightly more reasonable than for the opera, but be sure to book well ahead. The **English National Ballet** and visiting companies perform at the Coliseum from time to time, especially during the summer. **Sadler's Wells Theatre** (tel. 0171/278–8916) hosts regional ballet and international modern dance troupes. Prices here are reasonable.

Film Most West End movie theaters are in the area around Leicester Square and Piccadilly Circus. Tickets run from around £5 to £8. Matinees and Monday evenings are cheaper. Cinema clubs screen a wide range of films: classics, Continental, underground, rare, or underestimated masterpieces. A temporary membership fee is usually less than £1. One of the best-value clubs is the **National Film Theatre** (tel. 0171/928–3232), part of the South Bank arts complex.

Nightlife

London's night spots are legion, and there is space here to list only a few of the best known. For up-to-the-minute listings, buy *Time Out.*

Jazz **Bass Clef** (85 Coronet St., tel. 0171/729–2476), in an out-of-the-way warehouse on the northern edge of the City, (the nearest tube is Old Street), offers some of the best live jazz in town and a mainly vegetarian menu. **Ronnie Scott's** (47 Frith St., tel. 0171/439–0747) is the legendary Soho jazz club where a host of international performers have played, and still do so.

Nightclubs **Legends** (29 Old Burlington St., tel. 0171/437–9933) has an impressive high-tech interior; a large choice of cocktails is served at the upstairs bar, while the downstairs area is graced with a large cool dance floor and central bar. Glitzy **Stringfellows** (16 Upper St. Martin's Lane, tel. 0171/240–5534) has an Art Deco upstairs restaurant, mirrored walls, and a dazzling light show in the downstairs dance floor.
The Limelight (136 Shaftesbury Ave., tel. 0171/434–0572), in a converted church, is one of London's enduringly popular night spots, with lots of one-nighter shows and special events. It's liveliest on the weekend.
The Wag (33–35 Wardour St., W1, tel. 0171/437–5534) is loud, groovy, and young and changes according to which night it is and which DJ is spinning.

Discos **Camden Palace** (1A Camden High St., tel. 0171/387–0428) is perennially popular with both London and visiting youths. This multitier place, following a recent overhaul, has two major dance floors, plus at least three bars, and a colorful light show. American-style food is served.
Heaven (Under the Arches, Craven St., WC2, tel. 0171/839–3852) is a (mainly) gay club with flashy lazer lighting, loud sounds, and an enormous, frenetic dance floor.
The **Hippodrome** (Cranbourn St., tel. 0171/437–4311) is a hugely popular and lavish disco with live bands and dancing acts, a video screen, bars, and a restaurant.

Rock **The Forum** (9–17 Highgate Rd., tel. 0171/284–0303), an ex-ballroom, is the best venue for medium-to-big-name performers.
The Rock Garden (67 The Piazza, Covent Garden, tel. 0171/240–3961) is famous for encouraging younger talent; Talking Heads, U2,

and The Smiths are among those who played here while still virtually unknown. Music is in the standing-room-only basement, so eat
first in the American restaurant upstairs.
The Marquee (105 Charing Cross Rd., tel. 0171/437–6603), Soho's
original rock club, has moved house since its heyday; at least two live
bands perform every night.

Cabaret   The best comedy in town can be found in the **Comedy Store** (Haymarket House, Oxendon St., near Piccadilly Circus, tel. 01426/914433).
There are two shows, at 8 and midnight on Friday and Saturday, at 8
only Tuesday to Thursday.
Madame Jo Jo's (8 Brewer St., tel. 0171/734–2473) is possibly the
most fun of any London cabaret, with its outrageous, glittering drag
shows. The place is luxurious, and civilized. There are two shows, at
12:15 and 1:15 AM, and the food and drinks are reasonably priced.

Windsor to Stratford

The towns covered in this section can all be visited on a day-trip basis—with the possible exception of Stratford-upon-Avon. British
Rail seems determined to make Stratford—one of England's leading
tourist destinations—as difficult to reach as possible. Windsor, Oxford, and Bath, however, are great for a day's jaunt. The InterCity
trains are Britain's pride and joy. You can reach Bath from London,
for example, in just an hour and 10 minutes.

These excursions will allow you to explore historic townships, such
as Windsor, where the castle is still regularly used by the royal family; Oxford, home of the nation's oldest university; and Shakespeare's birthplace at Stratford-upon-Avon. Traveling south, you
come to Bath, whose 18th-century streets recall an age more elegant
than our own.

Getting Around

By Train   Suburban services run from London (Waterloo and Paddington stations) to Windsor. Regular fast trains run from Paddington to Oxford and Bath, and less frequent and slower services requiring at
least one change, to Stratford. For information, call 0171/262–6767.
An alternative route to Stratford is from London's Euston Station to
Coventry, from which there are hourly bus connections on the Stratford Blue line; call 01788/535555 for details.

By Bus   Regular long-distance services leave from Victoria Coach Station.
For information, call 0171/730–0202. The **Badgerline** bus company in
Bath has a series of **trails** that connect walking trails with bus routes
to make a super budget way of exploring the countryside.

Tourist Information

Bath (The Colonnades, 11–13 Bath St., tel. 01225/462831).
Oxford (The Old School, Gloucester Green, tel. 01865/726871).
Stratford (Bridgefoot, next to the canal bridge, tel. 01789/293127).
Windsor (Central Station, tel. 01753/852010).

Exploring Windsor to Stratford

Windsor   **Windsor,** some 40 kilometers (25 miles) west of London, has been a
royal citadel since the days of William the Conqueror in the 11th century. In the 14th century, Edward III revamped the old castle,
building the Norman gateway, the great round tower, and new
apartments. Almost every monarch since then has added new buildings or improved existing ones; over the centuries, the medieval fortification has been transformed into the lavish royal palace the
visitor sees today. Windsor Castle remains a favorite spot of Queen

Elizabeth and Prince Philip; they spend most weekends here, and there is a grand celebration with all the family at Christmas.

The terrible fire of November 1992, which started in the Queen's private chapel, totally gutted some of the **State Apartments.** Miraculously, a swift rescue effort meant that hardly any works of art were lost. The repairs are likely to last until 1999, though only two of the state rooms previously open to visitors were still closed at press time (summer 1995), and all of the other public areas are now open, including St. George's Chapel, and Queen Mary's Dolls' House. One interesting feature of a visit at this time is that you will be able to watch some of the expert work of restoration in progress.

St. George's Chapel, more than 71 meters (230 feet) long with two tiers of great windows and hundreds of gargoyles, buttresses, and pinnacles, is one of the noblest buildings in England. Inside, above the choir stalls, hang the banners, swords, and helmets of the Knights of the Order of the Garter, the most senior Order of Chivalry. The many monarchs buried in the chapel include Henry VIII and George VI, father of the present queen. The **State Apartments** indicate the magnificence of the queen's art collection; here hang paintings by such masters as Rubens, Van Dyck, and Holbein; drawings by Leonardo da Vinci; and Gobelin tapestries, among many other treasures. There are splendid views across to Windsor Great Park, the remains of a former royal hunting forest. Make time to view **Queen Mary's Dolls' House,** a charming toy country house with every detail complete, including electricity, running water, and miniature books on the library shelves. It was designed in 1921 by the architect Sir Edwin Lutyens for the present queen's grandmother. *Windsor Castle, tel. 01753/868286. Admission (including Precincts): £8 adults, £4 children, £5.50 senior citizens; Dolls' House viewable for extra £1 on the ticket price; Carriages admission: £1.60 adults, 80p children, £1.40 senior citizens. Open daily Mar.–Oct. 10–4 (last admission at 3); Nov.–Feb., 10–5:30 (last admission at 4).*

After you see the castle, stroll around the town and enjoy the shops; antiques are sold in cobbled Church Lane and Queen Charlotte Street.

A short walk over the river brings you to **Eton,** Windsor Castle's equally historic neighbor and home of the famous public school. (In Britain, so-called "public" schools are private and charge fees.) Classes still take place in the distinctive redbrick Tudor-style buildings; the oldest buildings are grouped around a quadrangle called School Yard. The **Museum of Eton Life** has displays on the school's history, and a guided tour is also available. *Brewhouse Yard, tel. 01753/671177. Admission: £2.30 adults, £1.60 children; with tour— £3.40 adults, £2.80 children. Open daily during term 2–4:30; 10:30– 4:30 on school holidays. Guided tours Mar.–Oct., daily at 2:15 and 3:15.*

Numbers in the margin correspond to points of interest on the Oxford map.

Oxford Continue along A4130 and A4070 northwest to **Oxford.** The surest way to absorb Oxford's unique blend of history and scholarliness is to wander around the tiny alleys that link the honey-color stone buildings topped by elegant "dreaming" spires, exploring the colleges where the undergraduates live and work. Oxford University, like Cambridge University, is not a single building but a collection of 35 independent colleges; many of their magnificent chapels and dining halls are open to visitors—times are displayed at the entrance

1 lodges. **Magdalen College** (pronounced "maudlin") is one of the most impressive, with more than 500-year-old cloisters and lawns leading

2 down to a deer park and the river Cherwell. **St. Edmund Hall,** the next college up the High Street, has one of the smallest and most

3 picturesque quadrangles, with an old well in the center. **Christ**

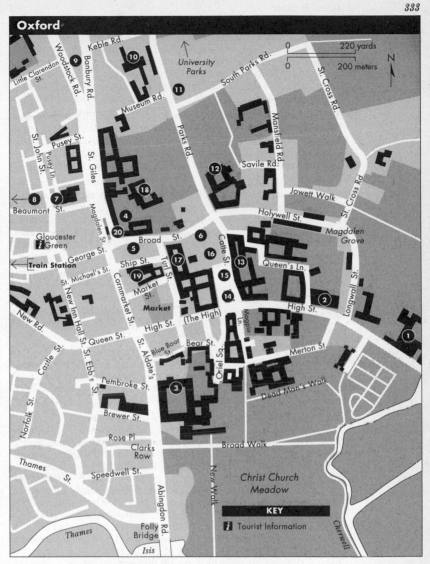

Oxford

Major Attractions
Ashmolean Museum, **7**
Balliol College, **4**
Christ Church, **3**
Magdalen College, **1**
Oxford Story, **5**
St. Edmund Hall, **2**
Sheldonian Theatre, **6**

Other Attractions
All Souls College, **13**
Bodleian Library, **16**
Exeter College, **17**
Jesus College, **19**
Keble College, **10**
Radcliffe Camera, **15**
St. Giles' Church, **9**
St. Mary Magdalen
Church, **20**

Trinity College, **18**
University Church
(St. Mary s), **14**
University Museum, **11**
Wadham College, **12**
Worcester College, **8**

Church, on St. Aldate's, has the largest quadrangle, known as Tom Quad; hanging in the medieval dining hall are portraits of former pupils, including John Wesley, William Penn, and no fewer than 14 prime ministers. The doors between the inner and outer quadrangles of **Balliol College,** on Broad Street, still bear the scorch marks from the flames that burned Archbishop Cranmer and Bishops Latimer and Ridley at the stake in 1555 for their Protestant beliefs.

❺ The **Oxford Story** on Broad Street is a dramatic multimedia presentation of the university's 800-year history, in which visitors travel through depictions of college life. *Broad St., tel. 01865/728822. Admission: £4.50 adults, £3.25 children, £3.95 senior citizens, £14 family ticket. Open Apr.–Oct., daily 9:30–5 (July and Aug. to 7), Nov.–Mar., 10–4.*

❻ Also on Broad Street is the **Sheldonian Theatre,** which St. Paul's architect Christopher Wren designed to look like a semi-circular Roman amphitheater; it's one of his earliest works. Graduation ceremonies are held here. *Broad St., tel. 01865/277299. Admission: 50p adults, 25p children. Open Mon.–Sat. 10–12:45 and 2–4:45; closes at 3:45 mid-Nov.–Feb.*

❼ The **Ashmolean Museum,** which you encounter by turning right out of Broad Street into Magdalen Street, then taking the first left, is Britain's oldest public museum, holding priceless collections of Egyptian, Greek, and Roman artifacts; Michelangelo drawings; and European silverware. *Beaumont St., tel. 01865/278000. Admission free. Open Tues.–Sat. 10–4, Sun. 2–4.*

For a relaxing walk, make for the banks of the river Cherwell, either through the University Parks area or through Magdalen College to Addison's Walk, and watch the undergraduates idly punting a summer's afternoon away. Or rent one of these narrow flat-bottom boats yourself. But be warned: Navigating is more difficult than it looks!

Blenheim Palace, about 13 kilometers (8 miles) north of Oxford on the A44 (Woodstock Road), is a vast mansion in neoclassical style built in the early 18th century by the architect Sir John Vanbrugh; it stands in 1,012 hectares (2,500 acres) of beautiful gardens landscaped later in the 18th century by "Capability" Brown, perhaps the most famous of all English landscape gardeners. The house was built for the soldier and statesman John Churchill, first duke of Marlborough, on land given to him by Queen Anne and with money voted him by Parliament on behalf of a "grateful nation" as a reward for his crushing defeat of the French at the Battle of Blenheim in 1704. The house is filled with fine paintings, tapestries, and furniture. Winston Churchill, a descendant of Marlborough, was born in the palace; some of his paintings are on display, and there is an exhibition devoted to his life. *Woodstock, tel. 01993/811091. Admission: £7 adults, £3.50 children 5–15, £4.90 senior citizens, £19 family ticket. Open mid-Mar.–Oct., 10:30–5:30. Grounds open all year 9–4:45 (admission free). Restaurant and cafeteria.*

Sir Winston Churchill (1874–1965) is buried in the nearby village of **Bladon.** His grave in the small tree-lined churchyard is all the more touching for its simplicity.

Stratford-upon-Avon Even without its most famous son, **Stratford-upon-Avon** would be worth visiting. The town's timbered buildings bear witness to its prosperity in the 16th century, when it was a thriving craft and trading center, and attractive 18th-century buildings are also of note.

Numbers in the margin correspond to points of interest on the Stratford-upon-Avon map.

The main places of Shakespearean interest are run by the **Shakespeare Birthplace Trust.** They all have similar opening times (mid-

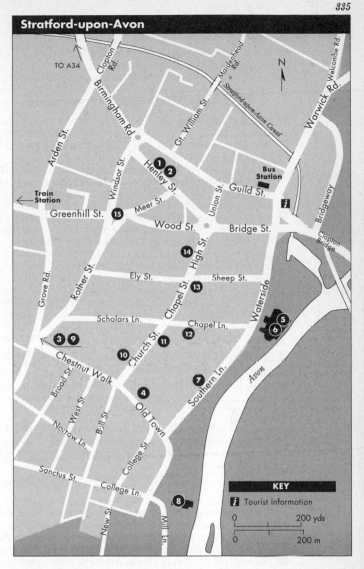

Stratford-upon-Avon

Major Attractions

Anne Hathaway's Cottage, **9**

Hall's Croft, **4**

Holy Trinity Church, **8**

Mary Arden's House, **3**

The Other Place, **7**

Royal Shakespeare Theatre, **5**

Shakespeare Centre, **1**

Shakespeare's Birthplace, **2**

Swan, **6**

Other Attractions

American Fountain, **15**

Grammar School and Guildhall, **11**

Guild Chapel, **12**

Harvard House, **14**

Shakespeare Institute, **10**

Town Hall, **13**

KEY

i Tourist Information

0 — 200 yds

0 — 200 m

Mar.–mid-Oct., Mon.–Sat. 9–6, Sun. 9:30–6; mid-Oct.–mid-Mar., Mon.–Sat. 9:30–4:30, Sun. 10–4:30 (last entry times always 30 min before closing), and you can get an inclusive ticket for them all—£8 adults, £3.60 children, £21 family ticket—or pay separate entry fees if you want to visit only one or two. The **Shakespeare Centre** and **Shakespeare's Birthplace** contain the costumes used in the BBC's dramatization of the plays and an exhibition of the playwright's life and work. *Henley St., tel. 01789/204016. A Shakespeare Birthplace Trust property.*

Two very different attractions reveal something of the times in which Shakespeare lived. Originally a farmhouse, the girlhood home of Shakespeare's mother, **Mary Arden's House,** is now an extensive museum of farming and country life. It was built in the 16th century and many of the original outbuildings are intact. There is also a falconry, with flying displays, and a new garden, planted with the trees mentioned in Shakespeare's plays. *Wilmcote (5.5 km [3.5 mi] northwest of Stratford, off A3400 and A46), tel. 01789/204016. Also* *reachable by train in a few mins from Stratford. A Shakespeare Birthplace Trust property.*

④ A complete contrast is **Hall's Croft,** a fine Tudor town house that was the home of Shakespeare's daughter Susanna and her doctor husband; it is furnished in the decor of the day, and the doctor's dispensary and consulting room can also be seen. *Old Town, tel. 01789/ 292107. A Shakespeare Birthplace Trust property.*

⑤ The **Royal Shakespeare Theatre** occupies a perfect position on the banks of the Avon—try to see a performance if you can. The company (always referred to as the RSC) performs several Shakespeare plays each season, as well as plays by a wide variety of other playwrights, between March and January. You can gain a fascinating insight into how the theater operates by joining one of the backstage tours taking place twice daily (four times on Sunday); call 01789/ 296655 for details. Beside the main theater there is the smaller
⑥ **Swan,** modeled on an Elizabethan theater, providing a very exciting auditorium for in-the-round staging, and a new auditorium for ex-
⑦ perimental productions, **The Other Place.** The Swan also provides entry to the RSC Collection, including paintings, props, and memorabilia, either visible on one of the backstage tours or on their own. For more information, telephone the number given above for the tours. It's best to book well in advance for RSC productions, but tickets for the day of performance are always available, and it is also worth asking if there are any returns. *Programs are available starting in February from the Royal Shakespeare Theatre, Stratford-upon-Avon, Warwickshire CV37 6BB, tel. 01789/295623.*

⑧ It is in **Holy Trinity Church,** close to the Royal Shakespeare Theatre, that Shakespeare and his wife are buried.

⑨ **Anne Hathaway's Cottage,** in Shottery on the edge of the town, is the early home of the playwright's wife. *A Shakespeare Birthplace Trust property.*

Bath Bath is a perfect 18th-century city, perhaps the best preserved in all Britain. It is a compact place, easy to explore on foot; the museums, elegant shops, and terraces of magnificent town houses are all close to each other.

Numbers in the margin correspond to points of interest on the Bath map.

It was the Romans who first took the waters at Bath, building a temple in honor of their goddess Minerva and a sophisticated series of baths to make full use of the curative hot springs. To this day, these springs gush from the earth at a constant temperature of 115.7°F
① (46.5°C). In the **Roman Baths Museum,** underneath the 18th-century Pump Room, you can see the excavated remains of almost the entire baths complex. *Abbey Churchyard, tel. 01225/477000, ext. 2785. Admission: £5 adults, £3 children, £13 family ticket. Combined ticket for Roman Baths and Costume Museum: £6.60 adults, £3.50 children, £16 family ticket. Open Apr.–Sept., daily 9–6; Oct.– Mar., Mon.–Sat. 9:30–5, Sun. 10:30–5.*

② Next to the Pump Room is the **Abbey,** built in the 15th century. There are superb fan-vaulted ceilings in the nave.

In the 18th century, Bath became the fashionable center for taking the waters. The architect John Wood created a harmonious city from the mellow local stone, building beautifully executed terraces, crescents, and villas. The heart of Georgian Bath is the perfectly
③ proportioned **Circus** and the Royal Crescent. On the corner, **No. 1**
④ **Royal Crescent** is furnished as it might have been when Beau Nash, the master of ceremonies and arbiter of 18th-century Bath society, lived in the city. *Tel. 01225/428126. Admission: £3 adults, £2.50 chil-*

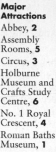

Major Attractions

Abbey, **2**

Assembly Rooms, **5**

Circus, **3**

Holburne Museum and Crafts Study Centre, **6**

No. 1 Royal Crescent, **4**

Roman Baths Museum, **1**

Other Attractions

Camden Works Museum, **7**

Carriage Museum, **8**

Octagon and National Centre of Photography, **10**

Pulteney Bridge, **11**

Sally Lunn's, **12**

Theatre Royal, **9**

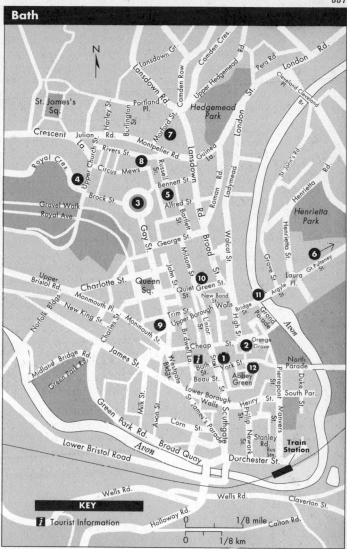

Bath

KEY

i Tourist Information

0 ————— 1/8 mile

0 ————— 1/8 km

dren and senior citizens. Open Mar.–Oct., Tues.–Sun. 10:30–5; Nov.–mid-Dec., Tues.–Sun 11–4.

⑤ Also near the Circus are the **Assembly Rooms,** frequently mentioned by Jane Austen in her novels of early 19th-century life. This neoclassical villa now houses a Museum of Costume, displaying dress styles from Beau Nash's day to the present. *Bennett St., tel. 01225/477000, ext. 2785. Admission: £3.20 adults, £2 children, £9 family ticket. Open Mon.–Sat. 10–5, Sun. 11–5.*

⑥ Across the Avon, in an elegant 18th-century building, is the **Holburne Museum and Crafts Study Centre,** which houses a superb collection of 17th- and 18th-century fine art and decorative arts. There are also works by 20th-century craftsmen in the study center. *Great Pulteney St., tel. 01225/466669. Admission: £3.50 adults, £1.50 children, £3 senior citizens, £7 family ticket. Open Easter–mid-Dec., Mon.–Sat. 11–5, Sun. 2:30–5:30; mid-Feb.–Easter, Tues.–Sat. 11–5, Sun. 2:30–6.*

Dining and Lodging

For details and price-category definitions, *see* Dining and Lodging *in* Staying in Great Britain, *above.*

Bath   **Number Five.** This candlelit bistro off Pulteney Bridge has a relaxed
Dining   ambience and offers simple pasta with olive oil and grilled eggplant or more elaborate dishes such as confit of duck or roast breast of chicken with sun-dried tomatoes. A BYOB option is offered on Mondays and Tuesdays. *5 Argyle St., tel. 01225/444499. DC, MC, V. Closed Sun., and Mon. lunch. $–$$*

Rascals. This is a good spot near the abbey for a meal and a break from sightseeing. In a network of cellar rooms, you can choose from a regularly changing menu or daily specials. There is a good choice of vegetarian dishes, and the desserts are rich and delicious. *8 Pierrepont Pl., tel. 01225/330201. MC, V. Closed Sun. lunch. $*

Theatre Vaults. These busy stone cellars house a very handy restaurant that serves light meals at lunchtime and early evening or full-scale dinner menus later. Try the rack of lamb or spinach lasagne. *Sawclose, tel. 01225/442265. AE, DC, MC, V. Closed Sun. $*

Lodging   **Paradise House.** This worthwhile B&B is about a 10-minute, uphill walk from the center of town. Its upstairs windows have great views over the city. Cheerfully decorated in soft greens and browns, pleasant fall shadings, this 1720 house has been restored and has open fires in winter and a garden in summer. A full breakfast is offered. All rooms have TV. *88 Holloway, BA2 4PX, tel. 01225/317723. 9 rooms, 7 with bath or shower. AE, MC, V. $$*

Pratt's. Just a few minutes' walk from the center of town and the main sights, Pratt's is a fine Georgian house. Once the home of novelist Sir Walter Scott, it is now a comfortable hotel with an innovative restaurant. *South Parade, BA2 4AB, tel. 01225/46041, fax 01225/448807. 46 rooms with bath. Facilities: restaurant. AE, DC, MC, V. $$*

Villa Magdala Hotel. This solid mid-Victorian house—named after a 1868 battle in Ethiopia—offers attractive views of Henrietta Park, across the road. The recently refurbished rooms cost from £58 (and up) a night, and some (for an extra charge) have four-poster beds; all have color TVs and phones. *Henrietta Rd., Bath BA2 6LX, tel. 01225/466329, fax 01225/483207. 17 rooms with bath. AE, MC, V. $*

Oxford   **Fifteen North Parade.** Just outside the city center, this is an inti-
Dining   mate, stylish restaurant with cane furniture and plants. The menu changes regularly and may feature lobster ravioli, or potted partridge. *15 North Parade, tel. 01865/513773. Reservations advised. MC, V. Closed Sun. evening and Mon. $$*

Munchy Munchy. A menu of spicy Malaysian dishes that changes three times weekly and a good selection of fresh fruit and vegetables make this a refreshing and popular spot. The surroundings are unpretentious, and the prices are reasonable. *6 Park End St., tel. 01865/245710. Reservations accepted. MC, V. Closed Sun., Mon., 2 wks in Aug. and Sept. and 2 wks in Dec. and Jan. $*

The Trout. This ivy-covered medieval pub, on the northern edge of Oxford, is a wonderful spot for a summer bar lunch. There are peacocks by the stream, and a tasty selection of both hot and cold dishes is available. Indoors is a beamed restaurant with slightly higher prices. *Godstow, tel. 01865/54485. ¢*

Lodging   **Cotswold House.** This popular B&B lies in the north of town, on the main A423 Banbury road. Inside the stone building the refurbished comfortable (no-smoking) rooms are furnished with attractive modern furniture. The owners, who really know the area, are pleased to help with tourism advice. Don't confuse it with the much more pricey Cotswold Lodge. *363 Banbury Rd., OX3 7SP, tel. 01865/310558. 6 rooms with bath. No credit cards. $*

Norham Guest House. This simple, very reasonably priced guest house, in a Victorian building, is in a conservation area—and thus is peaceful. The rooms are tastefully decorated and comfortable. All of them have tea and coffeemaking facilities and TVs. As with many guest houses now, smoking is not permitted within the building. Norham Guest House is on the north side of town and within an easy 15-minute walk of the town center. *16 Norham Rd., OX2 6SF, tel. 01865/515352. 8 rooms, 7 with bath or shower. No credit cards. $*

Pickwicks. Pickwicks is 1½ miles east of the town center, off the main A420, the London road. This quietly run inn, situated on a corner in its own garden, features standard rooms with TVs and tea and coffeemaking facilities. Evening meals are available on request. *17 London Rd., OX3 7SP, tel. 01865/750487, fax 01865/742208. 14 rooms, 10 with bath or shower. AE, MC, V. $*

Stratford **Box Tree Restaurant.** In the Royal Shakespeare Theatre, this ele-
Dining gant restaurant overlooks the river and is a favored spot for pre- and post-theater dining. Specialties include noisettes of lamb Box Tree and poached Scotch beef fillet. *Waterside, tel. 01789/293226. Reservations required. AE, DC, MC, V. Closed when theater is closed. $$*

The Opposition. The renovated Opposition is handy for the theater and caters to pre- and post-theater dining, as do all sensible restaurants in Stratford. It is extremely popular with the locals, so book in advance. The American and Continental dishes change constantly—if you're lucky there'll be Cajun chicken or courgette and aubergine lasagna on the menu. *13 Sheep St., tel. 01789/269980. Reservations advised. MC, V. $$*

The River Terrace. For less expensive fare at the theater, this spot provides informal meals and light refreshments. Hot dishes include lasagna and shepherd's pie, and there are also salads, cakes, and sandwiches. *Waterside, tel. 01789/293226. No reservations. No credit cards. $*

The Slug and Lettuce. Don't let the name put you off. This is a pine-paneled pub that serves excellent meals; the long-standing favorites are chicken breast baked in avocado and garlic and salmon escalope. *38 Guild St., tel. 01789/299700. Reservations accepted. MC, V. $*

Vintner's Wine Bar. This bar and restaurant—one of many on Sheep Street—features daily specials alongside the main menu, which has such delicious dishes as chicken breast stuffed with Parma ham and served with an apricot sauce. There are smoking and no-smoking sections. Before a performance the place gets very busy, indeed. *5 Sheep St., tel. 01789/297259. MC, V. $*

Lodging **Caterham House.** Built in 1830, this elegantly furnished building is in the center of town, close to the theater. Its rooms are individually decorated, featuring brass bedsteads and antiques. There is now a French restaurant, **Le Bonaparte,** attached, which has received plaudits. *58 Rother St., CV37 6LT, tel. 01789/267309, fax 01789/414836. 10 rooms with bath or shower. MC, V. $–$$*

Moonraker House. This distinctly upscale B&B, in the northwest section of town and near the rail station, is actually a complex of three white suburban houses. Rooms vary in both size and price, so you should be able to find something here even if you are on a tight budget. All rooms have TVs, hair dryers, and tea and coffeemakers, and all guests are invited to use the garden. *40 Alcester Rd., CV37 9DB, tel. 01789/299346, fax 01789/295504. 19 rooms with bath. MC, V. $*

Penryn House. This lodging is coveniently located halfway between the theater and Anne Hathaway's cottage and within an easy walk of both. The comfortably furnished rooms have TV, hair dryers, and tea and coffeemaking facilities. *126 Alcester Rd., CV37 0DP, tel. 01789/293718. 7 rooms, 5 with bath or shower. MC, V. ¢–$*

Windsor and **Watermans Arms.** A very pleasant pub near the Thames in Eton. It
Eton has an airy conservatory, partially uncovered for summer eating,
Dining and plenty of rowing decorations, oars and such. The attractively

presented bar food includes omelets and other hot dishes at reasonable prices. *Brocas St., tel. 01753/861001. $*

The Courtyard. The idyllic setting, near the river and castle, make this a pleasant spot for light lunches and teas. *8 King George Pl., tel. 01753/858338. Open daily 11:30–5. ¢*

The Dôme. Proximity to the castle, reasonable prices, and a varied French menu are reasons for having lunch here. Charcuterie, pâté, and salads, among other dishes, are available. *5 Thames St., tel. 01753/864405. AE, MC, V. ¢*

Lodging **Ye Harte and Garter.** Originally two Tudor taverns, this hotel was rebuilt during the last century. It is in a busy position immediately opposite the castle. *21 High St., Windsor, SL4 1LR, tel. 01753/863426, fax 01753/830527. 44 rooms, 42 with bath or shower. AE, DC, MC, V. $*

Cambridge

Cambridge, home of England's second-oldest university, is an ideal place to explore. Students began studying here in the early 13th century, and virtually every generation since then has produced fine buildings, often by the most distinguished architects of their day. The result is a compact gallery of the best of English architecture. There is also good shopping in the city, as well as relaxing riverside walks.

Getting Around

By Train Hourly trains from London's Liverpool Street Station take between 60 and 90 minutes to Cambridge; there's equally regular but generally slower service from London's King's Cross Station. For information, call 0171/928–5100. Cambridge is an easy day trip from London by train. It can be a long day, too, since the last train back leaves just before 11 PM.

By Bus There are 14 buses daily from Victoria Coach Station that take just under two hours. Tel. 0171/730–0202.

Tourist Information

Cambridge (Wheeler St., off King's Parade, tel. 01223/322640).

Exploring Cambridge

The university is in the very heart of **Cambridge.** It consists of a number of colleges, each of which is a separate institution with its own distinct character and traditions. Undergraduates join an individual college and are taught by dons attached to the college, who are known as "fellows." Each college is built around a series of courts, or quadrangles; because students and fellows live in these courts, access is sometimes restricted, especially during examination weeks from April through mid-June. Visitors are not normally allowed into college buildings other than chapels and halls. It's wisest to check first with the city tourist office which colleges are visitable.

Numbers in the margin correspond to points of interest on the Cambridge map.

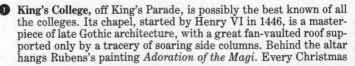 **King's College,** off King's Parade, is possibly the best known of all the colleges. Its chapel, started by Henry VI in 1446, is a masterpiece of late Gothic architecture, with a great fan-vaulted roof supported only by a tracery of soaring side columns. Behind the altar hangs Rubens's painting *Adoration of the Magi.* Every Christmas

Eve the college choir sings the Festival of Nine Lessons and Carols, which is broadcast all over the world.

King's runs down to the "Backs," the tree-shaded grounds on the banks of the river Cam, which is the background of many of the colleges. From King's make your way along the river and through the narrow lanes past **Clare College** and **Trinity Hall** to **Trinity.** This is the largest college, established by Henry VIII in 1546. It has a handsome 17th-century Great Court, around which are the chapel, hall, gates, and a library by Christopher Wren. In the massive gate house is Great Tom, a large clock that strikes each hour with high and low notes. Prince Charles was an undergraduate here during the late 1960s.

Beyond Trinity lies **St. John's,** the second-largest college. The white crenellations of the enormous mock-Gothic **New Court** of 1825 have earned it the nickname "the wedding cake." It is reached across a facsimile of the Bridge of Sighs in Venice. Behind St. John's is the oldest house in Cambridge, the 12th-century **Merton Hall.**

Across **Magdalene** (pronounced "maudlin") **Bridge** you come to **Magdalene College,** with its pretty redbrick courts. The **Pepys Library** contains the 17th-century diarist's own books and desk. *Admission free. Open Oct.–Mar., daily 2:30–3:30; Apr.–Sept., daily 11:30–12:30 and 2:30–3:30.*

Beyond Magdalene is **Kettle's Yard.** This was originally the home of Jim Ede, a connoisseur of 20th-century art. Here he displayed his collections to the public; a gallery extension now houses temporary exhibits. *Castle St., tel. 01223/352124. Admission free. House open Tues.–Sun. 2–4; gallery open Tues.–Sat. 12:30–5:30 (Thurs. to 7), Sun. 2–5:30.*

Returning the way you've just come, along the Backs from King's, you'll see **Queen's College,** where Isaac Newton's **Mathematical Bridge** crosses the river. This arched wooden structure was originally held together by gravitational force; when it was taken apart to see how Newton did it, no one could reconstruct it without using nails.

Back from the river, on Trumpington Street, sits **Pembroke College,** which contains some 14th-century buildings and a chapel by Wren, and **Peterhouse,** the oldest college, dating from 1281. Next to Peterhouse is the **Fitzwilliam Museum,** which contains outstanding art collections (including paintings by Constable, Gainsborough, and the French Impressionists) and antiquities (especially from ancient Egypt). *Trumpington St., tel. 01223/332900. Admission free. Open Tues.–Sat. 10–5, Sun. 2:15–5.*

Other colleges worth visiting include **Downing College,** which has a unique collection of neoclassical buildings dating from about 1800, and **Emmanuel College,** whose chapel and colonnade are by Christopher Wren. Emmanuel's spacious gardens have a pretty duck pond with several unusual breeds. Among the portraits of famous Emmanuel men hanging in the hall is one of John Harvard, founder of Harvard University.

If you have time, hire a punt at **Silver Street Bridge** or at **Magdalene Bridge** and navigate down past St. John's or upstream to **Grantchester,** the pretty village made famous by the Edwardian poet Rupert Brooke. On a sunny day, there's no better way to absorb Cambridge's unique atmosphere—somehow you will seem to have all the time in the world.

Dining and Lodging

For details and price-category definitions, *see* Dining and Lodging *in* Staying in Great Britain, *above.*

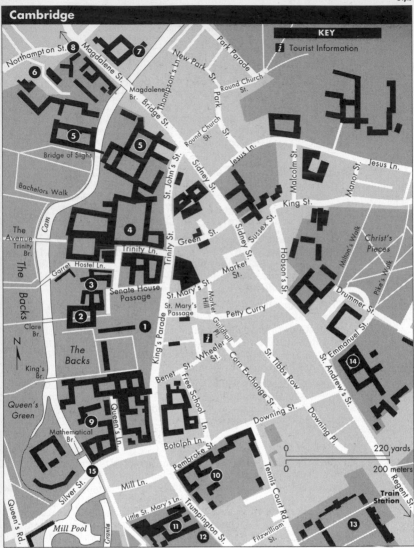

Cambridge

KEY

i Tourist Information

Clare College, **2**
Downing College, **13**
Emmanuel College, **14**
Fitzwilliam Museum, **12**
Kettle's Yard, **8**
King's College, **1**
Magdalene College, **7**
Merton Hall, **6**

Pembroke College, **10**
Peterhouse, **11**
Queen's College, **9**
St. John's, **5**
Silver Street Bridge, **15**
Trinity, **4**
Trinity Hall, **3**

Dining
$$

Charlie Chan. This is one of Cambridge's more exotic spots. The Chinese food is popular with undergrads, so there's a good-value set meal for around £27 for two. Downstairs is casual; upstairs is fancier. Dancing Friday and Saturday. *14 Regent St., tel. 01223/61763. Reservations advised. AE, MC, V.*

$$

Three Horseshoes. This is an early 19th-century thatched cottage with a recently added conservatory. A pub restaurant serves beautifully prepared grilled fish, and the conservatory menu offers traditional English fare and seafood, also beautifully presented. *Madingley, tel. 01954/210221 (3 mi southwest of Cambridge). AE, DC, MC, V.*

$$

Twenty-Two. This intimate restaurant occupies a modest house a half mile west of the city center. The proprietor cooks the set dinner, which features an eclectic and innovative assortment of international dishes, with an emphasis on fish and game. *22 Chesterton Rd., tel. 01223/351880. Reservations advised. AE, MC, V. Closed lunch, Sun. and Mon.*

¢

Hobbs Pavilion. This friendly creperie, near the colleges, is located in a former cricket pavilion (during spring and early summer, you can usually watch a game of cricket on the grounds). The menu offers a wide selection of savory and sweet crepes, which makes an ideal lunch. *Parker's Piece, Park Terr., tel. 01223/67480. No credit cards. Closed Sun., Mon. and mid-Aug.–mid-Sept.*

Lodging
$$

Arundel House. This hotel occupies a converted terrace of Victorian houses overlooking the river. The redecorated bedrooms are comfortably furnished with locally made mahogany furniture. *53 Chesterton Rd., CB4 3AN, tel. 01223/67701, fax 01223/67721. 105 rooms with bath or shower. Facilities: restaurant, bar, videos, garden. AE, DC, MC, V.*

$$

Centennial Hotel. The Centennial is conveniently located opposite the Botanical Gardens on the south side of town, near the station. All rooms have TVs and tea and coffeemaking facilities. There's an excellent restaurant serving table d'hôte and full à la carte menus, including assorted steaks and Aylesbury duckling with black cherry and brandy sauce. *63–71 Hills Rd., CB2 1PG, tel. 01223/314652. 26 rooms with bath. Facilities: restaurant, TV. AE, DC, MC, V.*

$–$$

Regency Guest House. This quiet guest house overlooks Parker's Piece, a central section of parkland. It's a large Victorian house, with simple, comfortably furnished rooms, of which some but not all have private bathrooms, though each has a wash basin and tea and coffeemaking facilities. This is a handy choice, both for its centrality and its reasonable prices. *7 Regent Terr., CB2 1AA, tel. 01223/329626, fax 01223/871816. 8 rooms. No credit cards.*

York

Once England's second city, the ancient town of York has survived the ravages of time, war, and industrialization to remain one of northern Europe's few preserved walled cities. It was King George VI, father of the present queen, who once remarked that the history of York is the history of England. Even in a brief visit to the city, you can see evidence of life from every era since the Romans, not only in museums but in the very streets and houses. On a more contemporary note, the city also boasts one of the most fashionable shopping centers in this part of the country.

York is surrounded by some of the grandest countryside England has to offer. A fertile plain dotted with ancient abbeys and grand aristocratic mansions leads westward to the hidden valleys and jagged, windswept tops of the Yorkshire Dales and northward to the brooding mass of the North York Moors. This is a land quite different from the south of England—friendlier, emptier, and less aggressively materialistic. No visitor to Britain should overlook it.

Getting Around

By Train Regular fast trains run from London's King's Cross Station to York. The trip takes around two hours. For information, call 0171/278–2477. York can be visited as a day trip from London, but only if you are prepared to make an early start. The last train leaves York at 9:40 in the evening, arriving in London at about midnight.

By Bus Regular long-distance buses leave from Victoria Coach Station. The trip takes 4½ hours. For information, call 0171/730–0202.

Tourist Information

There is a tourist information office at De Grey Rooms (Lendel Bridge, Exhibition Square, North Yorkshire Y01 2HB, tel. 01904/621756) and smaller ones at the York railway station (tel. 01904/643700) and 6 Rougier St. (tel. 01904/620557).

Exploring York

Numbers in the margin correspond to points of interest on the York map.

● York's greatest glory is the **Minster,** the largest Gothic church in England and one of the greatest in Europe. Take time to gaze at the soaring columns and intricate tracery of the 14th-century nave, the choir screen portraying the kings of England, and the rose window that commemorates the marriage of Henry VII and Elizabeth of York; it is just one of 128 stained-glass windows in the Minster. Visit the exquisite 13th-century **Chapter House** and the Roman and Saxon remains in the **Undercroft Museum and Treasury.** Climb the 275 steps of the **Central Tower** for an unrivaled view of the city and the countryside beyond. The **Crypt** is also worth a look, as it features some of the Minster's most venerable and valuable treasures. *York Minster Undercroft Museum and Treasury, Chapter House, and Central Tower, tel. 01904/624426. Admission: Foundations £1.80 adults, 70p children, £1.50 senior citizens, £4 family ticket; Chapter House 70p adults, 30p children; Central Tower £2 adults, £1 children and senior citizens; Crypt 60p adults, 30p children and senior citizens. Minster open summer daily 7–8:30, winter 7–5; Undercroft, Chapter House, Central Tower, and Crypt open Mon.–Sat. 10–6:30, Sun. 1–6:30.*

● At the **Jorvik Viking Centre,** south of the Minster through tiny medieval streets, you can take another journey into history—traveling in little "time cars" back to the sights, sounds, and even the smells of a Viking street, which archaeologists have re-created in astonishing detail. *Coppergate, tel. 01904/643211. Admission: £3.95 adults, £2 children, £3 senior citizens (Nov.–Mar. only). Open Apr.–Oct., daily 9–7; Nov.–Mar., daily 9–5:30.*

● Walk south down Castlegate and onto Tower Street, where you'll find the **Castle Museum,** housed in an 18th-century prison. It has a series of realistic period displays that bring the past to life. Highlights include a Victorian street scene, an 18th-century dining room, and a moorland farmer's cottage. Don't miss the Coppergate Helmet, one of only three Anglo-Saxon helmets ever found. The welcome tearoom serves drinks and simple snacks. *Clifford St., tel. 01904/653612. Admission: £4 adults, £2.90 children and senior citizens, £11 family ticket. Open Apr.–Oct., Mon.–Sat. 9:30–5:30, Sun. 10–5:30; Nov.–Mar., Mon.–Sat. 9:30–4, Sun. 10–4.*

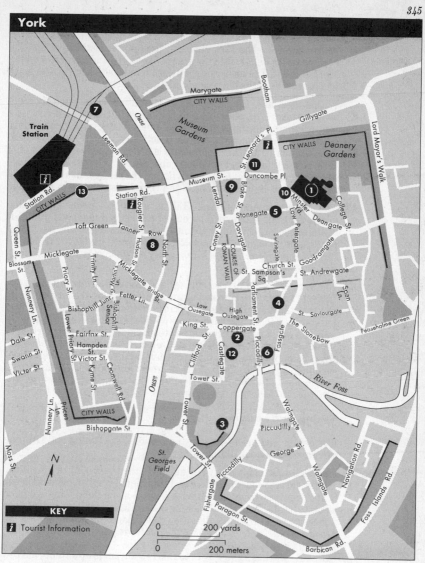

York

Major Attractions
Castle Museum, **3**
Jorvik Viking Centre, **2**
Merchant Adventurers'
Hall, **6**
Minster, **1**
National Railway
Museum, **7**
Shambles, **4**
Stonegate, **5**

Other Attractions
All Saints, **8**
Assembly Rooms, **9**
Cholera Burial
Ground, **13**
St-Michael-le-Belfry, **10**
Theater Royal, **11**
York Story
(Heritage Center), **12**

Even more than the wealth of museums, it is the streets and city walls that bring York's past to life. A walk along the **walls,** most of which date from the 13th century, though with extensive restoration, provides delightful views across rooftops and gardens and the Minster itself. The narrow paved path winds between various fortified gates where the old roads ran out of the city.

Within the walls, the narrow streets still follow the complex med-
④ ieval pattern. The **Shambles,** in the heart of this walled city, is a well-preserved example; the half-timbered shops and houses have such large overhangs that you can practically reach from one second-
⑤ floor window to another. **Stonegate** is a narrow pedestrian street of 18th-century (and earlier) shops and courts. Along a narrow passage off Stonegate, at 52A, you will find the remains of a 12th-century Norman stone house—one of the very few surviving in England.

⑥ The **Merchant Adventurers' Hall** is a superb medieval building (1357–68) built and owned by one of the richest medieval guilds; it contains the largest timber-framed hall in York. *Fossgate, tel. 01904/ 654818. Admission: £1.80 adults, 50p children under 15, £1.50 senior citizens. Open Mar.–Nov., daily 8:30–5; Nov.–Mar., Mon.– Sat. 8:30–3.*

⑦ One very different attraction is the **National Railway Museum,** the largest railway museum in the world, just outside the city walls, by the train station. It houses Britain's national collection of railway locomotives, including such giants of the steam era as *Mallard,* holder of the world speed record for a steam engine (126 mph), early rolling stock, and pioneer diesel and electric locomotives. There are lively changing exhibits, many of them hands-on, and a semipermanent display on the Channel Tunnel. *Leeman Rd., tel. 01904/621261. Admission: £4.20 adults, £2.10 children under 16, £2.80 senior citizens, £11.50 family ticket. Open Mon.–Sat. 10–6, Sun. 11–6.*

Dining and Lodging

For details and price-category definitions, *see* Dining and Lodging *in* Staying in Great Britain, *above.*

Dining **Four Seasons.** This cheery restaurant in the heart of York's medieval
$$ center serves homemade pies and traditional English meat dishes in a 16th-century beamed hall with a wood-block floor. This is a good spot to taste Yorkshire cooking and offers excellent-value light lunches; vegetarians will enjoy the cheese and lentil loaf. *45 Goodramgate, tel. 01904/633787. Reservations advised. AE, DC, MC, V. Open daily 10–10.*

$$ **Kites.** Be warned! The way in to this restaurant is up a steep, narrow staircase. But the slightly wacky food justifies the climb. Try chicken garda, filled with raisins, Parmesan and oregano, and served in a tamarind sauce. For dessert, the sumptuous bonoffi pie is a staple favorite. *13 Grape La., tel. 01904/640750. Reservations advised. AE, DC, MC, V. Closed Sun.*

$$ **Melton's.** The atmosphere in this restaurant, just 10 minutes' walk from the Minster, is simple, with bare tables, local art on the walls, and the kitchen open to view as you eat. The excellent seasonally changing menu, cooked up by Roux alumnus Michael Hjort, offers modern English, Continental, and fish dishes. Tuesday the menu focuses on fish, Wednesday on dessert, and Thursday on vegetarian fare. *7 Scarcroft Rd., tel. 01904/634341. Reservations advised. MC, V. Closed Sun. dinner, Mon. lunch, 3 wks at Christmas and 1 wk in Sept.*

$–$$ **Little Italy.** This cheery, bustling Italian-owned restaurant close to the Minster dishes out great pasta and pizza (the house special is a tasty concoction of mozzarella, mushrooms, prawns, garlic, and tomato), as well as veal, steaks, fresh fish, and seafood. The amaretto cheesecake is irresistible. *Goodramgate, tel. 01904/623539. Reservations advised Sat. and Sun. AE, DC, MC, V. Closed Mon. lunch and Tues. lunch.*

$ **Betty's.** This elegant restaurant and tea house, at the opposite end of Stonegate from the Minster, has been a York institution since 1912. Though it is best known for its teas and mouthwatering cakes (especially the "fat rascal," a plump bun bursting with cherries and nuts), it also has a wide selection of light meals (an inventive menu, from venison sausage with potatoes to gourmet toasted sandwiches), all served with old-fashioned style and refinement. Get a table on the upper floor if you can, next to the ceiling-to-floor picture windows, etched with Art Nouveau stained glass. Come early for dinner, as it closes at 9 PM. *6–8 St. Helen's Sq., tel. 01904/659142. MC, V.*

Lodging **Hobbits.** This is a quiet Edwardian guest house set in a peaceful cul-
$$ de-sac. It is in the northeast of the city, an easy 10-minute walk from the center. There are tea and coffeemaking facilities in all rooms, some of which are no-smoking, and TVs. *9 St. Peter's Grove, YO3 6AQ, tel. 01904/624538. 6 rooms with bath. Facilities: parking, garden. AE, MC, V.*

$ **Abbey Guest House.** This small, pretty guest house is 10 minutes' walk from the train station and town center. Spotlessly clean and with very friendly owners, it also enjoys a peaceful garden right on the river. Rooms have TVs and tea and coffeemaking facilities. *14 Earlsborough Terr., Marygate, YO3 7BQ, tel. 01904/627782. 7 rooms with basins. Facilities: babysitting service, parking, picnic lunches and evening meal on request. AE, MC, V.*

Edinburgh

Scotland and England *are* different—and let no Englishman tell you otherwise. Although the two nations have been united in a single state since 1707, Scotland retains its own marked political and social character, with, for instance, legal and educational systems quite distinct from those of England. And by virtue of its commanding geographic position, on top of a long-dead volcano, and the survival of a large number of outstanding buildings carrying echoes of the nation's history, Edinburgh proudly ranks among the world's greatest capital cities.

Getting Around

By Train Regular fast trains run from London's King's Cross Station to Edinburgh Waverley; the fastest journey time is about 4½ hours. For information in London, call 0171/278–2477; in Edinburgh, 0131/557–3000.

By Bus Regular services are operated by **Citylink Coaches** (0171/636–1921 and 0131/556–5717) and **Caledonian Express Stagecoach** (0171/930–5781 and 01738/33481) between Victoria Coach Station, London, and St. Andrew Square bus station, Edinburgh. The journey takes approximately eight to nine hours. Both **Lothian Region Transport** (deep-red-and-white buses) and **S.M.T.** (green buses) operate tours in and around Edinburgh. For information, call 0131/220–4111 (Lothian) or 0131/556–2515 (S.M.T). Tickets allowing unlimited travel on city buses for various periods are also available.

Tourist Information

City Information (3 Princes Street, tel. 0131/557–2727) is the main tourist center for Edinburgh. There is also a **tourist information desk** at the airport (tel. 0131/333–2167). The **Edinburgh Travel Cen-**

tre (Potterow Union, Bristo Sq., tel. 0131/668–2221) offers budget travel information for those going beyond Edinburgh.

Exploring Edinburgh

The key to understanding Edinburgh is to make the distinction between the Old and New Towns. Until the 18th century, the city was confined to the rocky crag on which its castle stands, straggling between the fortress at one end and the royal residence, the Palace of Holyroodhouse, at the other. In the 18th century, during a civilizing time of expansion known as the "Scottish Enlightenment," the city fathers fostered the construction of another Edinburgh, one a little to the north. This is the New Town, whose elegant squares, classical facades, wide streets, and harmonious proportions remain largely intact and lived-in today.

Numbers in the margin correspond to points of interest on the Edinburgh map.

The Royal Mile

Edinburgh Castle, the brooding symbol of Scotland's capital and the nation's martial past, dominates the city center. The castle's attractions include the city's oldest building—the 11th century **St. Margaret's Chapel;** the **Crown Room,** where the Regalia of Scotland are displayed (closed at press time); **Old Parliament Hall;** and **Queen Mary's Apartments,** where Mary, Queen of Scots, gave birth to the future King James VI of Scotland (who later became James I of England). In addition, there are excellent views. *Tel. 0131/244–3101. Admission: £5 adults, £1 children under 16, £3 senior citizens. Open Apr.–Sept., daily 9:30–5; Oct.–Mar., daily 9:30–4:15.*

❷ The **Royal Mile,** the backbone of the Old Town, starts immediately below the **Castle Esplanade,** the wide parade ground that hosts the annual Edinburgh Military Tattoo—a grand military display staged during a citywide festival every summer (*see below*). The Royal Mile consists of a number of streets, running into each other—**Castlehill, Lawnmarket, High Street,** and **Canongate**—leading downhill to the Palace of Holyroodhouse, home of the Royal Family when they visit Edinburgh. Tackle this walk in a leisurely style; the many original Old Town "closes," narrow alleyways enclosed by high tenement buildings, are rewarding to explore and give a real sense of the former life of the city.

❸ In Lawnmarket, the six-story tenement known as **Gladstone's Land** dates from 1620. It has a typical arcaded front and first-floor entrance and is furnished in the style of a merchant's house of the time; there are magnificent painted ceilings. *747B Lawnmarket, tel. 0131/ 226–5856. Admission: £2.50 adults, £1.30 children and senior citizens. Open Apr.–Oct., Mon.–Sat. 10–5, Sun. 2–5.*

❹ Close by is **Lady Stair's House,** a town dwelling of 1622 that now recalls Scotland's literary heritage with exhibits on Sir Walter Scott, Robert Louis Stevenson, and Robert Burns. *Lady Stair's Close, Lawnmarket, tel. 0131/225–2424, ext. 6593. Admission free. Open May–Sept., Mon.–Sat. 10–6; Oct.–Apr., Mon.–Sat. 10–5, Sun. 2–5 during the festival.*

❺ A heart shape set in the cobbles of the High Street marks the site of the **Tolbooth,** the center of city life until it was demolished in 1817.
❻ Nearby stands the **High Kirk of St. Giles,** Edinburgh's cathedral; parts of the church date from the 12th century, the choir from the 15th. *High St. Admission free. Open Mon.–Sat. 9–7, Sun. for services.*

❼ Farther down High Street you'll see **John Knox's House.** Its traditional connections with Scotland's celebrated religious reformer are tenuous, but it is said to be the only 15th-century house surviving in Scotland and gives a flavor of life in the Old Town during Knox's

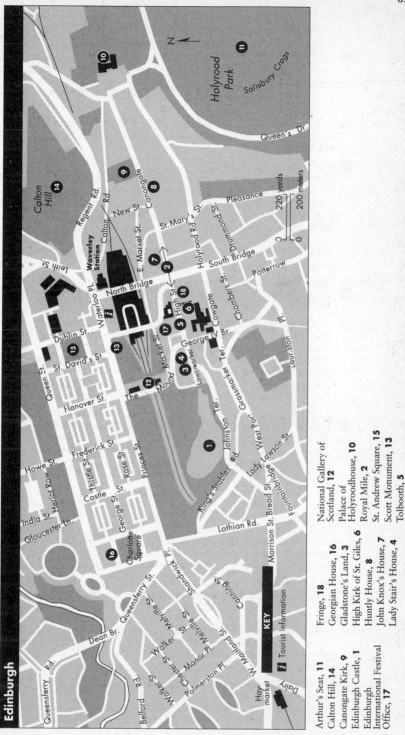

Edinburgh

Arthur's Seat, **11**
Calton Hill, **14**
Canongate Kirk, **9**
Edinburgh Castle, **1**
Edinburgh
International Festival
Office, **17**

Fringe, **18**
Georgian House, **16**
Gladstone's Land, **3**
High Kirk of St. Giles, **6**
Huntly House, **8**
John Knox's House, **7**
Lady Stair's House, **4**

National Gallery of
Scotland, **12**
Palace of
Holyroodhouse, **10**
Royal Mile, **2**
St. Andrew Square, **15**
Scott Monument, **13**
Tolbooth, **5**

KEY

i Tourist Information

time. *45 High St., tel. 0131/556–2647. Admission: £1.25 adults, 75p children, £1 senior citizens. Open Mon.–Sat. 10–5.*

8 **Canongate** was formerly an independent burgh, or trading community, outside the city walls of Edinburgh. **Huntly House,** built in 1570, is a museum featuring Edinburgh history and social life. *142 Canongate, tel. 0131/225–2424, ext. 6689. Admission free. Open June–Sept., Mon.–Sat. 10–6; Oct.–May, Mon.–Sat. 10–5, Sun. 2–5 during the festival.*

9 Some notable Scots are buried in the graveyard of the **Canongate Kirk** nearby, including the economist Adam Smith and the poet Robert Fergusson.

10 The **Palace of Holyroodhouse,** still the Royal Family's official residence in Scotland, was founded by King James IV at the end of the 15th century and was extensively remodeled by Charles II in 1671. The state apartments, with their collections of tapestries and paintings, can be visited. *Tel. 0131/556–7371. Admission: £3 adults, £1.50 children, £2.50 senior citizens, £7.50 family ticket. Open Apr.–Oct., Mon.–Sat. 9:30–5:15, Sun. 10:30–4:30; end Oct.–Mar., Mon.–Sat. 9:30–3:45, Sun. 10–3:45; closed during royal and state visits.*

11 The open grounds of **Holyrood Park** enclose Edinburgh's distinctive originally volcanic minimountain, **Arthur's Seat,** with steep slopes and miniature crags.

12 The **National Gallery of Scotland,** on the Mound, the street that joins the Old and New Towns, contains works by the Old Masters and the French Impressionists and has a good selection of Scottish paintings. This is one of Britain's best national galleries, small enough to be easily absorbed in one visit. *Tel. 0131/556–8921. Admission free; charge for special exhibitions. Open Mon.–Sat. 10–5, Sun. 2–5. Print Room, weekdays 10–12:30 and 2–4:30 by arrangement.*

13 To the east along Princes Street is the unmistakable soaring Gothic spire of the 62-meter- (200-foot-) high **Scott Monument,** built in the 1840s to commemorate the celebrated novelist of Scots history. There is a statue of Sir Walter and his dog within. The views from the top are well worth the 287-step climb. *Tel. 0131/225–2424. Admission: £1. Open Apr.–Sept., Mon.–Sat. 9–6; Oct.–Mar., Mon.–Sat. 9–3.*

14 There are more splendid views from **Calton Hill:** north across the Firth (or estuary) of Forth to the Lomond Hills of Fife and to the Pentland Hills that enfold the city from the south. Among the various monuments on Calton Hill are a partial reproduction of the **Parthenon** in Athens, begun in 1824 but left incomplete because the money ran out; the **Nelson Monument;** and the **Royal Observatory.**

15 Make your way to **St. Andrew Square;** then along George Street, where there is a wide choice of shops; and on to **Charlotte Square,** whose north side was designed by the great Scottish classical architect Robert Adam. The rooms of the elegant **Georgian House** are fur-**16** nished to show the domestic arrangements of a prosperous late-18th-century Edinburgh family. *7 Charlotte Sq., tel. 0131/225–2160. Admission: £2.40 adults, £1.20 children and senior citizens. Open Apr.–Oct., Mon.–Sat. 10–4:30, Sun. 2–4:30.*

Finally, a word about the **Edinburgh International Festival,** the annual celebration of music, dance, and drama that the city stages each summer from mid–late August, featuring international artists of the highest caliber. The **Festival Fringe,** the unruly child of the official festival, spills out of halls and theaters all over town, offering visitors a cornucopia of theatrical and musical events of all kinds—some so weird that they defy description. While the official festival is the place to see top-flight performances by established artists, at a Fringe event you may catch a new star, or a new art form, or a controversial new play in the making. Or then again, you may not; it's very much up to luck. Advance information, programs, and ticket sales for the festival are available from the **Edinburgh International Festival Office,** 21 Market St. (tel. 0131/226–4001); for the **Fringe,** from 180 High St. (tel. 0131/226–5257/5259).

Dining and Lodging

For details and price-category definitions, *see* Dining and Lodging *in* Staying in Great Britain, *above.*

Dining
$$

Jackson's Restaurant. Intimate and candlelit in a historic Old Town close, Jackson's offers good Scots fare. Aberdeen Angus steaks and Border lamb are excellent; there are vegetarian and seafood specialties, too. *2 Jackson Close, High St., tel. 0131/225–1793. Reservations advised. MC, V. Closed for lunch Sat. and Sun.*

$$ **L'Auberge.** An established restaurant, L'Auberge is comfortably old-fashioned and now has a new chef who worked in Atlanta. The French-style cuisine uses the best Scottish ingredients. Try the brill with oysters or the tender venison. *56–58 St. Mary's St., tel. 0131/556–5888. Reservations advised. AE, DC, MC, V.*

$$ **Martin's.** This is a good spot for imaginative vegetarian dishes and fresh seafood. Try the succulent halibut in a nettle sauce or pink sea trout cooked with seaweed. There's a good-value set lunch. *70 Rose St., tel 0131/225–3106. Reservations required. AE, DC, MC, V. Open lunch Tues.–Fri., dinner Tues.–Sat.*

$ **Henderson's Salad Table.** This friendly place claims to be the city's original vegetarian restaurant, long before such places became fashionable. Try the vegetarian haggis! *94 Hanover St., tel. 0131/225–2131. Reservations accepted. AE, DC, MC, V.*

$ **Howie's.** Howie's is a simple, neighborhood bistro, unlicensed, so you have to bring your own bottle. The steaks are tender Aberdeen beef, and the clientele is lively. *75 St. Leonard's St., tel. 0131/668–2917. MC, V. Open lunch Tues.–Fri. and Sun., dinner Tues.–Fri.*

$ **Pierre Victoire.** There are three branches of this popular bistro chain in Edinburgh. They are fairly chaotic, friendly, enjoyable eateries, serving healthy portions at low prices. The fish is especially good and is freshly caught—try the baked oysters with bacon and hollandaise. *38 Grassmarket, tel. 0131/226–2442; 10 Victoria St., tel. 0131/225–1721; and 18 Union St., tel. 0131/557–8451. Reservations haphazard. MC. Closed Sun.*

¢ **Guildford Arms.** This is one of the hundreds of Edinburgh pubs that serve acceptable bar food. It is decorated in molded plaster, mahogany, gilt, and velvet. There is bar food as well as more substantial fare, such as steaks and steamed fish. *West Register St., tel. 0132/556–4312. Bar open daily, restaurant closed Sun.*

¢ **Jolly Judge.** This atmospheric pub, in an old tenement, is in one of the oldest parts of town, just off the Royal Mile. There is basic bar food, with curries and lasagna, too. Beamed ceilings and a collection of foreign banknotes make this a pleasant place to eat. *James Court (beside 495 Lawnmarket), tel. 0131/225–2669. No main meals Sun. lunch.*

Lodging
$$

Albany Hotel. Three fine 18th-century houses with many original features have been carefully converted into a comfortable city-center hotel. There's a good restaurant in the basement. *39 Albany St., EH1 3QY, tel. 0131/556–0397, fax 0131/557–6633. 20 rooms with bath. AE, DC, MC.*

$$ **Brunswick.** This owner-run, Georgian guest house, convenient to the city center, has a friendly atmosphere and pleasant bedrooms, all with TVs and tea and coffeemaking facilities. *7 Brunswick St., EH7 5JB, tel. and fax 0131/556–1238. 10 rooms with shower. Closed Dec.–Feb. No credit cards.*

$$ **Bruntisfield Hotel.** All the rooms have their own style and character, with the lavish use of floral patterns and antiques. *68–74 Bruntisfield Pl., EH10 4HH, tel. 0131/229–1393. 53 rooms with bath. AE, DC, MC, V.*

$ **Dorstan Private Hotel.** A Victorian villa in a quiet area, the Dorstan has fully modernized rooms decorated in bright, country-cottage colors. *7 Priestfield Rd., EH16 5HJ, tel. 0131/667–6721, fax 0131/668–4644. 14 rooms, 9 with bath or shower. No credit cards.*

$ **Salisbury Guest House.** Another successful 18th-century building conversion, this quiet hotel is situated in a pleasant area. It's a good value and has a convenient location for city sightseeing. *45 Salisbury Rd., EH16 5AA, tel. 0131/667–1264. 13 rooms, 8 with bath. No credit cards.*

$ **Sibbet House.** This is a very elegant B&B, in the heart of the New Town, close to the National Portrait Gallery. The house was built in 1809 and has a lovely hanging staircase and many antiques. The rooms are large, and there is a big dining room for breakfast. *26 Northumberland St., EH3 6LS, tel. 0131/556–1078. 3 rooms with bath. MC, V.*

11 Greece

For centuries, Greece was a country of few material resources, poverty was borne with dignity, and a tradition of offering hospitality to strangers was upheld. Attitudes may have changed a bit as the Greek standard of living approaches that of other European Union countries, but the budget traveler is still made to feel welcome, particularly in out-of-the-way places in the countryside and on the islands.

You cannot travel far across the land here without meeting the sea or far across the sea without meeting one of Greece's roughly 2,000 islands. About the size of New York State, Greece has 15,019 kilometers (9,312 miles) of coastline, more than any other country of its size in the world. The sea is everywhere, not on three sides only but at every turn, reaching through the shoreline like a probing hand. The land itself is stunning, dotted with cypress groves, vineyards, and olive trees, carved into gentle bays or dramatic coves with startling white sand, rolling hills, and rugged mountain ranges that plunge straight into the sea. This natural beauty and the sharp, clear light of sun and sea, combined with plentiful archaeological treasures, make Greece one of the world's most inviting countries.

Poetry, music, architecture, politics, medicine, law—all had their Western birth here in Greece centuries ago, alongside the great heroes of mythology who still seem to haunt this sun-drenched land. Among the great mountains of mainland Greece are the cloud-capped peak of Mt. Olympus, fabled home of the Greek gods, and Mt. Parnassus, favorite haunt of the sun god Apollo and the nine Muses, goddesses of poetry and science. The remains of the ancient past—the Acropolis and the Parthenon, the temples of Delphi, the Tombs of the Kings in Mycenae—and a later procession of Byzantine churches, Crusader castles and fortresses, and Turkish mosques are spread throughout the countryside.

Of the hundreds of islands and islets scattered across the Aegean Sea in the east and the Ionian Sea in the west, fewer than 250 are still inhabited. This world of the farmer and seafarer has largely been replaced by the world of the tourist. More than 10 million vacationers

Greece

BULGARIA

Former Yugoslav Republic
of Macedonia

ALBANIA

Stavroúpoli

Sidirókastro
Séres
Philippi
Kilkis
Eleftheroúpoli
Amfípoli
Kava

E86
Edessa
Florina
Gianitsa
Alexandria
Thessaloniki
Ptolemaïda
Veria
E90
Néa
Thérmi
Apalonia
Vatoped
Polygyros
Katerini
Ormylia
Kastoria
Kozani
Gulf of
Thermaikos
Dafni
Iviri
Siatista
Mount
Athos
Kónitsa
Grevena
Olympus
E75
Kalithéa
Dalvinákio
Elassóna
Palioúri
Métsovo
Kalambaka
Tirnavos
Gulf of Kassandra
Igoumenitsa
Ioanina
Agia
Paramythia
Trikala
Larissa
Kerkira
Corfu

E951
Karditsa
Volos
Parga
Arta
Stavros
Farsala
SPORADE
Aliki
Almiros
Skiathos

Preveza
Lamia
Skópelos

Lefkas
Karpenissi
Skyros
Vassiliki

N
Agrinio
Orhomonós
Kymi
EVIA
Kephalonia
Ithaki
Itea
Delphi
Livadia
E75
Halkida
Lixouri
Sami
Messolongi
Nafpaktos
Galaxidi
Thebes
Patras
Gulf of Corinth
Kárystos
Diakofto
Megara

E55
Corinth
Athens
Killini
Nemea
Aegina
Piraeus
Kárystos
Loutra
Mycenae
Voula
Lavrio
Kéd
Zákynthos
Amalias
Argos
Nauplion
Poros
Sounio
Pyrgos
Olympia
Tripoli
Toló
Zákynthos
Kaiafas
Tripoli
Ermioni
Kythnos
Andritsena
Ydra
Kyparissia
PELOPONNESE
Spetses
Serifos
Messini
Sparta
Leonidio
Ionian Sea
Gargaliani
Kalamata
Mystras
Geraki
Mirtoan
Pilos
Skala
Kyparissi
Sea
Methoni
Koroni
Gythio
Monemvassia
Milos
Areopoli

Agía Pelagia
Kythira
Kythira

Mediterranean Sea
Haniá

0   100 miles
0   300 km
CRETE

Black Sea

THRACE   TURKEY

Kastaniés

Xanthi
Didymótiho

Avdira
Mákri   Alexandróupoli

Thassos

Samothrace

Istanbul

Sea of
Marmara

Troy

Límnos

Lesvos   Mytilíni

Plomári

TURKEY

Aegean Sea

Hios   Hios
Mésta
Pirgi

Izmir (Smyrna)

Ephesus

Andros
Andros

Tinos

Sámos   Sámos
Ikaria   Pythagorio

Agios
Kirykos

moupoli Tinos

Syros   Mykonos
Delos   Pátmos

Paros

Náxos

CYCLADES   Amorgós

Ios   Astypalea

Thira
Santorini Anafi

Leros
Kos

Bodrum
(Halicarnassus)
Kos

Nissyros   Symi

Tilos Kámiros   Rhodes

DODECANESE   Halki

Rhodes   Lindos

Sea of Crete

Kárpathos

Iraklio Mallia
Knossos

Phaestos   Ierapetra

Kassos

visit Greece each year, almost as many as the entire native population; in fact, tourism has overtaken shipping as the most important element in the nation's economy. On some of the islands, the impact of the annual influx of visitors has meant the building of a new Greece, more or less in their image. But traditionalism survives: Now, pubs and bars stand next door to *ouzeris*, discos are as popular as *kafeneia*, and pizza and hamburger joints compete with tavernas; once-idyllic beaches have become overcrowded and noisy, and fishing harbors have become flotilla sailing centers. Prices rose steeply after Greece joined the European Community (today's European Union) in 1981, and the simplicity and hardships of a peasant economy have largely disappeared from the islands' way of life.

Although mass tourism has taken over the main centers, it is still possible to strike out and find your own place among the smaller islands and the miles of beautiful mainland coastline. Except for some difficulty in finding accommodations (Greek families on vacation tend to fill the hotels in out-of-the-way places during high summer), this is the ideal way to see traditional Greece. Those who come only to worship the classical Greeks and gaze at their temples, seeing nothing but the glory that was, miss today's Greece. If you explore this fascinating country with open eyes, you'll enjoy it in all its forms: its slumbering cafés and buzzing tavernas; its elaborate religious rituals; its stark, bright beauty; and the generosity, curiosity, and kindness of its people.

Essential Information

Before You Go

When to Go Although the tourist season runs from May to October, the heat can be unpleasant in July and August, particularly in Athens. On the islands, a brisk northwesterly wind, the *meltemi*, can make life more comfortable. If you want to move about the country and avoid all the other tourists, the ideal months are May, June, and September. The winter months tend to be damp and cold virtually everywhere.

The following are the average daily maximum and minimum temperatures for Athens.

Jan.	55F	13C	May	77F	25C	Sept.	84F	29C
	44	6		61	16		67	19
Feb.	57F	14C	June	86F	30C	Oct.	75F	24C
	44	6		68	20		60	16
Mar.	60F	16C	July	92F	33C	Nov.	66F	19C
	46	8		73	23		53	12
Apr.	68F	20C	Aug.	92F	33C	Dec.	58F	15C
	52	11		73	23		47	8

Currency The Greek monetary unit is the drachma (dr.). Bank notes are in denominations of 50, 100, 500, 1,000, and 5,000 dr.; coins, 5, 10, 20, and 50. At press time (summer 1995), there were approximately 251 dr. to the U.S. dollar and 356 dr. to the pound sterling. Daily exchange rates are prominently displayed in banks. You'll get a better exchange rate at banks than from hotels or stores.

What It Will Cost Inflation in Greece is high—just under 11% a year—and fluctuations in currency make it impossible to do accurate budgeting long in advance, so keep an eye on the exchange rates before your vacation. On the whole, Greece offers good value compared with many other European countries. The values are especially good for modest hotels and restaurants, transportation, and entertainment.

There are few regional price differences for hotels and restaurants. A modest hotel in a small town will charge only slightly lower rates than a modest hotel in Athens, with the same range of amenities. The same is true of restaurants. The spread of tourism has made even the costlier Rhodes, Corfu, and Crete as affordable as many other islands. Car rentals are expensive in Greece, but taxis are inexpensive even for long-distance runs.

Sample Prices At a central-city café, you can expect to pay about 500 dr. for a cup of coffee or a bottle of beer, 300 dr. for a soft drink, and around 400 dr. for a toasted cheese sandwich. These prices can, of course, vary considerably from one place to another. A 1½-kilometer (1-mile) taxi ride costs about 300 dr.

Customs on Arrival You may take in one carton of cigarettes or cigars or ¼ pound of smoking tobacco, 1 liter of alcohol or 2 liters of wine, and gifts up to a total value of 51,000 dr. There's no duty on articles for personal use. The only restrictions applicable to tourists from EU countries are those for cigarettes, cigars, and tobacco. Foreign bank notes in excess of $2,500 must be declared for re-export. There are no restrictions on traveler's checks. Foreign visitors may take in 100,000 dr. in Greek currency and export up to 40,000 dr.

Language English is widely spoken in hotels and elsewhere, especially by young people, and even in out-of-the-way places someone is always happy to lend a helping hand.

In this guide, names are given in the Roman alphabet according to the Greek pronunciation except when there is a familiar English form, such as "Athens."

Getting Around

By Motorcycle and Bicycle Jeeps, dune buggies, bicycles, mopeds, and motorcycles can be rented on the islands. Use extreme caution. Crash helmets, though technically compulsory for motorcyclists, are not usually available, and injuries are common.

By Train Trains, although slow, are cheap and convenient, offering spectacular scenery on the route north to Thessaloniki and south to Mycenae. The main line runs north from Athens to the former Yugoslavia. It divides into three lines at Thessaloniki. The main line continues on to Belgrade, a second line goes east to the Turkish border and Istanbul, and a third line heads northeast to Bulgaria. The Peloponnese in the south is served by a narrow-gauge line dividing at Corinth into the Mycenae–Argos section and the Patra–Olympia–Kalamata section. For information, call 01/524–0601.

By Plane **Olympic Airways** (Syngrou 96, Athens, tel. 01/966–6666) has service between Athens and several cities and islands. Thessaloniki is also linked to the main islands, and there are several interisland connections. Reservations can be made by telephone daily from 7 AM to 10 PM. For information on arrivals and departures for Olympic Airways flights (West Terminal), call 01/936–3363; for other carriers (East Terminal), call 01/969–9466 or 01/969–9467.

By Bus Travel by bus is inexpensive, usually comfortable, and relatively fast. The journey from Athens to Thessaloniki, for example, takes roughly the same amount of time as the slow train, though the express covers the distance 1¼ hours faster. In the Peloponnese, however, buses are much faster than trains. Bus information and timetables are available at tourist information offices throughout Greece. Make reservations at least one day before your planned trip. Railway-operated buses leave from the Peloponnisos railway station in Athens. All other buses leave from one of two bus stations: Liossion 260—for central and eastern Greece and Evvia; Kifissou 100—for the Peloponnese and northwestern Greece.

By Boat There are frequent ferries and more expensive hydrofoils from Piraeus, the port of Athens, to the central and southern Aegean islands and Crete. Nearby islands are also served by hydrofoils and ferries from Rafina, east of Athens. Ships to other islands sail from ports nearer to them. Connections from Athens/Piraeus to the main island groups are good, connections from main islands to smaller ones within a group less so, and services between islands of different groups or areas—such as Rhodes and Crete—are less frequent. Travel agents and shipping offices in Athens and Piraeus and in the main towns on the islands have details. Buy your tickets two or three days in advance, especially if you are traveling in summer or taking a car, and reserve your return journey or continuation soon after you arrive.

Timetables change very frequently, and boats may be delayed by weather conditions, so your itinerary should allow for some flexibility.

Staying in Greece

Telephones
Local Calls

Many curbside kiosks have pay telephones for local calls only. You pay the kiosk owner 20 dr. per call after you've finished. It's easier, though, to buy a phone card from the Telecommunications Office (OTE), kiosks, or convenience shops and use it at the now ubiquitous card phones. If you're calling within Greece, the price is reduced by 30% daily 3 PM and 5 PM and on weekends from 3 PM Saturday to 9 AM Monday.

International Calls

Although you can buy phone cards with up to 5,000 dr. credit, if you plan to make and pay for several international calls, go to an OTE office, usually located in the center of towns and villages. There are several branches in Athens. Calls to the United States and Canada cost 348 dr. per minute during the day and 295 dr. nightly from 11 PM to 8 AM. Calls to Great Britain cost 159 dr. a minute but 120 dr. between 10 PM and 6 AM. There is a three-minute minimum charge for operator-assisted station-to-station calls and a four-minute minimum for person-to-person connections. To reach an **AT&T** long-distance operator, dial 00/800–1311; for **MCI,** 00/800–1211; **Sprint,** 00/800–1411.

Operators and Information

There are English-speaking operators on the International Exchange. Ask your hotel reception desk or an employee at the OTE for help in reaching one. It may take up to an hour for the international operator to connect your call.

Country Code

The country code for Greece is 30.

Mail
Postal Rates

Airmail letters or postcards for delivery within Europe cost 90 dr. for 20 grams and 180 dr. for 50 grams; for outside Europe, the cost is 120 dr. for 20 grams and 220 dr. for 50 grams. If you are mailing a package, you must take it, along with your wrapping materials, to the post office so it can be inspected. Parcels over a kilogram must be brought to the station at Mitropoleos 60.

Receiving Mail

You can have your mail sent to Poste Restante, Aeolou 100, Athens 10200 (take your passport to pick up your mail), or to American Express, Ermou 2, Athens 10225. For holders of American Express cards or traveler's checks, there is no charge for the service. Others pay 400 dr. for each pick-up.

Shopping

Prices quoted in shops include the VAT. There are no VAT refunds.

Bargaining

Prices in large stores are fixed. Bargaining may take place in small owner-managed souvenir and handicrafts shops. In flea markets, bargaining is expected.

Opening and Closing Times

The government has freed opening hours for shops and businesses under its program to liberalize the economy. As a result, office and shopping hours can vary considerably and may also change according to the season. Check with your hotel for up-to-the-minute information on opening and closing times. Below is a rough guide:

Banks. Banks are open weekdays 8–2, except Fridays, when they close at 1:30; they are closed weekends and public holidays. However, ATM machines are becoming more numerous throughout most cities.

Museums. Most major museums are open 8:30–3, with longer hours in summer; some smaller ones close earlier. Generally, museums are closed on Monday. Admission is free on Sunday and holidays. EU students enjoy free admission, students from other countries pay half the fee, and senior citizens often get a discount as well. Archaeological sites usually open at 8:30 and close at sunset during the summer, at 3 during the winter. Hours vary from one site to another and often change without notice; always check with tourist offices or travel agencies before visiting.

Post Offices. Except for the main offices at Aeolou 100 and on Syntagma Square (weekdays 7:30 AM–8 PM, Sat. 7:30–2, Sun. 9–1:30), most are open weekdays 8–2.

Shops. Most shops are open Tuesday, Thursday, and Friday 9–2 and 5:30–8; Monday, Wednesday, and Saturday 9–2. Supermarkets are open 8–8 on weekdays and 8–2 on Saturdays.

National Holidays
In 1996: January 1, January 6 (Epiphany), February 26 (Clean Monday), March 25 (Independence), April 12 (Good Friday), April 14 (Greek Easter Sunday), April 15 (Easter Monday), May 1 (Labor Day), June 2 (Pentecost), August 15 (Assumption), October 28 (Ochi Day), December 25–26. Changing holidays in 1997: March 10 (Clean Monday); April 25 (Good Friday); April 27 (Greek Easter Sunday); April 28 (Easter Monday); June 15 (Pentecost).

Dining
Greek cuisine cannot be compared to that of France, and few visitors would come to Greece for its food alone. You'll certainly be able to find a delicious and inexpensive meal, but don't look in hotel restaurants, where the menus often consist of bland, unimaginative international fare (although it's only here that you will find a reasonable prix-fixe menu). The principal elements of Greek cuisine are such vegetables as eggplants, tomatoes, and olives, fresh and inventively combined with lots of olive oil and such seasonings as lemon juice, garlic, basil, and oregano. While meat dishes are limited (pork, lamb, and chicken being the most common), fish is often the better, though more expensive, choice, particularly on the coast. Your best bet is to look for tavernas and *estiatoria* (restaurants) and choose the one frequented by the most Greeks. The *estiatorio* serves oven-baked dishes called *magirefta*, precooked and left to stand, while tavernas offer similar fare plus grilled meats and fish. Another alternative is an *ouzeri* or *mezedopolion*, where you can order several plates of appetizers instead of an entrée. The decor of these establishments may range from simple to sophisticated, with prices to match.

Traditional fast food in Greece consists of the gyro (slices of grilled lamb with tomato and onions in pita bread), souvlakia (shish kebab), and pastries filled with a variety of stuffings (spinach, cheese, or meat)—but hamburgers and pizzas can now be found even on the smaller islands.

Mealtimes
Lunch in Greek restaurants is served from 12:30 until 3. Dinner begins at about 9 and is served until 1 in Athens and until midnight outside Athens.

Precautions
Tap water is safe to drink everywhere, but it is often heavily chlorinated. Excellent bottled mineral water, such as Loutraki, is available.

What to Wear
Throughout the Greek islands you can dress informally for dinner, even at expensive restaurants. If you splurge in Athens, you may want to wear a jacket; otherwise, casual dress is fine.

Ratings Prices are per person and include a first course, main course, and dessert (generally fruit and cheese or a sweet pastry, such as baklava), and the 12%–15% service charge. Best bets are indicated by a star ★.

Category	Athens/ Thessaloniki	Other Areas
$$	3,500 dr.–6,000 dr.	2,500 dr.–5,000 dr.
$	2,000 dr.–3,500 dr.	1,800 dr.–2,500 dr.
¢	under 2,000 dr.	under 1,800 dr.

Lodging Most accommodations are in standard hotels, sometimes called motels. There are a number of "village" complexes, especially at the beaches, and as part of some hotels. On islands and at beach resorts, large hotels are complemented by family-run pensions and guest houses—usually clean, bright, and recently built—and self-catering apartment and bungalow complexes. In a very few places, there are state-organized "traditional settlements"—guest accommodations in buildings that are representative of the local architecture.

Greek hotels are classified as Deluxe, A, B, C, etc. For the budget traveler, a class-C Greek hotel usually offers the best value. In this guide, hotels are classified according to price: $$, $, and ¢. Within each category, quality can vary greatly, though the categories usually correspond to a price scale set by the government. Still, you may come across a C-class hotel that charges less than a D-class, depending on its facilities. If there are vacancies, keep in mind that, especially off-season, you can negotiate the price, depending on room vacancy. If a hotel is air-conditioned, this is indicated. All have been built or completely renovated during the past 20 years, and most have private baths.

Prices quoted by hotels usually include service, local taxes, and VAT. Some may also include breakfast. Prices quoted are for double occupancy. Single occupancy is slightly less. The official price should be posted on the back of the door or inside a closet. Booking a room at a $$ hotel through a travel agency can often reduce the price.

Ratings Prices quoted are for a double room in high season, including taxes and service, but not breakfast. Rates are the same throughout the country for each category. Best bets are indicated by a star ★.

Category	Cost
$$	15,000 dr.–23,000 dr.
$	9,000–15,000 dr.
¢	under 9,000 dr.

Tipping There are no absolute rules for tipping. In restaurants, cafés, and tavernas, in addition to the 15% service charge, you should leave a tip for the waiter of around 10% in the better restaurants. This should be left on the table for your waiter and not on the plate, where it will be taken by the head waiter. In hotels, tip porters 100 dr. per bag for carrying your luggage. Taxi drivers don't expect tips, but Greeks usually round off the fare. In live theaters, tip ushers 100 dr. if you are shown to your seat. In movie theaters, tip about 50 dr. if you receive a program from the usher.

Athens

Arriving and Departing

By Plane   Most visitors arrive by air at **Ellinikon Airport**, about 10 kilometers (6 miles) from the city center. All Olympic Airways flights, both international and domestic, use the West Terminal next to the ocean. All other flights arrive and depart from the East Terminal on the opposite side of the airport.

Between the
Airport and
Downtown   Bus service connects the two air terminals, Syntagma Square, Omonia Square, and Piraeus. Between the East Terminal and downtown, the express bus (No. 91) runs every 20 minutes 6 AM–12:30 AM; from the West Terminal, Bus 90 runs every 30 minutes 6:30 AM–9:30 PM. The night bus departs at irregular intervals; ask for a schedule from a Greek National Tourist Organization office. (*see* Important Addresses and Numbers, *below*). If you're traveling to the airport, you can catch either bus on Syntagma Square in front of the Bank of Macedonia Thrace or off Omonia Square on Stadiou Street. From both terminals to Karaiskaki Square in Piraeus and between the terminals, Bus 19 runs about every 50 minutes (5 AM–11:20 PM). A ticket costs 160 dr., or 200 dr. for night service. A taxi to the center of Athens costs about 1,300 dr.–1,600 dr., depending on the terminal. Taxi fare is 1,500 dr. to Piraeus and 900 dr. between terminals. The price goes up by about two-thirds from midnight until 5 AM.

By Train   Athens has two railway stations, side by side, not far from Omonia Square. International trains from the north arrive at, and depart from, **Stathmos Larissis** (tel. 01/823–7741). Take Trolley 1 from the terminal to get to Omonia Square. Trains from the Peloponnese use the marvelously ornate and old-fashioned **Stathmos Peloponnisos** (tel. 01/513–1601) next door. To get to Omonia and Syntagma Squares, take Bus 57. Since the phones are almost always busy and agents often don't speak English, it's easier to get information and buy tickets at a downtown railway office (Sina 6, tel. 01/362–4402 through 01/362–4406; Filellinon 17, tel. 01/323–6747; or Karolou 1, tel. 01/524–0646 through 01/524–0648).

By Bus   Greek buses arrive either at **Terminal A** (100 Kifissou, tel. 01/512–4910) or Terminal B (Liossion 260, tel. 01/831–7153). From Terminal A, take Bus 51 to Omonia; from Terminal B, take Bus 24 downtown. To go to the stations, catch Bus 51 at Zinonos and Menandrou streets off Omonia Square or Bus 24 on Amalias Avenue in front of the National Gardens. International buses drop their passengers off near Omonia or Syntagma Square or at the Stathmos Peloponnisos.

By Ship   Except for cruise ships, few passenger ships from other countries call at Piraeus, the port of Athens, 10 kilometers (6 miles) from Athens' center. If you do dock at the main port in Piraeus, you can take the nearby metro right into Omonia Square. The trip takes 20 minutes and costs 100 dr. Alternatively, you can take a taxi, which may well take longer because of traffic and will cost a great deal more, around 1,100 dr. If you arrive by hydrofoil in the smaller port of Zea Marina, take Bus 905 or Trolley 20 to the metro.

Getting Around

Many of the sights you'll want to see, and most of the hotels, cafés, and restaurants, are within a fairly small central area. It's easy to walk everywhere.

By Metro   An electric (partially underground) railway runs from Piraeus to Omonia Square and then on to Kifissia. It is not useful for getting around the central area. The standard fare is 75 dr. or 100 dr., depending on the distance. There are no special fares or day tickets for visitors, and there is, as yet, no public transport map.

By Bus The fare on blue buses and the roomier yellow trolley buses is 75 dr. Tickets should be purchased beforehand at one of the curbside kiosks or from booths at the main terminals. Be sure to validate your ticket when you enter by stamping it in the orange counter. Otherwise, if your ticket is spot-checked, you will have to pay a 1,500 dr. fine. Buses run from the center to all suburbs and suburban beaches until about midnight. For suburbs beyond central Kifissia, you have to change at Kifissia. Attica has an efficient bus network. Most buses to the east Attica coast, including those for Sounion (tel. 01/823–0179; 1,000 dr.) and Marathon (tel. 01/821–0872; 600 dr.), leave from the KTEL terminal, Platia Aigyptiou on Mavromateon, at the corner of Patission and Alexandras avenues.

Important Addresses and Numbers

Tourist Information There are **Greek National Tourist Offices (EOT)** at Karageorgi Servias 2, in the bank, tel. 01/322–2545; at East Ellinikon Airport, tel. 01/961–2722; and at Piraeus, EOT Building, 1st Floor, Zea Marina, tel. 01/413–5716.

Embassies **U.S.** (Vasilissis Sofias 91, tel. 01/721–2951). **Canadian** (Gennadiou 4, tel. 01/725–4011). **U.K.** (Ploutarchou 1, tel. 01/723–6211).

Emergencies **Police:** Tourist Police (tel. 171); Traffic Police (tel. 01/523–0111); and City Police (tel. 100). **Fire** (tel. 199). **Ambulance:** Tel. 166, but a taxi is often faster. **Doctors:** Not all hospitals are open nightly; dial 106 (in Greek) or check the English-language *Athens News*, which lists emergency hospitals daily in a section on the sports page. Any hotel will call one for you. You can also call your embassy. **Dentist:** Ask your hotel or embassy. **Pharmacies:** Many in the central area have someone who speaks English. Try **Marinopoulos** (Kanari 23, tel. 01/361–3051). For information on late-night pharmacies, dial 107 (Greek), or check the *Athens News*.

Exploring Athens

Athens is essentially a village that outgrew itself, spreading out from the original settlement at the foot of the Acropolis. Back in 1834, when it became the capital of modern Greece, the city had a population of fewer than 10,000. Now it houses more than a third of the Greek population—around 4 million. A modern concrete city has engulfed the old village and now sprawls for 388 square kilometers (244 square miles), covering almost all the surrounding plain from the sea to the encircling mountains.

The city is very crowded, very dusty, and overwhelmingly hot during the summer. It also has an appalling air-pollution problem, caused mainly by traffic fumes; in an attempt to lessen the congestion, it is forbidden to drive private cars in central Athens on alternate workdays. Despite the smog, heat, and dust, Athens is an experience not to be missed. It has a tangible vibrancy that makes it one of the most exciting cities in Europe, and the sprawling cement has failed to overwhelm the few striking and astonishing reminders of ancient Athens.

The central area of modern Athens is small, stretching from the Acropolis to Mt. Lycabettus, with its small white church on top. The layout is simple: Three parallel streets—Stadiou, Venizelou (commonly referred to as Panepistimiou), and Akademias—link two main squares—Syntagma and Omonia.

Numbers in the margin correspond to points of interest on the Athens map.

The Historic Heart

At the center of modern Athens is **Syntagma (Constitution) Square.** It has several leading hotels, airline and travel offices, and numerous cafés. Along one side of the square stands the **Parliament Building,** completed in 1838 as the royal palace for the new monarchy. In front of the palace, you can watch the changing of the vividly costumed **Evzone guard** at the Tomb of the Unknown Soldier. On Sundays there is a more elaborate ceremony at 11:15 AM. Amalias Avenue, leading out of Syntagma, will take you to the **National Gardens,** a large oasis in the vast sprawl of this largely concrete city.

Across the street, at the far end of the National Gardens, you will see the columns of the once-huge **Temple of Olympian Zeus.** This famous temple was begun in the 6th century BC, and when it was finally completed 700 years later, it exceeded in magnitude all other temples in Greece. It was destroyed during the invasion of the Goths in the 4th century, and today only the towering sun-browned columns remain. *Vasilissis Olgas 1, tel. 01/922–6330. Admission: 500 dr. Open Tues.–Sun. 8:30–2:45.*

Nearby stands **Hadrian's Arch,** built at the same time as the temple by the Roman emperor. It consists of a Roman archway, with a Greek superstructure of Corinthian pilasters. Visiting heads of state are officially welcomed here.

About three-quarters of a kilometer (a half mile) east, down Vasilissis Olgas Avenue, you'll come to **Panathenaic Stadium,** built for the first modern Olympic Games in 1896; it is a blindingly white, marble reconstruction of the ancient Roman stadium of Athens and can seat 80,000 spectators.

From Hadrian's Arch, take the avenue to the right, Dionysiou Areopagitou, a few blocks west to the **Theater of Dionysos,** built during the 6th century BC. Here the famous ancient dramas and comedies were originally performed in conjunction with bacchanalian feasts. *Tel. 01/322–4625. Admission: 500 dr. Open daily 8:30–2:45.*

A little higher up, on the right, you'll see the massive back wall of the much better preserved **Odeon of Herod Atticus,** built by the Romans during the 2nd century AD. Here, on pine-scented summer evenings, the **Athens Festival** takes place. It includes opera, ballet, drama, and concerts (*see* The Arts, *below*). *It is not otherwise open to the public.*

Beyond the theater, a steep, zigzag path leads to the **Acropolis.** After a 30-year building moratorium to commemorate the Persian wars, the Athenians built this complex during the 5th century BC to honor the goddess Athena, patron of the city. It is now undergoing conservation as part of an ambitious 20-year rescue plan launched with international support in 1983 by Greek architects. The first ruins you'll see are the **Propylaea,** the monumental gateway that led worshipers from the temporal world into the spiritual world of the sanctuary; now only the columns of Pentelic marble and a fragment of stone ceiling remain. Above, to the right, stands the graceful **Temple of Wingless Victory** (or Athena Nike), so called because the sculptor depicted the goddess of victory without her wings in order to prevent her from flying away. The elegant and architecturally complex **Erechtheion temple,** most sacred of the shrines of the Acropolis and later turned into a harem by the Turks, has now emerged from extensive repair work. Dull, heavy copies of the infinitely more beautiful Caryatids (draped maidens) now support the roof. The Acropolis Museum houses five of the six originals, their faces much damaged by acid rain. The sixth is in the British Museum in London.

The **Parthenon** dominates the Acropolis and indeed the Athens skyline. Designed by Ictinus, with Phidias as master sculptor, it is the most architecturally sophisticated temple of that period. Even with

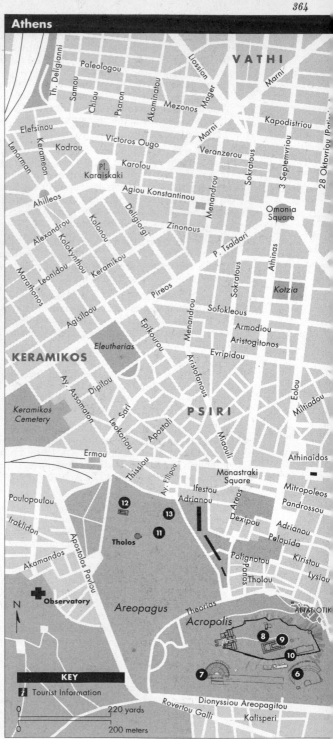

Athens

hordes of tourists wandering around the ruins, you can still feel a sense of wonder. It was completed in 438 BC. The architectural decorations were originally picked out in vivid red and blue paint, and the roof was of marble tiles, but time and neglect have given the marble pillars their golden-white shine, and the beauty of the building is all the more stark and striking. The British Museum houses the largest remaining part of the original 162-meter (523-foot) frieze (the Elgin Marbles). The building has 17 fluted columns along each side and eight at the ends, and these lean slightly inward and bulge to counterbalance cleverly the natural optical distortion. The Parthenon has had a checkered history: It was made into a brothel by the Romans, a church by the Christians, and a mosque by the Turks. The Turks also stored gunpowder in the Propylaea, and when it was hit by a Venetian bombardment in 1687, a fire raged for two days and 28 columns were blown out, leaving the Parthenon in its present condition. *Tel. 01/321–0219. Admission: joint ticket to Acropolis and museum 2,000 dr. Open weekdays 8–6:30 (8–4:30 in winter), weekends and holidays 8:30–2:30.*

⑩ The **Acropolis Museum,** just below the Parthenon, contains some superb sculptures from the Acropolis, including the Caryatids and a large collection of colored korai, (statues of women dedicated by worshipers to the goddess Athena, patron of the ancient city). *Tel. 01/323–6665. Admission: joint ticket to the Acropolis 2,000 dr. Open weekdays 8–6:30 (in winter 8–4:30), weekends and holidays 8–2:30.*

On Areopagus, the rocky outcrop facing the Acropolis, St. Paul preached to the Athenians; the road leading down between it and the hill of Pnyx is called Agiou Pavlou (St. Paul). To the right stands the ⑪ **Agora,** which means "marketplace," the civic center and focal point of community life in ancient Athens. The sprawling confusion of stones, slabs, and foundations is dominated by the best-preserved ⑫ temple in Greece, the **Hephaisteion** (often wrongly referred to as the Theseion), built during the 5th century BC. Nearby, the impressive Stoa of Attalus II, reconstructed by the American School of Classical Studies in Athens with the help of the Rockefeller Foundation, ⑬ houses the **Museum of the Agora Excavations.** *Tel. 01/321–0185. Admission: 1,200 dr. Open daily 8:30–7 (8:30–2:45 in winter).*

⑭ Next to the Agora you'll find **Plaka,** almost all that's left of 19th-century Athens. During the 1950s and '60s, the area became garish with neon as nightclubs moved in and residents moved out. Renovation in recent years has restored the Plaka, and it is one of the city's most charming quarters, with its winding lanes and pedestrian zones, neoclassical houses, and sights like the **Greek Folk Art Museum** (Kidathineon 17); the **Tower of the Winds** (a 1st-century-BC water clock near the Roman agora); and the Monument of Lysikrates (in a park off Lysikratous), which was awarded to the sponsor of an ancient play and is one of only two to survive. Above Plaka, at the base of the Acropolis, is **Anafiotika,** the closest thing you'll find to a village in Athens. To escape the city bustle, take some time to wander among its whitewashed, bougainvillea-framed houses and its tiny churches.

⑮ Below Plaka, in Cathedral Square, stands a charming 12th-century Byzantine church known as the Old or **Little Cathedral,** nestled below the vast structure of the 19th-century **Cathedral of Athens.** From here, a short walk up Mitropoleos will take you back to Syntagma.

Downtown Athens If you walk along Venizelou Avenue (Panepistimiou Avenue) from the square, you will pass, on the right, three imposing buildings in ⑯ ⑰ Classical style: the **Academy,** the **Senate House of the University,** and ⑱ the **National Library.** When you reach **Omonia Square,** a bedlam of touts and tourists, you are in the heart of downtown Athens.

⑲ Make time to see the **National Archaeological Museum.** Despite being somewhat off the tourist route, a good 10-minute walk north of Omonia Square, it is well worth the detour. This is by far the most important museum in Athens. It houses one of the most exciting collections of antiquity in the world, including sensational archaeological finds made by Heinrich Schliemann at Mycenae; 16th-century BC frescoes from the Akrotiri ruins on Santorini; and the 6½-foot-tall bronze sculpture *Poseidon,* an original work of circa 470 BC, possibly by the sculptor Kalamis, which was found in the sea off Cape Artemision in 1928. *Patission 44 (also known as 28 Oktovriou Ave.), tel. 01/821–7717. Admission: 2,000 dr. Open Mon. 11–5, Tues.–Fri. 8–7 (8–5 in winter), weekends and holidays 8:30–3.*

Alternatively, from Syntagma you can take Vasilissis Sofias Avenue ⑳ along the edge of the National Gardens to reach the **Evzone Guards' barracks.** From here you have several options. If you continue farther along Vasilissis Sofias, it will eventually take you to the Hilton Hotel and the U.S. Embassy. Or, turn right onto Herod Atticus, ㉑ which leads to the **Presidential Palace,** once used by Greece's kings after the restoration of 1935 and now by its head of state.

Or you can cross the street and turn up Neofytu Douka to the ㉒ **Museum of Cycladic Art.** The collection spans 5,000 years, with almost 100 exhibits of the Cycladic civilization (3,000 BC–2,000 BC), including many of the slim marble figurines that so fascinated artists like Picasso and Modigliani. *Neofytou Douka 4, tel. 01/722–8321. Admission: 400 dr. Open Mon. and Wed.–Fri. 10–4, Sat. 10–3.*

㉓ A little farther along Vasilissis Sofias is the **Byzantine Museum,** housed in an 1848 mansion that was built by an eccentric French aristocrat. Because the museum is undergoing renovation, not all its pieces are on display, but it has a unique collection of icons and the very beautiful 14th-century Byzantine embroidery of the body of Christ in gold, silver, yellow, and green. Sculptural fragments provide an excellent introduction to Byzantine architecture. *Vasilissis Sofias 22, tel. 01/721–1027. Admission: 500 dr. Open Tues.–Sun. 8:30–3.*

Kolonaki, the chic shopping district and one of the most fashionable ㉔ residential areas, occupies the lower slopes of **Mt. Lycabettus** and is only a 10-minute walk northeast of Syntagma; it's worth a stroll around if you enjoy window-shopping and people-watching. Three times the height of the Acropolis, Lycabettus can be reached by funicular railway from the top of Ploutarchou Street; Minibus 60 from Kolonaki Square will drop you at the station (fare: 400 dr. roundtrip; open daily 8:45 AM–12:45 AM, until 12:15 AM from October through March). The view from the top—pollution permitting—is the finest in Athens. You can see all Athens, Attica, the harbor, and the islands of Aegina and Poros laid out before you.

Shopping

Gift Ideas Better tourist shops sell copies of traditional Greek jewelry, silver filigree, enamel, Skyrian pottery, onyx ashtrays and dishes, woven bags, attractive rugs (including *flokates*—shaggy wool rugs, often brightly colored), good leather items, *koboloi* (worry beads) in amber or silver, and furs. Furs made from scraps are inexpensive. Some museums sell replicas of small items that are in their collections. Other shops sell dried fruit, packaged pistachios, and canned olives.

Shopping Areas The central shopping area lies between Syntagma and Omonia. The **Syntagma** area has good jewelers, shoe shops, and handicrafts and souvenir shops, especially along **Voukourestiou. Stadiou Street** is the best bet for men's clothing. Go to **Mitropoleos** for rugs and souvenirs. Ermou runs west to **Monastiraki,** a crowded market area popular with Athenians. Below the cathedral, **Pandrossou** has antiques, sandals (an especially good buy), and inexpensive souvenirs.

Flea Market The flea market, based on **Pandrossou** and **Ifestou streets,** operates on Sunday mornings and sells almost anything: secondhand clothes, daggers, cooking pots and pans, old books, guitars, bouzouki (stringed instruments), old furniture and carpets, and backgammon sets. Pontians—Greeks who lived in the former Soviet Union—sell Russian caviar, vodka, and table linen. However little it costs, you should haggle. Ifestou Street, where the coppersmiths have their shops, is more interesting on a weekday—and you can pick up copper wine jugs, candlesticks, cooking ware, etc., for next to nothing.

Dining

Be adventurous and go looking for the places that have at least half a dozen tables occupied by Athenians—they're discerning customers. For details and price-category definitions, *see* Lodging *in* Staying in Greece, *above.*

$$ **Apotsos.** A famous ouzerie, close to Syntagma Square but hidden away down an arcade, this is an echoing barn of a place—truly Athenian in atmosphere. Politicians, journalists, and artists gather here at lunchtime. As well as ouzo, wine and beer are served, along with dishes of *mezedes* (snacks for nibbling)—though three or four of these will add up to a substantial meal. The walls are decorated with old advertisements; the tabletops are of well-worn marble. *Panepistimiou 10, in the arcade, tel. 01/363-7046. No credit cards. Lunch only (11-5). Closed Sun.*

$$ **Kaldera.** Island specialties here include Chios *tsiro* salad (made with small, marinated fish resembling anchovies), *fava* (a dip made from mashed chick peas with pepper and tomato) from Santorini, and steaming hot mussels in mustard sauce from Skopelos. That's just for starters: For an entrée, try the *makaronada thalassina*—pasta with a jumble of crab, shrimp, and mussels—or any of the day's catch, fish straight from the Aegean. *Poseidonos 54, Palio Faliro, tel. 01/982-9647. Weekend reservations advised. AE, DC, MC, V.*

$$ **Kostoyiannis.** If you're looking for authenticity, this is the place to go. One of the oldest and most popular tavernas in the area, behind the National Archaeological Museum, it has an impressively wide range of Greek dishes—including excellent shrimp salad, stuffed mussels, rabbit *stifado* (a stew with onions), and sautéed brains. *Zaimi 37, tel. 01/821-2496. Reservations advised in summer. No credit cards. No lunch. Closed Sun. and Aug.*

$$ **Socrates' Prison.** Amiable owner Socrates eschews run-of-the-mill taverna fare for his own creations: pork rolls stuffed with carrots and celery in lemon sauce, zucchini with ham and bacon topped with béchamel, and his house salad—dill, carrots, olives, and eggs. It's ideal for a late dinner after a show at the nearby Herod Atticus theater. *Mitseon 20, Makriyanni, tel. 01/922-3434. Weekend reservations advised. V. Closed Sun. and latter ½ of Aug. No lunch.*

$$ **Vlassis.** Relying on recipes from Thrace, Roumeli, Thessaly, and the
★ islands, the cooks here whip up Greek home cooking in generous portions. Sample as much as possible by ordering several appetizers (there are more than 20, all reasonably priced). Musts are the fava dip and the octopus stifado, tender and sweet with lots of onions. Also good are the kebabs, the *seftalies* (a tasty mix of lamb liver bits and onions wrapped in intestines), and *katsiki ladorigani* (goat with oil and oregano). For dessert, the *galaktobouriko* (custard in phyllo) is delicious. *Armatolon and Klefton 20, Ambelokipi, tel. 01/642-5337. Reservations advised. No credit cards. Closed Sun. and July-Sept. No lunch.*

$$ **Xynos.** Enter a time warp in this Plaka taverna: Athens in the '50s. Nothing has changed much since then, including the excellent food. Start with the classic appetizer of stuffed grape leaves, then move

on to lamb *yiouvetsi*, made with tiny noodles called *kritharakia;* livers with sweetbreads in vinegar sauce and oregano; or *tsoutsoukakia*, spicy meat patties laced with cinnamon. Roving musicians charm the crowd of regulars as they croon ballads of yesteryear. *Aggelou Geronta 4, Plaka (entrance down walkway next to kafenion Glikis), tel. 01/322–1065. Reservations advised. No credit cards. Closed weekends and July. No lunch.*

$ **Eden.** This vegetarian restaurant, in a neoclassical Plaka house, serves vegetable pies and such hearty dishes as vegetable lasagna and spaghetti Bolognese with tofu—a delightful experience for those who are tired of seeing lamb roasted on a spit at every corner. *Lysiou 12, tel. 01/324–8858. AE, DC. Closed Tues.*

$ **Karavitis.** A neighborhood favorite, this taverna near the Olympic Stadium has outdoor garden seating in summer, in addition to a winter dining room decorated with huge wine barrels. All the classic Greek dishes are well prepared, including pungent *tzatziki* (yogurtgarlic dip), *bekri meze* (lamb chunks in a spicy red sauce), and *stamnaki* (beef baked in a clay pot). *Arktinou 35, tel. 01/721–5155. No credit cards. Closed a few days around Greek Easter. No lunch.*

$ **O Platanos.** Set in a picturesque corner of the Plaka, this is one of the
★ oldest tavernas in the area. It has a shady courtyard for outdoor dining. Don't miss the oven-baked potatoes, the roast lamb, and the exceptionally inexpensive but potent barrel retsina. Although the place is extremely friendly, not much English is spoken. *Diogenous 4, tel. 01/322–0666. No credit cards. Closed Sun.*

$ **Vasilenas.** This family-run taverna is probably still as good a bargain
★ now as it was 60 years ago. Come here ravenously hungry with friends, so you can do justice to the prix-fixe menu of 16 dishes. Zesty shrimp and prawn croquettes are two standouts, as is the dessert called *tiganites*, a fried bread filled with walnuts. *Etolikou 72, Agia Sofia, Piraeus, tel. 01/461–2457. Weekend and group reservations required. No credit cards. Closed Sun. and 3 wks in Aug. No lunch.*

¢ **Athinaikon.** After almost 60 years near the law courts, this renowned ouzeri moved, but is still a favorite of attorneys and local office workers. The variety and quality of the food—over 50 appetizers—more than compensate for the brusque service. Mussels are a specialty, along with grilled green peppers, crisp shrimp croquettes, fried calamari, and homemade halvah. *Themistokleous 2, tel. 01/388–8485. No credit cards. Closed Sun. and Aug.*

¢ **Leuka.** Start an evening of barhopping in Exarchia at this humble taverna that serves all the Greek classics. The grill offers souvlakia, tender pork chops, and lamb ribs sprinkled with oregano. Appetizers are numerous and include fava, garlicky lamb livers, marinated black-eyed peas, buttery giant beans called *gigantes*, and grilled green peppers. *Mavromichalis 121, Exarchia, tel. 01/361–4038. No credit cards. Closed Sun. and 3 wks in Aug. No lunch.*

¢ **Sigalas.** In the heart of Monastiraki, this classic tavern has been
★ keeping its customers happy since 1879. The decor is set by the charming painted wine barrels lining the walls and the photos of Greek film stars, and the food here is excellent. There are many magirefta on display—like pastitsio and beef *kokkinisto* (in red sauce)—but the best dish is the gyro platter, lamb roasted slowly on a spit, sliced and served in large portions with pita, tomatoes, and onions. Appetizers include fried eggplant—perfect with the creamy tzatziki, mini cheese pies with sesame seeds, mountain greens, and oven-baked potatoes the way Greek grandmothers make them. *Platia Monastiraki 2, tel. 01/321–3036. No credit cards.*

¢ **To Gerani.** Squeeze onto the balcony of this taverna, located in a Plaka house, and watch the tourists roam below. Waiters come by with appetizers for you to choose from—try the *bourekakia parmesana* (puff pastries) or the flaming village sausage—or order a hefty main dish like cuttlefish with spinach. The barrel wine is a delicious, unresinated red. *Tripodon 14, tel. 01/324–7605. No credit cards.*

Lodging

Since Athens is the starting point for so many travelers, its hotels are often full, so it's always advisable to reserve a room in advance. Which type of hotel you choose is really a matter of taste. Basically, the style of hotels in Athens can be divided into two neat brackets—traditional and modern—and these can be found both in the center of town, around Omonia and Syntagma Squares, and near the U.S. Embassy. For details and price-category definitions, *see* Lodging *in* Staying in Greece, *above.*

$$ **Acropolis View Hotel.** This hotel in a quiet neighborhood below the
★ Acropolis has a rooftop garden and agreeable rooms; those on the first, second, and fourth floor were recently renovated. Staff members in the homey lobby are efficient and friendly, and major sights lie just a stone's throw away. American breakfast (cornflakes, eggs, ham, bacon) is included in the price. *Webster 10, Acropolis, 11742, tel. 01/921–7303 through 01/921–7305, fax 01/923–0705. 32 rooms with bath. Facilities: bar (summer), air-conditioning. AE, MC.*

$$ **Astor.** The no-frills Astor is a good choice if you want to stay very close to Syntagma Square without paying a fortune. It offers convenience and the usual amenities—TV, room service—of a more expensive place. In 1995, the hotel installed new air-conditioning and elevators and outfitted rooms with more modern furniture. Request a room on the sixth floor or above for a memorable view of the Acropolis. Continental breakfast is included. *Karageorgi Servias 16, Syntagma, 10562, tel. 01/325–5111, fax 01/325–5115. 131 rooms with bath. Facilities: restaurant, bar, air-conditioning. AE, DC, V.*

$$ **Austria.** This small, unpretentious hotel on Filopappou Hill, opposite the Acropolis, is ideal as a base for exploring the heart of ancient Athens. Although it has no restaurant, it's at the low end of this price category and is well worth considering. Continental breakfast, included in the quoted rate, is not required (700 dr. per person). *Mouson 7, Filopappou, 11742, tel. 01/923–5151, fax 01/924–7350. 38 rooms with bath. Facilities: breakfast room, air-conditioning. AE, DC, MC, V.*

$$ **Lycabette.** The main draw of this hotel is its moderate price despite a location in the wealthy Kolonaki district, close to the city's sights and upscale boutiques. It has a friendly atmosphere, comfortable rooms with small balconies, and helpful staff. Ask for a room on the pedestrian zone, though even these can get noisy with motorcycles parking. If you book through a travel agency, the Continental breakfast will be obligatory (1,600 dr. per person), a shame when Jimmy's, a popular café, is just across the road. *Valaoritou 6, 10671, tel. 01/363–3514, fax 01/363–3518. 39 rooms with bath. Facilities: breakfast room, restaurant, air-conditioning. AE, DC, V.*

$$ **Plaka Hotel.** Convenient for sightseeing and the metro at Monastiraki Square, this hotel has a roof garden that offers a view across the red-tile roofs of the Plaka district to the Parthenon. Double-glazed windows cut down on the noise, as does the air-conditioning; the fifth and sixth floors are the quietest. All rooms have TV and are simply furnished; those in the back have Acropolis views. *Kapnikareas 7, 10556, tel. 01/322–2096/7/8, fax 01/322–2412. 67 rooms with bath or shower. Facilities: air-conditioning. AE, DC, MC, V.*

$$ **President.** Perhaps the most inexpensive A-class hotel in Athens, the President is a favorite with athletic teams and tourist groups. The rooms, though unexceptional, are quiet, air-conditioned, and have city views (the Acropolis is visible from the sixth floor and up). There are trolley and bus stops nearby for the 20-minute journey to the center. Continental breakfast is included. *Kifissias 43,*

Ambelokipi, 11523, tel. 01/692–4600, fax 01/692–4968. 513 rooms with bath. Facilities: restaurant, bar, grill, outdoor roof pool. AE, DC, MC, V.

$ **Acropolis House.** This landmark family-run villa in Plaka is popular with visiting students and faculty. Note Belle Epoque accents like the painting behind the reception desk. While the decor may be somewhat cluttered and the wallpaper elderly, this makes it all the more endearing to its clients, who feel the hotel's nurturing service and friendly atmosphere more than compensate. *Kodrou 6–8, Plaka, 10558, tel. 01/322–2344 or 01/322–6241, fax 01/324–4143. 23 rooms, 20 with bath. Facilities: TV room. V.*

$ **Aphrodite Hotel.** This is near Syntagma and perfectly comfortable, with quiet and tidy, if rather spare, rooms. With all the facilities of other, more costly hotels, it offers excellent value, with rates at the low end of the category. The gleaming white marble lobby ends in a bar, where guests often relax in the evenings. *Apollonos 21, Syntagma, 10557, tel. 01/323–4357/8/9, fax 01/322–5244. 84 rooms with bath. Facilities: bar, air-conditioning. AE, DC, MC, V.*

$ **Art Gallery Pension.** So named for the original Greek paintings on the wall, this upscale pension in Koukaki is a quiet and comfortable former family home. The rooms are spacious, with ceiling fans that work almost as well as air-conditioning, and the roof garden offers a view of the Acropolis, which is only a few minutes away by foot. *Erecthiou 5, Koukaki, 11742, tel. 01/923–8376 or 01/923–1933, fax 01/923–3025. 21 rooms with bath. Facilities: bar, roof garden. No credit cards. Closed Nov.–Feb.*

$ **Attalos Hotel.** The market area, where the Attalos is located, is full of life and color by day, but deserted at night. The hotel is pleasant and well run by owner Kostas Zissis, who goes out of his way to accommodate guests. One-half of the rooms have air-conditioning, and many have Acropolis views. Try to get a room on the fifth or sixth floor or at the back, where the street noise is less. *Athinas 29, Psiri, 10554, tel. 01/321–2801/2/3, fax 01/324–3124. 80 rooms with bath. Facilities: bar, roof garden (summer), air-conditioning. V.*

¢ **Erechtheion.** This very inexpensive, quiet hotel is close to the ancient sites, the subway, and the many bars and restaurants that make the Thission district popular. Rooms have carpeting, double-glazed windows, and except for the singles, an Acropolis view; the best are the corner rooms with balconies. *Flamarion 8, Thission, 11851, tel. 01/345–9606 or 01/345–9626, fax 01/346–2756. 22 rooms with bath. Facilities: dining room, air-conditioning in 10 rooms (1,400 dr. extra). AE, MC, V.*

¢ **Imperial Hotel.** Though not much to look at from the outside, this thoroughly old-fashioned hotel has large, spotless rooms, with a convivial atmosphere and balconies overlooking Cathedral Square. Front rooms from the second floor up have an Acropolis view, but those in the back are quieter. The best rooms are No. 46 and No. 47 on the top floor: incredible views, lots of sun, and very large balconies. The Monastiraki metro, Plaka, and Syntagma Square are 10 minutes away by foot. *Mitropoleos 46, Monastiraki, 10563, tel. 01/322–7617 or 01/322–7780. 21 rooms, 18 with bath. MC, V.*

¢ **Marble House.** This popular pension, in a cul-de-sac about a 15-minute walk from the Acropolis, has a steady, satisfied clientele even in winter, when it offers low monthly room rates (50,000 dr. plus electricity). Rooms are quiet, with ceiling fans and basic furniture. The international staff is always willing to help out, and the courtyard is a lovely place to read or relax. Take Trolleys 1, 5, or 9 from Syntagma and get off at the Zinni stop. *A. Zinni 35, Koukaki, 11741, tel. 01/923–4058 or 01/922–6461. 16 rooms, 12 with bath. Facilities: breakfast room. No credit cards.*

¢ **Museum Hotel.** At this friendly and efficiently run hotel, just behind the National Archaeological Museum in a middle-class residential area, you're likely to meet a distinguished archaeologist at breakfast in the cheerful café-bar. Rooms were newly painted in 1994 and most have balconies; choose one on the fifth floor to avoid street noise. *Bouboulinas 16, Exarchia, 10682, tel. 01/380–5611/2/3, fax 01/380–0507. 58 rooms with bath. AE, DC, V.*

¢ **Tempi Hotel.** Decorated with murals by visiting artists, this basic hotel built in 1960 offers standard rooms but great service from owners John and Katerina. Because the hotel is on a pedestrian zone, there isn't much street noise, and all front rooms have balconies overlooking tiny St. Irene's church. *Aeolou 29, Monastiraki, 10551, tel. 01/321–3175 or 01/324–2940, fax 01/325–4179. 24 rooms without bath, 6 with tub. Facilities: snack bar, laundry room. AE, V.*

The Arts

The **Athens Festival** runs from late June through September and includes concerts, recitals, opera, ballet, folk dancing, and drama. Performances are in various locations, including the open-air theater of Herodes Atticus at the foot of the Acropolis, nearby Philopappou Hill, and Mount Lycabettos. Tickets are available a few days before the performance from the festival box office in the arcade at Stadiou 4 (tel. 01/322–1459). Admission ranges from 1,500 dr. to 10,000 dr.

For those who are disappointed with the daytime view of the Acropolis, the **son-et-lumière** shows bring history to life. Performances are given nightly from April to October, in English, at 9 (the time is subject to change), and admission is 1,000 dr. adults, 500 dr. students. The entrance is on Dionysiou Areopagitou, opposite the Acropolis, and from your seat on the top of Filopappou Hill, you watch the changing lighting of the monuments.

The lively Dora Stratou Troupe performs Greek and Cypriot **folk dances** at its theater atop Filopappou hill from mid-May through mid-September. Daily performances begin at 10:15 PM; there are also earlier evening shows at 8:15 on Wednesday and Sunday. Tickets, which range from 1,900 dr. to 2,200 dr. (1,200 dr. for students; children under 7 free), can be purchased at the box office before the show. For information, call the theater at 01/921–4650 or the troupe's offices at 01/324–4395.

Cultural activity in the winter has improved enormously with the opening in 1991 of the **Megaron Athens Concert Hall** (Vasilissis Sofias and Kokkali, tel. 01/728–2333, fax 01/724–7409), with two auditoriums equipped with state-of-the-art acoustics. Daily listings are published for its September–May season in the *Athens News*, available in hotels and at many newsstands. *The Athenian* and the weekly *Greek News* also list concerts, exhibitions, and showings of films in English.

Opera The **Lyriki Skini Opera Company** has a winter season (Oct.–May) and a short ballet season with performances that aren't very good at the Olympia Theater (Akademias 59, tel. 01/361–2461). In summer it performs at the Herod Atticus Theater. The best seats cost about 7,000 dr.

Films Almost all movie theaters now show foreign films, usually managing to show the latest Hollywood offerings within a month or two of their New York and London openings. The *Athens News* and the *Greek News* list them in English. Downtown movie theaters are the most comfortable. Near Syntagma, try the **Astor** (Stadiou 28, tel. 01/323–1297) or the **Apollon** (Stadiou 19, tel. 01/323–6811), or, near Omonia, the **Ideal** (Panepistimiou 46, tel. 01/362–6720), which has the best seats in Athens. Unless they have air-conditioning, most cinemas close June–September, giving way to wonderful outdoor movie theaters, such as the **Thission** (Pavlou 7, tel. 01/342–0864 or 01/347–0980), where you have a view of the Acropolis as a backdrop, and **Cine Paris** (Kidathineon 22, tel. 01/322–2071) in Plaka. At both, the films change every few days, and you can order drinks from the bar during the screening.

Mycenae

Legend and history meet in Mycenae, where Agamemnon, Elektra, and Orestes played out their grim family tragedy. This city dominated the entire area from the 18th to the 12th century BC and may even have conquered Minoan Crete. According to Greek mythology, Paris, son of the king of Troy, abducted the beautiful Helen, wife of Menelaus, the king of Sparta. Agamemnon, the king of Mycenae, was Menelaus's brother. This led to the Trojan War in which Troy was defeated. The story of the war is told in Homer's *Iliad*. Following Heinrich Schliemann's discoveries of gold-filled graves and a royal palace during excavations in 1874, Mycenae has become a world-class archaeological site and, of all the sites in the Peloponnese, is most worthy of a visit.

Getting Around

The quickest way to reach Mycenae is by taking a bus for Argos or Nauplion and getting off at the Mycenae village turnoff. The train via Corinth offers an enjoyable, if slower, ride. Nauplion is the best place to stay; a local bus will take you there.

Tourist Information

Nauplion has a **Municipal Tourist Office** (25th Martiou across from OTE, tel. 0752/24 444); its **Tourist Police** are at Fotamara 16 (tel. 0752/28–131).

Exploring Mycenae

Mycenae, 44 kilometers (28 miles) from Corinth, was the fabulous stronghold of the Achaean kings of the 13th century BC. Destroyed in 468 BC, it was forgotten until 1874 when German archaeologist Heinrich Schliemann, who discovered the ruins of ancient Troy, uncovered the remains of this ancient fortress city. Mycenae was the seat of the doomed House of Atreus—of King Agamemnon and his wife, Clytemnestra, sister of Helen of Troy, and of their tragic children, Orestes and Elektra. When Schliemann uncovered six shaft graves (so named because the kings were buried standing up) of the royal circle, he was certain that one was the tomb of Agamemnon. The gold masks and diadems, daggers, jewelry, and other treasures found in the graves are now in the National Archaeological Museum in Athens; the new local museum is dedicated to archaeological studies. Along with the graves, you'll find the astounding beehive tombs built into the hillsides outside the reconstructed wall, the **Lion Gate,** dating from 1250 BC, and the castle ruins crowning the bleak hill, all remnants of the first great civilization in continental Europe. The tombs, the acropolis, the palace, and the museum can all be explored for the cost of admission. *Tel. 0751/76–585. Admission: 1,500 dr. Open weekdays 8–7 (8–5 in winter), weekends and holidays 8:30–3.*

Farther on is **Nauplion,** a picturesque town below the Venetian fortifications. Modern Greece's first king lived for a year or two within the walls of the higher fortress when Nafplio was the capital of Greece. His courtiers had to climb 999 steps to reach him; you can still climb the long staircase or drive up to the fortress. *Tel. 0752/28–036. Admission: 800 dr. Open weekdays 8–7 (8–4:45 in winter), weekends and holidays 8:30–2:45.*

The **Venetian naval arsenal** on the town square houses a museum crowded with Mycenaean finds, including items from Tiryns like a

7th-century BC gorgon mask. *Tel. 0752/27–502. Admission: 500 dr. Open Tues.–Sun. 8:30–3.*

Dining and Lodging

Nauplion
Dining

O Arapakos. Settle in on the waterfront and start with grilled octopus; then move on to *giouvetsi ton arapi* (lamb with potatoes, tomatoes, carrots, and eggplant) or *arnaki exohiko* (lamb stuffed with feta and potatoes). Fresh fish is also available, including charcoal-grilled sea bream and *bakaliaro skordalia* (dried cod fried and served with a dollop of garlic sauce). *Bouboulinas 81, tel. 0752/27–675. V. $$*

Savouras. Fresh seafood is served in this unpretentious taverna overlooking the bay; it is generally regarded as one of the best fish restaurants in the area, with such selections as red mullet, pandora, and dorado. *Bouboulinas 79, tel. 0752/27–704. No credit cards. $$*

★ **Ta Fanaria.** Sit at one of the tables in the narrow alley beside the restaurant and ask what's best that night. The restaurant is known for its *ladera*, vegetables cooked in olive oil, but equally delicious are the charcoal-grilled lamb ribs, lamb baked with vegetables like okra or green beans, and the *imam* (eggplant stuffed with onions). *Staikopoulos 13, tel. 0752/27–141. V. $*

Karamanlis. This simple taverna near the courthouse is crowded at lunch with civil servants who come for its tasty though limited number of magirefta. The light fish soup makes a good appetizer, followed by *yiouvelakia* (meat-rice balls) in egg-lemon sauce, baked potatoes, wild greens, and barrel wine. Fresh fish is also available at very good prices. *Bouboulinas 1, tel. 0752/27–668. No credit cards. ¢*

Lodging

Agamemnon. Located on the waterfront, this hotel has a large, cool lobby overhung with vines, a superb spot from which to watch the action. For those who don't mind the mandatory half board, this is a good deal, especially since many Nauplion restaurants tend to be higher priced. Most of the double rooms have marble terraces overlooking the water. *Akti Miaouli 3, 21100, tel. 0752/28–021, fax 0752/28–022. 40 rooms with bath. Facilities: restaurant, roof garden. No credit cards. Closed Nov.–mid-Dec. and Jan.–mid-Feb. $$*

Dioscouri. Located high up beneath the castle in the old town, with a fine view across the Nauplion gulf, this family-run hotel is cool and quiet. Continental breakfast is included. *Zigomala 7, 21100, tel. 0752/28–550, fax 0752/21–202. 50 rooms with shower. V. $*

King Otto. The best choice for those on a tight budget, this hotel reigns in a pale yellow neoclassical house. Rooms are simple: Only a few have a view of the fortress, and the bathrooms are shared, but there's a grand spiral staircase, the lemon-blossom-scented garden is ideal for breakfast, and the owner, who also runs the budget Leto in Nauplion, is a kindly gentleman who speaks English. *Farmakopoulou 4, 21100, tel. 0752/27585. 12 rooms without bath, 4 with tubs. No credit cards. Closed Nov.–Feb. ¢*

Mainland Greece

The dramatic rocky heights of mainland Greece provide an appropriate setting for man's attempt to approach divinity. The ancient Greeks placed their gods on snowcapped Mount Olympus and chose the precipitous slopes of Parnassus, "the navel of the universe," as the site for Delphi, the most important religious center of the ancient Greek world. In fact, many of mainland Greece's most memorable sights are closely connected with religion—including the remarkable Byzantine churches of Thessaloniki. Of course, there are remains of palaces and cities, but these do not have the impact of the great religious centers.

In this land of lonely mountain villages, narrow defiles, and dark woods, bands of *klephts* (a cross between brigands and guerrillas) earned their place in folk history and song during the long centuries of Turkish rule. The women of Souli, one of the mountain strongholds of the klephts, threw themselves dancing and singing over a cliff rather than be captured by the Turks. In these same mountains during the German occupation'of Greece during World War II, guerrilla bands descended to the valleys and plains to assault the occupying army and drive it from their land.

Farmers have flourished since Greece joined the European Union, and few villages, even those tucked away in the hills, are still poor and isolated. Despite the arrival of video clubs and discos, the traditional way of life still survives. This is a beautiful area to explore. The mainland Greeks see fewer tourists and have more time for those they do see, hotels are unlikely to be full, and the sights— steep, wooded mountains, cypress trees like candles, narrow gorges, the soaring monasteries of Meteora—are beautiful.

Getting Around

A one-day trip to Delphi is rushed; two days will give you more leisure time. Take the train or bus to Thessaloniki. In September, during the Thessaloniki International Trade Fair, there are no hotel rooms to be had; make reservations well in advance.

Tourist Information

In **Delphi,** visit the Delphi Tourist Office on Vasilissis Pavlou and Friderikis 12 for helpful service (tel. 0265/82–900); the Tourist Police is at Apollonos 40 (tel. 0265/82–220). In **Thessaloniki,** visit the Greek National Tourist Office (Mitropoleos 34 on Platia Aristotelous, tel. 031/222–935, or at the airport, tel. 031/417–170); here, the Tourist Police is at Dodekanissou 4 (tel. 031/254–871) and Taxiarchou 1, Kalamaria, (tel. 031/453–223). A very helpful travel agency is **Sismanidis Tours** (Egnatias 126, tel. 031/261–875 or 031/260–660, fax 031/265–930), which can book tours throughout northern Greece, as well as organize trips to Turkey and Bulgaria.

Exploring Mainland Greece

Delphi The ancient Greeks believed that **Delphi** was the center of the universe because two eagles released by the gods at opposite ends of Earth met here. For hundreds of years, the worship of Apollo and the pronouncements of the Oracle here made Delphi the most important religious center of ancient Greece. As you walk up the Sacred Way to the **Temple of Apollo,** the **theater,** and the **stadium,** you'll see Mount Parnassus above; silver-green olive trees below; and, in the distance, the blue Gulf of Itea. This is one of the most rugged and lonely sites in Greece, and one of the most striking; if you can get to the site in the early morning or evening, avoiding the busloads of tourists, you will feel the power and beauty of the place. You may even see an eagle or two. First excavated in 1892, most of the ruins date from the 5th to the 3rd century BC. *Tel. 0265/82–313. Admission: 1,200 dr. Open Tues.–Fri. 8–7 (7:30–5 in winter), Mon. 11–7 (11–5:30 in winter), weekends and holidays 8–3.*

Don't miss the famous bronze charioteer (early 5th century BC) in the **Delphi Museum.** Other interesting and beautiful works of art here include a statue of Antinoüs, Emperor Hadrian's lover; fragments of a 6th-century BC silver-plated bull, the largest example of an ancient statue in precious metal; the stone *omphalos*, representing the navel of the earth; fragments from the site's Sifnian Treasury that depict scenes from the Trojan war; and the statues of Kleobis and Viton. According to legend, they pulled their mother 80 kilometers (50 miles) by chariot to the Temple of Hera so she could worship, then died from exhaustion when Hera rewarded them with eternal sleep. It was said of them, "Those whom the gods love die young." *Tel. 0265/82–313. Admission: 1,200 dr. Open the same hrs as the archaeological site.*

Thessaloniki **Thessaloniki** is Greece's second-largest city, its second port after Piraeus, and the capital of northern Greece.

Although Thessaloniki still has some remains from the Roman period, the city is best known for its fine Byzantine churches. The city is compact enough for you to see the main sights on foot. Start at the 15th-century grayish **White Tower**, landmark and symbol of Thessaloniki, previously named "Tower of Blood," referring to its use as a prison. Now it houses a museum, with an exhibition on the history and art of Byzantine Thessaloniki, including pottery, mosaics, and ecclesiastical objects. *Pavlou Mela and Nikis, tel. 031/267–832. Admission: 800 dr. Open Tues.–Fri. 8–7 (8–5 in winter), Mon. 10:30–5, weekends 8:30–3.*

Then walk up Pavlou Mela toward Tsimiski, the elegant tree-lined shopping street, and cut across to the green-domed basilica-style church of **Aghia Sophia,** which dates from the 8th century and has beautifully preserved mosaics.

Walk to Egnatia, which partially traces the original Roman road leading from the Adriatic to the Bosphorous. Continue north along the **Roman Agora** (town center) to **Agios Dimitrios,** the town's principal church. Though it is only a replica of the original 7th-century church that burned down in 1917, it is adorned with many 8th-century mosaics that were in the original building. Follow Aghiou Dimitriou east to **Agios Georgios,** a rotunda built by Roman emperor Galerius as his tomb during the 4th century AD. His successor, Constantine the Great, the first Christian emperor, turned it into a church.

Return to Egnatia and the **Arch of the Emperor Galerius,** built shortly prior to the rotunda to commemorate the Roman victories of Emperor Galerius over forces in Persia, Armenia, and Mesopotamia. A short walk downhill toward the sea wall will bring you to the **Archaeological Museum.** Among its many beautiful objects are a huge bronze vase and a delicate, gold myrtle wreath from Derveni, as well as gold artifacts from recent excavations of the royal tombs of Vergina, including a 10-kilogram gold casket standing on lions' feet that contains bones thought to be those of Philip II, father of Alexander the Great. *Platia Hanth, tel. 031/830–538. Admission: 1,500 dr. Open Mon. 10:30–7 (10:30–5 in winter), Tues.–Fri. 8–7 (8–5 in winter), weekends and holidays 8:30–3.*

Dining and Lodging

For details and price-category definitions, *see* Dining and Lodging in Staying in Greece, *above.*

Delphi **Topiki Gefsi.** Local specialties, accompanied by a smattering of
Dining French dishes and a view over Delphi, is what this popular *mezedopolion* (a place serving appetizers) offers. In winter, warm yourself at the fireplace while listening to nightly piano music; in summer, dine on the veranda. Especially good are the *kokkora krasato* (rooster stewed in wine), *hortopites* (vegetable pies), and lamb *kleftiko* (baked in a pastry shell with vegetables). Another house speciality is *mides saganaki* (mussels in fried cheese). *Vas. Pavlou and Friderikis 19, tel. 0265/82–710, fax 0265/82–480. Reservations advised. AE, DC, MC, V. $$*
Vakhos. After opening in 1992, this restaurant quickly became a favorite with locals because of its excellent food and low prices. From the large veranda decorated with murals of Bacchus, for whom the

restaurant is named, you have a view of the Gulf of Itea; enjoy it with the local retsina, rooster stewed in wine, vegetable croquettes, the generous souvlakia, and, for the adventurous, boiled goat. There are also seven prix-fixe menus ranging from 1,000 dr. to 2,000 dr., including ouzo. Dessert is homemade *karidopita* (walnut cake drenched in syrup) or yogurt with preserves. *Apollonos 32, tel. 0265/82–448. V. Closed weekdays Nov.–mid-March except holidays.* ¢

Dining and Lodging **Kastalia.** Built to blend in with the other village houses and owned by the same people who opened Fedriades (*see below*), the hotel has simple rooms decorated with paintings of the area and views over Mt. Parnassos or down to Itea. Its restaurant, which is quite good, makes Greek dishes with a twist, like lamb *fricassee* with lettuce, rather than the typical cabbage. Be sure to try the local sweet cheese, *formaella. Vas. Pavlou and Friderikis 13, 33054, tel. 0265/ 82–205/6, fax 0265/82–208. 26 rooms with bath. Facilities: restaurant. AE, DC, MC, V. $$*

Lodging **Apollo.** The living room of this delightful family-run hotel has traditional wall hangings and old prints among its carefully selected furnishings. The light wood furniture in the cheerful bedrooms is set off by blue quilts and striped curtains. Many rooms have balconies with black-iron railings, and all have hair dryers and TVs; a full breakfast is included in the price. *Vas. Pavlou and Friderikis 59B, 33054, tel. 0265/82–580 or 0265/82–244, fax 0265/82–455. 21 rooms with bath. Facilities: bar, breakfast room, minibars, air-conditioning. MC, V. Closed weekdays Nov.–Mar. except holidays. $$*

★ **Fedriades.** Named after Delphi's famous rocks, the Fedriades, built in 1992, is one of the newer hotels in the area. The neoclassic exterior gives way to a light, airy lobby and rooms done in marble and wood, with views to the Gulf of Itea. *Main St., 33054, tel. 0265/82–919 or 0265/82–370, fax 0265/82–208. 24 rooms with bath. AE, DC, MC, V. $$*

★ **Acropole.** This friendly, family-run hotel has a garden and a spectacular view—bare mountainside and a sea of olive groves—so that guests feel as though they're completely secluded. All but a few rooms have balconies; 10 have air-conditioning, minibars, and TVs. *Filellinon 13, 33054, tel. 0265/82–675, fax 0265/83–171. 42 rooms with bath. Facilities: bar, breakfast room, TV lounge. AE, MC, V. $*

Hotel Delphi-Panorama. Living up to its name, the Panorama has a splendid view from its perch on the highest road in town. The spotless, cheerful rooms and very reasonable prices make up for nondescript furnishings. *Osios Loukas 47, 30054, tel. 0265/82–437 or 0265/ 82–061, fax 0265/82081. 20 rooms with bath. Facilities: breakfast room. MC, V. Closed Jan.–Feb. weekdays except holidays. $*

Hotel Dolphin. The rooms are truly tiny in this basic accommodation, probably the cheapest in all Delphi. But the warmth of the owners, who have run this hotel in their former home for years, provides a singular experience. The street is noisy, however, and the rooms are not equally pleasant, so carefully check what is available before moving in. *Dimou Frangou 4, 33054, tel. 0265/82–202. 13 rooms with bath. No credit cards.* ¢

Thessaloniki Dining **Krikelas.** A local landmark, this taverna has been serving classic Greek dishes for more than half a century. Its homemade eggplant dip has a faint smoky taste, and the gyros are heaped high with succulent lamb. You can even get *dordoumas*—a special kind of homemade ice cream topped with cherry syrup. In winter, Krikelas specializes in game like wild pig and venison; fresh fish is served year-round. *Ethnikis Antistasis 32, Kalamaria, tel. 031/451–690 or 031/451–289. Reservations advised. AE, DC, MC, V. $$*

O Ragias. Known for Macedonian cooking, this restaurant with a sea view offers unusual dishes like *yiaourtlou Ragias* (veal in yogurt-garlic sauce) and *hungar begiendi* (veal casserole with eggplant puree), grilled mussels, and for dessert, the Macedonian crepe with honey, walnuts, and ice cream. Except for Mondays, there is piano music nightly. *Nikis 13, tel. 031/279–993 or 031/227–468. AE, DC, MC. Closed Sun. No lunch. $$*

★ **O Kipos ton Pringipon.** The Milos enclave, where this ouzeri is located, is an entertaining place to spend an evening. The former mill complex in the city's slaughterhouse area was converted in the early 1990s into a nightlife center, with a café, bars playing everything from light jazz to heavy Greek music, and exhibition spaces for art and live performances. The "Princes' Garden" has traditional appetizers—saganaki and croquettes made with *kasseri* cheese—as well as such specialties as their own bekri meze. *Andrea Georgiou 56, Sfagia, tel. 031/251–838, 031/516–945, or 031/251–836. Reservations advised. No credit cards. $*

Ta Koumbarakia. A small ouzeri behind the church of the Metamorphosis (Transfiguration), this place is packed with students and locals working their way through the many mezedes, including marinated red peppers; village sausage; fava dip; and various fried hard cheeses like *kefalotiri*, served with lemon. Seafood—whitebait, swordfish, octopus, shrimp, and salted cod with garlic dip—and grilled meats are also available. *Egnatias 140, tel. 031/271–905 or 031/268–442. No credit cards. ¢–$*

Lodging **ABC.** This large hotel is centrally located, near the museum and the landmark White Tower. It offers the comforts of a more expensive hotel, with color TV and refrigerator in about half of the rooms. The owners have added various architectural touches to make every floor slightly different. Buffet breakfast is included. *Agelaki 41, 54621, tel. 031/265–421, fax 031/276–542. 101 rooms with shower. Facilities: TV room, coffee shop, air-conditioning. AE, DC, MC, V. $$*

Queen Olga Hotel. Though it's starting to show its age, this hotel is slowly being renovated. Its location near the International Fairgrounds and its helpful staff make it appealing to the budget-minded traveler. Rooms in the front have a sea view. *Vas. Olgas 44, 54641, tel. 031/824–621 through 031/824–629, fax 031/868–581. 148 rooms with bath. Facilities: restaurant, bar, minibars, air-conditioning. AE, MC, V. $$*

Pella. This quiet hotel between city hall and the Ministry of Northern Greece was renovated in 1992. It offers small but spotless rooms at very low prices, so book early. *Ionos Dragoumi 63, 54630, tel. 031/524–221, 031/524–222, or 031/524–224, fax 031/524–223. 79 rooms with bath. MC, V. $*

The Greek Islands

The islands of the Aegean have colorful legends of their own—the Minotaur in Crete; the lost continent of Atlantis, which some believe was Santorini; and the Colossus of Rhodes, to name a few. Each island has its own personality. Mykonos has windmills, dazzling whitewashed buildings, hundreds of tiny churches and chapels on golden hillsides, and small fishing harbors. Visitors to volcanic Santorini sail into what was once a vast volcanic crater and anchor near the island's forbidding cliffs. Crete, with its jagged mountain peaks, olive orchards, and vineyards, contains the remains of the Minoan civilization. In Rhodes, a bustling modern town surrounds a walled town with a medieval castle.

Getting Around

The simplest way to visit the Aegean Islands is by ferry from Piraeus, the port of Athens. There is also frequent air service from Athens, but most flights are fully booked year-round. It's vital to book well in advance and to confirm and reconfirm in order to be sure of your seat. (*See* Getting Around, By Boat, *in* Essential Information, *above*.)

Tourist Information

There are **Greek National Tourist Organization** offices on **Crete,** at Kriari 40, Hania (tel. 0821/26–426 or 031/92–943), and at Xanthoudidou 1, Heraklion, (tel. 081/244–462); and on **Rhodes,** at Archibishop Makarios and Papagou, Rhodes town (tel. 0241/23–655, 0241/23–255, or 0241/27–466). Much more helpful as well as closer to the Old Town is the **Rhodes Municipal Tourism Office** off Platia Rimini (tel. 0241/35–945; closed Nov.–Apr.) The **Tourist Police** are in Heraklion, Crete, at Dikaiosinis 10 (tel. 081/283–190) and in Hania at Karaiskaki 60 (tel. 0821/73–333); in **Mykonos** on the harbor where ferries arrive (tel. 0289/22–482); in **Santorini** near the town square in Thira (tel. 0286/22–649); and in **Rhodes** at Ethelondon Dodekanissou 45, New Town (tel. 0241/27–423).

Exploring the Greek Islands

Mykonos Cruise ships and car ferries to **Mykonos** leave from Piraeus or Rafina. As you sail to there, you will be able to see one of the great sights of Greece: the Temple of Poseidon looming on a hilltop at the edge of Cape Sounion, about two hours from the mainland.

Mykonos is the name of the island and also of its chief village—a colorful maze of narrow, paved streets lined with whitewashed houses, many with bright blue doors and shutters. Every morning, women scrub the sidewalks and streets in front of their homes, undaunted by the bustle of donkey traffic. During the 1960s, the bohemian jet set descended upon Mykonos, and most of the old houses along the waterfront are now restaurants, nightclubs, bars, and discos—both gay and straight, all blaring loud music into the wee hours; a quiet café or taverna is hard to find. Mykonos is still a favorite anchorage with yachting devotees, as well as being *the* holiday destination for the young, lively, and liberated—finding yourself either alone or attired on any of its beaches is unlikely.

Delos About 40 minutes by boat is the ancient isle of **Delos,** the legendary sanctuary of Apollo. Its **Terrace of the Lions,** a remarkable group of nine Naxian marble sculptures from the 7th century BC, is a must-see. Worth noting, too, are some of the houses of the Roman period, with their fine floor mosaics. The best of these mosaics are in **the Archaeological Museum.** *Tel. 0289/22–259. Admission to archaeological site (including museum entrance): 1,200 dr. Open Tues.–Sun. 8:30–3.*

Rhodes The large island of **Rhodes,** 170 kilometers (105 miles) southeast of Mykonos, is 11.2 kilometers (7 miles) off the coast of Turkey. The northern end of the island is one of Greece's major vacation centers, and the town of Rhodes is full of the trappings of tourism, mainly evident in the pubs and bars that cater to the large Western European market. The island as a whole is not particularly beautiful—most of the pine and cedar woods that covered its hilly center were destroyed by fire in 1987 and 1988—but it has fine beaches and an excellent climate. The town of Rhodes has an attractive harbor with fortifications; the gigantic bronze statue of the Colossus of Rhodes is said to have straddled the entrance, though archaeologists now dispute this. The old walled city, near the harbor, was built by crusaders—the Knights of St. John—who ruled the island from 1309 until they were defeated by the Turks in 1522. Within its fine medieval walls, on the Street of the Knights, stands the **Knights' Hospital,** now the Archaeological Museum, housing two famous statues of Aphrodite. *Tel. 0241/27–657. Admission: 800 dr. Open Tues.–Fri. 8:30–3 (8:30–7 in winter), weekends and holidays 8:30–3.*

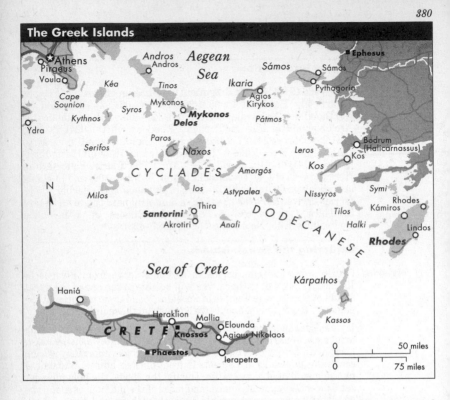

The Greek Islands

Aegean Sea

Athens, Piraeus, Voula, Cape Sounion, Kéa, Syros, Kythnos, Ydra, Serifos, Milos

Andros, Andros, Tinos, Mykonos, **Mykonos**, **Delos**, Paros, **Naxos**, Ikaria, Agios Kirykos, Pátmos, Leros, Amorgós, Ios, Astypalea, Thira, **Santorini**, Akrotiri, Anafi

Sámos, Sámos, Pythagorio, **Ephesus**

Bodrum (Halicarnassus), Kos, Kos, Nissyros, Symi, Tilos, Rhodes, Kámiros, Halki, Lindos, **Rhodes**

C Y C L A D E S

N

D O D E C A N E S E

Sea of Crete

Haniá, Heraklion, Mallia, Elounda, **Knossos**, Agios Nikolaos, **Phaestos**, Ierapetra

C R E T E

Kárpathos

Kassos

0 ——— 50 miles
0 ——— 75 miles

Another museum that merits a visit is the restored and moated medieval **Palace of the Grand Master.** Destroyed in 1856 by a gunpowder explosion, the palace was renovated by the Italians as a summer retreat for Mussolini. Note its splendid Hellenistic and Roman floor mosaics. *Tel. 0241/23–359. Admission: 1,200 dr. Open Tues.– Fri. 8:30–3 (8:30–7 in winter), weekends and holidays 8:30–3.*

About 60 kilometers (37 miles) by bus down the east coast is the enchanting village of **Lindos.** Walk up the steep hill to the ruins of the ancient **acropolis,** slowly being renovated. The sight of its beautiful colonnade with the sea far below is unforgettable. *Tel. 0244/31–258. Admission: 1,200 dr. Open Tues.–Sun. 8:30–3.*

Crete **Crete,** situated in the south Aegean and Greece's largest island, was the center of Europe's earliest civilization, the Minoan, which flourished from about 2000 BC to 1200 BC. It was struck a mortal blow by a devastating volcanic eruption on the neighboring island of Santorini (Thera) in about 1450 BC.

The most important Minoan remains are to be seen in the **Archaeological Museum** in Heraklion, Crete's largest city. The museum houses many Minoan treasures, including some highly sophisticated frescoes and elegant ceramics depicting Minoan life. *Plateia Eleftherias, tel. 081/226–092. Admission: 1,500 dr. Open Mon. 12–3, Tues.–Fri. 8–7 (8–5 in summer), weekends and holidays 8:30–3.*

Not far from Heraklion is the partly reconstructed **Palace of Knossos,** which will also give you a feeling for the Minoan world. Note the simple throne room, which contains the oldest throne in Europe, and the bathrooms with their efficient plumbing. The palace was the setting for the legend of the Minotaur, a monstrous offspring of Queen Pasiphae and a bull confined to the Labyrinth under the palace. *Tel. 081/231–940. Admission: 1,500 dr. Open Tues.–Sun. 8:30–3.*

In addition to archaeological treasures, Crete can boast beautiful mountain scenery and a large number of beach resorts along the north coast. One is **Mallia,** which contains the remains of another Minoan palace and has good sandy beaches. Two other beach resorts, **Ayios Nikolaos** and the nearby **Elounda,** are east of Iraklio. The south coast offers good, quieter beaches for those who want to get away from it all.

Santorini The best way to approach **Santorini** is to sail into its harbor, once the vast crater of its volcano, and dock beneath its black and red cliffs. In some parts, the cliffs rise nearly 310 meters (1,000 feet) above the sea. The play of light across them can produce strange color effects. The white houses and churches of the main town, **Thira,** cling to the rim in dazzling white contrast to the somber cliffs.

Most passenger ferries now use the new port, Athinios, where visitors are met by buses, taxis, and a gaggle of small-hotel owners hawking rooms. The bus ride into Thira takes about a half hour, and from there you can make connections to other towns on the island. Despite being packed with visitors in the summer, the tiny town is charming and has spectacular views. There's also **Oia,** the village at the northern tip where every tourist goes at least once to watch the sunset.

The island's volcano erupted during the 15th century BC, destroying its Minoan civilization. At **Akrotiri,** on the south end of Santorini, the remains of a Minoan city buried by lava are being excavated. The site, believed by some to be part of the legendary Atlantis, is open to the public. *Tel. 0286/81–366. Admission: 1,200 dr. Open Tues.–Fri. 8:30–3.*

At **Ancient Thira,** a clifftop on the east coast of the island, a well-preserved ancient town includes a theater and agora, houses, fortifications, and tombs. *No phone. Admission free. Open Tues.–Sun. 8:30–3.*

Dining and Lodging

For details and price-category definitions, *see* Dining *and* Lodging *in* Staying in Greece, *above.*

Crete **Kyriakos.** A popular taverna, with pink tablecloths and green
Dining chairs, Kyriakos offers a wide range of salads, fish dishes, and such Cretan specialties as snail stew with *pligouri* (cracked wheat), artichokes baked with tomatoes and fresh broad beans, and *tiropitakia,* pies with honey and the creamy, mild Cretan cheese *mizithra. Leoforos Dimokratias 53, tel. 081/224–649. AE, DC, MC, V. Closed Wed. and June 15–July 15. $$*
Minos Taverna. This is one of the many outdoor restaurants near the Venetian fountain. Good choices include lamb in yogurt, stifado, fresh seafood, stuffed squash blossoms (in season), and homemade *rizogalo* (rice pudding made from sheep's milk). Service is prompt and attentive. *Daedelou 10, tel. 081/244–827 or 081/246–466. AE, MC, V. Closed 2 months in winter, usually Nov.–Jan. $$*
★ **Vassilis.** Watch the boats bobbing along the jetty at this Cretan classic, which is crammed with memorabilia. Regional dishes include *koukouvayia* (a local roll soaked in wine, tomato, olive oil, and herbs) and lamb fricassee stewed with lettuce. The owners also make their own wine. *Nearchou 10, old harbor, Rethimno, tel. 0831/ 22–967 and 0831/52–135. AE, DC, MC, V. $$*

Lodging **Atrion.** This family-run hotel frequented by Dutch and Scandinavian tourists is in a quiet residential street close to the Historical Museum, a five-minute walk from the waterfront. Rooms are large, with balconies and TVs. Buffet breakfast is included. *Chronaki 9, Heraklion, 71202, tel. 081/242–830, fax 081/223–292. 61 rooms with* bath, 4 suites. Facilities: restaurant, bar, air-conditioning. AE, DC, MC, V. $$

Casa Delfino. In the heart of Hania's old town, this small, tranquil hotel was once part of a Venetian Renaissance palace. Rooms decorated in cool pastel colors with modern furniture surround a courtyard paved in pebble mosaic. The roof garden has a view over the harbor. *Theofanous 9, Palio Limani, Hania, 73131, tel. 0821/93–098 or 0821/87–400, fax 0821/96–500. 12 rooms with bath. Facilities: kitchenettes, air-conditioning. DC, MC, V. $$*

★ **Mediterranean.** This is another comfortable hotel in the center of Heraklion and 4.8 kilometers (3 miles) from the beach. There's a roof garden, and Continental breakfast is included in the price. *Smyrnis 1, 71201, tel. 081/289–331, fax 081/289–335. 55 rooms with bath. Facilities: restaurant, partially air-conditioned. AE, DC, MC, V. $$*

Rea. This comfortable hotel in Agios Nicolaos also offers outdoor dining and a roof garden with a view across the Mirabello Gulf. Buffet breakfast is included. *Marathonas and Milatou 10, 72100, tel. 0841/28–321, fax 0841/28–324. 110 rooms with bath. Facilities: restaurant with garden, bar. AE, DC, MC, V. $$*

Mykonos
Dining

Nikos. Sooner or later, everyone winds up eating here, and the owners always squeeze in one more table. Despite its small kitchen, the taverna produces consistently good food, with daily specials, including fresh fish. For those on a budget, the magirefta—moussaka, pastitsio, *briam* (like ratatouille)—are the best bet. *Harbor, tel. 0289/24–320. Closed Nov.–Feb. AE, V. $$*

Pilafas. This friendly taverna just behind the waterfront (follow the signs) is patronized by locals for its good grilled dishes, salads, and reasonably priced seafood. *Tel. 0289/24–120. No reservations. No credit cards. No lunch. $–$$*

Lodging
★

Kamari. This family-run hotel looks like new and is 4 kilometers (2½ miles) from Mykonos town, between two beaches, each a five-minute walk away. Recently the hotel added 11 more upscale rooms, with TVs, refrigerators, and air-conditioning. Buffet breakfast is included. *Platy Gialos, 84600, tel. 0289/23–424, 0289/23–982, or 0289/25–054; fax 0289/24–414. 55 rooms with bath. Facilities: bar, breakfast room, game room, airport shuttle. AE, DC, MC, V. $$*

Kouneni Hotel. The Kouneni is a comfortable family-run hotel in the town center, and it's quieter than most. It is set in a cool green garden, a rarity on Mykonos and the ideal place to linger over the Continental breakfast included in the price. Rooms are fairly large and the lounge is cozy. *Tria Pigadia, across from the public school, 84600, tel. 0289/22–301, fax 0289/26–559. 20 rooms with bath. Facilities: bar. No credit cards. $$*

Rhodes
Dining

Dinoris. Set in a great hall built in 1530 as a stable for the Knights of St. John, this establishment has long specialized in fish. For mezedes, try the variety platter, which includes *psarokeftedakia* (fish balls made from a secret recipe), as well as mussels, shrimp and lobster. Other dishes include the grilled prawns and sea urchin salad. *Platia Mouseou 14A, Rhodes Old Town, tel. 0241/25–824 or 0241/35–530. Garden reservations required. Summer weekend reservations advised. AE, MC, V. $$*

★ **Palia Istoria.** Ensconced in an old house with high ceilings, beautiful floors, and genteel murals, this mezedopolion is a visual treat. Begin your meal with a feta saganaki, very lightly fried with the potent red pepper *bukova*. Seafood starters are also excellent; try the scallops with mushrooms and artichokes baked in béchamel or the plump mussels served with piquant peppers. Entrées include tender pork in garlic and wine sauce and shrimp ouzo with orange juice. *Mitropoleos 108 and Dendrinou, Ammos Marasia area south of Old Town (about 850 dr. by taxi), tel. 0241/32–421. Reservations advised. MC, V. No lunch. $$*

Kavo d'Oro. This simple taverna is one of the few places in the Old

Town where you can get a solid, inexpensive meal. The fare includes roast chicken, roast lamb, and grilled meat. Especially good are the *papoutsakia*, eggplant "shoes" stuffed with mincemeat. The owner has a second taverna by the same name at Orfeous 40–42. *Parodos Sokratous 41 (the street behind Sokratous), Rhodes Old Town, tel. 0241/36–182. No credit cards. Closed Nov.–Mar. $*

Taverna Kostas. Though slightly more expensive than Kavo d'Oro, this is a good alternative in an area with overpriced food. *Dolmadakia* (stuffed grape leaves) have a tart egg-lemon sauce, the fried squid is plentiful, and the chicken souvlakia arrives tender and perfectly grilled. Other dishes include pork chops, swordfish, and a mixed seafood plate big enough for two. *Pythagora 62, Rhodes Old Town, tel. 0241/26–217. No credit cards. Closed Nov.–Mar. $*

Lodging **St. Nikolis Hotel.** Owned and run by an enterprising young couple, the St. Nikolis is within the Old Town but away from the most crowded tourist area. The rooms are small, outfitted with dark, rusticated furniture, and look out toward the spacious courtyard or the old city wall. A roof terrace lets you breakfast with a view over the entire town. The owner also has eight efficiency apartments, four with air-conditioning. Buffet breakfast is included. *Ippodamou 61, Rhodes Old Town, 85100, tel. 0241/34–561, 0241/36–238, or 0241/34–747, fax 0241/32–034. 10 rooms with bath, 8 apartments. Facilities: bar, breakfast room. AE, DC, MC, V. $$*

Hermes. Rooms at this family-run hotel close to the port were redone in 1994. Though the five in the back are quieter, all have double-glazed windows to cut down on noise. Ask for one with a view across the bay to the Turkish coast. *Plastira 7, 85100, tel. 0241/27–677, 0241/26–022, or 0241/23–723. 30 rooms with bath. Facilities: bar, breakfast room, air-conditioning. V. $*

Spartalis Hotel. Many rooms in this simple but lively hotel near the city's port have balconies overlooking the bay. Note that rooms on the street are noisy. *Plastira 2, 85100, tel. 0241/24–371/2, fax 0241/20–406. 79 rooms with bath. Facilities: bar, breakfast room. AE, DC, MC, V. $*

Pension Sofia. The Old Town is full of rooms to rent, but those at Sofia's, run by the same people that own Kavo d'Oro, are bright, pleasant, and framed by trailing jasmine; each has a small bath. *Aristofanous 27, Rhodes Old Town, 85100, tel. 0241/36–181. 10 rooms with bath. No credit cards. Closed Dec.–Mar. ¢*

Santorini **Camille Stefani.** This is one of the island's best restaurants, where
Dining you can enjoy seafood, Greek and Continental cuisine, and the local wines. A taste of the mellow Santorini Lava red wine, a product of the volcanic ash, is a must! *Main St., Thira, tel. 0286/22–265. Reservations advised. AE, MC, V. Closed Nov.–Mar. $$*

★ **Nikolas.** You can't go wrong at this simple taverna, one of the few places open in town during the winter. The menu, which changes daily, offers a limited but delicious choice of classic Greek dishes, such as beef stifado with pearl onions, stuffed cabbage rolls, and mountain greens. *Erithrou Stavrou, Thira, no phone. No credit cards. ¢–$*

Lodging **Matina.** Close to the beach at Kamari, this pleasant family-run hotel is set among vineyards. The rooms are priced at the low end of this category; about half have air-conditioning. *Kamari, 84700, tel. 0286/31–491 or 0286/32–275, fax 0286/31–860. 27 rooms with bath. Facilities: bar. AE, DC, MC, V. Closed mid-Nov.–mid-Mar. $$*

Panorama Hotel. Recently renovated, this family-run hotel in the center of Thira, the island's main town, has a fine view across the bay to the dormant volcano. *Thira, 84700, tel. 0286/22–479 or 0286/22–481, fax 0286/33–179. 24 rooms with bath. Facilities: restaurant, bar. AE, DC, MC, V. Closed Nov.–Mar. $$*

12 Holland

The innate common sense of the Dutch people assures that, no matter how sophisticated their cities seem to be at first glance, you always will find a choice of practically outfitted, quality hotels and restaurants at affordable prices, often in the same neighborhood as pricey, five-star establishments. This is, after all, a land of traders that has a long tradition of welcoming both lowly sailors and ship's captains.

Following World War II, tourist posters of Holland featured windmills, tulips, canals, and girls wearing lacy caps and clogs. These picturesque images are still to be found, certainly, but there is far more to this tiny country than these clichés portray. Remember, too, that this is the land of such creative geniuses as the painters Rembrandt, Hals, and Vermeer and the philosophers Descartes, Erasmus, and Spinoza.

The Netherlands (the country's proper name, though Holland remains in popular use) is one of Europe's smallest countries. It is also one of the world's most densely populated nations, with a population of around 15 million occupying a land area that is less than half the size of Maine—41,526 square kilometers (15,972 square miles), almost half of which has been reclaimed by the industrious Dutch from the North Sea. The nation's history has been dominated by continual resistance to two forces of invasion: the sea and successive foreign armies. Over the centuries, the Romans, Franks, Burgundians, Austrians, Spanish, English, French, and Germans have all tried to win and hold the Netherlands, but none has succeeded for long. These endless struggles against nature and enemies have molded the Dutch into a determined and independent nation, yet a remarkably tolerant one that is often at the forefront of many liberal social reforms and attitudes. Religious and political freedom are an essential part of Dutch life.

Amsterdam's medieval Nieuwe Kerk, both a church and a cultural center, embodies the Dutch spirit of practicality and social responsibility. It is also a sign of Amsterdam's cultural prominence. The city

Holland

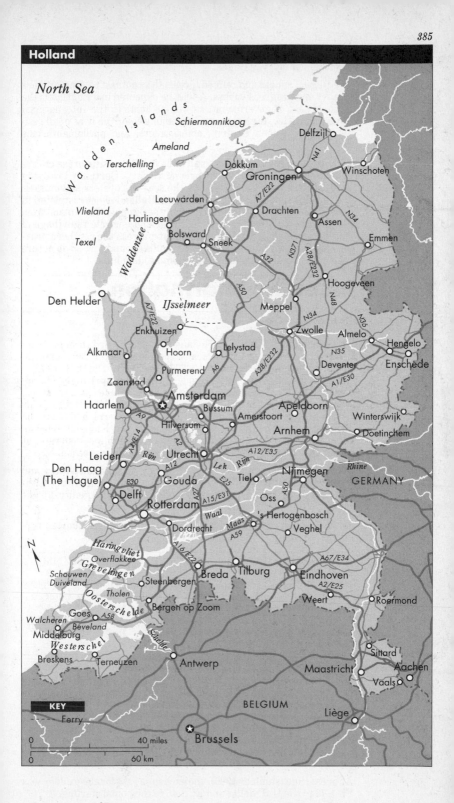

North Sea

Wadden Islands

Schiermonnikoog

Ameland

Terschelling

Vlieland

Texel

Waddenzee

Den Helder

Dokkum

Groningen

Delfzijl

Winschoten

Leeuwarden

Drachten

Assen

N34

Emmen

A7/E22

Harlingen

Bolsward

Sneek

A32

N371

N37

A28/E232

Hoogeveen

N48

N34

Meppel

A50

Zwolle

Almelo

N35

Hengelo

Enkhuizen

IJsselmeer

A7/E22

Alkmaar

Hoorn

Lelystad

A28/E232

Deventer

N35

Enschede

A1/E30

Purmerend

A6

Zaanstad

Haarlem

Amsterdam

Bussum

Amersfoort

Apeldoorn

Winterswijk

Doetinchem

Hilversum

A9

A2

A4/E19

Leiden

Rijn

Utrecht

A12/E35

Arnhem

Den Haag
(The Hague)

E30

A12

Lek

Rijn

Nijmegen

Rhine

GERMANY

Gouda

Tiel

A27

E25

Delft

Rotterdam

A15/E31

Oss

A50

's Hertogenbosch

Veghel

Waal

Dordrecht

Maas

A59

A16/E19

A16/E20

Haringvliet

Overflakkee

Grevelingen

Breda

Tilburg

Eindhoven

A67/E34

Schouwen/
Duiveland

Oosterschelde

Tholen

Steenbergen

Bergen op Zoom

Weert

A2/E25

Roermond

Walcheren

Goes

A58

Beveland

Middelburg

Westerschel

Schelde

Sittard

Breskens

Terneuzen

Antwerp

Maastricht

Aachen

Vaals

BELGIUM

Liège

KEY

Ferry

Brussels

0   40 miles
0   60 km

is now as famous for its jazz, modern art, and ballet as it is for its Rembrandts and van Goghs.

The Hague, sedate and refined, presents a contrast to Amsterdam's vitality and progressiveness. As can be expected in a city that is the national seat of government, as well as home to the International Court of Justice, diplomacy and ceremony color the lives of all residents, from Queen Beatrix, ambassadors, and parliamentarians downward.

Although the country is too small to have vast natural areas or dramatic landscapes, it offers surprising variety. Certainly low-lying Zeeland lives with the sea and on the sea—its oysters and mussels are world famous. And versatile North Holland is not restricted to sand dunes, bulb fields, and melancholy seascapes. (Just inland from Bergen-aan-Zee, deep woods and moorland encircle the village of Bergen, once an artists' enclave.) In and across the southern provinces of Holland, bulb fields and windmills abound, but so do nature reserves, inland lakes, lush valleys, and rolling hills.

Essential Information

Before You Go

When to Go The prime tourist season in Holland runs from April through October and peaks during school vacation periods (Easter, July, and August), when hotels may impose a 20% surcharge. Dutch bulb fields bloom from early April to the end of May—not surprisingly, the hotels tend to fill up then, too. June is the ideal time to catch the warm weather and miss the crowds, but every region of the Netherlands has its season. Delft is luminous after a winter storm, and fall in the Utrecht countryside can be as dramatic as in New England. Bargain rates are most likely to be found in winter, though weekend rates at business-oriented hotels are often a good deal in any season.

Climate Summers are generally warm, but beware of sudden showers and blustery coastal winds. Winters are chilly and wet, but are not without clear days. After a cloudburst, notice the watery quality of light that inspired Vermeer and other great Dutch painters.

The following are the average daily maximum and minimum temperatures for Amsterdam.

Jan.	40F	4C	**May**	61F	16C	**Sept.**	65F	18C
	34	1		50	10		56	13
Feb.	41F	5C	**June**	65F	18C	**Oct.**	56F	13C
	34	1		56	13		49	9
Mar.	47F	8C	**July**	70F	21C	**Nov.**	47F	8C
	38	3		59	15		41	5
Apr.	52F	11C	**Aug.**	68F	20C	**Dec.**	41F	5C
	43	6		59	15		36	2

Currency The unit of currency in Holland is the *guilder*, written as NLG (for Netherlands guilder), Fl., or simply F. (from the centuries-old term for the coinage, *florin*). Each guilder is divided into 100 cents. Bills are in denominations of 1,000, 250, 100, 50, 25, and 10 guilders. Denominations over 100 guilders are rarely seen, and many shops refuse to change them. Coins are 5, 2.5, and 1 guilder and 25, 10, and 5 cents. Be careful not to confuse the 2.5- and 1-guilder coins and the 5-guilder and 5-cent coins. Bills have a code of raised dots that can be identified by touch; this is for people who are blind.

At press time (summer 1995), the exchange rate for the guilder was Fl. 1.73 to the U.S. dollar and Fl. 2.46 to the pound sterling.

What It Will Cost Holland is a prosperous country with a high standard of living, so overall costs are similar to those in other northern European countries. Prices for hotels and other services in major cities are 10%–20% above those in rural areas. Amsterdam and The Hague are the most expensive. Hotel and restaurant service charges and the 6% value-added tax (VAT) are usually included in the prices quoted.

The cost of eating varies widely in Holland, from a snack in a bar or a modest restaurant offering a *dagschotel* (day special), or "tourist menu," at around Fl. 25 to the considerable expense of gourmet cuisine. A traditional Dutch breakfast is usually included in the overnight hotel price.

One cost advantage Holland has over other European countries is that because it is so small, traveling around is inexpensive—especially if you use the many price-saving transportation deals available.

Sample Prices Half-bottle of wine, Fl. 25; glass of beer, Fl. 3.50; cup of coffee, Fl. 2.75; ham and cheese sandwich, Fl. 5; 1-mile taxi ride, Fl. 10.

Museums The **Museumkaart,** which can be purchased from some museums and the local tourist office, provides a year's free or reduced admission to about 350 museums. It costs Fl. 45 for adults, Fl. 32.50 for senior citizens, Fl. 15 for persons 18 and under. A photo and passport are required for purchase. If your time is limited, you might want to check the list; not all museums participate.

Customs on Arrival For travelers arriving from a country that is not a member of the European Union (EU) or those coming from an EU country who have bought goods in a duty-free shop, the allowances are (1) 200 cigarettes or 50 cigars or 100 cigarillos or 250 grams of tobacco, (2) 1 liter of alcohol more than 22% by volume or 2 liters of liqueur wine or 2 liters of sparkling wine, (3) 50 grams of perfume or 25 centiliters of toilet water, and (4) other goods to the value of Fl. 380.

Since January 1, 1993, allowances for travelers within the EU member states have been effectively removed, provided that goods have been bought duty-paid (i.e., not in a duty-free shop) and are for personal use.

All personal items are considered duty-free, provided you take them with you when you leave Holland. Tobacco and alcohol allowances are for those 17 and older. There are no restrictions on the import and export of Dutch currency.

Language Dutch is a difficult language for foreigners, but luckily the Dutch are fine linguists, so almost everyone speaks at least some English, especially in larger cities and tourist centers.

Getting Around

By Train Fast, frequent, and comfortable trains operate throughout the country. All trains have first- and second-class cars, and many intercity trains have buffet or dining-car services. Intercity trains run every 30 minutes and regular trains run to the smaller towns at least once an hour. Sometimes one train contains two separate sections that divide during the trip, so be sure you are in the correct section for your destination.

Fares To get the best value out of rail travel, it is advisable to purchase one of the three available rail passes before you leave. The **Benelux Tourrail** gives you unlimited travel throughout Belgium, Holland, and Luxembourg on any five days within one month ($230 first class, $153 second class). A **Holland Rail Pass** (known in Holland as a EuroDomino Holland) ticket allows unlimited travel throughout Holland for 3, 5, or 10 days within any 30-day period (first class: 3-day, $84, 5-day $135, 10-day $250; second class: 3-day $64, 5-day

$100, 10-day $178). A **Rail Rover** entitles you to unlimited travel within Holland for seven consecutive days (first class $144, second class $96). A **Transport Link** ticket, which offers free travel on buses and trams as well, may be bought in conjunction with the Holland Rail Pass and the Rail Rover (with Holland Rail Pass: 3-day $12, 5-day $19, 10-day $31; with Rail Rover: $17).

Your rail pass is also valid on **Interliner,** a fast new bus network that operates 16 intercity lines between towns that have no direct rail link. The Netherlands Board of Tourism's (NBT) offices abroad have information on train services, as do overseas offices of Netherlands Railways. Your passport may be needed when you purchase these tickets. The Benelux Tourrail and the Rail Rover must be bought abroad, but the others are available in the Netherlands. **Dagtochtkaartjes** are special combined tickets covering train, boat, and bus trips. Ask about these fares at railway information bureaus or local tourist offices.

By Bus Holland has an excellent bus network between towns that are not connected by rail and also within towns. Bus excursions can be booked on the spot and at local tourist offices. In major cities, the best buy is a **strippenkaart** ticket (Fl. 11), which can be used for all bus, tram, and metro services. Each card has 15 strips, which are canceled by the driver as you enter the bus or by the stamping machine at each door of the tram. More than one person can travel on a strippenkaart—it just gets used up more quickly. A strippenkaart with 45 strips is available for Fl. 32.25. You can buy it at train stations, post offices, many newsagents, and some tourist offices or in Amsterdam at the GVB (national bus system) ticket office in the plaza in front of the central railway station. A one-day **dagkaart,** a travel-anywhere ticket, covers all urban bus/streetcar routes and costs Fl. 12 for one day, Fl. 16 for two days and Fl. 19.75 for three days.

By Bicycle Holland is a "cyclist-friendly" country with specially designated cycle paths, signs, and picnic areas. Bikes can usually be rented at train stations in most cities and towns, and Dutch trains are "cycle-friendly," too, with extra spacious entryways designed to accommodate bicycles (as well as wheelchairs). You will need an extra ticket for the bike, however. There are some restrictions on carrying bicycles on trains, so it is worthwhile to check first. The flat rate single fare to anywhere in the country is Fl. 10, but this can rise to Fl. 25 depending on the day of the week, the season, and what sort of ticket you hold. (Transporting a bike on Mondays and Fridays in July and August is the most expensive.) Rental costs for bicycles are around Fl. 10 per day or from Fl. 40 per week, plus a deposit of Fl. 50–Fl. 200. Many larger railway stations hire bicycles to holders of valid train tickets at Fl. 6 per day and Fl. 24 per week. Advice on rentals and routes is available from offices of the Netherlands Board of Tourism in North America or in Holland or from local tourist offices; cycling packages can be booked at the larger offices.

Staying in Holland

Telephones
Local Calls The telephone system in Holland is excellent and reliable. All towns and cities have area codes that are to be used only when you are calling from outside the area. Pay phones take 25¢, and Fl. 1 coins, though newer ones also accept other denominations. Increasingly, public phone booths are being converted to a phonecard system. Phone cards may be purchased from post offices, railway stations, and some newsagents for Fl. 5, Fl. 10, or Fl. 25. Lines at coin-operated boxes tend to be longer, so a phone card is worth the investment, especially if you intend to make international calls. For an English-speaking operator, dial 06–0410.

International Calls Direct-dial international calls can be made from any phone booth. Lower rates are charged from 7 PM to 10 AM weekdays and from 7 PM

Friday to 10 AM Monday. The average cost per minute to the United States is Fl. 1.70 (Fl. 1.50 nights and weekends). To reach an **AT&T** long-distance operator, dial 06/022–9111; for **MCI**, dial 06/022–9122; for **Sprint**, dial 000–999.

Country Code The country code for Holland is 31.

Mail The Dutch post office is as efficient as the telephone network. Air-
Postal Rates mail letters to the United States cost Fl. 1.60 for the first 20 grams; postcards cost Fl. 1; aerograms cost Fl. 1.30. Airmail letters to the United Kingdom cost Fl. 1 for the first 20 grams; postcards cost 80¢; aerograms cost Fl. 1.30.

Receiving Mail If you're uncertain where you'll be staying, have mail sent to Poste Restante, GPO, in major cities along your route, or to American Express offices, where a small charge will be made to non–American Express customers.

Shopping Purchases of goods in a single store in a single day amounting to Fl.
VAT Refunds 300 or more qualify for a value-added tax (VAT) refund of 17.5%, which can be claimed at the airport or main border crossing when you leave Holland or by mail. Ask the salesperson for a VAT refund form when you buy anything that may qualify.

Bargaining The prices in most shops are fixed, but you can try to bargain for items in any of the open-air markets.

Opening and **Banks.** Banks are open weekdays from 9 to 4. You can also change
Closing Times money at GWK border exchange offices at major railway stations and at the Schiphol Airport, which are open Monday–Saturday 8–8 and Sunday 10–4. GWK offices in major cities or at border checkpoints are open 24 hours. Many tourist offices exchange funds, too.

Museums. Most major museums now close on Monday, but not all, so check with local tourist offices. In rural areas, some museums close or operate shorter hours during winter. Usual hours are 10–5.

Shops. In general, shops are open weekdays from 8:30 or 9 to 5:30 or 6, but outside the cities, some close for lunch. Department stores and most shops, especially in shopping plazas (in The Hague and Amsterdam), do not open until 1 PM on Monday, and a few close one afternoon a week on whichever day they choose. Late-night shopping usually can be done until 9 PM on Thursday or Friday.

National In 1996: January 1; April 5–8 (Easter); April 30 (Queen's Day; shops
Holidays are open unless it falls on Sunday); May 5 (Liberation); May 16 (Ascension); May 26–27 (Pentecost); December 25–26. Changing holidays in 1997: March 28–31 (Easter); May 8: Ascension; May 18–19 (Pentecost).

Dining Of the many earthly pleasures the Dutch indulge, eating probably heads the list. There is a wide variety of cuisines from traditional Dutch to Indonesian—the influence of the former Dutch colony.

Breakfast tends to be hearty and substantial—traditionally including several varieties of bread, butter, jam, ham, cheese, boiled eggs, juice, and steaming coffee or tea. Dutch specialties for later meals include *erwtensoep*, a rich, thick pea soup with pieces of tangy sausage or pigs' knuckles, and *hutspot*, a meat, carrot, and potato stew; both are usually served only during winter. *Haring* (herring) is particularly popular, especially the "new herring" caught between May and September and served in brine, garnished with onions. If Dutch food begins to pall, try an Indonesian restaurant, where the chief dish is rijsttafel, a meal made up of 20 or more small dishes, many of which are hot and spicy.

The indigenous Dutch liquor is potent and warming *jenever* (gin), both "old" and "new." Dutch liqueurs and beers are also popular.

Mealtimes The Dutch tend to eat dinner around 6 or 7 PM, especially in the country and smaller cities, so many restaurants close at about 10 PM and accept final orders at 9. In larger cities dining hours vary, and some restaurants stay open until midnight.

What to Wear The Dutch are tolerant, and casual outfits are acceptable in most eateries except the very expensive.

Ratings Prices are per person, including three courses (appetizer, main course, and dessert), service, and sales tax but not drinks. For budget travelers, many restaurants offer a tourist menu at an officially controlled price, currently Fl. 25. Best bets are indicated by a star ★.

Category	Amsterdam	Other Areas
$$	Fl. 40–Fl. 70	Fl. 35–Fl. 55
$	Fl. 25–Fl. 40	Fl. 25–Fl. 35
¢	under Fl. 25	under Fl. 25

Lodging Holland offers a wide range of accommodations encompassing, at the less-expensive end of the spectrum, traditional, small-town hotels and family-run guest houses. For young or adventurous travelers, the provinces abound with modest hostels, camping grounds, and rural bungalows. Travelers with modest budgets may prefer to stay in friendly bed-and-breakfast establishments; these are in short supply and should be booked well in advance (if possible) or at local tourist offices.

Hotels Dutch hotels are generally clean, if not spotless, no matter how modest their facilities, and service is normally courteous and efficient. There are many moderate and inexpensive hotels, most of which are relatively small. In the provinces the range of accommodations is more limited, but there are pleasant, inexpensive, family-run hotels that are usually centrally located and offer a friendly atmosphere. Some have good—if modest—dining facilities. English is spoken or understood almost everywhere. Hotels usually quote room prices for double occupancy, and rates often include breakfast, service charges, and VAT.

To book hotels in advance, you can use the free **National Reservation Center** (Box 404, 2260 AK Leidschendam, tel. 070/3202500, fax 070/3202611). Alternatively, for a small fee, tourist offices can usually make reservations at short notice; bookings must be made in person, however.

Ratings Prices are for two people sharing a double room. Best bets are indicated by a star ★.

Category	Amsterdam	Other Areas
$$	Fl. 200–Fl. 300	Fl. 150–Fl. 200
$	Fl. 150–Fl. 200	Fl. 100–Fl. 150
¢	under Fl. 150	under Fl. 100

Tipping Hotels and restaurants almost always include 10%–15% service and VAT in their charges. Give a doorman Fl. 3 for calling a cab. Hat-check attendants expect at least 25¢, and washroom attendants get 50¢. Taxis in almost every town have a tip included in the meter charge, but you are expected to make up the fare to the nearest guilder nevertheless.

Amsterdam

Arriving and Departing

By Plane Most international flights arrive at Amsterdam's Schiphol Airport, one of Europe's finest. Immigration and customs formalities on arrival are relaxed, with no forms to be completed.

Between the The best transportation between the airport and the city center is
Airport and the direct rail link to the central station, where you can get a tram to
Downtown your hotel. The train runs every 10 to 15 minutes throughout the day and takes about half an hour. Second-class fare is Fl. 5.75.

By Train The city has excellent rail connections with the rest of Europe. Fast services link it to Paris, Brussels, Luxembourg, and Cologne. **Centraal Station** is conveniently located in the center of town.

Getting Around

By Bus, A zonal fare system is used. Tickets (starting at Fl. 3) are bought
Tram, from automatic dispensers on the metro or from the drivers on trams
and Metro and buses, or buy a money-saving **strippenkaart** (*see* Getting Around, By Bus, *in* Essential Information, *above*). Even simpler is the one-day **dagkaart**, which covers all city routes for Fl. 12. These discount tickets can be obtained from the main GVB ticket office in front of Centraal Station, along with route maps of the public transportation system. Water buses in the city center also have day cards. The **Canalbus**, which travels between the central station and the Rijksmuseum, is Fl. 22 for a hop-on, hop-off day card.

By Bicycle Rental bikes are readily available for around Fl. 10 per day with a Fl. 50–Fl. 200 deposit. Bikes are an excellent and inexpensive way to explore the city. Several rental companies are close to the central station, or ask at the tourist offices for details. Keep your bike locked at all times when not in use to ward off thieves, who can steal one in less than 30 seconds. Also check with the rental company about your liability under their insurance terms.

By Boat The **Museum Boat** (Stationsplein 8, tel. 020/6222181) combines a scenic view of the city with seven stops in the neighborhood of 20 museums. All-day tickets cost Fl. 19; a combination ticket (Fl. 35) includes admission to three museums.

On Foot Amsterdam is a small, congested city of narrow streets, which makes it ideal for exploring on foot. The tourist office issues seven excellent guides that detail walking tours around the center. The best are "The Jordaan," a stroll through the lively canalside district, and "Jewish Amsterdam," a walk past the remains of pre–World War II Jewish houses and synagogues.

Important Addresses and Numbers

Tourist There are two locations for the **VVV Amsterdam Tourist Office:** one
Information in front of Centraal Station (Stationsplein 10, in the Old Dutch Coffee House; open daily 9–5) and another at Leidseplein 1 (open fall–spring, daily 9–7; summer, daily 9–9). VVV is the Dutch acronym for tourist information offices; you'll see it on signposts throughout Holland. The general number for telephone inquiries is 06/34034066, but you are charged 75¢ per minute and kept waiting in an electronic line. The VVV reserves accommodations, tours, and entertainment, but reservations must be made in person.

Consulates **U.S.** (Museumplein 19, tel. 020/6645661). **Canadian** (7 Sophialaan, The Hague, tel. 070/3614111). **U.K.** (Koningslaan 44, tel. 020/6764343).

Emergencies The general number for emergencies is 06–11, but note direct numbers. **Police** (tel. 020/6222222); **Ambulance** (tel. 020/5555555); **Doctor Academisch Medisch Centrum** (Meibergdreef 9, tel. 020/5669111). **Central Medical Service** (tel. 06/35032042) will give you names of pharmacists and dentists as well as doctors. **Dentist Practice AOC** (W.G. Plein 167, tel. 020/6161234) is also open on weekends.

Exploring Amsterdam

Amsterdam is a gem of a city for the tourist. Small and densely packed with fine buildings, many dating from the 17th century or earlier, it is easily explored on foot or by bike. The old heart of the city consists of canals, with narrow streets radiating out like the spokes of a wheel. The hub of this wheel and the most convenient point to begin sightseeing is Centraal Station. Across the street, in the same building as the Old Dutch Coffee House, is a VVV tourist information office that offers helpful tourist advice.

Amsterdam's key points of interest can be covered within two or three days, with each walking itinerary taking in one or two of the important museums and galleries. The following exploration of the city center can be broken up into several sessions.

Around the *Numbers in the margin correspond to points of interest on the*
Dam *Amsterdam map.*

1 Start at the **Centraal Station** (Central Station). Designed by P. J.H. Cuijpers and built in 1884–89, it is a good example of Dutch architecture at its most flamboyant. The street directly in front of the station square is Prins Hendrikkade. To the left, a good vantage point
2 for viewing the station, is **St. Nicolaaskerk** (Church of St. Nicholas), consecrated in 1888.

Around the corner from St. Nicolaaskerk, facing the harbor, is the
3 **Schreierstoren** (Weepers' Tower), a lookout tower for women whose men were at sea. The tower was erected in 1480, and a tablet marks the point from which Henrik (aka Henry) Hudson set sail on the *Half Moon* on April 4, 1609, on a voyage that took him to what is now New York and the river that still bears his name. Today the Weepers' Tower is used as a combined reception and exhibition center, which includes a maritime bookshop.

Three blocks to the southwest along the Oudezijds Voorburgwal is
4 the **Museum Amstelkring,** whose facade carries the inscription "Ons Lieve Heer Op Solder" ("Our Dear Lord in the Attic"). In 1578 Amsterdam embraced Protestantism and outlawed the church of Rome. So great was the tolerance of the municipal authorities, however, that secret Catholic chapels were allowed to exist; at one time there were 62 in Amsterdam alone. One such chapel was established in the attics of these three neighboring canalside houses, built around 1661. The lower floors were used as ordinary dwellings, while services were held in the attics regularly until 1888, the year St. Nicolaaskerk was consecrated for Catholic worship. Of interest are the Baroque altar with its revolving tabernacle, the swinging pulpit that can be stowed out of sight, and the upstairs gallery. *Oudezijds Voorburgwal 40, tel. 020/6246604. Admission: Fl. 5. Open Mon.– Sat. 10–5, Sun. 1–5.*

5 Just beyond, you can see the **Oude Kerk,** the city's oldest church. Built during the 14th century but badly damaged by iconoclasts after the Reformation, the church still retains its original bell tower and a few remarkable stained-glass windows. From the tower, there is an engaging view of old Amsterdam stretching from St. Nicolaaskerk to medieval gables. Rembrandt's wife, Saskia, is buried here. *Admission Fl. 5. Open Apr.–Oct., Mon.–Sat. 11–5, Sun. 1:30–5; Nov.–Mar., Fri.–Sun. 1–5.*

This area, bordered by Amsterdam's two oldest canals (Oudezijds Voorburgwal and Oudezijds Achterburgwal), is the heart of the *rosse buurt,* the red-light district. In the windows at canal level, women in sheer lingerie slouch, stare, or do their nails. Although the area can be shocking, with its sex shops and porn shows, it is generally safe; however, midnight walks down dark side streets are not advised. If you do decide to explore the area, take care; purse snatchers and pickpockets are a problem.

⑥ Return to the Damrak and continue to the **Dam,** the broadest square in the old section of the town. It was here that the fishermen used to come to sell their catch. Today it is circled with shops and people and bisected with traffic; it is also a popular center for outdoor performers. At one side of the square you will notice a simple monument to Dutch victims of World War II. Eleven urns contain soil from the 11 provinces of Holland, while a 12th contains soil from the former Dutch East Indies, now Indonesia.

⑦ In a corner of the square is the **Nieuwe Kerk** (New Church). A huge Gothic church, it was gradually expanded until 1540, when it reached its present size. Gutted by fire in 1645, it was reconstructed in an imposing Renaissance style, as interpreted by strict Calvinists. The superb oak pulpit, the 14th-century nave, the stained-glass windows, and the great organ (1645) are all shown to great effect on national holidays, when the church is bedecked with flowers. As befits Holland's national church, the Nieuwe Kerk is the site of all inaugurations (as the Dutch call their coronations), including that of Queen Beatrix in 1980. But in democratic Dutch spirit, the church is also used as a meeting place and is the home of a lively café, temporary exhibitions, and concerts. *Dam, tel. 020/6268168. Admission free, except for special exhibitions (Fl. 12.50). Open daily 11–5; exhibitions daily 10–6.*

⑧ Dominating Dam Square is the **Het Koninklijk Paleis te Amsterdam** (Royal Palace), or **Dam Palace,** a vast, well-proportioned structure on Dam Square that was completed in 1655. It is built on 13,659 pilings sunk into the marshy soil. The great pedimental sculptures are an allegorical representation of Amsterdam surrounded by Neptune and mythological sea creatures. *Dam, tel. 020/6248698. Admission: Fl. 5. Open Tues., Wed., Thurs. 1–4. Daily noon–4 during Easter, summer, and fall holidays. Sometimes closed for state events.*

⑨ From behind the palace, Raadhuisstraat leads west across three canals to the **Westermarkt** and the **Westerkerk** (West Church), built in 1631. The church's 85-meter (275-foot) tower is the highest in the city. It also features an outstanding carillon. Rembrandt and his son Titus are buried in the church. During summer afternoons, you can climb to the top of the tower for a fine view over the city.

⑩ Opposite, at Westermarkt 6, is the house where Descartes, the great 17th-century French philosopher ("Cogito, ergo sum"—"I think, therefore I am"), lived in 1634. Another famous house lies farther down Prinsengracht. This is the **Anne Frank Huis** (Anne Frank House), immortalized by the poignant diary kept by the young Jewish girl from 1942 to 1944, when she and her family hid here from the German occupying forces. A small exhibition on the Holocaust is on display in the house. *Prinsengracht 263, tel. 020/5567100. Admission: Fl. 8. Open June–Aug., Mon.–Sat. 9–7, Sun. 10–7; Sept.–May, Mon.–Sat. 9–5, Sun. 10–5.*

⑪ Continuing across the Prinsengracht, you'll reach the **Noorderkerk,** built in 1623. In the square in front of the church, the Noorderplein, a bird market, is held every Saturday.

South of the Dam Turn down Kalverstraat, a shopping street leading from the Royal Palace. You will notice a striking Renaissance gate (1581) that

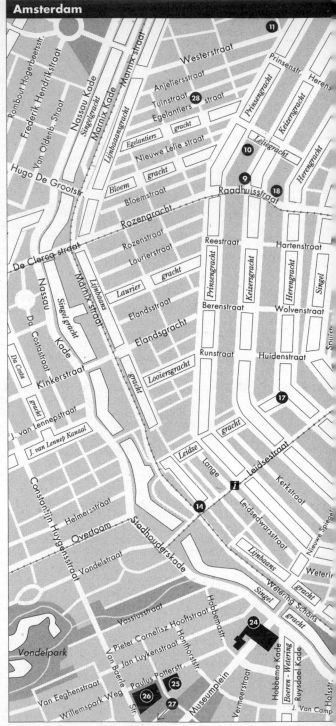

Amsterdam

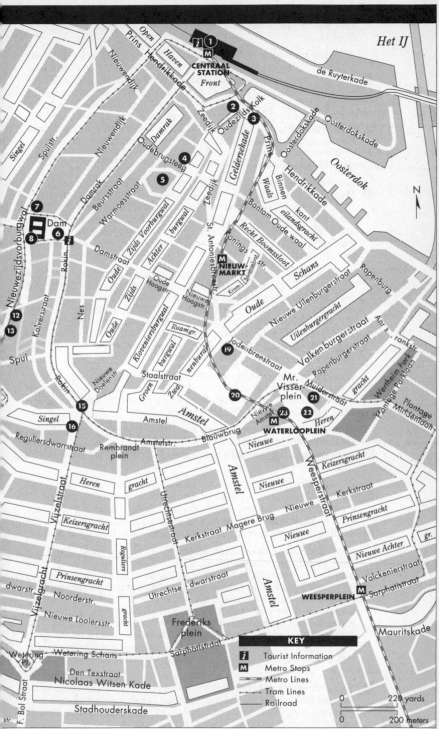

Het IJ

de Ruyterkade

CENTRAAL STATION Front

Open Haven Front

Prins Hendrikkade

Nieuwendijk

Oosterdokskade

Oosterdokskade

Oosterdok

N

Oudezijds Kolk

Zeedijk

Geldersekade

Prins Hendrikkade

Binnen Kant

Waals eilandsgracht

Bantam Oude waal

Recht Boomssloot

Konings str.

Schans

Rapenburg

Singel

Spuistr.

Damrak

Beursstraat

Warmoesstraat

Damrak

Oudebrugsteeg

Zeedijk

St. Antoniesbreestr.

NIEUW MARKT

Krom.

Oude

Nieuwe Uilenburgerstraat

Valkenburgerstraat

Uilenburgergracht

Papenburgergracht

Rapenburg

Anjaliersstr.

Wertheim Park Plantage Parklaan

Dam

Rokin

Damstraat

Zijds Voorburgwal

Achter burgwal

Oude

Zijds

Oude Hoogstr.

Nieuwe Hoogstr.

Kloveniersburgwal

Ruamgr.

nieuwgracht

Jodenbreestraat

Mr. Visserplein

Muiderstraat

Heren

Plantage Middenlaan

Nieuwezijdsvoorburgwal

Kalverstraat

Nes

Oude

Nieuwe Doelenstr.

Groen

Zwa

Staalstraat

Amstel

Amstel

Blauwbrug

Nieuwe Amstel

WATERLOOPLEIN

Keizersgracht

Kerkstraat

Spui

Rokin

Singel

Reguliersdwarsstraat

Rembrandt plein

Amstelstr.

Amstel

gracht

Utrechtsestraat

Amstel

Nieuwe

Nieuwe

Nieuwe

Nieuwe

Weesperstraat

Prinsengracht

Nieuwe Achter

Valckenierstraat

Vijzelstraat

Heren

Keizersgracht

Reguliers

Kerkstraat Magere Brug

Amstel

Weesperstraat

WEESPERPLEIN

Sarphatistraat

Vijzelgracht

Prinsengracht

Noorderstr.

Nieuwe Looiersstr.

gracht

Frederiks plein

Sarphatistraat

Mauritskade

dwarstr.

Wetering Pl

Wetering Schans

Den Texstraat

Nicolaas Witsen Kade

F. Bol Straat

Stadhouderskade

KEY

i Tourist Information
M Metro Stops
Metro Lines
Tram Lines
Railroad

0 220 yards
0 200 meters

guards a series of tranquil inner courtyards. In medieval times, this area was an island devoted to piety. Today the bordering canals are filled in.

The medieval doorway just around the corner in St. Luciensteeg leads to the former Burgerweeshuis (City Orphanage), once a nunnery but now the **Amsterdam Historisch Museum** (Museum of History). The museum traces the city's history from its origins as a fishing village through the 17th-century Golden Age of material and artistic wealth to the decline of the trading empire during the 18th century. The engrossing story unfolds through a display of old maps, documents, and paintings, often aided by a commentary in English. *Kalverstraat 92, tel. 020/5231822. Admission: Fl. 7.50. Open weekdays 10–5, weekends 11–5.*

A small passageway and courtyard link the museum with the **Begijnhof,** an enchanting, enclosed square of almshouses founded in 1346. The *beguines* were women who chose to lead a form of convent life, often taking the vow of chastity. The last beguine died in 1974, and her house, No. 26, has been preserved as she left it. No. 34, dating from the 15th century, is the oldest and the only one to keep its wooden Gothic facade.

In the center of the square is a church given to Amsterdam's English and Scottish Presbyterians more than 300 years ago. On the church wall and also in the chancel are tributes to the Pilgrim Fathers who sailed from Delftshaven to New York in 1620. Opposite the church is another of the city's secret Catholic chapels, built in 1671. *Admission to the Begijnhof is free, but as people still live here, access is restricted to weekdays 11–4. You are also requested to maintain the silence of the square.*

Continuing along Kalverstraat, you soon come to Spui, a lively square in the heart of the university area. It was a center for student rallies in revolutionary 1968. Now it is a center for bookstores and bars, including the cozy "brown cafés."

Beyond is the Singel Canal and, following the tram tracks, Leidsestraat, an important shopping street that terminates in the **Leidseplein,** a lively square that is one of the night-life centers of the city.

If you continue straight along Kalverstraat instead of turning at Spui, you'll soon reach the **Muntplein,** with its **Munttoren** (Mint Tower, built in 1620), a graceful structure whose clock and bells still seem to mirror the Golden Age. Beginning at the Muntplein is the floating **flower market** on the Singel Canal. *Open Mon.–Sat. 9:30–5.*

From the Singel, take Leidsestraat to the Herengracht, the city's most prestigious "Gentlemen's Canal." The stretch of canal from here to Huidenstraat is named the **Golden Bend** for its sumptuous patrician houses with double staircases and grand entrances. Seventeenth-century merchants moved here from the Amstel River to escape the disadvantageous by-products of their wealth: the noisy warehouses, the unpleasant smells from the breweries, and the risk of fire in the sugar refineries. These houses display the full range of Amsterdam facades: from neck, bell, and step gables to grander Louis XIV–style houses with elaborate cornices and frescoed ceilings.

Along Herengracht, parallel to the Westerkerk, is the **Nederlands Theater Instituut.** This theater museum is a dynamic find on such a genteel canal. Two frescoed Louis XIV–style merchants' houses form the backdrop for a history of the circus, opera, musicals, and drama. Miniature theaters and videos of stage productions are just two entertaining features. During the summer, the large garden is open for buffet lunches. *Herengracht 168, tel. 020/6235104. Admission: Fl. 5. Open weekdays 11–5, weekends 1–5.*

Jewish
Amsterdam
Take the Museum Boat or the metro from the central station to Waterlooplein and walk east to Jodenbreestraat. This is the heart of **Jodenbuurt,** the old Jewish district and an important area to all Amsterdammers. The original settlers here were wealthy Sephardic Jews from Spain and Portugal, later followed by poorer Ashkenazic refugees from Germany and Poland. At the turn of the century, this was a thriving community of Jewish diamond polishers, dyers, and merchants. During World War II, the corner of Jodenbreestraat marked the end of the *Joodse wijk* (Jewish neighborhood), by then an imposed ghetto. Although the character of the area was largely destroyed by highway construction in 1965, and more recently by construction of both the metro and the Muziektheater/Stadhuis, neighboring Muiderstraat has retained much of the original atmosphere. Notice the gateways decorated with pelicans, symbolizing great love; according to legend, the pelican will feed her starving young with her own blood.

From 1639 to 1658, Rembrandt lived at Jodenbreestraat No. 4, now ⑲ the **Museum Het Rembrandthuis** (Rembrandt's House). For more than 20 years, the ground floor was used by the artist as living quarters; the sunny upper floor was his studio. It is fascinating to visit, both as a record of life in 17th-century Amsterdam and as a sketch of Holland's most illustrious artist. It contains a superb collection of his etchings and engravings. From St. Antonies Sluis bridge, just by the house, there is a canal view that has barely changed since Rembrandt's time. *Jodenbreestraat 4–6, tel. 020/6249486. Admission: Fl. 7.50. Open Mon.–Sat. 10–5, Sun. 1–5.*

After visiting Rembrandt's House, walk back to the canal and go left to pass the Waterlooplein flea market. Ahead of you is the Amster- ⑳ dam **Muziektheater/Stadhuis** (Music Theater/Town Hall) complex, which presents an intriguing combination of bureaucracy and art. Amsterdammers come to the Town Hall section of the building by day to obtain driving licenses, to pick up welfare payments, and to be married. They return by night to the rounded part of the building facing the river to see opera and ballet by Holland's well-known performing companies. Feel free to wander into Town Hall (there are some interesting sculptures and other displays to see). Opera and ballet fans can go on a tour of the Muziektheater, which takes you around the dressing rooms, dance studios, and even the wig department. *Amstel 3, tel. 020/5518054. Admission: Fl. 8.50. Guided tours every Wed. and Sat. at 3.*

Walk through the flea market behind the Muziektheater, and across a busy traffic junction and you will come to the 17th-century ㉑ **Portugees Israelitische Synagogue** (Portuguese Israelite Synagogue). As one of Amsterdam's four neighboring synagogues, it was part of the largest Jewish religious complex in Europe. The austere interior is still intact, even if the building itself is marooned on a traffic island. *Mr. Visserplein 3, tel. 020/6245351. Admission Fl. 5. Open Apr.–Oct., Sun.–Fri. 10–4; Nov.–Mar., Mon.–Thurs. 10–4, Fri. 10–3, Sun. 10–12. Closed daily 12:30–1.*

Jonas Daniël Meijerplein is a square behind the synagogue. In the ㉒ center is a statue of the **Dokwerker** (Dockworker), a profession that has played a significant part in the city's history. The statue commemorates the 1942 strike by which Amsterdam dockworkers expressed their solidarity with persecuted Jews. A memorial march is held every year on February 25.

㉓ On the other side of the square is the intriguing **Joods Historisch Museum** (Jewish History Museum), set in a complex of three ancient synagogues. These synagogues once served a population of 100,000 Jews, which shrank to less than 10,000 after 1945. The new museum, founded by American and Dutch Jews, displays religious treasures in a clear cultural and historical context. Since the synagogues lost most of their treasures in the war, their architecture and history are more compelling than the individual exhibits. *Jonas Daniël Meijerplein 2–4, tel. 020/6269945. Admission: Fl. 7. Open daily 11–5.*

Instead of returning on foot, you can catch the Museum Boat from the Muziektheater to the central station or to a destination near your hotel. If you feel like a breath of fresh air, stroll along Nieuwe Herengracht, once known as the "Jewish Gentlemen's Canal." In Rembrandt's day, there were views of distant windjammers sailing into port, but today the canal is oddly deserted.

The Museum Quarter By crossing the bridge beyond the Leidseplein and walking a short distance to the left on Stadhouderskade, you'll find three of the most distinguished museums in Holland—the Rijksmuseum, the Stedelijk Museum, and the Rijksmuseum Vincent van Gogh. Of the three, the **Rijksmuseum** (State Museum), easily recognized by its towers, is the most important, so be sure to allow adequate time to explore it. It was founded in 1808, but the current, rather lavish, building dates from 1885. The museum contains significant collections of furniture, textiles, ceramics, sculpture, and prints, as well as Italian, Flemish, and Spanish paintings, many of which are of the highest quality. But the museum's fame rests on its unrivaled collection of 16th- and 17th-century Dutch masters. Of Rembrandt's masterpieces, make a point of seeing *The Nightwatch*, concealed during World War II in caves in Maastricht. The painting was misnamed because of its dull layers of varnish; in reality it depicts the Civil Guard in daylight. Also worth searching out are Frans Hals's family portraits and Jan Steen's drunken scenes, Van Ruysdael's romantic but menacing landscapes, and Vermeer's glimpses of everyday life bathed in his usual pale light. *Stadhouderskade 42, tel. 020/6732121. Admission: Fl. 12.50. Open Tues.–Sun. 10–5.*

㉕ A few blocks beyond is the **Rijksmuseum Vincent van Gogh** (Vincent van Gogh Museum). This museum contains the world's largest collection of the artist's works—200 paintings and 500 drawings—as well as works by some 50 other painters of the period. *Paulus Potterstraat 7, tel. 020/5705200. Admission: Fl. 10. Open daily 10–5.*

㉖ Next door is the **Stedelijk Museum** (Municipal Museum), with its neo-Renaissance facade that complements the Rijksmuseum's neo-Gothic turrets. The museum has a stimulating collection of modern art and ever-changing displays of contemporary art. Before viewing the works of Cézanne, Chagall, Kandinsky, and Mondrian, check the list of temporary exhibitions in Room 1. Museum policy is to trace the development of the artist, rather than merely to show a few masterpieces. Don't forget the museum's restaurant overlooking a garden filled with modern sculptures. *Paulus Potterstraat 13, tel. 020/5732911. Admission: Fl. 8. Open daily 11–5.*

㉗ Diagonally opposite the Stedelijk Museum, at the end of the broad Museumplein, is the **Concertgebouw,** home of the country's foremost orchestra, the world-renowned Concertgebouworkest. Many visiting orchestras also perform here. The building has two auditoriums, the smaller of which is used for chamber music and recitals.

The Jordaan One old part of Amsterdam that is certainly worth exploring is the ㉘ **Jordaan,** the area bordered by Herengracht, Lijnbaansgracht, Brouwersgracht, and Raadhuisstraat. The canals and side streets here are all named for flowers and plants. Indeed, at one time, when this was the French quarter of the city, the area was known as *le jardin* (the garden), a name that over the years has become Jordaan. The best time to explore this area is on a Sunday morning, when there are few cars and people about, or in the evening. This part of the town has attracted many artists and is something of a bohemian quarter, where rundown buildings are being renovated and converted into restaurants, antiques shops, boutiques, and galleries.

Shopping

Gift Ideas **Diamonds.** Since the 17th century, "Amsterdam cut" has been synonymous with perfection in the quality of diamonds. There is a cluster of diamond houses on the Rokin. Alternatively, try **Van Moppes Diamonds.** *Albert Cuypstraat 2–6, tel. 020/6761242. Open daily 9–5.*

Porcelain. The Dutch have been producing Delft, Makkum, and other fine porcelain for centuries. Try the **Focke and Meltzer** store near the Rijksmuseum (P.C. Hooftstraat 65–67, tel. 020/6642311).

Shopping Districts Amsterdam's chief shopping districts, which have largely been turned into pedestrianized areas, are the **Leidsestraat, Kalverstraat,** and **Nieuwendijk. Rokin,** hectic with traffic, houses a cluster of boutiques and renowned antiques shops. By contrast, some of the **Nieuwe Spiegelstraat**'s old curiosity shops sell a more inexpensive range. For trendy small boutiques and unusual crafts shops, locals browse through the Jordaan. For A to Z shopping in a wide variety of stores, the brand-new **Magna Plaza** shopping center, built in a glorious, former post office that's behind the royal palace, offers another alternative. When leaving Holland, remember that Schiphol Airport is Europe's best tax-free shopping center.

Department Stores **De Bijenkorf** (Dam Square), the city's number-one department store, is excellent for contemporary fashions and furnishings. Running a close second is **Vroom and Dreesman** (Kalverstraat 201), with well-stocked departments carrying all manner of goods.

Markets There is a lively open-air **flea market** on Waterlooplein around the Muziektheater (Mon.–Sat. 9:30–4). For antiques, especially silver and toys, you can try the **Antiekmarkt de Looier** (Elandsgracht 109, tel. 020/6249038; Sun.–Wed. 11–5, Thurs. 11–9). During the summer, art lovers can buy etchings, drawings, and watercolors at the Sunday **art markets** on Thorbeckeplein and the Spui.

Dining

Amsterdammers are less creatures of habit than are the Dutch in general. Even so, set menus and early dinners are preferred by these health-conscious citizens. For travelers on a diet or budget, the blue-and-white "Tourist Menu" sign guarantees an economical (Fl. 25) yet imaginative set menu created by the head chef. For traditionalists, the "Nederlands Dis" soup tureen sign is a promise of regional recipes and seasonal ingredients. "You can eat in any language" is the city's proud boast, so when Dutch restaurants are closed, Indonesian, Chinese, and Turkish restaurants are often open. Between meals, you can follow your nose to the nearest herring cart or drop into a cozy brown café for coffee and an apple tart. For details and price-category definitions, *see* Dining *in* Staying in Holland, *above.*

$$ **Albatross Seafood House.** This cheery, family-operated enterprise on the edge of the Jordaan is decked out with maritime flotsam and jetsam and offers the freshest of fish. You have a choice of Dutch specialties (such as stewed eel) as well as foreign favorites, including a delicious bouillabaisse. Even the simplest dishes are full of the subtle flavors of home cooking. The three-course set menus are an excellent value. *Westerstraat 264, tel. 020/6279932. Reservations advised. AE, DC, MC, V. Closed Sun. No lunch.*

$$ **Eerst Klas.** Amsterdam's best-kept secret is in the most public of places: the former first-class waiting room at the central train station. High ceilings, dark paneling, and soft lighting create a perfect hideaway. In the café section you can get well-priced snacks. The grills, salads, and fish dishes in the restaurant are a little more expensive. *Stationsplein 15, Spoer 2B, tel. 020/6250131. Reservations advised. Jacket and tie. AE, DC, MC, V.*

$$ **Haesje Claes.** Traditional Dutch food is served here in a traditional Dutch environment, with prices that are easy on the wallet. It sounds like a tourist's dream and, in ways, it is. There's a cozy feeling here and a relaxed simplicity. Menu choices can be as basic as liver and onions, as traditional as *stamppot* (mixed potatoes and sauerkraut), or as elaborate as fillet of salmon with lobster sauce. Although an à la carte meal would put this in the $ price category, there's a good three-course set menu for Fl. 25. *Spuistraat 273–275, tel. 020/6249998. Reservations advised. AE, DC, MC, V. Closed Sun. lunch.*

$$ **Rose's Cantina.** A perennial favorite of the arty set, students, and young professionals, Rose's Cantina offers spicy Tex-Mex food, lethal cocktails, and a high noise level. Pop in for a full meal, a plate of tacos, or a late afternoon drink. *Reguliersdwarsstraat 38, tel. 020/6259797. Weekend reservations required. AE, DC, MC, V.*

$$ **Speciaal.** Although set in the Jordaan area, this Indonesian restaurant is slightly off the beaten track. From the outside, the Speciaal looks very mundane, but inside, the soothing Indonesian prints, raffia work, and bamboo curtains create an intimate atmosphere. Along with the usual rijsttafel, chicken, fish, and egg dishes provide tasty variants on a sweet-and-sour theme. *Nieuwe Leliestraat 142, tel. 020/6249706. Reservations accepted. AE, MC, V.*

$$ **Toscanini.** This cavernous, noisy Italian restaurant with a bustling,
★ open kitchen has superb cuisine. Try the fresh pasta with game sauce, the scrumptious selection of antipasti, the rabbit, or fresh fish cooked with wine, basil, and tomato. Service is brisk, and the atmosphere friendly and relaxed. *Lindengracht 75, tel. 020/6232813. Reservations required. No credit cards. No lunch.*

$ **Blauwe Hollander.** The name is a bit of nonsense (it means Blue Dutchman), but the pricing strategy is not. This is a simple, straightforward sort of eatery, near the Leidseplein entertainment area. There's always a daily special as well as a variety of other meat-and-potato choices. The no-frills decor is traditional Dutch. *Leidsekruisstraat 28, tel. 020/6233014. Closed lunch. No credit cards.*

$ **Eettuin.** An "eating garden" in the heart of the artsy Jordaan area, the menu includes spare ribs, "house special" pork, and vegetarian dishes. Unusual for Europe is the salad bar. *Tweede Tuindwarsstraat 10, tel. 020/6237706. Reservations advised. No credit cards. No lunch.*

$ **Oud Holland.** This restaurant is in a convenient location for a night on the town—not far from the Leidseplein, yet just far enough from the red-light district. Oud Holland is one of the few Amsterdam restaurants to offer a tourist menu. A typical three-course meal is a game pâté followed by *pruttelpot* (a sweet beef stew cooked with apples) and tasty Dutch apple pie for dessert. A children's menu is also available. The heated terrace opens at 5 PM. *NZ Voorburgwal 105, tel. 020/6246848. Reservations accepted. AE, DC, MC, V.*

¢ **Bojo.** For cheap, authentic Indonesian food, this restaurant, in the Leidseplein area, offers a good deal; most dishes are less than Fl. 15. Enjoy the terrace during summer months. *L. Leidsedwarsstraat 51, tel. 020/6227434. No reservations. No credit cards. Open until 5:30 AM weekends.*

¢ **De Keuken van 1870.** You absolutely, positively can't get cheaper than this. Day menus are Fl. 11 and à la carte selections are only a few guilders more. The choices on any given night may be spare ribs, fried liver, or even jugged hare with peaches and cranberry, and every plate comes complete with vegetables and potato. The decor, if it can be called decor, is simple (like the soup kitchen this Keuken once was), but you come here for good eats, not ambience. *Spuistraat 4, tel. 020/6248965. No reservations. AE, DC, MC, V.*

¢ **Pancake Bakery.** Here is a chance to try a traditionally Dutch way of keeping eating costs down. The name of the game is pancakes—for every course including dessert, for which the topping can be ice cream, fruit, or liqueur. The Pancake Bakery is not far from Anne Frank Huis. *Prinsengracht 191, tel. 020/6251333. No reservations. No credit cards.*

Lodging

Accommodations are tight from Easter to summer, so early booking is advised if you wish to secure a popular hotel. The other snag is parking: Amsterdam is a pedestrian's paradise but a driver's nightmare. Since few hotels have parking lots, cars are best abandoned in a multistory parking ramp for the duration of your stay. Most tourists prefer to stay inside the concentric ring of canals, an atmospheric area of historic gable-roof merchants' houses. The quiet museum quarter is a convenient choice for the Rijksmuseum yet is near enough to the Vondelpark for light jogging. For details and price-category definitions, *see* Lodging *in* Staying in Holland, *above.*

$$ **Ambassade.** With its beautiful canalside location, its Louis XV–
★ style decoration, and its Oriental carpets, the Ambassade seems more like a stately home than a hotel. Service is attentive and room prices include breakfast. For other meals, the neighborhood has a good choice of restaurants. *Herengracht 341, tel. 020/6262333, fax 020/6245321. 49 rooms with bath. AE, DC, MC, V.*

$$ **Atlas Hotel.** Renowned for its friendly atmosphere, this small hotel has moderate-size rooms decorated in Art Nouveau style. It's also very handy for Museumplein, whose major museums are within easy walking distance. *Van Eeghenstraat 64, tel. 020/6766336, fax 020/6717633. 22 rooms with bath. Facilities: bar, restaurant. AE, DC, MC, V.*

$$ **Het Canal House.** The American owners of this canalside hotel opt to put antiques rather than televisions in the rooms. Spacious rooms overlook the canal or the illuminated garden. A hearty Dutch breakfast comes with the room. *Keizergracht 148, tel. 020/6225182, fax 020/6241317. 26 rooms with bath or shower. AE, DC, MC, V.*

$$ **Hotel de Filosoof.** In a quiet street near the Vondelpark, this hotel attracts artists, thinkers, and people looking for something a little different. Bona fide Amsterdam philosophers are regularly to be found in the comfy armchairs of the salon. Each room is decorated in a different cultural motif—there's an Aristotle room, and a Goethe room adorned with texts from *Faust. Anna van den Vondelstraat 6, tel. 020/6833013, fax 6853750. 29 rooms, 25 with bath. Facilities: bar. AE, MC, V.*

$$ **Hotel Toren.** The former home of Abraham Kuyper (founder of the Protestant University and a former prime minister of Holland), this delightful and large canal house was converted into a hotel in 1968 but retains some of its 17th-century splendor. Rooms range from the cheap-and-cheerful type to those with their own whirlpool bath. *Keizergracht 164, tel. 020/6226352, fax 020/6269705. 43 rooms with bath. AE, DC, MC, V.*

$ **Agora.** Near the Singel flower market, this small hotel, in an 18th-
★ century building, reflects the cheerful bustle of the surrounding neighborhood. The rooms are light and spacious, some decorated with vintage furniture; the best overlook the canal or the university. A considerate staff and comfortable accommodations ensure the hotel's popularity. Book well in advance. *Singel 462, tel. 020/6272200, fax 020/6272202. 15 rooms, 11 with bath or shower. AE, DC, MC, V.*

$ **Amstel Botel.** This floating hotel moored near Centraal Station is an appropriate place to stay in watery Amsterdam. The rooms are small, but the windows are large, offering fine views across the water to the city. Make sure you don't get a room on the land side of the vessel, or you'll end up staring at an ugly postal sorting office. *Oosterdokskade 224, tel. 020/6264247, fax 020/6391952. 176 rooms with shower. Facilities: bar. AE, DC, MC, V.*

$ **Hotel Seven Bridges.** Named for the scene beyond its front steps, this small canal-house hotel offers rooms decorated with individual flair. Oriental rugs are laid out on wooden floors, and there are comfy antique armchairs and custom-built marble washstands. The Rembrandtsplein is nearby. For a room with a stunning view, ask if one of the two large doubles is available. *Reguliersgracht 31, tel. 020/6231329. 6 rooms with bath. AE, MC, V.*

¢ **De La Haye.** There is a convivial mood in this simple little canal-house hotel, not far from the Leidseplein. The rooms are simple but clean and fresh. *Leidsegracht 114, tel. 020/6244044, fax 020/6835254. 9 rooms with bath. AE, V.*

¢ **Hotel Hoksbergen.** The public areas of this 300-year-old canal-house hotel were redecorated in 1994 with varnished pine furniture and soft colors. In 1995 and 1996, rooms will get the same simple treatment. The result is a hotel conveniently situated and easy on the pocket, with a quiet, unassuming atmosphere. *Singel 301, tel. 020/6266043, fax 020/6383479. 14 rooms with bath. AE, DC, MC, V.*

¢ **Quentin Hotel.** This small, family-run hotel, a stone's throw from hectic Leidseplein is simply decorated with plain colors and modern prints, and flooded with light through large windows. Renovations in 1994 meant that the rooms increased in number but decreased in size. The best rooms are the spacious corner ones that overlook a canal; those in the basement are less impressive. *Leidsekade 89, tel. 020/6262187, fax 020/6220121. 23 rooms, 15 with shower. AE, MC, V.*

The Arts

The arts flourish in tolerant and cosmopolitan Amsterdam. The best sources of information about performances are the monthly publications *Time Out Amsterdam* (in English) and *Uit Krant* (in Dutch) and the biweekly *What's On in Amsterdam*, which can be obtained from the VVV tourist office, where you can secure tickets for the more popular events. Tickets must be booked in person from Monday to Saturday, 10 to 4. You also can book at the **Amsterdam Uit Buro** (Stadsschouwburg, Leidseplein 26, tel. 020/62112111).

Classical Music Classical music is featured at the **Concertgebouw** (Concertgebouwplein 2–6), home of one of Europe's finest orchestras. A smaller auditorium in the same building is used for chamber music, recitals, and even jam sessions. While ticket prices for international orchestras are fairly high, most concerts are reasonably priced and the Wednesday lunchtime concerts are free. The box office is open from 9:30 to 7; you can make telephone bookings (020/6718345) from 10 to 5.

Opera and Ballet The Dutch national ballet and opera companies are housed in the new **Muziektheater** (tel. 020/6255455) on Waterlooplein. Guest companies from foreign countries perform there during the three-week Holland Festival in June.

Theater At the **Stalhouderij Theater** (1e Bloemdwarsstraat 4, tel. 020/6262282), an international cast performs a wide range of English-language plays in a former stable in the Jordaan. For experimental theater and colorful cabaret in Dutch, catch the shows at **Felix Meritis House** (Keizersgracht 324, tel. 020/6231311).

Nightlife

Amsterdam has a wide variety of discos, bars, and exotic shows. The more respectable—and expensive—after-dark activities are in and around Leidseplein and Rembrandtsplein; fleshier productions are on Oudezijds Achterburgwal and Thorbeckeplein. Names and locations change from year to year, but most bars and clubs are open every night from 5 PM to 2 AM or 4 AM. On weeknights, very few clubs charge admission, though the more lively ones sometimes ask for a "club membership" fee of Fl. 20 or more. Drink prices are, for the most part, not exorbitant. It is wise to steer clear of the area behind the central station at night.

Bars **Café Schiller,** a cozy, inexpensive bar on the Rembrandtsplein, has many of its original Art Deco fittings. In the first part of this century, it was a meeting place for Amsterdam's writers, artists, and music hall performers. Paintings by Frits Schiller, the first owner, still hang on the walls.

Jazz Clubs Set in a converted warehouse, the **BIMhuis** (Oude Schans 73–77, tel. 020/6233373; open Thurs.–Sat. from 9 PM) is currently the most fashionable jazz club. Ticket holders can sit in the adjoining BIMcafé and enjoy a magical view across Oude Schans to the port. If you long for good Dixieland jazz, go to **Joseph Lam Jazz Club** (Van Diemenstraat 242, tel. 020/6228086); it's only open on Saturdays.

Rock Clubs **Paradiso** (Weteringschans 6–8, tel. 020/6264521) is an Amsterdam institution that has become a vibrant venue for rock, New Age, and even contemporary classical music.

Dance Clubs Mostly hidden in cellars around the Leidseplein, the discos fill up after midnight. **Roxy** (Singel 465, tel. 020/6200354) is Holland's current hot spot, though if you're not a member you will have to be quite trendily dressed to get in. Also popular are **Escape** (Rembrandtsplein 11, tel. 020/6223542) and **It** (Amstelstraat 24, tel. 020/6250111), which is generally straight on Thursday and Sunday; gay Friday–Saturday. **Mazzo** (Rozengracht 114, tel. 020/6267500) uses dramatic lighting and slick videos to attract student poseurs, would-be musicians, and artists.

Casinos Blackjack, roulette, and slot machines have come lately—but not lightly—to the thrifty Dutch. Now everyone wants to play. At the elegant **Holland Casino** (Max Euweplein 62, tel. 020/6201006), just off Leidseplein, you'll need your passport to get in; the minimum age is 18.

Historic Holland

This circular itinerary can be followed either clockwise or counterclockwise, but whichever way you decide to follow it, you'll be sure to see some of Holland's most characteristic sights. There are the historic towns of Leiden and Utrecht and the major museums in Haarlem; in between these towns, you'll see some of Holland's windmill-dotted landscape and pass through centers of tulip growing and cheese production.

Getting Around

All the towns on the following itinerary can be reached by bus or train. From Amsterdam there are, for example, three direct trains per hour to Haarlem, Leiden, and Utrecht. Check with the VVV tourist office in Amsterdam for help in planning your trip or inquire at Centraal Station.

Tourist Information

Apeldoorn (Stationstraat 72, tel. 06/91681636).
Haarlem (Stationsplein 1, tel. 06/32024043).
Leiden (Stationsplein 210, tel. 071/146846).
Utrecht (Vredenburg 90, tel. 06/34034085).

Zandvoort (Schoolplein 1, tel. 02507/17947).

Exploring Historic Holland

Apeldoorn   Ninety kilometers (56 miles) east of Amsterdam is **Apeldoorn,** where the main attraction is the **Rijksmuseum Paleis Het Loo.** This former royal palace was built during the late 17th century for William III and has been beautifully restored to illustrate the domestic surroundings enjoyed by the House of Orange for more than three centuries. The museum, which is housed in the stables, has a fascinating collection of royal memorabilia, including cars and carriages, furniture and photographs, silver and ceramics. The formal gardens and the surrounding parkland offer attractive walks. *Koninklijk Park 1, tel. 055/212244. Admission: 12.50. Open Tues.–Sun. 10–5.*

Utrecht   The city of **Utrecht** is 72 kilometers (44 miles) west of Apeldoorn. The high gabled houses of the Nieuwegracht, the canals with their water gates, the 13th-century wharves and storage cellars of the Oudegracht, and the superb churches and museums are just some of the key attractions, most of which are situated around the main cathedral square. The **Domkerk** is a late-Gothic cathedral containing a series of fine stained-glass windows. The **Domtoren** (Dom Tower) opposite the building was connected to the cathedral until a hurricane hit in 1674. The bell tower is the tallest in the country, and it has 465 steep steps that lead to a magnificent view. A guide is essential in the labyrinth of steps and passageways. *Domplein, tel. 030/ 310403. Admission to Domkerk free; Fl. 2.25 for tour (on the hour). Open May–Sept., weekdays 10–5, Sat. 10–3:30, Sun. 2–4; Oct.– Apr., weekdays 11–4, Sat. 11–3:30, Sun. 2–4. Admission to Domtoren: Fl. 4. Open Apr.–Oct., weekdays 10–5, Sat. 12–5, Sun. 12–5; Nov.–Mar., Sat. 12–5, Sun. 12–5.*

Not far from the cathedral is the merry **Rijksmuseum van Speelklok tot Pierement** (National Museum of Mechanical Musical Instruments), devoted solely to music machines—from music boxes to street organs and even musical chairs. During the guided tour, music students play some of the instruments. The museum is housed in Utrecht's oldest parish church. *Buurkerkhof 10. Admission: Fl. 7.50. Open Tues.–Sat. 10–5, Sun. 1–5.*

Walk south out of Domplein, down Lange Nieuwstraat. Halfway down is the **Rijksmuseum Het Catharijneconvent.** In addition to its collection of holy relics and vestments, this museum contains the country's largest display of medieval art. *Nieuwe Gracht 63, tel. 030/ 317296. Admission: Fl. 5. Open Tues.–Fri. 10–5, weekends 11–5.*

There are more museums to be explored on Agnietenstraat, which crosses Lange Nieuwstraat. The **Centraal Museum** houses a rich collection of contemporary art and other city exhibits. Amid the clutter is an original Viking ship (discovered in 1930) and a 17th-century dollhouse complete with period furniture, porcelain, and miniature old masters. *Agnietenstraat 1, tel. 030/362362. Admission: Fl. 6. Open Tues.–Sat. 11–5, Sun. 1–5.*

An important part of the museum's collection is a house that is located a 15-minute walk away, in Utrecht's eastern suburbs; it is known as the **Rietveld Schröder House.** Designed in 1924 by the architect Gerrit Rietveld working with Truus Schröeder, this is considered to be the architectural pinnacle of the style known as de Stijl (The Style). The use of black and white along with primary colors (red, yellow, blue) and the definition of the interior space are unique and innovative even today. The experience of the house is, as one art historian phrased it, "like wandering into a Mondrian painting." The house was completely restored to its original condition in 1987; there is a guided tour through the rooms. *Prins Hendriklaan 50A,* *tel. 030/362310. Admission: Fl. 9. Open Wed.–Sat. 11–5, Sun. 12–5. Call for appointment.*

Leiden West of Utrecht is the ancient city of **Leiden,** renowned for its spirit of religious and intellectual tolerance and known for its university and royal connections. Start at **De Lakenhal,** built in 1639 for the city's cloth merchants and now an art gallery and cloth and antiques museum. Pride of place in the collection goes to the 16th- and 17th-century Dutch paintings, with works by Steen, Dou, and Rembrandt; and, above all, Lucas van Leyden's *Last Judgment*—the first great Renaissance painting in what is now the Netherlands. Other rooms are devoted to furniture and to the history of Leiden's medieval guilds: the drapers, tailors, and brewers. *Oude Singel 32, tel. 071/165361. Admission: Fl. 5. Open Tues.–Fri. 10–5, weekends noon–5.*

Near De Lakenhal is the **Molenmuseum de Valk** (Windmill Museum), housed in a windmill built in 1747, which was worked by 10 generations of millers until 1964. The seven floors still contain the original workings, an old forge, washrooms, and living quarters. On summer Saturdays the mill still turns—but for pleasure, not business. *2e Binnenvesstgracht 1, tel. 071/165353. Admission: Fl. 5. Open Tues.–Sat. 10–5, Sun. 1–5.*

Crossing the canal and walking into narrow, bustling Breestraat and then down the narrow Pieterskerk-Choorsteeg you'll come to the imposing **St. Pieterskerk,** with its memories of the Pilgrim Fathers who worshiped here and of their spiritual leader, John Robinson, who is buried here. A narrow street by the **Persijnhofje** almhouse, dating from 1683, takes you downhill and across the gracious Rapenburg Canal, crossed by triple-arched bridges and bordered by stately 18th-century houses. To the right is the **Rijksmuseum van Oudheden** (National Museum of Antiquities), the country's leading archaeological museum. The prize exhibit is the entire 1st-century AD Temple of Taffeh, donated by the Egyptian government. There is also a floor devoted to finds in the Netherlands. *Rapenburg 28, tel. 071/163163. Admission: Fl. 5; Fl. 3 surcharge for special exhibitions. Open Tues.–Sat. 10–5, Sun. noon–5.*

Continuing on, you find the **Academie** (university) and the **Hortus Botanicus** gardens. The university was founded by William the Silent as a reward to Leiden for its victory against the Spanish in the 1573–74 siege. During the war, the dikes were opened and the countryside flooded so that the rescuing navy could sail right up to the city walls. Founded in 1587, these botanical gardens are among the oldest in the world. The highlights are a faithful reconstruction of a 16th-century garden, the herb garden, the colorful orangery, and the ancient trees. *Rapenburg 73. Admission: Fl. 3.50. Open Apr.–Oct., Mon.–Sat. 9–5, Sun. 11–5; Nov.–Mar., weekdays 9–4:30.*

Haarlem With its secret inner courtyards and pointed gables, **Haarlem** can resemble a 17th-century canvas, even one painted by Frans Hals, the city's greatest painter. The area around the **Grote Markt,** the market square, provides an architectural stroll through the 17th and 18th centuries. Some of the facades are adorned with such homilies as "The body's sickness is a cure for the soul." Haarlem's religious faith can also be sensed in any of its 20 almshouses. The **Stadhuis** (Town Hall) was once a hunting lodge. Nearby is the **Vleeshal,** or meat market, which has an especially fine gabled front. It dates from the early 1600s and is now used as an art gallery and a museum of local history. *Lepelstraat. Admission: Fl. 4. Open Mon.–Sat. 11–5, Sun. 1–5.*

Across from the Vleeshal is the **Grote Kerk,** dedicated to St. Bavo. The church, built between 1400 and 1550, houses one of Europe's most famous organs. This massive instrument has 5,000 pipes, and both Mozart and Handel played on it. It is still used for concerts, and an annual organ festival is held here in July. Make your way down Damstraat, behind the Grote Kerk, and turn left at the **Waag** (Weigh House). On the left is the **Teylers Museum,** which claims to be the oldest museum in the country. It was founded by a wealthy merchant in 1778 as a museum of science and the arts; it now houses a fine collection of The Hague school of painting, as well as a collection of drawings and sketches by Michelangelo, Raphael, and other non-Dutch masters. Since the canvases in this building are lit by natural light, try to see the museum on a sunny day. *Spaarne 16, tel. 023/319010. Admission: Fl. 6.50. Open Tues.–Sat. 10–5, Sun. 1–5.*

Follow the Binnen Spaarn and turn right into Kampervest and then Gasthuisvest. On your right, in Groot Heiligland, you'll find the **Frans Hals Museum.** This museum, in what used to be a 17th-century hospice, contains a marvelous collection of the artist's work; his paintings of the guilds of Haarlem are particularly noteworthy. The museum also has works by Hals's contemporaries. *Groot Heiligland 62, tel. 023/319180. Admission: Fl. 7.50. Open Mon.–Sat. 11–5, Sun. 1–5.*

Dining and Lodging

In towns such as Apeldoorn and Gouda are bed-and-breakfast accommodations, booked through the VVV tourist office, an interesting choice for overnight visitors. Rooms in Utrecht are often in short supply, so book in advance or immediately upon arrival. For details and price-category definitions, *see* Dining and Lodging *in* Staying in Holland, *above.*

Apeldoorn **Hotel Berg en Bos.** If it were not for the flags and small covered en-
Lodging try, you might mistake this hotel on a quiet side street for a private house. While the rooms are not particularly large, they are neat, clean, and bright. There is also a homey lounge. *Aquamarijnstraat 58, tel. 055/552352, fax 055/554782. 17 rooms with bath. MC, V. ¢*
Hotel Pension Astra. As you might expect in a quiet residential city such as Apeldoorn, family-owned pensions abound. The Astra is just off the main road from the city center, the railway station, and Palace Het Loo. The rooms are tidy though not large, and have small private shower-baths. *Bas Backerlaan 12–14, tel. 055/223022, fax 055/223021. 26 rooms with bath. AE, DC, MC, V. ¢*

Leiden **Jill's.** A delightful, bright restaurant run by a cheerful staff and sit-
Dining uated just a few minutes' walk from the De Valk windmill, this is an attractive spot for a relaxing meal. A wide variety of set menus with Dutch, Italian, and Asian (especially Thai) influences offers something for nearly every palate. The fish cooked with ginger is especially tasty. *Morsstraat 6, tel. 071/143722. AE, DC, MC, V. ¢*
Annie's Verjaardag. A low-arched cellar full of cheery students and a canalside terrace make Annie's popular in all weather. Besides a modest but well-prepared selection of salads and baguettes, there's at least one substantial daily special, such as mussels or pork cooked with mustard and coriander. *Oude Rijn 1a, tel. 071/125737. No credit cards. ¢–$*

Dining and **Nieuw Minerva.** This family-run hotel is a conversion of eight 15th-
Lodging century buildings. While the original part of the hotel is decorated in Old Dutch style, the newer part is better equipped but has slightly less character. Many of the rooms overlook a quiet tributary of the Rhine. The restaurant caters to most tastes and pockets. The excellent three-course tourist menu offers vegetarian as well as meat and fish selections. A monthly menu is served with four or six courses of one's choice. Delicacies are also found on the à la carte menu. *Boommarkt 23, tel. 071/126358, fax 071/142674. 40 rooms, 30 with bath or shower. Facilities: restaurant. AE, DC, MC, V. $*

Lodging **Hotel De Doelen.** This small hotel is situated in a characteristic patrician house. The spartan decor is in keeping with the character of the 15th-century house, but the rooms are comfortable and much sought after. *Rapenburg 2, tel. 071/120527, fax 071/128453. 16 rooms with bath or shower. AE, DC, MC, V. $*

Utrecht **Polman's** With its lofty ceilings and early 20th-century fixtures,
Dining Polman's has been a grand café since long before *grande cafés* became the rage in Holland. The Art Deco decor is part of the joy of eating here. By choosing carefully from the menu, it is possible to limit the damage to your pocketbook. *Keistraat 2, tel. 030/313368. No credit cards. $$*

Town Castle Oudaen/"Between Heaven and Earth." In medieval times Utrecht's Oudegracht (Old Canal) was lined with many "town castles" such as this one, and some would say that along with the Domtoren, this is one of the finest examples of medieval architecture in Utrecht. You may be confused by the clublike atmosphere as you enter, but you'll find the dining room on the second floor (which may be why it is called "Between Heaven and Earth"). Another unique feature is that the owners brew their own beer in the basement and, in addition to serving it on tap, uses it as an ingredient in many of their dishes. *Oudegracht 99, tel. 030/311864. Reservations accepted. AE, DC, MC, V. No lunch (except café). $$*

★ **De Soepterrine.** This snug restaurant offers steaming bowls of homemade soup. Some 10 different varieties are made daily, usually including Dutch specialties such as thick *erwtensoep* (pea soup with sausages). Each bowl comes with crusty bread and herb butter. Quiches and generous salads fill up those extra corners. *Zakkendragerssteeg 40, tel. 030/317005. AE, MC, V. ¢*

Lodging **Malie.** The Malie hotel is on a quiet leafy street, a 15-minute walk from the old center. This small, friendly hotel has an attractive breakfast room overlooking the garden and terrace. *Maliestraat 2–4, tel. 030/316424, fax 030/340661. 29 rooms with bath or shower. Facilities: bar, breakfast room. AE, DC, MC, V. $$*

Hotel Ouwi. A friendly host is often the secret of an enjoyable visit to a city. You will find one here, along with a convenient neighborhood location just off a main bus route to the town center. The rooms are tidy and, while they vary in size, all are fairly roomy. *F. C. Dondersstraat 12, tel. 030/716303, fax 030/714619. 18 rooms with bath. No credit cards. ¢*

The Hague, Delft, and Rotterdam

Within this itinerary you can visit the Netherlands' most dignified and spacious city—the royal, diplomatic, and governmental seat of Den Haag (in English, The Hague)—and its close neighbor, the leading North Sea beach resort of Scheveningen. Also nearby are Delft, a historic city with many canals and ancient buildings, and the energetic and thoroughly modern international port city of Rotterdam, which is known to the Dutch as "Manhattan on the Maas," both for its office towers and its cultural attractions.

Getting Around

The Hague and Delft are each about 60 kilometers (37½ miles) southwest of Amsterdam and can be reached within less than an hour by fast and frequent trains. The heart of both towns is compact enough to be explored on foot. Scheveningen is reached from The Hague's center by bus or tram. Travelers will find public transportation more convenient than driving because of severe parking problems at the resort. The RET Metro is an easy-to-use option for getting around Rotterdam. There are two main branches (north–south and east–west), and they cross in the heart of the business district at a major transfer center, which connects one line to the other.

Tourist Information

Delft (Markt 85, tel. 015/126100).
The Hague (Babylon Center, Koningin Julianaplein 30, next to the central station, tel. 06/34035051).
Rotterdam (Coolsingel 67, in Centraal Station, tel. 06/34034065).
Scheveningen (Gevers Deynootweg 1134, tel. 06/34035051).

If you're planning to spend a few days in The Hague or Rotterdam, ask for the VVV brochure on city events and entertainment. Tickets for concerts and other entertainment can be reserved in person at the VVV tourist office.

Exploring The Hague, Delft, and Rotterdam

The Hague During the 17th century, when Dutch maritime power was at its zenith, **The Hague** was known as "The Whispering Gallery of Europe" because it was thought to be the secret manipulator of European politics. Although the Golden Age is over, The Hague remains a powerful world diplomatic capital, quietly boastful of its royal connections. It also is the seat of government for the Netherlands.

Its heart is the **Hofvijver** reflecting pool and the complex of gracious **Parliament Buildings** reflected in it. At the center of it all is the **Ridderzaal** (Knight's Hall). Inside are vast beams spanning a width of 18 meters (59 feet), flags, and stained-glass windows. A sense of history pervades the 13th-century great hall. It is now used mainly for ceremonies: Every year the queen's gilded coach brings her here to open Parliament. The two government chambers sit separately in buildings on either side of the Ridderzaal and can be visited by guided tour only when Parliament is not in session. Tours in English are conducted by Stichting Bezoekerscentrum Binnenhof, located just to the right of the Ridderzaal. Groups should book in advance. *Binnenhof 8a, tel. 070/3646144 (for tours; reservations required). Admission: tour Fl. 5.50, Parliament exhibition free. Open Mon.–Sat. 10–4.*

On the far side of the **Binnenhof,** the inner court of the Parliament complex, is a small, well-proportioned Dutch Renaissance building called the **Mauritshuis,** one of the finest small art museums in the world. This diminutive 17th-century palace contains a feast of art from the same period, including six Rembrandts; of these the most powerful is *The Anatomy Lesson of Dr. Tulp*, a theatrical work depicting a gruesome dissection of the lower arm. Also featured are Vermeer's celebrated *Girl Wearing a Turban* and his masterpiece, the glistening *View of Delft*, moodily emerging from a cloudburst. *Korte Vijverberg 8, tel. 070/3469244. Admission: Fl. 10. Open Tues.–Sat. 10–5, Sun. 11–5.*

The **Vredespaleis** (Peace Palace), near Laan van Meerdervoort, just to the northwest of the city center is a monument to world peace through negotiation. Following the first peace conference at The Hague in 1899, the Scottish American millionaire Andrew Carnegie donated $1.5 million for the construction of a building to house a proposed international court. The Dutch government donated the grounds, and other nations offered furnishings and decorations. Although it still looks like a dull multinational bank, the building has been improved by such gifts as Japanese wall hangings, a Danish fountain, and a grand staircase presented by The Hague. Today the **International Court of Justice,** consisting of 15 jurists, has its seat here. There are guided tours when the court is not in session. *Carnegieplein 2, tel. 070/3469680. Admission: Fl. 5. Open June–*

What to do when your *money* is done traveling before you are.

Don't worry. With **MoneyGram**,^{SM} your parents can send you money in usually 10 minutes or less to more than 19,000 locations in 80 countries. So if the money you need to see history becomes history, call us and we'll direct you to a **MoneyGram**^{SM} agent closest to you.

USA: **1-800-MONEYGRAM**
Germany: **0130-8-16629**

Canada: **1-800-933-3278**
England: **0800-89-7198**

France: **05-905311**
Spain: **900-96-1218**

or call collect **303-980-3340**

All the best trips start with **Fodor's**.

EXPLORING GUIDES

At last, the color of an art book combined with the usefulness of a complete guide.

"As stylish and attractive as any guide published." —*The New York Times*

"Worth reading before, during, and after a trip." —*The Philadelphia Inquirer*

More than 30 destinations available worldwide. $19.95 each.

BERKELEY GUIDES

The budget traveler's handbook

"Berkeley's scribes put the funk back in travel."
—*Time*

"Fresh, funny, and funky as well as useful."
—*The Boston Globe*

"Well-organized, clear and very easy to read."
—*America Online*

14 destinations worldwide. Priced between $13.00 - $19.50. ($17.95 - $27.00 Canada)

AFFORDABLES

"All the maps and itinerary ideas of Fodor's established gold guides with a bonus—shortcuts to savings." —*USA Today*

"Travelers with champagne tastes and beer budgets will welcome this series from Fodor's." —*Hartfort Courant*

"It's obvious these Fodor's folk have secrets we civilians don't." —*New York Daily News*

Also available: Florida, Europe, France, London, Paris. Priced between $11.00 - $18.00 ($14.50 - $24.00 Canada)

At bookstores, or call **1-800-533-6478**

Fodor's
The name that means smart travel.™

Sept., weekdays 10–4; Oct.–May, weekdays 10–3. Guided tours at 10, 11, 12, 3, and 4.

The nearby **Haags Gemeentemuseum** (Municipal Art Museum) is the home of the largest collection of Mondrians in the world, plus two vast collections of musical instruments—European and nonEuropean. The building itself is also fascinating. It was built in 1935 and is an example of the International Movement in modern architecture. *Stadhouderslaan 41, tel. 070/3512873. Admission: Fl. 8. Open Tues.–Sun. 11–5.*

Scheveningen is adjacent to The Hague along the North Sea coast. A fishing village since the 14th century, it became popular as a beach resort during the last century, when the grand **Kurhaus Hotel,** still a focal point of this beach community, was built. The beach itself, protected from tidal erosion by stone jetties, slopes gently into the North Sea in front of a high promenade whose function is to protect the boulevard and everything behind it from winter storms. The surface of the beach is fine sand, and you can bicycle or walk for miles to the north.

Part of the new design around the Kurhaus area includes the Golfbad, a surf pool complete with artificial waves. **The Pier,** completed in 1962, stretches 372 meters (1,200 feet) into the sea. Its four circular end buildings provide a sun terrace and restaurant, a 43-meter- (141-foot-) high observation tower, an amusement center with children's play area, and an underwater panorama. At 11 on summer evenings, the Pier is the scene of dramatic fireworks displays.

A newcomer to the beachfront is the **Sea Life Center,** an ingeniously designed aquarium complex that includes a transparent underwater tunnel. You walk through it as if you were on the sea floor, with sharks, rays, eels, and octopuses swimming inches above your head. *Strandweg 13, tel. 070/3542100. Admission: Fl. 13.50 adults, Fl. 8.50 children. Open Sept.–June, daily 10–6; July–Aug., daily 10–9.*

Delft Thirteen kilometers (8 miles) along the A13 from The Hague, you'll enter **Delft.** There is probably no town in the Netherlands that is more intimate, more attractive, or more traditional than this minimetropolis, whose famous blue-and-white earthenware is popular throughout the world. Compact and easy to explore, despite its web of canals, Delft is best discovered on foot—although canal boat excursions are available April through October, as are horse-drawn trams that leave from the marketplace.

In the marketplace, the only lively spot in this tranquil town, is the **Nieuwe Kerk** (New Church), built during the 14th century, with its piercing Gothic spire 108.5 meters (350 feet) high, a magnificent carillon of 48 bells, and the tomb of Prince William the Silent. Beneath this grotesque black marble sarcophagus is a crypt containing the remains of members of the Orange-Nassau line, including all members of the royal family since King William I ascended the throne during the mid-16th century. *Admission: Fl. 2.50. Tower: Fl. 2.50. Open Apr.–Oct., Mon.–Sat. 9–6; Nov.–Mar., Mon.–Sat. 11–4.*

Walk around the right side of the Nieuwe Kerk, then left at the back and along the Vrouwenregt canal for a few steps before taking another left turn into Voldersgracht. To the left, the backs of the houses rise straight from the water as you stroll to the end of the street, which is marked by the sculptured animal heads and outdoor stairs of the old **Meat Market** on the right. Cross the Wijnhaven and turn left along its far side to the Koornmarkt, a stately canal spanned by a high, arching bridge that is one of the hallmarks of Delft.

Turn right at the Peperstraat to reach the **Oude Delft,** the city's oldest waterway. A few blocks farther along the canal is the **Prinsenhof,** formerly the Convent of St. Agatha, founded in 1400. The chapel inside dates from 1471; its interior is remarkable for the wooden statues under the vaulting ribs. Today the Prinsenhof is a museum that tells the story of the liberation of the Netherlands after 80 years of Spanish occupation (1568–1648). For Dutch royalists, the spot is significant for the assassination of Prince William of Orange in 1584; the bullet holes can still be seen in the wall. *St. Agathaplein 1. Admission: Fl. 5. Open Tues.–Sat. 10–5, Sun. 1–5.*

Across the Oude Delft canal is the **Oude Kerk** (Old Church), a vast Gothic monument of the 13th century. Its beautiful tower, surmounted by a brick spire, leans somewhat alarmingly. *Heilige Geest Kerkhof, tel. 015/123015. Admission: Fl. 2.50. Open Apr.–Oct., Mon.–Sat. 10–5.*

While in Delft, you will want to see the famous local specialty— delftware. Decorated porcelain was brought to Holland from China on East India Company ships and was so much in demand that Dutch potters felt their livelihood was being threatened. They therefore set about creating pottery to rival Chinese porcelain. There are only two manufacturers that still make hand-painted delftware: **De Delftse Pauw** and the more famous "Royal" **De Porceleyne Fles.** *De Delftse Pauw: Delftweg 133, tel. 015/124920. Admission free. Open Apr.–mid–Oct., daily 9–4; mid–Oct.–Mar., weekdays 9–4, weekends 11–1. De Porceleyne Fles: Rotterdamsweg 196, tel. 015/560234. Admission: 2.50. Open Apr.–Oct., Mon.–Sat. 9–5, Sun. 10–4; Nov.–Mar., weekdays 9–5, Sat. 10–4.*

Rotterdam Thirteen kilometers (8 miles) farther along A13 is **Rotterdam,** one of the few thoroughly modern cities in the Netherlands and the site of the world's largest and busiest port. Art lovers know Rotterdam for its extensive and outstanding collection of art; philosophers recall it as the city of Erasmus. It is a major stop on the rock-and-roll concert circuit, and its soccer team is well known, but the city's main claim to fame is its extraordinary concentration of adventurous modern architecture.

The biggest surprise in Rotterdam is the remarkable 30-mile-long **Europoort,** which handles more than 250 million tons of cargo every year and more ships than any other port in the world. It is the delta for three of Europe's most important rivers (the Rhine, the Waal, and the Meuse/Maas) and a seemingly endless corridor of piers, warehouses, tank facilities, and efficiency. You can get to the piers at Willemsplein by tram or Metro (blue line to the Leuvehaven station) from the central station. A 1¼-hour harbor tour illuminates Rotterdam's vital role in world trade.

As an alternative to the boat tour, you also can survey the harbor from the vantage point of the **Euromast** observation tower. Get there via the metro red line to Dijkszicht. *Parkhaven 20, tel. 010/4364811. Admission: Fl. 14.50. Open Apr.–June and Sept., daily 10–7; July–Aug., Sun. and Mon. 10–7, Tues.–Sat. 10 AM–10:30 PM; Oct.–Mar., daily 10–5.*

After the harbor tour, walk down the boulevard past the metro station into Leuvehaven. On your right as you stroll along the inner harbor is **IMAX Rotterdam,** a gigantic theater in which films are projected onto a screen six stories high. There are earphones for English translation. *Leuvehaven 77, tel. 010/4048844. Admission: Fl. 15. Shows Tues.–Sun. 2, 3, 4, 5:45; Mon. also during holiday periods. Non-IMAX films (from the regular commercial circuit) shown daily 7:45 PM and 9:30 PM.*

Past the theater is a hodgepodge of cranes, barges, steamships, and old shipbuilding machines, even a steam-operated grain elevator.

What looks at quick glance to be a sort of maritime junkyard is in fact a work in progress: Volunteers are working daily to restore these vessels and machines. The whole operation is an open-air museum of shipbuilding, shipping, and communications that is part of the **Prins Hendrick Maritime Museum,** housed in a large gray building at the head of the quay. Also moored in this inner harbor adjacent to the museum is the historic 19th-century Royal Dutch Navy warship *De Buffel*. Within the museum are exhibits devoted to the history and activity of the great port outside. *Leuvehaven 1, tel. 010/4132680. Admission: Fl. 6. Open Tues.–Sat. 10–5, Sun. 11–5.*

From the nearby Churchillplein Metro station, take the red line toward Marconiplein to the first stop at Eendrachtsplein, where you will walk along the canal toward the park. As a welcome contrast to the industrial might of the Europoort and Holland's maritime history, the **Boymans–van Beuningen Museum** is an impressive refresher course in Western European art history. The collection includes paintings by many famous master painters, Dutch and otherwise, from the 14th century to the present day. There is an Old Arts section that includes the work of Brueghel, Bosch, and Rembrandt and a renowned print gallery with works by artists as varied as Dürer and Cézanne. Dali and Magritte mix with the Impressionists in the Modern Arts collection. *Mathenesserlaan 18–20, tel. 010/4419400. Admission: Fl. 7.50. Open Tues.–Sat. 10–5, Sun. 11–5.*

Beside this long-established museum is the **Nederlands Architectuurinstituut,** which houses changing exhibitions in the fields of architecture and design. Across the park is the recently built **Kunsthal,** which hosts all manner of major temporary exhibitions—from Andy Warhol retrospectives to rows of compact cars. *Nederlands Architectuurinstituut, Museumpark 25, tel. 010/ 4401200. Admission: 7.50. Open Tues.–Sat. 10–5, Sun. 11–5. Kunsthal, Westzeedijk 341, tel. 010/4400300. Admission: Fl. 10. Open Tues.–Sat. 10–5, Sun 11–5.*

Dining and Lodging

For details and price-category definitions, *see* Dining and Lodging in Staying in Holland, *above*.

Delft
Dining

Spijshuis De Dis. A favorite of the locals, this restaurant has a friendly staff who serve a host of typically Dutch delicacies. Seafood is a house specialty. The mussels with garlic sauce are delicious, and you can also get such delicacies as roast quail. A couple of set menus enable you to eat very reasonably indeed. *Beestenmarket 36, tel. 015/131782. Reservations recommended. AE, MC, V. $–$$*

Lodging

Hotel Leeuwenbrug. This traditional Dutch family-style hotel is on one of the prettiest canals in Delft. There are two buildings, one of which is simpler, with smaller, cheaper rooms; the annex is more contemporary and businesslike. Everyone enjoys breakfast overlooking the canal, however, and the rooms on the top floor of the annex overlook the city. *Koornmarkt 16, tel. 015/147741, fax 015/ 159759. 38 rooms with bath. AE, MC, V. $$*

Hotel De Kok. Conveniently near the railway station, this tidy little hotel is cozy and inviting. The rooms are spacious and bright and offer the sort of amenities you'd expect in a much larger hotel. There's a family-style lounge and, in summer, a garden terrace for guests. *Houttuinen 15, tel. and fax 015/122125. 14 rooms with shower. AE, DC, MC, V. $*

Dining and
Lodging
★

Hotel de Plataan. Converted in 1994 from a rather grand old post office building, Hotel de Plataan was decorated by a local artist in 1950s-style cream and green. The Moonlight Bridal Suite has a waterbed, bedside whirlpool bath, and murals inspired by fertility symbols. Most rooms have a kitchen nook where you can prepare your own breakfast. You can also take meals downstairs in Het Establissement, an excellent restaurant with meaty casseroles as well as imaginative vegetarian dishes. *Verwersdijk 48a, tel. 015/ 126046, fax 015/157327. 26 rooms with bath or shower. Facilities: restaurant (tel. 015/121687). AE, DC, MC, V. $*

Les Compagnons/Den Dulk. With three locations within a block of each other, this is a true family affair: The children operate the small, comfortable hotel on the market square; their father runs the small neighboring brasserie. You can't beat the location, directly on the historic market square. The rooms are bright and spiffy, and guests are given a discount for dinner at Dad's restaurant, which faces a canal and offers such temptations as cranberry pâté with Cumberland sauce. *Markt 61–65/Voldersgracht 17–18, tel. 015/ 140102, fax 015/120168. 16 rooms with bath. No lunch. AE, DC, MC, V. ¢–$*

The Hague
Dining

't Goude Hooft. The foundations of the building on the old vegetable market square date from the early 15th century, and town records show that ever since the 14th century there has been a tavern of essentially the same name on the very same spot. When the restaurant's promotions say that The Hague was built around it, it can be taken as truth. As may be expected, the ambience is totally Old Dutch; the menu, too, is traditional. There is a grand terrace café on the square in the summer months. *Groenmarkt 13, tel. 070/3469713. Reservations accepted. AE, DC, MC, V. $–$$*

Dining and Lodging

Hotel City. This small hotel a few minutes' walk from the Scheviningen beach has a sparkle and brightness that can be attributed as much to its cheerful owners as to its seaside-town location. The hotel is divided among several buildings, and the small restaurant has a bar and a sidewalk terrace. *Renbaanstraat 1–3/17–23, tel. 070/3557966, fax 070/3540503. 22 rooms with bath. Facilities: restaurant. AE, DC, MC, V. $*

Lodging

Hotel Petit. Not far from the Peace Palace and the Gemeentemuseum, this tidy little family hotel has spacious, bright, and attractive rooms equipped with tub and shower. *Groot Hertoginnelaan 42, tel. 070/3465500, fax 070/3463257. 20 rooms with bath or shower. Facilities: parking. AE, DC, MC, V. $$*

Rotterdam
Dining

Inn The Picture. Overlooking a large square, this trendy café offers a wide selection of typical Dutch fare. The salads are especially inviting. In the summer, tables offer a view of the passing crowds in the shopping district. *Karel Doormanstraat 294, tel. 010/4133204. AE, DC, MC, V. $$*

Zocher's. Resplendent beside a lake in the city's Maas Park, this airy 19th-century building has one of the most attractive positions—and the sunniest terrace—in town. In one wing, an expensive restaurant serves such dishes as guinea-fowl stuffed with salmon. In the café on the other side of the building, the same kitchen serves inexpensive, lighter meals. On Sundays the restaurant live classical music over breakfast. *Baden-Powelllaan 12, tel. 010/4364249. AE, MC, DC, V. Café $.*

Dining and Lodging

Hotel New York. For more than 90 years the twin towers of the Hotel New York have been a feature of Rotterdam's skyline. Before 1993, though, the building was the headquarters of the Holland-America Line. Today some rooms retain the original walnut paneling and Art Nouveau carpets, while others are modern in design and are hung with works by contemporary artists. Most have a veiw of the river and harbor. Downstairs, the huge café-restaurant (it seats 400) offers everything from English afternoon tea to a selection of five different types of oyster at the Oyster Bar; judicious selections can keep the price down. The hotel is 15 minutes' walk from the Rijnhaven metro station, or you can take one of the hotel's water taxis direct from Veerhaven or Leuvehaven. *Koninginnenhoofd 1,* tel. 010/4390500, fax 010/4842701. 73 rooms with bath. Facilities: restaurant, fitness room, meeting rooms. AE, MC, DC, V. $$

Lodging **Hotel van Walsum.** With typically Dutch regularity, the gregarious owner of this small hotel redecorates and refurbishes his rooms. Everything from the bath tiles to the bedspreads is redone in whatever that year's colors and textures happen to be. *Mathenessarlaan 199–201, tel. 010/4363275, fax 010/4364410. 26 rooms with bath. Facilities: restaurant, café. AE, DC, MC, V. $*

13 Hungary

Even under the reformist but now discredited communist regime, Hungary's stores were full of food and the latest fashions, and Hungarians enjoyed what they called "the happiest barracks in the bloc." Today, as the nation rebuilds in the spirit of freedom, comfortable accommodations, pleasant restaurants, and attractive shops are more plentiful than ever—and most prices still remain below Western European levels.

Nonetheless, Hungary's rush to modernize has not obliterated evidence of its past. Amenities are relatively modern, but the abundant Hapsburg architecture creates an aura of faded charm. Walk through the quiet back streets of Budapest on a foggy autumn morning or survey the majestic Danube from the city's Castle Hill on a summer day, and you'll quickly sense the sweep of Hungary's tumultuous history at the crossroads of Central Europe.

Hungarians struggled against foreign occupation for centuries: the Turks in the 17th century, the Hapsburgs in 1848, and the Soviet Union in 1956. Now at last, with the fall of the Iron Curtain, Hungarians once again control their own destinies.

Because Hungary is a small, agriculturally oriented country, visitors are often surprised by its grandeur and Old World charm, especially in the capital, Budapest, which bustles with life as never before. Hungarians like to complain about their economic problems, but they spare visitors bureaucratic hassles at the border and airport. Entry is easy and quick for westerners, most of whom no longer need visas. Gone are the days when visitors were forced to make daily currency exchanges and to register with local police on arrival.

Two rivers cross the country. The famous Duna (Danube) flows from the west through Budapest on its way to the southern frontier, while the smaller Tisza flows from the northeast across the Nagyalföld (Great Plain). What Hungary lacks in size, it makes up for in beauty and charm. Western Hungary is dominated by the largest lake in Central Europe, Lake Balaton. Although some overdevelopment has blighted its splendor, its shores are still lined with Baroque villages, relaxing spas, magnificent vineyards, and shaded

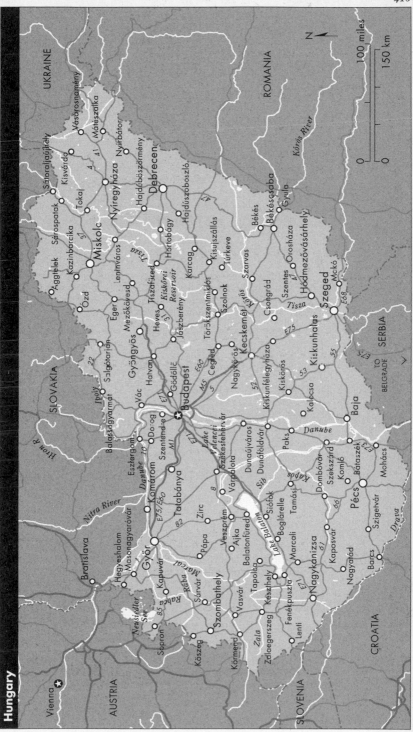

Hungary

garden restaurants serving the catch of the day. In eastern Hungary, the Nagyalföld offers visitors a chance to explore the folklore and customs of the Magyars (the Hungarians' name for themselves and their language). It is an area of spicy food, strong wine, and the proud *csikós* (horsemen). The unspoiled towns of the provincial areas are rich in history and culture.

Hungarians are known for their hospitality and love of talking to foreigners, although their strange language, which has no links to other European tongues, can be a problem. Today, however, everyone seems to be learning English, especially young people. Trying out a few words of German will delight the older generation. But what all Hungarians share is a deep love of music, and the calendar is star-studded with it, from Budapest's famous opera to its annual spring music festival and the serenades of gypsy violinists during evening meals.

Essential Information

Before You Go

When to Go Many of Hungary's major fairs and festivals take place in the spring and fall. During July and August, Budapest can be hot and the resorts at Lake Balaton crowded, so spring (May) and the end of summer (September) are the ideal times to visit.

Climate The following are average daily maximum and minimum temperatures for Budapest.

Jan.	34F	1C	May	72F	22C	Sept.	73F	23C
	25	- 4		52	11		54	12
Feb.	39F	4C	June	79F	26C	Oct.	61F	16C
	28	- 2		59	15		45	7
Mar.	50F	10C	July	82F	28C	Nov.	46F	8C
	36	2		61	16		37	3
Apr.	63F	17C	Aug.	81F	27C	Dec.	39F	4C
	45	7		61	16		30	- 1

Currency The unit of currency is the forint (Ft.), divided into 100 fillérs (f.). There are bills of 50, 100, 500, 1,000, and 5,000 forints and coins of 1, 2, 5, 10, and 20 forints and 10, 20, and 50 fillérs. A newly designed series of the coins—including new but rare 100- and 200-forint pieces—was introduced into the system in late 1993, precipitating mild confusion and general frustration with pay phones and other coin-operated machines that still accept only the old coins. Until the old coins are phased out entirely, it helps to know that *új* means "new" and *régi* means "old." The tourist exchange rate was approximately 149 to the dollar and 168 to the pound sterling at press time (summer 1995). Note that official exchange rates are adjusted at frequent intervals.

Hungary does not require you to change a certain sum of money for each day of your stay. Exchange money as you need it at banks, hotels, or travel offices, but take care not to change too much, because although in theory you can change back 50% of the original sum when you leave (up to U.S. $100), it may prove difficult in practice—at least until the forint becomes convertible.

Most credit cards are accepted, though don't rely on them in smaller towns or less expensive accommodations and restaurants. Eurocheque holders can cash personal checks in all banks and in most hotels. American Express has a full-service office in Budapest (V, Deák Ferenc utca 10, tel. 1/266–8680, 1/267–2024, or 1/267–2022; fax 1/267–2029), which also dispenses cash to its cardholders.

There is still a black market in hard currency, but changing money on the street is illegal and the bank rate almost always comes close. Stick with official exchange offices.

What It Will Cost Rates in Budapest's good-quality hotels are modest by Western standards. Even though the value-added tax (VAT) increases many of the prices in the service industry by up to 25%, and the annual inflation rate is more than 25%, enjoyable vacations with all the trimmings remain less expensive than in nearby Western cities like Vienna.

Sample Prices Cup of coffee, 60 Ft.; bottle of beer, 100 Ft.–120 Ft.; soft drinks, 20 Ft.–50 Ft.; ham sandwich, 100 Ft.; 1-mile taxi ride, 75 Ft.; museum admission, 50 Ft.–100 Ft.

Visas Only a valid passport is required of U.S., British, and Canadian citizens. For additional information, contact the Hungarian Embassy in the United States (3910 Shoemaker St., NW, Washington, DC 20008, tel. 202/362–6730) or Canada (7 Delaware Ave., Ottawa KP2 OZ2, Ontario, tel. 613/234–8316), or the Hungarian Consulate in London (35b Eaton Pl., London SW1 8BY, tel. 0171/235–2664).

Customs Objects for personal use may be imported freely. If you are over 16,
On Arrival you may also bring in 250 grams of tobacco, plus 2 liters of wine, 1 liter of spirits, and 250 grams of perfume. A customs charge is made on gifts valued in Hungary at more than 8,000 Ft.

On Departure Take care when you leave Hungary that you have the right documentation for exporting goods. Keep receipts of any items bought from Konsumtourist, Intertourist, or Képcsarnok Vállalat. A special permit is needed for works of art, antiques, or objects of museum value. You are entitled to a VAT refund on new goods (i.e., not works of art, antiques, or objects of museum value) valued at more than 25,000 Ft., including VAT. But pursuing it may rack up more frustration than money: Cash refunds are given only in forints, and you may find yourself in the airport minutes before boarding time with a handful of soft currency, of which no more than 1,000 forints may be taken out of the country. For more information., pick up a tax refund brochure from any tourist office or hotel, or contact **Intel Trade Rt.** (I Budapest, Csalogány u. 6–10, tel. 1/156–9800), or the **National Customs and Revenue Office** (VIII Budapest, Keleti train station arrivals area, tel. 1/114–0203 or 1/114–0280). If you have trouble communicating, ask Tourinform (tel. 1/117–9800) for some help.

Language Hungarian (Magyar) tends to look and sound intimidating to everyone at first because it is a non–Indo-European language. However, most people in the tourist trade, from bus drivers to waiters, speak some English or German.

Getting Around

By Train Travel by train from Budapest to other large cities or to Lake Balaton is cheap and efficient. Remember to take a *gyorsvonat* (express train) and not a *személyvonat* (local), which is extremely slow. A *helyjegy* (seat reservation), which costs about 45 Ft. (160 Ft. for intercity trains) and is sold up to 60 days in advance, is advisable for all express trains, especially for weekend travel in summer. It is also worth paying a little extra for first-class tickets.

Fares Only Hungarian citizens are entitled to student and senior citizen discounts. InterRail cards are available for those under 26, and the Rail Europe Senior Travel Pass entitles senior citizens to a 30% reduction on all trains. Snacks and drinks can be purchased on all express trains, but the supply often runs out, especially in summer, so pack a lunch just in case. For more rail travel information, contact the **MÁV Passenger Service** (Budapest VI, Andrássy út 35, tel. 1/ 322–8049 or 1/322–8275).

By Bus Long-distance buses link Budapest with many cities in Eastern and Western Europe. Services to the eastern part of the country leave from Népstadion station (tel. 1/252–0696). Buses to the west and south leave from the main Volán bus station at Erzsébet tér in the Inner City (tel. 1/118–2122). Although inexpensive, they tend to be crowded, so reserve your seat.

By Boat Hungary is well equipped with nautical transport, and Budapest is situated on a major international waterway—the Danube. Vienna is five hours away by hydrofoil, and many Hungarian resorts are accessible by hydrofoil or boat. For information about excursions or pleasure cruises, contact **MAHART Tours** (Budapest V, Belgrád rakpart, tel. 1/118–1704, 1/118–1586, or 1/118–1743) or **IBUSZ** (Hungarian Travel Bureau; Budapest VII, Károly körút 3/C, tel. 1/ 321–1000 or 1/321–2932).

By Bicycle A land of rolling hills and flat plains, Hungary lends itself to bicycling. A few of the larger train stations around Lake Balaton rent bicycles (in various states of repair) for about 200 Ft. a day, but the sad truth is that insurance difficulties have led to a serious, nationwide dearth of bicycle rental outlets. For the latest information about renting in Budapest, contact **Tourinform** (V, Sütő utca 2, tel. 1/117–9800). **IBUSZ Riding and Hobbies** department provides a variety of guided bicycle tours (Budapest V, Ferenciek tere 10, tel. 1/ 118–2967).

Staying in Hungary

Telephones Pay phones use 5-Ft. coins—the cost of a three-minute local call—
Local Calls and also accept 10- and 20-Ft. coins. At press time (spring 1995), pay phones had still not been converted to accept Hungary's new coins. Most towns in Hungary can be dialed directly—dial 06 and wait for the buzzing tone, then dial the local number. It is unnecessary to use the city code, 1, when dialing within Budapest. Gray card-operated telephones now outnumber coin-operated phones in Budapest and throughout the Balaton region. The cards—available at post offices and most newsstands and kiosks—come in units of 50 (250 Ft.) and 200 (600 Ft.) calls.

International Direct calls to foreign countries can be made from Budapest and all
Calls major provincial towns by dialing 00 and waiting for the international dialing tone; on pay phones, the initial charge is 20 Ft. To reach an **AT&T** long-distance operator, dial 00–800–01111; for **MCI,** dial 00–800–01411; for **Sprint,** dial 00–800–01877.

Operators International calls can be made through the operator by dialing 09; for operator-assisted calls within Hungary, dial 01. Be patient: The telephone system is antiquated, especially in the countryside.

Country Code The country code for Hungary is 36.

Information Dial 1/117–0170 for directory assistance. Some operators speak English and, depending on their mood, may assist you in English.

Mail The post offices at the Keleti (East) and Nyugati (West) train stations are open 24 hours.

Postal Rates An airmail postcard to the United States, the United Kingdom, and the rest of Western Europe costs 47 Ft., and an airmail letter costs from 67 Ft. Postcards to the United Kingdom and the rest of Western Europe cost 40 Ft., letters 60 Ft.

Receiving Mail A poste restante service, for general delivery, is available in Budapest. The address is Magyar Posta, H-1052 Budapest, Petőfi Sándor utca 17–19.

Opening and Closing Times

Banks are generally open weekdays 8–4; many close at noon on Fridays.

Museums. Most are open daily from 10 to 6 and are closed on Mondays.

Department stores are open weekdays 10–5 or 6, Saturday until 1. **Grocery stores** are generally open weekdays 7 or 8–7 and Saturday until 1; "nonstops" or *éjjeli-nappali* are open 24 hours.

National Holidays

In 1996: January 1, March 15 (Anniversary of 1848 Revolution), April 7 and 8 (Easter and Easter Monday); May 1 (Labor Day), June 26 and 27 (Pentecost), August 20 (St. Stephen's and Constitution Day), October 23 (1956 Revolution Day), December 25 and 26. Changing holidays in 1997: March 30 and 31 (Easter and Easter Monday); May 18 and 19 (Pentecost).

Dining

There are plenty of good, affordably priced restaurants offering a variety of Hungarian dishes. Meats, rich sauces, and creamy desserts predominate, but salads can be found, even out of season. There are self-service restaurants *(önkiszolgáló étterem)*, snack bars *(bistró* or *étel bár)*, buffets *(büfé)*, cafés *(eszpresszó)*, and bars *(drink-bár)*. The pastry shops *(cukrászda)* should not be missed.

In almost all restaurants, an inexpensive fixed-price lunch, called a *menü*, is available. It costs as little as 350 Ft. and includes soup or salad, an entrée, and a dessert.

What to Wear

A jacket is recommended in more expensive restaurants; otherwise casual dress is acceptable.

Mealtimes

Hungarians eat early—you risk off-hand service and cold food after 9 PM. Lunch, the main meal for many, is served from noon to 2.

Ratings

Prices are per person and include a first course, main course, and dessert, but no wine or tip. Prices in Budapest tend to be a good 30% higher than elsewhere in Hungary. Best bets are indicated by a star ★.

Category	Cost
$$	800 Ft.–1,200 Ft.
$	500 Ft.–800 Ft.
¢	under 500 Ft.

Lodging

Hotels

There are few expensive hotels outside Budapest, but the moderately priced hotels are generally comfortable and well run. An increasing number of inexpensive establishments—more numerous every year as Hungarians convert unused rooms or second apartments into rental units for tourists—have private baths, but even those that don't, usually have adequate plumbing.

Rentals

Apartments in Budapest and cottages at Lake Balaton are available for short- and long-term rental, and can often make the most economic lodging option for families—particularly for those who prefer to cook their own meals. Rates and reservations can be obtained from tourist offices in Hungary and abroad. A Budapest apartment may cost 5,000 Ft. a day and a luxury cottage for two on Lake Balaton costs around the same. Bookings can be made in Budapest at the IBUSZ on Petőfi tér 3 (tel. 1/118–5707 or 1/118–4842), which is open 24 hours a day, or through IBUSZ offices in the United States and Great Britain. (*See* Visitor Information *in* Chapter 1, The Gold Guide.) Some enterprising locals stand outside the IBUSZ office and offer tourists their apartments for lower rates, and are usually willing to bargain. If you choose this route, insist on seeing the place before you hand over any cash. Ask for a written agreement, and be sure to get the owner's contact telephone number and address should anything go wrong. Other rental agencies in Budapest include **Cooptourist** (I, Attila u. 107, tel. 1/175–2846 or 1/175–2937) and **Charles Apartments** (I, Hegyalja út 23, tel. 1/201–1796 or 1/212–3830).

Guest Houses   Also called pensions, these offer simple accommodations—well suited to young people on a budget. Many offer simple breakfast facilities. Arrangements can be made through local tourist offices or travel agents abroad.

In the provinces it is safe to accept rooms that you are offered directly: They will almost always be clean and in a relatively good neighborhood, and the prospective landlord will probably not cheat you. *Szoba kiadó* (or the German *Zimmer frei*) means "Room to Rent." The rate per night for a double room in Budapest or at Lake Balaton is around 1,500–2,000 Ft., which includes the use of a bathroom and sometimes breakfast. Reservations and referrals can also be made by any tourist office, and if you go that route, you have someone to complain to if things don't work out.

Camping   The 140 campsites in Hungary are open from May through September. As rates are no longer state-regulated, prices vary. An average is around 650 Ft. a day. There's usually a small charge for hot water and electricity plus an accommodations fee—around 100 Ft. per person per night. Children often get a 50% reduction. Camping is forbidden except in appointed areas. Information can be obtained through travel agencies or through the **Hungarian Camping and Caravanning Club** (Budapest VIII, Üllői út 6, tel. 1/133–6536), which publishes an informative brochure listing campsites and their facilities in English.

Ratings   The following price categories are in forints for a double room with bath and breakfast during the peak season (June through August); rates are even lower off-season (in Budapest, September through March; at Lake Balaton, in May and September) and in the countryside, sometimes less than 1,500 Ft. for two. For single rooms with bath, count on about 80% of the double-room rate. Best bets are indicated by a star ★.

Category	Budapest	Balaton
$$	8,000 Ft.–11,000 Ft.	3,500 Ft.–7,000 Ft.
$	3,000 Ft.–8,000 Ft.	2,500 Ft.–3,500 Ft.
¢	1,500 Ft.–3,000 Ft.	under 2,500 Ft.

During peak season, full board may be compulsory at some of the Lake Balaton hotels.

Tipping   Four decades of socialism didn't alter the Hungarian habit of tipping generously. Cloakroom and gas-pump attendants, hairdressers, waiters, and taxi drivers all expect tips. At least 10% should be added to a restaurant bill or taxi fare. If a gypsy band plays exclusively for your table, you can leave 100 Ft. in the plate discreetly provided for that purpose.

Budapest

Arriving and Departing

By Plane   Hungary's international airport, **Ferihegy** (tel. 1/157–9123), is about 22 kilometers (14 miles) southeast of the city. All **Malév** and **Lufthansa** flights operate from the new Terminal 2; other airlines use Terminal 1. For same-day flight information, call the airport authority (tel. 1/157–7155); you can also call for general information on arrivals (tel. 1/157–8406) and departures (tel. 1/157–8768). The staff takes its time to answer calls and may not be cordial; be prepared.

Between the Minibuses to and from Erzsébet tér station (Platform 1) in down-
Airport and town Budapest leave every half hour from 5:30 AM to 9 PM. The trip
Downtown takes 30–40 minutes (longer in rush hours) and costs 250 Ft. The modern minivans of the fast, friendly, and reliable LRI Airport Shuttle service (tel. 1/157–8555 or 1/157–6283) transport you to any destination in Budapest, door to door, for 800 Ft., even less than the least expensive taxi—and most employees speak English. At the airport, buy tickets at the LRI counter in the arrivals hall near the baggage claim; for your return trip, just call ahead for a pick-up. A taxi ride with an official airport taxi to the center of Budapest may cost about 2,000 Ft. and takes about the same time. Avoid drivers who offer their services before you are out of the arrivals lounge.

By Train There are three main train stations in Budapest: Keleti (East), Nyugati (West), and Déli (South). Trains from Vienna usually operate from the Keleti station, while those to the Balaton depart from the Déli.

By Bus Most buses to Budapest from the western region of Hungary, including those from Vienna, arrive at **Erzsébet tér** station.

Getting Around

Budapest is best explored on foot. The maps provided by tourist offices are not very detailed, so arm yourself with one from any of the bookshops in Váci utca or from downtown stationery shops and newsstands.

By Public The public transportation system—a metro (subway) with three
Transportation lines, buses, streetcars, and trolleybuses—is cheap, efficient, and simple to use but closes down around 11:30 PM. However, certain trams and buses run on a limited schedule all night. A day ticket *(napijegy)* costs 200 Ft. (three-day ticket, 400 Ft.) and allows unlimited travel on all services within the city limits. You can also buy tickets for single rides for 35 Ft. from metro stations or newsstands. You can travel on all trams and buses and on the subway with this ticket, but you can't change lines.

Bus, streetcar, trolleybus, and M1 metro tickets must be canceled on board—watch how other passengers do it; other metro tickets are canceled at station entrances. Don't get caught without a ticket: Spot checks are frequent, often targeting tourists, and you can be fined several hundred forints.

By Boat In summer the Budapest Transportation Authority runs a not-so-regular boat service that links the north and south of the city, stopping at points on both banks, including Margit-sziget (Margaret Island); contact Tourinform for current schedules. From May through October boats leave from the quay at Vigadó tér on 1½-hour cruises between the Árpád and Petőfi bridges. The trip, organized by **MAHART**, runs twice a day and costs around 400 Ft. (tel. 1/118–1704).

Important Addresses and Numbers

Tourist **Tourinform** (V, Sütő utca 2, tel. 1/1179–800) is open April–October
Information daily 8–8 and November–March weekdays 8–8, weekends 8–3. **IBUSZ Accommodation Office** (V, Petőfi tér 3, tel. 1/118–5707 or 1/118–4842) is open 24 hours. **Budapest Tourist** (V, Roosevelt tér 5, tel. 1/117–3555) is also helpful. The *Budapest Sun*, an English-language weekly newspaper that covers news, business, and culture, carries general orientation tips for tourists and listings of concerts, for-

eign-language films, and other cultural offerings;it's sold at newsstands and in hotels and bookstores.

Embassies **U.S.** V, Szabadság tér 12, (tel. 1/112–6450). **Canadian** XII, Budakeszi út 32, (tel. 1/275–1200). **U.K.** V, Harmincad utca 6, (tel. 1/266–2888).

Emergencies **Police** (tel. 07). **Ambulance** (tel. 04) or call **S.O.S.** (VIII, Kerepesi út 15, tel. 1/118–8212 or 1/118–8288), a 24-hour private ambulance service with English-speaking personnel. **Doctor:** Ask your hotel or embassy for recommendations or visit the **I.M.S.** (International Medical Services: XIII, Váci út 202, tel. 1/129–8423), a private clinic staffed by English-speaking doctors offering 24-hour medical service. U.S. and Canadian visitors are advised to take out full medical insurance. Because of an agreement between Hungary and Great Britain, U.K. visitors are covered for emergencies and essential treatment.

Travel **American Express** (V, Deák Ferenc utca 10, tel. 1/266–8680, 1/267–
Agencies 2024, or 1/267–2022; fax 1/267–2029). **Getz International** (V Falk Miksa utca 5, tel. 1/112–0645 or 1/112–0649; fax 1/112–1014). **Vista** (VII, Károly körút 21, tel. 1/269–6032, 1/342–9316, or 1/342–1534; fax 1/269–6031).

Exploring Budapest

Budapest, situated on both banks of the Danube, unites the colorful hills of Buda and the wide boulevards of Pest. Though it was the site of a Roman outpost in the 1st century, the city was not actually created until 1873, when the towns of Obuda, Pest, and Buda were joined. The cultural, political, intellectual, and commercial heart of the nation beats in Budapest; for the 20% of the nation's population who live in the capital, anywhere else is simply "the country."

Much of the charm of a visit to Budapest lies in unexpected glimpses into shadowy courtyards and in long vistas down sunlit cobbled streets. Although some 30,000 buildings were destroyed during World War II and in 1956, the past lingers on in the often-crumbling architectural details of the antique structures that remain and in the memories and lifestyles of Budapest's citizens.

The principal sights of the city fall roughly into three areas, each of which can be comfortably covered on foot. The Budapest hills are best explored by public transportation. Note that many street names have been changed to purge all reminders of the Communist regime. If the street you're looking for seems to have disappeared, ask any local—though he or she may well be as bewildered as you are.

Numbers in the margin correspond to points of interest on the Budapest map.

❶ Take a bus (No. 16 from **Erzsébet tér** or the *Várbusz*—castle minibus
❷ —from **Moszkva tér**) to **Dísz tér**, at the top of **Várhegy** (Castle Hill), where the painstaking work of reconstruction has been in progress since World War II. Having made their final stand in the Royal Palace itself, the Nazis left behind them a blackened wasteland. Under the rubble, archaeologists discovered the medieval foundations of the palace of King Matthias Corvinus, who, in the 15th century, presided over one of the most splendid courts in Europe.

❸ The **Királyi Palota** (Palace), now a vast museum complex and cultural center, can be reached on foot from Dísz tér—it is one block south—or by funicular railway *(Sikló)* from Clark Adám tér. The northern wing of the building was devoted to the **Legújabbkori Történeti Múzeum** (Museum of Contemporary History), but at press time (spring 1995), plans were underway to close it by 1996 and transfer the entire collection to the "most recent" end of the National Museum's epic Hungarian history exhibit. The central block houses the **Magyar Nemzeti Galéria** (Hungarian National Gallery), exhibiting a wide range of Hungarian fine art, from medieval paintings to modern sculpture. Names to look for are Munkácsy, a 19th-century Romantic painter, and Csontváry, an early Surrealist whom Picasso much admired. *Hungarian National Gallery: Buda Castle (Wing C), Dísz tér 17, tel. 1/175–7533. Admission: 50 Ft. adults, 20 Ft. children; free for all on Sat. Open Mar.–Nov., Tues.–Sun. 10–6; Dec.–Feb., Tues.–Sun. 10–4.*

The southern block contains the **Budapesti Történeti Múzeum** (Budapest History Museum). Down in the cellars are the original medieval vaults of the palace, portraits of King Matthias and his second wife, Beatrice of Aragon, and many late-14th-century statues that probably adorned the Renaissance palace. *Buda Castle (Wing E), Szent György tér 2, tel. 1/175–7533. Admission: 100 Ft. adults, 50 Ft. children. Open Mar.–Oct., Wed.–Mon. 10–6; Nov.–Dec., Wed.–Mon. 10–5; Jan.–Feb., Wed.–Mon. 10–4.*

❹ The **Mátyás templom** (Matthias Church), northeast of Dísz tér, with its distinctive patterned roof, dates from the 13th century. Built as a mosque by the occupying Turks, it was destroyed and reconstructed in the 19th century, only to be bombed during World War II. Only the south porch is from the original structure. The Hapsburg emperors, including Charles IV in 1916, were crowned kings of Hungary here. High mass is celebrated every Sunday at 10 AM with an orchestra and choir and organ concerts are often held in the summer on Fridays at 8 PM. *Szentháromság tér 2, tel. 361/155–5657. Open daily 7 AM–8 PM. Admission free, except during concerts. Tourists are asked to remain at the back of the church during services.*

❺ The turn-of-the-century **Halászbástya** (Fishermen's Bastion) is on your left as you leave the church. It was built as a lookout tower to protect what was once a thriving fishing settlement. Its neo-Romanesque columns and arches frame views over the city and river. Near the church, in Hess András tér, are remains of the oldest church on Castle Hill, built by Dominican friars in the 13th century. These have now been tastefully integrated into the modern Hilton hotel.

❻ The town houses lining the streets of the Castle District are largely occupied by offices, restaurants, and diplomatic residences, but the house where Beethoven stayed in 1800 is now the **Zenetörténeti Múzeum** (Museum of Music History), which hosts intimate classical music recitals and displays rare manuscripts and antique instruments. *I, Táncsics Mihály utca 7, tel. 1/175–9011. Admission: 40 Ft. Open mid-Mar.–mid-Nov., Mon. 4–8, Wed.–Sun. 10–6; mid-Nov.–mid-Mar., Mon. 3–6, Wed.–Sun. 10–5.*

❼ The remains of a **medieval synagogue** are also in the neighborhood and open to the public. On display are a number of objects related to the Jewish community, including religious inscriptions, frescoes, and tombstones dating from the 15th century. *I, Táncsics Mihály utca 26, tel. 361/155–8764. Admission: 40 Ft. adults, 20 Ft. children. Open May–Oct. 31., Tues.–Fri. 10–2, weekends 10–6.*

❽ The **Hadtörténeti Múzeum** (Museum of Military History) is at the far end of Castle Hill. The collection includes uniforms and regalia, many belonging to the Hungarian generals who took part in the abortive uprising against Austrian rule in 1848. Other exhibits trace the military history of Hungary from the original Magyar conquest in the 9th century through the period of Ottoman rule and right to the middle of this century. *Tóth Árpád sétány 40, tel. 1/156–9522 or 1/156–9770. Admission: 50 Ft.; free Sat. Open Mar.–Nov., Tues.–Sat. 9–5, Sun. 10–6; Dec.–Feb., Tues.–Sat. 10–4, Sun. 10–6.*

Állami Operház, **18**
Belvárosi plébánia templom, **12**
Dísz tér, **2**
Erzsébet tér, **1**
Hadtörténeti Múzeum, **8**
Halászbástya, **5**
Királyi Palota, **3**
Magyar Nemzeti Múzeum, **14**
Március 15 tér, **11**
Mátyás templom, **4**
Medieval synagogue, **7**
Mezőgazdasági Múzeum, **22**
Milleniumi Emlékmù, **19**
Mùcsarnok, **21**
Néprajzi Múzeum, **16**
Parliament, **15**
Roosevelt tér, **9**
Szépművészeti Múzeum, **20**
Szt. István Bazilika, **17**
Váci utca, **13**
Vigadó tér, **10**
Zenetörténeti Múzeum, **6**

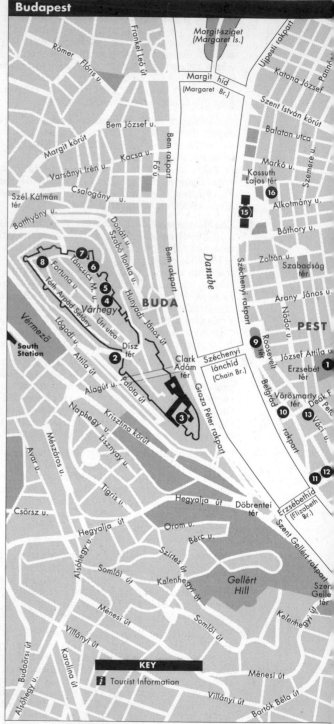

Budapest

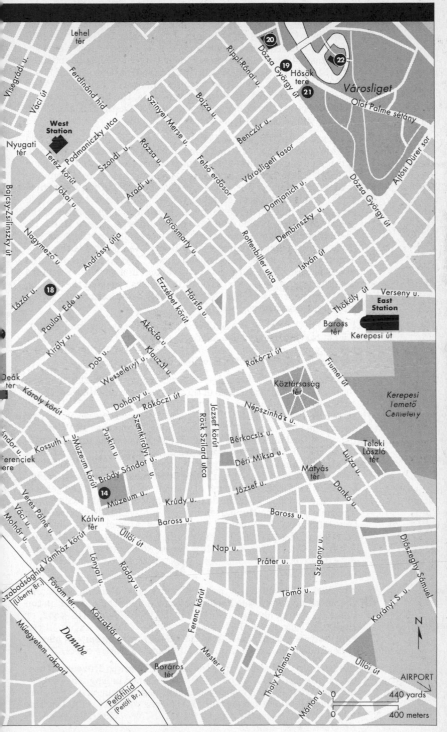

Lehel
tér

Rippl Rónai u.

Dózsa György út

20

19 Hősök
tere

22

Városliget

21

Olof Palme sétány

Váci út

Visegrádi u.

Ferdinánd híd

Szinyei Merse u.

Bajza u.

Benczúr u.

Arosi Dürer sor

West
Station

Nyugati
tér

Podmaniczky utca

Szondi u.

Rózsa u.

Felső erdősor

Városligeti fasor

Dózsa György út

Teréz körút

Jókai u.

Aradi u.

Vörösmarty u.

Damjanich u.

Bajcsy-Zsilinszky út

Nagymező u.

Andrássy útja

Dembinszky u.

Lázár u.

18

Paulay Ede u.

Erzsébet körút

Hársfa u.

Rottenbiller utca

István út

Thököly u.

Verseny u.

East
Station

Király u.

Dob u.

Klauzál u.

Rákóczi út

Baross
tér

Kerepesi út

Deák
tér

Károly körút

Wesselényi u.

Dohány u.

Rákóczi út

Szentkirályi u.

Köztársaság
tér

Népszínház u.

Fiumei út

Kerepesi
temető
Cemetery

sándor u.

ferenciek
ere

Kossuth L.

Múzeum körút

Puskin u.

Bródy Sándor u.

József körút

Rökk Szilárd utca

Bérkocsis u.

Déri Miksa u.

Mátyás
tér

Dankó u.

Luzsa u.

Telaki
László
tér

Veres Pálné u.

Váci u.

Molnár u.

14

Múzeum u.

Kálvin
tér

Krúdy u.

Baross u.

József u.

Baross u.

Nap u.

Práter u.

Szigony u.

Diószeghy Sámuel

Szabadsághíd
[Liberty Br.]

Fővám tér

Vámház körút

Lónyai u.

Ráday u.

Üllői út

Ferenc körút

Tömő u.

Korányi S. u.

N

Müegyetem rakpart

Danube

Közraktár u.

Boráros
tér

Petőfihíd
[Petőfi Br.]

Mester u.

Thaly Kálmán u.

Márton u.

Üllői út

AIRPORT

0   440 yards

0   400 meters

The Heart of the City

❾ Cross the **Széchenyi lánchíd** (Chain Bridge) from Clark Ádám tér to reach **Roosevelt tér** in Pest, with the 19th-century neo-classical Academy of Sciences on your left, and directly in front, the 1907 Gresham Palace, a crumbling temple to the age of Art Nouveau. Pest fans out from the **Belváros** (Inner City), which is bounded by the **Kiskörút** (Little Ring Road). The **Nagykörút** (Grand Ring Road) describes a wider semicircle from the Margaret Bridge to Petőfi Bridge. To your right, an elegant promenade, the **Korzó,** runs south along the river, providing postcard views of Castle Hill, the Chain Bridge, and Gellért Hill just across the Danube.

❿ A square called **Vigadó tér** is dominated by the Danube view and Vigadó concert hall, built in a Romantic mix of Byzantine, Moorish, and Romanesque styles, with Hungarian motifs thrown in for good measure. Liszt, Brahms, and Bartók all performed here. Completely destroyed during World War II, it has been rebuilt in its original **⑪** style. Another square, **Március 15 tér,** commemorates the 1848 struggle for independence from the Hapsburgs with a statue of the poet Petőfi Sándor, who died later in the uprising. Every March 15, the national holiday commemorating the revolution, the square is packed with patriotic Hungarians. Behind the square is the 12th-**⑫** century **Belvárosi plébánia templom** (Inner City Parish Church), the oldest in Pest. The church has been redone in a variety of western architectural styles; even Turkish influences, such as the Muslim prayer niche, remain. Liszt, who lived only a few yards away, often played the organ here.

⑬ Parallel to the Korzó, lies Budapest's most upscale shopping street, **Váci utca. Vörösmarty tér,** a handsome square in the heart of the Inner City, is a good spot to sit and relax. Street musicians and sidewalk cafés make it one of the liveliest places in Budapest.

⑭ A slight detour back down the river and deeper into Pest brings you to the stern, Classical edifice of the **Magyar Nemzeti Múzeum** (Hungarian National Museum), built between 1837 and 1847. On these steps, on March 15, 1848 Petőfi Sándor recited his revolutionary poem, the *"Nemzeti Dal"* ("National Song"), and the "12 Points," a list of political demands by young Hungarians calling upon the people to rise up against the Hapsburgs. Celebrations of the national holiday are held here every year on March 15. You'll find the museum's most sacred treasure, the **Szent Korona** (Korona)—a golden soufflé with a Byzantine band of enamel, pearl, and other gems—with other royal relics in the domed Hall of Honor off the main lobby. The museum's epic Hungarian history exhibit has been closed for renovations but is scheduled to reopen by August 1996, when the addition of the post-1989 exhibits will be complete. *IX, Múzeum körút 14–6, tel. 1/138–2122. Admission: 80 Ft. adults, 40 Ft. children. Open mid-Mar.–mid-Oct., Tues.–Sun. 10–6,; mid-Oct.–mid-March, Tues.–Sun. 10–5.*

⑮ North of Roosevelt tér is the riverfront's most striking landmark, the imposing neo-Gothic **Parliament,** now minus the red star on top (open for tours only; call IBUSZ, tel. 1/118–5776 or 1/118–4842, or Budapest Tourist, tel. 1/117–3555 or 1/118–1453). To its left sits an expressive statue of József Attila (1905–37), who, in spite of his early death, became known as one of Hungary's greatest poets.

⑯ Across from the Parliament is the majestic **Néprajzi Múzeum** (Museum of Ethnography), with exhibits—captioned in English—depicting folk traditions and such social customs as Hungarian costume and folklore. These are the authentic pieces you can't see at touristy folk shops. *V, Kossuth Lajos tér 12, tel. 1/132–6340. Admission: 80 Ft. Open Tues.–Sun. 10–6.*

⑰ Dark and massive, the 19th-century **Szt. István Bazilika** (St. Stephen's Basilica) is one of the chief landmarks of Pest. It was planned early in the 19th century as a neoclassical building, but was in the neo-Renaissance style by the time it was completed more than 50 years later. During World War II, the most precious documents from the Municipal Archives were placed in the cellar of the basilica—one of the few available bombproof sites. The mummified right hand of St. Stephen, Hungary's first king and patron saint, is preserved in the *Szent Jobb* chapel as a relic. *V, Szent István tér, tel. 361/117–2859. Open Mon.–Sat. 7 AM–7 PM, Sun. 1 PM–5 PM.*

Andrássy út runs 3.2 kilometers (2 miles) from the basilica to Hősök tere (Heroes' Square). About one quarter of the way up on the left, (18) at Hajós utca, is the **Állami Operaház** (State Opera House), with its statues of the Muses in the second-floor corner niches. Completed in 1884, it was the crowning achievement of architect Miklós Ybl. It has been restored to its original ornate glory—particularly inside—and has been spared attempts at modernization. Foreign-language tours, held daily at 3 and 4 PM, meet in front of the Opera House; but call ahead to confirm a tour is being given on the day you want to visit (tel. 1/131–2550 ext. 156). The cost is about 300 Ft. There are no performances in summer, except for the week-long BudaFest international ballet and opera festival in mid-August.

Heroes' In the center of Heroes' Square stands the 36.5-meter (118-foot)
Square and **Milleniumi Emlékmű** (Millenium Monument), begun in 1896 to com-
Városliget memorate the 1,000th anniversary of the Magyar Conquest. Statues
(19) of Prince Árpád and six other founders of the Magyar nation occupy the base of the monument, while Hungary's greatest rulers and princes are between the columns on either side.

(20) The **Szépművészeti Múzeum** (Fine Arts Museum) stands on one side of the square. Egyptian, Greek, and Roman artifacts dominate an entire section of the museum, and the collection of ceramics includes many rare pieces. The institution's largely unknown Spanish collection, which includes many works by El Greco and a magnificent painting by Velásquez, is considered the best of its kind outside Spain. *XIV, Dózsa György út 41, tel. 1/142–9759. Admission: 60 Ft. Open Tues.–Sun. 10–5:30; closed Jan.–Mar.*

After four years of being boarded up for exhaustive renovations, the (21) striking 1895 **Műcsarnok** (Art Gallery), on the other side of the square, reopened its doors to the public in March 1995 during the Budapest Spring Festival. Now, it again blesses Budapest with its magnificent visiting exhibitions of contemporary Hungarian and international art and its rich series of films, theater, and concerts. *XIV, Dózsa György út 37, tel. 1/267–8776 or 1/267–8777. Admission: 60 Ft. Open Tues.–Sun. 10–6.*

The **Városliget** (City Park) extends beyond the square; on the left as you enter it are the zoo, state circus, amusement park, and outdoor swimming pool of the Széchenyi mineral baths. On the right is the **Vajdahunyad Castle,** an art historian's Disneyland, created for the millennial celebration in 1896, that blends elements from all of Hungary's historic architectural past. Housed in one building is the (22) surprisingly interesting **Mezőgazdasági Múzeum** (Agricultural Museum), with displays on subjects including animal husbandry, forestry, and horticulture. *XIV, Városliget, Széchenyi Island, tel. 1/142–3198. Admission: 60 Ft.; Tues. free. Open Mar.–Nov., Tues.–Sat. 10–5, Sun. 10–6; Dec.–Feb., Tues.–Fri. 10–4, weekends 10–5.*

On the shores of the artificial lake stands the statue of George Washington, erected in 1906 from donations by Hungarians living in the United States. The **Olaf Palme sétány** (walk) is a pleasant route through the park.

Off the Beaten Track

A *libegő* (chair lift) will take you to the highest point in Budapest, **Jánoshegy** (János Hill), where you can climb a lookout tower for the best view of the city. *Take Bus 158 from Moszkva tér to the last stop, Zugligeti út. Tel. 1/156–7975 or 1/176–3764. Admission: 80 Ft. one way, 140 Ft. round-trip. Open mid-May–mid-Sept., daily 9–5; mid-Sept.–mid-May (depending on weather), daily 9:30–4. Closed alternate Mondays.*

For another good view, make the strenuous climb up the staircase that ascends the high cliff overlooking the Danube at the Buda end of the Szabadság Bridge. This will lead you to the *citadella* (fortress) crowning **Gellért-hegy** (Gellert Hill), named for an 11th-century bishop who was hurled to his death here by some pagan Magyars. During the Middle Ages the hill was associated with witches; nowadays there is a towering memorial to the liberation of Budapest by the Red Army.

Shopping

You'll find plenty of folk art and souvenir shops, foreign-language bookshops, and classical record shops in or around **Váci utca,** but a visit to some of the smaller, more typically Hungarian shops on **Erzsébet** and **Teréz boulevards, Kossuth Lajos utca** and to the modern **Skála-Metro** department store near the Nyugati train station may prove more interesting.

The magnificent **Vásárcsarnok** (Central Market Hall) (IX, Vámhaz Körút) was reopened in late 1994 after years of renovation—and disputes over who would foot the bill. The cavernous, three-story hall once again teems with shoppers browsing among stalls packed with salamis and red paprika chains, crusty bread, fresh fish, and other tastes of Hungary. Upstairs, you can buy folk embroideries and souvenirs.

Dining

Private restaurateurs are breathing excitement into the Budapest dining scene. You can choose among Chinese, Mexican, Italian, French, Indian, and other ethnic cuisines—there is even a vegetarian restaurant. Or you can stick to solid, traditional Hungarian fare as served in dozens of little restaurants scattered throughout the center of town, where you'll find Transylvanian folk art on the walls, linens with folk patterns on the tables, gypsy music in the air, and lots of heavy wood furniture and where a mere 200 Ft. will buy you a bowl of goulash or other hearty hot food. At most of the places listed below, there are less expensive options on the menus which make it possible to have a good meal for less than the price range indicated. For price-category definitions, *see* Dining *in* Staying in Hungary, *above.*

$$ **Cyrano.** Sophisticatedly chic but friendly, this young bistro just off
★ of Vörösmarty tér was a success the day it opened two years ago. A creative kitchen sends out elegantly presented Hungarian and Continental dishes, from standards such as goulash and chicken paprika to more eclectic specials like fried Camembert cheese with blueberry jam. *V, Kristóf tér 7–8, tel. 1/266–3096. Reservations advised. AE, MC.*

$$ **Fészek.** This elegant but casual Hungarian restaurant in the heart of downtown Pest is difficult to find, tucked as it is inside the nearly 100-year-old Fészek Artists Club. But the search is amply rewarded: a large, neoclassical dining room with an extensive, almost daunting, menu featuring all the Hungarian classics, with a variety of game dishes. *VII, Dob utca 55 (corner of Kertész utca), tel. 1/322–6043. Reservations accepted. 50 Ft. Artists Club cover charge. AE. Garden dining May–late summer.*

$ **Bohémtanya.** There's always a wait for a table at this lively hangout, but it pays to be patient. The reward: heaping plates of stuffed cabbage, fried pork chops filled with goose liver, and other Hungarian specialties. The trilingual menu is extra budget-conscious: Items are in order by price. *VI, Paulay Ede utca 6, tel. 1/322–1453. Reservations advised. No credit cards.*

$ **Tüköry Söröző.** Solid, hearty Hungarian fare comes in big portions at this popular downtown restaurant close to the Parliament. Red-checked tablecloths, low lighting, and dark wood booths give it a cozy, rustic atmosphere. Best bets include pork cutlets stuffed with savory liver or apples and cheese, washed down with a big mug of inexpensive beer. *V, Hold utca 15, tel. 361/269–5027. Reservations advised. No credit cards. Closed Sat. and Sun.*

¢ **Falafel Faloda.** This bright, modern spot, all mirrors, white tile, and light paneling, serves pita bread with plenty of fresh vegetables and salads to stuff into it—not always easy to find in these parts. *V, Paulay Ede utca 53, no phone. No reservations. No credit cards. Open Mon.–Fri. 10–8, Sat. 10–6.*

¢ **Marxim.** Just two years after the death of Socialism in Hungary, this pizza and pasta joint opened up to mock the old regime—and milk it for all it's worth. From the flashing red star above the door outside to the puns on the menu items, with names such as pizza *á la Anarchismo*, the theme of the place is "communist nostalgia." The pizzas and skinny calzones are tasty, but may take a while to arrive at your table when it's very busy. *II, Kisrókus utca 23, tel. 1/212–4183. AE, DC, V. Closed Sun. lunch.*

¢ **McDonald's.** Nowadays golden arches are all over town—but not one will you see in this dazzling Baroque and Belle Epoque spot in the old railroad station, possibly the world's most beautiful fast-food outlet. Only the smell tells you that yes, Virginia, this is the real thing. *VI, Teréz krt. 52, next to Nyugati station, 1/132–5970. No reservations. No credit cards.*

¢ **Szerb.** Down a sawdust-covered stairway, this lively cellar serves grilled meats on a skewer and other Serbian dishes for a song, along with giant pitchers of beer. *V, Nagy Ignác utca 16, tel. 1/269–3139. Reservations advised. AE, MC. Closed Sun. dinner.*

¢ **Vegetárium.** This oasis in a land of avid meat-eaters recently sold out a bit to carnivorousness by adding fish and poultry to its previously strictly vegetarian menu. But its offerings are still positively exotic for Hungary: brown rice and vegetables, tempura, and fresh salads, all lovingly prepared. *V Cukor utca 3, tel. 1/267–0322. Reservations advised. AE, DC, MC, V.*

Lodging

Some thirty million tourists come to Hungary each year, and the boom continues to encourage hotel building; yet there is sometimes a shortage of rooms, especially in summer.

If you arrive without a reservation, go to the IBUSZ travel office at Petőfi tér (tel. 1/118–5707) or to one of the tourist offices at any of the train stations or at the airport. For details and price-category definitions, *see* Lodging *in* Staying in Hungary, *above*.

$$ **Astoria.** Revolutionaries and intellectuals once gathered in the marble-and-gilt Art Deco lobby here. Recent renovations have not obscured the 82-year-old hotel's distinct charm, but have meant the addition of other comforts—most notably soundproofing, essential since the Astoria is located at the city's busiest intersection. *V, Kossuth Lajos utca 19, tel. 1/117–3411, fax 1/118–6798. 123 rooms with bath or shower, 5 suites. Facilities: restaurant, bar, café, nightclub, business center, conference room, parking. AE, DC, MC, V.*

$$ **Victoria.** The dark, stately Parliament building and city lights twin-
★ kling over the river can be seen from every room at this new hotel right on the Danube. The absence of conventions is a plus. *II, Bem rakpart, tel. 1/201–8644, fax 361/201–5816. 24 rooms with bath, 2*

with balcony; 1 suite. Facilities: 24-hr. room service, bar, sauna, conference room, garage. AE, DC, MC, V.

$ **Ifjúság.** The concrete "youth" hotel is a boxy remnant of socialist architecture, but the location—a quiet, residential street at the top of a hill in Buda, near Margaret Island, is a little special and the rooms are modern and clean. Ask for a room with a view, and you won't be sorry. *II, Zivatar utca 3, tel. 1/135–3331, fax 1/135–3989. 100 rooms with bath. Facilities: restaurant. AE, DC, MC, V.*

$ **Kulturinov.** One wing of what looks like a Gothic castle now houses basic budget accommodations. Rooms are clean, and the neighborhood—one of Budapest's most famous squares in the luxurious Castle District—is unbeatable. *I, Szentháromság tér 6, tel. 1/155–0122 or 1/175–1651, fax 1/175–1886. 17 rooms with 2 or 3 beds, all with shower. Facilities: snack bar, reading room. AE.*

$ **Medosz.** One of Budapest's better small hotels, the Medosz provides a central location near Oktogon, a major transport hub, and lovely Andrássy út; the Opera House and Liszt Ferenc Music Academy are a block away. Rooms are clean but very basic, with small, low beds; worn upholstery, and a leftover 1950s institutional feel. *VI, Jókai tér 9, tel. 1/153–1700 or 1/153–1434, fax 1/132–4316. 63 rooms with bath, 7 suites. Facilities: restaurant (for groups only). No credit cards.*

¢ **Park.** This establishment is centrally located across the street from Keleti station. The poet Allen Ginsberg once stayed here, and it has always been popular with young people. *VIII, Baross tér 10, tel. 1/113–1420. 170 rooms, 16 with bath. Facilities: restaurant, conference room, bar. AE, DC, MC, V.*

¢ **Citadella.** Built into a fortress on top of a hill overlooking the city, this small property is charming outside but militantly '60s-socialist inside, with its cotlike beds and bare walls. But it's airy, it's spotless, and the views are splendid. *XI, Citadella sétány, tel. 1/166–5794. 2 rooms with bath; 5 rooms with sink, 8 rooms with shower; 5 dormitory rooms. No credit cards.*

¢ **Korona Panzió.** This typical Hungarian guest house is in a quiet, tasteful residential area on the hill called Sas-hegy. All rooms have small balconies or terraces, and bedspreads with a folkloric motif and inexpensive rugs on the floors add a homey note. *XI, Sasadi út 127, tel. 1/186–2460 or 1/181–2788, fax 1/181–0781. 15 rooms and 3 apartments, all with bath or shower. Facilities: restaurant, parking. AE.*

The Arts

Budapest's English-language newspapers are the most up-to-date source for arts information. The *Budapest Sun's* "Style" section maps out the week's cultural goings-on. Hotels and tourist offices will provide you with a copy of the monthly publication *Programme*, which contains details of all cultural events in the city. Tickets are available from your hotel desk, the **Central Booking Agency** (Vörösmarty tér, tel. 1/117–6222), or from the **Central Theater Booking Office** (VI, Andrássy út 18, tel. 1/112–0000).

There are two opera houses, the **Magyar Állami Operaház** (Hungarian State Opera House) (VI, Andrássy út 22) and the **Erkel Színház** (Erkel Theater) (VIII, Köztársaság tér), for which dress can be informal, but many still choose to dress festively. Concerts are given all year at the **Academy of Music** on Liszt F. tér, the **Vigadó** on Vigadó tér, and at the **Old Academy of Music** on Vörösmarty út. Displays of Hungarian folk dancing are held at the **Cultural Center** on Corvin tér. There are also participatory folk dancing evenings, with instruction for beginners, at district cultural centers. Ask your hotel clerk to find out the latest programs at these popular centers.

Arts festivals fill the calendar beginning in early spring. The season's first and biggest, the **Budapest Spring Festival** (beginning early to mid-March), showcases Hungary's best opera, music, theater, dance, and fine arts, as well as major visiting foreign artists.

Nightlife

Budapest is a lively city by night. Establishments stay open late, and Western European–style *drink-bárs* have sprung up all over the city. As in many cities, the life of a nightspot in Budapest can be ephemeral. The following bars and clubs are popular and seem here to stay, but check the *Budapest Sun* and other local publications for the more transient "in" spots.

Bars and Clubs The **Jazz Café** hosts local jazz bands every night in a small basement space of neon blue lights and funky papier maché statues. *V, Ballasi Bálint utca 25, tel. 1/269–5506. Open Mon.–Sat. 5 PM–3 AM.*

Mad Block is a popular disco in the ornate Baroque theater that once housed the Moulin Rouge nightclub. Live bands play weeknights, but the disco on weekends is what draws the crowds. *VI, Nagymező utca 17, tel. 1/112–4492. Open daily 9 PM–6 AM.*

Made Inn Mine is a large bar and disco that hops with young local and international Beautiful People decked out in the latest MTV fashions. *VI, Andrássy út 112, tel. 1/111–3437. Open Sun.–Thurs. 8 PM–4 AM, Fri.–Sat. 8 PM–5 AM.*

Piaf is popular with arts sophisticates; it's classy and just a touch pretentious, with red velvet chairs and low, candlelit tables in cozy, brick rooms. The mood in the downstairs room tends to get more raucous. You have to ring the bell to get in. *VI, Nagymező utca 20, tel. 1/112–3823. Open daily 10 PM–5 AM (or when last person leaves).*

Lake Balaton

Lake Balaton, the largest lake in Central Europe, stretches 80 kilometers (50 miles) across western Hungary. It is within easy reach of Budapest by any means of transportation. Sometimes known as the nation's playground, it goes some way toward making up for Hungary's much-lamented lack of coastline. On its hilly northern shore, ideal for growing grapes, is **Balatonfüred,** the country's oldest and most famous spa town.

The national park on the Tihany Peninsula is just to the south, and regular boat service links Tihany and Balatonfüred with Siófok on the southern shore. This shore is not as attractive as the northern one—being flatter and more crowded with resorts, cottages, and high-rise hotels once used as Communist trade-union retreats. Still, it is worth visiting for its shallower—you can walk out for almost 2 kilometers (1¼ miles) before it deepens—warmer waters, which make it a better choice for swimming than other locations.

A circular tour taking in Veszprém, Balatonfüred, and Tihany could be managed in a day, but two days, with a night in Tihany or Balatonfüred, would be more relaxed.

The region gets more and more crowded every year (July and August are the busiest times), but a few steps along any side road will start you winding up picturesque hills dense with vineyards punctuated by old stone houses and wine cellars, leaving the bustle far below.

Getting Around

Trains from Budapest serve all the resorts on the northern shore; a separate line links the resorts of the southern shore. Road 71 runs along the northern shore; M7 covers the southern. Buses connect most resorts. Regular ferries link the major ones. On summer weekends, traffic can be heavy and driving slow around the lake. Book

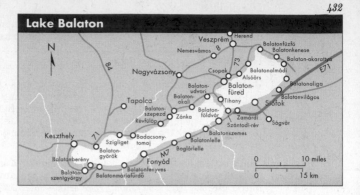

bus and train tickets in advance then. In winter, note that schedules are curtailed, so check before making plans.

Tourist Information

Budapest (Balatontourist, VIII, Üllői út 52/a, tel. 1/133–6982, fax 1/210–0363).
Balatonfüred (Balatontourist, Blaha L. utca 5, tel. 87/343–471 or 87/342–822, fax 87/343–435).
Tihany (Balatontourist, Kossuth utca 20, tel. 87/348–519).
Veszprém (Balatontourist, Kossuth Lajos utca 21, tel. 88/429–630).

Exploring Lake Balaton

Hilly **Veszprém** is the center of cultural life in the Balaton region. **Várhegy** (Castle Hill) is the most attractive part of town, north of Szabadság tér. **Hősök Kapuja** (Heroes' Gate), at the entrance to the Castle, houses a small exhibit on Hungary's history. Just past the gate and down a little alley to the left, is the **Tűztorony** (Fire Tower); note that the lower level is medieval while the upper stories are Baroque. There is a good view of the town and surrounding area from the balcony. *Exhibit admission: 10 Ft. Open May–Oct., Tues.– Sun. 10–6.*

Vár utca, the only street in the castle area, leads to a small square in front of the **Bishop's Palace** and **Cathedral;** outdoor concerts are held here in the summer. Vár utca continues past the square up to a terrace erected on the north staircase of the castle. Stand beside the modern statues of St. Stephen and his queen, Gizella, for a far-reaching view of the old quarter of town.

Balatonfüred, a spa and resort with good beaches, is about 20 kilometers (12 miles) from Veszprém. It is also one of the finest wine-growing areas of Hungary. Above the main square, where medicinal waters bubble up under a colonnaded pavilion, the hillsides are thick with vines.

A seven-minute boat trip takes you from Balatonfüred to the **Tihany Peninsula,** a national park rich in rare flora and fauna and an ideal place for strolling. From the ferry port, follow green markers to the springs (Oroszkút) or red ones to the top of **Csúcs-hegy,** a hill from which there is a good view of the lake.

The village of **Tihany,** with its famous **abbey,** is on the eastern shore. The abbey building houses a **museum** with exhibits related to the Balaton area. Also worth a look are the pink angels floating on the ceiling of the abbey church and the abbey organ, on which recitals are given in summer. *Batthyány utca 80, tel. 87/348–405. Admission: 20 Ft. Open Tues.–Sun. 10–6.*

Dining and Lodging

ABC convenience stores make picnics on the beach cheap and easy. And, although hotels can be expensive, it's relatively easy to line up rooms in private homes, which fall in the $ and ¢ price categories. For details and definitions, *see* Dining and Lodging *in* Staying in Hungary, *above*.

Balatonfüred
Dining

Baricska Csárda. From its perch on a hill at the southwestern end of town, this rambling, reed-thatched, rustic inn overlooks a smooth carpet of vineyards scarred only by the winding river. The hearty yet ambitious fare includes roasted trout and *fogas* (a freshwater fish particular to the Balaton region), creamy fish paprikás with gnocchi, and desserts crammed with sweet poppy-seed filling. *Baricska dülő, off Hwy. 71 (Széchenyi út) behind Shell station, tel. 87/343–105. Reservations advised. AE, V. Closed mid-Nov.–mid-Mar. $$*

Halászkert Etterem. The "Fisherman's Garden" restaurant, across a busy street from the beach, is famous for its grilled Balaton pike perch, cooked over an open flame, among other reasonably priced fish dishes. There's an outdoor dance floor. *Széchenyi 2, off Jókai Mór utca, tel. 87/343–039. Reservations advised for dinner July–Aug. AE, DC, MC, V. Closed Dec.–Feb. $*

Lodging

Margaręta. This attractive apartment-hotel stands on a low hill across the street from the lakefront highrise Hotel Marina and, unfortunately, behind a large gas station. It is smaller and more intimate than its neighbors, and its restaurant is popular locally. Each room has a kitchen, a balcony, a phone, a TV, and a radio. *Széchenyi út 29, tel. and fax 87/343–824. 52 rooms with bath. Facilities: restaurant, bar, snack bar, laundry facilities, parking. AE, DC, MC, V. Closed mid-Nov.–mid-Mar. (but open over New Year's holiday). $$*

Tihany
Dining

Halásztanya. The relaxed atmosphere and gypsy music in the evening help contribute to the popularity of the Halásztanya, set on a quaint, twisting, narrow street. The kitchen specializes in fish. *Visszhang utca 11, no tel. No reservations. Closed Nov.–Mar. $$*

Pál Csárda. Two thatched-roof cottages make up this simple restaurant, tucked away off a narrow street, where cold fruit soup and fish stew are the specialties. You can eat in the garden, which is decorated with gourds and strands of peppers, from which paprika is made. *Visszhang utca 19, no tel. No reservations. No credit cards. Closed Dec.–Mar. $$*

Lodging

Kolostor. The cozy, wood-panel rooms are built into an attic above a popular restaurant and brewery in the heart of Tihany village. *Kossuth utca 14, tel. 87/348–408. 7 rooms with bath. Facilities: breakfast room. No credit cards. $$*

Veszprém
Dining

Club Skorpio. This city-center eatery might look like an Alpine hut but the trilingual menu is top class and features grilled meats and such specialties as pheasant soup and steamed wild duck. *Virág Benedek utca 1/b, tel. 88/420–319. Reservations advised. No credit cards. $*

★ **Diana.** The Diana is just a little southwest of the town center, but worth the trip if you want to experience the old-fashioned charm of a small provincial Hungarian restaurant. The decor could be called "cozy traditional," and the fish and game specialties are perennial favorites. *József Attila utca 22, tel. 80/21–061. Reservations advised. No credit cards. $$*

Lodging

Veszprém. This modern, comfortable hotel, in the center of town, is in one of the less attractive buildings in Veszprém, but is convenient to all the major sights and to the bus station. *Budapesti utca 6, tel. 88/424–677, fax 88/424–076. 72 rooms, most with bath, 4 suites. Facilities: restaurant, café, bar, hairdresser. No credit cards. $*

14 Ireland

With its informal, unpretentious way of life, Ireland is an ideal destination for the budget traveler. Indeed, some of its best attractions—including its unspoiled scenery and unpolluted coast—are free. Ruined abbeys, medieval castles, and prehistoric remains are freely accessible, as are most of Dublin's galleries and museums. By staying in affordable bed-and-breakfasts, visitors can come to know firsthand the Irish and their way of life. Nightlife in Ireland consists of a visit to the local pub, where, for the price of a few drinks, you can enjoy performances by traditional musicians or take part in a sing-along.

Ireland, one of the westernmost countries in Europe, is a small island on which you are never more than an hour's drive from the sea. It's actually two countries in one. The northeast corner of the island, Northern Ireland, remains a part of the United Kingdom, while the Republic, with a population of only 3½ million, has been independent since 1921.

The Republic of Ireland is virtually free from the "troubles" that dominated Northern Ireland until the ceasefire of 1994. Over the past few years, millions of pounds have been spent upgrading tourist facilities, but the attractions of Ireland as a vacation destination remain the same as ever: those of a small, friendly country with a mild climate and a relaxed pace of life, where simple pleasures are found in its scenery, its historical heritage, its sporting opportunities, and the informal hospitality of its loquacious inhabitants.

Dublin, the capital, is a thriving modern city. It's a strikingly elegant city, too, a fact of which the Dubliners are well aware. Trinity College, Dublin Castle, and the magnificent public buildings and distinctive Georgian squares of the city have all been restored, allowing the elegance of 18th-century Dublin to emerge again after centuries of neglect.

The pace of life outside Dublin is even more relaxed. When a local was asked for the Irish-language equivalent of *mañana*, the reply came that there is no word in Irish to convey quite the same sense of urgency. An exaggeration, of course, but the farther you travel from the metropolis, the more you will be inclined to linger. Apart from such sporting attractions as championship golf, horse racing, deep-sea fishing, and angling, the thing to do in Ireland is to take it easy and look around you.

Essential Information

Before You Go

When to Go The main tourist season runs from June to mid-September. The attractions of Ireland are not as dependent on the weather as are those in most other northern European countries, and the scenery is just as attractive in the off-peak times of fall and spring. In all seasons the visitor can expect to encounter rain.

Climate Winters are mild though wet; summers can be warm and sunny, but there's always the risk of a sudden shower. No one ever went to Ireland for a suntan.

The following are the average daily maximum and minimum temperatures for Dublin.

Jan.	46F	8C	May	60F	15C	Sept.	63F	17C
	34	1		43	6		48	9
Feb.	47F	8C	June	65F	18C	Oct.	57F	14C
	35	2		48	9		43	6
Mar.	51F	11C	July	67F	19C	Nov.	51F	11C
	37	3		52	11		39	4
Apr.	55F	13C	Aug.	67F	19C	Dec.	47F	8C
	39	4		51	11		37	3

Currency The unit of currency in Ireland is the pound, or punt (pronounced poont), written as IR£ to avoid confusion with the pound sterling. The currency is divided into the same denominations as in Britain, with IR£1 divided into 100 pence (written *p*). There is likely to be some variance in the rates of exchange between Ireland and the United Kingdom (which includes Northern Ireland). Change U.K. pounds at a bank when you get to Ireland (pound coins not accepted); change Irish pounds before you leave.

U.S. dollars and British currency are accepted only in large hotels and shops licensed as bureaux de change. In general, visitors are expected to use Irish currency. Banks give the best rate of exchange. The rate of exchange at press time (summer 1995) was IR£.67 to the U.S. dollar and IR£.98 to the British pound sterling.

What It Will Cost Dublin is one of Europe's most expensive cities—an unfortunate state of affairs that manifests itself most obviously in hotel and restaurant rates. You can generally keep costs lower if you visit Ireland on a package tour. Alternatively, consider staying in a guest house or one of the multitude of bed-and-breakfasts; they provide an economical and atmospheric option (*see* Lodging *in* Staying in Ireland, *below*). The rest of the country—with the exception of the better-known hotels and restaurants—is less expensive than Dublin. That the Irish themselves complain bitterly about the high cost of living is partly attributable to the high rate of value-added tax (VAT)—a stinging 21% on "luxury" goods and 10% on hotel accommodations. Some sample costs make the point. For instance, while a double room in a moderate Dublin hotel will cost about IR£80, with breakfast sometimes another IR£7 per person, the current rate for a country B&B is around IR£15 per person. A modest small-town hotel will charge around IR£20 per person.

Sample Prices Cup of coffee, 70p; pint of beer, IR£2.00; Coca-Cola, 95p; ham sandwich, IR£1.80; 1-mile taxi ride, IR£3.50.

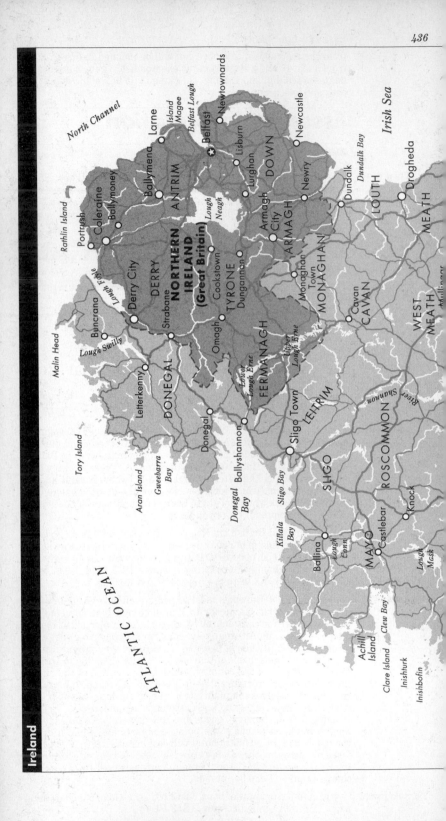

North Channel

Irish Sea

ATLANTIC OCEAN

Larne
Ballymena
Newtownards
Belfast Lough
Island Magee
Belfast
Lisburn
DOWN
Newcastle
Dundalk Bay
ANTRIM
Ballymoney
Portrush
Coleraine
Lurgan
Lough Neagh
Armagh City
ARMAGH
Newry
Dundalk
LOUTH
Drogheda
MEATH
Rathlin Island
Derry City
NORTHERN IRELAND (Great Britain)
Strabane
Cookstown
TYRONE
Dungannon
Monaghan Town
MONAGHAN
Malin Head
Buncrana
Lough Foyle
Omagh
Cavan
CAVAN
WEST MEATH
Mullingar
Lough Swilly
Letterkenny
DONEGAL
FERMANAGH
Lower Lough Erne
Upper Lough Erne
Tory Island
Donegal
Ballyshannon
Sligo Town
LEITRIM
River Shannon
Aran Island
Gweebarra Bay
Donegal Bay
Sligo Bay
SLIGO
ROSCOMMON
Killala Bay
Ballina
Lough Conn
MAYO
Castlebar
Knock
Lough Mask
Achill Island
Clew Bay
Clare Island
Inishturk
Inishbofin

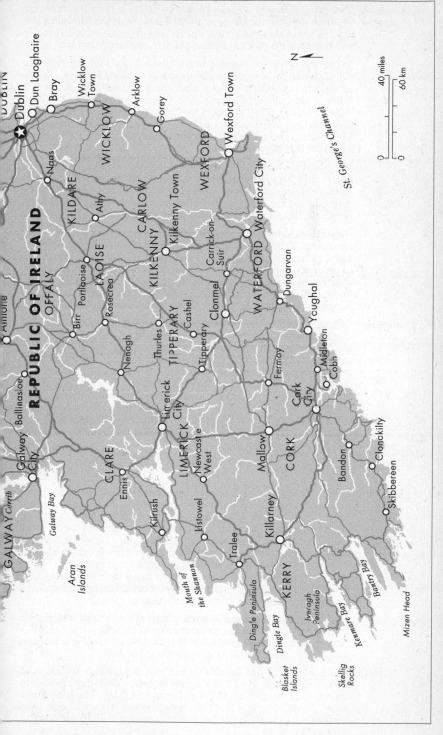

Customs on Arrival Two categories of duty-free allowance exist for travelers entering the Irish Republic: one for goods obtained outside the European Union (EU), on a ship or aircraft, or in a duty-free store within the EU and the other for goods bought in the EU, with duty and tax paid.

In the first category, you may import duty-free (1) 200 cigarettes or 100 cigarillos or 50 cigars or 250 grams of smoking tobacco, (2) 2 liters of wine and either 1 liter of alcoholic drink over 22% volume or 2 liters of alcoholic drink under 22% volume (sparkling or fortified wine included), (3) 50 grams of perfume and ¼ liter of toilet water, and (4) other goods to a value of IR£34 per person (IR£17 per person for travelers under 15 years of age); you may import 12 liters of beer as part of this allowance.

Duty-paid allowances increased substantially in 1993. Travelers are now entitled to purchase (1) 800 cigarettes, (2) 10 liters of spirits, (3) 45 liters of wine, and (4) 55 liters of beer. The allowances apply only to goods bought in shops in EU countries, including Britain and Northern Ireland, which already have the duty paid.

Goods that cannot be freely imported include firearms, ammunition, explosives, drugs (e.g., narcotics, amphetamines), drug paraphernalia, indecent or obscene books and pictures, oral smokeless tobacco products, meat and meat products, poultry and poultry products, plants and plant products (including shrubs, vegetables, fruit, bulbs, and seeds), domestic cats and dogs from outside the United Kingdom, and live animals from outside Northern Ireland.

Language Officially, Irish is the first language of the Republic, but the everyday language of the overwhelming majority of Irish people is English. Except for the northwest and Connemara, where many signs are not translated, most signs in the country are written in Irish with an English translation underneath. There is one important exception to this rule, with which all visitors should familiarize themselves: *Fir* (pronounced far) and *mná* (pronounced muh-*naw*) translate respectively into "men" and "women." The Gaelteacht (pronounced *Gale*-tockt)—areas in which Irish *is* the everyday language of most people—comprises only 6% of the land, and all its inhabitants are, in any case, bilingual.

Getting Around

By Train Iarnód Éireann (Irish Rail) and **Bus Éireann** (Irish Bus) are independent components of the state-owned public transportation company **Coras Iompair Éireann** (CIE). The rail network, although much cut back in the past 25 years, is still extensive, with main routes radiating from Dublin to Cork, Galway, Limerick, Tralee, Killarney, Westport, and Sligo; there is also a line for the north and Belfast. All trains are diesel; cars on principal expresses have air-conditioning. There are two classes on many trains—Super Standard (first class) and Standard (second class). Dining cars are carried on main expresses. There are no sleeping cars.

Speeds are slow in comparison with those of other European trains. Dublin, however, now has a modern commuter train—the DART—running south from the suburb of Howth through the city to Bray on the Wicklow coast, with many stops along the way.

Fares There is an eight-day **Rambler** ticket (rail and bus) for IR£78, valid for any eight days in a 15-day period. One- and four-day round-trip train tickets are also available at discounted rates. The **Irish Rover** ticket includes travel in Northern Ireland via rail, bus, and Ulsterbus; it costs IR£70 for 5 days' travel out of 15 consecutive days.

By Bus For the strictly independent traveler, the 15-day **Rambler** ticket gives unlimited travel by bus and is an excellent value at IR£95. It can be purchased from any city bus terminal or train-station ticket office and is valid for travel on any 15 days in a 30-day period. The provincial bus system operated by Bus Éireann is widespread—more so than the train system—although service can be infrequent in remote areas. But the routes cover the entire country and are often linked to the train services (*see* By Train, *above*, for details of combined train and bus discount tickets).

By Bicycle Biking can be a great way to get around Ireland. Details of bicycle rentals are available from Bord Fáilte (the Irish Tourist Board, pronounced Board *Fall*-cha). Rates average IR£7.50 per day or IR£35 per week. You must pay a IR£30 deposit. Be sure to make reservations, especially in July and August. If you rent a bike in the Republic, you may *not* take it into Northern Ireland; nor may you take a bike rented in Northern Ireland into the Republic.

Staying in Ireland

Telephones There are pay phones in all post offices and most hotels and bars, as
Local Calls well as in street booths. Local calls cost 20p for three minutes, calls within Ireland cost about 50p for three minutes, and calls to Britain cost about IR£1.75 for three minutes. Telephone cards are available from all post offices and most newsagents. Prices range from IR£2.00 for 10 Units to IR£8.00 for 50 Units. Card booths are as common as coin booths. Rates go down by about a third after 6 PM and all day Saturday and Sunday.

International For calls to the United States and Canada, dial 001 followed by the
Calls area code. For calls to the United Kingdom, dial 0044 followed by the number, dropping the beginning zero. To reach an **AT&T** long-distance operator, dial 1–800/550–000; for **MCI,** dial 1–800/551–001; and for **Sprint,** dial 1–800/552–001.

Country Code The country code for the Republic of Ireland is 353.

Mail Airmail rates to the United States, Canada, and the Commonwealth
Postal Rates are 52p for the first 10 grams, air letters 45p, and postcards 38p. Letters to Britain and continental Europe cost 32p, postcards 28p.

Receiving Mail A general delivery service is operated free of charge from Dublin's General Post Office (O'Connell St., Dublin 1, tel. 01/872–8888).

Shopping Visitors from outside Europe can take advantage of the "cash-back"
VAT Refunds system on value-added tax (VAT) if their purchases total more than IR£50. A cash-back voucher must be filled out by the retailer at the point of sale. The visitor pays the total gross price, including VAT, and receives green and yellow copies of the invoice; both must be retained. These copies are presented to and stamped by customs when you leave the country. Take the stamped form along to the cashier, and the VAT will be refunded.

Opening and **Banks** are open weekdays 10–4 and until 5 on selected days. In small
Closing Times towns they may close for lunch from 12:30–1:30.

Museums are usually open weekdays 10–5, Saturday 10–1, Sunday 2–5. Always make a point of checking, however, since hours can change unexpectedly.

Shops are open Monday–Saturday 9–5:30, closing earlier on Wednesday, Thursday, or Saturday, depending on the locality.

National For 1996: January 1; March 18 (St. Patrick's Day); April 5 (Good Fri-
Holidays day); April 8 (Easter Monday); May 1 (May Day); June 3 (Whit Monday); August 5 (August Holiday); October 28 (October Holiday); and December 25–26 (Christmas). Changing holidays for 1997: March 17 (St. Patrick's Day); March 28 (Good Friday); March 31 (Easter Monday); June 2 (Whit Monday); August 4 (August Holiday); October 27 (October Holiday). If you're planning a visit at Easter, remember

that theaters and movie houses are closed for the last three days of the preceding week.

Dining When it comes to food, Ireland has some of the best raw materials in the world: prime beef, locally raised lamb and pork, free-range poultry, game in season, abundant fresh seafood, and locally grown seasonal vegetables. Despite the near-legendary awfulness of much Irish cooking in the recent past, times are definitely changing, and a new generation of chefs is beginning to take greater advantage of this abundance of magnificent produce.

If your tastes run toward traditional Irish dishes, there are still a few old-fashioned restaurants serving substantial portions of excellent, if plain, home cooking. Look for boiled bacon and cabbage, Irish stew, and colcannon (cooked potatoes diced and fried in butter with onions and either cabbage or leeks and covered in thick cream just before serving). The best bet for daytime meals is "pub grub"—a choice of soup and soda bread, two or three hot dishes of the day, salad platters, or sandwiches. Most bars serve food, and many offer coffee and tea as an alternative to alcohol. Guinness, a dark beer, or "stout," brewed with malt, is the Irish national drink. Even if you never go out for a drink at home, you should visit at least one or two pubs in Ireland. The pub is one of the pillars of Irish society, worth visiting as much for entertainment and conversation as for drinking.

To help travelers on a budget, more than 360 restaurants participate in a *tourist menu* program. Three-course meals are offered at set prices ranging from about IR£7 to IR£14. Bord Fáilte's *Tourist Menu* leaflet (50p) gives full details. Most places limit the availability of this menu to lunchtime and early evening.

Mealtimes Breakfast is served between 8 and 10—earlier by special request only—and is a substantial meal of cereal, bacon, eggs, sausage, and toast. Lunch is eaten between 12:30 and 2. The old tradition of "high tea" taken around 5, followed by a light snack (supper) before bed, is still encountered in many Irish homes, including many bed-and-breakfasts. Elsewhere, however, it is generally assumed that you'll be eating between 7 and 9:30 and that this will be your main meal of the day.

What to Wear A jacket and tie or upscale casual dress are suggested for expensive restaurants. Otherwise, casual dress is acceptable.

Ratings Prices are per person and include a first course, a main course, and dessert, but no wine or tip. Sales tax at 10% is included in all Irish restaurant bills. A tip of 10% is adequate.

Category	Cost
$$	IR£16–IR£28
$	IR£12–IR£16
¢	under IR£12

Lodging Accommodations in Ireland range all the way from deluxe castles and renovated stately homes to thatched cottages and farmhouses to humble B&Bs. Standards everywhere are high, and they continue to rise. Pressure on hotel space reaches a peak between June and September, but it's a good idea to make reservations in advance at any time of the year. Rooms can be reserved directly from the United States; ask your travel agent for details. Bord Fáilte's Central Reservations Service (14 Upper O'Connell St., Dublin 1, tel. 01/874-7733, fax 01/874-3660) can make reservations, as can local tourist board offices.

NOW THE FASTEST WAY OVER THE CHANNEL MAY BE UNDER IT.

At speeds of up to 200 mph, the Eurostar train takes you from downtown London to downtown Paris in just 3 hours – the same amount of time it takes by plane. But without the hassles of cabs, traffic jams or weather delays.

What's more, Eurostar's first class service costs less than most airline business class trips.

And we're ready to go when you are – with at least 10 departures daily.

For information and reservations contact your travel agent or call **1-800-EUROSTAR**.

THE EUROSTAR TRAIN. THE BETTER WAY TO FLY ACROSS THE CHANNEL.

This guidebook teaches you how to budget your money.

This page is for slow learners.

We all make mistakes. So if you happen to find yourself making a costly one, call Western Union. With them, you can receive money from the States within minutes at any of our European locations. Plus, it's already been converted into the appropriate currency.

Just call our numbers in Austria 0222 892 0380, Belgium 02 753 2150, Denmark 800 107 11, Finland 9 800 20440, France 161 43 54 46 12, Germany 069 2648201, 0681 933 3328, Greece 01 687 3850, Ireland 1 800 395 395,* Italy 039 6 167016840, Netherlands 06 0566,* Poland 22 37 1826, Spain 93 301 1212, Sweden 020 741 742, United Kingdom 0 800 833 833,* or if you're in the United States 1 800 325 6000.*

And since nobody's perfect, you might want to keep these numbers in your wallet, for those times when nothing else is in there.

WESTERN UNION | MONEY TRANSFER®

The fastest way to send money worldwide.℠

Bord Fáilte has an official grading system and publishes a detailed price list of all approved accommodations, including hotels, guest houses, farmhouses, B&Bs, and hostels. No hotel may exceed this price without special authorization from Bord Fáilte; prices must also be displayed in every room. Don't hesitate to complain either to the manager or to Bord Fáilte, or both, if prices exceed this maximum.

In general, hotels charge per person. In most cases (but not all, especially in more expensive places), the price includes a full breakfast. VAT is included, but some hotels—again, usually the more expensive ones—add a 10–15% service charge. This should be mentioned in their price list. In $$ and $ hotels, be sure to specify whether you want a private bath or shower; the latter is cheaper. Off-season (October–May) prices are reduced by as much as 25%.

Guest Houses Some smaller hotels are graded as guest houses. To qualify, they must have at least five bedrooms. A few may have restaurants; those that do not will often provide evening meals by arrangement. Few will have a bar. Otherwise these rooms can be as comfortable as those of a regular hotel, and in major cities they offer very good value for the money, compared with the inexpensive hotels.

Bed-and- Bed-and-breakfast means just that. The bed can vary from a four-*Breakfasts* poster in the wing of a castle to a feather bed in a whitewashed farmhouse or the spare bedroom of a modern cottage. Rates are generally around IR£16 per person, though these can vary significantly. Although many larger B&Bs offer rooms with bath or shower, in some you'll have to use the bathroom in the hall and, in many cases, pay 50p–IR£1 extra for the privilege.

B&B accommodations can be booked for that night at local tourist information offices for a nominal fee. Most travelers do not bother booking a B&B in advance. They are so plentiful that it's often more fun to leave the decision open. But you should check in by at least 6 PM to obtain the best choice of rooms. Many B&Bs offer reductions for stays longer than two nights.

Hostels **An Oige** (The Irish Youth Hostels Association, pronounced on *Oy*-ga, 39 Mountjoy Sq., Dublin 1, tel. 01/836–3111) has a chain of 40 hostels. You must have an International Youth Hostel card to stay at one. All have a curfew and are closed 10 AM–5 PM. Charges for adults are IR£6 per night in city hostels and around IR£4 in rural ones.

About 100 other hostels are linked together in the **Association of Independent Hostels.** These are friendly, easygoing places with no curfew and no daytime closing rules. Most have private double rooms for around IR£6.50 per person per night and dormitory accommodations for about IR£5. Self-catering kitchens and hot showers are usually available. For a list of locations and facilities, write to Patrick O'Donnell, Dooey Hostel, Glencolumcille, Co. Donegal (tel. 073/30130).

Rentals In nearly 30 locations around Ireland, there are clusters of cottages for rent. The majority are built in traditional styles, but have central heating and all other conveniences. The average rent for a three-bedroom cottage equipped for six adults is around IR£250 in midseason; be sure to make reservations well in advance. Bord Fáilte's booklet *Self Catering* (IR£4) has full details.

Camping There are a variety of beautifully sited campgrounds and trailer parks, but be prepared for wet weather! Bord Fáilte publishes a useful booklet, *Caravan and Camping Guide* (IR£1).

Ratings Prices are for two people in a double room, based on high season (June to September) rates.

Category	Cost
$$	IR£70–IR£100
$	IR£50–IR£70
¢	under IR£50

Tipping Other than in upscale hotels and restaurants, the Irish are not really used to being tipped. Some hotels and restaurants will add a service charge of about 12% to your bill, so tipping isn't necessary unless you've received particularly good service.

Tip taxi drivers about 10% of the fare if the taxi has been using its meter. For longer journeys, where the fare is agreed in advance, a tip will not be expected unless some kind of commentary (solicited or not) has been provided. In luxury hotels, porters and bellhops will expect IR£1; elsewhere, 50p is adequate. Hairdressers normally expect a tip of about IR£1. You don't tip in pubs, but if there is waiter service in a bar or hotel lounge, leave about 20p.

Dublin

Arriving and Departing

By Plane All flights arrive at Dublin's Collinstown Airport, 10 kilometers (6 miles) north of town. For information on arrival and departure times, call individual airlines.

Between the Airport and Downtown Buses leave every 20 minutes from outside the Arrivals door for the central bus station in downtown Dublin. The ride takes about 30 minutes, depending on the traffic, and the fare is IR£2.50. A taxi ride into town will cost from IR£9 to IR£14, depending on the location of your hotel.

By Train There are three main stations. Heuston Station (at Kingsbridge) is the departure point for the south and southwest; Connolly Station (at Amiens Street), for Belfast, the east coast, and the west; Pearse Station (on Westland Row), for Bray and connections via Dun Laoghaire to the Liverpool/Holyhead ferries. Tel. 01/836–6222 for information.

By Bus The central bus station, Busaras, is at Store Street near the Custom House. Some buses terminate near O'Connell Bridge. Tel. 01/873–4222 for information on city services (Dublin Bus); tel. 01/836–6111 for express buses and provincial services (Bus Éireann).

By Car The main access route from the north is N1; from the west, N4; from the south and southwest, N7; from the east coast, N11. On all routes there are clearly marked signs indicating the center of the city: "An Lár."

Getting Around

Dublin is small as capital cities go—the downtown area is positively compact—and the best way to see the city and soak in the full flavor is on foot.

By Train An electric train commuter service, DART (Dublin Area Rapid Transit), serves the suburbs out to Howth, on the north side of the city, and to Bray, County Wicklow, on the south side. Fares are about the same as for buses. Street-direction signs to DART stations read Staisiun/Station. The **Irish Rail** office is at 35 Lower Abbey Street; for rail inquiries, tel. 01/836–6222.

By Bus Most city buses originate in or pass through the area of O'Connell Street and O'Connell Bridge. If the destination board indicates "An

Lár," that means that the bus is going to the city's central area. Timetables (IR£2) are available from the **Dublin Bus** office (59 Upper O'Connell St., tel. 01/873–4222) and give details of all routes, times of operation, and price codes. The minimum fare is 60p.

By Taxi Taxis do not generally cruise, but are located beside the central bus station, at train stations, at O'Connell Bridge, College Green, St. Stephens green, and near major hotels. They are not of a uniform type or color. Make sure the meter is on (unless you are on a long trip where the fare has already been agreed upon). The initial charge is IR£2; the fare is displayed in the cab. A 1-mile trip in city traffic costs about IR£3.50.

Important Addresses and Numbers

Tourist Information There is a tourist information office in the entrance hall of the **Bord Fáilte** headquarters (Baggot Street Bridge, tel. 01/676–5871); open weekdays 9–5. More conveniently located is the office at 14 Upper O'Connell St. (tel. 01/874–7733; open weekdays 9–5:30, Sat. 9–1). There is also an office at the airport (tel. 01/844–5387). From mid-June to September, there is an office at the Ferryport (Dun Laoghaire, tel. 01/280–6984).

Embassies U.S. (42 Elgin Rd., Ballsbridge, tel. 01/668–8777). **Canadian** (65 St. Stephen's Green, tel. 01/478–1988). **U.K.** (33 Merrion Rd., tel. 01/269–5211).

Emergencies Police (tel. 999). Ambulance (tel. 999). Doctor (tel. 01/679–0700). Dentist (tel. 01/679–4311).

Travel Agencies American Express (116 Grafton St., tel. 01/677–2874). Thomas Cook (118 Grafton St., tel. 01/677–1721).

Exploring Dublin

Numbers in the margin correspond to points of interest on the Dublin map.

Dublin is a small city with a population of just over 1 million. For all that, it has a distinctly cosmopolitan air, one that complements happily the individuality of the city and the courtesy and friendliness of its inhabitants. Most of the city's historically interesting buildings date from the 18th century, and, although many of its finer Georgian buildings disappeared in the overenthusiastic redevelopment of the '70s, enough remain, mainly south of the river, to recall the elegant Dublin of the past. The slums romanticized by writers Sean O'Casey and Brendan Behan have been virtually eradicated, but literary Dublin can still be recaptured by those who want to follow the footsteps of Leopold Bloom's progress, as described in James Joyce's *Ulysses*. And Trinity College, alma mater of Oscar Wilde, Jonathan Swift, and Samuel Beckett, among others, still provides a haven of tranquillity.

Dubliners are a talkative, self-confident people, eager to have visitors enjoy the pleasures of their city. You can meet a lively cross section of people in the city's numerous bars, probably the best places to sample the famous wit of the only city to have produced three winners of the Nobel Prize for Literature: William Butler Yeats, George Bernard Shaw, and Samuel Beckett.

O'Connell Street **❶** Begin your tour of Dublin at **O'Connell Bridge**, the city's most central landmark. Look closely and you will notice a strange feature: The bridge is wider than it is long. The north side of O'Connell Bridge is dominated by an elaborate memorial to Daniel O'Connell, "The Liberator," erected as a tribute to the great 19th-century orator's achievement in securing Catholic Emancipation in 1829. Today **O'Connell Street** is the city's main—though increasingly less ele-

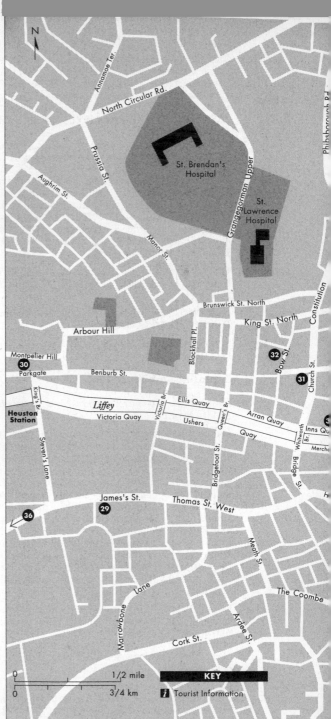

N

North Circular Rd.

Annamoe ter.

Phibsborough Rd.

Prussia St.

Aughrim St.

St. Brendan's Hospital

Grangegorman Upper

St. Lawrence Hospital

Manor St.

Brunswick St. North

King St. North

Constitution

Arbour Hill

Blackhall Pl.

Bow St.

Church St.

32

Montpelier Hill

30
Parkgate

Benburb St.

31

Liffey

Ellis Quay

King's Br.

Victoria Br.

Victoria Quay

Ushers

Queen's Br.

Arran Quay

Whitworth Br.

Inns Qu

Merche

Heuston Station

Steven's Lane

Quay

Bridgefoot St.

Bridge St.

James's St.

Thomas St. West

29

Meath St.

The Coombe

Lane

Marrowbone

Ardee St.

Cork St.

36

0 — 1/2 mile

0 — 3/4 km

KEY

i Tourist Information

gant—shopping area, though it seems decidedly parochial to anyone accustomed to Fifth Avenue or Rodeo Drive. Turn left just before the General Post Office and take a look at Henry Street. This pedestrians-only shopping area leads to the colorful **Moore Street Market,** where street vendors recall their most famous ancestor, Molly Malone, by singing their wares—mainly flowers and fruit—in the traditional Dublin style.

2 The **General Post Office,** known as the GPO, occupies a special place in Irish history. It was from the portico of its handsome classical facade that Padraig Pearse read the Proclamation of the Republic on Easter Monday, 1916. You can still see the scars of bullets on its pillars from the fighting that ensued. The GPO remains the focal point for political rallies and demonstrations even today and is used as a viewing stand for VIPs during the annual St. Patrick's Day Parade.

3 The **Gresham Hotel** has played a part in Dublin's history since 1817, although, along with the entire O'Connell Street area, it is less fashionable now than it was during the last century. Just south of the Gresham is the Bord Fáilte information office; drop in for a free street map, shopping guides, and information on all aspects of Dublin tourism. Opposite is the main office of Bus Éireann, which can supply bus timetables and information on excursions.

4 At the top of O'Connell Street is the **Rotunda,** the first maternity hospital in Europe, opened in 1755. Not much remains of the once-elegant Rotunda Assembly Rooms, a famous haunt of fashionable Dubliners until the middle of the last century. The **Gate Theater,** housed in an extension of the Rotunda Assembly Rooms, however, continues to attract crowds to its fine repertoire of classic Irish and European drama.

5 Beyond the Rotunda, you will have a fine vista of **Parnell Square,** one of Dublin's earliest Georgian squares. You will notice immediately that the first-floor windows of these elegant brick-face buildings are much larger than the others and that it is easy to look in from street level. This is more than simply the result of the architect's desire to achieve perfect proportions on the facades: These rooms were designed as reception rooms, and fashionable hostesses liked passersby to be able to peer in and admire the distinguished guests at their luxurious, candle-lit receptions.

6 **Charlemont House,** whose impressive Palladian facade dominates the top of Parnell Square, now houses the **Hugh Lane Municipal Gallery of Modern Art.** Sir Hugh Lane, a nephew of Lady Gregory, who was Yeats's curious, high-minded aristocratic patron, was a keen collector of Impressionist paintings. The gallery also contains some interesting works by Irish artists, including Yeats's brother Jack. *Parnell Sq., tel. 01/674–1903. Admission free. Open Tues.–Sat. 9:30–6, Sun. 11–5.*

7 The Parnell Square area is rich in literary associations, which are explained and illustrated in the **Dublin Writers Museum.** Opened in 1991 in two carefully restored 18th-century buildings, it contains paintings, letters, manuscripts, and photographs related to James Joyce, Sean O'Casey, George Bernard Shaw, W. B. Yeats, Brendan Behan, and others on permanent display. There are also temporary exhibitions, lectures, and readings, as well as a bookshop. *18–19 Parnell Sq. N, tel. 01/872–2077. Admission: IR£2.25. Open Mon.–Sat. 10–5, Sun. 1–5.*

8 Return to O'Connell Street, where a sign on the left will lead you to **St. Mary's Pro Cathedral,** the main Catholic church of Dublin. Try to catch the famous Palestrina Choir on Sunday at 11 AM. John McCormack is one of many famous voices to have sung with this exquisite en-

9 semble. The **Abbey Theatre,** a brick building dating from 1966, was given a much-needed new facade in 1991. It has some noteworthy portraits and mementos in the foyer. Seats are usually available at about IR£12, and with luck you may just have a wonderful evening. The luck element, unfortunately, must be stressed, since the Abbey has had both financial and artistic problems lately.

Trinity and Stephen's Green
⑩

It is only a short walk across O'Connell Bridge to **Parliament House.** Today this stately early 18th-century building is no more than a branch of the Bank of Ireland; originally, however, it housed the Irish Parliament. The original House of Lords, with its fine coffered ceiling and 1,233-piece Waterford glass chandelier, is open to the public during banking hours (weekdays 10–12:30 and 1:30–3). It's also worth taking a look at the main banking hall, whose judicial character—it was previously the Court of Requests—has been sensitively maintained.

⑪ Across the road is the facade of **Trinity College,** whose memorably atmospheric campus is a must for every visitor. Trinity College, Dublin (familiarly known as TCD), was founded by Elizabeth I in 1591 and offered a free education to Catholics—provided that they accepted the Protestant faith. As a legacy of this condition, right up until 1966, Catholics who wished to study at Trinity had to obtain a dispensation from their bishop or face excommunication. Today more than 70% of Trinity's students are Catholics, a clear indication of how far away those days seem to today's generation.

The facade, built between 1755 and 1759, consists of a magnificent portico with Corinthian columns. The design is repeated on the interior, so the view from outside the gates and from the quadrangle inside is the same. On the sweeping lawn in front of the facade are statues of two of the university's illustrious alumni—statesman Edward Burke and poet Oliver Goldsmith. Other famous students include the philosopher George Berkeley (who gave his name to the San Francisco area campus of the University of California), Jonathan Swift, Thomas Moore, Oscar Wilde, John Millington Synge, Henry Grattan, Wolfe Tone, Robert Emmet, Bram Stoker, Edward Carson, Douglas Hyde, and Samuel Beckett.

Ireland's largest collection of books and manuscripts is housed in **Trinity College Library.** There are 3 million volumes gathering dust here; about half a mile of new shelving has to be added every year to keep pace with acquisitions. The library is entered through the library shop. Its principal treasure is the **Book of Kells,** a beautifully illuminated manuscript of the Gospels dating from the 8th century. Because of the beauty and the fame of the Book of Kells, at peak hours you may have to wait in line to enter the library; it's less busy early in the day. Apart from the many treasures it contains, the aptly named **Long Room** is impressive in itself, stretching for 213 feet and housing 200,000 of the library's volumes, mostly manuscripts and old books. Originally it had a flat plaster ceiling, but the perennial need for more shelving resulted in a decision to raise the level of the roof and add the barrel-vaulted ceiling and the gallery bookcases. *Tel. 01/677–2941. Admission: IR£2.50. Open Mon.–Sat. 9:30–4:45, Sun. 12–5.*

A breath of fresh air will be welcome after the library, so when you're done admiring the award-winning modern architecture of the Berkeley Library and the Arts Building, pass through the gate to the sports grounds—rugby fields on your left, cricket on your right. Leave Trinity by the Lincoln Place Gate—a handy "back door."

⑫ Shoppers will find a detour along Nassau Street in order here. As well as being well endowed with bookstores, it contains the **Kilkenny Design Workshops,** which, besides selling the best in contemporary Irish design for the home, also holds regular exhibits of exciting new work by Irish craftsmen. *Open Mon.–Sat. 9–5.*

⑬ Nassau Street will lead you into **Merrion Square,** past a distinctive corner house that was the home of Oscar Wilde's parents. Merrion Square is one of the most pleasant in Dublin. Its flower gardens are well worth a visit in the summer months. Note the brightly colored front doors and the intricate fanlights above them—a distinctive feature of Dublin's domestic architecture.

⑭ The **National Gallery** is the first in a series of important buildings on the west side of the square. It is one of Europe's most agreeable and compact galleries, with more than 2,000 works on view, including a major collection of Irish landscape painting, 17th-century French works, paintings from the Italian and Spanish schools, and a collection of Dutch masters. *Merrion Sq., tel. 01/661–5133. Admission free. Open Mon.–Wed. and Fri.–Sat. 10–5:30, Thurs. 10–8:30, Sun. 2–5.*

⑮ Next door is **Leinster House,** seat of the Irish Parliament. This imposing 18th-century building has two facades: Its Merrion Square facade is designed in the style of a country house, while the other facade, in Kildare Street, is in the style of a town house. Visitors may be shown the house when Dail Éireann (pronounced "Dawl Erin"), the Irish Parliament, is not in session.

Stephen's Green, as it is always called by Dubliners, suffered more from the planning blight of the philistine '60s than did its neighbor, Merrion Square. An exception is the magnificent **Shelbourne Hotel,** which dominates the north side of the green. It is still as fashionable—and as expensive—as ever.

Time Out Budget-conscious visitors should put on their finery and try afternoon tea in the elegant splendor of the Shelbourne's **Lord Mayor's Room.** You can experience its old-fashioned luxury for around IR£10 (including sandwiches and cakes) per head.

---

⑯ ⑰ Around the corner on Kildare Street, the town-house facade of Leinster House is flanked by the **National Museum** and the **National Library,** each featuring a massive colonnaded rotunda entrance built in 1890. The museum (Admission: free. Open Tues.–Sat. 10–5, Sun. 2–5) houses a remarkable collection of Irish treasures from 6000 BC to the present, including the Tara Brooch, the Ardagh Chalice, and the Cross of Cong. Every major figure in modern Irish literature, from George Bernard Shaw onward, studied in the National Library at some point. In addition to a comprehensive collection of Irish authors, it contains extensive newspaper archives. *Kildare St., tel. 01/661–8811. Admission free, except for certain exhibits. Open Mon. 10–9, Tues.–Wed. 2–9, Thurs.–Fri. 10–5, Sat. 10–1.*

⑱ The **Genealogical Office**—the starting point for ancestor tracing—also incorporates the **Heraldic Museum,** which features displays of flags, coins, stamps, silver, and family crests that highlight the uses and development of heraldry in Ireland. *2 Kildare St., tel. 01/661–8811. Genealogical Office. Open weekdays 10–5. Heraldic Museum. Admission free. Open weekdays 10–12:30 and 2:30–4. Guided tours Mar.–Oct., cost IR£1.*

⑲ The **Royal Irish Academy,** on Dawson Street, is the country's leading learned society; it has many important manuscripts in its unmodernized 18th-century library (open Mon.–Fri. 9:30–5:15). Just below the academy is **Mansion House,** the official residence of the Lord Mayor of Dublin. Its Round Room was the location of the first assembly of Dail Éireann in January 1919.

⑳ **Grafton Street,** which runs between Stephen's Green and Trinity College, is the city's most upscale shopping street. Check out **Brown Thomas,** Ireland's most elegant and old-fashioned department store; it has an extremely good selection of sporting goods and Waterford crystal—an odd combination. Many of the more stylish boutiques are just off the main pedestrians-only areas, so be sure to poke around likely corners. Don't miss the **Powerscourt Town House,** an imaginative shopping arcade installed in and around the covered courtyard of an impressive 18th-century building. Nearby is the **Civic Museum,** which contains drawings, models, maps of Dublin, and other civic memorabilia. *58 S. William St., tel. 01/679–4260. Admission free. Open Tues.–Sat. 10–6, Sun. 11–2.*

A short walk from Stephen's Green will bring you to one of the smaller and more unusual gems of old Dublin, **Archbishop Marsh's Library.** It was built in 1701, and access is through a tiny but charming cottage garden. Its interior has been unchanged for more than 300 years and still contains "cages" into which scholars who wanted to peruse rare books were locked. (The cages were to discourage students who, often impecunious, may have been tempted to make the books their own.) *St. Patrick's Close, tel. 01/454–8511. Open Mon., Wed., and Fri. 10–12:45 and 2–4, Sat. 10:30–12:45.*

Opposite, on Patrick Street, is **St. Patrick's Cathedral.** Legend has it that St. Patrick baptized many converts at a well on the site of the cathedral in the 5th century. The building dates from 1190 and is mainly early English in style. At 93 meters (300 feet), it is the longest church in the country. Its history has not always been happy. In the 17th century, Oliver Cromwell, dour ruler of England and no friend of the Irish, had his troops stable their horses in the cathedral. It wasn't until the 19th century that restoration work to repair the damage was put in hand. St. Patrick's is the national cathedral of the Protestant Church of Ireland and has had many illustrious deans. The most famous was Jonathan Swift, author of *Gulliver's Travels,* who held office from 1713 to 1745. Swift's tomb is in the south aisle, and Dean Swift's corner at the top of the north transept contains his pulpit, his writing table and chair, his portrait, and his death mask. Memorials to many other celebrated figures from Ireland's past line the walls of St. Patrick's. *Patrick St., tel. 01/475–4817. Admission: IR£1.*

St. Patrick's originally stood outside the walls of Dublin. Its close neighbor, **Christ Church Cathedral** (Christ Church Rd.), on the other hand, stood just within the walls and belonged to the See of Dublin. It is for this reason that the city has two cathedrals so close to each other. Christ Church was founded in 1172 by Strongbow, a Norman baron and conqueror of Dublin for the English crown, and it took 50 years to build. Strongbow himself is buried in the cathedral beneath an impressive effigy. The vast and sturdy **crypt** is Dublin's oldest surviving structure and should not be missed.

Signs in the Christ Church area will lead you to **Dublin Castle.** Guided tours of the lavishly furnished state apartments are offered every half hour and provide one of the most enjoyable sightseeing experiences in town. Only fragments of the original 13th-century building survive; the elegant castle you see today is essentially an 18th-century building. The state apartments were formerly the residence of the English viceroys—the monarch's representative in Ireland—and are now used by the president of Ireland to entertain visiting heads of state. The state apartments are closed when in official use, so phone first to check. *Entrance off Dame St., tel. 01/677–7129. Admission: IR£2.50. Open weekdays 10–12:15 and 2–5, weekends 2–5.*

Step into the **City Hall** on Dame Street to admire the combination of grand classical ornament and understated Georgian simplicity in its circular main hall. It also contains a good example of the kind of gently curving Georgian staircase that is a typical feature of most large town houses in Dublin.

Between Dame Street and the river Liffey is the semipedestrianized area known as **Temple Bar,** which should interest anyone who wants to discover "young Dublin." The area is chock-full of innovative art galleries, inexpensive restaurants, and small, imaginative shops.

㉙ The **Guinness Brewery,** founded by Arthur Guinness in 1759, dominates the area to the west of Christ Church, covering 60 acres. Guinness is proud of its brewery and invites visitors to attend a 30-minute film shown in a converted hops store next door to the brewery itself. After the film, you can sample the famous black beverage. *Guinness Hop Store, Crane St., tel. 01/453–6700. Admission: IR£2.50. Open weekdays 10–3.*

Phoenix Park and the Liffey
㉚ Across the Liffey is **Phoenix Park,** 1,760 acres of green open space. Though the park is open to all, it has only two residents: the president of Ireland and the American ambassador. The park is dominated by a 64-meter- (205-foot-) high obelisk, a tribute to the first duke of Wellington. Sunday is the best time to visit: Games of cricket, soccer, polo, baseball, hurling—a combination of lacrosse, baseball, and field hockey—or Gaelic football will be in progress.

Returning to the city's central area along the north bank of the Liffey, you pass through a fairly run-down section that's scheduled for
㉛ major redevelopment. A diversion up Church Street to **St. Michan's** will be relished by those with a macabre turn of mind. Open coffins in the vaults beneath the church reveal mummified bodies, some more than 900 years old. The sexton, who can be found at the church gate on weekdays, will guide you around the church and crypt.

㉜ The **Irish Whiskey Corner** is just behind St. Michan's. A 90-year-old warehouse has been converted into a museum to introduce visitors to the pleasures of Irish whiskey. There's an audiovisual show and free tasting. *Bow St., tel. 01/872–5566. Admission: IR£3. Tours weekdays at 3:30, or by appointment.*

The Liffey has two of Dublin's most famous landmarks, both of them the work of 18th-century architect James Gandon and both among
㉝ the city's finest buildings. The first is the **Four Courts,** surmounted by a massive copper-covered dome, giving it a distinctive profile. It is the seat of the High Court of Justice of Ireland. The building was completed between 1786 and 1802, then gutted in the Civil War of the '20s; it has since been painstakingly restored. You will recognize
㉞ the same architect's hand in the **Custom House,** farther down the Liffey. Its graceful dome rises above a central portico, itself linked by arcades to the pavilions at either end. Behind this useful and elegant landmark is an altogether more workaday structure, the central bus station, known as Busaras.

Midway between Gandon's two masterpieces is the Metal Bridge,
㉟ otherwise known as the **Ha'penny Bridge,** so called because, until early in this century, a toll of a half-penny was charged to cross it. The poet W. B. Yeats was one among many Dubliners who found this too high a price to pay—more a matter of principle than of finance—and so made the detour via O'Connell Bridge. Today no such high-minded concern need prevent you from marching out to the middle of the bridge to admire the view up and down the Liffey as it wends its way through the city.

㊱ The **Royal Hospital Kilmainham** is a short ride by taxi or bus from the center; it's well worth the trip. The hospital is considered the most important 17th-century building in Ireland. It was completed in 1684 as a hospice—the original meaning of the term "hospital"—for veteran soldiers. Note especially the chapel with its magnificent Baroque ceiling. It also houses the **Irish Museum of Modern Art,** which opened in 1991. Parts of the old building, used as a national cultural center, are occasionally closed to the public. *Kilmainham La., tel. 01/671–8666. Guided tours: Sun. noon–5 and holidays 2–5; cost IR£2. Exhibitions: open Tues.–Sat. 2–5:30.*

Devotees of James Joyce may wish to take the DART train south to **Sandycove,** about 8 kilometers (5 miles) out of the city center. It was here, in a Martello tower (a circular fortification built by the British as a defense against possible invasion by Napoléon at the beginning of the 19th century), that the maverick Irish genius lived for some months in 1904. It now houses the **Joyce Museum.** *Sandycove Coast. Admission: IR£1.50 adults, 60p children. Open Apr.–Oct., Mon.– Sat. 10–1 and 2–5, Sun. 2:30–6. Also by appointment, tel. 01/280– 8571.*

Shopping

Shopping Districts The most sophisticated shopping area is around **Grafton Street.** The **St. Stephen's Green Center** contains 70 stores, large and small, in a vast Moorish-style glass-roof building on the Grafton Street corner. **Molesworth** and **Dawson Streets** are the places to browse for antiques; **Nassau** and **Dawson Streets,** for books; the smaller cross side streets for jewelry, art galleries, and old prints. The pedestrianized **Temple Bar** area, with its young, offbeat ambience, has a number of small art galleries, small specialty shops (including music and book stores), and inexpensive and adventurous clothing shops.

Department Stores The shops north of the river tend to be less expensive and less design conscious; chain stores and lackluster department stores make up the bulk of them. The **ILAC Shopping Center,** on Henry Street, is worth a look, however. **Clery's,** on O'Connell St. (directly opposite the GPO), was once the city's most fashionable department store and is still worth a visit, despite its rapidly aging decor. **Switzers** and **Brown Thomas** are Grafton Street's main department stores; the latter is Dublin's most elegantly decorated department store, with many international fashion labels on sale. **Arnotts,** on Henry Street, is Dublin's largest department store and has a good range of cut crystal. Visit **Kilkenny Design Workshops** on Nassau Street for the best selection of Irish designs for the home.

Tweeds and Woolens Ready-made tweeds for men can be found at **Kevin and Howlin,** on Nassau Street, and at **Cleo Ltd.,** on Kildare Street. The **Blarney Woollen Mills,** on Nassau Street, has a good selection of tweed, linen, and woolen sweaters in all price ranges. The **Woolen Mills,** at Ha'penny Bridge, has a good selection of handknits and other woolen sweaters at competitive prices.

Dining

The restaurant scene in Dublin has improved beyond recognition in recent years. Though no one is ever likely to confuse the place with, say, Paris, the days of chewy boiled meats and soggy, tasteless vegetables are long gone. Food still tends to be substantial rather than subtle, but more and more restaurants are at last taking advantage of the magnificent livestock and fish that Ireland has in such abundance. For details and price-category definitions, *see* Dining *in* Staying in Ireland, *above.*

$$ **Bad Ass Café.** Definitely one of Dublin's loudest restaurants, this barnlike place, situated in the trendy Temple Bar area, between the Central Bank and the Ha'penny Bridge, is always a fun place to eat. American-style fast food—burgers, chili, and pizzas—and the pounding rock music attract a lively crowd, both the young and the young at heart. Look out for the old-fashioned cash shuttles whizzing around the ceiling! *9–11 Crown Alley, tel. 01/671–2596. Reservations for large parties recommended. AE, MC, V.*

$$ **Dobbin's Wine Bistro.** Though Dobbin's aims at a French identity, with its red-and-white gingham tablecloths and sawdust-strewn slate floor, the cooking here is international and imaginative, with an emphasis on fresh Irish produce. Specialties are phyllo pastry with pepper and seafood filling, paupiettes of salmon and sole with spinach and dill sauce, and Szechuan boned crispy duck with an apple and plum sauce. *15 Stephen's La., tel. 01/876–4670. Reservations advised. AE, DC, MC, V. Closed Sun.*

$$ **Elephant and Castle.** The trendiest of the many eateries in the Temple Bar area, this small café's booths and tall stools are meant to recall the diners of 1950s teeny-bopper movies. Its menu is a bit more sophisticated than its decor: The menu includes a range of burgers (get 'em 10 different ways) and "New York style" open or triple-decker sandwiches. Spicy chicken wings in a basket, lime and coriander chicken, and steak are also popular choices. The Elephant is a favored hangout for Sunday brunch. The dessert list concentrates on large ice cream combinations. *18 Temple Bar, tel. 01/679–3121. No reservations. AE, DC, MC, V.*

$$ **La Pigalle.** This is a charming and unpretentious French restaurant in an old, crooked building that forms part of the archway leading to the Ha'penny Bridge. It is in the heart of the colorful Temple Bar area and very much part of the "scene." The decor is old-fashioned and well-worn, the atmosphere relaxed, and the authentically French food is presented on a menu that changes daily. Typical dishes include fresh asparagus tart, sea trout fillet with sorrel and muscadet, and duck breast with apple and calvados. *14 Temple Bar, tel. 01/671–9262. Reservations advised. MC, V. No lunch Sat. Closed Sun.*

$$ **Le Caprice.** This Italian restaurant, situated right in the city center, features white linen-covered tables amid lots of bric-a-brac and busy decorations. The place also has a real party atmosphere later in the evening when the pianist is in the right mood. The menu includes traditional Continental dishes, such as prawn cocktail, deep-fried scampi, and roast duckling *à l'orange,* as well as an interesting selection of authentic Italian dishes, including pasta and veal. *12 St. Andrew's St., tel. 01/679–4050. Reservations accepted. AE, DC, MC, V. Dinner only.*

$ **Cornucopia Wholefoods.** This vegetarian restaurant above a health-food shop provides good value for the money. The seating consists of bar stools at high, narrow, glass-top tables. It's popular with students from nearby Trinity College. The menu includes red lentil soup, avocado quiche, vegetarian spring roll, and vegetarian curry—all of them regular favorites. *19 Wicklow St., tel. 01/677–7583. No reservations. No credit cards. Closed Sun., Mon., and holidays.*

$ **Da Vicenza.** Watching the pizza dough being kneaded, rolled, topped off, and thrust into the brick oven will probably influence your menu choice here. The pizzas are indeed excellent, but the restaurant also offers interesting pasta combinations, fish, and steak. Dark blue blinds and drapery against natural stone and wood are the background for a venue that is popular with all age groups. *133 Upper Leeson St., tel. 01/660–9906. Reservations advised. AE, DC, MC, V.*

$ **Gallagher's Boxty House.** This highly original Irish eatery has a charming country ambience with antique pine furniture complementing the dark green decor. Boxty is a traditional Irish potato bread or cake that is served here as a pancake, thin enough to wrap around savory fillings, such as bacon and cabbage, chicken with leeks, and smoked fish. Follow these with brown bread and Bailey's ice cream or the superb bread-and-butter pudding. *20 Temple Bar, tel. 01/677–2762. No reservations. V. Closed Christmas and Good Friday.*

$ **Pasta Pasta.** This small, bright, and unpretentiously pretty Italian eatery serves combinations of pasta shapes and sauces plus a few Italian specials—medallions of pork *ai funghi* (with mushrooms), *escalope milanesa*—against a background of muted jazz-rock. It's excellent value. *27 Exchequer St., tel. 01/679–2565. Reservations advised for groups over 6 and on weekends. MC, V. Closed Sun.*

¢ **Bewley's.** This famous chain of coffeehouses is essential to Dublin's social fabric. Recent refurbishment restored the original turn-of-century style, with dark mahogany trim, stained-glass windows, and bentwood chairs, and put the motherly waitresses back into traditional black dresses with white aprons and headbands. Variations on the traditional Irish breakfast (eggs, bacon, sausage, black-and-white pudding, tomatoes, and mushrooms) are the thing to eat here—at any hour of the day. Other specialties include Bewley's 11 blends of tea and 15 blends of coffee, as well as home-baked scones, buns, and pastries. *Westmoreland St., Grafton St., South Great George's St., and suburban branches, tel. 01/677-6761 (head office). Open daily 8-6. No reservations. AE, DC, MC, V.*

¢ **Burdock's.** You'll find Burdock's in the heart of Viking Dublin, next door to the Lord Edward pub. Dublin's most famous fish and chipper sticks to the traditional method of frying in beef drippings over a coal fire. Waiting in line is all part of the fun. Since your meal should be eaten as soon as possible, the favored seating is on the steps of St. Patrick's Cathedral. *Werburgh St., tel. 01/479-3117. No credit cards. Dinner only. Closed Tues. and Sun.*

¢ **Captain America.** A surprise awaits you here at the top of a flight of stairs on fashionable Grafton Street. The collection of outrageous Americana strewn throughout is dominated by a replica of the Statue of Liberty that visibly shudders at the loud rock music. A wide selection of hamburgers graces the menu, plus beef tacos, burritos, enchiladas, and chili. *Grafton Court, Grafton St., tel. 01/671-5266. No reservations. AE, DC, MC, V.*

Pub Food All the pubs listed here serve food at lunchtime; some also have food in the early evening. They form an important part of the dining scene in Dublin and make a pleasant and informal alternative to a restaurant meal. In general, a one-course meal should not cost much more than IR£4–IR£5, but a full meal will put you in the lower range of the $$ category. In general, credit cards are not accepted.

Barry Fitzgerald's. Salads and a freshly cooked house special are available in the upstairs bar at lunch on weekdays. Pretheater dinners are served in the early evening. *90 Marlboro St., tel. 01/877-4082.*

Davy Byrne's. James Joyce immortalized Davy Byrne's in *Ulysses.* Nowadays it's more akin to a cocktail bar than a Dublin pub, but it's good for fresh and smoked salmon, salads, and a hot daily special. Food is available at lunchtime and in the early evening. *21 Duke St., tel. 01/671-1298.*

Kitty O'Shea's. Kitty O'Shea's cleverly, if a little artificially, re-creates the atmosphere of old Dublin. *23-25 Grand Canal St., tel. 01/660-9965. Reservations accepted for lunch and Sun. brunch.*

Thomas Read's. This new Continental-style bar offers a wide variety of lunch food, including hot bagels, danishes, and Parma ham. The coffees, especially the megaccino (a jumbo-size cappuccino), are particularly good. *Corner of Dame St. and Parliament St., tel. 01/677-2504.*

Old Stand. Located conveniently close to Grafton Street, the Old Stand offers grilled food, including steaks. *37 Exchequer St., tel. 01/677-0821.*

Lodging

Although only a few major hotels have opened in Dublin in the past few years, considerable investment in redevelopment, updating of facilities, and refurbishing of some of the older establishments is taking place. As in most major cities, there is a shortage of midrange accommodations. For value-for-the-money, try one of the registered guest houses; in most respects they are indistinguishable from small hotels. Most economical of all is the bed-and-breakfast. Both guest houses and B&Bs tend to be in suburban areas—generally a 10-minute bus ride from the center of the city. This is not a great drawback, and savings can be significant.

Bord Fáilte (14 Upper O'Connell St.) publishes a comprehensive booklet, *Guest Accommodation* (IR£4), that covers all approved possibilities in Dublin and the rest of the country, from the grandest hotel to the humblest B&B.

There is a VAT of 10% on hotel charges, which should be included in the quoted price. A service charge of 12–15% is also included and listed separately in the bills of top-grade hotels; elsewhere, check to see if the service is included. If it's not, a tip of between 10% and 15% is customary—if you think the service is worth it. For details and price-category definitions, *see* Lodging *in* Staying in Ireland, *above*.

$$ ★ **Ariel Guest House.** This is Dublin's leading guest house, just a block away from the elegant Berkeley Court and a 10-minute walk from Stephen's Green. The lobby lounge and restaurant of this Victorian villa are furnished with leather and mahogany heirlooms, as are most of the spacious bedrooms, 13 of which were added to the house in 1991. This is a good bet if you're in town for a leisurely, relaxing holiday. *52 Lansdowne Rd., Dublin 4, tel. 01/668–5512, fax 01/668–5845. 27 rooms with bath. Facilities: restaurant (wine license only), lounge, parking. AE, MC, V. Closed Dec. 21–Jan. 31.*

$$ **Ashling.** This family-run hotel sits on the edge of the river Liffey, close to Heuston Station. Some may find that the Ashling's relentlessly bright modern decor verges on the garish. It has a faithful following, however, not least because of its proximity to Phoenix Park and its friendly staff. The center of town is a brisk 10–15-minute walk away, taking in many famed landmarks en route. *Parkgate St., Dublin 1, tel. 01/677–2324, fax 01/679–3783. 56 rooms with bath. AE, DC, MC, V.*

$$ **Royal Dublin.** This centrally located Best Western hotel is just within the $$ category if you choose a "standard" room. Its modern facade dominates the top end of busy O'Connell Street. The interior incorporates part of a building that dates from 1752, providing an elegant and relaxing lounge area and restaurant. In contrast, Raffles Bar is a lively spot with a busy local trade. The rooms, decorated in pleasant pastel shades, are exceptionally well appointed by Dublin standards for this price range and have floor-to-ceiling windows. *40 Upper O'Connell St., Dublin 1, tel. 01/733666, fax 01/873–3666. 120 rooms with bath. Facilities: bar. AE, DC, MC, V.*

$$ **Tara Tower.** This modern, seven-story building is only a short walk from Booterstown DART station; from there it is less than a 10-minute ride to the city center. The bracing, seaside-suburban location is right across from a wild-bird sanctuary. Try to get a room facing the wide expanse of Dublin Bay; the view is striking. It's an informal, unpretentious place with attentive service. The bar and restaurant have been attractively refurbished with rustic woodwork. *Merrion Rd., Dublin 4, tel. 01/269–4666, fax 01/269–1027. 84 rooms with bath. Facilities: bar, restaurant, gift shop–newsagent. AE, DC, MC, V.*

$ **Clifton Court.** This is one of Dublin's most central hotels, on the banks of the Liffey just below O'Connell Bridge—but don't get any romantic ideas about the views. A four-lane traffic artery runs between the tall narrow building and the river, and most of the rooms overlook an internal service area. There is a busy bar on the ground floor and a busy restaurant in the basement. The rooms are small but well equipped for the price range. *O'Connell Bridge, Dublin 1, tel. 01/874–3535, fax 01/878–6698. 20 rooms, 13 with bath. Facilities: restaurant, bar. AE, DC, MC, V.*

$ **Kilronan House.** This guest house, a five-minute walk from St. Stephen's Green, is a favorite with vacationers. The large, late-19th-century terraced house is well converted, and the decor and furnishings are updated each year by the Murray family, who have run the place for the past 30 years. The bedrooms are pleasantly furnished with plush carpeting and pastel color walls. *70 Adelaide Rd., Dublin 2, tel. 01/475–5266, fax 01/478–2841. 10 rooms with bath. Facilities: restaurant (wine licence only). MC, V. Closed Dec. 21–Jan. 1.*

$ ★ **Maples House.** According to Bord Fáilte's complex grading system, Maples House is a guest house; to the rest of the world, however, it is definitely a small hotel. The lobby of this Edwardian house is decked out with oil paintings, Waterford crystal chandeliers, and a discreetly modern carpet and is dominated by a vast mirror-topped Victorian rococo sideboard that sets the tone for the ornate decor of the public rooms. The bedrooms are small but adequate, lacking the rococo splendor of the rest of the building. *Iona Rd., Glasnevin, tel. 01/830–3049, fax 01/830–3874. 21 rooms with bath. Facilities: grill restaurant and bar. AE, DC, MC, V. Closed Dec. 25, 26.*

¢ **Dublin International Youth Hostel.** Housed in a converted convent, it offers dormitory accommodations (up to 25 persons per room) and a few four-bed rooms. This is a spartan, inexpensive (around IR£6 per night) alternative to hotels; nonmembers of the international youth hosteling organization can stay for a small extra charge. The hostel is located north of Parnell Square, near the Mater Hospital. *61 Mountjoy St., Dublin 1, tel. 01/830–1766, fax 01/830–1600. 500 beds. No credit cards.*

¢ **The Gate.** Its location, atop O'Connell Street opposite the Gate Theatre, gives this hotel its name. Its raison d'être is a large, ground-floor nightclub-cum-disco, which is open on weekends. This need not bother residents, who have their own small but attractive lounge and restaurant at the top of the stairs. The rooms are plainly decorated and some overlook the busy life of Parnell Street. *80–81 Parnell St., Dublin 1, tel. 01/874 5253, fax 01/872–2940. 20 rooms, 18 with bath. Facilities: restaurant, bar. AE, DC, MC, V.*

¢ **Kelly's.** A small canopied door at street level labeled "Kelly's" is the only indication of this recently remodeled hotel that occupies the upper floors of a rambling old building. The tiny bar and the dining room are overdecorated in that mish-mash of styles with which veterans of budget European hotels will be only too familiar. The rooms vary in size and are furnished with only the basics (no TV or phone) and the plumbing gurgles at night, but the staff is friendly and helpful, and its central location (between Trinity College and Dublin Castle) makes an excellent touring base. *26 S. Great George's St., Dublin 2, tel. 01/677–9277, fax 01/671–3216. 23 rooms, 19 with bath. Facilities: dining room, bar. AE, DC, MC, V.*

¢ **Kinlay House.** This holiday hostel is an exception in that it has most of its beds in private rooms and only one dormitory. It is ideally located, a five-minute walk from the gates of Trinity College on the edge of the buzzing Temple Bar area. Prices rise in relation to your privacy, peaking at IR£16.50 (including Continental breakfast) for a single room. There are eight twin-bed rooms, and over 20 four- and six-bed rooms, some with private bathrooms. Tour groups and sports clubs take block bookings in winter, and in summer it is a favorite stopover for backpackers. Book well in advance to be sure of a place. *2–12 Lord Edward St., Dublin 2, tel. 01/679–6644, fax 01/679–7437. 149 beds; 84-bedrooms, 6 twins, 1 triplet, 2 singles, all with bath; 100 beds share 3 bath. MC, V.*

¢ **Mount Herbert Guest House.** Located close to the swank luxury hotels in the tree-lined inner suburb of Ballsbridge, a 10-minute bus ride from the city center, the Mount Herbert is popular with budget-minded American visitors in the high season. The bedrooms are small, but all have 10-channel TV and hair dryers. There is no bar on the premises, but there are plenty to choose from nearby. *7 Herbert Rd., Ballsbridge, tel. 01/668–4321, fax 01/660–7077. 88 rooms, 77 with bath. Facilities: restaurant (wine license only). AE, DC, MC, V.*

The Arts

The fortnightly magazine *In Dublin* contains comprehensive details of upcoming events, including ticket availability. In peak season, consult the free Bord Fáilte leaflet *Events of the Week*.

Theaters Ireland has a rich theatrical tradition. The **Abbey Theatre** (Lower Abbey St., tel. 01/478–7222) is the home of Ireland's national theater company, its name forever associated with J. M. Synge, William Butler Yeats, and Sean O'Casey. The **Peacock Theatre** is the Abbey's more experimental small stage. The **Gate** (Cavendish Row, Parnell Sq., tel. 01/874–4045) is an intimate spot for modern drama and plays by Irish writers. The **Gaiety** (South King St., tel. 01/677–1717) features musical comedy, opera, drama, and revues. The **Olympia** (Dame St., tel. 01/677–8962) has seasons of comedy, vaudeville, and ballet. The **Project Arts Centre** (39 E. Essex St., tel. 01/671–2321) is an established fringe theater. The **Tivoli** (Francis St., tel. 01/453–5998) also presents experimental productions. The new **National Concert Hall** (Earlsfort Terrace, tel. 01/671–1888), just off Stephen's Green, is the place to go for classical concerts.

Nightlife

Dublin does not have sophisticated nightclubs in the international sense. Instead, there is a choice of discos (often billed as nightclubs) and cabarets, catering mainly to visitors. There is also a very animated bar-pub scene—some places with live music and folksinging. No visit to this genial city will be complete without spending at least one evening exploring them.

Discos **Annabels** (Mespil Rd., tel. 01/660–5222) is a popular late-evening spot; so is **The Pink Elephant** (S. Frederick St., tel. 01/677–5876).

Cabarets The following all offer Irish cabaret, designed to give visitors a taste of Irish entertainment: **Braemor Rooms** (Churchtown, tel. 01/498–8664), **Burlington Hotel** (Upper Leeson St., tel. 01/660–5222, open May–Oct.), **Jury's Hotel** (Ballsbridge, tel. 01/660–5000, open May–mid-Oct.), and **Abbey Tavern** (Howth, Co. Dublin, tel. 01/839–0307).

Pubs Check advertisements in evening papers for "sessions" of folk, ballad, Irish traditional, or jazz music. The **Brazen Head** (20 Lower Bridge St., tel. 01/677–9549)—Dublin's oldest pub, dating from 1688—and **O'Donoghue's** (15 Merrion Row, tel. 01/661–4303) feature some form of musical entertainment on most nights. Several of Dublin's centrally located pubs are noted for their character and ambience; they're usually at their liveliest from 5 to 7 PM and again from 10. The **Bailey** (2 Duke St.) is mentioned in *Ulysses* (under its original name, Burton's) and retains something of its Edwardian character, while **William Ryan's** (28 Parkgate St.) is a beautifully preserved Victorian gem. **Henry Grattan** (47–48 Lower Baggot St.) is popular with the business and sporting crowd; **O'Neill's Lounge Bar** (37 Pearse St.) is always busy with students and faculty from nearby Trinity College; and the **Palace Bar** (21 Fleet St.) is a journalists' haunt. You can eavesdrop on Dublin's social elite and their hangers-on at the expensive **Horseshoe Bar** in the Shelbourne Hotel or bask in the theatrical atmosphere of **Neary's** (Chatham St.).

For details on pubs serving food, *see* Pub Food *under* Dining, *above*.

Cork

Many visitors find that Cork is closer to their idea of Ireland than is the bustling capital city, Dublin. You'll be amazed at the difference in accent only 254 kilometers (158 miles) down the road, and you'll appreciate the slower and friendlier way of life. Cork is the base for an excursion to the famous Blarney Stone, and it is also well worth taking a trip down its magnificent harbor to visit the port of Cobh.

Getting Around

By Train The terminus at Cork is Kent Station. There are direct services from Dublin and Tralee and a suburban line to Cobh (tel. 021/506–766 for information).

By Bus The main bus terminal in Cork is at Parnell Place (tel. 021/508–188).

By Bicycle Bicycles can be rented from **Isaacs** (48 MacCurtain St., Cork, tel. 021/505–399).

Guided Tours

CIE operates a number of trips from Parnell Place in Cork (tel. 021/506–066).

Tourist Information

Tourist House (Grand Parade, Cork, tel. 021/273–251, fax 021/273–504).

Exploring Cork

Cork is the major metropolis of the south and, with a population of about 127,000, the second largest city in Ireland. In the center of the city, the Lee divides in two, giving the city a profusion of picturesque quays and bridges. The name Cork derives from the Irish *corcaigh*, meaning marshy place. The city received its first charter in 1185 and grew rapidly in the 17th and 18th centuries with the expansion of its butter trade.

The main business and shopping center of Cork lies on the island created by the two diverging channels of the Lee, and most places of interest are within walking distance of the center. **Patrick Street** is the focal point of Cork. Here, you will find the city's most famous statue, that of **Father Theobald Mathew** (1790–1856), who led a nationwide temperance crusade, no small feat in a country as fond of a drink (or two) as this one. In the hilly area to the north of Patrick Street is the famous 120-foot **Shandon Steeple,** the bell tower of **St. Anne's Church.** It is shaped like a pepper pot and houses the bells immortalized in the song "The Bells of Shandon." Visitors can climb the tower; read the inscriptions on the bells; and, on request, have them rung over Cork.

Patrick Street is the main shopping area of Cork, and here you will find the city's two major department stores, **Roches** and **Cash's.** Cash's has a good selection of Waterford crystal. The liveliest place in town to shop is just off Patrick Street, to the west, near the city center parking lot, in the pedestrians-only **Paul Street** area. The **Meadows & Byrne** stocks the best in modern Irish design, including tableware, ceramics, knitwear, hand-woven tweeds, and high fashion. The **Donegal Shop,** in Paul Street Piazza, specializes in made-to-order tweed suits and rainwear. At the top of Paul Street is the **Crawford Art Gallery,** which has an excellent collection of 18th- and 19th-century prints and modern arts. *Emmet Place, tel. 021/273–377. Admission free. Open weekdays 10–5, Sat. 9–1.*

One of Cork's most famous sons was William Penn (1644–1718), founder of the Pennsylvania colony. He is only one of thousands who sailed from Cork's port, the Cove of Cork on Great Island, 24 kilometers (15 miles) down the harbor. **Cobh,** as it is known nowadays, can be reached by train from Kent Station, and the trip provides excellent views of the magnificent harbor. Cobh is an attractive hilly town dominated by its 19th-century **cathedral.** It was the first and last European port of call for transatlantic liners, one of which was the ill-fated *Titanic.* Cobh has other associations with shipwrecks: It was from here that destroyers were sent out in May 1915 to search for survivors of the *Lusitania,* torpedoed by a German submarine with the loss of 1,198 lives. Cobh's maritime past and its links with emigration are documented in a new IR£2 million heritage center known as **The Queenstown Project,** which opened in the town's old railway station in 1993. *Tel. 021/813–591. Admission: IR£3.50 adults, £2 children and senior citizens. Open Feb.–Nov., daily 10–6.*

Most visitors to Cork want to kiss the famous **Blarney Stone** in the hope of acquiring the "gift of gab." Blarney itself, 8 kilometers (5 miles) from Cork City, can be reached by the regular bus service from Parnell Bus Station. All that is left of **Blarney Castle** is its ruined central keep containing the celebrated stone. The stone is set in the battlements, and to kiss it, you must lie on the walk within the walls, lean your head back, and touch the stone with your lips. Nobody knows how the tradition originated, but Elizabeth I is credited with giving the word *blarney* to the language when, commenting on the unfulfilled promises of Cormac MacCarthy, Lord Blarney of the time, she remarked, "This is all Blarney; what he says, he never means." Adjoining the castle is a first-rate crafts shop. *Tel. 021/385–252. Admission: IR£3 adults, IR£1 children and senior citizens. Open Mon.–Sat. 9 to sundown, Sun. 9–5:30.*

Dining and Lodging

For details and price-category definitions, *see* Dining and Lodging *in* Staying in Ireland, *above.*

Dining **Jacques.** You will find this little place, on a side street behind the Im-
¢–$$ perial Hotel, to be an inexpensive self-service restaurant at lunch time and a more pricey, more intimate restaurant in the evenings. The owner-chef is famed for her imaginative use of Clonakilty black pudding (a local specialty related to the French *boudin* sausage) and her insistence on fresh local produce. She also serves vegetarian and gluten-free dishes. *9 Phoenix St., off Pembroke St., tel. 021/277–387. Open Mon. 9–5, Tues.–Sat. 9–10:30. Reservations evenings only. AE, DC, MC, V.*

$ **Cafe Paradiso.** This simple café-style restaurant near the university serves Mediterranean-style food that is so tasty even dedicated meat eaters forget it's vegetarian. Chef Denis Cotter is famous for his risottos with seasonal vegetables (pumpkin, radiccio) and *gougères* (pastry rings with savory fillings) and his excellent homemade desserts. *16 Lancaster Quay, Western Rd., tel. 021/277–939. Open Tues.–Sat., 12:30–10:30. Reservations advised. MC, V.*

$ **Gallery Cafe.** The food here is prepared by a team from Balleymaloe, one of Ireland's most famous country house hotels, and is the freshest and most elegant budget food in town, served amid statues and prints from the municipal art collection. *Crawford Gallery, Emmet Pl., tel. 021/274–415. Open Mon.–Fri. 12:30–4 and 7–9:45, Sat. 7–10. MC, V.*

$ **Isaac's.** In an old warehouse with cast-iron pillars, this popular brasserie-style spot has a lively Continental atmosphere echoed by the food, which combines Mediterranean influences with excellent local produce. It's worth a try, whatever your budget. *48*

MacCurtain St., tel. 021/503–805. Reservations advised weekends. MC, V.

¢ **Long Valley.** Resist the familiar neighborhood fast-food fare and try this extraordinary, mildly eccentric bar, which is just across from the General Post Office. Nip in for one of its amazing "doorstep" sandwiches, the meat freshly cut before your eyes from vast hunks of home-baked ham or hot salt beef. *Winthrop St., tel. 021/272–144. No reservations. No credit cards.*

Lodging **Arbutus Lodge.** This exceptionally comfortable hotel has an out-
$$ standing restaurant and panoramic views of the city and the river.
★ *Middle Glanmire Rd., Montenotte, tel. 021/501–237, fax 021/502–893. 20 rooms with bath. AE, DC, MC, V. Closed 1 wk at Christmas.*

$ **Jury's Inn.** Opened in 1994, the newest member of Jury's budget chain provides modern, well-equipped rooms in the city center that can accommodate three adults or two adults and two children. *Anderson's Quay, tel. 021/276–444, fax 021/276–144. 133 rooms with bath. AE, DC, MC, V.*

$ **Victoria Lodge.** Originally built in the early 20th century as a Capu-
★ chin monastery, this exceptionally well-appointed B&B is a five-minute drive from the town center; it is also on several bus routes. The rooms are simple but comfortable, with views over the lodge's own grounds. Breakfast is served in the spacious old refectory. *Victoria Cross, tel. 021/542–233, fax 021/542–233. 20 rooms with bath. Facilities: TV lounge. AE, MC, V.*

¢ **Gabriel House.** Convenient for both bus and train stations, this well-run Victorian guest house offers well-equipped rooms and boasts many satisfied customers. *Summerhill, St. Luke's, tel. 021/500–333, fax 021/500–178. 20 rooms with bath. AE, DC, MC, V.*

¢ **Sheila's Cork Tourist Hotel.** One of the easygoing chain of Independent Hostels with no petty rules, this is a popular economy stopover for backpackers. *Belgrave Pl. Wellington Rd., tel. 021/504–547, fax 500–940. 100 beds in dormitories, 20 in double rooms.*

Killarney

Killarney is one of the most scenic and beautiful parts of Ireland, where mountains and lakes combine with luxuriant vegetation to create unforgettable vistas: a deep blue sky reflected in the blue waters of the chain of lakes, surrounded by giant tangles of dark green foliage. Seasoned travelers have been captivated by Killarney ever since it was first "discovered" in the late 18th-century, and many visitors return year after year to relax in the balmy mountain air.

Getting Around

By Bus Buses offer a more flexible service than do trains; details are available from local tourist information offices.

By Bicycle You can rent bicycles from **O'Callaghan Bros.** (College St., Killarney, tel. 064/31175) and **D. O'Neill** (Plunkett St., Killarney, tel. 064/31970).

Tourist Information

All tourist information offices are open weekdays 9–6, Sat. 9–1.

Killarney (Town Hall, tel. 064/31633, fax 064/34506).
Shannon Airport (tel. 061/471664).

Exploring Killarney

Killarney itself is an undistinguished market town, well developed to handle the tourist trade that flourishes here in the peak season. To find the famous scenery, you must head out of town toward the lakes that lie in a valley running south between the mountains. Part of Killarney's lake district is within **Killarney National Park.** At the heart of the park is the 10,000-acre **Muckross Estate** (open daily, daylight hrs). Cars are not allowed in the estate, so if you don't want to walk, rent a bicycle in town or take a trip in a jaunting car—a small two-wheeled horse-drawn cart. At the center of the estate is **Muckross House,** a 19th-century manor that contains the **Kerry Folklife Center.** On the adjoining grounds is an Old World Farm. *Tel. 064/31440. Admission: IR£2.50 adults, IR£1 children. Open daily 9–5:30; July and Aug., daily 9–7.*

To get an idea of the splendor of the lakes and streams—of the massive glacial sandstone and limestone rocks and lush vegetation that characterize the Killarney district—take one of the day-long tours of the **Gap of Dunloe, the Upper Lake, Long Range, Middle** and **Lower lakes,** and **Ross Castle.** The central section, the Gap of Dunloe, is not suitable for cars, but horses and jaunting cars are available at **Kate Kearney's Cottage,** which marks the entrance to the gap.

The **Ring of Kerry** will add about 176 kilometers (110 miles) to your trip, but in good weather it provides a pleasant experience. All Killarney-based tour operators offer day trips of the Ring by coach or minibus. **Kenmare** is a small market town 34 kilometers (21 miles) from Killarney at the head of Kenmare Bay. Across the water, as you drive out along the Iveragh Peninsula, will be views of the gray-blue mountain ranges of the Beara Peninsula. **Sneem,** on the estuary of the river Ardsheelaun, is one of the prettiest villages in Ireland, although its English-style central green makes it an exception among Irish villages. Beyond the next village, Caherdaniel, is **Derrynane House,** home of the 19th-century politician and patriot Daniel O'Connell, "The Liberator," and completed by him in 1825. It still contains much of its original furniture. *Tel. 066/75113. Admission: IR£1 adults, 40p children and senior citizens. Open mid-June–Sept., daily 10–1 and 2–7; Oct.–mid-June, Tues.–Sat. 10–1, Sun. 2–5.*

If time and the weather are on your side, take an organized day tour by coach or minibus or an overnight trip on the regular bus service (July and August only) from Killarney to the **Dingle Peninsula**—one of the wildest and least spoiled regions of Ireland—taking in the **Connor Pass, Mount Brandon,** and **the Gallarus Oratory** and stopping at **Dunquin** to hear some of Ireland's best traditional musicians.

Dining and Lodging

For details and price-category definitions, *see* Dining and Lodging *in* Staying in Ireland, *above.*

Dingle **Beginish.** The best of several small but sophisticated restaurants in
Dining town, this relaxing place serves local meat and seafood in a generous version of nouvelle cuisine. *Green St., tel. 066/51588. AE, DC, MC, V. Closed Mon. and Nov. 1–Mar. $$*
The Islandman. This place is a combination of bar, bookshop, café, and restaurant, furnished in simple art-nouveau style. Snacks and light meals are served all day; the more serious dinner menu is worth lingering over. *Main St., tel. 066/51803. AE, DC, MC, V. ¢–$*

Dining and **Benner's.** This busy town-center hotel has been beautifully restored
Lodging with country-pine antique furniture in all bedrooms. *Main St., tel. 066/51638, fax 066/51412. 25 rooms with bath. Facilities: restaurant, 2 bars. AE, DC, MC, V. $$*

Lodging **The Alpine.** This modern three-story guest house, just outside Dingle town (a three-minute walk), is a better bet than most of the B&Bs in town; it has good ocean views from the front rooms. *Tel. 066/51250, fax 066/51966. 14 rooms with bath. MC, V. Closed Dec.–Feb. ¢*

Killarney
Dining
★

Gaby's. For simple and fresh seafood, Gaby's can't be beat. *17 High St., tel. 064/32519. AE, DC, MC, V. Closed Sun., Mon. lunch, and Dec.–mid-Mar. $$*

Strawberry Tree. A young and enthusiastic team of chefs prepares an imaginative nouvelle-cuisine-influenced menu from the freshest local ingredients, in this intimate, relaxing town-center restaurant. *24 Plunkett St., tel. 064/32688. Open 6:30–10:30. AE, DC, MC, V. Closed Dec. $$*

Bricín. This simple restaurant with exposed stone walls and bentwood chairs is above a crafts and book shop in the town center. Light lunches and homemade cakes are served during the day and a more serious menu featuring local steak, lamb, and salmon in the evening. *26 High St., tel. 064/34902. Open Mon.–Sat. 10–5 year-round; March–Oct. also 6–9:30. AE, MC, V. $*

Foley's. This popular eatery specializes in seafood, steaks, and Kerry mountain lamb. *23 High St., tel. 064/31217. AE, DC, MC, V. ¢*

Sheila's. This reliable, family-run restaurant has been feeding visitors to Killarney for over 30 years. It is brightly lit and simply furnished with pine tables and red paper mats, and the menu has a good selection of traditional Irish dishes, as well as international favorites like burgers and pizzas. *75 High St., tel. 064/31270. MC, V. ¢*

Dining and Lodging

Linden House. This family-run hotel is in a functional 1960s suburban home, a two-minute walk from the town center. The quietest rooms are in the back. *New Rd., tel. 064/31379, fax 064/31196. 20 rooms with bath. Facilities: restaurant (dinner only). Closed Dec.–end Jan. MC, V. ¢*

Lodging

Arbutus. Newly refurbished and centrally located, the Arbutus benefits from a lively bar and an Old World atmosphere. *College St., tel. 064/31037, fax 064/34033. 35 rooms with bath. AE, DC, MC, V. $$*

Kathleen's Country House. Situated on the Tralee Road, 2 kilometers (1 mile) outside town, this is an imaginatively designed modern guest house with spacious, prettily decorated rooms. The owner-manager, Kathleen, maintains exacting standards of comfort and cleanliness. *Tralee Rd., tel. 064/32810, fax 064/32340. 16 rooms with bath. MC, V. $*

Aghadoe House. This establishment is generally considered the Hilton of the Irish Youth Hostel Association's properties. The glorious Victorian-Gothic mansion, in its own lakeside grounds, is something of a tourist attraction in itself, and the views are better than in all but the most expensive hotels. *Aghadoe, tel. 064/31240, fax 064/34300. 220 dormitory beds. V. ¢*

An Sugan. A long-established member of the chain of Independent Hostels, this is the liveliest of the town center hostels, although, like all of them, it is small and rather cramped. The friendly restaurant, which often has live music, makes up for the lack of elbow room. *Lewis Rd., tel. 064/33104. 18 dormitory beds. No credit cards. ¢*

Lime Court. This comfortable, modern B&B is about five minutes' walk from the center of town on the way to Muckross Estate. Rooms have plain but comfortable modern furniture and small sitting areas. *Muckross Rd., tel. 064/34547, fax 064/34121. 11 rooms with bath. MC, V. ¢*

The Northwest

This route from Galway to Sligo takes you through the rugged landscape of Connemara to the fabled Yeats country in the northwest, passing some of the wildest and loneliest parts of Ireland. Galway still has a number of Irish-speaking residents, who contribute to its lively arts scene.

Getting Around

By Train Trains to Galway, Westport, and Sligo operate from Dublin's Heuston or Connolly (Sligo) stations. There is no train service north of Sligo.

By Bus Travel within the area is more flexible by bus; details are available from local tourist information offices.

By Car In Galway, cars can be rented from **Avis** (tel. 091/68886), **Budget** (tel. 091/66376), or **Murray's** (tel. 091/62222). Taxis do not operate on meters; agree on the fare beforehand.

By Bicycle You can rent bikes from **Celtic Cycles** (Victoria Pl., tel. 091/66606), **John Mannion** (Railway View, Clifden, tel. 095/21160), or **Gary's Cycles** (Quay St., Sligo, tel. 071/45418).

Tourist Information

All are open weekdays 9–6, Saturday 9–1.

Galway (off Eyre Sq., tel. 091/63081, fax 091/65201).
Sligo (Temple St., tel. 071/61201, fax 098/26709).

Exploring the Northwest

Galway City is the gateway to the ancient province of Connacht, the most westerly seaboard in Europe. Galway City was well established even before the Normans arrived in the 13th century, rebuilding the city walls and turning the little town into a flourishing port. Later its waterfront was frequented by Spanish grandees and traders. The salmon fishing in the river Corrib, which flows through the lower part of the town, is unsurpassed. In early summer, you can stand on the **Weir Bridge** beside the town's cathedral and watch thousands of salmon as they leap and twist through the narrow access to the inner lakes. **Lynch's Castle** in Shop Street, now a bank, is a good example of a 16th-century fortified house—fortified because the neighboring Irish tribes persistently raided Galway City, whose commercial life excluded them. Nowadays the liveliest part of town is around the area between **Eyre Square** (the town's center) and **Spanish Arch.** Galway is a compact city, best explored on foot.

On the west bank of the Corrib estuary, just outside the Galway town walls, is **Claddagh,** said to be the oldest fishing village in Ireland. **Salthill Promenade,** with its lively seaside amenities, is the traditional place "to sit and watch the moon rise over Claddagh, and see the sun go down on Galway Bay"—in the words of the city's most famous song.

County Sligo is noted for its seaside resorts, the famous golf course at Rosse's Point (just outside Sligo Town), and its links with Ireland's most famous 20th-century poet, William Butler Yeats, who is buried just north of **Sligo Town** at Drumcliffe. An important collection of paintings by the poet's brother, Jack B. Yeats, can be seen in the **Sligo Museum** (Stephen St., tel. 071/42212), which also has memorabilia of Yeats, the poet. Take a boat from Sligo up to **Lough Gill** and see the **Lake Isle of Innisfree** and other places immortalized in Yeats's poetry. His grave is found beneath the slopes of Ben Bulben, just north of the town. Nearby is **Lissadell House,** a substantial mansion dating from 1830 that features prominently in his writings. It was the home of Constance Gore-Booth, later Countess Markeviecz, who took part in the 1916 uprising. *Tel. 071/63150. Admission: IR£2 adults, 50p children. Open June–Sept., Mon.–Sat. 10:30–12 and 2–4:30.*

Dining and Lodging

For details and price-category definitions, *see* Dining and Lodging *in* Staying in Ireland, *above*.

Galway City
Dining

Malt House. This is a cheerful, relaxing pub-restaurant, hidden away in a shopping arcade. *Olde Malte Arcade, High St., tel. 091/63993. AE, DC, MC, V. Closed Sun., Oct.–Apr. $$*

Noctan's. This excellent, small French restaurant is situated above a popular pub. *17 Cross St., tel. 091/66172. MC, V. Dinner only. Closed Sun. $$*

Eyre House and Park Room Restaurants. Two family-oriented restaurants, one more formal, can be found behind a refurbished Victorian bar near the bus and rail stations. Both serve the same dishes, but the Park Room, at the back of the building, can cater to private functions. *Forster St., tel. 091/64924. AE, DC, MC, V. $*

Galway Bakery Company. The ground-floor coffee shop and the first-floor restaurant both offer excellent value in a bustling cosmopolitan atmosphere. The wide ranging menu includes steaks, seafood, and vegetarian dishes. *7 Williamsgate St., tel. 091/63087. AE, DC, MC, V. $*

McDonagh's Seafood Bar. Traditional fish and chips, Galway oysters, and steamed mussels are the chief attractions at this simple café-style restaurant. The premises are shared with a fish shop, so you can be sure the seafood is fresh. *Quay St., tel. 091/65001. AE, MC, V. ¢*

Lodging

Brennan's Yark. This stylish, modern hotel is an ingenious warehouse conversion in a four-story, stone-built building in the town center's lively dockside area. *Lower Merchant's Rd., tel. 091/68166, fax 091/68262. 24 rooms with bath. AE, DC, MC, V. $$*

Anno Santo. This is a small family-run hotel with rooms in a modern annex adjoining the original bungalow. It is about 300 meters (320 yards) from the sea on a residential road in the seaside suburb of Salthill. *Threadneedle Rd., Salthill, tel. 091/23011, fax 091/23011. 14 rooms with bath. AE, DC, MC, V. $*

Jury's Inn. This newly built town-center hotel beside the bubbling River Corrib offers good quality budget accommodation at a fixed price per room. *Quay St., tel. 091/66444, fax 091/68415. 128 rooms with bath. AE, DC, MC, V. $*

The Banba. All the rock-bottom hotels in Galway are clustered along the seafront in Salthill. This one is preferable because it does not have a nightclub, so your sleep is less likely to be disturbed. *Upper Salthill., tel. 091/21944, no fax. 29 rooms, 2 with bath. MC, V. ¢*

Sligo Town
Lodging

Silver Swan. In the town center overlooking the Garavogue River, this '60s-style hotel has recently been refurbished with pleasant dark-wood fittings. *Hyde Bridge, tel. 071/43231, fax 071/42232. 29 rooms with bath. AE, MC, V. $$*

Sligo Park. This is a modern two-story building, set in spacious grounds. *Pearse Rd., tel. 071/60291, fax 071/69556. 89 rooms with bath. Facilities: tennis court, indoor pool. AE, DC, MC, V. $$*

Southern. This solid, four-story, 19th-century hotel is set in its own pretty gardens. *Lord Edward St., tel. 071/62101, fax 071/60328. 50 rooms, most with bath. AE, DC, MC, V. $*

15 Italy

When it comes to great travel values, few European countries can beat Italy. It has great art, historic cities, dazzling landscapes, comfortable weather, delectable food and drink, and, of course, the very considerable charms of the Italians themselves. Even so, Italy has its drawbacks. For one, the days of laughably low-price hotels and inexpensive meals have gone forever. Italy may be an ancient land, but it is also a thoroughly modern nation with a high standard of living. Similarly, getting around in Italy, especially by air, can be expensive if you're not careful. But for anyone who is willing to shop around and compare prices and who is happy with honest comfort rather than five-star luxury, Italy can be surprisingly affordable.

In addition, much that is uniquely Italian is yours for the asking. After all, how much does it cost to look out over the Tuscan hills as the sun goes down on another glorious day, or to walk through the twisting streets of Venice, past ancient palaces and time-honored churches? How much does it cost to wander through the Roman Forum and ponder its lost glories? We're not suggesting you can live on art and beauty alone, but the cultural wealth of Italy makes it easier to save pennies for your real expenditures, such as dining and lodging. Chances are, too, that hotels and restaurants at the lower end of the price scale will let you discover the real spirit of Italy. Small inns with portraits of bewhiskered ancestors in the lobby, local *trattorie* where Italian families are sharing a meal: These are places where you can discover Italy at its most Italian.

The whole of Italy is one vast attraction, but the triangle of its most-visited cities—Rome (Roma), Florence (Firenze), and Venice (Venezia)—gives a good idea of the great variety to be found here. In Rome and Florence, especially, you can feel the uninterrupted flow of the ages, from the Classical era of the ancient Romans to the bustle and throb of contemporary life carried on in centuries-old settings. Venice, by contrast, seems suspended in time, the same today as it was when it held sway over the eastern Mediterranean and the Orient. Each of these cities presents a different aspect of the Italian character: the Baroque exuberance of Rome, Florence's serene stylishness, and the dreamy sensuality of Venice.

The uninhibited Italian lifestyle can be entertaining or irritating, depending on how you look at it. Rarely do things run like clockwork here; you are more likely to encounter unexplained delays and incomprehensible complications. Relax: There's usually something you can smile about even in the darkest circumstances.

Trying to soak in Italy's rich artistic heritage is a great challenge to tourists. The country's many museums and churches draw hordes of visitors, all wanting to see the same thing at the same time. From May through September, the Sistine Chapel, Michelangelo's *David*, St. Mark's Square, and other key sights are more often than not swamped by mobs of tourists. Try to see the highlights at off-peak times in the day. Off-season travel has significant advantages for the budget tourist. Not only are there fewer people competing for elbow room at the major sights, but costs may be lower, especially for value-conscious prepaid package tours and for special off-season discount plans offered locally.

Even in the major cities, Italians generally take a friendly interest in their visitors. Only the most blasé waiters and salespeople are less than courteous and helpful. However, the persistent attention Italian males pay to foreign females can be oppressive and annoying. If you're not interested, the best tactic is to ignore them. But do not ignore matters of personal security; in particular, always be on guard against pickpockets and purse snatchers in Rome and in Naples. Small cities and towns are usually safe.

Making the most of your time in Italy doesn't mean rushing through it. To gain a rich appreciation, don't try to see everything all at once. Do what you really want to do, and if that means skipping a museum to sit at a pretty café to enjoy the sunshine and a cappuccino, you're getting into the Italian spirit. Art—and life—are to be enjoyed, and the Italians can show you how.

Essential Information

Before You Go

When to Go The main tourist season in Italy runs from mid-April to the end of September. The best months for sightseeing are April, May, June, September, and October, when the weather is generally pleasant and not too hot. Foreign tourists crowd the major cities at Easter, when Italians flock to resorts and the countryside. Avoid traveling in August, when the heat can be oppressive and when vacationing Italians cram roads, trains, and planes, as well as beach and mountain resorts. Especially around the August 15 holiday, such cities as Rome and Milan are deserted, and many restaurants and shops close.

The hottest months are July and August, when brief afternoon thunderstorms are common in inland areas. Winters are relatively mild in most places on the tourist circuit, but there are always some rainy spells.

Although low-season rates do not apply at hotels in Rome, Florence, and Milan, you can save on hotel accommodations in Venice and in some summer resorts during their low seasons—the winter, early spring, and late-autumn months. Tourist boards and hotel associations in Florence and Venice often offer bargain packages during the winter that include special hotel rates and discounts in restaurants, shops, and museums. If business is slow, even hotels in Rome, Florence, and Milan may be willing to negotiate lower rates.

Italy

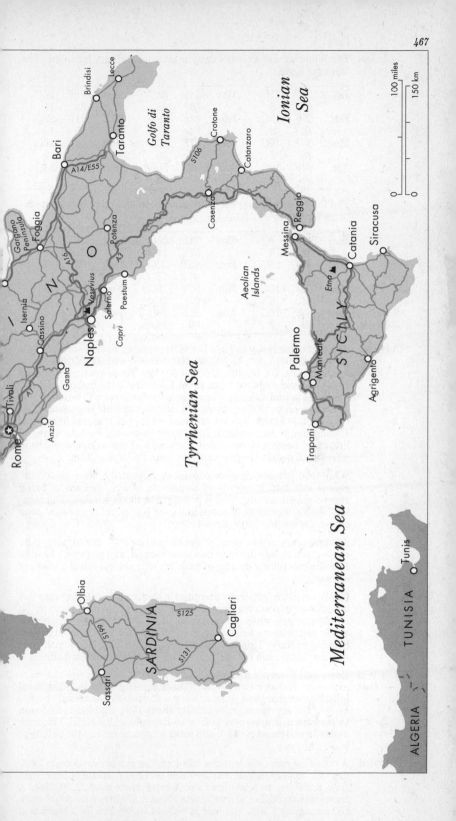

Climate   The following are average daily maximum and minimum temperatures for Rome.

Jan.	52F	11C	May	74F	23C	Sept.	79F	26C
	40	5		56	13		62	17
Feb.	55F	13C	June	82F	28C	Oct.	71F	22C
	42	6		63	17		55	13
Mar.	59F	15C	July	87F	30C	Nov.	61F	16C
	45	7		67	20		49	9
Apr.	66F	19C	Aug.	86F	30C	Dec.	55F	13C
	50	10		67	20		44	6

The following are average daily maximum and minimum temperatures for Milan.

Jan.	40F	5C	May	74F	23C	Sept.	75F	24C
	32	0		57	14		61	16
Feb.	46F	8C	June	80F	27C	Oct.	63F	17C
	35	2		63	17		52	11
Mar.	56F	13C	July	84F	29C	Nov.	51F	10C
	43	6		67	20		43	6
Apr.	65F	18C	Aug.	82F	28C	Dec.	43F	6C
	49	9		66	16		35	2

Currency   The unit of currency in Italy is the lira (plural, lire). There are bills of 1,000, 2,000, 5,000, 10,000, 50,000, 100,000, and 500,000 lire; coins are worth 10, 20, 50, 100, 200 and 500 lire. At press time (summer 1995), the exchange rate was about 1,590 lire to the dollar and 2,440 lire to the pound sterling. Sooner or later the zeros will be lopped off the lire in order to simplify money dealings and life in general. The long-heralded move has not yet been made, but it seems imminent. If and when it does come to pass, 5,000 lire would become 5 lire, 50 lire would become 50 centesimi. Both old and new values would be in effect until people became accustomed to the new system.

While the present system continues, especially when your purchases run into hundreds of thousands of lire, beware of being shortchanged, a dodge that is practiced at ticket windows and cashiers' desks, as well as in shops and even banks. *Always count your change before you leave the counter.*

Always carry some smaller-denomination bills for sundry purchases; you're less likely to be shortchanged, and you won't have to face the eye-rolling dismay of cashiers who are chronically short of change.

Credit cards are generally accepted in shops and hotels, but may not be welcome in restaurants, so always look for those little signs in the window or ask when you enter to avoid embarrassing situations. When you wish to leave a tip beyond the 15% service charge (*see* Staying in Italy, Tipping, *below*) that is usually included with your bill, leave it in cash rather than adding it to the credit card slip.

What It Will Cost   Rome and Florence and, especially, Milan and Venice are the more expensive Italian cities to visit. Taxes are usually included in hotel bills; a cover charge appears as a separate item in restaurant checks, as does the service charge, usually about 15%, if added. Admission to state-owned museums is free to European Union (EU) citizens under 18 and those over 60, and many museums extend the privilege to all visitors.

Sample Prices   A cup of espresso consumed while standing at a bar costs from 1,200 lire to 1,400 lire, triple that for table service. A bottle of beer costs from 2,200 lire to 3,500 lire, a soft drink costs about 2,200 lire. A *tramezzino* (small sandwich) costs about 2,200 lire, a more substantial one about 3,500. You will pay about 10,000 lire for a short taxi ride in Rome, less in Florence, more in Milan. Admission to a major museum is about 12,000 lire; a three-hour sightseeing tour, about 40,000 lire.

Customs on Arrival Two still cameras and one movie camera can be brought in duty-free. Travelers arriving in Italy from an EU country are allowed, duty-free, a total of 800 cigarettes (*or* 400 cigarillos *or* 400 cigars), 90 liters of still wine plus 10 liters of spirits over 22% volume if duty and taxes have been paid on them at the time of purchase. Visitors traveling directly from non-European countries are allowed 200 cigarettes and cigars or tobacco not exceeding 250 grams, 1 liter of spirits, and 2 liters of still wine.

Language Italy is accustomed to English-speaking tourists, and in major cities you will find that many people speak at least a little English. In smaller hotels and restaurants, a smattering of Italian comes in handy.

Getting Around

By Train The fastest trains on the FS (Ferrovie dello Stato), the state-owned railroad, are the ETR 450 trains, or *Pendolino*, for which you pay a supplement and for which seat reservations are required. Also fast are *Intercity* (IC) and *Eurocity* (EC) trains, for which you pay a supplement and for which reservations may be required and are always advisable. *Interregionale* trains usually make more stops and are a little slower. *Regionale* are the slowest of all. You can buy tickets and make seat reservations at travel agencies displaying the FS symbol, avoiding long lines at station ticket windows, up to two months in advance. Tickets for stops within a 100-kilometer (62-mile) range can be purchased at any *tabacchi* (tobacconist's shop) and at ticket machines in stations. They must be stamped in the yellow machines before you board the train. There is a refreshment service on all long-distance trains. Tap water on trains is not drinkable. Carry compact bags for easy overhead storage. Trains are very crowded at holiday times; always reserve.

By Plane Alitalia and domestic affiliate ATI, plus several privately owned companies such as Meridiana, provide service throughout Italy. Alitalia offers several types of discount fares; inquire at travel agencies or at Alitalia agencies in major cities.

By Bus An extensive network of bus routes provides service throughout Italy. Regional bus companies often provide the only means of getting to out-of-the-way places. Bus information is available at local tourist offices and travel agencies.

By Boat Ferries connect the mainland with all the major islands. Lake ferries connect the towns on the shores of the Italian lakes: Como, Maggiore, and Garda.

Staying in Italy

Telephones
Local Calls Pay phones take either 100-, 200-, or 500-lire coins, a *gettone* (token), or magnetic card. Some older phones take only tokens, which you insert in the slot before picking up the receiver; dial, and when your party answers, push the little knob on the slot to release the token and complete the connection. Tokens can be purchased from the token machine or from the cashier of the store, bar, or other facility where the phone is located. Local calls cost 200 lire. For *teleselezione* (long-distance direct dialing), place several coins in the slot; unused coins are returned when you push the large yellow knob. Buy magnetic cards at tobacconists, in 5,000- or 10,000-lire denominations. You can use them for any number of calls up to the equivalent of their face value.

International Calls To place international calls, it's best to go to the "Telefoni" telephone exchange, where the operator assigns you a booth, can help place your call, and will collect payment when you have finished. Telephone exchanges (usually marked Telecom) are found in all cities. The cheaper and easier option, however, will be to use your **AT&T, Sprint** or **MCI** calling card. For AT&T, dial access number 172–1011, for Sprint, dial access number 172–1877, and for MCI, dial access number 172–1022.

Operators and Information For Europe and the Mediterranean area, dial 15; for intercontinental service, dial 170.

Country Code The country code for Italy is 39.

Mail The Italian mail system is notoriously erratic and often excruciatingly slow. Allow up to 15 days for mail to and from the United States and Canada, almost as much to and from the United Kingdom, and much longer for postcards.

Postal Rates Airmail letters to the United States cost 1,250 lire for up to 20 grams; postcards with a short greeting and signature cost 1,000 lire, but cost letter rate if the message is lengthy. Airmail letters to the United Kingdom cost 750 lire, postcards 650 lire.

Receiving Mail You can have mail sent to American Express offices or to Italian post offices, marked "Fermo Posta" and addressed to you c/o Palazzo delle Poste, with the name of the city in which you will pick it up. In either case you must show your passport and pay a small fee.

Shopping Bargaining Most shops now have *prezzi fissi* (fixed prices), but you may be able to get a discount on a large purchase. Always bargain with a street vendor or at a market (except for food).

Opening and Closing Times **Banks** are open weekdays 8:30–1:30 and from 2:45 to 3:45.

Churches are usually open from early morning to noon or 12:30, when they close for about two hours or more, opening again in the afternoon until about 7 PM.

Museums. National museums are usually open until 2 and closed on Monday, but there are many exceptions. Other museums have entirely different hours, which may vary according to season. Archaeological sites are usually closed on Monday. At all museums and sites, ticket offices close an hour or so before official closing time. Always check with the local tourist office for current hours.

Shops are open, with individual variations, from 9 to 1 and from 3:30 or 4 to 7 or 7:30. They are open from Monday through Saturday, but close for a half day during the week; for example, in Rome most shops (except food shops) are closed on Monday morning or Saturday afternoon in July and August, though a 1995 ordinance allows flexibility. Some tourist-oriented shops are open all day, every day, as in Venice.

National Holidays In 1996: January 1, January 6 (Epiphany), April 7 and 8 (Easter Sunday and Monday), April 25 (Liberation Day), May 1 (May Day), August 15 (the religious feast of the Assumption, known as Ferragosto, when cities are literally deserted and most restaurants and shops are closed), November 1 (All Saints' Day), December 8 (Immaculate Conception), December 25 and 26. Changing holidays in 1997: March 30 and 31 (Easter Sunday and Monday).

Dining Generally speaking, a *ristorante* pays more attention to decor, service, and menu than does a trattoria, which is simpler and often family-run. An *osteria* used to be a lowly tavern, though now the term may be used to designate a chic and expensive eatery. A *tavola calda* offers hot dishes and snacks, with seating. A *rosticceria* has the same, to take out.

The menu is always posted in the window or just inside the door of an eating establishment. Check to see what is offered and note the charges for *coperto* (cover) and *servizio* (service), which will increase your check. A *menu turistico* includes taxes and service, but beverages are extra. When ordering, remember that seafood is usually pricey and that anything marked "s.q." (according to quantity) or "al hg." or "all'etto" (both referring to weight in hectograms) will invariably be expensive. To keep meal costs down, forego fruit or dessert, which you can pick up at a street market or local bakery for a better price. At lunchtime look for coffee bars with food counters selling cold or toasted sandwiches, or go to one of the ubiquitous pizza counters.

Mealtimes Lunch hour in Rome lasts from 1 to 3, dinner from 8 to 10. Service begins and ends a half hour earlier in Florence and Venice, later in the south. Practically all restaurants close one day a week; some close for winter or summer vacation.

What to Wear At some of the more stylish restaurants, a jacket is sometimes recommended. Otherwise, casual dress is appropriate.

Precautions Tap water is safe in large cities and almost everywhere else unless noted *Non Potabile*. Bottled mineral water is available everywhere, *gassata* (with bubbles) or *non gassata* (without). If you prefer tap water, ask for *acqua semplice* or *acqua di rubinetto*, a move that also means a lower restaurant check.

Ratings Prices are per person and include first course, main course, dessert or fruit, and house wine, where available. Best bets are indicated by a star ★.

Category	Rome, Milan	Other Areas
$$	35,000–45,000 lire	28,000–35,000 lire
$	28,000–35,000 lire	20,000–28,000 lire
¢	under 28,000 lire	under 20,000 lire

Lodging Italy, and especially the main tourist capitals of Rome, Florence, and Venice, offers a good choice of accommodations, but affordable hotels usually do not offer the amenities of comparably priced lodgings in other European capitals or the United States. They do, however, generally offer very clean accommodations. Inexpensive and budget hotels can be spartan, with basic furnishings and shower and toilets down the hall (showers may be the drain-in-the-floor type guaranteed to flood the bathroom). Hotels in the moderate, inexpensive, and budget categories are to some extent interchangeable, in that a room without bath in a superior category costs about the same as a room with bath in a lower one. Affordable hotels can often accommodate three or four people in a room, which makes the amount you pay per person a real bargain. Taxes and service are included in the room rate. Breakfast is an extra charge, and you can decline to take breakfast in the hotel, though the desk may not be happy about it; make this clear when booking or checking in. Air-conditioning, if available at all, may be an extra charge. In older hotels, room quality may be uneven; if you don't like the room you're given, ask for another. This applies to noise, too; some front rooms are bigger and have views but get street noise. Major cities have hotel reservation service booths in the rail stations. If you book a room through them, you pay a fee that is rebated on your hotel bill.

Hotels Italian hotels are officially classified from five-star (deluxe) to one-star (bed-and-breakfasts and small inns). Prices are established officially, and a rate card on the back of the door of your room or inside the closet door tells you exactly what you will pay for that particular room. Any variations are cause for complaint and should be reported to the local tourist office. The **Family Hotels** group (Via Faenza 77, 50123 Firenze, tel. 055/217975, fax 055/210101) includes small, independent, family-run hotels with affordable rates in many locations, including the major tourist cities. In Rome and elsewhere, institutions run by religious orders take paying guests—couples and families, as well as single men and women. Some require that guests take half board, and all have a nightly curfew, but otherwise no rules apply. Costs are low, accommodations are spotless, and the atmosphere is quiet and very cordial. For information, inquire at tourist information offices.

Camping Italy has a wide selection of campgrounds, and the Italians themselves are taking to camping by the thousands, which means that beach or mountain sites will be crammed in July and August. It's best to avoid these peak months. You need an international camping permit, and you can get a campsite directory by sending three international reply coupons to the **Federazione Italiana del Campeggio**, Casella Postale 23, 50100 Firenze, fax 055/882–5918.

Ratings The following price categories are determined by the cost of two people in a double room. Best bets are indicated by a star ★.

Category	Cost
$$	120,000–140,000 lire
$	90,000–120,000 lire
¢	under 90,000 lire

Tipping In restaurants, a 15% service charge is usually added to the total, but it doesn't all go to the waiter. In large cities and resorts it is customary to give the waiter a 5% tip in addition to the service charge shown on the check.

Charges for service are included in all hotel bills, but smaller tips to staff members are appreciated. In general, chambermaids should be given about 500–1,000 lire per day, 3,000 lire–4,000 lire per week.

Taxi drivers are happy with 5%. Porters at railroad stations and airports charge a fixed rate per suitcase; tip an additional 500 lire per person, more if the porter is very helpful. Tip guides about 2,000 lire per person for a half-day tour, more if they are very good.

Rome

Arriving and Departing

By Plane Rome's principal airport is at Fiumicino, 29 kilometers (18 miles) from the city. Though its official name is Leonardo da Vinci Airport, everybody calls it Fiumicino. For flight information, tel. 06/659-53640. The smaller airport of Ciampino is on the edge of Rome and is used as an alternative by international and domestic lines, especially for charter flights. For flight information, tel. 06/794941.

Between the To get to downtown Rome from Fiumicino airport, you have a choice
Airport and of two trains, either the Airport-Termini express or the FM1 train.
Downtown Inquire at the airport (at EPT or train information counters) as to which takes you closer to your hotel. The nonstop, hourly Airport-Termini express takes you to Track 22 at Termini station, Rome's main train terminal and hub of Metro and bus lines. The ride takes 30 minutes and tickets cost 12,000 lire. The other airport train, the FM1, runs every 20 minutes from the airport to Rome and beyond, to the suburb of Monterotondo. The main FM1 stops in Rome are at Trastevere, Ostiense and Tiburtina stations. At each of these stops you can find taxis, bus and/or Metro connections to various parts of

Rome. The ride to Tiburtina takes 40 minutes, and tickets cost 7,000 lire.

Ciampino is connected with the Anagnina station of the Metro Line A by ACOTRAL bus.

By Train Termini station is Rome's main train terminal, while Tiburtina and Ostiense stations serve some long-distance trains, many commuter trains, and the FM1 line to Fiumicino airport. For train information, try the English-speaking personnel at the Information Office in Termini or at any travel agency. Tickets and seats can be reserved and purchased at travel agencies bearing the FS (Ferrovie dello Stato) emblem. Short-distance tickets are also sold by tobacconists and at ticket machines in stations.

By Bus There is no central bus station in Rome; long-distance and suburban buses terminate either near Tiburtina station or near strategically located Metro stops.

Getting Around

The best way to see Rome is to choose an area or a sight that you particularly want to see, reach it by bus or Metro, then explore the area on foot, following one of our itineraries or improvising one to suit your mood and interests. Wear comfortable, sturdy shoes, preferably with thick rubber soles to cushion you against the cobblestones. Heed our advice on security and try to avoid the noise and polluted air of heavily trafficked streets, taking parallel byways whenever possible. **Secret Walks** (tel. 06/397–28728) conducts theme walks for small groups led by English-language connoisseurs of the city, at affordable fees.

You can buy transportation route maps at newsstands or get them free at EPT and municipal tourist information booths and at ATAC information and ticket booths.

Metrebus Rome's integrated Metrebus transportation system includes city buses and trams (ATAC), Metro and suburban trains and buses (COTRAL), and some other suburban trains run by the state railways (FS). For travel within the city limits, a ticket valid for 75 minutes on any combination of buses and trams and one entrance to the Metro costs 1,500 lire. You are supposed to date-stamp the ticket when you board the first vehicle, stamping it again when boarding for the last time within 75 minutes. Tickets are sold at tobacco counters, newsstands, some coffee bars, automatic ticket machines, and at ATAC and ACOTRAL ticket booths. A BIG tourist ticket, valid for one day on all public transportation, costs 6,000 lire. A weekly ticket (*Settimanale*, also known as CIS) costs 24,000 lire and can be purchased only at ATAC and Metro booths.

By Metro The subway, or Metro, provides the easiest and fastest way to get around. The Metro opens at 5:30 AM, and the last train leaves each terminal at 11:30 PM. Line A runs from the eastern part of the city to Termini station and past Piazza di Spagna and Piazzale Flaminio to Ottaviano, near St. Peter's and the Vatican Museums. Line B serves Termini, the Colosseum, and the Piramide station (air terminal).

By Bus Orange ATAC (tel. 06/4695–4444) city buses (and several streetcar lines) run from about 6 AM to midnight, with skeleton *notturno* services on main lines throughout the night. (Night service is being reorganized; check locally). When entering a bus, remember to board at the rear and exit at the middle. The most inexpensive organized English-language sightseeing tour of Rome is the three-hour bus tour run by ATAC. It costs 10,000 lire and leaves at least once daily (at 2:30 PM in winter, 3:30 PM in summer) from Piazza dei Cinquecento in front of Termini station; buy tickets at the ATAC booth there.

Rome Metro

By Bicycle Bikes provide a pleasant means of getting around when traffic isn't heavy. There are bike-rental shops at Via di Porta Castello 43, near St. Peter's, and at Piazza Navona 69, next to Bar Navona. Rental concessions are at the Piazza di Spagna and Piazza del Popolo Metro stops and at Largo San Silvestro and Largo Argentina. There are also two in Villa Borghese, at Viale della Pineta and Viale del Bambino on the Pincio.

By Moped You can rent a moped or scooter and mandatory helmet at **Scoot-a-Long** (Via Cavour 302, tel. 06/678–0206) or **St. Peter Moto** (Via di Porta Castello 43, tel. 06/687–5714).

Important Addresses and Numbers

Tourist Information The main **EPT** (Rome Provincial Tourist) office is at Via Parigi 5 (tel. 06/488–3748, open Mon.–Fri. 8:15–7:15, Sat. 8:15–1:15). There are also EPT booths at Termini station and Leonardo da Vinci Airport. Municipal tourist information booths are located at Largo Goldoni (corner of Via Condotti and Via del Corso in the Spanish Steps area), Via dei Fori Imperiali (opposite the Roman Forum), and Via Nazionale (at Palazzo degli Esposizioni). (Open Tues.–Sat. 10–6, Sun. 10–1.) A booth on the main floor of the **ENIT** (National Tourist Board) building at Via Marghera 2 (tel. 06/497–1222, open weekdays 9–1, Wed. also 4–6) can provide information on destinations in Italy outside Rome.

Consulates U.S. (Via Veneto 121, tel. 06/46741). **Canadian** (Via Zara 30, tel. 06/445981). **U.K.** (Via Venti Settembre 80a, tel. 06/482–5441).

Emergencies **Police** (tel. 06/4686), **Carabinieri** (tel. 06/112), **Ambulance** (tel. 118). **Doctor:** Call your consulate, the private **Salvator Mundi Hospital** (tel. 06/588961), or the **American Hospital** (tel. 06/22551), which has English-speaking staff members, for a recommendation.

Exploring Rome

Antiquity is taken for granted in Rome, where successive ages have piled the present on top of the past—building, layering, and overlapping their own particular segments of Rome's 2,500 years of history to form a remarkably varied urban complex. Most of the city's major sights are located in a fairly small area known as the *centro*, or center. At its heart lies ancient Rome, where the Forum and Colosseum stand. It was around this core that the other sections of the city grew up through the ages: medieval Rome, which covered the horn of land that pushes the Tiber toward the Vatican and extended across the river into Trastevere; and Renaissance Rome, which was erected upon medieval foundations and extended as far as the Vatican, creating beautiful villas on what was then the outskirts of the city.

The layout of the center is highly irregular, but several landmarks serve as orientation points: the Colosseum, the Pantheon and Piazza Navona, St. Peter's, the Spanish Steps, and Villa Borghese. You'll need a good map to find your way around; newsstands offer a wide choice. Energetic sightseers will walk a lot, a much more pleasant way to see the city now that some traffic has been barred from the center during the day; others may choose to take buses or the Metro. The important thing is to relax and enjoy Rome, taking time to savor its pleasures. If you are in Rome during a hot spell, do as the Romans do: Start out early in the morning, have a light lunch and a long siesta during the hottest hours, then resume sightseeing in the late afternoon and end your evening with a leisurely meal outdoors, refreshed by cold Frascati wine and the *ponentino*, the cool evening breeze.

Ancient Rome *Numbers in the margin correspond to points of interest on the Rome map.*

1 Start your first tour at the city's center, in **Piazza Venezia.** Behind the enormous marble monument honoring the first king of unified
2 Italy, Victor Emmanuel II, stands the **Campidoglio** (Capitol Square) on the Capitoline Hill. The majestic ramp and beautifully proportioned piazza are Michelangelo's handiwork, as are the three palaces. The **Palazzo Senatorio** at the center is still the ceremonial seat of Rome's city hall; it was built over the Tabularium, where ancient Rome's state archives were kept.

3 The palaces flanking the Palazzo Senatorio contain the **Capitoline Museums.** On the left, the **Museo Capitolino** holds some fine classical sculptures, including the *Dying Gaul*, the *Capitoline Venus*, and a fascinating series of portrait busts of ancient philosophers and em-
4 perors. In the courtyard of the **Palazzo dei Conservatori** on the right of the piazza, you can use the mammoth fragments of a colossal statue of the emperor Constantine as amusing props for snapshots. Inside you will find splendidly frescoed salons, as well as sculptures and paintings. *Piazza del Campidoglio, tel. 06/671–002475. Admission: 10,000 lire, free last Sun. of month. Open May–Sept., Tues. 9–1:30, 5–8; Wed.–Fri. 9–1:30; Sat. 9–1:30, 7:30–11:30; Sun. 9–1. Oct.–Apr., Tues. and Sat. 9–1:30, 5–8; Wed.–Fri. 9–1:30; Sun. 9–1.*

5 The Campidoglio is also the site of the very old **Aracoeli** church, which you can reach by way of the stairs on the far side of the Museo Capitolino. Stop in to see the medieval pavement, the Renaissance gilded ceiling that commemorates the victory of Lepanto, some Pinturicchio frescoes, and a much-revered wooden statue of the Holy Child. The Campidoglio gardens offer a splendid view of Roman antiquity, extending from the Palatine Hill on the right and across the original Roman Forum to Via dei Fori Imperiali on the

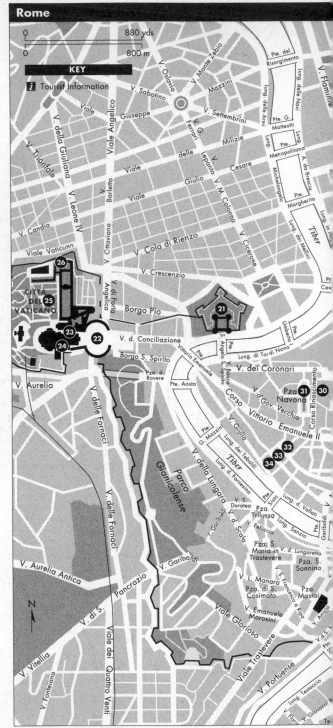

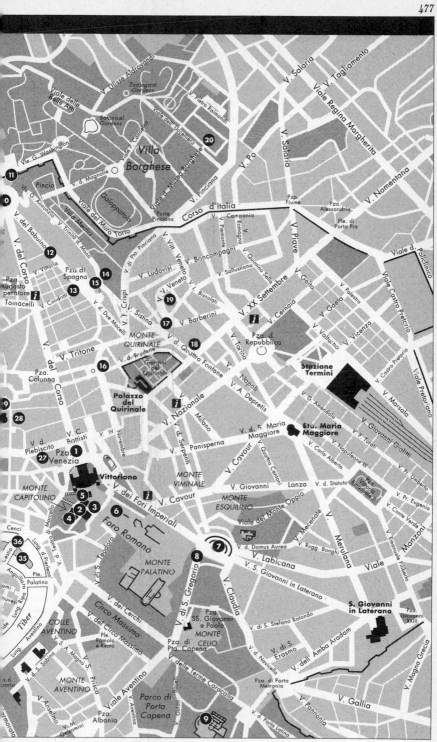

left, beyond which stretch the Imperial Fora that were built when the city outgrew the original one.

6 In the valley directly below, the **Roman Forum,** once only a marshy hollow, became the political, commercial, and social center of ancient Rome, studded with public meeting halls, shops, and temples. As Rome declined, these monuments lost their importance and eventually were destroyed by fire or the invasions of barbarians. Rubble accumulated, much of it was carted off by medieval homebuilders as construction material, and the site reverted to marshy pastureland; sporadic excavations began at the end of the 19th century.

You don't really have to try to make sense of the mass of marble fragments scattered over the area of the Roman Forum. Just consider that 2,000 years ago this was the center of the then-known world. Wander down the Via Sacra and climb the Palatine Hill, where the emperors had their palaces and where 16th-century cardinals strolled in elaborate Italian gardens. From the belvedere you have a good view of the Circus Maximus. *Entrances on Via dei Fori Imperiali, Piazza Santa Maria Nova and Via di San Gregorio, tel. 06/679–0110. Admission: 12,000 lire. Open Apr.–Sept., Mon.–Sat. 9–6, Sun. 9–1; Oct.–Mar., Mon.–Sat. 9–4, Sun. 9–1.*

Leave the Forum from the exit at Piazza Santa Maria Nova, near the **7** Arch of Titus, and head for the **Colosseum,** inaugurated in AD 80 with a program of games and shows that lasted 100 days. On opening day alone, 5,000 wild animals perished in the arena. The Colosseum could hold more than 50,000 spectators; it was faced with marble, decorated with stuccos, and had an ingenious system of awnings to provide shade. Try to see it both in daytime and at night, when yellow floodlights make it a magical sight. The Colosseum, by the way, takes its name from a colossal, 36-meter (115-foot) statue of Nero that stood nearby. You must pay a fee to explore the upper levels, where you can also see a scale model of the arena as it was in its heyday. *Piazza del Colosseo, tel. 06/700–4261. Admission: 8,000 lire to upper levels. Open Apr.–Sept., Mon., Tues., and Thurs.–Sat. 9–7, Sun. and Wed. 9–1; Oct.–Mar., Mon., Tues., Thurs.–Sat. 9–3.*

8 Stroll past the **Arch of Constantine.** The reliefs depict Constantine's victory over Maxentius at the Milvian Bridge. Just before this battle in AD 312, Constantine had a vision of a cross in the heavens and heard the words, "In this sign thou shalt conquer." The victory led not only to the construction of this majestic marble arch but, more important, was a turning point in the history of Christianity: Soon afterward a grateful Constantine decreed that it was a lawful religion and should be tolerated throughout the empire.

9 A fairly long but pleasant walk takes you to the **Baths of Caracalla,** which numbered among ancient Rome's most beautiful and luxurious, inaugurated by Caracalla in 217 and used until the 6th century. An ancient version of a swank athletic club, the baths were open to the public; citizens could bathe, socialize, and exercise in huge pools and richly decorated halls and libraries, now towering ruins. *Via delle Terme di Caracalla. Admission: 8,000 lire. Open Apr.–Sept., Tues.–Sat. 9–6, Sun. and Mon. 9–1; Oct.–Mar., Tues.–Sat. 9–3, Sun.–Mon. 9–1.*

Piazzas and **Piazza del Popolo** is one of Rome's most vast and airy squares, but
Fountains for many years it was just an exceptionally beautiful parking lot
10 with a 3,000-year-old obelisk in the middle. Now most traffic and parking has been barred, and the piazza is open to strollers. The
11 church of **Santa Maria del Popolo,** over in the corner of the piazza near the arch, stands out more, now that it has been cleaned, and is rich in art, including two stunning Caravaggios in the chapel to the left of the main altar.

⑫ If you're interested in antiques, stroll along **Via del Babuino.** If window-shopping suits your fancy, take Via del Corso and turn into **Via**
⑬ **Condotti,** Rome's most elegant and expensive shopping street. Here you can ogle fabulous jewelry, designer fashions, and accessories in the windows of Buccellati, Ferragamo, Valentino, Gucci, and Bulgari. The more-than-200-year-old **Antico Caffè Greco** is a Roman institution, the haunt of writers, artists, and well-groomed ladies toting Gucci shopping bags. With its small marble-topped tables and velour settees, it's a nostalgic sort of place—Goethe, Byron, and Liszt were regulars here, and even Buffalo Bill stopped in when his road show came to town. Whatever you have here should be ordered at the bar because table service is very expensive. *Via Condotti 86. Closed Sun.*

Via Condotti gives you a head-on view of the Spanish Steps in **Piazza**
⑭ **di Spagna** and of the church of **Trinità dei Monti.** In the center of the piazza is Bernini's **Fountain of the Barcaccia** (Old Boat), around which Romans and tourists cool themselves on hot summer nights.
⑮ The 200-year-old **Spanish Steps,** named for the Spanish Embassy to the Holy See, opposite the American Express office, is a popular rendezvous, especially for the young people who throng this area. On weekend afternoons, Via del Corso is packed wall-to-wall with teenagers, and the nearby McDonald's is a mob scene. In contrast, **Babington's Tea Room,** to the left of the Spanish Steps, is a stylish institution that caters to an upscale clientele.

To the right of the Spanish steps is the **Keats and Shelley Memorial House.** Once the home of these romantic poets, it's now a museum. *Piazza di Spagna 26, tel. 06/678–4235. Admission: 5,000 lire. Open June–Sept., weekdays 9–1 and 3–6; Oct.–May, weekdays 9–1 and 2:30–5:30.*

Head for Via del Tritone and cross this heavily trafficked shopping
⑯ street into narrow Via della Stamperia, which leads to the **Fountain of Trevi,** a spectacular fantasy of mythical sea creatures and cascades of splashing water. Legend has it that visitors must toss a coin into the fountain to ensure their return to Rome, but you'll have to force your way past crowds of tourists and aggressive souvenir vendors to do so. The fountain as you see it was completed in the mid-1700s, but there had been a drinking fountain on the site for centuries. Pope Urban VIII almost sparked a revolt when he slapped a tax on wine to cover the expenses of having the fountain repaired.

⑰ At the top of Via del Tritone, **Piazza Barberini** boasts two fountains by Bernini: the jaunty **Triton** in the middle of the square and the **Fountain of the Bees** at the corner of Via Veneto. Decorated with the heraldic Barberini bees, this shell-shape fountain bears an inscription that was immediately regarded as an unlucky omen by the superstitious Romans, for it erroneously stated that the fountain had been erected in the 22nd year of the reign of Pope Urban VIII, who had commissioned it, while, in fact, the 21st anniversary of his election was still some weeks away. The wrong numeral was hurriedly erased, but to no avail: Urban died eight days before the beginning of his 22nd year as pontiff.

⑱ A few steps up Via delle Quattro Fontane is **Palazzo Barberini,** Rome's most splendid 17th-century palace, now surrounded by rather unkempt gardens and occupied, in part, by the **Galleria Nazionale di Arte Antica.** Visit the latter to see Raphael's *Fornarina,* many other good paintings, some lavishly frescoed ceilings, and a charming suite of rooms decorated in 1782 on the occasion of the marriage of a Barberini heiress. *Via delle Quattro Fontane 13, tel. 06/481–4591. Admission: 8,000 lire. Open Tues.–Sat. 9–2, Sun. 9–1.*

⑲ One of Rome's oddest sights is the **crypt** of the **Church of Santa Maria della Concezione** on Via Veneto, just above the Fountain of the Bees. In four chapels under the main church, the skeletons and scattered bones of some 4,000 dead Capuchin monks are arranged in decorative motifs, a macabre practice peculiar to the bizarre Baroque Age. *Via Veneto 27, tel. 06/462850. Admission free, but a donation is encouraged. Open daily 9–noon and 3–6.*

The lower reaches of Via Veneto are quiet and sedate, but at the intersection with Via Bissolati, otherwise known as "Airline Row," the avenue comes to life. The big white palace on the right is the U.S. Embassy, and the even bigger white palace beyond it is the luxurious **Hotel Excelsior.** Together with Doney's next door and the Café de Paris across the street, the Excelsior was a landmark of La Dolce Vita, that effervescent period during the 1950s when movie stars, playboys, and exiled royalty played hide-and-seek with press agents and paparazzi, ducking in and out of nightclubs and hotel rooms along the Via Veneto. The atmosphere of the street is considerably more sober now, and its cafés cater more to tourists and expensive pickups than to barefoot cinema *contesse.*

㉑ Via Veneto ends at **Porta Pinciana,** a gate in the 12-mile stretch of defensive walls built by Emperor Aurelian in the 3rd century; 400 years later, when the Goths got too close for comfort, Belisarius reinforced the gate with two massive towers. Beyond is **Villa Borghese,** the most famous of Rome's parks, studded with tall pines that are gradually dying off as pollution and age take their toll. Inside the park, strike off to the right toward the **Galleria Borghese,** a pleasure palace created by Cardinal Scipione Borghese in 1613 as a showcase for his fabulous sculpture collection. In the throes of structural repairs for several years, the now-public gallery is, at press time, only partially open to visitors. It's still worth a visit to see the seductive reclining statue of Pauline Borghese by Canova and some extraordinary works by Bernini, among them the unforgettable *Apollo and Daphne,* in which marble is transformed into flesh and foliage. *During reconstruction, the entrance is on Via Raimondi, reached from Via Pinciana. Via Pinciana (Piazzale Museo Borghese–Villa Borghese), tel. 06/854–8577. Admission: 4,000 lire. Open Mon.–Sat. 9– 1:30, Sun. 9–1. (The gallery's picture collection, including some Caravaggios, has been moved to a former church in the huge San Michele a Ripa complex in Trastevere. Via di San Michele, tel. 06/ 58431. Admission: 4,000 lire. Open Tues.–Sat. 9–7, Sun., 9–1.)*

**Castle
Sant'Angelo,
St. Peter's,
Vatican
Museums
㉑** **Ponte Sant'Angelo,** the ancient bridge across the Tiber in front of Castel Sant'Angelo, is decorated with lovely Baroque angels designed by Bernini and offers fine views of the castle and of St. Peter's in the distance. **Castel Sant'Angelo,** a formidable fortress, was originally built as the tomb of Emperor Hadrian in the 2nd century AD. In its early days, it looked much like the **Augusteo,** or Tomb of Augustus, which still stands more or less in its original form across the river. Hadrian's Tomb was incorporated into the town walls and served as a military stronghold during the barbarian invasions. According to legend, it got its present name in the 6th century, when Pope Gregory the Great, passing by in a religious procession, saw an angel with a sword appear above the ramparts to signal the end of the plague that was raging. Enlarged and fortified, the castle became a refuge for the popes, who fled to it along the **Passetto,** an arcaded passageway that links it with the Vatican. Inside the castle you see ancient corridors, medieval cells and Renaissance salons, a museum of antique weapons, courtyards piled with stone cannonballs, and terraces with great views of the city. There's a pleasant bar with outdoor tables on one level. The highest terrace of all, under the newly restored bronze statue of the legendary angel, is the one from which Puccini's heroine, Tosca, threw herself. *Lungotevere Castello 50, tel. 06/687–5036. Admission: 8,000 lire. Open Mon.– Sat. 9–2, Sun. 9–noon. Closed 2nd Tues. and 2nd Fri. of month.*

Via della Conciliazione, the broad avenue leading to St. Peter's Basilica, was created by Mussolini's architects by razing blocks of old houses. This opened up a vista of the basilica, giving the eye time to adjust to its mammoth dimensions, and thereby spoiling the effect Bernini sought when he enclosed his vast square (which is really oval) in the embrace of huge quadruple colonnades. In **Piazza San** **Pietro** (St. Peter's Square), which has held up to 400,000 people at one time, look for the stone disks in the pavement halfway between the fountains and the obelisk. From these points the colonnades seem to be formed of a single row of columns all the way around.

When you enter Piazza San Pietro (completed in 1667), you are entering Vatican territory. Since the Lateran Treaty of 1929, **Vatican** **City** has been an independent and sovereign state, which covers about 44 hectares (108 acres) and is surrounded by thick, high walls. Its gates are watched over by the Swiss Guards, who still wear the colorful dress uniforms designed by Michelangelo. Sovereign of this little state is John Paul II, 264th Pope of the Roman Catholic Church. At noon on Sunday, the Pope appears at his third-floor study window in the **Vatican Palace,** to the right of the basilica, to bless the crowd in the square. (Note: Entry to St. Peter's and the Vatican Museums is barred to those wearing shorts, miniskirts, sleeveless T-shirts, and otherwise revealing clothing. Women should carry scarves to cover bare shoulders and upper arms or wear blouses that come to the elbow. Men should dress modestly, in slacks and shirts.)

St. Peter's Basilica is one of Rome's most impressive sights. It takes a while to absorb the sheer magnificence of it, however, and its rich decoration may not be to everyone's taste. Its size alone is overwhelming, and the basilica is best appreciated when providing the lustrous background for ecclesiastical ceremonies thronged with the faithful. The original basilica was built in the early 4th century AD by the emperor Constantine, over an earlier shrine that supposedly marked the burial place of St. Peter. After more than a thousand years, the old basilica was so decrepit it had to be torn down. The task of building a new, much larger one took almost 200 years and employed the architectural genius of Alberti, Bramante, Raphael, Peruzzi, Antonio Sangallo the Younger, and Michelangelo, who died before the dome he had planned could be completed. Finally, in 1626, St. Peter's Basilica was finished.

Free guided tours of the interior of St. Peter's are conducted in English by a volunteer group, usually at about 10 AM and about 3 PM. Inquire at the desk in the portico (daily 10–noon and 3–5).

The basilica is full of extraordinary works of art. Among the most famous is Michelangelo's *Pietà* (1498), seen in the first chapel on the right just as you enter from the square. Michelangelo has four *Pietà*s to his credit. The earliest and best known can be seen here. Two others are in Florence, and the fourth, the *Rondanini Pietà*, is in Milan.

At the end of the central aisle is the bronze statue of **St. Peter,** its foot worn by centuries of reverent kisses. Above the altar in the apse is the *Chair of St. Peter*, a bronze monument created by Bernini as a sort of combined throne and reliquary for a simple wood-and-ivory chair once believed to have belonged to St. Peter. An even more celebrated work is the bronze *baldacchino* (canopy) over the papal altar, which Bernini made with metal stripped from the portico of the Pantheon at the order of Pope Urban VIII, one of the powerful Roman Barberini family. His practice of plundering ancient monuments for material to implement his grandiose schemes inspired the famous quip, *"Quod non fecerunt barbari, fecerunt Barberini"* ("What the barbarians didn't do, the Barberini did").

As you stroll up and down the aisles and transepts, observe the fine mosaic copies of famous paintings above the altars, the monumental tombs and statues, and the fine stucco work. Stop at the **Treasury**

(Historical Museum), which contains some priceless liturgical objects.

The entrance to the **Vatican Grottoes** is in one of the huge piers at the crossing. It's best to leave this visit for last, as the grottoes' only exit takes you outside the church. The grottoes contain chapels and the tombs of many popes. They occupy the area of the original basilica, over the Early Christian cemetery, or necropolis, where evidence of what may be St. Peter's burial place has been found. You can book special tours of the excavations of the cemetery and the basilica's underpinnings.

In a courtyard on the right side of the basilica, at the exit of the Vatican Grottoes, is the entrance to the elevator up to the roof of the basilica. From here you can climb a short interior staircase to the base of the dome for an overhead view of the interior of the basilica. Only if you are in good shape should you attempt the strenuous and claustrophobic climb up the narrow, one-way stairs to the balcony of the lantern atop the dome, where the view embraces the Vatican Gardens as well as all of Rome. *St. Peter's Basilica, tel. 06/698–4466. Open daily 7–7. Treasury (Museo Storico-Artistico): entrance in Sacristy. Admission: 3,000 lire. Open Apr.–Sept., daily 9–6:30; Oct.–Mar., daily 9–5:30. Roof and Dome: entrance in the courtyard off the portico, on the right. Admission: 6,000 lire, including use of elevator to roof, 5,000 lire if you climb the spiral ramp on foot. Open Apr.–Sept., daily 8–6; Oct.–Mar., daily 8–5. Vatican Grottoes (Tombs of the Popes): entrance alternates among the piers at the crossing. Admission: free. Open Apr.–Sept., daily 7–6; Oct.–Mar., daily 7–5. Cemetery excavations: Apply a few days in advance or apply in the morning for the same day to Ufficio Scavi, left beyond the Arco delle Campane entrance to the Vatican, left of the basilica, tel. 06/698–5318. Admission: 10,000 lire for 2-hr guided visit, 6,000 lire with cassette tape. Ufficio Scavi office hrs: Mon.–Sat. 9–5; closed Sun. and religious holidays.*

For many visitors, a **papal audience** is the highlight of a trip to Rome. The Pope holds mass audiences on Wednesday morning; they take place in a modern audience hall (capacity 7,000) off the left-hand colonnade. You can also see the Pope on Sundays at noon when he appears at the window of the **Vatican Palace** (or of his summer residence at **Castel Gandolfo**) to bless the crowd and give a brief talk. *For audience tickets, apply in writing well in advance to the Papal Prefecture (Prefettura), 00120, Vatican City, indicating the date you prefer, your language, and your hotel in Rome, or go to the Prefettura (entrance through the Bronze Door in the right-hand colonnade, tel. 06/6982). Open Mon. and Tues. 9–1 for the Wed. audience. You can also pick up free tickets at the office of the North American College, Via dell'Umiltà 30 (tel. 06/678–9184).*

㉕ Guided minibus tours through the **Vatican Gardens** show you some attractive landscaping, a few historical monuments, and the Vatican mosaic school, which produced the mosaics decorating St. Peter's. These tours give you a different perspective on the basilica itself. *Tickets at information office, on the left side of St. Peter's Square, tel. 06/6988–4466. Open Mon.–Sat. 8:30–7. Garden tour cost: 16,000 lire. Available Mon., Tues., and Thurs.–Sat. All tours begin at 10 AM.*

From the information office in St. Peter's Square you can take a shuttle bus (cost: 2,000 lire) directly to the Vatican Museums. This operates every morning, except Wednesday and Sunday, and saves you the 15-minute walk that goes left from the square and continues along the Vatican walls.

㉖ The collections in the **Vatican Museums** cover nearly 8 kilometers (5 miles) of displays. If you have time, allow at least half a day for Castel Sant'Angelo and St. Peter's and another half day for the museums. Posters at the museum entrance plot out a choice of four color-coded itineraries; the shortest takes about 90 minutes, the longest more than four hours, depending on your rate of progress. All include the **Sistine Chapel.**

In 1508, Pope Julius II commissioned Michelangelo to fresco the more than 930 square meters (10,000 square feet) of the chapel's ceiling. For four years Michelangelo dedicated himself to painting over fresh plaster, and the result was his masterpiece. The cleaning of his frescoes on the ceiling and his *Last Judgment* on the wall over the altar have revealed their original and surprisingly brilliant colors.

You can try to avoid the tour groups by going early or late, allowing yourself enough time before the closing hour. In peak season, the crowds definitely detract from your appreciation of this outstanding artistic achievement. Buy an illustrated guide or rent a taped commentary in order to make sense of the figures on the ceiling. A pair of binoculars helps.

The Vatican collections are so rich that unless you are an expert in art history, you will probably want only to skim the surface, concentrating on a few pieces that strike your fancy. If you really want to see the museums thoroughly, you will have to come back again and again. Some of the highlights that may be of interest on your first tour include the *Laocoön,* the *Belvedere Torso,* and the *Apollo Belvedere,* which inspired Michelangelo. The Raphael Rooms are decorated with masterful frescoes, and there are more Raphaels in the Picture Gallery *(Pinacoteca).* At the Quattro Cancelli, near the entrance to the Picture Gallery, a rather spartan cafeteria provides basic nonalcoholic refreshments. *Viale Vaticano, tel. 06/6988-3333. Admission: 13,000 lire, free on last Sun. of the month. Open Easter period and July–Sept., weekdays 8:45–5, Sat. 8:45–2; Oct.–June, Mon.–Sat. 8:45–2. Ticket office closes 60 mins before museums close. Closed Sun., except last Sun. of the month, and on religious holidays. (There are many; check calendar at information office in St. Peter's Square.)*

Old Rome

㉗ Take Via del Plebiscito from Piazza Venezia to the huge **Church of the Gesù.** This paragon of Baroque style is the tangible symbol of the power of the Jesuits, who were a major force in the Counter-Reformation in Europe. Encrusted with gold and precious marbles, the Gesù has a fantastically painted ceiling that flows down over the pillars, merging with painted stucco figures to complete the three-dimensional illusion.

㉘ On your way to the Pantheon you will pass **Santa Maria Sopra Minerva,** a Gothic church built over a Roman temple. Inside there are some beautiful frescoes by Filippo Lippi; outside there is a charming elephant by Bernini with an obelisk on its back.

㉙ Originally built in 27 BC by Augustus's general Agrippa and rebuilt by Hadrian in the 2nd century AD, the **Pantheon** is one of Rome's most perfect, best-preserved, and perhaps least appreciated ancient monuments. Romans and tourists alike pay little attention to it, and on summer evenings it serves mainly as a backdrop for all the action in the square in front. It represents a fantastic feat of construction, however. The huge columns of the portico and the original bronze doors form the entrance to a majestic hall covered by the largest dome of its kind ever built, wider even than that of St. Peter's. In ancient times the entire interior was encrusted with rich decorations of gilt bronze and marble, plundered by later emperors and popes. *Piazza della Rotonda. Open Mon.–Sat. 9–2, Sun. 9–1.*

㉚ Stop in at the church of **San Luigi dei Francesi** on Via della Dogana Vecchia to see the three paintings by Caravaggio in the last chapel on the left; have a few hundred-lire coins handy for the light machine. The clergy of San Luigi considered the artist's roistering and unruly lifestyle scandalous enough, but his realistic treatment of sacred subjects was just too much for them. They rejected his first version of the altarpiece and weren't particularly happy with the other two works either. Thanks to the intercession of Caravaggio's patron, an influential cardinal, they were persuaded to keep them—a lucky thing, since they are now recognized to be among the artist's finest paintings. *Open Fri.–Wed. 7:30–12:30 and 3:30–7, Thurs. 7:30–12:30.*

㉛ Just beyond San Luigi is **Piazza Navona,** an elongated 17th-century piazza that traces the oval form of the underlying Circus of Diocletian. At the center, Bernini's lively **Fountain of the Four Rivers** is a showpiece. The four statues represent rivers in the four corners of the world: the Nile, with its face covered in allusion to its then-unknown source; the Ganges; the Danube; and the River Plate, with its hand raised. And here we have to give the lie to the legend that this was Bernini's mischievous dig at Borromini's design of the facade of the church of **Sant'Agnese in Agone,** from which the statue seems to be shrinking in horror. The fountain was created in 1651; work on the church's facade began some time later. The piazza dozes in the morning, when little groups of pensioners sun themselves on the stone benches and children pedal tricycles around the big fountain. In the late afternoon the sidewalk cafés fill up for the aperitif hour, and in the evening, especially in good weather, the piazza comes to life with a throng of street artists, vendors, tourists, and Romans out for their evening *passeggiata* (promenade). A good many of them stop at the **Tre Scalini** café (Piazza Navona 30) to treat themselves to a *tartufo,* a chocolate ice-cream specialty that was invented here. You may want to do the same, but order it at the counter, since table service is expensive at this and all cafés on the piazza.

㉜ Across Corso Vittorio is **Campo dei Fiori** (Field of Flowers), the site of a crowded and colorful daily morning market. The hooded bronze figure brooding over the piazza is philosopher Giordano Bruno, who was burned at the stake here for heresy. The adjacent **Piazza**
㉝ **Farnese,** with fountains made of Egyptian granite basins from the
㉞ Baths of Caracalla, is an airy setting for the **Palazzo Farnese,** now the French Embassy, one of the most beautiful of Rome's many Renaissance palaces. There are several others in the immediate area: **Palazzo Spada,** a Wedgwood kind of palace encrusted with stucco and statues; **Palazzo della Cancelleria,** a massive building that is now the Papal Chancellery, one of the many Vatican-owned buildings in Rome that enjoy extraterritorial privileges; and the fine old palaces along Via Giulia.

The area is one for browsing, through antiques shops and through streets where daily life takes place in a timeworn setting. Stroll along Via Arenula into a rather gloomy part of Rome, bounded by Piazza Campitelli and Lungotevere Cenci, the ancient Jewish ghetto. Among the most interesting sights here are the pretty **Fountain of the Tartarughe** (Turtles) on Piazza Mattei; the **Via Portico d'Ottavia,** with medieval inscriptions and friezes on the old buildings; and the **Teatro di Marcello,** a theater built by Julius Caesar to hold 20,000 spectators.

㉟ A pleasant place to end your walk is on **Tiberina Island.** To get there,
㊱ walk across the ancient **Fabricio Bridge,** built in 62 BC, the oldest bridge in the city.

 Ostia Antica   Make an excursion to **Ostia Antica,** the well-preserved ancient Roman port city near the sea, just as rewarding as an excursion to Pompeii. Pick up the pamphlet-guide at the Rome EPT office (Via Parigi 5). There is regular train service from the Ostiense station (Piramide Metro stop). *Via dei Romagnoli, Ostia Antica, tel. 06/ 565–1405. Admission: 8,000 lire. Open daily 9–2 hrs. before sunset.*

Shopping

Shopping is part of the fun of being in Rome, no matter what your budget. The best buys are leather goods of all kinds, from gloves to handbags and wallets to jackets; silk goods; and high-quality knitwear. Shops are closed on Sunday and on Monday morning; in July and August, they close on Saturday afternoon as well.

Prints A well-trained eye will spot some worthy old prints and minor antiques in the city's fascinating little shops. For prints, browse among the stalls at **Piazza Fontanella Borghese;** at **Casali,** Piazza della Rotonda 81a, at the Pantheon; and **Tanca,** Salita de' Crescenzi 10, also near the Pantheon.

Boutiques Lower-price fashions may be found on display at shops on **Via Frattina, Via del Corso, Via Ottaviano** (near St. Peter's), and around **San Giovanni in Laterano.**

Shopping In addition to those mentioned, Romans themselves do much of their
Districts shopping along **Via Cola di Rienzo** and **Via Nazionale.** The market booths on Via Sannio, near San Giovanni in Laterano, have good buys in new and second-hand clothing, though stocks vary.

Religious These abound in the shops around St. Peter's, on **Via di Porta Angeli-**
Articles **ca** and **Via della Conciliazione,** and in the souvenir shops tucked away on the roof and at the grottoes exit in St. Peter's itself.

Department You'll find a fairly broad selection of women's, men's, and children's
Stores fashions and accessories at the **Rinascente** stores on Piazza Colonna and at Piazza Fiume and at the **Coin** department store on Piazzale Appio near San Giovanni in Laterano. The **UPIM** and **Standa** chains have shops all over the city that offer medium-quality, low-price goods. The **Croff** chain features housewares.

Food and Flea The open-air markets at **Piazza Vittorio** and **Campo dei Fiori** are col-
Markets orful sights. The flea market held at **Porta Portese** on Sunday morning is stocked mainly with new or second-hand clothing. If you go, beware of pickpockets and purse snatchers.

Dining

There are plenty of fine restaurants in Rome serving various Italian regional cuisines and international specialties with a flourish of linen and silver, as well as a whopping *conto* (check) at the end. If you want family-style cooking and prices, try a trattoria, a usually smallish and unassuming, often family-run place. Fast-food places and Chinese restaurants are proliferating in Rome; very few of the latter can be recommended. Prix-fixe tourist menus can be scanty and unimaginative. The lunch hour in Rome lasts from about 1 to 3 PM, dinner from 8 or 8:30 to about 10:30, though some restaurants stay open much later. Romans love to eat out, so most restaurants, especially inexpensive and budget places, are jammed on weekend evenings. To get a table, you have to arrive 15–20 minutes before normal dining hours. During August many restaurants close for vacation.

For details and price-category definitions, *see* Dining *in* Staying in Italy, *above.*

$$ **Gemma alla Lupa.** As one of the the best trattorias in the Termini Station area, this is always crowded with regulars, so get there early to get a table. The specialties are typical Roman dishes, from pasta *all'amatriciana* (with tomato and bacon sauce) to *petto alla fornara* (roast veal breast with potatoes). *Via Marghera 39, tel. 06/ 491230. Reservations advised. No credit cards. Closed Sun.*

$$ **Grappolo d'Oro.** Located off Campo dei Fiori and near Piazza Navona, this trattoria is a favorite with locals and foreign residents, one of whom wrote it up in the *New Yorker* some years ago. Even with it's new-found fame, it hasn't changed. The owners are friendly

and patient, and the food is classic Roman trattoria fare. The daily special is usually a winner. *Piazza della Cancelleria 80, tel. 06/688–4118. Reservations advised for dinner. AE, MC, V. Closed Sun.*

$$ La Campana. An inconspicuous trattoria off Via della Scrofa, this has a long tradition of hospitality—there has been an inn on this spot since the 15th century. Now it's a classic Roman eating place, with friendly but businesslike waiters and a menu that offers Roman specialties, such as *vignarola* (sautéed fava beans, peas, and artichokes), rigatoni with prosciutto and tomato sauce, and *olivette di vitello* (tiny veal rolls, served with mashed potatoes). *Vicolo della Campana 18, tel. 06/686–7820. Dinner reservations advised. AE, V. Closed Mon. and Aug.*

$$ Le Maschere. This cellar restaurant, between Largo Argentina and
★ Piazza Campo dei Fiori, has lots of atmosphere and a lavish antipasto buffet. The decor is rustic, and the menu features southern Italian specialties, such as pasta with tomato and eggplant sauce, in addition to pizza. *Via Monte della Farina 29, tel. 06/687–9444. Reservations advised. AE, DC, MC, V. Open evenings only. Closed Mon. and mid-Aug.–mid-Sept.*

$$ Orso 80. A bustling trattoria in Old Rome, near Piazza Navona, it is known for a fabulous antipasto table. The egg pasta is freshly made, and the *bucatini all'amatriciana* (thick spaghetti with a tangy tomato and bacon sauce) is a classic Roman pasta. For dessert, try the ricotta cake, a Roman specialty. *Via dell'Orso 33, tel. 06/686–4904. Reservations advised. AE, DC, MC, V. Closed Mon. and Aug. 10–20.*

$$ Perilli. A traditional, wood-paneled trattoria that is an institution in Testaccio, the colorful working-class district near the Piramide and Ostiense stations. The cooking is quintessentialy Roman, from pasta *alla carbonars* (with bacon and egg) to *abbacchio* (roast baby lamb), or *trippa* (tripe) if you like it. *Via Marmorate 39, tel. 06/574–2415. Reservations not necessary. No credit cards. Closed Wed.*

$$ Pierluigi. Pierluigi, in the heart of Old Rome, is a longtime favorite. On busy evenings it's almost impossible to find a table, so make sure you reserve well in advance. Seafood predominates—but can be pricey; instead, try traditional Roman dishes, such as *orecchiette con broccoli* (disk-shaped pasta with greens) or just simple spaghetti. In warm weather ask for a table in the piazza. *Piazza dei Ricci 144, tel. 06/686–1302. Reservations advised. AE. Closed Mon. and 2 wks in Aug.*

$ Abruzzi. This simple trattoria, off Piazza Santi Apostoli near Piazza
★ Venezia, specializes in regional cooking of the Abruzzi, a mountainous region southeast of Rome. Specialties include *tonnarelli Abruzzi* (square-cut pasta with mushrooms, peas, and ham) and *abbacchio* (roast lamb). *Via del Vaccaro 1, tel. 06/679–3897. Lunch reservations advised. V. Closed Sat and Aug.*

$ Da Lucia. This family-run trattoria in Trastevere makes room for everyone by overflowing into the street in fair weather; you may have to wait for a table otherwise. The food is homey Roman. There are no menus, and the waiters recite the day's specials. But don't worry, they speak a little English. *Vicolo del Mattonato 2, tel. 06/580–3601. No credit cards. Closed Mon.*

$ Dino e Toni. A small trattoria on a shopping street close to the Vatican Museums, it offers cheese-filled *bocconcini* (cheese-filled pastry balls) as a starter, together with typical Roman pastas and main courses. *Via Leone IV 60, tel. 06/397–33284. Reservations advised for dinner. AE, DC, MC, V.*

$ Fratelli Menghi. A neighborhood trattoria that has been in the same family as long as anyone can remember, Fratelli Menghi produces typical Roman fare. There's usually a thick, hearty soup, such as minestrone; pasta *e ceci* (with chick peas); and other standbys, including *involtini* (meat roulades). *Via Flaminia 57, tel. 06/320–0803. No reservations. No credit cards. Closed Sun.*

$ Hostaria Farnese. This is a tiny trattoria between Campo dei Fiori and Piazza Farnese, in the heart of Old Rome. Papa serves, Mamma cooks, and depending on what they've picked up at the Campo dei Fiori market, you may find rigatoni with tuna and basil, spaghetti with vegetable sauce, *spezzatino* (stew), and other homey specialties. *Via dei Baullari 109, tel. 06/654-1595. Reservations advised. AE, V. Closed Thurs.*

$ Pollarola. Located near Piazza Navona and Campo dei Fiori, this typical Roman trattoria has flowers (artificial) on the tables and an antique Roman column embedded in the rear wall, evidence of its historic site. You can eat outdoors in fair weather. Try a pasta specialty, such as fettuccine *al gorgonzola* (noodles with creamy gorgonzola sauce), and a mixed plate from the temptingly fresh array of antipasti. The house wine, white or red, is good. *Piazza della Pollarola 24 (Campo dei Fiori), tel. 06/688-01654. Reservations advised for groups. AE, V. Closed Sun.*

$ Tavernetta. Its central location, between Trevi Fountain and the Spanish Steps, is convenient, and the economical tourist menu makes this a reliable place for a simple but satisfying meal. If you order à la carte, your check will be in the $$ range. *Via del Nazareno 3, tel. 06/679-3124. Reservations advised evenings. AE, DC, MC, V. Closed Mon. and Aug.*

$ Vecchia Roma da Severino. On Viale Manzoni, between Termini station and St. John Lateran, Severino is family run and serves specialties of the southern Italian region of Puglia, especially homemade pastas, hearty soups, and tasty vegetable dishes. *Viale Manzoni 52, tel. 06/495-8483. Reservations advised evenings. No credit cards. Closed Sun.*

¢ Augusto. Enjoy this one while you can. This classic type of neighborhood trattoria, with paper tablecloths and a limited menu of Roman dishes, is regrettably disappearing. This one is a favorite with foreign residents of the lively Trastevere district. *Piazza de' Renzi 15, tel. 06/580-3798. No reservations. No credit cards. Closed Sun.*

¢ Baffetto. Rome's best-known pizzeria is ultra-plain and very popular. You may have to wait for seating at one of the paper-covered tables, and you'll probably have to share it. *Bruschetta* (toast with olive oil) and *crostini* (mozzarella toast) are the only variations on the pizza theme. *Via del Governo Vecchio 114, tel. 06/686-1617. No reservations. No credit cards. Closed lunch, Sun., and Aug.*

¢ Birreria Tempera. This old-fashioned beer hall near Piazza Venezia is very busy at lunchtime. There's a good selection of salads and cold cuts, as well as pasta and daily specials. *Via San Marcello 19, tel. 06/678-6203. No reservations. No credit cards. Closed Sun. and Aug.*

¢ Cottini. On a corner of Piazza Santa Maria Maggiore, this reliable cafeteria-style restaurant, annexed to a large coffee bar, offers everything from salads to main courses and tempting desserts from the in-house bakery. *Via Merulana 287, tel. 06/474-0768. No reservations. No credit cards. Closed Mon.*

¢ Fagianetto. The reputation of this family-run trattoria near Termini station is as solid as the heavy wooden beams of the restaurant's ceiling. It has a regular neighborhood clientele but also satisfies tourists' appetites with a special menu for about 20,000 lire. The more imaginative à la carte menu is tempting, too. *Via Filippo Turati 21, tel. 06/446-7306. AE, DC, MC, V. Closed Mon.*

¢ L'Insalata Ricca. An informal place near Piazza Navona, it specializes in salads and basic pastas. No smoking here. If it's packed, as is often the case, try its sister restaurant, with the same name, at Piazza Pasquino 2 (closed Mon.). *Largo dei Chiavari 85, tel. 06/688-03656. Reservations advised evenings. No credit cards. Closed Wed.*

¢ La Caravella. The family that owns this wood-panel neighborhood trattoria handy to the Vatican Museums prides itself on pleasing tourists. You can lunch on pizza and a salad here, or delve into classic Roman dishes. *Via degli Scipioni 32 (corner Via Vespasiano, off Via*

Leone IV), tel. 06/397-26161. No reservations. AE, MC, V. Closed Thurs.

¢ **La Sagrestia.** Centrally located near the Pantheon, this tavern serves pizza, bean dishes, and 15 types of pasta. *Via del Seminario 89, tel. 06/679-7581. AE, DC, V. Closed Wed.*

Lodging

The list below covers mostly those hotels that are within walking distance of at least some sights and that are handy to public transportation. Rooms facing the street get traffic noise throughout the night, and few hotels in the lower categories have double glazing. Ask for a quiet room, or bring earplugs. Generally, rooms without bath in $ hotels cost as little as rooms in ¢ hotels and may offer more amenities.

We strongly recommend that you always make reservations in advance. Should you find yourself in the city without reservations, however, contact HR, **Hotel Reservation** service (tel. 06/699-1000; English-speaking operator available daily 7 AM–10 PM), with desks at Termini station and Fiumicino airport; or one of the following EPT offices: at Leonardo da Vinci Airport (tel. 06/601-1255); Termini train station (tel. 06/487-1270); or the main information office at Via Parigi 5 (tel. 06/488-3748), which is near Piazza della Repubblica. The Rome municipal tourist information booths (*see above*) also will help you find a room. Students can try the **Centro Turistico Studentesco** (CTS, information tel. 06/467-9271, or the main office, at Via Genova 16 tel. 06/46791).

For details and price-category definitions, *see* Lodging *in* Staying in Italy, *above*.

$$ **Alimandi.** Offering excellent value, this family-operated hotel is on a
★ side street just a block from the Vatican Museums entrance, in a neighborhood of moderately priced shops and trattorias. The spiffy lobby and ample lounges, a tavern for night owls, terraces and roof garden are some of the perks here. Rooms are well-furnished and many are spacious enough for extra beds. The few rooms without private bath are real bargains. *Via Tunisi 8, tel. 06/397-23948, fax 06/397-23943. 32 rooms, 26 with bath. Facilities: parking (extra charge). AE, MC, V.*

$$ **Margutta.** Centrally located near the Spanish Steps and Piazza del
★ Popolo, this small hotel has an unassuming lobby but bright, attractive bedrooms and modern baths. *Via Laurina 34, tel. 06/322-3674, fax 06/320-0395. 21 rooms with bath. AE, DC, MC, V.*

$$ **Montreal.** Don't let the run-down appearance of the building fool you. The Montreal, which is near Santa Maria Maggiore and Termini station, has a compact, tastefully decorated interior, with classical motifs and simple but attractive rooms on two floors. *Via Carlo Alberto 4, tel. 06/446-5522, fax 06/445-7797. 20 rooms with bath. AE, DC, MC, V.*

$$ **Parlamento.** In the heart of Rome's elegant shopping district, this small, well-kept hotel has a freshly refurbished look. It has a rooftop terrace and a friendly management. *Via delle Convertite 5, tel. and fax 06/678-7880. 22 rooms, 14 with bath. AE, MC, V.*

$$ **Romae.** Located in the better part of the Termini station neighborhood, it gives very good value in clean, airy rooms with amenities, such as satellite TV and hair dryers. The friendly management makes no extra charge for breakfast and offers special rates for families. *Via Palestro 49, tel. 06/446-3554, fax 06/446-3914. 20 rooms with bath. AE, MC, V.*

$$ **Santa Prisca.** This is a basic hotel in the Aventine neighborhood, adjacent to the Testaccio quarter's plentiful trattorie. It's run by nuns, and everything is clean and orderly. Meals are available. *Lar-*

go Manlio Gelsomini 25, tel. 06/575–0009, fax 06/574–6658. 45 rooms with shower. Facilities: restaurant, garden. No credit cards.

$$ Smeraldo. Near Largo Argentina, on a narrow byway in Old Roma, Smeraldo has a stylish entrance and bar-breakfast room paneled in decorative marble. Clean, sparingly furnished rooms have air-conditioning. Ask for a quiet room on the courtyard. Rates are slightly higher than $$ category. *Vicolo dei Chiodaroli 9, tel. 06/687–5929, fax 06/688–05495. 35 rooms, 22 with bath. AE, MC, V.*

$ Abruzzi. Rooms in this central hotel are tiny and dark, but almost all have a view of the Pantheon and its café-filled square, a Roman rendezvous in all seasons. The noise continues past midnight in summer, but that view is worth the aggravation. Bring earplugs. *Piazza della Rotonda 69, tel. 06/679–2021. 25 rooms without bath. No credit cards.*

$ Coronet. A small, comfortable hotel in an enviable location: It is in the 17th-century Palazzo Doria on central Via del Corso. The high-ceiling rooms are large and well furnished, and three have baths that are not new but clean and in good condition. Rooms on the palazzo courtyard are quieter. Hallways are worn, but the breakfast room is cheery. *Piazza Grazioli 5, tel. 06/699–22705, fax 06/699–22705. 13 rooms, 3 with bath. AE, MC, V.*

$ Lunetta. Located near Campo dei Fiori in the heart of Old Rome, this hotel has a drab entrance but spacious, even attractive rooms, a big plus at these rates. *Piazza del Paradiso 68, tel. 06/686–1080, fax 06/689–2028. 34 rooms, 18 with bath. No credit cards.*

$ Pomezia. On a side street near Campo dei Fiori, Pomezia occupies two floors of an old building. One floor has been renovated, and the rooms have new baths and good lighting; the other floor is drab, but rooms on both floors cost the same. *Via dei Chiavari 12, tel. and fax 06/686–1371. 22 rooms, 12 with bath. No credit cards.*

¢ Del Sole. The location near Campo dei Fiori's inexpensive eating spots, plus a relaxing living room and terrace are big advantages here. Most of the furniture is 1930's-style and bedrooms are small and basic; you'll have to take a room without bath to keep within ¢ range. *Via del Bisoione 76, tel. 06/688–06873, fax 06/689–3787. 80 rooms, 32 with bath. No credit cards.*

¢ Monaco. In a central residential neighborhood well provided with trattorias, the Monaco is simply furnished and kept scrupulously clean by Signora Maria and her family. The guests are mainly students; there is a midnight curfew. *Via Flavia 84, tel. 06/474–4335. 12 rooms, none with bath. No credit cards.*

The Arts

Pick up information on current events at EPT tourist offices. The bi-weekly booklet *Un Ospite a Roma*, free at some hotels and at EPT offices, is another source of information. Two periodicals in English, *Wanted in Rome* (1,000 lire) and *Metropolitan* (1,500 lire), available at centrally located newsstands, have listings of events. Also at newsstands you can buy *Roma c'è* (1,500 lire), with complete listings (plus handy bus information for each event) and "This Week in Rome" section in English. Tickets for opera, concerts, and ballet are sold at box offices only, just a few days before performances.

Opera The **Teatro dell'Opera** is on Via del Viminale (tel. 06/481–7003); its summer season from May through August it's famous for spectacular performances. Now that the Baths of Caracalla have been closed for such presentations, a promised new open-air venue should be ready by 1996 in Villa Pepoti, a parklike area adjacent to the ruins of the Baths. Tickets are on sale at the opera box office or at the box office at the summer venue.

Concerts The main concert hall is the **Accademia di Santa Cecilia** (box office, Via della Conciliazione 4, tel. 06/688–1044). The Santa Cecilia Symphony Orchestra has a summer season of concerts. For tickets to rock or pop concerts, try **Orbis** (Piazza Esquilino 37, tel. 06/474–4776) or Ricordi (Via del Corso 506, tel. 06/344104).

Film The only English-language movie theater in Rome is the **Pasquino** (Vicolo del Piede, just off Piazza Santa Maria in Trastevere, tel. 06/580–3622). Several other movie theaters show films in the original language on certain days of the week; the listings in *Roma c'è* are reliable.

Nightlife

Rome's "in" nightspots change like the flavor of the month, and many fade into oblivion after a brief moment of glory. The best sources for an up-to-date list are the weekly entertainment guide, "Trovaroma," published each Thursday in the Italian daily *La Repubblica* and *Roma c'è*.

Bars Informal wine bars are popular with young Romans. Near the Pantheon is **Spiriti** (Via Sant'Eustachio 5, tel. 06/689–2499). Another current favoriate near the Pantheon, a hub of after-dark activity, is **Antico Caffè della Pace** (Via della Pace 3, tel. 06/686–1216), open evenings only, until very late. **Birreria Marconi** (Via di Santa Prassede 9c, tel. 06/486636), near Santa Maria Maggiore, is a beer-hall pizzeria. For listings of pubs, see *Roma c'è*.

Discos and Nightclubs There's deafening disco music for an under-30s crowd at the **Big Bang** (entrance at Via Luciani 52, tel. 06/322–1251). Special events, such as beauty pageants and theme parties, are a feature, and there's a restaurant on the premises. **Alien** (Via Velletri 17, tel. 06/841–2212), near Piazza Fiume, features house music and theme nights; it's one of Rome's most popular clubs with the late-night crowd. **Piper 90** (Via Tagliamento 9, tel. 06/841–44590) has been a favorite for years, always on the cutting edge of the disco scene.

Florence

Arriving and Departing

By Plane The nearest, medium-size airport is the Galileo Galilei Airport at Pisa (tel. 050/500707), connected with Florence by train direct from the airport to the Santa Maria Novella Station. Service is hourly throughout the day and takes about 60 minutes. Some domestic and a few European flights use Florence's Peretola Airport (tel. 055/333498), connected by bus to the downtown area.

By Train The main train station is Santa Maria Novella Station, abbreviated SMN on signs. There is an Azienda Trasporti Autolinee Fiorentine (ATAF) city bus information booth across the street from the station (and at Piazza del Duomo 57/r). Inside the station is an Informazioni Turistiche Alberghiere (ITA) hotel association booth, where you can get hotel information and bookings.

By Bus The SITA bus terminal is on Via Santa Caterina da Siena, near Santa Maria Novella train station. The CAP bus terminal is at Via Nazionale 13, also near the station.

Getting Around

On Foot You can see most of Florence's major sights on foot, since they are packed into a relatively small area in the city center. Don't plan on using a car; most of the center is off-limits, and ATAF buses will take you where you want to go. Wear comfortable shoes, wander to your heart's content, and don't worry about finding your way around. There are so many landmarks that you cannot get lost for long. The system of street numbers is unusual, with commercial addresses written with a red "r" to distinguish them from residential addresses (32/r may be next to or even a block away from plain 32).

By Bus   ATAF city buses run from about 5:15 AM to 1 AM. Buy tickets before you board the bus; they are on sale singly or in books of five at many tobacco shops and newsstands. The cost is 1,400 lire for a ticket good for 60 minutes on all lines, 1,900 lire for 120 minutes. You can save by buying a multiple ticket (four 60-minute tickets) for 5,400 lire. An all-day ticket (*turistico*) costs 5,000 lire.

By Bicycle   You can rent a bicycle at **Alinari** (Via Guelfa 85/r, tel. 055/280500), Florence's largest rental service, with several strategic locations; at **Motorent** (Via San Zanobi 9/r, tel. 055/490113); and at city concessions in several locations, including Piazza della Stazione, Piazza Pitti, and Fortezza da Basso.

By Moped   For a moped, go to **Alinari** or to **Motorent** (*see* By Bicycle, *above*). Helmets are mandatory.

Important Addresses and Numbers

Tourist Information   The municipal tourist office is at Via Cavour 1/r (tel. 055/276–0382; open 8:30–7). There is an information office next to the train station and another near Piazza della Signoria, at Chiasso dei Baroncelli 17/r (tel. 055/230–2124). The **Azienda Promozione Turistica (APT)** tourist board has its headquarters and an information office at Via Manzoni 16 (tel. 055/234–6284; open Mon.–Sat. 8:30–1:30).

Consulates   **U.S.** (Lungarno Vespucci 38, tel. 055/239–8276). **U.K.** (Lungarno Corsini 2, tel. 055/284133).

Emergencies   **Police** (tel. 113). **Ambulance** (tel. 118, or 055/212222). **Doctor:** Call your consulate for recommendations, or call the **Tourist Medical Service** (tel. 055/475411), associated with IAMAT, for English-speaking medical assistance 24 hours a day.

Exploring Florence

Founded by Julius Caesar, Florence has the familiar grid pattern common to all Roman colonies. Except for the major monuments, which are appropriately imposing, the buildings are low and unpretentious. It is a small, compact city of ocher and gray stone and pale plaster; its narrow streets open unexpectedly into spacious squares populated by strollers and pigeons. At its best, it has a gracious and elegant air, though it can at times be a nightmare of mass tourism. Plan, if you can, to visit Florence in late fall, early spring, or even in winter, to avoid the crowds.

A visit to Florence is a visit to the living museum of the Italian Renaissance. The Renaissance began right here in Florence, and the city bears witness to the proud spirit and unparalleled genius of its artists and artisans. In fact, there is so much to see that it is best to savor a small part, rather than attempt to absorb it all in a muddled vision.

Numbers in the margin correspond to points of interest on the Florence map.

Piazza del Duomo and Piazza della Signoria
❶   The best place to begin a tour of Florence is **Piazza del Duomo,** where the cathedral, bell tower, and baptistry stand in the rather cramped square. The lofty **cathedral of Santa Maria del Fiore** is one of the longest in the world. Begun by master sculptor and architect Arnolfo di Cambio in 1296, its construction took 140 years to complete. Gothic architecture predominates; the facade was added in the 1870s but is based on Tuscan Gothic models. Inside, the church is cool and austere, a fine example of the architecture of the period. Among the sparse decorations, take a good look at the frescoes of equestrian monuments on the left wall; the one on the right is by

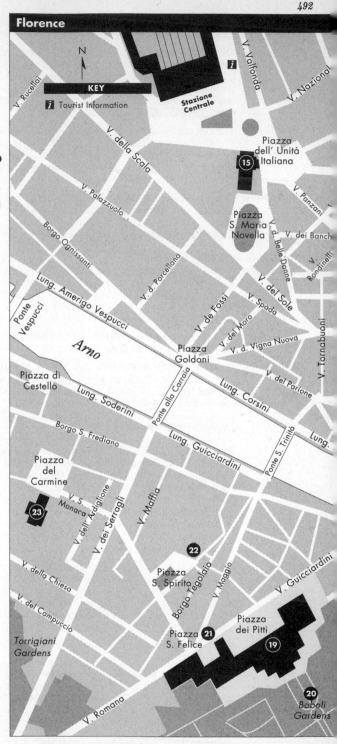

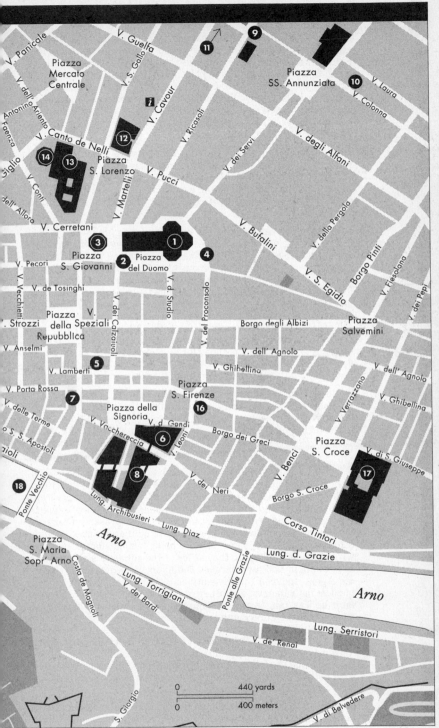

Paolo Uccello, the one on the left, by Andrea del Castagno. The dome frescoes by Vasari are upstaged by the dome itself, Brunelleschi's greatest architectural and technical achievement. It was also the inspiration of such later domes as Michelangelo's dome for St. Peter's in Rome and even the Capitol in Washington. You can climb to the cupola gallery, 463 fatiguing steps up between the two skins of the double dome, for a fine view of Florence and the surrounding hills. *Dome entrance is in the left aisle of the cathedral. Admission: 5,000 lire. Open Mon.–Sat. 10–5. Cathedral (a small admission fee may be charged for entrance to the Duomo) open Mon.–Sat. 10–5:30, Sun. 1–5.*

2 Next to the cathedral is Giotto's 14th-century **bell tower,** richly decorated with colored marble and fine sculptures (the originals are in the Museo dell'Opera del Duomo). The 414-step climb to the top is less strenuous than that to the cupola. *Piazza del Duomo. Admission: 5,000 lire. Open Mar.–Oct., daily 8:30–7; Nov.–Feb., daily 9–4:30.*

3 In front of the cathedral is the **baptistry** (open Mon.–Sat. 1–6:30, Sun. 9–1), one of the city's oldest and most beloved edifices, where, since the 11th century, Florentines have baptized their children. A gleaming copy of the most famous of the baptistry's three portals has been installed facing the cathedral, where Ghiberti's doors (dubbed "The Gate of Paradise" by Michelangelo) stood. Some of the **4** original panels have been removed to the **Museo dell'Opera del Duomo** (Cathedral Museum). The museum contains some superb sculptures by Donatello and Luca della Robbia—especially their *cantorie,* or choir decorations—as well as an unfinished *Pietà* by Michelangelo, which was intended for his own tomb. *Piazza del Duomo 9, tel. 055/230–2885. Admission: 5,000 lire. Open Mar.–Oct., Mon.–Sat. 9–6; Nov.–Feb., Mon.–Sat. 9–5:30.*

Stroll down fashionable Via Calzaiuoli to the church of **5** **Orsanmichele,** for centuries an odd combination of first-floor church and second-floor wheat granary. The statues (many of them copies) in the niches on the exterior constitute an anthology of the work of eminent Renaissance sculptors, including Donatello, Ghiberti, and Verrocchio, while the tabernacle inside is an extraordinary piece by Andrea Orcagna.

Continuing another two blocks along Via Calzaiuoli, you'll come upon **Piazza della Signoria,** the heart of Florence and the city's largest square. During the long and controversial process of replacing the paving stones over the past few years, well-preserved remnants of Roman and medieval Florence came to light and were thoroughly examined and photographed before being buried again and covered with the new paving. In the center of the square a slab marks the spot where in 1497 Savonarola—the Ayatollah Khomeini of the Middle Ages—induced the Florentines to burn their pictures, books, musical instruments, and other worldly objects—and where a year later he was hanged and then burned at the stake as a heretic. The square, the **Neptune Fountain** by Ammanati, and the surrounding cafés are popular gathering places for Florentines and for tourists who come to admire the massive **Palazzo della Signoria** (better **6** known as the **Palazzo Vecchio**), the copy of Michelangelo's *David* on its steps, and the frescoes and artworks in its impressive salons. *Piazza della Signoria, tel. 055/276–8465. Admission: 8,000 lire. Sun. free. Open Mon.–Wed., Fri., Sat. 9–7, Sun. 8–1.*

If you'd like to do a little shopping, make a brief detour off Piazza della Signoria to the **Loggia del Mercato Nuovo** on Via Calimala. It's **7** crammed with souvenirs and straw and leather goods at reasonable prices; bargaining is acceptable here. *Open Mon.–Sat. 8–7 (closed Mon. AM).*

8 If time is limited, this is your chance to visit the **Uffizi Gallery,** which houses Italy's most important collection of paintings. (Try to see it at a leisurely pace, though—it's too good to rush through!) The Uffizi Palace was built to house the administrative offices of the Medicis, onetime rulers of the city. Later their fabulous art collection was arranged in the Uffizi Gallery on the top floor, which was opened to the public in the 17th century—making this the world's first public gallery of modern times. The emphasis is on Italian art of the Gothic and Renaissance periods. Make sure you see the works by Giotto, and look for the Botticellis in Rooms X–XIV, Michelangelo's *Holy Family* in Room XXV, and the works by Raphael next door. In addition to its art treasures, the gallery offers a magnificent close-up view of Palazzo Vecchio's tower from the little coffee bar at the end of the corridor. *Loggiato Uffizi 6, tel. 055/23885. Admission: 12,000 lire. Open Tues.–Sat. 9–7, Sun. 9–1.*

Accademia, San Marco, San Lorenzo, Santa Maria Novella Start at the **Accademia Gallery,** and try to be first in line at opening time so you can get the full impact of Michelangelo's *David* without having to fight your way through the crowds. Skip the works in the exhibition halls leading to the *David;* they are of minor importance, and you'll gain a length on the tour groups. Michelangelo's statue is **9** a tour de force of artistic conception and technical ability, for he was using a piece of stone that had already been worked on by a lesser sculptor. Take time to see the forceful *Slaves,* also by Michelangelo; the roughhewn, unfinished surfaces contrast dramatically with the highly polished, meticulously carved *David.* Michelangelo left the *Slaves* "unfinished" as a symbolic gesture, to accentuate the figures' struggle to escape the bondage of stone. *Via Ricasoli 60, tel. 055/214375. Admission: 12,000 lire. Open Tues.–Sat. 9–7, Sun. 9–2.*

You can make a detour down Via Cesare Battisti to Piazza Santissima Annunziata to see the arcade of the **Ospedale degli Innocenti** (Hospital of the Innocents) by Brunelleschi, with charm-**10** ing roundels by Andrea della Robbia, and the **Museo Archeologico** (Archaeological Museum) on Via della Colonna, under the arch. It has some fine Etruscan and Roman antiquities and a pretty garden. *Via della Colonna 36, tel. 055/247–8641. Admission: 8,000 lire. Open Tues.–Sat. 9–2, Sun. 9–1.*

11 Retrace your steps to Piazza San Marco and the **Museo di San Marco,** housed in a 15th-century Dominican monastery. The unfortunate Savonarola meditated on the sins of the Florentines here, and Fra Angelico decorated many of the austere cells and corridors with his brilliantly colored frescoes of religious subjects. (Look for his masterpiece, *The Annunciation.*) Together with many of his paintings arranged on the ground floor, just off the little cloister, they form an interesting collection. *Piazza San Marco 1, tel. 055/238–8608. Admission: 8,000 lire. Open Tues.–Sat. 9–2, Sun. 9–1.*

12 Lined with shops, Via Cavour leads to **Palazzo Medici Riccardi,** a massive Renaissance mansion housing a chapel with Benozzo Gozzoli's glorious frescoes of the Journey of the Magi, a spectacular cavalcade with Lorenzo the Magnificent on a charger. *Via Cavour 1, tel. 055/276–0340. Admission: 6,000 lire. Open Mon.–Tues. and Thurs.–Sat. 9–1 and 3–6, Sun. 9–1.*

13 Turn right here to the elegant **Church of San Lorenzo,** with its Old Sacristy designed by Brunelleschi, and two pulpits by Donatello. Rounding the church, you'll find yourself in the midst of the sprawling **San Lorenzo Market,** dealing in everything and anything, including some interesting leather items. *Piazza San Lorenzo, Via dell'Ariento. Open Tues.–Sat. 8–7.*

14 Enter the **Medici Chapels** from Piazza Madonna degli Aldobrandini, behind San Lorenzo. These remarkable chapels contain the tombs of practically every member of the Medici family, and there were a lot of them, for they guided Florence's destiny from the 15th century to

1737. Cosimo I, a Medici whose acumen made him the richest man in Europe, is buried in the crypt of the Chapel of the Princes, and Donatello's tomb is next to that of his patron. The chapel upstairs is decorated in an eye-dazzling array of colored marble. In Michelangelo's New Sacristy, his tombs of Giuliano and Lorenzo de' Medici bear the justly famed statues of *Dawn* and *Dusk* and *Night* and *Day*. *Piazza Madonna degli Aldobrandini, tel. 055/213206. Admission: 9,000 lire. Open Tues.–Sun. 9–2.*

⑮ You can take either Via Panzani or Via del Melarancio to the large square next to the massive church of **Santa Maria Novella,** a handsome building in the Tuscan version of Gothic style. See it from the other end of Piazza Santa Maria Novella for the best view of its facade. Inside are some famous paintings, especially Masaccio's *Trinity*, a Giotto crucifix in the sacristy, and Ghirlandaio's frescoes in the apse. *Piazza Santa Maria Novella, tel. 055/210113. Open daily 7–11:30 and 3:30–6.*

Next door to the church is the entrance to the **Museo di Santa Maria Novella,** worth a visit for their serene atmosphere and the restored Paolo Uccello frescoes. *Piazza Santa Maria Novella 19, tel. 055/282187. Admission: 4,000 lire. Open Mon.–Thurs., Sat. 9–2, Sun. 8–1.*

⑯ Only a few blocks behind Piazza della Signoria is the **Bargello,** a fortresslike palace that served as the residence of Florence's chief magistrate in medieval times and later as a prison. Don't be put off by its grim look, for it now houses Florence's **Museo Nazionale** (National Museum), a treasure house of Italian Renaissance sculpture—it is to Renaissance sculpture what the Uffizi is to Renaissance painting. In a historically and visually interesting setting, it displays masterpieces by Donatello, Verrocchio, Michelangelo, and many other major sculptors, so don't shortchange yourself on time. *Via del Proconsolo 4, tel. 055/238–8606. Admission: 8,000 lire. Open Tues.–Sat. 9–2, Sun. 9–1.*

From Piazza San Firenze follow Via degli Anguillara or Borgo dei Greci toward Piazza Santa Croce. En route you'll pass close by **Vivoli,** which dispenses what many consider the best ice cream in Florence. (It's at Via Isole delle Stinche 7/r, on a little side street, the second left off Via degli Anguillara as you head toward Santa Croce.)

⑰ The mighty church of **Santa Croce** was begun in 1294; inside, Giotto's frescoes brighten two chapels, and monumental tombs of Michelangelo, Galileo, Machiavelli, and other Renaissance luminaries line the walls. In the adjacent museum, you can see what remains of a Giotto crucifix, irreparably damaged by a flood in 1966, when water rose to 16 feet in parts of the church. The **Pazzi Chapel** in the cloister is an architectural gem by Brunelleschi. *Piazza Santa Croce, tel. 055/244619. Church open Apr.–Sept., Mon.–Sat. 8–6:30, Sun. 8–12:30 and 3–6:30; Oct.–Mar., Mon.–Sat. 8–12:30 and 3–6:30, Sun. 3–6. Opera di Santa Croce (Museum and Pazzi Chapel), tel. 055/244619. Admission: 3,000 lire. Open Mar.–Sept., Thurs.–Tues. 10–12:30 and 2:30–6:30; Oct.–Feb., Thurs.–Tues. 10–12:30 and 3–5.*

The monastery of Santa Croce harbors a leather-working school and showroom, with entrances at Via San Giuseppe 5/r and Piazza Santa Croce 16. The entire Santa Croce area is known for its leather factories and inconspicuous shops selling gold and silver jewelry at prices much lower than those of the elegant jewelers near the Ponte Vecchio.

Ponte Vecchio, Oltrarno The **Ponte Vecchio,** Florence's oldest bridge, is the second bridge you'll encounter as you walk along the river toward the center. It seems to be just another street lined with goldsmiths' shops until

⑱ you get to the middle and catch a glimpse of the Arno flowing below. Spared during World War II by the retreating Germans (who blew up every other bridge in the city), it also survived the 1966 flood. It leads into the **Oltrarno district,** which has its own charm and still preserves much of the atmosphere of oldtime Florence, full of fascinating craft workshops.

But for the moment you should head straight down Via Guicciardini ⑲ to **Palazzo Pitti,** a 15th-century extravaganza that the Medicis acquired from the Pitti family shortly after the latter had gone deeply into debt to build it. Its long facade on the immense piazza was designed by Brunelleschi: Solid and severe, it looks like a Roman aqueduct turned into a palace. The palace houses several museums: One displays the fabulous Medici collection of objects in silver and gold; another is the **Gallery of Modern Art.** The most famous museum, though, is the **Palatine Gallery,** with an extraordinary collection of paintings, many hung frame-to-frame in a clear case of artistic overkill. Some are high up in dark corners, so try to go on a bright day. *Piazza dei Pitti, tel. 055/210323. Gallery of Modern Art. Admission: 4,000 lire. Palatine Gallery. Admission: 12,000 lire. Silver Museum. Admission: 8,000 lire (includes admission to the Porcelain Museum, if open, and Historical Costume Gallery). All open Tues.–Sat. 9–2, Sun. 9–1.*

⑳ Take time for a refreshing stroll in the **Boboli Gardens** behind Palazzo Pitti, a typical Italian garden laid out in 1550 for Cosimo Medici's wife, Eleanor of Toledo. *Piazza dei Pitti, tel. 055/213440. Admission 4,000 lire. Open daily Apr., May, and Sept., 9–6:30; June–Aug., 9–7:30; Oct. and Mar.–Apr., 9–5:30; Nov.–Feb., 9–4:30.*

In the far corner of Piazza dei Pitti, poets Elizabeth Barrett and ㉑ Robert Browning lived in the **Casa Guidi,** facing the smaller Piazza San Felice. *Piazza San Felice 8, tel. 055/284393. Admission free. Open by appointment.*

㉒ The church of **Santo Spirito** is important as one of Brunelleschi's finest architectural creations, and it contains some superb paintings, including a Filippino Lippi *Madonna.* Santo Spirito is the hub of a colorful neighborhood of artisans and intellectuals. An **outdoor market** enlivens the square every morning except Sunday. A crafts fair is held there on the second Sunday of the month.

Walk down Via Sant'Agostino and Via Santa Monaca to the church of ㉓ **Santa Maria del Carmine,** of no architectural interest but of immense significance in the history of Renaissance art. It contains the celebrated frescoes painted by Masaccio in the **Brancacci Chapel,** unveiled not long ago after a lengthy and meticulous restoration. The chapel was a classroom for such artistic giants as Botticelli, Leonardo da Vinci, Michelangelo, and Raphael, since they all came to study Masaccio's realistic use of light and perspective and his creation of space and depth. *Piazza del Carmine, tel. 055/212331. Admission: 5,000 lire. Open Mon. and Wed.–Sat. 10–5, Sun. 1–5.*

Take Bus 13 from the train station or cathedral up to Piazzale Michelangelo, then walk along Viale dei Colli and climb to **San Miniato al Monte,** a charming green-and-white marble Romanesque church full of artistic riches.

Shopping

Florence offers top quality for your money in leather goods, linens and upholstery fabrics, gold and silver jewelry, and cameos. Straw goods, gilded-wood trays and frames, hand-printed paper desk accessories, and ceramic objects make good inexpensive gifts. Many shops offer fine old prints.

Department Stores **UPIM,** in Piazza della Repubblica and various other locations, has inexpensive goods of all types.

Markets The big food market at **Piazza del Mercato Centrale** is open in the morning (Mon.–Sat.) and is worth a visit. The **San Lorenzo market** on Piazza San Lorenzo and Via dell'Ariento is a fine place to browse for buys in leather goods and souvenirs (open Tues. and Sat. 8–7; also Sun. in summer). The **Mercato Nuovo,** Via Calimala, which is sometimes called the **Mercato del Porcellino** because of the famous bronze statue of a boar at one side, is packed with stalls selling souvenirs and straw goods (open Tues.–Sat. 8–7; closed Sun. and Mon. morning in winter). There's a colorful neighborhood market at **Sant'Ambrogio,** Piazza Ghiberti (open Mon.–Sat. morning), and a permanent flea market at **Piazza Ciompi** (open Mon.–Sat. 9–1 and 4–7, Sun. 9–1 in summer).

Dining

Mealtimes in Florence are 12:30–2 and 7:30–9 or later. Many $$ and $ places are small, and you may have to share a table. Reservations are always advisable; to find a table at inexpensive places, get there early.

For details and price-category definitions, *see* Dining *in* Staying in Italy, *above.*

$$ **Angiolino.** You won't regret taking a meal at this bustling little
★ trattoria. Glowing with authentic atmosphere, Angiolino offers such Tuscan specialties as ribollita and juicy *bistecca alla fiorentina* (T-bone steak basted in olive oil and black pepper). The bistecca will push the bill up. *Via Santo Spirito 36/r, tel. 055/239–8976. Reservations advised in the evening. No credit cards. Closed Sun. dinner, Mon., and last 3 wks in July.*

$$ **Enzo e Piero.** Owners Enzo and Piero serve you in their neat, rustic-looking trattoria located near the train station. A neighborhood favorite, it's an enjoyable change from the city's more touristy eating places. Here you can choose among the day's specials, which may include tortellini and veal stew or other Tuscan dishes, especially roasted or grilled meat. The prix-fixe menu at about 20,000 lire is a bargain. A prominently displayed wine barrel confirms that the hosts take pride in serving good wine. *Via Faenza 105, tel. 055/214901. Reservations advised in evening. AE, DC, MC, V. Closed Sun.*

$$ **Il Fagioli.** This typical Florentine trattoria near Santa Croce has a simple decor and a menu in which such local dishes as *ribollita* (vegetable-and-bread soup) and involtini predominate. *Corso Tintori 47/r, tel. 055/244285. Reservations advised. No credit cards. Closed Sun. (also Sat. in summer), Aug., and Christmas Day.*

$$ **Mario da Ganino.** Highly informal, rustic, and cheerful, this trattoria greets you with a taste of mortadella and offers homemade pastas plus a heavenly cheesecake for dessert. It's tiny, seating only 35 but double that in summer at outdoor tables. *Piazza dei Cimatori 4/r, tel. 055/214125. Reservations advised. AE, DC. Closed Sun. and Aug. 15–25.*

$ **Acqua al Due.** At this tiny, popular restaurant near the Bargello, you can make a meal of pasta and find a really good hamburger. *Via dell'Acqua 2/r, tel. 055/284170. No reservations. AE, MC, V. Closed Mon. and Tues.*

$ **Del Carmine.** This typical neighborhood trattoria is a favorite discovery of tourists out to see the Masaccio frescoes in the church across the square. *Piazza del Carmine 18/r, tel. 055/218601. Reservations advised. AE, DC, MC, V. Closed Sun.*

$ **La Maremmana.** A display of fresh vegetables and fruit as you enter this popular trattoria near Santa Croce hints at what's on the menu. Authentic Tuscan cooking is served at long tables that you will probably be asked to share, in a wood-paneled dining room. The prix-fixe menu offers generous servings and good value. *Via dei Macci 77/r, tel. 055/241226. Reservations advised. MC, V. Closed Sun.*

$ **Le Mossacce.** A typical Florentine trattoria, located between the Duomo and Palazzo Vecchio, it serves a classic *ribollita* (vegetable-and-bread minestrone). Sitting at heavy wooden tables, you can watch the cook at work in the glassed-in kitchen. *Via del Proconsolo 55/r, tel. 055/294361. No reservations. AE, MC, V. Closed weekends and Aug.*

$ **Za-Za.** Its location within the heart of the bustling Mercato Centrale—Florence's main food market near San Lorenzo—guarantees the freshest of provisions at this informal place. Tourists and Italians mix at heavy trattoria tables under posters of movie stars to enjoy classic Florentine cooking. *Piazza Mercato Centrale 16/r, tel. 055/215411. Reservations advised. AE, DC, MC, V. Closed Sun. and Aug.*

¢ **Casalinga.** Loitering is discouraged in this bustling trattoria near the church of Santo Spirito, where there is always someone waiting for a seat at one of the communal tables. In a typically spare wood-paneled setting under high vaulted ceilings, you choose among pastas, such as *papardelle* (wide noodles), soups, and roasted meat. *Via dei Michelozzi 9, tel. 055/218624. No reservations. No credit cards. Closed Sat., Sun.*

¢ **Mario.** Clean and classic, this family-run trattoria, on a corner of Piazza del Mercato Centrale near San Lorenzo, offers genuine Florentine cooking and good house wine. *Via Rosina (Piazza del Mercato Centrale), tel. 2/055-218550. No credit cards. No dinner. Closed Sun.*

¢ **Nuti.** On a central street where there are plenty of other budget alternatives, Nuti is an old favorite, with minimal decor and good pizza, soups, and pasta. It's open all day until 1 AM. *Via Borgo San Lorenzo 22, tel. 055/210145. No reservations. No credit cards. Closed Mon.*

Lodging

What with mass tourism and trade fairs, rooms are at a premium in Florence for most of the year. Make reservations well in advance. If you arrive without a reservation, the ITA office in the railway station (open 8:20 AM–9 PM) can help you, but there may be a long line. Now that most traffic is banned in the downtown area, hotel rooms are quieter. Local traffic and motorcycles can still be bothersome, however, so check the decibel level before you settle in.

For details and price-category definitions, *see* Lodging *in* Staying in Italy, *above.* Keep in mind that rooms without bath in $ hotels can be had at ¢ rates.

$$ **Alessandra.** Only a block from the Ponte Vecchio, the Alessandra is clean and well kept, with large rooms and a friendly, English-speaking staff. Book well in advance. *Borgo Santi Apostoli 17, tel. 055/283438, fax 055/210619. 25 rooms, 18 with bath. MC, V.*

$$ **Apollo.** Fully renovated in 1995, and still under the same cordial, English-speaking management, the Apollo has added new comforts and conveniences for guests, including comfortable public rooms, an elevator, and a garage. Rooms are bright and spacious, with new bathrooms. The hotel is handy to the train station and to many sights. *Via Faenza 77, tel. 055/284119, fax 055/210101. 26 rooms with bath. AE, DC, MC, V.*

$$ ★ **Bellettini.** This central hotel occupies three floors (the top floor has two attractive rooms with a view) of a palazzo near the Duomo. The rooms are ample, with reproduction Venetian- or Tuscan-style furniture, and there are some authentic antiques and attractive art in the public rooms. The friendly family who runs it provides home-made cakes for breakfast, which is included in the low room rate, as

is air-conditioning. *Via dei Conti 7, tel. 055/213561, fax 055/283551. 28 rooms with bath. Facilities: bar, lounge. AE, DC, MC, V.*

$$ Liana. Located in a residential neighborhood, this small hotel is within walking distance of most sights. It's a dignified 19th-century town house with pleasant rooms overlooking the garden and bright new baths. *Via Vittorio Alfieri 18, tel. 055/245303, fax 055/234–4596. 26 rooms, 23 with bath. Facilities: parking lot, garden. AE, MC, V.*

$$ Nuova Italia. Near the train station, in a restored townhouse, this is a family-run hotel, bright with pictures and posters. The clean, ample rooms can accommodate extra beds, and rates include breakfast. *Via Faenza 26, tel. 055/268430, fax 055/210941. 20 rooms with bath. AE, DC, MC, V.*

$ Ausonia. A helpful young management and simple modern decor keynote this small hotel near the train station. Some rooms have private bath; those without are budget values. Special winter rates make it even more affordable. *Via Nazionale 24, tel. 055/496547, fax 055/496324. 20 rooms, 11 with bath. AE, MC, V.*

$ Azzi. Billed as "the inn of Artists," it has whimsically eccentric and old-fashioned decor, frayed around the edges but very clean. Rooms can accommodate several beds. Guests gather in the large living room or on a charming terrace. It is a favorite with musicians, performers, and students. *Via Faenza 56, tel. 055/213806. 12 rooms, 5 with bath. MC, V.*

$ Globus. The Globus has a handy location between the train station and the San Lorenzo market, where there are plenty of inexpensive eating places. There is a small, homey lounge. The hotel was renovated in 1992. *Via Sant'Antonino 24, tel. 055/211062. 21 rooms with bath. AE, MC, V.*

¢ Accademia. Near the train station and within walking distance of most sights, this is a simply furnished but comfortable family-run hotel. Guests mingle in the homey living room and large breakfast room. Rooms without bath are in the ¢ category. *Via Faenza 7, tel. 055/293451. 16 rooms, 9 with bath. V.*

¢ Mary. Located on a parklike square, the Mary is near the station and the San Marco museum. The rooms are simply furnished, and there are three flights of stairs to climb, but the proprietor couldn't be nicer (regulars say staying here is like staying at a friend's home). Rates are low for rooms without baths. *Piazza Indipendenza 5, tel. 055/496310. 12 rooms, 9 with bath. No credit cards.*

The Arts

For a list of events, pick up a *Florence Concierge Information* booklet from your hotel desk or the monthly information bulletin published by the **Comune Aperto** city information office (Via Cavour 1/r).

Music and Ballet Most major musical events are staged at the **Teatro Comunale** (Corso Italia 16, tel. 055/277–9236). The box office (closed Monday) is open from 9 to 1 and a half hour before performances. It's best to order your tickets by mail, however, since they're difficult to come by at the last minute. You can also order concert and ballet tickets through **Universalturismo** (Via degli Speziali 7/r, tel. 055/217241). **Amici della Musica** (Friends of Music) puts on a series of concerts at the **Teatro della Pergola** (box office, Via della Pergola 10r, tel. 055/247–9651). For program information, contact the Amici della Musica directly at Via Sirtori 49 (tel. 055/608420).

Nightlife

Other than strolling and hanging out in the cathedral square, Piazza della Signoria, and Piazzale Michelangelo, there's not much to do in Florence at night. Discos cost about 25,000 lire for entrance and a first drink. The most popular with a young international crowd are **Yab** (Via Sassetti 5/r, tel. 055/282018) and **Space Electronic** (Via Palazzuolo 37, tel. 055/239–3082). There are several beer halls, including **Be-Bop** (Via dei Servi 76/r), **Il Boccale** (Borgo Santi Apostoli 33/r), and **Nuti** (Via Borgo San Lorenzo 22), which stay open late.

Tuscany

Tuscany is a blend of rugged hills; fertile valleys; and long, sandy beaches that curve along the west coast of central Italy and fringe the pine-forested coastal plain of the Maremma. The gentle, cypress-studded green hills may seem familiar: Leonardo and Raphael often painted them in the backgrounds of their masterpieces. To most people, Tuscan art means Florence, but the other cities and towns of the region contain gems of art and architecture—the artists of the Middle Ages and the Renaissance took their work where they found it.

Getting Around

By Train The main train network connects Florence with Pisa and Florence with Arezzo, while a secondary line goes from Prato to the coast via Lucca. Trains also connect Siena with Pisa, via Empoli, in 2 hours.

By Bus The entire region is crisscrossed by bus lines, good alternatives to trains, especially for reaching Siena. Use local buses to tour the many pretty hill towns around Siena, such as San Gimignano, and then take a Tra-In or Lazzi bus from Siena to Arezzo, where you can get back onto the main Rome–Florence train line.

Guided Tours

American Express (Via Guicciardini 49/r, tel. 055/288751) is a member of a consortium operating one-day excursions to Siena and San Gimignano out of Florence.

Tourist Information

Lucca (Piazza Guidiccione 2, tel. 0583/491205).
Pisa (Piazza della Stazione 11, tel. 050/42291; Piazza del Duomo 8, tel. 050/560464).
Siena (Via di Città 43, tel. 0577/42209; Piazza del Campo 56, tel. 0577/280551).

Exploring Tuscany

Starting your excursions in Tuscany from Florence, you can go west, stopping if you like at Prato and Pistoia, workaday cities with a core of fine medieval buildings, to the historic cities of Lucca and Pisa. Make charming Lucca your base for an excursion to Pisa, which is only about 30 minutes away by bus or train. Heading south from Florence by bus, you can see some of the Chianti district and make Siena your base for excursions to San Gimignano and the unspoiled hill town of Montepulciano.

Lucca Less than 90 minutes from Florence by train or bus is **Lucca,** Puccini's hometown and a city well loved by sightseers who appreciate the careful upkeep of its medieval look. Though it hasn't the number of hotels and other tourist trappings that, say, Pisa does, for that very reason it's a pleasant alternative. You can easily make an excursion to Pisa from here by either train or bus—it's only 22 kilometers (14 miles) away. First enjoy the views of the city and countryside from the tree-planted 16th-century ramparts that encircle Lucca. Then explore the city's marvelously elaborate Romanesque churches, fronted with tiers and rows of columns, and looking suspiciously like oversize marble wedding cakes.

From vast **Piazza Napoleone,** a swing around the Old Town will take you past the 11th-century **Duomo** on Piazza San Martino, with its 15th-century tomb of Ilaria del Carretto by Jacopo della Quercia. Don't neglect a ramble through the **Piazza del Mercato,** which preserves the oval form of the Roman amphitheater over which it was built, or the three surrounding streets that are filled with atmosphere: **Via Battisti, Via Fillungo,** and **Via Guinigi.** In addition to the Duomo, Lucca has two other fine churches. **San Frediano** (Piazza San Frediano) is graced with an austere facade ornamented by 13th-century mosaic decoration. Inside, see the exquisite reliefs by Jacopo della Quercia in the last chapel on the left. **San Michele in Foro** (Piazza San Michele) is an exceptional example of the Pisan Romanesque style and decorative flair peculiar to Lucca: Note its facade, a marriage of arches and columns crowned by a statue of St. Michael.

Pisa **Pisa** is a dull, overcommercialized place, though even skeptics have to admit that the **Torre Pendente** (Leaning Tower) really is one of the world's more amazing sights. Theories vary as to whether the now-famous list is due to shifting foundations or to an amazing architectural feat by Bonanno Pisano (the first of three architects to work on the tower). Efforts to stabilize the tower have been successful, and by 1996 visitors should again be allowed to climb to the top, though on a limited basis. If you want a two-foot marble imitation of the Leaning Tower, perhaps even illuminated from within, this is your chance to grab one! *Campo dei Miracoli.*

Pisa's **Duomo** is elegantly simple, its facade decorated with geometric and animal shapes. The cavernous interior is supported by a series of 68 columns, while the pulpit is a fine example of Giovanni Pisano's work. Be sure to note the suspended lamp that hangs across from the pulpit; known as Galileo's Lamp, it's said to have inspired his theories on pendular motion. *Piazza del Duomo. Admission: 2,000 lire. Open Mon.–Sat. 10–5, Sun. 1–5.*

Also in Campo dei Miracoli are the **baptistery,** the **Camposanto** (cemetery), which has important frescoes, and the **Museo dell'Opera del Duomo,** with medieval sculpture. The baptistery was begun in 1153 but not completed until 1400, the Pisano family doing most of its decoration. Test out the excellent acoustics (occasionally the guard will slam the great doors shut and then sing a few notes—the resulting echo is very impressive and, costly, too, since he'll expect a tip). *Campo dei Miracoli. Admission to any two of above, 10,000 lire; admission to all three 15,000. Baptistery and Camposanto open Apr.– Sept., daily 8–7:40, Oct.–Mar., daily 9–5:40. Museo dell'Opera del Duomo, Via Arcivescovado, tel. 050/560547. Open daily 9–5:40.*

From Pisa you can take a train to Florence, where you can get an express bus or train for the approximately 90-minute trip to Siena. SITA buses are more convenient than the train, however, because you have to take a local bus from the Siena train station up to the town. SITA deposits passengers within walking distance of the sights.

Siena **Siena** is one of Italy's best-preserved medieval towns, rich both in works of art and in expensive antiques shops. The famous **Palio** is held here, a breakneck, 90-second horse race that takes place twice each year in the Piazza del Campo, on July 2 and August 16. Built on three hills, Siena is not an easy town to explore, for everything you'll want to see is either up or down a steep hill or stairway. But it is worth every ounce of effort. Siena really gives you an idea of what the Middle Ages must have been like: dark stone palaces that look like fortresses, Gothic church portals, and narrow streets opening out into airy squares.

Siena was a center of learning and art during the Middle Ages, and almost all the public buildings and churches in the town have enough artistic or historical merit to be worth visiting. Unlike most churches, Siena's **Duomo** has a mixture of religious and civic symbols ornamenting both its interior and exterior. The cathedral museum in the unfinished transept contains some fine works of art, notably a celebrated *Maestà* by Duccio di Buoninsegna. The animated frescoes of papal history in the Piccolomini Library (with an entrance off the left aisle of the cathedral) are credited to Pinturicchio and are worth seeking out. *Piazza del Duomo. Cathedral Museum. Admission: 5,000 lire. Open Mar. 14–Sept. 30, daily 9–7:30; Oct. 1–Nov. 3, daily 9–6; Nov. 4–Dec. 31, daily 9–1:30; Jan. 2–Mar. 13, daily 9–1. Library. Admission: 2,000 lire. Open mid-Mar.–Sept. 30, daily 9–7:30; Oct. 1–Nov. 3, daily 9–6:30; Nov. 4–Mar. 13, daily 10–1 and 2–5.*

Nearby, the fan-shape **Piazza del Campo** is Siena's main center of activity, with 11 streets leading into it. Farsighted planning has preserved it as a medieval showpiece, containing the 13th-century **Palazzo Pubblico** (City Hall) and the **Torre del Mangia** (Bell Tower). Try to visit both these buildings, the former for Lorenzetti's frescoes on the effects of good and bad government, the latter for the wonderful view (you'll have to climb 503 steps to reach it, however). *Piazza del Campo, tel. 0577/292111. Bell Tower. Admission: 5,000 lire. Open Mar. 15–Nov. 15, daily 10–one hr before sunset; Nov. 16–Mar. 14, daily 10–1. Palazzo Pubblico (Civic Museum). Admission: 6,000 lire. Open Mar. 15–Nov. 15, Mon.–Sat. 9–7, Sun. 9–1:30; Nov. 16–Mar. 13, daily 9–1:30.*

San Gimignano From Siena make an excursion to **San Gimignano**, about one hour by bus, changing at Poggibonsi. It is perhaps the most delightful of the Tuscan medieval hill towns with their timeless charm. There were once 79 tall towers here, symbols of power for the wealthy families of the Middle Ages. Thirteen are still standing, giving the town its unique skyline. The bus stops just outside the town gates, from which you can stroll down the main street to the picturesque Piazza della Cisterna.

Just around the corner is the church of the **Collegiata.** Its walls, and those of its chapel dedicated to Santa Fina, are decorated with radiant frescoes (have plenty of 100-lire coins for the light machines). From the steps of the church you can observe the town's countless crows as they circle the tall towers. In the pretty courtyard on the right as you descend the church stairs, there's a shop selling Tuscan and Deruta ceramics, which you'll also find in other shops along the Via San Giovanni. The excellent San Gimignano wine could be another souvenir of your visit; it's sold in gift cartons from just about every shop in town.

Dining and Lodging

For details and price-category definitions, *see* Dining and Lodging *in* Staying in Italy, *above.*

Lucca **Canuleia.** A small, popular trattoria between Via Mordini and Piaz-
Dining za Anfiteatro, the Canuleia serves typical Lucca fare, emphasizing vegetables in its minestrone and vegetarian lasagna. *Via Canuleia 14, tel. 0583/47470. Reservations advised. MC, V. Closed Sat., Sun., and Aug. $*
Giulio. Although it was recently renovated and enlarged, this classic trattoria hasn't changed its menu (a trove of local dishes) or its prices. *Via delle Conce 47, tel. 0583/55948. Reservations advised. No credit cards. Closed Sun. and Mon. $*

Lodging **Ilaria.** This small, family-run hotel sits in a pretty location on a minuscule canal within easy walking distance of the main sights. The rooms are smallish but fresh and functional. *Via del Fosso 20, tel. 0583/47558. 17 rooms, most with bath. AE, DC, MC, V. $*

Cinzia. On the upper floor of a centuries-old building, this small hotel is a favorite of budget-conscious Italians and foreigners. It offers basic rooms in a central location on a quiet street near the cathedral. *Via della Dogana 9, tel. 0583/41323. 12 rooms without bath. No credit cards. ¢*

Pisa
Dining

Bruno. A country-inn look, with beamed ceilings and soft lights, makes Bruno a pleasant place to lunch on classic Tuscan dishes, from *zuppa alla pisana* (vegetable soup) to *baccalà con porri* (cod with leeks). It's just outside the old city walls and only a short walk from the bell tower and cathedral. *Via Luigi Bianchi 12, tel. 050/560818. Reservations advised. AE, DC, MC, V. Closed Mon. dinner, Tues. $$*

Osteria dei Cavalieri. This tavern is in a medieval building off Piazza dei Cavalieri. It offers a one-course lunch and a range of vegetarian, meat and fish dishes. *Via San Frediano 16, tel. 050/580858. Reservations advised for dinner. AE, DC, MC, V. Closed Sat. lunch, Sun. and Aug. $$*

Lodging

Terminus Plaza. Conveniently located near the train station but across town from the famous tower, this is a basic commercial hotel. Ask for a quiet room away from the street. *Via Colombo 45, tel. and fax 050/500303. 52 rooms, most with bath. AE, DC, MC, V. $$*

Ariston. You couldn't ask for anything closer to the tower—it's practically outside the door of this smallish, simply furnished hotel. *Via Maffi 42, tel. 050/561834, fax 050/561891. 33 rooms, 23 with bath. DC, MC, V. $$*

San Gimignano
Dining

Il Pino. A trattoria that fills up fast with tourists at lunch time, it features ribollita and good beef dishes from the Chiana valley. *Via di San Matteo 31, tel. 0577/940415. Reservations advised. AE, DC, MC, V. Closed Thurs. $$*

Stella. Farm-fresh vegetables and the owner's own olive oil are part of the fare at this simple trattoria. *Via San Matteo 77, tel. 0577/940444. No reservations. AE, DC, MC, V. Closed Wed. and Jan. 6–Feb. 15. $$*

Siena
Dining
★

La Torre. The kitchen of this family-run trattoria, down the street from the Mangia Tower, is tucked into one corner of this brick-vaulted room, where the owner recites the day's menu and waits on tables. Try the homemade *pici*, the local pasta, and soups. The *arista* (roast pork) is redolent of herbs. *Via Salicotto 7, tel. 0577/287548. Reservations advised. No credit cards. Closed Thurs. and Aug. 14–31. $$*

La Grotta del Gallo Nero. At this wine cellar off Piazza del Campo, Chianti is king, and you can make a meal of *crostini* (toast with liver pâté) and local cheese. There are hot dishes, too. *Via del Porrione 65, tel. 0577/220446. No reservations. No credit cards. Closed Sun. $*

Le Tre Campane. Boasting a convenient location between Piazza del Campo and the Duomo, this small trattoria displays the colorful banners of Siena's 17 districts. Popular with the locals, it specializes in Tuscan fare and a *trittico* (trio) of pastas. *Piazzetta Bonelli, tel. 0577/286091. Reservations advised. No credit cards. Closed Tues. and Jan.–Feb. $*

Lodging

Chiusarelli. Near the SITA bus stop and within walking distance of Piazza del Campo, this hotel is in a well-kept, early 1900s villa with neoclassic columns and a small garden. The rooms are functional but airy. A downstairs restaurant caters to tour groups. *Viale Curtatone 9, tel. 0577/280562, fax 0577/271177. 50 rooms with bath. MC, V. $$*

Continentale. A block or so from Piazza del Campo, this old-fashioned hotel still has public rooms in the grand style of the days when Italian royalty visited in the early 1900s. The rooms are clean and quiet, and the location can't be beat. *Via Banchi di Sopra 85, tel. 0577/41451. 42 rooms, 27 with bath. AE, MC, V. $*

Lea. In a residential neighborhood separated by a ravine from the medieval center, Lea is an 18th-century villa with garden, transformed into an intimate family-run hotel. *Viale XXIV Maggio 10, tel. 0577/283207. 13 rooms with bath. No credit cards. $*

Tre Donzelle. This hotel, in the heart of Siena, off Piazza del Campo, has an unbeatable location that makes you feel a part of Sienese life. Tre Donzelle has basic modern furnishings; rooms without bath are a bargain. *Via delle Donzelle 5, tel. 0577/280358. 27 rooms, 7 with bath. No credit cards. ¢*

Milan

Arriving and Departing

As Lombardy's capital and the most important financial and commercial center in northern Italy, Milan is well connected with Rome and Florence by fast and frequent rail and air service, though the latter is often delayed in winter by heavy fog.

By Plane Linate Airport, 11 kilometers (7 miles) outside Milan, handles mainly domestic and European flights (tel. 02/7485–2200). Malpensa, 50 kilometers (30 miles) from the city, handles intercontinental flights (tel. 02/7485–2200).

Between the Buses connect both airports with Milan, stopping at the central sta-
Airport and tion and at the Porta Garibaldi station. The fare from Linate is 4,000
Downtown lire on the special airport bus or 1,400 lire on municipal Bus 73 (to Piazza San Babila); from Malpensa, 12,000 lire.

By Train The main train terminal is the central station in Piazzale Duca d'Aosta (tel. 02/67500). Several smaller stations handle commuter trains. There are several fast Intercity trains daily between Rome and Milan, stopping in Florence. A nonstop Intercity leaves from Rome or Milan morning and evening, taking about four hours to go between the two cities.

Getting Around

By Subway Milan's subway network, the Metropolitana, is modern, fast, and easy to use. "MM" signs mark Metropolitana stations. There are at present two lines, with another scheduled to open soon. The ATM (city transport authority) has an information office on the mezzanine of the Duomo Metro station (tel. 02/875495). Tickets are sold at newsstands at every stop and in ticket machines *for exact change only.* The fare is 1,400 lire, and the subway runs from 6:20 AM to midnight.

By Bus and Buy tickets at newsstands, tobacco shops, and bars. The fare is
Streetcar 1,400 lire. One ticket is valid for 75 minutes on all surface lines and one subway trip. Daily tickets valid for 24 hours on all public transportation lines are on sale at the Duomo Metro station ATM Information Office and at Stazione Centrale Metro station.

Tourist Information

APT information offices (Via Marconi 1, tel. 02/809662; Central Station, tel. 02/669–0432). **Municipal Information Office** (Galleria Vittorio Emanuele at the corner of Piazza della Scala, tel. 02/878363 and 62083101, open 8–8, closed Sun.).

Exploring Milan

Numbers in the margin correspond to points of interest on the Milan map.

❶ The center of Milan is the Piazza del Duomo. The massive **Duomo** is one of the largest churches in the world, a mountain of marble fretted with statues, spires, and flying buttresses. The interior is a more solemn Italian Gothic. Take the elevator or walk up 158 steps to the roof, from which—if it's a clear day—you can see over the city to the Lombard plain and the Alps beyond, all through an amazing array of spires and statues. The **Madonnina**, a gleaming gilt statue on the highest spire, is a Milan landmark. *Entrance to elevator and stairway outside the cathedral, to the right. Admission: stairs, 5,000 lire; elevator, 7,000 lire. Open Mar.–Oct., daily 9–5:45; Nov.–Feb., daily 9–4:30.*

Outside the cathedral to the right is the elegant, glass-roofed
❷ **Galleria,** where the Milanese and visitors stroll, window-shop, and sip pricey cappuccinos at trendy cafés. At the other end of the
❸ Galleria is **Piazza della Scala,** with Milan's city hall on one side and
❹ **Teatro alla Scala,** the world-famous opera house, opposite.

Via Verdi, flanking the opera house, leads to Via Brera, where the
❺ **Pinacoteca di Brera** houses one of Italy's great collections of paintings. Most are of a religious nature, confiscated in the 19th century when many religious orders were suppressed and their churches closed. *Via Brera 28, tel. 02/862634. Admission: 8,000 lire. Open Tues.–Sat. 9–5:30, Sun. 9–12:45. (Hrs may vary; check locally.)*

After an eyeful of artworks by Mantegna, Raphael, and many other Italian masters, stop at the pleasant café open to Brera visitors (just inside the entrance to the gallery) or explore the Brera neighborhood, dotted with art galleries, chic little restaurants, and such off-
❻ beat cafés as the **Jamaica** (Via Brera 26), once a bohemian hangout. Take Via dei Fiori Chiari in front of the Brera and keep going in the
❼ same direction to the moated **Castello Sforzesco,** a somewhat sinister 19th-century reconstruction of the imposing 15th-century fortress built by the Sforzas, who succeeded the Viscontis as lords of Milan in the 15th century. It now houses wide-ranging collections of sculptures, antiques, and ceramics, including Michelangelo's *Rondanini Pietà,* his last work, left unfinished at his death. *Piazza Castello, tel. 02/62083191. Admission free. Open Tues.–Sun. 9:30–5:30.*

From the vast residence of the Sforzas, it's not far to the church of
❽ **Santa Maria delle Grazie.** Although portions of the church were designed by Bramante, it plays second fiddle to the **Refectory** next door, where, over a three-year period, Leonardo da Vinci painted his megafamous fresco, *The Last Supper.* The fresco has suffered more than its share of disaster, beginning with the experiments of the artist, who used untested pigments that soon began to deteriorate. *The Last Supper* is now a mere shadow of its former self, despite meticulous restoration that proceeds at a snail's pace. To save what is left, visitors are limited in time and number, and you may have to wait in line to get a glimpse of this world-famous work. *Piazza Santa Maria delle Grazie 2, tel. 02/498–7588. Admission: 6,000 lire. Open Tues.–Sun. 8–2. (Hrs may vary; check locally.)*

If you are interested in medieval architecture, go to see the medieval
❾ church of **Sant'Ambrogio** (Piazza Sant'Ambrogio). Consecrated by St. Ambrose in AD 387, it's the model for all Lombard Romanesque churches and contains some ancient works of art, including a remarkable 9th-century altar in precious metals and enamels and some 5th-century mosaics. On December 7, the feast day of St. Ambrose, the streets around the church are the scene of a lively flea
 market. Another noteworthy church is **San Lorenzo Maggiore** (Corso di Porta Ticinese), with 16 ancient Roman columns in front

Milan

0   440 yards
400 meters

KEY

i Tourist Information

Castello Sforzesco, **7**
Corso Buenos Aires, **16**
Duomo, **1**
Galleria, **2**
Jamaica, **6**
Piazza della Scala, **3**

Pinacoteca di Brera, **5**
San Lorenzo
Maggiore, **10**
San Satiro, **11**
Santa Maria delle
Grazie, **8**
Sant'Ambrogio, **9**

Teatro alla Scala, **4**
Via Manzoni, **13**
Via Monte
Napoleone, **12**
Via Sant'Andrea, **15**
Via della Spiga, **14**

and some 4th-century mosaics in the Chapel of St. Aquilinus. The Navigli district near Porta Ticinese is a picturesque neighborhood with a canal, the Darsena, lined with quaint shops, cafés, and trattorias. Closer to Piazza del Duomo on Via Torino, the church of **San Satiro** is another architectural gem in which Bramante's perfect command of proportion and perspective, a characteristic of the Renaissance, made a small interior seem extraordinarily spacious and airy.

The **Peck** shops are only a few steps from San Satiro. The main store, at Via Spadari 9, is Italy's premiere gourmet delicatessen, and a satellite shop, at Via Cantu 3, offers an array of snacks to eat on the premises. But for fashion, Milan's most elegant shopping streets are beyond the Duomo—**Via Monte Napoleone, Via Manzoni, Via della Spiga,** and **Via Sant'Andrea.** Prices are stratospheric, so for bargains you'll have to go elsewhere. Make your way to **Corso Buenos Aires,** near the central station, which has hundreds more shops and accessible prices, too. You may also want to take in the huge outdoor market on **Viale Papiniano,** not far south of San Lorenzo Maggiore, if your visit includes a Tuesday or Saturday morning.

Dining

For details and price-category definitions, *see* Dining *in* Staying in Italy, *above.*

$$ **Dina e Pierino.** This busy and friendly trattoria in the Brera district has tables outdoors in fair weather and an inside dining room done in early 1900s style. The menu features Tuscan cuisine, including antipasto, gnocchi (potato dumplings) with butter and sage, and *panna cotta* (a delicate milk pudding) for dessert. *Via Marsala 2, tel. 02/659–9488. Reservations advised. D, MC, V. Closed Mon. and Aug.*

$$ **La Capanna.** A family-run trattoria with an upscale wine list, it is near the university and the Piola Metro stop. The menu offers classic Milanese dishes and some novelties, such as spaghetti *all'Attilio* (with a creamy sauce of basil, garlic, and sausage), as well as seafood. The *torta di mele* is the Italian version of homemade apple pie. *Via Donatello 9, tel. 02/294–00884. Reservations advised. AE, DC, MC, V. Closed Mon. evening, Sat., and Aug.*

$$ **Trattoria La Pesa.** This popular eating place is a little out of the way, but Milanese consider it worth the trip. It is near the De Angeli Metro and Bus 63 stops. The decor is straightforward trattoria style, and the menu features the specialties of Milan: *cotoletta* (breaded veal cutlet) and osso buco (braised veal shank). There is a special room for nonsmokers and a bargain prix-fixe lunch menu for about 14,000 lire. *Via Fantoni 26, corner Via Rembrandt, tel. 02/403–5907. Reservations advised in the evening. AE, DC, MC, V. Closed Mon. evening and Sun.*

$ **Abele.** Open only in the evening (until late), this trattoria is simple and usually crowded. The specialties of the house are a selection of risottos and meal-size salads. It is located off Viale Monza, near Piazzale Loreto (Pasteur M stop). *Via Temperanza 5, tel. 02/261–3855. Reservations advised. No credit cards. Closed Mon. and 2nd ½ July.*

$ **La Bruschetta.** A winning partnership of Tuscans and Neapolitans runs this tiny, busy, and first-class pizzeria near the Duomo. It features the obligatory wood-burning stove, so you can watch your pizza being cooked, though there are plenty of other dishes to choose from as well—try the spaghetti *alle cozze e vongole* (with clams and mussels). *Piazza Beccaria 12, tel. 02/8692494. Reservations advised, but service is so fast you don't have to wait long. No credit cards. Closed Mon., 3 wks in Aug.*

$ **La Giara.** The menu at this tavern with bare wooden tables and benches offers a limited selection of southern Italian specialties, notably a varied vegetable antipasto. Meat is grilled on a range at the front of the restaurant and served with crusty bread and dense olive oil from the Puglia region. La Giara is conveniently located in the vicinity of Piazzale Loreto. *Viale Monza 10, tel. 02/2614385. You may be asked to share a table. No credit cards. Closed Wed.*

$ **Taverna Moriggi.** This dusky, wood-paneled wine bar near the stock exchange serves a prix-fixe lunch for about 30,000 lire and cold cuts and cheeses in the evening. *Via Moriggi 8, tel. 02/864–50880. Reservations advised. D, MC, V. Closed Sat. lunch and Sun.*

¢ **Flash.** This is one of countless *paninoteche* (sandwich bars) where the Milanese eat economically. Here sandwiches are made in a tempting variety, and pizza and soup are served, as well. *Via Bergamini 1, no phone. No credit cards. Closed Sun.*

¢ ★ **Grand'Italia.** Big and busy, it's crowded at lunchtime with those who work in the Corso Garibaldi–Brera district. They stop in for a satisfying one-dish meal, whether that's pizza, focaccia (freshly baked flat bread) with sandwich fillings, or a prix-fixe lunch. The mood changes in the evening: Pizza is still available, but a full meal can be costly. *Via Palermo 5, tel. 02/877–759. Reservations accepted. Closed Tues. (except in Aug.)*

¢ ★ **Magenta.** Founded in 1908, Bar Magenta is a monument to Art Nouveau and is a Milanese classic. From late morning to 2 AM you can find thick, made-to-order *panini* (sandwiches) and other light snacks. At lunchtime it's a favorite with models and other fashion folk. *Via Carducci 13 at Corso Magenta, tel. 02/805–3808. No credit cards. Closed Mon.*

¢ ★ **Panino Giusto.** Some consider the sandwiches here the best in Milan. Try the Madeira, made with pâté, creamy Caprino cheese, and port wine. *Corso Garibaldi 125, 02/655–4728. No credit cards. Closed Sun. and Aug.*

¢ **Spaghetteria.** This restaurant in the Brera district is open only in the evening and offers an amazing number of pasta dishes. *Assaggini* means "samples," and if you order it you'll be able to taste several types of pasta for one low price. *Via Solferino 3, tel. 02/86462020. No reservations. AE, MC, V. Closed Mon.*

Lodging

Make reservations well in advance, particularly when trade fairs are on, which can be most of the year except for August (when many hotels close) and mid-December to mid-January. March and October are months with the highest concentration of fairs, and it's virtually impossible to find a room at this time.

For details and price-category definitions, *see* Lodging *in* Staying in Italy, *above.*

$$ **Città Studi.** This hotel is near the university and Piazzale Susa, some distance from the center, which you can reach by bus. It is functionally furnished in modern style. Most rooms have private showers; the few without showers are a bargain. *Via Saldini 24, tel. 02/744666, fax 02/713122. 45 rooms, 38 with shower. AE, MC, V.*

$$ **La Pace.** Near the Piazzale Loreto Metro station, La Pace has 19th-century-style furnishings, modern bedrooms, and a tiny garden. *Via Alfredo Catalani 69, tel. 02/261–9700, fax 02/261–12091. 20 rooms with bath. MC, V.*

$$ **London.** A 10-minute walk from the cathedral, the London is clean, with large rooms but cramped bathrooms. The friendly staff speaks English. *Via Rovello 3, tel. 02/720–20166, fax 02/805–7037. 29 rooms, 24 with bath. Closed Aug. and Dec. 23–Jan. 3. MC, V.*

$$ **San Francisco.** This hotel, near the Piazzale Piola Metro station, is modern in style, with functional furnishings, TV, and telephone in the rooms. It is family owned and managed and has one of Milan's "secret" inner gardens. *Viale Lombardia 55, tel. 02/236–1009, fax 02/266–80377. 31 rooms with bath. MC, V.*

$ **San Marco.** A small, quiet hotel near the Loreto Metro stop, it has clean bedrooms, a few without bath and therefore cheaper. American students are among its clientele. *Via Piccinni 25, tel. 02/295–16414, fax 02/295–13243. 11 rooms, 7 with bath. MC, V.*

¢ **Arthur.** Near the central train station, on a street where many 19th-century buildings have been converted to small hotels of various grades of acceptability, this hotel has large, clean rooms and faint touches of old-fashioned elegance at rock-bottom prices. *Via Lazzaretto 14, tel. 02/204–6294. 11 rooms, 7 with bath. No credit cards.*

¢ **Valley.** Close to the Central Station and Metro lines, the Valley is clean and conveniently located. The rooms are simply furnished, some of the staff speak English, and doubles with bath are available. *Via Soperga 19, tel. 02/669–2777, fax 56692777. 10 rooms, 8 with bath. No credit cards.*

¢ **Villa Mira.** Near the Loreto Metro stop, this family-run establishment is good value. All doubles have private bathrooms, and the rooms are spotless, though somewhat stark. *Via Sacchini 19, tel. 02/295–25618. 10 rooms, 8 with bath. No credit cards.*

The Arts

The most famous spectacle in Milan is the one at **La Scala,** which presents some of the world's most impressive operatic productions. The opera season begins early in December and ends in May. The concert season runs from May to the end of June and from September through November. There is a brief ballet season in September. Programs are available at principal travel agencies and tourist information offices in Italy and abroad. Tickets are usually hard to come by, but your hotel may be able to provide them. For information on schedules, ticket availability, and how to buy tickets, there is an Infotel Scala Service in operation (with English-speaking staff) at the ticket office (Teatro alla Scala, Ufficio Biglietteria, Via Filodrammatici 2, tel. 02/720–03744, daily, 10–7). Telephone bookings are not accepted. From abroad you can book in advance, within a short specified period some time before each presentation (these dates are published at the beginning of the season, and a certain percentage of tickets are set aside for this category of Postal Bookings, allocated on a first-come-first-served basis), applying for a reservation by mail or fax (transmitted 9–6 local time, with time and date of transmission, and sender's fax number indicated on the fax, to 02/877–996, or 8051625). You may also be able to book at CIT or other travel agencies (no more than 10 days before the performance). There is a 15% advance booking charge. Two hundred standing-room tickets in the two upper galleries go on sale 30 minutes before the start of each performance at the Biglietteria di Piazza Scala, to the left of the main entrance. These cost 10,000 lire.

Venice

Arriving and Departing

By Plane Marco Polo International Airport is situated about 10 kilometers (6 miles) northeast of the city on the mainland. For flight information, tel. 041/2609260.

Between the Airport and Downtown ATVO buses make the 25-minute trip in to Piazzale Roma, going through the city's unappealing outlying regions; the cost is around 5,000 lire. From Piazzale Roma visitors will most likely have to take a *vaporetto* (water bus) to their hotel (*see* Getting Around, *below*). The Cooperative San Marco motor launch is more costly (20,000 lire) and can be a more convenient way to reach the city, depending on where your hotel is located; it runs from the airport via the Lido, dropping passengers across the lagoon at Piazza San Marco. (It works on a limited schedule in winter.)

By Train Make sure your train goes all the way to Santa Lucia train station in Venice's northwest corner; some trains leave passengers at the Mestre station on the mainland, from which you must connect with the next train to Santa Lucia, remembering there is a *supplemento* (extra charge) for travelling on Intercity and Eurocity trains, and that if you get on one of these trains without having paid it in advance for this part of your journey, you are liable to a fairly hefty fine. For train information, tel. 041/715555, 7:15 AM–9:30 PM. The APT information booth (tel. 041/719078, open daily 8–8) and the baggage depot in the station are usually festooned with long lines of tourists. If you need a hotel room, go to the AVA (Venetian Hoteliers Association) (open daily Apr.–Oct., 8 AM–10 PM, Nov.–Mar., 8 AM–9:30 PM); there are others at the airport (open daily Apr.–Oct., 10–9, Nov.–Mar., 10:30–6:30) and at the city garage at Piazzale Roma (open daily, Apr.–Oct. 9 AM–10 PM, Nov.–Mar., 9–9). The deposit (15,000–60,000 lire, depending on the hotel category) is discounted on your hotel bill. Vaporetto landing stages are directly outside the station. *Make sure you know how to get to your hotel before you arrive.* You will probably have to walk some distance from the landing stage nearest your hotel; for this reason, try to obtain a map of Venice before arrival, and travel with a luggage cart—porters are hard to find and rates are quite high (15,000 lire for one bag and about 5,000 lire for each additional piece of luggage).

Getting Around

First-time visitors find that getting around Venice presents some unusual problems: the complexity of its layout (the city is made up of more than 100 islands linked by bridges); the bewildering unfamiliarity of waterborne transportation, the apparently illogical house-numbering system and duplication of street names in its six districts, and the necessity of walking whether you enjoy it or not. It's essential to have a good map showing all street names and water bus routes; buy the most detailed one you can find at any newsstand.

By Vaporetto ACTV water buses run the length of the Grand Canal and circle the city. There are several lines, some of which connect Venice with the major and minor islands in the lagoon; Line 1 is the Grand Canal local. Timetables are posted on all landing stages where ticket booths are located (open early morning–9 PM). Buy single tickets or books of 10 (the latter need to be stamped, before boarding, in the machine on the landing stage). The fare is 3,500 lire on most lines. A 24-hour tourist ticket costs 12,000 lire, while a three-day ticket costs 18,000 lire; these are especially worthwhile if you are planning to visit the islands of Murano, Burano, and Torcello. Vaporetti run every 10–20 minutes or so during the day; Line 1 runs every hour more or less between midnight and dawn. Landing stages are clearly marked with name and line number. Check before boarding that the boat is going in your direction.

By Traghetto Few tourists know about the two-man gondolas that ferry people across the Grand Canal at various fixed points. It's the cheapest and shortest gondola ride in Venice, and it can save a lot of walking. The fare is 600 lire, which you hand to one of the gondoliers when you get on. Look for "Traghetto" signs.

By Gondola If you feel like treating yourself to a gondola ride, make sure the gondolier understands that you want to see the *rii*, or smaller canals, as well as the Grand Canal. There's supposed to be a fixed minimum rate of about 80,000 lire for 50 minutes for up to five people. Come to terms with your gondolier *before* stepping into his boat.

On Foot This is the only way to reach many parts of Venice, so wear comfortable shoes. Invest in a good map that names all the streets and count on getting lost more than once.

Important Addresses and Numbers

Tourist Information The main Venice **APT Tourist Office** (tel. 041/522–6356, fax 5298730) is at Palazzetto Selva, on the waterfront near the San Marco vaporetto stop. It's open in summer and during Carnival every day except public holidays 9:30–1, 2–5; in winter Monday–Saturday 9–1, 2–4. There are APT information booths at the Santa Lucia station (tel. 041/719078) and on the Lido (Gran Viale S.M. Elisabetta 6A, tel. 041/526–5721, fax 041/529–8720).

In 1991 Venice Municipality's Youth Department launched a special scheme to help young visitors: "Rolling Venice," as it is somewhat oddly entitled, is open to everyone ages 14–29 and costs 5,000 lire to join (at Rolling Venice's offices at the Assessorato alla Gioventu, Corte Contarini 1529, behind the Piazza San Marco Post Office, tel. 041/2707650, open Mon.–Fri. 9:30–1, Tues. and Thurs. 3–5; Box Office, Calle Loredan 4127, off Campo San Luca, tel. 041/5239666, open Tues.–Fri. 3:30–7, Sat. 9:30–12:30; and from July to September at the Santa Lucia railway station). Benefits include a handy guidebook to the city and (sometimes substantial) discounts in hotels, restaurants, and shops and on ACTV vaporetto tickets. The Youth Department has also produced two useful leaflets, *Dormire Giovani* (*Accommodations for Young People*) and *Fuori Orario: di Notte a Venezia e Mestre* (Out of Hours: By Night in Venice and Mestre); *see* Nightlife, *below.*

Consulates There is no Canadian, U.K., or U.S. consular service in Venice. The nearest consulates for all three countries are in Milan: **Canadian,** Via Victor Pisani 19, tel. 02/6697451; **U.K.,** Via San Paolo 7, tel. 02/723001; **U.S.,** Via P. Amedeo 2/10, tel. 02/290351.

Emergencies **Carabinieri** (tel. 112). English-speaking officers are available 24 hours a day to deal with any kind of emergency. **Police** (tel. 113). **Ambulance** (tel. 041/523–0000). **Red Cross First Aid Station,** Piazza San Marco 55 (near Caffe Florian), open Monday–Saturday 8:30–1, tel. 041/5286346. **Doctor:** Your hotel should be able to offer advice, or else try the emergency room at Venice's hospital (tel. 041/523–0000).

Exploring Venice

Venice—La Serenissima, the Most Serene—is disorienting in its complexity, an extraordinary labyrinth of narrow streets and waterways, opening now and again onto some airy square or broad canal. The majority of its magnificent palazzi are slowly crumbling, yet somehow in Venice the shabby and the derelict create an effect of supreme beauty and charm, rather than one of horrible urban decay. The place is romantic, especially at night when the lights from the vaporetti and the stars overhead pick out the gargoyles and arches of the centuries-old facades. For hundreds of years Venice was the unrivaled mistress of trade between Europe and the Orient and the staunch bulwark of Christendom against the tide of Turkish expansion. Though the power and glory of its days as a wealthy city-republic are gone, the art and exotic aura remain.

To enjoy the city, you will have to come to terms with the crowds of day-trippers that take over the center, around San Marco, from May through September. Hot and sultry in the summer, Venice is much more welcoming in early spring and late fall. Romantics like it in the winter when prices are much lower, the streets are often deserted, and the sea mists impart a haunting melancholy to the *campi* (squares) and canals. Piazza San Marco (St. Mark's Square) is the pulse of Venice, but after joining with the crowds to visit the Basilica di San Marco and the Doge's Palace, strike out on your own and just follow where your feet take you—you won't be disappointed.

As part of a scheme begun in 1995 called *Dal Museo alla Città* (From Museum to City), to encourage visitors to seek out not only the artwork in museums but throughout the city Fabric proper—primarily in the churches and *scuole* (charitable confraternity halls) for which they were originally commissioned—over a dozen places, selected for their artistic interest, now have fixed visiting hours when tourists can be sure of finding the place open (and of not intruding on church services). At these times—given in the tours below as "Visiting hours"—there should always be someone to provide information and a free general leaflet plus an opportunity to buy post cards and booklets about these important sights.

Numbers in the margin correspond to points of interest on the Venice map.

Piazza San Marco and the Accademia

① Even the pigeons have to fight for space on **Piazza San Marco,** and pedestrian traffic jams clog the surrounding byways. Despite the crowds and because it is the most famous square in Venice, San Marco is the logical starting place of each of our various itineraries. The short side of the square, facing the Basilica of San Marco, is known as the Ala Napoleonica, a wing built by order of Napoléon to complete the much earlier buildings on either side of the square, enclosing it to form what he called "the most beautiful drawing room in all of Europe." Upstairs is the **Museo Correr,** with eclectic collections of historical objects and a picture gallery of fine 13th–17th-century paintings. *Piazza San Marco, Ala Napoleonica, tel. 041/ 522–5625. Admission: 8,000 lire. Open Apr.–Oct., Wed.–Mon. 10–5; Nov.–Mar., Wed.–Mon. 10–4.*

③ The **Basilica di San Marco** (St. Mark's Cathedral) was begun in the 11th century to hold the relics of St. Mark the Evangelist, the city's patron saint, and its richly decorated facade is surmounted by copies of the four famous gilded bronze horses (the originals are in the basilica's upstairs museum). Inside, golden mosaics sheathe walls and domes, lending an extraordinarily exotic aura, half Christian church, half Middle Eastern mosque. Be sure to see the **Pala d'Oro,** an eye-filling 10th-century altarpiece in gold and silver, studded with precious gems and enamels. From the atrium, climb the steep stairway to the museum: The bronze horses alone are worth the effort. *The Basilica is open from early morning, but tourist visits are allowed Mon.–Sat. 9:30–5, Sun. 2–5. No admission to those wearing shorts or other revealing clothing. Pala d'Oro and Treasury. Tel. 041/5225205. Admission: 3,000 lire. Open Apr.–Sept., Mon.– Sat. 9:30–5, Sun. 2–5; Oct.–Mar., Mon.–Sat. 10–4, Sun. 2–4, although these times may vary slightly. Gallery and Museum. Admission: 3,000 lire. Open Apr.–Sept., daily 9:30–5; Oct.–Mar., daily 10–4.*

④ Next to St. Mark's is the **Palazzo Ducale** (Doge's Palace), which, during Venice's prime, was the epicenter of the Serene Republic's great empire. More than just a palace, it was a combination White House, Senate, Supreme Court, torture chamber, and prison. The building's exterior is striking; the lower stories consist of two rows of fragile-seeming arches, while above rests a massive pink-and-white marble wall whose solidity is barely interrupted by its six great Gothic windows. The interior is a maze of vast halls, monumental staircases, secret corridors, state apartments, and the sinister prison cells and torture chamber. The palace is filled with frescoes, paintings, carvings, and a few examples of statuary by some of the Renaissance's greatest artists. Don't miss the famous view from the balcony, overlooking the piazza and St. Mark's Basin and the church of San Giorgio Maggiore across the lagoon. *Piazzetta*

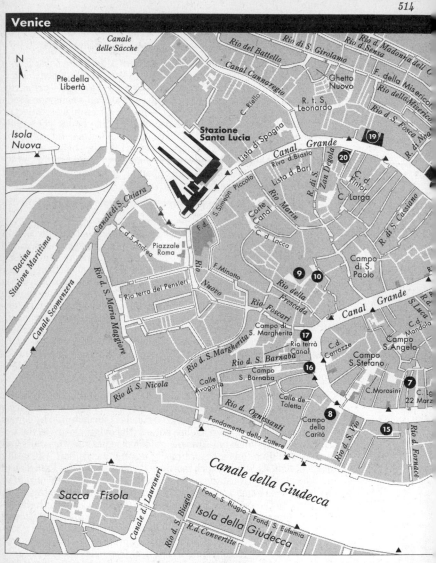

Venice

Canale delle Sacche

N

Pte. della Libertà

Isola Nuova

Bacino Stazione Marittima

Rio del Battello

Canal Cannaregio

Rio di S. Girolamo

Rio d. Sensa

Rio d. Madonna dell'U.

F. della Misericor.

Rio della Misericor.

Ghetto Nuovo

C. Riello

R. t. S. Leonardo

Rio d. S. Fosca

R. d. Nin

Stazione Santa Lucia

Lista di Spagna

Canal Grande

Riva d. Biasio

Rio d. Biasio

Zan Degola

Lista d. Bari

R. di S. Cassiano

C. d. Tintor

C. Larga

19

20

F. d. S. Simeon Piccolo

Corte Canal

Rio Marin

C. d. Lacca

Campo di S. Paolo

Canale di S. Chiara

C. d S. Andrea

Piazzale Roma

Rio terra dei Pensieri

Rio Nuovo

F. Minotto

Rio della Frescada

9 10

Canal Grande

Rio d. S. Maria Maggiore

Rio Foscari

Campo di S. Margherita

Rio terrà Canal

17

C. d. Carrozze

Campo S. Angelo

S. Luca

C. d. Mandola

Canale Scomenzera

Rio d. S. Margherita

Rio d. S. Barnaba

Campo S. Barnaba

16

Campo S. Stefano

Campo della Carità

Calle Avogaria

Calle de Toletta

8

Campo della Carità

7

C. Morosini

22 Marz

15

Rio d. Fornace

Rio di S. Nicola

Rio d. Ognissanti

Fondamenta della Zattere

Rio d. S. Vio

Canale della Giudecca

Sacca Fisola

Canale d. Lauraneri

Fond. S. Riagio

Fond. S. Eufemia

Isola della Giudecca

Rio d. S. Biagio

R. d. Convertite

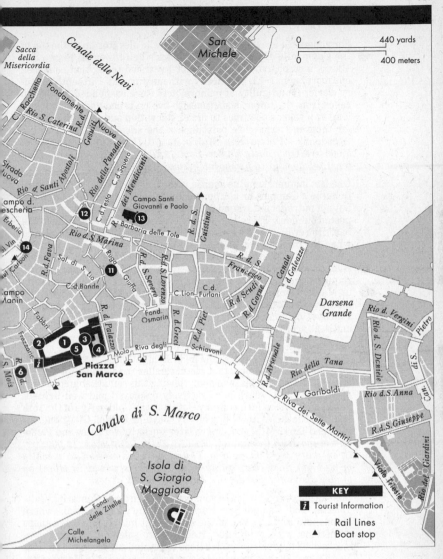

Sacca
della
Misericordia

Canale delle Navi

San
Michele

| 0 | 440 yards |
| 0 | 400 meters |

Cl. Racchetta

Fondamente

Rio S. Caterina

R.d.

Gesuiti Nuova

Rio della Panada

C.d. Testa

C.d. squero

dei Mendicanti

Campo Santi
Giovanni e Paolo

Barbaria delle Tole

Strada
Nuova

Rio d' Santi Apostoli

12

13

R.d.S. Marina

R. d. S.
Gustina

ampo d.
Pescheria

Erberia

14

R.d. Fava

Sal. di S. Lio

11

Rio d. S.
Francesco

Canale
d.Galeazze

Darsena
Grande

Rio d. Vergini

S. tp.
Pietra

el Vin

el Carbon

C.d. Bande

Rug.o Giuffa

R.d. S. Severo

R.d.S. Lorenzo

C. Lion

C.d.
Furlani

R.d. Scudi

R.d. Gorne

Rio d. S. Dentele

ampo
Manin

Fabbri

Fond.
Osmarin

R.d. Palazzo

R.d. Greci

R.d. Piet.

Schiavoni

Rio della Tana

Rio d. S. Anna

Frezzeria

2

1

5

3

4

Molo

Riva degli

i

6

R. d. Moss.

Piazza
San Marco

R.d. Arsenale

V. Garibaldi

Riva dei Sette Martiri

R.d.S. Giuseppe

Can.

Rio del Giardini

Viale Trieste

Canale di S. Marco

Fond.
delle Zitelle

Calle
Michelangelo

Isola di
S. Giorgio
Maggiore

KEY

i Tourist Information

—— Rail Lines

▲ Boat stop

San Marco, tel. 041/522–4951. Admission: 10,000 lire. Open daily Apr.–Oct., 9–7, Nov.–Mar., 9–4.

For a pigeon's-eye view of Venice, take the elevator up to the top of the **Campanile di San Marco** (St. Mark's bell tower) in Piazza San Marco, a reconstruction of the 1,000-year-old tower that collapsed one morning in 1912, practically without warning. Fifteenth-century clerics found guilty of immoral acts were suspended in wooden cages from the tower, sometimes to live on bread and water for as long as a year, sometimes to die of starvation and exposure. (Look for them in Carpaccio's paintings of the square that hang in the Accademia.) *Piazza San Marco, tel. 041/522–4064. Admission: 5,000 lire. Open daily Easter–Sept., 9:30–7; Oct., 10–6; Nov.–Easter, 10–4:30. Closed for maintenance most of Jan.*

One last landmark on the square is the *Caffè Florian*, a great place to nurse a Campari or a cappuccino (closed Wed.). Prices are high, but not outrageous (around $6 for a hot chocolate; there's a price list posted outside). There's no service charge if you drink sitting at the bar. However, there's an extra charge (about $3) if you're served when the orchestra is playing. If you succeed in denying yourself this pleasure, head west out of San Marco (with the facade of the basilica to your back), making your way past **San Moisè**'s elaborate Baroque facade and by the American Express office, on to Calle Larga 22 Marzo. Continue on to the church of **Santa Maria del Giglio,** behind the **Gritti Palace** hotel. Across the bridge behind the church, **Piazzesi,** on Campiello Feltrina, is famous for its handprinted paper and desk accessories.

Join the stream of pedestrians crossing the Grand Canal on the wooden **Accademia Bridge,** and head straight to the **Accademia Gallery,** Venice's most important picture gallery and a must for art lovers. Try to spend at least an hour viewing this remarkable collection of Venetian art, which is attractively displayed and well lighted. Works range from 14th-century Gothic to the Golden Age of the 15th and 16th centuries, including oils by Giovanni Bellini, Giorgione, Titian, and Tintoretto, and superb later works by Veronese and Tiepolo. *Campo della Carità, tel. 041/522–2247. Admission: 12,000 lire. Open daily 9–2, Tues. and Thurs. 9–7. Admission to recently opened top floor (displaying works previously held in store) by guided visit only. For details, telephone or ask at desk.*

Consulting your map, make your way through Calle Contarini, Calle Toletta, and Campo San Barnaba to Rio Terrà Canal, where **Mondonovo** ranks as one of the city's most interesting mask shops (Venetians, who originated Italy's most splendid carnival, love masks of all kinds, from gilded lions to painted sun faces and sinister death's heads). Just around the corner is Campo Santa Margherita, which has a homey feel.

Continue past Campo San Pantalon to Campo San Rocco, just beside the immense church of the Frari. In the 1500s, Tintoretto embellished the **Scuola di San Rocco** with more than 50 canvases; they are an impressive sight, dark paintings aglow with figures hurtling dramatically through space amid flashes of light and color. The *Crucifixion* in the Albergo (the room just off the great hall) is held to be his masterpiece. *Campo di San Rocco, tel. 041/523–4864. Admission: 8,000 lire. Open weekdays 9–5:30, Sat. and Sun. 10–4 in winter, 9–5:30 in summer.*

The church of Santa Maria Gloriosa dei Frari (known simply as the **Frari**) is one of Venice's most important churches, a vast soaring Gothic building of brick. Since it is the principal church of the Franciscans, its design is suitably austere to reflect that order's vows of poverty, though paradoxically it contains a number of the most sumptuous pictures in any Venetian church. Chief among them are the magnificent Titian altarpieces, notably the immense *Assump-*

tion of the Virgin over the main altar. Titian was buried here at the ripe old age of 88, the only one of 70,000 plague victims to be given a personal church burial. *Campo dei Frari. Admission: 1,000-lire. Visiting hrs: Mon.–Sat. 2:30–6.*

San Zanipolo and the Rialto Backtracking once again to Piazza San Marco, go to the arch under the Torre dell'Orologio (Clock Tower) and head northeast into the **Merceria,** one of Venice's busiest streets and, with the **Frezzeria** and **Calle dei Fabbri,** part of the shopping area that extends across the Grand Canal into the **Rialto district.** At Campo San Zulian, turn right into Calle della Guerra and Calle delle Bande to the graceful

⑪ white marble church of **Santa Maria Formosa;** it's situated right on a lively square (of the same name) with a few sidewalk cafés and a small vegetable market on weekday mornings.

Use your map to follow Calle Borgoloco into Campo San Marina, where you turn right, cross the little canal, and take Calle Castelli to

⑫ **Santa Maria dei Miracoli** (Campo dei Miracoli). Perfectly proportioned and sheathed in marble, this late-15th-century building embodies all the classical serenity of the early Renaissance. The interior is decorated with marble reliefs by the church's architect, Pietro Lombardo, and his son Tullio.

Retrace your steps along Calle Castelli and cross the bridge into Calle delle Erbe, following signs for "SS. Giovanni e Paolo." The

⑬ massive Dominican church of Santi Giovanni e Paolo—**San Zanipolo,** as it's known in the slurred Venetian dialect—is the rival of the Franciscan Frari. The church is a kind of pantheon of the doges (25 are buried here), and contains a wealth of artworks. (Visiting hrs: Mon.–Sat. 9–12 and 3–6.) Outside in the campo stands Verrocchio's equestrian statue of Colleoni, who fought for the Venetian cause in the mid-1400s.

Cross the canal in front of the church and continue along Calle Larga Giacinto Gallina, crossing a pair of bridges to Campiello Santa Maria Nova. Take Salizzada San Canciano to Salizzada San Giovanni Crisostomo to find yourself once again in the mainstream of

⑭ pedestrians winding their way to the **Rialto Bridge.** Street stalls hung with scarves and gondolier's hats signal that you are entering the heart of Venice's shopping district. Cross over the bridge, and you'll find yourself on the edge of the famous market. Try to visit the Rialto market when it's in full swing (Tuesday–Saturday mornings; Mondays are quiet because the fish market is closed), with fruit and vegetable vendors hawking their wares in a colorful and noisy jumble of sights and sounds. Not far beyond is the fish market, where you'll probably find sea creatures you've never seen before (and possibly won't want to see again). A left turn into Ruga Vecchia San Giovanni and Rughetta del Ravano will bring you face to face with scores of shops: At **La Scialuppa** (Calle Saoneri 2695) you'll find hand-carved wooden models of gondolas and their graceful oar locks known as *forcole.*

The Grand Canal Just off Piazzetta di San Marco (the square in front of the Doge's Palace) you can catch Vaporetto Line 1 at either the San Marco or San Zaccaria landing stages (on Riva degli Schiavoni), to set off on a boat tour along the **Grand Canal.** Serving as Venice's main thoroughfare, the canal winds in the shape of an "S" for more than 3½ kilometers (2 miles) through the heart of the city, past some 200 Gothic-Renaissance palaces. Although restrictions have been introduced to diminish the erosive effect of wash on buildings, this is still the route taken by vaporetti, gondolas, water taxis, mail boats, police boats, fire boats, ambulance boats, barges carrying provisions and building materials, bridal boats, and funeral boats. Your vaporetto tour provides a ringside view of Venice's beautiful, opulent palaces and a peek into the side streets and tiny canals where the Venetians go about their daily business. *Vaporetto Line 1. Cost: 3,500 lire.*

Departing from the San Marco landing, this tour passes first the **Accademia Gallery,** with its fine collection of 14th- to 18th-century ⑮ Venetian paintings (*see above*), then the **Peggy Guggenheim Museum,** in the late heiress's Palazzo Venier dei Leoni, which has an excellent modern art collection. *Entrance: Calle San Cristoforo, tel. 041/520–6288. Admission: 10,000 lire, Open Wed.–Mon. 11–6.*

⑯ Next you see the **Ca' Rezzonico,** built between the mid-17th and 18th centuries and now a museum of 18th-century Venetian paintings and ⑰ furniture, and the **Ca' Foscari,** a 15th-century Gothic building that was once the home of Doge Foscari, who was unwillingly deposed and died the following day. Today it's the headquarters of Venice's ⑱ university. **Ca' d'Oro,** farther along, is the most flowery palace on ⑲ the canal; it now houses the Galleria Franchetti. The **Palazzo Vendramin Calergi** is a Renaissance building where Wagner died in ⑳ 1883. It's also the winter home of the municipal casino. The **Fondaco dei Turchi** was an original Byzantine "house-warehouse" of a rich Venetian merchant, but the building has suffered some remodeling during the past 100 years and is now the Natural History Museum. *Ca' Foscari, tel. 041/5224543. Admission: 8,000 lire. Open Apr.– Oct., Sat.–Thurs. 10–5; Nov.–Mar., Sat.–Thurs. 10–4. Ca' d'Oro, tel. 041/5238790. Admission: 4,000 lire. Open daily 9–2. Fondaco dei Turchi, tel. 041/5240885. Admission: 5,000 lire. Open Tues.– Sat. 9–1.*

Shopping

Glass   Venetian glass is as famous as the city's gondolas, and almost every shop window displays it. There's a lot of cheap glass for sale; if you want something better, window shop at the top showrooms—**Venini** (Piazzetta dei Leoncini 314), **Pauly** (Calle dell' Ascensione 72, opposite the APT information office), **Salviati** (Piazza San Marco 78 and 110), and L'Isola (Campo San Moisè 1468)—and then look for similar pieces at lower-price shops between San Marco and the Rialto market. On the island of Murano, where prices are generally no lower than in Venice, **Domus** (Fondamenta dei Vetrai) has a good selection.

Shopping District   The main shopping area extends from Piazza San Marco through the Merceria and Calle dei Fabbri toward the Rialto.

Department Stores   The **Coin** store (off Campo San Bartolomeo) specializes in fashion and accessories. **Standa** has stores on Campo San Luca and Strada Nuova, where you can pick up medium-price goods of all kinds.

Dining

Venice is not a particularly cheap place to eat, but there are good restaurants, trattorias, and winebars where the prices are fair. Many trattorias have inexpensive prix-fixe menus, providing adequate if uninspired food for the money. There are also plenty of sandwich bars; pizzerias; and *bacari*, the typically Venetian wine bars, where you can order wine by the glass and snack on tidbits (which the Venetians call *cicchetti*) offered at the counter. In trattorias, save by ordering *acqua semplice* (tap water) instead of bottled mineral water and by choosing *vino sfuso* (a carafe of house wine) rather than bottled wine. City specialties include *pasta e fagioli;* risotto and all kinds of seafood; and the delicious *fegato alla veneziana*, thin strips of liver cooked with onions and served with grilled polenta (cornmeal cakes).

For details and price-category definitions, *see* Dining *in* Staying in Italy, *above.*

$$ **Alle Lanternine.** This friendly place in the Cannaregio quarter is especially nice in summer, when you dine outdoors. The menu offers a variety of fish and meat dishes and pizza, too. *Campiello della*

Chiesa 2134, tel. 041/721679. Reservations advised. AE, DC, MC, V. Closed Thurs.

$$ L'Incontro. ★ This trattoria near San Barnaba, handily situated about halfway between the Accademia Gallery and the Frari church, has won a faithful clientele of locals and visitors by offering good food (excellent meat—no fish) at reasonable prices. *Rio Terrà Canal 3062/a, tel. 041/522–2404. Reservations advised. MC, V. Closed Mon.*

$$ Metropole Buffet. ★ You can eat extremely well in comfort and style at the Hotel Metropole's prix-fixe buffet, which operates at lunchtime and in the evening. The price (around 50,000 lire) even includes a very palatable local white wine. Mineral water and coffee are extra. *Riva degli Schiavoni 4149, Castello, tel. 041/520–5044. Reservations advised. AE, DC, MC, V.*

$$ Al Tucano. This neighborhood trattoria conveniently close to St. Mark's is one of the rare reliable places to eat in the vicinity at affordable prices. It also serves pizza. *Ruga Giuffa 4835, tel. 041/520–0811. No reservations. No credit cards. Closed Thurs.*

$ Alla Fonte. This Sicilian-run pizzeria-trattoria, in a tiny square just off the waterfront, with tables outside in summer, offers a varied selection of good food at good prices—and excellent homemade ice cream. *Calle va in Crosera 3820 (off Campo Bandiera e Moro), Castello, tel. 041/523–8698. AE, MC, V. Closed Wed.*

$ Paradiso Perduto. Popular with young people, this informal wine bar in the Cannaregio quarter serves hot meals and is one of few such places in Venice to stay open late. Live music is usually featured at weekends. The menu changes daily, but pizza is served every day. *Fondamenta Misericordia 2540, tel. 041/720581. No reservations. No credit cards. Closed Wed.*

$ San Trovaso. A wide choice of Venetian dishes and pizzas, reliable house wines, and economical prix-fixe menus make this busy tavern near the Accademia Gallery a good value. *Fondamenta Priuli 1016 (Dorsoduro), tel. 041/520–3703. Reservations advised. AE, DC, MC, V. Closed Mon.*

¢ Boldrin. This cafeteria-style restaurant offers home cooking and a selection of pasta and meat dishes in a friendly atmosphere. It's near San Giovanni Crisostomo. *Salizzada San Canciano 5550, tel. 041/523–7859. No credit cards. No dinner. Closed Sun.*

¢ Sottoprova. In the Castello district, off the beaten track, this trattoria offers typical Venetian cooking and is popular with locals, especially in summer, when there are tables outdoors. The prix-fixe menu is an exceptional value. *Via Garibaldi 1698, tel. 041/520–6493. Reservations advised. AE, MC, V. Closed Tues.*

¢ Vino Vino. This is an informal annex of the upscale Antico Martini around the corner. A limited choice of reasonably priced dishes is available at mealtimes, and snacks are served throughout the day, 10 AM–1 AM. The wine list is impressive. *Calle del Cafetier 2007/A (San Fantin), tel. 041/523–7027. No reservations. AE, DC, MC, V. Closed Tues.*

Lodging

Venice is made up almost entirely of time-worn buildings, so it stands to reason that the majority of hotels are in renovated palaces. Renovations in most affordable hotels do not include the installation of elevators, so you will probably have to climb stairs. You are likely to find the rooms cramped and the furnishings simple. Inexpensive and budget hotels are essentially in the same one-star official category, the key distinction being whether you have a private bath (usually a shower) or not—doubles with bath fall into the inexpensive category, doubles without bath are budget. If you have not reserved your room, go to the AVA (Venetian Hoteliers Association) office at the train station, airport, or Piazzale Roma (*see* Arriving by Train, *above*). The main tourist season runs from mid-March through October, December 20 to New Year's Day, and the two-week Carnival period in February. Make reservations well in advance at all times, but especially for these periods.

$$ Bucintoro. This small, family-run hotel is right on the lagoon near the Arsenale, where the real *Bucintoro*, Venice's official and elaborate ceremonial boat, is kept. Every room has a water view, and rooms without private bath are a bargain. *Riva San Biagio 2135, Castello, tel. 041/522–3240, fax 041/523–5224. 28 rooms, 18 with bath. No credit cards. Closed Jan.–mid Feb.*

$$ Locanda Fiorita. This welcoming, small hotel is tucked away in a sunny little square (where breakfast is served in the summer), just off Campo Santo Stefano, near the Accademia Bridge. The rooms have beamed ceilings and are simply and unfussily furnished. *Campiello Nuovo 3457, San Marco, tel. 041/523–4754, fax 5228043. 10 rooms, 7 with shower. AE, MC, V. Closed 2 wks in Nov.–Dec.*

$$ Messner Dipendenza. Close to the Salute Church and the Guggenheim Collection, this annex of the more expensive Messner Hotel (just around the corner) is only a few minutes from Piazza San Marco by vaporetto or traghetto, yet it's in one of the most tranquil and attractive residential districts of the city. *Fondamenta di Ca' Bala', Dorsoduro 216/217, Dorsoduro, tel. 041/5227443, fax 5227266. 20 rooms, 15 with bath or shower. AE, DC, MC, V.*

$$ Riva. This pretty, recently refurbished hotel, close to San Marco, is at the junction of three canals in a picturesque spot. *Ponte dell'Angelo 5310, Castello, tel. 041/522–7034. 12 rooms, 10 with bath. No credit cards. Closed mid-Nov.–Feb. 1, except 2 wks at Christmas.*

$ Al Piave. You get clean, basic accommodations here, plus the convenience of being centrally located, near San Marco and Santa Maria Formosa. *Ruga Giuffa 4840, tel. 041/528–5174, fax 5288512. 12 rooms without bath. AE, MC, V. Closed Jan. 6–Feb. 1.*

$ Caneva. One of the larger inexpensive hotels, it has its own quiet courtyard, and rooms on one side overlook a canal. It is located between San Marco and the Rialto. *Calle Rio della Fava 5515, on calle to right of church of Fava, tel. 041/522–8118, fax 5208676. 23 rooms, 10 with bath. MC, V.*

$ Silva. This small hotel off Campo Santa Maria Formosa, close to San
★ Marco, is on a quiet canal. Low rates include breakfast; some rooms can accommodate an extra bed. *Fondamenta del Remedio 4423, tel. 041/522–7643, fax 041/528–6817. 25 rooms, 7 with bath. No credit cards. Closed mid-Nov.–beginning of Carnival.*

¢ Bernardi Semenzato. This particularly welcoming, small hotel is just
★ off Strada Nuova, and near Rialto. All the rooms in the main hotel were refurbished to a high standard in 1995, making the Bernardi a better value than ever. Prices are even lower in the nearby Annex (which includes a big room with a lovely canal view). *Calle dell'Oca 4366, Cannaregio, tel. 041/5227857, fax 031/5222424. 18 rooms, 11 with bath or shower (in main hotel); 7 rooms, 2 with bath or shower (in Annex). AE, MC, V. Closed 1st 2 wks of December.*

¢ Ca' Foscari. This is a pleasant little hotel between the university and the San Tomà landing on the Grand Canal. *Calle della Frescada 3887B, Dorsoduro, tel. and fax 041/522–5817. 10 rooms, 5 with bath or shower. No credit cards. Closed Dec.–Jan.*

¢ San Samuele. Centrally located (near Palazzo Grassi), this friendly, family-run hotel has attractive, sunny rooms. *Salizzada San Samuele 3358, San Marco, tel. 041/522–8045. 10 rooms, 2 with bath. No credit cards. Open all year.*

Hostels Foresteria Scuola Valdese. Near Campo Santa Maria Formosa and
¢ San Marco, this popular hostel is run by the Waldensian church, and offers dormitory beds for about 20,000 lire a night, including breakfast. There are also two big bedrooms, sleeping up to four, and two apartments with kitchens for up to six (for which you need to book well in advance). *Calle Lunga Santa Maria Formosa 5170, Castello,*

*tel. 041/5286797, fax 041/5286797. Telephone reservations accepted
9:30–1 and 6–8. No credit cards.*

¢ **Instituto Suore Canossiane.** This hostel, run by nuns, very close to
the main Giudecca vaporetto stop, is primarily for young women,
but older women are also accepted. It is open all day (with a 10:30 PM
curfew), and costs about 17,000 lire per night. *Ponte Piccolo 428,
Giudecca, tel. 041/5222157. No credit cards.*

¢ **Ostello (Youth Hostel).** This 273–bed hostel is on the Giudecca by the
Zitelle vaporetto stop, with a fine view of the city. Beds cost about
22,000 lire per night, including breakfast, but you have to leave the
hostel by 9:30 AM, and there's an 11:30 PM curfew. You need an IHYA
card, but this can be obtained on the spot. Bookings accepted only by
fax and letter. *Fondamenta delle Zitelle 86, Giudecca, tel. 041/
5238211, fax 5235689. No credit cards. Closed last 2 wks in Jan.*

There are several additional summer-only hostels, all listed in the
"Rolling Venice" leaflet *Dormire Giovane (Accommodations for
Young People)*, available free from the APT office (*see* Tourist Infor-
mation *in* Important Addresses and Numbers, *above*).

The Arts

For a program of events, pick up the free *Guest in Venice (Un Ospite
di Venezia)* booklet from the Assessorato al Turismo at Ca'
Giustianian (2nd Floor), Calle del Ridoto (close to Piazza San
Marco).

Concerts There are regular concerts at the Pietà Church, with an emphasis on
Vivaldi, and at San Stae and San Barnaba. Concerts are also held,
sometimes free, by visiting choirs and musicians, in other churches.
For information on these often short-notice events, ask at the APT
office and look out for posters on walls and in restaurants and shops.
The **Kele e Teo Agency** (Piazza San Marco 4930, tel. 041/520–8722)
and **Box Office** (Calle Loredan 4127, off Salizzada San Luca, tel. 041/
988369) handle tickets for many of the city's musical events.

Opera The season at **Teatro La Fenice** (Campo San Fantin, tel. 041/521–
0161, fax 041/522–1768) runs all year, except August, with an opera
in performance most months. The box office is open September to
July, Monday–Saturday 9:30–12:30 and 4–6, except when there's a
performance on Sunday, in which case the box office is open Sunday
and remains closed the following Monday. A 20% charge is levied on
all reservations made more than one week before the performance.

Nightlife

Dedicated nighthawks should get a copy of *Fuori Orario: di Notte a
Venezia e Mestre* (Out of Hours: By Night in Venice and a guide to
live music venues, discos, and late-night bars in and around Venice,
published by the Assessorato alla Gioventù, the Municipality's
Youth Department (Corte Contarini 1529, 4th Floor, near Piazza
San Marco), and available free at APT information offices (at pres-
ent, only in Italian, but with useful maps and easy-to-follow notes).
Night spots popular with young people are **Ai Canottieri**
(Fondamenta San Giobbe 690, Cannaregio, tel. 041/71548, live music
Thurs. and Sat., closed Sun. and in summer) and **Paradiso Perduto**
(Fondamenta Misericordia 2540, Cannaregio, tel. 041/720581, live
music Sun., closed Wed. and 1st ½ of Aug.).

Campania

As is to be expected in a region where extremes of wealth and poverty meet, the traveler in Campania (the region of Naples, Capri, and the Amalfi coast, among other sights) can find the level of comfort that suits his or her pocket. Between the slums of Naples and the villas of Capri, a variety of dining and accommodations options present themselves. On the whole, though, restaurants offer better value for your money than hotels. In Naples budget hotels tend to be on the sleazy side, but simple restaurants and pizzerias offer some of the best cooking available in the Italian south.

Once a cultural capital that rivaled Paris for its brillance and refinement, today's Napoli (Naples) is afflicted by acute urban decay and chronic delinquency that ranges from nefarious Mafia activities to bag-snatching perpetrated by thieves on scooters; though few visitors ever experience these directly, they cast a certain notoriety over this otherwise sunny, active city. But what really characterizes Naples—for other Italians as much as for tourists—is the combination of exuberance and cynicism in the local people, who have evolved a way of life that almost makes Naples a city foreign to Italians, with laws and customs all its own.

For those who would rather skip the stress of Naples, there are other practical bases. Transportation connections are good, and none of Campania's attractions is remote, from classical ruins by the acre to gorgeous scenery, all bathed in plenty of hot sun.

Sorrento is touristy but has some fine old hotels and beautiful views; it's a good base for a leisurely excursion to Pompeii. Capri is a pint-size paradise, though sometimes too crowded for comfort, while the Amalfi coast, which runs from Sorrento to Salerno, has some enchanting towns and spectacular scenery. A word of warning: Out-of-season travelers, who find prices considerably reduced in resorts such as Capri and the towns of the Amalfi coast, also find many establishments closed during winter.

Getting Around

By Plane There are several daily flights between Rome and Naples's Capodichino Airport (tel. 081/780–5763), 7 kilometers (4 miles) north of the downtown area. Bus 14 connects the airport with the center of town. During the summer months there's a direct helicopter service between Capodichino, Capri, and Ischia; for information, tel. 081/789–6273 or 081/584–1481.

By Train A great number of trains run between Rome and Naples every day; Intercity trains make the journey in less than two hours. The central station (tel. 081/553–3188) is at Piazza Garibaldi, but there are several smaller stations, also serving a network of suburban lines that connect the city with points of interest in Campania. The most useful line for excursions outside Naples is the **Circumvesuviana** (tel. 081/779–2444), which leaves from Piazza Garibaldi and takes in Ercolano (Herculaneum), Pompeii, and Sorrento. Other lines are the **Ferrovia Cumana** (tel. 081/551–3328) and the **Circumflegrea** (tel. 081/551–3328), both of which leave from the station in Piazza Montesanto.

By Subway The **Metropolitana** subway system can save hours of aggravation crossing the traffic-clogged city center. Be warned that service ends at around 11 PM.

By Bus Neapolitan buses and trams are unpredictable and often crowded, but they are convenient when walking becomes a chore or you need to travel between the station and the ferry-and-hydrofoil port. Useful services for this route are Nos. 1 (tram) and 150 (bus). Tickets

(1,000 lire per ride, 1,500 lire for a half day [until 2 PM or from 2 PM], or 2,500 lire for a ticket lasting the whole day) must be bought from ticket kiosks or tobacconists before boarding; punch them after you board.

Buses for the Amalfi coast leave from Naples, Salerno, and Sorrento. The trip can be unbearably slow in high season, but the cliff-hugging route is never dull. SITA buses leave Naples from Corso Arnaldo Lucci, beside the station, and from Via Pisanelli (tel. 081/552–2176), near Piazza Municipio. SITA buses from Salerno leave from Piazza Concordia, 100 meters straight out of the station, by the seafront. Tickets (5,000 lire to Sorrento, 2,400 lire to Amalfi) can be bought at the nearby office (tel. 089/791660). Departures are every hour or half hour. From Sorrento, SITA buses leave from outside the train station (hourly to Amalfi, 3,200 lire). For more detailed bus information, call the offices at Sorrento (tel. 081/878–1115) or Amalfi (tel. 089/871016).

By Boat Boats and hydrofoils for the islands, the Sorrento peninsula, and the Amalfi coast leave from the Molo Beverello, near Naples's Piazza Municipio. **Caremar** (tel. 081/551–3882), **Navigazione Libera del Golfo** (tel. 081/552–7209), and **Lauro** (tel. 081/551–3236) operate a frequent passenger and car ferry service, while hydrofoils of the **Caremar, Navigazione Libera,** and **Alilauro** (tel. 081/761–1004) lines leave from both Molo Beverello and the hydrofoil station at Mergellina pier, from which **SNAV** (tel. 081/761–2348) also operates.

Tourist Information

Capri (Marina Grande pier, tel. 081/837–0634; and Piazza Umberto I, Capri town, tel. 081/837–0686).
Naples. EPT Information Offices (Piazza dei Martiri 58, tel. 081/405311; central station, tel. 081/268779; Mergellina station, tel. 081/761–2102; and Capodichino Airport, tel. 081/780–5761). AAST Information Office (Piazza del Gesù, tel. 081/552–3328).
Sorrento (Via De Maio 35, tel. 081/807–4033).

Exploring Campania

Naples Founded by the Greeks, **Naples** became a playground of the Romans and was ruled thereafter by a succession of foreign dynasties, all of which left traces of their cultures in the city and its environs. The most splendid of these rulers were the Bourbons, who were responsible for much of what you will want to see in Naples, starting with the 17th-century **Palazzo Reale** (Royal Palace), still furnished in the lavish Baroque style that suited them so well. *Piazza del Plebiscito, tel. 081/413888. Admission: 8,000 lire. Open Apr.–Oct., Tues.–Sun. 9–7:30; Nov.–Mar., Tues.–Sun. 9–1:30.*

Across the way is the massive stone **Castel Nuovo,** which was built by the city's Aragon rulers in the 13th century. Also known as the Maschio Angioino, the impressive redoubt contains some sculptures and frescoes from the 14th and 15th centuries and an array of bronze and silver objects of limited interest. Walk up Via Toledo, also known as Via Roma. Make a detour to the right off Via Toledo to see the oddly faceted stone facade and elaborate Baroque interior of the church of the **Gesù** (Via Benedetto Croce) and, directly opposite, the church of **Santa Chiara,** built in the early 1300s in Provençal Gothic style. A favorite Neapolitan song celebrates the quiet beauty of its cloister, decorated in delicate floral tiles. *Castel Nuovo, admission: 5,000 lire. Open Mon.–Fri. 9–2, Sat. 9–1, closed Sun.*

Another detour off Via Toledo, to the left this time, takes you from **Piazza Dante** to the Montesanto funicular, which ascends to the Vomero hill, where you can see the bastions of **Castel Sant'Elmo** and visit the museum in the **Certosa di San Martino,** a Carthusian monastery restored in the 17th century. It contains an eclectic collection of

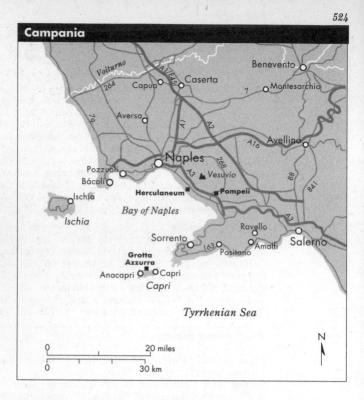

Neapolitan landscape paintings, royal carriages, and *presepi* (Christmas crèches). Check out the view from the balcony off room No. 25. *Certosa di San Martino, tel. 081/578–1769. Admission: 8,000 lire. Open Tues.–Sun. 9–2, Sun. 9–1.*

Return to Piazza Dante and follow Via Pessina (an extension of Via Toledo) to the **Museo Archeologico Nazionale.** Dusty and unkempt, the museum undergoes perpetual renovations, but it holds one of the world's great collections of antiquities. Greek and Roman sculptures, vividly colored mosaics, countless objects from Pompeii and Herculaneum, and an equestrian statue of the Roman emperor Nerva are all worth seeing. *Piazza Museo, tel. 081/440166. Admission: 12,000 lire. Open May–Sept., Mon.–Sat. 9–7, Sun. 9–1; Oct.–Apr., Mon.–Sat. 9–2, Sun. 9–1.*

About a mile north on the same road (reachable by bus), you'll come to the **Museo di Capodimonte,** housed in an 18th-century palace built by Bourbon king Charles III and surrounded by a vast park that must have been lovely when it was better cared for. In the picture gallery are some fine Renaissance paintings; climb the stairs to the terrace for a magnificent view of Naples and the bay. Downstairs you can visit the State Apartments and see the extensive collection of porcelain, much of it produced in the Bourbons' own factory right here on the grounds. *Parco di Capodimonte, tel. 081/744–1307. Admission: 12,000 lire. Open Apr.–Oct., Tues.–Sun. 9–7:30; Nov.–Mar., Tues.–Sun. 9–2.*

Herculaneum **Herculaneum** (Ercolano) lies 10 kilometers (6 miles) southeast of Naples. Reputed to have been founded by the legendary Hercules, the elite Roman resort was devastated by the same volcanic eruption that buried Pompeii in AD 79. Recent excavations have revealed that many died on the shore in an attempt to escape, as a slow-moving mud slide embalmed the entire town by covering it with an 11-meter-deep (35-foot-deep) blanket of volcanic ash and ooze. While that may have been unfortunate for Herculaneum's residents, it was fortunate for us. Herculaneum has been marvelously preserved for nearly two millennia! *Corso Ercolano, tel. 081/739–0963. Admission: 8,000 lire. Open daily 9–one hr before sunset (ticket office closes 2 hrs before sunset).*

Pompeii **Pompeii,** a larger community 12 kilometers (8 miles) farther to the east, lost even more residents. An estimated 2,000 of them perished on that fateful August day. The ancient city of Pompeii was much larger than Herculaneum, and excavations have progressed to a much greater extent (though the remains are not as well preserved, due to some 18th-century scavenging for museum-quality artworks, most of which you are able to see at Naples's Museo Archeologico Nazionale; *see above*). This prosperous Roman city had an extensive forum, lavish baths and temples, and patrician villas richly decorated with frescoes. It's worth buying a detailed guide of the site in order to give meaning and understanding to the ruins and their importance. Be sure to see the **Villa dei Misteri,** whose frescoes are in mint condition. Perhaps that is a slight exaggeration, but the paintings are so rich with detail and depth of color that one finds it difficult to believe that they are 1,900 years old. Have lots of small change handy to tip the guards at the more important houses so they will unlock the gates for you. *Pompeii Scavi, tel. 081/861–0744. Admission: 10,000 lire. Open daily 9–one hr before sunset.*

Sorrento Another 28 kilometers (18 miles) southwest is **Sorrento,** in the not-too-distant past a small, genteel resort for a fashionable elite. Now the town has spread out along the crest of its fabled cliffs. Once this was an area full of secret haunts for the few tourists who came for the beauty of this coastline, but it has now been discovered by the purveyors of package tours. In Sorrento's case, however, the change is not as grim as it sounds, since nothing can dim the delights of the marvelous climate and view of the Bay of Naples. For the best views go to the **Villa Comunale,** near the old church of **San Francesco** (in itself worth a visit), or to the terrace behind the **Museo Correale.** The museum, an attractive 18th-century villa, houses an interesting collection of decorative arts (furniture, china, and so on) and paintings of the Neapolitan school. *Via Correale. Admission: 5,000 lire; gardens only, 3,000 lire. Open Apr.–Sept., Mon. and Wed.–Sat. 9–12:30 and 4–6, Sun. 9–12:30; Oct.–Mar., Mon. and Wed.–Sat. 9–12 and 3–5, Sun. 9–12; closed Tues.*

Capri Sorrento makes a convenient jumping-off spot for a boat trip to **Capri.** No matter how many day-trippers crowd onto the island, no matter how touristy certain sections have become, Capri remains one of Italy's loveliest places. Incoming visitors disembark at Marina Grande, from which excursion boats leave for trips around the island and for the **Grotta Azzurra** (Blue Grotto). Be warned that the latter must rank as one of the country's all-time great rip-offs: Motorboat, rowboat, and grotto admissions are charged separately, and if there's a line of boats waiting, you'll have little time to enjoy the grotto's marvelous colors.

A cog railway or bus service takes you up to the town of Capri, where you can stroll through the **Piazzetta,** a choice place from which to watch the action and window-shop expensive boutiques on your way to the **Gardens of Augustus,** which have gorgeous views. The town of Capri is deliberately commercial and self-consciously picturesque. To get away from the crowds, hike to **Villa Jovis,** one of the many villas that Roman Emperor Tiberius built on the island, at the end of a lane that climbs steeply uphill. The walk takes about 45 minutes, with pretty views all the way and a final spectacular vista of the entire Bay of Naples and part of the Gulf of Salerno. *Via Tiberio. Admission: 4,000 lire. Open daily 9–one hr before sunset.*

Amalfi and Positano

From Sorrento, the coastal drive down to the resort town of Amalfi provides some of the most dramatic and beautiful scenery you'll find in all Italy. Hourly buses ply the twisting cliff-top road between Sorrento and Salerno. **Positano**'s jumble of pastel houses, topped by whitewashed cupolas, cling to the mountainside above the sea. The exhaustingly vertical town—the prettiest along this stretch of coast—attracts a sophisticated group of visitors and summer residents who find that its relaxed atmosphere more than compensates for the sheer effort of moving about its streets, most of which are stairways. This former fishing village now reaps the rewards of tourism and commercialized fashion; practically every other shop displays locally made casual wear. The beach is the town's focal point, with a little promenade and a multitude of café-restaurants.

Amalfi itself is a charming maze of covered alleys and narrow byways straggling up the steep mountainside. The piazza just below the cathedral forms the town's heart—a colorful assortment of pottery stalls, cafés, and postcard shops grouped around a venerable old fountain. The cathedral's exterior is its most impressive feature, so there's no need to climb all those stairs unless you really want to.

Ravello

Do not miss **Ravello,** 8 kilometers (5 miles) north of Amalfi, to which it's linked by an hourly bus, a 30-minute journey (board at the main bus-park on the seafront). Ravello is not actually on the coast, but on a high mountain bluff overlooking the sea. The road up to the village is a series of switchbacks, and the village itself clings precariously to the mountain spur. The village flourished during the 13th century and then fell into a tranquillity that has remained unchanged for the past six centuries. The center of the town is **Piazza Duomo,** with its cathedral, founded in 1087 and recently restored. Note its fine bronze 12th-century door and, just inside on the left, the pulpit with mosaics telling the story of Jonah and the whale. Look to the right as well and you will see another pulpit with fantastic carved animals.

To the right of the cathedral is the entrance to the 11th-century **Villa Rufolo.** The composer Richard Wagner once stayed in Ravello, and there is a Wagner festival every summer on the villa's garden terrace. There is a moorish cloister with interlacing pointed arches, beautiful gardens, an 11th-century tower, and a belvedere with a fine view of the coast. *Admission: 3,000 lire. Open summer, daily 9:30–1, 3–7:30; winter, daily 9:30–1, 2–4:30.*

Dining and Lodging

It is not hard to find good, cheap dining spots in Campania, although the smaller, trendier resorts cater to a more upscale crowd—in other words, the Amalfi coast towns and the islands make demands on your pocket. But even here, in summer especially, bargain prix-fixe menus can be found. Everywhere else, pizzerias and trattorias abound, and often the plainer they are, the better the fare.

With accommodations, the main problem is finding space in the high season, so call ahead. Most of the budget hotels in Naples and Salerno are located in the station areas; they tend to be dingy, if generally clean. In Naples, lodgings in the market zone around Piazza del Mercato south and west of the station are not recommended, although you may want to visit the area to lap up local color (hang onto your handbag!).

For details and price-category definitions, *see* Dining and Lodging *in* Staying in Italy, *above.*

Amalfi
Dining

La Caravella. Tucked away under some arches lining the coast road, the Caravella has a nondescript entrance but pleasant interior decorated in a medley of colors and paintings of old Amalfi. It's small and intimate, and proprietor Franco describes the cuisine as *"sfiziosa"* (taste tempting). Specialties include *scialatelli* (homemade pasta with shellfish sauce) and *pesce al limone* (fresh fish with lemon sauce). *Via M. Camera 12, tel. 089/871029. Reservations advised. AE, MC, V. Closed Tues. and Nov. 10–30. $$*

Lodging **Amalfi.** Up a flight of steps off the main Via Lorenzo d'Amalfi, this is one of the few inexpensive hotels in the city that stays open all year. The best features of this five-story hotel are the garden—where there are also a couple of guest rooms hidden away (Nos. 315 and 316) and the spacious roof-terrace with broad views over the town. In the summer guests are required to take half board, which will hike up the price. *Via dei Pastai 3, tel. 089/872440, fax 089/872250. 40 rooms with bath or shower. Facilities: bar, restaurant, garden. MC, V. $*

Capri **Al Grottino.** This small family-run restaurant, with a handy location
Dining near the Piazzetta, sports autographed photographs of celebrity
★ customers. House specialties are gnocchi with mozzarella and linguine *con gamberini* (with shrimp sauce). *Via Longano 27, tel. 081/837–0584. Dinner reservations advised. AE, MC, V. Closed Tues. and Nov. 3–Mar. 20. $$*

Da Gemma. One of Capri's favorite places for a homey atmosphere and a good meal, Da Gemma features *pappardelle all'aragosta* (egg noodles with lobster sauce) and fritto misto. If you're budgeting, don't order fish that you pay for by weight; it's always expensive. You can have pizza as a starter in the evening. *Via Madre Serafina 6, tel. 081/837–0461. Reservations advised. AE, DC, MC, V. Closed Mon. and Nov. $$*

La Capannina. Only a few steps away from Capri's social center, the Piazzetta, La Capannina has a delightful vine-hung courtyard for summer dining and a reputation as one of the island's best eating places. The antipasto features fried ravioli and eggplant stuffed with ricotta, and house specialties include chicken; scaloppine; and a refreshing, homemade lemon liqueur. *Via Botteghe 14, tel. 081/837–0732. Reservations advised. AE, MC, V. Closed Wed. (except during Aug.) and Nov.–mid-Mar. $$*

Lodging **La Tosca.** The Tosca is a tranquil haven from Capri's bustle and hard sell, a 10-minute walk from the center of town but only 20 minutes from the beach at Marina Piccola. The shady garden setting is pleasant, and all rooms are bright and airy—to enjoy the sea views, choose one with an attached bathroom. Book ahead for high season. *Via Birago, tel. 081/837–0989. 10 rooms, 6 with shower. No credit cards. Closed Jan. and Feb. $*

Stella Maris. In the heart of Capri town (right opposite the bus terminal), the Stella Maris is a good place for a day or two. The price you pay for the central location is a certain amount of noise and cramped rooms, though it's clean enough. Vacancies are limited in July and August. *Via Roma 27, tel. 081/837–0452, fax 081/378662. 10 rooms with bath. Facilities: bar. AE, V. $*

Villa Eva. A couple of kilometers outside Anacapri, Villa Eva is convenient to the beach and the Blue Grotto. Its large garden makes it ideal for families, which are welcomed by the friendly couple who run the place. Each bedroom is refreshingly different, and much of the solid rustic furniture was built by the artist-proprietor. It's open year-round—come in winter and you'll find fire on the hearth. To get here, take the Blue Grotto bus from Anacapri, or phone ahead to be picked up. *Via La Fabbrica 8, Anacapri, tel. and fax 081/837–2040. 10 rooms, 8 with bath or shower. No credit cards. ¢*

Naples **Ciro a Santa Brigida.** Centrally located off Via Toledo near the Cas-
Dining tel Nuovo, this no-frills place is a favorite with businesspeople, art-
★ ists, and journalists. Tables are arranged on two levels, and the decor is classic trattoria. This is the place to try traditional Neapolitan *sartù di riso* (a rich rice dish with meat and peas) and *melanzane* (eggplant) *alla parmigiana* or *scaloppe alla Ciro*, with prosciutto and mozzarella. There's pizza, too. *Via Santa Brigida 71, tel. 081/*

552–4072. Reservations advised. AE, DC, MC, V. Closed Sun. and 2 wks in Aug. $$

La Bersagliera. This restaurant has been making tourists happy for years, with a great location on the Santa Lucia waterfront, cheerful waiters, mandolin music, and good spaghetti *alla disgraziata* (with tomatoes, capers, and black olives) and mozzarella *in carrozza* (fried in batter). *Borgo Marinaro 10, tel. 081/764–6016. Reservations advised. AE, DC, MC, V. Closed Tues. $$*

Brandi. Where better to sample a pizza than at Brandi's, where a plaque on the wall commemorates the invention here, in 1889, of the famous pizza Margherita, named in honor of Queen Margherita di Savoia. Although Brandi offers a range of toppings, it would be a shame to miss the authentic article, the plain mozzarella-and-tomato pizza Margherita, to find out how it should be done. Popular with Neapolitans, Brandi also offers a more expensive, three-course menu. *Salita Sant'Anna di Palazzo 1, off Via Chiaia, tel. 081/416928. Reservations advised on weekends. Closed Mon. AE, DC, MC, V. ¢*

Lodging **San Pietro.** Just off Corso Umberto, at the Piazza Garibaldi end, the San Pietro is comfortable if rather gloomy. It's clean enough and convenient to the station and the market area. The rooms are old-fashioned, but the hotel's size ensures you will almost always find space here. *Via San Pietro ad Aram 18, tel. 081/286040, fax 081/553–5914. 54 rooms, 20 with bath or shower. Facilities: bar. AE, DC, MC, V. $*

Casanova. One of a wide selection of cheap hotels around Piazza Garibaldi and convenient to the station, the Casanova is cleaner than most in the area and has a relaxed and friendly management. The rooms are small and spartan but quiet, a big plus in Naples. The house dog, Zeus, enjoys a certain fame among the traveling community. *Via Venezia 2, tel. 081/268287, fax 081/554–3768. 18 rooms with bath. AE, DC, MC, V. ¢*

Ostello Mergellina. Inconvenient for the center, but by the same reckoning well out of the chaos of downtown Naples, this youth hostel is a good choice for those who want a guaranteed standard of cleanliness at a minimum cost. It is situated just behind Mergellina station, thus handy for the hydrofoil port. From Piazza Garibaldi, take the subway to Mergellina or jump on a 150 or 152 bus, or Trams 1 or 2. Single-sex dormitories accommodate a maximum of six people. The usual hostel restrictions apply: no admittance during the daytime and an 11:30 curfew. In high season there's sometimes a three-day maximum stay. Non-YH members can stay for an additional fee. *Salita della Grotta 23, tel. 081/761–2346, fax 081/761–2391. 200 beds. Facilities: restaurant. No credit cards. ¢*

Positano **Capurale.** Among all the popular restaurants on the beach prome-
Dining nade, Capurale (just around the corner) has the best food and lowest prices. Tables are set under vines on a breezy sidewalk in the summer, upstairs and indoors in winter. Spaghetti con melanzane and crepes *al formaggio* (cheese-filled) are good choices here. *Via Regina Giovanna 12, tel. 089/875374. Reservations advised for outdoor tables. AE, DC, MC, V. Closed Tues. (Nov.–Mar.). $$*

Lodging **Casa Guadagno.** Once you've found the Casa Guadagno, buried within Positano's steep network of stairs and alleys, you appreciate its advantages. The view from its terrace restaurant is one, its proximity to the beach, another (five minutes down, longer on the way back up!). It's small, but the rooms are adequately furnished, some with a balcony and all with a view. *Via Fornillo 22, tel. and fax 089/875042. 10 rooms, all with bath or shower. AE, DC, MC, V. $*

Italia. This tiny pensione is more a private house, really—but the vista from its windows and balconies keeps you from feeling cramped. The rooms are small, but there's a large *salone* overgrown with plants and flowers framing the view. Signora Durso, who runs the place, fusses over her guests, whom she provides with an indoor cooking area. *Via Pasitea 137, tel. 089/875024. 5 rooms with bath or shower. No credit cards. $*

Santa Caterina. There is more to this newly refurbished hotel than meets the eye. The rooms descend the steep slope on three levels, and each has a generous balcony or terrace that makes the most of the exquisite view of the town and seashore. On street level (the top floor) is an excellent fish restaurant, a favorite with locals. The beach is quite a hike—but that's Positano. *Via Pasitea 113, tel. 089/ 875019. 10 rooms with bath or shower. Facilities: bar, restaurant. AE, DC, MC, V. Closed Nov.–Mar. $*

Ravello
Lodging

Villa Amore. This family-run pensione, a 10-minute walk from the main Piazza Vescovado, is tidy and comfortable, and most rooms have exhilarating views. There's a garden and an air of utter tranquility, particularly at dusk, when the valley is tinged purple by glorious sunsets. The furnishings are modest but modern. Full board is available and may be required in summer. Book ahead if possible. *Via Santa Chiara, tel. 089/857135. 12 rooms with bath or shower. Facilities: bar, restaurant, garden. MC, V. $–$$*

Sorrento
Dining

Antica Trattoria. This is a homey, hospitable place with a garden for summer dining. The specialties of the house are a classic *pennette al profumo di bosco* (pasta with a creamy mushroom and ham sauce), fish (which can be expensive), and *gamberetti freschi Antica Trattoria* (prawns in a tomato sauce). *Via Giuliani 33, tel. 081/807– 1082. Dinner reservations advised. No credit cards. Closed Mon., Jan. 10–Feb. 10. $$*

La Belle Époque. Occupying a 19th-century villa perched on the edge of the vine-covered gorge of the Mulini, this is an elegant veranda restaurant. Try the *scialatelli Belle Époque* (homemade pasta with mozzarella and eggplant). *Via Fuorimura 7, tel. 081/ 878–1216. Reservations advised. AE, DC, MC, V. Closed Mon. $$*

★ **Parrucchiano.** One of the town's best and oldest, Parrucchiano features greenhouse-style dining rooms dripping with vines and dotted with plants. Among the antipasti, try the *panzarotti* (pastry crust filled with mozzarella and tomato) and for a main course, the *scalloppe alla sorrentina*, again with mozzarella and tomato. *Corso Italia 71, tel. 081/878–1321. Reservations advised. MC, V. Closed Wed. Nov.–May. $$*

Lodging

Eden. Eden occupies a fairly quiet but central location, with a garden and a pool. The bedrooms are bright but undistinguished; the lounge and lobby have more character. It's an unpretentious but friendly hotel, with some smaller rooms in the $ category. *Via Correale 25, tel. 081/878–1909, fax 081/807–2016. 60 rooms with bath. AE, MC, V. Closed Nov.–Feb. $$*

City. The central location and excellent value are the best reasons to stay in this small hostelry close to the bus and train stations. There is a bookshop and café downstairs, and the husband-and-wife team that manages the hotel is always ready with information and advice. *Corso Italia 221, tel. 081/877–2210, fax 081/877–2210. 13 rooms with shower. AE, MC, V. $*

Linda. With the City, this pensione is the only budget accommodation open all year. Bland but clean, it's just above the bus and railway station. *Via degli Aranci 125, tel. 081/878–2916. 13 rooms, 10 with shower. No credit cards. ¢*

16 Luxembourg

L uxembourg is going through the greatest period of prosperity
in its 1,000-plus-year history. But the budget traveler can find
a great deal of history, atmosphere, and good country cooking
despite the cosmopolitan metamorphosis taking place all around,
and the best Luxembourg has to offer can be easily attained on foot
by focusing on the capital, Luxembourg City.

One of the smallest countries in the United Nations, Luxembourg
measures only 2,587 square kilometers (999 square miles), less than
the size of Rhode Island. It is dwarfed by its neighbors—Germany,
Belgium, and France—yet from its history of invasion, occupation,
and siege, you might think those square miles were built over solid
gold. In fact, it was Luxembourg's very defenses against centuries
of attack that rendered it all the more desirable: From AD 963, when
Siegfried founded a castle on the high promontory of the Bock, the
once-grander duchy encased itself in layer upon layer of fortifications until by the mid-19th century, its very invulnerability was considered a threat to those not commanding its thick stone walls. After
successive invasions by Burgundians, the Spanish, the French, the
Austrians, the French again, the Dutch, and the Prussians, Luxembourg was ultimately dismantled in the name of peace, its neutrality
guaranteed by the 1867 Treaty of London, its function reduced to
that of a buffer zone. What remains of its walls, while impressive, is
only a reminder of what was one of the strongholds of Europe—the
"Gibraltar of the North."

Nowadays Luxembourg is besieged again, this time by bankers and
Eurocrats. The capital's boulevard Royal bristles with international
banks—enough to rival Switzerland—and just outside the old city,
a new colony has been seeded, populated by *fonctionnaires* for the
European Union, the heir to the Common Market. Fiercely protect-
ing its share of the expanding bureaucracy from competitive co-capi-
tals Strasbourg and Brussels, Luxembourg digs its heels in once
again, vying not only for political autonomy but for its newfound
prosperity and clout. In this it will be helped by the new president of
the union's powerful European Commission, Jacques Santer, who
was prime minister of Luxembourg for a decade. Thus the national

Luxembourg

motto takes on new meaning: *Mir wëlle bleiwe wat mir sin*, or "We want to stay what we are"—nowadays, a viable Grand Duchy in the heart of modern Europe.

Essential Information

Before You Go

When to Go   The main tourist season in Luxembourg is the same as in Belgium—early May to late September, with spring and fall being the nicest times. But temperatures in Luxembourg tend to be cooler than those in Belgium, particularly in the hilly north, where there is frequently snow in winter.

Climate   In general, temperatures in Luxembourg are moderate. It does drizzle frequently, however, so be sure to bring a raincoat.

The following are the average daily maximum and minimum temperatures for Luxembourg.

Jan.	37F	3C	May	65F	18C	Sept.	66F	19C
	29	– 1		46	8		50	10
Feb.	40F	4C	June	70F	21C	Oct.	56F	13C
	31	– 1		52	11		43	6
Mar.	49F	10C	July	73F	23C	Nov.	44F	7C
	35	1		55	13		37	3
Apr.	57F	14C	Aug.	71F	22C	Dec.	39F	4C
	40	4		54	12		32	0

Currency   In Luxembourg, as in Belgium, the unit of currency is the franc (abbreviated *Flux*). Luxembourg issues its own currency in bills of 100, 500, and 1,000 francs and coins of 1, 5, 20, and 50 francs. Belgian currency can be used freely in Luxembourg, and the two currencies have exactly the same value. However, Luxembourg currency is not valid in Belgium. At press time (summer 1995), the exchange rate was Flux 32 to the U.S. dollar, and Flux 45 to the pound sterling.

What It Will Cost Luxembourg is a developed and sophisticated country with a high standard and cost of living. Luxembourg City is an international banking center, and a number of European institutions are based there, a fact that tends to push prices slightly higher in the capital than in the countryside.

Sample Prices Cup of coffee, Flux 50; glass of beer, Flux 40–Flux 60; movie ticket, Flux 170–Flux 200; 3-mile taxi ride, Flux 600.

Customs on Arrival For information on customs regulations, *see* Essential Information *in* Chapter 3, Belgium.

Language Native Luxembourgers speak three languages fluently: Luxembourgish, German, and French. Many also speak English.

Staying in Luxembourg

Telephones You can find public phones both on the street and in city post offices.
Local Calls A local call costs about Flux 5 per three-minute period. (slightly more from restaurants and gas stations).

International Calls The cheapest way to make an international call is to dial direct from a public phone; in a post office, you may be required to make a deposit before the call. For operator-assisted calls, dial 0010. To reach an **AT&T** long-distance operator, dial 0800–0111; for *MCI*, dial 0800–0112; for **Sprint**, dial 0800–0115.

Country Code The country code for Luxembourg is 352.

Mail Airmail postcards and letters to the United States weighing less
Postal Rates than 20 grams cost Flux 22. Letters and postcards to the United Kingdom cost Flux 14.

Receiving Mail Holders of American Express cards or traveler's checks can have mail sent in care of American Express (34 av. de la Porte-Neuve, 2227 Luxembourg City).

Shopping Purchases of goods for export may qualify for a sales tax (VAT) re-
Sales Tax fund of 12%. Ask the shop to fill out a refund form. You must then
Refunds have the form stamped by customs officers on leaving either Luxembourg, Belgium, or Holland.

Opening and Closing Times **Banks** generally are open weekdays 8:30–noon and 1:30–4:30, though more and more remain open through the lunch hour.

Museums. Opening hours vary, so check individual listings. Many close on Monday, and most also close for lunch between noon and 2.

Shops. Large city department stores and shops are generally open weekdays, except Monday morning, and Saturday 9–noon and 2–6. A few small family businesses are open Sunday morning from 8 to noon.

National Holidays In 1996: January 1; February 19, 20 (Carnival); April 8 (Easter Monday); May 1 (Labor Day); May 16 (Ascension); May 27 (Pentecost Monday); June 23 (National Day); August 15 (Assumption Day); November 1 (All Saints' Day); November 2 (All Souls' Day); December 25, 26. Changing holidays in 1997: February 10 (Shrove Monday); March 31 (Easter Monday); May 8 (Ascension); May 19 (Pentecost Monday).

Dining Restaurants in Luxembourg offer their best deals at lunch, when you can find a plat du jour (one-course special) or *menu* (two or three courses) at bargain rates. Pizzerias offer an excellent and popular source of cheap food, with pasta, risotti, and wood-oven pizzas making a full meal. Light lunches—easy on the stomach if not always the wallet—can be found in chic pastry shops, where you point to the dishes in the display case (a slice of pâté *en croute*, an egg salad, a few small casseroles to be heated), then take your number to the *salon de consommation*, where your drink order will be taken and your meal served.

Mealtimes Most hotels serve breakfast until 10. Lunch hours are noon–2, sometimes extending until 3. Long accustomed to the Continental style of dining heavily at midday, business-conscious Luxembourgers now eat their main meal in the evening between 7 and 10.

Ratings Prices quoted here are per person and include a first course, main course, and dessert, but not wine. Best bets are indicated by a star ★.

Category	Cost
$$	Flux 750–Flux 1,500
$	Flux 450–Flux 750
¢	under Flux 450

Lodging
Hotels Most hotels in the capital are relatively modern and vary from the international style, mainly near the airport, to family-run establishments in town. As Luxembourg City is an important business center, many of its hotels offer reduced rates on weekends, particularly out of season.

Youth Hostels Inexpensive youth hostels are plentiful in Luxembourg. They are often set in ancient fortresses and castles. For information, contact **Centrale des Auberges de Jeunesse** (18 pl. d'Armes, L-1136, Luxembourg, tel. 225588).

Camping The Grand Duchy is probably the best-organized country in Europe for camping. It offers some 120 sites, all with full amenities and most with scenic views. Listings are published annually by the national tourist office (*see* Important Addresses and Numbers *in* Luxembourg City, *below*).

Ratings Price categories are determined by the cost of a double room (Continental breakfast is sometimes included in the room price). Best bets are indicated by a star ★.

Category	Cost
$$	Flux 2,500–Flux 4,500
$	Flux 1,700–Flux 2,500
¢	under Flux 1,700

Tipping In Luxembourg hotels and restaurants, taxes and service charges are included in the overall bill and it is not necessary to leave more. If you wish to, round off the sum to the nearest Flux 50 or Flux 100. Bellhops and doormen should receive between Flux 50 and Flux 100, depending on the grade of the hotel. At the movies, tip the usher Flux 20 if you are seated personally. In theaters, tip about Flux 20 for checking your coat, and the same to the program seller. In public washrooms, the attendant will usually expect Flux 10. Taxi drivers expect a tip; add about 15% to the amount on the meter.

Luxembourg City

Arriving and Departing

By Plane All international flights arrive at Luxembourg's Findel Airport, 6 kilometers (4 miles) from the city.

Between the Bus 9 leaves the airport at regular intervals for the bus depot, which
Airport and is next to the railway station. It stops in the city center en route.
Downtown Individual tickets cost Flux 35. A taxi will cost you Flux 700–Flux 800.

Getting Around

One of the best transportation options in Luxembourg is the **Oeko-Carnet**, a block of five one-day tickets good for unlimited transportation on trains and buses throughout the country. Cards are on sale, for Flux 540, at Gare Centrale (the main train station) in Luxembourg City, or at Aldringen Center, located underground in front of the central post office.

By Bus Luxembourg City has a highly efficient bus service. The blue-and-yellow buses outside the city train station will take you all around the city and to some of the outlying areas. Get details about services at the information counter in the station arrivals hall. Fares are low, but the best bet is to buy a 10-ride ticket (Flux 270), available from banks or from the bus station in the Aldringen Center. Other buses, connecting Luxembourg City with towns throughout the country, leave from Gare Centrale.

By Train Luxembourg is served by frequent direct trains from Paris and Brussels. From Paris, travel time is about four hours; from Brussels, just under three hours. From Amsterdam, the journey is via Brussels and takes about six hours. There are connections from most German cities via Koblenz. Outside Luxembourg City, three major train routes extend north, south, and east into the Moselle Valley. For all train information, phone 492424. All service is from Gare Centrale.

By Bicycle Bicycling is a popular sport in Luxembourg, and it is an excellent way to see the city and outlying regions. A brochure entitled "Cycling Tracks" is available from the Luxembourg National Tourist Office, Box 1001, L-1010 Luxembourg. Bikes can be rented in Luxembourg City at **Luxembourg DELTA** (8 Bisserwee, 4796–2383), from March 30 through October 31; in Reisdorf, Diekirch, and Echternach, rent bikes at the tourist office (**Syndicat d'Initiative**). Maps are available from local tourist offices.

Important Addresses and Numbers

Tourist The main **Luxembourg National Tourist Office (ONT)** in Luxem-
Information bourg City (Aerogare [Air Terminal] bus depot, place de la Gare, tel. 481199) is open daily (except Sun. Nov.–Mar.) 9–noon and 2–6:30 (July–mid-Sept., 9–7). The **Luxembourg City Tourist Office** (pl. d'Armes, tel. 222809) is open mid-September–mid-June, Monday–Saturday 9–1 and 2–6; mid-June–mid-September, weekdays 9–7, Saturday 9–1 and 2–7, Sunday 10–noon and 2–6.

Embassies U.S. (22 blvd. Emmanuel Servais, tel. 460123). U.K. (14 blvd. F. D. Roosevelt, tel. 229864). The Brussels embassy (av. de Tervuren 2, 1040 Brussels, tel. 00322/7410611) covers Luxembourg.

Emergencies Police (tel. 113). **Ambulance, Doctor, Dentist** (tel. 112). **Pharmacies** in Luxembourg stay open nights on a rotation system. Signs listing late-night facilities are posted outside each pharmacy.

Exploring Luxembourg City

Numbers in the margin correspond to points of interest on the Luxembourg City map.

This walk takes in the ancient fortifications and Old Town, with its cobbled streets and inviting public squares. In 1994 the United Nations Educational, Scientific, and Cultural Organization (UNESCO) declared these areas part of the world's architectural heritage.

❶ Start on the **Passerelle,** a 19th-century road bridge that links the station with the valley of the Pétrusse. The Pétrusse is more of a brook than a river and is now contained by concrete, but the valley has become a singularly beautiful park. From here you'll see the rocky ledges—partly natural, partly man-made—on which the city is perched.

At the cathedral end of the Passerelle, on the right, is the
❷ **Monument de la Solidarité Nationale** (National Monument to Luxembourg Unity). It was erected in 1971 to commemorate Luxembourg's sacrifices during World War II.

Follow the road along the remains of the old city fortifications,
❸ known as the **Citadelle du St-Esprit** (Citadel of the Holy Spirit). This 17th-century citadel was built by Vauban, the French military engineer, on the site of a former monastery. Ahead of you are the three spires of the cathedral.

Retrace your steps along the old city fortifications, cross boulevard
❹ F. D. Roosevelt, and continue on to the **place de la Constitution,** marked by the war memorial, the striking gilt *Gëlle Fra,* or Golden Woman. Here you'll find the entrance to the **Pétrusse Casemates,** ancient military tunnels carved into the bedrock. During the many phases of the fortress's construction, the rock itself was hollowed out to form a honeycomb of passages running for nearly 24 kilometers (15 miles) below the town. These were used both for storage and as a place of refuge when the city was under attack. Two sections of the passages are open to the public. These sections contain former barracks, cavernous abattoirs, bakeries, and a deep well. *Admission: Flux 50 adults, Flux 30 children. Open July–Sept.*

Take rue de l'Ancien Athénée alongside the former Jesuit college, now the National Library. In rue Notre-Dame, to your right, is the
❺ main entrance to the **Cathédrale Notre-Dame,** with its Baroque organ gallery and crypt containing the tomb of John the Blind, the 14th century king of Bohemia and count of Luxembourg. The roof of the main tower was rebuilt after a fire in 1985. *Open Easter–Oct., weekdays 10–5, Sat. 8–6, Sun. 10–6; Nov.–Easter, weekdays 10–11:30 and 2–5, Sat. 8–11:30 and 2–5, Sun. 10–5.*

Just east of the cathedral, past the handsome place Clairefontaine,
❻ you arrive at the new **Musée d'Histoire de la Ville de Luxembourg** (Luxembourg City Historical Museum), which opened in 1995. This interactive multimedia museum traces the development of the city over a thousand years and is partially underground, with the lowest five levels showing the town's preserved ancient stonework. A glass-wall elevator gives a wonderful view of the ravine from the upper floors. *38 rue du Marché-aux-Herbes. Open Tues.-Sun. 10–6 (Thurs. until 8). Admission and tel. not available at press time.*

A couple of blocks northwest via the rue du Fossé is place Guillaume, known locally as the Knuedler, a name derived from the girdle worn by Franciscan monks who once had a monastery on the site. On market days (Wednesday and Saturday mornings) the square is noisy and colorful.

The lively place d'Armes, with its cafés and restaurants, lies just beyond the place Guillaume. Open-air concerts are held every evening

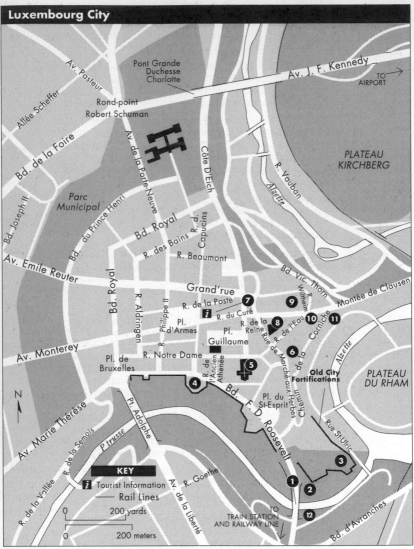

Luxembourg City

Pont Grande
Duchesse
Charlotte

Av. J. F. Kennedy

TO
AIRPORT

Av. Pasteur

Allée Scheffer

Rond-point
Robert Schuman

PLATEAU
KIRCHBERG

Bd. de la Foire

Av. de la Porte Neuve

Côte D'Eich

R. Vauban

Alzette

Bd. Joseph II

Parc
Municipal

Bd. du Prince Henri

Bd. Royal

R. d. Capucins

R. des Bains

R. Beaumont

Bd. Vic. Thorn

Montée de Clausen

Av. Emile Reuter

Bd. Royal

Grand'rue

R. de la Poste

7

9

Wilhelm

Corniche

R. Aldringen

Philippe II

R. du Curé

Pl.
d'Armes

R. de la
Reine

8

10

11

Av. Monterey

R. Notre Dame

Pl.
Guillaume

R. de l'Eau

Alzette

PLATEAU
DU RHAM

Pl. de
Bruxelles

R. de
l'Ancien
Athénée

5

6

Rue du Marché-aux-Herbes

Old City
Fortifications

4

Bd. F. D. Roosevelt

Pl. du
St-Esprit

Rue St-Ulric

Av. Marie Thérèse

Pl. Adolphe

P trusse

R. de la Semois

KEY

3

R. de la Vallée

Av. R. Goethe

1

2

TO
TRAIN STATION
AND RAILWAY LINE

12

Bd. d'Avranches

Av. de la Liberté

i Tourist Information

— Rail Lines

0   200 yards

0   200 meters

N

in summer. The town tourist office is located on the square, and on **(7)** rue du Curé there is a small museum that houses the **Maquette,** a model of the fortress at various stages of its construction: It provides a fascinating glimpse of the historical city. *Admission: Flux 40 adults, Flux 20 children. Open July–Aug. only, 10–12:30 and 2–6.*

(8) From place Guillaume, rue de la Reine leads to the **Grand Ducal Palace,** dating from the 16th century. Its elaborate macramé friezes display a Spanish-Moorish influence.

(9) On the left is the **Musée National** (National Museum), set in an attractive row of 16th-century houses. The collections shed light on daily life in this part of the world in Gallo-Roman and Frankish times. In the modern art collection, the major discovery for a visitor is the work of expressionist Joseph Kutter, probably Luxembourg's greatest artist. The museum also hosts the spectacular Bentinck-Thyssen collection of 15th- to 19th-century art, including works by Brueghel, Rembrandt, Canaletto, and other masters. *Admission free. Open Tues.–Fri. 10–4:45, Sat. 2–5:45, Sun. 10–11:45 and 2–5:45.*

(10) At the bottom of rue Wiltheim is the gate of the **Trois Tours** (Three Towers), the oldest of which was built around 1050. From here you can clearly see the source of Luxembourg's strength as a fortress.

(11) Facing the valley, to your right is the **Bock** promontory, the site of the earliest castle (AD 963) and always the duchy's most fortified point. From the Bock, steep cliffs plunge downward to the Alzette Valley. The Bock also has a series of passages similar to the Pétrusse Casemates. *Admission: Flux 50 adults, Flux 30 children. Open Mar.–Oct., daily 10–5.*

At the newly paved place du St-Esprit, take the elevator down to the Grund and turn right into the green Pétrusse Valley park. On **(12)** the left, the little **chapel of St-Quirin** is built into the rock near the Passerelle; the cave is known to have contained a chapel since the 4th century. At Pont Adolphe, walk back up to city level and you are suddenly face-to-face with the 20th century. The boulevard Royal, once the main moat of the fortress, is now Luxembourg's Wall Street, packed with the famous names of the international banking scene.

A longer walk takes you up the avenue de la Porte-Neuve to Rond-point Robert Schuman; turn right and cross the Pont Grande Duchesse Charlotte (with stunning views of the valley) to **Plateau Kirchberg,** a moonscape of modern architecture housing the European Court of Justice and various branches of the European Union. The most prominent structure—at 23 stories, Luxembourg's only skyscraper—is home to the secretariat of the European Parliament. The plateau is increasingly adorned with modern art and architecture. Works by Henry Moore and Lucien Wercollier stand outside the Court of Justice; there's a sculpture by Frank Stella in front of Frank Meier's Hypo Bank on rue Alphonse Weicker. German architect Gottfried Boehm's Deutsche Bank building on boulevard Konrad Adenauer surrounds a vast atrium, generally the site of modern art exhibitions.

Shopping

Luxembourg chocolates, called *knippercher*, are popular purchases, available from the best pastry shops. The Grand Duchy's most famous product is Villeroy and Boch porcelain, available in most gift shops here. Feast your eyes at the glossy main shop, located at 2 rue du Fossé, then buy—at a 20% discount—at the excellent second-quality factory outlet (330 rue Rollingergrund); the outlet will not ship, so weigh your purchases carefully.

Dining

French *cuisine bourgeoise*—steak, pork chops, veal with mushrooms, all served in generous portions, with heaps of *frites* (french fries) on the side—dominates local menus. Yet this tiny country has its own earthy specialties, fresh off the farm: *judd mat gardebounen* (salt pork with fava beans); *Eslecker ham* or *jambon d'Ardennes* (pearly-pink raw-smoked ham served cold with pickled onions); *choucroute* (sauerkraut); *treipen* (blood sausage); and batter-fried *merlan* (whiting). A few restaurants still feature them, though nowadays you're as likely to find Chinese, Thai, Japanese, Indian, and—leading the ethnic selection by several laps—Italian.

For details and price-category definitions, *see* Dining *in* Staying in Luxembourg, *above*.

$$ Ancre d'Or. ★ This tidy, friendly brasserie, just off the place Guillaume, serves a wide variety of old-time Luxembourgish specialties, as well as good cuisine bourgeoise. Try the judd mat gardebounen, kuddelfleck (breaded tripe), or rich blood sausages served with red cabbage and applesauce. The apple tart (Luxembourgish style, with custard base) is homemade. Portions are generous, service friendly, and the clientele local. *23 rue du Fossé, tel. 472973. Reservations advised at lunch. MC, V. Closed Sun.*

$$ Times. ★ On a pedestrian-only street of art galleries and boutiques, Times offers excellent value for the money. The narrow dining room, lined with glass and Canadian cherrywood, attracts artists and journalists. The cuisine is French with a Luxembourg accent, featuring ambitious creations like fillet of suckling pig cooked with tea, and five variations on the carpaccio theme. *8 rue Louvigny, tel. 222722. Reservations advised. AE, DC, MC, V. Closed Sun.*

$ Ems. Directly across the street from the train station, this lively establishment with vinyl booths and posted specials draws a loyal clientele for its vast portions of *moules* (mussels) in a rich wine-and-garlic broth, accompanied by frites and a bottle of sharp, cold Auxerrois or Rivaner (local white wines). For dessert, try one of the huge ice cream specialties. Food is served until 1 AM. *30 pl. de la Gare, tel. 487799. AE, DC, MC, V.*

$ Mousel's Cantine. ★ Directly adjoining the great Mousel brewery (there are beer taps that feed from tanks within), this fresh, comfortable café serves up heaping platters of local specialties—braised and grilled ham, sausage, sauerkraut, and fried potatoes—to be washed down with crockery steins of creamy *gezwickelte béier* (unfiltered beer). The front café is brighter, with sanded tabletops, but the tiny fluorescent-lit dining room has windows into the brewery. *46 montée de Clausen, tel. 470198. Reservations advised. MC, V. Closed Sun.*

¢ Taverne Bit. With sanded tabletops and dark-wood banquettes, this is a cozy and very local pub, where you can drink a *clensch* (stein) of draft Bitburger beer (from just across the German border) and have a plate of sausage with good potato salad; a plate of cold ham; or *kachkes*, the pungent local cheese spread, served with baked potatoes. *43 allée Scheffer, just off the Parking Glacis, tel. 460751. No credit cards. Closed Sat. PM, Sun.*

Lodging

Hotels in Luxembourg City are located in three main areas: the town center, the station area, and the area close to the airport. By far the largest number are around the station.

For details and price-category definitions, *see* Dining *in* Staying in Luxembourg, *above*.

$$ Arcotel, This airtight hotel, on he busy shopping street between the train station and the Old Town, provides a quiet haven. Decorated in shades of beige and rose, it offers extra comforts, such as hair dryers in the bathroom and drinks in the Bokhara-lined lounge, to make up for small rooms. The reception area is one flight up. *43 av. de la Gare, L-1611, tel.494001, fax 405624. 30 rooms with bath. Facilities: lobby lounge, breakfast room. AE, DC, MC, V.*

$$ Auberge du Coin. ★ At the edge of a quiet, dignified residential area but within easy reach of the station and the Old Town, this pleasant hotel was completely renovated in 1989 in pure "new Luxembourg" style—stone and terra-cotta floors, wood-framed double windows, polished oak, Oriental rugs, and tropical plants. The rooms are freshly furnished in bright knotty pine with new tile baths. There's a lovely French restaurant and a comfortable oak-and-stone bar as well. The nine-room matching annex down the street, which has no elevator, costs slightly less. *2 blvd. de la Pétrusse, L-2320, tel. 402101, fax 403666. 23 rooms with bath. Facilities: restaurant, bar. AE, DC, MC, V.*

$$ Italia. ★ This is a valuable and remarkably inexpensive find: a former private apartment converted into hotel rooms, some with plaster details and cabinetry left behind. The rooms are solid and freshly furnished, all with private tiled bathrooms. The somewhat-pricey restaurant downstairs is one of the city's better Italian eateries. *15–17 rue d'Anvers, L-1130, tel. 486626, fax 480807. 20 rooms with bath. Facilities: restaurant, bar, garden. AE, DC, MC, V.*

$$ Sieweburen. At the northwestern end of the city, this attractively rustic hotel dates from 1991; the clean, large rooms are furnished with wooden beds and armoires. There are woods in the back and a playground in front. The brasserie-style tavern, older than the rest of the property, is hugely popular, especially when the terrace is open. *36 rue des Septfontaines, tel. 442356, fax 442353. 13 rooms with bath. Facilities: restaurant, playground, parking. AE, DC, MC, V.*

$ Bristol. Though on a street near the train station that is lined with strip joints and flophouses (as well as legitimate shops and restaurants), this modest hotel offers comfortable, secure lodging and fresh decor. The lobby-bar is warm and familial, and the baths are newly refurbished. A few bathless rooms on the first and fourth floors go for bargain rates. *11 rue de Strasbourg, L-2561, tel. 485830, fax 486480. 30 rooms, 22 with shower/toilet. Facilities: bar for guests only. AE, DC, MC, V.*

¢ Auberge de Jeunesse Mansfeld. This youth hostel looks like a U.S. campus dorm, complete with rock music piped into the halls. It's a better choice than some of the more dubious hotels in the railway station area. There are three double rooms; others sleep four, six, or 20 dormitory style. New showers have been added on each floor. Breakfast is included in the room price, but sheets must be rented at Flux 120. *2 rue du Fort Olisy, tel. 226889, fax 223360. 312 beds. Facilities: restaurant, bar. MC, V.*

¢ Carlton. ★ In this vast 1918 hotel, buffered from the rue de Strasbourg scene by a rank of stores and opening onto a quiet inner court, budget travelers will find roomy, quiet quarters. The beveled glass, oak parquet, and terrazzo floors are original—but so are the toilets, all located down the hall. Each room has antique beds, floral-print comforters, and a sink; wood floors, despite creaks, are white-glove clean. *9 rue de Strasbourg, L-2561, tel. 484802, fax 486480. 50 rooms without toilet, 8 with shower. Facilities: breakfast room, bar. No credit cards.*

¢ Dauphin. Another budget option, this modern hotel offers plain, clean rooms with splashy '60s decor—daisy prints, linoleum—and private baths. Back rooms avoid heavy street noise. *42 av. de la Gare, tel 428282, fax 489661. 36 rooms with bath. Facilities: breakfast room. AE, DC, MC, V.*

17 Malta

For years, travelers to Malta and its two sister islands, Gozo and Comino, have enjoyed uncrowded and moderately priced seaside hotels and colorful taverns. The sunny climate finds many tourists spread out across the islands' golden sandy beaches, and the festive and hospitable residents happily welcome tourists.

For those interested in history and archaeology, tiny Malta—with only 28 kilometers (17 miles) between its two farthest points—displays the remains of a long and eventful history. Among the most fascinating ruins are Neolithic temples and stone megaliths left by prehistoric inhabitants. In AD 60, St. Paul, shipwrecked here, converted the people to Christianity. Other less welcome visitors, attracted by Malta's strategic position, conquered and ruled. These include the Phoenicians, Carthaginians, Romans, Arabs, Normans, and Aragonese.

The Knights of the Order of St. John of Jerusalem arrived here in 1530 after they had been driven from their stronghold on the island of Rhodes by the Ottoman emperor Suleyman the Magnificent. In 1565, with only a handful of men, the Knights held Malta against the Ottoman Turks in a dramatic and bloody siege. They ruled the islands until Napoleon arrived in 1798; their legacy includes massive fortifications, rich architecture, and the city of Valletta, Malta's capital.

The British drove the French out in 1800 and gave the island the distinctive British feel that it still retains. In 1942, during World War II, King George VI awarded the Maltese people the George Cross for their courage in withstanding repeated German and Italian attacks, especially from the air. Malta gained independence from Britain in 1964 and was declared a republic within the Commonwealth in 1974.

Malta

Mediterranean Sea

Essential Information

Before You Go

When to Go The archipelago is a year-round delight, but May through October is the time of the main tourist season. April and May are the months for spring freshness; the summer months can be very hot though sometimes tempered by sea breezes. August is just too hot for touring. If you visit in the winter, you'll find the climate pleasant and mild, but you may encounter sudden rainstorms.

Climate The following are the average daily maximum and minimum temperatures for Valletta.

Jan.	58F	14C	May	71F	22C	Sept.	81F	27C
	50	10		61	16		71	22
Feb.	59F	15C	June	79F	26C	Oct.	75F	24C
	51	10		67	19		66	19
Mar.	61F	16C	July	84F	29C	Nov.	67F	20C
	52	11		72	22		60	16
Apr.	65F	18C	Aug.	85F	29C	Dec.	61F	16C
	56	13		73	23		54	12

Currency The unit of currency is the Maltese lira (Lm), also sometimes referred to as the pound. It's divided into 100 cents, and the cents are divided into 10 mils, but in recent years the mils have dropped out of circulation. There are Lm 2, Lm 5, Lm 10, and Lm 20 bills; coins—1¢, 2¢, 5¢, 10¢, 25¢, 50¢, and Lm 1—are bronze and silver. At press time (summer 1995), the exchange rate was Lm .36 to the dollar and Lm .54 to the pound sterling.

What It Will Cost Malta is one of the cheapest holiday destinations in Europe, though with the rapid tourist development, prices are inevitably rising.

Prices tend to be uniform across the island, except in Sliema and Valletta, the capital, where they are slightly higher. There is now a 15% VAT on all purchases.

Sample Prices Cup of coffee, 25¢ (Maltese); bottle of beer, 25¢; Coca-Cola, 20¢.

Customs on Arrival You may bring into Malta, duty-free, 200 cigarettes, one bottle of liquor, one bottle of wine, and one bottle of perfume. You may bring in up to Lm 50 in currency.

Language Maltese and English are the official languages, and Italian is widely spoken as well.

Getting Around

By Bus Most routes throughout the island are via Valletta, which facilitates travel out of the capital but makes cross-country trips a bit longer. Public transportation is very inexpensive. Though some of the old green buses show their age, they are usually on time. Plans are in hand to renew the fleet and the shabby terminal at Valletta.

By Boat Daily car/passenger ferries operate year-round from Cirkewwa to Mġarr on Gozo. Telephone 243964 in Malta, 571884 in Cirkewwa, and 556114 or 556743 in Gozo for details. The crossing from Marfa to Mġarr in Gozo lasts 25 minutes, with shuttle service twice an hour in summer and every hour in winter. The round-trip fare is Lm 1.50 adults, 50¢ children. There is also one service daily from Pietà (near Valletta) to Gozo, leaving in the morning and taking an hour and 15 minutes each way. The fare from Mġarr (passenger plus car) is Lm 4.50. A daily ferry service links the tourist resort town of Sliema to Valletta.

By Helicopter **Malta Air Charter** (tel. 882916 or 882920) offers helicopter sightseeing tours and flies to and from Gozo several times daily. Flight time to Gozo is 10 minutes and costs Lm 17 round-trip (open return date) and Lm 15 (same-day return). Tours are 20 and 40 minutes and cost Lm 12 and Lm 20, respectively.

By Taxi There are plenty of metered taxis available, and fares are reasonable compared with those in other European countries. Be sure the meter is switched on when your trip starts, or bargain first. Tip the driver 10%.

Staying in Malta

Telephones
Local Calls There are no regional area codes in Malta. For a time check, dial 195; for flight inquiries, dial 249600.

International Calls There is direct dialing to most parts of the world from Malta. The overseas operator is 194; the international dialing access code is 00. You may place calls from the Overseas Telephone Division of Telemalta at St. Julian's, Qawra, St. Paul's Bay, Sliema, Valletta, and Luqa International Airport. For an **AT&T** long-distance operator, dial 0800–890110; public phones may require a deposit.

Country Code The country code for Malta is 356.

Mail Airmail letters to the United States cost 20¢; postcards 20¢. Airmail letters to the United Kingdom cost 14¢; postcards 14¢.

Opening and Closing Times Banks are open weekdays 8:30–12:45 (Tues. and Fri. 2:30–4, also), Saturday 8:30–noon (11:30 in summer). Banks in tourist areas are also open in the afternoon. The Airport Exchange is open 24 hours a day.

Museums run by the Museums Department are generally open mid-June through September, daily 8–2; October through mid-June, daily 8:30–5; closed holidays. In 1996: Valletta's museums are closed on

Sundays in August and September but are open in the afternoon on Tuesdays and Fridays.

Shops are open Monday–Saturday 9–1 and 4–7.

National Holidays January 1, February 10 (St. Paul's shipwreck), March 19 (St. Joseph's Day), March 31 (Freedom Day), April 5 (Good Friday), May 1 (Workers' Day), June 7 (Sette Giugno), June 29 (Sts. Peter and Paul), August 15 (Assumption, or Santa Marija), September 8 (Our Lady of Victories), September 21 (Independence Day), December 8 (Immaculate Conception), December 13 (Republic Day), December 25. Changing holidays in 1997: March 28 (Good Friday).

Dining There is a good choice of restaurants, ranging from expensive hotel restaurants to fast-food hamburger joints. Local specialties include *torta tal-lampuki* (dorado fish pie), *dentici* (sea bream), and tuna. *Minestra* is the local variant of minestrone soup, and the *timpana* (baked macaroni and meat) is filling. Rabbit, stewed or fried, is a national dish. Accompany your meal with the locally produced wine: Marsovin and Lachryma Vitis come in red or white. Maltese beers are excellent; highly popular are Cisk Lager and Hop Leaf. Try Kinnie, a local nonalcoholic drink.

Precautions The water in Malta is safe to drink, with the only drawback being its salty taste: Many prefer bottled mineral water.

What to Wear A jacket and tie are suggested for higher-priced restaurants. Otherwise, casual dress is acceptable.

Ratings Prices are for a three-course meal, not including wine, VAT, and tip. Best bets are indicated by a star ★.

Category	Cost*
$$	Lm 6–Lm 9
$	Lm 4–Lm 6
¢	under Lm 4

A 10% VAT is charged on meals eaten in all restaurants; 15% VAT on drinks.

Lodging Malta has a variety of lodgings, from deluxe modern hotels to modest guest houses. There are also self-contained complexes geared mainly to package tours.

Ratings Prices are for two people sharing a double room and exclude the 15% VAT.

Category	Cost
$$	Lm 12–Lm 22
$	Lm 6–Lm 12
¢	under Lm 6

Tipping A tip of 10% is expected when a service charge is not included.

Valletta

Arriving and Departing

By Plane There are no direct flights from the United States, but several airlines, including **Air Malta,** fly from London, Paris, Frankfurt, Athens, and Rome to Luqa Airport, 6 kilometers (4 miles) south of Valletta.

<table>
<tr><td>*Between the*
Airport and
Downtown</td><td>There is local bus service (Bus 8) that passes through the town of Luqa on its way to Valletta, with a stop in front of the airport. It operates every 10 or 15 minutes from 6 AM to 11 PM; the trip takes about 30 minutes, and the fare is about 10¢. Reasonably priced taxis are also available; approximate fares are listed by the taxi stand.</td></tr>
</table>

Important Addresses and Numbers

Tourist Information
Gozo (Mġarr Harbor, tel. 553343; Victoria, tel. 558106). **St. Julian's Bay** (Balluta Bay, tel. 342671 or 342672). **Sliema** (Bisazza St., tel. 313409). **Valletta** (1 City Gate Arcade, tel. 237747; Luqa Airport, tel. 249600; or 280 Republic St., tel. 224444 or 228282).

Embassies and High Commissions
U.S. Development House (St. Anne St., Floriana, tel. 243653). **British High Commission** (7 St. Anne St., Floriana, tel. 233134). **Canadian Embassy** (in Rome; via G. B. de Rossi 27, tel. 06/445981).

Emergencies
Hospital: St. Luke's (Gwardamangia, tel. 241251) or Craig Hospital (Gozo, tel. 556851). **Police** (tel. 191). **Ambulance** (tel. 196). **Fire Brigade** (tel. 199).

Exploring Valletta

The minicity of Valletta, with ornate palaces and museums, protected by massive honey-color fortifications, was built by the Knights of the Order of St. John who occupied the island from 1530 to 1798. The main entrance to the city is through the arched **City Gate** (where all bus routes end), which leads onto Republic Street, the spine of the city and the main shopping street. From Republic Street, other streets are laid out on a grid pattern.

Before setting out along Republic Street, stop at the tourist information office for maps, brochures, and a copy of *What's On.* Two blocks farther, on your left is the Auberge de Provence (the hostel of the knights from Provence), which now houses the **National Museum of Archaeology.** Its collection includes finds from Malta's many prehistoric sites—Tarxien, Hagar Qim, and the Hypogeum at Paola. You'll see pottery, statuettes, temple carvings, and, on the upper floor, finds from Punic and Roman tombs. *Republic St., tel. 225577. Admission: Lm 1. Open mid-June–July, daily 8–2; Aug.–Sept., Mon., Wed., Thurs., and Sat. 8–2, Tues. and Fri. 8–5; Oct.–mid-June, daily 8:30–5; closed holidays.*

From Republic Street, turn right at the Inter-Flora kiosk and head to St. John's Square. Dominating the square is **St. John's Co-Cathedral.** This was the Order of St. John's own church, completed in 1578. It is by far Malta's most important treasure. The cathedral **museum** includes the oratory in which hangs *The Beheading of St. John,* the masterpiece painted by Caravaggio when he was staying on Malta in 1608. In the museum, you'll find a rich collection of Flemish tapestries based on drawings by Poussin and Rubens, antique embroidered vestments, and illuminated manuscripts. *Museum admission: 60¢. Open weekdays 9:30–12:30 and 1:30–4:30, Sat. 9:30–12:30.*

While in St. John's Square, visit the **Government Craft Center,** which has a wide range of traditional, handmade goods. *Open weekdays 8:30–12:30 and 2–5.*

Continue along Republic Street to the **Grand Master's Palace,** where Malta's parliament sits. You can walk through the shady courtyards. Inside, friezes in the sumptuously decorated state apartments depict scenes from the history of the Knights. There is also a gallery with Gobelin tapestries. At the back of the building is the **Armoury of the Knights,** with displays of arms and armor down through the ages. *Republic St. Admission to state apartments and Armoury:*

Lm 1 each. Open mid-June–July, daily 8–2; Aug.–Sept., Mon., Wed., Thurs., and Sat. 8–2, Tues. and Fri. 8–5; Oct.–mid-June, 8:30–5; closed holidays.

Another building from the days of the Knights of Malta is the order's library, now the **National Library,** which stands on Republic Square, the most colorful part of the city. On Old Theatre Street, you can see the elegant **Manoel Theatre.** Built in 1731, it is said to be Europe's oldest theater still in operation.

Return to Republic Street and spend some time at Casa Rocca Piccola, a traditional 16th-century Maltese house. Continue to **Fort St. Elmo,** which was built by the Knights to defend the harbor. Today part of the fort houses the **War Museum,** with its collection of military objects largely related to Malta's role in World War II. Here you can see an Italian E-boat and the Gladiator *Faith,* one of three Gloster Gladiator biplanes that defended the island. The other two, *Hope* and *Charity,* were shot down in the air battles of 1940–41. *St. Elmo. Admission: Lm 1. Open mid-June–July, daily 8–2; Aug.–Sept., Mon., Wed., Thurs., and Sat. 8–2, Tues. and Fri. 8–5; closed holidays.*

Continue along the seawall to the **Hospital of the Order** at the end of Merchants Street. This gracious building has been converted into the Mediterranean Conference Center. For an excellent introduction to the island, see the "Malta Experience," a multimedia presentation on the history of Malta that is given here daily (admission: Lm 2). *Admission to center: 50¢.*

Follow the seawall past the siege bell memorial and climb up to the **Upper Barrakka Gardens.** Once part of the city's defenses, they're now a pleasant area from which to watch the comings and goings in the Grand Harbour. The Lascaris War Rooms, below, from which World War II operations were planned, are open to the public.

Then walk down to Merchants Street, which is dominated by an open-air market, where you can snap up some good bargains. Next, cut along South Street, across Republic Street, to the **National Museum of Fine Art.** The former 18th-century palace has paintings from the 15th century to the present day, including works by Tintoretto, Preti, and de Favray, as well as local artists. *South St., tel. 225769. Admission: Lm 1. Open mid-June–July, daily 8–2; Aug.–Sept., Mon., Wed., Thurs., and Sat. 8–2, Tues. and Fri. 8–5; Oct.–mid-June, daily 8:30–5; closed holidays.*

Dining

For details and price-category definitions, *see* Dining *in* Staying in Malta, *above.*

$$ ★ **Pappagall.** This restaurant in Valletta is popular with locals and visitors alike. Traditional Maltese food is featured, and the bustling atmosphere is warm and friendly. *Melita St., tel. 236195. Reservations advised. AE, DC, MC, V. Closed Sun.*

$$ **Scalini.** An attractive cellar restaurant with walls of Malta's golden limestone, it features seafood and Italian-style pastas. The prix-fixe menu is a good value. *32B South St., tel. 246221. Reservations advised. AE, DC, MC, V.*

$ **The Lantern.** This friendly spot is run by two brothers. The 18th-century town-house location may not win any design awards, but the food is delicious and served in a traditional Maltese atmosphere. *20 Sappers St., tel. 237521. Reservations advised. No credit cards.*

$ **Pizzeria Bologna.** A street-level establishment beside the Grand Master's Palace, serves delicious pizzas with an interesting choice of ingredients. *59B Republic St., tel. 238014. Open until 9.*

¢ **Galea Sluta.** Just inside the City Gate, this place is convenient for grabbing a quick snack before starting your tour of Valletta. It's especially known for its sweets. *City Gate, Republic St., tel. 225386. No reservations. No credit cards.*

¢ **Eddie's Cafè Regina.** At the Regina, you can eat outside and enjoy the city scene, or dine indoors in an informal yet elegant setting. Pizza, pastas, and salads are served. *9 Republic St., tel. 246454. No reservations. No credit cards.*

Lodging

For details and price-category definitions, *see* Lodging *in* Staying in Malta, *above.*

$$ **Castille.** For a touch of old Malta, stay at the Castille in what used to be a 16th-century palazzo. This is a gracious, comfortable, Old World hotel with a friendly, relaxed ambience. It has an ideal central location, close to the museums and the bus terminal. There's a good rooftop restaurant with an excellent prix-fixe menu offering several choices. A pianist plays most evenings during dinner, and the views across the harbor are stunning. *St. Paul St., tel. 243677 or 243673, fax 243679. 38 rooms with bath. Facilities: coffee shop–bar, pizzeria, restaurant, sun terrace. AE.*

$$ **Osborne.** Centrally located in Valletta, the Osborne has spacious rooms but undistinguished decor. Spend a few minutes in the rooftop lounge and enjoy the view. *South St., tel. 232128, fax 232120. 50 rooms with bath. Facilities: restaurant. AE, DC, MC, V.*

$ **Belmont.** An inexpensive but clean and functional hotel, it's close to the Sliema–St. Julian's seafront. *Mrabat St., St. Julian's, tel. 313077. 25 rooms with bath. Facilities: restaurant. No credit cards.*

$ **Mdina Hotel.** This is a good value close to the island's old capital, Mdina. It is not luxurious, but is quite comfortable nonetheless, with a full fitness center and an indoor pool. *196 Labour Ave., Rabat, tel. 453230, fax 455738. 40 rooms with bath. MC, V.*

¢ **British Hotel.** This old family hotel has a view of Malta's main seaport, and its restaurant specializes in Maltese dishes. Try stewed rabbit and octopus. *267 St. Ursula St., tel. 236019 or 224730, fax 239711. 46 rooms with bath. MC, V.*

¢ **Cerviola Hotel.** If you visit the fishing and resort town of Marsaskala, try this family-run hotel two blocks from the town promenade. Its restaurant serves Maltese food and fish, including rabbit stew and acciola (amberjack). *Tri-il-Qaliet, Marsaskala, tel. 823287, fax 822056. 32 rooms with bath. Facilities: restaurant. MC, V.*

18 Norway

Most visitors traveling to Norway for the first time usually have two preconceived notions: The temperature is cold year-round, and price levels are sky-high. They will be pleasantly surprised on both counts. The Gulf Stream makes the coastal waters ice-free all year. Winters do without the famous wind-chill factor, and summers are bearably warm with never-ending nights. Norway does not seem quite as expensive as it did a few years ago because low inflation and increased competition in the tourist industry have kept prices stable. And there are many ways to beat the high costs.

Norway has some of the most remote and dramatic scenery in Europe. Along the west coast, deep fjords knife into steep mountain ranges. Inland, cross-country ski trails follow frozen trout streams and downhill trails career through forests whose floors teem with wildflowers and berries during the summer. In older villages, wooden houses spill down toward docks where Viking ships—and later, whaling vessels—once were moored. Today the maritime horizon is dominated by tankers and derricks, for oil is now Norway's economic lifeblood. Fishing and timber, however, still provide many Norwegians with a stable income.

Inhabited since 1700 BC, Norway is today considered a peaceful nation. This was hardly so during the Viking period (the 9th and 10th centuries AD), when, apart from vicious infighting at home, the Vikings were marauding as far afield as Seville and Iceland. This fierce fighting spirit remained, despite Norway's subsequent centuries of subjugation by the Danes and Swedes. Independence came early this century but was put to the test during World War II, when the Germans occupied the country. Norwegian Resistance fighters rose to the challenge, eventually quashing Nazi efforts to develop atomic weapons.

The foundations for modern Norwegian culture were laid in the 19th century, during the period of union with Sweden, which lasted until 1905. Oslo blossomed at this time, and Norway produced its three greatest men of arts and letters: composer Edvard Grieg (1843–

Norway

0 — 200 miles
0 — 300 km

ATLANTIC
OCEAN

North Cape

Vardø
Vadsø
Hammerfest
Kirkenes
Alta
Masi
Tromsø

FINLAND

Norwegian
Sea

Bardu
Narvik

Vestfjorden

Bodø
Fauske
Saltdal

Arctic Circle
Mo-i-Rana
Umbukta

Sandnessjøen
Møsjøen

Brønnøysund

E6

SWEDEN

Gulf of Bothnia

Vikna
Namsos

Steinkjer

Trondheim
Meråker
Støren

Kristiansund N.

70 Oppdal
Røros
Tynset

Ålesund
9
Dombås
Otta

Nord fjord
Koppang

Florø
Jostedalsbreen
Rena
Lillehammer

Sognafjord
Lake
Mjøsa
Hamar

Voss
E16
Eidsvoll

Bergen
Hardangerfjord

40
Hønefoss
Oslo
Kongsberg
Sarpsborg
Drammen
Fredrikstad
Haugesund
11
Larvik
Oslofjord
Porsgrunn

Stavanger
Arendal
Sandnes
Evje
Grimstad
Skagerrak
Kattegat
Mandal
Kristiansand S.

Baltic Sea

N

1907), dramatist Henrik Ibsen (1828–1906), and painter Edvard Munch (1863–1944). The polar explorers Roald Amundsen and Fridtjof Nansen also lived during this period.

All other facts aside, Norway is most famous for its fjords, which were formed during an ice age a million years ago. The ice cap burrowed deep into existing mountain-bound riverbeds, creating enormous pressure. There was less pressure along the coast, so the entrances to most fjords are shallow, about 155 meters (508 feet), while inland depths reach 1,240 meters (4,067 feet). Although Norway's entire coastline is riddled with fjords, the most breathtaking sights are on the west coast between Stavanger and Trondheim.

Essential Information

Before You Go

When to Go Cross-country skiing was born in Norway, and the country remains an important winter sports center. While much of the terrain is dark and impassable through the winter, you can cross-country or downhill ski within Oslo's city limits. January, February, and early March are good skiing months, and hotel rooms are plentiful then. Avoid April, when sleet, rain, and countless thaws and refreezings may ruin the good skiing snow and leave the roads—and spirits—in bad shape. Bear in mind that the country virtually closes down for the five-day Easter holidays, when Norwegians make their annual migration to the mountains. If you plan to visit at this time, reserve well in advance. Hotels are more crowded and expensive during this period, but some offer discounts during the two weeks before Easter—which is a good time for skiing.

Summers are generally mild. Then there's the famous midnight sun: Even in the "southern" city of Oslo, night seems more like twilight around midnight, and dawn comes by 2 AM. The weather can be fickle, however, and rain gear and sturdy waterproof shoes are recommended even during the summer. The best times to avoid crowds in museums and on ferries are May and September; Norwegians themselves are on vacation in July and the first part of August.

Climate The following are the average daily maximum and minimum temperatures for Oslo.

Jan.	28F	− 2C	May	61F	16C	Sept.	60F	16C
	19	− 7		43	6		46	8
Feb.	30F	− 1C	June	68F	20C	Oct.	48F	9C
	19	− 7		50	10		38	3
Mar.	39F	4C	July	72F	22C	Nov.	38F	3C
	25	− 4		55	13		31	− 1
Apr.	50F	10C	Aug.	70F	21C	Dec.	32F	0C
	34	1		53	12		25	− 4

Currency The unit of currency in Norway is the krone, written as Kr. on price tags but as NOK by banks; in this book it appears as Nkr. It is divided into 100 øre. Bills of Nkr 50, 100, 200, 500, and 1,000 are in general use. Coins are 50 øre and 1, 5, 10, and 20 kroner. Credit cards are accepted in most hotels, stores, restaurants, and many gas stations and garages, but generally not in smaller shops and inns in rural areas. Banks charge per transaction, so it is more economical to change larger amounts of money or traveler's checks. The post office charges less. The exchange rate at press time (summer 1995) was Nkr 5.85 to the dollar and Nkr 9.71 to the pound sterling.

What It Will Cost Norway has a high standard—and cost—of living, but there are ways of saving money by taking advantage of some special offers for

accommodations and travel during the tourist season and on weekends throughout the year.

The **Oslo Card**—valid for one, two, or three days—entitles you to
free admission to museums and galleries and unlimited travel on vehicles operated by the Oslo Transport system and the Norwegian
Railways commuter trains within the city limits; free parking; free
admission to the Tusenfryd amusement park, various sights, public
swimming pools, and racetracks; and discounts at various stores,
movie theaters (May, June, and July), and sports centers. You can
get the card at Oslo's tourist information offices and hotels (*see* Important Addresses and Numbers *in* Oslo, *below*). A one-day card
costs Nkr 110 adults, Nkr 55 children; two days Nkr 190 adults, Nkr
80 children; three days Nkr 240 adults, Nkr 110 children.

Hotels in larger towns have special weekend and summer rates from
late June to early August, and some chains have their own discount
schemes—see Norway's annual accommodations guide. Discounts
in rural hotels are offered to guests staying several days; meals are
then included in the rate. Meals are generally expensive, so take the
hotel breakfast when it's offered. Alcohol is very expensive and is
sold only during strictly regulated hours.

Sample Prices Cup of coffee, Nkr 10–Nkr 20; bottle of beer, Nkr 30–Nkr 50; soft
drink, Nkr 15–Nkr 25; ham sandwich, Nkr 20–Nkr 40; 1-mile taxi
ride, Nkr 40 (for night rates, add 15%).

Customs on Residents of nonEuropean countries who are over 16 may import
Arrival duty-free into Norway 400 cigarettes or 500 grams of other tobacco
goods, souvenirs, and gifts to the value of Nkr 1,200. Residents of
European countries who are over 16 may import 200 cigarettes or
250 grams of tobacco or cigars, a small amount of perfume or eau de
cologne, and goods to the value of Nkr 1,200. Anyone over 20 may
bring in 1 liter of wine and 1 liter of liquor or 2 liters of wine and
beer.

Language In larger cities, on public transportation, and in most commercial
establishments, people speak English. Younger Norwegians generally speak it well; English is the main foreign language taught in
schools, and movies and cable TV reinforce its popularity.

There are two official forms of the Norwegian language plus many
dialects, so don't be disappointed if you've studied it but find that
you can't understand everyone. Typical of Scandinavian languages,
Norwegian's additional vowels—æ, ø, and å—come at the end of the
alphabet. Remember this when you're using alphabetical listings.

Getting Around

By Train Norwegian trains are punctual and comfortable, and most routes
are scenic. They fan out from Oslo and leave the coasts (except in the
south) to buses and ferries. Some express trains have observation
cars; the Oslo–Bergen route has a dining car, while all other long-
distance routes have buffet cars. Reservations are required on all
express (*ekspresstog*) services. The Oslo–Bergen route is superbly
scenic, while the Oslo–Trondheim–Bodø route takes you within the
Arctic Circle. The trains leave Oslo from Sentralstasjonen (Oslo S or
Central Station) on Jernbanetorget (at the beginning of Karl Johans
gate).

Fares Apart from the Europe-wide passes (EurailPass and InterRail), two
kinds of Scandinavian passes are available: **Nordturist** and
ScanRailpass. Nordturist allows unlimited travel in Norway, Sweden, Denmark, and Finland for 21 days. The cost is Nkr 1,980 (second class) or Nkr 2,640 (first class). Youths 12–25 years pay Nkr
1,470 and 1,980. Tickets are available through **NSB Travel**, the Norwegian State Railway (21–24 Cockspur St., London SW1Y 5DA, tel.

071/930–6666). In the United States, contact ScanAm (933 Highway 23, Pompton Plains, NJ 07444, tel. 201/835–7070 or 800/545–2204). ScanRail is a range of flexible railpasses offering a number of days' travel within a certain period in the four Scandinavian countries. These passes are available through **Rail Europe** (New York, tel. 914/ 682–2999) and **NSB Travel** (London). Credit-card payments are accepted. Minifares during off-peak times (green routes) are also available if seats are booked in advance.

By Plane The remoteness of so much of Norway means that air travel is a necessity for many inhabitants. The main Scandinavian airline, **SAS,** operates a network, along with **Braathens SAFE** and **Widerøe.** Fares are high, but the time saved makes it attractive if you are in a hurry. For longer distances, flying can be cheaper than driving a rented car and paying for gas and incidentals. Inquire about "Visit Norway" passes, which give you relatively cheap domestic-flight coupons (usually good only for summer travel). Norwegian airlines can be contacted at the following addresses: **SAS** (Oslo City, Stenersgate 1A, 0184 Oslo, tel. 67/596050 or 81/003300); **Braathens SAFE AS** (Haakon VII's gate 2, 0161 Oslo, tel. 67/597000 or 22/834470); **Norsk Air** (Torp Airport, Sandefjord, tel. 33/469000); and **Widerøes Flyveselskap AS** (Mustads vei 1, 0283 Oslo, tel. 22/736500).

By Bus The Norwegian bus network makes up for some of the limitations of the country's train system, and several of the routes are particularly scenic. For example, the north Norway bus service, starting at Fauske (on the train line to Bodø), goes right up to Kirkenes on the Russian-Norwegian border, covering the 1,000 kilometers (625 miles) within four days. Long-distance bus routes also connect Norway with all its Scandinavian neighbors. Most buses leave from Bussterminalen (Galleri Oslo, Schweigaardsgate 10, tel. 22/170166), close to Oslo Central Station.

By Ferry Norway's long, fjord-indented coastline is served by an intricate and essential network of ferries and passenger ships. A wide choice of services is available, from simple hops across fjords (saving many miles of traveling) and excursions among the thousands of islands to luxury cruises and long journeys the entire length of the coast. Most ferries carry cars. Reservations are required on ferry journeys of more than one day but are not needed for simple fjord crossings. Many ferries are small and have room for only a few cars, so book ahead if possible; this will allow you to drive onto the ferry ahead of the cars that are waiting in line. Fares and exact times of departures depend on the season and availability of ships. The main Norwegian travel office, Nortra (*see below*), has the most accurate information, or contact Norway Information Center (*see* Important Addresses and Numbers *in* Oslo, *below*).

One of the world's great sea voyages is onboard the mail-and-passenger ships called Hurtigruten, which run up the Norwegian coast from Bergen to Kirkenes, well above the Arctic Circle. For information about Hurtigruten, contact the **Bergen Line** (505 Fifth Avenue, New York, NY 10017, tel. 212/986–2711), or the Tromsø Main Office (tel. 77/686088).

Nortra (Nortravel Marketing) (Postboks 499, Sentrum, 0105 Oslo, tel. 22/427044, fax 22/336998) will answer your queries about long-distance travel.

Staying in Norway

Telephones Norway's phone system is not as expensive as one might fear. Domestic rates are reduced 5 PM–8 AM weekdays and all day on weekends. Avoid using room phones in hotels unless you're willing to pay a hefty service charge. Cheap rates for international calls apply only after 10 PM. In public booths, place coins in the phone before dialing. Unused coins are returned. The largest coins accepted are Nkr 10, with most older phones taking only Nkr 1 or Nkr 5 coins, so make sure you have enough small change. The minimum deposit is Nkr 3.

Local Calls The cost of calls within Norway varies according to distance: Within Oslo, the cost goes up according to the amount of time used after the three-minute flat fee. Check the Oslo phone book for dialing information.

International Calls To call North America, dial 095–1, then the area code and number. For the United Kingdom, dial 095–44, then the area code (minus the first 0) and number. (As of November 1, 1995, you'll need to dial 00 for an international connection.) To reach an **AT&T** long-distance operator, dial 180019011; for **MCI,** dial 180019912; and for **Sprint,** 180019877.

Operators and Information For local information, dial 180. For international information, dial 181.

Country code Norway's country code is 47.

Mail
Postal Rates Letters and postcards to the United States cost Nkr 5.50 for the first 20 grams. For the United Kingdom, the rate is Nkr 4.50 for the first 20 grams.

Receiving Mail Have letters marked "poste restante" after the name of the town, with the last name underlined. The service is free, and letters are directed to the nearest main post office. American Express offices (Winge—the agent for American Express—is located at Karl Johans gate 33–35, tel. 22/412030) will also hold mail (nonmembers pay a small charge on collection).

Shopping
VAT Refunds Much of the 23% Norwegian value-added tax (VAT) will be refunded to visitors who spend more than Nkr 300 in any single store. Ask for a special tax-free check and show your passport to confirm that you are not a resident. All purchases must be sealed and presented together with the tax-free check at the tax-free counter at ports, on ferries destined for abroad, and at airports and border posts. The VAT will be refunded, minus a service charge. General information about the tax-free system is available by calling tel. 67/149901.

Opening and Closing Times **Banks** are open weekdays 8:15–3:30; summer hours are 8:15–3. (All post offices change money.)

Museums are usually open Tuesday to Sunday 10–3 or 4. Many, but not all, are closed on Monday.

Shops. Though times vary, most shops are open weekdays 9 or 10–5 (Thursday until 7) and Saturday 9–1 or 2. Shopping malls are often open until 8 on weeknights.

National Holidays For 1996: January 1, April 4–8 (Easter), May 1 (Labor Day), May 16 (Ascension), May 17 (Constitution Day), May 26–27 (Pentecost), December 25–26. Changing holidays in 1997: March 27–31 (Easter), May 8 (Ascension), May 18–19 (Pentecost).

Dining The Norwegian diet is high in protein and starches. Breakfast is usually a large buffet of smoked fish, cheeses, sausage, cold meats, and whole-grain breads accompanied by tea, good coffee, or milk. Lunch is often similar to breakfast, or the famous, but not very filling, *smørbrød* open sandwich. Restaurant and hotel dinners are usually three-course meals, often starting with soup and ending with fresh fruit and berries. The main course may be salmon, trout, or other fish; alternatives can include lamb or pork, reindeer, or even ptarmigan. Remember that the most expensive part of eating is drinking (*see* What It Will Cost in Before You Go, *above*) and that liquor is not served on Sunday in most areas. One consolation is the quality of the water, which is still among the purest in the world despite the growing problem of acid rain.

What To Wear   Neat casual dress is appropriate in all but the most expensive Norwegian restaurants.

Mealtimes   Lunch is from noon to 3 at restaurants featuring a *koldtbord*, the famous Scandinavian buffet. Few Scandinavians ever partake of this, except when dining at mountain resorts. Most Scandinavians bring their own lunchboxes, consisting of open-face sandwiches. (Some hotels let guests pack their own lunches.) Dinner has traditionally been early, but in hotels and major restaurants it is now more often from 6 to 11. Some rural places still serve dinner from 4 to 7, however.

Ratings   Prices are per person and include a first course, main course, and dessert without wine or tip. Outside the major cities, prices are considerably less. Service is always included (*see* Tipping, *below*). Best bets are indicated by a star ★.

Category	Cost
$$	Nkr 125–Nkr 300
$	Nkr 85–Nkr 125
¢	under Nkr 85

Lodging   Accommodations in Norway are usually spotless, and smaller estab-
Hotels   lishments are often family-run. Service is thoughtful and considerate, right down to blackout curtains to block out the midnight sun. Passes are available for discounts in hotels. The **Scandinavia Bonus Pass,** costing approximately $25 and also valid in Denmark, Sweden, and Finland, gives discounts of up to 50% in 120 hotels during the summer (May 15–Oct. 1). In addition, children under 15 stay in their parents' room at no extra charge. It can also be used on weekends throughout the year. For full details, write to **Inter Nor Hotels** (Dronningensgate 40, 0154 Oslo, tel. 22/334200, fax 22/336906). Other chains' addresses are listed in Norway's accommodations guide, free from any tourist office. **Nordturist** passes (*see* Getting Around By Train, *above*) also offer discounts of about 40% in nearly 110 top hotels (Reso Hotels). Fjord Pass and Hotelexpress also entitle you to discounts at affiliated hotels.

Camping   Camping is a popular way of keeping down costs. There are more than 1,400 authorized campsites in the country, many set in spectacular surroundings. Prices vary according to the facilities provided: A family with a car and tent can expect to pay about Nkr 100 per night. Some campsites have log cabins available from about Nkr 250 per night. The *Camping Norway* guide is available from tourist offices, or go to **NAF** (the Norwegian Automobile Association), Storgaten 2, 0155 Oslo, tel. 22/341400.

Youth Hostels   There are about 90 youth hostels in Norway; some are schools or farms doing extra summer duty. Members of the Youth Hostel Association (YHA) get a discount, and there are no age restrictions. For a full list, write to **Norske Vandrerhjem (NoVa)** (Dronningensgate 26, 0154 Oslo, tel. 22/421410).

International YHA guides are available to members in the United Kingdom and North America. In the United States, contact **American Youth Hostels, Inc.** (733 15th St., NW, Suite 840, Washington, DC 20005, tel. 202/783–6161, fax 202/783–6171). In Canada, contact **Canadian Hostelling Association** (1600 James Naismith Dr., Suite 608, Gloucester, Ont. K1B 5N4, tel. 613/748–5638, fax 613/748–5750).

Rentals   Norwegians escape to mountain cabins whenever they have a chance. Stay in one for a week or two and you'll see why—magnificent scenery; pure air; edible wild berries; and the chance to hike, fish, or cross-country ski. For full details of this most popular Norwegian vacation, which includes accommodations in rented cabins, farms, or private homes, write to **Den Norske Hytteformidling A.S.**, Box 3404, Bjølsen, 0406 Oslo, tel. 22/356710. The brochure "Norsk Hytteferie" can be requested from tourist offices. An unusual alternative is to rent a *rorbu* (fisherman's dwelling) in the northerly Lofoten Islands. For information, contact **Destination Lofoten,** Box 210, N–8301 Svolvær, tel. 76/073000, fax 76/073001.

Ratings Prices are summer rates and are for two people in a double room with bath and include breakfast, service, and all taxes. Best bets are indicated by a star ★.

Category	Oslo	Other Areas
$$	Nkr 800–Nkr 1,000	Nkr 650–Nkr 850
$	Nkr 600–Nkr 800	Nkr 500–Nkr 650
¢	under Nkr 600	under Nkr 500

Tipping In Norway, a 10%–12% service charge is generally added to bills at hotels and restaurants. If you have had exceptional service, then give an additional 5% tip. It is not the custom to tip taxi drivers unless they help with luggage; porters at airports have set fees per bag, but the carts are free. If a doorman hails a taxi for you, you can give Nkr 5. On sightseeing tours, tip the guide Nkr 10–Nkr 15 if you are satisfied. Tip with local currency only; it is nearly impossible to exchange foreign coins. Even bills in small amounts present problems because of the transaction charge (usually Nkr 20).

Oslo

Arriving and Departing

By Plane Oslo Fornebu Airport on the edge of the fjord, about 20 minutes west of Oslo, has international and domestic services. Charter flights usually go to Gardermoen Airport, about 50 minutes north of Oslo.

Between the Buses from Bussterminalen (Galleri Oslo) to Fornebu leave every 15 *Airport and* minutes (starting at 6 AM) and run every half hour on weekends; the *Downtown* fare is Nkr 30. Alternatively, take Bus 31 from Jernbanetorget, marked "Snarøya." The fare is Nkr 20; the bus makes a round-trip once an hour. Buses meet flights to Gardermoen and take passengers to Oslo Central Station; the fare is Nkr 60.

By Train Trains on international or domestic long-distance and express routes arrive at Oslo Central Station. Suburban trains depart from Oslo Central Station, Stortinget, and National Theater Station.

Getting Around

By Public The best way to get around Oslo is by using the **Oslo Card** (*see* What **Transportation** It Will Cost *in* Before You Go, *above*), which offers unlimited travel for one, two, or three days on all Oslo's public transportation systems—bus, T-bane (the subway), streetcar, and even local ferries. You can buy the Oslo Card at Oslo tourist offices, from hotels, travel agents in Oslo, and larger stores (*see* Important Addresses and Numbers, *below*).

If you are using public transportation only occasionally, you can get tickets (adults Nkr 16, children Nkr 8) at bus and subway stops. For Nkr 35, the **Tourist Ticket** gives 24 hours' unlimited travel on any means of public transportation, including the summer ferries to

Bygdøy. The **Flexikort** gives you 10 subway, bus, or streetcar rides for Nkr 130, including transfers.

Important Addresses and Numbers

Tourist Information
Oslo Tourist Information Office (tel. 22/830050) is located at **Norway Information Center,** Vestbaneplassen 1, tel. 22/839100. (Open Oct. 1–Apr. 30, weekdays 9–4; May 1–May 31, daily 9–6; June 1–Aug. 31, daily 9–8; Sept. 1–Sept. 30, daily 9–4). **Oslo Central Station,** tel. 22/171124. Open daily 8 AM–11 PM. **Trafikanten,** Oslo Central Station, tel. 22/177030. Open daily 7 AM–8 PM.

Embassies
U.S. (Drammensveien 18, tel. 22/448550). **Canadian** (Oscarsgate 20, tel. 22/466955). **U.K.** (Thos. Heftyesgate 8, tel. 22/552400).

Emergencies
Police (Grønlandsleiret 44, tel. 22/669050, 24-hr service). **Ambulance:** 24-hour service (tel. 22/117070). **Dentist** (Oslo Kommunale Tannlegevakt, Tøyen Center, Kolstadsgate 18, Oslo 6, tel. 22/673000). Emergency treatment, weekdays 8 PM–11 PM, weekends and holidays 11 AM–2 PM.

Post Office
The main post office is at Dronningensgate 15. The **Telegraph Office** is at Kongensgate 21.

Exploring Oslo

Oslo is a small capital city, with a population of just under half a million. The downtown area is compact, but the geographic limits of Oslo spread out to include forests, fjords, and mountains, which give the city a pristine airiness that complements its urban amenities. Oslo has an excellent public transportation network. Explore downtown on foot, enjoying its jazz clubs and museums, then venture beyond via bus, streetcar, or train.

Numbers in the margin correspond to points of interest on the Oslo map.

Oslo's main street, **Karl Johans gate,** runs right through the center of town, from Oslo Central Station uphill to the Royal Palace. Half its length is closed to traffic, and it is in this section that you will find many of the city's shops and outdoor cafés.

1 Start at **Slottet** (the Royal Palace), the king's residence (not open to the public). The palace was built during the early 19th-century neoclassical style and is as sober, sturdy, and unpretentious as the Norwegian character. The surrounding park is open to the public. Time your visit to coincide with the changing of the guard (daily at 1:30). When the king is in residence (signaled by a red flag), the Royal Guard strikes up the band.

2 Walk down Karl Johans gate to the old **Universitet** (University), which is made up of the three big buildings on your left. The main hall of the university is decorated with murals by Edvard Munch (1863–1944), Norway's most famous artist. The hall (*aula*) is open only during July. The Nobel Peace Prize is presented there each year on December 10. *Admission to hall free. Open July, weekdays noon–2.*

3 Behind the University is **Nasjonalgalleriet** (the National Gallery), Norway's largest public gallery. It has a small but high-quality selection of paintings by European artists, but of particular interest is the collection of works by Norwegian artists. Edvard Munch is represented here, but most of his work is in the Munch Museum (*see below*), east of the center. *Universitetsgaten 13. Admission free. Open Mon., Wed., Fri. 10–4, Thurs. 10–8, Sat. and Sun. 11–3.*

4 The **Historisk Museum** (Historical Museum) is in back of the National Gallery. It features displays of daily life and art from the Viking

Oslo

KEY

i Tourist Information
──── Rail Lines

BYGDØY

Frognerkilen

Langvikbukta

Frogner Park

0   1 mile
0   1 km

N

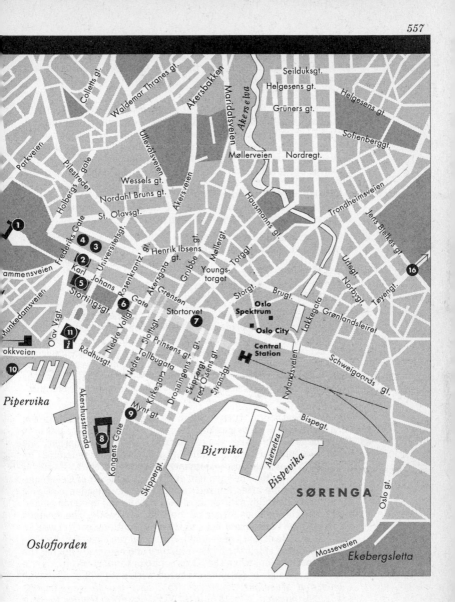

Colletts gt.
Waldemar Thranes gt.
Akersbakken
Seilduksgt.
Helgesens gt.
Grüners gt.
Maridalsveien
Helgesens gt.
Akerselva
Sofienberggt.
Ullevålsveien
Møllerveien Nordregt.
Parkveien
Pilestredet
Holbergs gate
Wessels gt.
Nordahl Bruns gt.
Akersveien
St. Olavsgt.
Hausmanns gt.
Trondheimsveien
Jens Bjelkes gt.

1

ammensveien
Frederiks Gate
4 3
Henrik Ibsens gt.
Universitetsgt.
2
Karl
5
Johans
Stortingsgt.
Munkedamsveien
Rosenkrantz' gt.
Akersgata
Grubbe gt.
Youngs-torget
Mellergt.
Torggt.
Urtegt.
Norbgt.
Teyengt.
16

Gate
6
Grensen
Stortorvet
Storgt.
Brugt.
Oslo Spektrum
Lakkegata
Grønlandsleiret

Olav V sgt.
7
Stortorvet
Oslo City

11
Rådhusgt.
Nedre Voligt.
Nedre Slotsgt.
Prinsens gt.
Central Station
Nylandsveien
Schweigaards gt.

okkveien
10
Pipervika
Akershusstranda
Tollbugata
Kirkegan
Dronningens gt.
Skippergt.
Fred Olsens gt.
Strandgt.
Bispegt.

Kongens Gate
9
Mynt gt.
8
Bjørvika
Akerselva
Bispevika

Skippergt.
SØRENGA
Oslo gt.

Oslofjorden
Mosseveien
Ekebergsletta

period, including treasures recovered from Viking ships. The Ethnographic Section houses a collection related to the great polar explorer Roald Amundsen, the first man to reach the South Pole.
*Frederiksgate 2. Admission free. Open summer, Tues.–Sun. 11–3;
winter, Tues.–Sun. 12–3.*

Return to Karl Johans gate and cross over for a closer look at
⑤ **Nationaltheatret** (the National Theater), watched over by the statues of Bjørnstjerne Bjørnson and Henrik Ibsen. Bjørnson was the
nationalist poet who wrote Norway's anthem. Internationally
lauded playwright Ibsen wrote *Peer Gynt* (he personally requested
Edvard Grieg's musical accompaniment), *A Doll's House,* and
Hedda Gabler, among others. He worried that his plays, packed
with allegory, myth, and sociological and emotional angst, might not
have appeal outside Norway. Instead, they were universally recognized and changed the face of modern theater.

⑥ At the far (eastern) end of the pond is the **Storting** (Parliament), a
bow-fronted yellow-brick building stretched across the block. It is
open to visitors by request when Parliament is not in session. A
guided tour takes visitors around the frescoed interior and into the
debating chamber. *Karl Johans gate 22, tel. 22/313050. Admission
free. Public gallery open weekdays 11–3.*

⑦ Karl Johans gate is closed to traffic near **Domkirken** (the Cathedral), with its staid, bronze door. The much-renovated cathedral,
consecrated in 1697, is modest by the standards of some other European capital cities, but the interior is rich with treasures, such as
the Baroque carved wooden altarpiece and pulpit. The ceiling frescoes by Hugo Louis Mohr were done after World War II. Behind the
cathedral is an area of arcades, small restaurants, and street musicians. *Stortorvet 1. Admission free. Open weekdays 10–3.*

Facing the cathedral, turn right at Kirkegata. Three blocks down,
turn right onto Rådhusgate and then almost immediately left onto
⑧ Kongens gate. This takes you to **Akershus Castle** on the harbor. The
castle was built during the Middle Ages, but was restored in 1527 by
Christian IV of Denmark—Denmark then ruled Norway—after it
was damaged by fire; he then laid out the present city of Oslo (nam-
ing it Christiania after himself) around his new residence. Oslo's
street plan still follows his design. Some rooms are open for guided
tours, and the grounds form a park around the castle. The grounds
also house the **Forsvarsmuseet** and **Hjemmefrontmuseet** (Norwegian
Defense and Resistance museums). Both give you a feel for the Norwegian fighting spirit throughout history and especially during the
German occupation, when the Nazis set up headquarters on this site
and had a number of patriots executed within its walls. *Akershus
Castle and Museums. Entrance from Festningsplassen, tel. 22/
412521. Admission: Nkr 15 adults, Nkr 5 children. Guided tours of
the castle, May–Sept., Mon.–Sat. 11, 1, and 3, Sun. 1 and 3. Museums open weekdays 10–4, Sun. 12:30–4.*

Just behind Akershus Castle, in the direction of Oslo Central Sta-
⑨ tion, is **Museet for Samtidskunst** (the Contemporary Art Museum),
housed in the Bank of Norway's old building. *Bankplassen 4, tel. 22/
335820. Admission free. Open Tues.–Fri. 11–7, Sat.–Sun. 11–4.*

Continue along the waterfront toward the central **harbor**—the
heart of Oslo and head of the fjord. Shops and cafés stay open late at
⑩ **Aker Brygge,** the new quayside shopping and cultural center, with a
theater, movie houses, and galleries among the shops, restaurants,
and cafés. You don't have to buy anything—just sit amid the fountains and statues and watch the portside activities.

⑪ The large redbrick **Rådhus** (City Hall) is on the waterfront, too.
Note the friezes in the courtyard, depicting scenes from Norwegian
folklore, then go inside and see murals depicting daily life in Nor-

way, historical events, and Resistance activities. You can set your watch by the astronomical clock in the inner courtyard. *Admission free. Open Mon.–Sat. 9:15–3:30. Tours Sat.–Thurs., 10, 12, 2.*

Norway Information Center is on the right side across the street when you face the harbor. From nearby Pipervika Bay, you can board a ferry in the summertime for the seven-minute crossing of the fjord to the **Bygdøy** peninsula, where there is a complex of seafaring museums. *Ferries run Apr.–Sept., at 15 past and 15 to each hr.* .

The first ferry stop is Dronningen. From here, walk up a well-marked road to the **Norsk Folkemuseum** (Norwegian Folk Museum), a large park where historic farmhouses, some of them centuries old, have been collected from all over the country and reassembled. A whole section of 19th-century Oslo was moved here, as was a 12th-century wooden stave church. There are displays of weaving and sheepshearing on Sunday, and throughout the park there are guides in period costume. *Museumsveien 10. Admission: Nkr 50 adults, Nkr 10 children. Open daily 10–4.*

Around the corner (signs will lead you) is the second museum. **Vikingskiphuset** (the Viking Ship Museum) contains 9th-century ships recovered from the fjord, where they had been ritually sunk while carrying the mortal remains of Viking kings and queens to the next world. Also on display are the treasures and jewelry that accompanied the royal bodies on their last voyage. The ornate craftsmanship evident in the ships and jewelry dispels any notion that the Vikings were skilled only in looting and pillaging. *Huk aveny 35. Admission: Nkr 20 adulls, Nkr 10 children. Open Nov.–Mar., daily 11–3; Apr. and Oct., daily 11–4; May–Aug., daily 9–6; Sept., daily 11–5.*

Reboard the ferry or follow signs for the 20-minute walk to the **Kon-Tiki Museum**, where the *Kon-Tiki* raft and the reed boat *RA II* are on view. Thor Heyerdahl made no concessions to the modern world when he used these boats to cross the Pacific *(Kon-Tiki)* and the Atlantic *(RA II). Admission: Nkr 25 adults, Nkr 10 children. Open Oct.–Mar., daily 10:30–4; Apr.–May 15 and Sept., daily 10:30–5; May 18–Aug. 31, daily 9–6.*

Directly across from the Kon-Tiki Museum is a large triangular building, **Fram-Museet.** This museum is devoted to the polar ship *Fram,* the sturdy wooden vessel that belonged to bipolar explorer Fridtjof Nansen. (It was also used by Amundsen.) In 1893 Nansen led an expedition that reached latitude 86°14′N, the most northerly latitude to have been reached at that time. The book *Farthest North* tells his story. (Active in Russian famine-relief work, Nansen received a Nobel Peace Prize in 1922.) You can board the ship and imagine yourself in one of the tiny berths, while outside a force-nine gale is blowing and the temperature is dozens of degrees below freezing. *Admission: Nkr 20 adults, Nkr 10 children. Open Apr., daily 11–2:45; May 1–15, daily 10–4:45; May 16–Sept., daily 9–5:45; Oct., daily 10–2:45; Nov., weekends; 11–2:45 Dec.–Mar., weekends 11–4.*

Back at City Hall, board Bus 29 to **Tøyen,** the area northeast of Oslo, where you'll find **Munch-Museet** (the Munch Museum). In 1940, four years before his death, Munch bequeathed much of his work to the city of Oslo; the museum opened in 1963, the centennial of his birth. Although only a fraction of its 22,000 items—books, paintings, drawings, prints, sculptures, and letters—are on display, you can still get a sense of the tortured expressionism that was to have such an effect on European painting. *Tøyengaten 53. Admission: Nkr 40 adults, Nkr 15 children. Open June–Sept. 15, Tues.–Sat. 10–6, Sun. noon–6; Sept. 16–May, Tues.–Sat. 10–4, Sun. noon–6.*

Shopping

Shopping Districts Many of the larger stores are between the Storting and the cathedral; much of this area is for pedestrians only. The **Basarhallene**, at the back of the cathedral, is an art and handicrafts boutique center. Oslo's newest shopping area is **Aker Brygge** (once a shipbuilding wharf). Right on the waterfront, it is a complex of stalls, offices, and garden cafés. Check out Bogstadveien/Hegdehaugsveien, which runs from Majorstua to Parkveien. This street offers a good selection of stores and has plenty of places to rest your tired feet and quench your thirst. Shops stay open until 5 PM (Thursday to 7 PM).

Department Stores and Malls Oslo's department stores, **Steen & Strøm** and **Christiania Glasmagasin**, are both in the shopping district near the cathedral. **Paléet** on Karl Johans gate is a new, elegant addition to Oslo's main street, with 40 shops and 10 restaurants. **Oslo City** (near Oslo Central Station) is the third-largest shopping Arcade in Oslo with 100 stores and businesses including a bank, a travel agency, and a medical center. *Open weekdays 9–8, Sat. 9–6.*

Dining

For details and price-category definitions, *see* Dining *in* Staying in Norway, *above.*

$$ **Brasserie Costa.** Costa is a trendy, Continental restaurant and bar with excellent pasta dishes that cost less in the bar. *Klingenberggate 4, tel. 22/424130. Reservations advised. AE, DC, MC, V.*

$$ **Det Gamle Raadhus.** The "old city hall," Oslo's oldest restaurant, is located in a building dating from 1641. Specialties include bacalao and shellfish casserole. *Nedre Slottsgate 1, tel. 22/420107. Reservations advised. AE, DC, MC, V. Closed Sun.*

$$ **Kastanjen.** The short menu at this neighborhood restaurant changes often and features all seasonal ingredients. The three-course prix-fixe dinner is an excellent value. *Bygdøy Allé 18, tel. 22/434467. Reservations recommended. AE, DC, MC, V. Closed Sun.*

$$ **Stefan.** The top-floor restaurant at the Stefan Hotel has the best lunch buffet in Oslo, with smoked, marinated, and pickled salmon; smoked reindeer; hot dishes; and homemade caramel pudding. *Stefan Hotel, Rosenkrantz' gate 1, tel. 22/429250. Lunch reservations required. AE, DC, MC, V.*

$$ **Theatercafeen.** This Oslo institution is the last Viennese-style café
★ in northern Europe and is a favorite with the literary and entertainment crowd. The daily menu is good value. Save room for dessert, which the pastry chef also makes for Norway's royal family. *Hotel Continental, Stortingsgata 24/26, tel. 22/419060. Reservations required. AE, DC, MC, V.*

$ **Albin Upp.** This cozy wine and snack bar is in a farmer's renovated
★ cottage, in a residential district about a 10-minute streetcar ride from town—catch the No. 1. Contemporary art is on display downstairs. *Briskebyveien 42, tel. 22/557192. No reservations. No credit cards. Lunch only. Closed weekends.*

$ **Felix.** This recently renovated day and night spot has marble-top tables and black café chairs, which create an informal atmosphere. Felix serves light meals and has extended opening hours. There's live music on weekends. *Drammensveien 30, tel. 22/442650. No reservations. AE, DC, MC, V.*

$ **Horgan's.** Among the excellent choices at this popular American restaurant and bar (it won Best Bar Award in 1992) are chicken Thai, fajitas, and potato skins. Heineken is on tap. *Hegdehaugsveien 24, tel. 22/608787. AE, DC, MC, V. Open 4 PM–1 AM.*

$ **Kaffistova.** This cafeteria serves Norwegian "country-style" cooking at reasonable prices. *Rosenkrantz' gate 8, tel. 22/429974. No reservations. AE, DC, MC, V.*

$ Lorry. This informal, funky restaurant was established in 1887 and still has its original interior. Lorry serves standard Norwegian food in a good atmosphere that's also a bit out of the ordinary. *Parkveien 12, tel. 22/696904. No reservations. AE, DC, MC, V.*

$ Vegeta. Next to the Nationaltheatret bus and streetcar station, this is a popular spot for hot and cold vegetarian meals and salads. It is a no-smoking restaurant. The all-you-can-eat specials offer top value. *Munkedamsveien 3B, tel. 22/834232. No reservations. No credit cards.*

¢ Beach Club. Looking for hard-to-find music? Beach Club is a quiet diner during the day and a rock café at night. The Club Burgers are famous, and prices start at about Nkr 50. *Bryggetorget 14, tel. 22/838382. No reservations. AE, DC, MC, V.*

¢ Eilefs Landhandleri. This is an untraditional restaurant made to look like an old-fashioned country store. The popular dishes start at Nkr 40. There's live music from 10 PM. *Kristian IVs gate 1, tel. 22/425347. No reservations. AE, DC, MC, V.*

¢ Olsens's Café. On Bogstadveien, this sunny yellow bohemian-style café has dishes that cost from Nkr 30 (there's a good quiche Lorraine). Keep yourself occupied with the many newspapers and backgammon and chessboards. *Bogstadveien 8 (entrance at Holtegata), tel. 22/690806. No reservations. No credit cards.*

¢ Tiffani. Tiffani is a two-story café with a basement and fireplace, plus friendly, good service. There's a variety of good homemade dishes served at breakfast, lunch, and dinner. *Behrensgate 2, tel. 22/434039. No reservations. No credit cards.*

Lodging

The tourist office's accommodations bureau (open daily 8 AM–11 PM) in Oslo Central Station can help you find reasonable rooms in hotels, pensions, and private homes. You must apply in person and pay a fee of Nkr 20 (Nkr 10 children) plus 10% of the room rate, which will be refunded when you check in. For details and price-category definitions, *see* Lodging *in* Staying in Norway, *above.*

$$ Bondeheimen. The most Norwegian hotel in town has modern, comfortable rooms and a staff that wears national costumes. *Rosenkrantz' gate 8, N–0159, tel. 22/429530, fax 22/419437. 76 rooms with bath or shower. AE, DC, MC, V.*

$$ Cecil Hotel. Built in 1989, just off Stortingsgata right in the heart of town, this hotel is a good value for the money. *Stortingsgata 8, N–0161, tel. 22/427000, fax 22/422670. 112 rooms with bath. Facilities: breakfast. AE, DC, MC, V.*

$$ Europa. This centrally located modern hotel is a moderately priced alternative to its expensive next-door neighbor, the SAS Scandinavia. The rooms are comfortable (all have color TV), and there are special reductions for children. *St. Olavs gate 31, N–0166, tel. 22/209990, fax 22/112727. 165 rooms with bath. AE, DC, MC, V.*

$$ Stefan. The service is cheerful and accommodating in this hotel in the center of Oslo. One of its main attractions is the popular restaurant on the top floor, with Oslo's best buffet lunch featuring traditional Norwegian dishes. *Rosenkrantz' gate 1, N–0159, tel. 22/429250, fax 22/337022. 130 rooms with bath or shower. Facilities: restaurant. AE, DC, MC, V.*

$$ Vika Atrium. This new, modern hotel is near City Hall and Aker Brygge. The restaurant serves breakfast, lunch, dinner, and a set à la carte menu that is available throughout the day. *Munkedamsveien 45, N–0121, tel. 22/833300, fax 22/830957. 79 rooms with bath. Facilities: restaurant. AE, DC, MC, V.*

$ Anker Hotel. This basic bed-and-breakfast has an awkward location, but the rooms are clean and airy. *Storgata 55, tel. 22/114005, N–0182, fax 22/110136. 120 rooms with bath. Facilities: breakfast room, free parking. AE, DC, MC, V.*

$ **Astoria.** This nicely renovated hotel is in the center of Oslo. *Dronningensgate 21, N–0154, tel. 22/420010, fax 22/425765. 132 rooms with bath. Facilities: breakfast room. AE, DC, MC, V.*

$ **Coch's Pensjonat.** Near the Royal Castle, Coch's is within walking distance of most of Oslo's attractions. The rooms are simple and clean with bathrooms and kitchenettes. Note that prices are lower for rooms with three to four beds. *Parkveien 25, N–0350, tel. 22/604836, fax 22/465402. 65 rooms, 50 with bath. V.*

$ **Gyldenløve.** Renovated in 1992, this central hotel offers good quality at a reasonable price and 160 well-equipped rooms. *Bogstadveien 20, N–0308, tel. 22/601090, fax 22/603390. 169 rooms with bath or shower. AE, DC, MC, V.*

$ **Munch Hotel.** This hotel, renovated in 1994, has large but rather basic rooms. It's a 10-minute walk from downtown. *Munchs gate 5, N–0130, tel. 22/424275, fax 22/206469. 180 rooms with shower. AE, DC, MC, V.*

¢ **Ami Hotel.** A comfortable, basic breakfast hotel, it is within walking distance from the downtown area. *Nordahl Brunsgate 9, N–0165, tel. 22/116110, fax 22/361801. 38 rooms, most with showers. Facilities: breakfast room. AE, DC, MC, V.*

¢ **Bogstad Camping.** By a lake with the same name and surrounded by golf courses and woodlands, this well-run camp has cabins. *Ankerveien 117, N–0757, tel. 22/507680, fax 22/500162. 16 cabins with bath. Facilities: cafeteria, laundry room. AE, MC, V.*

¢ **Oslo Vandrerhjem, Haraldsheim.** Close to public transport, this is a clean, well-run hostel. Rates are reduced for members of IYHF. Breakfast is served. *Haraldsheimveien 4, Box 41, Grefsen, N–0409, tel. 22/155043. 264 beds. No credit cards.*

The Arts

Considering the size of the city, Oslo has a surprisingly good artistic life. Consult the *Oslo Guide* or *Oslo This Week* for details. Winter is *the* cultural season, with the **Nationaltheatret** featuring modern plays (all in Norwegian), classics, and a good sampling of Ibsen. **Det Norske Teatret** (Kristian IVs gate 8), one of Europe's most modern theater complexes, features musicals and plays.

Oslo's modern **Konserthuset** (Concert Hall), at Munkedamsveien 14, is the home of the Oslo Philharmonic, famous for its recordings of Tchaikovsky's symphonies. A smaller hall in the same building is the setting for performances of chamber music and—in summer only—folk dancing, held Monday and Thursday at 9 in July and August. In addition to the **Museum of Contemporary Art,** there's a good modern collection at the **Henie-Onstad Kunstsenter** (Art Center) at Høvikodden. This center specializes in 20th-century art and was a gift from the Norwegian Olympic skater Sonja Henie and her husband, shipowner Niels Onstad. The center is open September–May, Tuesday–Friday 9–9, Saturday–Monday 11–5; June–August, weekends 11–7.

Nightlife

Karl Johans gate is a lively place into the wee hours. There are loads of music cafés and clubs, as well as more conventional night spots. Among the good ones is **Barock** (Universitetsgate 26, tel. 22/424420). **Cruise Kafé** (Aker Brygge 1, tel. 22/836430) is another hit. **Rockefeller** (Torggata 16—entrance from Mariboes gate, tel. 22/203232) draws crowds. **J Barbeint** (Drammensveien 20, tel. 22/445974) is also a good choice. Why not go to a movie? All films are screened in the original language with Norwegian subtitles. Tickets cost Nkr 45.

Bergen and Vicinity

To reach Bergen, you pass through the Telemark area, midway between Oslo and Bergen. This region is characterized by steep valleys, pine forests, lakes, and fast-flowing rivers that are full of trout. Bergen is also the gateway to the fabled land of the fjords.

Getting Around

By Plane Flesland Airport is about 40 miles from the center of Bergen. There is good airport bus service to the downtown area.

By Train The Oslo–Bergen train route passes through forests, mountains, and fjords and is the most spectacular in Norway.

By Bus Contact the Bergen Tourist Information Office (*see below*) about express or local bus service to and from Bergen.

When checking into your hotel, ask for **The Bergen Card,** which offers weekend discounts on buses, ferries, car rentals, theaters, and more.

Tourist Information

Bergen (Slottsgate 1, tel. 55/313860; Bryggen 7, tel. 55/321480).

Exploring Bergen

Bergen is Norway's second-largest city, with a population of 219,000. Before oil brought an influx of foreigners to Stavanger, it was the most international of the country's cities, having been an important trading and military center when Oslo was an obscure village. Bergen was a member of the medieval Hanseatic League and offered an ice-free harbor and convenient trading location on the west coast. Natives of Bergen still think of Oslo as a dour provincial town.

Founded in 1070, the town was first called Bjørgvin. Despite numerous fires, much of medieval Bergen has remained or been restored. Seven surrounding mountains set off the weathered wooden houses, cobbled streets, and Hanseatic-era warehouses of the **Bryggen** (harbor area).

The best way to get a feel for Bergen's medieval trading heyday is to visit the **Hanseatic Museum** on Bryggen, facing the bay. One of the oldest and best-preserved of Bergen's wooden buildings, it is furnished in 16th-century style. The guided tour is excellent. *Admission: Nkr 15 adults, Nkr 8 children. Open June–Aug., daily 10–5; May, Sept., daily 11–2; Oct.–Apr., Mon., Wed., Fri., Sun. 11–2.*

On the western end of the Vågen (bay) is the **Rosenkrantz Tower,** part of the **Bergenhus,** the 13th-century fortress guarding the harbor entrance. The tower and fortress were destroyed during World War II, but were meticulously restored during the '60s and are now rich with furnishings and household items from the 16th century. *Admission: Nkr 15 adults, Nkr 5 children. Open mid-May–mid-Sept., daily 10–4; mid-Sept.–mid-May, Sun. 12–3, or upon request.*

Across the Vågen is the **Nordnes peninsula,** where you can look back toward the city and the mountains beyond. Save time to meander through the winding side streets, intersected by broad *almenninger* (wide avenues built as protection against fires). For the best view of Bergen and its surroundings, take the funicular from the corner of Lille Øvregate and Vetrlidsalmenning. It climbs 310 meters (1,016 feet) to the top of **Fløyen,** one of the seven mountains guarding this ancient port. *Round-trip fare: Nkr 28 adults, Nkr 14 children.*

Troldhaugen manor on Nordås Lake, once home to Edvard Grieg, is now a museum and includes a new chamber music hall. Recitals are held each Wednesday and Sunday at 7:30 PM from late June through early August. *Troldhaugsveien, Hop, Bergen, tel. 55/911791. Admission: Nkr 30 adults, Nkr 15 children. Open May–Sept., daily 9:30–5:30.*

Excursions from Bergen

Lysøen Island Ole Bull was one of Norway's favorite musicians, and he passed many a violin-playing hour on **Lysøen Island,** the site of what was his villa. It is now a national monument, donated to Norway by his American granddaughter. Apart from Ole Bull memorabilia, there are 13 kilometers (8 miles) of nature trails. Ferries to Lysøen leave from Buena pier (Sørstraumen), 26 kilometers (16 miles) south of the center. Round-trip fare is Nkr 30 adults, Nkr 15 children. *Admission to villa (tel. 55/309077): Nkr 20 adults, Nkr 5 children. Open mid-May–early Sept., Mon.–Sat. 12–4, Sun. 11–5.*

Bergen is the start of fjord cruises of all descriptions. Crossing fjords is a necessary as well as a scenic way to travel in Norway. Hardangerfjord, Sognefjord, and Nordfjord are three of the deepest and most popular fjords. Details on cruises can be obtained from the Bergen Tourist Information Office.

Dining and Lodging

For details and price-category definitions, *see* Dining and Lodging *in* Staying in Norway, *above.* Best bets are indicated by a star ★.

Bergen **Banco Rotto.** This beautiful Art Deco building, formerly a bank, is
Dining now a reasonably priced café and restaurant, with dancing and a
★ late-night piano bar. *Vågsalmenningen 16, tel. 55/327520. AE, DC, MC, V. Open weekdays 11–4:30, Wed.–Sat. 7 PM–2:30 AM. $$*

Enhjørningen (Unicorn). One of Bergen's most popular seafood restaurants, Unicorn is in an old Hanseatic warehouse. *Bryggen, tel. 55/327919. Reservations required. AE, DC, MC, V. Open weekdays noon–midnight, closed Sun. $$*

Madam Felle. At Bryggen, Madam Felle serves very enjoyable light meals and snacks. Its Promenaden bar on the water, across the street, is the place to be on a sunny day. *Bryggen, tel. 55/543000. No reservations. AE, DC, MC, V. $$*

Michelangelo. A restaurant with Italian food and lots of atmosphere, Michelangelo serves up great pasta specialties. *Neumannsgate 25, tel. 55/900825 or 55/234004. Reservations required on weekends. AE, DC, MC, V. $$*

Pasta Sentralen. A cosy Italian restaurant frequented by students, this is a must if you're in search of hearty dishes at unbeatable prices. *Vestre Strandkai 6, tel. 55/960037. No credit cards. ¢*

Lodging **Augustin.** This small but excellent hotel in the center of town has a late–Art Nouveau character, complete with period furniture in the lobby. *C. Sundtsgate 24, N–5004, tel. 55/230025, fax 55/233130. 50 rooms with bath. AE, DC, MC, V. $$*

Bryggen Orion. Facing the harbor in the center of town, the hotel is surrounded by Bergen's most famous sights. *Bradbenken 3, N–5003, tel. 55/318080, fax 55/329414. 229 rooms with bath. Facilities: restaurant, bar, nightclub. AE, DC, MC, V. $$*

Myklebust Pensjonat. This tiny, popular, family-run lodge has a quiet, central location. *Rosenbergsgate 19, N–5015, tel. 55/901670. 5 double rooms, 2 with private bath. No credit cards. $*

Private accommodations are available as well, and range in price from Nkr 145–Nkr 170 for a single room to Nkr 235–Nkr 300 for a double. Apply in person at the Bergen Tourist Information Office.

19 Poland

Following the revolution of 1989, Poland offers the budget traveler more than ever. Despite rampant inflation and price hikes, the lifting of state controls on charges for accommodations and other services has made life much easier for the foreign visitor, and countrywide there is a far greater range of lodging and dining options.

Poland is rich in natural beauty and contrasts. Its landscape varies from rolling plains with slow-moving rivers, broad fields, and scattered villages to lakes, forests, and marshes in the north and jagged mountains in the south. This makes available a variety of low-cost touring possibilities. Every one of the major cities, with the exception of Kraków (Cracow) and Łódź, had to be rebuilt after the destruction of World War II. Particularly fine restoration work has been done on Warsaw's Old Town and in Gdańsk on the Baltic coast.

Poland never did fit into the mold of a Communist country. Through more than 40 years of Communist rule, most Poles remained devoutly Catholic. Both rural and urban life remain centered on the home and family, where old traditions are diligently upheld. Four-fifths of the country's farmland has remained privately owned, and since 1990 a major privatization drive has been under way in the rest of the economy.

Poland's geographic position between Germany and Russia has determined its history of almost continual war and struggle for independence since the late 18th century. More than 40 years of Communist rule left Poland in a serious economic crisis, and although Poland now has a non-Communist government, no one has simple answers to the country's complicated political and economic problems.

In spite of all this, the Polish people continue to be resilient, resourceful, and hopeful. Poles openly welcome visitors; their uninhibited hospitality makes them eager to please. It is easy to make friends here and to exchange views with strangers on trains and buses. Poles have a passionate interest in all things Western, from current affairs to the arts, clothes, and music.

Essential Information

Before You Go

When to Go The official tourist season runs from May through September. The best times for sightseeing are late spring and early fall. Major cultural events usually take place in the cities during the fall. The early spring is often wet and windy.

Below are the average daily maximum and minimum temperatures for Warsaw.

Jan.	32F	0C	**May**	67F	20C	**Sept.**	66F	19C
	22	- 6		48	9		49	10
Feb.	32F	0C	**June**	73F	23C	**Oct.**	55F	13C
	21	- 6		54	12		41	5
Mar.	42F	6C	**July**	75F	24C	**Nov.**	42F	6C
	28	- 2		58	16		33	1
Apr.	53F	12C	**Aug.**	73F	23C	**Dec.**	35F	2C
	37	3		56	14		28	- 3

Currency The monetary unit in Poland is the złoty (zł), which is divided into 100 groszy (gr). By 1994 inflation had driven the groszy, and coins in general, out of circulation; there were notes of 50, 100, 200, 500, 1,000, 2,000, 5,000, 10,000 20,000, 50,000, 100,000, 200,000, 500,000, 1,000,000, and 2,000,000 złotys. A currency reform in January 1995 knocked four naughts (or zeroes) off the numeration of the złoty and brought notes of 10, 20, 50, 100, and 200 złotys and coins of 1, 2, and 10 złotys and 1, 2, 5, 10, and 50 groszy. These are to circulate together with the old denominations until 1997. At press time (summer 1995), the bank exchange rate was about zł 2.4 (24,000) to the U.S. dollar and zł 3.9 (39,000) to the pound sterling. Since spring 1989, the złoty has been legally exchangeable at a free market rate in banks (*Bank Narodowy* and *Pekao* are the largest) and private exchange bureaus (*Kantor wymiany walut*), which sometimes offer slightly better rates than do the banks; kantor rates also vary, so it's worth shopping around. If you run out of złotys, you will find that Polish taxi drivers, waiters, and porters will usually accept dollars or any other Western currency. Money exchanged into złotys can be reconverted upon leaving the country.

Credit Cards American Express, Diners Club, MasterCard, and Visa are accepted in all Orbis hotels, in the better restaurants and nightclubs, and for other Orbis services. In small cafés and shops, credit cards may not be accepted.

What It Will Cost At press time (summer 1995), it was still illegal to import or export złotys. This may change if the Polish government goes through with plans to make the złoty fully convertible on the international market. Still, don't buy more złotys than you need, or you will have to go to the trouble of changing them back at the end of your trip.

Poland is now one of the more expensive countries of Eastern Europe, and inflation is still high by Western standards, despite the reforms of 1990. Prices are highest in the big cities, especially in Warsaw. The more you stray off the tourist track, the cheaper your vacation will be. The cost difference can sometimes be enormous. What you save in money, however, you may lose in quality of service.

Sample Prices A cup of coffee, zł 1.5–4.5 (15,000–45,000); a bottle of beer, zł 2–4.5 (20,000–45,000); a soft drink, zł 1–4.5 (10,000–45,000); a ham sandwich, zł 2–5 (20,000–50,000); 1-mile taxi ride, zł 3 (30,000).

Museums Admission fees to museums and other attractions are also rising in line with inflation and seem ever-changing. At press time (summer 1995), fees ranged from zł 1 (10,000) to zł 10 (100,000). Note that most museums offer free admission one day a week (usually Wednesday).

Visas U.S. and British citizens are no longer required to obtain visas for entry to Poland; Canadian citizens and citizens of other countries that have not yet abolished visas for Poles must pay the equivalent of $35 (more for multiple-entry visas). Apply at any Orbis office (the official Polish tourist agency), an affiliated travel agent, or from the Polish Consulate General in any country. Each visitor must complete three visa application forms and provide two photographs. Allow about two weeks for processing. Visas are issued for 90 days but can be extended in Poland, if necessary, either through the local county police headquarters or through Orbis.

You can contact the **Polish Consulate General** at the following addresses: **In the United States:** 233 Madison Ave., New York, NY 10016 (tel. 212/391–0844); 1530 North Lake Shore Dr., Chicago, IL 60610 (tel. 312/337–8166); 2224 Wyoming Ave., Washington, DC 20008 (tel. 202/234–2501). **In Canada:** 1500 Pine Ave., Montreal, Quebec H3G (tel. 514/937–9481); 2603 Lakeshore Blvd. W., Toronto, Ont. M8V 1G5 (tel. 416/252–5471). **In the United Kingdom:** 73 New Cavendish St., London W1 (tel. 0171/636–4533).

Customs on Arrival Persons over 17 may bring in duty-free: personal belongings, including musical instruments, typewriter, radio, 2 cameras with 24 rolls of film; up to 250 cigarettes or 50 cigars and 1 liter each of wine and spirits; and goods to the value of $200. Any amount of foreign currency may be brought in but must be declared on arrival.

Language Most older Poles know German; the younger generation usually knows some English. In the big cities you will find people who speak English, especially in hotels, but you may have difficulty in the provinces and countryside.

Getting Around

By Train Poland's PKP railway network is extensive and inexpensive. Most trains have first- and second-class accommodations, but Western visitors usually prefer to travel first-class; second-class is reasonably comfortable on intercity and express trains but can be cramped and uncomfortable on slow trains. The fastest trains are intercity and express trains, which require reservations. Some Orbis offices furnish information, reservations, and tickets. Overnight trains have first- and second-class sleeping cars and second-class couchettes. Most long-distance trains carry buffets, but the quality of the food is unpredictable and you may want to bring your own.

Fares Fares vary according to the speed at which a train travels: It is twice as expensive to travel on an express as on a local train. Note that your ticket is valid only for the day or days specified when you buy it; getting a refund is complicated, so it is best to plan carefully. Since a return ticket costs exactly twice the one-way fare, you may prefer to put off purchase until your plans are definite.

By Plane **LOT,** Poland's national airline, operates daily flights linking five main cities. Fares begin at about $60 round-trip and can be paid for in złotys. Tickets and information are available from LOT or Orbis offices. All flights booked through Orbis in the United Kingdom carry a discount, but it is cheaper to pay in local currency in Poland. Be sure to book well in advance, especially for the summer season.

By Bus Express bus services link all main cities as well as smaller towns and villages off the rail network. Buses are crowded; express buses are more expensive than trains, but local buses are inexpensive. PKS bus stations are usually located near railway stations. Tickets and information are best obtained from Orbis. Warsaw's central bus terminal is at aleje Jerozolimskie 144.

Staying in Poland

Telephones
Local Calls Public phone booths take tokens or coins for 20 gr (zł 2,000) for local calls and gr 5 (5,000), zł 1 (10,000), and zł 2 (20,000) for long-distance calls, which must be made from special booths, usually situated in post offices. Place a token in the groove on the side or top of the phone, lift the receiver, and dial the number. Many phones automatically absorb the token; in others you must push it into the machine when the call is answered. Card phones are being increasingly introduced and can be used for both local and long-distance calls. Cards cost zł 5 (50,000) and zł 10 (100,000) and are available at post offices and newspaper kiosks.

PARIS?
ROME?
WARSAW.

Don't just read about the changes in Eastern Europe. See them for yourself.
Stroll along the cobbled streets and vistas of Old Town. Enjoy coffee in the Old
Market square. And everywhere, experience a new birth of freedom
and enterprise in Warsaw, your best gateway to the splendors of Krakow,
Budapest, and Prague. Let us show you our passion for Poland.
With LOT Polish Airlines' Boeing 767s, the only non-stops to Warsaw, from New York,
Newark and Chicago, Business and Economy Class. Call your travel agent
today for new lower fares for the spring season, or call us direct at 1-800-223-0593.

T H E   P O L I S H   A I R L I N E

Reality check. Call home.

—— *AT&T USADirect® and World Connect®. The fast, easy way to call most anywhere.* ——

Take out AT&T Calling Card or your local calling card.** Lift phone. Dial AT&T Access Number
for country you're calling from. Connect to English-speaking operator or voice prompt.
Reach the States or over 200 countries. Talk. Say goodbye. Hang up. Resume vacation.

Austria*†††	022-903-011	Luxembourg	0-800-0111	Turkey*	00-800-1227
Belgium*	0-800-100-10	Netherlands*	06-022-9111	United Kingdom	0500-89-0011
Czech Republic*	00-420-00101	Norway	800-190-11		
Denmark	8001-0010	Poland†♦¹	0◊010-480-0111		
Finland	9800-100-10	Portugal†	05017-1-288		
France	19-0011	Romania*	01-800-4288		
Germany	0130-0010	Russia*†(Moscow)	155-5042		
Greece*	00-800-1311	Slovak Rep.*	00-420-00101		
Hungary*	00◊-800-01111	Spain●	900-99-00-11		
Ireland	1-800-550-000	Sweden	020-795-611		
Italy*	172-1011	Switzerland*	155-00-11		

AT&T
Your True Choice

**You can also call collect or use most U.S. local calling cards. Countries in bold face permit country-to-country calling in addition to calls to the U.S. World Connect® prices consist of USADirect® rates plus an additional charge based on the country you are calling. Collect calling available to the U.S. only. *Public phones require deposit of coin or phone card. † May not be available from every phone. ††† Public phone require local coin payment during call. ♦ Not available from public phones. ◊ Await second dial tone. ¹Dial 010-480-0111 from major Warsaw hotels. ●Calling available to most European countries. ©1995 AT&T

For a free wallet sized card of all AT&T Access Numbers, call: 1-800-241-5555.

International Post offices and first-class hotels have assigned booths, at which you
Calls pay after the completion of the call. To place an international call via
an **AT&T** operator, dial 0, wait for dial tone, then 010–480–0111;
from major hotels in Warsaw, dial 010–480–0111. To place a call via
MCI, dial 01–04–800–222; via **Sprint,** dial 0010–480–0115.

Country Code The country code for Poland is 48.

Information For general information (including international codes), dial 913.

Mail Airmail letters to the United States cost gr 85 (8,500); postcards, gr
Postal Rates 65 (6,500). Letters to the United Kingdom or Europe cost gr 65
(5,500); postcards, gr 55 (5,500). Post offices are open 8 AM–8 PM (except weekends). At least one post office is open 24 hours in every major
city. In Warsaw the post office is located at ulica Świętokrzyska 31.

Opening and **Banks** are open weekdays 8 or 9 AM–3 PM or 6 PM.
Closing Times
Museums. Hours vary greatly but are generally Tuesday–Sunday
9–5.

Shops. Food shops are open weekdays 7 AM–7 PM, Saturday 7 AM–1
PM. Other stores are open weekdays 11 AM–7 PM and Saturday 9 AM–1
PM; some food shops in all districts are now open on Sundays.

National In 1996: January 1, April 7 (Easter), May 1 (Labor Day), May 3
Holidays (Constitution Day), June 20 (Corpus Christi), August 15 (Feast of
the Assumption), November 1 (Remembrance), November 11 (re-
birth of Polish state, 1918), December 25–26. Changing holidays in
1997: March 30 (Easter), May 29 (Corpus Christi).

Dining There is a heavy emphasis on soups and meat (especially pork), as
well as freshwater fish. Much use is made of cream, and pastries are
rich and often delectable.

The most popular soup is *barszcz* (known to many Americans as
borscht), a clear beet soup often served with such Polish favorites as
sausage, cabbage, potatoes, sour cream, coarse rye bread, and beer.
Other dishes include pierogi (a kind of ravioli), which may be stuffed
with savory or sweet fillings; *gołąbki*, cabbage leaves stuffed with
minced meat; *bigos*, sauerkraut with meat and mushrooms; and
flaki, a select dish of tripe, served boiled or fried. Polish beer is
good; vodka is a specialty and is often downed before, with, and after meals.

There is an ever-widening selection of eating places, although—at
least in the cities—the top end of the price range is currently better
served than the lower end. The *bary mleczne* (milk bars) selling
cheap and healthy dairy and vegetable dishes are fast disappearing,
replaced by the ubiquitous pizza parlor. However, if you look hard,
you can still find one or two good, low-budget traditional eating
places in most towns. As elsewhere in Central Europe, cafés are a
way of life in Poland and are often stocked with delicious pastries
and ice cream.

Mealtimes At home, Poles eat late lunches and late suppers; the former is their
main meal. Many restaurants, however, especially in the provinces,
close around 9 PM. In cities, opening hours are later, and most hotel
restaurants serve the evening meal until 10:30.

Precautions Tap water is unsafe, so ask for mineral water. Beware of meat dishes
served in cheap snack bars. Avoid the food on trains.

What to Wear If you're splurging at an expensive restaurant in Warsaw or Kraków,
formal dress is appropriate. Casual dress is appropriate elsewhere.

Ratings Prices are for one person and include three courses and service but
no drinks. Best bets are indicated by a star ★.

Category	Warsaw	Other Areas
$$	zł 25–50 (250,000–500,000)	zł 20–40 (200,000–400,000)
$	zł 15–25 (150,000–250,000)	zł 10–20 (100,000–200,000)
¢	under zł 15 (150,000)	under zł 10 (100,000)

Lodging
Hotels Orbis hotels are usually very expensive (not to say overpriced) in cities and major tourist spots. But in out-of-the-way places—if you don't mind a room without a private bath—these hotels can be inexpensive. The standards of municipally owned hotels vary greatly, but some are very good, and you can occasionally find a real bargain. Dom Turysty hotels, run or licensed by the Polish Tourist Association, are usually unpretentiously comfortable but often have only a limited number of single and double rooms. Gromada, the cooperative, runs an excellent network of comfortable and inexpensive hotels with a reputation for good food. In many holiday resorts (Zakopane, Kraków, the Baltic coast) off-season prices can be as little as half those charged in full season; many hotels have now introduced a 20% weekend reduction.

Hostels The Polish Youth Hostels Association operates hostels at budget rate, zł 3.5 (35,000)–zł 8 (80,000) per night; in addition, hostels are open to people of all ages. Information is available from your local branch of the International Youth Hostel Association.

Roadside Inns A number of roadside inns, often very attractive, offer inexpensive food and a few guest rooms at moderate rates.

Private Accommodations Rooms can be arranged either in advance through Orbis or on the spot at the local tourist information office. Villas, lodges, rooms, or houses are available, and the prices are often negotiable. Rates vary from about $6 for a room to more than $150 for a villa.

Ratings The following chart is based on a rate for two people in a double room, with bath or shower and breakfast. These prices are in U.S. dollars. Best bets are indicated by a star ★.

Category	Cost
$$	$50–$100
$	$25–$50
¢	under $25

Tipping Waiters get a standard 10% of the bill. Hotel porters and doormen should get about zł 1 (10,000). In Warsaw and other big towns frequented by foreign tourists, waiters also often expect a tip to help find you a table. If you choose to tip in foreign currency (readily accepted), remember that $1 is about an hour's wage.

Warsaw

Arriving and Departing

By Plane All international flights arrive at Warsaw's Okęcie Airport (Port Lotniczy) just southwest of the city. Terminal 1 serves international flights from the West; Terminal 2 serves domestic and East European flights. For flight information, contact the airlines, or call the airport at tel. 02/650–42–20.

Between the LOT operates a regular bus service into Warsaw. In addition, Bus
Airport and 175 leaves every 10 minutes from the international terminal. The
Downtown trip takes about 15 minutes and the fare is gr 60 (6,000); after 11 PM,
it is raised to zł 2 (20,000).

By Train Trains to and from Western Europe arrive at Dworzec Centralny on
aleje Jerozolimskie in the center of town. For tickets and information, contact Orbis.

By Car There are seven main access routes to Warsaw, all leading to the center of the city. Drivers heading to or from the West will use the E8 or
E12 highways.

Getting Around

By Tram and These are often crowded, but they are the cheapest way of getting
Bus around. Trams and buses (including express buses) cost gr 60
(6,000). The bus fare goes up to zł 2 (20,000) between 11 PM and 5:30
AM. Tickets must be bought in advance from **Ruch** newsstands or
street vendors. You must cancel your own ticket in a machine on the
tram or bus when you get on; watch others do it.

Important Addresses and Numbers

Tourist The **Center for Tourist Information** is open 9–6 weekdays, 11–6
Information weekends; it is located at plac Zamkowy 1, tel. 02/635–18–81. **Orbis**
offices in Warsaw include ulica Bracka 16, tel. 022/26–02–71; and
ulica Marszałkowska 142, tel. 022/27–80–31 or 022/27–36–73.

Embassies U.S. (aleje Ujazdowskie 29–31, tel. 022/628–30–41). **Canadian** (ulica
Matejki 1/5, tel. 022/29–80–51). **U.K.** (aleje Róż 1, tel. 022/628–10–
01). **U.K. Consulate** (ul. Emilii Plater 28, tel. 02/625–30–30).

Emergencies **Police** (tel. 997). **Ambulance** (tel. 998). **Doctor** (tel. 998 or call your
embassy).

Travel **Thomas Cook,** ul. Nowy Świat 64, tel. 022/26–47–29.
Agencies

Guided Tours

Bus tours of the city depart in the morning and afternoon from the
major hotels. **Orbis** also has half-day excursions into the surrounding countryside. These usually include a meal and some form of traditional entertainment. Check for details with your hotel, the Orbis
office, or a tourist information office.

Exploring Warsaw

At the end of World War II, Warsaw lay in ruins, a victim of system-
atic Nazi destruction. Only one-third of its prewar population survived the horrors of German occupation. The experience has left its
mark on the city and is visible everywhere in the memorial plaques
describing mass executions of civilians and in the bullet holes on the
facades of buildings. Against all the odds, Warsaw's survivors have
rebuilt their historic city. The old districts have been painstakingly
reconstructed according to old prints and paintings, including those
of Belotto and Canaletto from the 18th century. The result, a city of
warm pastel colors, is remarkable.

Surrounding the old districts, however, is the modern Warsaw, built
since the war in utilitarian Socialist Realist style. Whether you like
it or not is your business, but it is worth noting as testimony to one
approach to urban life. The sights of Warsaw are all relatively close
to each other, making most attractions accessible by foot.

*Numbers in the margin correspond to points of interest on the War-
saw map.*

The Old Town A walking tour of the old historic district takes about two hours. Be-
① gin in the heart of the city at **plac Zamkowy** (Castle Square), where
you will see a slender column supporting the **statue of Zygmunt (Sig-
ismund) III Vasa,** the king who made Warsaw his capital in the early
17th century. It is the city's oldest monument and, symbolically, the
first to be rebuilt after the wartime devastation. Dominating the
② square is the **Zamek Królewski** (Royal Castle). Restoring the interi-
or was a herculean task, requiring workers to relearn traditional
skills, match ancient woods and fabrics, and even reopen abandoned
quarries to find just the right kind of stone. A visit is worthwhile,
despite the crowds. *Tel. 022/635–39–95. Admission: zł 8 (80,000)
adults, zł 4 (40,000) children; ½ price Sun. Open Tues.–Sat. 10–
2:30, Sun. 9–2:30.*

Enter the narrow streets of the **Old Town** (Stare Miasto), with its
colorful medieval houses, cobblestone alleys, uneven roofs, and
wrought-iron grillwork. On your right as you proceed along ulica
③ Świętojańska is the **Bazylika świętego Jana** (Cathedral of St. John),
the oldest church in Warsaw, dating from the 14th century. Several
④ Polish kings were crowned here. Soon you will reach the **Rynek
Starego Miasta** (Old Market Square), the charming and intimate
center of the Old Town. The old town hall, which once stood in the
middle, was pulled down in the 19th century. It was not replaced,
and today the square is full of open-air cafés, tubs of flowering
plants, and the inevitable artists displaying their talents for the
tourists. At night the brightly lighted Rynek (marketplace) is the
place to go for good food and atmosphere.

Continue along ulica Nowomiejska until you get to the imposing
⑤ redbrick **Barbakan,** a fine example of a 16th-century defensive fortification. From here you can see the partially restored town wall that
was built to enclose the Old Town and enjoy a splendid view of the
Vistula River, with the district of Praga on its east bank.

Follow the street called ulica Freta to Warsaw's **New Town** (Nowe
Miasto), which was founded at the turn of the 15th century. Rebuilt
after the war in 18th-century style, this district has a more elegant
⑥ and spacious feeling about it. Of interest here is the **Muzeum Marii
Skłodowskiej-Curie,** where the woman who discovered radium and
polonium was born. *Ul. Freta 16, tel. 022/31–80–92. Admission: zł 1
(10,000) adults, gr 50 (5,000) children. Open Tues.–Sat. 10–4:30,
Sun. 10–2:30.*

The Royal All towns with kings had their Royal Routes; the one in Warsaw
Way stretched south from Castle Square down Krakowskie Przedmieście, curving through Nowy Świat and on along aleje
⑦ Ujazdowskie to the **Pałac Belweder** (Belvedere Palace) and Łazienki
Park. Some of Warsaw's finest churches and palaces are found along
this route, as are the names of famous Poles. A few blocks south of
⑧ plac Zamkowy on Krakowskie Przedmieście, you'll come to **Warsaw**
⑨ **University** on your left. Farther down, on your right, the **Kościół
świętego Krzyża** (Holy Cross Church) contains a pillar in which the
heart of the great Polish composer Frédéric Chopin is entombed. As
you pass the statue of Nicolaus Copernicus, Poland's most famous
astronomer, you enter the busy Nowy Świat thoroughfare. Crossing aleje Jerozolimskie, on your left is the **former headquarters of the
Polish Communist party,** a large solid gray building typical of the
Socialist Realist architectural style, which now houses banks and
Poland's new stock exchange.

Aleje Ujazdowskie is considered by many locals to be Warsaw's finest
street. It is lined with magnificent buildings and has something of a
French flavor to it. A hundred years ago, this fashionable thoroughfare was thronged with fancy carriages and riders eager to see and
be seen. It is now a favorite with Sunday strollers. Down at its
southern end, before the name inexplicably changes to Belwed-

erska, the French-style landscaped **Park Łazienkowski** (Łazienki Park), with pavilions and a royal palace, stands in refreshing contrast to the bustling streets. The **Pałac Łazienkowski** (Łazienki Palace), a gem of Polish neoclassicism, was the private residence of Stanisław August Poniatowski, the last king of Poland. It overlooks a lake stocked with huge carp. At the impressionistic Chopin monument nearby, you can stop for a well-deserved rest and, on summer Sundays, listen to an open-air concert. *Tel. 02/621–62–41. Admission: zł 3 (30,000) adults, zł 1.5 (15,000) children. Open Tues.–Sat. 9:30–3.*

The Royal Route extends along ulica Belwederska, ulica Jana Sobieskiego, and aleja Wilanowska to **Wilanów,** 10 kilometers (6 miles) from the town center. This charming Baroque palace was the summer residence of King Jan III Sobieski, who, in 1683, stopped the Ottoman advance on Europe at the Battle of Vienna. The palace interior is open and houses antique furniture and a fine poster museum. *Ul. Wiertnicza 1, tel. 022/42–07–95. Admission: zł 3 (30,000) adults, zł 1.5 (15,000) children. Open Wed.–Mon. 10–2:30.*

Off the Beaten Track

Some 3 million Polish Jews were put to death by the Nazis during World War II, ending the enormous Jewish contribution to Polish culture, tradition, and achievement. A simple **Monument to the Heroes of the Warsaw Ghetto,** a slab of dark granite with a bronze basrelief, stands on ulica Zamenhofa in the Muranów district, the historic heart of the Jewish district before the war and ghetto under the Nazi regime. The Warsaw Ghetto uprising that broke out in April 1943 was put down with unbelievable ferocity, and the Muranów district was flattened. Today there are only bleak gray apartment blocks here.

With ironic humor, Warsaw locals tell you that the best vantage point from which to admire their city is atop the 37-story **Palace of Culture and Science.** Why? Because it is the only point from which you can't see the Palace of Culture and Science. This wedding-cakestyle skyscraper was a personal gift from Stalin. Although it is disliked by Poles as a symbol of Soviet domination, it does afford a panoramic view and is the best example in Warsaw of 1950s "Socialist Gothic" architecture. *Plac Defilad, tel. 02/050–07–77. Admission: zł 7.5 (75,000) adults, 2.5 (25,000) children. Open daily 9–5.*

Shopping

The most fashionable shopping streets, Nowy Świat and ulica Chmielna, are lined with elegant boutiques that are good for window-shopping—but if you want bargains, look elsewhere. Polish leather goods are of high quality and often substantially cheaper than those sold in the West; large specialty stores (for example at ulica Marszałkowska 83) are the best places to look. *Cepelia* stores (Plac Konstytucji 5, Rynek Starego Miasta 8/10) have a wide range of reasonably priced traditional handicrafts, such as hand-woven wool rugs, tapestries, amber jewelry, and carved-wood kitchenware. Polish crystal and glass are good buys; try the specialty store at ulica Piękna 26–34. State-owned department stores, **Junior** and **Centralne Domy Towarowe,** still survive in somewhat altered form on ulica Marszałkowska opposite the Palace of Culture and Science.

For the more adventurous there is a flea market, **Bazar Różyckiego,** on ulica Targowa 55, where you can find almost anything. Another market is now open daily at Stadion Dzięsięciolecia (Rondo Waszyngtona); here, visitors from all over Eastern Europe gather to sell their wares, often very cheaply—although you should inspect

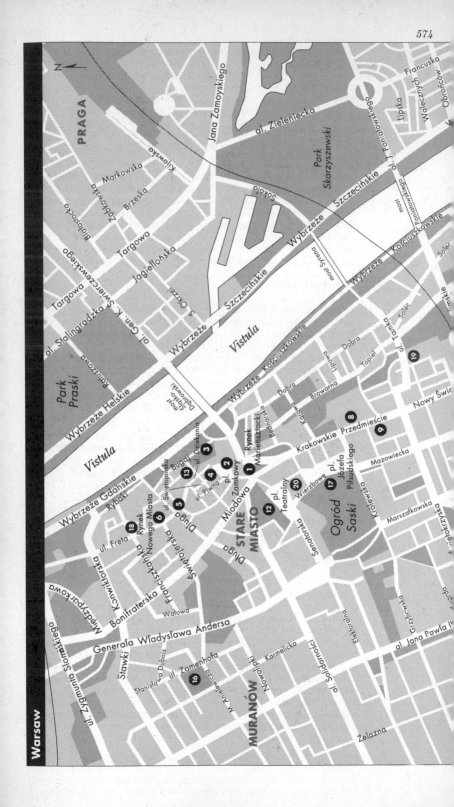

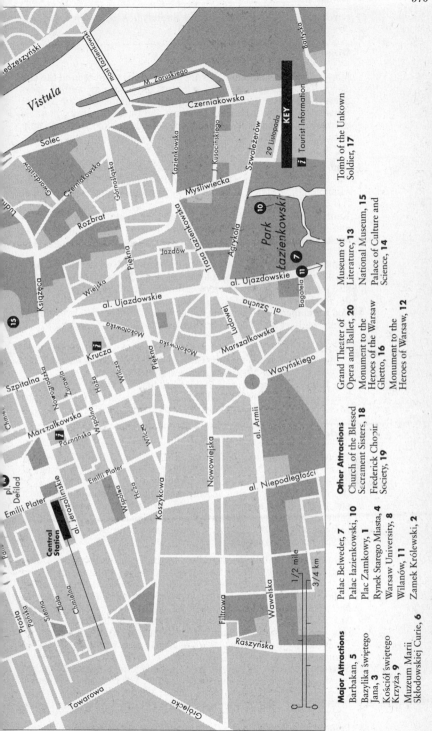

KEY

i Tourist Information

Major Attractions

Barbakan, **5**
Bazylika świętego
Jana, **3**
Kościół świętego
Krzyza, **9**
Muzeum Marii
Skłodowskiej Curie, **6**

Palac Belweder, **7**
Palac łazienkowski, **10**
Plac Zamkowy, **1**
Rynek Starego Miasta, **4**
Warsaw University, **8**
Wilanów, **11**
Zamek Królewski, **2**

Other Attractions

Church of the Blessed
Sacrament Sisters, **18**
Frederick Chopin
Society, **19**

Grand Theater of
Opera and Ballet, **20**
Monument to the
Heroes of the Warsaw
Ghetto, **16**
Monument to the
Heroes of Warsaw, **12**

Museum of
Literature, **13**
National Museum, **15**
Palace of Culture and
Science, **14**

Tomb of the Unkown
Soldier, **17**

purchases carefully. There is also a Sunday flea market at Koło (take Tram 24 to the terminal).

Dining

Many of Warsaw's restaurants are to be found in and around the Old Town. The setting is atmospheric, but the food may well be over-priced, so it is worth investigating what is available in other parts of town. Remember that in inexpensive and budget restaurants it is unlikely that English will be spoken; take along a dictionary to help with the menu. For details and price-category definitions, *see* Dining *in* Staying in Poland, *above.*

$$ Ambasador. This bright, well-lit restaurant, a stone's throw from the Polish parliament, specializes in Polish dishes. Try the grilled salmon. *Ul. Matejki 4, tel. 022/25–99–61. Reservations advised. AE, DC, MC, V.*

$$ Kamienne Schodki. This intimate, candlelit restaurant is located in one of the Market Square's medieval houses. Its main specialty is duck; also try the pastries. *Rynek Starego Miasta 26, tel. 022/31–08–22. Reservations advised. No credit cards.*

$$ Pod Samsonem. This small restaurant, decorated in wood, has a smoke-filled Warsaw atmosphere and friendly waitresses. The fish and pierogi are good when available. *Ul. Freta 3/5, tel. 022/31–17–88. Reservations accepted. No credit cards.*

$ Pod Retmanem. Wood trestle tables and folk decoration provide the
★ backdrop here for a solid, traditional meal. *Ul. Bednarska 9, tel. 022/26–87–58. Reservations accepted. No credit cards.*

$ Venetia. A clean, bright self-service restaurant with an imaginative menu. Try the *zupa chinska* (Chinese soup). *Ul. Jana Pawła II 35, tel. 022/32–56–49. No reservations. No credit cards.*

¢   Bar Kubuś. This small, self-service bar just off Nowy Świat is spot-less and serves excellent food to a faithful clientele. *Ul. Ordynacka 13, no phone. No reservations. No credit cards.*

Lodging

There is no off-season for tourism in Warsaw, and although five new hotels are currently under construction there is a great shortage of hotel beds that is expected to continue until the late 1990s. It is therefore difficult to find accommodations at the middle and lower end of the price range; book early. Private accommodations are sometimes cheaper and are available through the Center for Tourist Information. For details and price-category definitions, *see* Lodging *in* Staying in Poland, *above.*

$$ Dom Chłopa. Built in the late 1950s by the Gromada Peasants' Coop-erative, this hotel offers clean, cheerful, and reasonably priced ac-commodations in the center of Warsaw. *Plac Powstańców Warszawy 2, 00–030, tel. 022/27–49–43, fax 022/27–85–97. 160 rooms with bath. Facilities: restaurant. AE, DC, MC, V.*

$$ M.D.M. This Socialist Realist hotel, run by the municipal authori-ties, is on the main shopping thoroughfare and is clean, if shabby. *Plac Konstytucji 1, tel. 02/621–62–11, fax 02/621–41–73. 153 rooms, ⅓ with bath. Facilities: restaurant. AE, DC, MC, V.*

$$ Metropol. Built in 1965, this clean, modern hotel is right in the cen-ter of town. It's a good value for the money. The rooms have recently been renovated. *Al. Jerozolimskie 45, 00–024, tel. 02/621–43–54, fax 02/628–66–22. 175 rooms with bath. Facilities: restaurant, café. AE, DC, MC, V.*

$$ Polonia. The Art Nouveau Polonia was the only Warsaw hotel to sur-vive the Second World War intact—although renovation in the 1970s removed many of the original features. The hotel is central, comfort-able, and has a friendly staff. *Al. Jerozolimskie 45, tel. 022/628–72–*

41, fax 022/628–66–22. 234 rooms with bath. Facilities: restaurant. AE, DC, MC, V.

$ **Belfer.** Formerly owned by the schoolteachers' union, this hotel,
★ down by the banks of the Vistula, has comfortable if slightly drab rooms and is easily accessible from the city center. *Wybrzeze Kościuszkowskie 31, tel. and fax 022/625–26–00. 216 rooms, ⅓ with bath. Facilities: self-service restaurant. No credit cards.*

$ **Dom Turysty.** Run by the Polish Tourist Association until recently, this hotel has just been renovated and is now cheerfully furnished. *Krakowskie Przedmieście 4–6, tel. 022/26–00–71, fax 022/26–26–25. 63 rooms, some with bath. Facilities: self-service restaurant. AE, DC, MC, V.*

$ **Pensjonat Biała Dalia.** This small, privately owned pension in Konstancin Jeziorno, 24 kilometers (15 miles) from the center of Warsaw, stands in a beautifully kept garden. The rooms are elegantly furnished, clean, and comfortable. *Ul. Sobieskiego 24, Konstancin Jeziorno, tel. 022/56–33–70. 5 rooms with bath. Facilities: restaurant. No credit cards.*

¢ **Druh.** This 1960s five-story hotel (with no elevator), in Warsaw's Ochota district, belongs to the Boy Scouts' Association. It has a limited number of single and double rooms, which are clean, if spartan. *Ul. Niemcewicza 17, tel. 022/659–00–11, telex 022/81–23–08. 40 rooms. Facilities: self-service restaurant. No credit cards.*

¢ **Gromada Camp Site.** Open May–October, this campsite offers accommodation in wood chalets (bedding provided); it is five minutes by bus from the center of town. *Ul. Żwirki i Wigury 3–5, tel. 022/25–43–91. 60 chalets. Facilities: cafeteria. No credit cards.*

¢ **Uniwersytecki.** Taken over by the University of Warsaw in 1990 from the Central Committee of the Communist Party, this hotel gives priority to guests of the university, but there are usually a few rooms available for other visitors. *Ul. Belwederska 26–30, tel. 022/41–93–58. 90 rooms. Facilities: café-bar. No credit cards.*

The Arts

For information, buy the newspaper *Życie Warszawy* or *Gazeta Wyborcza* at Ruch newsstands. Tickets can be ordered by your Orbis hotel receptionist, through the tourist information center (pl. Zamkowy 1, tel. 02/635–1881), or at the ticket office on ulica Marszałkowska 104. Note that in the last hour before a performance most theaters and concert halls sell *wejściówka* (entry tickets) for as little as gr 50 (5,000), which entitle you to take any empty seat or sit on the floor.

Theaters There are 17 theaters in Warsaw, attesting to the popularity of this art form, but none offers English performances. **Teatr Narodowy,** opened in 1765 and the oldest in Poland, is on plac Teatralny; at press time it is closed for repairs after a major fire, but may be reopened during 1996. **Teatr Polski Kameralny** (ul. Foksal 16) has a small stage and is thus more intimate. **Współczesny** (ul. Mokotowska 13) shows contemporary works.

Concerts **The National Philharmonic** puts on the best concerts. The hall is on ulica Sienkiewicza 12. An excellent new concert hall, opened in 1992, is the **Studio Koncertowe Polskiego Radia,** ulica Woronicza 17. In the summer, free Chopin concerts take place both at the Chopin monument in **Łazienki Park** and each Sunday at **Żelazowa Wola,** the composer's birthplace, 58 kilometers (36 miles) outside Warsaw.

Opera **Teatr Wielki** (plac Teatralny) hosts the Grand Theater of Opera and Ballet. It has a superb operatic stage—one of the largest in Europe.

Nightlife

Cabaret The Victoria, Forum, Grand, Europejski, and Marriott hotels all have nightclubs that are popular with Westerners. The acts vary, so check listings in the press. These clubs also present striptease and jazz.

Bars Gwiazdeczka (ul. Piwna 42) is a noisy, hip, upscale joint, popular with chic young Warsovians. **Harenda** (Krakowskie Przedmieście 4/6), with an outdoor terrace in summer, is open until 4 AM.

Jazz Clubs **Akwarium** (ul. Emilii Platter) and **Wanda Warska's Modern Music Club** (Stare Miasto) are popular jazz clubs. A new jazz club that is winning a major following is **Jazz Club 77** at ulica Marszałkowska 77/79. Jazz musicians are booked frequently at the major hotels, too.

Discos Apart from the hotels, the most popular discos are **Hybrydy** (ul. Złota 7) and **Stodoła** (ul. Batorego 10).

Cafés Warsaw is filled with cafés *(kawiarnie)*, which move outdoors in the summer. They are popular meeting places and usually serve delicious coffee and pastries in the best Central European style.

Ambasador is an elegant and brightly lit café with a tree-lined terrace for summer visitors. *Ul. Matejki 4.*
Le Petit Trianon is a tiny, intimate 18th-century French-style restaurant and café. It is difficult to find a seat—but worth it once you do. *Ul. Piwna 40.*
Telimena is a small corner café with an art gallery on the ground floor. *Krakowskie Przedmieście 27.*
Trou Madame has a secluded setting in Łazienki Park.
Wilanowska is a café that has seen better days, but its crumbling elegance has a certain appeal. *Plac Trzech Krzyży 3.*

Kraków and Environs

Kraków (Cracow), seat of Poland's oldest university and once the capital of the country (before losing the honor to Warsaw in 1611), is one of the few Polish cities that escaped devastation during World War II. Hitler's armies were driven out before they had a chance to destroy it. Today Kraków's fine ramparts, towers, facades, and churches, illustrating seven centuries of Polish architecture, make it a major attraction for visitors. Its location—about 270 kilometers (160 miles) south of Warsaw—also makes it a good base for hiking and skiing trips in the mountains of southern Poland.

Also within exploring range from Kraków are the famous Polish shrine to the Virgin Mary at Częstochowa and, at Auschwitz (Oświęcim), the grim reminder of man's capacity for inhumanity.

Getting Around

Trains link Kraków with most major destinations in Poland; the station is in the city center near the Old Town, on ulica Pawia. The bus station is nearby.

Tourist Information

Kraków (ul. Pawia 8, tel. 012/22–95–10).
Częstochowa (al. Najświętszej Marii Panny 37/39, tel. 034/24–71–34).

Exploring Kraków

Numbers in the margin correspond to points of interest on the Kraków map.

Kraków's old city is ringed by a park called the **Planty**. The park replaced the old walls of the town, which were torn down in the mid-
❶ 19th century. Begin your tour at **Brama Floriańska** (St. Florian's Gate), which leads to the Old Town. The gate is guarded by an imposing 15th-century fortress called the **Barbakan**. Enter the city, passing along ulica Floriańska, the beginning of the Royal Route, where you should not pass up the chance to stop for refreshments at Kraków's most famous café, **Jama Michalikowa** (ul. Floriańska 8).

❷ Ulica Floriańska leads to the **Rynek Główny** (main market), one of the largest and finest Renaissance squares in Europe. The calm of this spacious square, with its pigeons and flower stalls, is interrupted every hour by four short bugle calls drifting down from the spire of the Church of the Virgin Mary. The plaintive notes recall a centuries-old tradition in memory of a trumpeter whose throat was pierced by a well-aimed enemy arrow as he was warning his fellow citizens of an impending Tartar attack. The square Gothic **Kościół**
❸ **Mariacki** (Church of the Virgin Mary) contains a 15th-century wooden altarpiece—the largest in the world—carved by Wit Stwosz (Veit Stos); the faces of the saints are reputedly those of Cracovian burghers. In the center of the square stands a covered market called
❹ **Sukiennice** (Cloth Hall), built in the 14th century but remodeled during the Renaissance. The ground floor is still in business, selling trinkets and folk art souvenirs. *Market open Mon.–Sat. 10–6, Sun. 10–5.*

From the Main Market, turn down ulica Świętej Anny to No. 8, the
❺ **Collegium Maius,** the oldest building of the famous **Jagiellonian University** (founded 1364). Its pride is the Italian-style arcaded courtyard. Inside is a museum where you can see the Copernicus globe, the first on which the American continents were shown, as well as astronomy instruments belonging to Kraków's most famous graduate. *Admission free. Courtyard open Mon.–Sat. 8–6. Museum shown by appointment only, 10–noon.*

Backtracking on ulica Świętej Anny will lead you to ulica Grodzka;
❻ make a right there and walk to the **Wawel Castle and Cathedral.** This impressive complex of Gothic and Renaissance buildings stands on fortifications dating as far back as the 8th century. Inside the castle is a museum with an exotic collection of Oriental tents that were captured from the Turks at the battle of Vienna in 1683 and rare 16th-century Flemish tapestries. Wawel Cathedral is where, until the 18th century, Polish kings were crowned and buried. Until 1978, the cathedral was the principal church of the see of Archbishop Karoł Wojtyla, now Pope John Paul II. *Ul. Grodzka, tel. 012/22–51–55. Castle. Admission: zł 5 (50,000) adults, zł 2.5 (25,000) children. Open Tues., Thurs., Sat., Sun. 9:30–3, Wed. and Fri. noon–6. Cathedral Museum. Admission: zł 2.5 (25,000). Open Tues.–Sun. 10–3.*

About 50 kilometers (30 miles) west of Kraków is Oświęcim, better known by its German name, **Auschwitz**. Here 4 million victims, mostly Jews, were executed by the Nazis in the Auschwitz and Birkenau concentration camps. Auschwitz is now a museum, with restored crematoria and barracks housing dramatic displays of Nazi atrocities. The buildings at Birkenau, a 15-minute walk away, have been left just as they were found in 1945 by the Soviet Army. Oświęcim itself is an industrial town with good connections from Kraków; buses and trains leave Kraków approximately every hour, and signs in Oświęcim direct visitors to the camp. *Auschwitz: admission free. Open Mar. and Nov., Tues.–Sun. 8–4; Apr. and Oct., Tues.–Sun. 8–5; May and Sept., daily 8–6; June–Aug., daily 8–7; Dec.–Feb., Tues.–Sun. 8–3. Birkenau: open 24 hrs.*

Wieliczka, about 8 kilometers (5 miles) southeast of Kraków, is the oldest salt mine in Europe, in operation since the end of the 13th cen-

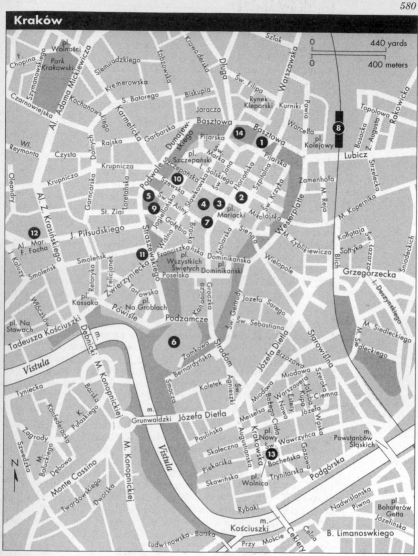

Kraków

Major Attractions
Brama Floriańska, **1**
Jagiellonian
University, **5**
Kościół Mariacki, **3**
Rynek Główny, **2**
Sukiennice, **4**
Wawel Castle and
Cathedral, **6**

Other Attractions
Central Station, **8**
Czartoryski Museum, **14**
Ethnographic
Museum, **13**
Helena Modrzejewska
Stary Theater, **10**

Jagiellonian University
Museum, **9**
K. Szymanowski State
Philharmonic Hall, **11**
National Museum, **12**
St. Adalbert
Romanesque Church, **7**

tury. It is famous for its magnificent underground chapel hewn in crystal rock, the **Chapel of the Blessed Kinga.** *Ul. Daniłowicza 10, tel. 012/22–08–52. Admission zł 10 (100,000) adults, 5 (50,000) children.*

Częstochowa, 120 kilometers (70 miles) from Kraków and reached by regular trains and buses, is the home of the holiest shrine in a country that is more than 90% Catholic. Inside the 14th-century **Pauline monastery** on Jasna Góra (Hill of Light) is the famous *Black Madonna*, a painting of Our Lady of Częstochowa attributed by legend to St. Luke. It was here that an invading Swedish army was halted in 1655 and finally driven out of the country. About 25 miles southwest of Kraków is the little town of **Wadowice,** birthplace of Pope John Paul II. *Wadowice Museum. Admission: zł 2 (20,000) adults, zł 1 (10,000) children. Open Tues.–Sat. 10–3, Sun. 10–5.*

Dining and Lodging

For details and price-category definitions, *see* Dining and Lodging *in* Staying in Poland, *above.*

Częstochowa **Polonia.** The Polonia makes a good base for exploring the Pauline
Lodging monastery, and since most of the other guests are pilgrims, the at-
$ mosphere is an interesting mixture of piety and good fun. *Ul. Piłsudskiego 9, tel. 034/24–40–67, fax 034/65–11–05. 62 rooms, most with bath or shower. No credit cards.*

Kraków **Balaton.** Sitting on benches at trestle tables, you can sample good
Dining Hungarian cuisine in this popular folksy restaurant. *Ul. Grodzka*
★ *37, tel. 012/22–04–69. Reservations accepted. AE, DC, MC, V.*
$$ **Kurza Stopka.** This crowded restaurant has a limited range of dishes, but the food is good and the service is friendly. *Plac Wszystkich Świętych 9, tel. 012/22–91–96. No reservations. No credit cards.*
¢ **Tunis Bar.** This busy, self-service bar offers delicious Tunisian dishes, which are slightly exotic for Kraków. *Plac Dominikański 1. No reservations. No credit cards.*

Lodging **Cracovia.** This large, five-story hotel, located near the center of
$$ town, is comfortable, if rather barrackslike. *Al. marszałka F. Focha, tel. 012/22–86–66, fax 012/21–95–86. 427 rooms with bath. Facilities: restaurant, night club. AE, DC, MC, V.*
$$ **Holiday Inn.** This was the first Holiday Inn in Eastern Europe. Rather bland, but comfortable, this high-rise establishment is pleasantly located near Kraków's Green Meadows. *Ul. Koniewa 7, tel. 012/37–50–44, fax 012/37–59–38. 310 rooms with bath. Facilities: restaurant, solarium, sauna, indoor pool. AE, DC, MC, V.*
$ **Dom Turysty.** This 1960s hotel stands opposite the Planty park, facing the walls of the Bernadine convent. The accommodations are standard but comfortable. *Westerplatte 15, tel. 012/22–95–66, fax 012/21–27–26. 129 rooms, ⅓ with bath. Facilities: self-service restaurant. No credit cards.*
$ **Hotel Pollera.** This 19th-century hotel, on the edge of the Old Town, has recently had a face-lift after being restored to private ownership. It is well located, and the management is keen to create a family atmosphere. *Ul. Szpitalna 40, tel. 012/22–10–44, fax 012/22–13–89. 77 rooms, ½ with bath. Facilities: restaurant. No credit cards.*
¢ **Europejski.** This small, older hotel, overlooking the Planty park, has seen better days, so make sure you see your room before you accept it. *Ul. Lubicz 5, tel. 012/22–09–11, fax 012/22–89–25. 55 rooms, most with bath. No credit cards.*
¢ **Warszawski.** This late-19th-century hotel opposite the main railway station has seen better days, although it is clean and the location is central. Take breakfast in the café next door. *Ul. Pawia 6, tel. and fax 012/22–06–22. No credit cards.*

Gdańsk and the North

In contrast to Kraków and the south, Poland north of Warsaw is the land of medieval castles and châteaus, dense forests and lakes, and beaches along the Baltic coast. Rail services in the region are good, although you may prefer going straight to Gdańsk and making excursions from there.

Getting Around

Gdańsk is a major transportation hub, with an airport just outside town (and good bus connections to downtown) and major road and rail connections with the rest of the country.

Tourist Information

Gdańsk (Ul. Heweliusza 8, tel. 058/31–03–38; Orbis, pl. Górskiego 1, tel. 058/31–49–44).
Ostróda (Orbis, ul. Czarnieckiego 10, tel. 088/35–57).
Płock (ul. Tuńska 4, tel. 024/226–00; Orbis, al. Jachowa 47, tel. 024/229–89).
Toruń (ul. Kopernika 27, tel. 056/272–99; Orbis, ul. Żeglarska 31, tel. 056/261–30).

Exploring Gdańsk and the North

Plock **Płock** is a day trip from Warsaw by PKS bus. Once you get through Płock's industrial area, you'll find a lovely medieval city that was, for a short time, capital of Poland. Worth seeing are the 12th-century cathedral, where two Polish kings are buried, and the dramatic 14th-century Teutonic castle. Continue through Włocławek to Toruń, where an overnight stay is recommended.

Toruń **Toruń,** birthplace of Nicolaus Copernicus, is also within easy reach (three hours) of Warsaw by train. It is an interesting medieval city that grew wealthy because of its location on the north–south trading route along the Vistula. Its old town district is a remarkably successful blend of Gothic buildings—churches, town hall, and burghers' homes—with Renaissance and Baroque patricians' houses. The Town Hall's Tower (1274) is the oldest in Poland. Don't leave without trying some of Toruń's famous gingerbread and honey cakes.

North from Toruń lie some of the oldest towns, castles, and churches in Poland. You should not miss **Malbork,** on the main rail route from Warsaw to Gdańsk (be sure your train stops there). This huge castle, 58 kilometers (36 miles) from Gdańsk, was one of the most powerful strongholds in medieval Europe. From 1308 to 1457, it was the residence of the Grand Masters of the Teutonic Order. The Teutonic Knights were a thorn in Poland's side until their defeat at the battle of Grunwald in 1410. Inside Malbork castle is a museum with beautiful examples of amber—including lumps as large as melons and pieces containing perfect specimens of prehistoric insects. *tel. 055/33–64. Open Tues.–Sat. 10–3, Sun. 10–5. Admission: zł 4.5 (45,000) adults, zł 3.5 (35,000) children.*

Gdańsk **Gdańsk,** once the free city of Danzig, is another of Poland's beautifully restored towns, displaying a rich heritage of Gothic, Renaissance, and Mannerist architecture. This is where the first shots of World War II were fired and where the free trade union Solidarity was born after strikes in 1980. The city's old town has a wonderful collection of historic houses and narrow streets. The splendid Długa and Długi Targ streets (best for shopping) form the axis of the city and are good starting points for walks into other districts. The evocative **Solidarity Monument** outside the Lenin shipyards was erected in honor of workers killed there by the regime during strikes in

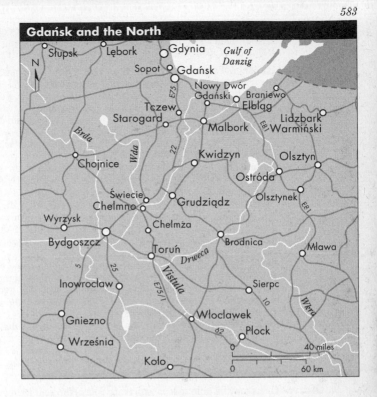

Gdańsk and the North

1970. The nearby town of **Sopot** is Poland's most popular seaside resort.

Most of the small towns in the scenic Mazurian lake district southeast of Gdańsk can be reached by public transport if you are persistent and have plenty of time to spare. The area is rich in nature and wildlife, as well as in places of historical interest.

Olsztyn and Olsztynek The medieval town of **Olsztyn,** once administered and fortified by Copernicus, is well worth a visit, as is **Olsztynek,** where the **Museum of Folk Buildings** has a collection of timber buildings from different parts of the country. The buildings include a small Mazurian thatch-roofed church, an inn, a mill, a forge, old windmills, and thatched cottages, some of which have been furnished in period style. *Tel. 089/19–24–64. Admission: zł 4 (40,000) adults, zł 2 (20,000) children. Open May–Sept., Tues.–Sun. 9–4; closed Mon.*

Both Olsztyn and Olsztynek can be reached by PKS bus from Warsaw or Gdańsk.

Dining and Lodging

For details and price-category definitions, *see* Dining and Lodging *in* Staying in Poland, *above.*

Gdańsk Dining
★
$$
Kaszubska. The specialties here come from Kashubia, the lake region west of the city. There are other good choices, but the smoked fish dishes are highly recommended. *Ul. Kartuska 76, tel. 058/32–06–02. Reservations advised. AE, DC, MC, V.*

$$
Pod Wieżą. This restaurant has a reputation for good meat dishes and generous portions. It's open to 2 AM. *Piwna 51, tel. 058/31–39–24. Reservations advised. AE, DC, MC, V.*

$
Jantar. This centrally located restaurant has a wide selection and friendly service. *Ul. Długi Targ 19, tel. 058/31–13–93. Reservations accepted. AE, DC, MC, V.*

¢ **Karczma Michał.** This dockside restaurant serves generous help-ings of good food in a bustling, cheerful atmosphere. *Ul. Jana z Kolna 8, tel. 058/31–05–35. No reservations. No credit cards.*

Lodging **Posejdon.** Though this modern hotel is a bit out of town, it is well
$$ equipped with leisure facilities. *Ul. Kapliczna 30, tel. 058/53–18–03, fax 058/53–02–28. 140 rooms with bath or shower. Facilities: so-larium, sauna, indoor pool, disco. AE, DC, MC, V.*

$ **Hotel Miramar.** This sea-view tourist hotel is clean and comfortable with easy transport links to Gdańsk. *Ul. Zamkowa Góra 25, Sopot, tel. 058/51–80–11, fax 058/51–51–64. 150 rooms, most with bath. Fa-cilities: restaurant. AE, DC, MC, V.*

$ **Jantar.** This small hotel is picturesquely situated in the heart of the Old Town—which largely compensates for the slightly shabby fur-nishings. *Ul. Długi Targ 19, tel. 058/31–27–16, fax 058/31–35–29. 42 rooms, ½ with bath. Facilities: restaurant. AE, DC, MC, V.*

$ **Maryla.** This pension, near Sopot's wooded northern beach, offers
★ homely comforts and is near public transport to Gdańsk. *Ul. Sępia 22, Sopot, tel. 058/51–00–34, fax 058/51–00–35. 16 rooms with bath. No credit cards.*

$ **Sopot.** With easy access to the Sopot beach and located on main bus and trolley-bus routes into Gdańsk, this hotel offers comfortable ac-commodations in three pavilions set in wooded grounds. *Ul. Haffnera 81–85, tel. 058/51–57–51, fax 058/51–32–96. 120 rooms, most with bath. No credit cards.*

¢ **Piast.** Attractively sited by the beach and woods of Gdańsk's north-ern Jelitkowo district, this small single-story hotel is a peaceful re-treat from the bustle of the city center. *Ul. Piastowska 199–201, tel. and fax 058/53–09–28. 68 rooms, most for three persons, none with bath. No credit cards.*

Olsztyn Orbis may be able to locate private rooms for you. Otherwise, there
Lodging is the **Orbis Novotel** (Ul. Sielska 4A, tel. 089/27–40–81, fax 089/27–54–03), which is $$.

Toruń **Polonia.** The Art Nouveau decor in this hotel restaurant has a cer-
Dining tain faded charm, and the food is plain and wholesome. The friendly
$$ new owner is renovating the place, which is a favorite of Polish fami-lies. *Plac Teatralny 5, tel. 056/230–28.*

$$ **Zajazd Staropolski.** This restaurant features excellent meat dishes and soups in a restored 17th-century interior. *Ul. Żeglarska 10/14, tel. 056/260–60. Reservations advised.*

$ **Wodnik.** This large café along the banks of the Vistula is very popu-lar with locals. *Blwd. Filadelfijski, tel. 056/287–55. No credit cards.*

Lodging **Kosmos.** A functional 1960s hotel, Kosmos is beginning to show
$ signs of wear and tear. It is situated near the river, in the city cen-ter. *Ul. Portowa 2, tel. 056/270–85. 180 rooms, most with bath or shower. AE, DC, MC, V.*

$ **Zajazd Staropolski.** This Gromada hotel, in a converted Renaissance
★ granary, has been recently redecorated and is homey and comfort-able. *Ul. Żeglarska 10–14, tel. 056/260–60, fax 056/253–84. 36 rooms with bath. AE, DC, MC, V.*

20 Portugal

First-time visitors to Portugal are often surprised by the relatively low cost of travel throughout the country. Although prices have been on the rise here for several years, especially in Lisbon, transportation, dining, and lodging rates remain among the lowest in Europe. Budget travelers in Portugal can indulge in the "good life" that is all too often prohibitively expensive in other European countries: Superb alfresco meals, fine wines, and comfortable accommodations in country inns and manor houses (some of historic importance) at nearly giveaway prices are a reality in Portugal. Café and restaurant meals, in particular, represent excellent values, and you should find the food fresh from the sea or market and prepared in portions so huge that you may consider ordering a *meia dose* (half-portion) or sharing an entrée with your companion.

Given its long Atlantic coastline, it isn't surprising that Portugal has been a maritime nation for most of its history. The valor of its seamen is well known; from the charting of the Azores archipelago in 1427 to the discovery of Japan in 1542, Portuguese explorers unlocked the major sea routes to southern Africa, India, the Far East, and the Americas. To commemorate this great era of exploration, a period that reached its height in the 15th century under the influence of Prince Henry the Navigator, the years 1988 to 2000 have been set aside for various celebrations throughout the country.

Despite its sailors' worldly adventures, Portugal itself has remained relatively undiscovered. Although it shares the Iberian Peninsula with Spain, it attracts far fewer visitors—a strange fact, because Portugal has much to recommend it to tourists: fine beaches, beautiful castles, charming fishing villages, excellent restaurants, and colorful folk traditions.

About the size of Indiana, Portugal is so small that its main attractions can be seen during a short visit; at the country's widest point the distance between the Atlantic and Spain is a mere 240 kilometers (150 miles). Short distances don't mean monotony, however, for this narrow coastal strip of land has more geographic and climatic variations than virtually any other nation in Western Europe.

Portugal

0 — 50 miles
0 — 50 km

N

ATLANTIC OCEAN

Minho
Valença
Viana do Castelo
Lima
Serra do Gerês N103
Bragança
Barcelos
Chaves
Braga
Guimarães *Tâmega*
Póvoa de Varzim
N15
Mirandela
Vila do Conde
Amarante
Vila Real
Sabor
Mogadouro
Oporto
Penafiel
Douro
Duoro
Espinho
Douro
Lamego
Oliveira dos Azeméis
Moimenta da Beira
Albergaria-a-Velha
S. Pedro do Sul
Vouga
Pinhel
Aveiro
Viseu
Mealhada
Sta. Comba Dão
Mira
Cantanhede
Mondego
Guarda
Coimbra
Figueira da Foz
Serra da Estrêla
Covilhã
Arganil
Fundão
EI/AI
Zêzere
N110
Pombal
Serra da Gardunha
Penamacor
N233
Leiria
Ourém
Proença-a-Nova
Nazaré
Batalha
Tomar
Castelo Branco
Alcobaça
Fátima
Tagus
Caldas da Rainha
Abrantes
Nisa
N118
Óbidos
Torres Novas
S P A I N
Aveiras de Cima
Santarém
Portalegre
Torres Vedras
Tejo
Mafra
Ponte de Sor
Sintra
Vila Franca de Xira
Sorraia
Avis
N8
Cascais
Lisbon
N10
Estoril
Arraiolos
Estremoz
Elvas
Seixal
Montemor-o-Novo
Sra. de Ossa
A2
Setúbal
Vila Viçosa
Guadiana
Cabo Espichel
Sado
Alcácer do Sal
Evora
Reguengos
N2
Ferreira do Alentejo
Moura
Sines
Beja
Cabo de Sines
Santiago do Cacém
Serpa
N122
EI
Castro Verde
Chança
Odemira
Ourique
Mértola
N120
Mira
Almodôvar
Guadiana
Monchique
A L G A R V E
Vila do Bispo
Portimão N125
Albufeira S. Bráz
Cabo de S. Vicente
Lagos
Tavira
Vila Real de S. António
Faro
Olhão

Although Portugal has seen numerous divisions in modern times, the country has traditionally been divided into six historic provinces. Most visitors head for the low-lying plains of the southern Algarve or the region around the Lisbon-Estoril coast, but as traditional tourist destinations become more crowded, adventurous travelers are trekking in other directions. The northern and central provinces—Minho, Beiras, and Trás-os-Montes—are largely unspoiled, full of tiny villages and splendid scenery. Getting around by public transportation is easy, too, and some of the views you'll get from the trains are among the most spectacular in Europe.

Observant visitors are likely to notice differences between Portugal's northern and southern regions and people. The northern character is decidedly more Celtic, while in the south, Moorish ancestry is apparent. But throughout the country, the Portuguese people are welcoming wherever you meet them.

For the purposes of this guide, we have concentrated our Exploring sections on the southern part of the country—the section most frequented by foreign visitors—including Lisbon—Portugal's sophisticated capital—and the Algarve.

Essential Information

Before You Go

When to Go The tourist season runs from spring through autumn, but some parts of the country—especially the Algarve, which boasts 3,000 hours of sunshine annually—are balmy even in winter. Hotel prices are greatly reduced between November and February, except in Lisbon where business visitors keep prices uniformly high throughout the year.

Climate Since Portugal's entire coast is on the Atlantic Ocean, the country's climate is temperate year-round. Portugal rarely suffers the extremes of heat that Mediterranean countries do. Even in August, the hottest month, the Algarve and the Alentejo are the only regions where the midday heat may be uncomfortable, but most travelers go to the Algarve and Alentejo beaches to swim and soak up the sun. What rain there is falls from November to March; December and January can be chilly outside the Algarve and very wet to the north, but there is no snow except in the mountains of the Serra da Estrela in the northeast. The almond blossoms and vivid wildflowers that cover the countryside start to bloom early in February. The dry months, June–September, can turn much of the landscape the tawny color of a lion's hide, but there is always a breeze in the evening in Lisbon, as well as along the Estoril coast west of the capital.

The following are the average daily maximum and minimum temperatures for Lisbon.

Jan.	57F	14C	May	71F	21C	Sept.	79F	26C
	46	8		55	13		62	17
Feb.	59F	15C	June	77F	25C	Oct.	72F	22C
	47	8		60	15		58	14
Mar.	63F	17C	July	81F	27C	Nov.	63F	17C
	50	10		63	17		52	11
Apr.	67F	20C	Aug.	82F	28C	Dec.	58F	15C
	53	12		63	17		47	9

Currency The unit of currency in Portugal is the *escudo*, which can be divided into 100 centavos. Escudos come in bills of 500$00, 1,000$00, 2,000$00, 5,000$00, and 10,000$00. (In Portugal the dollar sign stands between the escudo and the centavo.) Coins come in 1$00, 2$50, 5$00, 10$00, 20$00, 50$00, 100$00, and 200$00.

At press time (summer 1995), the exchange rate was 134$00 to the U.S. dollar and 226$00 to the pound sterling. Owing to the complications of dealing in millions of escudos, 1,000$00 is always called a *conto*, so 10,000$00 is referred to as 10 contos. Credit cards are accepted in all the larger shops and restaurants, as well as in hotels; however, better exchange rates are obtained in banks and *cambios* (exchange offices). However, there's a high commission charge on exchanging traveler's checks in Portugal—it's wise to take (and exchange) larger denominations. Short-changing is rare, but, as in every country, restaurant bills should be checked. Change in post offices and railway booking offices should also be counted. Shopkeepers are usually honest.

What It Will Cost While the cost of hotels and restaurants in Portugal is still reasonable, inflation is pushing prices up to levels approaching those found in the more affluent countries in northern Europe. Some of Portugal's best food bargains are to be enjoyed in its many simple seaside restaurants. The most expensive areas are Lisbon, the Algarve, and the tourist resort areas along the Tagus estuary. The least expensive areas are country towns, which all have reasonably priced hotels and *pensões*, or pensions, as well as numerous café-type restaurants. A sales, or value-added, tax (called IVA) of 16% is imposed on hotel and restaurant bills.

Sample Prices Cup of coffee, 150$00; bottle of beer, 150$00; soft drink, 175$00; bottle of house wine, 500$00–750$00; ham sandwich, 225$00; 1-mile taxi ride, 425$00; city bus ride, 150$00; museum entrance, 250$00–400$00.

Customs on Arrival Non–European-Union (EU) visitors over age 17 are allowed to bring the following items into Portugal duty-free: 200 cigarettes or 250 grams of tobacco, 1 liter of liquor (over 22% volume) or 2 liters (under 22% volume), 2 liters of wine, 100 ml of perfume, and a reasonable amount of personal effects (camera, binoculars, etc). There is no limit on money brought into the country. However, no more than 100,000$00 in Portuguese currency or the equivalent of 500,000$00 in foreign currency may be taken out without proof that an equal amount or more was brought into Portugal. Computerized customs services make random and often thorough checks on arrival.

Language Portuguese is easy to read by anyone with even slight knowledge of a Latin language, but it is difficult to pronounce and understand (most people speak quickly and elliptically). However, you will find that in the larger cities and major resorts many people, especially the young, speak English and, occasionally, French. In the country, people are so friendly and eager to be helpful that visitors can usually make themselves understood in sign language.

Getting Around

By Train The Portuguese railway system is surprisingly extensive for such a small country, and ticket prices are very reasonable. Trains are clean and leave on time, but there are few express runs except between Lisbon and Oporto (express trains take just over three hours for the 210-mile—or 338-kilometers—journey). Most trains have first- and second-class compartments; some of the Lisbon–Oporto expresses are first-class only; suburban lines around Lisbon have a single class. Tickets should be bought, and seats reserved if desired, at the stations or through travel agents, two or three days in advance. Advance reservations are essential on Lisbon–Oporto express trains. Timetables are mostly the same on Saturday and Sunday as on weekdays, except on suburban lines. **Wasteels–Expresso** (Av. António Augusto Aguiar 88, 1000 Lisbon, tel. 01/57965) is reliable for all local and international train tickets and reservations.

Special **tourist passes** can be obtained through travel agents or at main train stations. These are valid for periods of seven, 14, or 21 days for first- and second-class travel on any domestic train service; mileage is unlimited. At press time (summer 1995), the cost was 15,200$00 for seven days, 24,200$00 for 14 days, and 34,600$00 for 21 days. Child passes cost exactly half those amounts.

International trains to Madrid, Paris, and other parts of Europe depart from the Santa Apolonia Station in Lisbon and Campanhã in Oporto.

By Bus The main bus company, **Rodoviaria Nacional,** has passenger terminals in Lisbon (Av. Casal Ribeiro 18, tel. 01/545439), with regular bus services throughout Portugal. Several private companies offer luxury service between major cities. For information and reservations in Lisbon, contact the main tourist office (*see* Important Addresses and Numbers *in* Lisbon, *below*) or **Marcus & Harting** (Rossio 45–50, tel. 01/346–9271). Most long-distance buses have toilet facilities, and the fares are often cheaper than for trains.

By Boat Ferries across the river Tagus leave from Praça do Comércio, Cais do Sodré, and Belém. From April to October, a two-hour boat excursion leaves the ferry station at Praça do Comércio in Lisbon daily at 2:30 PM. The price is 3,500$00.

Boat trips on the river Douro (Oporto) are organized from May to October by **Porto Ferreira** (Rua da Cavalhosa, 19, Vila Nova de Gaia, Oporto, tel. 02/300866). They leave every day on the hour (10–6), except Saturday afternoon and Sunday. Overnight cruises are also available. Contact **Endouro** (Rua da Reboleira, 49 4000 Porto, tel. 02/208–4161, fax 02/317260).

By Bicycle **Cycling through the Centuries** (Box 877, San Antonio, FL 33576–0877, tel. 1–800/245–4226, fax 904/588–4158, or in Portugal, tel. 01/4862044, fax 01/4861409) offers bicycle tours in the Alentejo, Minho, and Algarve with accommodations in first-class hotels and romantic country inns. Each tour is accompanied by a guide, a mechanic, and a van for luggage.

Staying in Portugal

Telephones Pay phones take 10$00, 20$00, and 50$00 coins; 10$00 is the mini-
Local Calls mum payment for short local calls. Pay phones marked CREDIFONE will accept plastic phone cards, which can be purchased at post offices and most tobacconist shops.

International Long-distance calls cost less from 8 PM to 7 AM. Collect calls can also
Calls be made from post offices. Some telephone booths accept international calls. Access numbers to reach American long-distance operators are: for **AT&T,** 050–171288; for **MCI,** 0010–480–0112; for **Sprint,** 050–171877.

Country Code The country code for Portugal is 351.

Mail Postal rates, both domestic and foreign, increase twice a year. Country post offices close for lunch and at 6 PM on weekdays; they are not open on weekends. Main post offices in towns are open weekdays 8:30 to 6 with no midday closings. In Lisbon, the post office in the Praça dos Restauradores is open daily from 8 AM until 10 PM.

Receiving Mail Mail can be sent in care of American Express (Av. Duque de Loule 108, 1000 Lisbon, tel. 01/315–5877, fax 01/352–3227); there is no service charge. Main post offices also accept poste restante letters.

Shopping Bargaining is not common in city stores or shops, but it is sometimes possible in flea markets, antiques shops, and outdoor markets that sell fruit, vegetables, and household goods. The **Centro de Turismo Artesanato** (Rua Castilho 61, 1200 Lisbon, tel. 01/353–4879) will ship goods abroad even if they were not bought in Portugal. By air to the United States, parcels take about three weeks; by sea, two months.

IVA Refunds IVA is included in the price of goods, but the tax on items over a certain value can be reclaimed, although the methods are time-consuming. For Americans and other non-EU residents, the tax paid on individual items costing more than 10,000$00 can be reclaimed in cash on presentation of receipts and a special *Tax-free Shopping Check* to special departments in airports (in Lisbon, near Gate 23). You can also have the check stamped at any border crossing and receive the refund by mail or credit card. Shops specializing in IVA-refund purchases are clearly marked throughout the country, and shop assistants can help with the forms. For details consult the main tourist information center in Lisbon (*see* Important Addresses and Numbers *in* Lisbon, *below*).

Opening and Closing Times **Banks** are open weekdays 8:30 to 3 PM; they do not close for lunch. There are automatic currency-exchange machines in Lisbon in the Praça dos Restauradores and in major cities.

Museums are usually open 10–12:30 and 2–5. Most close on Sunday afternoon, and they are all closed on Monday. Most palaces close on Tuesday.

Shops are open weekdays 9–1 and 3–7, Saturdays 9–1. Shopping malls and supermarkets in Lisbon and other cities remain open until 10 PM or midnight and are often open on Sunday.

National Holidays In 1996: January 1 (New Year's), April 5 (Good Friday), April 25 (Anniversary of the Revolution), May 1 (Labor Day), June 2 (Corpus Christi), June 10 (National Day), August 15 (Assumption), October 5 (Day of the Republic), November 1 (All Saints' Day), December 1 (Independence Day), December 8 (Immaculate Conception), December 25. Changing holidays in 1997: March 28 (Good Friday), May 29 (Corpus Christi).

Dining Eating is taken quite seriously in Portugal, and, not surprisingly, seafood is a staple. Freshly caught lobster, crab, shrimp, tuna, sole, and squid are prepared in innumerable ways, but if you want to sample a little bit of everything, try *caldeirada,* a piquant stew made with whatever is freshest from the sea. In the Algarve, *cataplana* is a must: It's a mouthwatering mixture of clams, ham, tomatoes, onions, garlic, and herbs, named for the dish in which it is cooked. There are some excellent local wines, and in modest restaurants even the *vinho da casa* (house wine) is usually very good. Water is generally safe, but visitors may want to drink bottled water—*sem gas* for still, *com gas* for fizzy—from one of the many excellent Portuguese spas.

Mealtimes Lunch usually begins around 1 PM; dinner is served at about 8 PM.

What to Wear Except for the most elegant restaurants, where a jacket and tie are preferred, casual attire is acceptable for restaurants in all price categories.

Ratings Prices are per person, without alcohol. Taxes and service are usually included, but a tip of 5%–10% is always appreciated. All restaurants must post a menu with current prices in a window facing the street. Best bets are indicated by a star ★.

Category	Cost
$$	3,500$00–6,000$00
$	2,000$00–3,500$00
¢	under 2,000$00

Lodging Visitors have a wide choice of lodging in Portugal, which offers some of the lowest rates in Europe for accommodations. Hotels are graded from one to five stars, as are the smaller inns called *estalagems*, which usually provide breakfast only. *Pensões*—the mainstay of the budget traveler—go up to four stars and often include meals (though they don't usually insist that you take them). The state-subsidized *pousadas*, most of which are situated in castles or old monasteries or have been built where there is a particularly fine view, are five-star luxury properties. However, rates in winter drop by a few thousand escudos, making them by no means unaffordable. *Residencials* (between a pensão and a hotel) are located in most towns and larger villages; most rooms have private baths or showers, and breakfast is usually included in the charge. They are a good value, around 5,000$00–7,000$00, but usually they have only a few rooms from which to choose. Therefore, we don't review many residencials under Lodging, below. It's worth noting that room rates in all establishments drop considerably in low season—always check for discounts when traveling in the winter months.

A recent innovation is *Turismo no Espaço Rural* (Tourism in the Country), in which private homeowners all over the country offer visitors a room and breakfast (and sometimes provide dinner on request). This is an excellent way to experience life on a country estate or in a small village. Several agencies specializing in this field include Associação Portuguesa de Turismo de Habitação (Rua João Penha, 10, 1200 Lisbon, tel. 01/690549, fax 01/388–8115).

Tourist offices can help visitors with hotel or other reservations and will provide lists of the local hostelries without charge. In Lisbon, there's a hotel reservations desk at the airport and at the downtown tourist information center. Except for in Lisbon, few international chains have hotels in Portugal.

Camping Camping has become increasingly popular in Portugal in recent years, and there are now more than 150 campsites throughout the country offering a wide range of facilities. The best equipped have markets, swimming pools, and tennis courts. For additional information, contact **Federação Portuguesa de Campismo** (Ave. 5 Outubro 15-3, 1000 Lisbon, tel. 01/3152715).

Ratings Prices are for two people in a double room, based on high-season rates. Best bets are indicated by a star ★.

Category	Cost
$$	14,000$00–20,000$00
$	8,000$00–14,000$00
¢	under 8,000$00

Tipping In Portugal, modest tips are usually expected by those who render services. Service is included in bills at hotels and most restaurants. Otherwise tip 5%–10% on restaurant bills, except at inexpensive establishments, where you may just leave any coins given in change. Taxi drivers get 10%; movie and theater ushers who seat you, 50$00; train and airport porters, 100$00 per bag; service-station attendants, 20$00 for gas, 50$00 for checking tires and cleaning windshields; hairdressers, around 10%.

Lisbon

Arriving and Departing

By Plane   Lisbon's Portela Airport (tel. 01/802262) is only about 20 minutes from the city by bus or taxi.

Between the   There is a special bus service from the airport (7:30AM–10:30PM) ev-
Airport and   ery 20 minutes into the city center called the *Aerobus* (400$00), but
Downtown   taxis here are so much cheaper than in other European capitals that couples or groups would be wise to take a taxi straight to their destination. The cost into Lisbon is about 1,500$00–2,000$00, and to Estoril or Sintra, 6,000$00. There are no trains or subways between the airport and the city.

By Train   International trains from Paris and Madrid arrive at Santa Apolonia Station (tel. 01/8884025), just east of the city center. There is a tourist office at the station and plenty of taxis and porters. To get to the central Praça dos Restauradoes by public transport, take Bus 9, 39, or 46.

Getting Around

Lisbon is a hilly city, and the sidewalks are paved with cobblestones, so walking can be tiring, even when you're wearing comfortable shoes. Fortunately, Lisbon's tram service is one of the best in Europe, and buses go all over the city. A **Tourist Pass** for unlimited rides on the tram or bus costs 400$00 for one day's travel; four-day passes (1,350$00) and seven-day passes (2,050$00) are also valid on the metro. Passes can be purchased at the Cais do Sodré Station and other terminals. Otherwise there's a flat fare of 150$00 every time you ride a bus, tram, or *elevador* (funicular railway system).

By Tram and   Buses and trams operate from 6 AM to midnight. Try tram routes 12 or
Bus   28 for an inexpensive tour of the city; Nos. 15, 16, or 17 will take you to Belém; Buses 52 and 53 cross the Tagus bridge.

By Subway   The subway, called the Metropolitano, operates from 6:30 AM to 1 AM; it is modern and efficient but covers a limited route. You will find it convenient for transport to and from the Gulbenkian Foundation—watch out for pickpockets during rush hour. Tickets cost 65$00 if you buy them at the ticket office inside the station, 55$00 if you use the automatic ticket machine—instructions are in English. There are books of 10 tickets available, too, sold at a slight discount.

By Taxi   Taxis here are among the cheapest in Europe—even the tightest budget can allow for a few taxi rides around Lisbon. There are ranks in the main squares, and you can hail a cruising vehicle, though this can be difficult late at night. Taxis take up to four passengers at no extra charge. Rates start at 300$00.

Important Addresses and Numbers

Tourist   The main Lisbon tourist office (tel. 01/346–3314) is in the Palacio
Information   Foz, Praça dos Restauradores, at the Baixa end of the Avenida da Liberdade, the main artery of the city; open daily 9–8. The tourist office at Lisbon airport (tel. 01/849–3689) is open daily 6AM–2AM.

Embassies   U.S. (Av. Forças Armadas, tel. 01/726–6600); **Canadian** (Av. da Liberdade 144-3, tel. 01/3474892); **U.K.** (Rua S. Domingos à Lapa 37, tel. 01/3961191).

Emergencies   SOS Emergencies (tel. 115). Police (tel. 01/3466141). Ambulance (tel. 01/301–7777). Fire Brigade (tel. 01/606060). Doctor: British Hospital (Rua Saraiva de Carvalho 49, tel. 01/3955067). Pharmacies: open weekdays 9–1, 3007, Saturday 9–1.

Exploring Lisbon

North of the River Tagus estuary, spread out over a string of hills, Portugal's capital presents unending treats for the eye. Its wide boulevards are bordered by black-and-white mosaic sidewalks made up of tiny cobblestones called *calçada*. Modern, pastel-color apartment blocks vie for attention with Art Nouveau houses faced with decorative tiles. Winding, hilly streets provide scores of *miradouros*, natural vantage points that offer spectacular views of the river and city.

Lisbon is not a city that is easily explored on foot. The steep inclines of many streets present a tough challenge to the casual tourist, and visitors are often surprised to find that, because of the hills, places that appear to be close to one another on a map are actually on different levels. Yet the effort is worthwhile—judicious use of trams, a funicular railway, and the majestic city-center elevator make walking tours enjoyable even on the hottest summer day.

With a population of around a million, Lisbon is a small capital by European standards. Its center stretches north from the spacious Praça do Comércio, one of the largest riverside squares in Europe, to the Rossio, a smaller square lined by shops and sidewalk cafés. This district is known as the Baixa (Lower Town), and it is one of the earliest examples of town planning on a large scale. The grid of parallel streets between the two squares was built after an earthquake and tidal wave destroyed much of the city in 1755.

The Alfama, the old Moorish quarter that survived the earthquake, lies just to the east of the Baixa, while Belém, where many of the royal palaces and museums are situated, is about 5 kilometers (3 miles) to the west.

Numbers in the margin correspond to points of interest on the Lisbon map.

Castelo de São Jorge and the Alfama The Moors, who imposed their rule on most of the southern Iberian Peninsula during the 8th century, left their mark on Lisbon in many ways. The most visible examples are undoubtedly the imposing castle, set on one of the city's highest hills, and the Alfama, a district of narrow, twisting streets that wind their way up toward the castle. The best way to tour this area of Lisbon is to take a taxi—they're plentiful and cheap—to the castle and walk down; otherwise you'll have little energy left for sightseeing. Several trams also run to the Alfama: take the No. 28 from Rua Conceicão in the Baixa or the No. 12 from Largo Martim Monez, northwest of Rossio.

① Although the **Castelo de São Jorge** (St. George's Castle) is Moorish in construction, it stands on the site of a fortification used by the Visigoths in the 5th century. Today its idyllic atmosphere is shattered only by the shrieks of the many peacocks that strut through the grounds, a well-tended area that is also home to swans, turkeys, ducks, ravens, and other birds. The castle walls enclose an Arabian palace that formed the residence of the kings of Portugal until the 16th century; there is also a small village lived in by artists and craftspeople. Panoramic views of Lisbon can be seen from the castle walls, but visitors should take care, since the uneven, slippery surfaces have barely been touched for centuries. *Admission free. Open Apr.–Sept., daily 9–9; Oct.–Mar., daily 7–7.*

② After leaving the castle by its impressive gate, wander down through the warren of streets that make up the **Alfama.** This jumble of whitewashed houses, with their flower-laden balconies and red-tile roofs, managed to survive devastating earthquakes because it rests on foundations of dense bedrock. The Alfama district is a notorious place for getting lost in, but it's relatively compact and you'll keep coming upon the same main squares and streets. Find your way

to the Largo Rodrigues de Freitas, a street to the east of the castle,
then take a look at the **Museu da Marioneta** (Puppet Museum) at No.
19A (Admission: 300$00. Open Tues.–Sun. 10–1 and 2–6). From
there head south along the Rua de São Tome to the Largo das Portas
do Sol, where you'll find the **Museu de Artes Decorativas** (Museum of
Decorative Arts) in the Fundaçaõ Ricardo Espirito Santo (Admission: 500$00. Open Tues.–Sat. 10–5:30). More than 20 workshops
teach rare handicrafts, including bookbinding, ormulu, carving, and
cabinetmaking.

Head southwest past the Largo de Santa Luzia along the Rua do
Limoeiro, which eventually becomes the Rua Augusto Rosa. This
route takes you past the **Sé** (cathedral), which is also worth a visit.
Built in the 12th century, the Sé has an austere Romanesque interi-
or; its extremely thick walls bear witness to the fact that it also
served as a fortress. *Largo da Sé. Admission to cathedral free; cloister 300$00. Open daily 8:30–noon and 2–6.*

Continue northwest from the cathedral along the Rua de Santo António da Sé, turn left along the Rua da Conceiçao, then right and
north up the Rua Augusta. A 10-minute stroll along this street takes
you through the **Baixa,** which is also one of Lisbon's main shopping
and banking districts. Semipedestrianized, this old-fashioned area
boasts a small crafts market, some of the best shoe shops in Europe,
and a host of delicatessens selling anything from game birds to
queijo da serra—a delicious mountain cheese from the Serra da
Estrela range north of Lisbon.

Avenida da Liberdade Rua Augusta leads into the **Rossio,** Lisbon's principal square,
which, in turn, opens on its northwestern end into the Praça dos
Restauradores. This can be considered the beginning of modern Lisbon, for here the broad, tree-lined **Avenida da Liberdade** begins its
northwesterly ascent and ends just over 1.6 kilometers (1 mile) away
at the **Parque Eduardo VII** (Edward VII Park).

A leisurely stroll from the Praça dos Restauradores to the park
takes about 45 minutes. As you make your way up the Liberdade,
you'll find several cafés at its southern end serving coffee and cool
drinks. Most notable is the open-air *esplanada* (café), which faces
the main post office on the right. You'll also pass through a pleasant
mixture of ornate 19th-century architecture and Art Deco buildings
from the '30s—a marked contrast to the cool, green atmosphere of
the park itself. Rare flowers, trees, and shrubs thrive in the *estufa
fria* (cold greenhouse) and the *estufa quente* (hot greenhouse).
*Parque Eduardo VII. Admission to greenhouses: 75$00. Open win-
ter, daily 9–5; summer, daily 9–6.*

Turn right from the park and head north along the Avenida António
Augusto de Aguiar. A 15-minute walk will bring you to the busy
Praça de Espanha, to the right of which, in the Parque de Palhava, is
the renowned **Gulbenkian Foundation,** a cultural trust. The foundation's art center houses treasures that were collected by Armenian
oil magnate Calouste Gulbenkian and donated to the people of Portugal. The collection includes superb examples of Greek and Roman
coins, Persian carpets, Chinese porcelain, and paintings by such Old
Masters as Rembrandt and Rubens. *Av. de Berna 45, tel. 01/795-
0236. Admission: 200$00, free Sun. Open June–Sept., Tues.,
Thurs., Fri., and Sun. 10–5, Wed. and Sat. 2–7:30; Oct.–May,
Tues.–Sun. 10–5; closed Mon. year-round.*

Bairro Alto Lisbon's **Bairro Alto** (High District) is largely made up of 18th- and
19th-century buildings that house an intriguing mixture of restau-
rants, theaters, nightclubs, churches, bars, and antiques shops. The
best way to start a tour of this area is via the **Elevador da Glória** (funicular railway), located on the western side of Avenida da
Liberdade by the Praça dos Restauradores. The trip takes about a
minute and drops passengers at the São Pedro de Alcântara

Lisbon

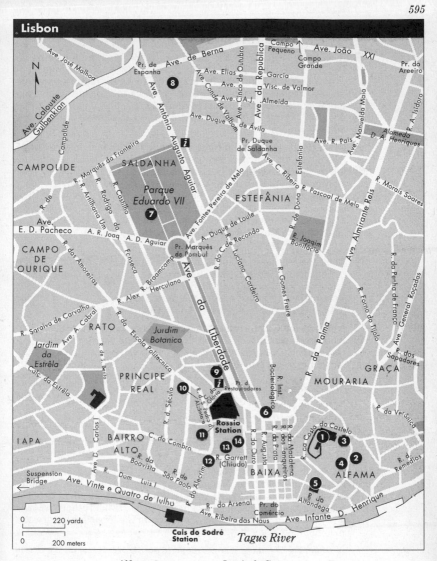

Alfama, **2**

Castelo de São Jorge, **1**

Elevador da Glória, **9**

Elevador de Santa Justa, **14**

Gulbenkian Foundation, **8**

Igreja do Carmo, **13**

Igreja de São Roque, **11**

Instituto do Vinho do Porto, **10**

Largo do Chiado, **12**

Museu de Artes Decorativas, **4**

Museu da Marioneta, **3**

Parque Eduardo VII, **7**

Rossio, **6**

Sé, **5**

miradouro, a viewpoint that looks toward the castle and the Alfama (Cost: 150$00. Open 7 AM–midnight).

⑩ Across the street from the miradouro is the **Instituto do Vinho do Porto** (Port Wine Institute), where, in its cozy, clublike lounge, visitors can sample more than 100 brands of Portugal's most famous beverage—from the extra-dry white varieties to the older, ruby-red vintages. *Rua S. Pedro de Alcântara 45, tel. 01/342–3307. Admission free. Prices of tastings vary, starting at 160$00. Open Mon.– Sat. 10–10.*

From the institute, turn right and walk down Rua de São Pedro de Alcântara. On your left is the Largo Trindade Coelho, site of the ⑪ highly decorative **Igreja de São Roque** (Church of São Roque). The church (open daily 8:30–6) is best known for the flamboyant 18th-century **Capela de São João Baptista** (Chapel of St. John the Baptist), but it is nonetheless a showpiece in its own right. The precious stones that adorn its walls were imported from Italy. Adjoining the church is the **Museu de Arte Sacra** (Museum of Sacred Art). *Admission: 250$00. Open Tues.–Sun. 10–5.*

⑫ Continue south down Rua da Misericórdia until you reach the **Largo do Chiado** on your left. The Chiado, once Lisbon's chic shopping district, was badly damaged by a fire in August 1988, but it still houses some of the city's most fashionable department stores. An ambitious building program is restoring the area's former glory.

North of the Chiado, on the Largo do Carmo, lies the partially ru-⑬ ined **Igreja do Carmo** (Carmo Church), one of the few older structures in the area to have survived the 1755 earthquake. Today open-air orchestral concerts are held beneath its majestic archways during the summer, and its sacristy houses an **archaeological museum.** *Museu Arqueologico. Largo do Carmo. Admission: 300$00. Open Oct.–Mar., Tues.–Sat. 10–1 and 2–5; Apr.–Sept., Tues.–Sat. 10–6.*

Return directly to the Praça dos Restauradores via the nearby ⑭ **Elevador de Santa Justa** (the Santa Justa funicular), which is enclosed in a Gothic tower created by Raul Mesnier, the Portuguese protégé of Gustave Eiffel. *Cost: 150$00. Open 7 AM–midnight.*

Belém To see the best examples of that uniquely Portuguese, late-Gothic architecture known as Manueline, head for Belém at the far southwestern edge of Lisbon. If you are traveling in a group of three or four, taxis are the cheapest means of transportation; otherwise take a No. 15, 16, or 17 tram from the Praça do Comércio for a more scenic, if bumpier, journey.

Numbers in the margin correspond to points of interest on the Belém map.

⑮ Trams Nos. 15 and 16 stop directly outside the **Mosteiro dos Jerónimos,** Belém's Hieronymite monastery, located in the Praça do Império. This impressive structure was conceived and planned by King Manuel I at the beginning of the 16th century to honor the discoveries of such great explorers as Vasco da Gama, who is buried here. Construction of the monastery began in 1502 and was largely financed by treasures brought back from the so-called *descobrimentos*—the "discoveries" made by the Portuguese in Africa, Asia, and South America. Don't miss the stunning double cloister with its arches and pillars heavily sculpted with marine motifs. *Admission to church free, cloisters 400$00. Open June–Sept., Tues.–Sun. 10–6:30; Oct.–May, Tues.–Sun. 10–1 and 2:30–5.*

⑯ The **Museu de Marinha** (Maritime Museum) is at the other end of the monastery. Its huge collection reflects Portugal's long seafaring tradition, and exhibitions range from early maps and navigational instruments to entire ships, including the sleek caravels that took

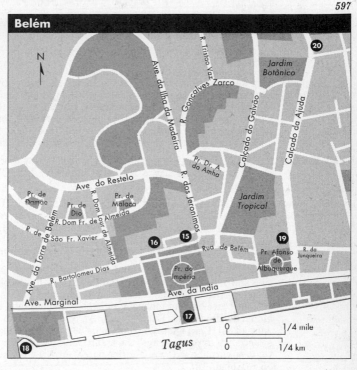

Portuguese explorers and traders around the globe. *Admission: 300$00, free Sun 10–12. Open Tues.–Sun. 10–5.*

Across from the monastery at the water's edge stands the **Monumento dos Descobrimentos** (Monument to the Discoveries). Built in 1960, this modern tribute to the seafaring explorers stands on what was the departure point of many of their voyages. An interesting mosaic, surrounded by an intricate wave pattern composed of black-and-white cobblestones, lies at the foot of the monument. *Admission for elevator: 275$00. Open Tues.–Sun. 9:30–7.*

A 15-minute walk west of the monument brings you to the **Torre de Belém** (the Belém Tower), another fine example of Manueline architecture with openwork balconies, loggia, and domed turrets. Although it was built in the early 16th century on an island in the middle of the River Tagus, today the tower stands near the north bank—the river's course has changed over the centuries. *Av. da Torre de Belém and Av. de India. Admission: June–Sept., 400$00; Oct.–May, 250$00. Open Tues.–Sun., 10–6:30 summer, 10–1 and 2:30–5 winter.*

Away from the Tagus and southeast of the monastery, on the Praça Afonso de Albuquerque, is the **Museu Nacional do Coches** (National Coach Museum), which houses one of the largest collections of coaches in the world. The oldest vehicle on display was made for Philip II of Spain in the late 16th century, but the most stunning exhibits are three golden Baroque coaches, created in Rome for King John V in 1716. *Admission: June–Sept. 400$00, Oct.–May 250$00; free Sun. Open summer, Tues.–Sun. 10–1 and 2:30–6:30; winter, Tues.–Sun. 10–1 and 2:30–5:30.*

Head north of the coach museum on Calçada da Ajuda to the **Palácio da Ajuda** (Ajuda Palace). Once a royal residence, this impressive building now contains a collection of 18th- and 19th-century paintings, furniture, and tapestries. *Largo da Ajuda. Admission:*

250$00; free Sun. 10–2. Guided tours arranged on request. Open Thurs.–Tues. 10–5. Closed Wed.

Shopping

Shopping Districts Fire destroyed much of Lisbon's choicest shopping street in 1988; however, an extensive reconstruction project is well under way. Another important shopping area is in the **Baixa** quarter (between the Rossio and the River Tagus). The blue-and-pink towers of the **Amoreiras,** a huge modern shopping center (open daily 9 AM–11 PM) on Avenida Engeneiro Duarte Pacheco, dominate the Lisbon skyline.

Flea Markets A **Feira da Ladra** (flea market) is held on Tuesday morning and all day Saturday in the Largo de Santa Clara behind the Church of São Vicente, near the Alfama district.

Gift Ideas *Leather Goods* Fine leather handbags and luggage are sold at **Galeão** (Rua Augusta 190) and at **Casa Canada** (Rua Augusta 232). Shoe stores abound in Lisbon, but they may have a limited selection of large sizes (the Portuguese have relatively small feet). Leather gloves can be purchased at a variety of specialty shops on Rua do Carmo and Rua Aurea.

Handicrafts **Viúva Lamego** (Largo do Intendente 25) has the largest selection of tiles and pottery, while **Fabrica Sant'Ana** (Rua do Alecrim 95), in the Chiado, sells wonderful hand-painted ceramics and tiles based on antique patterns. For embroidered goods and baskets, try **Casa Regional da Ilha Verde** (Rua Paiva de Andrade 4) or **Tito Cunha** (Rua Aurea 286). **Casa Quintão** (Rua Ivens 30), probably has the largest selection of *arraiolos* rugs, the traditional, hand-embroidered Portuguese carpets, in town. For fine porcelain, visit **Vista Alegre** (Largo do Chiado 18).

Jewelry and Antiques **Antonio da Silva** (Praça Luis de Camoes 40) at the top of the Chiado, specializes in antique silver and jewelry, as does **Barreto e Gonçalves** (Rua das Portas de Santo Antão 17). Most of the antiques shops are along the Rua Escola Politecnica, Dom Pedro IV, Rua da Misericordia, and Rua do Alecrim.

Look for characteristic Portuguese gold- and silver-filigree work at **Sarmento** (Rua Aurea 251).

Dining

For details and price-category definitions, *see* Dining *in* Staying in Portugal, *above.*

$$ **O Madeirense.** Lisbon's only Madeiran restaurant, this rustic-style room is set inside the Amoreiras shopping center. The *espedate* is famously traditional—a skewer of fillet steak hung above the table from a stand so that you can serve yourself at will. *Loja 3027, Amoreiras Shopping Center, Av. Eng. Duarte Pacheco, tel. 01/690827. Reservations advised. AE, DC, MC, V.*

$$ **Michel.** Innovative French cooking and an intimate atmosphere can be found in this attractive restaurant within the walls of St. George's castle. Choose from such dishes as bass fillet with champagne sauce, and the traditional *porco a alentejana* (pork with clams). *Largo S. Cruz do Castelo 5, tel. 01/886–4338. Reservations advised. AE, DC, MC, V. Closed Sat. lunch and Sun.*

$$ **Solmar.** Located near the Rossio, Lisbon's main square, this large restaurant is best known for its seafood and shellfish, but try the wild boar or venison in season. *Rua Portas de S. Antão 108, tel. 01/342–3371. AE, DC, MC, V.*

$ **Brasuca.** A comfortable Brazilian restaurant set in an old mansion on the edge of the Bairro Alto, the Brasuca serves a splendid *caipirinha* (rum cocktail), grills, and spicy meat stews. *Rua Joao Pereira da Rosa 7, tel. 01/342–8542. Reservations advised. AE, DC, MC, V. Closed Mon.*

$ **Cervejaria Trindade.** You get good value for your money at this large
★ restaurant, which has a garden and a cave-style wine cellar. *Rua
Nova da Trindade 20, tel. 01/342–3506. AE, DC, MC, V.*

$ **Farah's Tandoori.** What appears to be a simple Indian restaurant is
really one of the best in Lisbon. The good curries and Indian bread
are not to be missed. Two dining floors makes finding a table a manageable task. *Rua de Sant'Ana à Lapa 73, tel. 01/609219. MC, V.
Closed Tues.*

$ **O Alexandre.** This tiny restaurant in Belém has outdoor tables from
which diners, mostly locals, can soak up the superb view of the monastery. The seafood here is served on large platters, so bring your
appetite! Try the grilled *peixe espada* (scabbard fish) or one of the
more unusual squid or octopus dishes. Note that the restaurant
closes at 10 PM. *Rue Vieira Portuense 84, Belém, tel. 01/363–4454.
No reservations. MC, V. Closed Sat.*

$ **Ribadouro.** This bustling basement retaurant, facing the main ave-
nue, fills quickly with locals who come to sample the choice spread of
freshly prepared seafood. The surroundings are functional, not fancy, but the layout allows you to watch the chefs preparing crabs and
crayfish at the counter. Prices are even more reasonable if you eat at
the bar. *Av. da Liberdade 155, tel. 01/549411. Reservations advised.
AE, DC, MC, V.*

$ **Sua Excêlencia.** There's no menu in this cozy little restaurant in the
Lapa district. The English-speaking owner will personally talk you
through their outstanding Portuguese dishes, like the smoked
swordfish. *Rua do Conde 42, tel. 01/603614. Reservations advised.
MC, V. Closed Sept., Wed., and weekend lunch.*

¢ **Bonjardim.** Known locally as *Rei dos Frangos* (the King of Chick-
★ ens), the Bonjardim specializes in the spit-roasted variety. Just off
the Restauradores, it gets very crowded at peak hours. *Travesssa S.
Antão 11, tel. 01/342–7424. AE, DC, MC, V.*

¢ **Casa Faz Frio.** A traditional *adega* (wine cellar) on the edge of the
Bairro Alto, this restaurant is decorated with a sea of blue tiles and
bunches of garlic suspended from the ceiling. There's a changing
menu of Portuguese specialties, and all are good value. *Rua D. Pedro V 96–98, tel. 01/346 1860. No credit cards.*

¢ **O Cantinho do Aziz.** Hidden in the ring of tiny streets below the cas-
tle, this small, family-run Mozambican restaurant offers "Comida
Indio-Africana," plenty of rich curried meat and fish dishes served
with coconut-flavored rice. Climb the flight of steps from Poço do
Borratém, near Praça da Figueira, to find the entrance. *Rua de S.
Lourenço 3–5, tel. 01/876472. No credit cards. Closed Sun.*

Vá e Volta. This is a splendid place for one-plate budget Bairro Alto
fare—fried or grilled meat or fish dishes served with gusto. *Rua do
Diario de Noticias 100, tel. 01/342–7888. MC, V.*

Lodging

Lisbon has a good array of accommodations in all price categories,
ranging from major international chain hotels to charming little
family-run establishments. During peak season reservations should
be made well in advance. For details and price-category definitions,
see Lodging *in* Staying *in* Portugal, *above.*

$$ **Albergaria Senhora do Monte.** The rooms in this unpretentious little
★ hotel, in the oldest part of town near St. George's Castle, have ter-
races that offer some of the loveliest views of Lisbon, especially at
night when the castle and Carmo ruins in the middle distance are
softly illuminated. The top-floor grill has a picture window. The sur-
rounding neighborhood is quiet, and parking is available. *Calçada
do Monte 39, tel. 01/886–6002, fax 01/877783. 28 rooms with bath.
Facilities: restaurant, bar, grill. AE, DC, MC, V.*

$$ **Fenix.** At the top of Avenida da Liberdade, this recently remodeled
hotel has marble trappings in its bright, air-conditioned public

rooms, and large guest rooms with comfy armchairs. Its restaurant serves good Portuguese food. *Praça Marquês de Pombal 8, tel. 01/386–2121, fax 01/386–0131. 119 rooms with bath. Facilities: restaurant, bar, parking. AE, DC, MC, V.*

$$ Flamingo. Another good-value choice near the top of the Avenida da Liberdade, this hotel has a friendly staff and pleasant guest rooms, though the ones in the front tend to be noisy. There's a pay parking lot right next door, which is a bonus in this busy area. *Rua Castilho 41, tel. 01/386–2191, fax 01/386–2195. 39 rooms with bath. Facilities: restaurant, bar. AE, DC, MC, V.*

$$ Florida. This centrally located hotel has a pleasant atmosphere and guest rooms with marble-clad bathrooms. It's handily placed for downtown restaurants. *Rua Duque de Palmela 32, tel. 01/576145, fax 01/543584. 112 rooms with bath. Facilities: bar. AE, DC, MC, V.*

$$ Novotel Lisboa. There's an attentive staff and a quiet, welcoming at-
★ mosphere at this modern hotel near the U.S. Embassy. The public rooms are spacious and the guest rooms are spruce and comfortably equipped. *Av. Jose Malhoa, Lote 1642, tel. 01/726–6022, fax 01/726–6496. 246 rooms with bath. Facilities: restaurant, bar, pool, garage. AE, MC, V.*

$ Duas Nacões. You're paying for the superb location at this *pensão*— right in the heart of the Baixa—rather than for any particular facilities. The rooms here are plain and functional, though and there is a bar. Try to avoid booking any of the rooms facing the street—they can be noisy. *Rua da Vitória 41, tel. 01/346–0710. 66 rooms, 42 with bath. Facilities: bar. No credit cards.*

$ Hotel Borges. In the heart of the Chiado district, convenient for shopping, this dependable, old-fashioned hotel has good service and a charm that transcends its limited facilities. *Rua Garrett 108–110, tel. 01/346–1951, fax 01/342–6617. Facilities: breakfast room, bar. MC, V.*

$ Residencial Casa de S. Mamede. Halfway between the main avenue and Amoreiras shopping center, this attractive, old-fashioned residencial is a good value. If some of the guest rooms appear frayed at the edges then so be it: This is historic Europe at budget prices. *Rua da Escola Politecnica 159, tel. 01/396–3166, fax 01/395–1896. 30 rooms with bath. MC, V.*

¢ Pensão Arco Bandeira. It's reasonably quiet at this friendly pensão, despite its location at the bottom of the Rossio. The simple rooms and bathroom down the hall are spotless. *Rua dos Sapateiros 226–4, tel. 01/342–3478. 8 rooms. No credit cards.*

¢ Pensão Beira-Minho. The best rooms here have sweeping views over one of Lisbon's busiest squares, Praça da Figueira, so it's a good base for sightseeing in the city center. It's also just across from the Pastelaria Suiça, an excellent breakfast spot. *Praça da Figueira, 6–2, tel. 01/346–1846. 19 rooms, 12 with bath. No credit cards.*

¢ Pensão Ninho das Aguias. The location is what makes this place special: On the road below the castle, the pensão's attractive garden terrace has superb views over the city center. *Costa do Castelo 74, tel. 01/886–7008. 16 rooms, 6 with bath. No credit cards.*

¢ Residencial Florescente. One block from central Praça dos Restauradores, this is in a prime position. Rooms are spread across four floors—there's no elevator—and the best ones are airy and freshly painted, with their own bathroom and TV. Cheaper choices are not too impressive, so ask to see a selection, if necessary. *Rua Portas de Santo Antão 99, tel. 01/342–6609, fax 01/3423–7733. 100 rooms, 50 with bath. MC, V.*

The Arts

Two local newspaper supplements provide listings of music, theater, ballet, film, and other entertainment in Lisbon: *Sete*, published on Wednesdays, and *Sabado*, published on Fridays.

Plays are performed in Portuguese at the **Teatro Nacional de D. Maria II** (Praça Dom Pedro IV, tel. 01/342–2210) year-round except in July, and there are revues at small theaters in the Parque Mayer. Classical music, opera, and ballet are presented in the beautiful **Teatro Nacional de Opera de São Carlos** (Rua Serpa Pinto 9, tel. 01/346–5914). Classical music and ballet are also staged from autumn to summer by the **Fundação Calouste Gulbenkian** (Ave. Berna 45, tel. 01/793–5131). Of particular interest is the annual Early Music and Baroque Festival, held in churches and museums around Lisbon every spring. The new cultural center, the **Centro Cultural de Belém** (Av. da India, tel. 01/301–9606) at Belém, also hosts a full program of concerts and exhibitions—pick up a monthly program of events from the reception desk. The **Nova Filarmonica,** one of Portugal's national orchestras, performs concerts around the country throughout the year; consult local papers for details.

Nightlife

The most popular night spots in Lisbon are the *adegas tipicas* (wine cellars), where customers dine on Portuguese specialties, drink wine, and listen to *fado* (traditional Portuguese folk music), those haunting melodies unique to Portugal. Most of these establishments are scattered throughout the Alfama and Bairro Alto districts. Try the **Senhor Vinho** (Rua Meio a Lapa 18, tel. 01/397–7456. Closed Sun.), **Lisboa à Noite** (Rua das Gaveas 69, tel. 01/346–8557. Closed Sun.), or the **Machado** (Rua do Norte 91, tel. 01/346–0095. Closed Mon.). The singing starts at 10 PM, and reservations are advised. Lisbon's top spot for live jazz is **The Hot Clube** (Praça da Alegria 39, tel. 01/346–7369. Closed Sun. and Mon.), where sessions don't usually begin until 11 PM.

Bars and Discos The main areas for bars and discos are the Bairro Alto or along Avenida 24 de Julho, northwest of Cais do Sodre station. In the former, the best place to start is the refined **Instituto do Vinho do Porto** (Rua de São Pedro de Alcântara 45, tel. 01/347–5707), where you choose drinks from a menu of port wines. Also, **Cena de Copas** (Rua da Barroca 103–105, tel. 01/347–3372) is still loud and fashionable, while **Pavilhão Chines** (Rua Dom Pedro V 89, tel. 01/342–4729) is decorated with extraordinary bric-a-brac from around the world. Along Avenida 24 de Julho, current favorites include **Café 24 de Julho** (No. 114) and **Café Central** (No. 110), and the nearby **Kremlin** disco (Rua Escadinhas da Praia 5, tel. 01/608768) continues to attract the trendiest Lisboetas. **Trumps** (Rua Imprensa Nacional 104b, tel. 01/397–1059) is the city's biggest gay disco; **Memorial** (Rua Gustavo Sequeira 42, tel. 01/396–8891) is popular with both gay and lesbian visitors.

The Portuguese Riviera

Extending 32 kilometers (20 miles) west of Lisbon is a stretch of coastline known as the Portuguese Riviera. Over the years, the casino at Estoril and the beaches, both there and in Cascais, have provided playgrounds for the wealthy, as well as homes for expatriates and exiled European royalty. To the north of these towns lie the lush, green mountains of Sintra and to the northeast, the historic town of Queluz, dominated by its 18th-century rococo palace and formal gardens. Whether you stick to the coast or head for the mountains, you'll find the area is heavily populated with highly varied scenery and attractions.

The villas, châteaus, and luxury *quintas* (country properties) of Sintra contrast notably with Cascais and Estoril, where life revolves around the sea. Beaches here differ both in quality and cleanliness. Some display the blue Council of Europe flag, which signals a high standard of unpolluted water and sands, but others leave much to be desired. The waters off Cascais and Estoril are calmer, though sullied as a result of their proximity to the meeting of the sea and Lisbon's Tagus estuary. To the north, around Guincho's rocky promontory and the Praia de Maças coast, the Atlantic Ocean is often windswept and rough but provides good surfing, windsurfing, and scuba diving. The entire region offers comprehensive sports facilities: golf courses, horseback riding, fishing, tennis, squash, swimming, water sports, grand prix racing, mountain climbing, and country walking.

Getting Around

A commuter train leaves every quarter of an hour from Cais do Sodré Station in Lisbon for the trip to Estoril and then to Cascais, four stops farther. The 30-minute-total journey affords splendid sea views as it hugs the shore. A one-way ticket costs 160$00. Trains from Lisbon's Rossio station run every quarter of an hour to Queluz (145$00), taking 20 minutes, and on to Sintra (155$00), which takes 40 minutes.

Tourist Information

Cascais (Viscount Luz 14-r/c, tel. 01/4868204).
Estoril (Arcadas do Parque, tel. 01/4860113).
Sintra (Praça da Republica 3, tel. 01/9233919).

Exploring the Portuguese Riviera

Estoril Estoril is filled with grand homes and gardens, and many of its large mansions date from the last century when the resort was a favorite with the European aristocracy. Portugal's jet-set resort is expensive, with little in the way of sights. For those of us who weren't born with silver spoons in our mouths, people-watching is always a satisfying pastime, and one of the best places for it is on the **Tamariz esplanade,** especially from an alfresco restaurant. A palm-studded coastline, plush accommodations, sports facilities, and restaurants are among Estoril's other attractions, but it is perhaps best known for its **casino** (open 3PM–3AM) an excellent gambling hall and night spot that includes a restaurant, a bar, a theater, and an art gallery. A major open-air handicrafts and ceramics fair is held each summer (July–September), and many of the summer music festival concerts and ballets are staged here (a schedule is available at the tourist office).

Cascais Cascais lies less than 3.2 kilometers (2 miles) west of Estoril along the train route. A pretty but heavily developed tourist resort, it is packed with shopping centers, restaurants, movie theaters, and hotels. The three beaches are small and crowded: even so, there are still some sights worth seeing, including the **Igreja de Nossa Senhora da Assunção** (Church of Our Lady of the Assumption), which contains paintings by Portuguese artist Josefa de Óbidos. *Largo de Igreja. Admission free. Open daily 9–1 and 5–8.*

Opposite the church is one of the entrances to the **Parque do Marachal Carmona** (open daily 9–6), in which there's a shallow lake, a café, and a small zoo. Walk through the park to its southern edge and you'll find the **Museu Conde de Castro Guimarães** (Museum of the Counts of Castro Guimarães), a large stately home set in spacious grounds. It houses some good paintings, ceramics, furniture, and archaeological artifacts excavated locally. *Estrada da Boca do Inferno. Admission: 150$00, free Sun. Open Tues.–Sun. 11–12:30 and 2–5.*

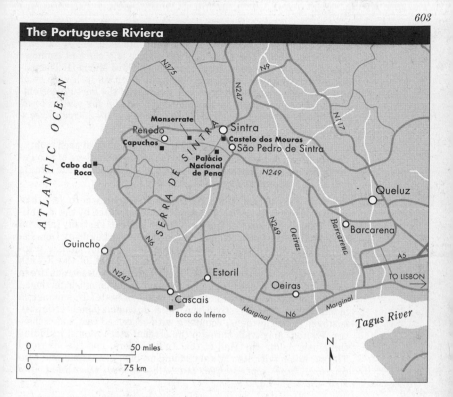

ATLANTIC OCEAN

N375 · N9 · N247 · N117 · N249 · N6 · N247 · A5

Monserrate · Renedo · Capuchos · Cabo da Roca · SERRA DE SINTRA · Sintra · Castelo dos Mouros · São Pedro de Sintra · Palácio Nacional de Pena · Queluz · Barcarena · Oeiras · Guincho · Estoril · Cascais · Boca do Inferno · Oeiras · Marginal · N6 · Marginal · TO LISBON · Tagus River

0 ___ 50 miles
0 ___ 75 km

N

Less than 2 kilometers (about 1¼ miles) out of the town center, in the direction of Guincho beach, lies the notorious **Boca do Inferno,** or Hell's Mouth. This rugged section of coastline is made up of numerous grottoes; visitors are able to see the full impact of the sea as it pounds into the walkways and viewing platforms. A path leads down to secluded spots on the rocks below.

Sintra Sintra, full of art, history, and architecture, is one of the country's oldest towns. This is where Portuguese kings and aristocrats formerly had their summer residences. At the center of the **Old Town** near the Hotel Tivoli Sintra stands the 14th-century **Palácio Nacional de Sintra** (Sintra Palace). This twin-chimneyed building, a combination of Moorish and Gothic architectural styles, was once the summer residence of the House of Avis, Portugal's royal lineage. Today it's a museum that houses some fine examples of mozarabic *azulejos* (handpainted tiles). *Admission: June–Sept. 400$00, Oct.– May 200$00, free Sun. morning. Open Mon., Tues., and Thurs.– Sun. 10–1 and 2–5.*

If you stand on the steps of the palace and look up toward the Sintra Mountains, you can spot the 8th-century ruins of the **Castelo dos Mouros** (Moors' Castle), which defied hundreds of invaders until it was finally conquered by Dom Afonso Henriques in 1147. For a closer look, follow the steep, partially cobbled road that leads up to the ruins; or, if you're a romantic, rent one of the horse and carriages outside the palace for the trip. From the castle's serrated walls, you can see why its Moorish architects chose the site: The panoramic views falling away on all sides are breathtaking. *Estrada da Pena, tel. 01/923–0137. Admission free. Open June–Sept., daily 10–6; Oct.–May, daily 10–5.*

Farther up the same road you'll reach the **Palácio Nacional de Pena** (the Pena Palace), a Wagnerian-style extravaganza built by the King Consort Ferdinand Saxe-Coburg in 1840. It is a cauldron of clashing styles, from Arabian to Victorian, and was home to the final kings of Portugal, the last of whom went into exile in 1910 after a republican revolt. The nucleus of the palace is a convent commissioned by Dom Fernando, consort to Queen Dona Maria II. The palace is surrounded by a splendid park filled with a lush variety of trees and flowers brought from every corner of the Portuguese empire by Dom Fernando in the 1840s. *Admission for guided tour: June–Sept. 400$00, Oct.–May 200$00, free Sun. 10–2. Open Tues.– Sun. 10–5.*

If you're in the area on the second or fourth Sunday of each month, visit the **Feira de Sintra** (Sintra Fair) in the nearby village of **São Pedro de Sintra,** 2 kilometers (about 1¼ miles) to the southeast. This is one of the best-known fairs in the country.

Queluz The train back to Lisbon will pass through **Queluz** where, less than half a mile from the train station, you'll be confronted by the magnificent **Palácio Nacional de Queluz** (Queluz Palace). Partially inspired by Versailles, this salmon-pink rococo palace was begun by Dom Pedro III in 1747 and took 40 years to complete. The formal landscaping and waterways that surround it are the work of the French designer Jean-Baptiste Robillon. Restored after a disastrous fire in 1934, the palace is used today for formal banquets, music festivals, and as accommodations for visiting heads of state. In summer, a month-long medieval festival, the **Noites de Queluz** (Queluz Nights), is staged in the gardens, complete with costumed cast and orchestra. Visitors may walk through the elegant state rooms, including the Music Salon, the Hall of the Ambassadors, and the mirrored Throne Room with its crystal chandeliers and gilt trimmings. *Admission: June–Sept. 400$00, Oct.–May 200$00. Open Mon. and Wed.–Sun. 10–1 and 2–5.*

Dining and Lodging

Budget travelers will find that dining and especially lodging along the Portuguese Riviera can run into quite a tidy sum—staying in Lisbon while making day trips into the area may be a less expensive alternative. For details and price-category definitions, *see* Dining and Lodging *in* Staying in Portugal, *above.*

Cascais **Beira Mar.** This well-established restaurant, behind the fish mar-
Dining ket, has a wide variety of fish and meat dishes. The atmosphere is comfortable and unpretentious. *Rua das Flores 6, tel. 01/483–0152. AE, DC, MC, V. Closed Tues. $$*
Dom Manolo. This is a bustling, unsophisticated, Spanish-owned grill-restaurant, where waiters charge back and forth delivering excellent spit-roasted chicken to a largely local clientele. *Av. Marginal 13, tel. 01/483–1126. No credit cards. ¢*

Lodging **Hotel Baia.** This modern hotel overlooks the glistening blue water of Cascais bay. The rooms are comfortable and well appointed; ask for one with a private balcony facing the sea. *Av. Marginal 2750, tel. 01/483–1033, fax 01/483–1095. 114 rooms with bath. Facilities: roof terrace, pool, restaurant, bar. AE, DC, MC, V. $$*

Estoril **Restaurante Frolic.** The Frolic is a friendly restaurant-bar next to
Dining Hotel Palácio with a covered outdoor terrace. Try the delectable cakes or stop longer for a Portuguese meal or a pizza. *Av. Clotilde, tel. 01/468–1219. AE, DC, MC, V. $*

Lodging **Hotel Lido.** On a quiet street well away from the beach overlooking the lush green hillside above Sintra, the Lido is justly popular for its good facilities, which include a pool and garden as well as a fine restaurant. The hotel is signposted from the casino—it's less suitable for visitors without a car since it's a steep 15-minute walk from the center of Estoril. *Rua do Alentejo 12, tel. 01/468–4123, fax 01/468–*

3665. 62 rooms with bath. Facilities: pool, restaurant, bar, garden, garage. AE, DC, MC, V. $$

Sintra
Dining

Alcobaça. This central restaurant offers excellent value for classic Portuguese home cooking. Try the grilled chicken or the *arroz de marisco* (seafood rice). It's a small, friendly, local place. *Rua das Padarias 7–11, tel. 01/923–1651. MC, V. $$*

Lodging

Hotel Central. Exuding a certain faded 19th-century charm, the Central was once *the* hotel in Sintra and the interior reflects those bygone days—a smell of polished wood prevails and Portuguese tiles and solid old furniture are everywhere. *Praça da República 35, tel. 01/923–0963. 14 rooms, 9 with bath. Facilities: restaurant, bar. AE, DC, MC, V. $$*

The Algarve

The Algarve, Portugal's southernmost holiday resort, encompasses some 240 kilometers (150 miles) of sun-drenched coast below the Serra de Monchique and the Serra do Caldeirão. It is the top destination for foreign visitors to Portugal. During the past three decades, this area, indelibly marked by centuries of Arab occupation, has been heavily developed in an effort to create a playground for international sun worshipers. Well known by Europeans as a holiday center of clean, sandy beaches; championship golf courses; and local color, this section of Portugal is only now being discovered by Americans. Although some parts of the coastline have been seriously overbuilt, there are still plenty of picturesque fishing villages and secluded beaches to leaven the concentration of hotels, casinos, disco nightclubs, and sports facilities.

This itinerary takes you to some of the most interesting and typical towns and villages in the Algarve, starting near the Portuguese border with Spain in the east and ending at the most southwesterly point of the European continent.

Getting Around

There is daily bus and rail service between Lisbon and several towns in the Algarve; the trip takes between four and six hours, depending on your destination. The best places to head are the main towns of Lagos and Faro; from here local rail and bus services serve most of the surrounding villages. Although the road and train do not run right along the immediate coast, it is generally a simple matter to walk to, or catch a bus to, the most popular beachside destinations.

Tourist Information

Local tourist offices can be found in the following towns: **Albufeira** (Rua 5 de Outubro, tel. 089/512144), **Faro** (Airport, tel. 089/818582; Rua da Misericorida 8/12, tel. 089/803604; **Lagos** (Largo Marquês de Pombal, tel. 082/763031), **Olhão** (Largo da Lagoa, tel. 089/713936), **Portimão** (Largo 1° de Dezembro, tel. 082/22065 or 082/23695), **Praia da Rocha** (Av. Tomás Cabreira, tel. 082/22290), **Sagres** (Promontório de Sagres, tel. 082/64125), **Silves** (Rua 25 de Abril, tel. 082/442255), **Tavira** (Praça da República, tel. 081/22511), **Vila Real de Santo António** (Praça Marquês de Pombal, tel. 081/44495; Frontier Tourist Post, tel. 081/43272).

Exploring the Algarve

Vila Real de Santo António is the easternmost town of the Algarve; its ferries (and a new suspension bridge) cross the River Guadiana to Ayamonte, the Spanish frontier town. Vila Real is worth noting for its design: Laid out on a grid, similar to that of Lisbon's Baixa sec-

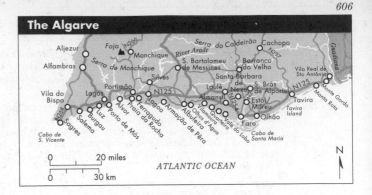

The Algarve

0   20 miles
0   30 km

ATLANTIC OCEAN

tion, it's considered a showcase of 18th-century Portuguese town planning. Aside from this, there's little reason to linger.

Tavira From Vila Real it's 40 minutes west by train to **Tavira**, which many people call the prettiest town in the Algarve. Situated at the mouth of the River Gilão, it is famous for its figs, arcaded streets, a seven-arched Roman bridge, old Moorish defense walls, and interesting churches. There are good sand beaches on nearby **Tavira Island**, which is reached by ferry (May–mid-Oct., every 30–60 mins; 150$00 round-trip) from the jetty at Quatro Águas, 2 kilometers (a little more than a mile) east of the town center; it's a 30-minute walk to the jetty. Another 22 kilometers (14 miles) west lies the fishing port and market town of **Olhão**. Founded in the 18th century, Olhão is notable for its North African–style architecture—cube-shape whitewashed buildings—and the best food markets in the Algarve.

Faro From Olhão it's just 9 kilometers (6 miles) to **Faro**, the provincial capital of the Algarve, located roughly at the center of the coast. When this city was finally taken by Afonso III in 1249, it ended the Arab domination of Portugal, and remnants of the medieval walls and gates that surrounded the city then can still be seen in the older district, the **Cidade Velha**. One of the gates, the **Arco da Vila**, with a white marble statue of St. Thomas Aquinas in a niche at the top, leads to the grand Largo de Sé. The **Gothic cathedral** here has a stunning interior decorated with 17th-century tiles (Admission free. Open weekdays 10–noon, Sat. at 5 for service, Sun. 8–1). There are also several fascinating museums in Faro, notably the **Museu do Etnografia Regional** (Algarve Ethnographic Museum) on Rua do Pé da Cruz, with good historical and folkloric displays (Admission: 150$00. Open weekdays 9–noon and 2–6); and the **Museu Maritimo** (Maritime Museum) on Rua Comunidade Lusiada near the yacht basin, next to the Hotel Eva (Admission: 150$00. Open Mon.– Sat. 10–11 and 2:30–4:30). The **Museu Municipal** (Municipal Museum) on Largo Afonso III has a section dedicated to the Roman remains found at Milreu (Admission: 150$00. Open Mon.–Sat. 9:30–noon and 2–5). There's a large sand beach on Faro Island, the **Praia de Faro**, which is connected to land by road (take Bus 16 from the stop opposite the town bus station).

Albufeira From Faro, regular buses and trains head west to **Albufeira**; there is a shuttle bus between the railroad station and town, 6 kilometers (about 3½ miles) to the south. At one time an attractive fishing village, Albufeira has long since mushroomed into the Algarve's largest and busiest resort, too brash for many. Even the dried-up riverbed has been turned into a parking lot. But with its steep, narrow streets and hundreds of whitewashed houses snuggled on the slopes of nearby hills, Albufeira still has a distinctly Moorish flavor. Its attractions include the lively fish market (held daily); interesting rock formations, caves, and grottoes along the beach; and plenty of nightlife.

Away from the coast, 25 kilometers (16 miles) to the west, is the hill town of **Silves.** Again, there's a connecting bus from the railroad station into town, 2 kilometers (about a mile) away. Once the Moorish capital of the Algarve, Silves lost its importance after it was almost completely destroyed by the 1755 earthquake. The 12th-century sandstone **fortress** (Admission free, always open), together with its impressive parapets, was restored in 1835 and still dominates the town. Below the fortress stands the 12th–13th-century **Santa Maria da Sé** (Cathedral of Saint Mary), which was built upon the site of a Moorish mosque. (Admission free. Church open daily 8:30–1 and 2:30–6.)

Portimão   From Silves it's only 10 kilometers (6 miles) to **Portimão,** the most important fishing port in the Algarve. There was a settlement here at the mouth of the river Arade even before the Romans arrived. This is a cheerful, busy town and a good center for shopping. Although the colorful fishing boats now unload their catch at a modern terminal across the river, the open-air restaurants along the quay are a pleasant place to sample the local specialty: charcoal-grilled sardines with chewy fresh bread and red wine. Across the bridge, in the fishing hamlet of **Ferragudo,** are the ruins of a 16th-century castle, and 3 kilometers (about 2 miles) south of Portimão is **Praia da Rocha,** to which there is regular bus service. Now dominated by high-rise apartments and hotels, this was the first resort in the Algarve to be developed.

The train and bus route continues west through **Lagos,** a busy fishing port with an attractive harbor and some startling cove beaches in the vicinity that attract a bustling holiday crowd. The 18th-century Baroque **Igreja de Santo António** (Church of Santo António), off Rua General Alberto Silveira, is renowned for its gilt, carved wood, and exuberant decoration. An amusing regional museum is alongside. (Admission 200$00. Open Tues–Sat. 9:30–12:30 and 2–5.) Lagos is the western terminal of the coastal railway that runs from Vila Real de Santo António, connecting with the Lisbon line at Tunes.

Sagres   After Lagos, the terrain along this route becomes more rugged. It is a 40-kilometer (25-mile) journey to the windy headland at **Sagres,** where Prince Henry established his famous school of navigation in the 15th century. The **Compass Rose,** made of stone and earth, in the courtyard of the **Forteleza de Sagres** (Sagres Fortress), was uncovered in this century, but is believed to have been used by Prince Henry in his calculations. The **Graça Chapel** is also inside the fortress (which is always open), as is a building believed to have been Henry's house.

There are spectacular views from here and from **Cabo de São Vicente** (Cape São Vicente) 6 kilometers (4 miles) to the west; it's a 90-minute walk. This point, the most southwesterly tip of the European continent, where the landmass juts into the rough waters of the Atlantic, is sometimes called *O Fim do Mundo,* "the end of the world." Admiral Nelson defeated the Spanish off this cape in 1797. The lighthouse at Cape São Vicente is said to have the strongest reflectors in Europe, casting a beam 96 kilometers (60 miles) out to sea; it is open to the public. It seems only appropriate that it was at this breathtaking spot that Vasco da Gama, Ferdinand Magellan, and other great explorers learned their craft 500 years ago.

Dining and Lodging

The accommodations listed below are only some of the many lodging possibilities in Algarve. Budget travelers are likely to be approached by people offering very reasonably priced rooms in private houses throughout Algarve's main towns and resorts. Though you should always ask to see the room before accepting, they are invariably clean and cheerful—even if they are small and share a bathroom. For details of other budget accommodations, it's always best to ask at the local tourist office—many maintain lists of pensões and will often book a room on your behalf (sometimes for a small fee). Finally, note that the more expensive hotels discount their rooms by as much as 40% during the winter months—so you may be pleasantly surprised by what you can afford. For details and price-category definitions, *see* Dining and Lodging *in* Staying in Portugal, *above*.

Albufeira
Dining
★

A Ruina. A big, rustic restaurant on the beach, built on several levels, this is the place for good views and charcoal-grilled seafood. *Cais Herculano, Praia dos Pescadores, tel. 089/512094. No credit cards. $$*

Lodging

Residencial Polona. Popular with European package operators, this is a good value. It's on a noisy central street of bars and restaurants, but the rooms are cheery, with private bathrooms, and the price includes breakfast. *Rua Cândido dos Reis 32, tel. 089/55859. 40 rooms with bath. Facilities: bar, breakfast room. MC, V. $$*

Caldas de Monchique
Dining and Lodging

Albergaria do Lageado. Right in the center of the spa town, this charming little inn has rather small guest rooms, though they are attractively furnished and some overlook the lush gardens. The traditionally tiled dining room serves good home cooking and there's a terrace for summer dining. *Caldas de Monchique, tel. 082/92616. 19 rooms with bath. Facilities: dining room, lounge, pool, gardens. No credit cards. Closed Nov.–Apr. $*

Faro
Dining

Dos Irmãos. This is a pretty, central restaurant with friendly staff, specializing in *cataplana* dishes. Save room for the homemade *pudim caseiro* (creme caramel). *Largo do Terreiro do Bispo 14–15, tel. 089/823337. MC, V. $*

Restaurante Adega Nova. This *adega* (wine cellar) serves excellent traditional dishes on massive wooden tables to mainly local clientele. *Rua Francisco Barreto 24, tel. 089/813433. No credit cards. $*

Café Aliança. This old-style coffee house, with outdoor seating facing the harbor, serves good snacks and sandwiches, as well as full meals. *Rua F. Gomes 7–11, tel. 089/801621. No credit cards. ¢*

Lodging

Hotel Eva. This well-appointed modern hotel block is on the main square overlooking the yacht basin. The best rooms overlook the sea, and there's a courtesy bus to the beach. *Av. da República, tel. 089/803354, fax 089/802304. 150 rooms with bath. Facilities: pool, restaurant, disco. AE, DC, MC, V. $$*

Casa de Lumena. This 150-year-old Faro mansion has been tastefully converted into a small hotel. Each room has its own ambience. *Praça Alexandre Herculano 27, tel. 089/801990, fax 089/804019. 12 rooms with bath. Facilities: restaurant, courtyard bar. AE, DC, MC, V. $*

Lagos
Dining

Dom Sebastião. Portuguese cooking and charcoal-grilled specials and fish are the main attractions at this cheerful restaurant. It has a wide range of Portuguese aged wines. *Rua 25 de Abril 20, tel. 082/762795. Reservations advised. AE, DC, MC, V. Closed Sun. in winter. $$*

Restaurante Piri-Piri. This small restaurant has a menu heavy with Portuguese specialties, including the spicy pork and chicken dishes that give the establishment its name. *Rua Afonso d' Almeida 10, tel. 082/763803. MC, V. ¢*

Lodging

Pensão Mar Azul. Though this pensão has an excellent central location, rooms facing the street can be noisy in high season. Accommodations are more than adequate, however—some guest quarters even have a terrace—and there's a comfortable lounge. *Rua 25 de*

Abril 13–1, tel. 082/769749 or 082/769143, fax 082/769960. 18 rooms, 17 with bath. ¢

Portimão **A Lanterna.** This well-run restaurant is located just over the bridge
Dining at Parchal, on the Ferragudo side. Its specialty is duck, but try the exceptional fish soup or smoked fish. *Tel. 082/23948. Reservations advised. MC, V. Closed Sun. $–$$*

Flor da Sardinha. This is one of several open-air eateries next to the bridge and by the fishing harbor. Fresh sardines grilled on ranges at the quayside are served to the crowds sitting at rows of informal plastic tables and chairs. *Cais da Lota, tel. 082/24862. No credit cards. ¢*

Praia da **Safari.** This lively Portuguese seafront restaurant has a distinctly
Rocha African flavor. Seafood and delicious Angolan recipes are the spe-
Dining cialties. *Rua António Feu, tel. 082/415540. Reservations advised. AE, DC, MC, V. $*

Silves **Churrasqueira Valdemar.** At this inexpensive grillroom on the river-
Dining front below the market, whole chickens are barbecued outside over charcoal. Eat under the stone arches and enjoy your *piri piri* (spicy) chicken with salad, fries, and local wine. *Facing the river, below the market. No tel. No credit cards. ¢*

Tavira **Restaurante Imperial.** The best restaurant on the riverfront, the Im-
Dining perial is well-known for its fish and seafood dishes, including clams and tuna, the local catch. *Rua José Pires Padinha 22–24, tel. 081/22306. Closed Wed. in winter. MC, V. $*

Vila Real de **Caves do Guadiana.** In a large, old-fashioned building facing the
Santo António fishing docks, this restaurant is well-known for its seafood and Por-
Dining tuguese specialties. *Av. República 90, tel. 081/44498. No reservations. DC, MC. Closed Thurs. $*

21 Romania

Romania is not the easiest destination for tourists, but it has advantages for the budget traveler. Few Romanians earn more than the equivalent of $70 a month, and costs of living are set accordingly. Visitors may tour the country cheaply and without restriction—through the stunning peaks and lush valleys of the Carpathian mountains, on hot Black Sea beaches, around the Moldavian wine-growing region with its many historic monasteries and folk traditions, and through Dracula's Transylvania, where Hungarian and German ethnic minorities maintain their old ways. People come each year from many countries for affordable Black Sea holidays and winter skiing in Sinaia; to view the historic buildings of the capital, Bucharest; or to stay in Europe's largest wetlands preserve, the Danube Delta, where traditional caviar-fishing communities live alongside pelicans and other rare species. Romanians are hospitable, although many regard Western visitors as opportunities to earn inflation-proof hard currency.

Visitors should use water purification tablets or boil their tap water, as hepatitis is a danger in Romania. All visitors should bring a supply of toilet paper to beat shortages; a flashlight for unlighted streets and corridors; and, in summer, insect repellent. Since medical facilities are primitive, it is best to bring along all medicines (including needles and syringes for injections).

It is always easiest, often cheapest, and usually safest to book either a package trip or a prepaid fly-drive tour with accommodation vouchers. These arrangements usually benefit from price discounts, guarantee at least minimum standards of quality, and assure greater security in a country that has experienced a major increase in street crime since the end of the Communist regime. More intrepid independent travelers need a good dose of caution (avoid isolated places and financial misunderstandings; don't travel alone), a phrase book, flexible standards and a flexible itinerary, and a good sense of humor to cope with the rip-offs, frustration, and discomforts most will experience. For many, discovering the numerous areas still untouched by modern ways is well worth the effort.

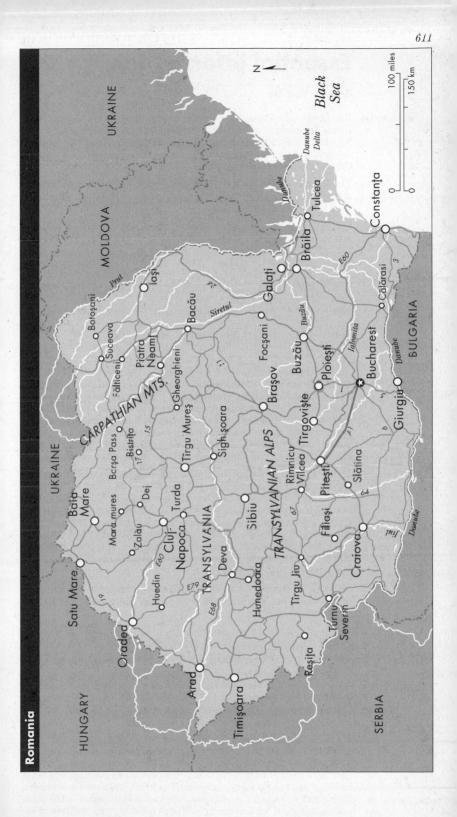

Essential Information

Before You Go

When to Go Bucharest, like Paris, is at its best during the spring and fall. The Black Sea resorts open in mid- to late May and close at the end of September. Winter ski resorts in the Carpathians are now well developed and increasingly popular, while the best time for touring the interior is late spring to fall.

Climate The Romanian climate is temperate and generally free of extremes, but snow as late as April is not unknown, and the lowlands can be very hot in midsummer.

The following are the average daily maximum and minimum temperatures for Bucharest.

Jan.	34F	1C	May	74F	23C	Sept.	78F	25C
	19	- 7		51	10		52	11
Feb.	38F	4C	June	81F	27C	Oct.	65F	18C
	23	- 5		57	14		43	6
Mar.	50F	10C	July	86F	30C	Nov.	49F	10C
	30	- 1		60	16		35	2
Apr.	64F	18C	Aug.	85F	30C	Dec.	39F	4C
	41	5		59	15		26	- 3

Currency The unit of currency is the *leu* (plural *lei*). There are coins of 1, 3, 5, 10, 20, 50, and 100 lei. Banknotes come in denominations of 100, 200, 500, 1,000, 5,000 and 10,000 lei. Coins of denominations smaller than 20 and 50 lei, which are for phones, are seldom used and not always accepted. The Romanian currency has dropped in value in recent years, causing frequent price rises; costs are therefore best calculated in hard currency. At press time (summer 1995), the exchange rate is 2,050 lei to the dollar and 3,250 lei to the pound sterling.

There is no longer an obligatory currency exchange, and an increasing number of licensed exchange offices (*casă de schimb*) have been competing to offer rates that are higher than the official rate and almost equal to those available on the illegal and risky black market. Retain your exchange receipts because you may need to prove your money was changed legally. Except for air tickets, by law foreigners must pay in lei, though hard currency is widely accepted. The local police rather than the financial police (*garda financiară*) are useful if you experience difficulty. You may not import or export lei.

Credit Cards Major credit cards are welcome in a number of major hotels and their restaurants, but are not accepted in most shops and independent restaurants.

What It Will Cost Prices of hotels and restaurants can be as expensive as those in Western Europe as far as the independent traveler is concerned. Those with prepaid arrangements, however, may have significant reductions.

Sample Prices Museum admission usually costs less than 50¢, a bottle of imported beer in a restaurant, around $2.50, or in a kiosk, about 75¢; a bottle of good local wine in a top restaurant, around $6. A 1-mile taxi ride will cost around 60¢.

Visas Visas are not required for United States citizens for stays of less than thirty days. The only requirement is a valid American passport, with an expiration date more than three months beyond departure date from Romania. All other visitors entering Romania must have a visa, but no formal applications or photographs are needed for British and Canadian citizens. The visa is stamped onto the passport and is valid for a minimum of three months from the date of entry into Romania. This visa can be issued from any Romanian diplomatic or consular office abroad, or at any Romanian customs station at the border of entry. For persons with prepaid hotel vouchers or for those on organized or escorted tours the visa fee is $1 or its equivalent (bring a copy of your voucher to the Romanian diplomatic or consular office, or send a copy of the hotel voucher when you order the visa by mail); the visa is free if you get it at the border (show your hotel/reservation voucher). For individual tourists without a hotel voucher, the visa fee is $22 at diplomatic offices and Otopeni, the Bucharest airport, or $15 at any other border point. For persons on business or study trips, the fee is $32 at diplomatic offices and Otopeni, or $25 at any other border point. Send the visa fee, a stamped, self-addressed envelope, and your passport to the relevant office: in **Canada,** Romanian Consulate (111 Peter St., Suite 530, Toronto, Ontario M5V 2H1, tel. 416/585–5802, fax 416/585–9117), Romanian Consulate (1111 Street Urbain, Suite M-01, Montreal, Quebec H2Z 1Y6, tel. 514/876–1793, fax 514/876–1797), or Embassy of Romania (655 Rideau St., Ottawa, Ontario K1N 6A3, tel. 613/789–3709, fax 613/789–4365); in the **United Kingdom,** Consular Section of the Romanian Embassy (4 Palace Green, London W84QD, tel. 0171/937–9667, fax 0171/937–8069). In the **United States,** questions on visas and passports can be addressed to: Embassy of Romania (1607 23rd St. NW, Washington DC 20008, tel. 202/387–6902, fax 202/232–4748) or Romanian Consulate (200 E. 38th St., New York, NY 10016, tel. 212/682–9122, fax 212/972–8463).

Customs You may bring in a personal computer and printer, two cameras, 20 rolls of film, one small camcorder/video camera or VCR, two rolls of video film, a typewriter, binoculars, a radio/tape recorder, a small television set, a bicycle, a stroller for a child, 200 cigarettes, 2 liters of liquor and 4 of wine or beer. Gifts are permitted, but you may be required to pay an import duty for some electronic goods; camping and sports equipment may be imported freely. Declare video cameras, personal computers, and expensive jewelry on arrival.

Souvenirs and gifts may be taken from Romania provided that their value is not more than half the amount of currency you have legally exchanged—so keep your receipts. In addition, you may export five paintings from the Plastic Artists' Union.

Language Romanian sounds appealingly familiar to anyone who speaks a smattering of French, Italian, or Spanish. French is widely spoken and understood in Romanian cities. Romanians involved with the tourist industry, in all hotels and major resorts, usually speak English.

Getting Around

By Train Romanian Railways (CFR) operates *expres, accelerat, rapide,* and *personal* trains; if possible, avoid the *personal* trains because they are very slow. Be sure the conductor doesn't mix up your ticket with someone else's when he checks it. Trains are inexpensive but are often crowded, with carriages in poor repair. First class is worth the extra cost. A *vagon de dormit* (sleeper) or cheap *cușeta,* with bunk beds, is available on longer journeys. It is always advisable to buy a seat reservation in advance, but you cannot buy the ticket itself at a train station more than one hour before departure. If your reserved seat is already occupied, it may have been sold twice. If you're in Bucharest, go either to a travel agency or to the Advance Reserve Office (Strada Domnița Anastasia 10–14, tel. 01/613–2642); for international destinations go to CFR International, (Bulevardul I.C. Brătianu 44, tel. 01/613–4008). You will be charged a small commission fee, but it is a less time-consuming process than buying your ticket at the railway station.

By Plane **Tarom** operates daily flights to major cities from Bucharest's Baneasa Airport. During the summer, additional flights link Constanţa with major cities, including Cluj and Iaşi. Be prepared for delays and cancellations. Prices average around $90 round-trip. External flights can be booked at the central reservations office (Strada Brezoianu 10) and at some major hotels. For domestic flights go to Piaţa Victoriei 1, (tel. 01/659–4125).

By Bus Bus stations, or *autogara*, are usually near train stations. Buses are generally crowded and far from luxurious. Tickets are sold at the stations up to two hours before departure.

By Boat Regular passenger services operate on various sections of the Danube; tickets are available at the ports (e.g. Giurgiu, Turnu Severin).

Staying in Romania

Telephones The system is antiquated and overextended; you may have to order and wait a long time for nonlocal calls. Coin-operated telephones at roadsides, airports, and train stations may work only for local calls. Older phones use a 20 lei coin, newer ones 50 and 100. It is less expensive to telephone from the post office than from hotels. Post offices have a waiting system whereby you order your call and pay at the counter. When your call is ready, the name of the town or country you are phoning is announced, together with the number of the cabin you should proceed to for your call. Private business services are opening in large towns, offering phone, fax, and telex facilities.

The area code for Bucharest is 01, and telephone numbers in the city have 2, 3, 6, or 7 as a prefix, followed by a six-digit number. Long-distance calls should be prefixed with a 0, as well as the former area code. For information dial the relevant area code, then 11515; in Bucharest it is 931 (A–L) and 932 (M–Z).

International In Bucharest international calls can be made from hotels, the train
Calls station, and the phone company building on Calea Victoriei. To call outside Romania, dial 00, then the country code and number. To reach an **AT&T** international operator, dial 01–800–4288; for **MCI,** dial 01–800–1800; for **Sprint,** dial 01–800–01–877.

Country Code Romania's telephone country code is 40.

Mail The central post office in Bucharest is at 10, Matei Millo and is open Monday through Thursday from 7:30 to 7:30, Fridays and Saturdays 8 to 2. The telephone section is open 24 hours.

Postal Rates Rates are increasing regularly in line with inflation, so check before you post.

Opening and **Banks** are open weekdays 9 to 12:30 or 1. Licensed exchange
Closing Times (schimb) bureaus are generally open weekday afternoons and Saturday mornings.

Museums and art galleries are usually open from 10 to 6, but it's best to check with local tourist offices. Most museums are closed on Monday, and some are also closed on Tuesday.

Shops are generally open Monday–Friday from 9 or 10 AM to 6 or 8 PM and shut between 1 and 3, though some food shops open earlier. Many shops are closed on Saturday afternoon.

National For 1996: January 1–2, April 8 (Easter Monday), May 1, December
Holidays 1, December 25, December 26, December 31. Changing holiday in 1997: March 31 (Easter Monday).

Dining Shortages have eased and poor standards have now improved sufficiently for the better hotels and restaurants to offer reasonable cuisine and menu choices. Traditional Romanian foods are *mamaliga* (corn porridge), *ciorbă* (slightly spicy and sour soup stock), and sheep cheeses. Overcharging is a hazard outside the bigger restaurants with printed menus. You can insist on seeing the prices, but small establishments may genuinely not have a menu prepared for just one or two dishes.

Mealtimes Outside Bucharest and the Black Sea and Carpathian resorts, many restaurants stop serving by 9 PM, although an increasing number have begun staying open until 11 PM or later. Restaurants usually open at midday.

Precautions The far less expensive *bufet expres* (beer and snack bar), *lacto vegetarian* snack bars, and *autoservire* (often serving meat) cannot always be recommended; the food may be inexpensive, but sanitary conditions may be poor. The best bet is often found at the better *cofetarie* (coffee shops). Romanian coffee is served with grounds; instant coffee is called *nes*. You may want to bring your own coffee whitener as milk is sometimes in short supply.

What to Wear There are no dress rules as such, but jacket and tie are advised for the best restaurants and business lunches and dinners. Casual, but conservative, dress is appropriate elsewhere.

Ratings Prices are per person and include first course, main course, and dessert, plus wine and tip. Because high inflation means that local prices frequently change, ratings are given in dollars, which remain reasonably constant. But your bill will be in lei. Best bets are indicated by a star ★.

Category	Cost
$$	over $20
$	$10–$20
¢	under $10

Lodging Prices are highly variable depending on booking arrangements. Prepaid arrangements through travel agencies abroad often benefit from discounted prices. Some schemes, such as fly-drive holidays, give bed-and-breakfast accommodation vouchers (these cannot be bought in Romania). Most places take vouchers. Otherwise, book accommodations directly with hotels or through tourism agencies. Some agencies deal only with their local areas; those spawned from the formerly monolithic national tourism office (ONT)—the *agenţia de turism*—and from the former youth tourism bureau, now known as the *Biroul de Turism Şi Tranzact, ii* (BTT), offer nationwide services. Travelers staying at less expensive hotels have sometimes encountered less than acceptable basic facilities and dangerous conditions. Rooms in private homes can be booked through many ONT offices and offer a good alternative to hotels.

Hotels The star system of hotel classification has been introduced in Romania. Standards of facilities, such as heat and hot water, should be inquired about in all categories. Ask at the front desk when hot water will be available. In principle, at least, all hotels leave a certain quota of rooms unoccupied until 8 PM for unexpected foreign visitors.

Camping There are more than 100 campsites in Romania; they provide an inexpensive way of exploring the country, but standards vary widely. Some offer reasonable bungalow accommodations and have showers with hot water at least some of the time. Others have no running water apart from a natural spring and very unpleasant toilets. Crime can also be a problem. Rates vary. Details are available from Romanian tourist offices abroad.

Ratings The following hotel price categories are for two people in a double room. Guests staying in single rooms are charged a supplement. Prices are estimates for high season. Because of inflation, ratings are given according to hard-currency equivalents—but you must usually pay in lei. (Note that hotels may insist on your buying lei from them to pay your bill, unless you can produce an exchange receipt to prove you changed your money legally.) Rates in Bucharest are much higher. No budget-level (¢) hotels are included because they carry health and safety risks. Best bets are indicated by a star ★.

Category	Cost
$$	$70–$125
$	under $70

Tipping A 12% service charge is added to meals at most restaurants. Elsewhere, a 10% tip is welcomed, and is expected by taxi drivers and porters.

Bucharest

Arriving and Departing

By Plane All international flights to Romania land at Bucharest's Otopeni Airport (tel. 01/633–3137), 16 kilometers (9 miles) north of the city.

Between the Express bus 783 leaves the airport every 30 minutes between 4 AM
Airport and and midnight, stopping in the main squares before terminating in
Downtown Piaţa Unirii. The journey takes an hour and costs 25¢. Your hotel can arrange transport by car from the airport. Taxi drivers at the airport seek business aggressively and usually demand payment in dollars. Note that the "official" fare is in lei, and the equivalent of about $12 with tip, so bargain.

By Train There are five main stations in Bucharest, though international lines operate from Gara de Nord (tel. 01/952). For tickets and information, go to the Advance Booking Office (Str. Domniţa Anastasia 10–14, tel. 01/613–2642). For international trains, go to CFR International (B-dul I.C. Brătianu 44, tel. 01/613–4008).

Getting Around

Bucharest is spacious and sprawling. Though the old heart of the city and the two main arteries running the length of it are best explored on foot, long, wide avenues and vast squares make some form of transportation necessary. New tourist maps are being printed and may be available at tourism agencies and hotels. It is generally safe on the streets at night, but watch out for vehicles and hidden potholes.

By Subway The subway system has four lines. Change, for admittance, is available from kiosks inside stations, and you may travel any distance. The present price is 100 lei (paid with two 50-lei coins). The system closes at midnight.

By Tram, These are uncomfortable, crowded, and infrequent, but service is
Bus, and extensive. A ticket valid for two trips of any length can be purchased
Trolley Bus from kiosks near bus stops or from tobacconists; validate your ticket when you board. There are also day and week passes *(abonaments)*, but more expensive *maxi taxis* (minibuses that stop on request) and express buses take fares on board. The system shuts down at midnight.

Important Addresses and Numbers

Tourist There are many new travel agencies in Bucharest and throughout
Information the country. The main branch of the **Romanian National Tourist Office (ONT)**, at 7 Boulevard General Magheru (tel. 01/312–2598, fax

01/312–2594), deals with all inquiries related to tourism (open weekdays 8–8, weekends 8–2). There are ONT offices at Otopeni Airport, open 24 hours, and at the Gara de Nord, open 8–8 Monday to Saturday. ONT is currently being broken up and privatized, so its office signs in most Romanian towns now read *Agenția de Turism*.

For information before your trip, write or call the Romanian National-al Tourist Office: **in the United States,** 342 Madison Ave., Suite 210, New York, NY 10016, tel. 212/697–6971, fax 212/697–6972; **in the United Kingdom,** 17 Nottingham Street, London W1M 3RD, tel. and fax 0171/224–3692.

Emergencies   Police: tel. 955. **Ambulance:** tel. 961. **Fire:** tel. 981.

Exploring Bucharest

The old story goes that a simple peasant named Bucur settled on the site upon which the city now stands. True or not, the name București was first officially used only in 1459, by none other than Vlad Țepeș, the real-life Dracula (sometimes known as Vlad the Impaler for his bloodthirsty habit of impaling unfortunate victims on wooden stakes). Two centuries later, this citadel on the Dimbovița (the river that flows through Bucharest) became the capital of Walachia, and after another 200 years, it was named the capital of Romania. The city gradually developed into a place of bustling trade and gracious living, with ornate and varied architecture; landscaped parks; busy, winding streets; and wide boulevards. It became known before the Second World War as the Paris of the Balkans; like Paris, Bucharest is still at its best in the spring, but its past glory is now only hinted at. The high-rise Intercontinental Hotel now dominates the main crossroads at Piața Universității; northward, up the main shopping streets of Bulevardul Nicolae Bălcescu, Bulevardul General Magheru, and Bulevardul Ana Ipătescu, only the occasional older building survives. However, along Calea Victoriei, a flavor of Bucharest's grander past can be savored, especially at the former royal palace opposite the Romanian senate (formerly Communist Party headquarters) in Piața Revoluției. Here, one also sees reminders of the December 1989 revolution, including the slow restoration of the domed National Library, gutted by fire, and bullet holes on walls nearby. Modest, touching monuments to the more than 1,000 people killed in the revolution can be found here, and Piața Universității has a wall still festooned with protest posters.

South along Calea Victoriei is the busy Lipscani trading district, a remnant of the old city that used to sprawl farther southward before it was bulldozed in Nicolae Ceaușescu's megalomaniacal drive to redevelop the capital. Piața Unirii was the hub of his enormously expensive and impractical vision, which involved the forced displacement of thousands of people and the demolition of many houses, churches, and synagogues. Cranes now stand eerily idle above unfinished tower blocks with colonnaded, white marble frontages. They flank a lengthy boulevard leading to the enormous, empty, and unfinished Palace of the People, second in size only to the Pentagon. With such a massive diversion of resources, it is not surprising that Bucharest is potholed and faded and suffers shortages and erratic services. But happily, the city continues to offer many places of historic interest, as well as movie houses, theaters, concert halls, and an opera house.

Numbers in the margin correspond to points of interest on the Bucharest map.

Historic   A tour of this city should start at the **Curtea Veche** (old Princely
Bucharest   Court) and the Lipscani District. The Princely Court now houses
❶   **Muzeul Curtea Veche-Palatul Voievodal,** a museum exhibiting the remains of the palace built by Vlad Țepeș during the 15th century. One

Bucharest

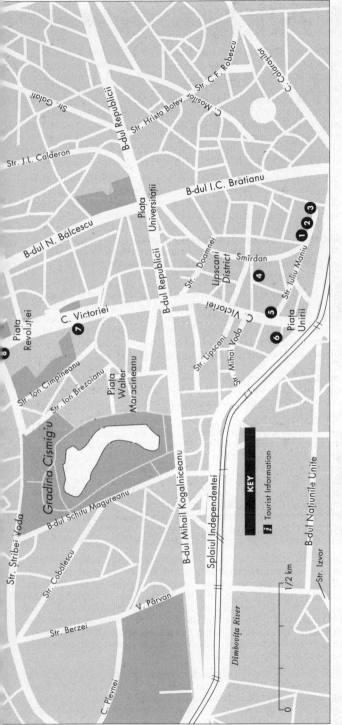

KEY

ℹ️ Tourist Information

Areul de Triumf, **12**
Ateneul Român, **9**
Biserica din Curtea Veche, **2**
Biserica Ortodoxă, **4**
Columna Traiană, **6**

Crețulescu Church, **7**
Curtea Veche, **1**
Hanul lui Manuc, **3**
Muzeul de Artă al României, **8**
Muzeul de Științe Naturale "Grigore Antipa," **10**

Muzeul Național de Istorie, **5**
Muzeul Satului Roman=sc, **13**
Muzeul Țăranului Român. **11**

section of the cellar wall presents the palace's history from the 15th century onward. *Str. Iuliu Maniu 31, tel. 01/614–0375. Admission: 900 lei. Open Tues.–Sun. 10–6.*

❷ The **Biserica din Curtea Veche** (Curtea Veche Church), beside the Princely Court, was founded during the 16th century and remains
❸ an important center of worship in the city. Nearby, **Hanul lui Manuc** (Manuc's Inn), a renovated 19th-century inn arranged in the traditional Romanian fashion around a courtyard, now houses a small hotel and restaurant. Manuc was a wealthy Armenian merchant who died in Russia by poisoning—at the hand of a famous French fortune-teller who, having forecast Manuc's death on a certain day, could not risk ruining her reputation. The 1812 Russian-Turkish Peace Treaty was signed here.

Nearby, **Lipscani** is a bustling area of narrow streets, open stalls, and small artisans' shops that combine to create the atmosphere of a
❹ bazaar. On Strada Stavropoleos, a small but exquisite **Biserica Ortodoxă** (Orthodox church) combines late Renaissance and Byzantine styles with elements of the Romanian folk-art style. Go inside to look at the superb wood and stone carving and a richly ornate iconostasis, the painted screen that partitions off the altar. Boxes on either side of the entrance contain votive candles—for the living on the left, for the "sleeping" on the right.

❺ At the end of the street is the **Muzeul Naţional de Istorie** (Romanian History Museum), which contains a vast collection of exhibits from neolithic to modern times. The Treasury, which can be visited and paid for separately, has a startling collection of objects in gold and precious stones—royal crowns, weapons, plates, and jewelry—dating from the 4th millennium BC through the 20th century. Opposite
❻ the Treasury is a full-size replica of **Columna Traiană** (Trajan's Column; the original is in Rome), commemorating a Roman victory over Dacia in AD 2. *Calea Victoriei 12, tel. 01/615–7056. Admission: 900 lei. Museum open Wed.–Sun. 10–4; Treasury, Tues.–Sun. 10–5, last admission at 4.*

Turning north along the Calea Victoriei, you'll pass a military club
❼ and academy before reaching the pretty little **Creţulescu Church** on your left. Built in 1722, the church and some of its original frescoes were restored during the 1930s. Immediately north is a massive building, once the royal palace and now the Palace of the Republic.
❽ The **Muzeul de Artă al României** (National Art Museum) is housed here, with its fine collection of Romanian art, including works by the world-famous sculptor Brâncuşi. The foreign section has a wonderful Brueghel collection and is well worth a visit. *Str. Ştirbei Vodă 1, tel. 01/615–5193. Admission: 1,000 lei. Open Wed.–Sun. 10–6.*

Opposite the palace, in Piaţa Revoluţiei, was the former headquarters of the Romanian Communist party. Before the revolution in December 1989, no one was allowed to walk in front of this building. During the uprising, the square was a major site of the fighting that destroyed the National Library, parts of the Palace, and the Cina
❾ restaurant next to the **Ateneul Român** (Romanian Athenaeum Concert Hall). The Ateneul, dating from 1888, with its Baroque dome and Greek columns, survived the upheavals and still houses the George Enescu Philharmonic Orchestra.

Follow Calea Victoriei as far as the Piaţa Victoriei. Opposite is the
❿ **Muzeul de Ştiinţe Naturale "Grigore Antipa"** (Natural History Museum), with its exceptional butterfly collection and the skeleton of *Dinotherium gigantissimum. Şoseaua Kiseleff 1, tel. 01/650–4710. Admission: 800 lei. Open Tues.–Sun. 10–5.*

Next door, in an imposing redbrick building, is the impressive
⓫ **Muzeul Ţăranului Român** (Museum of the Romanian Peasant). Reopened in 1990, it has an excellent collection of costumes, icons, car-

pets, and other artifacts from rural life, including two 19th-century churches. *Şoseaua Kiseleff 3, tel. 01/659–5655. Admission: 1,000 lei. Open Tues.–Sun. 10–6.*

Şoseaua Kiseleff, a pleasant tree-lined avenue, brings you to the **Arcul de Triumf,** built in 1922 to commemorate the Allied victory in World War I. Originally constructed of wood and stucco, it was rebuilt during the 1930s and carved by some of Romania's most talented sculptors.

Still farther north lies Herăstrău Park, accommodating the fascinating **Muzeul Satului Romanesc** (Village Museum), as well as Herăstrău Lake. The museum is outstanding, with more than 300 authentic, fully furnished peasants' houses in folk styles taken from all over Romania. *Şoseaua Kiseleff 28, tel. 01/617–1732. Admission: 1,000 lei. Open daily: fall and winter 8–4; spring and summer 10–7.*

Shopping

Gifts and Souvenirs   New private shops are bringing extra style and choice to Bucharest, but note the customs restrictions (*see* Customs *in* Before You Go, *above*). Keep receipts of all purchases, regardless of their legal export status. The **Apollo** gallery, in the National Theater building next to the Intercontinental Hotel, and the galleries in the fascinating **Hanul cu Tei,** off Strada Lipscani, sell art that you may legally take home with you.

Market   A main food market is in Piaţa Amzei, open seven days a week and best visited during the morning.

Dining

The restaurants of the better hotels are all recommended for a reasonable meal in pleasant surroundings. Some, like the **Balada,** at the top of the Intercontinental, offer a folklore show or live music. Although prices are not unreasonable, it is possible to rack up quite a total: Many restaurants have no menu, and waiters' recommendations can be expensive. Also note that most places will serve wine only by the bottle and not by the glass. For details and price-category definitions, *see* Dining *in* Staying in Romania, *above.*

$$ ★   **Dong Hai.** One of the more authentic recently opened Chinese restaurants in Bucharest, this one is in the Lipscani district. *Str. Blanari 14, tel. 01/615–6494. No credit cards.*

$$ ★   **Hanul lui Manuc** (Manue's Inn). Authentic Romanian cuisine is served in a beautifully restored 19th-century inn, which was built in the traditional Romanian fashion around a courtyard. *B-dul Iuliu Maniu 30, tel. 01/613–1415. Reservations advised. AE, DC, MC, V.*

$$ **Maramureş.** Mainly frequented by locals, it's tucked in a corner behind the Hotel Bucuresti. In summer and fall you can dine on typical Romanian dishes outside in small individual booths in a garden. *Str. G-ral Berthelot at corner of Str. T. Aman, tel. 01/664–4983. No credit cards.*

$ **Pani Pat.** If your weakness is delicious pastries, try the desserts at these take-out eateries. A selection of pizzas fills the main menu. *Str. C.A. Rossetti 1; Şos. Ştefan Cel Mare 4; B-dul N. Bălcescu near the Intercontinental hotel; and Calea Victoriei, 10 minutes' walk from Amzei market. No credit cards.*

$ **Quattro Stagione.** Connoisseurs say this is where you'll find the best pizza in Bucharest. *Piaţa Aviatorilor. No credit cards.*

$ **Spring Time.** The specialties here are Middle Eastern cakes and chicken sandwiches. *Piaţa Victoriei A6. No credit cards.*

¢   **Burger Ranch.** The nearest thing to McDonald's in Romania offers a large selection of burgers, fries, and salads. It has a large and well-lit seating area. *Piaţa Dorobanţi. No credit cards.*

¢ **OK Com SRL.** At this family-run restaurant you can eat good meals and enjoy the summer garden in season. *Across from Floreasca sports complex. No credit cards.*

Lodging

Hotels in Bucharest are often heavily booked during the tourist season. If you don't have reservations, the ONT office will be of help in suggesting available alternatives. For details and price-category definitions, *see* Lodging *in* Staying in Romania, *above.*

$$ **Ambassador.** The three-star, 13-story Ambassador was built in 1937 and enjoys a fine central location. Most rooms are comfortably furnished and there is a good café. *B-dul General Magheru 6–8, tel. 01/615–9080, fax 01/312–1239. 233 rooms with bath. Facilities: restaurant, café. AE, DC, MC, V.*

$$ **Lido.** Conveniently located in the center of the city, this prewar three-star hotel has been recently privatized and renovated to offer comfortable rooms and good facilities, including an outdoor swimming pool and a terrace. *B-dul Magheru 5, tel. 01/614–4930, fax 01/312–6544. 92 rooms with bath. Facilities: restaurant, bar, nightclub, outdoor pool, terrace. AE, DC, MC, V.*

$$ **Parc.** Near Herăstrău Park and the Flora Hotel, the Parc is modern and within easy reach of the airport; many guests stay here before moving on to the Black Sea resorts. There's a good restaurant that provides music every evening. *B-dul Poligrafiei 3, tel. 01/618–0950, fax 01/312–8419. 314 rooms with bath. Facilities: restaurant, pool, sauna, tennis. AE, DC, MC, V.*

$ **Capitol.** The circa 1900 Capitol is situated in a lively part of town near the Cişmigiu Gardens. In days gone by, it was the stomping ground of Bucharest's artists and writers. Today the Capitol is modernized and offers comfortable rooms. *Calea Victoriei 29, tel. 01/6158030, fax 01/312–4169. 70 rooms with bath. Facilities: restaurant. No credit cards.*

$ **Central.** This small hotel on a quiet side street in the middle of town near Cişmigiu gardens has recently been refurbished. *Strada Brezoianu 13, tel. 01/615–5637, fax 01/615–5635. 65 rooms. DC, MC, V.*

$ **Triumf.** This comfortable hotel is set on its own grounds slightly out-
★ side the city center near the Arcul de Triumf. Formerly the President, it used to serve only the Communist elite. This hotel is a good value; the more expensive rooms are miniapartments. *Soseaua Kiseleff 12, tel. 01/618–4110, fax 01/312–8411. 98 rooms, 49 with bath. Facilities: restaurant, bar, tennis court. No credit cards.*

The Arts

You can enjoy Bucharest's lively theater and music life at prices way below those in the West. Tickets can be obtained directly from the theater or hall or from your hotel (for a commission fee). Performances usually begin at 7 PM (6 in winter). **Opera Română** (The Opera House, B-dul Mihail Kogălniceanu 70) has some good productions, but don't expect the quality you'd find in Prague or Budapest. The **Teatrul de Operetă** (Operetta House) is now located at the **Teatrul National** (National Theater, B-dul N. Bălcescu 2), which also offers serious drama. For lighter entertainment, try the **Teatrul de Comedie** (Comedy Theater, Str. Mandinesti); despite the language barrier, there is often enough spectacle to ensure a good evening's entertainment. **Teatrul Tăndărică** (The Tandarica Puppet Theater, Calea Victoriei 50) has an international reputation, and the **Teatrul Evreesc de Stat** (State Jewish Theater, Str. Barasch 15) stages Yiddish-language performances. Don't miss the fine folkloric show at the **Rapsodia Română Artistic Ensemble** (Str. Lipscani 53).

The **Cinematica Romana** (Str. Eforie 5) runs a daily program of old, undubbed American and English films.

Nightlife

Increasing numbers of bars and restaurants stay open late. Coffee shops, however, are usually closed after 8 PM.

Nightclubs The **Lido, Ambassador,** and **Intercontinental** hotels have nightclubs with floor shows, and many others are popping up as well. **Vox Maris** (Piaţa Victoriei) is a late-night focus for disco lovers. **Salonul Spaniol** (116 Calea Victoriei) has a Spanish disco beat into the early hours. **Club A** (Str. Blanarii) is another late-night disco. **Şarpele Roşu** (Str. Icoanei Piaţa Galaţi), or "Red Snake," has a bohemian atmosphere, with Gypsy bands.

Cafés Cafés with outdoor terraces remain a feature of the city. Try the **Lido.** In winter, go to the excellent **Ana Café** (Str. Aviator Radu Beller 6), just north of Piata Dorobanţi.

22 Slovakia

Even if it had not developed separately for nearly a millennium under Hungarian and Hapsburg rule, the newly independent Slovak Republic (Slovensko) would be different from its Bohemian neighbor (*see* Chapter 5) in a great many respects. The mountains are higher here and the veneer is less sophisticated. The people seem more carefree, and the folk culture is particularly rich.

Although they speak a language closely related to Czech, the Slovaks have a strong sense of national identity, and indeed the two Slavic groups developed quite separately. United in the 9th century as part of the Great Moravian Empire, the Slovaks were conquered a century later by the Magyars and remained under Hungarian domination until 1918. After the Tartar invasions of the 13th century, many Saxons were invited to resettle the land, exploit the rich mineral resources, and thereby develop the economy. In the 15th and 16th centuries, Romanian shepherds migrated from Wallachia through the Carpathians into Slovakia, and the merging of these varied groups with the resident Slavs bequeathed to the region a rich folk culture and some unique forms of architecture, especially in the east.

Forty years of Communist rule left a clear mark on the capital city, Bratislava, hiding its ancient beauty with hulking, and now dilapidated, futurist structures. The picturesque streets of the Old Town, however, are now undergoing frenzied revitalization, and the city is filled with good concert halls, restaurants, and wine bars.

Most visitors head for the great peaks of the High Tatras. The smallest Alpine range in the world, the Tatras rise magnificently from the foothills of northern Slovakia. The tourist infrastructure here is very good, catering especially to hikers and skiers. Visitors who come to admire the peaks, however, often overlook the exquisite medieval towns of the Spiš in the plains and valleys below the Tatras and the beautiful 18th-century wood churches farther east.

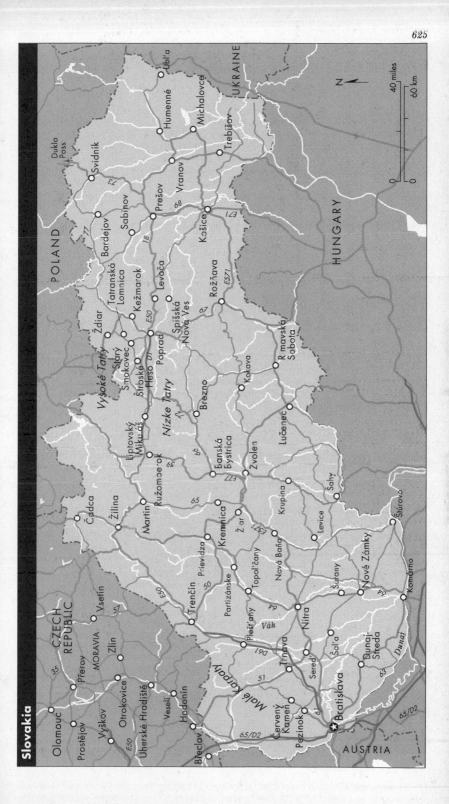

Slovakia

Essential Information

Before You Go

When to Go Organized sightseeing tours run from April or May through October. Some monuments, especially castles, either close entirely or open for shorter hours during the winter. Hotel rates drop during the off-season except during festivals. The High Tatra mountains come into their own in winter (Dec.–Feb.), when skiers from all over Eastern Europe crowd the slopes and resorts. If you're not into skiing, try visiting the mountains in late spring (May or June) or fall, when the colors are dazzling and you'll have the hotels and restaurants pretty much to yourself.

Climate The following are the average daily maximum and minimum temperatures for Bratislava.

Jan.	36F	2C	May	70F	21C	Sept.	72F	22C
	27	– 3		52	11		54	12
Feb.	39F	4C	June	75F	24C	Oct.	59F	15C
	28	– 2		57	14		45	7
Mar.	48F	9C	July	79F	26C	Nov.	46F	8C
	34	1		61	16		37	3
Apr.	61F	16C	Aug.	79F	26C	Dec.	39F	4C
	43	6		61	16		32	0

Currency The unit of currency in Slovakia is the crown, or slovenská koruna, written as Sk., and divided into 100 halér̆. There are bills of 10, 20, 50, 100, 500, and 1,000 Sk. and coins of 5, 10, 20, and 50 halér̆ and 1, 2, and 5 Sk.

At press time (summer 1995), the koruna was trading at around 30 Sk. to the American dollar and 48 Sk. to the pound.

Credit cards are widely accepted in establishments used by foreign tourists.

What It Will Cost Costs are highest in Bratislava and only slightly less in the High Tatra resorts and main spas, although even in those places you can now find bargain private accommodations. The prices at tourist resorts in the outlying areas and off the beaten track are incredibly low. The least expensive areas are central and eastern Slovakia.

Sample Prices Cup of coffee, 10 Sk.; beer (½ liter), 10 Sk.–15 Sk.; Coca-Cola, 10 Sk.–15 Sk.; ham sandwich, 15 Sk.; 1-mile taxi ride, 100 Sk.

Museums Admission to museums, galleries, and castles ranges from 5 Sk. to 50 Sk.

Visas U.S. and British citizens do not need visas to enter Slovakia. Visa requirements have been temporarily reintroduced for Canadian citizens; check whether this is still the case with the consulate. Apply to the Consulate of the Slovak Republic (50 Rideau Terrace, Ottawa, Ontario K1M 2A1, tel. 613/749–4442).

Customs *On Arrival* Valuable items should be entered on your customs declaration. You can bring in 250 cigarettes (or their equivalent in tobacco), 2 liters of wine, 1 liter of spirits, ½ liter of eau de cologne, and gifts to the value of 1,000 Sk.

On Departure Crystal not purchased with hard currency may be subject to a tax of 100% of its retail price. To be on the safe side, hang on to all receipts. Only antiques bought at specially designated shops may be exported.

Language English is spoken fairly widely among both the young and those associated with the tourist industry. You will come across English speakers elsewhere, though not frequently. German is widely understood throughout the country.

Getting Around

By Train Train service is erratic to all but the largest cities—**Poprad, Prešov, Košice,** and **Banská Bystrica.** Good, if slow, electric rail service, however, connects Poprad with the resorts of the **High Tatras.** If you're going just to the Tatras, you won't need any other kind of transportation.

By Bus Bus service in Bratislava is very cheap and reasonably frequent. You may have trouble reading the detailed information on the timetable, so try to ask if you're not sure where a particular bus is headed. The **CSAD** bus network in Slovakia is dense, linking all the towns on the tours given here.

Staying in Slovakia

Telephones These cost 2 Sk. from a pay phone. Lift the receiver, place the coin in
Local Calls the holder, dial, and insert the coin when your party picks up. Public phones are located on street corners; unfortunately, they're often out of order. Try asking in a hotel if you're stuck. If you are planning to make several local or out-of-town calls, it would be advisable to buy a phone card. They can be bought at most newsstands or at any post office and cost 150 Sk. for 75 local calls.

International There's automatic dialing to many countries, including those in
Calls North America and the United Kingdom. For international inquiries, dial 0132 for the United States, Canada, or the United Kingdom. To place a call via an **AT&T USA Direct** international operator, dial 00–420–00101; for **MCI,** dial 00–420–00112; for **Sprint,** dial 00–420–87187.

Country Code The country code for Slovakia is 42.

Mail Airmail letters to the United States and Canada cost 11 Sk. up to 10
Postal Rates grams, postcards 6 Sk. Airmail letters to the United Kingdom cost 8 Sk. up to 20 grams, postcards 5 Sk.

Receiving Mail Mail can be sent to Poste Restante at any main post office; there's no charge to claim it.

Opening and **Banks** are open weekdays 8–3. **Museums** are usually open Tues.–
Closing Times Sun. 10–5. **Shops** are generally open weekdays 9–6 (Thurs. 9–8); some close between noon and 2. Many are also open Sat. 9–noon (department stores, 9–4).

National January 1; April 17 (Easter Monday); May 1 (Labor Day); July 5
Holidays (Sts. Cyril and Methodius); August 29 (anniversary of the Slovak National Uprising); September 1 (Constitution Day); November 1 (All Saints' Day); December 24, 25. Changing holidays in 1997: March 31 (Easter Monday).

Dining The options in Slovakia include restaurants, wine cellars, the more down-to-earth beer taverns, cafeterias, and a growing number of coffee shops and snack bars. Most restaurants are remarkably reasonable, but privatization is beginning to push up prices in a few places.

The most typical main dish is roast pork (or duck or goose) with sauerkraut. Dumplings in various forms, generally with a rich gravy, accompany many dishes. Peppers are frequently used as well to spice up bland entrées. Look for *halušky*, a tasty Slovak noodle dish, usually served with sheep cheese. Fresh green vegetables and salads are still rare, but there are plenty of the pickled variety. Make sure to try *palačinky*, a delicious treat of crepes stuffed with fruit and ice cream or jam.

Mealtimes	Lunch is usually from 11:30 to 2 or 3; dinner from 6 to 9:30 or 10. Some places are open all day, and in Bratislava you may find it easier to find a table during off hours.
What to Wear	A jacket is suggested for higher-price restaurants. Otherwise, casual dress is acceptable.
Ratings	Prices are reasonable by American standards, even in the more expensive restaurants. The following prices are for meals made up of a first course, main course, and dessert (excluding wine and tip). Best bets are indicated by a star ★.

Category	Cost
$$	100 Sk.–250 Sk.
$	70 Sk.–100 Sk.
¢	under 70 Sk.

Lodging Travelers to Slovakia can choose from among hotels, motels, private accommodations, and campsites. Many older properties are gradually being renovated, and the best have great character and style. There is still an acute shortage of hotel rooms during the peak season, so make reservations well in advance. Many private room agencies are now in operation, and as long as you arrive before 9 PM, you should be able to get a room. The standards of facilities and services hardly match those in the West, so don't be surprised by faulty plumbing or indifferent reception clerks.

Hotels These are officially graded with from one to five stars. Many hotels used by foreign visitors—Interhotels—belong to **Satur (Slovak Travel Bureau and Tourist Office)** and are mainly in the three- to five-star categories. These will have all or some rooms with bath or shower. Satur (often still known by its former name **Čedok**) and tourist information services can also handle reservations for some non-Satur hotels, such as those run by Balnea (the spa treatment organization); CKM (the Youth Travel Bureau); and municipal organizations, some of which are excellent.

Hotel bills can be paid in crowns, though some hotels try to insist on hard currency.

Private Accommodations Satur and tourist information services can help you find a private room or an apartment in Bratislava and other larger cities. These accommodations are invariably cheaper (around $20) and often more comfortable than hotels, though you may have to sacrifice something in privacy. You can also wander the main roads looking for signs declaring "Room Free" or more frequently, in German, "Zimmer Frei" or "Privatzimmer."

Rates Prices are for double rooms, generally not including breakfast. Prices at the lower end of the scale apply to low season. At certain periods, such as Easter or during festivals, there may be an increase of 15%–25%. Best bets are indicated by a star ★.

Category	Cost
$$	450 Sk.–1,500 Sk.
$	350 Sk.–450 Sk.
¢	under 350 Sk.

Tipping Small sums of hard currency will certainly be most welcome. To reward good service in a restaurant, round up the bill to the nearest multiple of 10; 10% is considered appropriate on very large tabs. Tip porters who bring bags to your rooms 20 Sk. For room service, a 20

Sk. tip is enough. In taxis, round up the bill by 10%. Give tour guides and helpful concierges between 20 Sk. and 30 Sk. for services rendered.

Bratislava

Arriving and Departing

By Plane As few international airlines land in Bratislava, the most convenient international airport is in Vienna, approximately 50 kilometers (30 miles) away. Four buses a day stop at Schwechat en route to Bratislava, or you could even take a taxi; the journey takes just over an hour, depending on the border crossing. From Prague's Ruzyně Airport you can take a ČSA flight to Bratislava for less than 1,000 Sk.; the flight takes about an hour.

If time is a factor during your stay in Slovakia, flying may be an option to consider for reaching the relatively far-flung Tatras and eastern Slovakia. ČSA has reasonably priced daily flights from Prague to Poprad (the regional airport for the Tatras) and flies twice daily from Prague to Košice via Bratislava. For further information, contact the ČSA offices in Prague (tel. 02/2146), Poprad (tel. 092/24190), or Košice (tel. 095/22578).

By Train Reasonably efficient train service connects Prague and Bratislava. Trains leave from Prague's main station (Hlavní nádraží), and the journey takes between five to six hours depending on the train. There are four trains a day to and from Vienna, with the journey lasting just over an hour.

By Bus There are numerous buses from Prague to Bratislava; the journey costs less than 200 Sk. and takes about five hours. From Vienna, there are four buses a day from Autobusbahnhof Wien Mitte. The journey takes between 1½ and two hours. The **Autobus Stanica** in Bratislava is just outside the center; you can take Trolleybus 217 to Mierové námestie or Bus 107 to the Castle (Hrad).

By Car There are good freeways from Prague to Bratislava via Brno (D1 and D2); the 315-kilometer (203-mile) journey takes about 3½ hours. From Vienna, take the A4 and then Route 8 to Bratislava. The 60-kilometer (37-mile) trip will take about 1½ hours.

Getting Around

By Car Bratislava is not a good city for drivers, and finding a parking space can be a problem; hence, for touring the republic's capital, walking is the best option. If you do need to rent a car, you can do so either at Satur or at the Hotel Forum.

By Bus Bus service in Bratislava is very cheap and reasonably frequent, and you can use it with confidence to reach any of the main sights.

Important Addresses and Numbers

Tourist Information Bratislava has its own tourist information service, **Bratislava Tourist Information (BIS)** (Panská 18, tel. 333715 or 07/334370). The office is in the Old Town, a few steps down from Hlavné Námestie, and can supply visitors with information on accommodations. It's open weekdays 8–4:30 (8–6 in summer) and Saturday 8–1. With 54 offices throughout the country, **Satur Tours and Travel** is the largest travel agency in Slovakia. The main office is in Bratislava (Jesenské 5, tel. 07/367613 or 07/367624, fax 07/368624; open weekdays 9–6, Sat. 9–noon). Although a travel agent more than a tourist information office, Satur can supply you with hotel and tour information, and book air, rail, and bus tickets. Satur's U.S. representative is **Slovakia**

Travel Service, 10 East 40th Street, Suite 3601, New York, NY 10016, tel. 212/213–3865, fax 212/213–4461.

Emergencies **Police:** tel. 158. **Ambulance:** tel. 155.

Late-Night Pharmacies *(lekárna)* take turns staying open late or on Sunday.
Pharmacies Look for the list posted on the front door of each pharmacy. For after-hours service, ring the bell; you will be served through a little hatch-door.

Guided Tours

The best tours of Bratislava are offered by **BIS** (*see* Tourist Information, *above*), although out of the summer season they are given only in German and only on weekends. These tours start at 2 PM at the National Theater; they last two hours and cost 270 Sk. per person. **Satur** offers tours from May through September on Wednesday and Saturday, starting at 1:45 from the Hotel Devín (Riečna ul. 4, tel. 07/330851). You can combine these tours with an afternoon tour of the Small Carpathians (departing at 4:45 PM, also from the Devín), which includes dinner at the Zochová Chata. Satur can also arrange an individual guide at a cost of around 150 Sk.

Exploring Bratislava

Many visitors are disappointed by **Bratislava.** Expecting a Slovak version of Prague, they discover instead a rather shabby city that seems to embody more the previous regime's blind faith in modernity than the stormy history of this once Hungarian and now Slovak capital. Originally settled by a variety of Celts and Romans, the city became part of the Great Moravian Empire under Prince Břetislav. After a short period under the Bohemian Přemysl princes, Bratislava was brought into the Hungarian kingdom by Stephan I at the end of the 10th century. The Hungarians called it Pozsony; the German settlers, Pressburg; and the original Slovaks called it Bratislava, after Prince Břetislav.

Numbers in the margin correspond to points of interest on the Bratislava map.

❶ Begin your tour of the city at the modern square **Námestie SNP.** An abbreviation for *Slovenské Národné Povstanie* (Slovak National Uprising), these three letters appear on streets, squares, bridges, and posters throughout Slovakia. This anti-Nazi resistance movement involved partisan fighting, organized partly but not exclusively by the Communists, in Slovakia's mountainous areas during the final years of the war.

❷ From here walk up toward **Hurbanovo námestie.** Across the road, unobtrusively located between a large shoe store and a bookshop, is the enchanting entrance to the old town. A small bridge, decorated with wrought-iron railings and statues of St. John Nepomuk and St. Michael, takes you over the old moat, now blossoming with trees and fountains, into the intricate barbican, a set of gates and houses that made up the medieval fortifications. After going through the first archway, you come to the narrow **Michalská ulica;** in front of you is
❸ the **Michalská brána** (Michael's Gate), the last remaining of the original three city gates.

❹ A little farther down Michalská ulica, on the right, is the **Palác Uhorskej kráľ'ovskej komory** (Hungarian Royal Chamber), a Baroque palace that housed the Hungarian nobles' parliament from 1802 until 1848; it is now used as the University Library. Go through the arched passageway at the back of this building, and you'll emerge in a tiny square dominated by the **Church and Convent of the Poor Clares.** Follow Farská ulica up to the corner, and turn left on **Kapitulská ulica,** noticing the ground stone depicting two kissing

Bratislava

⑤ lizards. At the bottom of the street is the side wall of the **Dóm svätého Martina** (St. Martin's Cathedral). Construction of this massive plain Gothic church, with its 280-foot steeple twinkling with gold trim, began in the 14th century. Between the 16th and 19th centuries, the cathedral saw the coronation of 17 Hungarian royals. You can enter the church through a door on this side (Kapitulská ulica).

⑥ As you leave the church and walk around to the front, the freeway leading to the futuristic spaceship bridge, **Most SNP**, is the first thing you see. Follow the steps under the passageway and up the other side in the direction of the castle.

⑦ Continue up the steps, through a Gothic arched gateway built in 1480, until you reach the **Hrad** (castle) area. The original fortifications date from the 9th century. The Hungarian kings expanded the castle into a large royal residence, and the Hapsburgs turned it into a very successful defense against the Turks. Its current design, square with four corner towers, stems from the 17th century, although the existing castle had to be completely rebuilt after a disastrous fire in 1811. In the castle, you'll find the **Slovenské národné múzeum** (Slovak National Museum). The exhibits cover glassmaking, medieval warfare, and coinmaking. *Zámocká ul., tel. 07/ 332985. Admission: 40 Sk. adults, 10 Sk. children and students. Open Tues.–Sun., 10–5.*

⑧ Leave the castle by the same route, but instead of climbing the last stairs by the Arkadia restaurant, continue down the old-world Beblaveho ulica. Continue along **Židovská ulica**. The name, Jews' Street, marks this area as the former Jewish ghetto. Walk up Židovská until you come to a thin concrete bridge that connects with the reconstructed city walls across the freeway. Across the road you'll find steps leading down into the Old Town. Go through the Františkánske námestie into the adjoining square, **Hlavné námestie**, which is lined with old houses and palaces representing the spectrum of architectural styles from Gothic (No. 2), through Baroque (No. 4) and Rococo (No. 7), to a wonderfully decorative example of Art Nouveau at No. 10. To your immediate left as you come into the ⑨ square is the richly decorated **Jezuitský kostol** (Jesuit Church). Next door is the colorful agglomeration of old bits and pieces that makes ⑩ up the **Stará radnica** (Old Town Hall). Walk through the arched passageway into a wonderfully cheery Renaissance courtyard with romantic arcades and gables. Toward the back of the courtyard, you'll find the entrance to the **Mestské múzeum** (City Museum), which documents Bratislava's varied past. *Primaciálne nám., tel. 07/334742. Admission: 10 Sk. adults, 5 Sk. children and students. Open Tues.– Sun. 10–5.*

Leaving the back entrance of the Old Town Hall, you come to the **Primaciálne námestie** (Primates' Square), with the glorious pale ⑪ pink, classical elegance of the **Primaciálny palác** (Primates' Palace). If the building is open, go up to the dazzling hall of mirrors. In this room, Napoléon and Hapsburg Emperor Franz I signed the Bratislava Peace of 1805, following Napoléon's victory at the Battle of Austerlitz.

Dining and Lodging

For details and price-category definitions, *see* Dining and Lodging *in* Staying in Slovakia, *above*.

Dining **Klaštorná vináreň.** Old Town dining can be a delight in the vaulted
$$ cellars of this old monastery. The spiciness of Slovak cooking comes alive in dishes like *Čikós tokáň*, a fiery mixture of pork, onions, and peppers. Wash it down with a glass of mellow red wine and a fire hose. *Bravcové ražníci* is milder, a tender pork shish kebab and fried potatoes. *Františkanská ul. 1, tel. 07/330430. Reservations advised. No credit cards. Closed Sun.*

$$ **Modrá Hviezda.** The best of a new breed of small, privately owned wine cellars, the "Blue Star" eschews the international standards in favor of regional Slovak fare. Be sure to try the *bryndza* (baked sheep-cheese) pie and the tasty goulash. *Beblavého 14, tel. 07/332747. Reservations advised. No credit cards.*

$ **Stará Sladovňa.** This mammoth beer hall is known lovingly, and fittingly, as "Mamut" to Bratislavans. Locals come here for the Bohemian beer on tap and for inexpensive, filling meals. The place seats almost 2,000, so don't worry about reservations. *Cintorínska ul. 32, tel. 07/324050. No credit cards.*

$ **Veľkí Františkáni.** Trendy and popular with foreigners, this large restaurant and wine cellar features local wine from barrels; you can also listen to music and enjoy your drink outdoors in summer. *Františkánske nám. 10, tel. 07/333073. No reservations. AE, MC.*

¢ **Blankyt.** This little mom-and-pop shop serves homemade halušky at rock-bottom prices. Wash down your meal with the house white at around 8 Sk. a glass. The dingy atmosphere here actually lends to the charm. *Obchodná ul. 48, tel. 07/332248. Closed Sun. No credit cards.*

¢ **Presporská Kúria.** This casual pub, and restaurant features a large outdoor patio. Buffet serves fried chicken, fish, or cauliflower salad, with chips, pastries, and beer at rock-bottom prices. *Dunajská 21, tel. 07/367981. No credit cards.*

Lodging **Bratislava.** Depressing but suitably clean, this 1970s-style block ho-
$$ tel is in the suburb of Ružinov. The well-appointed rooms, each equipped with a TV and a shiny bath, are actually good value for the money. The staff is friendly. *Urxová ul. 9, tel. 07/239000, fax 07/236420. From the center of town, take Bus 34 or Tram 8. 344 rooms with bath. Facilities: restaurant, snack bar, lounge. AE, DC, MC, V.*

¢ **Flóra.** One of the cheapest deals around is located in the outskirts near Zlaté Piesky (Golden Sands) lake and recreational area and is convenient for sports but for little else. Although it's small and a little run-down, the Flóra has a friendly management who know some English and German. Doubles are cheap and fill up quickly in summer. Bring toilet paper—not all bathrooms have it. *Senecká cesta, tel. 07/214154 or 07/214122, fax 07/257945. From train station take Tram 2 to last stop. 20 rooms with bath. Facilities: restaurant. No credit cards.*

Eastern Slovakia

Most visitors head for the great peaks of the High Tatras, with their excellent tourist facilities, and this is where most tours will take you. The mountains *are* spectacular, but also worth seeing are the exquisite medieval towns of **Spiš** in the plains and valleys below the High Tatras and the beautiful 18th-century country churches farther east. Away from main centers, these areas are short on tourist amenities, so if creature comforts are important to you, stick to the Tatras.

Getting Around

By Plane ČSA's 40-minute flights from Bratislava to Poprad connect with services from Prague once or twice daily and are very reasonable.

By Train Train service is erratic to all but the largest cities—**Poprad, Prešov, Košice,** and **Banská Bystrica.** (Bratislava to Poprad by express train takes four hours.) Good, if slow, electric rail service, however, connects Poprad with the resorts of the **High Tatras.** If you're going just to the Tatras, you won't need any other kind of transportation.

By Bus The ČSAD bus network is dense, linking all the towns mentioned in Exploring Eastern Slovakia, *below.* Leave a couple of extra days, however, to compensate for infrequent service to smaller towns. Consult local timetables or the ČSAD office in Bratislava for specific information.

Guided Tours

Satur's seven-day **Grand Tour of Slovakia,** which leaves from Bratislava every other Saturday from June through September, stops in the High Tatras, Kežmarok, Košice, and Banská Bystrica. The tour includes all meals and accommodations. For more information, contact the Satur office in Bratislava (tel. 07/367613).

Slovair offers a novel biplane flight over the Tatras from Poprad airport. Contact the Satur office in Poprad (tel. 092/23651). The Satur office in Starý Smokovec (tel. 0969/2417) is also helpful in arranging tours of the Tatras and the surrounding area.

Tourist Information

Bratislava (Panská 18, tel. 07/333715).
Bardejov (Radnické nám. 21, tel. 0935/3271).
Prešov (Hlavná 8, tel. 091/731113).
Smokovec (Starý Smokovec V/22, tel. 0969/3127174).
Žilina (Burianová medzienka 4, tel. 089/23171).
Košice (Hlavná 8, tel. 095/186)

Exploring Eastern Slovakia

Whether you travel by bus or train, your route will follow the Vah Valley for most of the way to **Poprad,** a transit point for Slovakia's most magnificent natural treasure, the High Tatras. Though Poprad

The Tatras and Eastern Slovakia

itself is a dreary place, its suburb of **Spišská Sobota,** reached by Bus 2, 3, or 4, is a little gem. It was one of 24 small Gothic towns in a medieval region known as **Spiš.** Steep shingled roofs, high timber-framed gables, and brick-arched doorways are the main features of the rich merchants' dwellings, usually grouped around a main square dominated by a Gothic church, often with a separate Renaissance bell tower. Keep in mind the name Pavol of Levoča, one of the great woodcarvers of the 16th century. The main altar in Sv. Juraj (the Church of St. George) is his work. The **museum** is worth a visit. *Admission: 4 Sk. Open Mon.–Sat. 9–4.*

Both an electric train network and a winding highway link Poprad with the resorts spread about on the lower slopes of the High Tatras. **Štrbské Pleso** is the highest of the towns and the best launching point for mountain excursions. A rewarding two-hour trek of moderate difficulty leads from here to **Popradské Pleso,** one of dozens of tiny, isolated Alpine lakes that dot the Tatras. **Smokovec** is really three resorts in one (Starý, Nový, and Horný) and has the most varied amenities. For the most effortless high-level trip, though, go to **Tatranská Lomnica,** from which a two-stage cable car will take you via Skalnaté Pleso to Lomnický štít, which, at 8,635 feet high, is the second-highest peak in the range. From Skalnaté Pleso, you can take the red-marked Magistrale trail down to **Hrebienok,** where you can board a funicular and ride down to Stary Smokovec. The **Museum of the Tatra National Park** at Tatranská Lomnica offers an excellent introduction to the area's natural and human history. *Admission: 6 Sk., 2 Sk. for children. Open weekdays 8:30–noon and 1–5, weekends 8–noon.*

Leave Poprad on Highway 18 east. Restoration work on **Levoča,** the most famous of the Spiš towns, is well under way, and the overlays of Renaissance on Gothic are extremely satisfying to the eye (note especially Nos. 43, 45, 47, and 49 on the main square). Pavol of Levoča's work on the main altar of **Sv. Jakub** (the Church of St.

James) on the main square is both monumental in size and exquisite in its detail.

The surrounding countryside is dotted with more medieval towns. About 16 kilometers (10 miles) to the east, the massive, partly restored ruins of **Spiš Castle,** above Spišské Podhradie, dominate the surrounding pastures and orchards. Some of **Prešov's** fortifications survive, and its spindle-shape main square is lined with buildings in the Gothic, Renaissance, and Baroque styles. You have now left Spiš and entered **Šariš,** a region whose proximity to the Orthodox east has left a unique legacy of both Greek Orthodox and Catholic (Uniate) churches.

Bardejov is a splendid walled town and makes the best center from which to set out on a journey of exploration, as long as you're prepared to get lost along some rough minor roads while seeking out the 17th- and 18th-century wooden churches of **Bodružal, Ladomirová, Mirola,** and **Šemetkovce**—and the right person to open them up for you. You'll find these churches east and northeast of **Svidník,** near the border with Poland (follow the road to the Dukla Pass). These churches jostle for attention with the dramatic collection of Nazi and Soviet tanks and planes dotted around this area to commemorate the fighting that took place in 1944.

Dining and Lodging

For details and price-category definitions, *see* Dining and Lodging *in* Staying in Slovakia, *above.*

Bardejov
Lodging

Minerál. This rather sterile modern hotel lies in a quiet location in the spa town of Bardejovské kúpele, 3½ miles from Bardejov proper. *Bardejovské kúpele, tel. 0935/4122, fax 0935/4124. 60 rooms with shower. Facilities: tennis courts. No credit cards. $$*

Smokovec
Dining

Tatranská kúria. The Tatranská's rustic decor and Slovak specialties will provide some insight into local life. Dishes include *rezeň kúria* (pork cutlets with a cheese and ham filling in a cheese pastry) and *bryndzové pirohy* (cheese-filled pastry served with cream and bacon). *Starý Smokovec, tel. 0969/2806. No credit cards. Closes early. $$*

Lodging

Villa Dr. Szontagh. Away from the action in Nový Smokovec, this steepled chalet, formerly known as the Tokajík, offers mostly peace and quiet. The darkly furnished rooms and public areas are well maintained, and the courtly staff goes out of its way to please. *Nový Smokovec, tel. 0969/2061, fax 0969/2062. 11 rooms with bath. Facilities: restaurant, wine cellar. Breakfast not included. V. $$*

Tatranská
Lomnica
Dining

Zbojnícka koliba. This tavern offers a small range of Slovak specialties prepared over an open fire, amid rustic decor and accompanied by folk music. *Near Grandhotel Praha, tel. 0969/967630. No credit cards. Dinner only. Closed Sun. $$*

Lodging

Grandhotel Praha. A renovated turn-of-the-century building, the Grandhotel has large, comfortable rooms decorated with a traditional touch. The restaurant has an air of elegance that is unusual in Slovakia. *Tel. 0969/967941, fax 0969/967891. 92 rooms with bath. Facilities: restaurant, nightclub. AE, DC, MC, V. $$*

23 Spain

The Spain that for generations attracted penurious adventure-seekers has all but disappeared. With the country's admission to the European Union (EU)—formally completed in 1992—life has become as expensive as in most of the peninsula's western European neighbors. Spain still offers great rewards to the intrepid budget traveler, but don't expect to find great deals in the main cities or in tourist-saturated areas, such as the Costa del Sol. Travel to Seville and Barcelona grew especially pricey in 1992, when those cities hosted the International Exposition and the Olympic Games; prices receded somewhat in 1993, and then climbed again in 1994 and 1995, with the biggest hikes at coastal resorts and in the Balearic and Canary Islands. There are occasional bargains (many unadvertised), especially on weekends in Madrid and Barcelona. Trips to lesser-known towns and the countryside will reward the traveler with lower prices and fewer crowds. Some areas are package-vacation destinations suffering from overdevelopment and mass tourism; elsewhere you'll find sophisticated European cities, romantic hilltop villages, and a magnificent Moorish legacy (contact the National Tourist Office of Spain about its "Andalus Legacy" program that features 10 tourism routes through the south's most picturesque and historic villages).

If it's beaches you're after, there is the jet-set Costa del Sol in the south or San Sebastián in the Basque country. Farther west is the resort city of Santander and the port La Coruña, a long-standing favorite of British visitors. In the east is the Costa Brava, while to the south, around Alicante, is the Costa Blanca, with its most popular (and occasionally wild) tourist center at Benidorm. Perhaps the number-one tourist attraction in Spain is the Alhambra, in Granada. Following close behind are the Mosque of Córdoba and the Alcázar and cathedral of Seville. Àvila is a historic walled town and Madrid, the capital, contains some of the greatest art collections in the world. Toledo, home of El Greco and boasting a cathedral, synagogues, and startling views, is one of Spain's greatest treasures. Finally, Barcelona, an architecture student's dream, has a charm and vitality quite its own.

Essential Information

Before You Go

When to Go The tourist season runs from Easter to mid-October. The best months for sightseeing are May, June, September, and early October, when the weather is usually pleasant and sunny without being unbearably hot. During July and August, try to avoid Madrid or the inland cities of Andalucía, where the heat can be stifling and many places close down at 1 PM. If you visit Spain in high summer, the best bet is to head for the coastal resorts or to mountain regions, such as the Pyrenees or Picos de Europa. The one exception to Spain's high summer temperatures is the north coast, where the climate is similar to that of northern Europe. The high season, when hotels are significantly more expensive, is usually in summer, although there are exceptions.

Visitors should be aware of the seasonal events that can clog parts of the country, reserving in advance if traveling during peak periods. Easter is always a busy time, especially in Madrid; Barcelona; and the main Andalucían cities of Seville, Córdoba, Granada, Málaga, and the Costa del Sol resorts. July and August, when most Spaniards and other Europeans take their annual vacations, see the heaviest crowds, particularly in coastal resorts. Holiday weekends are naturally busy, and major fiestas, such as Pamplona's bull runnings, make advance booking essential and cause prices to soar. Off-season travel offers fewer crowds and lower rates in many hotels.

Climate The following are the average daily maximum and minimum temperatures for Madrid.

Jan.	47F	9C	May	70F	21C	Sept.	77F	25C
	35	2		50	10		57	14
Feb.	52F	11C	June	80F	27C	Oct.	65F	18C
	36	2		58	15		49	10
Mar.	59F	15C	July	87F	31C	Nov.	55F	13C
	41	5		63	17		42	5
Apr.	65F	18C	Aug.	85F	30C	Dec.	48F	9C
	45	7		63	17		36	2

Currency The unit of currency in Spain is the peseta. There are bills of 500, 1,000, 2,000, 5,000, and 10,000 ptas. Coins are 1 pta., 5, 25, 50, 100, 200, and 500 ptas. The 2- and 10-pta. coins and the old 100-pta. bills are rare but still legal tender. Note that pay phones in Spain won't accept the new, smaller 5- and 25-pta. coins first minted in 1991. At press time (summer 1995), the exchange rate was about 111 ptas. to the U.S. dollar and 184 ptas. to the pound sterling.

Credit Cards Most hotels, restaurants, and stores (though not gas stations) accept payment by credit card. Visa is the most widely accepted piece of plastic, followed by MasterCard (called EuroCard in Spain). More expensive establishments may also take American Express and Diners Club.

Changing Money The word to look for is *Cambio* (exchange). Most Spanish banks take a 1½% commission, though some less scrupulous places charge more; always check because rates can vary greatly. To change money in a bank, you need your passport and a lot of patience because filling out the forms takes time. Hotels offer rates lower than banks, but they rarely make a commission, so you may well break even. Restaurants and stores, with the exception of those catering to the tour bus trade, do not usually accept payment by dollars or traveler's checks. If you have a credit card with a personal identification number (PIN), you can withdraw cash at most Spanish banks' cash machines.

Bay of Biscay

El Ferrol

La Coruña

Villalba

Ribadeo

Luarca

Gijón

Ribadesella

Santander

Santiago de
Compostela

Lugo

Oviedo

Cangas
de Onis

Mieres

PICOS DE
EUROPA

Bilba

Muros

Orense

Ponferrada

León

Burgos

Pontevedra

Vigo

Tui/Túy

Astorga

Benavente

Palencia

CANTABRIAN MTS.

Zamora

Tordesillas

Valladolid

Duero

Salamanca

Adanero

Segovia

SIERRA DE GUAD

Ciudad
Rodrigo

Avila

El Escorial

Guado

MADRI

PORTUGAL

Plasencia

SIERRA DE GREDOS

Toledo

Aranjuez

Tajo

Talavera
de la Reina

Alcázar
San Ju

Guadalupe

Cáceres

Trujillo

Guadiana

Ciudad
Real

Abenójar

Valdepeñas

Mérida

Badajaz

Almadén

Jerez de los
Caballeros

Zafra

Fregenal
de la Sierra

Córdoba

SIERRA MORENA

Bailén

Linares

Baeza

Aroche

Jaén

Seville

Guadalquivir

Ecija

Baena

Guadix

Huelva

Carmona

Lucena

Granada

SIERR

*Gulf of
Cadiz*

Sanlúcar de
Barrameda

Antequera

Loja

COSTA DE LA LUZ

Ronda

Nerja

Cádiz

Jerez de
la Frontera

Torremolinos

Málaga

Motril

*ATLANTIC
OCEAN*

Estepona

Marbella

Fuengirola

COSTA DEL SOL

Algeciras

Gibraltar

TO CANARY
ISLANDS

Strait of Gibraltar

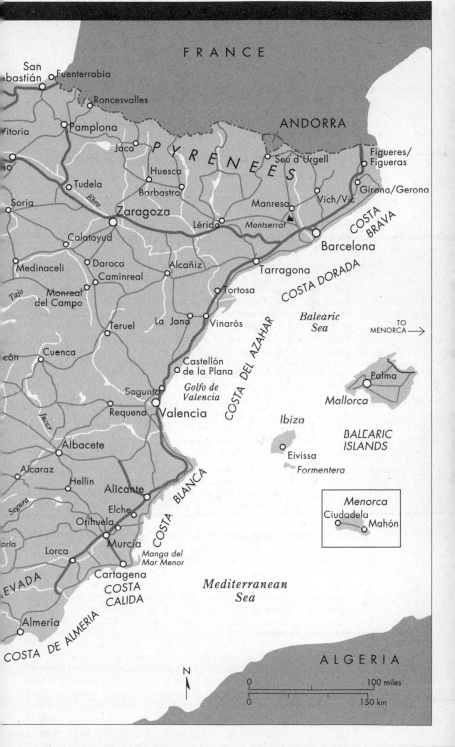

Currency Regulations Visitors may take any amount of foreign currency in bills or traveler's checks into Spain as well as any amount of pesetas. When leaving Spain, you may take out only 100,000 ptas. per person in Spanish bank notes and foreign currency up to the equivalent of 500,000 ptas, unless you can prove you declared the excess at customs on entering the country.

What It Will Cost Prices rose fast during the first decade of Spain's democracy, and the nation's inflation rate was one of the highest in Europe. By the 1990s, however, inflation had been curbed; in 1994, it was running at a little over 5%. Generally speaking, the cost of living in Spain is now on a par with that of most other western European countries, although the weakness of the peseta has helped Americans' buying power somewhat. Hotels are relatively expensive, sometimes shockingly so, especially in Seville, Barcelona, and Madrid. Dining out generally is not expensive; even with constantly rising prices, inexpensive restaurants abound. Snacks in cafés and bars are moderate to expensive by American standards, and alcohol is generally reasonable, except for cocktails in hotel bars. Trains and long-distance buses are relatively inexpensive. City subways and buses are a very good value.

Taxes A value-added tax, known as IVA, was introduced in 1986 when Spain joined the EU. IVA is levied at 6% on most goods and services, but it's 7% on hotels and 15% on car rentals. IVA is always included in the purchase price of goods in stores, but for hotels and car rentals, the tax will be added to your bill. Many restaurants include IVA in their menu prices, but plenty—usually the more expensive ones—do not. Large stores, such as the Corte Inglés and Galerías Preciados, operate a tax refund plan for foreign visitors who are not EU nationals; but to qualify for this refund, you need to spend at least 48,000 ptas. in any one store and, in theory, on any one item. There is no airport tax in Spain.

Sample Prices A cup of coffee will cost around 125 ptas., a Coca-Cola 150 ptas., bottled beer 150 ptas., a small draught beer 100 ptas., a glass of wine in a bar 100 ptas., an American-style cocktail 400 ptas., a ham sandwich 300 ptas., an ice-cream cone about 150 ptas., a local bus or subway ride 125 ptas., and a 1-mile taxi ride about 400 ptas.

Language In major cities and coastal resorts you should have no trouble finding people who speak English. In such places, reception staff in hotels of three or more stars are required to speak English. Don't expect the person in the street or the bus driver to speak English, although they may.

Visitors may be surprised to find that Spanish is not the principal language of many regions of Spain. The Basques speak Euskera; in Catalunya (Catalonia), where Barcelona is located, you'll hear Catalan; in Galicia, Gallego; and in Valencia, Valenciana. While almost everyone in these regions also speaks Spanish, local radio and TV broadcasts are often in these other languages, as well as road signs, menus, and other printed material you will encounter.

Getting Around

Between cities, your best options are trains and buses—flying is convenient but expensive. Subways in the major cities are generally excellent, city buses a little harder to figure out. In emergencies, taxicabs are still a good deal, although you can get caught in traffic jams where you sit while the meter ticks on inexorably.

By Train The Spanish railroad system, known usually by its initials RENFE, has greatly improved in recent years. Air-conditioned trains are now widespread but by no means universal. Most overnight trains have first- and second-class sleeping cars and second-class *literas* (couchettes). Dining, buffet, and refreshment services are available on most long-distance trains. There are various types of trains— *Talgo*, ELT (electric unit expresses), TER (diesel rail cars), and ordinary *expresos* and *rápidos*. Fares are determined by the kind of train you travel on and not just by the distance traveled. Talgos are by far the quickest, most comfortable, and the most expensive trains; *expresos* and *rápidos* are the slowest and cheapest of the long-distance services. In spring 1992, a high-speed train, referred to as the AVE (Alto Velocidad Español), began service between Madrid and Seville, reducing travel time between these cities from six to 2½ hours (fares vary, but the AVE can cost almost as much as flying). A few lines, such as the narrow-gauge FEVE routes along the north coast from San Sebastián to El Ferrol and on the Costa Blanca around Alicante, do not belong to the national RENFE network, and international rail passes are not valid on these lines.

Ticket Purchase and Seat Reservation
Tickets can be bought from any station (regardless of your point of departure) and from downtown RENFE offices and travel agents displaying the blue and yellow RENFE sign. The latter are often best in the busy holiday season. At stations, buy your advance tickets from the window marked LARGO RECORRIDO, VENTA ANTICIPADA (Long Distance, Advance Sales). Seat reservations can be made up to 60 days in advance and are obligatory on all the better long-distance services.

Fare Savers
The **RENFE Tourist Card** is an unlimited-kilometers pass, valid for 3, 5, or 10 days' travel, and can be bought by anyone who lives outside Spain. It is available for first- or second-class travel and can be purchased from selected travel agencies and main railroad stations abroad; and in Spain, at RENFE travel offices and the stations of Madrid, Barcelona, Port Bou, and Irún. At press time (summer 1995) the second-class pass cost 15,650 ptas. for three days, 24,955 ptas. for five days, and 44,020 ptas. for 10 days. RENFE has no representative in the United States.

If you plan to travel to other countries in Europe, you may want to invest in a **EurailPass** or a **Eurail FlexiPass** (*see* Getting Around by Train *in* Chapter 1).

Blue Days *(Días Azules)* leaflets are available from RENFE offices and stations and show those days of the year (approximately 270) when you can travel at reduced rates. Be warned, though, that some of these bargains may apply only to Spaniards or to foreigners officially resident in Spain.

By Plane
Iberia and its subsidiary **Aviaco** operate a wide network of domestic flights, linking all the main cities and the Balearic Islands. Distances are great and internal airfares are high by U.S. standards, although deregulation is pushing prices lower. Flights from the mainland to the Balearics are heavily booked in summer, and the Madrid–Málaga route is frequently overbooked at Easter and in high season. A frequent shuttle service operates between Madrid and Barcelona. Iberia has its own offices in most major Spanish cities and acts as agent for Aviaco. In Madrid, Iberia headquarters are at Velázquez 130 (tel. 91/411–1011 for domestic reservations, 91/329–4353 for international, or call Infoiberia for flight information, tel. 91/329–5767). Flights can also be booked at most travel agencies. Air Europa (tel. 91/305–5130) offers slightly cheaper service between Madrid and Barcelona as well as flights to the Canary Islands. For information on other airlines' flights to and within Spain, call the airline itself, or call the airport (tel. 91/205–8343) and ask for your airline.

By Bus
Spain has an excellent bus network, but there is no national or nationwide bus company. The network simply consists of numerous private regional bus companies *(empresas)*, and there are therefore no comprehensive bus passes. Some of the buses on major routes are now quite luxurious, although this is not always the case in rural areas. Buses tend to be more frequent than trains, are sometimes

cheaper, and often allow you to see more of the countryside. On major routes and at holiday times, it is advisable to buy your ticket a day or two in advance. Some cities have central bus stations, but in many, including Madrid and Barcelona, buses leave from various boarding points. Always check with the local tourist office. Bus stations, unlike train stations, usually provide luggage-storage facilities.

Staying in Spain

Telephones
Local Calls
Pay phones are supposed to work with coins of 25 and either 50 or 100 ptas. (smaller 5- and 25-pta. coins do not work in the machines). Twenty-five ptas. is the minimum for short local calls. In the older gray phones, place several coins in the slot or in the groove on top of the phone, lift the receiver, and dial the number. Coins then fall into the machine as needed. In the newer green phones, place several coins in the slot, watch the display unit, and feed as needed. These phones take 100-pta. coins. Area codes, necessary when calling another province from within Spain, always begin with 9 and are different for each province. In Madrid province, the code is 91; in Cantabria, it's 942. If you're dialing from outside the country, drop the 9.

International Calls
Calling abroad is best done from the *Telefónica*, a telephone office found in all sizable towns, where an operator assigns you a private booth and collects payment at the end of the call. This is by far the least expensive way of making international calls. You can also call from any pay phone marked *Teléfono Internacional.* These phones are feasible for very short transatlantic calls, but you'll need a large handful of 25-, 50- and 100-pta. coins. Use 50-pta. (or 100-pta. if the phone takes them) coins initially, then coins of any denomination to prolong your call. Dial 07 for international, wait for the tone to change, then 1 for the United States, 0101 for Canada, or 44 for the United Kingdom, followed by the area code and number. For calls to the United Kingdom, omit the initial 0 from the area code.

Country Code
Spain's country code is 34.

Operators and Information
For the operator and information for any part of Spain, dial 003. To make collect calls from Madrid, dial 008 for Europe and 005 for the rest of the world. From most other places in Spain, dial 9198 for Europe and 9191 for the rest of the world. In the Catalan provinces, dial 9398 for Europe and 9391 for the rest of the world. U.S. long-distance companies now have special access numbers: **AT&T** (tel. 900/99–00–11), **MCI** (900/99–00–14), **Sprint** (900/99–00–13).

Mail
Postal Rates
To the United States, airmail letters up to 15 grams and postcards each cost 90 ptas. at press time (summer 1995). To the United Kingdom and other EU countries, letters up to 20 grams and postcards each cost 62 ptas. To non–EU European countries, letters and postcards up to 20 grams cost 80 ptas. If you wish to expedite your overseas mail, send it *Urgente* for 170 ptas. over the regular airmail cost. Within Spain, letters and postcards each cost 30 ptas.; within a city in Spain, letters and postcards cost 19 ptas. Mailboxes are yellow with red stripes, and the slot marked "Extranjero" is the one for mail going abroad. Buy your stamps *(sellos)* at a post office *(correos)* or in a tobacco shop *(estanco).*

Receiving Mail
If you're uncertain where you'll be staying, have mail sent to American Express or to the Poste Restante *(Lista de Correos)* of the local post office. To claim your mail, you'll need to show your passport. The Spanish mail is notoriously slow and not always very efficient.

Shopping
Sales Tax Refunds
If you purchase goods up to a value of 48,000 ptas. or more in any one store (and in theory this should be on only *one* item), you are entitled to a refund of the IVA tax paid (usually 6% but more in the case of certain luxury goods), provided you leave Spain within three

months. You will be given two copies of the sales invoice, which you must present at customs together with the goods as you leave Spain. Once the invoice has been stamped by customs, mail the blue copy back to the store, which will then mail your tax refund to you. If you are leaving via the airports of Madrid, Barcelona, Málaga or Palma de Mallorca, you can get your tax refund immediately from the Banco Exterior de España in the airport. The above does not apply to residents of EU countries, who must claim their IVA refund through customs in their own country. The Corte Inglés and Galerías Preciados department stores operate the above system, but don't be surprised if other stores are unfamiliar with the tax-refund procedure and do not have the necessary forms.

Bargaining Prices in city stores and produce markets are fixed; bargaining is possible only in flea markets; some antiques stores; and with gypsy vendors, with whom it is *essential*, though you'd do best to turn them down flat because their goods are almost always fake and grossly overpriced.

Opening and Closing Times **Banks** are open Monday through Saturday 9–2 from October to June; during the summer months they are closed on Saturdays.

Museums and churches. Opening times vary. Most are open in the morning, and most museums close one day a week, often Monday.

Post offices. These are usually open weekdays 9–2, but times can vary; check locally.

Stores are open weekdays from 9 or 10 until 1:30 or 2, then again in the afternoon from around 4 to 7 in winter, and 5 to 8 in summer. In some cities, especially in summer, stores close on Saturday afternoon. The Corte Inglés and Galerías Preciados department stores in major cities are open continuously from 10 to 8, and some stores in tourist resorts also stay open through the siesta.

National Holidays In 1996: January 1, January 6 (Epiphany), March 19 (St. Joseph), March 31 (Holy Thursday), April 5 (Good Friday), April 7 (Easter), May 1 (May Day), June 2 (Corpus Christi), July 25 (St. James), August 15 (Assumption), October 12 (National Day), November 1 (All Saints' Day), December 6 (Constitution), December 8 (Immaculate Conception), December 25. Other holidays include May 2 (in the province of Madrid) and June 24 (St. John). These holidays are not celebrated in every region; always check locally. Changing holidays in 1997: March 28 (Good Friday), March 30 (Easter), May 29 (Corpus Christi).

Dining Visitors have a choice of restaurants, tapas bars, and cafés. Restaurants are strictly for lunch and dinner; they do not serve breakfast. Tapas bars are ideal for a glass of wine or beer accompanied by an array of savory tidbits (tapas). Cafés, called *cafeterías*, are basically coffee houses serving snacks; light meals; tapas; pastries; and coffee, tea, and alcoholic drinks. They also serve breakfast and are perfect for afternoon tea.

Mealtimes Mealtimes in Spain are much later than in any other European country. Lunch begins between 1 and 2:30, with 2 being the usual time, and 3 more normal on Sunday. Dinner is usually available from 8:30 onward, but 10 PM is the usual time in the larger cities and resorts. Lunch is the main meal, not dinner. Tapas bars are busiest between noon and 2 and from 8 PM on. Cafés are usually open from around 8 AM to midnight.

Precautions Tap water is safe to drink in all but the remotest villages (in Madrid, tap water, from the surrounding Guadarrama Mountains, is excellent; in Barcelona, it's safe but tastes terrible). However, most Spaniards drink bottled mineral water; ask for either *agua sin gas* (without bubbles) or *agua con gas* (with). A good paella should be served only at lunchtime and should be prepared to order (usually 30 minutes); beware the all-too-cheap version.

Typical Dishes Paella—a mixture of saffron-flavored rice with seafood, chicken, and vegetables—is Spain's national dish. *Tortilla,* a thick potato and egg omelet, is a national snack, and is eaten hot or cold alone or as a sandwich. Gazpacho, a cold soup usually made of crushed garlic, tomatoes, and olive oil and garnished with diced vegetables, is a traditional Andalucían dish and is served mainly in summer. The Basque Country and Galicia are the gourmet regions of Spain, and both serve outstanding fish and seafood. Asturias is famous for its *fabadas* (bean stews), cider, and dairy products; Extremadura for its hams and sausages; and Castile for its roasts, especially *cochinillo* (suckling pig), *cordero asado* (roast lamb), and *perdiz* (partridge). The best wines are those from the Rioja and Penedés regions. Valdepeñas is a pleasant table wine, and most places serve a perfectly acceptable house wine called *vino de la casa.* Sherries from Jerez de la Frontera make fine aperitifs; ask for a *fino* or a *manzanilla;* both are dry. In summer you can try *horchata,* a sweet white drink made from ground nuts, or *granizados de limón* or *de café,* lemon juice or coffee served over crushed ice. *Un café solo* is a small, black, strong coffee, and *café con leche* is espresso diluted with hot milk; weak black American-style coffee is hard to come by.

What to Wear Casual dress is almost always appropriate; you'll need a jacket and tie for only the most expensive restaurants. However, shorts are often frowned upon in cities.

Ratings Spanish restaurants are officially classified from five forks down to one fork, with most places falling into the two- or three-fork category. In our rating system, prices are per person and include a first course, main course, and dessert, but not wine or tip. Sales tax (IVA) is usually included in the menu price; check the menu for *IVA incluído* or *IVA no incluído.* When it's not included, an additional 7% will be added to your bill. Most restaurants offer a prix-fixe menu called a *menú del día;* however, this is often offered only at lunch, and at dinner tends to be merely a reheated midday offering. This is usually the cheapest way of eating; à la carte dining is more expensive. Service charges are never added to your bill; leave around 10%, less in inexpensive restaurants and bars. Major centers, such as Madrid, Barcelona, Marbella, and Seville, tend to be a bit more expensive. Best bets are indicated by a star ★.

Category	Cost
$$	3,500 ptas.–6,500 ptas.
$	2,000 ptas.–3,500 ptas.
¢	under 2,000 ptas.

Lodging Spain has a wide range of accommodations, including luxury palaces, medieval monasteries, converted 19th-century houses, modern hotels, high-rises on the coasts, and inexpensive hostels in family homes. All hotels and hostels are listed with their rates in the annual *Guía de Hoteles,* available from bookstores and kiosks for around 1000 ptas., or you can see a copy in local tourist offices. Rates are always quoted per room, not per person. Single occupancy of a double room costs 80% of the normal price. Breakfast is rarely included in the quoted room rate; always check. The quality of rooms, particularly in older properties, can be uneven; always ask to see your room *before* you sign the acceptance slip. If you want a private bathroom in a less expensive hotel, state your preference for shower or bathtub; the latter usually costs more, though many hotels have both. Local tourist offices will provide you with a list of accommodations in their region, but they are not allowed to make reservations for you. In Madrid and Barcelona, hotel booking agencies are found at the airports and railroad stations.

Hotels and Hostels Hotels are officially classified from five stars (the highest) to one star, hostels from three stars to one star. Good, inexpensive lodging can be found at hostels, which in Spain are usually family homes converted to provide accommodations (though they are frequently comfortable and modern midsize hotels). If an "R" appears on the blue hotel or hostel plaque, the hotel is classified as a *residencia*, and full dining services are not provided, though breakfast and cafeteria facilities may be available. A three-star hostel usually equates with a two-star hotel; two- and one-star hostels offer simple, basic accommodations. The main hotel chains are Husa, Iberotel Melia, Sol, Tryp, and the state-run *paradores* (tourist hotels). Holiday Inn, InterContinental, and Forte also own some of the best hotels in Madrid, Barcelona, and Seville; only these and the paradors have any special character. The others mostly provide clean, comfortable accommodations in the two- to four-star range. The cost of lodging in Spain varies wildly according to place and season, so you're wise *always* to inquire before booking.

In many hotels rates vary fairly dramatically according to the time of year. The hotel year is divided into *estación alta, media,* and *baja* (high, mid, and low season); high season usually covers the summer and Easter and Christmas periods, plus the major fiestas. IVA is rarely included in the quoted room rates, so be prepared for an additional 7% to be added to your bill. Service charges are never included.

Paradors There are about 100 state-owned-and-run paradors, many of which are located in magnificent medieval castles or convents or in places of great natural beauty. Most of these fall into the four-star category and are priced accordingly. Most have restaurants that specialize in local regional cuisine and serve a full breakfast. The most popular paradors (Granada's San Francisco parador, for example) are booked far in advance, and many close for a month or two in winter (January or February) for renovations. While the paradors aren't cheap, they're a wonderful treat—and far less expensive than anything comparable in the United States or western Europe. For more information or to make reservations, contact **Spain:** Paradores (Requena 3, 28013 Madrid, tel. 91/559–0069, fax 91/559–3223; in Spain, the toll-free number is 90/108–686; **Great Britain:** Keytel International (402 Edgware Rd., London, W2 1ED, tel. 0171/402–8182); or **United States:** Marketing Ahead, Inc. (433 Fifth Ave., New York, NY 10016, tel. 212/686–9213).

Camping There are approximately 530 campsites in Spain, with the highest concentration along the Mediterranean coast. The season runs from April to October, though some sites are open year-round. Sites are listed in the annual publication *Guía de Campings,* available from bookstores or local tourist offices, and further details are available from the Spanish National Tourist Office. Reservations for the most popular seaside sites can be made either directly with the site or through camping reservations at Federación Española de Campings (Príncipe de Vergara 85, 2° Dcha, 28006 Madrid, tel. 91/562–9994).

Ratings Prices are for two people in a double room and do not include breakfast. Best bets are indicated by a star ★.

Category	Major City	Other Areas
$$	10,000–15,000 ptas.	8,000–12,000 ptas.
$	5,500–10,000 ptas.	5,000–8,000 ptas.
¢	under 5,500 ptas.	under 5,000 ptas.

Tipping Spaniards appreciate being tipped, though the practice is becoming less widespread. Restaurants and hotels are by law not allowed to add a service charge to your bill, though confusingly your bill for both will most likely say *servicios e impuestos incluídos* (service and tax included). Ignore this unhelpful piece of advice and leave 10% in most restaurants where you have had a full meal; in humbler eating places, bars, and cafés, 5%–10% is enough, or you can round out the bill to the nearest 100 ptas. A cocktail waiter in a hotel will expect at least 30 ptas. a drink, maybe 50 ptas. in a luxury establishment. Tip taxi drivers about 10% when they use the meter, otherwise *nothing*—they'll have seen to it themselves. Gas-station attendants get no tip for pumping gas, but they get about 50 ptas. for checking tires and oil and cleaning windshields. Train and airport porters usually operate on a fixed rate of about 60 ptas.–100 ptas. a bag. Coat-check attendants get 25 ptas.–50 ptas., and restroom attendants get 10 ptas.–25 ptas. In top hotels doormen get 100 ptas.–150 ptas. for carrying bags to the check-in counter or for hailing taxis, and bellhops get 100 ptas. for room service or for each bag they carry to your room. In moderate hotels about 50 ptas. is adequate for the same services. Leave your chambermaid about 300 ptas. for a week's stay. There's no need to tip for just a couple of nights.

Madrid

Arriving and Departing

By Plane All international and domestic flights arrive at Madrid's **Barajas Airport** (tel. 91/305–8343), 16 kilometers (10 miles) northeast of town just off the N-II Barcelona highway. For information on arrival and departure times, call **Inforiberia** (tel. 91/329–5767) or the airline concerned.

Between the Buses leave the national and international terminals every 15 min-
Airport and utes from 5:40 AM to 2 AM for the downtown terminal at Plaza de Colón
Downtown just off the Paseo de la Castellana. The ride takes about 20 minutes and the fare at press time was 325 ptas. Most city hotels are then only a short taxi ride away. The fastest and most expensive route into town (usually around 1,500 ptas., but up to 2,000 ptas. plus tip in traffic) is by taxi. Pay what is on the meter plus 350 ptas. surcharge and 150 ptas. for each suitcase.

By Train Madrid has three railroad stations. **Chamartín,** in the northern suburbs beyond the Plaza de Castilla, is the main station, with trains to France and the north (including Barcelona, Segovia, El Escorial, Santiago, and La Coruña). Most trains to Valencia, Alicante, and Andalucía now leave from here, too, but stop at **Atocha station,** at the southern end of Paseo del Prado on the Glorieta del Emperador Carlos V. Also departing from Atocha, where a new station was built in 1989, are trains to Toledo, Granada, Extremadura, and Lisbon. In 1992, a convenient new metro stop (Atocha RENFE) was opened in Atocha station, connecting it to the city subway system. The old Atocha station, designed by Eiffel, was reopened in 1992 as the Madrid terminal for the new high-speed rail service to Seville (AVE). **Norte** (or Príncipe Pío), on Paseo de la Florida, in the west of town below the Plaza de España, is the departure point for local trains to the Madrid suburbs.

For all train information, call RENFE (tel. 91/563–0202, in Spanish and English), or go to its offices at Alcalá 4, or on the second floor of Torre de Madrid in the Plaza de España, right above the main tourist office (open weekdays 9–7, Sat. 9:30–1:30). There's another RENFE office at Barajas Airport in the International Arrivals

Hall, or you can purchase tickets at any of the three main stations, or from travel agents displaying the blue-and-yellow RENFE sign.

By Bus Madrid has no central bus station. The two main bus stations are the **Estación del Sur** (Canarias 17, tel. 91/468–4200), nearest metro Palos de la Frontera, for buses to Toledo, La Mancha, Alicante, and Andalucía, and **Auto-Rés** (Plaza Conde de Casal 6, tel. 91/551–7200), nearest metro Conde de Casal, for buses to Extremadura, Cuenca, Salamanca, Valladolid, Valencia, and Zamora. Auto-Rés has a central ticket and information office at Salud 19 near the Hotel Arosa, just off Gran Vía. Buses to other destinations leave from various points, so check with the tourist office. The Basque country and most of north central Spain is served by Auto Continental (Alenza 20, nearest metro Ríos Rosas, tel. 91/533–0400). For Ávila, Segovia, and La Granja, Empresa La Sepulvedana (tel. 91/527–9537) leaves from Paseo de la Florida 11, next to the Norte station, a few steps from the Norte metro stop. Empresa Herranz (tel. 91/543–3645 or 91/543–8167), serving San Lorenzo de El Escorial and the Valley of the Fallen, departs from the base of Calle Fernandez de los Ríos, a few yards from the Moncloa metro stop. La Veloz (Av. Mediterraneo 49, tel. 91/409–7602) serves Chinchón.

Getting Around

Madrid is a fairly compact city, and most of the main sights can be visited on foot. But if you're staying in one of the modern hotels in the north of town off the Castellana, you may well need to use the bus or subway (metro). The metro is efficient, inexpensive, and easy to use; buses are priced identically, but are generally harder to use (an exception may be the buses that run up and down the Castellana, a useful route). As a rough guide, the walk from the Prado to the Royal Palace at a comfortable sightseeing pace but without stopping takes around 30 minutes; from Plaza del Callao on Gran Vía to the Plaza Mayor, it takes about 15 minutes.

By Metro The subway offers the simplest and quickest means of transport and is open from 6 AM to 1:30 AM. Metro maps are available from ticket offices, hotels, and tourist offices. The fare is 125 ptas. a ride. Savings can be made by buying a *taco* of 10 tickets for 625 ptas. Keep some change (5, 25, 50, and 100 ptas.) handy for the ticket machines, especially after 10 PM; the machines give change and are handy for beating often long lines for tickets.

By Bus City buses are red and run from 6 AM to midnight (though check, as some stop earlier). Again there is a flat-fare system, with each ride costing 125 ptas. The smaller, yellow microbuses also cost 125 ptas. and are slightly faster. Route plans are displayed at bus stops *(paradas)*, and a map of the entire system is available from EMT (Empresa Municipal de Transportes) booths on Plaza de la Cibeles, Callao, or Puerta del Sol. Savings can be made by buying a **Bonobus** (625 ptas.), good for 10 rides, from EMT booths, most newsstands, tobacco shops, or any branch of the Caja de Ahorros de Madrid.

Important Addresses and Numbers

Tourist Information The main Madrid tourist office (tel. 91/541–2325) is on the ground floor of the Torre de Madrid in Plaza de España, near the beginning of Calle de la Princesa, and is open weekdays 9–7, Saturdays 9:30–1:30. Another Madrid Provincial Tourist Office (Duque de Medinacelli 2, tel. 91/429–4951) is conveniently located on a small street across from the Palace Hotel. The much less useful municipal tourist office is at Plaza Mayor 3 (tel. 91/266–5477) and is open weekdays 10–8, Saturdays 10–2. A third office is in the International Arrivals Hall of Barajas Airport (tel. 91/305–8656) and is open weekdays 8–8, Saturdays 9–1.

Madrid Metro

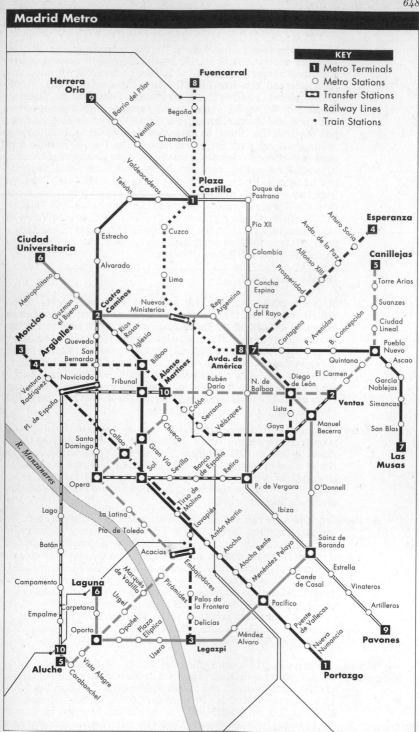

KEY

1 Metro Terminals
○ Metro Stations
⊂⊃ Transfer Stations
— Railway Lines
• Train Stations

Embassies **U.S.** (Serrano 75, tel. 91/577–4000), **Canadian** (Núñez de Balboa 35, tel. 91/431–4300), **U.K.** (Fernando el Santo 16, tel. 91/319–0200).

Emergencies **Police** (National Police, tel. 091; Municipal Police, tel. 092; Main Police [Policía Nacional] Station, Puerta del Sol 7, tel. 91/522–0435). To report lost passports, go to Los Madrazos 9, just off the top of Paseo del Prado (tel. 91/521–9350). **Ambulance** tel. 91/522–2222 or 91/588–4400. **Doctor:** Your hotel reception will contact the nearest doctor for you. Emergency clinics: **Hospital 12 de Octubre** (Av. Córdoba, tel. 91/390–8000) and **La Paz Ciudad Sanitaria** (Paseo de la Castellana 261, tel. 91/358–2600). English-speaking doctors are available at Conde de Aranda 7 (tel. 91/435–1595). **Pharmacies:** A list of pharmacies open 24 hours (*farmacias de guardia*) is published daily in *El Pais.* Hotel receptions usually have a copy. **Company** (Puerta del Sol 14, tel. 91/521–3625) has English-speaking pharmacists.

Airlines **Iberia** (Goya 29, tel. 91/581–8155; for flight information, call Inforiberia, tel. 91/411–2545), **British Airways** (Serrano 60, 5th floor, tel. 91/431–7575), and **TWA** (Plaza de Colón 2, tel. 91/410–6007 or 91/410–6012). United (Goya 6, tel. 91/578–0177).

Exploring Madrid

Numbers in the margin correspond to points of interest on the Madrid map.

You can walk the following route in a day, or even half a day if you stop only to visit the Prado and Royal Palace. Two days should give you time for browsing. Begin in the Plaza Atocha, more properly known as the Glorieta del Emperador Carlos V, at the bottom of the Paseo del Prado, and check out what's showing in the **Reina Sofía Arts Center,** opened by Queen Sofía in 1986. This converted hospital, home of art and sculpture exhibitions and symbol of Madrid's new cultural pride, is fast becoming one of Europe's most dynamic venues—a Madrileño rival to Paris's Pompidou Center. The center's status as an important art repository rose in 1992 when it acquired from the Prado Picasso's *Guernica,* the artist's monumental expression of anguish and outrage at the German bombing of a Basque town in 1937. The main entrance is on Calle de Santa Isabel 52. *Tel. 91/467–5062. Admission: 400 ptas., free Sat. (2:30–9) and Sun. Open Mon., Wed.–Sat. 10 AM–9 PM; Sun. 10 AM–2:30 PM; closed Tues.*

Walk up Paseo del Prado to Madrid's number-one sight, the famous **Prado Museum,** one of the world's most important art galleries. Plan on spending at least 1½ days here, though it will take at least two full days to view its treasures properly. Brace yourself for the crowds. The greatest treasures—the Velázquez, Murillo, Zurbarán, El Greco, and Goya galleries—are all on the upstairs floor. Two of the best works are Velázquez's *Surrender of Breda* and his most famous work, *Las Meninas,* which dominates the room where it hangs. The Goya galleries contain the artist's none-too-flattering royal portraits (Goya believed in painting the truth); his exquisitely beautiful *Marquesa de Santa Cruz;* and his famous *Naked Maja* and *Clothed Maja,* for which the 13th duchess of Alba was said to have posed. Goya's most moving works, the *Second of May* and the *Fusillade of Moncloa* or *Third of May,* vividly depict the sufferings of Madrid patriots at the hands of Napoléon's invading troops in 1808. Before you leave, feast your eyes on the fantastic flights of fancy of Hieronymus Bosch's *Garden of Earthly Delights* and his triptych *The Hay Wagon,* both downstairs on the ground floor. *Paseo del Prado s/n, tel. 91/420–2836. Admission: 400 ptas. Open Tues.–Sat. 9–7, Sun. 9–2.*

Across the street is the **Ritz,** the grand old lady of Madrid's hotels, built in 1910 by Alfonso XIII when he realized that his capital had no hotels elegant enough to accommodate the guests at his wedding in

Major Attractions

Cibeles Fountain, 7
Convento de las
Descalzas Reales, 10
Museo Thyssen–
Bornemiza, 4
Palacio Real, 13
Parque del Retiro, 5
Plaza de la Villa, 12
Plaza Mayor, 11
Prado Museum, 2
Puerta de Alcalá, 6
Puerta del Sol, 9
Real Academia de
San Fernando, 8
Reina Sofía Arts
Center, 1
Ritz, 3
Royal Carriage
Museum, 14

Other Attractions

Biblioteca Nacional, 19
Municipal Museum, 16
Museo Arqueológico, 20
Museo de Artes
Decorativas, 21
Museo de Cera
(Wax Museum), 18
Museo Romántico, 17
Torre de Madrid, 15

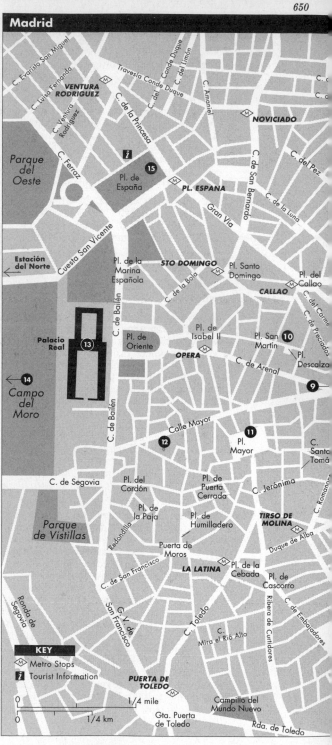

Madrid

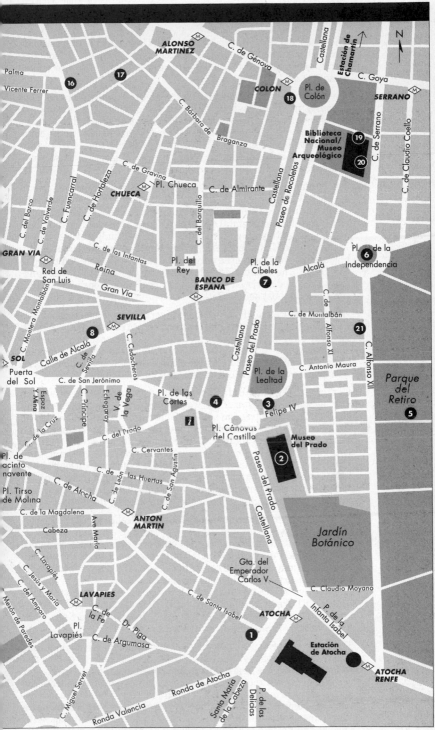

Palma

Vicente Ferrer

ALONSO MARTINEZ

C. de Génova

Estación de Chamartín

N

C. Goya

COLON

Pl. de Colón

SERRANO

C. de Serrano

C. de Claudio Coello

C. Bárbara de Braganza

CHUECA

C. de Gravina

Pl. Chueca

C. de Almirante

Castellana

Paseo de Recoletos

Biblioteca Nacional/ Museo Arqueológico

C. del Barco

C. de Valverde

C. Fuencarral

C. de Hortaleza

C. del Barquillo

GRAN VIA

C. de las Infantas

Reina

Pl. del Rey

Pl. de la Cibeles

Alcalá

Pl. de la Independencia

Red de San Luis

C. Montera

Montalbán

Gran Vía

BANCO DE ESPAÑA

C. de Montalbán

C. de Alfonso XI

SEVILLA

C. de Sevilla

C. Cadacheros

Castellana

Paseo del Prado

Pl. de la Lealtad

C. Antonio Maura

C. de Alfonso XII

Parque del Retiro

SOL

Calle de Alcalá

Puerta del Sol

Espoz y Mina

C. de San Jerónimo

C. Príncipe

Echegaray

V. de la Vega

C. del Prado

Pl. de las Cortes

Felipe IV

Museo del Prado

C. de la Cruz

Pl. de acinto navente

C. Cervantes

C. de León

las Huertas

C. de San Agustín

Pl. Cánovas del Castillo

Pl. Tirso de Molina

C. de Atocha

ANTON MARTIN

C. de la Magdalena

Cabeza

Ave María

Jardín Botánico

C. Lavapiés

C. Jesús y María

C. del Amparo

Mesón de Paredes

LAVAPIES

C. de la Fe

Dr. Piga

Pl. Lavapiés

C. de Argumosa

C. de Santa Isabel

Gta. del Emperador Carlos V

C. Claudio Moyano

ATOCHA

P. de la Infanta Isabel

C. Miguel Servet

Ronda de Atocha

Santa María de la Cabeza

P. de las Delicias

Estación de Atocha

ATOCHA RENFE

Ronda Valencia

1906. The Ritz garden is a delightfully aristocratic place to lunch in summer—men always need ties.

The **Casón del Buen Retiro,** entrance on Calle Alfonso XII, is an annex of the Prado that contains 19th-century Spanish art, including works by Sorolla and Rusiñol. *Open same hrs as Prado and visited on same ticket.*

❹ The **Museo Thyssen-Bornemiza,** north on the Paseo del Prado, has a formerly privately owned collection of paintings that attempt to trace the history of Western art with examples from all the important movements. Impressionism—the only such display in the country—is well represented. The setting for the museum itself is beautiful: It is housed in the Villahermosa Palace, which was elegantly renovated to be airy and light-filled.

❺ The **Parque del Retiro,** once a royal retreat, is today Madrid's prettiest park. Visit the beautiful rose garden, **La Rosaleda,** and enjoy the many statues and fountains. You can rent a rowboat on **El Estanque,** gaze up at the monumental **statue to Alfonso XII,** one of Spain's least notable kings though you wouldn't think so to judge by its size, or wonder at the **Monument to the Fallen Angel**—Madrid claims the dubious privilege of being the only capital to have a statue dedicated to the Devil. The **Palacio de Velázquez** and the beautiful steel-and-glass **Palacio de Cristal,** built as a tropical plant house in the 19th century, now host art exhibits.

❻ Leaving the Retiro via its northwest corner, you come to the Plaza de la Independencia, dominated by the **Puerta de Alcalá,** a grandiose gateway built in 1779 for Charles III. A customs post once stood beside the gate, as did the old bullring until it was moved to its present site at Ventas in the 1920s. At the turn of the century, the Puerta de Alcalá more or less marked the eastern limits of Madrid.

❼ Continue to the **Plaza de la Cibeles,** one of the great landmarks of the city, at the intersection of its two main arteries, the Castellana and Calle de Alcalá. If you can see it through the roar and fumes of the thundering traffic, the square's center is the **Cibeles Fountain,** the unofficial emblem of Madrid. Cybele, the Greek goddess of fertility, languidly rides her lion-drawn chariot, overlooked by the mighty **Palacio de Comunicaciones,** a splendidly pompous cathedral-like building often jokingly dubbed Our Lady of Communications. In fact, it's the main post office, erected in 1918. The famous goddess looks her best at night, when she's illuminated by floodlights.

❽ Now head down the long and busy Calle de Alcalá toward the Puerta del Sol, resisting the temptation to turn right up the Gran Vía, which beckons temptingly with its mile of stores and cafés. Before you reach the Puerta del Sol, art lovers may want to step inside the **Real Academia de San Fernando** at Alcalá 13. This recently refurbished fine-arts gallery boasts an art collection second in Madrid only to the Prado's and features all the great Spanish masters: Velázquez, El Greco, Murillo, Zurbarán, Ribera, and Goya. *Alcalá 13, tel. 91/532–1546. Admission: 200 ptas., free Sat. and Sun. Open Tues.–Fri. 9–7; Sat., Sun., and Mon. 9–3.*

❾ The **Puerta del Sol** is at the very heart of Madrid. Its name means Gate of the Sun, though the old gate disappeared long ago. It's easy to feel you're at the heart of things here—indeed, of all Spain—for the kilometer distances for the whole nation are measured from the zero marker in front of the Police Headquarters. The square was expertly revamped in 1986 and now accommodates both a copy of **La Mariblanca** (a statue that 250 years ago adorned a fountain here) and, at the bottom of Calle Carmen, the much-loved **statue of the bear and *madroño*** (strawberry tree). The Puerta del Sol is inextricably linked with the history of Madrid and of the nation. Here, half a century ago, a generation of literati gathered in the long-gone cafés to thrash out the burning issues of the day, and if you can cast your thoughts back almost 200 years, you can conjure up the heroic deeds of the patriots' uprising, immortalized by Goya in the *Second of May*.

This is a good place to break the tour if you've had enough sightseeing for one day. Head north up Preciados or Montera for some of the busiest and best shopping streets in the city or southeast toward Plaza Santa Ana for tavern-hopping in Old Madrid.

⑩ The **Convento de las Descalzas Reales** on Plaza Descalzas Reales just above Arenal was founded by Juana de Austria, daughter of Charles V, and is still inhabited by nuns. Over the centuries the nuns, daughters of the royal and noble, endowed the convent with an enormous wealth of jewels, religious ornaments, superb Flemish tapestries, and the works of such great masters as Titian and Rubens. A bit off the main tourist track, it's one of Madrid's better-kept secrets. Your ticket includes admission to the nearby, but less interesting, **Convento de la Encarnación.** *Plaza de las Descalzas Reales, tel. 91/559-7404. Admission: 600 ptas. Guided Spanish-language tours only. Open Tues.–Thurs., Sat. 10:30–12:30 and 4–5:30; Fri. 10:30–12:30; Sun. 11–1:30.*

⑪ Walk up **Calle Mayor,** the Main Street of Old Madrid, past the shops full of religious statues and satins for bishops' robes, to the **Plaza Mayor,** the capital's greatest architectural showpiece. It was built in 1617–19 for Philip III—that's Philip on the horse in the middle. The plaza has witnessed the canonization of saints, burning of heretics, fireworks, and bullfights and is still one of the great gathering places of Madrid.

⑫ If you're here in the morning, take a look inside the 19th-century steel-and-glass San Miguel market, a colorful provisions market, before continuing down Calle Mayor to the **Plaza de la Villa.** The square's notable cluster of buildings includes some of the oldest houses in Madrid. The **Casa de la Villa,** the Madrid city hall, was built in 1644 and has also served as the city prison and the mayor's home. Its sumptuous salons are now open to the public on Mondays at 5 PM. The free guided visits are usually in Spanish, but English tours can be arranged with advance notice. An archway joins the Casa de la Villa to the **Casa Cisneros,** a palace built in 1537 for the nephew of Cardinal Cisneros, primate of Spain and infamous inquisitor general. Across the square, the **Torre de Lujanes** is one of the oldest buildings in Madrid. It once imprisoned Francis I of France, archenemy of the Emperor Charles V.

⑬ The last stop on the tour, but Madrid's second most important sight, is the **Palacio Real** (Royal Palace). This magnificent granite and limestone residence was begun by Philip V, the first Bourbon king of Spain, who was always homesick for his beloved Versailles, the opulence and splendor of which he did his best to emulate. His efforts were successful, to judge by the 2,800 rooms with their lavish Rococo decorations, precious carpets, porcelain, timepieces, mirrors, and chandeliers. From 1764, when Charles III first moved in, till the coming of the Second Republic and the abdication of Alfonso XIII in 1931, the Royal Palace proved a very stylish abode for Spanish monarchs. Today King Juan Carlos, who lives in the far less ostentatious Zarzuela Palace outside Madrid, uses it only for official state functions. Allow 1½–2 hours for a visit that includes the Royal Carriage Museum (*see below*), Royal Pharmacy, and other outbuildings. *Bailén s/n, tel. 91/559-7404. Admission: 800 ptas. Open Mon.–Sat. 9:30–5, Sun. 9–2.*

⑭ The **Royal Carriage Museum,** which belongs to the palace (and has the same hours) but has a separate entrance on Paseo Vírgen del Puerto, can be visited only on an all-inclusive ticket. One of its highlights is the wedding carriage of Alfonso XIII and his English bride,

Victoria Eugenia, granddaughter of Queen Victoria. The carriage was damaged by a bomb thrown at it in the Calle Mayor during the royal wedding procession in 1906; another is the chair that carried the gout-stricken old Emperor Charles V to his retirement at the remote monastery of Yuste.

Shopping

Gift Ideas There are no special regional crafts associated with Madrid itself, but traditional Spanish goods are on sale in many stores. The **Corte Inglés** and **Galerías Preciados** department stores both stock good displays of Lladró porcelain. They also carry fans, but for really superb examples, try the long-established **Casa Diego** in Puerta del Sol. Two stores opposite the Prado on Plaza Cánovas del Castillo, **Artesanía Toledana** and **El Escudo de Toledo,** have a wide selection of souvenirs, especially Toledo swords, inlaid marquetry ware, and pottery. Carefully selected handicrafts from all over Spain—ceramics, furniture, glassware, rugs, embroidery, and more—are sold at **Artespaña** (Gran Vía 32, and Hermosilla 14), a government-run crafts store.

Antiques The main areas to see are the Plaza de las Cortes, the Carrera San Jerónimo, and the Rastro flea market, along the Ribera de Curtidores and the courtyards just off it.

Shopping Districts The main shopping area in the heart of Madrid is around the pedestrian streets of **Preciados** and **Montera,** between Puerta del Sol and Plaza Callao on Gran Vía. **Calle Mayor** and the streets to the east of **Plaza Mayor** are lined with fascinating old-fashioned stores straight out of the 19th century.

Department Stores **El Corte Inglés** is the biggest and most successful Spanish chain store. Its main branch is on Preciados, just off the Puerta del Sol. **Galerías Preciados,** its main rival, is on Plaza del Callao right off Gran Vía. Both stores are open Monday–Saturday 10–8, and neither closes for the siesta.

Flea Markets The **Rastro,** Madrid's most famous flea market, operates on Sundays from 9 to 2 around the Plaza del Cascorro and the Ribera de Curtidores. A **stamp and coin** market is held on Sunday mornings in the Plaza Mayor, and there's a **secondhand book** market most days on the Cuesta Claudio Moyano near Atocha Station.

Bullfighting

The Madrid bullfighting season runs from March to October. Fights are held on Sunday and sometimes also on Thursday; starting times vary between 4:30 and 7 PM. The pinnacle of the spectacle may be seen during the three weeks of daily bullfights held during the San Isidro festivals in May. The bullring is at Las Ventas (formally known as the Plaza de Toros Monumental), Alcalá 237 (metro Ventas). You can buy your ticket there on the day of the fight or, with a 20% surcharge, at the agencies that line Calle Victoria, just off Carrera San Jerónimo and Puerta del Sol.

Dining

For details and price-category definitions, *see* Dining *in* Staying in Spain, *above.*

$$ **Botín.** Madrid's oldest and most famous restaurant, just off the Plaza Mayor, has been catering to diners since 1725. Its decor and food are traditionally Castilian. *Cochinillo* (suckling pig) and *cordero asado* (roast lamb) are its specialties. It was a favorite with Hemingway; today it's very touristy and a bit overrated, but fun. Insist on the *cueva* or upstairs dining room. *Cuchilleros 17, tel. 91/366–4217. Reservations advised, especially at night. AE, DC, MC, V.*

$$ **Carmencita.** Dating from 1850, this charming restaurant is small and intimate, with ceramic wall tiles, brass hat racks, and photos of bullfighters. The menu recounts the famous who have dined here and their life stories. The cuisine is part traditional, part nouvelle, with an emphasis on *pasteles* (a kind of mousse), both savory and sweet. *Libertad 16, on the corner of San Marcos in the Chueca area above Gran Vía; tel. 91/531–6612. Reservations advised. AE, DC, MC, V. Closed Sat. lunch and Sun.*

$$ **Casa Ciriaco.** In this atmospheric old standby, only a few paces from the Plaza Mayor and city hall, the Madrid of 50 years ago lives on. You won't find many foreigners here—just businesspeople and locals enjoying traditional Spanish cooking and delicious *fresones* (strawberries) for dessert. *Mayor 84, tel. 91/548–0620. Reservations accepted. No credit cards. Closed Wed. and Aug.*

$$ **Fuente Real.** Dining here is like eating in a turn-of-the-century
★ home. Tucked away between Mayor and Arenal, it's brimming with personal mementos, such as antique dolls, Indian figures, and Mexican Christmas decorations. The cuisine is French and Spanish with an emphasis on high-quality meats and crepes. Try the *pastel de espinacas* (spinach mousse) or *crêpes de puerros* (leeks). *Fuentes 1, tel. 91/559–6613. AE, MC, V. Closed Sun. eve. and Mon.*

$$ **La Barraca.** A Valencian restaurant with cheerful blue-and-white decor, colorful windowboxes, and ceramic tiles, this is the place to go for a wonderful choice of paellas. Located just off Gran Vía (Alcalá end), behind Loewe, it's popular with businesspeople and foreign visitors. Try the paella *reina* or the paella *de mariscos. Reina 29, tel. 91/532–7154. Reservations advised. AE, DC, MC, V.*

$ **Casa Mingo.** Resembling an Austrian cider tavern, Casa Mingo is built into a stone wall beneath the Estación del Norte train station. It's a bustling place where you'll share long plank tables with other diners; the only dishes offered are succulent roast chicken, salad, and sausages, all to be washed down with *sidra* (hard cider). In summer small tables are set up on the sidewalk. *Paseo de la Florida 2, tel. 91/547–7918. No reservations. No credit cards.*

$ **El Cuchi.** "Hemingway *never* ate here" is the sign that will lure you
★ inside this colorful tavern at the bottom of the Cuchilleros, steps off the Plaza Mayor. A fun-packed experience awaits. The ceilings are plastered with photos of Mexican revolutionaries, huge blackboards announce the menu and list the calories in the irresistible desserts, and home-baked rolls are lowered in baskets from the ceiling to your table. Salads are on the house. El Cuchi stays open all afternoon, unusual in Spain. *Cuchilleros 3, tel. 91/366–4424. Reservations advised. AE, DC, MC, V.*

$ **Puebla.** Although the dining room decor lacks charm (fake wood beams fool no one), you'd be hard-pressed to find better-prepared food at such affordable prices anywhere in Madrid. Puebla opened in 1992 and is always crowded with bankers and politicians from nearby Cortes. There are two prices for the menú del día, with more than a dozen choices in each. Be sure to try the *berenjenas a la romana* (batter-fried eggplant) if it's offered. The soups are always great, and other dishes include roast lamb, trout, calamari, and chicken. *Ventura de la Vega 12, tel. 91/429–6713. AE, MC, V, DC. Closed Sun.*

¢ **Sanabresa.** You can tell by the clientele what a find this is: a demanding crowd of working men and women and penurious dance students from the nearby flamenco school. The menu is classic Spanish fare, with wholesome meals like the *pechuga villaroy* (breaded roast chicken with white sauce) and paella. If you arrive later than 1:30, you'll wait in line for lunch. *Amor de Díos 12, no phone. No credit cards. Closed Sun. eve. and Aug.*

¢ **Zara.** Here's one of the finest gastronomic expressions of Madrid's Cuban community, second in size only to Miami's. Low prices and hearty Cuban specialties have made this small restaurant an extremely popular lunch spot—so popular you should plan on getting there before 1:30 for lunch. It's a dim room, without natural light and crowded with tables, but the animated talk of Cuban expatriates gives it great life. *Infantas 5, tel. 91/532–2074. AE, DC, MC, V. Closed weekends and Aug.*

Lodging

Affordable hotels in the midst of all the sights and shops are mostly located in 19th-century houses, a great many of which are now small, inexpensive hostels. It's still possible to find a decent, if tiny, room in one of these for less than $20, but you'll have to hunt for it. The scores of such hostels close to the Puerta del Sol and the Plaza Santa Ana are not listed here—their few rooms are snapped up quickly and are impossible to reserve in advance. You can inquire upon arrival, but be prepared with alternatives, especially during high tourist season.

Most of the newer hotels that conform to American standards of comfort are in the northern part of town on either side of the Castellana and are a short metro or bus ride from the center. There are hotel reservation desks in the national and international terminals of the airport and at Chamartín station (tel. 91/315–7894). Or you can contact **La Brújula** (tel. 91/559–9705) on the sixth floor of the Torre de Madrid in Plaza de España, which is open 9–9. It has English-speaking staff and can book hotels all over Spain for a fee of 250 ptas.

For details and price-category definitions, *see* Lodging *in* Staying in Spain, *above.*

$$ Atlantico. Don't be put off by the location on a noisy stretch of Gran Via, or by the rather shabby third-floor lobby. Bright, clean accommodations at good prices is what Atlantico is all about. Rooms are small but comfortable, with fabric wall-coverings and new furniture. All have tile baths. A member of the Best Western chain, this hotel is a favorite with British travelers and is almost always full, so it's a good idea to book well in advance. *Gran Vía 38, 28013, tel. 91/ 522–6480, fax 91/531–0210. 60 rooms. AE, MC, V.*

$$ Capitol. If you like being right in the center of things, then this hotel on the Plaza Callao is for you. It's an older hotel, but four floors have been renovated; the rooms on these floors are more comfortable, but also 30% more expensive. There's a well-decorated reception area and a pleasant cafeteria for breakfast. *Gran Vía 41, tel. 91/521– 8391, fax 91/547–1238. 145 rooms. AE, DC, V.*

$$ Carlos V. For those who like to be right in the center of things, this classic hotel in a quiet pedestrian zone is a good option. A suit of armor decorates the tiny lobby, while crystal chandeliers add elegance to a second-floor guest lounge. All rooms are bright and carpeted. *Maestro Victoria 5, 28013, tel. 91/531–3761. 67 rooms. AE, MC, V.*

$$ Paris. Overlooking the Puerta del Sol, the Paris is a stylish hotel full of old-fashioned appeal. It has an impressive turn-of-the-century lobby and a restaurant where you can dine for around 1,500 ptas. Recently refurbished, the hotel has managed to retain its character while adding modern amenities. *Alcalá 2, tel. 91/521–6496, fax 91/ 531–0188. 114 rooms. Facilities: Restaurant. MC, V.*

$ Cliper. This simple hotel offers good value for the cost-conscious traveler. It's tucked away in a side street off the central part of Gran Vía between Callao and Red San Luis. *Chinchilla 6, tel. 91/531– 1700. 52 rooms. AE, MC, V.*

$ ★ Inglés. The exterior may seem shabby but don't be deterred. The Inglés is a long-standing budget favorite. Its rooms are comfortable, with good facilities, and the location is a real bonus: You're a short walk from the Puerta del Sol one way and from the Prado, the other; inexpensive restaurants and atmospheric bars are right at hand. *Echegaray 10, tel. 91/429–6551, fax 91/420–2423, fax 91/420–2423. 58 rooms. Facilities: Cafeteria, bar, exercise room, parking (fee). AE, DC, MC, V.*

$ **Hotel Mora.** Directly across the Paseo del Prado from the Botanical Gardens, the Mora underwent a complete renovation in 1994 and now has a sparkling faux-marble lobby and bright, carpeted hallways. Guest rooms are modestly decorated but large and comfortable; those on the street side have great views of the gardens and the Prado (they're also fairly quiet, thanks to the double-pane windows). *Paseo del Prado 32, 28014, tel. 91/420–1569, fax 91/420–0564. 61 rooms. AE, DC, MC, V.*

$ **Ramón de la Cruz.** If you don't mind a longish metro ride from the center of town, this medium-size hotel is a find. The rooms are large, with modern bathrooms, and the lobby is spacious, with stone floors. Given Madrid prices, it's a bargain. *Don Ramón de la Cruz 94, tel. 91/401–7200, fax 91/402–2126. 103 rooms. Facilities: Cafeteria. MC, V.*

¢ **Lisboa.** Clean, small, and central, the Lisboa has for years been a well-kept secret just off the Plaza de Santa Ana. It offers no frills but it's in a good location on a busy bar and restaurant street. The rooms tend to vary greatly in size and quality. Most of them are sparsely furnished, with tile floors and papered walls, but they are clean and functional. There's a tiny lobby. *Ventura de la Vega 17, tel. 91/429–9894. 22 rooms. AE, DC, MC, V.*

Bars and Cafés

Bars **The Mesones.** The most traditional and colorful taverns are on Cuchilleros and Cava San Miguel, just west of Plaza Mayor, where you'll find a whole array of mesones with names like **Tortilla**, **Champiñón**, and **Huevo**.

Old Madrid. Wander the narrow streets between Puerta del Sol and Plaza Santa Ana, which are packed with traditional tapas bars. Favorites here are the **Cervecería Alemana**, Plaza Santa Ana 6, a beer hall founded more than 100 years ago by Germans and patronized, inevitably, by Hemingway; **Los Gabrieles**, Echegaray 17, with magnificent ceramic decor; **La Trucha**, Manuel Fernández y González 3, with loads of atmosphere; and **Viva Madrid**, Fernández y González 7, a lovely old bar.

Calle Huertas. Fashionable wine bars with turn-of-the-century decor and chamber or guitar music, often live, line this street. **La Fídula** at No. 57 and **El Hecho** at No. 56 are two of the best.

Plaza Santa Barbara. This area, just off Alonso Martínez, is packed with fashionable bars and beer halls. Stroll along Santa Teresa, Orellana, Campoamor, or Fernando VI and take your pick. The **Cervecería Santa Barbara,** in the plaza itself, is one of the most colorful, a popular beer hall with a good range of tapas.

Cafés If you like cafés with an old-fashioned atmosphere, dark wooden counters, brass pumps, and marble-top tables, try any of the following: **Café Comercial**, Glorieta de Bilbao 7; **Café Gijón**, Paseo de Recoletos 21, a former literary hangout and the most famous of the cafés of old, now one of the many café-terraces that line the Castellana; **Café León**, Alcalá 57, just up from Cibeles; and **El Espejo**, Paseo de Recoletos 31, with art-nouveau decor and an outdoor terrace in summer.

The Arts

Details of all cultural events are listed in the daily newspaper *El País* or in the weekly *Guía del Ocio*.

Concerts The main concert hall for classical music is the **Auditorio Nacional de Madrid** (tel. 91/337–0100), Príncipe de Vergara 146 (metro, Cruz del Royo).

Zarzuela and Dance Zarzuela, a combination of light opera and dance ideal for non-Spanish speakers, is held at the **Teatro Nacional Lírico de la Zarzuela**, Jovellanos 4, tel. 91/429–8225. The season runs from October to July.

Theater If language is no problem, check out the fringe theaters in Lavapiés and the **Centro Cultural de la Villa** (tel. 91/575–6080) beneath the Plaza Colón and the open-air events in the Retiro Park. Other leading theaters—you'll also need reasonable Spanish—include the **Círculo de Bellas Artes,** Marqués de Casa Riera 2, just off Alcalá 42 (tel. 91/531–7700); the **Teatro Español,** Príncipe 25 on Plaza Santa Ana (tel. 91/429–0318) for Spanish classics; and the **Teatro María Guerrero,** Tamayo y Baus 4 (tel. 91/310–2949), home of the Centro Dramático Nacional, for plays by García Lorca. Most theaters have two curtains, at 7 and 10:30 PM, and close on Mondays. Tickets are inexpensive and often easy to come by on the night of performance.

Films Foreign films are mostly dubbed into Spanish, but movies in English are listed in *El País* or *Guía del Ocio* under "V.O.," meaning *versión original*. A dozen or so theaters now show films in English; some of the best bets are **Alphaville** and **Cines Renoir,** both in Martín de los Heros, just off Plaza España, and the **Filmoteca Español** (Santa Isabel 3), a city-run institution where first-rate V.O. films change daily.

Nightlife

Cabaret **Florida Park** (tel. 91/573–7805), in the Retiro Park, offers dinner and a show that often features ballet, Spanish dance, or flamenco and is open Monday to Saturday from 9:30 PM with shows at 10:45 PM. **Berlin** (Costanilla de San Pedro 11, tel. 91/366–2034) opens at 9:30 PM for a dinner that is good by most cabaret standards, followed by a show and dancing until 4 AM. **La Scala** (Rosario Pino 7, tel. 91/571–4411), in the Meliá Castilla hotel, is Madrid's top nightclub, with dinner, dancing, cabaret at 8:30, and a second, less expensive show around midnight. This is the one visited by most night tours.

Flamenco Madrid offers the widest choice of flamenco shows in Spain; some are good, but many are aimed at the tourist trade. Dinner tends to be mediocre and overpriced, but it ensures the best seats; otherwise, opt for the show and a drink *(consumición)* only, usually starting around 11 PM and costing around 3,000 ptas.–3,500 ptas. **Arco de Cuchilleros** (Cuchilleros 7, tel. 91/366–5867), behind the Plaza Mayor, is one of the better, cheaper ones. **Café de Chinitas** (Torija 7, tel. 91/547–1502) and **Corral de la Morería** (Morería 17, tel. 91/365–8446) are two of the more authentic places where well-known troupes perform. Another choice is **Corral de la Pacheca** (Juan Ramón Jiménez 26, tel. 91/458–1113). **Zambra** (Velázquez 8, tel. 91/435–5164), in the Hotel Wellington, is one of the smartest (jacket and tie essential), with a good show and dinner served into the small hours.

Jazz The leading club of the moment is **Café Central** (Plaza de Angel 10), followed by **Clamores** (Albuquerque 14). Others include **Café Jazz Populart** (Huertas 22) and **El Despertar** (Torrecilla del Leal 18). Excellent jazz frequently comes to Madrid as part of city-hosted seasonal festivals; check the local press for listings and venues.

Casino **Madrid's Casino** (tel. 91/859–0312) is 28 kilometers (17 miles) out at Torrelodones on the N-VI road to La Coruña. *Open 5 PM–4 AM. Free transportation service from Plaza de España 6.*

Madrid Environs

The beauty of the historic cities surrounding Madrid and the role they have played in their country's history rank them among Spain's most worthwhile sights. Ancient Toledo, the great palace-monastery of El Escorial, the sturdy medieval walls of Ávila, and the magnificent Plaza Mayor of the old university town of Salamanca all lie within an hour or so from the capital.

It's possible to visit all the towns below, with the exception of Salamanca, on day trips from Madrid—either by bus or train, or by organized tour (inquire at any travel agency). But you'll find it far more rewarding to spend a night or two in your destination cities. Long after the day-trippers have gone home, you discover the real charm of these small provincial towns and wander at leisure throughout their medieval streets. In some cases, you'll have to return to Madrid to visit another one of the outlying towns; in others, there's direct service, usually by bus.

Getting There

Trains to Toledo leave from Madrid's Atocha Station (metro: Atocha-RENFE); to Salamanca, El Escorial, and Ávila from Chamartín (metro: Chamartín). Madrid has no central bus station, and buses are generally less popular than trains. La Sepulvedana (Paseo de la Florida 11, near the Norte station, tel. 91/527–9537) serves Ávila; Estación del Sur (Canarias 17, tel. 91/468–4200) has buses to Toledo; Auto-Rés (Plaza Conde de Casal 6, tel. 91/551–7200) serves Salamanca; and Herranz (tel. 91/543–3645) has buses for the Escorial and Valley of the Fallen that depart regularly from Calle Fernándo de los Ríos (metro: Moncloa).

Getting Around

There's a direct train from Madrid, making stops in El Escorial, Ávila, and Salamanca; another line goes to Toledo. Tourist offices can help you with schedules. Toledo's bus station is on the Ronda de Castilla la Mancha (tel. 925/215850) just off the road to Madrid; Ávila's bus station is on Avenida de Madrid (tel. 920/220154); and Salamanca's is at Filiberto Villalobos 73 (tel. 923/236717). Regional train stations are all a bit of a walk from the city centers.

Tourist Information

Ávila (Plaza de la Catedral 4, tel. 920/211387); open weekdays 8–3 and 4–6 (5–7 in summer), Saturday 9–1:30.
El Escorial (Floridablanca 10, tel. 91/8901554); open weekdays 9–2 and 3–5, Saturday 9–1:45.
Salamanca (Casa de las Conchas, Rua Mayor 70, tel. 923/270340); open weekdays 9:30–2 and 4:30–8, Saturday 10–2. There's also an information booth on the Plaza Mayor (market side).
Toledo (Puerta Nueva de Bisagra tel. 925/220843); open weekdays 9–2 and 4–6, Saturday 9:30–1:30.

Exploring the Madrid Environs

The following includes tours of Toledo, El Escorial, the Valley of the Fallen, Ávila, and Salamanca. You'll want to work out the best mode of transportation according to the towns you intend to visit.

Toledo   By bus or train, the trip to **Toledo** is drab and industrial. But after about 90 minutes of travel, the unforgettable silhouette of Toledo suddenly rises before you, the imposing bulk of the Alcazar and the slender spire of the cathedral dominating the skyline. This former capital, where Moors, Jews, and Christians once lived in harmony, is now a living national monument, depicting all the elements of Spanish civilization in hand-carved, sun-mellowed stone. For a stunning view and to capture the beauty of Toledo as El Greco knew it, begin with a panoramic drive around the Carretera de Circunvalación, crossing over the Alcántara bridge and returning by way of the bridge of San Martín. As you gaze at the city rising like an island in its own bend of the Tagus, reflect how little the city skyline has changed in the four centuries since El Greco painted *Storm Over Toledo.*

Toledo is a small city steeped in history and full of magnificent buildings. It was the capital of Spain under both Moors and Christians until some whim caused Philip II to move his capital to Madrid in 1561. Begin your visit with a drink in one of the many terrace cafés on the central **Plaza Zocodover**, study a map, and try to get your bearings, for a veritable labyrinth confronts you as you try to find your way to Toledo's great treasures. While here, search the square's pastry shops for the typical marzipan candies *(mazapanes)* of Toledo.

Begin your tour with a visit to the 13th-century **Cathedral**, seat of the Cardinal Primate of Spain, and one of the great cathedrals of Spain. Somber but elaborate, it blazes with jeweled chalices, gorgeous ecclesiastical vestments, historic tapestries, some 750 stained-glass windows, and paintings by Tintoretto, Titian, Murillo, El Greco, Velázquez, and Goya. The cathedral has two surprises: a **Mozarabic chapel**, where Mass is still celebrated on Sundays according to an ancient Mozarabic rite handed down from the days of the Visigoths (AD 419–711), and its unique **Transparente,** an extravagent Baroque roof that gives a theatrical glimpse into heaven as the sunlight pours down through a mass of figures and clouds. *Admission: 400 ptas. Open Tues.–Sat. 10:30–1 and 3:30–6 (7 in summer), Sun. 10:30–1:00 and 4–6, closed Mon.*

En route to the real jewel of Toledo, the **Chapel of Santo Tomé,** you'll pass a host of souvenir shops on Calle Santo Tomé, bursting with damascene knives and swords, blue-and-yellow pottery from nearby Talavera, and El Greco reproductions. In the tiny chapel that houses El Greco's masterpiece, *The Burial of the Count of Orgaz*, you can capture the true spirit of the Greek painter who adopted Spain, and in particular Toledo, as his home. Do you recognize the sixth man from the left among the painting's earthly contingent? Or the young boy in the left-hand corner? The first is El Greco himself, the second his son Jorge Manuel—see 1578, the year of his birth, embroidered on his handkerchief. *Admission: 100 ptas. Open daily 10–1:45 and 3:30–5:45 (6:45 in summer).*

Not far away is **El Greco's House,** a replica containing copies of his works. *Tel. 925/224046. Closed for restoration until 1990.*

The splendid **Sinagoga del Tránsito** stands on the corner of Samuel Levi and Reyes Católicos. Commissioned in 1366 by Samuel Levi, chancellor to Pedro the Cruel, the synagogue shows Christian and Moorish as well as Jewish influences in its architecture and decoration—look at the stars of David interspersed with the arms of Castile and León. There's also a small **Sephardic Museum** chronicling the life of Toledo's former Jewish community. *Admission: 400 ptas. Open Tues.–Sat. 10–2 and 4–6, Sun. 10–2.*

Another synagogue, the incongruously named **Santa María la Blanca** (it was given as a church to the Knights of Calatrava in 1405), is just along the street. Its history may have been Jewish and Christian, but its architecture is definitely Moorish, for it resembles a mosque with five naves, horseshoe arches, and capitals decorated with texts from the Koran. *Admission: 100 ptas. Open daily 10–2 and 3:30–6 (7 in summer).*

Across the road is **San Juan de los Reyes,** a beautiful Gothic church begun by Ferdinand and Isabella in 1476. Wander around its fine cloisters and don't miss the iron manacles on the outer walls; they were placed there by Christians freed by the Moors. The Catholic Kings originally intended to be buried here, but then their great triumph at Granada in 1492 changed their plans. *Admission: 100 ptas. Open daily 10–1:30 and 3:30–5:45 (6:45 in summer).*

El Escorial In the foothills of the Guadarrama Mountains, 50 kilometers (31 miles) to the northwest of Madrid (an easy day trip by bus or train) and 120 kilometers (74 miles) from Toledo, lies **San Lorenzo de El Escorial,** burial place of Spanish kings and queens. The **Monastery,** built by the religious fanatic Philip II as a memorial to his father, Charles V, is a vast rectangular edifice, conceived and executed with a monotonous magnificence worthy of the Spanish royal necropolis. It was designed by Juan de Herrera, Spain's greatest Renaissance architect. The **Royal Pantheon** contains the tombs of monarchs from Charles V to Alfonso XIII, grandfather of Juan Carlos, and those of their consorts. Only two kings are missing, Philip V, who chose to be buried in his beloved La Granja, and Ferdinand VI, buried in Madrid. In the **Pantheon of the Infantes** rest the 60 royal children who died in infancy and those queens who bore no heirs. The lavishly bejeweled tomb here belongs to Don Juan, bastard son of Charles V and half brother of Philip II, dashing hero and victor of the Battle of Lepanto. The monastery's other highlights are the magnificent **Library of Philip II,** with 40,000 rare volumes and 2,700 illuminated manuscripts, including the diary of Santa Teresa, and the **Royal Apartments.** Contrast the spartan private apartment of Philip II and the simple bedroom in which he died in 1598 with the beautiful carpets, porcelain, and tapestries with which his less austere successors embellished the rest of his somber monastery-palace. *Tel. 91/890–5905. Admission: 800 ptas. for whole complex, including Casita del Príncipe. Open Tues.–Sun. 10–6 (7 in summer). Last entry is 45 mins. before closing time.*

The **Valley of the Fallen** is easily reached by bus from Madrid; many tours to the Escorial include a visit to the Valley of the Fallen. This vast basilica, hewn out of sheer granite, was built by General Franco between 1940 and 1959 as a monument to the dead of Spain's Civil War of 1936–39. Buried here are 43,000 war dead; José Antonio Primo de Rivera, founder of the Falangists and early martyr of the war; and Franco himself, who died in 1975. A funicular to the top of the monument costs 200 ptas. *Tel. 91/890–5611. Admission: 400 ptas. Open Tues.–Sun. 10–7 (6 in winter); closed Mon.*

Ávila Ávila, almost 1,240 meters (4,000 feet) above sea level, is the highest provincial capital in Spain. Alfonso VI and his son-in-law, Count Raimundo de Borgoña, rebuilt the town and walls in 1090, bringing it permanently under Christian control. It is these walls, the most complete military installations of their kind in Spain, that give Ávila its special medieval quality. Thick and solid, with 88 towers tufted with numerous untidy storks' nests, they stretch for 2½ kilometers (1½ miles) around the entire city and make an ideal focus for the start of your visit. For a superb overall view and photo spot, drive out to the **Cuatro Postes,** three-quarters of a kilometer (half a mile) out on the road to Salamanca.

The personality of Santa Teresa the Mystic, to whom the city is dedicated, lives today as vividly as it did in the 16th century. Several religious institutions associated with the life of the saint are open to visitors, the most popular of which is the **Convent of Santa Teresa,** which stands on the site of her birthplace. There's an ornate Baroque chapel, a small gift shop, and a museum with some of her relics: her rosary, books, walking stick, a sole of her sandal, and her finger wearing her wedding ring. *At Plaza de la Santa, just inside the southern gate, tel. 920/21130. Open daily 9:30–1:30 and 3:30–8.*

Ávila's other ecclesiastical monuments are far older and more rewarding than those that commemorate the saint. The impregnable hulk of the **cathedral** is in many ways more akin to a fortress than a house of God. Though of Romanesque origin—the Romanesque sections are recognizable by their red-and-white brickwork—it is usually claimed as Spain's first Gothic cathedral. Inside, the ornate alabaster tomb of Cardinal Alonso de Madrigal, a 15th-century bishop whose swarthy complexion earned him the nickname of "El Tostado" (the toasted one), is thought to be the work of Domenico Fancelli, who also sculpted the tomb of Prince Juan in Santo Tomás and the sepulchers of the Catholic Kings in Granada's Royal Chapel. *Tel. 920/211641. Admission free. Cathedral open daily summer 10–1 and 3:30–7; winter 10–2. Admission: 200 ptas.*

Salamanca Farthest from Madrid of the towns we have visited, **Salamanca** is an ancient city, and your first glimpse of it is bound to be unforgettable. Beside the road flows the Tormes River and beyond it rise the old houses of the city and the golden walls, turrets, and domes of the Plateresque cathedrals. "Plateresque" comes from *plata* (silver) and implies that the stone is chiseled and engraved as intricately as that delicate metal. A superb example of this style is the facade of the Dominican **Monastery of San Esteban** (150 ptas.; open daily 9–1 and 4–7, 5–8 in summer), which you'll pass on your way to the cathedrals. The **old cathedral** far outshines its younger sister, the **new cathedral,** in beauty. (The new cathedral's funds ran out during construction—1513–1733—leaving a rather bare interior.) Inside the sturdy Romanesque walls of the old cathedral, built between 1102 and 1160, your attention will be drawn to Nicolás Florentino's stunning altarpiece with 53 brightly painted panels. Don't miss the splendid **cloisters,** which now house a worthwhile collection of religious art, and the **Degree Chapel,** where anxious students sought inspiration on the night before their final exams. *New cathedral free; old cathedral and cloisters 200 ptas. Open daily 10–2 and 4–7.*

Founded by Alfonso IX in 1218, **Salamanca University** is to Spain what Oxford University is to England. On its famous **doorway** in the Patio de las Escuelas, a profusion of Plateresque carving surrounds the medallions of Ferdinand and Isabella. See if you can find the famous frog and skull, said to bring good luck to students in their examinations. Inside, the **lecture room** of Fray Luis de León has remained untouched since the days of the great scholar, and the prestigious **library** boasts some 50,000 parchment and leather-bound volumes. *Tel. 923/294400, ext. 1150. Library admission: 200 ptas. Open Mon.–Sat. 9:30–1:30 and 4–6, Sun. 10–1.*

Now make for Salamanca's greatest jewel, the elegant 18th-century **Plaza Mayor.** Here you can browse in stores offering typical *charro* jewelry (silver and black flowerheads), head down the steps to the market in search of colorful tapas bars, or simply relax in an outdoor café. In this, the city's crowning glory and the most exquisite square in Spain, you've found the perfect place to end your tour of Salamanca and Castile.

Dining and Lodging

For details and price-category definitions, *see* Dining and Lodging *in* Staying in Spain, *above.*

Ávila **El Fogón de Santa Teresa.** Traditional Castilian roasts, lamb chops,
Dining and trout are featured on the menu of this attractive restaurant in the vaults of the Palacio de Valderrábanos. *Alemania 3, tel. 920/211023. AE, DC, MC, V. $$*

★ **El Rastro.** This ancient inn, tucked into the city walls, is Ávila's most atmospheric place to dine. Local specialties include Ávila's famous veal *(ternera)* and *yemas de Santa Teresa,* a dessert made from candied egg yolks. *Plaza del Rastro 1, tel. 920/211218. AE, DC, MC, V. $$*

El Torreón. Castilian specialties are served in this typical mesón, situated in the basement of the old Velada Palace, opposite the cathedral. *Tostado 1, tel. 920/213171. AE, MC, V. $$*

Lodging **Don Carmelo.** This functional, modern, and comfortable hotel, close to the station, is Ávila's best moderate bet. *Paseo Don Carmelo 30, tel. 920/228050. 60 rooms. V. $$*

Las Cancelas. In the heart of the old city, this 14-room hostel—which even has its own elevator—is a good economical choice, although you'll have to share a bathroom. Every room has a view of the street. *Cruz Vieja 6, 920/212249. 14 rooms. V. $*

Continental. Many of the rooms in this aging but still-charming hotel on the Plaza de la Catedral have remarkable views of the cathedral. The rooms are large, if somewhat fading. *Plaza de la Catedral 6, tel. 920/211502. 57 rooms. AE, MC, V. ¢*

El Escorial **El Candil.** One of the best of the many middle-range restaurants in
Dining El Escorial, El Candil is situated above a bar on the corner of Plaza San Lorenzo on the village's main street. In summer you can dine outdoors in the square, a delightful spot. *Reina Victoria 12, tel. 91/890–4103. AE, DC, MC, V. $$*

Mesón de la Cueva. Founded in 1768, this atmospheric mesón has several small, rustic dining rooms. This inn is a must for ambience, and the food is good, too. *San Antón 4, tel. 91/890–1516. Reservations advised on weekends. AE, DC, MC, V. $$*

Cafeteria del Arte. Just a few steps from El Escorial monastery, this restaurant-café is a perfect spot for a light meal or snack. It's part of a complex that includes the much more formal Carillon restaurant and the Hotel Florida. One delightful regional dish is the *chocolate con picatostas* (hot chocolate with toasted bread). *Floridablanca 14, tel. 91/890–1520. AE, MC, V. ¢*

Lodging **Miranda Suizo.** Rooms are comfortable in this charming old hotel on the main street, and the hotel café, with its dark wood fittings and marble tables, is right out of the 19th century. *Floridablanca 20, tel. 91/890–4711, fax 91/8904358. 47 rooms. AE, DC, MC, V. $$*

Salamanca **Chapeau.** This chic spot offers both meat and fish, carefully roasted
Dining in its wood-fired ovens. Try the *pimientos rellenos* (stuffed peppers)
★ and orange mousse for dessert. *Gran Vía 20, tel. 923/271833. Reservations advised. AE, DC, MC, V. Closed Sun. in summer. $$*

El Mesón. There's plenty of colorful atmosphere and good traditional Castilian food in this typical mesón, just off the Plaza Mayor, beside the Gran Hotel. *Plaza Poeta Iglesias 10, tel. 923/217222. AE, MC, V. Closed Jan. $$*

Río de la Plata. This small, atmospheric restaurant, close to El Mesón and the Gran Hotel, serves superb *farinato* sausage; it's a great find. *Plaza del Peso 1, tel. 923/219005. AE, MC, V. Closed Mon., July. $$*

El Bardo. Students and others daily pack this popular Salamanca restaurant, a bustling place with three wood-and-stone dining rooms. Both a regular and a vegetarian menú del día are offered—exceedingly unusual for Spain. Other specialties prepared by the friendly owners include the house salad and a fine *crema de champiñon* (mushroom soup). *Compania 8, tel. 923/219089. V. ¢*

Lodging **Castellano III.** Overlooking the Alamedilla Park, just a few minutes' walk from the center, this comfortable, modern hotel is considered the best medium-price hotel in town. *San Francisco Javier 2, tel. 923/261611, fax 923/266741. 73 rooms. AE, MC, V. $$*

Condal. This is a functional but comfortable hotel in a central location just off Calle Azafranal, two minutes from the Plaza Mayor. *Santa Eulalia 3–5, tel. 923/218400. 70 rooms. AE, DC, MC, V. $*

Tormes. This is a clean, well-kept family hostel with a TV lounge and a central location—a good choice for basic accommodations. *Rua Mayor 20, tel. 923/219683. 12 rooms. No credit cards. $*

Toledo **Asador Adolfo.** This restaurant near the cathedral is well known for
Dining its good service and good food—Try the superb roast meat and the
★ *pimentos del piquillo rellenos de pescado* (peppers stuffed with fish). *Calle de la Granada 6, tel. 925/227321. AE, DC, MC, V. Closed Sun. eve. $$*

Casa Aurelio. There are two branches of this popular restaurant, both around the corner from the cathedral. Try the partridge or quail. *Sinagoga 6, tel. 925/221392, and Sinagoga 1, tel. 925/221392. AE, DC, MC, V. Closed Wed. $$*

Los Cuatro Tiempos. The picturesque downstairs bar, decorated with ceramic tiles, is an ideal place for a tapas before you head upstairs for a traditional Toledo meal. *Sixto Ramón Parro 7, tel. 925/223782. MC, V. $–$$*

Transito. If you're in the mood for some benchmark Castilian specialties—*sopa castellana* and *ternera asada* (roast veal) among them—this large restaurant, just a few yards from the Santa Maria la Blanca synagogue, facing Plaza de Barrionuevos, is a popular spot. *Reyes Católicos 7, tel. 925/225623. AE, DC, MC, V. $*

Lodging **Alfonso VI.** This pleasant modern hotel has Castilian-style decor
★ and is conveniently located in the center of town by the Alcázar. *Gen. Moscardó 2, tel. 925/222600, fax 925/214458. 80 rooms. AE, DC, MC, V. $$*

Carlos V. No hotel in town enjoys such a convenient location as this one, halfway between the Alcázar and the main square. It stands on a delightful square of its own, with an excellent view of the town. The staff is exceptionally friendly, and the entire hotel was renovated in 1992—including the addition of a Mudejar-style restaurant. *Plaza Horno de los Vizcochos, tel. 925/222100. 55 rooms. AE, MC, V. $$*

María Cristina. You'll pass this comfortable new hotel on your way from Madrid. Located beside the bullring, it provides excellent facilities. Its El Abside restaurant is fast gaining in prestige. *Marqués de Mendigorría 1, tel. 925/213202. 65 rooms. AE, V. $$*

Barcelona

Arriving and Departing

By Plane All international and domestic flights arrive at **El Prat de Llobregat** airport, 14 kilometers (8½ miles) south of Barcelona, just off the main highway to Castelldefels and Sitges. For information on arrival and departure times, call the airport (tel. 93/478–5000 ext. 2086 or 478–5032) or Iberia information (tel. 93/412–5667).

Between the The airport–city train leaves every 30 minutes between 6:30 AM and
Airport and 11 PM and reaches the Barcelona Central (Sants) Station in 15 minutes;
Downtown a new extension now carries you to the Plaça de Catalunya, at the head of the Ramblas, in the heart of the old city. Taxis will then take you to your hotel. The Aerobus service connects the airport with Plaza Catalunya every 15 minutes between 6:25 AM and 11 PM; pay the driver the fare of 450 ptas. RENFE provides a bus service to the Central Station during the night hours. A cab from the airport to your hotel, including airport and luggage surcharges, will cost about 2,000 ptas.

By Train The old Terminal (or **França**) Station on Avenida Marquès de l'Argentera reopened in 1992 after major renovations and now serves as the main terminal for trains to France and some express trains to points in Spain. The Central (**Sants**) Station on Plaça Paisos Catalans, which was a long-distance station while França was under renovation, now serves suburban destinations, as well as most cities in Spain. Inquire at the tourist office to find out which station you need. Many long-distance trains also stop at the **Passeig de Gràcia** underground station at the junction of Aragó. This station is closer to the Plaça de Catalunya and Ramblas area than is Central (Sants), but though tickets and information are available here, luggage carts and taxi ranks are not. Check with tourist offices for current travel information and phone numbers. For RENFE information, call 93/490–0202 (24 hours).

By Bus Barcelona has no central bus station, but many buses operate from the old Estació Vilanova (or Norte) at the end of Avenida Vilanova. **Julià,** Ronda Universitat 5, runs buses to Zaragoza and Montserrat; and **Alsina Graëlls,** Ronda Universitat 4, to Lérida and Andorra.

Getting Around

Modern Barcelona above the Plaça de Catalunya is built mostly on a grid system, though there's no helpful numbering system as in the United States. The Old Town, from the Plaça de Catalunya to the port, is a warren of narrow streets, however, and you'll need a good street map to get around. Most sightseeing can be done on foot—you won't have any other choice in the Gothic Quarter—but you'll need to use the metro or buses to link sightseeing areas.

By Metro The subway is the fastest way of getting around, as well as the easiest to use. You pay a flat fare of 135 ptas., no matter how far you travel, or purchase a **targeta multiviatge,** good for 10 rides (600 ptas.). Plans of the system are available from main metro stations or from branches of the Caixa savings bank.

By Bus City buses run from about 5:30 or 6 AM to 10:30 PM, though some stop earlier. Again, there's a flat-fare system (135 ptas.). Plans of the routes followed are displayed at bus stops. A reduced-rate targeta multiviatge, good for 10 rides (600 ptas.), can be purchased at the transport kiosk on Plaça de Catalunya.

By Cable Car and Funicular Montjuïc Funicular is a cog railroad that runs from the junction of Avenida Parallel and Nou de la Rambla to the Miramar Amusement Park on Montjuïc. It runs only when the amusement park is open (11–8:15 in winter, noon–2:45 and 4:30–9:25 in summer). A cable car (*telefèric*) then runs from the amusement park up to Montjuïc Castle (noon–8 daily in summer; winter, weekends only, 11–7:30).

A **Transbordador Aeri Harbor Cable Car** runs from Miramar on Montjuïc, across the harbor to the Torre de Jaume I on Barcelona *moll* (quay), and on to the Torre de Sant Sebastià at the end of Passeig Joan de Borbó in Barceloneta. You can board at either stage. *Fare 850 ptas. (1000 ptas. round-trip). Operates Oct.–June, weekdays noon to 5:45, weekends noon to 6:15; June–Oct., daily 11 to 9.*

To reach Tibidabo summit, take either Bus 58 or the Ferrocarrils de la Generalitat train from Plaça de Catalunya to Avenida Tibidabo, then the *tramvía blau* (blue tram) to Peu del Funicular, and the Tibidabo Funicular from there to the Tibidabo Fairground. The funicular runs every half hour from 7:15 AM to 9:45 PM.

By Boat **Golondrinas** harbor boats operate short harbor trips from the Portal de la Pau near the Columbus Monument between 10 AM and 1:30 PM weekends only in winter, daily in summer between 10 AM and 8 PM.

Important Addresses and Numbers

Tourist Information The city's three main tourist offices are at **Central** (Sants) train station (tel. 93/491–4431, open daily 8–8), the **França** train station (tel. 93/319–5758, open daily 8–8), and at the **airport** (tel. 93/478–4704, open Mon.–Sat. 9:30–8).

Information on the province and city can be found at the useful office at Gran Vía 658 (tel. 93/301–7443; open weekdays 9–7, Sat. 9–2).

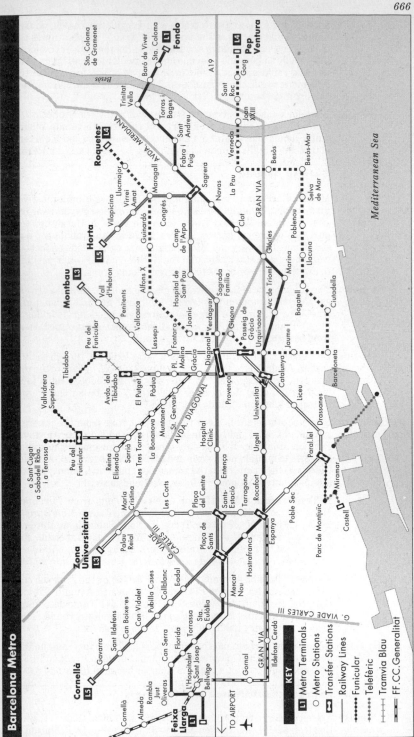

During special events and conferences, a tourist office is open at the **Palav de Congressos** (Av. Maria Cristina, tel. 93/423–3101, ext. 8356); a small office with some pamphlets and maps is found at the **Ajuntament** (Plaça Sant Jaume, tel. 93/402–7000, ext. 433, open daily 9–8 in summer), and cultural information is available during the summer months at the **Palau de la Virreina** (Ramblas 99, tel. 93/301–7775, open Mon.–Sat. 9–9; Sun. 10–2).

American Visitors' Bureau (Gran Vía 591 between Rambla de Catalunya and Balmes, 3rd Floor, tel. 93/301–0150 or 301–0032).

Consulates **U.S.** (Paseo Reina Elisenda de Moncada 23, tel. 93/280–2227), **Canadian** (Vía Augusta 125, tel. 93/209–0634), **U.K.** (Diagonal 477, tel. 93/419–9044).

Emergencies **Police** (National Police, tel. 091; Municipal Police, tel. 092; Main Police [Policía Nacional] Station, Vía Laietana 43, tel. 93/301–6666). **Medical emergencies:** (tel. 061). **On-duty pharmacies:** (tel. 010). **Tourist Attention:** (La Rambla 43, tel. 93/301–9060) is a 24-hour service offered by the police department for crime victims.

Exploring Barcelona

Numbers in the margin correspond to points of interest on the Barcelona map.

Barcelona, capital of Catalonia and Madrid's great rival as one of Spain's two largest cities, thrives on its business acumen and industrial muscle. Its hardworking citizens are proud of and use their own language—with street names, museum exhibits, newspapers, radio programs, and movies all in Catalan (*see* Language *in* Essential Information, *above*). A recent milestone was the realization of their long-cherished goal to host the Olympic Games, held in Barcelona in summer 1992 after a massive building program. The games' legacy to the city includes a vastly improved ring road and several other highways; four new beaches and an entire new neighborhood in what used to be the rundown industrial neighborhood of Barceloneta, near the port; an adjoining marina; and a new sports stadium and pools on the hill of Montjuïc. This thriving metropolis also has a rich history and an abundance of sights. Few places can rival the narrow alleys of its Gothic Quarter for medieval atmosphere, the elegance and distinction of its Modernista Eixample area, or the fantasies of Gaudí's whimsical imagination.

It should take you two full days of sightseeing to complete the following tour. The first part covers the Gothic Quarter, the Picasso Museum, and the Ramblas. The second part takes you to Passeig de Gràcia, the Sagrada Familia, and Montjuïc.

❶ Start on Plaça de la Seu, where on Sunday morning the citizens of Barcelona gather to dance the *Sardana*, a symbol of Catalan identity. Step inside the magnificent Gothic **Catedral**, built between 1298 and 1450, though the spire and Gothic facade were not added until 1892. Highlights are the beautifully carved **choir stalls**, Santa Eulalia's tomb in the crypt, the battle-scarred crucifix from Don Juan's galley in the **Lepanto Chapel**, and the cloisters. *Tel. 93/315–1554. Admission free. Open daily 7:45–1:30 and 4–7:45.*

❷ Around the corner, at Plaza Sant Iu 6, is the **Museu Frederic Marès**, where you can browse for hours among the miscellany of sculptor-collector Frederic Marès. On display is everything from polychrome crucifixes to hat pins, pipes, and walking sticks. *Tel. 93/310–5800. Admission: 350 ptas., Wed. ½ price; 1st Sun. of every month free. Open Tues.–Sat. 10–5, Sun. 10–2; closed Mon.*

❸ The neighboring **Plaça del Rei** embodies the very essence of the Gothic Quarter. Legend has it that after Columbus's first voyage to America, the Catholic Kings received him in the **Saló de Tinell**, a

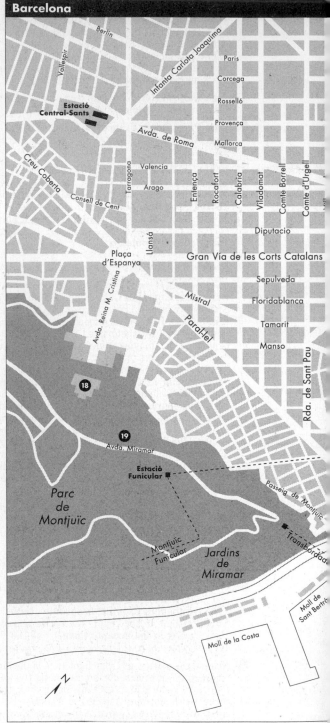

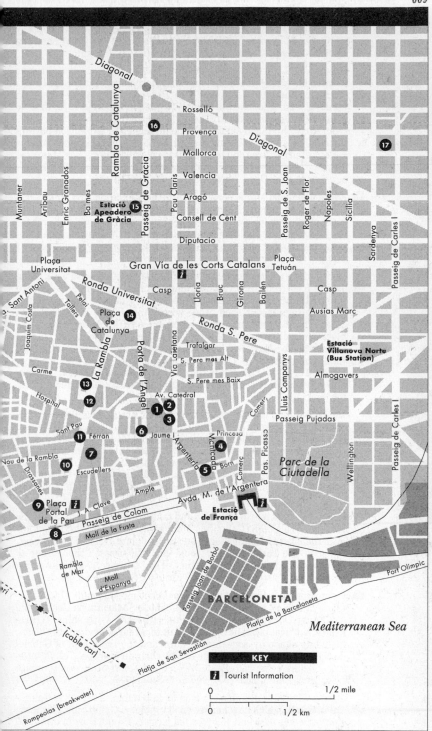

magnificent banqueting hall built in 1362. Other ancient buildings around the square are the **Lieutenant's Palace;** the 14th-century **Chapel of St. Agatha,** built right into the Roman city wall; and the **Padellás Palace,** which houses the City History Museum.

④ Cross Vía Laietana, walk down Princesa, and turn right into Montcada, where you come to one of Barcelona's most popular attractions, the **Museu Picasso.** Two 15th-century palaces provide a striking setting for the collections donated in 1963 and 1970, first by Picasso's secretary, then by the artist himself. The collection ranges from early childhood sketches done in Málaga to exhibition posters done in Paris shortly before his death. Of particular interest are his Blue Period pictures and his variations on Velázquez's *Las Meninas*. *Tel. 93/319–6310. Admission: 500 ptas., Wed. ½ price, 1st Sun. every month free. Open Tues.–Sat. 10–8, Sun. 10–3.*

⑤ **Santa María del Mar** is considered the best example of a Mediterranean Gothic church. It was built between 1329 and 1383 in fulfillment of a vow made a century earlier by Jaume I to build a church for the Virgin of the Sailors. Its simple beauty is enhanced by a stunning rose window and magnificent soaring columns. *Open daily 8–1 and 4–7:30.*

⑥ Continue up Carrer Argentería, cross Vía Laietana, and walk along Jaume I till you come to **Plaça Sant Jaume,** an impressive square built in the 1840s in the heart of the Gothic Quarter. The two imposing buildings facing each other across the square are very much older. The 15th-century **Ajuntament,** or City Hall, has an impressive black-and-gold mural (1928) by Josep María Sert (who also painted the murals for New York's Waldorf Astoria) and the famous **Saló de Cent,** from which the Council of One Hundred ruled the city from 1372 to 1714. The **Palau de la Generalitat,** seat of the Catalan Regional Government, is a 15th-century palace open to the public on Sunday mornings only.

⑦ Continue along the Carrer Ferrán, with its attractive 19th-century shops and numerous Moderniste touches, to the **Plaça Reial.** Here in this splendid, if rather dilapidated, 19th-century square, arcaded houses overlook the wrought-iron **Fountain of the Three Graces** and lampposts designed by a young Gaudí in 1879. Watch out for drug pushers here; the safest and most colorful time to come is on a Sunday morning when crowds gather at the stamp and coin stalls and listen to soap-box orators.

⑧ Head to the bottom of Ramblas and take an elevator to the top of the **Monument a Colon** (Columbus Monument) for a breathtaking view over the city. Columbus faces out to sea, pointing, ironically, east. (Nearby you can board the cable car that crosses the harbor to Montjuïc.) *Admission: 350 ptas., Wed. ½ price, 1st Sun. every month free. Open Tues.–Sat. 10–2 and 3:30–6:30, Sun. 10–7.*

⑨ Our next stop is the **Museu Marítim** (Maritime Museum), (Plaça Portal de la Pau 1), housed in the 13th-century Atarazanas Reales, the old Royal Dockyards. The museum is packed with ships; figureheads; nautical paraphernalia; and several early navigation charts, including a map by Amerigo Vespucci and the 1439 chart of Gabriel de Valseca from Mallorca, the oldest chart in Europe. *Tel. 93/318–3245. Admission: 350 ptas., Wed. ½ price, 1st Sun. every month free. Open Tues.–Sat. 10–2 and 4–7, Sun. 10–2.*

⑩ Turn back up the Ramblas to Nou de la Rambla. At No. 3 is Gaudí's **Palau Güell,** which now houses an art gallery. Gaudí built this mansion between 1885 and 1890 for his patron, Count Eusebi de Güell, and it's the only one of his houses that is readily open to the public. *Admission: 350 ptas. Open Tues.–Sat. 11–2 and 5–8.*

⑪ Our next landmark, the **Gran Teatre del Liceu,** Barcelona's famous opera house, was tragically gutted by fire in early 1994. Until recently one of the oldest and most beautiful opera houses in the world, the Liceu is being restored and is expected to open again in 1997. *Visits to certain halls and rooms that were not damaged can be arranged (tel. 93/318–9122).*

⑫ This next stretch of the **Ramblas** is one of the most fascinating. The colorful paving stones on the Plaça de la Boquería were designed by Joan Miró. Glance up at the swirling Moderniste dragon and the Art Nouveau street lamps. Then take a look inside the bustling **Boquería Market** and the **Antigua Casa Figueras**, a vintage pastry shop on the corner of Petxina, with a splendid mosaic facade.

⑬ The **Palau de la Virreina** was built by a viceroy from Peru in 1778. It's recently been converted into a major exhibition center, and you should check to see what's showing while you're in town. *Rambla de las Flores 99, tel. 93/301–7775. Admission: 300 ptas. Open Tues.– Sat. 10–2 and 4:30–9, Sun. 10–2, Mon. 4:30–9. Last entrance 30 mins. before closing.*

On the next block is the 18th-century **Church of Betlem** (Bethlehem) and, opposite, the handsome ocher Baroque **Palau de Moja,** built in 1702.

⑭ The final stretch of the Ramblas brings us out onto the busy **Plaça de Catalunya,** the frantic business center and transport hub of the modern city. The first stage of the tour ends here. You may want to head for the Corte Inglés department store across the square or for any of the stores on the nearby **Porta de l'Angel.** Alternatively, you can relax on the terrace of the ancient **Café Zurich** at the head of the Rambla or stop at the colorful beer hall, the **Cervecería,** opposite the Hostal Continental.

Above the Plaça de Catalunya you come into modern Barcelona and an elegant area known as the **Eixample,** which was laid out in the late 19th century as part of the city's expansion scheme. Much of the building here was done at the height of the **Moderniste** movement, a Spanish and mainly Catalan offshoot of Art Nouveau, whose leading exponents were the architects Antoni Gaudí, Domènech i Montaner, and Puig i Cadafalch. The principal thoroughfares of the Eixample are the Rambla de Catalunya and the Passeig de Gràcia, where some of the city's most elegant shops and cafés are found. Modernista houses are one of Barcelona's special drawing cards, so walk up

⑮ **Passeig de Gràcia** until you come to the **Manzana de la Discòrdia,** or Block of Discord, between Consell de Cent and Aragó. Its name is a pun on the word *manzana,* which means both "block" and "apple." The houses here are quite fantastic: The floral **Casa Lleó Morera** at No. 35 is by Domènech i Montaner. The pseudo-Gothic **Casa Amatller** at No. 41 is by Puig i Cadafalch. At No. 43 is Gaudí's **Casa Batlló.** Farther along the street on the right, on the corner of

⑯ Provença, is Gaudí's **Casa Milà** (Passeig de Gràcia 92), more often known as **La Pedrera** (which, along with Casa Batlló, was dramatically spruced up in conjunction with the 1992 Olympics). Its remarkable curving stone facade with ornamental balconies actually ripples its way around the corner of the block.

Now take the metro at Diagonal directly to Barcelona's most eccen-

⑰ tric landmark, Gaudí's **Temple Expiatori de la Sagrada Família** (Holy Family). Far from finished at his death in 1926—Gaudí was run over by a tram and died in a pauper's hospital—this striking creation will cause consternation or wonder, shrieks of protest or cries of rapture. In 1936, during the Civil War, the citizens of Barcelona loved their crazy temple enough to spare it from the flames that engulfed all their other churches except the cathedral. An elevator takes visitors to the top of one of the towers for a magnificent view of the city. Gaudí is buried in the crypt. *Tel. 93/455–0247. Admission: 800 ptas. Open Sept.–May, daily 9–7; June–Aug., daily 9–9.*

Back across town to the south, the hill of **Montjuïc** was named for the Jewish community that once lived on its slopes. Montjuïc is home to a castle, an amusement park, several delightful gardens, a model Spanish village, an illuminated fountain, the recently rebuilt Mies van der Rohe Pavilion, and a cluster of museums—all of which could keep you busy for a day or more. This was the principal venue for the 1992 Olympics.

⑱ One of the leading attractions here is the **Museu d'Art Catalunya** (Museum of Catalan Art) in the Palau Nacional atop a long flight of steps. The collection of Romanesque and Gothic art treasures—medieval frescoes and altarpieces, mostly from small churches and chapels in the Pyrenees—is simply staggering. Just three rooms were open at press time, but the entire museum is expected to open after extensive renovations by late 1995; ask at the tourist office for current information.

⑲ Nearby is the **Miró Foundation,** a gift from the artist Joan Miró to his native city. One of Barcelona's most exciting contemporary galleries, it has several exhibition areas, many of them devoted to Miró's works. Miró himself now rests in the cemetery on the southern slopes of Montjuïc. *Tel. 93/329–1908. Admission: 750 ptas. Open Tues.–Sat. 11–7 (9:30 on Thurs.), Sun. 10:30–2:30.*

Shopping

Gift Ideas If you're into fashion and jewelry, then you've come to the right place because Barcelona makes all the headlines on Spain's booming fashion front. **Xavier Roca i Coll,** Sant Pere mes Baix 24, just off Laietana, specializes in silver models of Barcelona's buildings.

Barcelona and Catalonia have passed along a playful sense of design ever since Antoni Gaudí began shocking civilians over a century ago. Stores and boutiques specializing in design items (jewelry, furnishings, knickknacks) include **Gimeno** (Passeig de Gracia 102), **Vinçon** (Passeig de Gracia 96), **Bd** (Barcelona Design, at Mallorca 291–293), and **Dos i Una** (Rosselló 275).

Antiques Carrer de la Palla and Banys Nous in the Gothic Quarter are lined with antiques shops, where you'll find old maps, books, paintings, and furniture. An **antiques market** is held every Thursday morning in Plaça Nova in front of the cathedral. The **Centre d'Antiquaris,** Passeig de Gràcia 57, has some 75 antiques stores. **Gothsland,** Consell de Cent 331, specializes in Moderniste designs.

Shopping Districts Elegant shopping districts are the Passeig de Gràcia, Rambla de Catalunya, and the Diagonal. For more affordable, more old-fashioned, and typically Spanish-style shops, explore the area between Ramblas and Vía Laietana, especially around C. Ferran.

Department Stores **El Corte Inglés** is on the Plaça de Catalunya 14 (tel. 93/302–1212) and at Diagonal 617 (tel. 93/419–2828) near María Cristina metro. **Galerías Preciados** is at Porta de l'Angel 19 just off the Plaça de Catalunya; Diagonal 471 on the Plaça Francesc Macià; and Avenida Meridiana 352. All are open Monday to Saturday 10–8.

Food and Flea Markets The **Boquería** or **Sant Josep Market** on the Ramblas between Carme and Hospital is a superb, colorful food market, held every day except Sunday. **Els Encants,** Barcelona's wild and woolly Flea Market, is held every Monday, Wednesday, Friday, and Saturday at the end of Dos de Maig on the Plaça Glòries Catalanes. There's an **artists' market** in the Placeta del Pi just off Ramblas and Boquería on Saturday mornings.

Bullfighting

Barcelona has two bullrings, the **Arènes Monumental** on Gran Vía and Carles I, and the smaller, rarely used, **Arènes las Arenas** on the Plaça d'Espanya. Bullfights are held on Sundays between March and October; check the newspaper for details. The official ticket office, where there is no markup on tickets, is at Muntaner 24 (tel. 93/453–3821) near Gran Vía. There's a **Bullfighting Museum** at the Monumental ring, open March–October, daily 10–1 and 5:30–7.

Bars and Cafés

Cafés and Tearooms Zurich (Plaça de Catalunya 35), on the corner of Pelai, is one of the oldest and most traditional cafés, perfect for watching the world go by. **The Croissant Show** (Santa Anna 10 just off Ramblas), is a small coffee and pastry shop, ideal for a quick mid-morning or afternoon break. **Carrer Petritxol** (from Portaferrissa to Plaça del Pi) is lined with *chocolaterías*, tearooms, and art galleries. Also, try the **Café de l'Estiu** in the Museu Marés (Plaça Sant Iu), a café-terrace open from nine to midnight.

Tapas Bars Barcelona is rich in tapa opportunities. **Cal Pep** (Plaça de les Olles 8) is one of the best, near the Picasso Museum and Santa Maria del Mar. The counter is the best place to be, even if you have to wait for a few minutes. **Casa Tejada** (Tenor Viñas 3) is at the other end of town near Plaça Francesc Macià. **Bar Tomás** (Major de Sarrià 49) in Sarrià has the best potatoes and *allioli* in town. **Carrer de la Mercé** (from the main post office at the bottom of Via Laietana to the Capitanía General army headquarters in Plaça de la Mercé) is also lined with options.

Cocktail Bars These places are both popular and plentiful everywhere, but the two best areas are the **Passeig del Born**, which is near the Picasso Museum and very fashionable with the affluent young, and in the **Eixample**, near Passeig de Gràcia.

Champagne Bars *Xampanyerías*, serving sparkling Catalan *cava*, are popular all over town and are something of a Barcelona specialty. Try **Brut** (Trompetas 3), in the Picasso Museum area; **La Cava del Palau** (Verdaguer i Callis 10), near the Palau de la Música; **La Folie** (Bailén 169), one of the best; or **La Xampanyería** (Provença 236), on the corner of Enric Granados.

Special Cafés **Els Quatre Gats** (Montsiò 5, off Porta de l'Angel) is a reconstruction of the original café that opened in 1897, and a real Barcelona institution. Literary discussions, jazz, and classical music recitals take place in this café where Picasso held his first show, Albéniz and Granados played their piano compositions, and Ramón Casas painted two of its original murals. **Café de l'Opera** (Ramblas 74), right opposite the Liceu, is a long-standing Barcelona tradition, ideal for a coffee or drink at any time of day.

Dining

For details and price-category definitions, *see* Dining *in* Staying in Spain, *above.*

$$ **Can Culleretes.** This picturesque old restaurant began life as a pastry shop in 1786, and it is one of the most atmospheric and reasonably priced finds in Barcelona. Located on an alleyway between Ferran and Boquería, its three dining rooms are decorated with photos of visiting celebrities. It serves real Catalan cooking and is very much a family concern; don't be put off by the street life that may be raging outside. *Quintana 5, tel. 93/317–3022. Reservations accepted. AE, MC, V. Closed Sun. eve. and Mon.*

$$ Los Caracoles. Just below the Plaça Reial is a restaurant that caters to tourists but has real atmosphere. Its walls are hung thick with photos of bullfighters and visiting celebrities; its specialties are mussels; paella; and, of course, snails (*caracoles*). *Escudellers 14, tel. 93/309–3185. Reservations accepted. AE, DC, MC, V.*

$$ Set Portes. ★ With plenty of Old World charm, this delightful restaurant near the waterfront has been going strong since 1836. The cooking is Catalan, the portions are enormous, and the specialties are paella *de pescado* (with fish) and *zarzuela set portes* (seafood casserole). *Passeig Isabel II 14, tel. 93/315–3910. Reservations advised on weekends. AE, DC, MC, V.*

$$ Sopeta Una. ★ Dining in this delightful small restaurant with old-fashioned decor and intimate atmosphere is more like eating in a private home. The menu is in Catalan, all the dishes are Catalan, and the atmosphere is very genteel. For dessert, try the traditional Catalan *música*—a plate of raisins, almonds, and dried fruit served with a glass of muscatel. It's near the Palau de la Música; don't be put off by the narrow street. *Verdaguer i Callis 6, tel. 93/319–6131. Reservations accepted. V. Closed Sun., and Mon. AM.*

$ Agut. ★ Simple, hearty Catalan fare awaits you in this lively and usually packed restaurant in the lower reaches of the Gothic Quarter. Founded in 1924, its popularity has never waned. Simple home-style cooking features the full repertory of Catalan recipes. *Gignàs 16, tel. 93/315–1709. AE, MC, V.*

$ Egipte. This small, friendly restaurant is hidden away in a very convenient location behind the Boquería Market. Its traditional Catalan home cooking; huge desserts; and swift, personable service all contribute to its popularity and good value. A new branch of Egipte, Egipte Rambla (Rambla 79, tel. 93/317–9545), has standard urban-modern decor. *Jerusalem 3, tel. 93/317–7480. AE, DC, MC, V. Closed Sun.*

$ Pitarra. Writers, politicians, artists, and intellectuals have crowded this excellent restaurant since 1890. It's named after the Barcelona poet Federico Soler, whose pen name was Pitarra, and run today with loving care by brothers Marc and Jaume Roig. The food is a delight: *salmon ahumado* (salmon smoked in the restaurant's own smoker), *jamón de pato* (duck fillets), tuna cooked in a squid ink sauce, and *oca a la catalana* (goose with pears). *Carrer d'Avinyo 56, tel. 93/301–1647. AE, DC, MC, V. Closed Sun. and Aug.*

¢ La Fonda. This is one of three Camós family restaurants offering simple, well-prepared cuisine in elegant surroundings at astonishingly low prices. The other two locations are in neighboring Plaça Reial: **Les Quinze Nits** (Plaça Reial 6) and **Hostal de Rita** (Carrer Aragó 279). It is best to be early (1:00 for lunch, 8:00 for dinner); no reservations are accepted and long lines tend to develop. *Escudellers 10, tel. 93/301–7515. AE, DC, MC, V. Closed Dec. 25.*

Lodging

For a city of its size and importance, Barcelona has long been underendowed with hotels. The 1992 Olympic Games, however, brought with them some new hotels—generally of the featureless modern variety—and spurred the renovation and cleaning up of most of the older ones. Hotels in the Ramblas and Gothic Quarter have plenty of Old World charm, but are less strong on creature comforts; those in the Eixample are mostly '50s or '60s buildings, often recently renovated; and the newest hotels are found out along the Diagonal or beyond, in the residential district of Sarriá. There are hotel reservation desks at the airport and Sants Central Station.

For details and price-category definitions, *see* Lodging *in* Staying in Spain, *above*.

$$ Gran Vía. Architectural features are the special charm of this 19th-century mansion, close to the main tourist office. The original chapel has been preserved, and you can have breakfast in a hall of mirrors, climb its Moderniste staircase, and call from elaborate Belle Epoque phone booths. *Gran Vía 642, tel. 93/318–1900, fax 93/318–9997. 53 rooms with bath. Facilities: Breakfast room, parking (fee). AE, DC, MC, V.*

$$ ★ **Oriente.** Barcelona's oldest hotel opened in 1843. Its public rooms are a delight—the ballroom and dining rooms have lost none of their 19th-century magnificence—though the bedrooms have undergone a rather featureless renovation. It's located just below the Liceu, and its terrace café is the perfect place for a drink. *Ramblas 45, tel. 93/302–2558. 142 rooms with bath. Restaurant, bar. AE, DC, MC, V.*

$ **Continental.** Something of a legend among cost-conscious travelers, this comfortable hostel, with canopied balconies, stands at the top of Ramblas, just below Plaça Catalunya. The rooms are homey and comfortable, the staff is friendly, and the location is ideal. Buffet breakfasts are a plus. *Rambla 136, tel. 93/301–2570, fax 93/302–7360. 35 rooms. AE, DC, MC, V.*

$ **España.** The Domenech i Montaner–designed Moderniste interior renders this hotel a bargain for those who put architectural style on a par with comfort. The high-ceiling downstairs features a breakfast room decorated with mermaids, elaborate woodwork, and an Art Nouveau chimney in the cafeteria. The rooms have been renovated and the neighborhood looks worse than it is. *Sant Pau 9, tel. 93/318–1758, fax 93/317–1134. 65 rooms. Facilities: Restaurant. AE, DC, MC, V.*

$ **Jardí.** With views over the traffic-free and charming Placeta del Pi, this recently renovated gem offers great value. Try to get a corner room, or at least an exterior with a view of the Esglesia del Pi rose window. *Plaça Sant Josep Oriol 1, 08002, tel. 93/301–5900, fax 93/318–3664. 40 rooms with bath. AE, DC, MC, V.*

$ **Paseo de Gracia.** This is one of those rare hostels with good-quality plain carpets and sturdy wooden furniture adorning the soft-color bedrooms. Add to this the location on the handsomest of Eixample's boulevards, and you have an excellent option, if you want to stay uptown. Half the rooms have superb rooftop terraces, with great views up to Tibidabo. *Passeig de Gracia 102, tel. 93/215–5828 and 93/215–5824; fax 93/215–3724. 55 rooms. AE, DC, MC, V.*

¢ **Alberg Mare de Deu de Montserrat.** This elegant Moderniste building above the Parc Güell is a youth hostel but cheerfully accepts others, albeit at slightly higher rates. Rooms with six beds are ideal for families. The location is a little out of the way, but with Parc Güell for a garden who could ask for more? *Passeig Nostra Senyora del Coll, 41–51, 08023, tel. 93/210–5151, fax 93/483–8350. For reservations call 93/483–8363. MC, V.*

The Arts

To find out what's on in town, look in the daily papers or in the weekly *Guía del Ocio*, available from newsstands all over town. *Actes a la Ciutat* is a weekly list of cultural events published by the Ajuntament and available from its information office on Plaça Sant Jaume or at La Virreina, La Rambla 99.

Concerts Catalans are great music lovers, and their main concert hall is **Palau de la Música** (Sant Francesc de Paula 2, tel. 93/268–1000). The ticket office is open weekdays 11–1 and 5–8 and Saturdays 5–8. Sunday morning concerts are a popular tradition. Tickets are reasonable and can often be purchased just before the concert.

Opera The **Gran Teatre del Liceu** was one of the world's finest opera houses, considered by many to be second only to Milan's La Scala. Since the Liceu was destroyed by fire in 1994, opera performances have been held at the Palau Sant Jordi (the indoor Olympic installation on Montjuïc), at the Teatre Victoria, and at the Palau de la Música.

Check listings for performance and ticket information. *Liceu tours and information: tel. 93/318–9277.*

Dance L'Espai de Dansa i Música de la Generalitat de Catalunya, known as **L'Espai** (the Space) (Travesera de Gràcia 63, tel. 93/201–2906) is Barcelona's prime dance venue. **El Mercat de les Flors** (Lleida 59, tel. 93/426–1875) also programs dance as well as theater, as does the **Teatre Victoria** (Av. Parallel 67, tel. 93/443–2929).

Theater Most theater performances are in Catalan, but Barcelona is also known for experimental theater and for its mime troupes, such as Els Joglars and La Claca. **Teatre Lliure** (Montseny 47, in Gràcia, tel. 93/218–9251), **Mercat de les Flors** (*see*, Dance, *above*), **Teatre Romea** (Hospital 51, tel. 93/317–7189), **Teatre Tivoli** (Casp 10, tel. 93/412–2063), and **Teatre Poliorama** (Rambla Estudios 115, tel. 93/317–7599) are the leading modern theaters.

Film Major films can be found in their original languages: Look for listings followed by *v.o.* **The Filmoteca** (Av. Sarrià 33, tel. 93/430–5007) often has English-language films in its schedule.

Nightlife

Cabaret **Belle Epoque** (Muntaner 246, tel. 93/209–7385) is a beautifully decorated music hall with the most sophisticated shows. **El Mediévolo** (Gran Vía 459, tel. 93/243–1566) has medieval feasts and entertainment; it's all geared to tourists but fun.

Jazz Clubs Try **Harlem Jazz Club** (Contessa de Sobradiel 8, tel. 93/310–0755), **La Cova del Drac** (Vallmajor 33, tel. 93/200–7032), and **Jamboree-Jazz & Dance Club** (Plaça Reial 17, tel. 93/301–7564).

Rock Check out **Zeleste** (Almogávares 122). Major concerts are usually held in sports stadiums; keep an eye out for posters.

Flamenco The best place is **El Patio Andaluz** (Aribau 242, tel. 93/209–3378). **El Cordobés** (Ramblas 35, tel. 93/317–6853) is aimed at tour groups but can be fun. **Los Tarantos** (Plaça Reial 17, tel. 93/318–3067) is currently the hottest flamenco place in town.

Casino The **Gran Casino de Barcelona** (tel. 93/893–3866), 42 kilometers (26 miles) south in Sant Pere de Ribes, near Sitges, also has a dance hall and some excellent international shows in a 19th-century atmosphere. Jacket and tie are essential.

Ports and Beaches

The Barcelona waterfront has undergone a major overhaul since 1992. The **Port Vell** (Old Port) now includes an extension of the Rambla, the **Rambla de Mar,** crossing the inner harbor from just below the Columbus monument. This boardwalk connects the Rambla with the Moll d'Espanya, where a shopping mall, a dozen restaurants, an aquarium, a cinema complex, and Barcelona's two yacht clubs are located. A walk around the Port Vell leads past the marina to Passeig Joan de Borbon, both lined with restaurants and outdoor tables. From here, you can go south out to sea along the rompeolas, a 2-mile excursion, or north (left) down the San Sebastian beach to the Passeig Maritim that leads down to the **Port Olimpic.** This new complex has a choked yacht basin, and dozens of bars and other booming nightlife. Except for the colorful inner streets of Barceloneta, the traditional fishermen's quarter, all of this new construction is devoid of character.

Take the Golondrina boat to the end of the breakwater and walk into Barceloneta for a paella; the rest is generic entertainment aimed not so much at visitors as at local weekenders. The beaches that stretch down to and past the Port Olimpic are much improved although generally dusty and crowded. The water quality is erratic.

Moorish Spain

Stretching from the dark mountains of the Sierra Morena in the north, west to the plains of the Guadalquivir valley, and south to the mighty snowcapped Sierra Nevada, Andalucía rings with echoes of the Moors. In the kingdom they called Al-Andalus, these Muslim invaders from North Africa dwelt for almost 800 years, from their first conquest of Spanish soil (Gibraltar) in 711 to their expulsion from Granada in 1492. And to this day the cities and landscapes of Andalucía are rich in their legacy. The great Mosque of Córdoba; the magical Alhambra Palace in Granada; and the Giralda tower, landmark of Seville, were the inspired creations of Moorish architects and craftsmen working at the behest of Al-Andalus's Arab emirs. The brilliant white villages with narrow streets and sturdy-walled houses clustered round cool inner patios; the whitewashed facades with heavily grilled windows; and the deep wailing song of Andalucía's flamenco, so reminiscent of the muezzin's call to prayer, all stem from centuries of Moorish occupation.

Getting There

Seville, Córdoba, and Granada all lie on direct train routes from Madrid. Service is frequent from both Chamartín and Atocha stations in Madrid and includes overnight trains; slower, day trains; and express talgos. In addition, the high-speed AVE train connecting Seville and Atocha Station began service in 1992 on an entirely new track; it's very expensive, but has cut traveling time on that route from 5½–6 hours to about 2½ hours. Most bus service from Madrid to Moorish Spain operates out of the Estación del Sur (*see* Madrid Arriving and Departing, *above*).

Getting Around

Seville and Córdoba are linked by direct train service. Buses are a better choice between Seville and Granada and between Córdoba and Granada because trains are relatively slow and infrequent and often involve a time-consuming change. **Seville**'s older bus station (tel. 95/441–7111) is between José María Osborne and Manuel Vazquez Sagastizabal; a new bus station is closer to downtown (Arjona, next to the Cachorro Bridge, tel. 95/490–8040). Check with the tourist office to determine which one you'll need. The city also has a spanking new train station, Santa Justa (tel. 95/454–0202), built in conjunction with the 1992 International Exposition. In **Granada**, the main bus station is Alsina Gräells (Camino de Ronda 97, tel. 958/251358); the train station is at the end of Avenida Andaluces (RENFE office, Reyes Católicos 63, tel. 958/271272). **Córdoba** has no central bus depot, so check at the tourist office for the appropriate company. The long-distance train station is on Glorieta Conde de Guadalorce (RENFE office, Ronda de los Tejares 10, tel. 957/475884).

Tourist Information

Córdoba (Plaza de Judá Leví, tel. 957/200522, and the much less useful office at Palacio de Congresos y Exposiciones, Torrijos 10, tel. 957/471235).
Granada (Plaza Mariana Pineda 10, tel. 958/226688, and Libreros 2, tel. 958/225990).
Seville (Av. Constitución 21B, tel. 95/422–1404, not far from the cathedral and Archives of the Indies, and the smaller office at Costurero de la Reina, Paseo de las Delícias 9, tel. 95/423–4465).

Exploring Moorish Spain

Our tour begins in Seville and continues to Córdoba and Granada. Seville and Granada are relatively expensive cities—Seville, especially, after its hotels and restaurants boosted prices for Expo '92— but Córdoba retains a provincial feel and, with a few exceptions, prices to match.

The downside to a visit here, especially to Seville, is that petty crime, much of it directed against tourists, is rife. Purse snatching and thefts from cars, frequently when drivers are in them, are depressingly familiar. *Always* keep your car doors *and* trunk locked. *Never* leave any valuables in your car. Leave your passport, traveler's checks, and credit cards in your hotel's safe, *never* in your room. Don't carry expensive cameras or wear jewelry. Take only the minimum amount of cash with you. There comes a point, however—your bag is snatched, for example—when all the precautions in the world will prove inadequate. If you're unlucky, it's an equally depressing fact that the police, again especially in Seville, have adopted a distinctly casual attitude to such thefts and often combine indifference to beleaguered tourists with rudeness in about equal measure. Frankly, there's little you can do except remain calm.

Numbers in the margin correspond to points of interest on the Seville map.

Seville Lying on the banks of the Guadalquivir, **Seville**—Spain's fourth-largest city and capital of Andalucía—is one of the most beautiful and romantic cities in Europe. Here in this city of the sensuous Carmen and the amorous Don Juan, famed for the spectacle of its Holy Week processions and April Fair, you'll come close to the spiritual heart of Moorish Andalucía.

You'll also find some dramatic improvements, courtesy of the International Exposition hosted by the city in 1992. They include the development of La Cartuja Island, where the fairgrounds were built and where a new science theme park opened in 1995; seven new bridges and the new riverfront esplanade; the new Maestranza opera house, built on the river; new roads in the city and throughout the region; and a new railroad station and bus station.

❶ Start your visit in the **Catedral,** begun in 1402, a century and a half after St. Ferdinand delivered Seville from the Moors. This great Gothic edifice, which took just over a century to build, is traditionally described in superlatives. It's the biggest and highest cathedral in Spain, the largest Gothic building in the world, and the world's third-largest church after St. Peter's in Rome and St. Paul's in London. And it boasts the world's largest carved wooden altarpiece. Despite such impressive statistics, the inside can be dark and gloomy, with too many overly ornate Baroque trappings. But seek out the beautiful Virgins by Murillo and Zurbarán and reflect on the history enshrined in these walls. In a silver urn before the high altar rest the precious relics of Seville's liberator, St. Ferdinand, said to have died from excessive fasting, and down in the crypt are the tombs of his descendants Pedro the Cruel, founder of the Alcázar, and his mistress María de Padilla. But above all, you'll want to pay your respects to Christopher Columbus, whose mortal vestiges are enshrined in a flamboyant mausoleum in the south aisle. Borne aloft by statues representing the four medieval kingdoms of Spain, it's to be hoped that the great voyager has found peace at last after the transatlantic quarrels that carried his body from Valladolid to Santo Domingo and from Havana to Seville. *Admission: 550 ptas. Open Mon.–Sat. 10–5, Sun. 2–4. Cathedral also open for Mass.*

Every day the bell that summons the faithful to prayer rings out from a Moorish minaret, relic of the Arab mosque whose admirable tower of Abu Yakoub the Sevillians could not bring themselves to de-

Seville

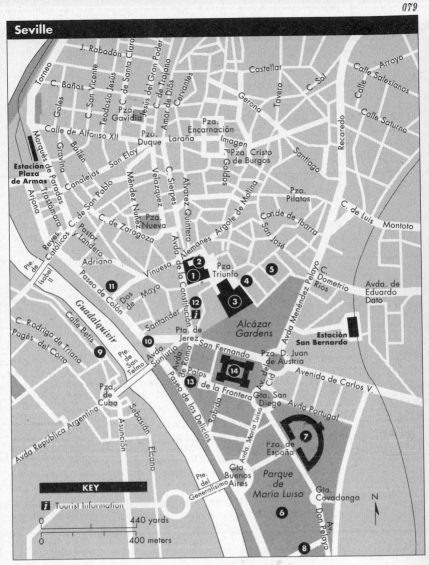

KEY

ℹ️ Tourist Information

0   440 yards

0   400 meters

N

Major Attractions

Alcázar, **3**

Barrio de Santa Cruz, **5**

Calle Betis, **9**

Catedral, **1**

Giralda, **2**

Maestranza Bullring, **11**

Parque de María Luisa, **6**

Patio de las Banderas, **4**

Plaza de America, **8**

Plaza de España, **7**

Torre de Oro, **10**

Other Attractions

Museo Arte Comtemporaneo, **12**

San Telmo Palace, **13**

Tobacco Factory (University), **14**

stroy. Topped in 1565–68 by a bell tower and weather vane and ❷ called the **Giralda,** this splendid example of Moorish art is one of the marvels of Seville. In place of steps, a gently sloping ramp climbs to the viewing platform 71 meters (230 feet) above Seville's rooftops. St. Ferdinand is said to have ridden his horse to the top to admire the view of the city he had conquered. Seven centuries later your view of the Golden Tower and shimmering Guadalquivir River will be equally breathtaking. Try, too, to see the Giralda at night when the floodlights cast a new magic on this gem of Islamic art. *Open same hrs as Cathedral and visited on same ticket. Admission to Giralda only: 250 ptas.*

❸ The high fortified walls of the **Alcázar** belie the exquisite delicacy of the palace's interior. It was built by Pedro the Cruel—so known because he murdered his stepmother and four of his half-brothers—who lived here with his mistress María de Padilla from 1350 to 1369. Don't mistake this for a genuine Moorish palace, as it was built more than 100 years after the reconquest of Seville; rather, its style is Mudéjar—built by Moorish craftsmen working under orders of a Christian king. The Catholic Kings (Ferdinand and Isabella), whose only son, Prince Juan, was born in the Alcázar in 1478, added a wing to serve as administration center for their New World empire, and Charles V enlarged it further for his marriage celebrations in 1526. Pedro's Mudéjar palace surrounds the beautiful **Patio de las Doncellas** (Court of the Damsels), whose name pays tribute to the annual gift of 100 virgins to the Moorish sultans whose palace once stood on the site. Resplendent with the most delicate of lacelike stucco and gleaming *azulejo* (tile) decorations, it is immediately reminiscent of Granada's Alhambra and is, in fact, the work of Granada craftsmen. Opening off this are the apartments of María de Padilla, whose hold over her lover, and seemingly her courtiers, too, was so great that they apparently vied with one another to drink her bath water!

The **Alcázar Gardens** are fragrant with jasmine and myrtle, an orange tree said to have been planted by Pedro the Cruel, and a lily pond well stocked with fat, contented goldfish. The end of your visit ❹ brings you to the **Patio de las Banderas** for an unrivaled view of the Giralda. *Palace and gardens admission: 600 ptas. Open Tues.–Sat. 10:30–5, Sun. 10–1.*

❺ The **Barrio de Santa Cruz,** with its twisting alleyways, cobbled squares, and whitewashed houses, is a perfect setting for an operetta. Once the home of Seville's Jews, it was much favored by 17th-century noblemen and today boasts some of the most expensive properties in Seville. All the romantic images you've ever had of Spain will come to life here: Every house gleams white or deep ocher yellow; wrought-iron grilles adorn the windows, and every balcony and patio is bedecked with geraniums and petunias. You'll find the most beautiful patio at Callejón del Agua 12. Ancient bars nestle side by side with antiques shops. Don't miss the famous **Casa Román** bar in Plaza de los Venerables Sacerdotes, with its ceilings hung thick with some of the best hams in Seville, or the **Hostería del Laurel** next door, where in summer you can dine in one of the loveliest squares in the city. Souvenir and ceramics shops surround the **Plaza Doña Elvira,** where the young of Seville gather to play guitars around the fountain and azulejo benches. And in the **Plaza Alianza,** with its well-stocked antiques shops and **John Fulton gallery** (Fulton is the only American ever to qualify as a full-fledged bullfighter), stop a moment and admire the simplicity of the crucifix on the wall, framed in a profusion of bougainvillea.

Walk or, better still, hire a horse carriage from the Plaza Virgen de ❻ los Reyes, below the Giralda, and visit the **Parque de María Luisa,** whose gardens are a delightful blend of formal design and wild vegetation, shady walkways and sequestered nooks. In the 1920s the park was redesigned to form the site of the 1929 Hispanic-American exhibition, and the impressive villas you see here today are the fair's

❼ remaining pavilions. Visit the monumental **Plaza de España,** whose grandiose pavilion of Spain was the centerpiece of the exhibition. At the opposite end of the park you can feed the hundreds of white

❽ doves that gather round the fountains of the lovely **Plaza de America;** it's a magical spot to while away the sleepy hours of the siesta.

❾ An early evening stroll along the **Calle Betis,** on the far side of the Guadalquivir, is a delight few foreigners know about. Between the San Telmo and Isabel II bridges, the vista of the sparkling water,

❿ the palm-lined banks, and the silhouette of the **Torre de Oro** (Golden Tower, built 1220; admission: 100 ptas., open Tues.–Fri. 10–2,

⓫ weekends 11–2) and the **Maestranza Bullring** (built 1760–63), one of Spain's oldest, is simply stunning (admission for plaza tours and bullfighting museum: 250 ptas.; open Mon.–Sat. 10–1:30).

Numbers in the margin correspond to points of interest on the Córdoba map.

Córdoba Ancient **Córdoba,** city of the caliphs, is one of Spain's oldest cities and the greatest embodiment of Moorish heritage in all Andalucía. From the 8th to the 11th centuries, the Moorish emirs and Caliphs of the West held court here, and it became one of the Western world's greatest centers of art, culture, and learning. Moors, Christians, and Jews lived together in harmony within its walls. Two of Córdoba's most famous native sons were Averröes, the great Arab scientist, and Maimónides, the notable Jewish doctor and philoso-

❶ pher. But above all, Córdoba is known for its famous **Mezquita** (Mosque), one of the finest built by the Moors. Its founder was Abd ar-Rahman I (756–788), and it was completed by Al Mansur (976–1002) around the year 987. As you step inside you'll come face to face with a forest of gleaming pillars of precious marble, jasper, and onyx, rising to a roof of red-and-white horseshoe arches, one of the most characteristic traits of Moorish architecture. Not even the heavy Baroque cathedral that Charles V so mistakenly built in its midst—and later regretted—can detract from the overpowering impact and mystery wrought by the art of these Moorish craftsmen of a thousand years ago. It was indeed a fitting setting for the original copy of the Koran and a bone from the arm of the Prophet Mohammed, holy relics once housed in the Mezquita that were responsible for bringing thousands of pilgrims to its doors in the great years before St. Ferdinand reconquered Córdoba for the Christians in 1236. In Moorish times, the mosque opened onto the **Orange Tree Courtyard,** where the faithful performed their ablutions before worshiping, and the bell tower, which you can climb for a magnificent view of the city, served as the mosque's minaret. *Tel. 957–470512. Admission: 700 ptas. Open daily May–Sept., 10–7; Oct.–Apr., 10–5.*

Near the mosque, the streets of Torrijos, Cardenal Herrero, and Deanes are lined with tempting souvenir shops specializing in local handicrafts, especially the filigree silver and embossed leather for which Córdoba is famous. In her niche on Cardenal Herrero, the

❷ **Virgen de los Faroles** (Virgin of Lanterns) stands demurely behind a lantern-hung grille, rather like a lovely lady awaiting a serenade. In a narrow alleyway off to your left is the **Callejón de las Flores,** its houses decked with hanging flower baskets. Now make your way

❸ ❹ westward to the old **Judería,** or Jewish quarter. On the **Plaza Judá Leví** you'll find the municipal tourist office. A few paces down, on Calle Manríquez, is another outstanding patio open to visitors.

❺ Overlooking the Plaza Maimónides (or Bulas) is the **Museo Taurino** (Museum of Bullfighting), housed in two delightful old mansions. You'll see a well-displayed collection of memorabilia, paintings, and posters by early 20th-century Córdoban artists and rooms dedicated

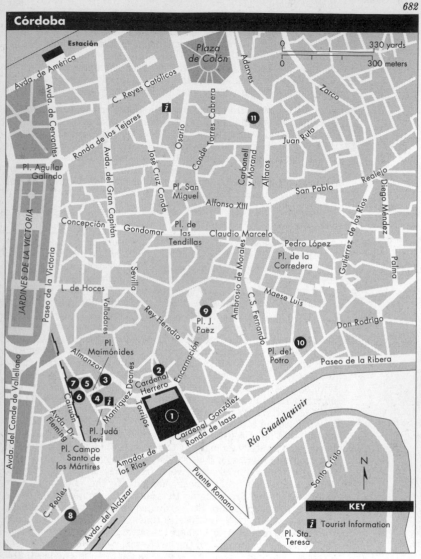

Córdoba

Major Attractions
Judería, **3**
Maimónides Statue, **6**
Mezquita, **1**
Museo Taurino, **5**
Plaza Judá Leví, **4**
Synagogue, **7**
Virgen de los Faroles, **2**

Other Attractions
Alcázar, **8**
Cristo de los Faroles, **11**
Museo Arqueológico, **9**
Museo de Bellas
Artes, **10**

to great Córdoban *toreros*—even the hide of the bull that killed the legendary Manolete in 1947. *Tel. 957/472000, ext. 211. Admission: 400 ptas. Open Tues.–Sat. 9:30–1:30 and 5–8 (4–7 in winter); Sun. 9:30–1:30; closed Mon.*

⑥ A moving **statue** of the great Jewish philosopher **Maimónides** stands in the Plaza Tiberiades. A few paces along Judíos, you come to the
⑦ only **synagogue** in Andalucía to have survived the expulsion of the Jews in 1492. It's one of only three remaining synagogues in Spain—the other two are in Toledo—built before 1492, and it boasts some fine Hebrew and Mudéjar stucco tracery and a women's gallery. *Tel. 957/298133. Admission: 50 ptas. Open Tues.–Sat. 10–2 and 3:30–5:30, Sun. 10–1:30.*

Across the way is the courtyard of El Zoco, a former Arab souk, with some pleasant shops and stalls, and sometimes a bar open in summer.

Numbers in the margin correspond to points of interest on the Granada map.

Granada The city of **Granada** rises majestically on three hills dwarfed by the mighty snowcapped peaks of the Sierra Nevada, which boasts the highest roads in Europe. Atop one of these hills the pink-gold palace of the Alhambra, at once splendidly imposing yet infinitely delicate, gazes out across the rooftops and gypsy caves of the Sacromonte to the fertile *vega* rich in orchards, tobacco fields, and poplar groves. Granada, the last stronghold of the Moors and the most treasured of all their cities, fell finally to the Catholic Kings in January 1492. For Ferdinand and Isabella their conquest of Granada was the fulfill-ment of a long-cherished dream to rid Spain of the Infidel, and here
① they built the flamboyant **Capilla Real** (Royal Chapel), where they have lain side by side since 1521, later joined by their daughter Juana la Loca. Begin your tour in the nearby Plaza de Bib-Rambla, a pleasant square with flower stalls and outdoor cafés in summer, then
② pay a quick visit to the huge Renaissance **catedral,** commissioned in 1521 by Charles V, who thought the Royal Chapel "too small for so much glory" and determined to house his illustrious grandparents somewhere more worthy. But his ambitions came to little, for Gra-nada Cathedral is a grandiose and gloomy monument, not completed until 1714, and is far surpassed in beauty and historic value by the neighboring Royal Chapel, which, despite the great emperor's plans, still houses the tombs of his grandparents and mother. *Tel. 958/229239. Admission: 200 ptas. each. Royal chapel and cathedral open daily 10:30–1 and 4–7 (3:30–6 in winter).*

③ The adjacent streets of the **Alcaicería,** the old Arab silk exchange, will prove a haven for souvenir hunters. Here you can find any num-ber of local handicrafts inspired by Granada's Moorish heritage: brass and copperware, green and blue Fajalauza pottery, wooden boxes, tables and chess sets inlaid with mother of pearl, and woven goods from the villages of the Alpujarras in which the colors green, red, and black predominate. Across the Gran Vía de Colón, Granada's main shopping street, the narrow streets begin to wind
④ up the slopes of the **Albaicín,** the old Moorish quarter, which is now a fascinating mixture of dilapidated white houses and beautiful *cármenes,* luxurious villas with fragrant gardens. Few visitors find
⑤ their way to the balcony of **San Nicolás Church,** which affords an un-forgettable view of the Alhambra, particularly when it is floodlit at night.

⑥ The Cuesta de Gomérez climbs steeply to the **Alhambra precincts,** where the Duke of Wellington planted shady elms and Washington Irving tarried among the gypsies from whom he learned the Moor-ish legends so evocatively recounted in his *Tales of the Alhambra.*
⑦ Above the **Puerta de la Justicia** the hand of Fatima, her fingers evok-ing the five laws of the Koran, beckons you inside the mystical Al-

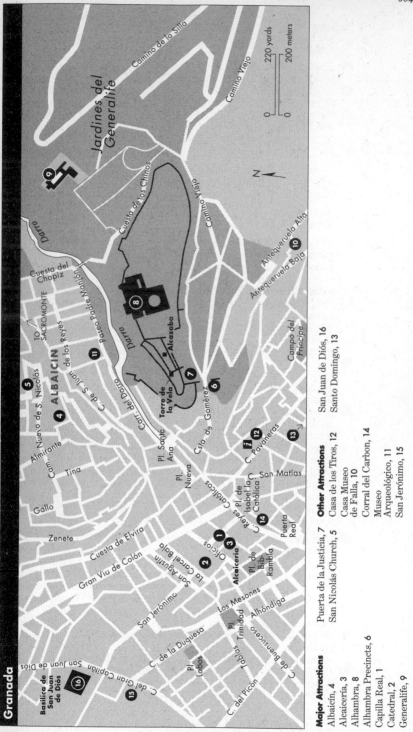

Granada

684

Major Attractions

Albaicín, 4
Alcaicería, 3
Alhambra, 8
Alhambra Precincts, 6
Capilla Real, 1
Catedral, 2
Generalife, 9

Puerta de la Justicia, 7
San Nizolás Church, 5

Other Attractions

Casa de los Tiros, 12
Casa Museo
de Falla, 10
Corral del Carbon, 14
Museo
Arqueológico, 11
San Jerónimo, 15

San Juan de Diós, 16
Santo Domingo, 13

hambra, the most imposing and infinitely beautiful of all Andalucía's
❽ Moorish monuments. The history of the **Alhambra** is woven through
the centuries. Once you are inside its famous courts, the legends of
the Patio of the Lions, the Hall of the Two Sisters, and the murder of
the Abencerrajes spring to life in a profusion of lacy walls, frothy
stucco, gleaming tiles, and ornate domed ceilings. Here in this realm
of myrtles and fountains, festooned arches and mysterious inscriptions, every corner holds its secret. Here the emirs installed their
harems, accorded their favorites the most lavish courts, and bathed
in marble baths. In the midst of so much that is delicate the Baroque
palace of Charles V would seem an intrusion, heavy and incongru-
ous, were it not for the splendid acoustics that make it a perfect setting for Granada's summer music festival.

❾ Wisteria, jasmine, and roses line your route to the **Generalife**, the
nearby summer palace of the caliphs, where crystal drops shower
from slender fountains against a background of stately cypresses.
The view of the white, clustered houses of the Albaicín; the
Sacromonte riddled with gypsy caves; and the imposing bulk of the
Alhambra towering above the tiled roofs of the city will etch on your
memory an indelible image of this most beautiful setting and greatest Moorish legacy. *Admission to Alhambra and Generalife: 525
ptas. Free Sun. after 3. Open Nov.–Feb., daily 9–6, Mar.–Oct., daily 9–8. Floodlit visits daily 10 PM–midnight (8–10 PM in winter).
Ticket office closes 45 mins. before closing times above.*

Dining and Lodging

For details and price-category definitions, *see* Dining and Lodging
in Staying in Spain, *above.*

Córdoba
Dining
★

La Almudaina. This attractive restaurant is located in a 15th-centu-
ry house and former school that overlooks the Alcázar at the entrance to the Judería. It has an Andalucían patio, and the decor and
cooking are both typical of Córdoba. *Campo Santo de los Mártires 1,
tel. 957/474342. AE, DC, MC, V. No dinner Sun. $$*

El Cardenal. Close to the mosque, beside the Marisa hotel, this res-
taurant, in the heart of Córdoba's tourist center, offers a stylish set-
ting for lunch or dinner. A marble staircase with Oriental carpets
leads up to the second-floor dining room. Good food and professional
service complement the cool, agreeable atmosphere. *Cardenal
Herrero 14, tel. 957/480346. AE, DC, MC, V. Closed Mon. in winter,
no dinner Sun. $$*

★ **El Churrasco.** This atmospheric restaurant with a patio is famous
for its grilled meat dishes. Specialties are, of course, *churrasco,* a
pork dish in pepper sauce, and an excellent salmorejo. *Romero 16,
tel. 957/290817. AE, DC, MC, V. Closed Aug. $$*

Federación de Peñas. You'll find this popular budget restaurant on
one of the main thoroughfares of the old town, halfway between the
mosque and the Plaza Tendillas. You can eat traditional Spanish fare
at one of several outdoor tables in the spacious courtyard, graced
with a fountain and surrounded by horseshoe arches, or inside, in a
pretty room with dark green cloths and linen. *Conde de Luque 8, tel.
957/476698. MC, V. $*

Mesón El Burladero. Off a small patio at the end of an alley off
Deanes, this is a typical mesón, decorated with bullfight posters,
stags' heads, stuffed birds, and a boar's head. Try the *menú Manole-
te,* which includes concoctions such as *revuelto de la casa* (a scram-
bled egg dish). *Calleja la Hoguera 5, tel. 957/472719. AE, DC, MC,
V. $*

Benítez. Located in a residential neighborhood that's a brisk 15-
minute walk from the mosque, this large, marble-floor eatery offers
even better prices if you eat at the counter. This pleasant spot fea-
tures a dozen very inexpensive combination plates. *Gran Capitán
25, no phone. AE, DC, MC, V. ¢*

Lodging **El Califa.** This is a small, modern hotel in a reasonably quiet, central location in the heart of the old city. It accepts no tour groups, only individual guests, and is a comfortable place to stay, with the sights and shops close at hand. *Lope de Hoces 14, tel. 957/299400. 65 rooms. Facilities: Cafeteria, bar. MC, V. $$*

Marisa. A charming old Andalucían house whose location in the heart of the old town overlooking the mosque's Patio de los Naranjos is its prime virtue. You'll find the decor quaint and charming and the rates reasonable. *Cardenal Herrero 6, tel. 957/473142. 28 rooms. MC, V. $$*

Antonio Machado. On a pretty little street above the Mosque, this hostel is typically Moorish, with its small, flower-bedecked interior courtyard, pleasant rooms overlooking the street, and friendly family of proprietors. You'll have to share a bath, however. *Buen Pastor 4, tel. 957/204959. 10 rooms. AE, MC, V. $*

Granada **Sevilla.** This is a very atmospheric, colorful restaurant in the
Dining Alcaicería beside the cathedral. There's a superb tapas bar at the entrance, and the dining room is picturesque but rather small and crowded. The menu tends to be tourist oriented, but try the *sopa Sevillana* (fish soup). *Oficios 12, tel. 958/221223. AE, DC, MC, V. Closed Sun. $$*

★ **El Macasar.** In a small house on Alhambra hill, with extraordinary views over Granada, this restaurant has served exquisitely delicate food with a nouvelle touch since 1991. Normally run-of-the-mill dishes like *sopa obispo* (soup with chicken, duck, and ham) and *pollo campero de frutas* (chicken prepared in fruit) come alive in owner Rosario Lopez Tamayo's five-table dining room. *Aire Alta de San Cecilio 4, on a narrow street below the Alhambra Palace Hotel, tel. 958/227811. No credit cards. Reservations advised weekend evenings. Closed Sun. and Mon. $–$$*

Alacena de las Monjas. In the heart of town, by the Casa de los Tiros, this restaurant ("The Nun's Closet") has a short menu of regional dishes and wines. Meaty stews are prevalent in winter. If you're in a more adventurous mood, try the *lomos de salmon en salsa de naranja y estagon* (salmon in orange and tarragon sauce). *Plaza Padre Suarez, tel. 958/224028. AE, V. Closed Sun. and Mon. $*

Los Manueles. This old inn is one of Granada's long-standing traditions. The walls are decorated with ceramic tiles, and the ceiling is hung with hams. There's lots of atmosphere, good old-fashioned service, and plenty of traditional Granada cooking. *Zaragoza 2, tel. 958/223413. AE, DC, MC, V. $*

Torres Bermejas. A functional, good-value restaurant at the base of the Alhambra hill, this typically Spanish restaurant offers good deals on such standards as paella for two. A fine steak (*solomillo*) will cost you less than $15. The dining room is at the back of the long wooden bar. *Plaza Nueva 6, tel. 958/223116. AE, DC, MC, V. Closed Sun. ¢*

Lodging **América.** A simple but charming hotel within the Alhambra precincts, the América is very popular, so you'll need to reserve a room months ahead. The location is magnificent, and guests can linger over breakfast on a delightful patio. *Real de la Alhambra 53, tel. 958/227471. 14 rooms. No credit cards. Closed Nov.–Feb. Facilities: Restaurant. $$*

Britz. Housed in a clean, pleasant building, this small hotel is conveniently located at the base of the Alhambra hill and close to downtown attractions—a good, cheap bet all around. *Plaza Nueva y Gomerez 1, tel. 958/223652. 22 rooms. MC, V. $$*

Juan Miguel. This comfortable, modern hotel right in the center of town opened in 1987. The rooms are well equipped, service is professional, and there's a good restaurant. *Acera del Darro 24, tel. 958/258912. 66 rooms. AE, DC, MC, V. $$*

Inglaterra. Set in a period house just two blocks above the Gran Vía de Colón in the heart of town, this is a hotel that will appeal to those who prefer Old World charm to creature comforts, though accommodations are perfectly adequate for the reasonable rates. *Cetti Meriem 6, tel. 958/221559, fax 958/221586. 36 rooms. AE, DC, MC, V. $*

Navarro Ramos. Perhaps the best deal among the hostales that line the main road up to the Alhambra, this 16-room hotel (six with private bath) in an old apartment building is very clean, well maintained, and friendly. The rooms are unusually large and pleasant for this price range. *Cuesta de Gomérez 21, tel. 958/250555. 15 rooms. No credit cards. No reservations. ¢*

Seville
Dining

El Bacalao. This popular fish restaurant, opposite the church of Santa Catalina, is in an Andalucían house decorated with ceramic tiles. As its name suggests, the house specialty is *bacalao* (cod); try the bacalao *con arroz* (with rice) or the bacalao *al pilpil* (fried). *Plaza Ponce de León 15, tel. 95/421–6670. Reservations advised. Closed Sun. $$*

Enrique Becerra. This small intimate restaurant, in an old Andalucían house just off the Plaza Nueva, is well known for its Andalucían cuisine. *Gamazo 2, tel. 95/421–3049. Reservations advised. AE, DC, MC, V. Closed Sun. $$*

La Isla. Located in the center of town between the cathedral and the Convent of La Caridad, La Isla has long been famous for its superb seafood and paella. *Arfe 25, tel. 95/421–5376. AE, DC, MC, V. Closed Mon. and Aug. $$*

★ **La Judería.** This bright, modern restaurant near the Hotel Fernando III is fast gaining recognition for the quality of its Andalucían and international cuisine and for its reasonable prices. Fish dishes from the north of Spain and meat from Ávila are specialties. Try *cordero lechal* (roast baby lamb) or *urta a la roteña* (a fish dish unique to Rota). *Cano y Cueto 13, tel. 95/441–2052. Reservations required. AE, DC, MC, V. Closed Sun. in Aug. $$*

★ **Mesón Don Raimundo.** In an old convent close to the cathedral, the atmosphere and decor are deliberately Sevillian. Its bar is the perfect place to sample a *fino* and some splendid tapas, and the restaurant, when not catering to tour groups, is one of Seville's most delightful. *Argote de Molina 26, tel. 95/422–3355. Reservations advised. AE, DC, MC, V. No Sun. dinner. $$*

La Cueva del Pez de Espada. The Swordfish's Cave is a colorful, somewhat tourist-oriented restaurant just off the Plaza Doña Elvira. The tables have bright red cloths, and the white walls are hung with cheerful oil paintings, ceramic tiles, trailing plants, and other typical Sevillian paraphernalia. The service is friendly and helpful, and an English-language menu offers a good choice of traditional Spanish meat and fish dishes. *Rodrigo Caro 18, tel. 95/421–3143. AE, DC, MC, V. $*

Las Escobas. Located a few steps from the Giralda, this atmospheric restaurant with azulejo wainscoting, coffered ceilings, and other classic Andalucían touches, claims to have first opened in 1386. It also counts such illustrious former patrons as Cervantes, Lord Byron, Lope de Vega, and a host of other literary luminaries. Today, it serves inexpensive Sevillian staples, such as gazpacho *andaluz* and *pescaito frito sevillano* (fried fish plate). *Alvarez Quintero 62, tel. 95/421–4479. MC, V. $*

Mesón Castellano. This recently refurbished, old Sevillian house opposite the church of San José is an ideal place for lunch after a morning's shopping on Calle Sierpes. Specialties are Castilian meat dishes, at reasonable prices. *Jovellanos 6, tel. 95/421–4028. Open for lunch only. AE, DC, MC, V. Closed Sun. $*

Girarda. A family-run hotel (*see below*) that doubles as a charming, tiny restaurant. *Justin de Neve 8, tel. 95/421–5113. ¢*

Lodging

Bécquer. This functional, modern hotel with attentive service is convenient to the shopping center and offers comfortable, if unexciting, accommodations. It's one of the best moderate bets, with a parking garage but no restaurant. *Reyes Católicos 4, tel. 95/422–8900, fax 95/421–4400. 126 rooms. facilities: Bar, breakfast room. AE, DC, MC, V. $$*

Giralda. Modernized and extensively renovated, this is a comfortable, functional hotel with spacious, light rooms decorated in typical Castilian style. In a cul-de-sac off Avenida Menéndez Pelayo, it lies on the edge of the old city; rooms on the fifth floor are best. *Sierra Nevada 3, tel. 95/441–6661, fax 95/441–9352. 107 rooms. Facilities: Restaurant, bar, meeting rooms. AE, DC, MC, V. $$*

La Rábida. With lots of delightful 19th-century touches, this is a charming old-fashioned hotel in the center of town. *Castelar 24, tel. 95/422–0960. 87 rooms. Facilities: Restaurant, bar. AE, MC, V. $$*

Girarda. One of several very basic family-run hotels in the Barrio Santa Cruz, the Girarda is in an old, Moorish-style building with a colorful interior patio that also serves as a restaurant. *Justin de Neve 8, tel. 95/421–5113. 5 rooms. AE, MC, V. $*

Goya. This charming hostel is centrally located near the cathedral and the Barrio Santa Cruz and has a typically Sevillian lobby with iron grillwork and abundant flowers decorating the covered courtyard. The rooms are large, with only two facing the sometimes noisy street. *Mateos Gagos 31, tel. 95/421–1170. 20 rooms. No credit cards. $*

Internacional. Well maintained and charming, this Old World hotel lies in the narrow streets of the old town near Casa Pilatos. *Aguilas 17, tel. 95/421–3207. 26 rooms. $*

Monreal. In a pedestrian alley in the Barrio Santa Cruz, the Monreal offers a spacious lobby and some large rooms for prices that won't break you. There's a family-run restaurant in the azulejo-decorated lobby, and the rooms (only five with full bath) are well kept. *Rodrigo Caro 8, tel. 95/421–4166. 21 rooms. No credit cards. $*

Murillo. This picturesque hotel, in the heart of the Barrio Santa Cruz, was redecorated in 1987. The rooms are simple and small, but the setting is a virtue. You can't reach the hotel by car, but porters with trolleys will fetch your luggage from your taxi. *Lope de Rueda 7, tel. 95/421–6095, fax 95/421–9616. 61 rooms, 30 with bath, 31 with shower. Facilities: Bar, breakfast room. AE, DC, MC, V. $*

The Arts and Nightlife

Granada
Flamenco
There are several "impromptu" flamenco shows in the caves of the Sacromonte, but these can be dismally bad and little more than tourist rip-offs. Go only if accompanied by Spanish friends who know their way around. **Jardines Neptuno** (Calle Neptuno, tel. 958/522533) is a regular but colorful flamenco club that caters largely to tourists. **Reina Mora** (Mirador de San Cristobal, tel. 958/272228), though somewhat smaller than Jardines Neptuno, offers regular flamenco shows known as *tablaos*. Both can be booked through your hotel.

Seville
Flamenco
Regular flamenco clubs cater largely to tourists, but their shows are colorful and offer a good introduction for the uninitiated. **El Arenal** (Rodo 7, tel. 95/421–6492) is a flamenco club in the back of the picturesque Mesón Dos de Mayo. **Los Gallos** (Plaza Santa Cruz 11, tel. 95/421–6981) is a small intimate club in the heart of the Barrio Santa Cruz offering fairly authentic flamenco. There are shows of flamenco and other regional dances nightly at **El Patio Sevillano** (Paseo de Colón, tel. 95/421–4120), which caters largely to tour groups.

Bullfights
Corridas take place at the Maestranza bullring on Paseo de Colón, usually on Sundays from Easter to October. The best are during the April Fair. Tickets can be bought in advance from the windows at the ring (one of the oldest and most picturesque in Spain) or from the kiosks in Calle Sierpes (these charge a commission). The ring and a bullfighting museum may be visited year-round (admission: 250 ptas.; open Mon.–Sat. 10–1:30; tel. 95/422–4577).

Costa del Sol

What were impoverished fishing villages in the 1950s are now retirement villages and package-tour meccas for northern Europeans and Americans. Despite the abuses of this naturally lovely area during the boom years of the 1960s and '70s and the continuing brashness of the resorts that cater to the package-tour trade, the Costa del Sol has managed to preserve at least some semblance of charm. Behind the hideous concrete monsters—some of which are now being demolished—you'll come across old cottages and villas set in gardens that blossom with jasmine and bougainvillea. The sun still sets over miles of beaches and the lights of small fishing craft still twinkle in the distance. Most of your time should be devoted to indolence—sunbathing and swimming (though not in the polluted Mediterranean; all hotels have pools for this reason). When you need something to do, you can head inland to the historic town of Ronda and the perched white villages of Andalucía. You can also make a day trip to Gibraltar or Tangier.

Getting There

Daily Iberia and Aviaco flights connect Málaga with Madrid and Barcelona. Iberia (tel. 95/213–6166/67), British Airways, and charter services like Dan Air offer frequent service from London; most other major European cities also have direct air links. You'll have to make connections in Madrid for all flights from the United States. Málaga's airport (tel. 95/224–0000) is 12 kilometers (7 miles) west of the city, but there are city buses every 20 minutes (fare: 115 ptas., 6:30 AM–midnight); the **Portillo** bus company (tel. 95/236–0191) has frequent service to Torremolinos. A useful suburban train serving Málaga, Torremolinos, and Fuengirola also stops at the airport every half hour. From Madrid, Málaga is easily reached by a half dozen rapid trains a day.

Getting Around

Buses are the best way of getting around the Costa del Sol (as well as reaching it from Seville or Granada). Málaga's long-distance station is on the Paseo de los Tilos (tel. 95/235–0061); nearby, on Muelle de Heredía, a smaller station serves suburban destinations. The main bus company is **Portillo** (Córdoba 7, tel. 95/236–0091), serving the Costa del Sol. **Alsina Gräells** (Plaza de Toros Vieja, 95/231–8295) has service to Granada, Córdoba, Seville, and Nerja. In Torremolinos, Fuengirola, and Marbella, buses operate out of Portillo stations. The train station in Málaga (Explanada de la Estación, tel. 95/236–0202) is a 15-minute walk from the town center, across the river. The **RENFE** office (Strachan 2, tel. 95/221–4127) is more convenient for tickets and information.

Tourist Information

The most helpful tourist offices, by far, are in Málaga and Marbella. The Málaga office covers the entire province.

Estepona (Paseo Marítimo Pedro Manrique, tel. 95/280–0913).
Fuengirola (Av. Jesús Santos Rein 6, tel. 95/246–7457).
Gibraltar (On Cathedral Square, tel. 9567/74950).
Málaga (Pasaje de Chinitas 4, tel. 95/221–3445, and at the airport in both national and international terminals).
Marbella (Miguel Cano 1, tel. 95/277–1442).
Nerja (Puerta del Mar 2, tel. 95/252–1531).
Ronda (Plaza de España 1, tel. 95/287–1272).
Torremolinos (Guetaria 517, tel. 95/238–1578).

Exploring the Costa del Sol

You'll find it quite easy to get around the well-linked Costa del Sol by public transportation; inquire at helpful local tourist offices if you need assistance. The tour below includes visits to Málaga, Torremolinos, Benalmádena, Fuengirola, Mijas, Marbella, Ronda, Estepona, and Gibraltar. Of those, only Ronda and Mijas are set back from the coast, but both towns are quite accustomed to tourists and easily reached by public transportation from most coastal towns.

Málaga is a busy port city with ancient streets and lovely villas set among exotic foliage, but it has little to recommend it to the overnight visitor. The central Plaza de la Marina, overlooking the port, is a pleasant place for a drink. The main shops are along the Calle Marqués de Larios.

The **Alcazaba** is a fortress begun in the 8th century when Málaga was the most important port of the Moorish kingdom. The ruins of the Roman amphitheater at its entrance were uncovered when the fort was restored. The inner palace dates from the 11th century when, for a short period after the breakup of the Caliphate of the West in Córdoba, it became the residence of the Moorish emirs. Today you'll find the **Archaeological Museum** here and a good collection of Moorish art. *Tel. 95/222-0043. Admission: 30 ptas. Open Mon.-Sat. 11-2 and 5-8 (4-7 in winter), Sun. 10-2.*

Energetic souls can climb through the Alcazaba gardens to the summit of **Gibralfaro.** Others can drive by way of Calle Victoria or take the parador minibus that leaves roughly every 1½ hours from near the cathedral on Molina Lario. The Gibralfaro fortifications were built for Yusuf I in the 14th century. The Moors called it Jebelfaro, which means "rock of the lighthouse," after the beacon that stood here to guide ships into the harbor and warn of invasions by pirates. Today the beacon has gone, but there's a small parador that makes a delightful place for a drink or a meal and has some stunning views.

Your first glimpse of **Torremolinos,** the ocean of concrete blocks that form its outskirts, makes it difficult to grasp that as recently as the early 1960s this was an inconsequential fishing village. Today, this grossly overdeveloped resort is a prime example of 20th-century tourism run riot. The town center, with its brash Nogalera Plaza, is full of overpriced bars and restaurants. Much more attractive is the district of La Carihuela, farther west, below the Avenida Carlota Alexandra. You'll find some old fishermen's cottages here, a few excellent seafood restaurants, and a traffic-free esplanade for an enjoyable stroll on a summer evening.

West of Torremolinos are the similar but more staid resorts of **Benalmádena** and **Fuengirola,** both retirement havens for British and American senior citizens. Frequent buses from Fuengirola, Marbella, or Málaga will take you up into the mountains to the picturesque—and overphotographed—village of **Mijas.** Though the vast tourist-oriented main square may seem like an extension of the Costa's tawdry bazaar, there are hillside streets of whitewashed houses where you'll discover an authentic village atmosphere that has changed little since the days before the tourist boom of the 1960s. Visit the bullring, the nearby church, and the chapel of Mijas's patroness, the Virgen de la Peña (to the side of the main square), and enjoy shopping for good-quality gifts and souvenirs.

Marbella is the most fashionable and sedate resort area along the coast. It does have a certain Florida-land-boom feel to it, but development has been controlled, and Marbella will, let's hope, never turn into another Torremolinos. The town's charming old Moorish quarter may be crowded with up-market boutiques and a modern, T-shirt-and-fudge section along the main drag, but when people

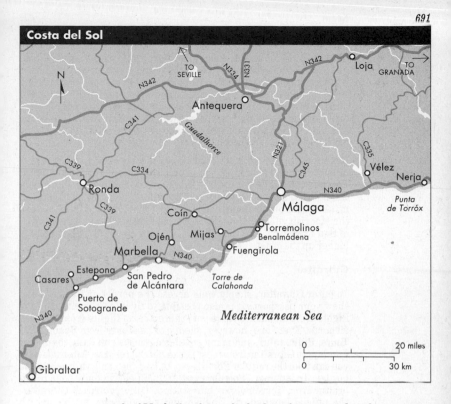

Costa del Sol

TO SEVILLE · TO GRANADA · Loja · Antequera · *Guadalhorce* · Vélez · Nerja · Ronda · Punta de Torróx · Coín · **Málaga** · Ojén · Mijas · Torremolinos · Benalmádena · Marbella · Fuengirola · Casares · Estepona · San Pedro de Alcántara · Torre de Calahonda · Puerto de Sotogrande · *Mediterranean Sea* · Gibraltar

0   20 miles
0   30 km

speak of Marbella, they refer both to the town and to the resorts—some more exclusive than others—stretching 16 kilometers (10 miles) or so on either side of town, between the highway and the beach. If you're vacationing in southern Spain, this is the place to stay. There's championship golf and tennis, fashionable waterfront cafés, and trendy shopping arcades.

The coastal highway outside Marbella, known locally as the Golden Mile, with its mosque, Arab banks, and residence of King Fahd of Saudi Arabia, proclaims the ever-growing influence of wealthy Arabs in this playground of the rich. In **Puerto Banús** (accessible by city buses; inquire at the tourist office), Marbella's plush marina, with its flashy yachts, fashionable people, and expensive restaurants, the glittering parade outshines even St. Tropez in ritzy glamour.

Ronda is reached via a spectacular mountain road from the coast. One of the oldest towns in Spain and the last stronghold of the legendary Andalucían bandits, Ronda's most dramatic feature is its ravine, known as **El Tajo**, which is 279 meters (900 feet) across and divides the old Moorish town from the "new town" of El Mercadillo. Spanning the gorge is the **Puente Nuevo,** an amazing architectural feat built between 1755 and 1793. Its parapet offers dizzying views of the River Guadalevin way below. Countless people have plunged to their death from this bridge, including its own architect, who accidentally fell over while inspecting his work, and numerous victims of the Civil War of 1936–39 who were hurled into the ravine—an episode recounted in Hemingway's *For Whom the Bell Tolls*. Ronda is visited more for its setting, breathtaking views, and ancient houses than for any particular monument. Stroll the old streets of **La Ciudad;** drop in at the historic **Reina Victoria** hotel, built by the English from Gibraltar as a fashionable resting place on their Algeciras to Bobadilla railroad line; and visit the **bullring,** one of the earliest and most beautiful rings in Spain. Here Ronda's most famous native son,

Pedro Romero (1754–1839), father of modern bullfighting, is said to have killed 5,600 bulls during his 30-year career, and in the **Bull-fighting Museum** you can see posters dating from the very first fights held in the ring in May 1785. The ring is privately owned now, but three to four fights a year are still held in the summer months. Tickets are exceedingly difficult to come by (tel. 95/287–4132, admission to ring and museum: 200 ptas., open daily 10–6:30, 7 in summer). Above all, don't miss the cliff-top walk and the gardens of the **Alameda del Tajo,** where you can contemplate one of the most dramatic views in all Andalucía.

Returning to the coast, the next town is **Estepona,** which until recently marked the end of the urban sprawl of the Costa del Sol. Estepona lacks the hideous high rises of Torremolinos and Fuengirola, and set back from the main highway, it's not hard to make out the old fishing village this once was. Wander the streets of the Moorish village, around the central food market and the **Church of San Francisco,** and you'll find a pleasant contrast to the excesses higher up the coast.

Gibraltar

To enter **Gibraltar,** simply walk across the border at La Línea and show your passport. It is also possible to fly into Gibraltar on daily flights from London but, as yet, there are no flights from Spanish airports. There are, however, plenty of bus tours from Spain. **Juliá Tours, Pullmantur,** and many smaller agencies run daily tours (not Sunday) to Gibraltar from most Costa del Sol resorts. Alternatively, you can take the regular **Portillo** bus to La Línea and walk across the border. In summer, **Portillo** runs an inexpensive daily tour to Gibraltar from Torremolinos bus station. Once you reach Gibraltar, the official language is English and the currency is the British pound sterling, though pesetas are also accepted.

The Rock of Gibraltar acquired its name in AD 711 when it was captured by the Moorish chieftain Tarik at the start of the Arab invasion of Spain. It became known as Jebel Tarik (Rock of Tarik), later corrupted to Gibraltar. After successive periods of Moorish and Spanish domination, Gibraltar was captured by an Anglo-Dutch fleet in 1704 and ceded to the British by the Treaty of Utrecht in 1713. This tiny British colony, whose impressive silhouette dominates the straits between Spain and Morocco, is a rock just 5⅘ kilometers (3⅞ miles) long, three-quarter kilometers (half a mile) wide, and 425 meters (1,369 feet) high.

On entering Gibraltar you have a choice. You can either plunge straight into exploring Gibraltar town or opt for a tour around the Rock. Several minibus tours are available, some at the point of entry that crosses the Gibraltar Airport's runway. Inquire at the tourist office for details.

Numbers in the margin correspond to points of interest on the Gibraltar map.

The minibus tour around the Rock is best begun on the eastern side. As you enter Gibraltar, you'll turn left down Devil's Tower Road and ❶ drive as far as **Catalan Bay,** a small fishing village founded by Genoese settlers in the 18th century and now one of the Rock's most picturesque resorts. The road continues on beneath water catchments ❷ that supply the colony's drinking water to another resort, **Sandy Bay,** and then plunges through the Dudley Ward Tunnel to bring you ❸ out at the Rock's most southerly tip, **Europa Point.** The view here is remarkable, across the Straits to the coast of Morocco, 22½ kilometers (14 miles) away. You are standing on what in ancient times was called one of the two Pillars of Hercules. Across the water in Morocco, a mountain between the cities of Ceuta and Tangier formed the

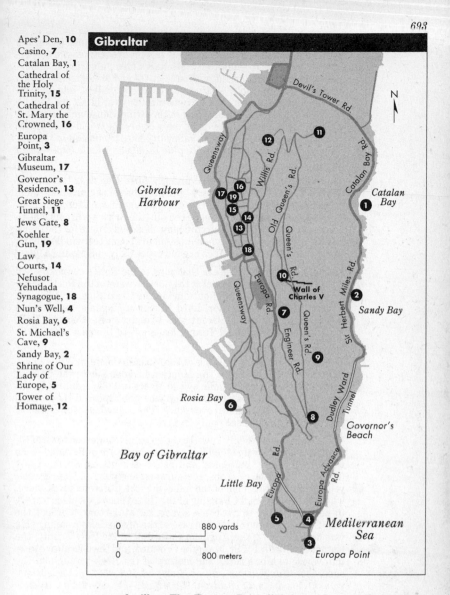

Gibraltar

second pillar. The Europa Point lighthouse has stood above the meeting point of the Atlantic and the Mediterranean since 1841. Plaques explain the history of the gun installations here, and, near-by on Europa Flats, you can see the **Nun's Well,** an ancient Moorish cistern, and the **Shrine of Our Lady of Europe,** venerated by sailors since 1462.

Europa Road winds its way high on the western slopes above **Rosia Bay,** to which Nelson's flagship, HMS *Victory,* was towed after the Battle of Trafalgar in 1805. Aboard were the dead of the battle, who are now buried in Trafalgar Cemetery on the southern edge of town, and the body of Admiral Nelson himself, preserved in a barrel of rum. He was then taken to London for burial.

Europa Road continues to the **casino** (tel. 9567/76666, open daily 9 PM–4 AM) above the Alameda Gardens. Make a sharp right here up En-gineer Road to **Jews Gate,** an unbeatable lookout point over the docks and Bay of Gibraltar to Algeciras in Spain. Here you gain access to the **Upper Nature Preserve,** which includes St. Michael's Cave, the Ape's Den, the Great Siege Tunnel, and the Moorish castle (*see below*). Queens Road leads to **St. Michael's Cave,** a series of underground chambers adorned with stalactites and stalagmites, which provides an admirable setting for concerts, ballet, and drama. Sound-and-light shows are held here most days at 11 AM and 4 PM. A skull of Neanderthal Woman (now in the British Museum in London) was found in the caves some eight years *before* the world-famous discovery in Germany's Neander Valley in 1856. *Admission to the preserve, including all sites: £4.50, plus £1.50 per vehicle. Open daily 10–6.*

(10) Down Old Queen's Road you'll find the **Apes' Den** near the **Wall of Charles V.** The famous Barbary apes are a breed of cinnamon-color, tailless monkeys, natives of the Atlas Mountains in Morocco. Legend holds that as long as the apes remain, the British will continue to hold the Rock. Winston Churchill himself issued orders for the maintenance of the ape colony when its numbers began to dwindle during World War II. Today the apes are fed twice daily at 8 AM and 4 PM.

Passing beneath the cable car that runs to the Rock's summit, you'll **(11)** ascend the **Great Siege Tunnel** at the northern end of the Rock. These huge galleries were carved out during the Great Siege of 1779–83. Here, in 1878, the governor, Lord Napier of Magdala, entertained ex-President Ulysses S. Grant at a banquet in **St. George's Hall.** From here, the **Holyland Tunnel** leads out to the east side of the Rock above Catalan Bay.

The last stop before the town is at the **Moorish Castle** on Willis Road. Built by the successors of the Moorish invader Tarik, the present **(12) Tower of Homage** was rebuilt by the Moors in 1333. Admiral Rooke hoisted the British flag from its top when he captured the Rock in 1704, and here it has flown ever since. The castle has been closed to the public and can be seen only from the outside.

Willis Road leads steeply down to the colorful, congested town of Gibraltar, where the dignified Regency architecture of Britain blends with the shutters, balconies, and patios of southern Spain. Apart from the attraction of shops, restaurants, and pubs on Main Street, **(13)** you'll want to visit some of the following: the **Governor's Residence,** where the ceremonial Changing of the Guard once took place weekly (it now occurs four to five times a year; ask at the tourist office); the **(14)** **Law Courts,** where the famous case of the *Mary Celeste* sailing ship **(15)** was heard in 1872; the Anglican **Cathedral of the Holy Trinity;** the **(16) (17)** Catholic **Cathedral of St. Mary the Crowned;** and the **Gibraltar Museum,** whose exhibits recall the history of the Rock throughout the ages. *Gibraltar Museum, Bomb House La., tel. 9567–74289. Admission: £1.50 adults, £1 children. Open Mon.–Fri. 10–6, Sat. 10–2.*

(18) Finally, the **Nefusot Yehudada Synagogue** on Line Wall Road is worth a look for its inspired architecture, and, if you're interested in **(19)** guns, the **Koehler Gun** in **Casemates Square** at the northern end of Main Street is an impressive example of the type of gun developed during the Great Siege.

Dining and Lodging

For details and price-category definitions, *see* Dining and Lodging *in* Staying in Spain, *above.*

Estepona   **Antonio.** Head for the patio of this prize-winning restaurant, if you *Dining*   can beat the crowds of locals who flock to the place. Try the *ensalada* ★   *de pimientos asados* (roast pepper salad) or the *fritura malaguena* (fried fish Málaga style). *Puerto Deportivo, tel. 95/280–1142. Reservations advised. DC, MC, V. $$*

  Costa del Sol. This friendly French bistro offers French and Spanish dishes in an informal setting. French favorites include bouillabaisse and duck in orange sauce. It's on a side street beside the Portillo bus station. *San Roque s/n, tel. 95/2801101. AE, DC, MC, V. Closed Mon. lunch and Sun. $*

Lodging **Santa Marta.** This is a small, quiet hotel with just 37 rooms in chalet bungalows set in a large, peaceful garden. Some rooms are a little faded after 30 years, but the tranquil setting is a plus. Good lunches are served by the pool. *Rte. N340, km 173, tel. 95/288–8180. 37 rooms. AE, MC, V. Closed Oct.–Mar. $$*

Gibraltar **Country Cottage.** Opposite the Catholic cathedral, this is the place
Dining to go for a taste of Old England. Enjoy steak-and-kidney pie, Angus steak, and roast beef, by candlelight. *13 Giro's Passage, tel. 9567/70084. Reservations advised. AE, MC, V. Closed Sun. $$*

Ye Olde Rock. A changing menu of pub fare is offered at this colorful spot on McKintosh Square. *Tel. 9567/71804. No credit cards. ¢*

Lodging **Bristol.** This colonial-style hotel is just off Gibraltar's main street, right in the heart of town. The rooms are large and comfortable, and the tropical garden is a real haven for those guests who want to relax in peaceful isolation. *10 Cathedral Sq., tel. 9567/76800. 60 rooms. Facilities: Breakfast room, bar, pool. AE, DC, MC, V. $$*

Miss Serruya Guest House. Miss Serruya rents four quite luxurious rooms (one of them really a small apartment) in her renovated 1850 frame house, one of Gibraltar's old aristocratic residences. *92/1A Irish Town, tel. 9567/73220. 4 rooms. No credit cards. $*

Málaga **Rincón de Mata.** This is one of the best of the many restaurants in the
Dining pedestrian shopping streets between Calle Larios and Calle Nueva. Its menu is more original than most. In summer, there are tables outside on the sidewalk. *Esparteros 8, tel. 95/222–3135. V. $$*

Rincón de la Catedral. This beautiful restaurant in a beautiful setting directly faces the cathedral. In an atmosphere of elegant wood, rafter-hung ham, and fresh flowers, try specialties such as *brochetas de rape con gambas* (kebabs with angler and prawns) or the relatively expensive *solomillo a la pimienta verde* (pork steak in green pepper sauce). *Canon 7, tel. 95/260–0518. AE, MC, V. Closed Sun. $–$$*

La Cancela. This is a colorful restaurant in the center of town, just off Calle Granada. Dine indoors or alfresco. *Denís Belgrano 5, tel. 95/222–3125. AE, DC, MC, V. Closed Wed. $*

La Buena Sombra. Hung with caricatures of famous Spanish personalities, this spot abutting the cathedral is usually packed with locals enjoying hearty regional fare like *pescado frito* (fried fish). Its daily special is an excellent value. *Cañon 3, tel. 95/222–6230. No credit cards. ¢–$*

Don Jamón. You'll dine on a landing above the bar at Don Jamón, which features a wide offering of traditional Castilian dishes. Try the *conejo a la castellana* (rabbit in sauce), roast chicken, paella, or *morcilla* (blood sausage). Heads of boar and deer and roof-hung hams give the place a hunter ambience. *Strachan 5, tel. 95/222–1343. No credit cards. ¢*

Lodging **Las Vegas.** In a pleasant part of town, just east of the center, this hotel has a dining room overlooking the Paseo Marítimo, an outdoor pool, and a large leafy garden. Rooms at the back enjoy a good view of the ocean. *Paseo de Sancha 22, tel. 95/221–7712. 100 rooms. Facilities: Restaurant, bar, pool. AE, DC, MC, V. $$*

Carlos Quinto. Slightly faded but well-run and clean, this hotel is a few steps from the cathedral in the heart of old Málaga. All rooms have either a shower or full bath, and some offer television. *Cister 10, tel. 95/221–5120. 53 rooms. AE, DC, MC, V. $*

Victoria. This small, recently renovated hostel in an old house just off Calle Larios offers excellent budget accommodations in a convenient central location. *Sancha de Lara 3, tel. 95/222–4223. 13 rooms. AE, V. $*

Chinitas. A giant sign on the Plaza Constitución points the way to

Hostal Chinitas. After climbing a rather gruff set of stairs, you'll find a charming home, hung with pictures and inhabited by a cheerful family. *Pasaje de Chinitas 2–2, tel. 95/221–4683. 4 rooms. No credit cards. ¢*

Marbella
Dining

La Tricycleta. In an old house in the center of town, this English-owned restaurant is a local institution. Have a drink beside a log fire at the downstairs bar, then dine upstairs or outside on the rooftop patio when it's warm. *Buitrago 14, tel. 95/277–7800. Reservations advised in summer. AE, MC, V. Closed Sun. $$*

Meson del Pasaje. A warren of small dining rooms and bars awaits you in this old house just off the Plaza Naranjos. The decor is Victorian, with Spanish touches. The menu features a wide variety of pastas. *Pasaje 5, tel. 95/277–1261. Reservations advised in summer. V. Closed summer lunch. $*

Meson del Pollo. This small, sunny, "house of chicken" illustrates how Marbella, despite tourism, remains truly Spanish. Porcelain lampshades, azulejo tiles, a dozen tables, and the scents of roasting chicken fill this popular lunch spot. Try the *pollo a la sevillana* dinner (roast chicken with squid, fried potatoes, salad, and cider) or sample tapas of octopus or meatballs. *Antonio Martín, across from the El Fuerte Hotel, no phone. No credit cards. $*

Guerola. At this small restaurant, the food is good, homemade, and inexpensive. Stop for a tapa at the bar. The gazpacho is tasty, and so is the *fritura variada* (fried fish assortment). *Padre Enrique Cantos 4, 95/277–0007. AE, MC, V. ¢*

Lodging

El Fuerte. This is the best of the few hotels in the center of Marbella, with simple, adequate rooms. It's in a 1950s-type building in the midst of a large garden with an outdoor pool. *Avda. El Fuerte, tel. 95/286–1500. 263 rooms. Facilities: Outdoor and indoor pools, tennis. AE, DC, V. $$*

Finlandia. If you're looking for clean, inexpensive accommodations in the heart of town, try this simple white hostel on a quiet residential street. The atmosphere is friendly and informal, with a small bar and TV lounge in the lobby. The large rooms have balconies. *Finlandia s/n, tel. 95/277–0700. 10 rooms. MC, V. $*

Paco. On a quiet and pretty white street above the main road, the Hostal Paco is another good find in the old town (unfortunately, it's closed October–April). Many of the rooms have small balconies on the three-story building front. *Peral 16, tel. 95/277–1200. 25 rooms. No credit cards. ¢–$*

Pilar. This may be the best find in Marbella: a cheerful, relatively large and charming hotel in a central location—and very fairly priced to boot. It was taken over in 1992 by a Scot, Michael Wright, a former butler and master of guest houses in Edinburgh. It's clean and intimate and includes such delightful surprises as a log fire in winter. *Mesoncillo 4, 95/282–9936. 17 rooms. No credit cards. ¢*

Mijas
Dining

La Reja. This charming restaurant has two dining rooms overlooking the main square of Plaza Virgen de la Peña. There's an atmospheric bar and an inexpensive pizzeria, too. *Caños 9, tel. 95/248–5068. Reservations accepted. AE, DC, MC, V. Closed Mon. $$*

Mirlo Blanco. Here you can sample Basque specialties, such as *txangurro* (crab) and *merluza a la vasca* (hake with asparagus, eggs, and clam sauce). *Plaza Constitución 13, tel. 95/248–5700. Reservations accepted. AE, DC, MC, V. $$*

El Horno. You'll have a choice in summer of where to eat: out in the pedestrian alley where you enter or inside in a dining room with spectacular views of the main plaza. There's a wide range of traditional Spanish fare here, more unusual dishes like spaghetti *bolognese*, (with meat sauce) and a variety of sandwiches. *Loscaños 13, tel. 95/248–5097. MC, V. $*

Lodging

Luque. There is no inexpensive lodging in Mijas, but just a few miles away and reachable by hourly bus service connecting Marbella and

Mijas, you'll find this serene and charming hotel. The family that runs it keeps the seven rooms spotless, and many of them face out onto the Plaza Andalucía, a small plaza dotted with palm trees. *Plaza Andalucía 4, enter from the main road, Benalmádena, tel. 95/244–8197. 7 rooms. No credit cards. ¢*

Ronda
Dining

Pedro Romero. Because of its location opposite the bullring, this restaurant is, not surprisingly, packed with colorful taurine decor. Among the traditional regional recipes worth trying is the *sopa de mesón*—the soup of the house. *Virgen de la Paz 18, tel. 95/287–1110. AE, DC, MC, V. $$*

Hermanos Macias. In summer, if you dine on the terrace out front, you'll be looking down an alley at the main entrance to the bullring. Inside, there's a dark and moody dining room with a Moorish feel. Service is attentive, and the food is good. *Pedro Romero s/n, tel. 95/287–4238. AE, DC, MC, V. $*

Mesón Santiago. This typical Andalucían mesón with colorful decor opens for lunch only and has a pleasant, recently renovated outdoor patio. It serves hearty portions of home-cooked food—but be prepared for long waits. *Marina 3, tel. 95/287–1559. MC, V. $*

Flores. This very Spanish restaurant, with a large, bare dining room, faces the bullring. *Vírgen de la Paz 9, tel. 95/287–1040. MC, V. ¢*

Lodging

Polo. A cozy, old-fashioned hotel in the center of town, Polo sports a reasonably priced restaurant. The staff is friendly and the rooms simple but comfortable. *Mariano Soubiron 8, tel. 95/287–2447. 33 rooms. Facilities: Restaurant. AE, DC, V. $$*

La Española. Starkly simple rooms, sometimes a bit cold but clean, are in a building with dramatic views of the rocky and wild countryside upon which Ronda is built. *Jose Aparicio 3, tel. 95/287–1052. 20 rooms. No credit cards. ¢*

Torremolinos
Dining

Casa Guaquin. Casa Guaquin is widely known as the best seafood restaurant in the region. Changing daily catches are served on a seaside patio alongside such menu stalwarts as *coquillas al ajillo* (sea cockles in garlic sauce). *Paseo Maritimo 63, tel. 95/238–4530. AE, V. Closed Thurs. $$*

El Roqueo. Owned by a former fisherman, this is one of the locals' favorite Carihuela fish restaurants. Ingredients are always fresh and the prices are very reasonable. *Carmen 35, tel. 95/238–4946. AE, V. Closed Tues. and Nov. $$*

Juan. This is a good place to enjoy seafood in summer, with a sunny outdoor patio facing the sea. The specialties include the great Costa del Sol standbys: *sopa de mariscos* (shellfish soup), *dorada al horno* (oven-roasted giltheads), and *fritura malagueña. Paseo Marítimo 29, La Carihuela, tel. 95/238–5656. AE, DC, MC, V. $$*

Lodging

Tropicana. Located on the beach at the far end of the Carihuela is this comfortable, relaxing resort hotel. Several good restaurants are nearby. *Trópico 6, tel. 95/238–6600, fax 95/238–0568. 86 rooms. Facilities: pool. AE, DC, MC, V. $$*

Pizarro. If you want to stay right downtown, this modern hotel just off the Plaza Andalucía is a good choice. It's well maintained and comes with a functional restaurant and bar. It's a 15-minute walk to the beach. *Pasaje Pizarro s/n, tel. 95/238–7167. 49 rooms. No credit cards. $–$$*

★ **Miami.** Set in an old Andalucían villa in a shady garden to the west of the Carihuela, this is something of a find amid the ocean of concrete blocks. *Aladino 14, tel. 95/238–5255. 29 rooms. facilities: Pool. No credit cards. $*

Marloy. Near the Pizarro, the Pensión Marloy offers very cheap rooms that are clean but in need of sprucing-up. The street can be noisy. *Cruz 6, tel. 95/238–7820. 28 rooms. No credit cards. ¢*

24 Sweden

Less expensive ways of visiting Sweden are available to the traveler who takes the trouble to do a little research. Major hotel chain discounts and packages, youth hostels, special rail passes, and carefully selected restaurants and hotels are among the many ways visitors can substantially cut costs in Sweden. Because of its size—450,707 square kilometers (173,349 square miles), approximately that of California—a visit to Sweden is wisely limited to a region or two. But no matter where you go in this sparsely populated country of vast spaces and pristine forests, unspoiled lakes and churning rivers, jagged coastlines and countless archipelagoes, the visit is well worth the price of admission. The distances are considerable, especially by European standards—almost 1,600 kilometers (1,000 miles) as the crow flies, from north to south. The 2,128-kilometer (1,330-mile) train journey from Trelleborg, in the far south, through endless birch forests to Riksgränsen, in the Arctic north, is said to be the world's longest stretch of continuously electrified railroad.

This chapter concentrates on the more densely populated southern part of the country—essentially the area dominated by the two largest cities, Stockholm and Gothenburg.

The Swedish Travel and Tourism Council, a privately supported tourism corporation that replaced the Swedish Tourist Board in 1992, is mounting a more vigorous effort to market the country to overseas visitors. Until recently, Sweden's image did not keep pace with reality, and that, too, is expected to change under the new tourism organization. Though it is widely accepted that prices in Sweden are higher than in other European countries, an effort has been made to bring prices in line, an effort that in part reflects the fact that Sweden joined the European Union in 1995. The government reduced the value-added tax (Moms) on transportation, food, restaurants, and hotels from 25% to 21% (it was as low as 18% in 1992), and a whole generation of restaurateurs with a Continental outlook is introducing affordable dishes utilizing Swedish ingredients. Indeed, those who visit Sweden today will be surprised by the breadth and quality of the cuisine, as well as the high standards of

Sweden

N

0   50 miles

75 km

Norwegian Sea

Kiruna

Gällivare

Luleälven

Jokkmokk

400

Arjeplog

Töre

Torneå

Tärnaby

Arvidsjaur

Kalix

E79

Sorsele

95

Piteå

Luleå

Storuman

Lycksele

Skellefteå

342

Åsele

92

Umeå

Strömsund

60

Åre

Östersund

E75

Tännäs

Sundsvall

FINLAND

84

Ljungan

Gulf of Bothnia

Idre

Hudiksvall

70

Bollnäs

Mora

Söderhamn

Klarälven

Falun

Gävle

80

Borlänge

Avesta

Fagersta

Uppsala

Karlstad

Västerås

E4

E18

Mellerud

Örebro

Mälaren

★ Stockholm

Gulf of Finland

Strömstad

Vänern

NORWAY

Uddevalla

Trollhättan

Norrköping

Gotska Sandön

ESTONIA

Göteborg

Vättern

Linköping

Baltic Sea

40

Jönköping

Borås

Nässjö

E66

Visby

Gulf of Riga

Falkenberg

E6

Värnamo

Oskarshamn

Gotland

Halmstad

Växjö

23

Kalmar

Öland

LATVIA

Helsingborg

Karlskrona

Malmö

Kristianstad

LITHUANIA

DENMARK

Trelleborg

Ystad

lodging. Even the most modest establishments are spotlessly clean, and you will be given a warm welcome (almost certainly in excellent English, too).

Sweden's cities make the most of their natural settings and are carefully planned, with an emphasis on light and open spaces. Stockholm, one of the most beautiful of European capitals, is the major attraction, though Gothenburg, on the west coast, and Malmö, just across the sound from Denmark, are worthy of short visits as well.

Essential Information

Before You Go

When to Go Although the peak tourist season runs from June through August, Sweden has extended the season to run from mid-May to mid-September, in an effort to encourage visitors from abroad. Nevertheless, many visitor attractions do not start operating until mid-June and then suddenly restrict their opening times or close down altogether in midAugust, when the Swedes' own vacation season ends and the children return to school. The weather can also be magnificent in the spring and fall, and there are plenty of tourists who would like to do some sightseeing when there are fewer people around.

The concentrated nature of the Swedes' own vacation period can sometimes make it difficult to get hotel reservations during July and early August. On the other hand, the big city hotels, which cater mainly to business travelers, reduce their rates drastically in summer, when their ordinary clients are on vacation. Check with your travel agent or the tourist information center, **Next Stop Sweden** (Box 3030, 103 61 Stockholm, tel. 08/725–5500, fax 08/725–5531). **Upptäck Sverige Resor** (Discover Sweden Travel Agency, Sveavägen 16, Stockholm, tel. 08/791–8085) has well-priced seasonal package tours.

Climate Like the rest of northern Europe, Sweden has unpredictable summer weather, but it is more likely to be rainy on the west coast than on the east. When the sun shines, the climate is usually agreeable; it is rarely unbearably hot. In Stockholm it never really gets dark in midsummer, while in the far north, above the Arctic Circle, the sun doesn't set between the end of May and the middle of July.

The following are the average daily maximum and minimum temperatures for Stockholm.

Jan.	30F	– 1C	May	58F	14C	Sept.	60F	15C
	23	– 5		43	6		49	9
Feb.	30F	– 1C	June	67F	19C	Oct.	49F	9C
	22	– 5		51	11		41	5
Mar.	37F	3C	July	71F	22C	Nov.	40F	5C
	26	– 4		57	14		34	1
Apr.	47F	8C	Aug.	68F	20C	Dec.	35F	3C
	34	1		55	13		28	– 2

Currency The unit of currency in Sweden is the krona (plural kronor), which is divided into 100 öre and is written as Skr, SEK or kr. Coins come in values of 50 öre and 1, 5, and 10 kronor, while bills come in denominations of 20, 100, 500, and 1,000 Skr. Traveler's checks and foreign currency can be exchanged at banks all over Sweden and at post offices bearing the NB Exchange sign. At press time (summer 1995), the exchange rate was 7.45 kronor to the dollar and 11.76 kronor to the pound sterling.

What It Will Cost Sweden is an expensive country. Hotel prices are above the European average, but, as in most countries, the most expensive hotels are found in major cities, such as Stockholm and Gothenburg. Restaurant prices are generally fairly high, but there are bargains to be had: Look for the *dagens rätt* (dish of the day) in many city restaurants. This costs about Skr 40–Skr 65 and can include a main dish, salad, soft drink, bread and butter, and coffee.

Many hotels have special low summer rates and cut costs on weekends in winter. Because of heavy taxes and excise duties, liquor prices are among the highest in Europe. It pays to take in your maximum duty-free allowance. Value-added tax (Moms) is imposed on most goods and services at a rate of 25%; the rate is 21% for food, hotels, restaurants, and transportation. You can avoid most of the tax on goods if you take advantage of the tax-free shopping service offered at more than 13,000 stores throughout the country (*see* Shopping *in* Staying in Sweden, *below*).

Sample Prices Cup of coffee, Skr 10–Skr 15; bottle of beer, Skr 30–Skr 40; Coca-Cola, Skr 12–Skr 15; ham sandwich, Skr 25–Skr 35; 1-mile taxi ride, Skr 70 (depending on the taxi company).

Customs on Arrival Travelers from the United States may import duty-free: 1 liter of liquor *or* 2 liters of fortified wine; 2 liters of wine; 15 liters of beer; 200 cigarettes *or* 100 cigarillos *or* 50 cigars *or* 250 grams of tobacco; 50 grams of perfume; 0.25 liter of aftershave; and other goods up to the value of Skr 1,700. Travelers from the United Kingdom or other European Union countries may import duty-free: 1 liter of liquor *or* 3 liters of fortified wine; 5 liters of wine; 15 liters of beer; 300 cigarettes *or* 150 cigarillos *or* 75 cigars *or* 400 grams of tobacco; and other goods, including perfume and aftershave, of any value. Duties are applied according to the traveler's point of origin, not citizenship— for example, if a U.S. citizen traveling from New York to Sweden were to break the trip for a few days in London, then the more generous U.K. limitations would be applied. There are no limits on the amount of foreign currency that can be imported or exported.

Language Virtually all Swedes you are likely to meet will speak English, for it is a mandatory subject in all schools and is the main foreign language that Swedish children learn. Some of the older people you meet in the rural areas may not be quite so familiar with English, but you'll soon find someone who can help out. Swedish is one of the Germanic languages and is similar to Danish and Norwegian. Grammatically it is easier than German, although pronunciation can pose some problems. Also, the letters å, ä, and ö rank as separate letters in the Swedish alphabet and come at the end after *Z*. So if you're looking up a Mr. Ängelholm in a Swedish telephone book, you'll find him near the end. Another oddity in the phone book is that *v* and *w* are interchangeable; Wittström, for example, comes before Vittviks, not after.

Getting Around

By Train Sweden's rail network, mostly electrified, is highly efficient, and trains operate frequently, particularly on the main routes linking Stockholm with Gothenburg and Malmö, on which there is frequent service. First- and second-class cars are provided on all main routes, and sleeping cars are available in both classes on overnight trains. On virtually all long-distance trains, there is a buffet or dining car. Seat reservations are always advisable, and on some trains—indicated with R, IN, or IC on the timetable—they are compulsory. Reservations can be made right up to departure time at a cost of Skr 30 per seat (tel. 020/757575).

Fares On certain trains, listed as "Low price" or "Red" departures, fares are reduced by 50% (25% on Tuesdays, Wednesdays, Thursdays, and Saturdays). To enjoy these rates, passengers must purchase the *Reslustkort* (Desire-to-Travel card), which costs Skr 150. Passengers paying low fares cannot make stopovers, and the tickets are valid for only 36 hours.

Contact the Swedish rail network for a special pass called the **Scan Rail Pass,** which allows for free rail travel anywhere in Scandinavia. The 21-day pass costs Skr 2,250, or Skr 1,700 if you're under 26, for second-class train travel and can also be used for free travel or 50% discounts on certain bus and ferry services. Also available is the *Norden Special,* which offers reduced rates on round-trip fares between Stockholm and Oslo (Skr 780), Stockholm and Copenhagen (Skr 795), and Gothenburg and Oslo (Skr 485). For more information, contact any local railway station or *Statens Jarnvagar* (SJ) (tel. 020/757575).

By Plane Sweden's domestic air network is highly developed. Most major cities are served by **SAS** (Scandinavian Airlines, tel. 020/727000). From Stockholm, there are services to about 30 points around the country. SAS offers cut-rate round-trip "Jackpot" fares every day of the week on selected flights, and these fares are available on most services during the peak tourist season, from late June to mid-August.

By Bus Sweden has an excellent network of express bus services that provides an inexpensive and relatively speedy way of getting around the country. **Swebus** (tel. 031/103285 in Gothenburg or 08/237190 in Stockholm) offers daily bus services from most major Swedish cities to various parts of Sweden. A number of other private companies operate weekend-only services on additional routes. In the far north of Sweden, post buses delivering mail to remote areas also carry passengers and provide an offbeat and inexpensive way of seeing the countryside.

By Boat The classic boat trip in Sweden is the four-day journey along the Göta Canal between Gothenburg and Stockholm, operated by **Göta Kanal** (Gothenburg, tel. 031/806315, fax 031/158311).

By Bicycle Cycling is a popular activity in Sweden, and the country's uncongested roads make it ideal for extended bike tours. Bicycles can be rented throughout the country; inquire at the local tourist information office. Rental costs average around SEK 80 per day or SEK 400 per week. The **Swedish Touring Club** (STF) in Stockholm (Drottninggatan 31–33, tel. 08/790–3100) can give you information about cycling packages that include bike rental, overnight accommodations, and meals. **Cykelfrämjandet** (tel. 08/321680, fax 08/310305) has an English-language guide to cycling trips.

Staying in Sweden

Telephones
Local Calls Sweden has plenty of pay phones, found in special offices marked Tele or Telebutik. To make calls from a pay phone, you should have Skr 1 or Skr 5 coins available. For a local call, you need two Skr 1 coins. You can also purchase a *telefonkort* (telephone card) from a *Telebutik, pressbyrå,* or hospital for Skr 30, Skr 55, or Skr 95, which works out to be cheaper if you make numerous domestic calls. Telephone numbers beginning with 020 are toll-free within Sweden.

International Calls These can be made from any pay phone. For calls to the United States and Canada, dial 009, then 1 (the country code), then wait for a second dial tone before dialing the area code and number. When dialing the United Kingdom, omit the initial zero on area codes (for Central London you would dial 009 followed by 44, wait for the second tone, then dial 171 and the local number). To reach an **AT&T** long-distance operator, dial 020/795611; for **MCI**, dial 020/795922; and for **Sprint** 020/799011.

Operators and Information	For international calls, the operator assistance number is 0018; directory assistance is 07977. Within Sweden, dial 90130 for operator assistance and 07975 for directory assistance.
Country Code	If you're calling Sweden from another country, the country code is 46.
Mail *Postal Rates*	Airmail letters and postcards to the United States and Canada weighing less than 20 grams cost Skr 7.50. Postcards and letters within Europe cost Skr 6.
Receiving Mail	If you're uncertain where you will be staying, have your mail sent to Poste Restante, S-101 10 Stockholm. Collection is at the Central Post Office (Vasagatan 28–32, tel. 08/781–2040). A Poste Restante service is also offered to its clients by American Express (Birger Jarlsgatan 1, tel. 08/235330).
Shopping	Swedish goods have earned an international reputation for elegance and quality, and any visitor to the country should spend some time exploring the many impressive shops and department stores. The midsummer tourist season is as good a time as any to go shopping, for that is when many stores have their annual sales. The best buys are to be found in glassware, stainless steel, pottery and ceramics, leather goods, and textiles. You will find a wide selection of goods available in such major stores as **NK, Åhléns,** and **PUB,** which have branches all over the country.

High-quality furniture is a Swedish specialty, and it is worthwhile visiting one of the many branches of **IKEA,** a shop usually located on the outskirts of major towns. IKEA's prices are extremely competitive, and the company also operates an export service. An IKEA shuttle bus operates between Sweden House and one of its Stockholm stores. For glassware at bargain prices, head for the "Kingdom of Crystal" area (*see* Gothenburg and the Glass Country, *below*). All the major glassworks, including **Orrefors** and **Kosta Boda,** have large factory outlets where you can pick up "seconds" (normally indistinguishable from the perfect product) at only a fraction of the normal retail price. In country areas, look for the local **Hemslöjd** craft centers, featuring high-quality clothing and needlework items.

VAT Refunds	About 13,000 Swedish shops—1,000 in Stockholm alone—participate in the tax-free shopping service for visitors, enabling you to claim a refund on most of the Moms that you have paid. Shops taking part in the scheme display a distinctive black, blue, and yellow sticker in the window. (Some stores offer the service only on purchases worth more than Skr 200.) Whenever you make a purchase in a participating store, you are given a "tax-free shopping check" equivalent to the tax paid, less a handling charge. This check can be cashed when you leave Sweden, either at the airport or aboard ferries. You should have your passport with you when you make your purchase and when you claim your refund.
Opening and Closing Times	**Banks** are open weekdays 9:30–3, but some stay open until 5:30 in some larger cities. Banks at Stockholm's Arlanda Airport and Gothenburg's Landvetter Airport open every day, with extended hours. "Forex" currency-exchange offices operate in downtown Stockholm, Gothenburg, and Malmö, also with extended hours.

Museums. Hours vary widely, but museums are typically open weekdays 10–4 or 10–5. Many are also open on weekends but may close on Monday.

Shops are generally open weekdays 9 or 9:30–6 and Saturday 9–1 or 9–4. Some large department stores stay open until 8 or 10 on certain evenings, and some are also open on Sunday 12–4 in the major cities. Many supermarkets open on Sunday.

National Holidays	In 1996: January 1, January 6 (Epiphany), April 5 (Good Friday), April 8 (Easter Monday), May 1 (Labor Day), May 16 (Ascension),

May 26, 27 (Pentecost), June 22 (Midsummer's Day), November 2 (All Saints' Day), December 25, 26. Changing holidays in 1997: March 28 (Good Friday), March 31 (Easter Monday), May 8 (Ascension), May 18, 19 (Pentecost), June 20 (Midsummer's Day).

Dining Swedish cuisine has lately become much more cosmopolitan. The inevitable fast-food outlets, such as McDonald's and Burger King, have come on the scene, as well as Clock, the homegrown version. But there is also a good range of more conventional restaurants, including less expensive places where you can pick up a somewhat cheaper lunch or snack. Snacks can also be enjoyed in a *Konditori*, which offers inexpensive sandwiches, pastries, and pies with coffee, tea, or soft drinks.

Many restaurants all over the country specialize in *Husmanskost*— literally "home cooking"—which is based on traditional Swedish recipes.

Sweden is best known for its *smörgåsbord*, a word whose correct pronunciation defeats non-Swedes. It consists of a tempting buffet of hot and cold dishes, usually with a strong emphasis on seafood, notably herring, prepared in a wide variety of ways. Authentic smörgåsbord can be enjoyed all over the country, but the best is found in the many inns in Skåne, where you can eat as much as you want for about Skr 300. Many Swedish hotels serve a lavish smörgåsbord-style breakfast, often included in the room price. Do justice to your breakfast and you'll probably want to skip lunch!

Mealtimes The Swedes tend to eat early. Restaurants start serving lunch at about 11 AM, and outside the main cities you may find that they close quite early in the evening (often by 9) or may not even open at all for dinner. In major cities, especially on weekends, it's advisable to make reservations for any dinner plans.

What to Wear Except for the most formal restaurants, where a jacket and tie are preferable, casual—or casual chic—attire is perfectly acceptable for restaurants in all price categories. Swedish dress, however, like other Europeans', tends to be a bit more formal and a bit less flamboyant than that of Americans.

Ratings With the exception of the budget category, prices are per person and include a first course, main course (Swedes tend to skip desserts), and service charge, but no drinks. Service charges and Moms are included in the meal, so there is no need to tip. Restaurants in the budget category tend to offer simpler meals that don't usually include more than a main dish with bread, salad, coffee, and a beverage. Best bets are indicated by a star ★.

Category	Cost
$$	Skr 120–Skr 250
$	Skr 80–Skr 120
¢	under Skr 80

Lodging Sweden offers a wide range of accommodations, from simple village rooms and campsites to top-class hotels of the highest international standard. Except at the major hotels in the larger cities that cater mainly to business clientele, rates are fairly reasonable. Prices are normally on a per-room basis and include all taxes and service and usually breakfast. Apart from the more modest inns and the cheapest budget establishments, private baths and showers are standard features, although it is just as well to double-check when making your reservation. Budget hotels are typically small, family-run establishments offering basic accommodations with access to showers and baths. These hotels generally do not offer any additional facilities. Whatever their size, virtually all Swedish hotels provide scrupulously clean accommodations and courteous service. In Stockholm, there is a hotel reservation office—**Hotellcentralen** (tel. 08/240880, fax 08/791–8666)—at the central train station and at the Stockholm Tourist Center in Sweden House. In other areas, local tourist offices will help you with hotel reservations. A number of farms throughout Sweden offer accommodations, normally on a bed-and-breakfast basis, with self-catering facilities for cooking and other meals. A list of farm and cottage accommodations in Sweden is available from most regional tourist offices, or by contacting the **Federation of Swedish Farmers** (LRF, Bo på Lantgård, 105 33 Stockholm, tel. 08/787–5000).

Biltur-Logi (Go-as-You-Please) (S–793 70 Tällberg, Sweden, tel. 0247/50925, fax 0247/50925) is a hotel pass that offers discount rates to some 100 hotels and bed-and-breakfasts throughout Sweden. With a Skr 65 pass, you have a choice of rooms ranging from Skr 158 per person for a modest room to Skr 198 per person for a room with a bathroom or shower.

Hotels You can get a good idea of the facilities and prices at a particular hotel by consulting the official annual guide, *Hotels in Sweden*, obtainable free of charge from the Swedish Travel and Tourism Council (Box 101 34, S–121 28 Stockholm–Globen, tel. 08/725–5500, fax 08/649–8882). There is a fair selection of hotels in all price categories in every town and city, though major international chains, such as Sheraton and Best Western, have made only small inroads in Sweden thus far. The main homegrown chains are Scandic and RESO. The Sweden Hotels group has about 100 independently owned hotels and offers a central reservation office (tel. 08/789–8900). The group also has its own classification scheme—A, B, or C—based on the facilities available at each establishment.

House-Rental In Sweden, these are popular among other Europeans, particularly
Vacations the British and Germans. There are about 250 chalet villages with amenities, such as grocery stores, restaurants, saunas, and tennis courts. You can often arrange such accommodations on the spot at local tourist information offices.

Camping Camping is also popular in Sweden. There are about 750 officially approved sites throughout the country, most located next to the sea or a lake and offering such activities as windsurfing, riding, and tennis. They are generally open between June 1 and September 1, though some are available year round. The Swedish Campsite Owners' Association publishes, in English, an abbreviated list of sites; it is available free of charge from SCR, Box 255, S–451 17 Uddevalla (tel. 0522/39345).

Ratings Prices are for two people in a double room, with tax and breakfast included, based on summer-season rates. Best bets are indicated by a star ★.

Category	Cost
$$	Skr 725–Skr 970
$	Skr 600–Skr 725
¢	under Skr 600

Tipping Unlike some countries, Sweden cannot be described as "the land of the outstretched palm"—probably because earnings are relatively high anyway, and hotel and restaurant staff do not depend on their tips for their existence. Taxi drivers do not expect a tip. Usually the fee for checking coats is set between Skr 6 and Skr 15; this fee is required in some restaurants whether or not you want to leave your coat.

Stockholm

Arriving and Departing

By Plane All international flights arrive at Arlanda Airport, 40 kilometers (25 miles) north of the city. The airport is linked to Stockholm by a fast freeway. For information on arrival and departure times, call the individual airlines.

Between the Airport and Downtown Buses leave both the international and domestic terminals every 10–15 minutes, from 6:30 AM to 11 PM, and run to the city terminal at Klarabergsviadukten next to the central train station. The bus costs Skr 50 per person. A bus-taxi package is available (tel. 08/670–1010) for Skr 120 per person inside city limits and Skr 180 anywhere in the Stockholm area; additional passengers in a group pay only the bus portion of the fare.

By Train All major domestic and international services arrive at Stockholm Central Station on Vasagatan, in the heart of the city. This is also the terminal for local commuter services. For 24-hour train information, tel. 020/757575; if you get a recording, try 08/762–2580 for domestic travel or 08/696–7540 for international travel. At the station there is a ticket and information office where you can make seat or sleeping-car reservations. An automatic ticket-issuing machine is also available. Seat reservations on the regular train cost Skr 30, couchettes Skr 85, and beds from Skr 130 to Skr 295.

By Bus Long-distance buses, from such places as Härnösand and Sundsvall, arrive at Norra Bantorget, a few blocks north of the central train station, and all others at Klarabergsviadukten, just beside it. Bus tickets can also be bought at the railroad reservations office.

Getting Around

The most cost-effective way of getting around Stockholm is to use a **Stockholmskort** (Key to Stockholm card). Besides giving unlimited transportation on city subway, bus, and rail services, it offers free admission to 50 museums and several sightseeing trips. The card costs Skr 175 for 24 hours, Skr 350 for two days, and Skr 525 for three days. It is available from the tourist center at Sweden House, by Kungsträdgården, and at the Hotellcentralen accommodations bureau at the central train station.

Maps and timetables for all city transportation networks are available from the Stockholm Transit Authority (SL) information desks at Sergels Torg, the central train station, and Slussen in Gamla Stan. You can also obtain information by phone (tel. 08/600–1000).

By Bus and Subway The Stockholm Transit Authority (SL) operates both the bus and subway systems. Tickets for the two networks are interchangeable.

The subway system, known as T-banan (the *T* stands for tunnel), is the easiest and fastest way of getting around the city. Some of the stations offer permanent art exhibitions. Station entrances are marked with a blue T on a white background. The T-banan has about 100 stations and covers more than 60 route-miles. Trains run frequently between 5 AM and 2 AM.

Tickets are available at ticket counters, but it is cheaper to buy the SL Tourist Card, a significant savings compared with buying separate tickets each time you travel. The cards, valid on both bus and subway and in some cases including free entry to an array of museums and sights, are available at Pressbyrån newsstands and SL information desks. A card for the entire Greater Stockholm area costs Skr 54 for 25 hours or Skr 107 for 72 hours. People under 18 or over 65 pay Skr 33 for one day and Skr 70 for three days. Also available from the Pressbyrån newsstands are Skr 85 coupons, good for at least 10 bus and subway rides in the central zone.

The Stockholm bus network services not only within the central area but also to out-oftown points of interest, such as Waxholm, with its historic fortress, and Gustavsberg, with its well-known porcelain factory. Within Greater Stockholm, buses run throughout the night.

By Train SL operates conventional train services from Stockholm Central Station to a number of nearby points, including Nynäshamn, a departure point for ferries to the island of Gotland. Trains also run from the Slussen station to the fashionable seaside resort of Saltsjöbaden.

Important Addresses and Numbers

Tourist Information The main tourist center is at **Sweden House** (Kungsträdgården, tel. 08/789–2490). During the peak tourist season (June through August), it is open weekdays 8–6; weekends 9–5. The current off-season hours are 9–6 and 10–3, respectively. Besides providing information, it is the main ticket center for sightseeing excursions. There are also information centers at the central train station, in the City Hall (summer only), and in the Kaknäs TV Tower. When planning an independent visit to any of the tourist attractions in Stockholm, be sure to call ahead because opening times and prices are subject to change.

For information about Sweden, contact **Next Stop Sweden** (Box 3030, 103 61 Stockholm, tel. 08/725–5500, fax 08/725–5531). Once you're in Sweden, you might also pay a visit to *Upptäck Sverige Resor (Discover Sweden)* Travel Agency, Sveavägen 16, tel. 08/791–8085, fax 08/791–8889) for a wide selection of well-priced seasonal package tours throughout Sweden.

Embassies **U.S.** (Strandvägen 101, tel. 08/783–5300). **Canadian** (Tegelbacken 4, tel. 08/613–9900). **U.K.** (Skarpogatan 6–8, tel. 08/671–9000).

Emergencies **Police** (tel. 08/769–3000; emergencies only: 90000). **Ambulance** (tel. 90000). **Doctor** (Medical Care Information, tel. 08/644–9200)—travelers can get hospital attention in the district where they are staying or can contact the private clinic, **City Akuten** (tel. 08/411–7102). **Dentist** (8 AM–9 PM tel. 08/654–1117, 9 PM–8 AM tel. 08/644–9200). **Twenty-four-hour Pharmacy: C. W. Scheele** (tel. 08/218934); all pharmacies are indicated by the sign *Apoteket*.

Travel Agencies **American Express** (Birger Jarlsgatan 1, tel. 08/679–5200, fax 08/611–6214). **Thomas Cook** (Kottbygatan 5, Kista, tel. 08/632–2200).

Exploring Stockholm

Numbers in the margin correspond to points of interest on the Stockholm map.

Because Stockholm's main attractions are concentrated in a relatively small area, the city itself can be explored in several days. But if you want to take advantage of some of the full-day excursions offered, it is worthwhile to devote a full week to your visit.

The city of Stockholm, built on 14 small islands among open bays and narrow channels, has been dubbed the "Venice of the North." It is a handsome, civilized city, full of parks, squares, and airy boulevards, yet it is also a bustling, modern metropolis. Glass-and-steel skyscrapers abound, but in the center you are never more than five minutes' walk from twisting, medieval streets and waterside walks.

City Hall and the Old Town Anyone in Stockholm with limited time should give priority to a tour of **Gamla Stan** (the Old Town), a labyrinth of narrow, medieval streets, alleys, and quiet squares just south of the city center. From the central station, take Vasagatan down to the waterfront. Ideally, you should devote an entire day to this district, but it's worthwhile starting with a detour, along the quay and across Stadshusbron to the modern-day **City Hall,** constructed in 1923 and now one of the symbols of Stockholm. Lavish mosaics decorate the walls of the **Golden Hall,** and the **Prince's Gallery** features a collection of large murals by Prince Eugene, brother of King Gustav V. Take the elevator and stairway to the top of the 106-meter (348-foot) tower for a magnificent view of the city. *Tel. 08/785–9074. Admission: Skr 30. Tours daily at 10 and noon; also at 11 and 2 in summer. Tower admission: Skr 15. Tower open May–Sept., daily 10–4:30.*

Retrace your steps over Stadshusbron and head for the stairway leading up from the quay onto the footbridge. As you cross into the Old Town, the first thing you'll see is the magnificent **Riddarholm Church,** where a host of Swedish kings are buried. *Tel. 08/789–8500. Admission: Skr 10. Open May–Aug, daily 10–3; Sept., Wed. and weekends noon–3.*

From there proceed across Riddarhusbron to the **Royal Palace,** preferably by noon, when you can see the colorful changing-of-the-guard ceremony. The smartly dressed guards seem superfluous, since tourists wander at will into the castle courtyard and around the grounds. Several separate attractions are open to the public. Be sure to visit the **Royal Armory,** with its outstanding collection of weaponry and royal regalia. The **Treasury** houses the Swedish crown jewels, including the regalia used for the coronation of King Erik XIV in 1561. You can also visit the **State Apartments,** where the king swears in each successive government. *Tel. 08/789–8500. Admission: Skr 50 for Armory; Skr 30 for Treasury; Skr 30 for State Apartments. Call ahead for opening hrs, since they are subject to change.*

From the palace, stroll down **Västerlånggatan,** one of two main shopping streets in the Old Town. This popular shopping area brims with boutiques and antiques shops. Walk down to the Skeppsbron waterfront, then head back toward the center over the Ström bridge, where anglers cast for salmon. If you feel like a rest, stop off at **Kungsträdgården** and watch the world go by. Originally built as a royal kitchen garden, the property was turned into a public park in 1562. During the summer, entertainment and activities abound, and you can catch a glimpse of local people playing open-air chess with giant chessmen.

Djurgården Be sure to spend at least a day visiting the large island of **Djurgården.** Although it's only a short walk from the city center, the most pleasant way to approach it is by ferry from Skeppsbron, in the Old Town. The ferries drop you off near two of Stockholm's best-known attractions, the Vasa Museum and Gröna Lund Tivoli. Or you might want to take the reinstated streetcar, which runs along refurbished tracks from Norrmalmstorg, near the city center, to **Prince Eugene's Waldemarsudde,** an art museum in the former summer residence of a Swedish prince, on a peninsula in Djurgården, tel. 08/662–2800. The *Vasa,* a restored 17th-century warship, is one of the oldest preserved war vessels in the world and has become Sweden's most popular tourist sight. She sank ignominiously in Stockholm Harbor on her maiden voyage in 1628, reportedly because she was not carrying sufficient ballast. Recovered in 1961, she has been restored to her original appearance and has now been moved into a spectacular new museum, the **Vasamuseet,** which opened in 1990. It features guided tours, films, and displays. *Gälarvarvet, tel. 08/666–4800. Admission: Skr 45 adults, Skr 30 students, children under 7 free. Open Thurs.–Tues. 10–5, Wed. 10–8.*

Gröna Lund Tivoli, Stockholm's version of the famous Copenhagen amusement park, is a favorite family attraction, with hair-raising roller coasters as well as tamer delights. *Tel. 08/670–7600. Open late Apr. to early Sept. Call for prices and opening hrs, since they are subject to change.*

⑦ Just across the road is **Skansen,** a large, open-air folk museum consisting of 150 reconstructed traditional buildings from Sweden's different regions. Here you can see a variety of handicraft displays and demonstrations. There is also an attractive open-air zoo—with many native Scandinavian species, such as lynxes, wolves, and brown bears—as well as an excellent aquarium and a carnival area for children. *Tel. 08/442–8000. Open year-round. Call for prices and opening hrs, as these are subject to change.*

From Skansen, head back toward the city center. Just before the
⑧ Djurgård bridge, you come to the **Nordic Museum,** which, like Skansen, provides an insight into the way Swedish people have lived over the past 500 years. The collection includes displays of peasant costumes, folk art, and Lapp culture. Families with children should visit the delightful "village life" play area on the ground floor. *Tel. 08/666–4600. Admission: Skr 40 adults, Skr 10 children. Open Tues.–Sun. 11–5.*

⑨ Once you're back on the "mainland," drop into the **Museum of National Antiquities.** Though its name is uninspiring, it houses some remarkable Viking gold and silver treasures. **The Royal Cabinet of Coin,** in the same building, boasts the world's largest coin. *Narvavägen 13–17. Tel. 08/783–9400. Admission: Skr 55. Call the museum for opening hrs.*

Stockholm Environs

The region surrounding Stockholm offers many attractions that can easily be seen on day trips out of the capital. Most sights in the Stockholm environs can be visited inexpensively by using the SL (Stockholm Local Traffic) bus and/or subway system (tel. 08/600–1000) or by taking a boat or ferry. If you have a Stockholmskortet (Key to Stockholm card), you are entitled to free travel on SL's subways and buses, and reduced fares on other means of transportation.

Nearby **Drottningholm Slott,** a Baroque castle whose spectacular gardens were influenced by those at Versailles, can be reached by a combined subway and bus trip. Take the subway to Brommaplan and then any 300 bus (301, 323, and so on). The one-way cost is Skr 26. A more spectacular approach is by ferry, which costs only Skr 70 round-trip. The ferry (available Apr. 29–Sept. 3) leaves from in front of city hall in Stockholm.

One "must" is the trip to the majestic 16th-century **Gripsholm Castle,** at Mariefred, on the southern side of Lake Mälaren and about 64 kilometers (40 miles) from Stockholm. Gripsholm, with its drawbridge and four massive round towers, is one of Sweden's most romantic castles. There was a castle on the site as early as the 1380s, but it was destroyed, and King Gustav Vasa had the present building erected in 1577. Today the castle is best known for housing the Swedish state collection of portraits and is one of the largest galleries in the world, with some 3,400 paintings. *Tel. 0159/10194. Admission: Skr 30. Open Apr.–Sept., Tue.–Sun. 10–3.*

Mariefred can be reached by bus from the Liljeholmen subway stop for Skr 40, or by SJ train-bus from Central Station for Skr 80. But the most pleasant way of traveling to Gripsholm from Stockholm is on the vintage steamer *Mariefred,* the last coal-fired ship on Lake Mälaren. Departures, between mid-June and late August, are from the city hall, daily except Monday at 10 AM, returning from Mariefred at 4:30. The journey takes 3½ hours each way, and there is a restaurant on board. *Tel. 08/669–8850. Round-trip fare: Skr 140.*

Major Attractions
City Hall, **1**
Gröna Lund Tivoli, **6**
Kungsträdgården, **4**
Museum of National
Antiquities, **9**
Nordic Museum, **8**
Riddarholm Church, **2**
Royal Palace, **3**
Skansen, **7**
Vasamuseet, **5**

Other Attractions
Cathedral, **22**
Concert Hall, **12**
House of Nobles, **20**
Kaknäs TV Tower, **15**
Kulturhuset, **23**
Museum of Far
Eastern Antiquities, **18**
Museum of Modern
Art, **14**
National Museum, **16**

NK, **24**
Parliament, **21**
Prince Eugene s
Waldemarsudde, **25**
Royal Dramatic
Theater, **11**
Royal Library, **13**
Royal Opera House, **17**
Stock Exchange,**10**
Supreme Court, **19**

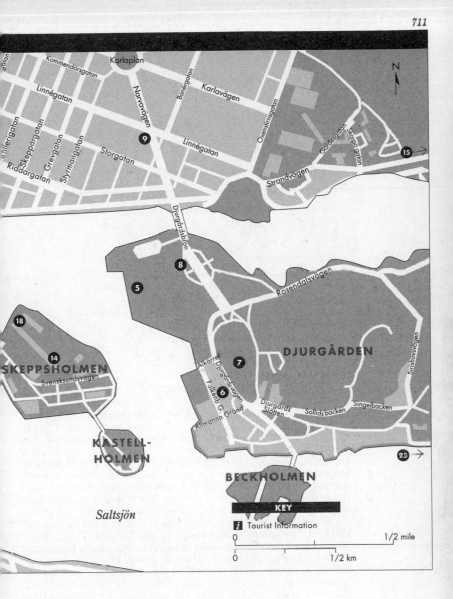

N

Kommendörsgatan
Karlaplan
Linnégatan
Millergatan
Skeppargatan
Grevgatan
Riddargatan
Styrmangatan
Storgatan
Narvavägen
Banérgatan
Karlavägen
Linnégatan
Oxenstiernsgatan
Gärdesgatan
Starpsgatan

9

15 →

Strandvägen

Djurgårdsbron

8

5

Rosendalsvägen

18

14

SKEPPSHOLMEN

Svensksundsvägen

Alkärret

Djurgårdsvägen

7

DJURGÅRDEN

Sirishovsvägen

Falkenb G.

6

Djurgårds
Slätten

Sollidsbacken

Singelbacken

Allmanna Gränd

25 →

KASTELL-
HOLMEN

BECKHOLMEN

KEY

Saltsjön

i Tourist Information

0 _____ 1/2 mile

0 _____ 1/2 km

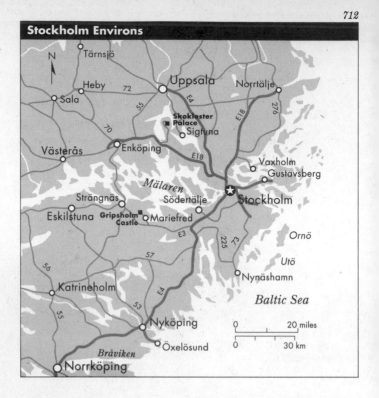

Stockholm Environs

Another popular boat trip goes to **Skokloster Palace,** about 70 kilometers (44 miles) from Stockholm. Departures are from the city hall bridge (Stadshusbron) daily, except Monday and Friday, between early June and mid-August. The route follows the narrow inlets of Lake Mälaren along the "Royal Waterway" and stops at **Sigtuna,** an ancient trading center. You can get off the boat here; visit the town, which has medieval ruins and an 18th-century town hall; and catch the boat again on the return journey. But it is also worthwhile to stay on board and continue to Skokloster, an impressive palace dating from the 1650s. Built by the Swedish field marshal Carl Gustav Wrangel, it contains many of his trophies from the Thirty Years' War. Other attractions include what is reckoned to be the largest private collection of arms in the world, as well as some magnificent Gobelin tapestries. Next door to the palace is a motor museum that houses Sweden's largest collection of vintage cars and motorcycles. The round-trip boat fare is Skr 165, and there is a restaurant and cafeteria on board. The castle is also reachable via Uppsala by taking the SJ train from Stockholm's Central Station and then the 894 bus to Skokloster—a time-consuming trip but well worth it if you want to take in the sights of Uppsala. The round-trip fare to Uppsala is Skr 110. *Admission to Skokloster Palace: Skr 40 (free with Key to Stockholm card). Open daily 11–4. Admission to motor museum: Skr 35 (free with Key to Stockholm card). Open daily noon–6.*

Shopping

Gift Ideas   Stockholm is an ideal place to find items that reflect the best in Swedish design and elegance, particularly glass, porcelain, furs, handicrafts, home furnishings, and leather goods. The quality is uniformly high, and you can take advantage of the tax-free shopping service in most stores (*see* Shopping *in* Staying in Sweden, *above*).

Department Stores	The largest is **NK** (Hamngatan 18–20, tel. 08/762–8000), where you can find just about anything. A less expensive store is **PUB** (Hötorget, tel. 08/791–6000). **Åhléns City,** (Klarabergsgatan) is moderate. All three are open on Sunday.
Shopping Districts	The center of Stockholm's shopping activity has shifted from Kungsgatan to Hamngatan, a wide boulevard along which a huge, covered shopping complex called **Gallerian** has been built. The **Old Town** area is best for handicrafts, antiquarian bookshops, and art shops.
Food and Flea Markets	One of the biggest flea markets in northern Europe is in the parking garage at **Skärholmen** shopping center, a 20-minute subway ride from the downtown area. Market hours are weekdays 11–6, Saturday 9–3, Sunday 10–3, with an entry fee of Skr 10 on weekends. Superior food markets can be found on Östermalmstorg and Hötorget.
Glassware	For the best buys, try **Nordiska Kristall,** at Kungsgatan 9. **Rosenthal Studio-Haus,** at Birger Jarlsgatan 6, operates its own shipping service. **Arioso,** at Västerlånggatan 59 in the Old Town, is good for modern crystal and ceramics. **Önskebutiken,** on the corner of Kungsgatan and Sveavägen, specializes in crystal as well as porcelain.
Handicrafts	**Stockholms Läns Hemslöjdsförening** (Drottninggatan 14, tel. 08/761–1717) has a wide selection of Swedish folk costumes and handicraft souvenirs from different parts of Sweden.

Dining

For details and price-category descriptions, *see* Dining *in* Staying in Sweden, *above.*

$$ Bakfickan. ★ The name means "hip pocket" and is appropriate because this restaurant is tucked around the back of the Opera House complex. It's particularly popular at lunchtime, offering Swedish home cooking and a range of daily dishes. Counter and table service are available. *Operahuset, tel. 08/207745. No reservations. AE, DC, MC, V. Closed Sun. and major holidays.*

$$ Cassi. This centrally located restaurant, with an espresso bar dominating the front room, specializes in French cuisine at reasonable prices. *Narvavägen 30, tel. 08/661–7461. DC, MC, V. Closed Sat., Christmas and New Year's Day.*

$$ Eriks Bakficka. An extremely popular dining spot among local residents, this unpretentious eatery serves a wide variety of Swedish dishes. The 120-seat restaurant is a block from the elegant waterside street Strandvägen, a few steps down from street level. *Frederikshovsgatan 4, tel. 08/660–1599. Reservations advised. AE, DC, MC, V. Closed weekends in July and major holidays.*

$$ Gondolen. Suspended under the gangway of the *Katarina* elevator at Slussen, Gondolen offers a magnificent view over the harbor, Lake Mälaren, and the Baltic Sea. The cuisine is international, and a range of prix-fixe menus is available. *Stadsgården 6, tel. 08/641–7090. Reservations advised. AE, DC, MC, V. Closed Sun. and major holidays.*

$$ Martini. You can't get more central than Martini, a popular Italian restaurant and great people-watching hangout. The terrace is open during the summer, when people line up to get a seat. The main restaurant is below street level, but the decor is light and the atmosphere is bustling. *Norrmalmstorg 4, tel. 08/679–8220. Reservations advised. AE, DC, MC, V. Closed Christmas–New Year's Day.*

$ Open Gate. ★ Near the Slussen locks, on the south side of Stockholm Harbor, this is a popular, trendy, Art Deco, Italian-style trattoria. Pasta dishes are the house specialty. *Högbergsgatan 40, tel. 08/643–9776. No reservations. AE, DC, MC, V.*

$ Ortagården. This vegetarian, no-smoking restaurant is one floor up from the Östermalmshallen market hall. It offers an attractive buf-

fet, with soups, salads, hot dishes, and homemade bread—not to
mention the 5-kronor bottomless cup of coffee—served in a turn-of-
the-century atmosphere. *Nybrogatan 31, tel. 08/662–1728. AE,
MC, V. Closed major holidays.*

¢ **Belvéns Restaurant.** A small, family-run restaurant a block east of
Kungliga Humlegården, Belvéns offers a surprisingly wide variety
of tasty dishes at low prices. Usually crowded at dinner, this quaint
restaurant has a dozen or so tables with red-and-white checked tablecloths. *Kommendörsgatan 7, tel. 08/662–5487. Reservations advised. AE, DC, MC, V. Closed Sun. and Christmas–New Year's
Day.*

Lodging

Stockholm has plenty of hotels in most price brackets, although relatively few in the $ or ¢ categories. Many hotels cut their rates in the
summer season, however, when business travelers are on vacation.
The major hotel chains also have a number of bargain packages available on weekends throughout the year and daily during the summer.

More than 50 hotels offer the "Stockholm Package," providing accommodations for one night, costing between Skr 360 and Skr 760
per person, including breakfast and a Stockholmskoret card (Key to
Stockholm) (*see* Getting Around, *above*). The package is available
June through mid-August, at Christmas and Easter, and Thursday
through Monday year-round; get details from the **Stockholm Information Service** (Excursion Shop, Box 7542, S-103 93 Stockholm tel.
08/789–2490). The package can also be reserved through travel
agents or through **Hotellcentralen** (tel. 08/240880, fax 08/791–8666).

If you arrive in Stockholm without a hotel reservation, the
Hotellcentralen in the central train station will arrange accommodations for you. The office is open November–March, weekdays 8–5
and weekends 8–2; April and October, daily 8–5; May and September, daily 8–7; and June–August, daily 7 AM–9 PM; telephone reservations can be made after 9 AM. There is a reservations office in
Sweden House (*see* Important Addresses and Numbers, *above*) as
well. There's a small fee for each reservation, but advance telephone
reservations are free. Or phone one of the central reservations offices run by the major hotel groups: RESO (tel. 08/720–8100), Scandic (tel. 08/610–5050), Sweden Hotels (tel. 08/798–8900), or Best
Western (tel. 08/330600 or 020/792752).

For details and price-category definitions, *see* Lodging *in* Staying in
Sweden, *above*.

$$ **Alexandra.** Although it is in the Södermalm area, to the south of the
Old Town, the Alexandra is only five minutes by subway from the
city center. It is a small modern hotel, opened in the early 1970s and
renovated in 1988. Only breakfast is served. *Magnus Ladulåsgatan
42, S–111 46, tel. 08/840320, fax 08/720–5353. 85 rooms with bath.
Facilities: sauna, no-smoking rooms. AE, DC, MC, V. Closed
Christmas.*

$$ **Gamla Stan.** A quiet, cozy hotel in one of Old Town's 17th-century
houses, the Gamla Stan was renovated in 1986, and each room is
uniquely decorated. *Lilla Nygatan 25, S–111 28, tel. 08/244450, fax
08/216483. 51 rooms with shower. Facilities: no-smoking floor. AE,
DC, MC, V. Closed Christmas–New Year's Day.*

$ **Birger Jarl.** A short subway ride from the city center, Birger Jarl is a
modern, characteristically Scandinavian hotel that opened in 1974.
The coffee shop closes in summer. *Tulegatan 8, S–104 32, tel. 08/
151020, fax 08/673–7366. 225 rooms with bath. Facilities: coffee
shop, no-smoking rooms, sauna. AE, DC, MC, V. Closed Christmas–New Year.*

$ **City.** A large, modern hotel built in the 1940s but completely rebuilt
in 1984, City is near the center of town and the Hötorget market. It

is owned by the Salvation Army, so alcohol is not served. Breakfast is served in the atrium Winter Garden. *Slöjdgatan 7, S–111 81, tel. 08/222240, fax 08/208224. 290 rooms with bath. Facilities: restaurant, no-smoking rooms, sauna. AE, DC, MC, V. Closed Christmas–New Year's Day.*

$ **Gustav af Klint.** A "hotel ship" moored at Stadsgården quay, near Slussen subway station, the Gustav af Klint is divided into two sections—a hotel and a hostel. It was refurbished in 1989. There is a cafeteria and a restaurant, and you can dine on the deck in summer. Breakfast, at Skr 40, is not included. *Stadsgårdskajen 153, S–116 45, tel. 08/640–4077, fax 08/640–6416. 14 cabins with showers. 80 hostel beds. Facilities: restaurant, cafeteria. AE, MC, V. Closed Christmas and New Year's Day.*

$ **Långholmen.** This former prison, built in 1724, was converted into a combined hotel and hostel in 1989. It is on the island of Långholmen, which has popular bathing beaches and a Prison Museum. The inn next door, serves Swedish home cooking, the Jail Pub offers light snacks, and a garden restaurant operates in summer. *Långholmen, Box 9116, S–102 72, tel. 08/668–0500, fax 08/841096. 101 rooms with shower. Facilities: mini-golf course, boule court, no-smoking rooms. AE, DC, MC, V. Closed Christmas–New Year's Day.*

$ **Stockholm.** This hotel has an unusual location—the upper floors of a downtown office building. The mainly modern decor is offset by traditional Swedish furnishings that help create its family atmosphere. Breakfast is the only meal served. *Norrmalmstorg 1, S–111 46, tel. 08/678–1320, fax 08/611–2103. 93 rooms with bath. AE, DC, MC, V. Closed Christmas–New Year's Day.*

¢ **Queen's Hotel.** Located on Drottninggatan, Stockholm's major shopping street, the family-run Queen's Hotel is a 5- to 10-minute walk from Stockholm's central train station and interesting sights in the downtown area. The hotel recently added 10 modern hotel rooms, all with showers, telephone, and TV. *Drottninggatan 71A, S–111 36, tel. 08/249460, fax 08/217620. 30 rooms with shower. AE, MC, V. Closed Christmas–New Year's Day.*

¢ **Wasa Park.** A clean, family-run hotel, the Wasa Park is convenient for travelers coming into Stockholm from the airport (the airport shuttle bus regularly stops in front of the building before going on to Stockholm's central train station). The hotel is convenient to the subway station and city bus lines. *St. Eriks Plan 1, S–113 20, tel. 08/340285, fax 08/309422. 16 rooms. MC, V.*

The Arts

Stockholm's main theater and concert season runs from September through May or June, so there are not many major performances during the height of the tourist season. But for a list of events, pick up the free booklet *Stockholm This Week*, available from hotels and tourist information offices. You can get last-minute tickets to theaters and shows at the **Box Office**, a cut-price ticket booth on Norrmalmstorg Square. Tickets sold here are priced 25% below box office rates. The booth is open Monday to Friday 10–6 and Saturday 10–3. The **Biljettdirekt** desk in Sweden House also handles ticket sales for most of the shows in town.

Concerts During the summer, free concerts are given in many city parks. Check the Events section of *Stockholm This Week* for listings.

Theater Stockholm has about 20 top-rank theaters, but dramatic productions are unlikely to interest those who don't understand Swedish. A better option is to go to a musical; several city theaters hold regular performances. Productions by the English Theatre Company are occasionally staged at the **Vasan** (Vasagatan 19, tel. 08/102363).

Film English and American films predominate, and they are screened with the original soundtrack and Swedish subtitles. Programs are listed in the local evening newspapers, though titles are usually in Swedish. Movie buffs should visit **Filmstaden** (Film City) (Mäster Samuelsgatan 25, tel. 08/840500), where 15 cinemas under one roof show a variety of films from noon until midnight. Bear in mind that most, if not all, cinemas take reservations over the phone, so it's best to do so or you may find a show sold out well ahead of time.

Nightlife

Cabaret Stockholm's largest nightclub, **Börsen** (Jakobsgatan 6, tel. 08/787–8500), offers high-quality Swedish and international cabaret shows. Another popular spot is the **Cabaret Club** (Barnhusgatan 12, tel. 08/411–0608); although it can accommodate 450 guests, reservations are advised.

Bars and Nightclubs **Café Opera** (Operahuset, tel. 08/411–0026) is a popular meeting place for young and old; at the waterfront end of Kungsträgården, it has the longest bar in town, plus dining and roulette and dancing after midnight. **Riche** (Birger Jarlsgatan 4, tel. 08/611–8450) is another popular watering hole in the city center. Piano bars are also an important part of the Stockholm scene. Try the **Anglais Bar** at the Hotel Anglais (Humlegårdsgatan 23, tel. 08/614–1600). The **Clipper Club** is at the Hotel Reisen (Skeppsbron 12–14, tel. 08/223260). Not to be forgotten is the restaurant–bar **Berns' Salonger** (Berzelii Park 9, tel. 08/614–0550); worth a visit is the Red Room, a private dining room on the second floor, where playwright August Strindberg once held court.

Pubs Irish pubs are trendy with the happy-hour crowd. **Limerick** (Tegnérgatan 10, tel. 08/673–4398) is a leader. **Dubliner** (Birger Jarlspassagen, tel. 08/679–7707) draws Irish beer lovers. **Bagpiper's Inn** (Rörstrandsgatan 21, tel. 08/311855) is among the best.

Jazz Clubs **Fasching** (Kungsgatan 63, tel. 08/216267) is Stockholm's largest, with a jazz lunch weekdays and soul music Saturday nights. Another popular spot is **Stampen** (Stora Nygatan 5, tel. 08/205793); get here in good time if you want a seat, and phone first to be sure the establishment hasn't been reserved for a private party.

Discos **Galaxy** (Strömsborg, tel. 08/215400) is one of the most popular night spots, catering to a variety of musical tastes; there is an outdoor bar and dining area in summer. Try also **Downtown** (Norrlandsgatan 5A, tel. 08/411–9488). **Karlsson** (Kungsgatan 65, tel. 08/411–9298) is another good choice.

Gothenburg and the Glass Country

For many visitors traveling to Sweden by ferry, Gothenburg (Göteborg in Swedish) is the port of arrival. If you arrive in Stockholm, don't miss making a side trip to this great shipping city and Sweden's scenic western coast. This itinerary combines a western trip with a route through the Glass Country.

Getting Around

The route can be followed by train. Regular trains for Gothenburg depart from Stockholm's central train station about every hour, and normal travel time is about four and a half hours. Seat reservations are compulsory on all trains to Gothenburg. There are also hourly flights to Gothenburg from Stockholm's Arlanda Airport between 7 AM and 10 PM on weekdays, slightly less frequently on weekends. The trip by air takes 55 minutes.

For getting around the city of Gothenburg itself, the best transportation option for the visitor is the **Göteborgskort** (Key to Gothenburg card), similar to the Key to Stockholm card. This entitles the user to free travel on all public transportation, free parking, and free admission to the Liseberg amusement park and all city museums. Prices for the card are Skr 120 for one day, Skr 200 for two days, and Skr 250 for three days. Children under 18 can purchase cards for Skr 60 for one day, Skr 100 for two days, and Skr 140 for three days.

Tourist Information

Gothenburg (Kungsportsplatsen 2, tel. 031/100740).
Växjö (Kronobergsgatan 8, tel. 0470/41410).

Exploring Gothenburg and the Glass Country

Visitors arriving in **Gothenburg** often go straight through the city in their haste to reach their coastal vacation spots, but it is well worth spending a day or two exploring this attractive harbor city. A quayside jungle of cranes and warehouses attests to the city's industrial might, yet within 10 minutes' walk of the waterfront is an elegant, modern city of broad avenues, green parks, and gardens. It is an easy city to explore. Most of the major attractions are within walking distance of each other, and there is an excellent streetcar network. In the summer, you can even take a sightseeing trip on a vintage open-air streetcar.

Gothenburg's development was pioneered mainly by British merchants in the 19th century, when it acquired the nickname "Little London." But a more accurate name would have been "Little Amsterdam," for the city was designed during the 17th century by Dutch architects, who gave it its extensive network of straight streets divided by canals. There is only one major canal today, but you can explore it on one of the popular "Paddan" sightseeing boats. The boats got their nickname, Swedish for toad, because of their short, squat shape, necessary for negotiating the city's 20 low bridges. You embark for the one-hour tour at the **Paddan terminal** at Kungsportsplatsen. *Fare: Skr 60. Departures: late Apr.–late June and mid-Aug.–early Sept., daily 10–5; late June–mid-Aug., daily 10–9; early Sept.–Oct. 1, daily 12–3; closed Oct.–Apr. Check with Gothenburg tourist information for specific dates.*

The hub of Gothenburg is **Kungsportsavenyn,** better known as "The Avenue." It is a broad, tree-lined boulevard flanked with elegant shops, restaurants, and sidewalk cafés. During the summer it has a distinctly Parisian air. The avenue ends at **Götaplatsen** (Göta Square), home of the municipal theater, concert hall, and library (where there's an excellent selection of English-language newspapers). Just off the avenue is **Trädgårdsföreningen,** an attractive park with a magnificent Palm House that was built in 1878 and a Butterfly House featuring 40 different species. *Admission to park: Skr 10. Open year-round. Admission to Palm House: Skr 25. Open Apr., Tues.–Sun. 10–4; May and Sept., daily 10–4; June–Aug., daily 10–5; Oct.–Mar., Tues.–Sun. 10–3. Admission to Butterfly House (tel. 031/611911): Skr 25. Open same hrs as Palm House.*

If you're interested in shopping, the best place to go is **Nordstan,** a covered complex of shops near the central train station. Many of its businesses participate in the tax-free shopping service.

In the harbor near the Nordstan shopping complex, you will find the new **Maritime Center** (Packhuskajen 8, tel. 031/101035). The center houses a historic collection of ships, including a destroyer, a lightship, a trawler, and tugboats. *Admission: Skr 35. Open Mar.–Apr. and Sept.–Nov., daily 10–4; May–June, daily 10–6; July–Aug., daily 10–9.*

Kronoberg County's main town and the best center for exploring Sweden's Glass Country is **Växjö**. It is also an important sightseeing destination for some 10,000 American visitors each year, for it was from this area that their Swedish ancestors set sail during the 19th century. The **Emigrants' House** (tel. 0470/20120), in the town center, tells the story of the migration, during which close to one million Swedes—one-quarter of the entire population—departed for the promised land. The museum exhibits provide a vivid sense of the rigorous journey, and an archive room and research center allow American visitors to trace their ancestry. On the second Sunday in August, Växjö celebrates "Minnesota Day." Swedes and Swedish-Americans come together to commemorate their common heritage with American-style square dancing and other festivities.

Many of Sweden's most famous glassworks are within easy reach of Växjö, and it is usually possible to take an organized sightseeing tour of the facilities. Inquire at the tourist office for information. The manufacture of Swedish glass dates from 1556, when Venetian glassblowers were first invited to the Swedish court. But it was another 200 years before glass manufacturing became a real Swedish industry. This area was chosen for its dense forest, which offered plentiful wood supplies for heating the furnaces. All the major Swedish glass companies, including **Orrefors** and **Kosta Boda,** still have their works in this area, and all of them are open to the public. They also have shops where you can pick up near-perfect seconds at bargain prices. *Open weekdays 9–6, Sat. 9–3, Sun. noon–4 (no glass manufacturing on Sat. and Sun. in winter).*

To return to Stockholm from Växjö, catch the train to Alvesta (the service runs about five times a day) and change there for Stockholm. The journey takes about five and a half hours. For information call 0470/53230. SAS operates several flights per day to Stockholm from Växjö airport, located about 8 kilometers (5 miles) from the town center. The trip takes about 40 minutes. For information call 020/727000.

Dining and Lodging

For details and price-category definitions, *see* Dining and Lodging *in* Staying in Sweden, *above.*

Gothenburg
Dining

Åtta Glas. A casual and lively restaurant located on what was formerly a barge, Åtta Glas offers excellent views of the river and of Kungsportsbron, a bridge spanning the center of town. The second floor has a bar that is especially popular with a younger crowd on weekends. The two standard specials—*oxfilé* (beef fillet) and grilled salmon—are the best deals (Skr 69), and a children's menu, which includes ice cream, is popular with families. *Kungsportsbron, tel. 031/136015. Reservations advised. AE, DC, MC, V. Splurge.*
Weise. A centrally located restaurant with a German beer-cellar atmosphere, Weise was once a haunt of local painters and intellectuals and still retains something of that ambience. The tables and chairs date from 1892. It specializes in traditional Swedish home cooking, serving such dishes as pork and brown beans. *Drottninggatan 23, tel. 031/131402. Reservations advised. AE, DC, MC, V. $$*

Lodging

Liseberg Heden. Not far from the famous Liseberg amusement park, Liseberg Heden is a popular, modern family hotel. *Sten Sturegatan, tel. 031/200280, fax 031/165283. 160 rooms with bath. Facilities: restaurant, sauna, no-smoking rooms. AE, DC, MC, V. Closed Christmas–New Year's Day. $$*
Maria Erikssons Pensionat. Occupying an old, elegant building with high ceilings in the center of the city, the small Maria Erikssons Pensionat is a traditional Gothenburg hotel. The rooms feature old wooden furniture. Breakfast is not included. *Chalmersgatan 27A,*

tel. 031/207030, fax 031/166463. 12 rooms, some with showers. Facilities: no-smoking rooms. AE, MC, V. ¢

Växjö **Esplanad.** Centrally located, Esplanad is a small, family hotel offer-
Lodging ing basic amenities. Only breakfast is served. *Norra Esplanaden 21A, tel. 0470/22580, fax 0470/26226. 27 rooms, most with shower. Facilities: no-smoking rooms. MC, V. Closed Christmas–New Year's Day. $*

Solvikens Pensionat. A family-run hotel 15 miles south of Växjö, Solvikens Pensionat is situated on Lake Torsjön. A new hotel and annex offer basic accommodations. A French cook offers three meals a day to guests of the hotel. *Ingelstad, tel. 0470/38280, fax 0470/30141. 21 rooms, some with shower. MC, V. Closed Christmas and Midsummer weekend. ¢*

25 Switzerland

Switzerland's political isolation, prosperity, and ruthless efficiency have produced a standard of living that is sometimes dauntingly high. But careful planning can open up much of the country's best: rustic coziness, medieval charm, magnificent Alpine wilderness. "Rustic" in Switzerland doesn't mean Turkish toilets and sagging mattresses; the Swiss keep their coziness under strict control. An electric eye may beam open the sliding glass door into that firelit, wood-raftered *Stübli* (pub), and your knotty-pine hotel room is likely to have state-of-the-art bedding and an all-tile bath. That is the paradox of the Swiss, whose aesthetic pitches high-tech efficiency against bucolic Alpine tranquillity. Fiercely devout, rigorously clean, prompt as their world-renowned watches, the Swiss measure liquors with scientific precision into glasses marked for one or two centiliters, and the local wines come in sized carafes that are reminiscent of laboratory beakers. And as for passion—well, the "double" beds have separate mattresses and sheets that tuck firmly down the middle. (Foreigners with more lusty Latin tastes may request a French—that is, a standard double—bed.) Switzerland is a country of contrasts: While cowbells tinkle on the slopes of Klewenalp, the hum of commerce in Zürich isn't far away. As befurred and bejeweled socialites shop in Geneva, across the country in Appenzell women stand beside their husbands on the Landsgemeinde-Platz to raise their hands in the local vote—a right they didn't win until 1990.

Switzerland comprises most of the attractions of its larger European neighbors—Alpine grandeur, urban sophistication, ancient villages, scintillating ski slopes, and all-around artistic excellence. It's the heart of the Reformation, the homeland of William Tell; its cities are full of historic landmarks, its countryside strewn with castles. The varied cuisine reflects an ethnic mix, with three distinct cultures dominating: French in the southwest, Italian in the southeast, and German—a 70% majority—in the north and east.

All these assets have combined to create a major center of tourism, and the Swiss are happy to pave the way. A welcoming if reserved people, most of them well versed in English, they have earned their

Switzerland

age-old reputation as fine hosts. Their hotels and inns are famous for cleanliness and efficiency, but travelers pay exorbitant prices for these basics. The high value of the Swiss franc to the U.S. dollar requires that frugality be the guiding motto.

Essential Information

Before You Go

When to Go There's always something happening—it just depends on what you want. Winter sports begin around Christmas and usually last until mid-April, depending on the state of the snow. The countryside is a delight in spring when the wild flowers are in bloom, and the fall colors rival those in New England. In the Ticino (the Italian-speaking area) and around Lake Geneva (Lac Léman), summer stays late. There is often sparkling weather in September and October, and the popular resorts are less crowded then. After that, though, beware: They may close up altogether in November and May. Always check with the local tourist office.

Climate Summer is generally warm and sunny, though the higher you go, of course, the cooler it gets, especially at night. Winter is cold everywhere: In low-lying areas the weather is frequently damp and overcast, while in the Alps there are often brilliantly clear days, but it is guaranteed to be cold and snowy—especially above 1,400 meters (4,600 feet). Summer or winter, some areas of Switzerland are prone to an Alpine wind that blows from the south and is known as the *Föhn*. This gives rise to clear but rather oppressive weather, which the Swiss claim causes headaches.

The only exception to the general weather patterns is the Ticino. Here, protected by the Alps, the weather is positively Mediterranean; even in winter, it is significantly warmer than elsewhere.

The following are the average daily maximum and minimum temperatures for Zürich.

Jan.	36F	2C	May	67F	19C	Sept.	69F	20C
	26	- 3		47	8		51	11
Feb.	41F	5C	June	73F	23C	Oct.	57F	14C
	28	- 2		53	12		43	6
Mar.	51F	11C	July	76F	25C	Nov.	45F	7C
	34	1		56	14		35	2
Apr.	59F	15C	Aug.	75F	24C	Dec.	37F	3C
	40	4		56	14		29	- 2

Currency The unit of currency is the Swiss franc (Fr.), divided into 100 rappen (known as centimes in French-speaking areas). There are coins of 5, 10, 20, and 50 rappen and of 1, 2, and 5 francs. The bills are of 10, 20, 50, 100, 500, and 1,000 francs.

At press time (summer 1995), the Swiss franc stood at 1.28 to the dollar and 1.86 to the pound sterling.

All banks will change your money, though many impose a minimum and a slight fee. Traveler's checks get a better exchange rate, as do cash advances on major credit cards. Main airports and train stations have exchange offices (*bureaux de change*) that are open longer hours than banks and often offer equally good rates of exchange. Most hotels and some restaurants will change money but usually at a far less favorable rate. Most major credit cards are generally, though not universally, accepted at hotels, restaurants, and shops.

What It Will Switzerland is very expensive, especially for visitors spending dol-
Cost lars. It's extremely rare to find even the simplest hotel room for less than 100 SF (at press time, $83 or £53), and hot meals start at 15 SF

($12.50 or £7.95). Renting a holiday apartment or chalet can save on restaurant costs, but you may find yourself paying inflated prices in resort grocery stores. For instance, three raw sausage kebabs recently cost 22 SF in Gstaad. When possible, steer away from the flashier resorts and budget for limited stays in the biggest cities (Geneva, Zürich, Basel). And take chances off the beaten track: Many of Switzerland's most atmospheric restaurants and inns lie outside the developed tourist centers. If you really need to watch your budget, settle for rooms with bathrooms down the hall: You'll still have a sink to call your own and will save about 30%. Calculate the cost of novelty-transit excursions carefully; those cable cars, funiculars, and cog-rail trains cost a lot to build, inspect, and maintain, and rides are priced accordingly.

Sample Prices Cup of coffee, 3 SF; bottle of beer, 3 SF; Coca-Cola, 3 SF; ham sandwich, 7 SF; a 1-mile taxi ride, 10 SF (except in Geneva, Lugano, or Zürich).

Customs on Arrival There are two levels of duty-free allowance for visitors to Switzerland. Residents of non-European countries may import 400 cigarettes or 100 cigars or 500 grams of tobacco, plus 2 liters of alcoholic beverage below 15% and 1 liter of alcoholic beverage in excess of 15%. Residents of European countries may import 200 cigarettes or 50 cigars or 250 grams of tobacco, plus 2 liters of alcoholic beverage below 15% and 1 liter of alcoholic beverage in excess of 15%. These allowances apply only to those aged 17 and above.

There are no restrictions on the import or export of any currency.

Language French is spoken in the southwest, around Lake Geneva, and in the cantons of Fribourg, Neuchâtel, Jura, Vaud, and the western portion of Valais; Italian is spoken in the Ticino, and lilting dialects of German are spoken everywhere else—in more than 70% of the country, in fact. The Romance language called Romansch has regained a firm foothold throughout the Upper and Lower Engadine regions of the canton Graubünden, where it takes the form of five dialects. English, however, is spoken widely. Many public signs are in English, as well as in the regional language, and all hotels, restaurants, tourist offices, train stations, banks, and shops will have someone who can speak English comfortably.

Getting Around

By Plane Swissair connects the cities of Zürich, Basel, and Geneva. The airline (Box 845, New York, NY 10102, tel. 800/688–7947) offers flexible packages from April through October for the independent traveler who flies at least one way between North America and Europe on Swissair or Delta. "The Swiss Travel Invention" allows visitors to tailor-fit their Swiss holiday to include hotels, car rentals, rail vacations, and guided tours at great savings. Swissair also offers personalized ski packages consisting of round-trip flights, surface travel by rail or bus, and hotels.

By Train Switzerland's trains are among Europe's finest. Generally, they are swift (except through the mountains), immaculate, and unnervingly punctual. Don't linger between international connections: The Swiss don't wait for languorous travelers. If you plan to use the trains extensively, get the official timetable *(Offizieles Kursbuch),* which costs 26 SF. A small, pocket-size version *(Fribo)* covers key intercity connections and costs 10.80 SF. A useful booklet called "Switzerland by Rail," available from the Swiss National Tourist Office (SNTO), describes 20 excursions that can be made by public transportation, and includes timetables for the best train connections to Zürich and Geneva airports. Apply for tickets through your travel agent or *Rail Europe* (tel. 800/438–7245).

Trains described as Inter-City or Express, the fastest, stop only at principal towns. A *Regionalzug* is a local train and often affords the most spectacular views. Meals, snacks, and drinks are provided on most main services. Seat reservations are useful during rush hours and high season, especially on international trains.

Fares There are numerous concessions for visitors. The **Swiss Pass,** the best value, offers unlimited travel on Swiss Federal Railways, postal buses, lake steamers, and the local bus and tram service of 30 cities. It also gives reductions on many privately owned railways, cable cars, and mountain railways. It's available from the Swiss National Tourist Office and from travel agents outside Switzerland. The card is valid for eight days (cost 264 SF), 15 days (306 SF), or one month (420 SF). There is also a three-day **Flexi Pass** (210 SF), which offers the same unlimited travel options of a regular Swiss Pass for any three days within a 15-day period. Prices are for second-class travel; first-class travel costs about 40% more.

Within some popular tourist areas, **Regional Holiday Season Tickets,** issued for 15 days, give five days of free travel by train, postal buses, steamers, and mountain railways, with half fare for the rest of the validity of the card. Central Switzerland offers a similar pass for seven days, with two days of free travel. Prices vary widely, depending upon the region and period of validity, but if you like to cover a lot of ground, they do assure you of savings over full fare. Increasingly popular with tourists is a **Swiss Half-Fare Travel Card,** which allows half-fare travel for 30 days (90 SF) or one year (150 SF).

The new **Swiss Card,** which can be purchased in the United States through RailEurope (226–230 Westchester Ave., White Plains, NY 10604, tel. 914/682–5172 or 800/345–1990) and at train stations at the Zürich and Geneva airports and in Basel, is valid for 30 days and grants full round-trip travel from your arrival point to any destination in the country, plus a half-price reduction on any further excursions during your stay (170 SF first class, 140 SF second class). For more information about train travel in Switzerland, get the free "Swiss Travel System" or "Discover Switzerland" brochures from the SNTO.

For 20 SF per bag round-trip, travelers holding tickets or passes on Swiss Federal Railways can forward their luggage to their final destination—and make stops en route unencumbered.

By Bus Switzerland's famous yellow postal buses link main cities with villages off the beaten track. Both postal and city buses follow posted schedules to the minute; free timetables can be picked up at any post office.

The Swiss Pass (*see above*) gives unlimited travel on the postal buses. The **Postal Coach Weekly Card** gives unlimited travel within certain regions where train travel is limited and can be bought at local post offices.

The postbuses pay special attention to hikers. You can get a free booklet, "The Best River and Lakeside Walks," from the SNTO. The booklet describes 28 walks you can enjoy by hopping on and off postal buses. Most walks take around three hours.

By Boat Drifting across a Swiss lake and stopping off here and there at picturesque villages nestling by the water makes a relaxing day's excursion, especially if you are lucky enough to catch one of the elegant old paddle steamers. Trips are scheduled on most of the lakes, with increased service in summer. Unlimited travel is free to holders of the **Swiss Pass** (*see above*). For those not traveling by train, there is also a **Swiss Boat Pass,** which allows half-fare travel on all lake steamers for the entire year (35 SF, May 1–Oct. 31).

By Bicycle Bikes can be rented at all train stations and returned to any station. Rates are 19 SF per day or 76 SF per week for a conventional bike. Families can rent bikes for a single fee of 48 SF per day, depending on the region, or for 208 SF per week; groups get reductions according to the number of bikes involved. Reservations are necessary by 6 PM the day before use by individuals and a week ahead for groups. **Touring Club Suisse** (9 rue Pierre Fatio, CH-1211 Geneva 3, tel. 022/7371212) also rents bikes from its local offices at prices ranging from 14 SF to 24 SF per day.

Staying in Switzerland

Telephones There is direct dialing to every location in Switzerland. For local and
Local Calls international codes, consult the pink pages at the front of the telephone book.

International You can dial most international numbers direct from Switzerland,
Calls adding a 00 before the country's code. If you want a number that cannot be reached directly, dial 114 for a connection. Dial 191 for international numbers and information. To call the United States directly, dial 55–0011 for an **AT&T** operator, 155–0222 for an **MCI** operator, or 155–9777 for a **Sprint** operator. It's cheapest to use the booths in train stations and post offices; calls made from hotels cost a great deal more. Rates are lower between 5 PM and 7 PM, after 9 PM, and on weekends. Calls to the United States cost 1.80 SF per minute, to the United Kingdom 1 SF per minute.

Operators and All telephone operators speak English, and instructions are printed
Information in English in all telephone booths.

Country Code The country code for Switzerland is 41.

Mail Mail rates are divided into first class (air mail) and second class (sur-
Postal Rates face). Letters and post cards to the United States up to 20 grams cost 1.80 SF first class, .90 SF second class; to the United Kingdom, 1 SF first class, .80 SF second class.

Receiving Mail If you're uncertain where you'll be staying, you can have your mail, marked Poste Restante or Postlagernd, sent to any post office in Switzerland. The sender's name and address must be on the back, and you'll need proof of identity to collect it. American Express cardholders can also have their mail sent to American Express for a small fee.

Shopping A 6.5% value-added tax (VAT) on all goods is included in the price.
VAT Refunds Nonresidents who have spent at least 500 SF at one time at a particular store may claim a VAT refund at the time of purchase, or the shop will send the refund to your home. In order to qualify, sign a form at the time of purchase and present it to Swiss customs on departure.

Bargaining Don't try bargaining: Except at the humblest flea market, it just doesn't work. As with everything in Switzerland, prices are efficiently controlled.

Opening and **Banks** are open weekdays 8:30–4:30 or 5.
Closing Times
Museums. Museum times vary considerably, though many close on Monday. Check locally.

Shops are generally open 8–noon and 1:30–6:30. Some close at 4 on Saturday, and some are closed Monday morning. In cities, many large stores do not close for lunch.

National In 1996: January 1, 2; April 5 (Good Friday); April 7, 8 (Easter); May
Holidays 16 (Ascension); May 26 (Pentecost Sunday); August 1 (National Day); December 25, 26. May 1 (Labor Day) is also celebrated, though not throughout the country. Changing holidays in 1997:

March 28 (Good Friday); March 30, 31 (Easter); May 16 (Ascension); May 18 (Pentecost Sunday).

Dining Options range from luxury establishments to modest cafés, *Stübli* (pubs), and restaurants specializing in local cuisine.

Because the Swiss are so good at preparing everyone else's cuisine, it is sometimes said that they have none of their own, but there definitely is a distinct and characteristic Swiss cuisine. Switzerland is the home of great cheeses—Gruyère, Emmentaler, Appenzeller, and Vacherin—which form the basis of many dishes. *Raclette* is cheese melted over a fire and served with potatoes and pickles, *Rösti* are hash-brown potatoes, and fondue is a bubbling pot of melted cheeses flavored with garlic and kirsch, into which you dip chunks of bread. Other Swiss specialties to look for are *Geschnetzeltes Kalbfleisch* (veal bits in cream sauce), polenta (cornmeal mush) in the Italian region, and fine game in autumn. A wide variety of Swiss sausages make both filling and inexpensive meals, and in every region the breads are varied and superb.

Mealtimes At home, the main Swiss meal of the day is lunch, with a snack in the evening. Restaurants, however, are open at midday and during the evening; often limited menus are offered all day. Watch for *Tagesteller* or *menus* (prix-fixe lunches), which enable you to experience the best restaurants without paying high à la carte rates.

What to Wear Jacket and tie are suggested for some restaurants in the $$ category; casual dress is acceptable elsewhere.

Ratings Prices are per person, without wine or coffee, but including tip and taxes. Best bets are indicated by a star ★.

Category	Zürich/Geneva	Other Areas
$$	35 SF–50 SF	30 SF–50 SF
$	20 SF–35 SF	20 SF–30 SF
¢	under 20 SF	under 20 SF

Lodging Switzerland's accommodations cover a broad range, from the most luxurious hotels to the more economical rooms in private homes. Pick up the *Schweizer Hotelführer (Swiss Hotel Guide)* from the SNTO before you leave home. The guide is free and lists all the members of the Swiss Hotel Association (comprising nearly 90% of the nation's accommodations); it tells you everything you'll want to know.

Most hotel rooms today have private bath and shower; those that don't are usually considerably cheaper. Single rooms are generally about two-thirds the price of doubles, but this can vary considerably. Remember that the no-nonsense Swiss sleep in separate beds or, at best, a double with separate bedding. If you prefer more sociable arrangements, ask for the rare "matrimonial" or "French" bed. Service charges and taxes are included in the price quoted and the bill you pay. Breakfast is included unless there is a clear notice to the contrary. In resorts especially, half pension (choice of a noon or evening meal) may be included in the room price. If you choose to eat à la carte or elsewhere, the management will generally reduce your price. Give them plenty of notice, however.

All major towns and train stations have hotel-finding services, which sometimes charge a small fee. Local tourist offices will also help.

Hotels Hotels are graded from one star (the lowest) to five stars. Always confirm what you are paying before you register, and check the posted price when you get to your room. Major credit cards are generally accepted, but, again, make sure beforehand.

The Check-In E and G Hotels are small hotels, boardinghouses, and mountain lodges that offer comfortable and often charming accommodations at reasonable prices. Details are available from the SNTO, which also offers pamphlets recommending family hotels and a list of hotels and restaurants that cater specifically to Jewish travelers.

Country Inns Country inns offer clean, comfortable, and hospitable accommodations, often in areas of great scenic beauty. Many are in the $ category and are a good value.

Rentals Switzerland has literally thousands of furnished chalets. Off-season, per-day prices are around 50 SF per person for four sharing a chalet. In peak season, prices would be at least twice that. Deluxe chalets cost much more. For more information, pick up an illustrated brochure from the **Swiss Touring Club** (9 rue Pierre Fatio, CH-1211 Geneva 3) or from **Uto-Ring AG** (Beethovenstr. 24, CH-8002 Zürich). Or contact **Interhome** in the United States (36 Carlos Dr., Fairfield, NJ 07006) or in Britain (383 Richmond Rd., Twickenham, Middlesex TW1 2EF). You may save considerably if you write directly to the village or resort you wish to rent in, specifying your projected dates and number of beds required: Prices may start at around 20 SF per person without an agency's commission.

Ratings Prices are for two people in a double room with bath or shower, including taxes, service charges, and breakfast. Budget hotels do not have baths or toilets in rooms. Best bets are indicated by a star ★.

Category	Zürich/Geneva	Other Areas
$$	150 SF–250 SF	125 SF–200 SF
$	110 SF–150 SF	90 SF–125 SF
¢	under 110 SF	under 90 SF

Tipping Although restaurants include service charges of 15% with the taxes in your hotel and restaurant bill, you will be expected to leave a small additional tip: 1 SF or 2 SF per person for a modest meal, 5 SF for a first-class meal, and 10 SF at any exclusive gastronomic establishment. When possible, tip in cash rather than on the credit-card slip. Elsewhere, give bathroom attendants 1 SF and hotel maids 2 SF. Theater and opera-house ushers get 2 SF for showing you to your seat and selling you a program. Hotel porters and doormen should get about 1 SF per bag.

Zürich

Arriving and Departing

By Plane Kloten (tel. 01/8121212) is Switzerland's most important airport and is among the most sophisticated in the world. Several airlines fly directly from major cities in the United States, Canada, and the United Kingdom.

Swissair flies nonstop from New York, Chicago, Toronto, Montreal, Atlanta, Los Angeles, and Boston. "Fly Rail Baggage" allows Swissair passengers departing Switzerland to check their bags at any of 120 rail or postal bus stations throughout the country; the luggage is automatically transferred to the airplane. At eight Swiss railway stations, passengers may complete all check-in procedures for Swissair flights, boarding-pass issuance as well as baggage forwarding.

<table>
<tr><td>*Between the Airport and Downtown*</td><td>Beneath the air terminals, there's a train station with an efficient, direct service into the Hauptbahnhof (main station) in the center of Zürich. Fast trains run every 20 minutes, and the trip takes about 10 minutes. The fare is 4.80 SF and the ticket office is in the airport. There are express trains to most Swiss cities at least every hour. Trains run from 6 AM to midnight.</td></tr>
<tr><td>**By Train**</td><td>There are straightforward connections and several express routes leading directly into Zürich's Hauptbahnhof from Basel, Geneva (Genève), Bern (Berne), and Lugano, as well as from other major European cities.</td></tr>
</table>

Getting Around

Although Zürich is Switzerland's largest city, it has a population of only 362,000 and is not large by European standards. That's one of its nicest features: You can explore it comfortably on foot.

By Bus and Streetcar The city's transportation network is excellent. **VBZ Züri-Line** (Zürich Public Transport) buses run from 5:30 AM to midnight, every six minutes on all routes at peak hours, and about every 12 minutes at other times. Before you board the bus or train, you must buy your ticket from the automatic vending machines (instructions appear in English) found at every stop. A ticket for all travel for 24 hours is a good buy at 6.40 SF. Free route plans are available from VBZ offices.

Important Addresses and Numbers

Tourist Information The tourist office is located at Bahnhofplatz 15 (Main Station), tel. 01/2114000. *Open Apr.–Oct., weekdays 8:30 AM–9:30 PM, weekends 8:30 AM–8:30 PM; Nov.–Mar., Mon.–Fri. 8:30–7:30, weekends 8:30–6:30.*

Consulates U.S. (Zollikerstr. 141, tel. 01/4222566). U.K. (Dufourstr. 56, tel. 01/2611520).

Emergencies **Police** (tel. 117). **Ambulance** (tel. 144). **Doctor/Dentist** (tel. 01/2614700).

Exploring Zürich

Zürich is not at all what you'd expect. Stroll around on a fine spring day and you'll ask yourself if this can really be one of the great business centers of the world: The lake glistening and blue in the sun, the sidewalk cafés, the swans gliding in to land on the river, the hushed and haunted old squares of medieval guildhouses, the elegant shops. There's not a gnome (a mocking nickname for a Swiss banker) in sight, not a worried business frown to be seen. The point is that for all its economic importance, Zürich is a place where people enjoy life. Hardworking, inventive, serious when need be, the Swiss love the good things in life, and they have the money to enjoy them.

Numbers in the margin correspond to points of interest on the Zürich map.

Collect your map from the tourist office (Bahnhofplatz 15), then start your walk from the nearby **Bahnhofstrasse**, famous for its shops and cafés and as the center of the banking network, though you'd be unlikely to guess it. Take Rennweg on your left, and then turn left again into the Fortunagasse, a quaint medieval street leading to the **Lindenhof**, a square where there are remains of Zürich's Roman origins. The fountain commemorates the ingenuity of the Zürich women who, when the city was besieged by the Hapsburgs in 1292, donned armor and marched around the walls. The invaders thought they were reinforcements and beat a hasty retreat.

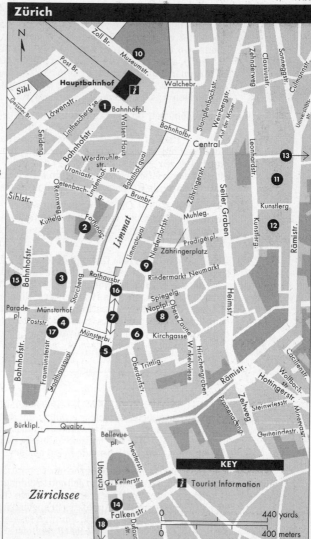

③ An alley on the right leads to a picturesque square dating from the Middle Ages, with the **Peterskirche**, Zürich's oldest parish church (13th century), which also happens to have the largest clockface in Europe. Walk down to the river and follow it to the 13th century **④ Fraumünster** (church), which has modern stained-glass windows by Chagall. There are two handsome guildhalls nearby: the **Zunfthaus zur Waag**, the hall of the linen weavers (Münsterhof 8), built in 1637, and the **Zunfthaus zur Meise** (Münsterhof 20), built during the 18th century for the wine merchants.

Continue along Bahnhofstrasse to Bürkliplatz and cross the **Quai Bridge** to take in the impressive views of the lake and town. Now **⑤** head left to the **Wasserkirche** (Water Church), dating from the 15th century and a lovely example of late-Gothic architecture. It is attached to the **Helmhaus**, originally an 18th-century cloth market.

⑥ Now turn right toward the **Grossmünster** church, which dates from the 11th century. During the 3rd century AD, St. Felix and his sister

Regula were martyred by the Romans. Legend maintains that having been beheaded, they then walked up the hill carrying their heads and collapsed on the spot where the Grossmünster now stands. On the south tower you can see a statue of Charlemagne (768–814), emperor of the West. During the 16th century, the Zürich reformer Huldrych Zwingli preached sermons here that were so threatening in their promise of fire and brimstone that Martin Luther himself was frightened.

7 Back at the river on the **Limmatquai** are some of Zürich's most enchanting old buildings. Today most of them are restaurants. In the **Haus zum Ruden,** a 13th-century noblemen's hall, you will eat under a 300-year-old wooden ceiling. Other notable buildings here are the **Zunfthaus zur Saffran,** built in 1723 for haberdashers, and the **Zunfthaus zur Zimmerleuten,** built in 1708 for carpenters. The 17th-century Baroque **Rathaus** (Town Hall) is nearby.

8 Turn right into the **Old Town,** and you will enter a maze of fascinating medieval streets where time seems to have stood still. The Rindermarkt, Napfplatz, and Kirchgasse all have their charming old houses.

9 Head back to the river through **Niederdorf,** Zürich's nightlife district, and cross the bridge to the Hauptbahnhof. On the northern
10 edge of the Hauptbahnhof, go to the **Schweizerisches Landesmuseum,** housed in a curious 19th-century building, for a look at Swiss history. There are fascinating pre-Romanesque and Romanesque church art, glass paintings from the 15th to the 17th century, splendid ceramic stoves, gold and silver from Celtic times, and weapons from many ages. *Museumstr. 2, tel. 01/2186565. Admission free. Open Tues.–Sun. 10–5.*

Shopping

Gift Ideas Typical Swiss products, all of the highest quality, include watches in all price categories, clocks, jewelry, music boxes, embroidered goods, wood carvings, and the famous multiblade Swiss army pocket knife. You'll also find fine household linens, delicate cotton or woolen underthings, and Zürich-made Fogal hosiery.

Shopping The **Bahnhofstrasse** is one of the most bountiful shopping streets in
Districts Switzerland. Here you'll find **Jelmoli** (Seidengasse 1), Switzerland's largest department store, carrying a wide range of tasteful Swiss goods. **Heimatwerk** (Bahnhofstr. 2) specializes in handmade Swiss crafts, all of excellent quality. For high fashion, go to **Trois Pommes** (Storchengasse 6/7) and **Grieder** (Bahnhofstr. 30), and for the finest porcelain, glass, and silverware, visit **Sequin-Dormann** (Bahnhofstr. 69a). If you have a sweet tooth, stock up on truffles at **Sprüngli** (Paradepl.), or **Teuscher** (Old Town 9).

In the **Old Town** and off the **Limmatquai,** you'll find boutiques, antiques shops, bookstores, and galleries in picturesque byways. The **Löwenstrasse** has a diversity of upscale shops; the **Langstrasse** is another good shopping area and often has slightly lower prices. Under the central train station, **Shopville** offers a variety of middle-class stores and snack bars.

Food and Flea In many parts of town, there are lively markets where fruit, vegeta-
Markets bles, and flowers are competitively priced. The best are at **Bürkliplatz, Helvetiaplatz,** and **Milkbuckstrasse** (open Tues. and Fri. 6 AM–11 AM) and at **Marktplatz,** on the way to the airport (open Wed. and Sat. 6 AM–11 AM).

At Bürkliplatz, at the lake end of the Bahnhofstrasse, there's a flea market that's open May through October, and a curio market is held at **Rosenhof** every Thursday and Saturday between April and Christmas.

Dining

You're likely to be served seconds in Zürich's generous restaurants, where the rest of your Rösti and Geschnetzeltes Kalbfleisch nach Zürcher Art (veal, Zurich-style) simmer in copper pans by your table while you relish the hefty first portion. This is a Germanic city, after all, though its status as a minor world capital means that most international cuisines are represented as well. But brace yourself: The cash register rings portentously when the waiter places your order. Watch for posted *Tagesteller* specials, a good source of savings. For details and price-category definitions, *see* Dining *in* Staying in Switzerland, *above*.

$$ Oepfelchammer. This was once the haunt of Zürich's beloved writer
★ Gottfried Keller, and, recently restored, it still draws unpretentious literati. One room's a dark and graffiti-scribbled bar, with sagging timbers and slanting floors; the other's a welcoming little dining room, with carved oak paneling, a coffered ceiling, and pink damask linens. The traditional meats—calf's liver, veal, tripe in white wine sauce—come in generous portions; salads are fresh and seasonal. It's always packed, and service can be slow, so stake out a table and spend the evening. *Rindermarkt 12, tel. 01/2512336. Reservations advised. MC, V. Closed Sun.*

$$ Zunfthaus zur Schmiden. The sense of history and the magnificent mix of Gothic wood, leaded glass, and tile stoves justify a visit to this popular landmark, the guildhouse of blacksmiths and barbers since 1412. All the classics are served in enormous portions, and there's a considerable selection of alternatives, fish among them. The guild's own house wine is fine. *Marktgasse 20, tel. 01/2515287. Reservations advised. AE, DC, MC, V.*

$ Bierhalle Kropf. Under the giant boar's head and century-old murals
★ that have been recently restored, businesspeople, workers, and shoppers crowd shared tables to feast on generous hot dishes and a great selection of sausages. The *Leberknödli* (liver dumplings) are tasty, *Apfelköchli* (fried apple slices) tender and sweet, and the bread chewy and delicious—though you pay for every chunk you eat. The bustle, clatter, and wisecracking waitresses make for a lively, sociable experience. *In Gassen 16, tel. 01/2211805. Reservations advised. AE, DC, MC, V.*

$ Zeughauskeller. Built as an arsenal in 1487, this enormous stone-
★ and-beam hall offers hearty meat platters and a variety of beers and wines amid comfortable and friendly chaos. They're not unaccustomed to tourists, but locals consider this their home away from home. *Bahnhofstr. 28 (at Paradeplatz), tel. 01/2112690. Reservations advised at lunch. No credit cards.*

¢ Hiltl Vegi. As the German world takes its cholesterol count, more and more vegetarian restaurants are catching on, including this popular old landmark, founded in the late 19th century. The atmosphere these days is all contemporary, with color photos posted of daily specials, which include soups, curries, and variations on ratatouille. *Sihlstrasse 28, tel. 01/2213870. No credit cards.*

¢ Odeon. A pre-Revolutionary Lenin once nursed a coffee and read the
★ house's daily papers in this historic café-restaurant, whose atmosphere is as Parisian as it gets in this Prussian town. Now the crowd is just as intense, and a tonic air of counterculture chic mixes with the no-filter cigarette smoke. You can nurse a coffee, too, or have a plate of pasta, a sandwich, or dessert from the limited menu. The restaurant is open daily to 2 AM, weekends to 4 AM. *Am Bellevue, tel. 01/2511650. AE, DC, MC, V.*

¢ Rheinfelder Bierhaus. Mixed parties of workers, bikers, shoppers, and tourists squeeze into every wooden table at this dark, smoky spot, a solid old institution in the Niederdorf area. There's rich *Rindpfeffer* (preserved beef stew) with homemade *Spätzli* (tiny dumplings), tender liver with Rösti, sausage standards, and, incongruously, once a month the chef's pride: a freshly homemade paella. *Marktgasse 19, tel. 01/2512991. No credit cards.*

Lodging

Zürich has an enormous range of hotels, from some of the most chic and prestigious in the country to modest guest houses. Prices tend to be higher than anywhere else in Europe, but you can be sure that you will get what you pay for: Quality and good service are guaranteed. For details and price-category definitions, *see* Lodging *in* Staying in Switzerland, *above.*

$$ ★ **Rössli.** Young, trendy, and completely high-tech, this hip new spot in Oberdorf, near the Grossmünster, offers a refreshing antidote to Zürich's medievalism. Decor is white-on-white, with metallic-tiled baths, vivid lithographs, and splashy fabrics; hair dryers, robes, and fax connections keep services above average, especially for the price. The adjoining bar is very popular with young locals. *Rössligasse 7, CH-8001, tel. 01/2522121, fax 01/2522131. 12 rooms with bath. Facilities: bar. AE, DC, MC, V.*

$$ ★ **Sonnenberg.** If you're traveling by car and want to avoid the urban rush, escape to this hillside refuge east of town. There are breathtaking views of the city, lake, and mountains and landscaped grounds with a lovely terrace restaurant. The wood, stone, and beam decor reinforces the resort atmosphere. It's run by the friendly Wismer family. Take Tram 3 or 8 to Klusplatz, then walk 10 minutes uphill. *Aurorastr. 98, CH-8030, tel. 01/2620062, fax 01/2620633. 35 rooms with bath. Facilities: restaurant, café. AE, DC, MC, V.*

$$ **Wellenberg.** Another effort at high style but not as effective as the Rössli, this new, central hotel sports a postmodern retro look, with burled wood, black lacquer, Art Deco travel posters, and Hollywood photos. The rooms are relatively roomy, if occasionally garish, and the location—on Niederdorf's Hirschenplatz—is superb. The staff is especially friendly to overseas visitors. *Niederdorfstr. 10, CH-8001, tel. 01/2624300, fax 01/2513130. 46 rooms with bath. AE, DC, MC, V.*

$ ★ **Linde Oberstrasse.** Near the university in a sterile residential area, this small hotel, built as a guildhouse in 1628, offers a handful of modest but agreeable rooms. The decor has been comfortably modernized, and though baths are down the hall, there is a sink, a TV, and a minibar in each room to compensate. The restaurant is comfortable and, though renovated to dated-modern style, maintains its traditional atmosphere and solid menu. *Universitätstr. 91, CH-8033, tel. 01/3622109. 10 rooms without bath. Facilities: restaurant, minibar. AE, DC, MC, V.*

$ **Vorderer Sternen.** On the edge of the Old Town and near the lake, this plain but adequate establishment takes in the bustle (and noise) of the city. It's steps from the opera house, theaters, art galleries, cinemas, and a shopping area; it's also close to the Bellevueplatz tram junction. There's a dependable and popular restaurant downstairs with moderate standards; none of the rooms has a bathroom. *Theaterstr. 22, CH-8001, tel. 01/2514949, fax 01/2529063. 15 rooms without bath. Facilities: restaurant. AE, DC, MC, V.*

¢ ★ **Italia.** This cozy Old World family hotel, located far west of the river in a barren but perfectly safe neighborhood, spills over with doilies, overstuffed chairs, and mismatched antiques. Rooms have sinks only, but there's a big, homey bathroom on each floor, and prices are rock-bottom. The Papagni family runs the restaurant downstairs, a picture of leather and wood, and in summer serves crowds under the chestnut pollards in the garden outside. To get there, take Bus 31 from the train station to Kanonengasse. *Zeughausstrasse 61, CH-8004, tel. 01/2410555. 36 rooms, none with bath. Facilities: restaurant. No credit cards.*

¢ **St. Georges.** In this simple former pension, the lobby and breakfast room are fresh and bright, but the rooms and corridors are considerably more spare, with toothpaste-green walls, red linoleum, and pine furniture dating from the 1960s. Rooms with shower cost 40% more than those without. Take Tram 3 or 14 from the station to Stauffacher; it's another five minutes on foot. *Weberstrasse 11, CH-8004, tel. 01/2411144, fax 01/2411142. 44 rooms, half with private bath. Facilities: breakfast room. AE, DC, MC, V.*

The Arts

Pick up *Zürich News*, published each week by the tourist office, to find out what's going on. Ticket reservations can be made through the **Billetzentrale** (Werdmühleplatz, tel. 01/2212283; open weekdays 10–6:30, Sat. 10–2). **Musik Hug** (Limmatquai 26, tel. 01/2212540) and **Jecklin** (Rämistr. 30, tel. 01/2617733) are good ticket sources as well.

The **Zürich Tonhalle Orchestra** (Claridenstr. 7, tel. 01/2063434) ranks among Europe's best. The **Opernhaus** (Falkenstr., tel. 01/2620909) is renowned for its adventurous opera, operetta, and ballet productions. The **Schauspielhaus** (Rämistr. 34, tel. 01/2511111) is one of the finest German-speaking theaters in the world. Zürich has 40 movie theaters, with English-language films appearing regularly.

Nightlife

Zürich has a lively nightlife scene, largely centered in the Niederdorf, parallel to the Limmat, across from the Hauptbahnhof. Many spots are short-lived, so check in advance. Informal dress is acceptable in most places, but again, check to make sure. The hotel porter is a good source of information.

Bars and Lounges   The narrow bar at the **Kronenhalle** (Rämistr. 4, tel. 01/2511597) draws mobs of well-heeled locals and internationals for its prize-winning cocktails. The **Jules Verne Panorama Bar** (Uraniahaus, tel. 01/2111155) offers cocktails with a wraparound view of downtown Zürich. **Champagnertreff** in the Hotel Central (Central 1, tel. 01/2515555) is a popular Deco-look piano bar with several champagnes available by the glass. **Odeon** (Am Bellevue, tel. 01/2511650) serves a young, arty set until 4 AM. Some beer halls, including **Bierhalle Kropf** (In Gassen 16, tel. 01/2211805) and **Zeughauskeller** (Bahnhofstr. 28, tel. 01/2112690), serve draft beers in an old-Zürich atmosphere.

Cabaret/ Nightclubs   There's a variety show (dancers, magicians) at **Polygon** (Marktgasse 17, tel. 01/2521110). There are strip shows all over town, as well as the traditional nightclub atmosphere at **Le Privé** (Stauffacherstr. 106, tel. 01/2416487), **Moulin Rouge** (Mühlegasse 14, tel. 01/2620730), and the slightly more sophisticated **Terrace** (Limmatquai 3, tel. 01/2511074). Expect high prices at all of the above.

Discos   **Mascotte** (Theaterstr. 10, tel. 01/2524481) is, at the moment, popular with all ages on weeknights, but caters to young crowds on weekends. **Nautic Club** (Wythenquai 61, tel. 01/2026676) opens onto the lakefront in summer. **Le Petit Prince** (Bleicherweg 21, tel. 01/2011739) attracts an upscale crowd. **Birdwatcher's Club** (Schützengasse 16, tel. 01/2115058) requires jackets and a membership card. Even more exclusive is **Diagonal,** at the Hotel Baur au Lac (Talstr. 1, tel. 01/2117396), where you must be a hotel guest—or the guest of one. **Joker** (Gotthardstrasse 5, tel. 01/2063666) has live bands—folk, rock, and tango.

Jazz   **Casa Bar** (Münstergasse 30, tel. 01/2612002) is the exclusive domain of jazz, with music until 2 AM.

Excursion from Zürich: Liechtenstein

For an international day trip out of Zürich, dip a toe into tiny Liechtenstein: There isn't room for much more. Just 80 kilometers (50 miles) southeast on the Austrian border, this miniature principality covers a scant 158 square kilometers (61 square miles). An independent nation since 1719, Liechtenstein has a customs union with Switzerland, which means they share trains, currency, and diplomats—but not stamps, which is why collectors prize the local releases. It's easiest to get there by car, since Liechtenstein is so small that Swiss trains pass through without stopping. If you're using a train pass, ride to Sargans or Buchs and take a postbus across the border to Liechtenstein's capital, Vaduz.

Tourist Information
The principal tourist office in Liechtenstein is at Städtle 37, Box 139, FL 9490, Vaduz, tel. 075/2321443. It's open weekdays 8–noon and 1:30–5.

Exploring Liechtenstein
Green and mountainous, its Rhine shores lined with vineyards, greater Liechtenstein is best seen by car. But if you're on foot, you won't be stuck: The postbuses are prompt and take you everywhere at a scenic snail's pace.

In fairy-tale **Vaduz,** Prince Johannes Adam Pius still lives in **Vaduz Castle,** a massive 16th-century fortress perched high on the cliff over the city. Only honored guests of the prince tour the castle's interior, but its exterior and the views from the grounds are worth the climb. In the modern center of town, head for the tourist information office to have your passport stamped with the Liechtenstein crown. Upstairs, the **Prince's Art Gallery and the State Art Collection** display Flemish masters. *Städtle 37, tel. 075/2322341. Admission: 5 SF adults, 2 SF children. Open Apr.–Oct.; daily 10–noon and 1:30–5:30; Nov.–Mar., daily 10–noon and 1:30–5.*

On the same floor, the **Postage Stamp Museum** attracts philatelists from all over the world to see the 300 frames of beautifully designed—and relatively rare—stamps. Place subscriptions here for future first-day covers. *Städtle 37, tel. 075/2366109. Admission free. Open Apr.–Oct., daily 1:30–5:30; Nov.–Mar., 10–noon and 1:30–5.*

Next, move on to the **Liechtenstein National Museum** (closed until mid-1997), which houses historical artifacts, church carvings, ancient coins, and arms from the prince's collection. *Städtle 43, tel. 075/22310. Admission: 2 SF. Open May–Oct., daily 10–noon and 1:30–5:30; Nov.–Apr., Tues.–Sun. 2–5:30.*

In **Schaan,** just north of Vaduz, visit the Roman excavations and the parish church built on the foundations of a Roman fort. Or drive up to the chalets of picturesque **Triesenberg** for spectacular views of the Rhine Valley. Higher still, **Malbun** is a sundrenched ski bowl with comfortable slopes and a low-key family ambience.

Dining
For details and price-category definitions, *see* Dining *in* Staying in Switzerland, *above.*

$ ★ **Wirthschaft zum Löwen.** Though there's plenty of French, Swiss, and Austrian influence, Liechtenstein has a cuisine of its own, and this is the place to try it. In a wood-shingled farmhouse on the Austrian border, the friendly Biedermann family serves tender homemade *Schwartenmagen* (the pressed pork-mold unfortunately known as headcheese in English), pungent *Sauerkäse* (sour cheese), and *Käseknöpfli* (cheese dumplings), plus lovely meats and the local crusty, chewy bread. Try the area's wines and the automatic snuff machine. *FL-9488 Schellenberg, tel. 075/3731162. Reservations advised. V.*

Lodging
For details and price-category definitions, *see* Lodging in Staying in Switzerland, *above.*

$$ **Engel.** Directly on the main tourist street, its café bulging with bus-tour crowds, this simple hotel-restaurant manages to maintain a local, comfortable ambience. The Huber family oversees the easy-going pub downstairs; the restaurant upstairs serves Chinese food. The rooms were renovated in 1991. *Städtle 13, tel. 075/2320313, fax 075/2331159. 17 rooms with bath. Facilities: restaurant, café. AE, DC, MC, V.*

$ **Alpenhotel.** Well above the mists of the Rhine in sunny Malbun, this 82-year-old chalet has been remodeled and a modern wing added. The old rooms are small and cozy; the higher-price new rooms are modern and spare. The Vögeli family's welcoming smiles and good food have made it a Liechtenstein institution. *FL-9497 Tel. 075/2631181, fax 075/2639646. 25 rooms with bath. Facilities: restaurant, café, indoor pool. AE, DC, MC, V.*

Geneva

Arriving and Departing

By Plane Cointrin (tel. 022/7993111), Geneva's airport, is served by several airlines that fly directly from New York, Toronto, and London. Swissair also has flights from Chicago and Los Angeles.

Swissair ticketholders departing from Cointrin can check their luggage through to their final destination from 120 rail and postal bus stations and at eight train stations also get their boarding passes.

Between the Airport and Downtown Cointrin has a direct rail link with Cornavin (tel. 022/7316450), the city's main train station, which is located in the center of town. Trains run about every 10 minutes from 5:30 AM to midnight. The trip takes about six minutes, and the fare is 4.40 SF for second class.

There is regular city bus service from the airport to the center of Geneva. The bus takes about 20 minutes, and the fare is 2 SF. Some hotels have their own bus service.

By Train All services—domestic and international—use Cornavin Station in the center of the city. For information, dial 022/7316450.

By Bus Buses generally arrive at and depart from the bus station at place Dorcière, behind the English church in the city center.

Getting Around

By Bus and Streetcar There are scheduled services by local buses and trains every few minutes on all routes. Before you board, you must buy your ticket (2 SF) from the machines at the stops (they have English instructions). Save money and buy a ticket covering unlimited travel all day within the city center for 6 SF. If you have a **Swiss Pass,** you can travel free (*see* Getting Around Switzerland by Train, *above*).

Tourist Information

The **Office du Tourisme de Genève** (Cornavin Station, Case Postale 440, CH-1211, tel. 022/7385200; open mid-Sept.–mid-June, Mon.–Sat. 9–6; late June–early Sept., weekdays 8–8, weekends 8–6). For information by mail, contact their administrative branch at 1 rue de la Tour de l'Ile, Case Postale 5230, CH-1211 Genève. **Thomas Cook** (64 rue de Lausanne, tel. 022/7324555).

Exploring Geneva

Draped at the foot of the Juras and the Alps on the westernmost tip of Lake Geneva (or Lac Léman, as the natives know it), Geneva is the most cosmopolitan and graceful of Swiss cities and the stronghold of the French-speaking territory. Just a stone's throw from the French border and 160 kilometers (100 miles) or so from Lyon, its grand mansarded mansions stand guard beside the river Rhône, where yachts bob, gulls dive, and Rolls-Royces purr beside manicured promenades. The combination of Swiss efficiency and French savoir faire gives the city a chic polish, and the infusion of international blood from the United Nations adds a heterogeneity that is rare in cities with a population of only 160,000.

A Roman seat for 500 years (from 120 BC), then home to early Burgundians, Geneva flourished under bishop-princes into the 11th century, fending off the greedy dukes of Savoy in conflicts that lasted into the 17th century. Under the guiding fervor of Calvin, Geneva rejected Catholicism and became a stronghold of Protestant reforms. In 1798 it fell to the French, but joined the Swiss Confederation as a canton in 1815, shortly after Napoleon's defeat. The French accent remains nonetheless.

Numbers in the margin correspond to points of interest on the Geneva map.

Start your walk from Gare de Cornavin (Cornavin Station) and head
❶ down the rue du Mont-Blanc to the **Pont du Mont-Blanc,** which spans the westernmost point of Lac Léman as it squeezes back into the Rhône. From the middle of the bridge (if it's clear) you can see the snowy peak of Mont Blanc itself, and from March to October you'll have a fine view of the **Jet d'Eau,** Europe's highest fountain, gushing 145 meters (475 feet) into the air.

Back at the foot of the bridge, turn right onto quai du Mont-Blanc to
❷ reach the **Monument Brunswick,** the high-Victorian tomb of a duke of Brunswick who left his fortune to Geneva in 1873. Just north are the city's grandest hotels, overlooking a manicured garden walk and the embarkation points for excursion boats. If you continue north a considerable distance through elegant parks and turn inland on the
❸ avenue de la Paix, you'll reach the enormous **International Complex,** where the Palais des Nations houses the European seat of the United Nations. (You can also reach it by taking Bus 8 or F from the train station.)

Or turn left from the Pont du Mont-Blanc and walk down the elegant
❹ quai des Bergues. In the center of the Rhône is **Ile J.J. Rousseau** (Rousseau Island), with a statue of the Swiss-born philosopher.
❺ Turn left onto the **Pont de l'Ile,** where the tall Tour de l'Ile, once a medieval prison, houses the tourist office. Turn left again and cross the place Bel-Air, the center of the business and banking district,
❻ and follow the rue de la Corraterie to the **place Neuve.** Here you'll see the **Grand Théâtre,** which hosts opera, ballet, and sometimes the Orchestre de la Suisse Romande (it also performs at nearby Victoria Hall), and the **Conservatoire de Musique.** Also at this address is the **Musée Rath,** with top-notch temporary exhibitions. *Tel. 022/ 3105270. Admission and hrs vary; check local listings. Open Tues.– Sun. 10–noon and 2–6; also Wed. evening 8–10.*

Above the ancient ramparts on your left are some of the wealthiest old homes in Geneva. Enter the gated park before you, the promenade des Bastions, site of the university, and keep left until you see
❼ the famous **Monument de la Réformation,** which pays homage to such Protestant pioneers as Bèze, Calvin, Farel, and Knox. Passing the uphill ramp and continuing to the farther rear gate, take the park exit just beyond the monument and turn left on the rue St-Leger, passing through the ivy-covered arch and winding into the **Vieille Ville,** or Old Town.

When you reach the ancient place du Bourg-de-Four, once a Roman forum, you can turn right on rue des Chaudronniers and head for the
❽ **Musée d'Art et Histoire** (Museum of Art and History), which has a

fine collection of paintings, sculpture, and archaeological relics. *2 rue Charles-Galland, tel. 022/3114340. Admission free. Open Tues.–Sun. 10–5.*

⑨
⑩ Just beyond are the spiraling cupolas of the **Eglise Russe** (Russian Church) and the **Collection Baur** of Oriental arts. *8 rue Munier-Romilly, tel. 022/3461729. Admission: 5 SF. Open Tues.–Sun. 2–6.*

⑪ Alternatively, from the place du Bourg-de-Four, head left up any number of narrow streets and stairs toward the **Cathédrale St-Pierre,** done in a schizophrenic mix of Classical and Gothic styles. Under its nave (and entered from outside) is one of the biggest archaeological digs in Europe, a massive excavation of the cathedral's early Christian predecessors, now restored as a stunning maze of backlit walkways over mosaics, baptisteries, and ancient foundations. *Tel. 022/7385650. Admission to site: 5 SF. Open Tues.–Sun. 10–1 and 2–6.*

⑫ Calvin worshiped in the cathedral; he made the **Temple de l'Auditoire,** a small Gothic church just south of the cathedral toward place du Bourg-de-Four, into his lecture hall, where he taught missionaries his doctrines of reform. *Place de la Taconnerie, tel. 022/738-5650. Open Oct.–May, weekdays 9–noon and 2–5, Sat. 9:30–12:30 and 2–5, Sun. 2–5; June–Sept., weekdays 9–noon and 2–6, Sat. 9:30–12:30 and 2–6, Sun. 2–6. English-speaking hostess available Sun. and Mon.*

⑬ Behind the Temple de l'Auditoire, on the rue de l'Hôtel de Ville, is the 16th-century **Hôtel de Ville,** where in 1864, in the Alabama Hall, 16 countries signed the Geneva Convention and laid the foundations for the International Red Cross. *Individual visits by request. Guided group tours by advance arrangement, tel. 022/3272202.*

The winding, cobbled streets leading from the cathedral down to the modern city are lined with antiques shops, galleries, and unique but often expensive boutiques. The medieval Grand' Rue is the oldest in Geneva, the rue de l'Hôtel de Ville features lovely 17th-century homes, and the rue Jean Calvin has noble mansions of the 18th century (No. 11 is on the site of Calvin's house). No. 6 on the rue du
⑭ Puits-St-Pierre is the **Maison Tavel,** the oldest building in town and home of an intimate re-creation of daily life and urban history. *Tel. 022/3102900. Admission free. Open Tues.–Sun. 10–5.*

Down the hill, plunge back into the new city and one of the most luxurious shopping districts in Europe, which stretches temptingly between the quai Général-Guisan, rue du Rhône, rue de la Croix d'Or, and rue du Marché. It's tough enough to resist top name pret-a-porter (ready-to-wear clothing), dazzling jewelry and watches, luscious chocolates, and luxurious furs and leathers, but the glittering bou-
⑮ tiques of the new three-story **Confédération-Centre**—where all the above are concentrated with a vengeance—could melt the strongest resolve. Escape across the quai, head back toward the lake, and
⑯ come to your senses in the **Jardin Anglais,** where the famous floral clock will tell you that it's time to stop.

Dining

$$ **Boeuf Rouge.** Despite its decor—a consciously contrived send-up of
★ a Lyonnais bistro, jam-packed with kitschy ceramics and Art Nouveau posters—this cozy and popular spot delivers the real thing: rich, unadulterated Lyon cuisine, from the bacon, egg, and greens *salade Lyonnaise* to the homemade *boudin blanc,* a delicate, pistachio-studded white sausage in morel cream sauce. There's sausage with lentils, too, and duck pâté served with a crock of *cornichons* and authentic *tarte tatin.* Service—by the proprietors and the chef himself—is flamboyant (they present all dishes on a flower-crowded tray before serving tableside), but the ambience is relaxed. *17 rue*

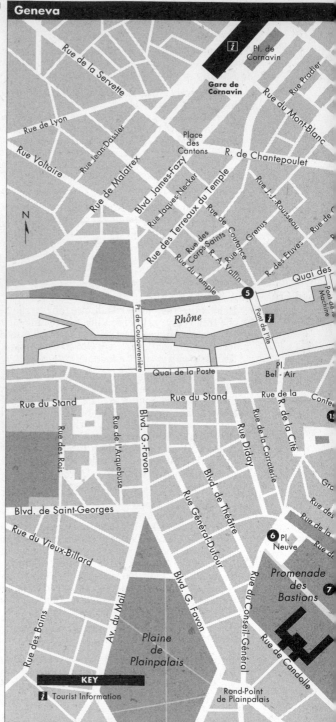

Geneva

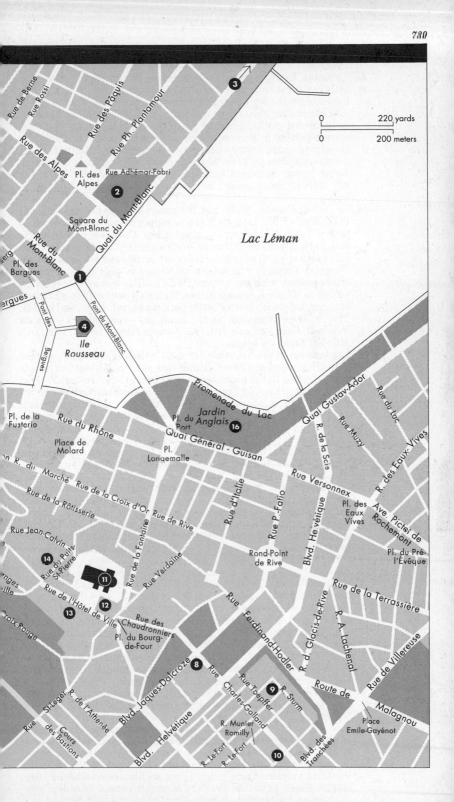

3

0   220 yards

0   200 meters

Rue de Berne

Rue Rossi

Rue des Pâquis

Rue Ph. Plantamour

Rue des Alpes

Rue Adhémar-Fabri

Pl. des Alpes

2

Square du Mont-Blanc

Quai du Mont-Blanc

Lac Léman

Rue du Mont-Blanc

berg

Pl. des Bergues

1

Pont des Bergues

ergues

Pont du Mont-Blanc

4

Ile Rousseau

Promenade du Lac

Pl. de la Fusterio

Rue du Rhône

Pl. du Port

Jardin Anglais

16

Quai Gustav-Ador

Rue du Lac

Place de Molard

Quai Général - Guisan

Pl. Longemalle

R. de la Scie

Rue Muzy

R. des Eaux-Vives

en R. du Marché

Rue de la Croix d'Or

Rue de Rive

Rue Versonnex

Rue de la Rôtisserie

Rue d'Italie

Rue P.-Falio

Pl. des Eaux Vives

Ave. Pictet de Rochemont

Rue Jean-Calvin

Rue de la Fontaine

Rue Verdaine

Rond-Point de Rive

Blvd. Helvétique

Pl. du Pré- l'Évêque

14

Rue du Puits- St-Pierre

11

12

Rue de l'Hôtel de Ville

Rue de la Terrassière

13

Rue des Chaudronniers

Pl. du Bourg- de-Four

Rue Ferdinand-Hodler

R. d. Glacis-de-Rive

R. A. Lachenal

Rue de Villereuse

Croix-Rouge

8

Rue Jaques-Dalcroze

Rue Charles-Galland

Rue Toepffer

R. Sturm

9

Route de

St-Léger R. de l'Athénée

Blvd. Jaques-Dalcroze

Blvd. Helvétique

R. Munier Romilly

Place Emile-Gayénot

Malagnou

Cours des Bastions

R.-Le-Fort

R.-Le-Fort

10

Blvd. des Tranchées

Alfred-Vincent, tel. 022/7327537. Reservations advised. V. Closed weekends.

$$ La Favola. Run by a young Ticinese couple from Locarno, this quirky
★ little restaurant may be the most picturesque in town. The tiny dining room, at the top of a vertiginous spiral staircase, strikes a delicate balance between rustic and fussy, with its lace window panels, embroidered cloths, polished parquet, and rough-beamed ceiling sponge-painted in Roman shades of ochre and rust. The food finds the same delicate balance between country simple and city chic: carpaccio with olive paste or white truffles, ravioli of duck à l'orange. Lunch menus represent excellent value. *15 rue Jean Calvin, tel. 022/3117437. Reservations advised. No credit cards. Closed weekends.*

$$ Le Pied-de-Cochon. While visiting antiques shops and art galleries in the Vielle Ville, stop for lunch or supper in this old bistro, which retains its original beams and zinc-top bar. Crowded, noisy, smoky, and lively, it faces the Palais de Justice and shelters famous lawyers who plead celebrated causes; there are artists and workers as well. The good, simple fare includes *pieds de cochon* (pigs' feet), of course, either grilled, with mushrooms, with lentils, or *dessossés* (boned), as well as simple Lyonnais dishes, including *petit salé* (pork belly), ham, grilled *andouillettes* (little pork sausages), tripe, and salads. The ambience is *sympa*, as the locals say—congenial. *4 place du Bourg-de-Four, tel. 022/3104797. Reservations advised. AE, DC, MC, V. Closed weekends.*

$ Les Armures. If you have only one meal in Geneva and want well-pre-
★ pared Swiss food in a cheerful ambience at reasonable prices, this is your best bet. In the picturesque and historic Les Armures hotel at the summit of the Old Town and two steps from the Cathédrale St-Pierre, it offers several dining halls, all decorated with authentic arms from the Middle Ages. The broad menu of Swiss specialties ranges from fondue to *choucroute* to *Rösti*, but some of the dishes are pure Genevois. There also are inexpensive pizzas and a good selection of salads. Everyone comes here, from workers to politicians. *1 rue du Puits-St-Pierre, tel. 022/3103442. Reservations advised. AE, DC, MC, V.*

$ L'Echalotte. Big and brightly lit, with warm polished wood banquettes and paper mats, this is a casual, comfortable meeting place with a generous, impulsive menu; fixed-price meals may offer a choice of no fewer than six first courses and three seconds. Cooking is eclectic and homey (turkey with chestnuts, zucchini flan, lemon bavarian), and everything is highly seasoned and served with casual flair. *17 rue des Rois, tel. 022/3205999. No credit cards. Closed weekends.*

¢ Manora/Placette. There's nothing of Old Geneva in this Swiss Woolworth's, but you *will* find much of New Geneva, crowding elbow to elbow around the islands in the store's cafeteria to fill trays with fresh-cooked chicken curry, grilled chops, cheese tarts, fruits, salads, and pastries. Portions are generous, ingredients and preparation straightforward (some dishes are browned before your eyes in industrial-size woks), and prices are rock-bottom. It's upstairs in the department store, but attractive and welcoming nonetheless. *6 rue Cornavin, tel. 022/7313146. No credit cards.*

¢ Taverne de la Madeleine. Tucked into the commercial maze between
★ the rue de la Croix-d'Or and the old town, near l'Eglise de la Madeleine, this casual, alcohol-free café run by the city's temperance league claims to be the oldest eatery in Geneva. The business folk who insist on a pitcher of Fendant with their meals go elsewhere—which leaves all the more room for you to relax over homemade choucroute, perch, or fresh-baked fruit tarts in the charming Victorian upstairs dining room. There are big, fresh salads and vegetarian plates, as well as a variety of freshly brewed loose-leaf teas. In summer, the terrace—overlooking the *place*—is in demand, and dinners are served until up to 10 o'clock; the rest of the year, the

kitchen closes at 7. *20 rue Toutes-âmes, tel. 022/3106070. Reservations advised. No credit cards.*

Lodging

For details and price-category definitions, *see* Lodging *in* Staying in Switzerland, *above.*

$$ d'Allèves. On a quiet square between the station and the Right Bank, this simple hotel has been lovingly crowded with the art and antiques collection of the owner, and done in a kind of dark elegance no longer in vogue (velour, red carpet, chenille). *13 Rue Kléberg, CH-1211, tel. 022/7321530, fax 7383266. 80 beds. Facilities: restaurant, café. AE, DC, MC, V.*

$$ International et Terminus. Although it's in the busy station area, this modest lodging has warm public areas scattered with antiques and fresh-looking rooms with clean, neutral decor. The restaurant is moderate, and there's a terrace café. The rooms without bath cost considerably less. *Rue des Alpes 20, CH-1201, tel. 022/7328095, fax 7321843. 83 beds. Facilities: restaurant, café. AE, DC, MC, V.*

$$ Montana. Following a slick renovation inside and out, rooms in this
★ station-area property are snazzily decorated in taupe and salmon and have double-glazed windows and bright tile baths. Only breakfast is served. *23 rue des Alpes, CH-1201, tel. 022/7320840. 70 beds. Facilities: breakfast room. AE, DC, MC, V.*

$$ Strasbourg-Univers. A stylish oasis in the slightly sleazy train-station neighborhood, this just-renovated spot offers sleek decor, convenience, and four-star quality at a three-star price. The new look is marble and faux exotic wood; a few older, less flashy rooms, redone eight years ago, still don't show the wear. *10 rue Pradier, CH-1201, tel. 022/7322562, fax 7384208. 58 rooms with bath or shower. AE, DC, MC, V.*

$$ Touring-Balance. Renovations have given this 19th-century hotel a
★ modern, contemporary look; ask to stay in the slick, solid, high-tech rooms on the higher floors, where gallery-quality lithos hang. The restaurant offers a straightforward French menu, with entrès at around 45 SF. You can't beat this location for shopping and sightseeing. *13 pl. Longemalle, tel. 022/3104045, fax 022/3104039. 60 rooms with bath. Facilities: restaurant, café. AE, DC, MC, V.*

$ De la Cloche. This once-luxurious walk-up apartment house has
★ tidy, tasteful new decor and a quiet courtyard setting. Good-size rooms share a bath down the hall. The price may be the lowest in town. *6 rue de la Cloche, CH-1201, tel. 022/7329481, fax 022/738–1612. 8 rooms without shower. Facilities: breakfast served in rooms. No credit cards.*

$ Des Tourelles. Once worthy of a czar, now host to the backpacking crowd, this fading Victorian offers enormous baywindowed corner rooms, many with marble fireplaces, French doors, and views over the Rhône. Several rooms have been renovated to include a modern shower and toilet, and those on the street side have double-glazed windows to keep the street noise out. The staff is young and friendly, and the breakfast—included in the price of a night—is an all-you-can-eat backpacker's delight. *2 blvd. James-Fazy, CH-1201, tel. 022/7324423, fax 7327620. 25 rooms, some with shower. AE, DC, MC, V.*

¢ Central. The location at the top of an anonymous, urban building on a
★ back shopping street is unpromising. But this bargain hotel merits the ride to the top floor: The rooms are freshly decorated with nice carpet and gleaming tile baths. The lake is just four minutes away, and the staff is friendly and helpful. Only breakfast is served. *2 rue de la Rôtisserie, CH-1204, tel. 022/3114594, fax 3107825. 40 beds. Facilities: breakfast room. No credit cards.*

¢ St. Gervais. This budget inn on a historic block in the Right Bank
★ town center has atticlike rooms that are neat, tidy, quaint, and well

maintained, with fresh linens on the beds and framed prints on the walls. Families should ask for the large, old room with ancient beams. A tiny pub on the ground floor serves snacks. *20 rue Corps-Saints, CH-1201, tel. 022/7324572. 52 beds, 2 with bath. Facilities: café. AE, MC, V.*

Luzern

Arriving and Departing

By Plane The nearest international airport is **Kloten** in **Zürich,** approximately 54 kilometers (33 miles) from Luzern. **Swissair** flies in most often from the United States and the United Kingdom. Easy rail connections, departing hourly, whisk you on to Luzern within 50 minutes.

By Train Luzern functions as a rail crossroads, with express trains connecting hourly from Zürich and every two hours from Geneva, the latter with a change at Bern. For rail information, call the station (tel. 041/213111).

Getting Around

Luzern's modest scale allows you to explore most of the city easily on foot, but you will want to resort to mass transit to visit far-flung attractions like the Verkehrshaus (Transit Museum) and nearby Alpine viewpoints.

By Bus The city bus system offers easy access throughout the urban area. If you're staying in a Luzern hotel, you will be eligible for a special **Guest-Ticket,** offering unlimited rides for two days for a minimal fee of 5 SF.

By Boat It would be a shame to see this city only from the shore; some of its most impressive landscapes can be seen from the decks of one of the cruise ships that ply the Vierwaldstättersee (Lake Lucerne). The boats of the **Schiffahrtsgesellschaft des Vierwaldstättersees** (tel. 041/404540) operate on a standardized, mass-transit-style schedule, criss-crossing the lake and stopping at scenic resorts and historic sites. Rides are included in a **Swiss Pass** or **Swiss Boat Pass** (*see* Getting Around *in* Essential Information, *above*).

Important Addresses and Numbers

Tourist Information The city tourist office, near the Bahnhof (Frankenstrasse 1, tel. 041/517171), offers information April–October, weekdays 8:30–6, Saturday 9–5, Sunday 9–1; and November–March, weekdays 8:30–noon and 2–6, Saturday 9–1. There is also an accommodations service. The tourist office offers a two-hour guided walking tour of Luzern, departing from the office daily at 9:30; from May through September, there are 2 PM tours as well. The 15-SF price includes a drink.

Emergencies **Police** (tel. 117). **Medical, dental, and pharmacy referral** (tel. 111).

Exploring Luzern

Numbers in the margin correspond to points of interest on the Luzern map.

Where the River Reuss flows out of the Vierwaldstättersee, Luzern's Old Town straddles the narrowed waters with the greater concentration of city life lying on the river's right bank. To get a feel for this riverfront center, start at the right-bank end of the prominent **Kapellbrücke,** with its flanking water tower. Stay on this side for the moment and head down the **Rathausquai,** lined with hotels and cafés on the right, a sloping reinforced bank on the left. Facing the end of a modern bridge (the Rathaus-Steg) stands the **Altes Rathaus** (Old Town Hall), built between 1599 and 1606 in the late-Renaissance style.

❶ Just to the right of the Rathaus, the **Am Rhyn-Haus** (Am Rhyn House), also known as the Picasso Museum, contains an impressive collection of late paintings by Picasso. *Furrengasse, tel. 041/511773. Admission: 5 SF adults, 3 SF students. Open daily 11–1 and 2–4.*

Turn right and climb the stairs past the ornately frescoed **Zunfthaus zu Pfistern,** a guildhall dating from the late 15th and early 16th century, to the Kornmarkt, former site of the local grain market. Cross the square and cut left into the **Weinmarkt,** the loveliest of Luzern's several squares. Its Gothic central fountain depicts St. Mauritius, patron saint of warriors, and its surrounding buildings are flamboyantly frescoed in 16th-century style.

Leave the square from its west end, turn right on Kramgasse, and ❷ cross the Mühlenplatz to the **Spreuerbrücke,** a narrow, weathered all-wood covered bridge dating from 1408. Its interior gables frame a series of eerie, well-preserved paintings (by Kaspar Meglinger) of the Dance of Death; they date from the 17th century, though their style and inspiration—tracing to the plague that devastated Luzern and all of Europe in the 14th century—is medieval.

At the other end of the bridge, on the left bank, stands the stylish ❸ **Historisches Museum** (Historical Museum). Its exhibitions of city sculptures, Swiss arms and flags, and reconstructed rooms depict rural and urban life. The late-Gothic building itself was an armory, dating from 1567. *Pfistergasse 24, tel. 041/245424. Admission: 4 SF. Open Tues.–Fri. 10–noon and 2–5, weekends 10–5.*

From the end of the Spreuerbrücke, cut back upstream along Pfistergasse and turn left on Bahnhofstrasse to reach the Baroque ❹ **Jesuitenkirche** (Jesuit Church), constructed 1667–78. Its symmetrical entrance is flanked by two onion-dome towers, added in 1893. Do not fail to go inside: Its vast interior, restored to mint condition, is a rococo explosion of gilt, marble, and epic frescoes.

Continue past the Rathaus-Steg bridge, but before you enter the ❺ **Kapellbrücke** (Chapel Bridge), take a look at its exterior from the right. It snakes diagonally across the water and, when it was built in the early 14th century, served as the division between the lake and the river. Its shingled roof and grand stone water tower (now housing a souvenir stand) are to Luzern what the Matterhorn is to Zermatt—but considerably more vulnerable, as a 1993 fire proved: Almost 80% of this fragile monument was destroyed, including many of the 17th-century paintings inside. The bridge has been rebuilt, and the original paintings are being restored and will soon be displayed in a local museum. If you walk the length of this dark, creaky landmark you'll see polychrome copies of the 112 gable panels painted by Heinrich Wägmann in the 17th century, depicting Luzern and Swiss history, stories of St. Leodegar and St. Mauritius, Luzern's patron saints, and coats of arms from local patrician families.

Now break away from the Old Town and work through thick pedestrian and bus traffic at Schwanenplatz to Schweizerhofquai. Turn left on Zürichstrasse or Löwenstrasse and continue to Löwenplatz, which is dominated by an enormous conical wooden structure, like a remnant of a Victorian world's fair. That's its spirit: The ❻ **Bourbaki-Panorama** was created between 1876 and 1878 as a genuine, step-right-up tourist attraction: The conical roof covers a sweeping, wraparound epic painting of the French Army of the East retreating into Switzerland at Verrières—a famous episode in the Franco-Prussian War. There's a recorded commentary in the lan-

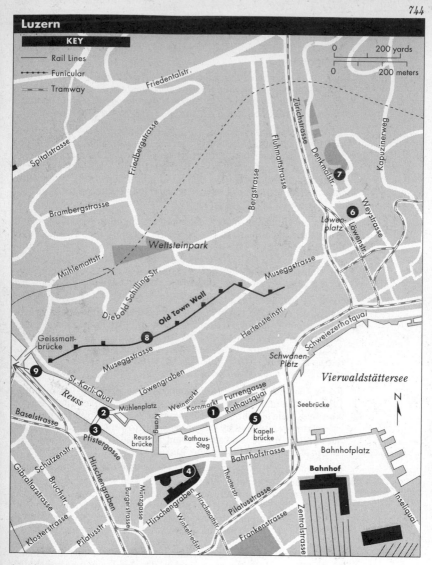

Luzern

KEY
— Rail Lines
••••• Funicular
—••— Tramway

Vierwaldstättersee

Am Rhyn-Haus, **1**   Kapellbrücke, **5**
Bourbaki-Panorama, **6**   Löwendenkmal, **7**
Château Gütsch, **9**   Spreuerbrücke, **2**
Historisches   Zytturm, **8**
Museum, **3**
Jesuitenkirche, **4**

guage of visitors present; majority rules. *Löwenplatz, tel. 041/ 529942. Admission: 3 SF. Open May–Sept., daily 9–6; Mar.–Apr. and Oct., daily 9–5.*

 Just beyond lies yet another 19th-century wonder, a Luzern landmark that is certainly one of the world's most evocative public sculptures: the **Löwendenkmal** (Lion Monument). Designed by Danish sculptor Berthel Thorwaldsen and carved out of a sheer sandstone face by Lucas Ahorn of Konstanz, it's a simple image of a dying lion, his chin sagging on his shield, a broken stump of spear in his side. It commemorates the 760 Swiss guards and their officers who died defending Louis XVI of France at the Tuileries in Paris in 1792. The Latin inscription translates: "To the bravery and fidelity of the Swiss."

Return down Löwenstrasse and, at Löwenplatz, turn right on Museggstrasse. This long street cuts through an original city gate and runs parallel to the **watchtowers** and **crenellated walls** of old Luzern, constructed around 1400. The clock in the **Zytturm,** the fourth of the towers, was made in Basel in 1385 and still keeps time.

For a bird's-eye view of the city, its wooden bridges, the ramparts, the river, and the lake, take the funicular (2 SF) off Baselstrasse to the **Château Gütsch,** where you can have drinks on the terrace.

Shopping

Luzern offers a good concentration of general Swiss goods. At **Sturzenegger** (Schwanenplatz 7, tel. 041/511958), you'll find fine St.-Gallen-made linens and embroidered niceties. **Mühlebach & Birrer** (Kapellplatz, tel. 041/516673) has a selection of Alpen-style (though Austrian-made) Geiger clothing (boiled woolen jackets, edelweiss-embroidered sweaters) as well as Swiss-made handkerchiefs. **Schmid-Linder** (Denkmalstrasse 9, tel. 041/514346) sells a comprehensive line of Swiss kitsch: cuckoo clocks, cowbells, embroidery, and a large stock of wood carvings from Brienz, in the Berner Oberland. **Innerschweizer Heimatwerk** (Franziskanerplatz 14, tel. 041/236944) sells nothing but goods—most of them contemporary rather than traditional-Swiss—made in the region by independent craftspeople, from handweaving to ceramics and wooden toys. Watch dealers are unusually competitive, and the two enormous patriarchs of the business **Gübelin** (Schweizerhofquai, tel. 041/515142) and **Bucherer** (Schwanenplatz, tel. 041/437700) advertise heavily and offer inexpensive souvenirs to lure shoppers into their luxurious showrooms. Watch for closeouts on out-of-date models.

Dining

Rooted in the German territory of Switzerland and the surrounding farmlands, Central Switzerland's native cuisine is down-home and hearty. Luzern takes pride in its *Kügelipastetli,* puffed pastry nests filled with tiny veal meatballs, chicken or sweetbreads, mushrooms, cream sauce, and occasionally raisins. Watch for lake fish such as *Egli* (perch), *Hecht* (pike), *Forellen* (trout), and *Felchen* (whitefish). Though most often served baked or fried, a Luzern tradition offers them sautéed and sauced with tomatoes, mushrooms, and capers. After your meal here, watch for two rural specialties from the region's orchards: dried pears poached in sweetened red Dole (a Swiss wine), and coffee laced with *Träsch,* a harsh schnapps blended from the dregs of other eaux-de-vie; for the latter, the locals leave their spoon in the stemmed cup as they drink—and never seem to poke themselves in the eye.

$$ Galliker. Step past the ancient facade into an all-wood room roaring
★ with local action, where Luzerners drink, smoke, and wallow in their culinary roots like puppies in mud. Brisk, motherly waitresses

serve up the dishes Mutti used to make: Fresh *Kutteln* (tripe) in rich white wine sauce with cumin seeds to cut the offal taste; real *Kalbskopf* (chopped fresh veal head) served with heaps of green onions and warm vinaigrette; authentic Luzerner Kügelipastetli; and their famous simmered-beef pot-au-feu, served only on Tuesday, Wednesday, and Saturday. Desserts may include dried pears steeped in pinot noir. The list of local schnapps is enormous. Tables form elbow-to-elbow ranks, and neighbors wish each other *Guten Appetit. Schützenstrasse 1, tel. 041/221002. Reservations advised. AE, MC, V. Closed Sun., Mon., mid-July–mid-Aug.*

$$ ★ **La Vague** (Hotel Des Balances). This chic bistro, sharing a sleek, open Deco/Post-Modern room with a much more expensive restaurant, offers a combination as desirable as it is rare: soigné decor, a shimmering riverside view, and adventurous, worldly, informed cuisine that features (believe it or not) local fish. Italian influence inspires a delectable *fritto misto* (mixed batter-fry) of perch, trout, and pike. *Weinmarkt, tel. 041/511851. Reservations advised. AE, DC, MC, V.*

$$ ★ **Wilden Mann.** You may choose the ancient original Burgerstube, all dark beams and family crests, its origins as a rest stop for St. Gotthard travelers traced back to 1517; or you may opt for the more formal adjoining Liedertafel dining room, with wainscoting, vaulting, and candlelight. On either side, the menu and prices are the same (with additional soup, salad, and sausage options in the small dining room in back—and the cooking is outstanding. *Bahnhofstr. 30, tel. 041/231666. Reservations advised. AE, DC, MC, V.*

$ **Rebstock/Hofstube.** At the opposite end of the culinary spectrum from Galliker (*see above*), this up-to-date kitchen offers modern, international fare, including rabbit, lamb, Asian, and vegetarian specialties. But you're still in Switzerland: The chewy breads, baked up the street in loaves as big as couch cushions, are so beautiful they display them as objets d'art. The lively bentwood brasserie hums with locals lunching by the bar, while the more formal, old-style restaurant glows with wood and brass under a low beam-and-herringbone-parquet ceiling. On sunny days and summer nights, the outdoor terrace café fills with basking locals and tourists taking in fine views of the Hofkirche next door. *St.-Leodegarstrasse 3, tel. 041/513581. Reservations advised. AE, DC, MC, V.*

$ **Zur Pfistern.** One of the architectural focal points of the old town waterfront, this floridly decorated old guildhouse—its origins trace back to 1341—offers a good selection of cheap one-plate meals in addition to higher-price standards. Lake fish and *Pastetli* (savory puffed pastry dishes) are good local options. Inside, its woody-pub ambience can be slightly stuffy, but summer travelers take note: The small first-floor balcony may provide the best seat in town for a postcard waterfront overview. Chestnut-shaded tables are strewn directly along the waterfront in the thick of the strolling crowds. *Kornmarkt 4, tel. 041/513650. AE, DC, MC, V.*

Lodging

Luzern is more than a good representative Swiss city, with a mix of cosmopolitan features and medieval atmosphere: It's also a convenient home base for excursions around the lake and nearby mountains. Unlike most Swiss cities, Luzern has high and low seasons, and drops prices by as much as 25% in winter.

$$ **Des Alpes.** With a terrific riverfront location in the bustling heart of town, this historic hotel has been completely renovated inside to look like a laminate-and-vinyl chain motel. Rooms are generously proportioned, tidy, and sleek; front doubles, several with balconies, overlook the water and promenade. Cheaper back rooms face the Old Town. *Rathausquai 5, CH-6003, tel. 041/515825, fax*

041/517451. 45 rooms with bath. Facilities: restaurant, café. AE, DC, MC, V.

$$ Goldener Stern. Clean, plain, and pleasant, this former wine cellar has restored its fine 17th-century exterior and redecked its restaurant to present an upscale face to the world. Modern rooms are softened with pretty, pristine linens; windows are double-glazed, some looking over the Franciscan church. The Stübli is popular with locals. *Burgerstrasse 35, CH-6003, tel. 041/230891, fax 041/230891. 30 beds. Facilities: restaurant, pub. AE, MC, V.*

$$ Zum Weissen Kreuz. Now renovated and upgraded, this former bargain hotel on the waterfront is slick, bright, and airtight, with tile, ★ stucco, oak, and pine to soften modern edges. Some rooms face the lake, others the old town. *Furrengasse 19, CH-6003, tel. 041/514040, fax 041/514060. 22 rooms with bath. AE, DC, MC, V.*

$ Schlüssel. On the Franziskanerplatz, with several rooms looking over the Franciscan church and fountain, this spare, no-nonsense little lodging attracts young bargain hunters. It's a pleasant combination of tidy new touches (quarry tile, white paint) and antiquity: You can have breakfast in a low, cross-vaulted "crypt" and admire the fine old lobby beams. *Franziskanerplatz 12, CH-6003, tel. 041/231061, fax 041/231021. 11 rooms, most with bath. MC, V.*

¢ SSR Touristen. Despite its friendly collegiate atmosphere, this ★ cheery dormlike spot is anything but a backpackers' flophouse. It has a terrific setting over the Reuss, around the corner from the Old Town. Its spare modern structure is brightened with fresh, trendy colors and framed prints. The staff is young and helpful, and the coed four-bed dorms (sex-segregated in high season) draw sociable travelers for rock-bottom prices. Rooms available with or without bath. *St. Karliquai, tel. 041/512474, fax 041/528414. 100 beds. AE, DC, MC, V.*

The Arts

Luzern hosts the **International Music Festival** for three weeks in August every year. Performances take place at the **Kunsthaus** (Frohburgstr. 6, tel. 041/233880). For further information, contact Internationale Musikfestwochen (Postfach, CH-6002, Luzern, tel. 041/235272). The **Allgemeine Musikgesellschaft Luzern** (AML), the local orchestra in residence, offers a season of concerts from October through June, also in the Kunsthaus.

Nightlife

Bars and Lounges **Des Balances** hotel has a hip, upscale piano bar (Metzgerrainle 7, tel. 041/511851), and **Château Gütsch** draws a sedate dinner-and-dancing crowd. **Mr. Pickwick** (Rathausquai 6, tel. 041/515927) is a Swiss version of an English pub.

Casinos The most sophisticated nightlife in Luzern is found in the **Casino** (Haldenstr. 6, tel. 041/512751), on the northern shore by the grand hotels. You can play boule in the Gambling Room (5 SF federally-imposed betting limit), dance in the **Babilonia** club, watch a strip show in the **Red Rose**, or have a Swiss meal in **Le Chalet** while watching a folklore display.

Discos **Flora Club** (Seidenhofstr. 5, tel. 041/244444) mixes dancing with folklore shows.

Folklore Besides the shows at Flora Club and the casino, there are performances at the **Stadtkeller** (Sternenplatz 3, tel. 041/514733) that transport you to the Valais—cheese specialties, yodelers, dirndled dancers, and all. A phenomenon called the **Night Boat,** which sails from Landungsbrücke 6 every evening at 8:45 from May through September, offers meals, drinks, and a folklore show during a pleasant lake cruise.

Lugano

Arriving and Departing

By Plane There are short connecting flights by **Crossair**—the Swiss domestic network—to Lugano Airport (tel. 091/505001) from Zürich, Geneva, Basel, and Bern, as well as from Paris, Nice, Rome, Florence, and Venice. The nearest intercontinental airport is at Milan, Italy, about 56 kilometers (35 miles) away.

Between the There is no longer a regular bus service between the local airport
Airport and and central Lugano, 7 kilometers (4 miles) away; taxis, costing
Downtown about 25 SF to the center, are the only option.

By Train There's a train from Zürich seven minutes past every hour, and the trip takes about three hours. If you're coming from Geneva, you can catch the Milan express at various times, changing at Domodossola and Bellinzona. Daytime, there's a train 30 minutes past every hour from Milan's Centrale Station; the trip takes about 1½ hours. Always keep passports handy and confirm times with the SNTO. For train information in Lugano, tel. 091/226502.

Getting Around

By Bus Well-integrated services run regularly on all local routes. You must buy your ticket from the machine at the stop before you board. Remember that with a **Swiss Pass** you'll be able to travel free.

By Train With or without a Swiss Pass, get a **Regional Holiday Season Ticket** for Lugano from the tourist office. This ticket gives unlimited free travel for seven consecutive days on most rail and steamer routes and a 50% or 25% discount on longer trips. It costs 78 SF for adults (68 SF for holders of a Swiss Pass) and 39 SF for children six through 16. The newest version offers any three out of seven days free on most routes, with 50% or 25% reductions on the remaining four days. Its price is 60 SF for adults, 50 SF for Swiss Pass holders, and 30 SF for children.

Tourist Information

Ente Turistico Lugano (riva Albertolli 5, CH-6901, tel. 091/214664) is open weekdays 9–6 (July–September to 6:30) and, from April–October, Saturday 9–5.

Exploring Lugano

Its sparkling bay, with dark, conical mountains rising from the beautiful Lago di Lugano, has earned Lugano the nickname "Rio of the Old World." The largest city in the Ticino—the Italian-speaking corner of Switzerland—Lugano has not escaped some of the inevitable overdevelopment of a successful resort town. There's thick traffic, right up to the waterfront; much of it manic Italian-style, and it has more than its share of concrete waterfront high-rise hotels, with balconies skewed to claim rooms with a view no matter what the aesthetic cost. But the view from the waterfront is unforgettable, the boulevards are fashionable, and the old quarter is still reminiscent of sleepy old towns in Italy.

Numbers in the margin correspond to points of interest on the Lugano map.

Start your walk under the broad porticoes of the tourist office and cross over to the tree-lined promenade, where you can stroll along the waterfront and take in stunning mountain views. Palm trees, pollards, and funeral cypresses—the standard greenery of Italian

lake resorts—are everywhere. Head left along the waterfront and
❶ into the **Parco Civico** (City Park), full of cacti, exotic shrubs, and
more than 1,000 varieties of roses. There's an aviary, a tiny "deer
zoo," and a fine view of the bay from its peninsula. The **Villa Ciani,**
temporarily closed for renovations, contains paintings and sculpture from Tintoretto to Giacometti.

❷ There's also the canton's **Museum of Natural History,** which contains
exhibits on animals, plants, and mushrooms. *Viale Cattaneo 4, tel.*
091/237827. Admission free. Open Tues.–Sat. 9–noon and 2–5.

❸ If you continue left along the waterfront, you'll find the **Lido,** with a
stretch of sandy beach, several swimming pools, and a restaurant.
Admission: 5 SF adults, 2 SF children 2–14.

Or follow the promenade right until you reach the **Imbarcadero
Centrale,** where steamers launch into the bay, and turn inland to the
❹ **Piazza della Riforma,** the scene of Lugano's vigorous Italian life,
where the modish locals socialize in outdoor cafés. From here, enter
the **Old Town** and follow the steep, narrow streets lined with chic
Italian clothing shops and small markets offering pungent local
cheeses and porcini mushrooms. Swiss culture asserts itself only at
lunch stands, where *panini* (small sandwiches) are made not only of
prosciutto, tuna, or mozzarella, but of sauerkraut and sausage as
well.

❺ On the street of the same name, you'll find the **Cathedral San Lorenzo,** with its graceful Renaissance facade and noteworthy frescoes inside. Then shop your way down the Via Nassa until you reach the
❻ **Church of Santa Maria degli Angioli** in Piazza Luini, started in 1455.
Within, you'll find a splendid fresco of the *Passion and Crucifixion*
by Bernardino Luini (1475–1532).

❼ Across the street, the waterfront **Giardino Belvedere** (Belvedere
Gardens) frame 12 modern sculptures with palms, camelias, olean-
ders, and magnolias. At the far end, to your right, there's **public
bathing** on the Riva Caccia. *Admission (bathing): 5 SF, 3 SF children. Open mid-May–mid-Sept.*

If you want to see more of Lugano's luxurious parklands, take the
funicular from the Old Town to the train station: Behind the station,
❽ deer greet you as you enter the floral **Parco Tassino.** Or take Bus 2
❾ east to the San Domenico stop in Castagnola to reach the **Parco degli
Ulivi** (Olive Park), where you can climb the olive-lined slopes of
Monte Brè for views of the surrounding mountains.

❿ The dust has finally settled at the **Villa Favorita,** owned by art baron
and *real* Baron Heinrich von Thyssen, and you'll find the villa not
only completely renovated but also with a portion of its magnificent
art collection back on the walls. In a controversial bidding war,
much of the collection was transferred to Madrid—at least temporarily—but a significant display of 19th- and 20th-century paintings
and watercolors from Europe and America remains, shown to better
advantage than ever in the renewed space. Artists represented include Thomas Hart Benton, Giorgio de Chirico, Frederic Church,
Lucien Freud, Edward Hopper, Franz Marc, Jackson Pollock, and
Andrew Wyeth. *Strada Castagnola, tel. 091/516152. Admission: 14
SF. Open Easter–Oct., Tues.–Sun. 10–5.*

Dining

The Ticinese were once poor mountain people, so their cuisine
shares the earthy delights of the Piemontese: polenta (cornmeal
mush), gnocchi (potato-base dumplings), game, and mushrooms.
But as in all prosperous resorts, the mink-and-Vuarnets set draws
the best in upmarket international cooking. Prix-fixe lunches are almost always cheaper, so dine as the Luganese do—before your sies-

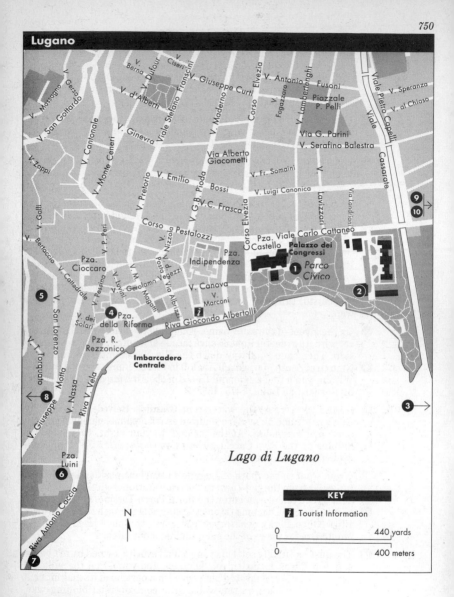

Lugano

Lago di Lugano

KEY

i Tourist Information

0 ——————————— 440 yards
0 ——————————— 400 meters

N

Cathedral San
Lorenzo, **5**
Church of Santa Maria
degli Angioli, **6**
Giardino Belvedere, **7**
Lido, **3**
Museum of Natural
History, **2**

Parco Civico, **1**
Parco Tassino, **8**
Parco degli Ulivi, **9**
Piazza della Riforma, **4**
Villa Favorita, **10**

ta. That way you can sleep off the fruity local merlot wine before the requisite *passeggiata* (afternoon stroll). For details and price-category definitions, *see* Dining *in* Staying in Switzerland, *above.*

$$ Al Barilotto. ★ Despite its generic pizzeria decor and American-style salad bar, this restaurant draws local crowds for grilled meats, homemade pasta, and wood-oven pizza. Take Bus 10 from the center. *Hôtel de la Paix, Via Cattori 18, tel. 091/542331. Reservations advised. AE, DC, MC, V.*

$ Sayonara. There's nothing Japanese about it: This is a modern urban pizzeria whose several rooms are crowded at lunchtime with a mix of tourists and shoppers. The old copper polenta pot stirs automatically year-round, with polenta offered in several combinations, one of them with mountain hare. *Via F. Soave 10, tel. 091/220170. AE, DC, MC, V.*

$ La Tinera. ★ This tiny taverna crowds loyal locals, tourists, and families onto wooden benches for authentic regional specialties, hearty meats, and pastas. Regional wine is served in traditional ceramic bowls. This taverna is tucked down an alley off Via Pessina in the Old Town. *Via dei Gorini 2, tel. 091/235219. Reservations advised. AE, DC, MC, V.*

¢ Federale. You may choose to spend the whole afternoon at this popular outdoor café-bar, which offers light meals and cheap daily specials, as well as drinks, to the diverse and often glamorous crowds who all face forward, as if an audience for the real-life theater passing by. Homemade pastas include gnocchi *alla romana* (flour dumplings, not the traditional potato version). *Piazza Riforma 9, tel. 091/239175. No credit cards.*

Lodging

Since this is a summer resort, many hotels close for the winter, so call ahead. For details and price-category definitions, *see* Lodging *in* Staying in Switzerland, *above.*

$$ Alba. ★ This solid little hotel, with landscaped grounds and an interior that is lavish in the extreme, is ideal for lovers with a sense of camp or honeymooners looking for romantic privacy. Mirrors, gilt, plush, and crystal fill the public areas, and the beds are all ruffles and swags. The garden is studded with palms, a lovely place for a drink. *Via delle Scuole 11, CH-6902, tel. 091/9943731, fax 9944523. 25 rooms with bath. Facilities: restaurant, bar. AE, DC, MC, V.*

$$ International au Lac. This is a big, old-fashioned, friendly city hotel, half a block from the lake, with many lake-view rooms. It's next to Santa Maria degli Angioli, on the edge of the shopping district and the Old Town. *Via Nassa 68, CH-6901, tel. 091/227541, fax 227544. 86 rooms with bath. Facilities: restaurant. AE, DC, MC, V.*

$$ Park-Hotel Nizza. ★ This former villa, modernized in 1974, affords panoramic views from its spot on the lower slopes of San Salvatore, well above the lake, and thus is an uphill hike from town. The mostly small rooms are decorated with antique reproductions; you don't pay extra for rooms with lake views. An ultramodern bar overlooks the lake, and a good restaurant serves vegetables and even wine made from grapes from the hotel's own garden. There's a shuttle service to Paradiso. *Via Guidino 14, CH-6902, tel. 091/541771, fax 541773. 30 rooms with bath. Facilities: restaurant, bar, outdoor pool. AE, DC, MC, V.*

$ Flora. ★ Though it's one of the cheapest hotels in town, this 70-year-old lodging has been reasonably well maintained. The room decor is minimal, a holdover of the '60s (red-orange prints, wood-grain Formica), and the once-elegant dining hall has seen better days. But some rooms have balconies, and there's a sheltered garden terrace that's lovely on balmy nights. *Via Geretta 16, CH-6902, tel. 091/9941671, fax 091/9942738. 33 rooms with bath. Facilities: restaurant, bar, outdoor pool. AE, DC, MC, V.*

$ **San Carlo.** The San Carlo offers one of the better deals in a high-price town: It's small, clean, freshly furnished, and right on the main shopping street, a block from the waterfront. There are no frills, but the friendly atmosphere compensates. *Via Nassa 28, CH-6902, tel. 091/9227107, fax 091/9228022. 22 rooms with bath. Facilities: breakfast. AE, DC, MC, V.*

¢ **Rex.** Although its comforts are minimal and its location strictly urban, this no-nonsense shelter is convenient—near museums, parks, beaches, and bus lines. Only breakfast is served. *11 Viale Cattaneo, CH-6900, tel. 091/227608. 30 beds. Facilities: breakfast room. AE, DC, MC, V.*

Bern

Arriving and Departing

By Plane **Belp** (tel. 9613411) is a small airport, 9 kilometers (6 miles) south of the city, with flights from London, Paris, Nice, Venice, and Lugano. A bus from the airport to the train station costs 12 SF, a taxi about 35 SF.

By Train Bern is a major link between Geneva, Zürich, and Basel, with fast connections running usually every hour from the enormous central station. The high-speed French TGV gets to Paris in 4½ hours.

Getting Around

By Bus and Streetcar Bern is a small, concentrated city, and it's easy to get around on foot. There are 6½ kilometers (4 miles) of covered shopping arcades in the center. Bus and tram service is excellent, however, if you don't feel like walking. Fares range from 1.50 SF to 2.40 SF. Buy individual tickets from the dispenser at the tram or bus stop; the posted map will tell you the cost. Tourist cards for unlimited rides are available at 5 SF for one day, 7 SF for two, and 10 SF for three. Buy them at the Bahnhof tourist office or from the public-transportation ticket office in the subway leading down to the main station (take the escalator in front of Loeb's department store and turn right through the Christoffel Tower). A **Swiss Pass** allows you to travel free.

Important Addresses and Numbers

Tourist Information The tourist office is located at Bahnhofplatz (main station, tel. 031/3116611); it's open May–June, daily 9–8:30; October–May, Monday–Saturday 9–6:30; and Sunday 10–5.

Embassies **U.S.** (Jubiläumsstr. 93, tel. 031/3517011). **Canadian** (88 Kirchenfeldstr., tel. 031/3526381). **U.K.** (Thunstr. 50, tel. 031/3525021).

Emergencies **Police** (tel. 117). **Ambulance** (tel. 144). **Doctor/Dentist** (tel. 3119211).

Exploring Bern

No cosmopolitan nonsense here: The local specialties are fatback and sauerkraut, the annual fair features the humble onion, and the president takes the tram to work. Walking down broad, medieval streets past squares teeming with farmers' markets and cafés full of shirt-sleeved politicos, you may forget that Bern is the federal capital—indeed, the geographic and political hub—of a sophisticated, modern, and prosperous nation.

Numbers in the margin correspond to points of interest on the Bern map.

❶ ❷ Start on the busy **Bahnhofplatz** in front of the grand old Schweizerhof hotel, facing the station. To your left is the **Heilig-**

geistkirche (Church of the Holy Spirit), finished in 1729 and contrasting sharply with both the modern and the medieval in Bern.

Head right up Bollwerk and turn right into Kleeplatz and
❸ Hodlerstrasse, where you'll come to the **Kunstmuseum Bern** (Bern Art Museum) on your left. Originally dedicated to Swiss art, it houses an exceptional group of works by Ferdinand Hodler, including some enormous, striking allegories; there are landscapes and portraits as well. But the concentration is no longer entirely Swiss, and early Bern masters mingle with Fra Angelico, and Böcklin and Anker share space with artists of the caliber of Cézanne, Rouault, and Picasso. The museum's pride—and its justified claim to fame—is its collection of more than 2,000 works by Paul Klee, who spent years in Bern. *Hodlerstrasse 8–12, tel. 031/220944. Admission: 6 SF. Open Tues. 10–9; Wed.–Sun. 10–5.*

Walk down Spitalgasse outside the arcades to see some of the city's stunning architecture; inside the sheltered walkways are modern shops and cafés.

❹ Head for the **Bagpiper**, the first of the city's many signature foun-
❺ tains erected between 1539 and 1546, and the **Käfigturm** (prison gate), which dates from the 13th and 14th centuries. There's a small museum of economic and cultural life inside. *Tel. 031/3112306. Admission free. Open Tues.–Sun. 10–1 and 2–6, also Thurs. 6–9.*

❻ Continue down Marktgasse past the **Anna Seilerbrunnen** and
❼ **Schützenbrunnen** (Anna Seiler and Marksman Fountains) to the
❽ **Zeitglockenturm** (clock tower), built as a city gate in 1191 but transformed by the addition of an astronomical clock in 1530. To your
❾ right is the Theaterplatz, to your left the **Kindlifresserbrunnen** (Ogre Fountain) and the Kornhausplatz, where you will see the im-
❿ posing 18th-century **Kornhaus** (granary), its magnificent vaulted cellar a popular beer hall today. Now walk past the clock tower and observe the clock from the east side. At four minutes before every hour, you can see the famous mechanical puppet bears perform their ancient dance.

Continue down Kramgasse, past fine 18th-century houses and the
⓫ ⓬ **Zähringerbrunnen** and **Simsonbrunnen** (Zähringer and Samson Fountains). Turn left at the next small intersection and head for
⓭ Rathausplatz, with its **Vennerbrunnen** (Ensign Fountain), and the
⓮ late-Gothic **Rathaus** (city hall), where the city and cantonal government meet.

Head back to the main route, here named Gerechtigkeitsgasse, and
⓯ continue past the **Gerechtigkeitsbrunnen** (Justice Fountain) and lovely patrician houses. Artisan shops, galleries, and antiquaries line this leg of the endless arcades. Turn left at the bottom and head down the steep Nydegg Stalden through one of the city's oldest sec-
⓰ tions, past **Läuferbrunnen** (Messenger Fountain), to the river Aare. Here the **Nydeggkirche** (Nydegg Church), on the right, was built from 1341 to 1571 on the foundations of Berchtold V's ruined fortress.

Cross the river by the Untertorbrücke Bridge, then turn right and climb up to the **Nydeggbrücke** Bridge. Here you'll find the
⓱ **Bärengraben** (bear pits), where Bern keeps its famous live mascots. According to legend, Berchtold named the town after the first animal he killed while hunting—a bear, since the woods were thick with them.

Now cross the bridge and head back into town, turning left up
⓲ Junkerngasse to the magnificent Gothic **Münster** (cathedral), begun in 1421. It features a fine portal (1490) depicting the *Last Judgment*, recently restored and repainted in extravagant hues. There also are stunning stained-glass windows, both originals and period reproductions.

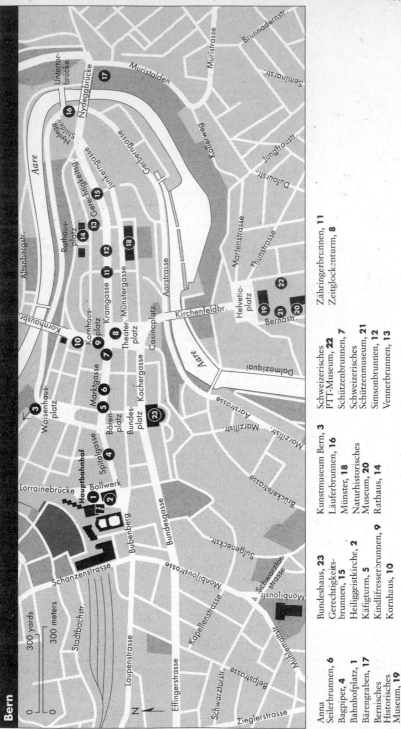

Bern

Anna
Seilerbrunnen, **6**
Bagpiper, **4**
Bahnhofplatz, **1**
Bärengraben, **17**
Bernisches
Historisches
Museum, **19**

Bundeshaus, **23**
Gerechtigkeits-
brunnen, **15**
Heiliggeistkirche, **2**
Käfigturm, **5**
Kindlifresserbrunnen, **9**
Kornhaus, **10**

Kunstmuseum Bern, **3**
Läuferbrunnen, **16**
Münster, **18**
Naturhistorisches
Museum, **20**
Rathaus, **14**

Schweizerisches
PTT-Museum, **22**
Schützenbrunnen, **7**
Schweizerisches
Schützenmuseum, **21**
Simsonbrunnen, **12**
Vennerbrunnen, **13**

Zähringerbrunnen, **11**
Zeitglockenturm, **8**

Arty boutiques line the Münstergasse, leading to the **Casino,** which houses a concert hall and restaurants, but no casino. If you head even farther south (across the river yet again), you'll find Helvetiaplatz, a historic square surrounded by museums. The

⑲ **Bernisches Historisches Museum** (Bern Historical Museum) has a prehistoric collection, 15th-century Flemish tapestries, and Bernese sculptures. Its fine Islamic holdings are imaginatively displayed. *Helvetiaplatz 5, tel. 031/3511811. Admission: 5 SF. Open Tues.–Sun. 10–5.*

⑳ The **Naturhistorisches Museum,** one of Europe's major natural history museums, has enormous wildlife dioramas and a splendid collection of Alpine minerals. *Bernastr. 15, tel. 031/3507111. Admission: 3 SF. Open Mon. 2–5, Tues.–Sat. 9–5, and Sun. 10–5.*

㉑ The **Schweizerisches Schützenmuseum** (Swiss Shooting Museum) traces the development of firearms from 1817 and celebrates Swiss marksmanship beyond the apple-splitting accuracy of William Tell. *Bernastr. 5, tel. 031/3510127. Admission free. Open Tues.–Sat. 2–4, Sun. 10–noon and 2–4.*

㉒ The **Schweizerisches PTT–Museum** (Swiss Postal and Telecommunications Museum), now housed in its striking new building behind the Bernisches Historisches Museum, offers detailed documents, art, and artifacts of early technology to trace the history of the mail system in Switzerland, from Roman messengers to telegraph and radio. *Helvetiastr. 16, tel. 031/3387777. Admission: 2 SF adults. Open Tues.–Sun. 10–5.*

Alternatively, head back from the casino on Kochergasse past the enormous domed **Bundeshaus** (Capitol). By night, be sure to stick to

㉓ Kochergasse instead of the riverview promenade behind the capitol building; some visitors have been annoyed by obvious drug traffic.

Dining

While Bern teeters between two cultures politically, Teutonic conquers Gallic when it comes to cuisine. Dining in Bern is usually a down-to-earth affair, with Italian home cooking running a close second to the local standard fare of meat and potatoes. Specialties include the famous *Bernerplatte* (sauerkraut with boiled beef, fatty pork, sausages, ham, and tongue), *Buurehamme* (hot smoked ham), and *Ratsherrentopf* (Rösti with roast veal, beef, liver, and sausage). Coffee and *Kuchen* (pastry) are standard four-o'clock fare.

For details and price-category definitions, *see* Dining *in* Staying in Switzerland, *above.*

$$ **Della Casa.** You can stay downstairs in the steamy, rowdy Stübli,
★ where necktied businessmen roll up their sleeves and play cards, or head up to the linen-and-silver restaurant, where they leave their jackets on. It's an unofficial Parliament headquarters and serves generous portions of local and Italian specialties—including a good Bernerplatte. *Schauplatzgasse 16, tel. 031/3112142. Reservations advised. DC, MC, V. No credit cards downstairs.*

$$ **Lorenzini.** In a town where the cozy and the stuffy hold sway, this
★ hip, bright spot stands apart. Delicious homemade pasta and changing menus featuring the specialties of different Italian regions are served with authentic, contemporary flair. *Marktgass-Passage 3, tel. 031/3117850. Reservations advised. DC, MC, V.*

$$ **Zunft zu Webern.** Founded as a weavers' guildhouse and built in 1704, this classic building has been renovated on the ground floor in a slick but traditional style, with gleaming new wood and bright lighting. Its culinary style is simple but sophisticated, and it serves generous portions of reinterpreted standards, such as lamb stew with saffron. *Gerechtigkeitsgasse 68, tel. 031/3114258. MC, V.*

$ Brasserie zum Bärengraben. Directly across from the bear pits, this
★ popular, easygoing little local institution, with the thinnest veneer
of a French accent, serves inexpensive lunches to shoppers, tourists, businesspeople, and retirees, who settle in with a newspaper
and a *dezi* (deciliter) of wine. The menu offers many old-style favorites—*Kalbskopf am Vinaigrette* (chopped veal head in vinaigrette),
pig's feet, stuffed cabbage—and wonderful pastries. *Muristalden
1, tel. 031/3314218. Reservations advised. No credit cards.*

$ Harmonie. Run by the same family since 1900, this leaded-glass and
old-wood café-restaurant serves inexpensive basics: fondue, sau-
sage-and-Rösti, *Käseschnitte* (cheese toast), and *bauern* omelets
(farm-style, with bacon, potatoes, onions, and herbs). It's lively,
very friendly, and welcoming to foreigners if a little dingy.
Hotelgasse 3, tel. 031/3113840. No credit cards.

¢ Klötzlikeller. A cozy muraled wine cellar, this is much more intimate
★ than the famous Kornhauskeller and just as lovely. Dating from
1635, when there were as many as 250 wine bars in Rome, this is one
of the few places where you can still taste the limited wine of Bern,
which is sold by the glass. There's also a good, if limited, menu of
meat specialties. *Gerechtigkeitsgasse 62, tel. 031/3117456. AE, MC,
V.*

¢ Kornhauskeller. This spectacular vaulted old wine cellar, under the
★ Kornhaus granary, is now a popular beer hall with live music on
weekends. Drinkers and revelers take tables in the upstairs galleries while diners in the vast main hall below gaze up at the ceiling
frescoes. The Swiss fare satisfies the largest of appetites, but the
historic ambience is the real reason to come. *Kornhausplatz 18, tel.
031/3111133. AE, DC, MC, V.*

Lodging

For details and price-category definitions, *see* Lodging *in* Staying in
Switzerland, *above.*

$$ Goldener Adler. The exterior of this 1764 building is a magnificent
★ patrician town house, but its interior is modern and modest, with
linoleum-floor baths and severe Formica furniture. The ambience is
comfortable and familial nonetheless: The same family has run the
place for more than 100 years. *Gerechtigkeitsgasse 7, CH-3011, tel.
031/3111725, fax 3113761. 40 rooms with bath. Facilities: restau-
rant. café. AE, DC, MC, V.*

$$ Krebs. A classic, small, Swiss hotel, Krebs is impeccable and solid,
★ managed with an eye on every detail. The spare decor is warmed
with wood and made comfortable by the personal, friendly service of
the Buri family. A handful of inexpensive rooms without bath offer
excellent value. *Genfergasse 8, CH-3001, tel. 031/3114942, fax
3111035. 44 rooms, 41 with shower. Facilities: restaurant. AE, DC,
MC, V.*

$ Glocke. Though it's very plain and slightly shabby, there's a young,
friendly management here and two lively restaurants, one a "Swiss
Chalet," with dancing and folklore shows, the other Italian. The
rooms have a fresh paint job, tile baths, and homey, unmatched tow-
els. A few rooms without baths cost even less. *Rathausgasse 75, CH-
3011, tel. 031/3113771, fax 3111008. 20 rooms, some with bath. Facilities: 2 restaurants, entertainment. AE, DC, MC, V.*

$ Goldener Schlüssel. This is a bright, tidy spot with its abundance of
wood, crisp linens, and tiled baths. It's in the heart of the Old Town,
so the rooms are quieter in the back. The two good restaurants serve
Swiss and international specialties. Rooms without baths are a bargain. *Rathausgasse 72, CH-3011, tel. 031/3110216, fax 3115688. 29
rooms, some with shower. Facilities: 2 restaurants. DC, MC, V.*

$ Hospiz zur Heimat. The elegant 18th-century exterior promises bet-
★ ter than the dormitory gloom inside, but the baths are new, the
rooms are immaculate, and the Old Town location is excellent.

Gerechtigkeitsgasse 50, CH-3011, tel. 031/3110436, fax 3123386. 40 rooms, some with bath. Facilities: breakfast room. AE, DC, MC, V.

¢ **Marthahaus.** Take Bus 20 over the Kornhaus Bridge to this spare, old-style pension in a residential neighborhood north of the Old Town. Rates are low and the service is friendly. *Wyttenbachstrasse 22a, CH-3013, tel. 031/3324135. 40 rooms without bath. Facilities: breakfast room. No credit cards.*

26 Turkey

Turkey is one place to which the term "East meets West" really applies, both literally and figuratively. It is in Turkey's largest city, Istanbul, that the continents of Europe and Asia meet, separated only by the Bosphorus, which flows 29 kilometers (18 miles) from the Black Sea to the Sea of Marmara. Turkey is also a perfect destination for the budget traveler. It's a country where good food and clean lodging can be found for very reasonable prices.

Although most of Turkey's landmass is in Asia, Turkey has faced West politically since 1923, when Mustapha Kemal, better known as Atatürk, founded the modern republic. He transformed the remnants of the shattered Ottoman Empire into a secular state with a Western outlook. So thorough was this changeover—culturally, politically, and economically—that in 1987, 49 years after Atatürk's death, Turkey applied to the European Community (EC) for full membership. It has been a member of the North Atlantic Treaty Organization (NATO) since 1952.

For 16 centuries Istanbul, originally known as Byzantium, played a major part in world politics, first as the capital of the Eastern Roman Empire, when it was known as Constantinople, then, as capital of the Ottoman Empire, the most powerful Islamic empire in the world, when it was renamed Istanbul. Atatürk moved the capital to Ankara at the inception of the Turkish Republic.

The legacy of the Greeks, Romans, Ottomans, and numerous other civilizations has made the country a vast outdoor museum. The most spectacular of the reconstructed classical sites are along the western Aegean coast and the southwest Mediterranean coast, which are lined with magnificent sandy beaches and sleepy little fishing villages, as well as busy holiday spots with sophisticated facilities for travelers.

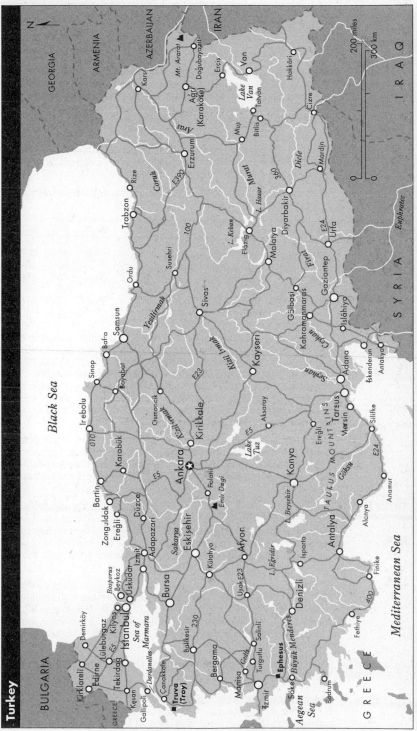

Turkey

Essential Information

Before You Go

When to Go The height of the tourist season runs from April through October. July and August are the busiest and warmest months. April through June and September and October are the best months to visit archaeological sites or Istanbul and the Marmara area because the days are cooler and the crowds are smaller.

Climate The Mediterranean and Aegean coasts have mild winters and hot summers. You can swim in the sea from late April through October. The Black Sea coast is mild and damp, with a rainfall of 228 centimeters (90 inches) a year.

The following are the average daily maximum and minimum temperatures for Istanbul.

Jan.	46F	8C	May	69F	21C	Sept.	76F	24C
	37	3		53	12		61	16
Feb.	47F	9C	June	77F	25C	Oct.	68F	20C
	36	2		60	16		55	13
Mar.	51F	11C	July	82F	28C	Nov.	59F	15C
	38	3		65	18		48	9
Apr.	60F	16C	Aug.	82F	28C	Dec.	51F	11C
	45	7		66	19		41	5

Currency The monetary unit is the Turkish lira (TL), which comes in bank notes of 20,000, 50,000, 100,000, 250,000, 500,000 and 1,000,000. Coins come in denominations of 500, 1,000, 2,500, 5,000, and 10,000. At press time (summer 1995), the exchange rate was 40,000 TL to the dollar and 70,220 TL to the pound sterling. Major credit cards and traveler's checks are widely accepted in hotels, shops, and expensive restaurants in cities and resorts, but rarely in villages and small shops and restaurants.

Be certain to retain your original exchange slips when you convert money into Turkish lira—you will need them to reconvert the money. Because the Turkish lira is worth a lot less than the dollar or most other foreign currencies, it's best to convert only what you plan to spend.

What It Will Cost Turkey is the least expensive of the Mediterranean countries. Although inflation hovers between 50% and 70%, frequent small devaluations of the lira keep prices fairly stable when measured against foreign currencies. Prices in this chapter are quoted in dollars, which indicate the real cost to the tourist more accurately than do the constantly increasing lira prices.

Sample Prices Coffee can range from about 30¢ to $2.50 a cup, depending on whether it's the less expensive Turkish coffee or American-style coffee and whether it's served in a luxury hotel or a café; tea, 20¢ to $2.50 a glass; local beer, $1–$3; soft drinks, $1–$4; lamb shish kebab, $1.50–$7; taxi, less than $1 for 1 mile (prices are 50% higher between midnight and 6 AM).

Customs on Arrival Turkish customs officials rarely look through tourists' luggage on arrival. You are allowed to take in 400 cigarettes, 50 cigars, 200 grams of tobacco, 1.5 kilograms of instant coffee, 500 grams of tea, and 2.5 liters of alcohol. An additional 600 cigarettes, 100 cigars, or 500 grams of tobacco may be imported if purchased at the Turkish duty-free shops on arrival. Register all valuable personal items in your passport on entry.

Language Atatürk launched language reforms that replaced Arabic script with the Latin-based alphabet. English and German are widely spoken in cities and resorts. In the villages or in remote areas, you'll have a hard time finding anyone who speaks anything but Turkish.

Getting Around

By Train Although there are express trains in Turkey, the term is usually a misnomer. The best daily trains between İstanbul and Ankara are the *Fatih Expres* and the *Başkent Expres*. The overnight *Yatakli Ankara Expres* has luxurious sleeper cars, while the *Anadolu Expres* offers cheaper bunk beds. A sleeper travels between İstanbul and Pamukkale and Izmir and Ankara. Daily trains run between Sîrkeci station and Edirne. Dining cars on some trains have waiter service and serve surprisingly good and inexpensive food.

Fares Train fares tend to be less expensive than bus fares. Seats on the best trains, as well as those with sleeping berths, should be booked in advance. Round-trip fares are cheaper than two one-way fares. There are 10% student discounts (30% December–May) and 30% discounts for groups of 24 or more. In railroad stations, buy tickets at windows marked "Anahat Giseleri." Travel agencies carrying the TCDD (State Railways) sign, and post offices sell train tickets also.

By Bus Buses, which are run by private companies, are much faster than trains and provide excellent, inexpensive service. Buses are available, virtually around the clock, between all cities and towns. They are fairly comfortable and many are air-conditioned. Companies have their own fixed fares for different routes. Istanbul to Ankara, for instance, varies from $8 to $13; Istanbul to Izmir varies from $11 to $16. *Su* (bottled water) is included in the fare. You can purchase tickets at stands in a town's *otogar* (central bus terminal) or at branch offices in city centers. All seats are reserved. Fares vary among the competing companies, but most buses between major cities are double-deckers and have toilets. Companies, such as Varan, Ulusoy, and Pamukkale, offer no-smoking seating. For very short trips or for getting around within a city, take minibuses or a *dolmuş* (shared taxi). Both are inexpensive and comfortable.

By Plane Turkish Airlines (THY) operates an extensive domestic network. There are at least nine flights daily on weekdays between Istanbul and Ankara. During the summer, many flights between the cities and coastal resorts are added. Try to arrive at the airport at least 45 minutes before your flight because security checks, which are rigidly enforced without exception, can be time-consuming. Checked luggage is placed on trolleys on the tarmac and must be identified by boarding passengers before it is put on the plane. Unidentified luggage is left behind and checked for bombs or firearms.

THY offers several discounts on domestic flights: 10% for family members, including spouses; 50% for children under 13; 90% for children under two; and 50% for sports groups of seven or more. The THY sales office is at Taksim Square (tel. 212/252–1106; reservations by phone, tel. 212/663–6363).

Staying in Turkey

Telephones Note: All telephone numbers in Turkey now have seven local digits plus three-digit city codes. Intercity calls are preceded by 0.

Most pay phones are yellow, push-button models, although a few older, operator-controlled telephones are still in use. Multilingual directions are posted in phone booths.

Local Calls Public phones use *jetons* (tokens), which can be purchased for 2,000 TL at post offices and street booths. If you need operator assistance for long-distance calls within Turkey, dial 131. For intercity automatic calls, dial 0, then dial the city code and the number. Jetons are available for 8,000 TL for long-distance calls. Far more practical than the jetons are telephone cards, available at post offices for 48,000 TL, 96,000 TL, and 160,000 TL.

Telephone numbers in European and Asian Istanbul have been assigned different codes: The code for European Istanbul (for numbers beginning with 2, 5, or 6) is 0/212; for Asian Istanbul, dial 0/216 for local numbers beginning with 3 or 4.

International Calls For all international calls dial 00, then dial the country code, area or city code, and the number. You can use the higher-price cards for this, or reach an international operator by dialing 132. To reach an **AT&T** long distance operator, dial 00800-12277, for **MCI**, dial 00800-11177, and for **Sprint**, 00800-14477.

Country Code The country code for Turkey is 90.

Mail Post offices are painted bright yellow and have PTT (Post, Telegraph, and Telephone) signs on the front. The major ones are open Monday–Saturday from 8 AM to 9 PM, Sundays from 9 to 7. Smaller branches open Monday–Saturday 8:30–5.

Receiving Mail If you're uncertain where you'll be staying, have mail sent to Post Restante, Merkez Postanesi (central post office) in the town of your choice.

Shopping
Bargaining The best part of shopping in Turkey is visiting the *bedestans* (bazaars), all brimming with copper and brassware items, hand-painted ceramics, alabaster and onyx goods, fabrics, and richly colored carpets. The key word for shopping in the bazaars is "bargain." You must be willing to bargain, and bargain hard. It's great fun once you get the hang of it. As a rule of thumb, offer 50% less after you're given the initial price and be prepared to go up by about 25% to 30% of the first asking price. It's both bad manners and bad business to underbid grossly or to start bargaining if you're not serious about buying. Outside the bazaars prices are usually fixed, although in resort areas some shopkeepers may be willing to bargain if you ask for a "better price." Part of the fun of roaming through the bazaars is having a free glass of *çay* (tea), which vendors will offer you whether you're a serious shopper or just browsing. Beware of antiques: Chances are you will end up with an expensive fake, but even if you do find the genuine article, it's illegal to export antiques of any type.

VAT Refunds Value-added tax (VAT) is nearly always included in the price. You can claim back the VAT if you buy articles from authorized shops. The net total value of articles subject to VAT on your invoice must be over $22, and these articles must be exported within three months of purchase. The invoice must be stamped by customs. If the VAT to be refunded is less than $22, you can obtain it from a bank outside customs boundaries where the dealer has an account. Otherwise, mail the stamped invoice back to the dealer within one month of departure and the dealer will send back a check.

Opening and Closing Times **Banks** are open weekdays, 8:30–noon and 1:30–5.

Mosques are usually open to the public, except during *namaz* (prayer hours), which are observed five times a day. These times are based on the position of the sun, so they vary throughout the seasons. Prayers last 30–40 minutes.

Museums are generally open Tuesday–Sunday, 9:30–4:30, and closed Monday. Palaces, open the same hours, are closed Thursday instead of Monday.

Shops are closed daily from 1 PM to 2 PM and all day Sunday. Generally they're open Monday–Saturday, 9:30–1 and 2–7.

National Holidays In 1996: January 1; February 20–22 (S'eker Bayram, "sugar feast," a three-day feast marking the end of Ramadan); April 23 (National Sovereignty and Children's Day); April 28–May 1 (Kurban Bayram, an important sacrificial feast celebrating Abraham's willingness to sacrifice his son to God); May 19 (National Youth and Sports Day); August 30 (Victory Day); October 28–29 (Republic Day); November 10 (Atatürk's Commemoration). Changing holidays in 1997: February 9–11 (S'eker Bayram), April 18–21 (Kurban Bayram).

Dining The Turkish people are justly proud of their cuisine. The old cliché about it being hard to find a bad meal in Paris more aptly describes Istanbul, where the tiniest little hole-in-the-wall serves delicious food. The dishes are also extremely healthy, full of fresh vegetables, yogurt, legumes, and grains, not to mention fresh seafood, roast lamb, and kebabs made of lamb, beef, or chicken. Because Turkey is predominantly Muslim, pork is not readily available. But there's plenty of alcohol, including local beer and wine, which are excellent and inexpensive. The most popular local beer is Efes Pilsen. The national alcoholic drink, *raki*, is made from grapes and aniseed. Turks mix it with water or ice and sip it throughout their meal or serve it as an aperitif.

Hotel restaurants have English-language menus and usually serve a bland version of Continental cuisine. Far more adventurous and tasty are meals in *restorans* and in *lokantas* (Turkish restaurants). Most lokantas do not have menus because they serve only what's fresh and in season, which varies daily. At lokantas, you simply sit back and let the waiter bring food to your table, beginning with a tray of *mezes* (appetizers). You point to the dishes that look inviting and take as many as you want. Then you select your main course from fresh meat or fish—displayed in glass-covered refrigerated units—which is then cooked to order or from a steam table laden with casseroles and stews. For lighter meals there are *kebabs*, tiny restaurants specializing in kebabs served with salad and yogurt, and *pidecis*, selling *pides*, a pizzalike snack on flat bread, topped with butter, cheese, egg, or ground lamb and baked in a wood-fired oven.

What to Wear Except for very expensive restaurants, where formal dress is appropriate, informal dress is acceptable at restaurants in all price categories.

Precautions Tap water is heavily chlorinated and supposedly safe to drink in cities and resorts. It's best to play it safe, however, and drink *maden suyu* (bottled mineral water) or *şişe suyu* (bottled water), which is better tasting and inexpensive.

Ratings Prices are per person and include an appetizer, main course, and dessert. Wine and gratuities are not included. Best bets are indicated by a star ★.

Category	Major Cities	Other Areas
$$	$12–$25	$10–$20
$	$8–$12	$6–$10
¢	under $8	under $6

Lodging Hotels are officially classified in Turkey as HL (luxury), H1 to H5 (first to fifth class); motels, M1 to M2 (first to second class); and P, *pansiyons* (guest houses). The classification is misleading because the lack of a restaurant or a lounge automatically relegates the establishment to the bottom of the ratings. A lower-grade hotel may actually be far more charming and comfortable than one with a higher rating. There are also many local establishments that are licensed but not included in the official ratings list. You can obtain their names from local tourist offices.

Accommodations range from international luxury chains in Istanbul, Ankara, and Izmir to comfortable, family-run pansiyons. Plan ahead for the peak summer season, when resort hotels are often booked solid by tour companies. Turkey does not have central hotel reservations offices.

Rates vary from $10 to more than $200 a night for a double room. In the less expensive hotels, the plumbing and furnishings will probably leave much to be desired. You can find very acceptable, clean double rooms with a bath for between $30 and $70, with breakfast included. Room rates are displayed in the reception area. It is accepted practice in Turkey to ask to see the room in advance.

Ratings Prices are for two people in a double room, including 20% VAT and a 10–15% service charge. Best bets are indicated by a star ★.

Category	Major Cities	Other Areas
$$	$60–$100	$50–$100
$	$35–$60	$30–$50
¢	under $35	under $30

Tipping Except at inexpensive restaurants, a 10% to 15% charge is added to the bill. Since the money does not necessarily find its way to the waiter, leave an additional 10% on the table or hand it to the waiter. In the top restaurants, waiters expect tips of between 10% and 15%. Hotel porters expect between $2 and $5, and the chambermaid, about $2 a day. Taxi drivers don't expect tips, although they are becoming accustomed to foreigners giving them something. Round off the fare to the nearest 500 TL. At Turkish baths, the staff who attends you expects to share a tip of 30% to 35% of the bill.

Istanbul

Arriving and Departing

By Plane All international and domestic flights arrive at Istanbul's Atatürk Airport. For arrival and departure information, call the individual airline or the airport's information desk (tel. 212/663–6400).

Between the Airport and Downtown Shuttle buses run between the airport's international and domestic terminals to the Turkish Airlines (THY) terminal in downtown Istanbul, at Meşrutiyet Caddesi, near the Galata Tower. Buses depart for the airport at the same address every hour from 6 AM to 11 PM. After that, departure time depends on the number of passengers. Allow at least 45 minutes for the bus ride. Plan to be at the airport two hours before your international flight because of the lengthy security and check-in procedures. The ride from the airport into town takes from 30 to 40 minutes, depending on traffic. Taxis charge about $15 to Taksim Square and $11 to Sultanahmet.

By Train Trains from the west arrive at Sirkeci station (tel. 212/527–0050 or 0051) in Old Istanbul. Eastbound trains to Anatolia depart from Haydarpasa station (tel. 216/348–8020) on the Asian side.

By Bus The final destination for most buses arriving in Istanbul is the newly built Esenler terminal, northwest of the city center. Given the relatively remote location of this modern complex, it is a good idea to make use of the company minibus services to centers such as Aksaray and Taksim. If you are travelling light you can brave the rapid train (*hızlı tren*) to Aksaray. A few buses from Anatolia arrive at Harem terminal, on the eastern shore of the Bosphorus. Some bus companies have *servis arabasi* (minibus services) to the hotel areas of Taksim Square and Aksaray. If you arrive with baggage, it is much easier to take a taxi, which will cost about $8 to Taksim from the bus terminals and about $5 to Old Istanbul.

Getting Around

The best way to get around all the magnificent monuments in Sultanahmet in Old Istanbul is to walk. They're all within easy distance of each other, along streets filled with peddlers, shoeshine boys, children playing, and craftsmen working. To get to other areas, you can take a bus or one of the many ferries that steam between the Asian and European continents. Sea buses (Deniz Otobüsü) running between continents as well as to destinations such as the Princes' Islands, are fast and efficient. Dolmuş vehicles and taxis are plentiful, inexpensive, and more comfortable than city buses. A new tram system runs from Topkapi via Sultanahmet to Sirkeci, but it's usually too crowded. There's no subway system, but there is the Tünel, a tiny underground train that's handy for getting up the steep hill from Karaköy to the bottom of Istiklal Caddesi. It runs every 10 minutes and costs about 25¢.

By Bus Buy a ticket before boarding a bus. You can buy tickets, individually or in books of 10, at ticket stands around the city. Shoeshine boys or men on the street will also sell them to you for a few cents more. Fares are about 25¢ per ride. On the privatized orange buses (Halk Otobüsü), as well as on the city's new double-deckers, tickets are purchased on boarding. The London style double-deckers operate a scenic route between Sultanahmet and Emirgan on the Bosphorus.

By Dolmuş These are shared taxis that stop at one of the blue-and-white dolmuş signs. The destination is shown either on a roof sign or a card in the front window. Many of them are classic American cars from the '50s.

By Taxi Taxis are inexpensive. Since most drivers do not speak English and may not know the street names, write down the street you want, the nearby main streets, and the name of the area. Taxis are metered. Although tipping is not expected, you should round off the fare to the nearest 5,000 TL.

By Boat For a fun and inexpensive ride, take the *Anadolu Kavaği* boat along the Bosporus to its mouth at the Black Sea. The boat leaves year-round from the Eminönü Docks, next to the Galata Bridge on the Old Istanbul side, at 10:30 AM and 1:30 PM, with two extra trips on weekdays and four extra trips on Sundays from April to September. The fare is $6 (round-trip). The trip takes one hour and 45 minutes one way. You can disembark at any of the stops and return by land if you wish. Regular ferries depart from Kabataş Dock, near Dolmabahçe Palace on the European side, to Üsküdar on the Asian side and from Eminönü Docks 1 and 2, near Sirkeci station.

Important Addresses and Numbers

Tourist Information Official tourist information offices are at **Atatürk Airport** (tel. 212/663–6400); the **Hilton Hotel** (tel. 212/233–0592); **Karaköy Yolcu Salonu,** International Maritime Passenger Terminal (tel. 212/249–5776); and in a pavilion in the **Sultanamet** district of Old Istanbul (Divan Yolu Cad. 3, tel. 212/518–1802 or 212/518–8754).

Consulates U.S. (Meşrutiyet Caddesi 147, Tepebaşi, Beyoğlu, tel. 212/251–3602). **Canadian** (Büyükdere Cad. 107/3, Bengün Han, tel. 212/272–5174). **U.K.** (Meşrutiyet Cad.34, Tepebaşi, Beyoğlu, tel. 212/293–7540).

Emergencies **Tourism Police** (tel. 212/527–4503). **Ambulance** (tel. 112). **Doctors:** For an English-speaking doctor, call the American Hospital (Güzelbahçe Sok. 20, Nişantaşi, tel. 212/231–4050/69) or International Hospital (Yeşilyurt, tel. 212/663–3000).

Exploring Istanbul

Istanbul is a noisy, chaotic, and exciting city, where spires and domes of mosques and medieval palaces dominate the skyline. At dawn, when the call to the muezzin's prayer rebounds from ancient minarets, many people are making their way home from the nightclubs and bars, while others are kneeling on their prayer rugs, facing Mecca.

Ironically, Istanbul's Asian side is filled with Western-style sprawling suburbs, while its European side contains Old Istanbul—an Oriental wonderland of mosques, opulent palaces, and crowded bazaars. The Golden Horn, an inlet 6½ kilometers (4 miles) long, flows off the Bosphorus on the European side, separating Old Istanbul from New Town. The center of New Town is Beyoğlu, a modern district filled with hotels, banks, and shops grouped around Taksim Square. There are three bridges spanning the Golden Horn: the Atatürk, the Galata, and the Haliç. The historic Galata Bridge, which has been replaced by a modern drawbridge, is a central landmark and a good place to get your bearings. From here, you can see the city's layout and its seven hills. The bridge will also give you a taste of Istanbul's frenetic street life. It's filled with peddlers selling everything from pistachio nuts and spices to curly-toed slippers fancy enough for a sultan; fishermen grill their catch on coal braziers and sell them to passersby. None of this sits well with motorists, who blast their horns constantly, usually to no avail. If you want to orient yourself in a quieter way, take a boat trip from the docks on the Eminönü side of the Galata Bridge up the Bosporus.

Numbers in the margin correspond to points of interest on the Istanbul map.

Old Istanbul (Sultanahmet)
❶ The number-one attraction in Istanbul is **Topkapı Palace** (Topkapı Saray), on Seraglio Point in Old Istanbul, known as Sultanahmet. The palace, which dates from the 15th century, was the residence of a number of sultans and their harems until the mid-19th century. In order to avoid the crowds, try to get there by 9 AM, when the gates open. If you're arriving by taxi, tell the driver you want the Topkapı *Saray* (palace) in Sultanahmet, or you could end up at the remains of the former Topkapı bus terminal on the outskirts of town.

Sultan Mehmet II built the first palace during the 1450s, shortly after the Ottoman conquest of Constantinople. Over the centuries, sultan after sultan added ever more elaborate architectural fantasies, until the palace eventually ended up with more than four courtyards and some 5,000 residents, many of them concubines and eunuchs. Topkapı was the residence and center of bloodshed and drama for the Ottoman rulers until the 1850s, when Sultan Abdül Mecit moved with his harem to the European-style Dolmabahçe Palace farther up the Bosphorus coast.

❷ In Topkapı's outer courtyard are the **Church of St. Irene** (Aya Irini), open only during festival days for concerts, and the **Court of the Janissaries** (Merasim Avlusu), originally for members of the sultan's **❸** elite guard.

Adjacent to the ticket office is the **Bab-i-Selam** (Gate of Salutation), built in 1524 by Suleyman the Magnificent, who was the only person allowed to pass through it. From the towers on either side, prisoners were kept until they were executed beside the fountain outside the gate in the first courtyard. In the second courtyard, amid the rose gardens, is the **Divan-i-Humayun,** the assembly room of the council of state, once presided over by the grand vizir (prime minister). The sultan would sit behind a latticed window, hidden by a curtain so no one would know when he was listening, although occasionally he would pull the curtain aside to comment.

One of the most popular tours in Topkapı is the **Harem,** a maze of nearly 400 halls, terraces, rooms, wings, and apartments grouped around the sultan's private quarters on the west side of the second courtyard. Forty rooms have been meticulously restored and are open to the public. Next to the entrance are the quarters of the eunuchs and about 200 of the lesser concubines, who were lodged in tiny cubicles, as cramped and uncomfortable as the main rooms of the Harem are large and opulent. Tours begin about every half hour. *Admission: $1.*

In the third courtyard is the **Treasury** (Hazine Dairesi), four rooms filled with jewels, including two uncut emeralds, each weighing 3½ kilograms (7.7 pounds), that once hung from the ceiling. Here, too, you will be dazzled by the emerald dagger used in the movie *Topkapı* and the 84-carat "Spoonmaker" diamond that, according to legend, was found by a pauper and traded for three wooden spoons.

In the fourth and last courtyard of the Topkapı Palace are small, elegant summer houses; mosques; fountains; and reflecting pools, scattered amid the gardens on different levels. Here you will find the **Erivan Kiosk,** also known as the Revan Kiosk, built by Murat IV in 1636 to commemorate his capture of Rivan in the Caucasus. In another kiosk in the gardens, called the **Golden Cage** (Iftariye), the closest relatives of the reigning sultan lived in strict confinement under what amounted to house arrest. The custom began during the 1800s after the old custom of murdering all possible rivals to the throne had been abandoned. The confinement of the heirs apparently helped keep the peace, but it deprived them of any chance to prepare themselves for the formidable task of ruling a great empire. *Topkapı Palace. Admission: $4, harem $1. Open Wed.–Mon. 9:30– 5:30.*

④ To the left as you enter the outer courtyard, a lane slopes downhill to three museums grouped together: the **Archaeological Museum** (Arkeoloji Müzesi), which houses a fine collection of Greek and Roman antiquities, including finds from Ephesus and Troy; the **Museum of the Ancient Orient** (Eski Şark Eserleri Müzesi), with Sumerian, Babylonian, and Hittite treasures; and the **Tiled Pavilion** (Çinili Köşkü), which houses ceramics from the early Seljuk and Osmanli empires. The admission price covers all three museums. *Admission: $2.50. Open Tues.–Sun. 9:30–5.*

⑤ Just outside the walls of Topkapı Palace is **Hagia Sophia** (Church of the Divine Wisdom), one of the world's greatest examples of Byzantine architecture. Built in AD 532 under the supervision of Emperor Justinian, it took 10,000 men and six years to complete. Hagia Sophia is made of ivory from Asia, marble from Egypt, and columns from the ruins of Ephesus. The dome, one of the most magnificent in the world, was also the world's largest until the dome at St. Peter's Basilica was built in Rome 1,000 years later. Hagia Sophia was the cathedral of Constantinople for 900 years, surviving earthquakes and looting Crusaders until 1453, when it was converted into a mosque by Mehmet the Conqueror. Minarets were added by succeeding sultans. Hagia Sophia originally had many mosaics depicting Christian scenes, which were plastered over by Suleyman I, who felt they were inappropriate for a mosque. In 1935, Atatürk converted Hagia Sophia into a museum. Shortly after that, American archaeologists discovered the mosaics, which were restored and are now on display. *Ayasofya Meydani. Admission: $4. Open Tues.–Sun. 9:30–5:00.*

⑥ Across from Hagia Sophia is the **Blue Mosque** (Sultan Ahmet Camii), with its shimmering blue tiles, 260 stained-glass windows, and six minarets, as grand and beautiful a monument to Islam as Hagia Sophia was to Christianity. Mehmet Aga, also known as Sedefkar (Worker of Mother of Pearl) built the mosque during the reign of Sultan Ahmet I in eight years, beginning in 1609, nearly

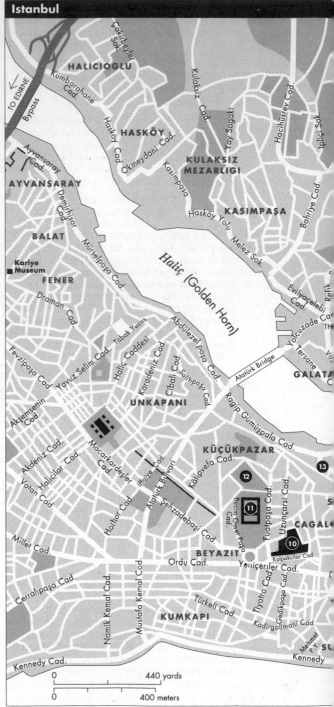

Archaeological
Museum, **4**
Blue Mosque, **6**
Church of St. Irene, **2**
Cistern Basilica, **9**
Court of the
Janissaries, **3**
Dolmabahçe
Mosque, **16**
Dolmabahçe Palace, **17**
Egyptian Bazaar, **13**
Flower Market, **15**
Galata Tower, **14**
Grand Bazaar, **10**
Hagia Sofia, **5**
Hippodrome, **7**
Istanbul University, **11**
Museum of Turkish
and Islamic Arts, **8**
Süleymaniye
Mosque, **12**
Topkapi Palace, **1**

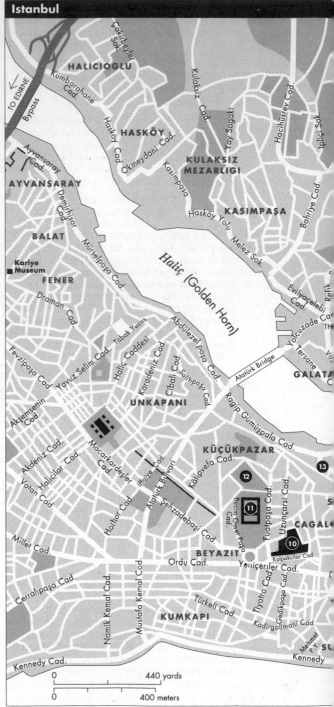

Istanbul

HALICIOĞLU

TO EDIRNE
Bypass

HASKÖY

KULAKSIZ
MEZARLIĞI

AYVANSARAY

KASIMPAŞA

BALAT

Kariye
Museum

FENER

Haliç (Golden Horn)

Atatürk Bridge

GALATA

UNKAPANI

KÜÇÜKPAZAR

⑫

⑬

⑪

CAĞAL

⑩

BEYAZIT

Ordu Cad.

Yeniçeriler Cad.

KUMKAPI

Kennedy Cad.

| 0 | | 440 yards |
| 0 | | 400 meters |

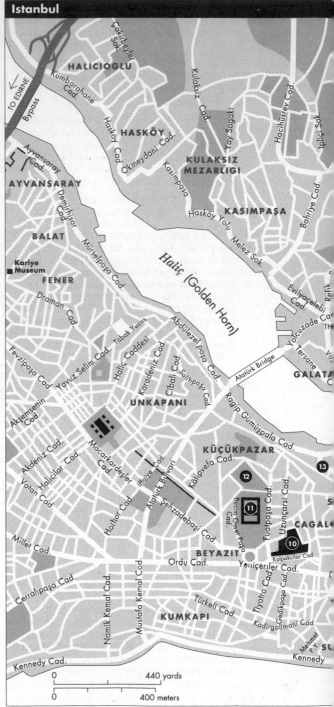
768

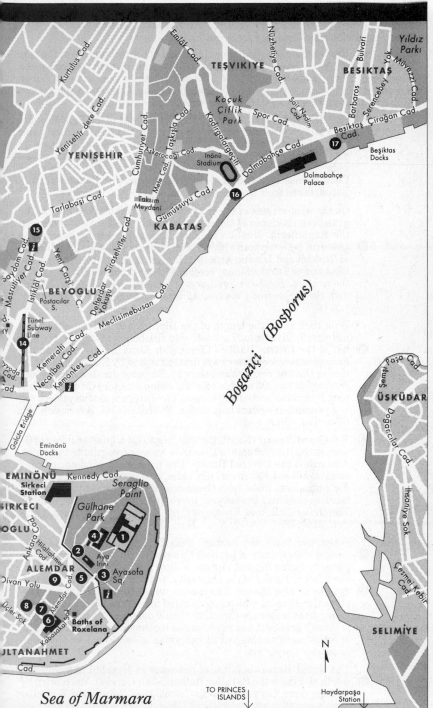

Kurtuluş Cad.

Emlâk Cad.

Nüzhetiye Cad.

Yıldız Parkı

TEŞVİKİYE

Bulvari

BEŞİKTAŞ

Yok.

Müvezzi Cad.

Barbaros

Şair Nedim

Koçuk Çiflik Park

Serencebey

Spor Cad.

Yenişehir dere Cad.

Askerocağı Cad.

Taşkışla Cad.

Kadırgalargeçiti

Beşiktaş Cad.

Çirağan Cad.

YENİŞEHİR

Cumhuriyet Cad.

Meta Cad.

İnönü Stadium

Dolmabahçe Cad.

17

Beşiktaş Docks

Dolmabahçe Palace

Tarlabaşı Cad.

Taksim Meydani

Gümüşsuyu Cad.

KABATAS

16

15

Saydam Cad.

Mesruiyet Cad.

Yeni Çarşı

Siraselviler Cad.

Sıraselviler Cad.

BEYOGLU

Postacılar S.

Defterdar Yokuşu

Meclisimebusan Cad.

Bogaziçi (Bosporus)

Şemsi Paşa Cad.

14

Tünel Subway Line

Kemeraltı Cad.

Necatibey Cad.

Kemankeş Cad.

ÜSKÜDAR

Dogacılar Cad.

yoda Cad.

ad.

i

Galota Bridge

Eminönü Docks

İhsaniye Sok.

EMİNÖNÜ

Kennedy Cad.

Seraglio Point

Sirkeci Station

ŞİRKECİ

Gülhane Park

OGLU

Ankara Cad.

Hilaliahmer Cad.

4

1

2

ALEMDAR

9

Aya İrini

5

3

Ayasofa Sa

Divan Yolu

Alemdar Cad.

i

Çeşmi Kebir Cad.

Üçler Sok.

8

7

6

Kabasakal Sok.

Baths of Roxelana

SELİMİYE

JLTANAHMET

Cad.

N

Sea of Marmara

TO PRINCES ISLANDS

Haydarpaşa Station

1,100 years after the completion of Hagia Sophia. His goal was to surpass Justinian's masterpiece, and many in the world believe he succeeded.

Press through the throng of touts and enter the mosque at the side entrance that faces Hagia Sophia. You must remove your shoes and leave them at the entrance. Immodest clothing is not allowed, but an attendant at the door will lend you a robe if he thinks you are not dressed appropriately. *Admission free. Open daily 9–5.*

❼ The **Hippodrome** is a long park directly in front of the Blue Mosque. As a Roman stadium with 100,000 seats, it was once the focal point for public entertainment, including chariot races and circuses. It was also the site of many riots and public executions. What remain today are an **Egyptian Obelisk** (Dikilitas), the **Column of Constantinos** (Örme Sütun), and the **Serpentine Column** (Yilanli Sütun) taken from the Temple of Apollo at Delphi in Greece.

On the western side of the Hippodrome is **Ibrahim Paşa Palace,** the grandiose residence of the son-in-law and grand vizir of Suleyman the Magnificent. Ibrahim Paşa was executed when he became too
❽ powerful for Suleyman's liking. The palace now houses the **Museum of Turkish and Islamic Arts,** which gives a superb insight into the lifestyles of Turks of every level of society, from the 8th century to the present. *Şifahane Sok., across from the Blue Mosque, in line with the Serpentine Column. Admission: $2.50. Open Tues.–Sun. 9:30–5.*

Walk back along the length of the Hippodrome and cross the busy main road, Divanyolu. Turn left onto Hilaliahmer Caddesi. On your
❾ left is the **Cistern Basilica** (Yerebatan Sarayi). This is an underground network of waterways first excavated by Emperor Constantine in the 3rd century and then by Emperor Justinian in the 6th century. It has 336 marble columns rising 8 meters (26 feet) to support Byzantine arches and domes. The cistern was always kept full as a precaution against long sieges. *Yerebatan Cad. Admission: $2. Open Wed.–Mon. 9–5.*

❿ The **Grand Bazaar** (Kapali Carsişi) lies about a quarter mile northwest of the Hippodrome (a 15-minute walk or five-minute taxi ride). Also called the Covered Bazaar, this maze of 65 winding, covered streets, hides 4,000 shops, tiny cafés, and restaurants. It's a shopper's paradise, filled with thousands of curios, including carpets, fabrics, clothing, brassware, icons, furniture, and gold jewelry. *Yeniçeriler Cad. and Fuatpaşa Cad. Admission free. Open Apr.– Oct., Mon.–Sat. 8:30–7; Nov.–Mar., Mon.–Sat. 8:30–6:30.*

When you leave the bazaar, cross Fuatpaşa Caddesi and walk
⓫ around the grounds of **Istanbul University,** which has a magnificent gateway facing Beyazit Square. Follow Besim Ömer Paşa Caddesi, the western border of the university, to the right to the 16th-centu-
⓬ ry **Süleymaniye Mosque.** The mosque was designed by Sinan, the architectural genius who masterminded more than 350 buildings and monuments under the direction of Suleyman the Magnificent. This is Sinan's grandest and most famous monument, and the burial site of both himself and his patron, Suleyman. *Admission free. Open daily outside prayer hrs.*

⓭ The Grand Bazaar isn't the only bazaar in Istanbul. Another one worth visiting is the **Egyptian Bazaar** (Misir Carsişi). You reach it by walking down Çarşi Caddesi to Çakmakçilar Yokuşu and Firincilar Sokak, and then into Sabunchani Sokak, where you will see the back of the bazaar. It was built in the 17th century as a means of rental income for the upkeep of the Yeni Mosque. The bazaar was once a vast pharmacy, filled with burlap bags overflowing with herbs and spices for folk remedies. Today, you're more likely to see bags full of fruit, nuts, Royal Jelly from the beehives of the Aegean coast, and white sacks spilling over with culinary spices. Nearby are the equally colorful array of fruit and fish markets. *Next to Yeni Cami. Open Mon.–Sat. 8–7.*

New Town New Town is the area on the northern shore of the Golden Horn, the waterway that cuts through Istanbul and divides Europe from Asia.

⑭ The area's most prominent landmark is the **Galata Tower,** built by the Genoese in 1349 as part of their fortifications. In this century, it served as a fire lookout until 1960. Today it houses a restaurant and nightclub (*see* Nightlife, *below*), and a daytime viewing tower. *Büyük Hendek Cad. Admission: $1. Open daily 9–8.*

⑮ North of the tower is the **Flower Market** (Çiçek Pasaji), off Istiklâl Caddesi, a lively blend of flower stalls, tiny restaurants, bars, and street musicians.

⑯ Next head for **Dolmabahçe Mosque** and **Dolmabahçe Palace,** which are reached by following Istiklâl Caddesi to Taksim Square and then taking Gümüssuyu Caddesi around the square to a junction. You will see the Dolmabahçe Mosque on your right and the clock tower and gateway to Dolmabahçe Palace on your left. The mosque is a separate building from the palace. It was founded by Valide Sultan Bezmialem, mother of Abdül Mecit I, and was completed in 1853. *Admission free. Open daily outside prayer hrs.*

⑰ The **Dolmabahçe Palace** was also built in 1853 and, until the declaration of the modern republic in 1923, was the residence of the last sultans of the Ottoman Empire. It was also the residence of Atatürk, who died here in 1938. The palace, floodlit at night, is an extraordinary mixture of Hindu, Turkish, and European styles of architecture and interior design. Queen Victoria's contribution to the lavishness was a chandelier weighing 4½ tons. Guided tours of the palace take about 80 minutes. *Gümüssuyu Cad. Admission: $4.80. Open Apr.–Oct., 9–4; Nov.–Mar., 9–3. Closed Mon. and Thurs.*

Shopping

Gift Ideas The **Grand Bazaar** (*see* Exploring Istanbul, *above*) is a treasure trove of all things Turkish—carpets, brass, copper, jewelry, textiles, and leather goods.

Stores Stores and boutiques are located in New Town on such streets as **Istiklâl Caddesi,** which runs off Taksim Square, and **Rumeli, Halaskargazi,** and **Valikonagi Caddeleri,** north of the Hilton Hotel. Two streets in the Kadiköy area that offer good shopping are **Bağdat** and **Bahariye Caddeleri. Ataköy Shopping and Tourism Center** is a large shopping and leisure mall near the airport. It's a good place for children, too. Akmerkez, a luxurious mall in the posher Etiler district carries a variety of designer ware and also has a great movie theater.

Markets **Balikpazari** (fish market) is in Beyoğlu Caddesi, off Istiklâl Caddesi. Despite its name, you will find anything connected with food at this market. A **flea market** is held in Beyazit Square, near the Grand Bazaar, every Sunday. A crafts market, with street entertainment, is open on Sundays along the Bosporus at Ortaköy. A weekend crafts market is also held on Bekar Sokak, off Istiklal Caddesi.

Dining

Istanbul has a wide range of eating establishments, with prices to match. Most of the major hotels have dining rooms serving rather bland international cuisine. It's far more rewarding to eat in Turkish restaurants. For details and price-category definitions, *see* Dining *in* Staying in Turkey, *above.*

$$ Borsa Lokantasi. This unpretentious restaurant serves some of the
★ best food in Turkey. The baked lamb in eggplant purée and the
stuffed artichokes are not to be missed. *Yaliköskü Cad. Yaliköskü
Han 60–62, Eminönü, tel. 212/522–4173. No credit cards. Lunch
only. Closed Sun. Another branch at Halaskargazi Cad. 90/1,
Osmanbey, tel. 212/232–4200. AE, DC, MC, V.*

$$ Dört Mevsim. Located in a large Victorian building, Dört Mevsim is
noted for its blend of Turkish and French cuisine and for its owners,
Gay and Musa, an Anglo-Turkish couple who opened it in 1965. On
any given day, you'll find them in the kitchen overseeing such delights as shrimp in cognac sauce and baked marinated lamb. *Istiklâl
Cad. 509, Beyoğlu, tel. 212/245–8941. Reservations advised. AE,
DC, MC, V. Closed Sun.*

$$ Dunya. The frenetic pedestrian traffic of the adjacent Ortakoy
Square and waiters balancing appetizer trays is countered by the
picturesque Bosphorus view, which on summer nights includes
many passing pleasure boats. The grilled *cupra* (bream) is a must,
while mezes are always fresh and sumptuous. *Salhane Sokak 10,
Ortakoy, tel. 212/258–6358. Reservations advised. No credit cards.*

$$ Pandeli. Excellent food is served in this frenetic turn-of-the-century
restaurant adorned with domed alcoves. It's two flights of stairs
above the arched gateway to the Egyptian Bazaar. *Misir Carsisi,
Eminönü, tel. 212/527–3909. AE, DC, MC, V. Lunch only. Closed
Sun.*

$ Hacibaba. This is a large, cheerful-looking place, with a terrace
overlooking a churchyard. Fish, meat, and a wide variety of vegetable dishes are on display for your selection. Before you choose your
main course, you'll be offered a tray of appetizers that can be a meal
in themselves. *Istiklal Cad. 49, Taksim, tel. 212/244–1886. Reservations advised. AE, DC, MC, V.*

$ Haci Salih. A tiny, family-run restaurant, Haci Salih has only 10 ta-
★ bles, so you may have to line up and wait—but it's worth it. Traditional Turkish food is the fare here, with special emphasis on
vegetable dishes and lamb. Alcohol is not served, but you can bring
your own. *Anadolu Han 201, off Istiklal Cad., tel. 212/243–4528.
Reservations sometimes accepted. No credit cards. Lunch only.
Closed Sun.*

$ Rejans. Founded by two Russians and a Crimean fleeing the Bolshe-
vik revolution, this restaurant offers traditional East European decor and excellent Russian food and vodka, served by eccentric old
waiters. *Istiklâl Cad., Olivo Geçidi 15, Galatasaray, tel. 212/244–
1610. Reservations required. V. Closed Sun.*

$ Yakup. This cheery hole-in-the-wall is smoky and filled with locals
rather than tourists, and it can get loud, especially if there's a soccer
match on television. From the stuffed peppers to the octopus salad,
the mezes are several notches above average. *Asmali Mescit Sok.
35–37, Beyoglu, tel. 212/249–2925. Reservations advised on weekends. AE, MC, V.*

¢ Cennet. The main culinary attraction at this traditional style restaurant in the center of the sightseeing area are the *gozleme* and *cig
borek*, deep-fried and grilled pastries prepared on site by women
from Anatolia. Dishes such as shish kebab and stewed meats are also
available. *Divan Yolu Caddesi 90, Cemberlitas, tel. 212/513–1416.
V.*

¢ Taş Plak. Located centrally right off Istiklal Caddesi, this is a smallish meyhane which gets its name from the gramophone records of
days gone by. The walls are decorated with old record jackets and
photographs of Istanbul before cars and television. Appetizers such
as eggplant salad and *haydari* (a spiced yogurt dip), and *coban
kavurma* (sautéed lamb with green pepper and spices) are served to
the tune of piped-in or live music. *Istiklal Caddesi, Acara Sokak 6,
Beyoglu, tel. 212/251–1139. Reservations advised. DC, V.*

Lodging

The top hotels are mainly around Taksim Square in New Town. Hotels generally include the 15% VAT and a service charge of 10–15% in the rate. Modern, middle-range hotels usually have a friendly staff, which compensates for the generally bland architecture and interiors. In Old Istanbul, the Aksaray, Laleli, Sultanahmet, and Beyazit areas have many conveniently located, inexpensive small hotels and family-run pansiyons. Istanbul has a chronic shortage of beds, so plan ahead. For details and price-category definitions, *see* Lodging *in* Staying in Turkey, *above*.

$$ **Barut's Guesthouse.** Quiet and secluded and in the heart of Old Istanbul, Barut's has a roof terrace overlooking the Sea of Marmara. ★ The friendly artist-owners keep an art gallery in the foyer. *Ishakpaşa Cad. 8, Sultanahmet, tel. 212/516–0357, fax 212/516– 2944. 23 rooms with bath. MC, V.*

$$ **Ibrahim Pasa Oteli.** This exquisitely renovated old Turkish house, in the historic Sultanahmet neighborhood, has panoramic views of the Bosphorus and Sultanahmet square. It's the right place if you want to treat yourself. *Terzihane Sok. 5, Sultanahmet, tel. 212/518–0394 or 518/0395, fax. 212/518–4457. 19 rooms with bath. Facilities: restaurant, bar. MC, V.*

$ **Richmond.** This hotel is in a charming renovated turn-of-the-century building in the vicinity of many of the city's consulates. Rooms have carpeted comfort and some have views of the Bosphorus. Downstairs is the Lebon patisserie, which is a remake of the 19th century pastry shop that once operated there. *Istiklal Caddesi 445, tel. 212/252–5460, fax 212/252–9707. 101 rooms with bath. AE, V.*

$ **Berk Guest House.** Clean and exceptionally comfortable, this is run by an English-speaking couple, Güngör and Nevin Evrensel. Two rooms have balconies overlooking a garden. *Kutlugün Sok. 27, Cankurtaran, Sultanahmet, tel. 212/516–9671, fax 212/517–7715. 7 rooms with bath. No credit cards.*

$ **Hotel Nomade.** This Sultanahmet pansiyon offers a congenial and personal atmosphere, comfortable beds in small rooms, and low prices. The building is a restored, five-story Ottoman house, decorated with kilims and folk crafts. The roof-garden bar and terrace have wonderful views of all Sultanahmet. *Ticarethane Sok. 7, Sultanahmet, tel. 212/511–1296, fax 212/513–2404. 12 rooms, some with shared bath. AE, MC, V.*

¢ **Hanedan Hostel.** A very clean hostel, run by a Finnish-Turkish couple, popularity makes reservations here a must in peak season. The terrace café and rooms offer uninterrupted views of the Bosphorus, as well as of the Blue Mosque and the Aghia Sophia. The owners, who run a carpet shop nearby, will help you find a good bargain and avoid traps. *Akbıyık Cad., Adliye Sok. 3, Sultanahmet, tel. 212/ 516–4869. 13 rooms, 2 with bath. AE, DC, MC, V.*

¢ **Hotel Empress Zoe.** Named after an empress who ruled Byzantium in the 11th century, this unique and comfortable inn is decorated with murals and paintings of that period. The rooms are furnished with colorful textiles and have cool marble bathrooms. Some have views of the Marmara Sea. The American owner, Ann Nevans, runs the place in style and helps out with personalized itineraries around the nearby Sultanahmet sites. *Akbiyik Cad., Adliye Sok. 10, Sultanahmet, tel. 212/518–2504, fax 212/518–5699. 12 rooms with bath. MC, V.*

¢ **Plaza.** This somewhat run-down hotel, with upstairs rooms overlooking the Bosphorus, is cheap and conveniently located near Taksim. It was recently expanded. Rooms without views are cheaper. *Arslanyatağı Sok. 19, Taksim, tel. 212/245–3273, fax 212/293– 7040. 25 rooms with bath. MC, V.*

¢ **Side Pansiyon.** The three Kiğili brothers who run this popular pansiyon in a restored house are expanding it into a hotel. The rooms

are modest; some have private baths. *Utangaç Sok., 20
Sultanahmet, tel. 212/517–6590, fax 212/517–6590. 30 rooms, 10
with bath. No credit cards.*

The Arts

Entertainment in Istanbul ranges from the **Istanbul International
Festival**—held late June through mid-July and attracting internationally renowned artists and performers—to local folklore and theatrical groups, some amateur, some professional. Because there is
no central ticket agency, ask your hotel to help you. You can also pick
up tickets at the box office or through a local tourist office.

For tickets to the Istanbul International Festival, apply to the **Istanbul Foundation for Culture and Arts** (Kültür ve Sanat Vakfi). Performances, which include modern and classical music, ballet, opera,
and theater, are given throughout the city in historic buildings, such
as St. Irene Church and Rumeli Castle. The highlight of the festival
is the performance of Mozart's opera *Abduction from the Seraglio,*
at Topkapı Palace, the site that inspired the opera.

Concerts Tickets for performances at the main concert hall, **Atatürk Kültür
Merkezi,** are available from the box office at Taksim Square (tel. 212/
251–5600). From October through May, the **Istanbul State Symphony** gives performances here. It's also the location for ballet and
dance companies.

Nightlife

Bars and **Beyoglu Pub & Restaurant** (Istiklal Caddesi 140/17, Beyoglu, tel.
Nightclubs 212/252–3842) is behind an arcade off Istiklal in a pleasant garden
and is usually full of moviegoers. Open noon to 2 AM. **Kepkedi Bar**
(Birinci Cad. 17/1, Arnavutkoy, tel. 212/263–3234) is a waterfront
bar where cat lovers, among others, congregate for drinks and live
music. The bar's name means "very cat."

Orient Express Bar (Pera Palace Hotel, Meşrutiyet Cad. 98,
Tepebaşi, tel. 212/251–4560) distills the atmosphere of old Istanbul
with the lingering presence of the rich, powerful, and famous (from
Atatürk to Italian king Victor Emmanuel to Josephine Baker) who
once played here.

A well-established nightclub is **Kervansaray** (Cumhuriyet Cad. 30,
Elmadağ, tel. 212/247–1630), where you can dine, dance, and watch
belly-dancing shows. Open daily 8 PM–midnight. **Galata Tower**
(Kuledibi, tel. 212/245–1160) offers dinner between 8:30 and 10,
with a Turkish show and dancing from 10 PM to 1 AM.

Jazz **Hayal Kahvesi** (Büyük Parmakkapi Sok. 19, Beyoğlu, tel. 212/244-
2558) is a bohemian side-street bar with wood furniture and lace curtains. Local groups perform jazz, blues, and rock.

Discos The hottest place in town is **2019** (Oto Sanayi Sitesi, Maslak tel. 212/
285–1896), an outdoor junk yard turned disco, reminiscent of a Mad
Max movie. A chic disco with space-age decor and a hip atmosphere
is **Juliana's,** which also offers live music (Swissotel The Bosphorus,
Macka, tel. 212/259–0940), open nightly 8 PM–4 AM.

The Aegean Coast

Some of the finest reconstructed Greek and Roman cities, including
the fabled Pergamum, Ephesus, Aphrodisias, and Troy, are to be
found in this region of Turkey. Bright yellow road signs pointing to
historical sites or to those currently undergoing excavation are
everywhere here. There are so many Greek and Roman ruins, in

fact, that some haven't yet been excavated and others are going to seed.

Grand or small, all the sites are steeped in atmosphere and are best explored early in the morning or late in the afternoon, when there are fewer crowds. You can escape the heat of the day on one of the sandy beaches that line the coast.

Getting Around

The E24 from Çanakkale follows the coast until it turns inland at Kuşadasi to meet the Mediterranean again at Antalya. All the towns on the itinerary are served by direct bus routes, and there are connecting services to the ancient sites.

Tourist Information

Contact the tourist office in each town for names of travel agencies and licensed tour guides.

Ayvalik (Yat Limani Karşisi, tel. 266/312–2122).
Bursa (Ulu Cami Parki, Atatürk Cad. 1, tel. 224/221–2359).
Çanakkale (Iskele Meyd. 67, tel. 286/217–1187).
İzmir (Atatürk Cad. 418, Alsancak, tel. 232/422–0207; Gaziosmanpasa Bul. 1/C, tel. 232/484–2147).
Kuşadasi (Iskele Meyd., tel. 256/614–1103).

Exploring the Aegean Coast

Bursa **Bursa,** the first capital of the Ottoman Empire, is known as Yeşil (Green) Bursa, not only because of its many trees and parks but also because of its **Yeşil Cami** (Green Mosque) and **Yeşil Turbe** (Green Mausoleum). Both the mosque and mausoleum derive their names from the green tiles that line the interior of the buildings. They are located opposite each other on Yeşil Caddesi (Green Avenue). *Admission free. Open daily outside prayer hrs.*

The town square is called **Heykel,** which means "statue," and is named for its statue of Atatürk. Off Heykel, along Atatürk Caddesi, is the **Ulu Cami** (Great Mosque), with its distinctive silhouette of 20 domes. *Admission free. Open daily outside prayer hrs.*

Troy Long thought to be simply an imaginary city from Homer's *Iliad*, Troy was excavated in the 1870s by Heinrich Schliemann, a German amateur archaeologist who also found the remains of nine successive civilizations, one on top of the other, dating back 5,000 years. Considering Troy's fame, the site is surprisingly small. It's best to take a guided tour to appreciate fully the significance of this discovery and the unwavering passion of the man who proved that Troy was not just another ancient myth. *Admission: $2.50. Open daily 8–7.*

The E24 highway leads around the **Gulf of Edremit,** a glorious area of olive groves, pine forests, and small seaside resorts. **Ayvalik,** 5 kilometers (3 miles) off the main bus route, between Çanakkale and İzmir, is an ideal place to stay while visiting the ruins of ancient Pergamum, 40 kilometers (24 miles) away.

Pergamum **Pergamum** is reached by driving southeast along E24 following the signs toward Bergama, the modern-day name of the ancient Greek-Roman site. If you're traveling by bus, be certain it is going all the way to Bergama, or you'll find yourself dropped off at the turn-in, 8 kilometers (5 miles) from the site.

Because the ruins of Pergamum are spread out over several miles, it's best to take a taxi from one site to the next. The most noteworthy places are the Asklepieion, the Ethnological Museum, the Red Hall,

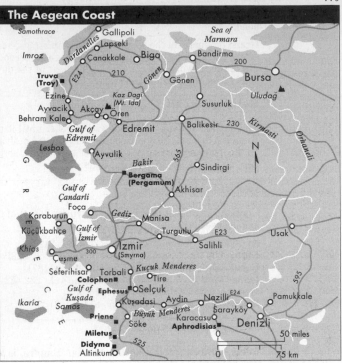

The Aegean Coast

and the **Acropolis.** *Admission: $2.50. Open Apr.–Oct., daily 8:30–6:30; Nov.–Mar., daily 8:30–5:30.*

Pergamum's glory peaked during the Greek Attalid dynasty (241–133 BC), when it was one of the world's most magnificent architectural and artistic centers—especially so under the rule of Eumenes II, who lavished his great wealth on the city. Greek rule continued until 133 BC, when the mad Attalus III died, bequeathing the entire kingdom to Rome.

The most famous building at the acropolis is the **library,** which once contained a collection of 200,000 books, all on papyrus. The library's collection was second only to the one in Alexandria, Egypt. When the troops of Julius Caesar burned down the library in Alexandria, Mark Antony consoled Cleopatra by shipping the entire collection of books from Pergamum to Alexandria. These, too, went up in flames 400 years later, in wars between Muslims and Christians.

İzmir The coastal area between Bergama and İzmir, 104 kilometers (64 miles), was once thick with ancient Greek settlements. Today only İzmir remains. Called Smyrna by the Greeks, it was a vital trading port that was often ravaged by wars and earthquakes. İzmir was completely destroyed by a fire in 1922 following Turkey's War of Independence against Greece. The war was a bloody battle to win back the Aegean coast, which had been given to the Greeks in the 1920 Treaty of Sèvres. Atatürk was in İzmir helping to celebrate the victory when celebrations soon turned to horror as the fire engulfed the city.

The city was quickly rebuilt, and it then became known by its Turkish name, İzmir. It's a lively, modern city filled with wide boulevards and apartment houses and office buildings. On top of İzmir's highest hill is the **Kadifekale** (Velvet Fortress), built in the 3rd century BC by Lysimachos. It is easily reached by dolmuş and is one of the few ancient ruins that was not destroyed in the fire. At the foot of the hill is the restored **Agora,** the market of ancient Smyrna. The modern-day marketplace is in **Konak Square,** a maze of tiny streets filled with shops and covered stalls. *Open 8–8. Closed Sun.*

Kuşadasi **Kuşadasi,** about 80 kilometers (50 miles) south of İzmir on Route 300, has grown since the late 1970s from a fishing village into a sprawling, hyperactive town geared to serving thousands of tourists who visit the nearby ruins and beaches.

Ephesus The major attraction near Kuşadasi is **Ephesus,** a city created by the Ionians in the 11th century BC and now one of the grandest reconstructed ancient sites in the world. It is the showpiece of Aegean archaeology. Ephesus was a powerful trading port and the sacred center for the cult of Artemis, Greek goddess of chastity, the moon, and hunting. The Ionians built a temple in her honor, one of the Seven Wonders of the Ancient World. During the Roman period, it became a shrine for the Roman goddess Diana. Today waterlogged foundations are all that remain of the temple.

Some of the splendors you can see here include the two-story **Library of Celsus;** houses of noblemen, with their terraces and courtyards; a 25,000-seat **amphitheater,** still used today during the Selçuk Ephesus Festival of Culture and Art; remains of the municipal baths; and a brothel. *Admission: $5.50. Admission to the houses on the slopes: $1.50. Open daily 8:30–6 (summer), 8:30–5 (winter).*

Selçuk On Ayasoluk Hill in **Selçuk,** 4 kilometers (2½ miles) from Ephesus, is the restored **Basilica of St. John** (St. Jean Aniti), containing the tomb of the apostle. Near the entrance to the basilica is the **Ephesus Museum,** with two statues of Artemis. The museum also has marvelous frescoes and mosaics among its treasures. *Admission: $2.50. Basilica and museum open Tues.–Sun. 8:30–6.*

St. Paul and St. John preached in both Ephesus and Selçuk and changed the cult of Artemis into the cult of the Virgin Mary. **Meryemana,** 5 kilometers (3 miles) from Ephesus, has the **House of Mary,** thought to have been the place where St. John took the mother of Jesus after the crucifixion and where some believe she ascended to heaven. *Admission $1.20. Open daily 7:30–sunset.*

Priene and Priene and Miletus, 40 kilometers (25 miles) from Kuşadasi, are sis-
Miletus ter cities, also founded by the Ionians in 11 BC. Nearby is **Didyma,** a holy sanctuary dedicated to Apollo. **Priene,** on top of a steep hill, was an artistic and cultural center. Its main attraction is the **Temple of Athena,** a spectacular sight, with its five fluted columns and its backdrop of mountains and the fertile plains of the Meander River. You can also see the city's small amphitheater, gymnasium, council chambers, marketplace, and stadium. *Admission: $1.20. Open daily 8:30–6.*

Nearby, **Miletus,** once a prosperous port, was the first Greek city to use coins for money. It also became an Ionian intellectual center and home to such philosophers as Thales, Anaximander, and Anaximenes, all of whom made contributions to mathematics and the natural sciences.

The city's most magnificent building is the **Great Theater,** a remarkably intact 25,000-seat amphitheater built by the Ionians and kept up by the Romans. Climb to the highest seats in the amphitheater for a view across the city to the bay. *Admission: ruins $1.20, museum $1.20. Open Tues.–Sun. 8:30–6.*

The temple of **Didyma** is reached by a 32-kilometer (20-mile) road called the **Sacred Way,** starting from Miletus at the bay. The temple's oracles were as revered as those of Delphi. Fragments of bas-relief include a gigantic head of Medusa and a small statue of Poseidon and his wife, Amphitrite. *Admission: $1.20. Open daily 8:30–6.*

Dining and Lodging

For details and price-category definitions, *see* Dining and Lodging *in* Staying in Turkey, *above.*

Ayvalik   **Büyük Berk.** This modern hotel is part of a larger complex on
Lodging   Ayvalik's best beach, about 3½ kilometers (2 miles) from the center
of town. *Sarimsakli Mev., tel. 266/324–1045, fax 266/324–1194. 180 rooms with bath. Facilities: outdoor pool, restaurant, disco. No credit cards. $$*
Ankara Oteli. On Sarimsakli beach, just a few feet from the surf, the Ankara Oteli gives excellent value for the money. *Sarimsakli Mev., tel. 266/324–1195, fax 266/324–1048. 104 rooms with bath. Facilities: restaurant, café, bar, game room. No credit cards. $*

Bursa   **Cumurcul.** This old house, converted into a restaurant, is a local fa-
Dining   vorite. Grilled meats and fish are both attentively prepared.
Çekirge Cad. tel. 224/235–3707. Reservations advised. V. $$
Kebabci Iskender. Bursa is famous for the dish served here: *Iskender Kebap,* slivers of skewer-grilled meat served with a rich tomato sauce, and yogurt. *Unlu Cad. 7, Heykel, tel. 224/221–4615. No credit cards. $*

Lodging   **Artiç Hotel.** The greatest advantage of this hotel is that it's both central and cheap. It's also a good base for sightseeing. *Ulu Camii Karşisi, tel. 224/224–5505, fax 224/224–5509. 70 rooms with bath. V. $*

★   **Ilman Oteli.** This 30-year-old hotel stands in a garden across from the Kültür Park. *Çekirge Cad. 45, tel. 224/220–6590. 28 rooms with bath. No credit cards. ¢*

Çanakkale,   **Büyük Truva.** Near the center of Çanakkale, the Truva is an excel-
Troy, and   lent base for sightseeing. *Kayserili Ahmet Pasa Cad. Kordonboyu,*
Gallipoli   *tel. 286/217–1024, fax 286/217–0903. 66 rooms with bath. No credit*
Lodging   *cards. $$*
Akol. This modern, new hotel is on the waterfront in Çanakkale; ask for a room with a terrace overlooking the Dardenelles. *Kordonboyu, tel. 286/217–9456, fax 286/217–2897. 138 rooms with bath. Facilities: bar, restaurant, disco, outdoor pool, meeting room. AE, MC, V. ¢*
Tusan. Surrounded by a pine forest on a beach at Güzelyali, north of Troy, the Tusan is one of the most popular hotels in the area. Be certain to reserve well in advance. *Güzelyali, tel. 286/232–8273, fax 286/232–8226. 64 rooms with bath. Facilities: restaurant, bar, disco. MC, V. Closed Oct.–Feb. ¢*

İzmir   **Kismet.** Tastefully decorated, the Kismet is a quiet, comfortable ho-
Lodging   tel with friendly service. *1377 Sok. 9, tel. 232/463–3853, fax 232/ 421–4856. 68 rooms with bath. Facilities: restaurant, bar, sauna. AE, MC, V. $$*

Kuşadasi   **Ada Restaurant.** The setting for this expansive outdoor restaurant is
Dining   a terrace on Guvercinada, the small island attached to Kusadasi.
★   Fresh bass, turbot, as well as kebabs and appetizers are displayed at the entrance. *Guvercin Adasi, tel. 256/614–1725. Reservations advised for groups. AE, MC, V. $*

★   **Ali Baba Restaurant.** Adjacent to the Kuşadasi port, this restaurant prides itself on its fish and salads. You choose and bargain for your fish, which can then be grilled, steamed, or salted. *Belediye Turistik Carsisi, tel. 256/614–1551. MC, V. $*

Lodging   **Efe Oteli.** All the rooms in this small, centrally located hotel have a sea view. Reserve in advance during high season. *Güvercin Ada Cad. 37, tel. 256/614–3660, fax 256/614–3662. 44 rooms with bath. Facilities: restaurant, bar. AE, MC, V. $*
Liman Hotel. Opened in 1993, this whitewashed building has black cast-iron balconies and black window frames. The front rooms over-

look panoramic views of the town and the port. The staff are very friendly. *Kibris Cad., Buyral Sok. 4, tel. and fax 256/612–3149. 16 rooms with shower. Facilities: café, bar. No credit cards. $*

Selçuk
Lodging

Kale Han. Located in a refurbished stone inn, Kale Han is one of the nicest hotels in town managed by a welcoming family. Rooms are simple, with bare, whitewashed walls and dark timber beams. The restaurant serves excellent food round the clock. *Atatürk Cad. 49, tel. 5451/6154, fax 5451/2169. 50 rooms with shower. MC, V. $*

Hulya. This is a pleasant, family-run pansiyon, where one of the family members is a fisherman who sometimes brings in some of his daily catch. The down-to-earth owners serve meals in the lemon-blossom-scented courtyard. *Atatürk Cad., Ozgur Sok. 15, tel. 232/892–2120. No credit cards. ¢*

Index

NOTES

NOTES

NOTES

NOTES

NOTES

NOTES

NOTES

NOTES

Fodor's Travel Publications

Available at bookstores everywhere, or call 1–800–533–6478, 24 hours a day.

Gold Guides

U.S.

Alaska

Arizona

Boston

California

Cape Cod, Martha's Vineyard, Nantucket

The Carolinas & the Georgia Coast

Chicago

Colorado

Florida

Hawaii

Las Vegas, Reno, Tahoe

Los Angeles

Maine, Vermont, New Hampshire

Maui

Miami & the Keys

New England

New Orleans

New York City

Pacific North Coast

Philadelphia & the Pennsylvania Dutch Country

The Rockies

San Diego

San Francisco

Santa Fe, Taos, Albuquerque

Seattle & Vancouver

The South

U.S. & British Virgin Islands

USA

Virginia & Maryland

Waikiki

Washington, D.C.

Foreign

Australia & New Zealand

Austria

The Bahamas

Barbados

Bermuda

Brazil

Budapest

Canada

Cancún, Cozumel, Yucatán Peninsula

Caribbean

China

Costa Rica, Belize, Guatemala

The Czech Republic & Slovakia

Eastern Europe

Egypt

Europe

Florence, Tuscany & Umbria

France

Germany

Great Britain

Greece

Hong Kong

India

Ireland

Israel

Italy

Japan

Kenya & Tanzania

Korea

London

Madrid & Barcelona

Mexico

Montréal & Québec City

Morocco

Moscow, St. Petersburg, Kiev

The Netherlands, Belgium & Luxembourg

New Zealand

Norway

Nova Scotia, New Brunswick, Prince Edward Island

Paris

Portugal

Provence & the Riviera

Scandinavia

Scotland

Singapore

South America

South Pacific

Southeast Asia

Spain

Sweden

Switzerland

Thailand

Tokyo

Toronto

Turkey

Vienna & the Danube

Fodor's Special-Interest Guides

Branson

Caribbean Ports of Call

The Complete Guide to America's National Parks

Condé Nast Traveler Caribbean Resort and Cruise Ship Finder

Cruises and Ports of Call

Fodor's London Companion

France by Train

Halliday's New England Food Explorer

Healthy Escapes

Italy by Train

Kodak Guide to Shooting Great Travel Pictures

Shadow Traffic's New York Shortcuts and Traffic Tips

Sunday in New York

Sunday in San Francisco

Walt Disney World, Universal Studios and Orlando

Walt Disney World for Adults

Where Should We Take the Kids? California

Where Should We Take the Kids? Northeast

Special Series

Affordables
Caribbean
Europe
Florida
France
Germany
Great Britain
Italy
London
Paris

Fodor's Bed & Breakfasts and Country Inns
America's Best B&Bs
California's Best B&Bs
Canada's Great Country Inns
Cottages, B&Bs and Country Inns of England and Wales
The Mid-Atlantic's Best B&Bs
New England's Best B&Bs
The Pacific Northwest's Best B&Bs
The South's Best B&Bs
The Southwest's Best B&Bs
The Upper Great Lakes' Best B&Bs

The Berkeley Guides
California
Central America
Eastern Europe
Europe
France
Germany & Austria
Great Britain & Ireland
Italy
London
Mexico

Pacific Northwest & Alaska
Paris
San Francisco

Compass American Guides
Arizona
Canada
Chicago
Colorado
Hawaii
Hollywood
Las Vegas
Maine
Manhattan
Montana
New Mexico
New Orleans
Oregon
San Francisco
South Carolina
South Dakota
Texas
Utah
Virginia
Washington
Wine Country
Wisconsin
Wyoming

Fodor's Español
California
Caribe Occidental
Caribe Oriental
Gran Bretaña
Londres
Mexico
Nueva York
Paris

Fodor's Exploring Guides
Australia
Boston & New England

Britain
California
Caribbean
China
Florence & Tuscany
Florida
France
Germany
Ireland
Italy
London
Mexico
Moscow & St. Petersburg
New York City
Paris
Prague
Provence
Rome
San Francisco
Scotland
Singapore & Malaysia
Spain
Thailand
Turkey
Venice

Fodor's Flashmaps
Boston
New York
San Francisco
Washington, D.C.

Fodor's Pocket Guides
Acapulco
Atlanta
Barbados
Jamaica
London
New York City
Paris
Prague
Puerto Rico

Rome
San Francisco
Washington, D.C.

Rivages Guides
Bed and Breakfasts of Character and Charm in France
Hotels and Country Inns of Character and Charm in France
Hotels and Country Inns of Character and Charm in Italy

Short Escapes
Country Getaways in Britain
Country Getaways in France
Country Getaways Near New York City

Fodor's Sports
Golf Digest's Best Places to Play
Skiing USA
USA Today
The Complete Four Sport Stadium Guide

Fodor's Vacation Planners
Great American Learning Vacations
Great American Sports & Adventure Vacations
Great American Vacations
National Parks and Seashores of the East
National Parks of the West